M000311736

ASHE Reader Series on Community Colleges

Fourth Edition

Edited by
Eboni M. Zamani-Gallaher, Jaime Lester, Debra D. Bragg,
and Linda Serra Hagedorn

Foreword by
George R. Boggs

Series Editor
Jerlando F.L. Jackson, University of Wisconsin

Pearson Learning Solutions, 501 Boylston Street, Suite 900, Boston, MA 02116
A Pearson Education Company
www.pearsoned.com

Printed in the United States of America

1 2 3 4 5 6 7 8 9 10 V0ZN 18 17 16 15 14

000200010271892525

JH/JL

ISBN 10: 1-269-90554-6
ISBN 13: 978-1-269-90554-1

TABLE OF CONTENTS

COPYRIGHT ACKNOWLEDGMENTS   IX

ADVISORY BOARD   XIII

FOREWORD | GEORGE R. BOGGS, PRESIDENT AND CEO EMERITUS   XIV
OF THE AMERICAN ASSOCIATION OF COMMUNITY COLLEGES (AACC)

**SECTION I: HISTORICAL FOUNDATIONS, THEORETICAL   1
PERSPECTIVES, AND SOCIOLOGICAL APPROACHES**

CHAPTER 1

THE CASE FOR THE COMMUNITY COLLEGE | ARTHUR M. COHEN   5

CHAPTER 2

THE RHETORIC OF PROFESSIONAL EDUCATORS AND THE DEFINITION OF PUBLIC JUNIOR COLLEGES   16
FROM 1900 TO 1940 | JOHN H. FRYE

CHAPTER 3

EDITOR'S CHOICE ESSAY: REMEMBERING RAYMOND J. YOUNG AND THE GRASS-ROOTS DEVELOPMENT   23
OF COMMUNITY COLLEGES FROM 1950 TO 1976 | STEPHEN G. KATSINAS

CHAPTER 4

THE "COOLING-OUT" FUNCTION IN HIGHER EDUCATION | BURTON R. CLARK   39

CHAPTER 5

COMMUNITY COLLEGES AND THE AMERICAN SOCIAL ORDER | S. BRINT AND J. KARABEL   46

CHAPTER 6

THE COMMUNITY COLLEGE: THE IMPACT, ORIGIN, AND FUTURE OF A CONTRADICTORY INSTITUTION | 58
KEVIN J. DOUGHERTY

**SECTION II: DIVERGENT GOALS AND INSTITUTIONAL   69
DIVERSITY AMONG TWO-YEAR INSTITUTIONS**

CHAPTER 7

RETHINKING AND REFRAMING THE CARNEGIE CLASSIFICATION | ALEXANDER C. MCCORMICK   73
AND CHUN-MEI ZHAO

CHAPTER 8

PROMOTING ACCESS AND EQUITY THROUGH MINORITY-SERVING AND WOMEN'S INSTITUTIONS | 80
STEVEN R. ARAGON AND EBONI M. ZAMANI

CHAPTER 9

COMMUNITY COLLEGE MISSION IN HISTORICAL PERSPECTIVE | KEN MEIER   93

CHAPTER 10

THE BENEFITS OF ATTENDING COMMUNITY COLLEGE: A REVIEW OF THE EVIDENCE | CLIVE R.   107
BELFIELD AND THOMAS BAILEY

CHAPTER 11

INSTITUTIONAL AMBIGUITY: CONTINUED STRUGGLES OF THE CONTRADICTORY COLLEGE | J. M.
BEACH   125

CHAPTER 12

STATEWIDE GOVERNANCE STRUCTURES AND TWO-YEAR COLLEGES | RICHARD C. RICHARDSON, JR.   142
AND GERARDO E. DE LOS SANTOS

SECTION III: ORGANIZATION, ADMINISTRATIVE   153
LEADERSHIP, AND FINANCE

CHAPTER 13

EMERGING DEFINITIONS OF LEADERSHIP IN HIGHER EDUCATION: NEW VISIONS OF LEADERSHIP OR 157
SAME OLD "HERO" LEADER? | PAMELA L. EDDY AND KIM VANDERLINDEN

CHAPTER 14

REVISIONING LEADERSHIP IN COMMUNITY COLLEGES | MARILYN J. AMEY AND SUSAN B. TWOMBLY   172

CHAPTER 15

TRUSTEES' PERCEPTIONS OF THE DESIRED QUALIFICATIONS FOR THE NEXT GENERATION OF   188
COMMUNITY COLLEGE PRESIDENTS | KATHLEEN PLINSKE AND WALTER J. PACKARD

CHAPTER 16

EQUITY AND EFFICIENCY OF COMMUNITY COLLEGE APPROPRIATIONS: THE ROLE OF LOCAL   204
FINANCING | ALICIA C. DOWD AND JOHN L. GRANT

CHAPTER 17

DOING MORE WITH LESS: THE INEQUITABLE FUNDING OF COMMUNITY COLLEGES | CHRISTOPHER M. 223
MULLIN

CHAPTER 18

THE MOVING TARGET: STUDENT FINANCIAL AID AND COMMUNITY COLLEGE STUDENT RETENTION | 232
MICHAEL A. KENNAMER, STEPHEN G. KATSINAS, AND RANDALL E. SCHUMACKER

SECTION IV: THE INSTRUCTIONAL CORE – COMMUNITY   245
COLLEGE FACULTY

CHAPTER 19

COMMUNITY COLLEGE FACULTY: WHAT WE KNOW AND NEED TO KNOW | SUSAN TWOMBLY AND   249
BARBARA K. TOWNSEND

CHAPTER 20

PERFORMING GENDER IN THE WORKPLACE: GENDER SOCIALIZATION, POWER, AND IDENTITY AMONG   262
WOMEN FACULTY MEMBERS | JAIME LESTER

CHAPTER 21

STRATEGIES FOR FACULTY-STUDENT ENGAGEMENT: HOW COMMUNITY COLLEGE FACULTY ENGAGE   281
LATINO STUDENTS | BRENT D. CEJDA AND RICHARD E. HOOVER

CHAPTER 22

RECRUITING AND RETAINING RURAL COMMUNITY COLLEGE FACULTY | JOHN P. MURRAY   294

CHAPTER 23

UNINTENDED CONSEQUENCES: EXAMINING THE EFFECT OF PART-TIME FACULTY MEMBERS ON   300
ASSOCIATE'S DEGREE COMPLETION | AUDREY J. JAEGER AND M. KEVIN EAGAN JR.

CHAPTER 24

A COMPARISON OF FACTORS THAT PREDICT THE SATISFACTION OF COMMUNITY COLLEGE FACULTY BY   318
GENDER | DUANE AKROYD, SUSAN BRACKEN, AND CRYSTAL CHAMBERS

CHAPTER 25

PURPLE IS TO LAVENDER: WOMANISM, RESISTANCE, AND THE POLITICS OF NAMING | DIMPAL JAIN   330
AND CAROLINE TURNER

SECTION V: DIVERSE STUDENTS AT TWO-YEAR INSTITUTIONS OF   343
HIGHER LEARNING

CHAPTER 26

RESEARCH ON RACE AND ETHNIC RELATIONS AMONG COMMUNITY COLLEGE STUDENTS | WILLIAM   347
MAXWELL AND DIANE SHAMMAS

CHAPTER 27

LEAVING THE 2-YEAR COLLEGE: PREDICTORS OF BLACK MALE COLLEGIAN DEPARTURE | J. LUKE   358
WOOD

CHAPTER 28

HISPANIC STUDENT SUCCESS: FACTORS INFLUENCING THE PERSISTENCE AND TRANSFER DECISIONS OF   373
LATINO COMMUNITY COLLEGE STUDENTS ENROLLED IN DEVELOPMENTAL EDUCATION | GLORIA
CRISP AND AMAURY NORA

CHAPTER 29

FOLLOWING THEIR EVERY MOVE: AN INVESTIGATION OF SOCIAL-CLASS DIFFERENCES IN COLLEGE   391
PATHWAYS | SARA GOLDRICK-RAB

CHAPTER 30

PERCEPTIONS OF CAMPUS CLIMATE AND ENGAGEMENT FOR LESBIAN, GAY, BISEXUAL, AND   408
TRANSGENDER COMMUNITY COLLEGE STUDENTS | CRYSTAL KIEKEL

CHAPTER 31

STUDENTS WITH DISABILITIES AT 2-YEAR INSTITUTIONS IN THE UNITED STATES: FACTORS RELATED TO   411
SUCCESS | KETEVAN MAMISEISHVILI AND LYNN C. KOCH

SECTION VI: CAREER-TECHNICAL AND WORKFORCE EDUCATION   425

CHAPTER 32

THE COMMUNITY COLLEGE: EDUCATING STUDENTS AT THE MARGIN BETWEEN COLLEGE AND WORK | 429
THOMAS J. KANE AND CECILIA ELENA ROUSE

CHAPTER 33

CAREER AND TECHNICAL EDUCATION: OLD DEBATES, PERSISTENT CHALLENGES IN COMMUNITY   447
COLLEGES | DEBRA D. BRAGG

CHAPTER 34

SOCIO-ACADEMIC INTEGRATIVE MOMENTS: RETHINKING ACADEMIC AND SOCIAL INTEGRATION   461
AMONG TWO-YEAR COLLEGE STUDENTS IN CAREER-RELATED PROGRAMS | REGINA DEIL-AMEN

CHAPTER 35

TEACHING BY CHOICE: COMMUNITY COLLEGES EXPAND K-12 STEM PATHWAYS AND PRACTICES | 485
MADELINE PATTON

CHAPTER 36

THE COMMUNITY COLLEGE BACCALAUREATE IN THE U.S.: MODELS, PROGRAMS, AND ISSUES | 493
DEBORAH L. FLOYD

CHAPTER 37

UPDATE ON THE COMMUNITY COLLEGE BACCALAUREATE: EVOLVING TRENDS AND ISSUES | ALENE   505
BYCER RUSSELL

SECTION VII: COMMUNITY COLLEGE TRANSFER   517

CHAPTER 38

THE COMMUNITY COLLEGE TRANSFER CALCULATOR: IDENTIFYING THE COURSE-TAKING PATTERNS   521
THAT PREDICT TRANSFER | LINDA SERRA HAGEDORN, ALBERTO CABRERA, AND GEORGE PRATHER

CHAPTER 39

"A HAND HOLD FOR A LITTLE BIT": FACTORS FACILITATING THE SUCCESS OF COMMUNITY COLLEGE   541
TRANSFER STUDENTS TO A LARGE RESEARCH UNIVERSITY | BARBARA K. TOWNSEND AND KRISTIN
WILSON

CHAPTER 40

TRANSFER ACCESS FROM COMMUNITY COLLEGES AND THE DISTRIBUTION OF ELITE HIGHER   556
EDUCATION | ALICIA C. DOWD, JOHN J. CHESLOCK, AND TATIANA MELGUIZO

CHAPTER 41

ADJUSTMENT OF COMMUNITY COLLEGE STUDENTS AT A FOUR-YEAR UNIVERSITY: ROLE AND   577
RELEVANCE OF TRANSFER STUDENT CAPITAL FOR STUDENT RETENTION | FRANKIE SANTOS LAANAN,
SOKO S. STAROBIN, AND LATRICE E. EGGLESTON

CHAPTER 42

AN INVESTIGATION OF CRITICAL MASS: THE ROLE OF LATINO REPRESENTATION IN THE SUCCESS OF   606
URBAN COMMUNITY COLLEGE STUDENTS | LINDA SERRA HAGEDORN, WINNY (YANFANG) CHI,
RITA M. CEPEDA, AND MELISSA MCLAIN

SECTION VIII: REMEDIATION AND DEVELOPMENTAL EDUCATION   621

CHAPTER 43

DOES MATHEMATICS REMEDIATION WORK? A COMPARATIVE ANALYSIS OF ACADEMIC ATTAINMENT   625
AMONG COMMUNITY COLLEGE STUDENTS | PETER RILEY BAHR

CHAPTER 44

REFERRAL, ENROLLMENT, AND COMPLETION IN DEVELOPMENTAL EDUCATION SEQUENCES IN   653
COMMUNITY COLLEGES | THOMAS BAILEY, DONG WOOK JEONG, AND SUNG-WOO CHO

CHAPTER 45

THE LOCATION OF DEVELOPMENTAL EDUCATION IN COMMUNITY COLLEGES: A DISCUSSION OF THE   674
MERITS OF MAINSTREAMING VS. CENTRALIZATION | DOLORES PERIN

CHAPTER 46

THE SOCIAL PREREQUISITES OF SUCCESS: CAN COLLEGE STRUCTURE REDUCE THE NEED FOR SOCIAL   684
KNOW-HOW? | REGINA DEIL-AMEN AND JAMES E. ROSENBAUM

CHAPTER 47

IS DEVELOPMENTAL EDUCATION HELPING COMMUNITY COLLEGE STUDENTS PERSIST?: A CRITICAL   701
REVIEW OF THE LITERATURE | TATIANA MELGUIZO, JOHANNES BOS, AND GEORGE PRATHER

SECTION IX: GLOBALIZATION, TECHNOLOGY, AND POLICY ISSUES   711
FACING 21ST CENTURY COMMUNITY COLLEGES

CHAPTER 48

GOVERNMENTAL POLICIES AFFECTING COMMUNITY COLLEGES: A HISTORICAL PERSPECTIVE | 715
ARTHUR M. COHEN

CHAPTER 49

PUBLIC POLICY, COMMUNITY COLLEGES, AND THE PATH TO GLOBALIZATION | JOHN S. LEVIN   729

CHAPTER 50

GLOBALIZATION AND COMMUNITY COLLEGE MODEL DEVELOPMENT | ROSALIND LATINER RABY   746

CHAPTER 51

ONLINE EDUCATION AND ORGANIZATIONAL CHANGE | REGINA L. GARZA MITCHELL   760

CHAPTER 52

DELICATE ENGAGEMENT: THE LIVED EXPERIENCE OF COMMUNITY COLLEGE STUDENTS ENROLLED IN   773
HIGH-RISK ONLINE COURSES | CYNTHIA S. BAMBARA, CLIFFORD P. HARBOUR, TIMOTHY GRAY
DAVIES, AND SUSAN ATHEY

APPENDIX A: LIST OF RECOMMENDED WORKS   785

APPENDIX B: WEB-BASED RESOURCES   802

ABOUT THE EDITORS   812

COPYRIGHT ACKNOWLEDGMENTS

ADVISORY BOARD

FOREWORD

The Editors of the Fourth Edition of the *ASHE Reader Series on Community Colleges* have compiled a very comprehensive series of articles that cover a wide range of issues, many of which have been the subject of debate from the very founding of community colleges in the United States. From the beginning, community college leaders have exhibited a passion that is unmatched elsewhere in American higher education; many even refer to community colleges as "democracy's colleges" and the development of the institutions as "the Community College Movement." Early leaders, like Raymond Young (profiled in the chapter by Katsinas) are admired for their pioneering work to establish community college systems. However, as the authors of the *Reader* make clear, community colleges are not without their critics—and interpretation of the research about their impact on students and American society is not conclusive.

Arguably, community colleges have made laudable contributions in spite of the lower funding streams from state and federal expenditures. Community college funding models are a local development and usually involve cost sharing among students, localities, and states. In their chapter, Dowd and Grant discuss typical community college funding patterns. Outside of financial aid, the federal government provides only a small portion of funding to community colleges. Mullen contends, community colleges receive much less funding than any other segment of higher education and spend a much greater percentage of their resources on instruction.

In terms of governance, community colleges vary widely from state to state, and as Richardson and de Los Santos point out, governance structures are complex and dynamic. Moreover, they can affect coordination of a state's higher education systems and determine the ease of student transfer between institutions in a state. Cohen provides a good perspective on how state governmental policies have affected the development of community colleges and how two-year institutions of learning are steered.

Community college leadership and leadership styles have changed over time. Eddy and VanDerLinden discuss how the "great man" or "hero" style of leadership has given way to team leadership, transformative leadership, and inclusive leadership. Leadership styles also differ by gender and position within the organization. Amey and Twombly review the styles of leaders during the early years of community colleges. Plinske and Packard provide a trustee perspective on leadership characteristics with their chapter on desired qualifications of presidents.

Authors in this volume point out how community colleges have been labeled as buffers for universities, places where minority and low-income students can be educated or trained without being a burden on the more elite universities. Community colleges also have been criticized for their contradictory missions and for channeling minorities into workforce programs rather than academic transfer programs. As Dougherty points out, the "open door," low tuition, and wide distribution of the colleges have yielded significant access to higher education, but that doesn't necessarily lead to success. Clark's chapter introduces the concept that community colleges serve a "cooling out" function, lowering student aspirations and tracking them into less demanding majors. In fact, several studies have shown that students who start in community colleges are less likely to receive a baccalaureate than those who start in universities. Cohen points out in Chapter One, the higher education choice for many students has been community colleges or nothing; however, as noted by Belfield and Bailey, the benefits of community college attendance outweigh not earning an associate's degree as community college degrees result in positive earnings gains for completers.

Community colleges are often judged on the effectiveness of their transfer programs. However, as the *Reader* authors point out, the effectiveness of the transfer function depends as much on the policies and practices of the four-year institution as it does on the strength of the community college programs. For instance, Hagedorn, Cabrera, and Prather introduce the Community College Transfer Calculator as a tool for assisting community college students, faculty, and academic advisors with predicting the likelihood of transfer based on class scheduling and course taking. However, the authors also note the value-add of the "Calculator" by informing database decision-making and enrollment management. Townsend and Wilson found that transfer students are often ignored in four-year retention efforts. Laanan, Starobin, and Eggleston point out barriers to successful transfer and make recommendations to improve the success of transfer students. Dowd, Cheslock, and Melguizo indicate that elite four-year institutions can increase their enrollment of low-income transfer students through renewed emphasis on recruitment, admissions, counseling, and curricular structures.

Several of the *Reader* authors describe community college faculty, curricular matters, and other issues that involve the faculty. Twombly and Townsend point out that community college faculty generally do not get enough respect, and that more needs to be researched about their issues. Lester discussed gender expectations and the degree of representation of women across departments. Akroyd, Bracken, and Chambers compare factors that affect satisfaction of community college faculty. Cejda and Hoover discuss how important it is for faculty to be sensitive to Hispanic culture and to understand preferred student learning styles. Murray addresses the difficulty that rural community colleges have in attracting and retaining qualified faculty. Jaeger and Eagan found a modest negative effect on student completion based upon the part-time status of faculty.

Community college faculties have been on the front line in utilizing new technology in their teaching. Several of the *Reader* authors review how community college faculty use distance learning technologies and how the use differs based upon gender, discipline, and whether the faculty member is full- or part-time. Barnbara, Harbour, Davies, and Athey discuss the advantages and disadvantages of online education for students. Garza notes how organizational change presented in alternate modes of program delivery, which include online modules, have steadily grown. Subsequently, another emerging trend is the evolution of the community college baccalaureate, which is considered by some to be a departure in the mission of community colleges.

Classifying community colleges is a challenge because of their wide variety and the responsiveness of the curriculum to local needs. Meier refers to mission relative to the social origins, context, and ideological assumptions upon which the modern community college social movement has evolved. McCormick argues that community colleges need to be differentiated; and should not all fit into a single Carnegie classification. However, the missions are moving targets, changing over time, even to the extent of offering baccalaureates. A growing number of community colleges are offering baccalaureates, and this trend is likely to continue. Some see the trend as mission creep and worry that over time community colleges will lose their emphasis on serving the most at-risk students. Others such as Floyd and Russell in their respective chapters say that offering the baccalaureate is just another way that community colleges meet the higher education of students and communities and the needs of local industry for advanced employee skills.

Although American community colleges trace their roots to the junior college, which offered the first two years of a traditional college education, workforce preparation has emerged as an important mission for the institutions. Several of the *Reader* authors address the growth of and support for these programs and how effective they are in increasing wages. Deil-Amen sheds light on the social and academic integration of students who participate in career-related education programs finding that academic integration was more significant than social integration, which was often unrelated to student persistence. The extent to which students can persist and navigate between college and work is at the center of Kane and Rouse's chapter. The authors asserts that current labor market conditions could result in significant increases in demand for postsecondary education with community colleges absorbing much of the increase in enrollment given the need for high skill, high demand labor, particularly in science, technology, engineering, and mathematics (STEM) fields.

One of the most challenging issues in improving student success rates is dealing with students who are not prepared for college (see Melguizo, Bos, & Prather). Developmental education is the subject of a significant amount of research and an area where many new strategies are being tested. The *Reader* authors thoroughly examine important aspects of developmental education and its outcomes. As Bahr points out, if students remediate their weaknesses successfully, they succeed at similar rates to those who need no remediation. The problem is that the majority do not remediate successfully. Bailey, Jeong, and Cho document the general lack of success in developmental education programs. Perin reviews one of the most contentious issues: whether developmental education should be centralized in its own department or mainstreamed in regular academic departments. Whichever way a college chooses to structure its development education programs, it is important to align the content with college-level courses and to provide individualized attention and supplemental tutoring to the students.

Many of the chapters discuss community college students, their wide diversity, and their different pathways. As Goldrick-Rab points out, today's students are more mobile than ever, attending more than one higher education institution on their way to a degree or credential. However, she also points out that attendance patterns and completion rates differ by socio-economic status. Students who are continuously enrolled and do not "stop out" are much more likely to complete a degree. Dougherty points out that success rates for all students can be improved through better academic and social integration, points also made by Deil-Amen. Dougherty recommends learning communities, freshman seminars, improved advising, and work with high schools to improve readiness skills. Hagedorn, Cabrera, and Prather discuss the use of a "transfer calculator" to advise students on ways to increase transfer likelihood.

Other authors also address the issue of student success. Deil-Amen and Rosenbaum discuss social prerequisites for success and point out that community colleges could be more successful with their students if they adopted some of the practices of the for-profit occupational colleges. In particular, they argue for clear structure, improved counseling, monitoring of progress, better information, and assisting students with external pressures. Kennamer, Katsinas, and Schumacker address the importance of financial aid to retention, but find that tuition increases have overwhelmed modest increases in federal financial aid. Hagedorn, Chi, Cepeda, and McLain found that a "critical mass" of Latino faculty and students at an institution was an important factor that affected the academic success of Latino students.

Maxwell and Shammas shed light on the importance of race and ethnic relations among community college students. Several authors discuss the issues surrounding campus climate and the unique experiences that certain groups of community college students have—Black males (Wood), Hispanics (Crisp and Nora), LGBTQ students (Kiekel), and students with disabilities (Mamiseishvili and Koch). What seems to be common is that student success can be enhanced by improved sensitivity, responsive student support services for diverse groups, increasing financial and academic support, encouragement, in addition to assisting students to deal with family and job responsibilities.

There are many roles and responsibilities that community college students juggle. The borders of their local context broaden as they take their newly attained skills into the labor market and/or transfer to a four-year institution. Hence, in an increasingly global and interconnected world, it has become important to provide community college students with a global education. Beach declares that global responsiveness was one of the most dramatic new trends among community colleges in the 1990s. Community colleges have been active in internationalizing their curricula and in providing students experiences with other cultures. While community colleges are a U. S. invention, several other countries have taken note of the significant effect that community colleges in the U.S. have had on both individual opportunity and economic development. Many have developed or are developing institutions based upon the American model. Raby and Levin have described the paths toward globalization in their chapters.

The fourth edition of the *ASHE Reader Series on Community Colleges* is a significant resource for those who study American higher education, especially community colleges, but it is also a wonderful text for educators and leaders of higher education institutions. The articles and research reports provide an important picture of the development of community colleges, the missions that guide them, the challenges they face, the students they serve, and the faculty and leaders who serve them. As the articles point out, not everyone agrees about the issues and how they should be addressed. All of us in higher education are still learning, and the *Reader* is an important resource for us as we continue to study and learn how to be more effective.

—George R. Boggs

SECTION I

HISTORICAL FOUNDATIONS, THEORETICAL PERSPECTIVES, AND SOCIOLOGICAL APPROACHES

SECTION I: HISTORICAL FOUNDATIONS, THEORETICAL PERSPECTIVES, AND SOCIOLOGICAL APPROACHES

The *ASHE Reader Series on Community Colleges* serves as a seminal collection of readings providing sound, wide-ranging, sought after works that explore the multitude of facets of two-year colleges. The *Community College Reader* has been a central resource and primary text in graduate programs countrywide, offering courses and programs in community college leadership and higher education administration. In the years since the publication of the *Third Edition* in 2006, there have been numerous advances in leadership approaches, theoretical and conceptual frameworks, and empirical studies regarding community colleges, their constituents, and related outcomes.

The body of research produced during the release of the current edition is vast and rich. The corpus of extant literature available in this *Fourth Edition* provides readers with a compendium of works that underscore the historical significance and contemporary importance of American community colleges. This collection blends theory and practice in describing the status, scope and effectiveness of services, programs, policies, and best practices in community college education that appeal to practitioners, intellectuals, and scholars-in-training. The *Fourth Edition* continues the tradition of prior *Readers* to include historical antecedents, classical models, and traditional frameworks germane to community colleges. In addition, this edition will maintain the custom of including research that seamlessly weaves the classics and foundations while offering contemporary synthesis of the two-year collegiate context.

To begin to understand these colleges, readers should review the historical accounts of their development, functions, and arguments of their benefit (or lack thereof) to society. Section I of the *Reader* provides multiple chapters that give historical context to community colleges and the sociological contradictions that scholars have and continue to address. The first chapter of this section, authored by Cohen, a luminary in the field of community college research, sets out to make the "case" for community college—to argue that community colleges have value to individuals, communities, and society writ large. Cohen tackles topics that range from occupational education to minority student success and concludes that colleges could be strengthened through state level fiscal policies that promote associate degree completion, focus on workforce development or occupational programs, and promoting student transfer.

Frye, in Chapter Two, continues the discussion of the historical and contemporary role of community colleges with concentration on four decades (i.e., the period from 1900 to 1940), when these institutions were created. The attention in this chapter is on two major models for community colleges. One is the model that community colleges create access to higher education for those who would otherwise be denied it, and the other is that a community college should offer a terminal or complete higher education credential. The author concludes with a discussion of the relevance of these two models to contemporary community colleges and to federal and state policy.

Chapter Three, authored by Katsinas, focuses on the role of one individual, Raymond Young, who played a significant role in the post-World War II development of community colleges. The focus of this chapter is the grassroots citizen's participatory studies, created by Young, that led to the establishment of over 60 community colleges over a twenty-year period. This chapter highlights the importance of citizen participation and local and state levels in the creation of higher education. Even as the article shares how community colleges must assume key leadership roles in the reconstruction of American society, one of the more controversial articles of its time, Clark, in Chapter Four, suggests that community colleges have long been "cooling out" student aspirations and perpetuating the social order of the status quo. Clark asserts that some institutions of higher education, specifically community colleges, create a system that reduces expectation on individual effort through an avoidance of standards, agents of consolation, and gradual disengagement, to name a few. The chapter discusses the consequences of such a system in the context of higher education's role in supporting a democracy.

Brint and Karabel in Chapter Five present an institutional model inspired by sociological traditions of organizational analyses. Their model focuses on the relationship between organizational development, in this case the expansion of community colleges, and structural constraints. The authors' argument focuses specifically on the vocationalization of community college and the relative subordinate position of community colleges within the higher education sector.

In the last chapter, Dougherty focuses on what he calls the contradictory roles of community colleges—a host of different and incompatible social functions that community colleges have taken on over time. The functions include college transfer, remedial education, continuing education, and general education among others. His historical analysis discusses why and how community colleges have adopted what some call "mission creep." The chapter concludes with a discussion of the future of community colleges.

CHAPTER 1

THE CASE FOR THE COMMUNITY COLLEGE

ARTHUR M. COHEN
UNIVERSITY OF CALIFORNIA, LOS ANGELES

The American public community colleges were established to accommodate the twentieth-century drive for more years of education. Located in every state, they enroll 5 million students, two-thirds of whom attend part time. Their occupational programs lead toward both immediate employment, as in clerical work, and higher-status careers, such as those in the health and engineering technologies that may require additional schooling. Their transfer function is indistinct because the data and definitions are not stable and because their students have variant goals. The colleges could be strengthened if the states developed fiscal incentives to be awarded to institutions that increased their proportion of students who gained associate degrees, entered employment in the field for which they were prepared, and/or matriculated at a four-year college or university.

Why did community colleges flourish when students' desires for higher education opportunity could have been met by expanding the state universities? This article traces the development of community colleges, analyzes their major curricular functions, and discusses their contributions to schooling in America.

Why Community Colleges?

Many interpretations have been offered to account for the rise of community colleges. One contention is that the colleges were sponsored by the upper classes who wanted to maintain their social position by supporting an institution that would "reproduce existing social relations" (Karabel 1986, p. 18). The proponents of that position point to the differential rates of progress made by upper-class and lower-class youths and conclude therefore that the colleges were designed to serve as "one more barrier put between the poor and the disenfranchised and the decent and respectable stake in the social system which they seek" (Zwerling 1976, p. xvii). This thesis is especially appealing to those who seek institutional and political villains to account for a class-based society and for the inequitable distribution of attainments among different ethnic and socioeconomic groups.

A thesis that attributes the rise of the colleges to a combination of social and political forces was advanced by Rubinson (1986). He contended that an alliance between working-class groups, professional educators, and middle-class reformers was able to fend off the desire of the business classes to limit and stratify education. The working class has always supported publicly funded education forms that allow for progression to higher levels of schooling and that have a common curriculum, not just a vocational orientation. Therefore, the community colleges have emphasized both occupational studies and a collegiate curriculum that is modeled on the lower division of universities, complete with academic discipline-dominated courses and faculty members.

A different explanation connects the basic support for the colleges more directly to the professional educators. Since the colleges provide the less qualified students with the less prestigious curricula, they have allowed the universities to distance themselves from the students whom they did not wish to serve and the programs they did not wish to offer; thus, the universities sponsored community college development in their own interest. A complementary position is that public school officials and local community leaders advocated community colleges for the prestige and higher-status professional positions they yielded (see Dougherty 1988). According to these theses, the education community itself created the colleges and built the political coalitions necessary to sustain their support.

Brint and Karabel (1989) have extended the thesis that the professional educators determined community college directions. They argue that the transformation of the colleges from prebaccalaureate to occupational training institutions in the 1970s was occasioned less by student demands for job-relevant education than it was by college leaders seeking a secure niche in the structure of higher education. Accordingly, the leaders lobbied for funds for occupational programs, built corporate training connections, and sought the part-time, older, less highly motivated students to fit those curricula.

It is difficult to reject any thesis because few serious scholars have studied community colleges, and little information is available on the mechanisms by which any of these forces have been able to affect college development. A conspiracy of the elite, a populist alliance, or a clique of professional educators—all are plausible. But regardless of their ontogeny, the colleges have become part of the formal education structure in America, thriving on the educative tasks that the other postsecondary institutions had not undertaken. Three-fourths of the colleges' incomes derive from public appropriations. The colleges live in a political arena.

The community college in America is any institution accredited to award the associate degree as its highest degree. Although the private junior colleges and the two-year proprietary schools are included in that definition, the 1,050 publicly supported comprehensive institutions are the dominant form; hence, this discussion concentrates on them. Located in every state, these colleges provide nearly 5 million students with occupational programs, the first two years of baccalaureate studies, basic skills development, and a variety of special interest courses.

The students enrolled in community colleges exhibit a variety of goals and characteristics. Thirty-six percent enroll to gain transferable credits, and 33 percent want job-entry skills. The other primary reasons for attending include upgrading in a job the student already holds (15 percent), personal interest (14 percent), and gaining basic skills (3 percent). The students' median age is 25; the modal age is 19. Women outnumber men 56 to 44 percent.[1]

In general, the students differ in several ways from their counterparts in universities. They are less academically able: only 9 percent of the 1980 high school seniors with an "A" average entered community colleges compared with 44 percent who entered public four-year colleges; in 1988, 24 percent of the freshmen entering all colleges and universities had "A" averages in high school whereas 12 percent of the community college matriculants were "A" students (Astin et al. 1988). Community college students tend to come from lower-income families: according to surveys conducted by the National Center for Education Statistics (NCES) in the 1980s, 46 percent of the college-going students from the lowest socioeconomic status (SES) quartile entered community colleges (West 1989). And they are more likely to be ethnic minorities. With 37 percent of the total enrollment in American higher education, the colleges enroll 43 percent of the blacks, 55 percent of the Hispanics, 56 percent of the Native Americans, and 42 percent of the Asians.

The community colleges are open-access institutions, enrolling anyone for virtually any purpose. Accordingly, relatively few of their students complete programs. Because the colleges provide occupational courses in both highly structured career programs and in general skills areas, their contribution to labor force development is varied. Because they encourage students to attend part-time (67 percent do), their matriculants take longer to attain their goals. Because few of the colleges have residence halls, their students commute from the local neighborhoods, dropping in or out as work schedules and family responsibilities dictate; 70 percent of their students hold

ARTHUR M. COHEN is professor of higher education at the University of California, Los Angeles. He is the director of the ERIC Clearinghouse for Junior Colleges and president of the Center for the Study of Community Colleges.

off-campus jobs. Accordingly, when the students' degree-completion or high-status job-entry rates are compared with those of other types of colleges and universities, the community colleges fall short.

Why Occupational Studies?

The role of community colleges can best be understood by analyzing their two major curricular functions: occupational and transfer-related studies. The vocationalization of higher education dates to the rise of the universities and their attendant professional schools late in the nineteenth century. The small academies of the pre—Civil War era grew into universities with student bodies numbering in the tens of thousands only when they incorporated schools of law, medicine, engineering, architecture, and numerous other professions. The latter-day state colleges developed curricula in the professions of lesser status: accountancy, teaching, agriculture. The community colleges of the second half of the twentieth century built programs in nursing, office skills, computer applications, and in the trades that had not yet attained even semiprofessional status. This three-tiered structure of higher education, matching the status order of the workplace, was reflected also in the socioeconomic status of the students attending each type of institution and in the magnitude of the resources that each group was able to command.

The perception that higher education is particularly to be used for occupational training is pervasive among students in all types of institutions. According to Cooperative Institutional Research Program data (Astin et al. 1988), 86 percent of the entering freshmen in two-year colleges noted "get a better job" as a very important reason in deciding to go to college, but 81 percent of matriculants in four-year colleges and universities gave the same reason. Similarly, although 77 percent of two-year college entrants gave "make more money" as an important reason, 70 percent of the freshmen at four-year colleges and universities said the same thing. However, because the community college job-entry programs are of one- or two-year duration, they attract many students with short-term practical goals. Occupational studies in community colleges account for more than one-third of the enrollments and more than two-thirds of the 450,000 associate degrees that the colleges award each year (Cohen and Brawer 1989, p. 210).

Some critics are concerned that the community college career programs channel students untowardly. On the first page of their book on higher education in the cities, Richardson and Bender (1987) state, "There is growing evidence that the policy decision made by many states in the 1960s to rely on community colleges as the primary access point for urban minorities has produced side effects that now threaten some of the hoped-for outcomes. ... There has been little change in economic and social class mobility for minorities *because their curriculum choices have been so concentrated in the career and vocational areas*" (p. 1, emphasis added). It is obviously misleading to categorize career programs as a unitary group because there are high- and low-status programs, programs preparing people for areas of high demand such as health care and electronics technology and those such as office work or data processing for which the market is not as distinct. But these are labor market, not educative, phenomena.

The critics also view with alarm the high dropout rates in community colleges without acknowledging that program completion is an institutional artifact. To the student who seeks a job in the field, completing the program becomes irrelevant as soon as a job is available; the categories "graduate" and "dropout" lose much of their force when viewed in this light. Students who leave programs before graduation and enter employment in the field for which they are prepared and students who graduate but do not obtain employment because they have entered related baccalaureate programs must be considered as program successes.

Occupational education as a stepping stone to the baccalaureate is an important part of its value. In a California statewide study, 25 percent of students enrolled in career curricula said they intended to transfer (Hunter and Sheldon 1980), and a national study found 26 percent of the students in vocational programs and/or classes planning to transfer (Palmer 1987, p. 134). Regardless of their intentions when they enrolled, 40 percent of the Los Rios (California) Community College District career program graduates transferred (Lee 1984), as did 36 percent of the William Rainey Harper College (Illinois) career alumni (Lucas 1988), 11 percent of the graduates of the technical institute and the six vocational-technical colleges in New Hampshire (New Hampshire State Department of Postsecondary Vocational- Technical Education 1988), 14 percent of the career program graduates in Illinois (Illinois Community College Board 1987), and 27 percent of the career program graduates in Maryland (Maryland State Board for Community Colleges 1988). Many of the graduates were employed in their field of study and pursuing further education simultaneously.

Within the colleges, the organization of occupational programs reflects both the belief that separate curricular tracks are the best way to accommodate the varying educational objectives and characteristics of the students and the way that the programs are funded. However, Palmer (1987) concluded that the organization of career education as a separate curricular track stems from several viewpoints other than student intentions. First is a "political agenda" held by state legislators and college planners who assume that occupational programs serve students whose primary educational objective is to gain skills allowing them to enter the work force. Second is a "terminal education agenda" that sees occupational studies as a way of serving academically less able students who are not likely to obtain the baccalaureate. The third is an "economic agenda," which holds that occupational studies improve the economy through labor force development and thus serve society. These three agendas, embedded in the history of the community college, have been put forth by American Association of Community and Junior Colleges leaders from Eells (1941) to Parnell (1985). A fourth agenda, the "hidden agenda," has been postulated by other commentators who charge that occupational programs channel low-income and minority students away from academic studies and the upward social mobility attendant thereon.

The career programs in community colleges may have been furthered by leaders who subscribed to those beliefs, but the agendas do not accurately reflect what the curricula do. Occupational programs are not exclusively related to the work force or the economy: they actually serve people with a wide range of abilities and goals, including students who wish to obtain skills for their personal interest. Palmer rejected the charge that community college students are counseled into career programs on the basis of their academic ability, hence their socioeconomic status. His analysis showed that the enrollment patterns in high-status and low-status occupational classes deviate considerably from what would be expected if curricular tracking were efficiently carried out. He found low-income students enrolling in high-status and low-status program areas in almost equal numbers. And he found highly self-confident students as likely to enroll in low-status program areas as students with below-average self-ratings of ability were to enroll in high-status programs.

In summation, an oversimplified view of career education as a track leading away from the baccalaureate leads to several errors. It neglects the extent to which occupational classes serve avocational or community service functions. It increases the likelihood of confounding curricular content with student intentions. It suggests that career education serves an ever-changing middle-level portion of the job market that supposedly requires some college study but not the baccalaureate, thus ignoring the high transfer rates exhibited by career program graduates. And it perpetuates the myth that career studies are the exclusive domain of the low-ability or low-income students. The problem with transfer from community colleges is not with career education; it is with the policies supporting the idea that the institution is a passive resource available to all who would drop in at any time during their lifetime to take a course in whatever interests them.

The Transfer Function

Preparing students to transfer to four-year colleges and universities has been a primary function of the two-year colleges since they began. But few colleges maintain data on the number of their students who transfer. Two major reasons account for this lack: the college leaders have always feared the untoward comparisons that are often made between the progress of their students and those who begin as freshmen in the selective four-year institutions, and the colleges receive funding based on the number of students who take classes, not on the number who complete programs or go on to further education. Hence, there are no incentives to produce the data. Even the definitions of transfer are unclear. Is a high school graduate who takes a summer class at the community college before matriculating as a university freshman in the fall a transfer? Is a university underclassman who takes classes at the local community college from time to time a transfer? How many units must a community college student complete before matriculating at a university to be called a transfer? How should those students who stop out of the education system for a few years before transferring be counted? If the universities accepted as transfers only those students who had completed associate degree requirements, the inconsistencies in data and definitions would be readily resolved. But the system is fluid, the definitions are variable, and any estimates of transfer rates are just that—estimates.

Even when data are available, the transfer rates vary depending on the definitions employed. Flaherty (1989) reported an 11.6 percent transfer rate for the colleges in Illinois at the same time that the Chancellor's Office of the California Community Colleges (1989) found a 42.6 percent transfer rate for the California colleges. Are the two systems that disparate? Of course not. Both reports relied on cross-sectional data that were calculated differently. Flaherty divided the number of students transferring to an Illinois college or university in 1988 by the total enrollment in "prebaccalaureate programs" during the previous fall. The Chancellor's Office divided the number transferring in 1988-89 by the "number of California high school graduates who entered community colleges three years prior to transfer" (p. 12). As for national figures, Adelman (1988) used National Longitudinal Study (NLS) data and reported that "1 out of 5 individuals who attend two-year colleges eventually attends a four-year college . . . . This is the true 'de facto' transfer rate." Another national study used as a denominator the number of students entering the community college with no prior college experience and attaining at least 12 credits, and as a numerator the number of that group who transferred any time in the ensuing five years. Based on preliminary data from 39 colleges, that mode of calculation yielded a transfer rate of around 23 percent nationwide (Center for the Study of Community Colleges 1990).

In general, however, if the purpose of the collegiate enterprise is to pass most students through to the baccalaureate degree, the community college is a failure by design. It encourages part-time and commuter attendance patterns. Most of its students matriculate with no intention of transferring; many already have higher degrees, and many more seek basic literacy training or rapidly attainable job-entry or job-upgrading skills. The students enrolling in community colleges are somewhat less likely to attain baccalaureate degrees within four or five years than those entering as freshmen in four-year colleges and institutions. The part-time attendance pattern certainly accounts for some of the difference. And since few community college students are resident on campus and few have on-campus jobs, they tend to be less involved with their collegiate studies.

The mere fact that community college matriculants must transfer from one institution to another before obtaining the baccalaureate accounts for some of the shortfall. It is somewhat analogous to the difference between a nonstop flight and one in which the passengers must change planes before reaching their destination. Many things might happen to cause the latter group to miss their connecting flight. So it is with students who must move from one institution to another: they take jobs instead; they cannot readily leave their hometown to go to the university; they find it convenient to stop out of formal education and get on with other aspects of their life.

Chance plays a role in progress toward the baccalaureate. In 1988, because of a sudden surge in applications, the University of California turned away around 10,000 qualified candidates for its freshman class. Many of these young people had to begin their higher education careers in one of the state's community colleges. Undoubtedly, their baccalaureate attainment rate will be slightly lower because of the difficulties they will encounter when they eventually transfer: loss of credits; adjusting to different campuses, academic calendars, and faculty expectations; and less opportunity for on-campus housing and jobs. And some of them may not transfer at all.

The data available on student transfer tell only part of the colleges' contributions to student progress. The Maricopa (Arizona) Community College District offers a case in point. Among its 60,000 students are 7,000 who were formerly enrolled in Arizona State University, and 8,700 of that university's students previously attended the local community colleges. An additional 3,900 students are taking classes at both institutions concurrently. Forty-five percent of the high school graduates in the Phoenix metropolitan area enter one of the local community colleges (de los Santos 1989). In sum, nearly 20,000 students in Phoenix are being, or have been, assisted toward the baccalaureate by the Maricopa District. Whether they actually attain it depends on many factors, few of them within the colleges' control.

Elsewhere, some of the community colleges have attempted to increase their transfer rates by monitoring student progress, providing information on transfer opportunities, enforcing course prerequisites, holding special group meetings for prospective transfers, and similar interventions. One of the most powerful aids to transfer is a set of inter-institutional agreements erected program-by-program so that students who want to obtain bachelor's degrees in certain fields are encouraged to begin at the local community college, with the assurance that the curricula articulate and that a place in the university's junior class will be available to them. Another stimulant to student progress, pioneered by Miami-Dade (Florida) Community College, is not to allow students to take more than four classes unless they have been tested, placed, and matriculated in an associate-degree program.

Since the 1960s, the community colleges have been stimulated to develop occupational programs by an influx of state and federal funds. More recently, many states have begun encouraging the colleges to increase the flow of students toward the baccalaureate. In 1987, California set aside $3 million for transfer centers in 20 colleges; Colorado and Michigan mandated articulated plans between community colleges and public universities; New Jersey awarded special funds to its colleges to recruit minority students who sought transfer; and Ohio awarded funds for colleges that would promote such activities (Center for the Study of Community Colleges 1987). Illinois has numerous special programs to enhance minority student progress through the community colleges, including recruiting and counseling high school students, offering basic skills activities for adults, connecting the community colleges with elementary schools, and providing intramural support groups (Illinois Community College Board 1989).

These types of transfer-directed activities, including many that the Ford Foundation has supported, have been summarized in many works including Cohen et al. (1985), Donovan et al. (1987), and Richardson and Bender (1987). They can be encapsulated with the statement that the community college staff members must identify the potential transfers early and monitor their progress, making frequent direct contact with them until they complete their studies and enter the universities. This takes a form of dedication to student achievement that stands in contradistinction to the more common laissez-faire approach to program completion. But the colleges cannot have it both ways: they cannot sit by and allow students to take a random walk through the curriculum and at the same time further student progress toward the baccalaureate.

College Contributions

Various dilemmas plague the study of any college's contributions. First is the question of individual gain versus social value. Is it sufficient for an institution to provide an avenue of mobility for its matriculants? Or should it be held accountable for the influence it has on the broader society, such as the extent to which it tends to equalize incomes or enhance economic development in its region? A second concern relates to the inquirer's perspective. External critics filter information through their own preconceptions, often using data selectively to warrant their conclusions. And internal studies of college effects, conducted by the institutions' managers, tend to deny any finding that might be interpreted negatively. The limitations inherent in social science research also come into play: incomplete data, confounding variables, the impossibility of randomizing the population, and inadequate statistical techniques, to name a few.

All these limitations are revealed in considering community college contributions. One line of study attempts to calculate the economic impact that is attributable to direct expenditures by the college itself, and by its students and employees. Findings are usually that the college returns around $2.50 to $3.00 for each dollar it receives. But the data used in such calculations are selected so that the outcome is assuredly positive: bank deposits, personal expenditures, and institutional purchases in a community invariably grow when a college is established, and they go up as the college's income increases. The same holds true for any establishment: prisons, military bases, hospitals. Still, such studies appear from time to time (see, e.g., Johnson County Community [1985] and Winter [1988]) and are sometimes publicized as though they were reports of the college's contributions to economic development.

The rate of return to people who attend community colleges is occasionally studied, usually by deducting forgone earnings and other costs of college from anticipated lifetime personal income. Blair and Finn (1981) estimated the 20-year and 30-year earnings of graduates of associate degree technician programs nationally, compared them with those of college dropouts, and concluded that the graduates enjoyed a 14 percent higher rate of return. Romano (1985) reviewed several studies and reported that the graduates of two-year programs seem to be headed toward higher earnings than those students who have attended college but not completed a program, but lower earnings than those who have completed the baccalaureate.

The higher-education researchers more frequently address college contributions to individual mobility by correlating the type of college attended with student progress through the graded educational system or with subsequent income or job status. These linear-flow models yield few definitive statements, primarily because student demographics and predispositions interact with college location, regional employment opportunities, and other uncontrollable factors so that only a small portion of the variance can be attributed to the college's effects. For example, using data from the Cooperative Institutional Research Program's survey of college freshmen and subsequent follow-ups, Astin (1983) has calculated institutional effects by controlling for up to 100 variables. He concludes that "a baccalaureate-oriented freshman who enrolls initially at a community college has a 16 percent better chance of becoming a dropout than a comparable student (in terms of entering characteristics) who enrolls at a public four-year college" (p. 125). However, he points out that much of the differential rate is due to the fact that few community colleges have on-campus residents and that community college students tend to work more hours per week outside school and take fewer classes. After equating for students who work or who reside away from home, Astin finds that the discrepancy between expected and actual dropout rates among community college entrants drops to 7 percent.

Several analysts have made similar calculations using data from the 1972 NLS of high school seniors. Velez (1985) used the NLS 1976 follow-up, which showed 42 percent of the four-year college entrants and 12 percent of the two-year college entrants completing the baccalaureate, and concluded that where one began college had an important effect on attainment. He also noted that "living quarters had the largest significant effect on the probability of finishing college" and that "students who had work-study jobs had a 23 percent higher probability of finishing college" (p. 197). Pascarella et al. (1986) used NLS data to calculate student progress after nine years. They found 14 variables accounting for 17 percent of the variance in persistence and 24 percent of the variance in baccalaureate attainment. Anderson (1981) ran 26 variables and found that community college entrants were less likely to persist through the sophomore year. She acknowledged, "It is true that these variables explain only a small proportion of the variance in persistence . . . . The intervening variables included in the models mediated only a small proportion of the effects of college, work, and residence" (pp. 13-14). And all the analyses founder on the elusive fact that a sizable proportion of the people attending community colleges are not seeking formal credentials: they want what they can use in the labor market or in their avocational pursuits and leave when they have attained it.

What Happens to the Minorities?

The difficulty in disaggregating the effects of community colleges from the characteristics of the students who enter them is magnified in the attempts to describe the community colleges' special effects on minority students. Nationwide, 47 percent of the minority students in postsecondary education are in community colleges. Forty-one percent of the Hispanics and 24 percent of the blacks who enter college immediately following high school begin in a community college (Horn and Carroll 1989). The minorities constitute 24 percent of all community college enrollments (as compared with around 15 percent in the senior institutions). These enrollments are close to parity with the student groups' proportions of the local population. In Illinois, for example, 15.2 percent of the high school graduation class of 1985 were black and 16.8 percent of the state's community college students were black (Illinois Community College Board 1986). Minorities constituted 9.1 percent of the population of Kansas and 9.3 percent of that state's community college students (Kansas State Department of Education 1986); the figures for California are 32.4 and 34.3 percent, respectively (Field Research Corporation 1984). Single college data also reflect this pattern; in 1986, Laredo (Texas) Junior College, in a city where 93 percent of the population was Hispanic, counted 88 percent of the students as Hispanic, and Southwestern College had a student body that was 31 percent Hispanic in a California city where 32 percent of the population was Hispanic (Rendon et al. 1988). Community colleges in cities with high proportions of minorities—Chicago, Cleveland, El Paso, Los Angeles, Miami, New York, Phoenix—enroll sizable numbers of minority students. The evidence of neighborhood attendance is revealed where the community college has several campuses in the same city: at East Los Angeles College in the mid-1980s, 65 percent of the students were Hispanic; at Los Angeles Southwest College, 87 percent were black; and at Los Angeles Pierce College, 75 percent were white. This pattern is not confined to the cities; community colleges in rural areas with high minority populations, as in many areas of Mississippi, Texas, and California, similarly attract large numbers of minorities.

The question of whether the community colleges have enhanced or retarded progress for minority students has been debated at length; see, for example, Astin (1982), Cohen (1988), Orfield and Paul (1987–88), and Richardson and Bender (1987). Those who say that the community colleges have assisted minority students point to their ease of access, low tuition, and minimal entrance requirements. They note the numerous programs that provide special services to minority students, and they applaud the efforts made to recruit them. Their most telling argument is that a sizable percentage of those students would not be in college at all were it not for the community colleges.

However, several analysts have charged that minority students who begin in community colleges will do less well than those of equal ability who begin in the senior institutions and that this differential is greater for them than it is for the majority students. These detractors have taken the position that because students who begin at a community college are less likely to obtain baccalaureate degrees, minorities are actually harmed by the two-year institutions. What is the evidence? The best estimates suggest that white students, who constitute 75 percent of the community college enrollment, obtain 85 percent of the associate degrees; black students, 13 percent of the enrollment, obtain 8 percent of the associate degrees; and Hispanic students, 6 percent of enrollment, obtain 4 percent of the degrees (Asian and unclassified students account for the remainder). These figures suggest not only differential achievement but also the imprecision of the term "minority student."

The lower graduation rates for minorities should be viewed in the light of the community colleges' effects on all their students. Anderson reported that the institutional characteristics most influential in reducing bachelor's degree attainment at community colleges were "expenditures per student, percentage of lower SES, and percentage of part-time students, total enrollment, percentage of majors offered in vocational areas, and mean SAT score" (1981, p. 3). She, along with Astin (1982) and Velez (1985), also acknowledged that the depressing effect that community colleges have on baccalaureate attainment seems to affect white students at least as much as, if not more than, it affects black students of comparable ability and aspiration. The surveys conducted by the NCES in the 1980s show whites and Hispanics as nearly equivalent in their degree completion rates, with blacks lagging far behind (Horn and Carroll 1989).

Whom do the community colleges best serve? If all colleges and universities drew their students at random from the nation's pool of potential college goers each year, the value imputed to attending high-status institutions would quickly shrink as Yale, Michigan, and Berkeley struggled to educate students with a wide range of abilities and commitment to collegiate work. But, realistically, college effects relate quite closely to their admissions criteria, and the open-access community colleges suffer by comparison with the selective institutions. For most of the community college students, *the choice is not between the community college and a senior residential institution; it is between the local college and nothing.* Therefore, comparisons of relative progress are useful only to the extent that they guide changes in institutional policy.

Some major changes must be made, most of them at the state level, if the community colleges are to come anywhere near parity in the proportion of their entering students who go on to receive the baccalaureate. As a beginning, the states should enforce compacts to the effect that any student who completes an associate degree program is guaranteed admission to the public universities with no loss of credit, set aside special funds to be awarded to community colleges that increase their percentage of transfers, develop common course numbering systems so that each student's transcript does not have to be reviewed separately, and maintain a common student data base so that progress can be monitored. Whether the rationale centers on social justice or on the need for a better-educated work force, the community colleges should be supported to the extent that they enhance student development. That suggests maintaining open access but at the same time effecting measures that encourage program completion.

Notes

The points cited in this article have been elaborated in the second edition of *The American Community College*, by Arthur M. Cohen and Florence B. Brawer, published by Jossey-Bass, San Francisco, 1989.

1. These data were obtained by asking 7,558 students enrolled in a sample of 548 college-credit classes in 95 community colleges across the nation, "What is the primary reason you are attending this college at this time?" (Palmer 1987).

References

Adelman, C. "Transfer Rates and the Going Mythologies: A Look at Community College Patterns." *Change* 20 (1988): 38–41.

Anderson, K. L. "Post–High School Experiences and College Attrition." *Sociology of Education* 54 (1981): 1–15.

Astin, A. W. *Minorities in American Higher Education: Recent Trends, Current Prospects, Recommendations.* San Francisco: Jossey-Bass, 1982.

Astin, A. W. "Strengthening Transfer Programs." In *Issues for Community College Leaders in a New Era*, edited by G. B. Vaughan. San Francisco: Jossey-Bass, 1983.

Astin, A. W., K. C. Green, W. S. Korn, M. Schalit, and E. R. Berz. *The American Freshman: National Norms for Fall 1988.* Washington, D.C.: American Council on Education, Higher Education Research Institute, Los Angeles, 1988. (ERIC Document Reproduction Service no. ED 303 133)

Blair, L. M., and M. G. Finn. "The Returns to the Associate Degree for Technicians." *Journal of Human Resources* 16 (1981): 449–58.

Brint, S., and J. Karabel. *The Diverted Dream: Community Colleges and the Promise of Educational Opportunity in America, 1900–1985.* New York: Oxford University Press, 1989.

Center for the Study of Community Colleges. "Community College Involvement in the Education of Adults: Survey of State Directors regarding Populations Served and Funding Sources." Center for the Study of Community Colleges, Los Angeles, 1987.

Center for the Study of Community Colleges. "Defining and Promoting Transfer from Community Colleges." Center for the Study of Community Colleges, Los Angeles, 1990.

Chancellor's Office of the California Community Colleges. "Community College Transfer Performance." Chancellor's Office of the California Community Colleges, Sacramento, 1989.

Cohen, A. M. "Degree Achievement by Minorities in Community Colleges." *Review of Higher Education* 11 (1988): 383–402.

Cohen, A. M., and F. B. Brawer. *The Collegiate Function of Community Colleges.* San Francisco: Jossey-Bass, 1987.

Cohen, A. M., and F. B. Brawer. *The American Community College*, 2d ed. San Francisco: Jossey-Bass, 1989.

Cohen, A. M., F. B. Brawer, and E. M. Bensimon. "Transfer Education in American Community Colleges: Report to the Ford Foundation." Los Angeles: Center for the Study of Community Colleges, 1985. (ERIC Document Re-production Service no. ED 255 250)

de los Santos, A. G., Jr. "Changes in Credit Hour Distribution." Phoenix: Maricopa Community Colleges, 1989. (ERIC Document Reproduction Service no. ED 307 918)

Donovan, R. A., B. Schair-Peleg, and B. Forer. "Transfer: Making It Work: A Community College Report." Washington, D.C.: American Association of Community and Junior Colleges, 1987. (ERIC Document Reproduction Service no. ED 281 579)

Dougherty, K. "Educational Policy-making and the Relative Autonomy of the State: The Case of Occupational Education in the Community College." *Sociological Forum* 3 (1988): 400–432.

Eells, W. C. *Present Status of Junior College Terminal Education.* Washington, D.C.: American Association of Junior Colleges, 1941.

Field Research Corporation. "Student Socioeconomic Characteristics, Spring 1984: First Phase of Fee-Impact Survey." San Francisco: Field Research Corporation, 1984. (ERIC Document Reproduction Service no. ED 283 567)

Flaherty, R. "2-Year Colleges Fail Test," *Chicago Sun-Times,* November 12, 1989.

Horn, L., and C. D. Carroll. *Enrollment, Completion, Attrition, and Vocational Course-taking Patterns in Postsecondary Education: A Comparison of 1972 and 1980 High School Graduates Entering Two-Year Institutions.* Report CS 89-360. Washington, D.C.: National Center for Education Statistics, 1989.

Hunter, R., and M. S. Sheldon. "Statewide Longitudinal Study: Report on Academic Year 1979–80." Part 3, "Fall Results." Woodland Hills, Calif.: Los Angeles Pierce College, 1980. (ERIC Document Reproduction Service no. ED 188 714)

Illinois Community College Board. "Minority Student Participation: Illinois Public Community College System, Fiscal Years 1983 through 1986." Springfield: Illinois Community College Board, 1986. (ERIC Document Reproduction Service no. ED 275 360)

Illinois Community College Board. "Follow-Up Study of Students Who Completed Community College Occupational Programs during Fiscal Years 1983–1985." Springfield: Illinois Community College Board, 1987. (ERIC Document Reproduction Service no. ED 282 614)

Illinois Community College Board. "Special Programs for Minority Students at Illinois Community Colleges." Springfield: Illinois Community College Board, 1989. (ERIC Document Reproduction Service no. ED 302 312)

Johnson County Community College. "The Economic Impact of the Kansas Community Colleges on the Counties and the State of Kansas, Fiscal 1983–84." Overland Park, Kans.: Office of Institutional Research, 1985. (ERIC Document Reproduction Service no. ED 262 845)

Kansas State Department of Education. "Minority Student Enrollment in Kansas Community Colleges." Topeka: Kansas State Department of Education, 1986. (ERIC Document Reproduction Service no. ED 273 220)

Karabel, J. "Community Colleges and Social Stratification." In *The Community College and Its Critics.* New Directions for Community Colleges, no. 54, edited by L. S. Zwerling. San Francisco: Jossey-Bass, 1986.

Lee, B. S. "Follow-Up of Occupational Education Students: Los Rios Community College District, Spring 1983." Sacramento, Calif.: Los Rios Community College District, 1984. (ERIC Document Reproduction Service no. ED 241 099)

Lucas, J. A. "Follow-Up Study of 1986 Harper Career Alumni." Research Report Series, vol. 16, no. 9. Palatine, Ill.: Office of Planning and Research, William Rainey Harper College, 1988. (ERIC Document Reproduction Service no. ED 291 456)

Maryland State Board for Community Colleges. "Performance Profile, Maryland Community Colleges." Annapolis: Maryland State Board for Community Colleges, 1988. (ERIC Document Reproduction Service no. ED 297 807)

New Hampshire State Department of Postsecondary Vocational-Technical Education. "Graduate Placement Report, Annual Summary: Class of 1987, New Hampshire Vocational-Technical Colleges and New Hampshire Technical Institute." Concord: New Hampshire State Department of Postsecondary Vocational-Technical Education, 1988. (ERIC Document Reproduction Service no. ED 279 483)

Orfield, G., and F. Paul. "Declines in Minority Access: A Tale of Five Cities." *Educational Record* 68, no. 4, 69, no. 1 (1987-88): 56–62.

Palmer, J. "The Characteristics and Educational Objectives of Students Served by Community College Vocational Curricula." Ph.D. dissertation, University of California, Los Angeles, Graduate School of Education, 1987.

Parnell, D. *Associate Degree Preferred.* Washington, D.C.: American Association of Community and Junior Colleges, 1985. (ERIC Document Reproduction Service no. ED 255 266)

Pascarella, E. T., J. C. Smart, and C. A. Ethington. "Long-Term Persistence of Two-Year College Students." Paper presented at the annual meeting of the Association for the Study of Higher Education, San Antonio, Tex., February 1986. (ERIC Document Reproduction Service no. ED 268 900)

Rendon, L. I., M. J. Justiz, and P. Resta. "Transfer Education in Southwest Border Community Colleges." Columbia: University of South Carolina, Department of Educational Leadership and Policies, 1988. (ERIC Document Reproduction Service no. ED 296 748)

Richardson, R. C.,Jr., and L. W. Bender. *Fostering Minority Access and Achievement in Higher Education: The Role of Urban Community Colleges and Universities*. San Francisco: Jossey-Bass, 1987.

Romano, R. M. "What Is the Economic Pay-Off to a Community College Degree?" Working Paper Series no. 3-85. Binghamton, N.Y.: Broome Community College, Institute for Community College Research, 1985. (ERIC Document Reproduction Service no. ED 262 839)

Rubinson, R. "Class Formation, Politics, and Institutions: Schooling in the United States." *American Journal of Sociology* 92 (1986): 519–48.

Velez, W. "Finishing College: The Effects of College Type." *Sociology of Education* 58 (1985): 191–200.

West, J. *The Postsecondary Vocational Education of 1980 High School Seniors: The Two-Year Associate of Arts Degree*. Report CS 89-610. Washington, D.C.: National Center for Education Statistics (ED), Office of Educational Research and Improvement, 1989.

Winter, G. M. *The Economic Impact of SUNY's Community Colleges on the State of New York*. Albany: State University of New York, Two-Year College Development Center, 1988. (ERIC Document Reproduction Service no. ED 292 493)

Zwerling, L. S. *Second Best: The Crisis of the Community College*. New York: McGraw-Hill, 1976.

CHAPTER 2

THE RHETORIC OF PROFESSIONAL EDUCATORS AND THE DEFINITION OF PUBLIC JUNIOR COLLEGES FROM 1900 TO 1940

JOHN H. FRYE

The place of the two-year college in the American educational system has been problematic from the beginning. Considering the pattern of development in American education from the Colonial period, this is not surprising. Four-year baccalaureate colleges actually emerged before the system of common schools, particularly high schools, developed. The pattern of secondary schools (comprising academies, various types of seminaries, and Latin, commercial, or English high schools) showed various tendencies over two centuries in terms of their organization and relationships with colleges. By 1900, the relationship between public high schools and colleges was fairly well fixed in practice and, for professionals, as an educational model. When the public two-year junior college emerged in the first decade of the twentieth century, it had to be introduced as a novel and intrusive institution.

Much ink was spilled on its definition. Two major appraisals of its role appeared over the first decades of its existence. In one model, it served as an opportunity mechanism allowing access to higher education for those who would otherwise be denied it. The second model arose from a contradictory view that the two-year college was or should be terminal. Because these two views have diametrically different consequences for policies within two-year schools, the failure to close this definitional gap is a remarkable state of affairs.

In the 90-year history of the public two-year college, the relative emphasis on these two roles has varied. The national leadership has emphasized one or the other at various times, while often speaking as if there were no conflict at all in the conceptualization of two-year institutions. In practice, two-year colleges have generally employed both models, so characteristically they provide both transfer programs and occupational programs.

Because of this dichotomy of emphasis for two-year colleges, internal conflicts arise, the public vision of them is muddled, and relations with universities and secondary schools are strained. The failure of the leadership to deal with this issue explicitly and coherently arises from a basic conflict in American society. While we value opportunity and individual advancement, we also value stability and hierarchy. Such values have made it difficult to articulate certain kinds of problems in education, and the two-year college is at the crux of the social mobility/social stability dilemma.

Professional and Public Rhetoric

Professional groups develop cultures and ideologies that serve their needs as a group, while their rhetoric tends to focus on the services provided to their clients. Professional faculty and staff in community colleges share this characteristic with other educators and professional groups in general. The difficulties experienced by contemporary community colleges in clearly conveying their institutional purposes to the public mind can be attributed, in part, to the phenomenon that professional interests and public interests may vary, while the professional rhetoric employed tends to minimize any apparent conflict.

The first 40 years of the two-year college movement illustrates this point clearly. The national leaders of the two-year college movement employed a rhetoric of public service. They also intended to develop the terminal function of the junior college as the dominant one. This was not a popular view with the general public, who supported the junior college as a source of upward mobility through access to higher education. The complex interactions among the national leadership, local presidents and their staffs, and students and their families revealed limits on the influence of the educational elite.

If the junior college is viewed as an example of educational reform, the limits on reform inherent in the American educational system are apparent. With no central control at the national level and little at the state level, the two-year public college emerged with a character of its own, distinct from the vision developed by its national leadership.

While educators may be considered to be a professional level group by virtue of their educational and social standing, they differ from members of other professions in substantive ways. First of all, they provide a public service as opposed to the individual or personal services provided by lawyers, doctors, accountants, and the like. Secondly, educators, as professionals, generally operate under the aegis of a bureaucracy—common school, two-year college, or university—in contrast to more traditional professions. As a result, career paths for educators differ from those for practitioners in professions, and hierarchy is inherent in their functioning. Age grading implies a hierarchy from graded common schools to university. And within levels of institutions, a clear status hierarchy of institutions has been pervasive in the twentieth century. Moreover, managing education has had higher prestige than teaching, with some qualifications made for the university.

Within the broad occupational field of education, "stepladdering" to a higher position (both within institutional levels and between levels) is generally financially rewarding and socially fulfilling. For the two-year colleges arising in the first years of the twentieth century, the issue of hierarchy was particularly acute. This was true both within the profession of education and in its larger social context as related to students. The idea of terminal education promoted by the junior college national leadership related directly to the issue of social hierarchy, and the examination of the literature and data on this issue reveals social conflict within and outside the educational system.

Methodology

There is a vast literature on education in the United States. Books, articles, speeches, annual reports, statistical information, and other materials abound. The sources are not only individual writers but associations, committees, and foundations with an interest in education. From 1930 on, the American Association of Junior Colleges (now the American Association of Community Colleges) has had its own journal, the *Junior College Journal* (which has modified its name several times to the current title, the *Community College Journal*). It included not only standard articles but anecdotal reports, excerpts from speeches and other journals, and news items on individual colleges. The *Journal* was controlled by a small group of prominent national figures in the junior college movement and reflected their point of view (Brick, 1964, pp. 103-109). Comparing the policy promoted by the national leadership in the *Journal* and elsewhere with the actual practices of junior colleges reveals a marked incongruity between leadership rhetoric and the reality of public junior colleges.

Professional Careers and the Leadership of the Junior College Movement

As a new educational institution, the junior college opened new career opportunities for individuals in the early twentieth century. This opportunity arose at a time when numerous new specialized occupations and professions were arising as industry and business expanded and opportunity in agriculture declined (Ben-David, 1963- 64). In general, education grew in size and complexity, particularly in high schools and lower grades. In this period, the university also underwent some expansion and continued to refine its function as a center for research and policy development. University specialists in education became particularly influential. When the American Association of Junior Colleges was founded in 1920, the pattern of organizational leaders forming intimate associations with university specialists was already well established. By 1930, when the first issue of the *Junior College Journal* was published, a leadership elite of association figures and professors of education was already well developed. The same pattern of speaking, writing, and employment brokering, typical of elite figures in other fields, characterized the junior college national leadership as well (Brick, 1964, pp. 24-51).

By 1930, this leadership was almost uniform in promoting the junior college as a two-year terminal institution (Frye, 1992, pp. 48-65). While no leadership figure insisted on excluding the transfer function altogether, national leaders made it clear that the primary purpose of the college should be to educate students who would not go on to earn baccalaureate degrees. This position had to do with their social outlook as well as structural problems they faced within the educational system.

Like most educators, the junior college leadership expressed conservative views and perceived that the structure of society was naturally hierarchical. The university was thought to be an appropriate institution for the education of the national political and social elite. The majority of youth, however, could not aspire to this level and should not weaken the system by flooding into the university. On the other hand, the rising complexity of social and economic life seemed to justify the need for more education than twelve years in order to meet skilled work-force needs and local leadership requirements.

The public junior college usually was associated with a local high school and, as the thirteenth and fourteenth years, was frequently assumed to be an extension of the high school. This position was reinforced by such university leaders as William Rainey Harper, who argued that the freshman and sophomore years were secondary in nature and that the university might be better off without them (Blauch, 1923). Few of the personnel in the junior college movement, either national leaders or local figures, had begun careers in the university. Almost without exception, they arose from secondary or even elementary school careers (Frye, 1992, pp. 89-92).

By promoting junior colleges as terminal institutions, the leadership satisfied not only its ideological perception of evolving American society, but the career aspirations of junior college staff as well. If junior colleges were mainly for university transfer, the numbers of potential students would be small and career opportunities would be limited. On the other hand, as terminal institutions, junior colleges could be designed for most, if not all, high school students and the numbers and resulting career opportunities would be much greater.

The leadership developed a rationale for the terminal program that included the idea that a group of occupations could be labeled the "semiprofessions." The junior college should educate for this level. This category was thought to reside between artisan and professional levels, but a successful definition or even an agreed-upon list of occupations for the semiprofessions was never achieved. The leadership was anxious to avoid the perception that terminal education was trade or vocational training because of the low social standing of such programs. They frequently spoke of terminal cultural courses and education for "social intelligence" (Carnegie Foundation, 1932; Eells, 1941).

The association with secondary education provided numerous positive advantages from the perspective of the leadership. With some distaste, one university leader observed the tendency of junior college leaders to "exploit...numbers," emphasize growth, and promote secondary "attitudes" (Kelly, 1932, p. 93). By connecting with the high school, growth for the junior college appeared inevitable as high school enrollments were growing prodigiously. Moreover, the social outlook of the leadership, with its hierarchial bent, was satisfied with a position in the system that allowed their institution to focus on a middle social level of education and hence confirm their own social views. As one writer observed with considerable candor, it was better for the junior college to be the top of the secondary system rather than the bottom of the higher education system (Proctor, 1932, p. 203). While the potential for growth and the security inherent in the public secondary system were positive attractions for the leadership, strong negative pressures from colleges and universities posed a threat if the transfer functions were emphasized.

Although leaders such as Harper at the University of Chicago theorized about a European model for the university that would cut off the freshman and sophomore years, this idea never got far. President Angell of Yale University talked about this "venerable" proposal and its lip service, but noted that it failed in practice ("President Angell's Opinion," 1933, p. 190; "Retain Lower Division," 1932, p. 384). Lower division students were as financial tv important to universities then as they are now. University leaders, especially baccalaureate college presidents, were hostile to public junior colleges as competitors even for freshman and sophomore students.

Criticism of junior colleges by university leaders was common. They attacked the presumed poor quality of teaching, inadequate facilities, and, in general, the "high-schoolishness" of such an undertaking (Bishop, 1932, p. 325). However, as a place for a different kind of student, one not desired as a student at the university in any case, the junior college had its place.

Robert Sproul, president of the University of California, set out this position with greater clarity and direction than most of his peers. For Sproul, the problem was more critical because of the size of the junior college system in California. In an address, later amplified into an article for the *Junior College Journal*, Sproul argued that the junior college had a place in the educational system, but, in his view, this was to get students to their life's work sooner and not to the university. Junior colleges "masquerading" as four-year schools "are subversive of the best interests of democracy" (1931, p.276). The purpose of the university is to produce the "aristocracy" of democracy. From the junior colleges should come not "agricultural scientists" but "farmers," not engineers but "skilled mechanics." Producing "non-commissioned officers in the great adventure of modern business" should be the junior college' chief goal (p.278).

In the course of his article, Sproul quoted several national leaders of the junior college movement to support his position. In fact, his statements reflect the purposes and goals of the national leadership. The reservations and criticisms of university leaders were one of the reasons the national junior college leadership figures supported the terminal program. Many junior college leadership figures were university professors. In addition, university presidents and staff were highly influential with state legislators. In any case, the relationship between the national leadership of junior colleges and universities was intimate. Making enemies of universities would have been dangerous institutionally, and the personal careers of junior college leaders could have been injured by animosity from figures so powerful.

The leadership proposal to emphasize terminal education for the junior college appeared to solve the problem of place for the junior college in the educational system. It appeared to ensure large-scale and long-term growth and as a result create significant career opportunities for professionals in the field. The social function of the institution was explained in terms of semiprofessional occupations, social efficiency, and good citizenship. University opposition was at least muted by this position, and it was argued that the leadership position was based on a carefully thought out, planned program relating the junior college to the overall scheme of education in America.

The difficulty with the leadership's proposed program was that no one followed it. Students ignored terminal programs. The public was indifferent to the concept. Semiprofessions never achieved meaningful recognition as categories of occupations in the larger world. Students enrolled in transfer programs in consistent majorities and transferred to universities regardless of whether their programs were terminal or transfer by design. Local presidents might pay lip service to the idea of terminal education, but they ignored it in practice and did everything in their power to distance themselves and their institutions from high school and secondary education (Frye, 1992, pp. 87-95).

After 1940, the rhetoric of semiprofessions, social efficiency, education for life, and other progressive education terminology began to disappear from the junior college literature. With the changes in higher education after World War II, a different approach and rhetoric came to dominate the junior college literature.

Professional Staff in the Local Colleges and Popular Aspirations

In Sproul's article, as noted earlier, he had cause to observe the extreme sensitivity of junior college staff to criticism from university figures. They became "enraged," he said, at the "mildest criticism" (Sproul, 1931, p. 274). The literature is filled with evidence that faculty and staff at local junior colleges were not interested in programs of terminal education, if they were not actively hostile to them. Local presidents and staff actively sought physical and administrative separation from high schools, and dreaded possible unification into high school extension systems (Bailey, 1936). It is not surprising that local faculty and staff wished to associate themselves and their institutions with the higher status of universities and baccalaureate colleges rather than with secondary schools. One wag observed the secret desire of every high school principal to be known as a (junior) college president and every high school teacher to be known as a "college" professor (Holiday, 1929, p. 887). The sensitivity to criticism, rejection of the terminal emphasis, and the association with secondary schools by local staff demonstrate the concerns they had with social and professional status.

The literature is replete with grousing and complaints from the national leadership that progress was not being made with regard to the terminal function of the junior college (Douglass, 1928; Medsker, 1938; Potts, 1935). Educators who dealt with the public in organizing junior colleges gave little attention to terminal education. Public relations staff members emphasized attracting the best students, and consultants who helped to organize new colleges ignored the terminal concept almost entirely (O'Brien, 1928; Vande Bogart, 1932).

The difference between leadership rhetoric and local junior colleges' catalogs on the subject of terminal education is likewise striking. Catalogs intended for public consumption invariably emphasized the first two years of university work over terminal education. The terminal function was often ignored in catalogs (Koos, 1921).

The geographic distribution of public junior colleges also contradicted the premise of those promoting terminal education. Before 1940, public junior colleges were largely restricted to states in the Mississippi Valley, Texas, and California. They clearly served primarily a university transfer function. Urban eastern states, where semi-professional courses might have been expected to have their greatest appeal, generally did not establish two-year public colleges until well after World War II (Frye, 1992, pp. 74-80).

Students perceived the junior college as representing the first two years of higher education. Even when enrolled in "terminal" programs, students seemed to have no understanding of the concept, intended to transfer, and indeed did transfer in substantial numbers (Frye, 1992, pp. 104-109). The evidence makes it clear that the institution offered at least the hope of upward social mobility. In all the voluminous literature produced by the leadership, nowhere was evidence produced that the general public endorsed or accepted the idea that the junior college should emphasize educational preparation for second-level social and occupational positions ("Objectives...," 1935). In this respect, the terminal education program was related conceptually to the issue of tracking in the high school, and the issue reflected many of the attendant difficulties associated with tracking in terms of the potential for parental opposition. Hence, junior college movement leaders ignored terminal education when promoting local colleges to local audiences, but they employed the concept in literature aimed at professional educators.

Local junior college faculty and staff rejected the terminal emphasis, as did students, parents, and local citizens in general. An emphasis on terminal education lowered the status of local faculty and staff. It undoubtedly would have been difficult for local presidents to promote their colleges had they emphasized the terminal, two-year, secondary nature of their offerings as advocated by the national leadership. The gap described here between leadership theory and local practice illustrates both the underlying social conflict within a profession that was itself stratified but theoretically had "democratic" goals. The rhetoric of the national leadership could not be sustained in this environment. Whether the ideology that underlay this rhetoric was modified also is not so clear. But, after World War II, the rhetoric of terminal education was gradually replaced by a guidance-centered student development model. Numerous critics have argued that the two-year college continues to track students out of higher education, which was the explicit goal of the national leadership before 1940 (Astin, 1977; Brint & Karabel, 1989: Pincus, 1980).

Impact/Conclusion

The definition of the two-year public college is not much clearer today than it was before 1940. The debate over its function and success continues. The large portion of culturally diverse, nontraditional students who begin their postsecondary education in the community college has made this debate even more acute. The commitment to equality and access (that is, social mobility) continues to frustrate leaders and the public.

The solution of the national leadership before 1940, which accepted social inequality and proposed that the junior college serve a stratification function, was as unacceptable then as it is now. On balance, it would appear that the leadership goal of terminal education had rather little effect on the course of junior college development.

Without a centralized national structure, individual two-year colleges continued to verbalize the transfer and social opportunity functions popular on the local level. In American society, where social stratification is accepted but opportunity is demanded, the denouement of the conflict between national leadership theory and local experience exemplifies a mechanism for handling socially charged questions. The professional group modified its rhetoric to accommodate popular values.

The gap between professional and popular rhetoric and ideologies can result in lost opportunities, debilitating confusion, and misdirection on both local and national levels. In the case considered here, the impact of the conflict appears limited except for the loss of opportunity that a different approach might have offered, but this cannot be measured. To a degree, national junior college leaders have achieved their goal of maintaining credibility with universities by promoting terminal education, while local developments have satisfied local demands for access to higher education in a more traditional frame of reference. The conflict illustrated here may be a paradigm for the failures and successes of general educational reform in the United States. The distance between professional rhetoric and local concern is a factor that needs to be evaluated in relationship to educational change.

References

Astin, Alexander. (1977). *Four critical years: effects of college on beliefs, attitudes and knowledge*. San Francisco: Jossey-Bass.

Bailey, Floyd P. (1936). Adaption to changing community needs. *Junior College Journal, 6*, 230–223.

Ben-David, Joseph. (1963-64). Professions in the class system of present day societies. *Current Sociology, 12*, 318–325.

Bishop, Ralph T. (1932). Junior college: Objections and dangers. *Junior College Journal, 2*, 318–325.

Blauch, L.E. (1923). Reorganization on European lines appears Imminent. *School Life, 9*, 77–79.

Brick, Michael. (1964). *Forum and focus of the junior college movement: The American Association of Junior Colleges*. New York: Teacher's College.

Brint, Steven and Karabel, Jerome. (1989). *The diverted dream: Community colleges and the promise of educational opportunity in America, 1990-1985*. New York: Oxford University Press.

Carnegie Foundation for the Advancement of Teaching. (1932). *State of higher education in California*. Sacramento: State of California.

Douglass, Aurbrey A. (1928). Curriculum determinants in the junior college. *California Quarterly of Secondary Education, 4*, 437–44.

Dr. Kelly speaks. (1932). *Junior College Journal, 3*, 93.

Eells, W.C. (1941). *Why junior college terminal education*. Washington, DC: American Association of Junior Colleges.

Frye, John H. (1992). *The vision of the public junior college, 1900-1940: Professional goals and popular aspirations*. New York: Greenwood Press.

Holiday, Carl. (1929). This junior college movement. *School and Society, 3*, 887-888.

Koos, Leonard. (1921). Current conceptions of the special purposes of the junior college. *School Review, 29*, 520–529.

Medsker, Leland. (1938). Chicago faces the issue on terminal courses. *Junior College Journal, 9*, 109.

Objectives in Duluth. (1935). *Junior College Journal, 6,* 43.

O'Brien, F.P. (1928). Conditions which justify establishing a junior college. *School Review, 34,* 128–137.

Pincus, Fred L. (1980). The false promises of community colleges, class conflict and vocational education. *Harvard Educational, 50,* 332–361.

Potts, Alfred, II. (1935). Selection of students for terminal courses. *Junior College Journal, 5,* 426.

President Angell's Opinion. (1933). *Junior College Journal, 3,* 190.

Proctor, William. (1932). Time to take account of stock (editorial). *Junior College Journal, 2,* 303.

Retain lower division. (1932). *Junior College Journal, 2,* 384.

Sproul, Robert Gordon. (1931). Certain aspects of the junior college. *Junior College Journal, 1,* 274–280.

Vande Bogart, G.H. (1932). Public relations of the junior college. *Junior College Journal, 2,* 357–395.

John H. Frye teaches history at Triton College, River Grove, Illinois.

CHAPTER 3

REMEMBERING RAYMOND J. YOUNG AND THE GRASS-ROOTS DEVELOPMENT OF COMMUNITY COLLEGES FROM 1950 TO 1976

STEPHEN G. KATSINAS
UNIVERSITY OF ALABAMA

Raymond J. Young (1923–2007) played a key role in the post–World War II development of community colleges in Illinois, Michigan, Ohio, and elsewhere. This article describes his scholarly and professional contributions in developing "bottom-up," grassroots citizen's participatory studies that led to the establishment of 60 community colleges in 33 states between 1955 and 1976.

Keywords: community college establishment, community college governance, citizen's studies

This article reviews the scholarly and professional contributions of Raymond J. Young (1923–2007) to the field of community college education. Young and community colleges are inextricably intertwined, as he observed when speaking to students from 24 doctoral programs at the 1994 graduate student seminar of the Council for the Study of Community Colleges:

> In my career I've probably written as many words about community colleges as anybody else, but much of my work was not formally published. Most of the 50-plus participatory studies I've been involved in resulted in 300-page documents, done in such a fashion as to meet the specific needs of the situation. I was out in the field making a difference. (Wright & Katsinas, 1994, p. 3)

Raymond J. Young *was* out in the field, attempting to make a difference. A review of newspaper clippings in his personal files after his death in February 2007, along with an examination of the unpublished interviews I conducted with him, reveal that he helped to establish or significantly expand some 60 two-year colleges by directing or codirecting citizen's participatory studies that gauged the demand for community college services in specific geographic areas (counties, metropolitan areas, and regions). These 60 colleges are located in 19 states; just more than half (33) are located in Illinois, Michigan, and Ohio. According to data provided by the Carnegie Foundation for the Advancement of Teaching (2007), the combined unduplicated headcount enrollment of these 60 colleges in 2003-2004 was in excess of 400,000 students. In addition, Young held academic positions at five universities as well as a professional position in the private sector.

A review of his scholarly writings reveals four phases in his long career. The first occurred from 1947 to 1955, when he completed his graduate degrees and subsequently held appointments at Oklahoma State University (1950 to 1953) and the University of Oklahoma (1953 to 1955). At this time, few programs in higher education existed, and early junior college scholars, including Young, regularly taught in secondary education administration programs (Young, 2002). Young's formal education and extensive scholarly and professional field work in both secondary education and junior colleges prepared him for the second phase of his career, from 1955 to 1976. At the Universities of

Illinois (1955 to 1958) and Michigan (1958 tp 1967), and then as an educational consultant with Arthur D. Little, Inc. (1968 to 1976), he led and wrote the citizen's participatory studies mentioned above. This was followed by a fruitful third period at Washington State University (1976 to 1986), when his work on the establishment of community colleges was largely concluded and when his scholarship focused on a variety of issues, including reading programs in schools (Young, 1987–1988, 1988), community college trustees (Young & Thompson,1982), community education programs (Young & Jones, 1982), occupational education at community colleges (Thompson & Young, 1990), and summer-school practices at colleges and universities (Young, 1989a, 1989b, 1989c; Young & McDougall, 1982, 1985, 1987, 1988, 1991). While at Washington State University, Young also reflected on his experience as both a buyer and seller of consultative services (Young, 1982), examining such issues as community needs surveys (Young, 1985–1986), community opinion cluster surveys (Young, 1986a), and community needs in rural areas (Young, 1986b). The final and fourth period of his professional life entailed an active retirement, during which he published a number of reflection pieces on the postwar era of community college establishment, attended annual conferences of the Council for the Study of Community Colleges (an organization he helped to establish), and served as a contributing editor for the *Community College Journal of Research and Practice* until his death in 2007.

This essay focuses on Young's experiences during the first two phases of his career, examining the formative experiences that shaped his thinking about community colleges and detailing his subsequent approach to grass-roots field work on citizen's participatory studies. At a time when community colleges are taken for granted as a well-established sector of American higher education, examining Young's career during the growth years of the community college movement offers an important reminder of the work that was undertaken at the local and state levels to create this higher education sector and enhance and extend opportunities for postsecondary education.

Formative Experiences in Kansas, Colorado, and Oklahoma, 1947 to 1955

After service in World War II, during which his Army unit liberated a Nazi death camp, Young used his GI Bill education benefits to complete his formal education. He earned his associate's degree at Iola Junior College (now Allen County Community College) and his bachelor's (1948) and master's (1949) degrees at Kansas State Teachers College–Pittsburg (KSTC-P), where his thesis examined practices in secondary school libraries in eight Kansas school districts (Young, 1949), a subject of interest 35 years later (Young & Berger, 1983).

While at KSTC-P, Young took a course titled "The Junior College" from William A. Black, an early junior college scholar. It is likely that he assisted Black in organizing a conference on junior colleges at which Harl Douglas, Dean of the College of Education at the University of Colorado, was a featured speaker. Young would soon earn his doctorate at Colorado and subsequently assume the position of assistant professor of secondary education at Oklahoma A&M College (now Oklahoma State University) in the fall of 1950. A 1952 article, "How Well Do We Teach?" in *The Journal of Teacher Education* lists his title there as "Coordinator of Student Teaching" (Young, 1952a, p. 214). Just as junior colleges in the period from 1930 to 1950 grew from secondary schools, so too did university level programs related to junior college education flow from school leadership preparation programs. Young would have significant teaching, research, and service activities related to elementary and secondary education until 1958, when he joined the newly established Center for the Study of Higher and Postsecondary Education at the University of Michigan, and could focus solely on community college issues.

Young's Dissertation and Its Influence

Young's 1950 doctoral dissertation, *An Analysis and Evaluation of General Legislation Pertaining to Public Junior Colleges*, is seminal to understanding his later efforts to start junior colleges. Endorsed by the Research Committee of the American Association of Junior Colleges (AAJC; Young, 2002), it begins with a review of demographic, economic, social, technological, and political data from the U.S. Bureau of the Census, the federal National Economic Bureau, and other sources. From this analysis, which foreshadowed his citizen's participation studies, Young concluded that prospects for the future development of junior colleges were bright. He cited AAJC data to show the tremendous growth in the three preceding decades, from 74 junior colleges in 1915 to 645 in 1950, and he noted that the rise of public junior colleges was evident: By 1948-1949, when the number of public junior colleges exceeded the number of private junior colleges for the first time, enrollment at public junior colleges averaged 1,063 students per institution, compared to 346 at the private junior colleges (Young, 1950). The positive trends were unmistakable.

Young's dissertation then analyzed the general legislative provisions for public junior colleges in all 26 of the 48 states that had them as of January 1950 (Young, 1950). In all but 4 of these states—California, Mississippi, New York, and Texas—public junior colleges were legally a part of the secondary school systems. Most were organized and governed by local school districts, employing the 6-4-4 curriculum espoused by Koos (1924). The analysis of general legislative provisions for public junior colleges in the 26 states was used to develop a comprehensive survey that assessed attitudes of respondents on the following issues: (a) appropriate requirements for establishing junior colleges; (b) procedures used to legally form junior colleges and to create colleges within a single jurisdiction (county or school district); (c) policies for creating regional junior college districts across jurisdictions, be they counties or school districts; (d) technical issues regarding the elections and petitions required to establish junior colleges; (e) support for buildings and equipment; (f) faculty issues, especially certifications; (g) college supervision, governance, and control; (h) the role of the state in oversight, inspection, and accreditation; (i) admission and graduation policies; (j) finance issues, including state aid, county and district taxation, tuition and fees, and transportation; (k) curriculum; and (l) policies and procedures to disband or discontinue junior colleges. Two groups were surveyed: (a) deans, presidents, or school superintendents from the 269 member public junior colleges of the AAJC, of which 170 (62%) responded; and (b) a jury of experts that included George F. Zook, C. C. Colvert, Jesse P. Bogue, S. V. Martorana, L. V. Koos, James W. Reynolds, John W. Harbeson, Galen Jones, and Charles Simms (Young, 1950). Reflecting on the superintendents' responses decades later, Young wrote that in "some communities the junior college was the object of community pride and joy, and in others, monies were perceived as being diverted from the lower levels to support the junior college" (Young, 2002, p. 560).

Young's dissertation thoroughly familiarized him with state junior college enabling legislation and with the general status of junior colleges in the United States at that time. It is interesting to note that in his first *Junior College Journal* article, in 1951, although he was not yet ready to call for the formal separation of public junior colleges from school districts, he observed that the

> signs of the times point unerringly toward a greater need for attention to the junior colleges as an extension of secondary education and its promise for aiding in the solution of social and educational problems of the greatest magnitude. (Young, 1951a, p. 446)

He found a haphazard state of affairs in which "each section of the United States [was] groping its way to general legislative enactments that provide for the public junior college" (Young, 1951a, p. 446). Still, he noted, some significant trends could be observed, concluding,

> Public junior colleges should be legally a part of the public school system, and the state department of education should exercise the same general supervision and inspection over them as it does over the other units of the public school district. (Young, 1951a, p. 450)

This call for state oversight was, he noted years later, "virtually unanimous" among experts in the field (Young, 2002, p. 569), yet this was a time when nearly half the states lacked both junior college enabling legislation and state financial support for the students attending junior colleges. Young argued for state laws that would help in "(1) enlarging junior college districts and (2) unifying levels of support and control" (Young, 1951b, p. 72). He also called for laws that would "include provisions enabling . . . two or more contiguous counties or districts, whether in the same county or not, to cooperate in establishing a junior college" (Young, 1951b, p. 72).

Young reported that 8 of the 20 states in the North Central Association of Colleges and Secondary Schools had no general legislative provisions at all concerning junior colleges (Young, 1952b), and he predicted that expanding demands for higher education made "improved types of legal enactments . . . more critical" (Young, 1952b, p. 293).

Young's "bottom-up" philosophical approach to establishing new junior colleges had also been largely formed, emphasizing local elections to show support after well-planned research studies of area needs had been conducted. To be successful, he argued,

> the public junior college must have the support of the people within its immediate area. . . . A new district should be established by vote in every case. . . . State law should require a survey to be made under the auspices of the state department of education or state board of education to determine the need, ability, facilities, and prospective attendance of the proposed district or districts. . . . A scientific state education survey concerning post high school education needs of youth and adults and out-of-school youth should be made by competent impartial committee members of the state who know junior colleges. (Young, 1951b, p. 74)

In another 1951 article published in *The School Review*, Young noted that the

> local school board should administer and exercise general supervision over the junior college through the superintendent of schools, or the principal of the high school, or both, under the jurisdiction of the state superintendent of education or state board of education. (Young, 1951c, p. 487)

He also offered this distinction between junior and community colleges: "If a junior college is a 'community college,' then the local patrons, governing board, and community should be free, within limits, to exercise control and supervision of the local junior college" (Young, 1951c, p 488).

An Emphasis on Community Involvement

Young's continuing thinking about the formation of local educational institutions is evident in *The School and the Community: Educational and Public Relations*, which he coedited with J. E. Grinnell of Indiana State Teacher's College in 1955. The five chapters he wrote included two (Chapters 1 and 5) that were quite relevant to his future field work with community leaders in establishing and expanding junior colleges. Young's philosophy can be observed in the first chapter, "The Problem of School and Community Relationships":

> The school as a social institution was developed and maintained to provide educative experiences delegated to it by society. As such, it has no vested interests. Inasmuch as an institution in a democracy should be maintained to serve the ends of man individually and collectively, the school, as a social institution, should, in so far as it can, contribute leadership in effective desired changes consistent with the democratic philosophy. The obvious conclusion seems to be that the *most desirable situation results when representative members of society, including school personnel, work cooperatively to define the social goals of education and to study their application to school work*. The democratic group process, based on interaction and widespread participation and involvement, the proper use of planning techniques and group discussion techniques, is the process by which social goals are most appropriately defined. (Young, 1955a, p. 5)

If one substitutes "junior college" for "school" in the above quotation, Young's philosophy of good college leadership can be observed. He decried the "ivory tower approach" to school leadership in which "'administrators who follow the line of least resistance' are afraid of the democratic approach to solving problems" (Young, 1955a, p. 16). He went on to argue:

> In such communities, contacts between the school and community have consisted largely of required official reports, attractive eye-catchers, such as slogans and well-staged athletic events, and commencements designed to secure complacency or support. There is an absence of community participation, and public confidence has been maintained through low taxes, a quiescent attitude, and a hope that nothing will happen to disturb the status quo. The athletic contests and other display activities designed to direct public attention away from the educational program promote community indifference to the larger and more satisfying objectives for which public education exists. (Young, 1955a, pp. 16-17)

Chapter 5, "Unofficial Influences on the Schools," is also revealing in light of Young's subsequent field work with noneducators to establish junior colleges. It is clear that he gained much from the extensive literature review he wrote for this chapter. He categorized "unofficial local community influences" and "unofficial larger community influences," with the former category including local professional education groups and associations, patriotic organizations, individual laymen, enthusiasts for a cause, religious organizations, local professional and vocational groups, and local business and industry. Local professional education associations, he maintained,

> can provide genuine leadership in the formulation of school policies and programs [by] training community leadership . . . , analyzing issues . . . , and collecting or preparing data. . . . Patriotic organizations can serve as members of community planning councils and be involved in lay discussion meetings on school program planning. (Young, 1955b, p. 90)

Young noted that although educators do not feel that they are "expert" enough to comment on banking, auto mechanics, dentistry, or legal issues, professionals outside of the field of education often feel that they possess the expertise needed to comment on educational issues. Periodic "town hall" meetings are a good way to deal with these individuals, he argued (Young, 1955b, p. 91). "Enthusiasts for a cause,"Young continued, are "often labeled 'cranks,' 'crackpots,' or 'rabble-rousers,' who often distribute handbills, pamphlets, and write strongly worded letters to the newspaper editor or school superintendent" (Young, 1955b, p. 91). Young suggested that the best approach may be "to invite them, subsequent to an audience with the school superintendent, to present views at a regular school board meeting . . . , [a procedure] that can be characterized by 'attentive listening,' so that these individuals can fulfill their primary wish 'to be heard'" (Young, 1955b, p. 91). In his future work in local communities, Young would deliberately involve, wherever possible, potential critics of junior college formation in his citizen's participatory studies (Wright & Katsinas, 1994).

   In short, Young passionately believed that public schools and community colleges existed to promote "bottom-up" participatory democracy and regional economic development. He had personally fought in a war against dictatorship, and, in his view, educational institutions should not represent the views of any narrow group. Educational leaders thus needed practical skills to broadly involve diverse people and interests in the democratic process of creating and sustaining institutions of public education. Young noted the need to positively channel the involvement of professional groups:

> Especially to be avoided are the efforts of such a group as the local medical association to influence instruction relative to the social and political aspects of medical service. . . . Perhaps the best way to deal with the influences . . . is to put them to work in school initiated committees. (Young, 1955b, pp. 91-92)

Young (1955b, p. 92) believed that communities are "vitally influenced by local business and industry," which are "the heaviest sustainers of payrolls and employment opportunities, [and] which youth obviously would care greatly about." The recognition that educational institutions should aspire to more than this function (i.e., preparing individuals for employment in large businesses) led him to suggest a careful inventory of community assets that involved school and business groups, and that clearly focused on the educational heritage of a community, to ensure that the community would value its schools over time.

   Young (1955b) also argued that many educators were unaware of unofficial influences on the state and national levels. He listed national or regional professional education associations, textbook publishing companies, production and distributing corporations, patriotic organizations, colleges and universities, examination systems, professional journals and magazines for laymen, pressures for contest participation, accrediting groups, and widespread attacks on modern education. His appreciation of the power of these unofficial influences was acute:

> In many instances, the curriculum is essentially prescribed by what is in the textbooks. Almost complete reliance on the textbook is still a common practice by thousands of teachers. Inadvertently, then, the textbooks become a dominating influence. America's textbook companies are aware of their strategic roles. (Young, 1955b, p. 93)

Young objected to the negative influence of the examination systems in New York, where

> entire classes are subjected to the Regents' examinations, often without regard to the appropriateness for individual pupils concerned. In many communities, teachers who question these demonstrations are looked upon with suspicion by laymen and occasionally school administrators as well. The first accusation is that the teacher is lowering standards or that he is afraid to let the pupils show in this

way what he has taught them. . . . If newly appointed teachers wish to be reappointed . . . , the safest way does not include a challenge to the local examination system. (Young, 1955b, p. 95)

School Curriculum Improvement in Oklahoma

Finally, Young's formative work in Oklahoma included leadership of the statewide Oklahoma Secondary School Curriculum Improvement Commission (Oklahoma Secondary School Curriculum Improvement Commission and Oklahoma State Department of Education, 1953; Young 1955c). Beginning in 1953, Young directed or commissioned 10 studies of Oklahoma's educational problems covering the following issues: (a) holding power (i.e., retention) of secondary school youth; (b) follow-up studies of graduates and nongraduates; (c) youth needs and problems; (d) faculty, student, and lay person's beliefs; (e) participation in extracurricular activities; (f) community needs and characteristics; (g) incidental expenses involved in school attendance; (h) evaluation of instructional programs; (i) guides to assist in studies; and (j) other projects. These studies motivated him to learn good methodological approaches for researching the first three items, which later helped him assess community needs in the citizen's participatory studies he would soon direct. His perspectives on items d and f, and his approach to item h, were later seen in how he used economic, demographic, and sociological data to assess the need for new junior colleges (Young, 1955c).

The initial phase of Young's career thus prepared him well for the work that was to come in establishing junior and community colleges. Work on his UNC dissertation familiarized him with general enabling law for junior colleges and with the leading scholars in the field. His direction of statewide studies in Oklahoma on key secondary school issues such as finance, organization, educational programs, and governance attracted the interest of educators at the University of Illinois. He would draw on all of these experiences as his career unfolded.

Young and Community College Establishment and Expansion, 1955 to 1976

While at the University of Illinois (1955 to 1958) and subsequently as a professor at the University of Michigan (1958 to 1969) and as an educational consultant at Arthur D. Little, Inc. (1968 to 1976), Young made notable contributions during the "baby-boom" growth era of American higher education. His work can be divided into three distinct yet interrelated strains: community college establishment, leadership development, and analysis and study of the role of community colleges in community services.

Community College Establishment in Illinois

Young's work related to secondary school issues centered on expanding postsecondary educational opportunities for high school youths. As acting coordinator of research for *The Caldron*, the publication of the Illinois Council on Educational Administration (ICEA), an organization composed entirely of K–12 educators, he wrote an article titled, "Is there educational waste of Illinois human resources?" The article (Young, 1957c) reported data for all 102 Illinois counties on the numbers of public and private high school graduates enrolling in higher education, the proportion of high-ability Illinois youths with plans to attend college, and adult educational attainment levels. Young found a "low desire among high ability youth" to enroll in college, resulting in low rates of college attendance. He added, "If low desire is associated with low economic conditions, the implication would be for greater exploration of scholarships, loans, or part-time job opportunities on college campuses" (Young, 1957c, p. 31).

In an interview I conducted with him 44 years later, Young recalled that in 1955 all 16 Illinois public junior colleges were housed in high schools, and their deans were an assortment of high school administrators, football coaches, and guidance counselors. Illinois did not have a centralized K–12 system on which 2-year colleges could build, and few of the colleges were accredited (Krebs,

Katsinas, & Johnson, 1999). Less than half of the junior colleges in the region covered by the North Central Association (NCA) of Colleges and Schools were accredited, leading Young to chair the Subcommittee on Junior College Problems of the NCA Committee on Research and Service. The report he authored on behalf of the subcommittee called for an "expanded definition of 'community'" that moved beyond a single school district to a larger geographical region that could more adequately fund expensive postsecondary occupational curricula and an enlarged, democratizing transfer function (Young, 1962b, p. 327). Young's work with the NCA included research and training sessions for new junior college administrators and trustees that began in 1957 (Young, 1996). Gaining accreditation as colleges was important in the process of separating community colleges from secondary schools.

Young's initial Illinois studies in 1955 recommended the separation of both Thornton Junior College (Harvey, Illinois) and Belleville Area Junior College (Belleville, Illinois) from their local high school districts. He worked directly with citizens' groups in both areas to develop feasibility studies for new junior colleges (Krebs et.al, 1999). In an address to the fall 1955 meeting of the Illinois Junior College Association,Young for the first time recommended separation throughout the state, a suggestion that

> was not well received. . . . Many influential members of the group had at stake both their professional employment and matters of personal status in the communities they served. Additionally, the junior colleges had provided the secondary districts with a supplemental revenue stream that generated profits far beyond the costs associated with operation of the two-year programs. (Krebs et al., 1999, p. 25)

Young also recommended sound planning in the establishment of separate junior colleges, a theme emphasized by leading experts at the time, including L. V. Koos, S. V. Martorana, and James Wattenbarger (Young, 2002). Writing in 1996, Young recalled that up until the mid-1950s, 2-year college establishment had been

> erratic, haphazard, and largely without plan. College establishment was subject to the special economic and altruistic motives of local communities, the political whims of legislators, and the missionary work of a few public university personnel. . . . Legislators in a few states had foreseen the possibility that too many financially and educationally inefficient two-year colleges might be established if local community aspirations guided the burgeoning two-year college movement. But with the exception of California, local colleges were established in the absence of an overall plan for higher education or two-year college development. (Young, 1996, pp. 5-6).

On March 3, 1956, Young was invited by the superintendent of Wood River, Illinois, to a meeting with school leaders and board members to discuss the possibility of a new public junior college. No institutions of public higher education existed on the Illinois side of the Mississippi River across from St. Louis; the nearest were nearly two hours away—Centralia Junior College and Southern Illinois University. Illinois law at that time permitted junior college establishment if the school district had obtained permission from the state superintendent of public instruction, if the district served a population of at least 10,000, and if the local citizenry had approved creating the college in an election (Young, 2002). The Wood River school leaders were advised that "there should be a study of the need for programs, potential enrollments, facility requirements, and cost of operation, and capital requirements" prior to asking taxpayers in an election to fund the college (Young, 2002, p. 561). Young also advised that the nearby town of Alton be included, so that the minimum population requirement would be met (Young, 2002).

As Young recalled in 2002, he then contacted university personnel, including L.V. Koos, Hugh Stickler, Ralph Fields, and S.V. Martorana, and a few superintendents from large districts, to see if any comprehensive studies to assess program and community needs had been completed; none were found. Ralph Berdie had assessed the educational intentions and occupational aspirations of Minnesota high school juniors and seniors, and Harold Reese had studied methods of projecting junior college enrollments in his Pennsylvania State University doctoral dissertation; both had created instruments that Young would borrow and modify (Young, 2002). E. K. Fretwell's dissertation, published by Teacher's College Press in 1954 as the book *Founding Public Junior Colleges: Local Initiative in Six Communities*, suggested specific criteria by which new colleges should be established. Young concluded that "no one in the United States was known to have previously conducted a comprehensive citizen's participatory study for the establishment of a public junior college" (Young, 2002, p. 561).

Young would evaluate all these criteria scientifically in his first citizen's participatory study, which helped the Illinois communities of Wood River and Alton assess the potential "draw" for a new college (Young, 1957a). On September 20, 1956, a meeting was held in Wood River at which the various subcommittees were charged with their assignments, and the study was completed the following spring. The very public nature of Young's bottom-up planning studies, which were part of a process under Illinois law that required an election authorizing the establishment of a locally governed community college district and a subsequent election to pass a tax levy for the new college, made them easy targets for schoolmen and university leaders with other agendas. His work in Wood River was spoiled when "the president of a major state university" (Southern Illinois University President Delyte W. Morris) spoke to community leaders shortly before the authorizing election and announced the establishment of a new branch campus (Young, 2002, p. 562). The authorizing election was narrowly lost (Young, 2002) despite Young's argument that the presence of junior colleges and universities in the same community would help enrollments at both (Wright & Katsinas, 1994). Nearly two decades later, Lewis and Clark College, today a leading transfer student feeder to Southern Illinois University at Edwardsville, was established.

Despite this defeat, important lessons were learned. First, data gathering instruments needed to assess if Fretwell's college establishment criteria had been met were field tested (Young, 2002). Second, Young discovered that people would drive about as far to obtain a community college education as they would to purchase a durable good, such as a washing machine, refrigerator, or automobile (Wright & Katsinas, 1994). This finding—some five decades before rural development experts were writing about the "new regionalism" for rural development—led him to propose a regional delivery model for new junior colleges across rural downstate Illinois that was based on the establishment of junior college districts serving multiple counties or school districts (Young, 1957b). Third, Young gained an understanding of the importance of citizen perceptions. He noted:

> In those days of the late 1950s and early 1960s, it was necessary to persuade and convince citizens in an area that they needed a two-year college if they were to vote favorably for one. The best method to neutralize dissent and of persuasion was the involvement approach to determining if conditions supported the notion of a new public college in their midst, particularly if an election to create the institution and tax themselves was needed. (Young, 2002, p. 562)

The lessons learned in Wood River would be quickly applied elsewhere. By 1957, Young had helped establish new colleges in Freeport (Highland Community College) and Canton (Spoon River Community College; Krebs et al., 1999; Young, 2002). His focus soon shifted to the state level, as the coming baby-boom generation of college students would overwhelm the haphazard planning that had occurred to date. This is reflected in a November 1961 speech to the Annual Conference on Higher Education in Michigan, in which he called attention to the need to educate many more Americans (Young, 1961b). He made the same argument in a 1962 article in *College and University*:

> The extent to which youth are not *all* being educated to a level of which they are capable through an educational program appropriate to both their interests and the demands of society is the extent to which there is loss of human potential. Some study groups have declared that approximately half the nation's youth could pursue successfully at least two years of post-high school education, and over a third could profitably complete a degree program. The facts show that only 35-40 per cent of youth graduating from high school are taking advantage of further education. Only about half of the top quarter in academic ability are receiving further education. The problem is magnified when one realizes that in some communities no more than ten per cent of the high school graduates pursue further education. (Young, 1962a, p. 62)

Financial considerations were the top reason high school graduates did not attend, Young argued, followed by the influences of the parents and the influences of peers (Young, 1962a). Institutions needed to conduct follow-up studies of these and other related issues (Young, 1961a; Young, 1962b). These same reasons for not attending college sound all too familiar today.

In 1957, one of Young's seminal works appeared—a report titled "The Community-Junior College" (Young, 1957b), published as Chapter 7 of the 1957 report of the Illinois Commission on Higher Education, *Illinois Looks to the Future in Higher Education* (Illinois Commission on Higher Education, 1957). Based on his rigorous analysis of demographic data, this chapter included two maps of Illinois, one with the 16 municipally controlled junior colleges that then existed and a second with potential locations for new junior colleges (Young, 1957b). To avoid university opposition, downstate cities that hosted universities, including Champaign–Urbana (University of Illinois), Bloomington–Normal (Illinois State University), and Carbondale (Southern Illinois University) were deliberately excluded, despite the fact that Young—even at this time—believed these communities needed junior colleges (Krebs et al., 1999; Young, 2002). With few exceptions, today's current map of Illinois's community colleges looks remarkably similar to the map proposed by Young in 1957. Fifty years later, the annual report cards issued by the National Center for Public Policy and Higher Education consistently award Illinois the grade of A for participation, a measure based on the opportunities young adults have for college and on the enrollment of both young adults and working-age adults in college (National Center for Public Policy and Higher Education, n.d., p. 18).

The Commission proposed a comprehensive, accessible statewide network of community colleges for the Land of Lincoln. Drawing heavily on Young's analysis of the minimum number of students (1,000) needed to offer a comprehensive program, the Commission recommended 10 potential locations for new junior colleges under the then-current $100-per-student state aid funding formula. These locations were Decatur, East St. Louis, Maywood, Peoria, Quincy, Rockford, Skokie, Waukegan, Winnetka, and Wood River. If the formula could be raised to $200 per student, an additional 11 cities could be considered as potential locations for junior colleges: Aurora, Blue Island, Chicago Heights, Sterling, Downers Grove, Elmwood Park, Evergreen Park, Freeport, Galesburg, Kankakee, and Wheaton (Illinois Commission on Higher Education, 1957, p. 18). Young, through his statewide planning in Illinois, was the first to propose that a minimum enrollment of 1,000 students was needed to establish a junior college. Young reflected on this in 2002:

> Much lower levels, in the neighborhood of 200 and 300 students, had been previously advocated by Koos, Eells, and others. In . . . 1958, S.V. Martorana, who had recently joined the U.S. Office of Education, was selected to conduct the two-year college portion of a comprehensive statewide study of higher education in Michigan. . . . Martorana telephoned [me] to check on the criteria used in . . . Illinois . . . and agreed that a 1,000 minimum prospective enrollment was indeed the most desirable minimum. From that time forward, the 1,000 minimum prospective enrollment came to be used by state-level planners as kind of a "birth-control" related to the establishment of smaller institutions. (Young, 2002, p. 565).

Young's memories of this 1,000 minimum enrollment figure were confirmed by Martorana in their meetings with graduate students at the 1994 meeting of the Council for the Study of Community Colleges (Wright & Katsinas, 1994).

The very title of his 1959 *Junior College Journal* article, "Survey of Junior College Possibilities: A State Responsibility," shows how Young had come to believe in the primary role of the states in extending universal education to Grades 13 and 14 (Young, 1959). Young and other experts of his era knew that if the state had already agreed on the policy goal of expanding access statewide to the 13th and 14th year, and if the state had authorized and formalized the role of the state superintendent to develop an appropriate process to bring this about, local school district leaders would feel less pressure to "hold on" to current junior college arrangements and otherwise repress the establishment of new junior college districts that were independent of the schools. "Fearing a topsy-turvy, unmanaged explosion of two-year college development, state-level educational agencies were urged to take responsibility for orderly college development based upon empirically determined community needs" (Young, 1996, p. 7). This was behind his 1955 call to separate junior colleges from school districts, as well as his meetings in 1959 to encourage Illinois State Superintendent of Public Instruction Wilkins to hire a full-time staff member to oversee junior college development (Krebs et al., 1999; Young, 2002). Young now referred to the institutions as "community-junior colleges" (Young, 1959, p. 245).

Young's frustration with the opposition he encountered, his belief that he had done about all he could in Illinois after helping to write a statewide plan, and his desire to be in a position to spend even more time on the establishment of community colleges and on the preparation of trained personnel for these new and expanding institutions, led him to accept an appointment at the University of Michigan. At Michigan's Center for the Study of Higher and Postsecondary Education, he would enjoy a lower teaching load, substantial support and freedom to do his work in the field, and, for the first time in his career, no responsibilities related to secondary education.

Leadership Development and Community College Establishment in Michigan and Ohio

Soon after his arrival at Michigan, Young was one of four consultants in a 1960 citizen's advisory study of the need for community colleges in the six-county metropolitan area of Detroit (Nurnberger, 1960). A follow-up to S.V. Martorana's (1957) statewide study, it began by repeating Martorana's suggestion that 10 additional community college campuses were needed in southeast Michigan, including three in the city of Detroit, three elsewhere in Wayne County, two in Oakland County, one in Macomb County, and one in Monroe County (Nurnberger, 1960). However, Recommendation 4 of the report stated that each of the six counties should have a community college district, and the "controlling board of each district should be The County Board of Education" (Nurnberger, 1960, p. 3). In his personal copy of this report, Young used a thick red pencil to underline Chairman Thomas S. Nurnberger's forward that "It did not ask [the consultants] to endorse any of its conclusions." In his own handwriting Young noted that "*none* of [the consultants] agreed with [the] conclusions and recommendations." Despite this opposition, Young was involved in studies to establish new community colleges in Michigan that included Delta College, Lake Michigan College, Mid-Michigan Community College, Monroe County Community College, Montcalm Community College, Schoolcraft College, and Wayne County Community College.

Young was also extensively involved in community college establishment in nearby Ohio. Ohio's 1961 enabling law allowed each county to either create new institutions or contract with universities to establish five types of 2-year colleges: (a) community colleges with local tax support and elected trustees, (b) state community colleges without local taxation and with trustees appointed by the governor, (c) technical colleges with no local taxation and with trustees appointed by the governor, (d) university 2-year branch campuses, and (e) university 2-year colleges operated on university campuses. Young worked in 44 of Ohio's 88 counties (Katsinas, Colon, Johnson, Sanders, & Thompson, 1999, p. 90). He directed or participated in citizen's participatory studies to establish Cuyahoga Community College and Sinclair Community College, the state's two largest 2-year colleges, as well as Lorain County Community College, Lakeland Community College, and Rio Grande College. Young helped to establish five of the six community colleges in Ohio that have local funding.

As had occurred in Illinois, Ohio universities used the public nature of the citizen's participatory study process to thwart the establishment of community colleges by influencing county officials who were enamored with the idea of bringing a university to their local communities. For example, Mahoning and Columbiana counties both established branch campuses after university officials made the false but alluring case that they would not "cost" local taxpayers anything. The "cost" of the establishment of branch campuses in these counties and across the state (rather than community colleges) was instead borne by students and their families through higher university-level tuition (Katsinas, Colon, et al., 1999), with the long-term result of lower rates of college attendance and graduation (Katsinas, Johnson, & Snider, 1999). Young recounted university-based opposition at a July 1963 hearing at which recommendations

> growing out of the Lorain County Citizen's Participatory Study I had directed were hotly contested by representatives of Ohio State University, and afterwards I was asked, "Why didn't I go back and *stay* in Michigan?" Someone even called the president's office at the University of Michigan to ask if they knew I was in Ohio—fortunately, they did know." (Katsinas, Colon et al., 1999, p. 90)

Young's work in college establishment accelerated further when he accepted a full-time position in 1968 to direct the education consulting division of Arthur D. Little, Inc. (ADL). No longer required to direct dissertations and teach, Young directed a statewide study in 1970 on behalf of ADL for the

Ohio Board of Regents in response to the public outcry over unbridled competition for students and wasteful overlapping of services. Titled *A Proposed Plan for Meeting Ohio's Need for Two-Year Post-High School Education*, it acknowledged that "a lack of coordination" and "considerable overlap exists" (Young, 1970a, p. 1). It noted that "considerable disagreement, misunderstanding, and differences of opinion exist in Ohio regarding the missions of public university branches, technical institutes, and community colleges," and the report further maintained that the "separation of values fostered by a tri-part post-high school system is inconsistent with the realities of American democratic life" (Young, 1970a, p. 2). Young argued that university branches often failed to be oriented to community needs and that technical institutes needed a broader curriculum that included general education for transfer, as well as community educational and cultural programs. He proposed that the technical institutes should become comprehensive community colleges serving specific state-assigned regions (Young, 1970a). Some three decades later, when the *Community College Journal of Research and Practice* published a series of special issues on community college history in 1999, Ohio still possessed 27 two-year university branch campuses that charged the same tuition as the mother universities and 23 independently governed colleges, of which six were community colleges with local tax support, nine were state community colleges with no local support, and eight were state technical colleges that also received no local tax support (Katsinas, Colon, et al., 1999). Ohio also had much lower rates of educational attainment in the adult population than Illinois and Michigan (Katsinas, Johnson, et al., 1999), a fact that motivated the Ohio Board of Regents to encourage its technical colleges to convert to state community colleges offering general education for transfer (Katsinas, Colon, et al., 1999). Access to 2-year general education had been solely a function of where one was born or resided. Full-time equivalent enrollment at Owens Community College in suburban Toledo jumped by 43% from 1993 to 1998 after conversion (Katsinas, Colon, et al., 1999).

On behalf of ADL, Young also directed a study to guide the future expansion of the Kansas City Metropolitan Junior College District (Young, 1973b). The final report included 100 tables and six figures dealing with a variety of demographic, social, and economic data, as well as data related to educational aspirations and projections of future student needs. At the CSCC Graduate Student Seminar in 1994, Young recalled that

> over 200 citizens participated. They were chosen to broadly represent the rank and file of the Kansas City population. Over a period of eight months, we identified the key informal leaders in the community, and involved them in an educational process. We tried to ensure that some of our worst critics were involved at the beginning, because if you could convince *them*, you might have a chance of convincing everyone. (Wright & Katsinas, 1994, p. 3)

In addition to this work within the United States, Young directed studies of educational organizations in other nations while at ADL, including a proposed national management information system for higher education in Holland (Young, 1970b), and a study of postsecondary programs, services, and institutions for Algeria (Young, 1976). He was also involved in studies in Sweden, Yugoslavia, Denmark, and Greece.

New Leaders for New Institutions

Young's involvement in preparing professionally trained leaders for separately accredited community colleges also expanded, and these efforts were often intertwined with his work on the establishment of colleges (Young, 1996). Major foundation interest in supporting community college leadership preparation programs, Young recalled, may have emanated from concerns expressed in the early 1950s by the Carnegie Foundation for the Advancement of Teaching that there was a need to prepare and upgrade the skills of those leading the expanding number of colleges and universities. "Using community colleges to extend access to postsecondary education for adults would later become a long-term agenda item for Kellogg, Ford, and other philanthropic foundations" (Young, 1996, p. 9).

In the 1958-1959 academic year, Young joined his University of Michigan colleagues, former AAJC Executive Secretary Jesse Bogue and Algo Henderson, at several conferences convened by the

W. K. Kellogg Foundation to discuss expanding graduate programs in the face of the coming leadership shortage (Young, 1996, 2002; see also Meek & Morgan, 1977). C. C. Colvert and James Reynolds also attended. Young believed that Kellogg's center for the improvement of secondary school administration, which was housed at the University of Texas and with which Reynolds had been involved, was a model for Kellogg's subsequent work with community colleges:

> The record of effectiveness of the Texas center, along with the records of some of the 22 other funded centers, inspired confidence in the ability of philanthropic assistance to foster improvement in educational leadership. . . . Grants were made to ten universities located in California, Florida, Michigan, New York, and Texas. Almost a decade later, grants were made to the Universities of Colorado and Washington. All these grants provided legitimacy to graduate programs in higher education and community college leadership, a point that cannot be overstated, given the traditional emphasis of colleges of education on elementary and secondary education. (Young, 1996, pp. 9-10)

Young authored the University of Michigan proposal to the W. K. Kellogg Foundation, and he believed that the Kellogg programs made six key contributions to the field. First, through preservice preparation and inservice programs, Kellogg genuinely cared about providing quality 2-year college leadership in a broad manner spanning the university preparation programs, state agencies, and the colleges themselves. Second, Kellogg recognized that a diversity of approaches would be needed, and that by bringing the program directors together periodically, innovations could be widely shared. Third, the role of the funded programs was not just to meet the leadership shortage, but, rather, to encourage universities to test various approaches and formats. Fourth, the Foundation promoted voluntary interinstitutional university cooperation related to program planning, while requiring collaboration (with funding as incentive). Fifth, it hoped that an organization, like the University Council for Educational Administration with its focus on K–12 leadership, might emerge in the postsecondary arena. Sixth, graduate programs might become institutionalized in terms of financial support once the Kellogg funding ran out. "Time has demonstrated that this [final] objective was only partially achieved," Young noted in 1996 (p. 7).

The need for expanded opportunities for graduate study in community college leadership was sharply felt by Young and his colleagues. During the postwar era of community college establishment, it was not uncommon for professors to receive telephone calls from desperate presidents of newly created institutions asking, "Who can you send me to be dean?" (Wright & Katsinas, 1994, p. 18). In their February 1961 report of a national survey of public and private junior college business offices, Young and J. J. Hines predicted a rising demand for business managers coinciding with the trend toward locally controlled public junior colleges as regional institutions that served more than one school district or county (Young & Hines, 1961). Young's work with Kellogg coincided with his involvement in the formation of the Council for Universities and Colleges (Young, 2002; see also Meek & Morgan, 1977). Today called the Council for the Study of Community Colleges, it is the oldest affiliated council of the American Association of Community Colleges. Young remained active in it until his death, attending each of the organization's first 49 annual meetings, and speaking at each of the Council's graduate student seminars held from 1994 through 2002.

Young's Evolving Thinking on Community Colleges

Young was so consumed with work in the field, heading citizen's participatory studies after joining Arthur D. Little, Inc., that he had little time to publish articles or books. Although he had authored 23 journal articles, book chapters, and books, along with two coauthored articles from 1950 to 1963, he did not author a single refereed journal article from 1964 until after he left ADL in 1976. Yet he produced a large body of work that included 60 institutional studies as well as state studies in Connecticut, Illinois, Iowa, Louisiana, Michigan, Ohio, Nevada, and, in 1972, the District of Columbia. As a consequence, Young's views on community colleges changed during the 1955 to 1976 period, a time of great social unrest in the United States and around the world. Student demonstrations occurred in Mexico, and Charles de Gaulle resigned following student protests in France. Young had long been attuned to the need for civil rights and full equality for African Americans, and to the cause of human rights in general. While at the University of Oklahoma, President George Cross asked him to serve as the doctoral student advisor for George W. McLaurin, an African American who had gained admission to the Graduate School of Education following his successful suit against the Oklahoma State Regents for Higher Education, which was decided by the U.S. Supreme Court on June 5, 1950. This case, which preceded the landmark 1954 *Brown* decision, was one of a series launched by the NAACP Legal Defense Fund under the leadership of its director, Thurgood Marshall, to knock down "separate-but-equal" policies in graduate and professional education. In addition, Young was a charter member of the United States Holocaust Museum; a picture Young took as a staff sergeant liberating the first Nazi death camp discovered by the advancing western Allies is displayed as a poster at the museum. He also was a strong supporter of the Southern Poverty Law Center.

Young's evolving views on the future of community colleges were influenced by his own past and by the events of the times. By 1955, Young no longer believed junior colleges could fulfill their potential without separation from elementary and secondary school districts. By the 1970s, like many others, Young believed that a transformation of American society was needed, and that the new community colleges had to shoulder their share of the load as change agents. A 1973 keynote speech at a conference sponsored by the Center for the Study of Higher Education at Pennsylvania State University was quite revealing. Young discussed changing notions of the concept of community, changing notions of community human service leadership, and the interorganizational composition of communities. He argued that a new role was needed:

> Almost since I can remember, I have heard that one major function of a relatively new community-based organization, the public community college, now in the backyard of most communities of any size, was to provide human services of an educational nature which would enhance the life of people in their sphere of influence and also the general community. For the most part, I am still waiting. (Young, 1973a, pp. 19-20)

Most of these efforts have been superficial, he maintained, only scratching the surface of needed services in their communities. He went on to say:

> Generally, community colleges that have sought to provide services beyond the offering of courses in the traditional (extension) mode have done so outside of community human services structures and have, more often than not, been hampered by archaic state level funding policies and provisions that do not recognize some method for equating these services for funding purposes. . . . In the future, community colleges in this country are going to have to consider themselves community service agencies rather than primarily as institutions of higher education. . . . Community colleges must assume a key leadership role in the reconstruction of American society in cooperation with other institutions. . . . They must quit thinking of themselves as primarily a sector of higher education and develop as their primary role the role of community leadership. This view will be most unpopular with some of my colleagues who have devoted much effort over the years, on the defensive, trying to prove that the first two years of community colleges were as good as the first to years of a four-year college or university—and that they were respectable places for students to go. I was once caught up in this effort with my blinders on. For more than a decade we have heard how the community college could be a catalyst for a community. . . . While this more passive, coordinative role will still be the one possible in various communities, time and conditions call for a role for community development, improvement, and reconstruction. (Young, 1973a, pp. 25-26)

Young's belief in the importance of the community services mission of community colleges presages the modern role of the community college in workforce training. As early as 1963, he included adult education programs and classes, public affairs, community development, and counseling in his definition of community services (Young, 1963). Writing in 1973, however, it is easy to see that his view of this function had expanded:

> The services dimension for a community college derives its legitimacy, as does the institution itself, from its educational role. A community college is not after all a governing agency, a social welfare agency, a museum, a social club, a religious institution, a voluntary association, an employment agency, a theater, or a labor union. Community colleges are educational institutions. Community human services which they can provide are legitimate only to the extent that they represent an extension or expansion of the educational resources directed toward the economic, social, cultural, and civic needs of the people the college serves. The community college cannot always be a "prime mover" for change, for its role may often be a coordinative or supportive one. It will sometimes need to assume a "partnership" role in personal and community development. (Young, 1973a, pp. 25-26)

Summary and Discussion

This article has reviewed the scholarship and contributions to the field of the late Raymond J. Young. It did not attempt to provide a comprehensive review of the factors that caused states such as Illinois, Michigan, and Ohio to establish 2-year colleges in the manner that they did. Instead, the efforts of one man, and what shaped his pioneering contributions during the "baby-boom" establishment era, have been examined. Yet, it is no overstatement to say that from 1955 to 1976, Young spent as much time in the field, visiting and working with community leaders, as did any of the other pioneers of that era, including S. V. Martorana, James L. Wattenbarger, and C. C. Colvert. His efforts helped to start or expand 60 colleges, develop plans for community college systems in seven states, and assist in the ongoing development of postsecondary education issues in five nations. All of this work required, as he himself noted, "personal zeal and missionary spirit" (Young, 2002, p. 560).

At the time of Young's work on community college establishment, the state role in providing universal access was not well defined in its legal, financial, or programmatic dimensions. What factors caused states like Illinois to create a statewide network of comprehensive community colleges, whereas Ohio failed to do so? Further "bottom-up" histories are needed. This is particularly true today, as the flaws inherent in poorly planned systems are being exposed by the combined impacts of "Tidal-Wave II" enrollments and state budget cuts (Katsinas, 2005). As Young noted in the closing paragraph of the final journal article he wrote:

The need for future community college leaders to have a solid grounding in research methods that allow for the scientific collection of many aspects related to community needs assessment has never been greater. . . . If the college is to truly *serve* the community, it must *know* the community, and therefore leaders should know rigorous research and survey methodologies to comprehensively assess community needs. (Young, 2002, p. 572)

References

Carnegie Foundation for the Advancement of Teaching. (2007). *Basic classification tables*. Retrieved December 26, 2007, from http://www.carnegiefoundation.org/classifications/index.asp?key=805

Fretwell, E. K. (1954). *Founding public junior colleges*. New York: Teacher's College, Columbia University.

Grinnell, J. E., & Young, R. J. (Eds.). (1955). *The school and the community; educational and public relations*. New York: Roland Press Company.

Illinois Commission on Higher Education. (1957). *Illinois looks to the future in higher education: Report to the governor and legislature of the state of Illinois*. Springfield, IL: Author.

Katsinas, S. G. (2005). Increased competition for scarce state dollars. In S. G. Katsinas & J. C. Palmer (Eds.), *Sustaining financial support for community colleges* (New Directions for Community Colleges, No. 132, pp. 19–32). San Francisco: Jossey Bass, Winter.

Katsinas, S. G., Colon, D. M., Johnson, J. L., Sanders, E. Y., & Thompson, D. (1999). The development of two-year colleges in Ohio: The tension between state and local area interests. *Community College Journal of Research and Practice, 23,* 79–105.

Katsinas, S. G., Johnson, J. L., & Snider, L. G. (1999), Two-year college development in five Midwestern states: An introduction and overview. *Community College Journal of Research and Practice, 23,* 1–18.

Koos, L. V. (1924). *The junior college*. Minneapolis, MN: University of Minnesota Press.

Krebs, P., Katsinas, S. G., & Johnson, J. L. (1999). Illinois community colleges: Their history and system. *Community College Journal of Research and Practice, 23,* 19–41.

Martorana, S. V. (1957). *The community college in Michigan*. Lansing, MI: Michigan Legislative Study Committee on Higher Education.

Meek, D., & Morgan, D. A. (1977). *Council of Universities and Colleges: An introductory history*. Tucson, AZ: Higher Education Program, University of Arizona.

National Center for Public Policy and Higher Education. (n.d.). *Measuring up 2006: The national report card for higher education*. San Jose, CA: Author. Retrieved December 12, 2007, from http://measuringup.higheredu-cation.org/_docs/2006/NationalReport_2006.pdf

Nurnberger, T. S. (1960). *Six county study of community college needs, citizen's advisory council final report*. Detroit, MI: Citizen's Advisory Council.

Oklahoma Secondary School Curriculum Improvement Commission and Oklahoma State Department of Education. (1953). *A guide for the improvement of curriculum in Oklahoma secondary schools* (Bulletin No. 1). Oklahoma City, OK: State Superintendent of Education.

Thompson, L. F., & Young, R. J. (1990). Accomplishment of selected occupational programs in community colleges. *Community College Review, 18*(2), 41–46.

Wright, D., & Katsinas, S. G. (1994, April). *Community college pioneers: S.V. "Marty" Martorana, James L. Wattenbarger, and Raymond J. Young, notes from the graduate student seminar of the Council of Universities and Colleges.* Unpublished manuscript.

Young, R. J. (1949). An *evaluation of administrative practitioners concerning secondary school libraries*. Unpublished master's thesis, Kansas State Teachers College at Pittsburg.

Young, R. J. (1950). *An analysis and evaluation of general legislation pertaining to public junior colleges.* Unpublished doctoral dissertation, University of Colorado at Boulder.

Young, R. J. (1951a). Junior college prospects and a guide for its legal propagation. *Junior College Journal, (21)*8, 444–452.

Young, R. J. (1951b). School district re-organization and the public junior college. *Junior College Journal, 22*(2), 72–75.

Young, R. J. (1951c). Junior-college supervision and control. *The School Review, 59,* 485–488.

Young, R. J. (1952a). How well do we teach? *The Journal of Teacher Education, 3,* 214–216.

Young, R. J. (1952b). General legislative needs for the public junior college in the North Central Association area. *North Central Association Quarterly, 26,* 287–294.

Young, R. J. (1955a). The problem of school and community relationships. In J. E. Grinnell & R. J. Young, (Eds.), *The school and the community; educational and public relations* (pp. 3–17). New York: Roland Press Company.

Young, R. J. (1955b). Unofficial influences on the schools. In J. E. Grinnell & R. J. Young (Eds.), *The school and the community; educational and public relations* (pp. 88–101). New York: Roland Press Company.

Young, R. J. (1955c). The curriculum improvement movement in Oklahoma. *National Association of Secondary School Principals Bulletin, 39*(214), 16–25.

Young, R. J. (1957a). *Citizen's survey of community college possibilities: A survey of the East Alton-Wood River, Illinois High School District.* Urbana, IL: Office of Field Services, College of Education, University of Illinois.

Young, R. J. (1957b). The community-junior college. In *Illinois looks to the future in higher education: Report to the governor and legislature of the state of Illinois* (pp. 97–149). Springfield, IL: Illinois Commission on Higher Education.

Young, R. J. (1957c). Is there educational waste of Illinois human resources? *The Caldron, 3*(1), 7–40.

Young, R. J. (1959). Survey of junior college possibilities: A state responsibility. *Junior College Journal, 29*(5), 245–253.

Young, R. J. (1961a). Improvement through introspection: Are self-studies essential? *Junior College Journal, 32*(1), 29–34.

Young, R. J. (1961b). What surveys show about characteristics, motivations, and educational aspirations of youth. In *Proceedings of the Annual Conference on Higher Education in Michigan, November 14 and 15, 1961* (pp.40–48). Ann Arbor, MI: Center for the Study of Higher and Postsecondary Education, University of Michigan.

Young, R. J. (1962a). What surveys show about characteristics, motivations, and educational aspirations of youth for college. *College and University, 38*(2), 61–67.

Young, R. J. (1962b). Crucial times for North Central area junior college involvement, a report of the Subcommittee on Junior College Problems, Committee on Current Problems, Commission on Research and Services. *North Central Association Quarterly, 36,* 323–387.

Young, R. J. (1963). The American junior college, a modern development in higher education. *Michigan Quarterly Review, 64*(36), 41–47.

Young, R. J. (1970a). *A proposed plan for meeting Ohio's need for two-year post-high school education: Consultant's Report to the Ohio Board of Regents by Arthur D. Little.* Unpublished manuscript.

Young, R. J. (1970b). *Feasibility study of a data comparison system for academic institutions in Holland: Report prepared for the Committee of Presidents-Curator by Arthur D. Little, Inc.* Unpublished manuscript.

Young, R. J. (1973a). Concentration on cooperation: Everyone's duty, each one's goal. In S. V. Martorana & J. O. Hammons (Eds.), *State-local agency and community college cooperation for community improvement: A conference of state and local officials in the middle states (proceedings)* (pp. 16–26). University Park, PA: Center for the Study of Higher Education, The Pennsylvania State University.

Young, R. J. (1973b). *Progress and prospect: A study of the Kansas City Metropolitan Junior College District; A report to the Board of Trustees.* Unpublished manuscript.

Young, R. J. (1976). *Strategies pur le Developpement du Systeme d'Education Post-Secondaire en Algerie: Rapport prepare pour Le Minestere de l'Enseignement Suerieur et de la recherche Scientfiique.* Unpublished manuscript.

Young, R. J. (1982). Both sides of the management coin. *Community College Review, 10*(2), 19–25.

Young, R. J. (1985–1986). Methodology for community educational study: How appropriate is cluster sampling? *Journal of Experimental Education, 54,* 114–117.

Young, R. J. (1986a). Discovering community opinion. *Community Services Catalyst, 16*(4), 11–14.

Young, R. J. (1986b). Assessment of public opinion on school issues: A critique. *The Rural Educator, 9*(3), 12–24.

Young, R. J. (1987–1988). Structural features of a good secondary school reading program: Thoughts for school administrators. *National Forum of Educational Administration and Supervision Journal, 4,* 157–170.

Young, R. J. (1988). Administrative intervention—An integral aspect of the reading program. *National Association of Secondary School Principals Bulletin, 72*(508), 89–94.

Young, R. J. (1989a). The good old summertime in public two-year colleges. *Community Services Catalyst, 19*(2), 9–15.

Young, R. J. (1989b). *Summer sessions in public two-year colleges* (ERIC Document No. ED304202). Pullman, WA: Washington State University.

Young, R. J. (1989c). Factors associated with creativity: Educational programming for summer terms. *Continuing Higher Education Review, 53,* 27–34.

Young, R. J. (1996). Legacy of the Post-WWII growth years for community college leadership programs. In J. C. Palmer & S. G. Katsinas (Eds.), *Sustaining financial support for community colleges* (New Directions for Community Colleges, No. 132; pp. 5–14). San Francisco: Jossey Bass.

Young, R. J. (2002). From persuasion to accommodation in public two-year college development. *Community College Journal of Research and Practice, 26,* 559–572.

Young, R. J., & Berger, D. F. (1983). Evaluation of a year-round junior high school operation. *National Association of Secondary School Principals Bulletin, 67*(459), 53–59.

Young, R. J., & Hines, J. J. (1961). Business management in selected junior colleges. *School Business Affairs, 17*(2), 5–18.

Young, R. J., & Jones, H. M. (1982). State governance structures for community education. *Community Services Catalyst, 12*(4), 15–20.

Young, R. J., & McDougall, W. P. (1982). *Relationships of selected factors to summer session organizations* (ERIC Document No. ED215734). Pullman, WA: Washington State University.

Young, R. J., & McDougall, W. P. (1985). *Recent changes in summer sessions of U.S. And Canadian colleges and universities* (ERIC Document No. ED279264). Pullman, WA: Washington State University.

Young, R. J., & McDougall, W. P. (1987). Comparison of university summer session characteristics in Canada and the United States. *Canadian Journal of University Continuing Education, 13,* 16–31.

Young, R. J., & McDougall, W. P. (1988). Trends in university summer sessions. *The Journal of Higher Education, 59,* 39–53.

Young, R. J., & McDougall, W. P. (1991). *Summer sessions in colleges and universities: Perspectives, practices, problems, and prospects* (ERIC Document No. ED370493). St. Louis: North American Association of Summer Sessions.

Young, R. J., & Thompson, M. J. (1982). A study of relationships between characteristics of elected and appointed trustees and their beliefs. *Community/Junior College Quarterly of Research and Practice, 6,* 121–128.

Stephen G. Katsinas is director of the Education Policy Center at The University of Alabama, and Professor of Higher Education. He has personally visited more than 350 community colleges in 36 states over the past two decades, and has written extensively on policy, governance, economic development, and rural issues. With Vincent Lacey and David Hardy, he coauthored the new *2005 Basic Classifications of Associate's Colleges* published by the Carnegie Foundation for the Advancement of Teaching in February 2006.

CHAPTER 4

THE "COOLING-OUT" FUNCTION IN HIGHER EDUCATION[1]

BURTON R. CLARK

Abstract. The wide gap found in many democratic institutions between culturally encouraged aspiration and institutionally provided means of achievement leads to the failure of many participants. Such a situation exists in American higher education. Certain social units ameliorate the consequent stress by redefining failure and providing for a "soft" denial; they perform a "cooling-out" function. The junior college especially plays this role. The cooling-out process observed in one college includes features likely to be found in other settings: substitute achievement, gradual disengagement, denial, consolation, and avoidance of standards.

A major problem of democratic society is inconsistency between encouragement to achieve and the realities of limited opportunity. Democracy asks individuals to act as if social mobility were universally possible; status is to be won by individual effort, and rewards are to accrue to those who try. But democratic societies also need selective training institutions, and hierarchical work organizations permit increasingly fewer persons to succeed at ascending levels. Situations of opportunity are also situations of denial and failure. Thus democratic societies need not only to motivate achievement but also to mollify those denied it in order to sustain motivation in the face of disappointment and to deflect resentment. In the modern mass democracy, with its large-scale organization, elaborated ideologies of equal access and participation, and minimal commitment to social origin as a basis for status, the task becomes critical.

The problem of blocked opportunity has been approached sociologically through means-ends analysis. Merton and others have called attention to the phenomenon of dissociation between culturally instilled goals and institutionally provided means of realization; discrepancy between ends and means is seen as a basic social source of individual frustration and recalcitrance.[2] We shall here extend means-ends analysis in another direction, to the responses of organized groups to means-ends disparities, in particular focusing attention on ameliorative processes that lessen the strains of dissociation. We shall do so by analyzing the most prevalent type of dissociation between aspirations and avenues in American education, specifying the structure and processes that reduce the stress of structural disparity and individual denial. Certain components of American higher education perform what may be called the cooling-out function,[3] and it is to these that attention will be drawn.

The Ends-Means Disjuncture

In American higher education the aspirations of the multitude are encouraged by "open-door" admission to public-supported colleges. The means of moving upward in status and of maintaining high status now include some years in college, and a college education is a prerequisite of the better positions in business and the professions. The trend is toward an ever tighter connection between higher education and higher occupations, as increased specialization and professionalization insure that more persons will need more preparation. The high-school graduate, seeing college as essential to success, will seek to enter some college, regardless of his record in high school.

A second and allied source of public interest in unlimited entry into college is the ideology of equal opportunity.[4] Strictly interpreted, equality of opportunity means selection according to ability, without regard to extraneous considerations. Popularly interpreted, however, equal opportunity in obtaining a college education is widely taken to mean unlimited access to some form of college: in California, for example, state educational authorities maintain that high-school graduates who cannot qualify for the state university or state college should still have the "opportunity of attending a publicly supported institution of higher education," this being "an essential part of the state's goal of guaranteeing equal educational opportunities to all its citizens."[5] To deny access to college is then to deny equal opportunity. Higher education should make a seat available without judgment on past performance.

Many other features of current American life encourage college-going. School officials are reluctant to establish early critical hurdles for the young, as is done in Europe. With little enforced screening in the pre-college years, vocational choice and educational selection are postponed to the college years or later. In addition, the United States, a wealthy country, is readily supporting a large complex of colleges, and its expanding economy requires more specialists. Recently, a national concern that man-power be fully utilized has encouraged the extending of college training to more and different kinds of students. Going to college is also in some segments of society the thing to do; as a last resort, it is more attractive than the army or a job. Thus ethical and practical urges together encourage the high-school graduate to believe that college is both a necessity and a right; similarly, parents and elected officials incline toward legislation and admission practices that insure entry for large numbers; and educational authorities find the need and justification for easy admission.

Even where pressures have been decisive in widening admission policy, however, the system of higher education has continued to be shaped partly by other interests. The practices of public colleges are influenced by the academic personnel, the organizational requirements of colleges, and external pressures other than those behind the open door. Standards of performance and graduation are maintained. A commitment to standards is encouraged by a set of values in which the status of a college, as defined by academicians and a large body of educated laymen, is closely linked to the perceived quality of faculty, student body, and curriculum. The raising of standards is supported by the faculty's desire to work with promising students and to enjoy membership in an enterprise of reputed quality—college authorities find low standards and poor students a handicap in competing with other colleges for such resources as able faculty as well as for academic status. The wish is widespread that college education be of the highest quality for the preparation of leaders in public affairs, business, and the professions. In brief, the institutional means of the students' progress toward college graduation and subsequent goals are shaped in large part by a commitment to quality embodied in college staffs, traditions, and images.

The conflict between open-door admission and performance of high quality often means a wide discrepancy between the hopes of entering students and the means of their realization. Students who pursue ends for which a college education is required but who have little academic ability gain admission into colleges only to encounter standards of performance they cannot meet. As a result, while some students of low promise are successful, for large numbers failure is inevitable and *structured*. The denial is delayed, taking place within the college instead of at the edge of the system. It requires that many colleges handle the student who intends to complete college and has been allowed to become involved but whose destiny is to fail.

Responses to Disjuncture

What is done with the student whose destiny will normally be early termination? One answer is unequivocal dismissal. This "hard" response is found in the state university that bows to pressure for broad admission but then protects standards by heavy drop-out. In the first year it weeds out many of the incompetent, who may number a third or more of the entering class.[6] The response of the college is hard in that failure is clearly defined as such. Failure is public; the student often returns home. This abrupt change in status and in access to the means of achievement may occur simultaneously in a large college or university for hundreds, and sometimes thousands, of students after the first semester and at the end of the freshman year. The delayed denial is often viewed on the outside as heartless, a slaughter of the innocents.[7] This excites public pressure and anxiety, and apparently the practice cannot be extended indefinitely as the demand for admission to college increases.

A second answer is to sidetrack unpromising students rather than have them fail. This is the "soft" response: never to dismiss a student but to provide him with an alternative. One form of it in some state universities is the detour to an extension division or a general college, which has the advantage of appearing not very different from the main road. Sometimes "easy" fields of study, such as education, business administration, and social science, are used as alternatives to dismissal.[8] The major form of the soft response is not found in the four-year college or university, however, but in the college that specializes in handling students who will soon be leaving—typically, the two-year public junior college.

In most states where the two-year college is a part of higher education, the students likely to be caught in the means-ends disjuncture are assigned to it in large numbers. In California, where there are over sixty public two-year colleges in a diversified system that includes the state university and numerous four-year state colleges, the junior college is unselective in admissions and by law, custom, and self-conception accepts all who wish to enter.[9] It is tuition-free, local, and under local control. Most of its entering students want to try for the baccalaureate degree, transferring to a "senior" college after one or two years. About two-thirds of the students in the junior colleges of the state are in programs that permit transferring; but, of these, only about one-third actually transfer to a four-year college.[10] The remainder, or two out of three of the professed transfer students, are "latent terminal students": their announced intention and program of study entails four years of college, but in reality their work terminates in the junior college. Constituting about half of all the students in the California junior colleges, and somewhere between one-third and one-half of junior college students nationally,[11] these students cannot be ignored by the colleges. Understanding their careers is important to understanding modern higher education.

The Reorienting Process

This type of student in the junior college is handled by being moved out of a transfer major to a one- or two-year program of vocational, business, or semiprofessional training. This calls for the relinquishing of his original intention, and he is induced to accept a substitute that has lower status in both the college and society in general.

In one junior college[12] the initial move in a cooling-out process is pre-entrance testing: low scores on achievement tests lead poorly qualified students into remedial classes. Assignment to remedial work casts doubt and slows the student's movement into bona fide transfer courses. The remedial courses are, in effect, a subcollege. The student's achievement scores are made part of a counseling folder that will become increasingly significant to him. An objective record of ability and performance begins to accumulate.

A second step is a counseling interview before the beginning of the first semester, and before all subsequent semesters for returning students. "At this interview the counselor assists the student to choose the proper courses in light of his objective, his test scores, the high school record and test records from his previous schools."[13] Assistance in choosing "the proper courses" is gentle at first. Of the common case of the student who wants to be an engineer but who is not a promising candidate, a counselor said: "I never openly countermand his choice, but edge him toward a terminal program by gradually laying out the facts of life." Counselors may become more severe later when grades provide a talking point and when the student knows that he is in trouble. In the earlier counseling the desire of the student has much weight; the counselor limits himself to giving advice and stating the probability of success. The advice is entered in the counseling record that shadows the student.

A third and major step in reorienting the latent terminal student is a special course entitled "Orientation to College," mandatory for entering students. All sections of it are taught by teacher-counselors who comprise the counseling staff, and one of its purposes is "to assist students in evaluating their own abilities, interests, and aptitudes; in assaying their vocational choices in light of this evaluation; and in making educational plans to implement their choices." A major section of it takes up vocational planning; vocational tests are given at a time when opportunities and requirements in various fields of work are discussed. The tests include the "Lee Thorpe Interest Inventory" ("given to all students for motivating a self-appraisal of vocational choice") and the "Strong Interest Inventory" ("for all who are undecided about choice or who show disparity between accomplishment and vocational choice"). Mechanical and clerical aptitude tests are taken by all. The aptitudes are directly related to the college's terminal programs, with special tests, such as a pre-engineering ability test, being given according to need. Then an "occupational paper is required of all students for their chosen occupation"; in it the student writes on the required training and education and makes a "self-appraisal of fitness."

Tests and papers are then used in class discussion and counseling interviews, in which the students themselves arrange and work with a counselor's folder and a student test profile and, in so doing, are repeatedly confronted by the accumulating evidence—the test scores, course grades, recommendations of teachers and counselors. This procedure is intended to heighten self-awareness of capacity in relation to choice and hence to strike particularly at the latent terminal student. The teacher-counselors are urged constantly to "be alert to the problem of unrealistic vocational goals" and to "help students to accept their limitations and strive for success in other worthwhile objectives that are within their grasp." The orientation class was considered a good place "to talk tough," to explain in an *impersonal* way the facts of life for the overambitious student. Talking tough to a whole group is part of a soft treatment of the individual.

Following the vocational counseling, the orientation course turns to "building an educational program," to study of the requirements for graduation of the college in transfer and terminal curriculum, and to planning of a four-semester program. The students also become acquainted with the requirements of the colleges to which they hope to transfer, here contemplating additional hurdles such as the entrance examinations of other colleges. Again, the hard facts of the road ahead are brought to bear on self-appraisal.

If he wishes, the latent terminal student may ignore the counselor's advice and the test scores. While in the counseling class, he is also in other courses, and he can wait to see what happens. Adverse counseling advice and poor test scores may not shut off his hope of completing college; when this is the case, the deterrent will be encountered in the regular classes. Here the student is divested of expectations, lingering from high school, that he will automatically pass and, hopefully, automatically be transferred. Then, receiving low grades, he is thrown back into the counseling orbit, a fourth step in his reorientation and a move justified by his actual accomplishment. The following indicates the nature of the referral system:

Need for Improvement Notices are issued by instructors to students who are doing unsatisfactory work. The carbon copy of the notice is given to the counselor who will be available for conference with the student. The responsibility lies with the student to see his counselor. However, experiences hows that some counselees are unable to be sufficiently self-directive to seek aid. The counselor should, in such cases, send for the student, using the Request for Conference blank. If the student fails to respond to the Request for Conferences lip, this may become a disciplinary matter and should be referred to the deans.

After a conference has been held, the Need for Improvement notices are filed in the student's folder. *This may be important* in case of a complaint concerning the fairness of a final grade.[14]

This directs the student to more advice and self-assessment, as soon and as often as he has classroom difficulty. The carbon-copy routine makes it certain that, if he does not seek advice, advice will seek him. The paper work and bureaucratic procedure have the purpose of recording referral and advice in black and white, where they may later be appealed to impersonally. As put in an unpublished report of the college, the overaspiring student and the one who seems to be in the wrong program require "skillful and delicate handling. An accumulation of pertinent factual information may serve to fortify the objectivity of the student-counselor relationship." While the counselor advises delicately and patiently, but persistently, the student is confronted with the record with increasing frequency.

A fifth step, one necessary for many in the throes of discouragement, is probation: "Students [whose] grade point averages fall below 2.0 [C] in any semester will, upon recommendation by the Scholarship Committee, be placed on probationary standing." A second failure places the student on second probation, and a third may mean that he will be advised to withdraw from the college altogether. The procedure is not designed to rid the college of a large number of students, for they may continue on probation for three consecutive semesters; its purpose is not to provide a status halfway out of the college but to "assist the student to seek an objective (major field) at a level on which he can succeed."[15] An important effect of probation is its slow killing-off of the lingering hopes of the most stubborn latent terminal students. A "transfer student" must have a C average to receive the Associate in Arts (a two-year degree) offered by the junior college, but no minimum average is set for terminal students. More important, four-year colleges require a C average or higher for the transfer student. Thus probationary status is the final blow to hopes of transferring and, indeed, even to graduating from the junior college under a transfer-student label. The point is reached where the student must permit himself to be reclassified or else drop out. In this college, 30 per cent of the students enrolled at the end of the spring semester, 1955-56, who returned the following fall were on probation; three out of four of these were transfer students in name.[16]

This sequence of procedures is a specific process of cooling-out;[17] its effect, at the best, is to let down hopes gently and unexplosively. Through it students who are fail-ing or barely passing find their occupational and academic future being redefined. Along the way, teacher-counselors urge the latent terminal student to give up his plan of transferring and stand ready to console him in accepting a terminal curriculum. The drawn-out denial when it is effective is in place of a personal, hard "No"; instead, the student is brought to realize, finally, that it is best to ease himself out of the competition to transfer.

Cooling-Out Features

In the cooling-out process in the junior college are several features which are likely to be found in other settings where failure or denial is the effect of a structured discrepancy between ends and means, the responsible operatives or "coolers" cannot leave the scene or hide their identities, and the disappointment is threatening in some way to those responsible for it. At work and in training institutions this is common. The features are:

1. *Alternative achievement.*—Substitute avenues may be made to appear not too different from what is given up, particularly as to status. The person destined to be denied or who fails is invited to interpret the second effort as more appropriate to his particular talent and is made to see that it will be the less frustrating. Here one does not fail but rectifies a mistake. The substitute status reflects less unfavorably on personal capacity than does being dismissed and forced to leave the scene. The terminal student in the junior college may appear not very different from the transfer student—an "engineering aide," for example, instead of an "engineer"—and to be proceeding to something with a status of its own. Failure in college can be treated as if it did not happen; so, too, can poor performance in industry.[18]

2. *Gradual disengagement.*—By a gradual series of steps, movement to a goal may be stalled, self-assessment encouraged, and evidence produced of performance. This leads toward the available alternatives at little cost. It also keeps the person in a counseling milieu in which advice is furnished, whether actively sought or not. Compared with the original hopes, however, it is a deteriorating situation. If the individual does not give up peacefully, he will be in trouble.

3. *Objective denial.*—Reorientation is, finally, confrontation by the facts. A record of poor performance helps to detach the organization and its agents from the emotional aspects of the cooling-out work. In a sense, the overaspiring student in the junior college confronts himself, as he lives with the accumulating evidence, instead of the organization. The college offers opportunity; it is the record that forces denial. Record-keeping and other bureaucratic procedures appeal to universal criteria and reduce the influence of personal ties, and the personnel are thereby protected. Modern personnel record-keeping, in general, has the function of documenting denial.

4. *Agents of consolation.*—Counselors are available who are patient with the overambitious and who work to change their intentions. They believe in the value of the alternative careers, though of lower social status, and are practiced in consoling. In college and in other settings counseling is to reduce aspiration as well as to define and to help fulfil it. The teacher-counselor in the "soft" junior college is in contrast to the scholar in the "hard" college who simply gives a low grade to the failing student.

5. *Avoidance of standards.*—A cooling-out process avoids appealing to standards that are ambiguous to begin with. While a "hard" attitude toward failure generally allows a single set of criteria, a "soft" treatment assumes that many kinds of ability are valuable, each in its place. Proper classification and placement are then paramount, while standards become relative.

Importance of Concealment

For an organization and its agents one dilemma of a cooling-out role is that it must be kept reasonably away from public scrutiny and not clearly perceived or understood by prospective clientele. Should it become obvious, the organization's ability to perform it would be impaired. If high-school seniors and their families were to define the junior college as a place which diverts college-bound students, a probable consequence would be a turning-away from the junior college and increased pressure for admission to the four-year colleges and universities that are otherwise protected to some degree. This would, of course, render superfluous the part now played by the junior college in the division of labor among colleges.

The cooling-out function of the junior college is kept hidden, for one thing, as other functions are highlighted. The junior college stresses "the transfer function," "the terminal function," etc., not that of transforming transfer into terminal students; indeed, it is widely identified as principally a transfer station. The other side of cooling-out is the successful performance in junior college of students who did poorly in high school or who have overcome socioeconomic handicaps, for they are drawn into higher education rather than taken out of it. Advocates of the junior college point to this salvaging of talented manpower, otherwise lost to the community and nation. It is indeed a function of the open door to let hidden talent be uncovered.

Then, too, cooling-out itself is reinterpreted so as to appeal widely. The junior college may be viewed as a place where all high-school graduates have the opportunity to explore possible careers and find the type of education appropriate to their individual ability; in short, as a place where everyone is admitted and everyone succeeds. As described by the former president of the University of California:

> A prime virtue of the junior college, I think, is that most of its students succeed in what they set out to accomplish, and cross the finish line before they grow weary of the race. After two years in a course that they have chosen, they can go out prepared for activities that satisfy them, instead of being branded as failures. Thus the broadest possible opportunity may be provided for the largest number to make an honest try at further education with some possibility of success and with no route to a desired goal completely barred to them.[19]

The students themselves help to keep this function concealed by wishful unawareness. Those who cannot enter other colleges but still hope to complete four years will be motivated at first not to admit the cooling-out process to consciousness. Once exposed to it, they again will be led not to acknowledge it, and so they are saved insult to their self-image.

In summary, the cooling-out process in higher education is one whereby systematic discrepancy between aspiration and avenue is covered over and stress for the individual and the system is minimized. The provision of readily available alternative achievements in itself is an important device for alleviating the stress consequent on failure and so preventing anomic and deviant behavior. The general result of cooling-out processes is that society can continue to encourage maximum effort without major disturbance from unfulfilled promises and expectations.

UNIVERSITY OF CALIFORNIA, BERKELEY

Notes

1. Revised and extended version of paper read at the Fifty-fourth Annual Meeting of the American Sociological Association, Chicago, September 3–5, 1959. I am indebted to Erving Goffman and Martin A. Trow for criticism and to Sheldon Messinger for extended conceptual and editorial comment.

2. "Aberrant behavior may be regarded sociologically as a symptom of dissociation between culturally prescribed aspirations and socially structured avenues for realizing these aspirations" (Robert K. Merton, "Social Structure and Anomie," in *Social Theory and Social Structure* [rev. ed.; Glencoe, Ill.: Free Press, 1957], p. 134). See also Herbert H. Hyman, "The Value Systems of Different Classes: A Social Psychological Contribution to the Analysis of Stratification," in Reinhard Bendix and Seymour M. Lipset (eds.), *Class, Status and Power: A Reader in Social Stratification* (Glencoe, Ill.: Free Press, 1953), pp. 426–42; and the papers by Robert Dubin, Richard A. Cloward, Robert K. Merton, and Dorothy L. Meier, and Wendell Bell, in *American Sociological Review*, Vol. XXIV (April, 1959).

3. I am indebted to Erving Goffman's original statement of the cooling-out conception. See his "Cooling the Mark Out: Some Aspects of Adaptation to Failure," *Psychiatry*, XV (November, 1952), 451–63. Sheldon Messinger called the relevance of this concept to my attention.

4. Seymour Martin Lipset and Reinhard Bendix, *Social Mobility in Industrial Society* (Berkeley: University of California Press, 1959), pp. 78–101.

5. *A Study of the Need for Additional Centers of Public Higher Education in California* (Sacramento: California State Department of Education, 1957), p. 128. For somewhat similar interpretations by educators and laymen nationally see Francis J. Brown (ed.), *Approaching Equality of Opportunity in Higher Education* (Washington, D.C.: American Council on Education, 1955), and the President's Committee on Education beyond the High School, *Second Report to the President* (Washington, D.C.: Government Printing Office, 1957).

6. One national report showed that one out of eight entering students (12.5 per cent) in publicly controlled colleges does not remain beyond the first term or semester; one out of three (31 per cent) is out by the end of the first year; and about one out of two (46.6 per cent) leaves within the first two years. In state universities alone, about one out of four withdraws in the first year and 40 per cent in two years (Robert E. Iffert, *Retention and Withdrawal of College Students* [Washington, D.C.: Department of Health, Education, and Welfare, 1958], pp. 15–20). Students withdraw for many reasons, but scholastic aptitude is related to their staying power: "A sizeable number of students of medium ability enter college, but . . . few if any of them remain longer than two years" (*A Restudy of the Needs of California in Higher Education* [Sacramento: California State Department of Education, 1955], p. 120).

7. Robert L. Kelly, *The American Colleges and the Social Order* (New York: Macmillan Co., 1940), pp. 220–21.

8. One study has noted that on many campuses the business school serves "as a dumping ground for students who cannot make the grade in engineering or some branch of the liberal arts," this being a consequence of lower promotion standards than are found in most other branches of the university (Frank C. Pierson, *The Education of American Businessmen* [New York: McGraw-Hill Book Co., 1959], p. 63). Pierson also summarizes data on intelligence of students by field of study which indicate that education, business, and social science rank near the bottom in quality of students (*ibid.*, pp. 65–72).

9. Burton R. Clark, *The Open Door College: A Case Study* (New York: McGraw-Hill Book Co., 1960), pp. 44–45.

10. *Ibid.*, p. 116.

11. Leland L. Medsker, *The Junior College: Progress and Prospect* (New York: McGraw-Hill Book Co., 1960), chap. iv.

12. San Jose City College, San Jose, Calif. For the larger study see Clark, *op. cit.*

13. San Jose Junior College, Handbook for Counselors, 1957–58, p. 2. Statements in quotation marks in the next few paragraphs are cited from this.

14. *Ibid.*, p. 20.

15. Statement taken from unpublished material.

16. San Jose Junior College, "Digest of Analysis of the Records of 468 Students Placed on Probation for the Fall Semester, 1956," September 3, 1956.

17. Goffman's original statement of the concept of cooling-out referred to how the disappointing of expectations is handled by the disappointed person and especially by those responsible for the disappointment. Although his main illustration was the confidence game, where facts and potential achievement are deliberately misrepresented to the "mark" (the victim) by operators of the game, Goffman also applied the concept to failure in which those responsible act in good faith (*op. cit., passim*). "Cooling-out" is a widely useful idea when used to refer to a function that may vary in deliberateness.

18. *Ibid.*, p. 457; cf. Perrin Stryker, "How To Fire an Executive," *Fortune*, L (October, 1954), 116–17 and 178–92.

19. Robert Gordon Sproul, "Many Millions More," *Educational Record*, XXXIX (April, 1958), 102.

CHAPTER 5

COMMUNITY COLLEGES AND THE AMERICAN SOCIAL ORDER

S. BRINT AND J. KARABEL

From the earliest days of the Republic, Americans have possessed an abiding faith that theirs is a land of opportunity. For unlike the class-bound societies of Europe, America was seen as a place of limitless opportunities, a place where hard work and ability would receive their just reward. From Thomas Jefferson's "natural aristocracy of talent" to Ronald Reagan's "opportunity society," the belief that America was—and should remain—a land where individuals of ambition and talent could rise as far as their capacities would take them has been central to the national identity. Abraham Lincoln expressed this deeply rooted national commitment to equality of opportunity succinctly when, in a special message to Congress shortly after the onset of the Civil War, he described as a "leading object of the government for whose existence we contend" to "afford all an unfettered start, and a fair chance in the race of life."[1]

Throughout much of the nineteenth century, the belief that the United States was a nation blessed with unique opportunities for individual advancement was widespread among Americans and Europeans alike. The cornerstone of this belief was a relatively wide distribution of property (generally limited, to be sure, to adult white males) and apparently abundant opportunities in commerce and agriculture to accumulate more. But with the rise of mammoth corporations and the closing of the frontier in the decades after the Civil War, the fate of the "self-made man"—that heroic figure who, though of modest origins, triumphed in the competitive marketplace through sheer skill and determination—came to be questioned. In particular, the fundamental changes then occurring in the American economy—the growth of huge industrial enterprises, the concentration of propertyless workers in the nation's cities, and the emergence of monopolies—made the image of the hardworking stockboy who rose to the top seem more and more like a relic of a vanished era. The unprecedented spate of success books that appeared between 1880 and 1885 (books bearing such titles as *The Law of Success, The Art of Money Getting. The Royal Road to Wealth,* and *The Secret of Success in Life)* provide eloquent, if indirect, testimony to the depth of the ideological crisis then facing the nation.[2]

Clearly, if belief in the American dream of individual advancement was to survive under the dramatically changed economic and social conditions of the late nineteenth century, new pathways to success had to be created. No less a figure than the great steel magnate Andrew Carnegie recognized this. Indeed, in 1885, just one year before the bitter labor struggle that culminated in the famous Haymarket affair, Carnegie conceded in a speech to the students of Curry Commercial College in Pittsburgh that the growth of "immense concerns " had made it "harder and harder . . . for a young man without capital to get a start for himself." A year later, in his widely read book, *Triumphant Democracy,* Carnegie forthrightly acknowledged that opportunities to rise from "rags to riches " had declined with the rise of the giant corporation (Carnegie 1886; Perkinson 1977, pp. 120–121).

Carnegie's solution to the problems posed by the great concentration of wealth was not, however, its redistribution, as was being called for by an increasing number of Americans. On the contrary, in 1889, Carnegie wrote that the "Socialist or Anarchist" who proposes such solutions "is to be regarded as attacking the foundation upon which civilization itself rests." Nevertheless, the man of wealth has a responsibility to administer it in the interest of all so as to promote "the reconciliation of the rich and poor." Perhaps the most effective means of doing so, Carnegie suggested, was to follow the example of such educational benefactors as Peter Cooper and Leland Stanford. The result of such judicious and far-sighted philanthropy would be, he noted, the construction of "ladders upon which the aspiring can rise" (Carnegie 1889, pp. 656, 660, 663).

Yet when Carnegie wrote, the nation's educational institutions were poorly suited to provide such ladders of ascent. In 1890, the average American had not been educated beyond the fifth grade. Moreover, the prevailing assumption—among both businessmen and the population at large—was that an ordinary common school training would provide the skills necessary for economic advancement. The nation's colleges and universities, still largely encrusted by traditional notions of cultural transmission and professional training, stood well to the side of the pathways to business success. As late as 1900, 84 percent of the prominent businessmen listed in *Who's Who in America* had not been educated beyond high school (Wyllie 1954, p. 95). In the late nineteenth century, getting ahead in America thus largely remained a matter of skill in the marketplace, not in the classroom.

If education remained peripheral to the attainment of the American dream, this was in part because, as late as 1890, there was a sense in which no educational system as such had yet been constructed. To be sure, the widely accessible common school had been one of the distinguishing features of American democracy, and one of its tasks was to provide those who attended it with the tools for economic success. But the primary purpose of the common school had been to train citizens for life in a democratic society, not to select workers and employees for their future positions in an increasingly complex and hierarchical division of labor. For this task, a differentiated rather than a common educational system needed to be constructed whose hierarchical divisions would mirror those of the larger society.

The "ladders of ascent" that Carnegie advocated presupposed basic structural changes in the organization of American education. The loose array of high schools, colleges, universities, and professional schools attended in the late nineteenth century by the increasing, though still limited, numbers of students who continued beyond elementary school was not really a system at all. There was not even a clear sequential relationship among the various types of educational institutions. Professional schools did not require the completion of four years of college, and colleges did not require the completion of four years of high school (Collins 1979, pp. 109–130). As a consequence, high schools, colleges, and professional schools sometimes even competed for the same students.[3] For its part, business was largely contemptuous of the diplomas awarded by high schools and especially colleges; in fact, many businessmen contended that college training was positively harmful to young men, in that it made them unfit for the harsh and practical world of commerce and industry (Wyllie 1954, pp. 101–105).

Yet despite the chaotic and relatively undifferentiated organization of American education in 1890, by 1920 the outlines of the orderly and highly stratified educational system that remains with us today were already visible.[4] The emergence of a hierarchically differentiated educational system closely linked to the labor market provided an alternative pathway to success in an era when the traditional image of the self-made man who rose to riches through success in the competitive marketplace was becoming less and less plausible. The creation of "ladders of ascent" through education thus gave new life to the American ideology of equality of opportunity at the very moment when fundamental changes in the economy threatened to destroy it.

In a context of increasing inequality between rich and poor and growing challenges to the established order, the importance of a new pathway to economic advancement is difficult to overestimate. America's large and open educational system now provided an alternative means of getting ahead. Vast inequalities of wealth, status, and power though there might be, the ladders of opportunity created by the new educational system helped the United States retain its national identity as a land of unparalleled opportunities for individual advancement.

Today, the idea that the education system in general, and higher education in particular, should provide ladders of upward mobility is so familiar as to be taken for granted. Yet viewed from a comparative perspective, the emphasis in the United States on individual mobility through education is quite remarkable.[5] To this day, no other society—not Japan, not Canada, not Sweden—sends as many of its young people to colleges and universities as the United States does (Organization for Economic Cooperation and Development 1983). *The vast and expensive system of educational pathways to success that has been constructed in this country is both the institutional embodiment of this commitment to the ideology of equality of opportunity and a constant source of reinforcement of this ideology.* The shape of today's enormous system of colleges and universities—a system in which in recent years almost half the nation's young people have participated—is incomprehensible apart from this commitment.

Central to this distinctive system of higher education is an institution—the two-year junior college (or community college, as it came to be called)—that came into being just when the American educational system was being transformed so as to provide new ladders of ascent. The two-year college, whose pattern of historical development will be the subject of this book, has from its very origins at the turn of the century reflected both the egalitarian promise of the world's first modern democracy and the constraints of its dynamic capitalist economy. Enrolling fewer than ten thousand students in 1920, the American junior college had by 1980 grown to enroll well over four million students (Eells 1931a. p. 70; U.S. Bureau of the Census 1987. p. 138).[6] The most successful institutional innovation in twentieth-century American higher education, the two-year college has in recent years spread beyond the United States and established roots in a growing number of foreign countries, among them Japan, Canada, and Yugoslavia

Community Colleges and Democratic Ideology

With over one-half of all college freshmen now enrolled in two-year institutions (U.S. Department of Education 1986. p. 111), the community college has come to be an integral feature of America's educational landscape. Yet as recently as 1900, the junior college was no more than a dream in the minds of a few administrators at a handful of America's leading universities. Enrolling under 2 percent of all college freshman in 1920 (U.S. Office of Education 1944, pp. 4, 6), the year in which the American Association of Junior Colleges (AAJC) was founded, the junior college came to play an increasingly pivotal role in the transformation of the nation's system of colleges and universities. Perhaps more than any other segment of postsecondary education, the community college was at the forefront of the postwar demographic expansion that changed the face of American higher education.

The transformation of American higher education was organizational as well as demographic. For the birth of the two-year college marked the arrival of an entirely new organizational form in the complex ecological structure of American postsecondary education. In terms of sheer numbers, no other twentieth-century organizational innovation in higher education even begins to approach the success of the two-year college, which grew from a single college in 1901 to over 1,200 institutions in 1980, representing almost 40 percent of America's 3,231 colleges. In 1984, over 4.5 million students were enrolled in two-year colleges nationwide (U.S. Bureau of the Census 1987, p. 138).

When the junior college first appeared, the outlines of a hierarchical system of colleges and universities were already becoming visible. Nonetheless, the emergence of the junior college fundamentally altered the shape of American higher education, for it introduced a new tier into the existing hierarchy. Thus the two year institution was not simply another of the many lower-status colleges that dotted America's educational landscape; it was a different type of institution altogether. Unlike even the humblest four-year institution, it failed to offer what had come to be considered the sine qua non of being an "authentic" college—the bachelor's degree.

What was behind the birth of this new institutional form with roots in both secondary and higher education? What explains the extraordinary growth of the two-year college during the twentieth century? And why has the provision of terminal vocational education—a function that, as we shall see, was for decades peripheral to the mission of the junior college—come to occupy an increasingly central place in the community college? The answers to these questions require an understanding of the peculiar political and ideological role that education has come to play in American life.

American Education and the Management of Ambition

All industrial societies face the problem of allocating qualified individuals into a division of labor characterized by structured inequalities of income, status, and power. Since occupying the superordinate positions in such systems provides a variety of material and psychological gratifications not available to those who occupy subordinate positions, the number of individuals who aspire to privileged places in the division of labor not surprisingly tends to surpass, often by a considerable margin, the number of such slots that are available. In advanced industrial societies, all of which have renounced to one or another degree the ideologies that have historically legitimated the hereditary transmission of positions, this problem of a discrepancy between ambition and the capacity of the opportunity structure to satisfy it is endemic. All such societies face, therefore, a problem in what might be called the *management of ambition*.[7]

In the United States, the management of ambition is a particularly serious dilemma, for success—as Robert Merton (1968, pp. 185–214) and others have pointed out—is supposed to be within the grasp of every individual, no matter how humble his (and, more recently, her) background.[8] Moreover, ambition and hard work have been held in more unambiguously high regard in America—a society that was bourgeois in its very origin—than in many European societies, with their aristocratic residues. From Benjamin Franklin to Norman Vincent Peale, the desire to succeed and the willingness to work hard to do so have been seen by Americans as among the highest moral virtues. One consequence of this belief that the "race of life" is both open and well worth winning is that more Americans from subordinate social groups harbor aspirations of making it to the top.

To be sure, not all Americans have joined the race to get ahead. Educational and occupational aspirations are systematically related to social class (Kerckhoff 1974, Spenner and Featherman 1978), and some segments of the population, especially in the racial ghettos of the nation's inner cities, have withdrawn from the competition all together (Ogbu 1978, 1983).[9] Even among those individuals who do harbor hopes of upward mobility, the depth of their commitment is highly variable and shifts in aspirations are common. Upward mobility has real social and psychological costs, and not everyone is willing—or able—to pay them. For many Americans, hopes of a "better life" crumble in the face of obstacles; consigned to low-status jobs, they nonetheless find fulfillment in the private sphere of family and friends. Moreover, aspirations to move ahead are often accompanied by a belief in the legitimacy of inequalities that are based on genuine differences in ability and effort[10] —*and* by doubts about whether one measures up.

The problem of managing ambition is particularly difficult in the United States. In 1980, for example, over half of high school seniors "planned" (not "aspired to") careers in professional/technical jobs. But in that same year, only 13 percent of the labor force was employed in such jobs (Wagenaar 1984). Even if one assumes that there will be a considerable increase in the number of such jobs in the future and that there is significant uncertainty in many of these "plans," it seems clear nonetheless that American society generates far more ambition than its structure of opportunity can satisfy.

As early as the 1830s, there was a powerful popular demand for free schooling, although it should be noted that the early workingmen 's organization of New York, Boston, and Philadelphia looked on the provision of free, public education not as a way of getting ahead but as indispensable to the exercise of their rights as democratic citizens (Welter 1962, pp. 46–47).[11] By the middle of the nineteenth century, free elementary education in America's "common schools" had become a reality in many states. Much as the early granting of "universal" suffrage (limited in fact to white males) promoted the incorporation of American working people into the existing political order, so too did the early provision of free public schools (Katznelson and Weir 1985).

As schools became more relevant to economic success and correspondingly more attractive to ambitious young men and women during the early twentieth century, popular demand for the expansion of education intensified. Between 1920 and 1940, over 20 percent of the age-eligible (fourteen to seventeen) population in the United States was enrolled in secondary schools; in eleven European countries, including Great Britain, France, Germany, and Sweden, the proportions nowhere surpassed 8 percent (Rubinson 1986, p. 522). The same pattern could also be seen in rates of attendance in higher education. An examination of statistics regarding college enrollments in twenty-two countries, including Japan and Russia as well as the major nations of Western and Central Europe, reveals that no country enrolled even half as many students as did the United States during the period 1913 and 1948 (Ben-David 1966, p. 464). From a sheer demographic perspective, then, the educational system has nowhere been as central to the life experiences of the population as it has been in the United States.

In light of the extraordinary emphasis in the United States on individual economic success and on the role of education as a pathway to it, it is hardly surprising that there has been such a powerful demand from below to expand the educational system. What is perhaps more difficult to understand is the readiness of the state to provide the additional years of schooling demanded by the populace. After all, one can well imagine the state trying to control public expenditures by limiting the amount of education. Yet for the most part, governing elites have joined in a broad national consensus that favored the construction of an educational system of unparalleled dimensions.

There have been many sources of elite support for the expansion of education, among them adherence to the classic Jeffersonian view that a democratic citizenry must be an educated one, and a related commitment to the task of nation building (Meyer et al. 1979). But also critical, we wish to suggest, has been the implicit recognition that a society that promises its subordinate classes unique opportunities for individual advancement needs to offer well-developed channels of upward mobility.

No one could deny the inequalities of wealth and power in the United States. But what made these inequalities tolerable, perhaps, was that everyone—or so the national ideology claimed—had a chance to advance as far as his ability and ambition would take him. And once education became established as the principal vehicle of this advancement, it became politically difficult for any group to oppose its expansion.

The result of this interplay of popular demand and elite response was the creation of a huge but highly differentiated educational system, with unequaled numbers of students enrolled in it. America's commitment to the idea of equal opportunity guaranteed that there would be a tremendous amount of ambition for upward mobility among the masses; somehow the educational system would have to find a way to manage the aspirations that its own relative openness had helped arouse. The junior college was to play a critical role in this process, and it is to the complex pressures it has faced both to extend and to limit opportunity that we now turn.

The Contradictory Pressures Facing the Junior College

From its very beginnings, the junior college has been subjected to contradictory pressures rooted in its strategic location in the educational system in a society that is both democratic and highly stratified. Its growth in substantial part a product of the responsiveness of a democratic state to demand from below for the extension of educational opportunity, the junior college's trajectory has also been shaped by the need to select and sort students destined to occupy different positions in the job structure of a capitalist economy. In the popular mind—and in the eyes of the many dedicated and idealistic men and women who have worked in the nation's two-year institutions—the fundamental task of the junior college has been to "democratize" American higher education, by offering to those formerly excluded an opportunity to attend college. But the junior college has also faced enormous pressure to limit this opportunity, for the number of students wishing to obtain a bachelor's degree—and the type of professional or managerial job to which it has customarily led—has generally been far greater than the capacity of the economy to absorb them. Poised between a burgeoning system of secondary education and a highly stratified structure of economic opportunity, the junior college was located at the very point where the aspirations generated by American democracy clashed head on with the realities of its class structure.

Like the American high school, the community college over the course of its history has attempted to perform a number of conflicting tasks: to extend opportunity and to serve as an agent of educational and social selection, to promote social equality and to increase economic efficiency, to provide students with a common cultural heritage and to sort them into a specialized curriculum, to respond to the demands of subordinate groups for equal education and to answer the pressures of employers and state planners for differentiated education, and to provide a general education for citizens in a democratic society and technical training for workers in an advanced industrial economy.[12]

Burton Clark, in a seminal article on "The 'Cooling-Out' Function in Higher Education," put the dilemma facing the junior college well: "a major problem of democratic society is inconsistency between encouragement to achieve and the realities of limited opportunity" (Clark 1961, p. 513). By virtue of its position in the structure of educational and social stratification, the junior college has confronted the necessity of diverting the aspirations of students who wish to join the professional and managerial upper middle class, but who are typically destined by the structure of opportunity to occupy more modest positions. In such a situation, Clark notes bluntly, "for large numbers failure is inevitable and *structured*" (Clark 1961, p. 515. emphasis his).

The junior college has thus been founded on a paradox: the immense popular support that it has enjoyed has been based on its link to four-year colleges and universities, but one of its primary tasks from the outset has been to restrict the number of its students who transfer to such institutions. Indeed, the administrators of elite universities who developed the idea of the junior college (and who later gave the fledgling organizational form crucial sponsorship) did so with the hope that it would enable them to divert from their own doors the growing number of students clamoring for access to higher education. These university administrators recognized that the democratic character of American culture and politics demanded that access to higher education be broad; in the absence of alternative institutions, masses of ill-prepared students would, they feared, be clamoring at their gates.[13]

The junior college thus focused in its early years on offering transfer courses. The reason was simple: Students who attended two-year institutions did so on the basis of their claim to be "real" colleges, and the only way to make this claim convincing was for them to offer liberal arts courses that would in fact receive academic credit in four-year institutions. For the first three decades of their existence, the junior colleges thus concentrated on constructing preparatory programs that, as the catalogues of the two-year institutions were fond of characterizing them, were of "strictly collegiate grade."

There was almost a missionary zeal among the predominantly small-town Protestant men who presided over the early junior college movement; their task as they saw it was to bring the blessings of expanded educational opportunity to the people. Proudly referring to their institutions as "democracy's colleges," they viewed the two-year institution as giving thousands of worthy students who would otherwise have been excluded a chance to attend higher education. Yet they were also aware that the educational and occupational aspirations of their students outran their objective possibilities by a substantial margin; while some of their students had great academic promise, well under half of them, they knew, would ever enter a four-year college or university. Something other than college preparatory courses, therefore, would have to be provided for them if they were to receive an education appropriate for their future place in the division of labor.

The solution that the leaders of the junior college movement devised bore a striking resemblance to the one developed earlier by the administrators of secondary education at the point when the high school was transformed from an elite to a mass institution: the creation of a separate vocational education track. The underlying logic of the vocational solution is perhaps best captured in a speech given in 1908 by Dean James Russell of Teachers College, Columbia University, to a meeting of the National Education Association. Entitling his presentation "Democracy and Education: Equal Opportunity for All," Russell asked:

> How can a nation endure that deliberately seeks to raise ambitions and aspirations in the oncoming generations which in the nature of events cannot possibly be fulfilled? If the chief object of government be to promote civil order and social stability, how can we justify our practice in schooling the masses in precisely the same manner as we do those who are to be our leaders? (quoted in Nasaw 1979, p. 131)

Russell's answer was unequivocal: The ideal of equal education would have to be forsaken, for only *differentiated education*—education that fit students for their different vocational futures—was truly democratic. Paradoxically, then, if mass education were to realize the promise of democracy, separate vocational tracks had to be created.

In a society that generated far more ambition for upward mobility than its structure of opportunity could possibly satisfy, the logic of vocationalism, whether at the level of secondary or higher education, was compelling. The United States was, after all, a class-stratified society, and there was something potentially threatening to the established order about organizing the educational system so as to arouse high hopes, only to shatter them later. At the same time, however, the political costs of turning back the popular demand for expanded schooling were prohibitive in a nation placing so much stress on equality of opportunity. What vocationalism promised to do was to resolve this dilemma by, on the one hand, accepting the democratic pressure from below to provide access to new levels of education while, on the other hand, differentiating the curriculum to accommodate the realities of the economic division of labor. The aspirations of the masses for upward mobility through education would not, advocates of vocationalization claimed, thereby be dashed; instead, they would be rechanneled in more "realistic" directions.[14]

The leaders of the junior college movement enthusiastically embraced the logic of vocationalism and, by the 1930s, had come to define the decided lack of student enthusiasm for anything other than college-transfer programs as the principal problem facing the two-year institution. Their arguments in favor of expanding terminal vocational education in the junior college were essentially identical to those used by advocates of vocational education in the high school: Not everyone could be a member of the elite; vocational programs would reduce the high dropout rate; and occupational training would guarantee that students would leave the educational system with marketable skills.

At times, junior college leaders were remarkably forthright about the fate that awaited these students in the labor market. For example, Walter Crosby Eells, founder of the *Junior College Journal* and executive secretary of the American Association of Junior Colleges from 1938 to 1945, noted that while universities tend to train leaders, democratic societies also needed "educated followership" and so proposed junior college terminal education as a particularly effective vehicle for training such followers (Eells 1941b, p. 29). Under Eells's leadership, by 1940 a consensus had been reached among key junior college leaders that between two-thirds and three-fourths of junior college students should be enrolled in terminal vocational education programs.

Yet the junior college leaders who advocated vocationalization faced a formidable obstacle: the widespread and persistent lack of interest among their own students. Despite encouragement from local administrators and counselors, no more than 25 to 30 percent of junior college students had ever enrolled in vocational programs. Their chances of getting ahead in a nation increasingly obsessed with educational credentials depended, they believed, on transferring to a four-year institution. The students realized that junior college occupied the bottom rung of higher education's structure. But as long as they were enrolled in college-parallel transfer programs, the possibility that they could obtain a professional or upper managerial job survived. Faced with the energetic efforts of junior college administrators to expand occupational education, the students—many of whom were of modest social origins—sensed that the attempt to vocationalize their institutions threatened to divert them from their educational and occupational aspirations.

This pattern of student opposition to vocational programs continued after World War II. The enrollment target of vocational education advocates remained two-thirds to three-quarters of junior college students, but at no time from the mid-1940s to the late 1960s did the proportion of two-year college students in the vocational track surpass one-third of the entire enrollment. Remarkably, this pattern of resistance to vocational education continued despite a dramatic increase in the number of students enrolled in community colleges, from just over 200,000 students in 1948 to almost 1.3 million in 1968 (U.S. Bureau of the Census, 1975, p. 383). Throughout this period, approximately two-thirds of community college students continued to be enrolled in college preparatory programs; of these, fewer than half ever transferred to a four-year institution (Medsker 1960, Medsker and Tillery 1971).

After decades of student resistance, enrollments in community college vocational programs finally surged after 1970, following a decline in the market for college graduates. By the mid-1970s, the percentage of students in programs specifically designed to provide occupational training had risen to at least 50 percent, and by 1980, the proportion had grown to approximately 70 percent.[15] Simultaneously, transfer rates fell drastically (Baron 1982, Cohen and Brawer 1982, Friedlander 1980, Lombardi 1979).

Although it would be misleading to hearken back to a mythical "golden age" when the junior college catapulted the majority of its students onto the pathway of educational and occupational success, the community college has historically provided a ladder of upward mobility to at least some of its students.[16] Especially in an institution that claimed as its *raison d'être* the democratization of American higher education, the sharp rise in vocational enrollments and the corresponding decline in the rate of transfer warrant careful examination. Increasingly, it seems, the community college has become a vocational-training institution, more and more divorced from the rest of academia, with potentially serious consequences for the life chances of its students.[17]

Curricular Change in the Community College

Observers of the transformation of the community college from an institution oriented to college-preparatory transfer programs to one emphasizing terminal vocational training have tended to focus on one of two forces as the principal cause: either the changing preference of student "consumers" of community college education or, alternatively, the decisive influence of business elites. In the first, which might be called the *consumer-choice model*, institutions of higher education are regarded as responding exclusively to students' curricular preferences: what the consumers of higher education demand, they receive. In the second, which we shall refer to as the *business-domination model*, the curricular offerings of the community colleges are seen as reflecting the imprint of powerful business interests, which prefer programs that provide them with technically trained workers. Drawing, respectively, on classical liberal and Marxist approaches to the problem of institutional change, each of these models provides a theoretically plausible explanation for the trajectory of community college development, and, accordingly, commands our attention.

The Consumer-Choice and Business-Domination Models

The consumer-choice model is an application of the more general "'rational-choice" model of human behavior popular among economists (see, for example, Becker 1983) and an increasing number of social scientists in neighboring disciplines. This model sees students' preferences as based on perceptions of the labor market "returns" that are yielded by different programs (Freeman 1971, 1976). According to this perspective, the enormous growth in community college vocational programs reflects the shift in the preference of hundreds of thousands of educational consumers. The aggregate consequence of all these individual shifts is the increasing predominance of occupational training in the two-year colleges.

The consumer-choice model views students as highly rational economic maximizers.[18] They wish to obtain the highest possible rates of return for the lowest cost in time, effort, and expense. Consequently, as the rate of return to liberal arts education begins to decline and opportunities for relatively high returns to low-cost vocational education increase, students make the rational choice: they begin to invest more heavily in vocational education, and colleges in turn expand their vocational course offerings to meet the increased demand. Especially in light of the widely publicized decline in the early 1970s in the economic returns for a college degree, the consumer-choice model offers a parsimonious explanation of the community college's vocationalization.

The unit of analysis in the consumer-choice model is not the group or the institution but, rather, the individual. As with the other approaches embodying "methodological individualism," the underlying assumption of this model is that social processes can be reduced to individuals' preferences and activities (Lukes 1968).

The other explanation of the community colleges' vocationalization, the business-domination model, emphasizes the power of large corporations to shape the educational system to serve their own interests. This perspective is in many ways an application to education of a broader Marxist "instrumentalist" theory of the role of the state in advanced capitalist societies.[19] Advocates of this view see the rise of vocationalism as primarily caused by the active intervention of business in shaping the community college's curricular offerings. Seeing in vocational education an opportunity to train at public expense a labor force of narrowly educated but technically competent middle-level specialists, big business has moved—through private donations, control of boards of trustees, and influence on trendsetting private foundations—to tailor the community college to its particular needs. In the business-domination model, the primary unit of analysis is social class, viewed in the Marxist framework as embedded in a capitalist mode of production.

Given the historical enthusiasm of the business community for vocational training (Lazerson and Grubb 1974) and its often-expressed concern in recent years about the tendency of four-year colleges and universities to produce masses of "overeducated" workers, the role attributed by the business-domination model to large corporations in the process of vocationalization seems plausible. According to this perspective, community colleges are seen as eager "to do the errands of business interests," having " no broader conception of education . . . than one that narrowly serves these interests" (Pincus and Houston 1978, p. 14). Bowles and Gintis, authors of *Schooling in Capitalist America,* believe that the increasingly vocationalized community college is well designed to produce that particular combination of technical competence and social acquiescence that is required to occupy skilled but powerless positions in the corporate economy: "The social relationships of the community college classroom increasingly resemble the formal hierarchical impersonality of the office or the uniform processing of the production line" (Bowles and Gintis 1976, p. 212).[20]

Both the consumer-choice and the business-domination perspectives capture something important, we believe, about the forces shaping community college development. Market forces have influenced student preferences, and the downturn in the labor market for college graduates in the early 1970s was indeed a major factor in the rapid community college vocationalization of the following years. And especially since the mid-1970s business has influenced (occasionally directly, but more often indirectly) the shape and content of the curricula from which community college students select their programs.

Today student "consumers" eagerly enroll in community college occupational programs that they hope will lead them into relatively high-paying, secure jobs with opportunities for advancement. These choices, though based, we shall argue, on imperfect labor market information, are in part logical responses to the overcrowded market for college-trained persons and the difficulties of competing in such a market. The programs in which these occupational students enroll, in turn, are determined in part by industry's needs for particular types of "middle-level" manpower.

We believe that the indirect influence of business on community college curricula has always been great. The colleges have for some time sought to keep pace with manpower developments in the private economy. Indeed, the more enterprising two-year college administrators have studied regional and national labor projections almost as if they were sacred texts. Arthur Cohen, now director of the ERIC Clearinghouse for Junior Colleges at the University of California at Los Angeles, was hardly exaggerating when he wrote that "when corporate managers . . . announce a need for skilled workers . . . college administrators trip over each other in their haste to organize a new curriculum" (Cohen 1971, p. 6).

Yet despite the consumer-choice and business-domination models' contributions to our understanding of recent developments in the community college, neither is an adequate guide to the past. Rather, they are most useful for the period since 1970, the year of the first signs of decline in the labor market for college graduates—and of little help for the period before that year. Since some of the most influential community college officials have been attempting to vocationalize their institutions since at least 1930, that leaves forty years of history almost entirely unaccounted for by either model. Moreover, we shall argue, neither model captures some of the key dynamics of the process of vocationalization since 1970.

Before 1970, our study reveals, neither students nor businessmen were very interested in vocational programs. Most students (and their families) desired the prestige of a baccalaureate degree and resisted terminal vocational training. But despite the students' overwhelming preference for liberal arts programs, the leaders of the American Association of Junior Colleges and their allies pursued a policy of vocationalization for over four decades before there was any notable shift in the students' preferences. This policy decision cannot be explained by the consumer-choice model.

Similarly, most members of the business elite were indifferent to community colleges before the late 1960s. Indeed, for almost another decade after that, business interest in the community colleges remained modest and picked up only in the late 1970s, after the colleges had already become predominantly vocational institutions. The indifference of business people to programs ostensibly developed in their interests cannot be readily explained by the business-domination model. An adequate explanation of the community college's transformation thus requires a fundamental theoretical reformulation.

Toward an Institutional Approach

The framework that we propose to account for the transformation of American community colleges may be called, albeit with some oversimplification, an *institutional model*. Inspired in part by the classical sociological tradition in the study of organizations,[21] this approach can, we believe, illuminate processes of social change beyond the specific case of education. Perhaps the model's most fundamental feature is that it takes as its starting point organizations themselves, which are seen as pursuing their own distinct interests. Within this framework, special attention is focused upon "organizational fields" (e.g., education, medicine, journalism), which may be defined as being composed of "those organizations that, in the aggregate, constitute a recognized area of institutional life: key suppliers, resource and product consumers, regulatory agencies, and other organizations that produce similar services or products" (DiMaggio and Powell 1938, p. 148).[22] Relations among organizations within the same field are often—but not always—competitive; accordingly, understanding the historical trajectory of a particular organization generally requires an analysis of its relationship to other organizations offering similar services. The dynamics of specific institutions, in turn, are rooted in their relationships to other major institutions. For example, the educational system must be analyzed in relation to the state and the economy. If the focus of the consumer-choice and the business-domination models is on the individual and the class respectively, the focus of this approach will be, accordingly, on the institution.

According to this perspective, neither the consumer-choice nor the business-domination model pays sufficient attention to the beliefs and activities of the administrators and professionals who typically have the power to define what is in the "interest" of the organizations over which they preside. Much of our analysis will focus, therefore, on explaining why these administrators chose to vocationalize despite what we shall document was the opposition of the student consumers (an opposition that casts doubt on the consumer-choice model) and the indifference of potential sponsors in the business corporations (which in turn undermines the business-domination model). Our analysis assesses the beliefs and organizational interests of those who pursued the vocationalization policy and the techniques they used to implement this policy over time. It also examines the forces, both external and internal to the community college movement, that facilitated or hindered implementation of the policy at different historical moments.

In skeletal from, our basic argument is that the *community colleges chose to vocationalize themselves, but they did so under conditions of powerful structural constraints.* Foremost among these constraints was the subordinate position of the community college in the larger structure of educational and social stratification. Put more concretely, junior colleges were hampered by their subordinate position in relation to that of the older and more prestigious four-year colleges and universities and, correspondingly, a subordinate position in the associated competition to place their graduates into desirable positions in the labor market.

Perhaps the best way to capture this dual structural subordination is to think of the structure of stratification faced by community colleges in terms of two parallel but distinct components—one a structure of labor market stratification and the other a structure of institutional stratification in higher education. From this perspective, educational institutions may be viewed as competing for training markets—the right to be the preferred pathway from which employers hire prospective employees. Access to the most desirable training markets—those leading to high-level professional and managerial jobs—is, and has been for decades, dominated by four-year colleges and, at the highest levels, by elite graduate and professional schools. Community colleges, by their very location in the structure of higher education, were badly situated to compete with better-established institutions for these training markets. Indeed, it is not an exaggeration to say that by the time that two-year colleges established a major presence in higher education, the best training markets were effectively monopolized by rival institutions.

Training markets are critical to the well-being of higher-education institutions. In general, those that have captured the best markets—for example, the top law, medical, and management schools—are the institutions with the most resources, the greatest prestige, and the most intense competition for entry. Viewed historically, community colleges had lost the most strategic sectors of this market before they could enter the competition. The best that the community colleges could hope to do, therefore, was to try to situate themselves favorably for the next available market niche. Therein resided the powerful organizational appeal of the two-year college's long-standing vocationalization project, a project that, as we shall show, had become widely accepted among community college administrators long before there was any decline in the demand for graduates of four-year colleges or any demand for vocational programs from the community college students themselves.

Because of their precarious position in the competition for training markets, community colleges tried desperately to fit themselves to the needs of business despite the absence of direct business interest in the colleges. Indeed, far from imposing on the community colleges a desire for a cheap docile labor force trained at public expense, as the business-domination model would have it, big business remained indifferent to the community colleges for the first sixty years of their existence. Yet because of the structural location of business in the larger political economy—and, in particular, its control of jobs—community colleges had little choice but to take into account the interests of their students' future employers. Thus business exerted a profound influence over the direction of community college affairs and pushed them in the direction of vocationalization without any direct action whatsoever. This capacity to exert influence in the absence of direct intervention reflects the *structural power* of business.[23]

Reduced to its essentials, then, our argument is that the community colleges found themselves in a situation of structured subordination with respect to both other higher-education institutions and business. Within the constraints of this dual subordination, the vocationalization project was a means of striking the best available bargain. We refer in the text to this deference to the perceived needs of more powerful institutions—even when such institutions made no conscious efforts to control their affairs—as *anticipatory subordination*.

This anticipatory subordination was rooted in the recognition by the community colleges that if they tried to compete with the existing better-endowed, higher-status institutions on their own terrain, they would face certain defeat. A far better strategy, it was determined after much internal debate with the junior college movement, was to try to capture an unexploited—albeit less glamorous—market in which they would not compete directly with institutions with superior resources. In return for accepting a subordination that was, in any case, inherent in their structural location, the community colleges would use vocationalization to bring a stable flow of resources linked to a distinctive function, a unique institutional identity, and above all, a secure—indeed, expanding—market niche. Only the students' resistance stood in the way of this project's realization.

The following text refers to content found in *The Diverted Dream: Community Colleges and the Promise of Educational Opportunity in America*, by S. Brint and J. Karabel, 1989.

The Outline of This Volume

Our study of the American junior college is divided into two sections. Part I, which includes Chapters 2 through 4, is a historical analysis of the origins of the two-year institution, its growth and development, and its transformation into a predominantly vocational institution. The focus of Part I is on developments at the national level, and it attempts to trace the spread of junior colleges during this century from a few states in the Midwest and West to every corner of the United States. We shall pay particular attention in Part One to the trajectory of junior college development in the state that for decades was the uncontested leader of the national movement: California. For California was not only the first state to develop a coherent "master plan" for higher education; as late as 1968, it enrolled over one-third of all the junior college students nationwide (Carnegie Commission 1970, p. 59)[24]

Part II, which covers Chapter 5 through 7, is a detailed case study of the development of community colleges in Massachusetts. The history of junior colleges in this state encapsulates, in telescoped fashion, developments at the national level. Founded initially as institutions primarily devoted to the provision of liberal arts–transfer programs, Massachusetts's community colleges were transformed during the 1970s into overwhelmingly vocational institutions. Broadly representative of national trends over the past two decades, the case of Massachusetts's community colleges will illuminate the dynamics which have led to the triumph of vocationalism in so many other states.[25]

We have included both national-level and state-level studies because of our conviction that each is critical to understanding junior college development. The study of national-level events is crucial for tracing the rise to prominence of the two-year college. By 1920, with the founding of the AAJC, the junior college movement had become nationwide, and developments in national institutions often had major consequences for two-year colleges at state and local levels. In particular, the national level was where the campaign for vocationalization originated and gained momentum; indeed, it is hard to imagine that the "comprehensive model" of the community college, with its strong emphasis on vocational programs, would have been embraced by state systems from Florida to Washington without the help of such national organizations as the American Association of Junior Colleges and the Carnegie Foundation.

Yet an analysis of national-level forces and developments can tell us only part of the story of the two-year colleges' transformation. Although it can illuminate the historical evolution of program preferences, it cannot give us a detailed account of the reactions to these preferences at the state and local levels, the independent sources of change at these levels, or the means through which policy preferences were implemented on specific community college campuses. Such issues require both archival data and field work for the purposes of examining processes of change in state coordinating bodies and on individual community college campuses. A case study was thus necessary, we believed, to complement and give texture to our broader analysis of national trends, and it is for this reason that we examined the rise and transformation of Massachusetts community colleges.

Finally, in the last chapter, we attempt to bring together the findings of our national-level study and our case study of Massachusetts and to identify the theoretical implications of our investigation. The development of junior colleges reveals much about not only the educational system but also the character of American society: the two-year college has been a distinctively American creation, and nowhere else has it attained such prominence. How and why this peculiar institution developed—and through what processes it was fundamentally transformed—will be the subject of the remainder of the book.

CHAPTER 6

THE COMMUNITY COLLEGE: THE IMPACT, ORIGIN, AND FUTURE OF A CONTRADICTORY INSTITUTION

KEVIN J. DOUGHERTY

Kevin Dougherty discusses the development of the community college and its role in American society. In doing so, he explores what he calls "the contradictory roles" of community colleges and considers the future of this important, but often neglected, part of higher education. As you read through this reading, consider how community colleges came to be and how educational trajectories and future work careers are shaped by the type of educational institution you attend.

Questions to consider for this reading:

1. What are the functions of community colleges? In what sense are they contradictory?
2. What is the role of community colleges in maintaining inequality in society?
3. How did business and government affect the growth of community colleges and how was their impact different from that on research universities?

Community colleges are one of the most important sectors of U.S. higher education. They are important because of their great number, their critical role in providing college opportunity (especially for nontraditional students), and the essential role that they play in providing postsecondary vocational training. These public two-year colleges—numbering 1,032 in 2007—comprise one-quarter of all higher educational institutions in the United States (U.S. National Center for Education Statistics, 2009, table 266). Community colleges enroll over one-third of all college students (some 6.3 million in fall 2007). This enrollment share is even greater for nontraditional students, whether older, part-time, minority, or disadvantaged (U.S. National Center for Education Statistics, 2009, tables 192, 227). Finally, community colleges are important as key sources of postsecondary vocational education. Vocational enrollees at community colleges comprise over half of all students in all forms of postsecondary vocational training and provide a large share of our nation's graduates in such important occupations as nursing, computer operations, and auto repair (Cohen & Brawer, 2008; Dougherty & Bakia, 2000; Grubb, 1996, pp. 54–56).

Yet, because of this very importance, community colleges are contradictory institutions. Community colleges have taken on a host of different social functions, but some of these functions are partially incompatible. In this piece I explore these contradictory functions in closer detail and trace their historical origins.

Author's Note: I would like to thank Regina Deil-Amen, Floyd Hammack, James Jacobs, Vanessa Smith Moresi, and Joan Spade for their comments on this chapter as it has evolved over the years.

For an updated version of this reading, refer to Kevin J. Dougherty and Vanessa S. Morest, "The Community College: The Impacts, Origins, and Futures of a Contradictory Institution," pp. 372-383 in Jeanne H. Ballantine and Joan Z. Spade (eds.), *Schools and Society*, 5th ed., Sage, 2015.

Contradictory Functions and Impacts

Most community colleges are "comprehensive" institutions, offering a wide variety of programs to a diverse clientele. In most community colleges, a majority of students are enrolled in workforce preparation and economic development programs. However, three-quarters of all first-time community college students (including adults) aspire to get at least a baccalaureate degree and one-quarter transfer to a four-year college within five years of entering a community college (McCormick, 1997, pp. 32, 41).[1] In addition, community colleges operate sizable programs in remedial education, adult education, and community services (such as concerts and day camps) (Cohen & Brawer, 2008). Examining these functions in greater detail allows us to better understand the ways in which they are compatible or incompatible, synergistic, or contradictory.

College Access and Opportunity

The community college is a central avenue into higher education and toward the baccalaureate degree, particularly for working class, nonwhite, and female students. Many baccalaureate recipients, particularly in states such as California and Florida, got their start at community colleges. In fact, several studies find that states and localities that are highly endowed with community colleges have significantly higher rates of college attendance and baccalaureate attainment than states and localities with a smaller community college presence (Dougherty, 1994, pp. 50–51; Rouse, 1998).

Several features of community colleges make them great avenues of college access. Community colleges are widely distributed across the country, located in urban, suburban, and rural areas. They are cheaper to attend than four-year colleges. Their tuitions are usually low and dormitory residence is not necessary because the colleges are nearby. And because of their open-door admissions ideal, they are more willing to take "nontraditional" students: high school dropouts, vocational aspirants, and adults interested in leisure education.

However, despite the community college's success in widening college access, there is concern about its role in providing college success. Many students entering the community college do not leave it either with a degree in hand or having transferred to another institution. Among students who entered a community college in fall 2003 and were followed up three years later, 45% had left higher education without a degree of any kind (Horn, 2009, pp. 22-23).

In explaining this high dropout rate, it is important to acknowledge that community college students tend to come from less advantaged backgrounds and be less prepared academically than four-year college entrants. However, it is also important to acknowledge the important role of *institutional* factors. Community colleges are less able to academically and socially integrate their students into the life of the college through such means as on-campus housing (Dougherty 1994, chap. 4; 2002, pp. 317-318). Moreover, community college faculty are less able to engage students because so many are part time. In fall 2007, 69% of all faculty in public two-year colleges were part-timers (National Center for Education Statistics, 2009, table 245). In studies that control for various student and institutional characteristics, there is evidence that higher proportions of part-time faculty in community colleges are associated with lower rates of student retention (Calcagno, Bailey, Jenkins, Kienzl, & Leinbach, 2008; Jaeger & Eagan, 2009). Finally, community colleges often do not adequately meet the needs of their students for extensive program and career advice (Rosenbaum, Deil-Amen, & Person, 2006).

Preparation for the Baccalaureate (College Transfer)

Historically, one of the leading roles of the community college has been to provide access to the baccalaureate. Originally, this took the role of fostering transfer to four-year colleges but in recent years, community colleges have begun increasingly to offer their own baccalaureate degrees (Floyd, Skolnik, & Walker, 2005). But despite the long-standing nature of this role of the community college, it has been fraught with controversy.

Many different studies find that entering a community college rather than a four-year college significantly lowers the probability that a student will attain a baccalaureate degree. Clearly, this gap in baccalaureate attainment could be simply due to the fact that community college students *on average* tend to be less well off, less prepared academically, and less ambitious educationally and occupationally than are four-year college entrants. But even when we compare community college entrants and four-year college entrants with the same family background, academic aptitude, high school grades, and educational and occupational aspirations, the community college entrants on average attain about 15% *fewer* baccalaureate degrees than their four-year college peers. This baccalaureate gap even holds in studies that systematically address issues of selection bias through the use of instrumental variables analysis or propensity score analysis (Alfonso, 2006; Dougherty, 1994, pp. 52–61; Doyle, 2008; Long & Kurlaender, 2009; Pascarella & Terenzini, 2005, p. 376). How do we explain this?

On closer inspection we find that—quite apart from the qualities students bring to college—entering the community college puts obstacles in the way of the pursuit of the baccalaureate degree. All other things being equal, baccalaureate aspirants who begin at a community college are more likely than comparable four-year college entrants to drop out during the first two years of college and not move on to become juniors at a four-year college.[2] As we have seen above, community college students more often drop out in the first two years of college because community colleges are less able to academically and socially integrate their students into the life of the college. In addition, fewer community college students go on to the junior year at four-year colleges because, in comparison to four-year college entrants, they receive weaker encouragement to pursue a bachelor's degree, less adequate   financial aid, and less interest by four-year colleges in admitting them to popular campuses and programs (Dougherty, 2002, pp. 315-323). This lack of transfer to universities is more pronounced among students who are lower in socioeconomic status, nonwhite, and older (Cabrera, Burkum, & LaNasa, 2005; Dougherty & Kienzl, 2006).

Workforce Preparation and Economic Development

The community college role in workforce preparation and economic development ranges from preparing students for their first job to retraining unemployed workers and welfare recipients, upgrading the skills of employed workers, assisting owners of small businesses, and helping communities with economic development planning (Dougherty & Bakia, 2000; Cohen & Brawer, 2008, chap. 8; Grubb, 1996; Jacobs & Dougherty, 2006).

In terms of initial job preparation, community colleges play a central role in supplying trained workers for "middle level" or "semiprofessional" occupations such as nurses, computer operators, and auto mechanics. In fact, about one-fifth of recent labor force entrants began at a community college (Grubb, 1996, pp. 54–56). These vocational graduates receive substantial economic payoffs. For example, students earning a vocational associate's degree from a community college earn 15% to 30% more in annual income than high school graduates of similar race and ethnicity, parental education, marital status, and job experience (Grubb, 2002; Marcotte, Bailey, Borkoski, & Kienzl, 2005).[3] In fact, there are community college vocational programs—particularly in nursing and certain technical fields—whose graduates earn more than many bachelor's degree holders. As a result, for many less privileged students who are only able to pursue short-term degrees, vocational education has emerged as a viable path to success (Deil-Amen & Deluca, 2010).

Still, the economic payoffs to community college degrees are, on average, not as good as those for baccalaureate degrees. Looking across all fields of study, the average baccalaureate degree pays about 40% to 50% more than the average high school degree, considerably more than the average vocational or academic associate's degree (Grubb, 2002; Marcotte et al., 2005). Moreover, community college students who pursue a vocational degree are significantly less likely to eventually transfer to pursue a baccalaureate degree, even when one controls for family background, educational aspirations, and high school preparation (Dougherty & Kienzl, 2006).

The community college's role in job retraining, small business assistance, and economic development planning—though less heralded than its role in job preparation—is important. Today, almost all community colleges retrain workers for new jobs or new tasks in existing jobs. In addition, many colleges assist small business owners by sponsoring small business development centers or simply offering courses that provide advice and training in management and personnel practices, marketing, finance, procuring contracts with government agencies, introducing new production technologies and work practices, and adapting to new government regulations. Finally, community colleges promote economic development by assisting local economic development planning efforts (Dougherty & Bakia, 2000).

While the community college's role in workforce preparation and economic development is very useful, it also can cause the community college considerable difficulties. Community colleges with very active workforce preparation programs can lose money on unpopular training programs flood the market with too many graduates, provoke criticism by competing training providers, and give employers too much influence over the college curriculum (Dougherty, 1994; Dougherty & Bakia, 2000). Moreover, an active workforce preparation effort can interfere with other functions of the community college such as preparing students for transfer to four-year colleges and providing students with a general education

Remedial Education

From the beginning, community colleges have been gateways into higher education for students whom four-year colleges would turn away as unprepared for college. As a result, community colleges have long provided remedial education to many of their students (Cohen & Brawer 2008). In 2000, 42% of freshmen in public two-year colleges were officially enrolled in remedial courses either in reading, writing, or arithmetic, as compared to 28% of college students generally (U.S. National Center for Education Statistics, 2003, p. 18). This remedial role grew during the 1990s as state legislators and four-year college boards pushed to have remedial education reduced or even eliminated at four-year colleges and relegated instead to community colleges (Shaw, 1997). This diversion of remediation into the community college poses a deep dilemma, one rooted in the contradictory effects of the community college. On the one hand, academically unprepared students pushed into community colleges may attain more education by perhaps receiving better remediation and occupational education than they would at four-year colleges. (However, there is no conclusive evidence that this is the case.[4]) But on the other hand, their long-run educational attainment may be harmed by receiving less assistance in pursuing a baccalaureate degree.

Adult, Continuing Education, and Community Education

Adult, continuing, and community education (ACCE) is a catchall including vocational improvement and retraining for those already working, high school completion and adult literacy improvement, personal development and recreational courses, and community services such as arts events.

Adult-education students are a key community college constituency. Many adult students enter the community college to take high school equivalency (GED), adult basic education (ABE), and English as a second language (ESL) courses. It is estimated that 33% of adult-education enrollees are in community colleges and such students make up 7% of total credit and non-credit FTE enrollments in community colleges. About three-quarters of these community college adult-education students are in the bottom half in socioeconomic status and about half are non-white (Grubb, Badway, & Bell, 2003, p. 223; Prince & Jenkins, 2005). Despite the hopes for adult-education programs, there is little evidence that they bring significant income benefits if they do not lead to a degree (Grubb et al., 2003, pp. 229–233; Prince & Jenkins, 2005, pp. 5–6, 21). A study of first-time adult students entering Washington State community colleges in the late 1990s (the majority of whom did not have high school diplomas) found that the income payoff only becomes significant if students accrue at least a year's worth of credits and a credential. Unfortunately, the same study found that five years after entering the community college only 58% of adult education students had acquired *any* college credits (with only 13% of ESL entrants doing so) (Prince & Jenkins, 2005, pp. 13–16, 23).

The ACCE divisions of community colleges are often their most dynamic because community colleges can more easily develop new course offerings in this area because the courses usually do not carry credit and therefore are less subject to state regulation. Community colleges can use noncredit offerings to learn more about the demands of the labor market, particularly in fast changing technology fields, and then develop similar credit-bearing courses (Dougherty & Bakia, 2000; Downey, Pusser, & Turner, 2006; Van Noy, Jacobs, Korey, Bailey, & Hughes, 2008). However, ACCE divisions of community colleges usually are not well funded, with state funding often being absent or paying less per student than state funding for regular, credit-bearing academic and occupational programs (Cohen & Brawer, 2008, chap. 10; Grubb et al., 2003; Van Noy et al., 2008). In part because of this, ACCE courses, particularly in adult education, are often criticized for being of poor quality because they rely on too many part-time faculty and provide inadequate student support services (Grubb et al., 2003).

General Education

Community colleges have made a major commitment to general education, whether defined as transmitting a common culture or fostering skills of broad utility in a person's life, such as critical thinking and communication skills (Higginbotham & Romano, 2006). Unfortunately, this commitment is partially contradicted by the community college's other commitments, particularly to occupational education. An analysis of the catalogs of 32 community colleges found that all of them had some kind of general education requirement for their transfer programs and at least 90% had a general education requirement for their nontransfer programs. But though these figures are impressive, they also exaggerate the actual degree to which community college students receive a general education. For example, among the 90% of those 32 community colleges that had core curriculum requirements for their nontransfer programs, only half required taking even one course in U.S. government and only one-fifth required a course in ethnic studies or multiculturalism (Zeszotarski, 1999).

These apparent gaps in the provision of general education are not surprising because community colleges face great difficulties in providing general education for all their students. The rise of occupational education has meant that community colleges now enroll many students whose primary purpose is likely to be preparation for a job rather than preparation for a variety of life roles. This problem is exacerbated if employers are paying for the training. Contract training programs typically are narrowly focused on providing skills and usually devote little or no attention to broader social knowledge and life skills. Finally, it is easier for public authorities to hold community colleges accountable for inculcating work skills than general learning (Dougherty, 2002, pp. 333–338; Higginbotham & Romano, 2006).

The Origins and Later Development of Community Colleges

Befitting their multiple and contradictory functions, community colleges have had equally mixed and contrasting origins. This is rarely acknowledged in the standard accounts of how community colleges were founded and later developed. Typically, these conventional accounts state that the community college was founded in response to calls by students, parents, and publicly interested educators and government officials for more college opportunities. And later, community colleges moved from an emphasis on academic education to a stress on occupational education primarily in response to the needs of students and employers for vocational training (Cohen & Brawer, 2008).

But other observers—particularly sociologists—have pointed out how these conventional chronicles miss much of the real history of the community college. For example, while these accounts mention the key role of state universities, they often misanalyze it. The state universities pushed the founding of community colleges not just to expand college opportunity, as is typically claimed, but also to keep the universities academically selective by channeling less able students toward the community colleges. Moreover, the universities unwittingly spurred the vocationalization of the community college by monopolizing greater status as "senior" colleges that trained for the most prestigious professional and managerial occupations. In order to escape the status of "junior" colleges, community colleges began in the 1920s to carve out an independent role as suppliers of a distinct training market of their own the "middle level" or semiprofessional occupations such as technicians, nurses, etc. (Brint & Karabel, 1989; Dougherty, 1994).

Local and state government officials also played a key role in the establishment and later vocationalization of community colleges, motivated not just by a sincere belief in educational opportunity but also by self-interest. At the local level, school superintendents and high school principals were the prime instigators of local drives to found community colleges. While they were certainly moved by a commitment to expand college opportunity, they were also driven by the desires to earn prestige as college founders and to secure jobs as presidents of the new colleges (Dougherty, 1994).

At the state level, governors, state legislators, and state education departments strongly pushed the expansion and later vocationalization of community colleges. Again, their support was prompted by more than just a desire to widen college access. State officials were mindful that building more community colleges, rather than expanding existing four-year colleges, could meet the great demand for college access in the 1960s and 1970s at a much lower cost to state government. Unlike the four-year colleges, community colleges would not require expensive dormitories, libraries, and research facilities. These savings would translate either into lower taxes or more state funds for other politically popular programs, both of which would make elected government officials more popular. In addition, community colleges, because of their strong commitment to vocational and technical education, could help stimulate the growth of state economies by attracting business firms with the carrot of publicly subsidized training of employees. This economic growth in turn would enhance the reelection chances of officials when they ran again for political office (Dougherty, 1994).

Business firms usually did not play a powerful *direct* role in founding or vocationalizing community colleges. But business played a powerful *indirect* role, based on business's central position within the United States' economic and ideological systems. Economically, business controls jobs and investment capital. Hence, in order to get their graduates access to the jobs employers control, community college officials on their own initiative will develop occupational programs that employers find useful, even without business demand for such programs (Brint & Karabel, 1989; Dougherty, 1994). Business also owns investment capital and thus largely controls the pace and distribution of economic growth. Realizing that capital investment is key to economic growth and therefore their own political prospects, elected officials have taken the initiative to offer business publicly subsidized vocational education in order to secure business investment in their jurisdictions. Ideologically, business influences government officials because those officials subscribe to values and beliefs—such as that economic growth is vital and that this growth must come primarily through an expansion of jobs in the private rather than public sector—that have made them ready to serve business interests (Dougherty, 1994).[5]

From Complex Origins to Contradictory Effects

An awareness of the community college's complex origins allows us to see how community colleges have come to powerfully hinder the baccalaureate opportunities of their students without this necessarily being an intended result. Because they lack dormitories, community colleges are less likely to keep their students in college by enmeshing them in a vibrant campus social life. But the reason community colleges lack dormitories is because this made the colleges cheaper to operate, a potent consideration in the minds of the local educators founding them and the state officials financing them. Because community colleges are heavily vocational, this may lead their transfer rate to be lower than it might otherwise be.[6] But a major reason community colleges are so strongly vocational is that this was a means of meeting elected officials' desire for economic investment and community college officials' desire for political support from business and jobs for their graduates. Finally, because community colleges are two-year schools, students are discouraged from pursuing a baccalaureate degree because they have to transfer to separate four-year institutions with different academic standards. But the reason community colleges are two-year schools is largely because university heads did not want the competition of many more four-year schools, state officials did not want the financial burden of a myriad four-year colleges, and local educators felt two-year colleges would be easier to establish and be staffed by local educators. The precipitate of these many different interests is an institutional structure that, unfortunately and largely unintentionally, often subverts the educational ambitions of baccalaureate aspirants entering community college, even as it opens up opportunities for students with nonbaccalaureate ambitions. In short, the complex origins of the community college have created a contradictory institution: one serving many, often conflicting, missions.

What Can Community Colleges Do to Improve Student Success?

Many of the difficulties the community college encounters are out of its control, lying in the nature of its students (who typically are less well off and less prepared than four-year college students) and the community college's very structure as a two-year nonresidential institution. Still, there is much community colleges can do to improve success rates for their students. They can reduce the number who leave without a degree by improving the academic and social integration of students and their academic achievement by creating learning communities and freshman seminars, employing more full-time faculty, improving advising and retention services particularly for minority students, working with high schools to improve the skills students enter college with, and developing more effective and transparent remedial education (Bailey, 2009; Bailey, Calcagno, Calcagno, Leinbach, & Kienzl, 2006; Dougherty, 2002, pp. 324–325; Jenkins, 2006; Kirst & Venezia, 2006; O'Gara, Karp, & Hughes, 2009; Rosenbaum et al., 2006; Scrivener et al., 2008; Zeidenberg, Jenkins, & Calcagno, 2007). Community colleges can increase transfer rates by encouraging transfer aspirations through better transfer advising, working to facilitate the transfer of course credits (especially for occupational students), and pushing state governments to provide financial aid specifically for transfer students (Bahr, 2008; Dougherty, 2002, pp. 325–328; Ignash & Kotun, 2005; Moore, Shulock, & Jensen, 2009).[7] In addition to these operational reforms, community colleges can also consider more far-reaching structural reforms, particularly themselves offering baccalaureate degrees rather than requiring students to engage in the often difficult process of transferring to a four-year college (Dougherty, 2002, pp. 328–330; Floyd et al., 2005).[8]

The Future of the Community College

The community college will not remain static. It will continue to change, perhaps sharply, due to its diffuse institutional mission and high responsiveness to its economic, social, and political environments (Townsend & Dougherty, 2006). As our economy globalizes, skilled and semiskilled jobs in offices and factories continue to be eliminated or moved abroad and class inequality increases. In response, community colleges are being asked to revamp their job preparation and economic development efforts to put more emphasis on high skilled jobs, including ones requiring baccalaureate degrees (Levin, 2001). Yet at the same time, community colleges still feel they should meet the needs of the many people who require remedial and adult basic education and preparation for semiskilled jobs (Jacobs & Dougherty, 2006). Meanwhile, as states conclude that their economies need more baccalaureate degree holders, community colleges are increasingly being asked by state officials to replace the more expensive public universities as the main site for the first two years of baccalaureate education (Wellman, 2002). But even as they respond to these demands, community colleges face increasing difficulties getting enough funds from state governments and rising competition from other colleges, whether four-year colleges offering continuing education or for profit colleges offering occupational education with higher placement rates than community colleges typically produce (Bailey, 2006; Kenton, Huba, Schuh, & Shelley, 2005; Rosenbaum et al., 2006). As the focus for these many cross-pressures emanating from a socially stratified and conflictual society, the community college will continue to be an important, but also contradictory, institution.

Notes

1. These figures overstate the baccalaureate ambitions of community college students. Many of those holding baccalaureate ambitions are in no hurry to realize them. Moreover, for a good many, this ambition is not founded on a very solid basis. However, it is still important to realize that many students who enter community college, even if with the intention of securing vocational training, do hope to eventually get a baccalaureate degree.

2. Data from the 1980s indicated that baccalaureate attainment of community college transfer students was undercut as well by higher rates of attrition in the junior and senior year than was the case for students who had started at four-year colleges as freshmen. However, studies based on data from the 1990s apparently find that this is no longer the case (Melguizo & Dowd, 2009).

3. Lower degrees receive smaller payoffs. Students receiving one-year certificates outpace high school graduates by only about 10% in annual earnings, and students who attend community college but do not receive a certificate or degree lead high school graduates by only 5% to 10% in earnings for every year of community college. Moreover, the payoff to a given community college credential varies by the student's social background, major, and job placement. For example, women make more from associate's degrees and certificates than do men but make less when they have secured no credential. The payoff is considerably higher for associate's degrees in engineering and computers, business, and (for women) health than in education or humanities. Finally, community college students get much better returns if they find employment in fields related to their training, than if they do not (Grubb, 1996, pp. 90, 95, 99, 102; Grubb, 2002).

4. Despite the importance of remedial education, we have little hard data on how well community colleges actually remediate. A number of studies have found small positive impacts of community college developmental education but the areas of impact (whether grades on subsequent nonremedial courses, completing a degree, or transferring to a four-year college) are not consistent across studies. In addition, there is no consensus on what forms of developmental education are most effective (Bailey, 2009; Dougherty, 2002, pp. 311–312; Perin, 2006).

5. The argument laid out in the preceding paragraphs is indebted to the theory of the state in political sociology and institutional theory in the sociology of organizations. For more on these theoretical roots, see Dougherty (1994) and Brint and Karabel (1989).

6. There is some debate over how much transfer rates are negatively affected by whether a community college is high in the proportion of its students and degrees that are in vocational fields. Compare Dougherty (1994, pp. 93–97) and Dougherty and Kienzl (2006) to Roksa (2006). In any case, the growing push to facilitate the transfer of occupational credits and degrees will help reduce the negative impact of the vocational emphasis of community colleges on transfer rates.

7. It bears noting that studies of the impact of state policies to facilitate transfer and articulation do not find that seemingly stronger policies lead to higher rates of transfer or even lesser credit loss. However, the studies conducted so far have had to cope with less than ideal data so there is a need for further studies in this area (Roksa, 2009).

8. Community colleges in 14 states have begun to offer their own baccalaureate degrees (Dougherty, 2002, pp. 329–330; Floyd et al., 2005). In Florida, over a third of community colleges offer baccalaureate degrees, primarily in education, business management, nursing, and health care administration (Community College Baccalaureate Association, 2010).

References

Alfonso, M. (2006). The impact of community college attendance on baccalaureate attainment. *Research in Higher Education, 47*(8), 873–903.

Bahr, P. R. (2008). Cooling out in the community college: What is the effect of academic advising on students' chances of success? *Research in Higher Education, 49*(8), 704–732.

Bailey, T. (2006). Increasing competition and the growth of the for profits. In T. Bailey & V. S. Morest (Eds.), *Defending the community college equity agenda* (pp. 87–109). Baltimore: Johns Hopkins University Press.

Bailey, T. (2009). Challenge and opportunity: Rethinking the role and function of developmental education in community college. In C. P. Harbour & P. L. Farrell (Eds.), *Contemporary issues in institutional ethics: New directions for community colleges #148* (pp. 11–30). San Francisco: Jossey-Bass.

Bailey, T., Calcagno, J. C., Jenkins, D., Leinbach, T., & Kienzl, G. (2006). Is student right-to-know all you should know? An analysis of community college graduation rates. *Research in Higher Education, 47*(3), 491–519.

Brint, S. G., & Karabel, J. B. (1989). *The diverted dream.* New York: Oxford University Books.

Cabrera, A. F., Burkum, K. R., & LaNasa, S. M. (2005). Pathways to a four-year degree. In A. Seidman (Ed.), *College student retention: Formula for student success* (pp. 155–214). Westport, CT: Praeger.

Calcagno, J.C., Bailey, T., Jenkins, D., Kienzl, G., & Leinbach, T. (2008). Community college student success: What institutional characteristics make a difference? *Economics of Education Review, 27*(6), 632–645.

Cohen, A. C., & Brawer, F. B. (2008). *The American community college* (5th ed.). San Francisco: Jossey-Bass.

Community College Baccalaureate Association. (2010). *Baccalaureate conferring locations.* Fort Myers, FL: Author. Retrieved from http://www.accbd.org/resources/baccalaureate-conferring-locations/

Deil-Amen, R., & Deluca, S. (2010). The underserved third: How our educational structures populate an educational underclass. *Journal of Education for Students Placed at Risk, 15*(1/2), 27–50.

Dougherty, K. J. (1994). *The contradictory college: The conflicting origins, impacts, and futures of the community college.* Albany: State University of New York Press.

Dougherty, K. J. (2002). The evolving role of the community college: Policy issues and research questions. In J. Smart & W. Tierney (Eds.), *Higher education: Handbook of theory and research,* Vol. 17. (pp. 295–348). Dordrecht, Netherlands: Kluwer.

Dougherty, K. J., & Bakia, M. F. (2000). Community colleges and contract training: Content, origins, and impacts. *Teachers College Record, 102*(1), 198–244.

Dougherty, K. J., & Kienzl, G. (2006). It's not enough to get through the open door: Inequalities by social background in transfer from community colleges to four-year colleges. *Teachers College Record, 108*(3), 452–487.

Downey, J., Pusser, B., & Turner, K. (2006). Competing missions: Balancing entrepreneurialism with community responsiveness in community college continuing education divisions. In B. T. Townsend & K. J. Dougherty (Eds.), *Community college missions in the 21st century: New directions for community colleges #136* (pp. 75–82). San Francisco: Jossey-Bass.

Doyle, W. R. (2008). The effect of community college enrollment on bachelor's degree completion. *Economics of Education Review. 28*(2), 199–206

Floyd, D. F., Skolnik, M., & Walker, K. (Eds.). (2005). *The community college baccalaureate.* Sterling VA: Stylus Press.

Grubb, W. N. (1996). *Working in the middle.* San Francisco: Jossey-Bass.

Grubb, W. N. (2002). Learning and earning in the middle, Part I: National studies of pre-baccalaureate education. *Economics of Education Review 21*(4), 299–321.

Grubb, W. N., Badway, N., & Bell. D. (2003). Community colleges and the equity agenda: The potential of non-credit education. *Annals of the American Academy of Social and Political Science, 586*(1), 218–240.

Higginbotham, G. H., & Romano, R. M. (2006). Appraising the efficacy of civic education at the community college. In B. T. Townsend & K. J· Dougherty (Eds.), *Community college missions in the 21st century: New directions for community colleges #136* (pp. 23–32). San Francisco Jossey-Bass.

Horn, L. (2009). *On track to complete? A taxonomy of beginning community college students and their outcomes 3 years after enrolling: 2003–04 through 2006. Statistical analysis report* (NCES 2009–152). Washington, DC: Government Printing Office

Ignash, J. M., & Kotun, D. (2005). Results of a national study of transfer in occupational/technical degrees: Policies and practices. *Journal of Applied Research in the Community College 12*(2), 109–120.

Jacobs, J., & Dougherty, K. J. (2006). The uncertain future of the workforce development mission of community colleges. In B. T. Townsend & K. J. Dougherty (Eds.), *Community college missions in the 21st century: New directions for* community *colleges #136* (pp. 53–62). San Francisco Jossey-Bass.

Jaeger, A. J., & Eagan, M. K. (2009). Unintended consequences: Examining the effect of part-time faculty members on associate's degree completion. *Community College Review, 36*(3), 167–194.

Jenkms, D. (2006). *What community college management practices are effective in promoting student success?* New York: Columbia University, Teachers College, Community College Research Center. Retrieved from http://ccrc.tc.columbia edu/ Publication.asp?UID=4I 9

Kenton, C. P., Huba,. M. E., Schuh, J. H., & Shelley, M.C: (2005). Financing community colleges: A longitudinal study of 11 states. *Community College Journal of Research and Practice, 29*(2), 109–122.

Kirst, M., & Venezia, A. (Eds.). (2006). *From high school to college: Improving opportunities for* success *in post-secondary education.* San Francisco: Jossey-Bass.

Levin, J. (200I). *Globalizing the community college* New York: Palgrave.

Long, B. T., & Kurlaender, M. (2009). Do community colleges provide a viable pathway to a baccalaureate degree? *Educational Evaluation and Policy Analysis, 31*(1), 30–53.

Marcotte, D. E., Bailey, T., Borkoski, C., & Kienzl, G. S. (2005). The returns of a community college education: Evidence from the national education longitudinal survey. *Educational Evaluation and Policy Analysis, 27*(2), 157–175.

McCormick, A. (1997). *Transfer behavior among beginning postsecondary students: 1989–94* (NCES 97–266). Washington, DC: U.S. National Center for Education Statistics.

Melguizo, T., & Dowd, A C. (2009). Baccalaureate success of transfers and rising 4-year college juniors. *Teachers College Record, 111*(1), 55–89.

Moore, C., Shulock, N., & Jensen, C (2009). Creating *a student-centered transfer process in California: Lessons from other states.* Sacramento: California State University, Institute for Higher Education Leadership & Policy.

O'Gara, L., Karp, M. M., & Hughes, K. L. (2009). Student success courses in the community college: An exploratory study of student perspectives. *Community College Review, 36*(3), 195–218.

Pascarella, E. T., & Terenzini, P. T. (2005). *How college affects students* (2nd ed.). San Francisco: Jossey-Bass.

Perin, D. (2006). Can community colleges protect both access and standards? The problem of remediation. *Teachers College Record, 108*(3), 339–373.

Prince, D., & Jenkins, D. (2005). *Building pathways to success for low-skill adult students: Lessons for community college policy and practice from a statewide longitudinal tracking study.* New York: Columbia University, Teachers College, Community College Research Center. Retrieved from http:/ccrc.tc.columbia.edu/Content ByType.asp?t=l

Roksa, J. (2006). Does the vocational focus of community colleges hinder students' educational attainment? *Review of Higher Education, 29*(4), 499–526.

Roksa, J. (2009). Building bridges for student success: Are higher education articulation policies effective? *Teachers College Record, 111*(10), 2444–2478.

Rosenbaum, J. E., Deil-Amen, R., & Person, A. E. (2006). *After admission: From college access to college success.* New York: Russell Sage Foundation.

Rouse, C. E. (1998). Do two-year colleges increase overall educational attainment? Evidence from the states. *Journal of Policy Analysis and Management, 17*(4), 595–620.

Scrivener, S., Bloom, D., LeBlanc, A., Paxson, C., Rouse, C. E., & Sommo, C. (2008). *A good start: Two-year effects of a freshmen learning community program at Kingsborough Community College.* New York: MDRC. Retrieved from http:// www.mdrc.org/publications/473/full.pdf

Shaw, K. M. (1997). Remedial education as ideological battleground: Emerging remedial education policies in the community college. *Educational Evaluation and Policy Analysis, 19*(3), 284–296.

Townsend, B. T., & Dougherty, K. J. (Eds.). (2006). *Community college missions in the 21st century: New directions for community colleges #136.* San Francisco: Jossey-Bass.

Van Noy, M., Jacobs, J., Korey, S., Bailey, T., & Hughes, K. L. (2008). *The landscape of noncredit workforce education: State policies and community college practice* (Issue Brief 38). New York: Community College Research Center, Teachers College, Columbia University. Retrieved from http:// ccrc.tc.columbia.edu/Publication.asp?uid=634

U.S. National Center for Education Statistics. (2003). *Remedial education at degree granting postsecondary institutions in fall 2000* (NCES 2004-010). Washington, DC: Government Printing Office.

U.S. National Center for Education Statistics. (2009). *Digest of education statistics, 2009.* Washington, DC: Government Printing Office.

Wellman, J. V. (2002). *State policy and community college-baccalaureate transfer.* San Jose, CA: National Center for Public Policy and Higher Education.

Zeidenberg, M., Jenkins, D., & Calcagno. J. C. (2007). *Do student success courses actually help community college students succeed?* (CCRC Brief#36). New York: Community College Research Center, Teachers College, Columbia University. Retrieved from http://ccrc.tc.columbia.edu/Publication.asp? uid=667

Zeszotarski, P. (1999). Dimensions of general education requirements. In G. Schuyler (Ed.), *Trends in community college curriculum. New directions for community colleges #108* (pp. 39–48). San Francisco: Jossey-Bass.

SECTION II

DIVERGENT GOALS AND INSTITUTIONAL DIVERSITY AMONG TWO-YEAR INSTITUTIONS

SECTION II: DIVERGENT GOALS AND INSTITUTIONAL DIVERSITY AMONG TWO-YEAR INSTITUTIONS

This section examines important contextual dimensions associated with community colleges in the United States. Though the diversity of institutional type, governing bodies and structures, and declared and operating missions is less fully articulated in the literature than the four-year baccalaureate sector, community colleges represent an extremely diverse segment of higher education in the United States. Whether examining location (rurality vs. urbanicity), degree-granting authority (associate vs. baccalaureate), governance (federal, segmented vs. unified) or other features, it is important to understand the vastly different ways community colleges are manifested across the nation's 50-state landscape. The articles chosen for this section give readers a sense of the rich diversity of community colleges in the United States, and the unfortunate misunderstandings that emerge when the literature characterizes all community colleges in any one stereotypical way.

In the first chapter, McCormick and Zhao provide a historical backdrop on "The Carnegie Classification," showing how the rubric has evolved since its first iteration in 1971, which introduced the groupings that have had staying power in the nation's conception of higher education institution types. The authors help readers understand changes in the classification system that occurred over time and laid the groundwork for the newest classification that is searchable via the web and offers a broader and more flexible system than was evident in the past.

In the second chapter of this section, Aragon and Zamani examine postsecondary access and promoting an equity agenda for diverse collegians at special population colleges. The authors share the origins and missions of minority-serving institutions, paying particular attention to address the differential attendance patterns of students of color at particular types of colleges (i.e., critical mass at Historically Black Colleges/Universities, Hispanic-serving Institutions, and Tribal Colleges). Additionally, Aragon and Zamani note higher education enrollments by race/ethnicity and gender illustrate increasing numbers of female students across racial/ethnic groups attend community colleges, particularly in lieu of the higher costs of attendance at privately controlled minority-serving institutions. However, less prominent in number are institutions that are hybrids in that they are community colleges that were originated to serve the needs of particular minorities (i.e., women, Blacks, and Native Americans). The authors situate the importance of institutional type and mission in creating inclusive campus environments for women and racially/ethnically diverse collegians as cultural congruence and person-environment fit contribute to successful matriculation of underserved, underrepresented students.

Chapter Nine shifts from classification of higher education institution types and special population colleges to community college missions. Meier sheds light on the mission problem relative to ambiguity of institutional mission within the community college sector. However, Meir argues that the purpose of the community college has historically shifted as two-year colleges have sought to be flexible and adaptive to the changing social and economic contexts.

The fourth chapter, by authors Belfield and Bailey, provides a review of the literature on earnings gains as benefits of community college attendance and completion, illustrating community colleges as a public and individual good (e.g., gains in general well-being, improved health behaviors, less reliance on public assistance, lower probability of criminal involvement, as well as economic gains). The manner in which earnings gains are calculated is complex, yielding variable gains across subgroups of community college degree recipients with some groups experiencing greater advantages than others.

In Chapter Eleven, Beach also situates community colleges in the political landscape of public education that positions these institutions on the bottom rung (or nearly so) of higher education and therefore chronically under-resourced and at the mercy of policymakers and politicians. He offers a critic essay on community colleges using historical, sociological, political, and economic lenses. His writing echoes the scholarship of Brint and Karabel (1989) in *The Diverted Dream* and Dougherty (1994) in *The Contradictory College* to catalog the accomplishments, shortcomings, and untapped potential of comprehensive community colleges in the United States.

Richardson, Jr. and de la Santos lift the discussion of community college type and mission to the state level in Chapter Twelve. Their writing points to variation in state governance of two-year colleges, both reflecting upon and contributing to variation in two-year institutions evidenced in earlier chapters in this section of the *Reader*. Various configurations and authority of governing boards are categorized in this chapter, along with a discussion of how these approaches may enhance partnerships with K-12 education but compete with the four-year baccalaureate-granting sector. The necessity for community colleges to use state and local fiscal resources strategically and garner greater federal support is also discussed.

Taken together, these chapters provide a richly nuanced depiction of community colleges historically and contemporarily. They make clear the importance of understanding the geographic, political, sociological, and economic context in which community colleges operate.

CHAPTER 7

RETHINKING AND REFRAMING THE CARNEGIE CLASSIFICATION

ALEXANDER C. MCCORMICK AND CHUN-MEI ZHAO

The Carnegie Commission on Higher Education was established by The Carnegie Foundation for the Advancement of Teaching in 1967 to study and make recommendations regarding the major issues facing U.S. higher education. The commission soon confronted a problem: no extant classification system differentiated colleges and universities along the dimensions that were most relevant to its work. So in 1970 the commission developed a new classification scheme to meet its analytic needs. Three years later, it published classification listings of colleges and universities to "be helpful to many individuals and organizations that are engaged in research on higher education." The rest, as they say, is history.

Clark Kerr headed the Carnegie Commission when it created the classification system, so it is not surprising that the scheme bore marked similarities to another element of the Kerr legacy, the mission differentiation embedded in the 1960 California Master Plan for Higher Education. Indeed, one goal of the new system was to call attention to—and emphasize the importance of—the considerable institutional diversity of U.S. higher education. The classification provided a way to represent that diversity by grouping roughly comparable institutions into meaningful, analytically manageable categories. It enabled researchers to make reasonable comparisons among "similar" institutions and to contrast them with groups of "different" ones.

In describing the new system, Kerr wrote that the commission sought to create categories that would be "relatively homogeneous with respect to the functions of the institutions as well as with respect to characteristics of students and faculty members." In other words, institutions were grouped according to what they did and who taught whom. Operationally, this was achieved by looking at empirical data on the type and number of degrees awarded, federal research funding, curricular specialization, and (for undergraduate colleges only) admissions selectivity and the preparation of future PhD recipients.

The result was a classification organized by degree level and specialization: doctorate-granting universities, master's-level institutions (called comprehensive colleges), undergraduate liberal arts colleges, two-year colleges, and specialized institutions, with all but the two-year colleges further broken into subcategories (see Table 1). The nation's high-status research universities were clustered together, as were the most prestigious liberal arts colleges. This fact, combined with the new classification's pedigree, may have influenced its broad acceptance: these groupings seemed reasonable and reflected the conventional wisdom—they made sense.

Alexander C. McCormick is a senior scholar at The Carnegie Foundation for the Advancement of Teaching where he directs the Carnegie Classification project and the Foundation's survey research program. Chun-Mei-Zhao is a research scholar at The Carnegie Foundation for the Advancement of Teaching

TABLE 1

The First Carnegie Classification (1971)

1. **Doctoral-Granting Institutions**
   Heavy emphasis on research
   Moderate emphasis on research
   Moderate emphasis on doctoral programs
   Limited emphasis on doctoral programs
2. **Comprehensive Colleges**
   Comprehensive colleges I
   Comprehensive colleges II
3. **Liberal Arts Colleges**
   Liberal arts colleges—Selectivity I
   Liberal arts colleges—Selectivity II
4. **All Two-Year Colleges and Institutes**
5. **Professional Schools and Other Specialized Institutions**
   Theological seminaries, bible colleges, and other institutions offering degrees in religion
   Medical schools and medical centers
   Other separate health professional schools
   Schools of engineering and technology
   Schools of business and management
   Schools of art, music, and design, etc.
   Schools of law
   Teachers colleges
   Other specialized institutions

Source: Carnegie Commission on Higher Education, New Student and New Place.

What has come to be known as "The Carnegie Classification" was not intended to be the last word on institutional differentiation, as suggested by the humble article in the title *A Classification of Institutions of Higher Education* (1973). But the higher education research community readily adopted the new system, and it soon became the dominant—arguably the default—way that researchers characterized and controlled for differences in institutional mission.

The first commission report to use the classification framework, published even before Carnegie listed institutions within the categories, was *New Students and New Places* (1971). This was an analysis of future demand for higher education that established parameters for growth of existing institutions and called for the establishment of new, accessible community colleges and comprehensive colleges, especially in metropolitan areas. In projecting the future needs of higher education, the commission wrote, "We find no need whatsoever in the foreseeable future for any more research-type universities granting the PhD." Instead, the report urged "preserving and even increasing the diversity of institutions of higher education by type and by program [and] resisting homogenization." A special irony of the Carnegie Classification—which called attention to institutional diversity—is the homogenizing influence it has had, as many institutions have sought to "move up" the classification system for inclusion among "research-type" universities.

The classification's use soon reached beyond the research community—many others saw value in a classification system created and maintained by an independent, reputable agent such as the Carnegie Commission and its parent organization, The Carnegie Foundation for the Advancement of Teaching. Thus by what is largely an accident of history, the Foundation became the custodian of a classification system that has been used to describe, characterize, and categorize colleges and universities for over 30 years, and its category labels are firmly established in the vernacular of higher education. The Foundation has taken on a sometimes enviable, sometimes controversial, sometimes uncomfortable role as the arbiter of institutional classification and comparison.

Since its publication in 1973, the Carnegie Classification has been updated four times to take account of changes in both the constellation of institutions (the result of openings, closings, and mergers) and within the institutions themselves (the result of changes in offerings and activities). Successive editions have revealed the changing contours of U.S. higher education over time—although longitudinal analysis must be approached with care due to the many incremental changes to categories and category definitions that have been made since 1973.

Over the last few years, the Foundation has been engaged in a comprehensive reexamination of this system and of its own role as classifier. In the following pages, we explore some key issues related to classification, how it is understood and used, and how it might move forward. We begin with a brief discussion of classification in general, then we shift to the specific case of classifying colleges and universities. We conclude with a discussion of the Carnegie Classification's future prospects.

Classification in the Abstract

Classification is a ubiquitous human activity, an essential part of how we perceive and make sense of the world. It helps us collect, organize, store, and retrieve complex information. For instance, when asked to describe someone, we may say he (not she) is of medium height, in his mid-30s, with brown eyes, short curly hair, and a slender build. This short description is full of classification choices, but other contexts might call for entirely different choices. In an emergency room, for instance, many of these features might be ignored in favor of other characteristics that would lead to a diagnostic classification: consciousness, pupil dilation, shallowness of breath, and coherence of speech, to name a few.

In this sense, classification is a way of seeing, a social practice that directs attention toward selected characteristics and away from others (see the Bowker and Star volume in Resources). Classifications based on different criteria represent different perspectives on or approaches to understanding a phenomenon. No absolute standard for the "best" solution exists; rather, the value of a classification is closely linked to its intended use. Thus in a library, classification according to subject matter is far more useful than other possible approaches, such as grouping books by paper type, typeface, number of pages, or jacket design (some of which might be entirely appropriate in a different context, such as a museum collection).

While classification's power to facilitate the analysis of complex phenomena by reducing cognitive complexity may be welcome, there are dangers associated with the process. A significant one is reification, whereby categories representing conceptual constructs come to be viewed as empirically "real" and "natural." In addition, a dominant classification may channel people's perceptions and limit the consideration of other perspectives. Classification also tends to be retrospective, based on observations from the past. And it is static rather than dynamic: the fixed categories of a classification or fixed classifications of individual entities may not keep up with phenomena that are subject to change over time.

Classification also can involve trade-offs among conflicting goals. For example, choosing the number of classification categories is a matter of judgment that involves a tension between precision and parsimony. As categories are defined more precisely, the number of categories increases, as does homogeneity within them, while the size of the group within each category declines. Favoring parsimony yields more manageable and more easily comprehended classifications made up of fewer categories but with more members and more variation within the categories.

In the end, the value of a classification is best judged pragmatically. To form a useful classification we must take multiple factors into account, such as the classification's purpose, the nature of entities to be classified, the available classification criteria, and the degree of differentiation required. Do its groupings make sense? Does it focus attention on the "right" similarities and differences for its purposes? Does it lead to new and valuable insights? Does it advance knowledge and understanding?

Classification of Colleges and Universities: Issues and Challenges

We now turn to the specific case of classifying colleges and universities, focusing on what we consider to be some fundamental issues confronted by classifiers and the classified.

Although the Carnegie Classification was created for research purposes with particular analytic needs in mind, it has evolved into a sort of general-purpose classification employed by a wide range of users for a variety of applications. Now commonly used by institutional personnel, state systems, foundations, membership organizations, news magazines, and others, it is so highly institutionalized that it is often invoked without explanation or rationale. As its use has extended beyond the realm of aggregate-level policy analysis and academic research, it has attracted the interest of stakeholders such as administrative leaders, faculty, trustees, state boards, accreditors, and legislators. This has led to a corresponding expansion of ideas regarding what the classification is or ought to be, and in many cases the ideas of the various users and stakeholders are in conflict.

For instance, some classification users want it to remain fixed in overall structure and classification criteria, in the interest of studying long-term trends: change in the landscape of U.S. higher education, change at individual institutions, faculty career mobility, patterns of education participation, and so on. Others want it to evolve to accommodate new developments, such as new organizational forms, new (or newly salient) priorities, new methods of participation and delivery, and new types of students.

Some want the classification to represent the status-and-resource hierarchy that exists in higher education, while others want it to disrupt that hierarchy. In many cases, calls to disrupt hierarchy implicitly or explicitly seek to establish a new hierarchy in its place, and the Carnegie Classification is seen as a powerful platform for doing so. Some object that the classification appears to privilege one element of institutional mission, knowledge production (and by extension certain types of institutions), over others judged equally or more important, which would call for a change in emphasis, while others see an emphasis on knowledge creation as important in generating social and political

TABLE 2

Other Classifications of Colleges and Universities

1. **From *The Academic Marketplace* by Theodore Caplow and Reece McGee (1958)**
   Major League
   Minor League
   Bush League
   Academic Siberia
2. **From *Change* "Landscape" Columns (1997, 1998, & 2001) by Robert Zemsky and Colleagues**
   - Four-year colleges and universities
   Medallion
   Name Brand
   Good Buy
   Good Opportunity
   User-Friendly/Convenience
   - Two-year colleges
   Degree Focus
   Course Focus
   Mixed Focus
3. **Southern Regional Education Board (2003)**
   Four-Year 1 through 4
   Two-Year with Bachelor's
   Two-Year 1 through 3
   Technical Institute or College 1 and 2
   Technical Institute or College—size unknown (Specialized)
4. **AAUP Salary Survey (2005)**
   Category I (Doctoral)
   Category IIA (Master's)
   Category IIB (Baccalaureate)
   Category III (Two-Year Institutions with Academic Ranks)
   Category IV (Two-Year Institutions without Academic Ranks)

Source: Carnegie Commission on Higher Education, New Students and New Places.

support for university-based research (and research universities). Both groups see the classification as playing an important symbolic role in advancing their priorities, which may also be related to strategic goals of individual institutions.

Significant problems arise when classification is seen as an adequate representation of an institution's identity or character. Colleges and universities are complex organizations that differ on many more dimensions than the handful of attributes used to define the classification's categories, and of course the very act of asserting similarity among institutions runs counter to the rhetoric of distinctiveness on our campuses. More important, the host of intangibles that constitute institutional identity could not possibly be incorporated into an empirically based classification system.

The Carnegie Classification has always been based on secondary analysis of numerical data collected by other organizations. It has never involved site visits, interviews with knowledgeable informants, or content analyses of institutional documents. In short, it has used *none* of the techniques more typical of the labor-intensive accreditation process, which would be required for an in-depth assessment of an institution's identity or ethos. Nevertheless, conspicuous misalignment between an institution's self-proclaimed identity or mission and its Carnegie Classification can affect relations with important constituencies, adding to the tension surrounding classification (and consequent demands for accommodation).

This points to the need for classifiers to select labels carefully and then clearly explain what they signify. When category labels mirror broad cultural categories within higher education—such as "research university" and "liberal arts college"—classification and identity are easily confused. Classifiers should also try to anticipate how labels may be adapted or abbreviated in general use. For example, in 2000 the Carnegie Foundation abolished the former Research Universities I & II and Doctoral Universities I & II categories in favor of two categories, one including universities that award the doctorate in relatively large numbers across a wide range of fields (Doctoral/Research Universities—Extensive) and the other containing universities that award the doctorate in smaller numbers or in a more limited set of fields (Intensive). We failed to anticipate that the new categories might be shortened to "research-extensive" and "research-intensive," leading to confusion with a widely used term of art, the "research-intensive university"—a term generally applied to universities that we labeled "extensive" and rarely to those we called "intensive."

In some cases, concerns arise from the use of the classification by third parties. Foundations sometimes use the classification as an eligibility criterion for grant programs; some states use the classification (or a derivative system) in their funding formulas; and in its annual college rankings, *U.S. News & World Report* bases its comparison groups on categories of the classification. With each of these, an institution can have a very tangible interest in maintaining or changing its classification, and the stakes can be high. This places the Carnegie Foundation in a very uncomfortable position, torn between the desires to preserve the integrity of its classification and to avoid indirectly harming institutions.

The point of the foregoing discussion is not to generate sympathy or make excuses for what are seen as shortcomings or biases of the Carnegie Classification. It is to emphasize that no classification can be perfectly neutral or objective—it necessarily reflects decisions about what is important and meaningful (subject to the constraints of available data on which to base a classification). Neither can the assessment of a classification system—whether it is good or bad, whether it makes important and meaningful distinctions—be neutral or objective. For these reasons, some measure of dissatisfaction with a classification that is so widely and prominently used for so many purposes is inevitable.

Moving the Carnegie Classification Forward

As readers of this magazine probably know, a substantially revised version of the Classification will be released in November 2005. Indeed, by the time this issue goes to press, draft versions should already have received attention and public discussion (for details, visit **www.carnegiefoundation .org/classification**).

Some of the changes will, as in the past, acknowledge the evolution of higher education. For instance, the increasing size and complexity of the community college sector will be reflected in a further differentiation of that group, and we will use a multi-measure index in the research category.

Most important though are three major innovations. First, instead of a single framework to represent similarity and difference among institutions, we will provide a set of independent, parallel classification frameworks—distinct lenses through which to view similarities and differences. We all know that colleges and universities resemble and differ from one another along many dimensions. To the extent that the Carnegie Classification has been a dominant framework for conceiving of similarity and difference, it may have impeded recognition of this simple and important truth.

A second innovation will add considerable power to the first. We will provide a set of Web-based tools that will enable users to manipulate the new classification in various ways: to generate lists of subsets of institutions (for example, public institutions, minority-serving institutions, and land-grant institutions); to combine categories of a given classification scheme; and most importantly, to examine points of intersection in the new classification schemes. This opens the possibility of much more sophisticated and specialized analysis, and we expect that it will lead to new and sometimes surprising insights as well.

Einstein is reported to have said, "Not everything that can be counted counts, and not everything that counts can be counted." This points to the single most significant constraint in the classification enterprise: We are limited to criteria that can be captured by empirical data, and short of a massive investment in new data collection (with added burden for institutional respondents), we are limited to currently available national data. Historically, the Carnegie Classification has used data collected by the U.S. Department of Education, the National Science Foundation, and the College Board. As a result, many important aspects of similarity and difference are simply unavailable for use in classification.

In response to this problem, our third innovation will create a middle ground that we hope will enable us to fill some of the gaps in the national data. We are developing a set of "elective" classifications that will depend on voluntary participation by institutions. In relaxing the requirement that all institutions must be classified (and thus that we must have data for all institutions), we open the possibility for special-purpose classifications involving only those institutions willing to make special efforts at additional documentation.

The first of these will focus on institutions with special commitments in the area of community engagement. A pilot project is underway to develop a framework for documenting the various ways institutions are engaged with their communities for mutual benefit, a project that will result in a preliminary classification scheme for participating institutions. In this work we are capitalizing on related efforts by other organizations, such as the Big 10 Committee on Institutional Cooperation; the National Association of State Universities and Land-Grant Colleges Council on Extension, Continuing Education, and Public Service; and Campus Compact. A second elective project will focus on institutional efforts to assess and improve undergraduate education. These are early steps to fill in important gaps in the national data, and if promising they will be incorporated into future classification efforts.

It is important to note that we do not see this revision of the classification as an end point. As noted earlier in this article, the true test of a classification system is in its use. As the new schemes are put to use, combined, and shared, we will learn which have the greatest utility and what modifications are required. Further refinements may be necessary before the promise of the new Carnegie Classification approaches can be realized.

These changes promise more flexibility for classification users. In a sense, the Carnegie Foundation is ceding some of its authority as national arbiter of institutional categorization, similarity, and difference, and it is our hope that this will lead to valuable insights and new perspectives. With the additional flexibility comes responsibility: classification users will need to make choices about what dimensions of comparison are most relevant to a given use, and they will have to justify these choices. In this way, the classification will need to be used reflectively rather than reflexively.

By broadening the range of available classifications and introducing the possibility of hybrid classifications created on the fly, we will give up the simpler language and mutually exclusive framework that we have been accustomed to. But as any linguist can tell you, language is constantly evolving and adapting, and this should be true of the language we use to describe and understand colleges and universities.

Resources

- Carnegie Classification Web pages: **www.carnegiefoundation.org/classification**
- Bailey, K.D., *Typologies and Taxonomies: An Introduction to Classification Techniques*, Thousand Oaks, CA: Sage Publications, 1994.
- Bowker, G.C., and S.L. Star, *Sorting Things Out: Classification and Its Consequences, Cambridge*, MA: MIT Press, 2000.
- Carnegie Commission on Higher Education, *New Students and New Places: Policies for the Future Growth and Development of American Higher Education*, New York: McGraw-Hill, 1971.
- Carnegie Commission on Higher Education, *A Classification of Institutions of Higher Education*, Berkeley, CA, 1973.
- Carnegie Foundation for the Advancement of Teacher, *The Carnegie Classification of Institutions of Higher Education*, 2000 edition, Menlo Park, CA, 2001.
- Kwasnik, B.H., "The Role of Classification in Knowledge Representation and Discovery," *Library Trends*, Vol. 48, No. 1, pp. 22-47, 1999.

CHAPTER 8

PROMOTING ACCESS AND EQUITY THROUGH MINORITY-SERVING AND WOMEN'S INSTITUTIONS

STEVEN R. ARAGON & EBONI M. ZAMANI

Introduction

During the last decade, minority-serving and women's institutions in the United States have experienced a resurgence in both enrollment and prominence. As recently as the early 1980s, these schools—particularly historically Black colleges and universities—experienced stagnant and even declining enrollment as well as a general loss of visibility as providers of educational opportunity for underserved populations. Today, minority-serving and women's colleges and universities are a major component in the postsecondary education of minority and female students.

In many ways, the newfound stature of minority-serving institutions should come as no surprise. The nonwhite population of the United States, and of American higher education, is growing at record rates. As a result of this growth, the higher education establishment and nonminority institutions have been challenged to pay increased attention to this evolving group of schools. What is surprising about this resurgence, however, is that little of the growth has been the result of coordinated efforts on the part of these institutions to work together and seek common goals (Merisotis & O'Brien, 1998). In a range of arenas, most noticeably in federal government support for developing institutions, minority-serving institutions are in competition for limited resources. Yet despite this competitive pressure, minority-serving institutions have prospered, not only in terms of student enrollments but also in political recognition and in the success of the students they educate.

This chapter is intended to serve as a primer on the growing group of minority-serving institutions, with the goal of educating leaders at mainstream institutions, analysts, and the minority-serving institutions themselves about the distinct purposes and common goals of these institutions. An increased understanding of minority-serving institutions and of their roles in educating underserved populations is important as the nation's demographic profile becomes increasingly diverse.

Minority-serving institutions are defined in this chapter primarily as those colleges and universities that are designated as historically Black colleges and universities (HBCUs), tribal colleges, Hispanic-serving institutions (HSIs) and women's colleges. These designations have been accorded through various federal policies and programs designed to encourage the development and growth of the institutions. As this chapter points out, the history, purposes, and operating structures of these institutions vary considerably. Yet despite their differences, minority-serving institutions share many goals related to educating underserved populations. These common goals make it important to understand the shared visions and missions of these institutions, and candidly to air their unique roles and concerns as they build for the future.

Background

Although the last four decades have brought improved social status and access to education for ethnic minorities, African Americans, Hispanics, Asians/Pacific Islanders and American Indians/Alaska Natives are still disenfranchised (Aragon, 2000). According to researchers, minority students are more likely than their White counterparts to be at risk of academic failure at the elementary, secondary, and postsecondary levels (O'Brien & Zudak, 1998; Rendon & Hope, 1996). The risk factors associated with not completing a postsecondary program include delayed enrollment, part-time attendance, being self-supporting, single-parent status, full-time work schedules, caring for a dependent, and holding a GED certificate. According to a National Postsecondary Student Aid Study (as reported by O'Brien & Zudak, 1998), 27% of Hispanic students, 31% of African American students, and 35% of American Indian/Alaska Native students have four or more of these risk factors, compared with 22% of White students. Another potential risk for minority students is that they often break new ground as the first in their families to attend college. While these data represent the averages for the different groups of students, enormous diversity exists within these four populations.

Today, racial and ethnic minorities make up about 28% of the U.S. population (U.S. Bureau of the Census, 1998). According to the U.S. Bureau of the Census (1996a) projections, by 2050 minorities will make up about 47% of the U.S. population. The implications of neglecting to better understand and address the learning needs of people of color for society, in general, and adult education, in particular, are staggering. Briscoe and Ross (1989) note that

> it is likely that young people will leave school early, will never participate fully in society or in the decision-making processes of government, and that they will neither enjoy the benefits of good health, nor experience the upward mobility needed as adults to make them full contributors and partners in shaping and participating in the larger society. (p . 586)

A decade later, these issues have yet to be resolved (O'Brien & Zudak, 1998; Rendon & Hope, 1996).

Today's Demographics

Students of color account for almost one-quarter (24.8%) of postsecondary education enrollment, with African Americans representing approximately 12%, Hispanics 9%, Asians/Pacific Islanders 3%, and American Indians/Alaska Natives 8% (O'Brien & Zudak, 1998). During the period between 1988 and 1997, enrollment of minority students across all institutions of higher education had a change of 57.2%, while White (non-Hispanic) enrollment saw a negative 0.2% change (American Council on Education, 2000). As a result of these demographic changes within society at large and institutions of higher education specifically, the term minority is losing its statistical meaning, as a new student majority rapidly emerges, comprising, collectively, African Americans, Hispanics/Latinos, Asians/Pacific Islanders, and American Indians/Alaska Natives (Rendon & Hope, 1996).

It is important, however, to keep in mind that within American higher education, community colleges play a significant role in providing educational access and opportunity to minority students. Each fall, approximately half of all minority undergraduates enrolled in higher education attend a community college. Arguably, community college campuses reflect the diversity of the American population. Enrolled students, are of all ages and from different cultural and ethnic backgrounds. In fact, among minorities, community colleges are typically the schools of choice (American Association of Community Colleges, 1998).

According to the American Association of Community Colleges, these institutions saw an increase in enrollments of minority students between 1992 and 1997 (American Association of Community Colleges, 2000). The American Council on Education (2000) reports a 56.1% change in the enrollment of minority students in four-year institutions between 1988 and 1997. The community college saw a slightly higher percentage change (58.5%) in the enrollment of minority students during this same period.

Environment: The Influence of Institutional Type and Mission

The institutional mission reflects the intentions and direction of a college that involves establishing a statement of purpose that will endure and distinguishes types of institutions (Peeke, 1994). Community college missions have a uniqueness that sets them apart from senior institutions with regard to more than just the highest degree conferred. Referred to as the "people's colleges," two-year institutions were designed to extend higher education opportunities through a system of open admissions that has aided numerous first-generation, underprepared, financially wrought, and underrepresented college-bound students (Cohen & Brawer, 1996; Richardson & Skinner, 1992). However, within the two-year sector are institutions with dual missions, 1) open door admittance; and 2) serving a specific marginalized group. Because many American educational institutions did not voluntarily seek diversity among its participants, special focus colleges emerged (Townsend, 1999). Hence, minority-serving, two- and four-year institutions originated out of efforts to assist in navigating the terrain of racial tensions and gender disparities within education as well as within a larger societal context

Community colleges provide routes to baccalaureate degrees by filling existing gaps in educational access for those who may not have other options for postsecondary attendance. Baccalaureate aspirants entering two-year colleges often differ from students attending four-year colleges or universities with regard to precollegiate preparation (Dougherty, 1987; Richardson & Bender, 1987). Thus, the role of admissions and enrollment in two- and four-year institutions of higher education varies due to divergent settings (Adelman, 1999).

Community colleges have a unique purpose, yet are still similar to four-year institutions. In addressing the varying missions, functions, students, and curricula of community colleges, Katsinas (1993) developed a community college classification system comprised of fourteen distinct types. The various types of community colleges include:

- institutions with comprehensive offerings located in rural areas;
- suburban colleges with an emphasis on liberal arts and transfer;
- urban/inner city colleges with a focus on vocational courses and school-to-work;
- metropolitan college districts with centralized and decentralized governance;
- colleges in close proximity to residential universities;
- mixture of the above categories;
- predominately Hispanic-serving institutions;
- historically Black two-year colleges;
- tribal community colleges;
- colleges devoted only to general education and transfer;
- exclusively technical colleges;
- non-profit private institutions (sectarian and non-sectarian);
- private proprietary colleges;
- community colleges administered directly by four-year institutions.

Institutional type and mission largely influence campus environments, and are important factors in students actualizing the aspirations to earn baccalaureate degrees. Among recipients of community college degrees, larger numbers of women receive associate degrees and certificates while a greater number of White students in general are awarded two-year degrees and certificates. Although roughly 25% of two-year collegians intend to obtain a certificate or associate degree without aspirations for the baccalaureate or beyond, many others intend to transfer to senior institutions. In underscoring the desire for higher degrees within the United States, one-fifth of the population has attained a bachelor's degree or higher.

Still, institutions also vary in accordance with how they are controlled. Privately controlled institutions foster student development, retention, and degree attainment (Astin, Tsui, & Avalos, 1996). Notably, the vast numbers of minority-serving institutions are privately governed. In terms of community colleges, there remain small enclaves of historically Black and women's two-year institutions of which many are private colleges. These institutions have unique campus climate and distinct missions to serve special populations. Various institutions of higher learning illustrate aspects of the interconnectedness of culture, identity, and schooling in accord with the tailored aims of their college and constituencies (Rhoads, 1999; Rhoads & Valadez, 1996). Not only does racial and ethnic cultural pluralism (i.e., diversity) shape campus climates, but the institutional type and heterogeneity of student gender, age, and status of enrollment level do as well.

Participation of African Americans and Women in Higher Education

The United States is becoming increasingly multiethnic and changing demographics suggest that during the twenty-first century the term minority will no longer be an appropriate designation as racially diverse groups will collectively represent the majority of the U.S. population (U.S. Bureau of the Census, 1996a). As higher education is commonly thought to be the great societal equalizer, there are differenetial rates of progression to college by race or ethnicity with substantially higher rates of White high school graduates attending college than African Americans (Solomon & Wingard, 1991). High school completion rates and patterns of postsecondary enrollment among African Americans have fallen in part to a host of factors such as college costs, academic preparedness, and proximity that affect access to higher education (Benjamin, 1996).

With regard to higher education participation, over the last 20 years community colleges have traditionally enrolled higher proportions of African American students than four-year colleges and universities (Rendon & Garza, 1996; Rendon & Matthews, 1994; Solomon & Wingard, 1991). Baccalaureate-degree granting institutions' total enrollment in 1997 comprised 10% African American students while community colleges' total enrollment consisted of 11% African American (National Center for Educational Statistics, 1999). At present, the majority of educational opportunities for students of color are at community colleges as they enroll almost half of all African American collegians (Rendon & Hope, 1996; Townsend, 2000).

Considering higher education participation by gender, nearly two-thirds of African American undergraduates are women. While the majority of African Americans are in two-year institutions, 58% of all community college students are women (Horn & Maw, 1995; American Association of Community Colleges, 2000). Roughly two-thirds of community college students are part-time attendees, of which a significant number are women, many who are not traditional college age (i.e., 18-24) students (Jacobs, 1999; National Center for Educational Statistics, 1997; American Association of Community Colleges, 2000). Full-time, baccalaureate degree aspirants attending two-year institutions are twice as likely as part-timers to transfer to a four-year college or university within five years (National Center for Educational Statistics, 1997).Therefore, the racial/ethnic background, gender and enrollment status of community college students relate to the orientation of those attending, campus climate, institutional culture, and student outcomes.

Clearly, issues revolving around race and gender affect campus climate differently across institutional contexts given the unique student compositions of the various colleges and universities. As such, the remainder of this chapter addresses the defining mission and characteristics of two-year institutions. More specifically, the following section gives attention to the multi-faceted nature of American community colleges founded to further postsecondary educational attainment among underrepresented, disenfranchised African Americans and women.

Historical Origins and Unique Missions: Two- and Four-Year Black Colleges

Education has long been viewed as the gateway to upward mobility and economic independence. Not limited to the area of education, the history of African Americans in the United States is replete with instances of overt discriminatory treatment along color lines. Unlike other racial/ethnic groups, many African Americans did not immigrate to the United States, but were brought to this country against their will and sold into slavery (Bennett, 1988; Bonacich, 1989). Treated as subhuman, traditional practice was to keep African Americans from receiving schooling.

While very few White institutions admitted African Americans in the late nineteenth century, the few that did were located in the North and most African Americans were in the South (Guyden,

1999). Though against the law to educate persons of African descent, abolitionists and missionaries founded schools for African Americans during the late 1800s in an effort to extend postsecondary opportunities to those with collegiate aspirations (Gayden, 1999). Several educational foundations were established for African Americans between the Civil War and World War I (Bowman, 1992). With the second Morrill Act of 1890, public land-grant institutions of higher learning were established for African Americans, which launched legal racial separation of colleges and universities, particularly in the south.

Often referred to as 'Historically Black Colleges and Universities' (HBCUs), the curriculum initially had a vocational emphasis that later evolved to include and promote general/liberal arts studies (Gayden, 1999). By 1900, roughly 100 HBCUs had been established, the majority as four-year institutions (Townsend, 1999). Despite institutional attrition at present there still exist approximately 107 HBCUs in the United States comprising 9% of baccalaureate-granting institutions, many which are privately controlled (Bowman, 1992; Hope, 1996). Although 75% of African American students attend predominately White institutions (PWIs), HBCUs have consistently produced slightly over one-third of African American bachelor degree recipients, outproducing other institutional types (Chideya, 1995; Hope, 1996). For that reason, there are significant differences in the educational outcomes for African American students at traditional Black colleges and universities versus PWIs (Jackson & Swan, 1991).

Similar to historically Black four-year institutions, Black two-year colleges carried the same charge of providing ex-slaves educational opportunities. Most two- and four-year Black institutions of higher learning were church affiliated colleges and many were extensions of segregated secondary schools (Guyden, 1999; Hope, 1996). In describing characteristics of HBCUs in general, Clayton (1979) reported that 42% of Black colleges are located in cities with fewer than 50,000 people; many that are religious-affiliated are Methodist; and 84% of those accredited are in the southern association. Different from historically Black four-year colleges and universities, the development of Black two-year institutions was an outgrowth of the twentieth century (Townsend, 1999). Lane (1933, in Guyden, 1999), made an early attempt to provide a portrait of historically Black two-year colleges, noting that these institutions largely promoted a liberal arts curriculum with the purpose of encouraging transfer in pursuit of baccalaureate degrees. For that reason, degrees conferred at four-year institutions held more prestige, placing little emphasis on vocational education within Black two-year colleges irrespective of open admissions policies as the general rule for each tier.

As the educational aspirations and academic needs of African American students' further convoluted attempts to equalize postsecondary schooling, various threats to the existence of HBCUs, particularly two-year institutions, arose. While at one time well over 100 Black colleges were two-year institutions or provided two-year curriculums, by the late 1970s severe declines were witnessed (Guyden, 1999; Historically Black colleges and universities fact book, 1983). By 1997, only fourteen historically Black, two-year institutions remained, most located in the Southeast. Attendance at eleven of these institutions range from just short of 200 students to over 1,700[1] (Townsend, 1999).

Unfortunately, due to the higher costs of a private college education, many African American students cannot afford to attend these institutions specifically founded to foster their educational attainment, as nearly two-thirds are privately controlled (Hope, 1996). In contrast to those educated in public HBCUs, African American private college students have degree aspirations that exceed the baccalaureate level, higher grade point averages, and better academic progression (Davis & Nettles, 1987; Horn & Maw, 1995). Although both public and private HBCUs combined account for less than 9% of postsecondary institutions, publicly controlled PWIs, particularly public two-year colleges, may be the first-choice, or only option, for postsecondary attendance among low-income and first generation students in pursuit of the baccalaureate degree.

Predominantly Black institutions (PBIs) have emerged which, unlike HBCUs, were not originally erected with the sole purpose of educating African Americans, but arose from traditional White institutions that, over time, witnessed growth in African American student attendees who comprise at least 50% of total enrollment (Gayden, 1999; Townsend, 1999). While HBCUs are geographically located primarily in the Southern states, in contrast, PBIs are often in major cities. Likewise, two-year PBIs are metropolitan community colleges with 50% or greater African American enrollment; whereas Black-serving institutions have student bodies that enroll between 25% to 49% African Americans (Townsend, 1999). While the majority of students at historically Black and predominantly Black two-year colleges are African American, the same degree of diversity does not exist in terms of faculty at these institutions as over one-quarter are White (Foster, Guyden, & Miller 1999).

Given the relatively small number of Black community colleges, both historically Black and predominantly White institutions of higher learning (particularly PWIs enrolling one-quarter or more African Americans) should work cooperatively to address high attrition, low rates of transfer, declines in the number of associate degrees awarded to African Americans, and subsequent transition to the baccalaureate (Simmons & Jackson, 1988). Relative to college choice, cost and location are major factors for African Americans considering higher learning. Due to lower tuition rates, institutions that are within an individual's financial reach and in close proximity are commonly community colleges.

Many urban community colleges boast large enrollments and research has noted that the size and level of an institution can adversely impact student aspirations (Carter, 1999). Irrespective of the tier, large student enrollments hinder students' level of comfort within the institutional environment, preventing them from self-actualizing, thereby slowing their academic progression (Attinasi, as cited in Carter, 1999). Critics contend that community colleges are not the optimal environment for those seeking baccalaureate degree completion (Brint & Karabel, 1989; Clark, 1960; Karabel, 1986; Dougherty, 1987, 1994; Pascarella et al., 1998; Pincus & Archer, 1989; Whitaker & Pascarella, 1994). Nonetheless, African American and female students are commonly left little choice in utilizing two-year institutions as the conduit to a bachelor' s degree.

Providing Educational Access for American Indians: The Tribal College

In a relatively short period of time, tribal colleges have improved the educational opportunities of American Indian students who otherwise might not have participated in higher education. These schools are unique institutions that blend the traditional community college goals of local economic development, workforce training, and preparation for continuing education with a combination of supplemental student support, cultural preservation and enhancement, and community outreach. As Boyer (1997) notes in his report on American Indian Colleges, "tribal colleges establish a learning environment that supports students who had come to view failure as the norm"(p. 4). These schools have succeeded despite a host of obstacles that include a chronic lack of funding, dilapidated facilities, and the low-income levels and poor academic preparation of many of their students (Boyer, 1997).

Probably the most important function of the tribal college is the access it provides for students – especially local ones – who otherwise would not participate in higher education (Boyer, 1997). To help students with their family responsibilities, colleges such as Fond du Lac, Little Big Horn, and Fort Peck operate on-site day care centers for the children of students, and these centers are often available to the wider community as well (American Indian College Fund, 1996). Besides their open admissions policies and convenient locations, some colleges offer transportation to and from isolated parts of the reservation, while others have decentralized their campuses – in effect "moving classes to the students" (Cahape & Howley, 1992, p. 98). For example, Bay Mills Community College has offered classes at each of the twelve reservations in Michigan since 1984; Oglala Lakota has established a college center in each of the nine districts of the Pine Ridge reservation; and Sitting Bull College operates an innovative adult learning program that features a mobile classroom to serve outlying districts (American Indian College Fund, 1996).

Because tribal colleges often serve academically unprepared students who are forced to deal with family responsibilities, financial difficulties, and other problems, providing access is not enough (Cunningham & Parker, 1998). The colleges, therefore, continue supporting their students after enrollment by offering tutoring programs that build basic skills, General Education Development (GED) instruction, as well as active counseling programs for students. Faculties consciously try to develop self-esteem in students as "the greatest obstacle is often psychological – the belief that higher education is something foreign and intimidating" (Boyer, 1997, p. 58). In addition, many tribal colleges work with local four-year institutions to ensure that courses are comparable and that the transfer process goes smoothly for those students who decide to continue their education. For example, the College of the Menominee Nation has articulation agreements with the University of Wisconsin at Stevens Point and Green Bay and Wisconsin's Technical Colleges in Wausau, Appleton, and Green Bay, to facilitate student transfers (American Indian College Fund, 1996).

Tribal colleges also utilize distance learning to encourage access and persistence toward a degree. All tribal colleges participate in a network that allows them to increase the number of courses they can offer by downloading them from other sites via satellite. Several of the colleges – including Lac Courte Oreilles and Blackfeet – offer courses from state institutions through video, audio, and other digital communications, thereby providing students with the opportunity to complete undergraduate degrees without leaving the reservation.

Hispanic-Serving Institutions: High-Serving Institutions

In order to understand the barriers that are involved in educating the U.S. Hispanic population, it is important to realize that Hispanics are, by no means, a homogeneous group. The use of the term *Hispanic* – and, more recently, *Latino* – within the United States are both umbrella terms that represent many national races, cultures, and origins. These individuals represent descendants of pre-Columbian inhabitants of the Americas to the offspring of migratory streams to the Spanish-speaking New World. The United States' Hispanic population also includes sixth- and seventh generation U.S. citizens.

The continued influx of Hispanics has perpetuated the division between the dominant Anglo culture and the ethnic and socioeconomic stereotypes of Hispanics as newly arrived, non-English-speaking, illegal aliens. According to the President's Advisory Commission on Educational Excellence for Hispanic Americans (1996), approximately 64% of the Hispanic population in the United States is made up of U.S. born citizens. While a growing number of Hispanics have achieved economic success in the United States and interact with ease in English-speaking circles, Hispanics are often portrayed in the media and in public discourse as unassimilated, undereducated, child-laden, and menially employed.

Although Hispanics are the fastest growing minority in the United States, their numbers at all levels of the educational system in this country have not kept pace with their population growth. Dropout rates for Hispanics are higher and occur earlier than for other ethnic groups. The President's Advisory Commission on Educational Excellence for Hispanic Americans (1996) reports that "40% of 16- to 24-year-old Hispanic dropouts left school with less than a 9th grade education, compared with 13% of White dropouts and 11% of Black dropouts" (p. 26). The National Education Goals Panel (1996) points out that in 1995 the disparity between Whites and Hispanics with regard to high school completion was 27%, while it was 5% between Whites and Blacks. Disparities in college completion rates between Whites and Hispanics are also growing. In 1992, the gap between the proportions of Hispanic and White high school graduates who completed a college degree was 15%; in 1996, the gap was 21%.

Within less than a decade, however, Hispanic enrollment in postsecondary institutions nearly doubled from 520,000 in 1992 to 1,045,600 in 1997. Hispanic students account for 9% of the nation's fifteen million students in postsecondary institutions (O'Brien & Zudak, 1998), up from 4.5% in 1985. According to the U.S. Department of Education's Fact Sheet on Title III Institutions (1998), more than half of Hispanics in postsecondary education are concentrated in about 177 institutions with 25% or more Hispanic enrollment

An Overview of HSIs. The term *Hispanic-serving institution* (HSI) is a relatively recent educational classification that has yet to be uniformly defined. "The most frequently used criterion to identity HSIs is a Hispanic student enrollment of 25% or more" (Benitez, 1998, p. 59). Title III of the Higher Education Act (MEA) of 1965 provides the most important, as well as the most restrictive, legal definition of a HSI (U.S Department of Education, 1997). Title III authorized federal aid programs to institutions that served large numbers of needy and underrepresented students. According to Title III, Section 312 of the HEA, to be eligible for aid, institutions must meet the following criteria:

- Cannot be for-profit;
- Must offer at least two-year academic programs that lead to a degree;

- Must be accredited by an accrediting agency or association recognized by the Secretary of Education;
- Must have a high enrollment of economically needy students; and
- Must have low-average education expenditures.

In addition to meeting these criteria, to be recognized as an HSI an institution must:

- Have at least 25% Hispanic undergraduate full-time-equivalent (FTE) student enrollment;
- Provide assurances that no less than 50% of its Hispanic students are low-income individuals and first-generation college students; and
- Provide assurances that an additional 25% of its Hispanic students are low-income individuals or first-generation college students.

Other entities including the White House Initiative on Educational Excellence for Hispanic Americans and the Hispanic Association of Colleges and Universities employ criteria that are similar to, but less exacting than, Title III to identify HSIs. They define HSIs as accredited degree-granting public or private non-profit institutions of higher education with at least 25% Hispanic student enrollment. This definition increases the number of HSIs from 131 to 177, based on Integrated Postsecondary Education Data System (IPEDS) for 1995-96. This definition, however, does not have legal status. Federal agencies and other funding sources tend to rely on existing statutes when developing policy directives and funding priorities. "At present, the only statutory references to HSIs is the REA Title III definition" (Benitez, 1998, p. 60).

The development of most HSIs has taken place within the last three decades. This development is closely related to two extraordinary quantitative increases that have brought about qualitative changes in education in the United States – a large increase in federal funding, and a dramatic increase in the Hispanic population of the United States. The great increase in need-based federal student aid that followed the passage in 1965 of the Higher Education Act (HEA) allowed more student access to postsecondary education. Far more important than Title III to the development of HSIs and other minority serving institutions were the programs that were created under Title IV of the HEA. Title IV established the Basic Educational Opportunity Grants, which later became Pell grants, as well as college work-study and guaranteed student loan programs. Federal student grants, along with the movement for open admissions, were the keys to the gates of higher education for U.S. minority populations.

Today's Profile of the HSI. The most frequent type of institution among HSIs is a public two-year community college that is greatly dependent on state and federal funds, and that has a limited budget with almost no endowment. According to the U. S. Department of Education (1997):

- The total revenues of HSIs are 42%, or $5,742, less per FTE student than at other institutions;
- Endowment revenues at HSIs per FTE student are 91% less than at other institutions;
- HSIs spend 43% less on instruction per FTE student than other schools;
- HSIs spend 51% less on academic support functions (i.e., libraries, curriculum development, etc.) per FTE student than other schools; and
- HSIs spend 27% less on student services (guidance, counseling, financial aid administration, etc.) per FTE student than other schools.

The financial condition of a large number of HSIs is precarious. Many HSIs are underequipped, understaffed, unable to competitively hire, develop baccalaureate or graduate programs, maintain modern research facilities, or offer high-tech learning and working environments. Given this current picture, one wonders whether Hispanic students are better off at HSIs than at other institutions that are stronger financially and academically. However, it is important to consider the profile of today's typical Hispanic student.

Hispanic students tend to be enrolled part-time in an associate or nondegree program near their home. They often receive federal student aid mainly in the form of Pell grants and must work in order to stay in school. Hispanic students usually take longer than Whites to complete a degree and are 33% more likely than Whites to drop out before completing a bachelor's degree

(U.S. Department of Education, 1997). Financial factors, including tuition costs, availability of financial aid, and nearness to home are major considerations for Hispanic students when choosing a school.

HSIs are both relatively inexpensive and close to home for most Hispanic students. Despite their limitations, the rate of completion for Hispanic students at HSIs is higher than at majority institutions. According to the U.S. Department of Education (1997), "whereas 32% of all Hispanic students in higher education are enrolled at [Title III] HSIs, Hispanic students at HSIs earn 47% of the associate degrees and 48% of the bachelor's degrees awarded to Hispanic students nationwide" (p. 2). HSIs figure prominently as part of the top one hundred schools that grant the highest number of bachelor degrees to Hispanics. However, they lose ground at the masters' level and practically disappear from the doctoral listing. As noted earlier, most HSIs offer only undergraduate degrees and most are two-year institutions.

HSIs have begun to use statistics to request increased government funding as well as to gain credibility as a successful educational alternative for minorities. Not exclusively Hispanic, a large number of HSIs also serve other minority populations, with more than 65% of the students enrolled at HSIs belonging to diverse minority groups (U.S. Department of Education, 1998).

Not all HSIs were were originally founded as Hispanic-serving insititutions. Migratory and demographic shifts have helped to redefine the student population at many campuses throughout the United States. This means that HSIs were not necessarily designed or staffed with a Hispanic student population in mind. It may be argued that the fact that an institution enrolls large numbers of Hispanic students need not imply or assure that it is geared to their educational needs. A closer examination of individual institutions is required to ascertain their effectiveness, taking into account their mission, student populations, academic offerings and achievements, faculty and staff profiles, student support services, funding sources, and funding priorities.

Nevertheless, it is still fair to say that HSIs as a group are presently at the front line of American postsecondary education. They are dealing with the population mix that will dominate the twenty-first century, and appear to be doing better than any groups' institutions at meeting the educational needs of Hispanics. Whether their efforts and resources suffice to meet the challenge of educating Hispanics in the United States is another question. HSIs, at present, are seriously underfunded, and most do not go beyond the undergraduate level. That is not sufficient to serve the needs of the population, or of the nation in the future.

Many HSIs are part of community college systems and are assigned their mandates and funds by a central administrative office, which, in turn, answers to city authorities or state legislatures. Thus, the level of funding most HSIs receive is tied to the political process at the local, state, and federal levels and ebb and flow of the clout and networking skills of the representatives of Hispanic communities.

Evolution and Challenges in Continuance of Two-year Women's Colleges

Prior to the nineteenth century, women were educationally disadvantaged as societal roles dictated that only White men should receive formal postsecondary education. Participation of women of Anglo decent in higher education was witnessed as early as 1749 via women's seminaries (Kelly, 1987; Schuman & Olufs, 1995). However, it was not until the early 1800s that the educational training of White women gained social acceptance. More significant, by 1920 women made up 47% of college undergraduates (Lerner, 1993).

During the 1930s there were 211 two- and four-year women's colleges, accounting for 16% of all higher education institutions. It is estimated that as many as 80 two-year women's colleges existed in 1940, the majority religiously affiliated and privately controlled (Wolf-Wendel & Pedigo, 1999). Moreover, between 1930 and 1976, 40% of women's colleges were two-year institutions (Wolf-Wendel & Pedigo, 1999).

Wolf-Wendel and Pedigo (1999) reported that there were 252 women's colleges in 1960, but by 1993 roughly two-thirds of institutions for women had disappeared. The institution of choice during the first half of the 1900s in the Northeast and South, women's colleges began to lose momentum with the growth of coeducational institutions, especially public colleges and universities (Townsend, 1999; Wolf-Wendel & Pedigo, 1999). Women's colleges also reached a stalemate in terms of further development and longevity due to many becoming four-year institutions (Schultz & Stickler, 1965).

Two-year colleges specifically for women were thought appropriate as women frequently stayed home while pursuing additional education. However, Solomon (1985) suggested that two-year women's colleges were enacted as a means of stratifying educational opportunity by gender. In other words, men would be able to attend senior level institutions leading to higher degrees while women would have less access to four-year colleges and universities.

Presently, the majority of college students earning two-year and bachelors degrees are female (Jacobs, 1999). Similar to persons of color, women are overrepresented in community colleges in general, concurring with Solomon's assertions regarding the educational stratification of women in higher education (Jacobs, 1999; American Association of Community Colleges, 2000). Although the majority of women attend coeducational institutions of higher learning, as of 1997 there were over 80 women's colleges, of which only five were two-year institutions.

In contrast to two-year Black colleges, less has been written about two-year womens' institutions of higher learning. Existing literature on women's colleges is contradictory regarding the effects of single-sex postsecondary education on student outcomes. Some researchers (Miller-Bernal, 1989; Riordan, 1994; Smith, 1990) contend there are significant positive effects while others insist women's colleges bear no influence on student outcomes (Gose, 1995; Stoecker & Pascarella, 1991). Robinson (1990) suggests that at the core of single-sex education for women are leadership and self-esteem building skills that are generally negated in coeducational college choices. Hence, women's colleges can provide particularly laudable contributions in the personal and professional development of female students. However, given declining enrollments at single-sex institutions and the virtual extinction of two-year women's colleges, the extent to which collegiate education of this kind can be nurtured is daunting (Gose, 1995; Perry, 2000).

Conclusion

Minority-serving institutions (MSI) have clearly helped to fulfill the vast educational needs of a growing number of language and cultural minorities. Their convergent strengths have supported the economic development and social mobility of people of color and women as mainstream institutions historically have provided similar opportunities for the majority population. MSIs collectively share a number of characteristics that have contributed significantly to the educational development of racial and ethnic groups in the United States. Included among these strengths are:

- Their collective, targeted missions;
- The significant number of degrees conferred each year;
- Culturally based educational efforts;
- Various leadership opportunities;
- Independent and self-sufficient daily operations; and
- Educational, economic, and community development endeavors.

The stated missions of these schools address the issues that form a well-recited litany of the failures that characterize many mainstream institutions in their attempts to educate minorities and women. Recognizing that mainstream institutions were built for nonminority populations and women, MSIs have attempted to structure and organize education experiences for students within their own social and cultural contexts.

Notes

1. As reported, enrollment information was not provided for three institutions as they were community colleges with one or more branch campuses.

References

Adelman, C. (1999). *Answers in the toolbox: Academic intensity, attendance patterns, and bachelor's degree attainment.* Washington, DC: U. S. Department of Education.

American Association of Community Colleges. (2000). *National profile of community colleges: 'Trends and statistics (3rd ed).* Washington; DC: Community College Press.

American Association of Community Colleges. (1998). *Pocket profile of community colleges: Trends and statistics 1997–1998.* Washington, DC: Community College Press.

American Council on Education. (2000). *Minorities in higher education 1999-2000.* Washington, DC: American Council on Education.

American Indian College Fund (AICF). (1996, November). *Unpublished profiles of tribal colleges.*

Aragon, S, R, (Ed.). (2000). *Beyond access: Methods and models for increasing retention and learning among minority students.* San Francisco: Jessey-Bass.

Astin, A.W, Tsui, L. & Avalos, J. (1996). *Degree attainment rates at American colleges and universities: Effects of race, gender, and institutional type.* Los Angeles; CA: Higher Education Research Institute, University of California, Los Angeles.

Benjamin, M. (1996). *Cultural diversity, educational equity, and the transformation of higher education: Group profiles as a guide to policy and programming.* Westport; CT: Greenwood.

Benitez, M. (1998). Hispanic-serving institutions: Challenges and opportunities. In J.P. Merisotis & C. T. O'Brien (eds.) *Minority-serving institutions: Distinct purposes, common goals* (pp. 57–68). San Francisco: Jossey-Bass.

Bennett, L. Jr. (1988). *Before the Mayflower: A history of black America,* (6th ed.) New York: Penguin Books.

Bonacich, E. (1989). Inequality in America: The failure of the American system for people of color. *Sociological Spectrum, 9,* 77–101.

Bowman, J. W. (1992). *America's black colleges: The comprehensive guide to historically & predominantly black 4-year colleges and universities.* Pasadena, CA: Sandcastle Publishing.

Boyer, P. (1997). *Native American colleges: Progress and prospects.* Princeton, NJ: Carnegie Foundation for the Advancement of Teaching.

Brint, S. & Karabel, J. (1989). American education, merito-cratic ideology, and the legitimization of; inequality: The community college and the problem of American exceptionalism. *Higher Education, 18,* 725–735.

Briscoe, D. B., & Ross, J. M. (1989). Racial and ethnic minorities and adult education. In S. B, Merriam and P. M. Cunningham (eds.), *Handbook of Adult and Continuing Education* (pp. 583-598). San Francisco: Jossey-Bass.

Cahape, P., & Howley, C. B. (eds.). (1992). *Indian nationals at risk: Listening to the people.* Summaries of papers commissions by the Indian Nationals at Risk Task Force of the U.S. Department of Education. Charleston, WV: Clearinghouse on Rural Education and Small Schools.

Carter, D. F. (1999). The impact of institutional choice and environments on African-American and White students' degree expectations. *Research in Higher Education, 40,* 17–41.

Chideya, F. (1995). *Don't believe the hype: Fighting cultural misinformation about African Americans.* New York: Penguin.

Cohen, A. M. & Brawer, F B. (1996). *The American community college* (3rd ed.). San Francisco, CA: Jessey-Bass.

Clark, B. (1960). The "cooling out" function in higher education. *American Journal of Sociology, 65,* 569–576.

Clayton, R. (1979). *Some characteristics of the historically black colleges.* (ED176651)

Cunningham, A. F, & Parker, C. (1998). Tribal colleges as community institutions and resources. In J. P. Merisotis, & C. T. O'Brien (eds.), *Minority-serving institutions: Distinct purposes, common goals* (pp. 45-56). San Francisco: Jossey-Bass.

Davis, J. E. & Nettles, M. T. (1987). *Academic progression of students at public and private historically black colleges.* Paper presented at the Annual Meeting of the Association for the Study of Higher Education, San Diego, CA. (ED281462).

Dougherty, K. (1987). The effects of community colleges: Aid or hindrance to socioeconomic attainment? *Sociology of Education, 60,* 86-103.

Dougherty, K. J. (1994). *The contradictory college: The conflicting origins, impacts, and future of the community college.* New York: State University of New York.

Foster, L., Guyden, J. A., & Miller, A. L. (1999). *Affirmed action: Essays on the academic and social lives of white faculty members at historically black colleges and universities.* New York: Rowman & Littlefield.

Gose, B. (1995,Februrary). Second thoughts at women's colleges. *Chronicle of Higher Education, 41*(22), A22..24.

Guyden, J. A. (l999). Two-year historically black colleges. In B. K. Townsend (Ed.), *Two-year colleges for women and minorities: Enabling access to the baccalaureate* (pp. 85-112). New York: Palmer Press.

Historically black colleges and universities fact book, Volume 1: Junior & Community Colleges (1983) Washington, DC: Federal Government, Division of Black American Affairs.

Hoffman, C. M. & Associates (1996). *Historically black colleges .and universities, 1976-1994.* Washington, DC: U.S. Government Printing Office. (ED399897)

Hope, R.O. (1996). Revitalizing minority colleges and universities: In. L. I. Rendon & R. O. Hope(eds.), *Educating a new majority: Transforming America's educational system for diversity,* (pp. 390–402). San Franeisco, CA: Jessey-Bass.

Horn, L. & Maw, C. (1995). *Minority undergraduate participation in postsecondary education: A statistical report.* Toronto, Ontario: Council of Ontario Universities. (ERIC Document Reproduction Service No. ED383267).

Jacobs, J. A. (1999).·Gender and the stratification of colleges. *The Journal of Higher Education, 70* (2), 161–187.

Jackson, K.W. & Swan, L. A. (1991). Institutional and individual factors affecting black undergraduate student performance: Campus race and student gender. In W. R. Allen, E. G. Epps, & N. Z. Haniff (eds.), *College in black and white: African American students in predominantly white and in historically black public universities* (pp. 127–141). New York: SUNY.

Karabel, J. (1986). Community colleges and social stratification in the 1980s. *New Directions for Community Colleges, 54,* 13–30.

Katsinas, S. G. (1993, April)). *Toward a classification system for community colleges.* Paper presented at Annual Meeting of the Council of Universities and Colleges Portland, OR.

Kelly, D. K. (1987). *The nineteenth century experience of women college students: A profile of the women and their motivations.* (ED292745)

Lerner, G. (1993). *The creation of feminist consciousness: From the middle ages to eighteen-seventy.* New York: Oxford University Press.

Merisotis, J. P. & O'Brien, C. T. (eds.). (1998). *Minority-serving institutions: Distinct purposes, common goals.* San Francisco: Jossey-Bass.

Miller-Bernal, L. (1989). College experiences and sex-role attitudes: Does a women's college make a difference? *Youth and Society, 20*(4), 363–387.

National Center for Educational Statistics (1997). *Transfer behavior among beginning post secondary students: 1989-94.* Washington, DC: U.S. Department of Education, Office of Educational Research and Improvement.

National Center for Educational Statistics (1999). *Integrated postsecondary education data system (IPEDS) fall enrollment survey.* Washington, DC: U. S. Department of Education.

National Education Goals Panel. (1996). *The national education goals report: Building a nation of learners.* Washington, DC: Government Printing Office.

O'Brien, E. M., & Zudak, C. (1998). Minority-serving institutions: An overview. In J. P. Merisotis & C. T. O'Brien (eds.), *Minority-serving institutions: Distinct purposes, common goals* (pp. 5-15). San Francisco: Jossey-Bass.

Pascarella, E. T., Edison, M., Nora, A., Hagedorn, L. S., & Terenzini, P. T. (1998). Does community college attendance versus four-year college attendance influence students' educational plans? *Journal of College Student Development, 39*(2), 179–193.

Peeke, G. (1994). *Mission and change: Institutional mission and its application to the management of further and higher education.* Bristol, PA: SRHE & Open University Press.

Perry, P. (2000). *Culture at the crossroads: The education of women: Is there a future for women's colleges in the new millennium?* Paper presented at the Technological Education and National Development (TEND) Conference, Abu Dhabi, United Arab Emirates. (ERIC Document Reproduction Service No. ED447279).

Pincus, F. & Archer, E. (1989). *Bridges to opportunity: Are community colleges meeting the transfer needs of minority students?* New York: Academy for Educational Development and College Entrance Examination Board.

President's Advisory Commission on Educational Excellence for Hispanic Americans. (1996). *Our nation on the fault line: Hispanic American education.* Washington, DC: Government Printing Office.

Quality Education for Minorities Project (1990). *Education that works.* Cambridge. MA: MIT.

Rendon, L. I. & Matthews, T. B. (1994). Success of community college students: Current Issues. In J. L. Ratcliff, S. Schwarz, & L. H. Ebbers (eds.), *Community Colleges: ASHE Reader Series* (pp. 343–353). Needham Heights, MA: Simon & Schuster Custom Publishing.

Rendon, L. I. & Garza, H. (1996): Closing the gap between two- and four-year institutions. In L. I. Rendon & R. O. Hope (eds.), *Educating a new majority: Transforming America's educational system for diversity* (pp. 289–308). San Francisco, CA: Jessey-Bass.

Rendon, L. I., & Hope, R. O. (1996). An educational system in crisis. In L. I. Rendon & R. O. Hope (eds.), *Educating a new majority: Transforming America's educational system for diversity* (pp. 1–32). San Francisco: Jossey-Bass.

Rhoads, R. A. (1999). The politics of culture and identity: Contrasting images of multiculturalism and monoculturalism. In K. M. Shaw, J. R. Valadez, & R. A. Rhoads (eds.), *Community colleges as cultural texts: Qualitative explorations of organizational student culture* (pp. 103-124). New York: State University of New York Press, Albany.

Rhoads, R. A & Valadez, J. R. (1996). *Democracy, multiculturalism, and the community college: A critical perspective.* New York: Garland.

Richardson, R. C. & Bender, L. W. (1987). *Fostering minority access and achievement in higher education: The role of urban community colleges and universities.* San Francisco, CA: Jossey-Bass.

Richardson, R. C. & Skinner, E. F. (1992). Helping first generation minority students achieve degrees. *New Directions for Community Colleges, 80,* 29–43.

Riordan, C. (1994). The value of attending a women's college: Education, occupation, and income benefits. *Journal of Higher Education, 65*(4), 486–510.

Robinson, P. W. (1990). *A study of declining enrollment trends in women's colleges in America; and the impact of Brenau College: Emergence of higher education in America.* (ED323863)

Schultz, R. E. & Stickler, W H. (1965). Vertical extension of academic programs in institutions of higher education. *Educational Record,* 231–241.

Schuman, D. & Olufs, D. (1995). *Diversity on campus.* Boston, MA: Allyn & Bacon.

Simmons, B. R. & Jackson, A. (1988, March). *Fostering black student enrollment at community colleges and historically black colleges in the same service area.* Pager presented at the National Association for Equal Opportunity in Higher Education, Conference, Washington, DC. (ED301240)

Smith, D. (1990). Women's colleges and coed colleges: Is there a difference for women? *Journal of Higher Education, 61*(2), 181–97.

Solomon, B. M. (9185). *In the company of educated women: A history of women and higher education in America.* New Haven, CT: Yale University Press.

Solomon, L. C. & Wingard, T. L. (1991). The changing demographics: Problems and opportunities. In P. G. Altbach and K. Lomotey (eds.), *The racial crisis in American higher education* (pp. 19–42). Albany, NY: SUNY Press.

Stoecker, J. L. & Pascarella, E. T. (1991). Women's colleges and women's career attainments revisited. *Journal of Higher Education, 62*(4), 394–406.

Townsend, B. K. (1999). Collective and distinctive patterns of two-year special focus colleges. In B. K. Townsend (ed.), *Two-year colleges for women and minorities: Enabling access to the baccalaureate* (pp. 3–42). New York: Falmer Press.

Townsend, B. K. (2000). Integrating nonminority instructors into the minority environment. In S. R. Aragon (Ed.), *Beyond access: Methods and models for increasing retention and learning among minority students* (pp . 85–93). San Francisco: Jossey-Bass.

U. S. Bureau of Census. (1996a). *Current population reports* (pp.1).Washington, DC: U.S. Department of Commerce.

U. S. Bureau of Census. (1996b). *Population projections of the United States by age, sex, race, and Hispanic origin: 1995 to 2050.* Washington, DC: U. S. Department of Commerce.

U. S. Bureau of Census. (1998). *Age, sex, race, and Hispanic origin reports* (pp. 2-3). Washington, DC: U.S. Department of Commerce.

U. S. Department of Education. (1998). *Fact sheet: Title III institutions.* Washington, DC: Government Printing Office.

U. S. Department of Education. (1997). *Hispanic-serving institutions: An analysis of higher education institutions eligible for the Hispanic-serving institutions program, title III of the higher education act of 1965, as amended.* Unpublished paper.

Whitaker, D. G. & Pascarella, E. T. (1994). Two-year college attendance and socioeconomic attainment. *Journal of Higher Education, 65*(2); 194–210.

Wolf-Wendel, L. & Pedigo, S. (1999). Two-year women's colleges: Silenced; fading, and almost forgotten. In B. K. Townsend (Ed.), *Two-year colleges for women and minorities: Enabling access to the baccalaureate* (pp. 43–83). New York: Falmer Press.

CHAPTER 9

COMMUNITY COLLEGE MISSION IN HISTORICAL PERSPECTIVE

KEN MEIER

The Mission Problem

Understanding historical context is essential for demystifying the community college mission and the discourses surrounding it. Terms such as "community college mission" or "junior college philosophy" have been undertheorized by scholars. Community college mission discussions often lack precision. In mission debates variant categories and levels of analysis tend to elide differences of meaning or intent, depending on the theoretical stance, rhetorical strategy, or the professional or social interests of the observer or practitioner (Levin, 1998; Meier, 2008).

There is a history of ambiguity, even confusion, regarding the mission and purposes of the colleges (Breneman & Nelson, 1981; Cross, 1985; Levin, 2000). John Frye remarks that the first junior colleges were "accompanied by no clear mission, set of criteria, nor theoretical framework" (Frye, 1992, p. 1). Employing content analysis of the publications of 56 colleges for the year 1920-1921, an early junior college scholar identified at least 21 distinct educational and social purposes for the colleges (Koos, 1925). Later scholars worried that the colleges lacked a "plausible categorical imperative" (Cohen, 1977, p. 74).

The Carnegie Commission on Higher Education notes that the "most striking structural development in higher education has been the phenomenal growth of the community college." The Commission adds, "[t]he roles of the community college are so diverse as to be bewildering" (Olgivie & Raines, 1971, p. v). Multiple roles and shifting institutional identity are reflected in organizational rituals of public community colleges devoted to "reforming," "renewing," "revitalizing," "reassessing," and "revisiting" the mission (Tillery & Deegan, 1985). Burton Clark views uncertainty about the junior-community college mission as a consequence of open-access and weak institutional connection to the organizational field of higher education: "[T]he building of a communicable and socially acceptable identity is *the* problem resulting from the character of the unselective junior college" (Clark, 1960, p. 171, emphasis in original).

The "academic revolution" of the 20th century defined a mission for the research university focused on the troika of research, teaching, and public service (Jencks & Riesman, 1968). There has never been a similar degree of consensus among practitioners, policy-makers, or university scholars in respect to the community college mission (Breneman & Nelson, 1981). A barrier to theoretical consensus is that some scholars evaluate these community-based, open-access organizations by the standards of selective universities (Frye, 1994).

Another challenge to theorizing the mission is the wide diversity of institutions, communities, and state-level governance systems that exists across the community college organizational field. National mission discourses often overlook community contexts that shape the enacted missions of individual colleges. Arizona Eastern College is a small historically Mormon-led college in Safford, Arizona. It defines and enacts the mission for its relatively homogeneous community and students differently compared to La Guardia Community College in Queens with its 50,000 students from over 160 countries speaking more than 110 native languages (Meier, 2008; Mellow & Heelan, 2008). Reconciling the missions of such different institutions requires both historical understanding and theoretical suppleness. Finally, the volatility of the U.S. social and economic context dictates that community colleges tack and wend continually in response to the frequent and sometimes conflicting gales directed at them from the state, business, labor markets, and local communities (Cohen & Brawer, 2008; Levin, 2001).

A common conception among scholars is that the colleges are "non-specialized by design, their mandate is to offer a comprehensive curriculum and to serve a wide range of community needs" (Owen, 1995, p. 145). The rub is what this means in either theory or practice. Openness, access, and responsiveness amount to a stance, perspective, or attitude rather than constituting either a theory or a purposeful program that differentiates a college from, say, a shopping mall or a theme park. The perennial focus on "inputs" by practitioners begs the question of measurable institutional outcomes.

The idea of comprehensiveness tied to open-access emerged in part from California junior college developments during the depression and World War II (Brossman & Roberts, 1973; Witt, Wattenbarger, Gollattscheck, & Suppinger, 1994). The comprehensive mission gained national currency by the 1960s. The conventional definition of the community college mission incorporates those educational functions that comprise "five traditional community college programs" (Cross, 1985, p. 36). These include: (1) collegiate and transfer education; (2) vocational education; (3) developmental or compensatory education; (4) general education; and (5) community education and service. Some practitioners include guidance and student development in the list of functions (Collins & Collins, 1971). By the 1990s, a "new function" was added to the mix—community economic and workforce development (Dougherty & Bakia, 1999).

One group of scholar-practitioners contends that flux, change, and "multi-variance" are defining characteristics of the colleges and their mission (Blocker, Plummer, & Richardson, 1965). Mutability is a frequently observed characteristic of the mission: "[Community colleges] change frequently, seeking new programs and clients" (Cohen & Brawer, 2008, p. 41). Mission opportunism may lead to muddled institutional identity: "[The] definition of the two year college is not much clearer today than it was before 1940" (Frye, 1991, p. 12).

It is not unusual for community colleges to ignore their publicly expressed missions in response to perceived community needs or demands, external policy signals from the state or federal governments, an enticing revenue stream, or social and economic change. In the restless pursuit of new opportunities, the colleges ignore the history and traditions of higher education: "Unlike four-year colleges and universities, community colleges are non-traditional or untraditional: they do not even adhere to their own traditions. They make and remake themselves" (Levin, 1998, p. 2).

Some observers perceive frenetic activity and weak traditions as symptoms of an inadequately realized "institutionalization project" (DiMaggio, 1988). Others explain mission drift and organizational ambiguity as a consequence of: (1) pioneering on the frontiers of community economic development and social responsibility (Vaughan, 1991); (2) self-aggrandizing behaviors of relatively autonomous professional elites (Dougherty, 1994); (3) cutting-edge entrepreneurial enterprise and technological innovation (O'Banion, 1997); (4) tracking and diverting student ambitions (Brint & Karabel, 1989); and (5) cultural dynamics and adaptive behaviors that maintain and reproduce community college identity (Levin, 1998).

Conceptual Framework

Historical and organizational analyses are necessary for assessing the relative merits of competing perspectives on the mission and the community college *qua* institution. This chapter is the result of nearly two decades of investigation into community college history. It conceptualizes the community college mission as an historically contingent social and educational process that is structured by the needs of local communities, student demands, and regional and national imperatives for economic and workforce development (Gleazer, 1994; Ratcliff, 1994). Multiple missions and influences dictate organizational behavior that is often at variance with traditional higher education.

Community college leaders equate non-traditional practice with institutional virtue. Loath to seek a lesser place within the higher education hierarchy, community college leaders assert a community college identity that is "neither the penthouse for the high school nor the first two floors of the senior institution" (Gleazer, 1958, p. 486).

The historical junior-community college mission is more intelligible when analyzed across four theoretical domains: the philosophical, functional, empirical, and formative missions. The philosophical mission is expressed or implied in vision and values statements. It communicates the social and educational purposes of the community college in a democratic society. Historically these philosophical values include student-centeredness, community service, lifelong learning, equity, opportunity, social justice, open access, education for citizenship, and even spirituality (Meier, 2008).

The functional or operational mission is generally articulated in formal college mission and purposes statements. It is reflected in the curriculum and "core" programs that characterize the comprehensive community college. The classic functions are transfer general education, career and technical education, developmental education, student development, and community and cultural programming (Bogue, 1950).

The summative or empirical mission is enacted at the level of the academic schedule and daily organizational commitments and activities of the colleges. It constitutes concrete, replicated organizational behavior. It encompasses the educational, fiscal, and political decisions that shape educational practices and outcomes. This is the nexus at which institutional structures connect to the purposeful professional activity of faculty and the educational and social engagement of students and community. This substantive mission is reflected in measurable organizational outcomes.

The formative or social mission is conceptualized as the long-term effects of more than one thousand public colleges on local communities, higher education, and U.S. society in general. This is the domain in which practitioners, stakeholders, policy-makers, critics, and scholars contend over the efficacy of the community college in U.S. society and as an institution of higher education. Perceived gaps between the philosophical mission and the formative mission are a matter of ideological and theoretical contest to validate or invalidate the community college as an educational institution.

Almost by definition, formal community colleges mission statements are influenced by the expectations of external constituencies: "[M]issions exist at the interface between an institution and its environment" (Richardson & Doucette, 1984, p. 12). The publicly stated mission of an organization is one matter, but the enacted or empirical mission may be quite another as the organization is shaped by and responds to its social and economic environment. Organizational theory provides insights regarding the environmental context of mission enactment.

Resource dependency theory (Pfeffer & Salancik, 1978) frames organizations as open systems influenced decisively by the environment. They are "quasi-markets" that struggle for limited organizational autonomy. Threats and opportunities are defined by influences emanating from broader organizational fields: "The key to organizational survival is the ability to acquire and maintain resources" (Pfeffer & Salancik, 1978, p. 2). Transactions within and between organizational fields in pursuit of marginal dollars and increments of political capital tend to structure organizational behavior.

Institutional theory explains organizational activity and outcomes as nested within networked organizational fields. Organizational forms with similar social, political, or economic purposes take on the characteristics of institutions by emulating each other. Institutional environments comprise historical and cultural as well as technical and economic dimensions: "[O]rganizations compete not just for resources and customers, but for political power and institutional legitimacy, for social as well as economic fitness" (DiMaggio & Powell, 1983, p. 150). Insights from organization theory provide nuances and context for explaining the historical development of the community college mission.

Historiography of the Public Community College

Junior-community college historical research is a relatively underdeveloped field. Practitioners take little interest in their history; individual colleges devote little time and few resources to the preservation of institutional memory. Academic researchers who examine the history of the colleges often evidence ideological assumptions that bias their perceptions of the community mission and outcomes (Pedersen, 2000).

John Frye argues that community college historical writing is mostly "descriptive and promotional," and when it "touches on theory or general models . . . it tends to vagueness and imprecision" (1992, p. 6).

> [It] is very rare for any writer on the junior college to show a serious historical interest in the origins of the movement. Typically a few generalizations are made as to formative figures, usually prominent personalities in higher education, who played a role in initiating the movement. This outline information is passed from author to author in those few introductory or survey studies of the junior college. (Frye, 1992, p. 5)

A relative paucity of accurate historical information leads researchers on the colleges to make assumptions about the mission and history of these institutions that will not stand the test of rigorous theoretical interrogation. The following discussion addresses the contributions and limitations of the most important historical works in the field.

America's Community Colleges: The First Century (Witt et al., 1994), published by the American Association of Community Colleges (AACC), attempts to survey the entire history of community colleges. The authors celebrate rather than critically analyze the movement. The book is ebullient about community college growth without paying much attention to the quality of its outcomes. As community college boosters, they ignore critical research on the colleges. Their work provides a useful state-level chronology ofthe historical development of community college systems. An important contribution is an extended analysis ofjunior college developments during World War II. The authors also make a significant point that has not been theorized by community college scholars: community colleges constitute the "only sector of higher education to be called a movement" (Witt et al., 1994, p. xviii).

Brick (1964) provides a shrewd history of the American Association of Junior Colleges (AAJC) to 1960. Brick describes the AAJC as "forum and focus" of the movement. He is one of the first community college historians to employ primary material and careful document analysis to explain community college history from a national perspective. This is an important synthesis of AAJC history to 1960.

Utilizing secondary sources, Tillery and Deegan (1985) develop a brief, schematic history of the community college mission from the founding of the first public junior college in 1901 through the "fourth generation" comprehensive community college that reached "maturity" by the 1980s. They provide a useful typology of community college history as experiencing four discrete stages of development. The primary historical purpose is their establishment of a context for understanding the future trajectory of institutional mission. They predict presciently that the emerging "fifth generation" college will be driven increasingly by the imperatives of economic development and competition in the new postindustrial economy, high technology and computer-based information systems, and heightened external demands for institutional accountability.

Ratcliff (1987) makes a persuasive case that the "first" public junior colleges emerged as a result of broad social and economic forces spawned by the second industrial revolution (*circa* 1870-1920) and its aftermath. Interest group politics grounded in local economic aspirations drove early junior college development rather than visionary leaders. In a later article, Ratcliff (1994, p. 4) identifies "seven streams of educational innovation" that influenced the historical development of the comprehensive community college: (1) "local community boosterism"; (2) "rise of the research university"; (3) "restructuring and expansion of the public educational system" in tandem with the second industrial revolution; (4) "professionalization of teacher education"; (5) "the vocational education movement"; (6) "the rise of adult, continuing, and community education"; and, (7) "open public access to higher education." Taken together, Tillery and Deegan and Ratcliff identify the social and intellectual forces that shaped the institutional development of the colleges.

Dougherty (1994) employs historical analysis in conjunction with case-study materials and national university transfer data to develop a "state-relativist" interpretation of leadership ideology and interests. He argues that a community of interest among educational policy-makers and institutional leaders has been the driving force in shaping and even deforming the community college mission. He perceives an unforced choice on the part of community college leadership to shift the institution away from transfer education to vocational programming. The shift in mission negatively affects the life chances of students while marginalizing the colleges as institutions of higher education. Based on his reading of student transfer data, he makes policy arguments for eliminating the community college as an independent higher education sector.

As prelude to a case study of "vocationalization" in the Massachusetts community college system, Brint and Karabel (1989, 1991) offer a critical, historically informed "institutional-conflict analysis" of the origins and "hidden significance" of the vocational mission. Community colleges sort and track students along class lines primarily, diverting students from liberal transfer education into less prestigious vocational programs. By diverting these students from collegiate to vocational education, community colleges acquire a secure market niche and modicum of influence within the organizational field of higher education. Community college leaders practice "anticipatory subordination" to corporations, labor markets, and elite university opinion. These activities further the professional interests of community college leaders who are rewarded by policy-makers and corporations for "managing the ambitions" of students. Though marred by ideological bias in data collection and analysis, this is one of the most important contributions to the historical sociology of the colleges.

Frye (1992) examines the "vision of the public junior college" from 1900 to 1940. He exposes the irony of a national leadership that, while legitimizing and popularizing the junior college ideal among policy-makers and university elites, was frequently ignored in educational aspirations and practice by both local practitioners and students (1991, 1992). Junior college leaders developed a strategy to acquire social legitimacy and stability through the acquisition of new markets outside the purview of traditional higher education. They sought to popularize the concepts of terminal education and paraprofessional training in the junior college. Frye offers a well-informed practitioner's analysis of the vision and early mission of the public junior college.

Gregory Goodwin's dissertation (1971) on the formation and development of community college ideology is a critical history of the movement told from the perspective of the most widely published AAJC leaders prior to the 1960s. Goodwin offers a penetrating analysis validated by immense research in the primary documents of the national movement. He describes a social and educational reform movement that was for many years "more of an idea than institution" (Goodwin, 1971, p. 189). For the junior college founders, according to Goodwin, the road to individual achievement and discipline was through the classroom. This work has been appropriated by a number of subsequent community college historians. It remains one of the most important works in the field.

Collectively these works establish that there were several broad goals for the early national junior college movement: (1) to capture growing educational and training markets within the increasingly complex ecology of the U.S. education system (Brint & Karabel, 1989); (2) to secure professional respect, personal advancement, and institutional support from policy-makers, stakeholders, and the educational community as a whole (Frye, 1992); (3) to advance a moderate social/educational reform agenda that would support both social order and democratic social progress (Goodwin, 1971); and (4) to support open-access to higher education and "short-cycle needs" of diverse clientele (Ratcliff, 1994). For Edmund Gleazer, historical analysis of the community college mission reveals the "search for [community college] institutional freedom to determine its program and to look to the community [and its needs] as the arbiter of the suitability of its programs rather than the universities" (1994, p. 19).

Social Context of Public Junior College Development

In community college lore, the first public junior college was founded in 1901 at Joliet, Illinois. Six decades later junior colleges had achieved a ubiquitous national presence. Cohen argues, "[t]he foremost impetus for their growth was the pressure for further education occasioned by the rising numbers of high school graduates" (1998, p. 112). The public high school movement (and eventually the junior college) was stimulated by the education and training requirements of a new corporate industrial order.

During the "Second Industrial Revolution" (circa 1870-1930), the U.S. witnessed a series of complementary economic, social, and technological innovations so extensive that each has been characterized as a revolution: (1) an economic revolution that shifted most of the nation in less than three generations from a predominantly agrarian and more or less craft-based economy comprised of both market and subsistence sectors to a corporate, globalizing economy; (2) an energy revolution that moved most of the country and eventually the world from animal, human, wind, water, and timber sources of power to more productive carboniferous and petroleum-based technologies; (3) a demographic and urban revolution that grew the U.S. population almost exponentially, concentrating it around more socially complex industrial centers and away from the rural hinterland or from Europe; and (4) a techno-science, engineering revolution that was both stimulus and consequence of the other interrelated movements (Williams, 2002).

These innovations led to the creation of a new mass consumption society and a growing middle class that demanded more educational services and credentials to provide them with relative economic security in the increasingly competitive industrial society. Professionals and white-collar workers required higher levels of literacy, numeracy, and communication skills for occupational success than previous generations. University administrators, scholars, practitioners, and community boosters proposed the junior college as a solution to the education and training requirements of the new order (Frye, 1992; Ratcliff, 1994).

Social Origins and Ideological Assumptions of Junior College Founders

Prior to World War II, university leaders and scholars dominated the junior college movement, theoretically and ideologically. The AAJC attracted a strong group of advocates and theorists to articulate the vision and multiple purposes of the junior-community college (Goodwin, 1973). The professors and practitioners who led the movement came from predominantly small-town, Protestant evangelical backgrounds. Some were ordained ministers and a significant number of the most prominent national leaders held doctorates in education from elite universities such as Chicago, Michigan, Berkeley, Stanford, and Harvard. In their minds, Christianity, educational opportunity, and democracy constituted a unified social philosophy. Edmund Gleazer, who dominated the AAJC for two decades, personifies the evangelical subtext of the movement. The former street preacher also possessed a glittering Harvard doctorate. He proclaimed the open door college as Christian revelation: "We have borrowed from John the Revelator a phrase of almost 20 centuries ago, conceived high on the steep slopes of the Island of Patmos: 'Behold, I have set before thee an open door'" (Gleazer, 1970, p. 49).

Movement leaders developed a variety of justifications for the junior college. These included educational opportunity and socialization for democratic citizenship, social adjustment and social solidarity, strengthening secondary education, training middle-level managers and semi-professionals for a rapidly industrializing society, family health and social hygiene, supporting upward mobility for deserving "bright boys" from the lower orders, facilitating university matriculation, providing general education to the masses, and contributing to social stability and economic development by matching students with labor market niches congruent with their intellectual and emotional development (Goodwin, 1971; Koos, 1924). The leaders believed that education informed by spiritual and moderately democratic values was the most efficient method for addressing social and economic problems. In Gregory Goodwin's words, junior college leaders viewed "the basic mission of the community-junior college as a panacea for social ills" (Goodwin, 1973, p. 13).

The Quest for an Institutional Framework

Scholars often perceive unity of purpose in the early junior college movement. Some contend that the *raison d'être* of the early public junior colleges was the collegiate transfer function. Shaw and London (2001) assert that the first junior colleges were "originally developed to deliver the equivalent of the first two years of a baccalaureate education" (p. 91). Cohen and Brawer counter that all the elements—academic transfer programs, vocational-technical education, continuing education, developmental education, and community service—of the comprehensive mission "have been present in public colleges from the beginning" (2008, p. 22).

The AAJC was established in 1920. The first issue of the *Junior College Journal*, the association's trade publication, appeared in 1930. With the advent of the *Journal* the AAJC presented itself as an energetic national educational movement that attempted to guide local junior college initiatives. The AAJC sought to establish a coherent institutional identity and compelling social purpose for the colleges. This was a major challenge for a small, scattered educational movement that was more of a dream than a national educational reality. Frye notes, "One is hard pressed to establish an unambiguous purpose for the first public junior college at Joliet, Illinois, or elsewhere" (1992, p. 1).

The AAJC convention in 1922 gave the impression of national unity with its masthead resolution: "The junior college is an institution offering two years of instruction of strictly collegiate grade" (AAJC, 1922). Three years later the AAJC expanded the functional mission to include terminal vocational and paraprofessional training (Thornton, 1972). Multiple functions were present in practice and theory from the inception of the movement. Researchers who focus on the transfer function as the master function of the junior colleges overlook institutional nuances at peril of historical accuracy.

Merton Hill's (1938) longitudinal analysis of the curricula of 39 California public junior colleges confirms multiple functions by the 1930s. Most California colleges were engaged in some vocational, developmental, cultural, and adult programming from their inception. Vocational education increased significantly at a number of colleges during the Depression and was the dominant function for several large urban colleges. Generally speaking, close proximity of a college to a university and an expanding industrial labor market pushed it toward vocational education. More isolated rural colleges with weak local labor markets tended to focus on the terminal general education and transfer functions (Hill, 1938).

Institution building and diversification were challenging processes. As late as 1945, the incoming AAJC President Lawrence L. Bethel bemoaned institutional disorder. Lack of consistency among junior colleges was revealed at state meetings: "Institutions that operated within a stone's throw of each other spoke almost a different language" (1945a, p. 393). For a movement that prided itself on being "sanely progressive" and fostering "social intelligence" disunity was disturbingly inefficient (Goodwin, 1971).

Social Origins of the Comprehensive Community College Concept

By the mid-1930s, a new perspective on the mission and purposes of the junior college in an increasingly complex, but troubled, industrial society developed in regions such as the Mississippi Valley, Texas, and California. These were areas where populist and progressive sentiments were closely allied with frontier traditions; this political context was tied to a significant degree of insulation from university influence due to the paucity of four-year collegiate institutions compared to the Upper Midwest and the Northeast (Frye, 1992). California practitioners in particular attempted to shift the philosophical mission to lifelong learning, adult education, and community service (Hayden, 1939; Hill, 1938). Clearly there were regional differences in the development of these institutions. Connections to local communities, student academic preferences, and local labor markets, rather than a national movement, were the primary mission drivers (Frye, 1992).

The economic and social crisis of the Great Depression stimulated community alignment nationally. Edmund Gleazer credits Byron Hollinshead's article in the *Journal* (1936) as a path-breaking redefinition of the junior college as a "community college" focused on meeting community needs.

Hollinshead would soon become president of the AAJC. Gleazer sees this article as the intellectual genesis of the comprehensive mission, which "anticipated the marketing approach of the present as did his view on close relationships with the high schools and other community institutions" (Gleazer, 1994, p. 18).

These developments widened the purposes of the institution. Young, rising AAJC leaders expanded the definition of collegiate education. They focused on the ideals of lifelong learning and community service as plausible social justification for a community college that moved beyond the restrictions of the extended high school model. Advocates of a new kind of community college argued that "considering education as a lifelong process is the most important function of the junior college as a community institution" (Hayden, 1939, p. 72). Stimulated by economic crisis and galvanized by New Deal idealism, new leaders reframed the junior college as a local consensus social movement dedicated to providing educational and community services that would blunt the impact of the Depression by wedding mission outcomes to community development: "The junior college which attacks vigorously the problems of the social reconstruction must be a part of the community, warmed or chilled by the same breezes which warm or chill a community" (Kelley, 1936, p. 428). The lifelong education and community service perspective reflected and reinforced the drift in the movement from older progressive notions of social engineering to more liberal-democratic models of social mobilization paralleling the politics of New Deal America. The emerging community college ideology advocated for a comprehensive, fungible mission to address the political conflicts and social problems of the 1930s and ultimately mobilization for war (Goodwin, 1973; Meier, 2008).

The new outlook undermined traditional conceptions of the university patriarchs who sought to restrict the junior college to teaching an extended high school curriculum and socializing youth (Koos, 1924). New AAJC leaders argued that educational services should be accessible to all adults who could profit from the community college experience (President's Commission on Higher Education, 1947a). They asserted the legitimacy of vocational education as an integral element of higher education. AAJC President Bethel defended vocational education through a witty observation on one of the long-standing canards in community college curriculum—cosmetology as higher education:

> Perhaps someday we may regard the art of beautifying a lady's face of collegiate importance equal to the science of engineering. I suspect that it is not so much *what* is taught that makes a curriculum collegiate or sub-collegiate, but instead *how* it is taught and to *whom* it is taught. (1945b, p. 103, emphasis in original)

AAJC leaders, who came up through local colleges that thrived in spite of Depression and war, talked excitedly about meeting community needs. As Thornton observed, "The emphasis in the community junior college is on providing legitimate educational services, rather than conforming to preconceived notions of what is or is not collegiate subject matter, or of who is or is not college material" (Thornton, 1972, p. 277).

In 1939 the *Journal* published a polemic in favor of the community-based comprehensive mission, "Junior College as a Community Institution" (Hayden, 1939). Its author was a Santa Monica College faculty member and past president of the Southern California Junior College Association. Hayden re-imagined the junior college movement as an educational reform movement that employed the curriculum and faculty to "mold public sentiment." The two most important mechanisms for changing public perceptions and effecting local social reform were a "planned public education campaign" and "a program for adult education" (Hayden, 1939, p. 73). The philosophical turn to lifelong learning, community service, and democratic, popular higher education positioned the junior college to expand its social reach and market.

Legitimating the Comprehensive Mission

Junior college practitioners, including those most committed to the vocational project, were quite willing to defend the collegiate and transfer functions in the face of any overt threat from their university brethren. John W. Harberson, principal of Pasadena Junior College, is a case in point. Brint and Karabel label him as the most prominent and effective diverter of potential junior college transfer students into vocational tracks (1989, pp. 54-61). Yet, in 1942 Harberson penned a doughty defense of the "Preparatory Objective of the Junior College." In a lead editorial of the *Journal*, Harberson implored his colleagues not to ignore the transfer function as they once did the terminal function, since "25 to 30 percent of the [junior college] student population can and should continue their education in higher institutions and they comprise too important and sizable a group to disregard" (Harberson, 1942, p. 180).

> [T]he universities are taking advantage of the present emphasis on terminal education to proclaim to the world, by inference at least, that in its post-high school training of non-university preparatory students the junior college has at last found its true role and the university preparatory function should be surrendered exclusively to the standard college . . . [The junior college] can and must, if it continues to merit the financial support of all the people, prepare the potential university student for specialization, research or professional study. (Harberson, 1942, pp. 179-180)

Harberson's position was axiomatic to practitioners. The history of the junior-community college movement witnesses the tenacity of its leaders to neither abandon a market nor cede institutional autonomy without a struggle. Community college leaders possess an abiding professional and institutional interest in defending multiple missions and functions.

The historical literature of the community colleges devotes scant attention to the role of the colleges in World War II. The usual compressed narrative slides quickly over the draft and declining enrollments and then to the almost giddy reactions of national and local leaders to the G.I. Bill and the 1947 Truman Commission Report (Brint & Karabel, 1989). The most informative discussion of the wartime junior college focuses on the rapid shift to short-term job training, extended adult education, and development of patriotic non-credit courses." The new curriculum ranged from aviation to victory gardens, cartography to riveting, nursing to do-it-yourself functions. These observers note that the sudden shift in emphasis from liberal arts transfer courses to vocational and short-cycle occupational training focused on adult part-time students "had a profound effect on the future mission of American junior colleges" (Witt et al., 1994, pp. 119-121).

Early in the war, Leland Medsker, a prominent junior college administrator and scholar, observed that "several factors seem to make [the junior college] position strategic" for anticipating postwar needs.

> Probably no type of accredited institution is less hampered by tradition and by orthodox methods . . .
> It is or can be a local institution [with the] experience and ability to deal with all types of students regardless of ability, background, or educational and vocational ambitions. (Medsker, 1943, pp. 19, 38)

Throughout the war, the AAJC hyped successful experiments in short-term training with an eye to strengthening postwar junior college vocational programs in the name of meeting the demands and expectations of their communities (Eells, 1944a, 1944b).

Postwar Community College

At the end of World War II, the junior college movement possessed an articulate national leadership and hundreds of vigorous local colleges (Goodwin, 1971). The movement took advantage of postwar prosperity to expand its reach and influence. Widespread liberal optimism about higher education's potential to stimulate economic growth, strengthen democracy, mitigate class and racial conflict, and to provide Cold War ideological munitions to the nation provided a cultural context supportive of junior college expansion (Meier, 2008).

Postwar explosion of the community college was tied closely to Federal public policy. Initiatives such as the G.I. Bill and the Truman Commission permanently altered the educational landscape by creating a social perception that "college attendance was a right not a privilege" (Vaughan, 1984, p. 25). The comprehensive community college ideal extolled in the Commission report and junior colleges' responsiveness to veteran demands for higher education and workforce training helped to shape the growing national perception of higher education as a necessary public good. Much has been made in the literature of the dual impact of the G.I. Bill and Truman Commission on the growth of the national movement (Brint & Karabel, 1989; Vaughan, 1984; Witt et al., 1994). Of the two federal initiatives, the G.I. Bill had the greatest direct impact on the development of the community college mission. Junior college enrollments doubled to more than 500,000 students between 1944 and 1947. By 1946, more than 40% of all junior college students were veterans. At least 58 new public colleges were established during the decade after the war (Witt et al., 1994).

Community college leaders appreciated the symmetry between their liberal consensus politics and the aims of the G.I. Bill. They relished the opportunity to mobilize massive federal and state resources in pursuit of patriotic aims. Even though the AAJC had virtually no influence on shaping veterans' policy at the national level, local junior colleges proved to be adroit opportunists in taking advantage of the windfall. The emphasis on technical-vocational training during the war positioned the colleges to accept and serve "a more diverse group of students, thereby helping to move the public junior college in the direction of open access" (Vaughan, 1984, p. 25). The arrival of hundreds of thousands of non-traditional students reinforced community college commitment to lifelong learning and adult education, presenting a vista of almost limitless educational markets in the future (Martorana, 1946).

The President's Commission on Higher Education (Truman Commission) recommended that a community college be established within commuting distance of nearly all Americans (1947b, pp. 6-7). The comprehensive ideal promised a spectrum of educational services extending from transfer education and vocational training to adult education and community service programs. It addressed the burgeoning public demand for accessible higher education services and credentials.

The Commission Report emphasized skills training and workforce development. The relative privileging of community colleges is explicable as an economic policy initiative. The Commission asserted that junior colleges "must prepare [their] students to live a rich and satisfying life, part of which involves earning a living" (President's Commission on Higher Education, 1947b, pp. 6-7). The Commission promoted the junior college role in university-level transfer education as well.

In 1948, the California Association of Junior Colleges (CAJC) influenced the "Strayer Report" (Deutsch, Aubrey, & Strayer, 1948) to incorporate the outlines of its version of the comprehensive functional mission and the values of its philosophical mission. These became models for the national movement. The Strayer Report anticipated the 1960 California Master Plan for Higher Education. It outlined the comprehensive community college mission in the following terms: "Terminal Education, General Education, Orientation and Guidance, Lower Division Training, Adult Education, Removal of Matriculation Difficulties." Underpinning this functional mission was a broader philosophical and social mission. The CAJC expressed its commitment to this social mission by articulating a set of values intended to rationalize the comprehensive mission.

> 1. The junior college is committed to the democratic way of life; 2. The junior college recognizes the individual man as the highest value of the world and universe; 3. The junior college is committed to the policy of granting to the individual man the maximum amount of freedom, personal initiative, and adventure consistent with equal opportunities on the part of his fellows; 4. The junior college is committed to the policy of providing for all the children of all the people, a post-high-school education which will meet their needs. (Deutschet al., 1948, pp. 6-7)

A key AAJC/CAJC postwar goal was to accelerate the junior college organizational transition from extended secondary education while redefining its place in higher education.

Following the CAJC example, Jesse Bogue, executive leader of the AAJC, promulgated a synthesis of the comprehensive, open-access mission in his influential book, *The Community College* (1950). He emphasized the importance of becoming a community-based institution independent of both high schools and direct university influence: "Community colleges must strike out boldly, demonstrate that they are not bound by tradition or the desire to ape senior colleges for the sake of a totally false notion of academic respectability, and do the job" (Bogue, 1950, p. 313). Bogue's synthesis of 50 years of junior-community college development established the model for a comprehensive, community-based, fungible mission that remains dominant in practitioner ideology to this day.

Conclusion

By the 1960s the G.I. Bill, U.S. economic growth, and baby boom demographics helped to establish the comprehensive, open-access college as a national postsecondary education institution. The movement took great pride in the spectacle of a new college being created almost every week in this decade (Witt et al., 1994). Community college leadership side-stepped issues of educational quality and institutional outcomes by emphasizing access, innovation, and growth, equating these organizational attributes with the democratizing mission of the "People's Colleges." They assumed the new institutions must be heading in the right direction because the colleges mirrored the U.S. business model of success—more customers, new markets, bigger profits (Meier, 2008).

Leaders in the 1960s shared a tacit consensus that "the community college was philosophically and economically constituted to be all things to all people" (Vaughan, 1984, p. 38). John Lombardi, President of Los Angeles City College, advanced the ideal of a comprehensive mission with permeable boundaries. He endorsed the comments of prominent political leaders calling for expanded college missions.

> A junior college should be, according to Governor Terry Sanford of North Carolina, an institution which undertakes everything not being taken care of elsewhere. Lest there be any doubt, Governor Sanford spelled out activities such as education of the illiterates, uplifting the underprivileged, retraining the unemployed—a truly comprehensive institution. Senator Walter Stierns of California urged the junior college to undertake the task of preparing Americans for recreational and leisure activities. Secretary of Labor Willard Wirtz looks to the junior college for aid in solving unemployment. (Lombardi, 1964, p. 8)

This outline of a "truly comprehensive institution" was enough of an identity for many community college leaders. But knowledgeable practitioners understood that continual mission expansion opened them to charges by academic critics that "the many qualifications to the definition [of identity and mission] may leave the impression that the community junior college is an entirely amorphous institution, so fluid and adaptable as to lack character and defy consistent definition" (Thornton, 1972, p. 279). There was also the perennial challenge of taking on "new missions without the resources to fund new programs or to integrate them with the existing institution" (Rosenbaum, Deil-Amen, & Person, 2006, p. 1). The most important question was posed by Martorana and Kuhns (1988, p. 230): "Can institutions defined only by access and growth continue to maintain themselves?"

The closing theoretical point is that historically community college organizational behavior tends to mirror social and economic change rather than leading it (Levin, 2000). Changes in mission focus are adaptive behaviors structured by rapid alterations in the social and economic logic of both the public and private sectors. Responding to massive changes in postwar U.S., community colleges reacted reflexively by pursuing new initiatives that might give them a competitive advantage in the education and training marketplace. As suggested by both resource dependency theory (Pfeffer & Salancik, 1978) and institutional theory (DiMaggio & Powell, 1983), all organizations compete for economic survival and social fitness. Their history suggests that community colleges will continue to seek presumed advantages within economic trends and changing labor markets, while continuing their embrace of a fungible, comprehensive mission (Meier, 2008). Multiple missions and multiple identities are inherent in the organizational and social design of community colleges.

Questions for Discussion

1. What justifies the view that the community college and its predecessor, the junior college, was a social movement?

2. Are there examples from the present that indicate that the community college continues as a social movement?

3. What are the four domains of community/junior college mission?

4. What are examples of the expression of mission within each domain?

References

American Association of Junior Colleges (AAJC). (1922). *Report of the American Association of Junior Colleges in annual session*. Washington, DC: Author.

Bailey, F. (1967). *Santa Rosa junior college, 1918–1957: A personal history*. Santa Rosa, CA: Santa Rosa College.

Bergquist, W. (1998). The postmodern challenge: Changing our community colleges. In J. Levin (Ed.), *Organizational change in the community college: A ripple or a sea change. New Directions for Community Colleges, no. 102* (pp. 87–98). San Francisco, CA: Jossey-Bass.

Bethel, L. (1945a). Power of coordinated effort. *Junior College Journal, 15*(9), 391–394.

Bethel, L. (1945b). What are 'these institutions'? *Junior College Journal, 16*(3), 101–105.

Blocker, C., Plummer, R., & Richardson, R. (1965). *The two-year college: A social synthesis*. Englewood Cliff, NJ: Prentice-Hall.

Bogue, J. (1950). *The community college*. New York, NY: McGraw-Hill.

Breneman, D., & Nelson, S. (1981). *Financing community colleges: An economic perspective*. Washington, DC: Brookings Institute.

Brick, M. (1964). *Forum and focus for the junior college movement: The American Association of Junior Colleges*. New York, NY: Teachers College, Columbia University.

Brint, S., & Karabel, J. (1989). *The diverted dream: Community colleges and the promise of education opportunity in America, 1900-1985*. New York, NY: Oxford University Press.

Brint, S., & Karabel, J. (1991). Institutional origins and transformations: The case of American community colleges. In W. Powell & P. DiMaggio (Eds.), *The new institutionalism in organizational analysis* (pp. 337–360). Chicago, IL: University of Chicago.

Brossman, S., & Roberts, M. (1973). *The California community colleges*. Palo Alto, CA: First Educational publications.

Brothers, E. (1934). The new deal and the junior college. *Junior College Journal, 5*(1), 5.

Clark, B. (1960). *The open door college: A case study*. New York, NY: McGraw-Hill.

Clowes, D., & Towles, D. (1985). Lessons from fifty years: Analysis of the association's journal provides insight into shifting leadership interests. *Community, Technical, and Junior College Journal, 55*(1), 28–32.

Cohen, A. (1977). The social equalization fantasy. *Community College Review, 5*(2), 74–82.

Cohen, A. (1998). *The shaping of American higher education: Emergence and growth of the contemporary system*. San Francisco, CA: Jossey-Bass.

Cohen, A. M., & Brawer, F. B. (1994). The changing environment: Contexts, concepts, and crises. In A. M. Cohen & F. B. Brawer (Eds.), *Managing community colleges*. San Francisco, CA: Jossey-Bass.

Cohen, A. M., & Brawer, F. B. (2008). *The American community college* (5th ed.). San Francisco, CA: Jossey-Bass.

Cohen, A. M., Lombardi, J., & Brawer, F. B. (1975). *College responses to community demands*. San Francisco, CA: Jossey-Bass.

Collins, C., & Collins, J. (1971). The case for the community college: Basic assumptions. In W. Olgive & M. Raines (Eds.), *Perspectives on the community-junior college* (pp. 139–148). New York, NY: Appleton-Century-Crofts.

Cross, K. (1985). Determining missions and priorities for the fifth generation. In W. Deegan, D. Tilllery, & Associates (Eds.), *Renewing the American community college*. San Francisco, CA: Jossey-Bass.

Deutsch, M., Aubrey, A., & Strayer, D. (1948). *A report of a survey of the needs of California higher education*. Berkeley: University of California Press.

DiMaggio, P. (1988). Interest and agency in institutional theory. In L. Zucker (Ed.), *Institutional patterns and organizations: Culture and environment* (pp. 3–21). Cambridge, MA: Ballinger.

DiMaggio, P., & Powell, W. (1983). The iron cage revisited: Institutional isomorphism and collective rationality in organizational fields. *American sociological Review, 47*(2), 147–160.

Dougherty, K. (1994). *The contradictory college: Conflict origins, impacts, and futures of the community college*. Albany, NY: State University of New York Press.

Dougherty, K., & Bakia, M. (1999). *The new economic development role of the community college*. New York, NY: Community College Research Center, Teachers College, Columbia University.

Eells, W. (1931). The junior college—What manner of child shall this be? *Junior College Journal, 1*(5), 309–328.

Frye, J. (1991). *Conflicting voices in the definition of the junior/community college*. Los Angeles, CA: ERIC Clearinghouse for Junior Colleges (ERIC Document Reproduction Service No. ED 337228).

Frye, J. (1992). *The vision of the public junior college, 1900-1940.* New York, NY: Greenwood Press.

Frye, J. (1994). Educational paradigms in the professional literature of the community college. In J. Smart (Ed.), *Higher education: Handbook of theory and research* (Vol. X, pp. 181–224). New York, NY: Agathon Press.

Gleazer, E. (1958). The junior college—Bigger! Better? *Junior College Journal, 28*(9), 484–487.

Gleazer, E. (1970). The community college issue of the 1970s. *Educational Record, 51*(1), 47–52.

Gleazer, E. (1980). *The community college. Values, vision, and vitality.* Washington, DC: American Association of Junior Colleges.

Gleazer, E. (1994). Evolution of junior colleges into community colleges. In G. Baker (Ed.), *A handbook on the community college in America.* Westport, CN: Greenwood Press.

Goodwin, G. (1971). *The historical development of the community-junior college ideology: An analysis and interpretation of the writings of selected community-junior college leaders from 1890-1970.* (Unpublished doctoral dissertation.) University of Illinois, Urbana-Champaign, 1L.

Goodwin, G. (1973). *A social panacea: A history of community college ideology.* Los Angeles, CA: ERIC Clearinghouse for Junior Colleges (ERIC Document Reproduction Service No. ED093427).

Grubb, W., & Lazerson, M. (2004). *The education gospel: The economic power of schooling.* Cambridge, MA: Harvard University Press.

Harberson, J. (1942). Preparatory objective of the junior college. *Junior College Journal, 13*(4), 179–180.

Hayden, S. (1939). Junior college as a community institution. *Junior College Journal, 10*(2), 70–73.

Hill, M. (Ed.). (1938). *The functioning of the California public junior college: A symposium.* Berkeley: University of California Press, Works Progress Administration.

Hollinshead, B. (1936). The community junior college program. *Junior College Journal, 7*(3), 111–116.

Jencks, C., & Riesman, D. (1968). *The academic revolution.* Garden City, NY: Doubleday.

Kelley, F. (1936). The junior college and social reconstruction. *Junior College Journal, 6*(8), 428.

Koos, L. (1924). *The junior college.* Minneapolis: University of Minnesota.

Koos, L. (1925). *The junior college movement.* New York, NY: AMS.

Koos, L. (1927a). Conditions favor integration of junior colleges with high schools. *School Life, 12*(9), 164.

Koos, L. (1927b). The junior college curriculum. *The School Review, 35*(9), 657–672.

Levin, J. (1998). Organizational change and the community college. In J. Levin (Ed.), *Organizational change in the community college: A ripple* or *a sea change? New Directions in Community Colleges, no. 102* (pp. 1–4). San Francisco, CA: Jossey-Bass.

Levin, J. (2000). The revised institution: The community college mission at the end of the twentieth century. *Community College Review, 28*(2), 1–24.

Levin, J. (2001). *Globalizing the community college: Strategies for change in the twenty-first century.* New York, NY: Palgrave Macmillan.

Lombardi, J. (1964). Emergent issues in administration. *Junior College Journal, 35*(3), 4–8.

Martorana, S. (1946). Implications of wartime adjustments for junior colleges. *Junior College Journal, 17*(1), 11–17.

Martorana, S., & Khuns, E. (1988). Community colleges, local and regional development, and the drift toward communiversity. In Eaton (Ed.), *Colleges of choice: The enabling impact of the community college* (pp. 230–247). New York, NY: ACE, Macmillan.

Medsker, L. (1943). The wartime role of our junior colleges. *The School Executive, 62*(5), 18–19.

Meier, K. (2008). *The community college mission: History and theory, 1930-2000.* (Unpublished doctoral dissertation.) University of Arizona, Tucson, AZ.

Mellow, G., & Heelan, C. (2008). *Minding the dream: The process and practice of the American community college.* New York, NY: Rowman & Littlefield Publishers, Inc.

Nelson, J., & Cooperman, D. (1998). Out of utopia: The paradox of postindustrialization. *The Sociological Quarterly, 39*(4), 583–596.

O'Banion, T. (1997). *A learning college for the 21st century.* Phoenix, AZ: Oryx Press.

Ogilivie, W., & Raines, M. (1971). *Perspectives on the community-junior college: Selected readings.* New York, NY: Appleton-Century-Crofts.

Owen, S. (1995). Organizational culture and community colleges. In J. Dennison (Ed.), *Educational leadership in community colleges: Canada's community colleges at the crossroads* (pp. 141–168). Vancouver, BC: University of British Columbia Press.

Pedersen, R. (2000). *The origins and development of the early public junior college: 1900-1940.* (Unpublished doctoral dissertation.) Columbia University, New York.

Pfeffer, J., & Salancik, G. (1978). *The external control of organizations: A resource dependence perspective.* New York, NY: Harper and Row.

Presidents Commission on Higher Education: (1947a). *Higher education for American democracy: Volume I, Establishing the goals.* Washington, DC: Government Printing Office.

President's Commission on Higher Education. (1947b). *Higher education for American democracy: Volume III, Organizing higher education.* Washington, DC: Government Printing Office.

Ratcliff, J. (1987). 'First' public junior colleges in an age of reform. *Journal of Higher Education, 58*(2), 151–180.

Ratcliff, J. (1994). Seven streams in the historical development of the modern American community college. In G. Baker III (Ed.), *A handbook on the community college in America* (pp. 1–16). Westport, CT: Greenwood Press.

Richardson, R., & Doucette, D. (1984). *An empirical model for formulating operational missions of community colleges.* Paper presented at the American Educational Research Association, New Orleans.

Rosenbaum, J., Deil-Amen, R., & Person, A. (2006). *After admission: From college access to college success.* New York, NY: Russell Sage Foundation.

Shaw, K., & London, H. (2001). Culture and ideology in keeping transfer commitment: Three community colleges. *The Review of Higher Education, 25*(1), 91–114.

Thornton, J. (1972). *The community junior college* (2nd ed.). New York, NY: John Wiley & Sons.

Tillery, D., & Deegan, W. (1985). The evolution of two-year colleges through four generations. In D. Tillery & W. Deegan (Eds.), *Renewing the American community college* (pp. 3–33). San Francisco, CA: Jossey-Bass.

Vaughan, G. (1984). Forging the community college mission. *Educational Record, 65*(3), 24-29.

Vaughan, G. (1991). *Institutions on the edge: America's community colleges.* Los Angeles, CA: ERIC Clearing house for Junior Colleges (ERIC Document Reproduction Service No. ED 338270).

Vinen, R. (2001). *History in fragments: Europe in the twentieth century.* London: De Capo Press.

Williams, R. (2002). *Retooling: A historian confronts technological change.* Cambridge, MA: MIT Press.

Winter, C. (1964). *History of the junior college movement in California.* Sacramento: Bureau of Junior College Education, California State Department of Education.

Witt, A., Wattenbarger, J., Gollattscheck, J., & Suppiger, J. (1994). *America's community colleges: The first century.* Washington, DC: Community College Press.

CHAPTER 10

THE BENEFITS OF ATTENDING COMMUNITY COLLEGE: A REVIEW OF THE EVIDENCE

CLIVE R. BELFIELD[1] AND THOMAS BAILEY[2]

Abstract. This article reviews the existing literature on the economic and other benefits of attending community college. First, the article reports on the earnings gains across all students and reviews the evidence for subgroups by gender, minority status, and credits accumulated. The article then reviews the methodological challenges associated with calculating earnings gains from attending a community college. Despite these challenges, the evidence for the significant earnings gains from community college attendance appears to be compelling. The second part of the article reviews the literature on a broader spectrum of gains, such as health, crime, and welfare reliance. This literature is very limited and potentially offers an important area for further research to establish the full returns from community college attendance.

Keywords: economic research, educational attainment, outcomes of education, income, welfare recipients, crime

This article reviews the literature on the education-earnings premium for students who attend community colleges. The research evidence on the earnings gains from additional education is substantial (see Rouse, 2007), yet relatively few studies have focused specifically on the community college sector. Specific attention is warranted, because the sector is extremely heterogeneous, with many institutional types, varied program offerings, and multiple student pathways. Also, a review of this literature is timely in light of two countervailing developments. One is an increasingly skeptical commentary on the expense of attending a 4-year college (e.g., Steinberg, 2010). The other is the recent claim that many students are "undermatched" and should enroll at a 4-year college instead of a community college (Bowen, Chingos, & McPherson, 2009).[1]

As well, it is important not to present a narrow picture of the consequences of going to a community college. A growing body of research has identified large benefits of education beyond those found in the labor market (e.g., Attewell & Lavin, 2007; Belfield & Levin, 2007). This review covers such benefits of community college attendance, including changes in health status, well-being, criminal activity and incarceration, and welfare reliance. It may be that these benefits are as large as the earnings gains (as suggested by Wolfe & Zuvekas, 1997); if so, current policy discussions on community college attendance are missing half of the picture.

Thus, the earnings gains and benefits are the full set of advantages from attending community college. It is against these full benefits that enrollees should consider the costs of attendance (such as tuition and foregone earnings) when deciding on whether to enroll, for what award, and for how

---

[1]Queens College, City University of New York, Flushing
[2]Columbia University, New York, NY

long. The goal of this review is to set out systematically what is known about the labor market and other advantages of community college attendance and to highlight areas where more research would be beneficial. Methodological and data quality issues that researchers have faced are also considered. In these respects, this review updates and expands on two earlier reviews by Grubb (2002a, 2002b), although our interpretations are based on the original sources directly.

Evidence Base

The goal here is to set out the evidence in the research literature on the benefits of attending community college. The literature uses many terms to describe these benefits. In this review, the evidence is summarized in terms of gains in earnings that derive from attending community college over not attending community college. Specifically, all the literature is reported in terms of annual earnings gains (advantages or premiums) in percentage terms (e.g., a student who completes an associate's degree earns x% more than a person who did not choose to enroll). The gains are reported for earnings, not wages; differences in hours of work are therefore accounted for.[2] As such, the gains reflect both higher productivity and greater labor market participation or employment. This is appropriate insofar as more education increases the likelihood that a person will be employed as well as have a higher wage. Of course, these earnings advantages should be set against the costs of tuition and lost earnings while in college; this allows for calculation of the "returns" or net gains to community college.[3] However, these costs are often unavailable and will vary significantly depending on the students' enrollment choices and pathways. Therefore, this review is restricted to reporting the gross advantages or gains from community college attendance.

Notwithstanding the mass of evidence on the gains from education, research on the labor market advantages of community college attendance per se is relatively limited. One reason why there are so few directly pertinent studies is that the research literature typically analyzes education in units that are not straightforwardly interpreted in relation to community college attendance. Much of the literature estimates the gains to education in terms of years accumulated. If it is assumed that attending community college is equivalent to two additional years of education, and that the effects of education are linear across all years of education, it is possible to include all of this relevant literature. Other studies do report earnings gains by education level, but they typically classify higher education levels as either *any college graduate* or *some college* versus *bachelor's degree*. Clearly, *any college graduate* will combine graduates from all institutions. The *some college* classification, which typically includes persons with associate's degrees, is the most applicable for community college students, but it will include many persons who fail to complete a bachelor's degree from a 4-year college. Also, significant proportions of community college students progress through to complete bachelor's degrees.[4] Thus, this review of evidence focuses primarily on the studies that specifically examine community college students.

The search strategy used to identify relevant research evidence included a keyword search of the Web of Science database (specifically, the ERIC, JSTOR, and ProQuest databases); citation tracking from key publications; specific author searches; and a "hand search" of relevant journals (including *Economics of Education Review*, *Journal of Labor Economics*, and *Educational Evaluation and Policy Analysis*). The search was restricted to studies published after 1980 (the review that follows also includes two very recent unpublished studies).

The studies itemized below represent the best available evidence; that is, research that rates highest on a set of methodological criteria. The primary methodological criterion relates to the likelihood that the research has established a causal link. The general methodological hierarchy favors random assignment, followed by natural experiments or other situations in which some students are constrained in their enrollment choices (e.g., by the availability of a college nearby). However, almost all studies in this field are fundamentally correlation studies; any methodological rating should therefore be based on the quality of baseline data, the extent of adjustment for covariates, and how selection into the community college was modeled. (Some of the studies do model how students might face differential costs of accessing the community college in a "quasi-experimental" fashion). The greater the extent to which these studies can address these issues, the closer they come to approximating a causal effect. A secondary methodological criterion might relate to the quality of the data used in the study; more recent data sets with formal sampling frames were preferred.

Although the methods used in these studies cannot establish causality, the research findings summarized below may still be regarded as strong or compelling. Many studies have investigated whether education coefficients in Mincerian earnings equations are biased.[5] These biases might include *ability bias* (i.e., observed earnings premiums are actually a return to innate ability not education); *selection bias*, in that differences in earnings are conditional on (unobservable) individual choices about college or about where to work after college; *imputation bias* in matching individuals to earnings profiles; *misreporting bias* on occupations; and *sampling or measurement error*. For a detailed treatment of each bias, see, respectively, Arcidiacono (2004); Dahl (2002), and Black, Kolesnikova, and Taylor (2009); Bollinger and Hirsch (2006); Abraham and Spletzer (2009); and Schmitt and Baker (2006).

In their reviews for the general labor market, both Card (1999) and Rouse (2007) concluded that at least some of these biases do not significantly distort the results obtained from simple earnings functions and that many studies include controls for ability—another potentially biasing factor. Nevertheless, although this conclusion might be valid in general, it may not be valid for estimating gains to particular subgroups, such as sex or race. Some of the subgroup gains may therefore be biased upward or downward. For example, findings from a recent investigation by Hamermesh and Donald (2008) suggest that sampling or nonresponse bias is significant in estimations of the impact of college major on earnings. Perhaps more importantly, most studies do not adjust for failure to complete community college programs but typically estimate the effect of community college on those who have actually completed these programs. Thus, they are not *ex ante* (or "intention-to-treat") estimates of the earnings gains. However, few of the studies adjust directly for employment probabilities or for "full-wage" effects. If community college attendance increases the probability of employment (as seems likely if attendance increases productivity), then the earnings gains should be adjusted upward to account for the higher probability of being employed. Similarly, if community college attendance increases the probability of receiving fringe benefits at work (such as a health plan or pension contribution), this too should be counted as part of the full earnings gain.

Earnings Gains from Community College Attendance

Aggregate Gains

There is strong evidence that associate's degrees and years of community college education yield extra earnings compared to high school graduation. There is also evidence that vocational certificates and basic credits contribute positively to subsequent earnings. This evidence is summarized in Tables 1 and 2. The evidence is reported as percentage differences in annual earnings across educational categories; as such, they do not need to be adjusted for inflation.

Almost all studies have found positive earnings gains from an associate's degree, with an average estimate across the studies of 13% for males and 22% for females. (The lowest estimates—by Ishikawa and Ryan [2002]—control for literacy skills, which are highly correlated with education levels). However, these estimates rely on data from only five surveys, with seven studies using data from the National Longitudinal Study of Youth, 1979 (NLSY79). Nevertheless, very similar estimates were found in the one econometrically similar study that looks at community college attendance using administrative data maintained by the state of Washington on displaced workers (Jacobson, LaLonde, & Sullivan, 2005a).

Similarly, almost all studies have found gains to credits or years of study at community college that do not lead to a completed degree. The average earnings gain for attending community college without obtaining a credential is estimated at 9% for males and 10% for females. In addition, Heckman, Lochner, and Todd (2008) used Census data to calculate the internal rate of return to progressing from 12 to 14 years of schooling for males; this progression path is close to that from community college. Overall, they estimated that the gains to two more years of schooling beyond high school were between 8% and 19% in 2000 (see Table 3). In addition, research has found that earnings

TABLE 1

Earnings Premiums to Associate's Degrees, by Gender

Source	Data set	Earnings Premiums (%)	
		Male	Female
Kane and Rouse (1995a, 1995b)	National Longitudinal Survey of the High School Class of 1972 (NLS72)	8	29
Kane and Rouse (1995a, 1995b)	National Longitudinal Survey of Youth, 1979 (NLSY79)	29	36
Hollenbeck (1993)	NLS72	−1	12
Grubb (1993, 1995)[a]	NLS72	0	10
Grubb (1993, 1995)[b]	NLS72	4	3
Jaeger and Page (1996)[a]	Current Population Survey, 1991 (CPS91)	8	31
Jaeger and Page 1996)[b]	CPS91	20	23
Grubb (1997)	Survey of Income and Program Participation (SIPP)	18	23
Surette (2001)	NLSY79	7	13
Leigh and Gill 1997)	NLSY79	24	29
Gill and Leigh 2000)	NLSY79	13	21
Averett and Dalessandro (2001)[c]	NLSY79	18	19
Averett and Dalessandro (2001)[d]	NLSY79	19	33
Ishikawa and Ryan (2002)[c]	National Adult Literacy Survey (NALS)	2	5
Ishikawa and Ryan (2002)[d]	NALS	−1	0
Ishikawa and Ryan (2002)[e]	NALS	6	3
Gill and Leigh (2003)	NLSY79	22	29
Light and Strayer (2004)[f]	NLSY79	19	19
Bailey et al. (2004)	High School and Beyond (HS&B) (HS&B) Survey	12	47
Marcotte et al. (2005)	National Education Longitudinal Study of 1988 (NELS)	17	40
Jepsen et al. (2009)	KY administrative data	20	39
Unweighted average		13	22

Source: Grubb (2002a, pp. 305-306) and original sources.

Note: Studies cited use annual earnings measures (various dates).

a. Vocational-occupational programs.

b. Academic programs.

c. Whites.

d. Blacks.

e. Hispanics.

f. Hourly earnings.

gains rise with the numbers of credits accumulated (see appendix Tables A1, A2, and A3) and that earnings gains are found for a semester's worth of credits or more (Jacobson, Lalonde, & Sullivan, 2005b); but below this amount, there is no earnings advantage (Jepsen, Troske, & Coomes, 2009).[6]

Finally, despite recent emphasis on stronger links between community colleges and their local labor markets, only two studies (Grubb, 1997; Marcotte, Bailey, Borkoski, & Kienzl, 2005) have reported on the earnings effects from vocational certificates. Both studies found significant earnings gains ranging from 7% to 24%.

Earnings Gains by Subgroup

Gender. Earnings gains from community college are much higher for females than for males. Table 1 shows this differential, which is evident at the associate's degree level for graduation, and for

TABLE 2

Earnings Premiums to Vocational Certification and Credits or Years Completed Without Credentials

Source	Data set	Earnings premiums (%)	
		Male	Female
Premiums to vocational certificate			
Grubb (1997)	SIPP	8	20
Marcotte et al. (2005)	NELS	7	24
Jepsen et al. (2009)[a]	KY administrative data	22	41
Jepsen et al. (2009)[b]	KY administrative data	9	3
Premiums to credits or years completed without credentials			
Grubb (1993, 1995)[c]	NLS72	4	2
Grubb (1993, 1995)[d]	NLS72	2	0
Kane and Rouse (1995b)	NLS72	6	7
Jaeger and Page (1996)	CPS91	9	9
Leigh and Gill (1997)[e]	NLSY79	21	4
Grubb (1997)	SIPP	7	22
Gill and Leigh (2000)	NLSY79	15	8
Surette (2001)[f]	NLSY79	12	13
Averett and Dalessandro (2001)[g]	NLSY79	6	11
Averett and Dalessandro (2001)[h]	NLSY79	20	18
Bailey et al. (2004)	HS&B	0	14
Marcotte et al. (2005)	NELS	6	9
Jacobson et al. (2005a)[i]	WA administrative data	9	11
Jacobson et al. (2005a)[j]	WA administrative data	12	15

Source: Grubb (2002a, pp. 305-306) and original sources.

Note: Studies cited use annual earnings measures (various dates). KY refers to unemployment and college administrative data from Kentucky. WA refers to unemployment insurance and college administrative data from Washington state. In addition to the studies noted here, Light and Strayer (2004), analyzing NLSY79 data, calculated an overall earnings premium of 9% for men and women combined.

a. Diploma.

b. Certificate, any subject.

c. Vocational only.

d. Academic only.

e. Two-year college with no credential.

f. Hourly earnings.

g. Whites only.

h. Blacks only.

i. Age 35 or older.

j. Under 35 years of age.

credits obtained without a credential. Gill and Leigh (2000) found that this male–female gap remains stable as community college graduates gain experience in the labor market.

Age. There is also evidence that older college enrollees get less of an earnings advantage than younger enrollees. Using unemployment insurance (UI) data from Washington state in the 1990s, Jacobson, LaLonde, and Sullivan (2005a) estimated gains by age stemming from the community college attendance of displaced workers. The earnings gains were 7% to 16% per year for males less than 35 years of age but ranged from 3% to 14% for males aged more than 34; the rates for females in these age categories were 11% to 18% and 6% to 15%, respectively. Using UI data from Kentucky in the 2000s, Jepsen et al. (2009) also found positive earnings effects for degrees, diplomas, and certificates that decrease with age. Using data from the National Education Longitudinal Study (NELS), Bailey, Kienzl, and Marcotte (2004) estimated an earnings effect of community college attendance

TABLE 3

Internal Rates of Return by Years of Schooling

Year	Internal rates of return (%) to advancing from 12 years of schooling to 14 years of schooling		Internal rates of return (%) to advancing from 14 years of schooling to 16 years of schooling	
	White males	Black males	White males	Black males
1960	6-12	5-11	12-25	10-25
1970	6-13	7-12	13-24	12-23
1980	5-11	8-12	11-21	12-31
1990	7-14	15-18	14-26	16-35
2000	8-14	15-19	14-29	18-31

Source: Data are from Heckman et al. (2008, pp. 12-14).

Note: Data reflect Mincerian earnings equations estimated using Census data. Ranges depend on specification of Mincerian earnings equation. Tuition costs are excluded. The internal rate of return refers to the value that equalizes the present value stream of benefits with the present value of costs.

that is zero or even negative for older workers. Using NLSY79 data, Light (1995) found smaller advantages to schooling for males who drop out and then reenter formal education. However, earnings gaps by education do grow with age: Using the Census Bureau's Current Population Survey (CPS) data from 1998 to 2003 as well as NLSY79 data, Heckman and Lafontaine (2006) found much higher earnings gaps for persons aged 30 to 39 than for those aged 20 to 29.

Race. Earnings gains may also vary by race, but the evidence for this is not consistent. On balance, the most that one might say is that minority students may experience higher earnings gains from community college attendance. Averett and Dalessandro (2001) reported higher estimates for Blacks than for Whites, either from an associate's degree or from credits accumulated. Gill and Leigh (2003) also reported generally higher earnings gains for Blacks either from completion of a program or transfer from a community college to obtain a bachelor's degree. In addition, Heckman et al. (2008) reported that Black males experienced larger earnings gains by advancing from 12 to 14 years of schooling than did White males (Table 3), and Heckman and LaFontaine (2006) reported higher gains to years of education for Blacks using a range of data sets.

However, using the National Adult Literacy Survey (NALS) database, Ishikawa and Ryan (2002) reported very mixed results (although their model specification differed from the norm). They found that Blacks earned the lowest gains for post–high school vocational training, associate's degrees, and completing some college (controlling for literacy levels in adulthood); but they also found that Hispanic males had higher gains than White males and that Hispanic females had lower gains than White females. In addition, Jaeger and Page (1996) similarly found that the highest gains accrued to White females, with other groups having lower gains.

Immigrants. No U.S. study has looked at labor market advantages to immigrants over domestic-born community college students.[7] However, the college–high school wage premium for foreign-born persons appears to be at least as high as, and probably higher than, the wage premium of U.S.-born workers. Using CPS data from 1998 to 2003, Heckman and LaFontaine (2006) reported that male and female foreign-born college graduates earned, respectively, 57% and 61% more than male and female foreign-born high school graduates. Using NALS data from 1992, the authors estimated the differences at 41% and 56% (males and females, respectively).

Subjects of Study. The earnings gains to education vary significantly across the students' chosen subjects of study. Broadly, studies have found higher gains to quantitative and vocational subjects than to other disciplines. Using UI data from Washington state in the 1990s, Jacobson et al. (2005a) estimated returns of 10% per year for students in quantitative or technically oriented vocational courses and 3% to 5% for less quantitative courses (e.g., sales and service, social sciences or humanities, and basic skills). Jepsen et al. (2009) found that the highest gains were linked to associate's degrees in vocational subjects, with health degrees at the top, followed by other vocational degrees, degrees in business subjects, and then degrees in humanities disciplines (with the last being, in some cases, not significantly different from zero). Using 1984, 1987, and 1990 data from the Survey of Income and Program Participation (SIPP), Grubb (1997) also reported advantages by subject of study. For certificates, gains were highest in health, business and vocational-technical courses. For associate's degrees, gains were highest in health and quantitative courses (business, mathematics and science, and engineering and computers). Gill and Leigh (2000) reported mixed results, albeit with few differences across subjects: Gains were lower for males in business and education, higher for females in sciences. Similarly, mixed evidence was reported by Jaeger and Page (1996) across occupational versus academic associate's degrees.[8] Based on state administrative data from California, Texas, and Washington state, Grubb (2002b) reported unadjusted salaries by field of study for community college students 3 years after graduation. Raw salaries were highest in more technical fields and in nursing. Finally, Jacobson and Mokher (2009) reported unadjusted salaries in Florida and estimated that, relative to students with a 2-year credential in the humanities, health fields paid 42% more, vocational-technical fields paid 20% more, and science-related fields paid 13% more.[9]

It appears that the higher earnings gains to vocational subjects are genuine, but two cautions should be noted. First, vocational subjects often lead to licensure or certification in a trade or profession, and it may be the license or certificate that is being rewarded. Of course, if the licensing or certification system is demanded by consumers as a way to guarantee quality of service, then these earnings gains are still real (rather than reflecting a restrictive practice in the labor market). Second, courses that lead to licensing or trade certification (or any formal work-related training) may differ in duration or flexibility from other courses leading to associate's or bachelor's degrees. Clearly, shorter courses would yield higher net returns for a given earnings gain. This consideration might bias the returns even more toward vocational courses if they are shorter, offered at more convenient times outside the working day, or linked with job placements.

Findings over time. Finally, there is evidence that the earning premiums to education have grown over recent decades. Using SIPP data, Grubb (1997) calculated earnings gains over high school graduates from 1984 through to 1990 (see appendix Table A2). Labor market advantages to bachelor's degrees and vocational certificates grew over the 6-year period, but gains to associate's degrees fell slightly. Also, the evidence from Marcotte et al. (2005) shows higher gains using the more recent NELS data set. This evidence is consistent with the general literature on the labor market advantages of education. Using Census data, Heckman et al. (2008) reported internal rates of return for White and Black males from the 1960s to the 2000s (see Table 3). For White males going from 12 to 14 years of schooling, the rates were a few percentage points higher for more recent cohorts; for Black males, the returns to two more years of schooling grew substantially more. Using CPS data from 1979 to 2002, Fortin (2006) identified a growing college–high school earnings premium over the period from 1980 to 2000 for both males and females. Also using CPS data from 1970 to 1997, Card and Lemieux (2001) similarly showed a growing college–high school earnings premium over time and across age cohorts; that is, gains for persons of a given age were higher in 1994 than they were in 1967.

Sheepskin Effects

A proportion of the earnings gains may reflect the possession of a credential (a *sheepskin effect*) rather than necessarily any additional skills. Unfortunately, it is often difficult to estimate the size of this sheepskin effect because of data limitations. It is rare for surveys to ask individuals for both years of education attained and terminal qualification earned, such that the two might be distinguished.[10]

Using the Current Population Survey from 1991 to 1992, Jaeger and Page (1996) estimated sheepskin effects across levels of higher education.[11] Without accounting for sheepskin effects, the study found that a White male with 14 years of education earned 18% more than a White male who was a high school graduate. However, taking out the sheepskin effect reduced that premium to 5%, with the remainder (13%) attributable to the credential. Using NLSY79 data on earnings in 1996, Gill and Leigh (2003) estimated the gains to students who enroll at 2-year colleges. Students who completed an associate's degree earned 11% more than students who enrolled but who did not complete an associate's degree. In their response to Grubb (1993), Kane and Rouse (1995b) tested for the equivalence of 2 years of community college against an associate's degree using data from the National Longitudinal Survey of the High School Class of 1972 (NLS-72). In all specifications, they failed to reject the hypothesis of equivalence, indicating that sheepskin effects were not evident.

Finally, Bailey et al. (2004) tested for sheepskin effects for certificates, associate's degrees, and bachelor's degrees using NELS data. They found that—for females—the earnings of certificate holders were not statistically greater than the earnings of comparable students with equivalent coursework but no certificate. (For males, they found no earnings gain from certification.) For associate's degrees, Bailey et al. found sheepskin effects for female students studying occupational subjects, but no sheepskin effects for men. Last, Bailey et al. did not find evidence of sheepskin effects for bachelor's degrees.

Overall, the research consensus appears to be that there are sheepskin effects but that these effects are not always evident, that they vary across levels of education and by sex, and that they do not eliminate the earnings gains from years of noncredentialed college attainment.

Transfer Effects

The question of whether students gain from starting in a community college or lose out because they are diverted from attending a 4-year college—"democratization" versus "diversion"—has received considerable attention in the literature. Both forces appear to be influential.

Some students might have been better off attending a 4-year college initially. Early literature found a small diversion effect (Rouse, 1995); subsequent studies have found a larger diversion effect in terms of reduced attainment or degree completion (Alfonso, 2006; Bowen et al., 2009; Long & Kurlaender, 2008; Reynolds, 2006; Sandy, Gonzalez, & Hilmer, 2006). But the tremendous methodological challenge is in isolating—from the large and heterogeneous pool of community college attendees—the students who genuinely should have begun at a 4-year college.

Moreover, the democratization effect is also strong for the general student population. Many students have no intention of completing a 4-year degree and want to enroll in (shorter) vocational or technical courses that lead to certification. As noted above, many of these courses yield high earnings gains.

For this review, the focus is on the economic gains from community college attendance. Thus, the democratization and diversion effects should be interpreted in terms of how they affect earnings, not completion or attainment effects.[12]

Extant research indicates that in terms of postcollege earnings, transfer students do not fully catch up with students who attend a 4-year college throughout. A student who "should" have gone to a 4-year college in his or her first year therefore loses out. Using NLSY79, Gill and Leigh (2003) estimated that community college transfer students who completed a bachelor's degree earned less than students who enrolled in a 4-year college throughout. Using NELS data, Reynolds (2006) also found a significant earnings penalty for those starting at a 2-year college. But the extent of the disparity may not be great: Using the Baccalaureate and Beyond (B&B) Survey, Hilmer (2002) reported little or no difference in the earnings gains that might be attributed to transfer from a relatively low quality 4-year institution (as measured by selectivity in terms of student ACT or SAT scores) to a higher quality 4-year institution.

Moreover, it is not obvious which students "should" have gone to a 4-year college from the start. Many students—including those at flagship 4-year colleges—are not certain about their college decisions. They may be unsure of their own ability, of the academic standards of the college, or of the quality of human capital that the college is producing (leaving aside the social environment). Because the community college is relatively inexpensive, and because many students may be risk averse (i.e., wishing to avoid failing courses more than they value getting high grades), it may make

TABLE 4

Earnings Gains for Community College Students Over High School

	Earnings gains (%) for students who enroll in terminal training programs	Earnings gains (%) for students who transfer to complete a bachelor's degree
Aggregate	38-68	64-85
White male	31-60	50-69
White female	34-64	73-94
Black male	45-77	57-76
Hispanic male	38-69	62-82

Source: Gill and Leigh (2003, pp. 149-150).

Note: Gill and Leigh used the NLSY79 data set in their analysis. The earnings gains were calculated from unconditional and conditional log points and reflect earnings in 1996.

sense for many of them to start at community college. This will give students the opportunity to become more sure about their decision, with the option to transfer to a 4-year college if they ultimately decide to do so. This is the *option value* of starting out at a community college (Kane & Rouse, 1995a). As more information is revealed—either about one's own aptitude or college quality—the student may transfer to a 4-year college if desirable. Critically, the "diversion" argument assumes that the option value for those starting at a community college is very low or negative (i.e., students gain very little or indeed lose out by not starting out at a 4-year college).

For the option value to be very low, several conditions must hold. First, the expense of attending community college must not differ much from that of attending a 4-year college. Second, the barriers to transferring out of community college must be high. Third, for students who do transfer, their earnings gains (a) must not exceed those of students who stayed behind and did not transfer, and (b) must be far below the earnings gains of equivalent students who started at a 4-year college. Overall, these assumptions seem more wrong than right. Community college tuition is considerably lower than that of 4-year, bachelor's-degree-granting colleges. Certainly, many students do transfer from community colleges to 4-year colleges. Finally, the evidence indicates that students who transfer and then obtain advanced credentials obtain higher earnings advantages than those who do not transfer. (This is assumption "a" as noted in the previous paragraph; assumption "b" is not strongly evident: Transfers students only lose out a small percentage to those who start at a 4-year institution.) Using NLSY79 data on earnings in 1996, Gill and Leigh (2003) estimated the gains for students who enrolled at a 2-year college and then transferred to complete a bachelor's degree. These students earned 22% more than all 2-year enrollees (see Table 4 for more detailed data from this study). Using NLSY79 data on earnings from 1979 to 1996, Light and Strayer (2004) estimated that students who initially enrolled at a 2-year college and then completed a bachelor's degree earned 23% to 43% more than high school graduates; this rate was greater than the rate experienced by those who earned associate's degrees only.[13] The advantage of transferring may also be inferred from Hilmer (2002). Using the Baccalaureate & Beyond data set, Hilmer found that the quality of both institutions (original and terminal) mattered for earnings; when community college students transfer up to a higher quality institution (i.e., to an institution that is more selective), their earnings should rise also.[14]

Other Benefits of Community College Attendance

In addition to private earnings gains from community college attendance, there are also likely to be additional economic benefits. These benefits might include gains in health and general economic well-being (e.g., through improved consumption efficiency or assortative mating), as well as benefits from lower welfare reliance and lower involvement in the criminal justice system; in turn, this accumulation of advantage might lead to higher levels of subjective well-being. Potentially, these benefits may be monetized and added either to the private earnings gains or counted as part of the social benefit of community college attendance. Yet these gains are rarely discussed by policymakers, despite the fact that they may be as large as the earnings gains and—from an economic perspective— equally valid.[15] As a point of caution, it is possible that some of these benefits are included in the earnings gains. For example, healthier workers may be more productive. But many studies of health gains do control for labor market status.

The research literature on these benefits is much smaller and more disparate than the literature on earnings gains; it is particularly scarce with regard to studies specifically on the benefits from community college attendance. Generally, this literature adopts the same method used to estimate earnings gains (regression analysis controlling for covariates) but with little scrutiny of possible estimation biases. However, many of these benefits are strongly correlated with income, so it may be appropriate to infer an indirect, income-driven impact from community college attendance. Finally, as with research on earnings, it may be possible to infer benefits of community college attendance from estimates of the benefits derived either from persons with additional years of schooling (again, if the effect of education is linear in years of schooling) or from the general college-educated population (adjusting for expected graduation rates, college quality, or attenuation, if any, of the effect of education after high school).

Here the summary is restricted to three domains—health, welfare, and crime. Notably, there appear to be no studies that have examined whether community college raises subjective well-being.[16]

Health Status

The association between years of education and health status and health behaviors is extremely strong. Using the National Health Interview Surveys from 1990 to 2000, Cutler and Lleras-Muney (2010) estimated the health impacts of additional years of education (controlling for covariates). Each additional year of education reduced the probability of smoking by 3 percentage points, of being obese by 1.4 percentage points, and of being a heavy drinker by 1.8 percentage points. Years of education were also positively associated with a range of health behaviors (wearing a seat belt, mammogram testing, getting a colonoscopy, and getting a flu shot). Moreover, many of these indicators appear to be linear with years of education, such that they can be applied to community college attendance.

Education appears to be positively associated with other health indicators, but the evidence base is not conclusive. Lleras-Muney (2005) found strong evidence that education reduces mortality, but this evidence was based on an examination of the relationship between mortality and changes in state laws raising the levels of compulsory schooling. Using data from the National Longitudinal Mortality Study (NLMS) covering the years 1979 to 1989, Backlund, Sorlie, and Johnson (1999) concluded that there is no difference in death rates and mortality rates between high school graduates and those with some college (but no degree). Finally, research suggests that mothers with a college education are also more likely to promote health in their children. Using SIPP data, Cheng (2006) found that mothers with more education were more likely to have taken their children to the physician or dentist and to have used a prescription (but the data only made distinctions between mothers with at least some college education, whether they graduated or not, mothers with a high school diploma, and mothers who had not obtained a high school diploma).

Welfare Receipt

It is likely that community college attendance and graduation reduces welfare reliance, if only through their effect in raising income. However, because very few college graduates receive welfare, they are typically grouped with persons with "some college" in analyses of the impact of education on the receipt of welfare. Using CPS data, Waldfogel, Garfinkel, and Kelly (2007) reported lower reliance on housing assistance (by 34%) and food stamps (by 22%) for those with some college education or above relative to high school graduates. For females, Grogger (2004) calculated that welfare spells for those with some college education or above were 15% lower than those who are high school graduates. Using data from the Panel Study of Income Dynamics, Rank and Hirschl (2005) tracked food stamp reliance by education level over time; but their estimates were for dropouts versus the rest of the population. More apposite is recent research by London (2006), who used SIPP and NLSY data to track employment and welfare for females who were attending college during a welfare spell. After a welfare spell, those who had graduated from college during their welfare spell were much more likely than those who had not attended college to be employed and to avoid subsequent welfare or family poverty. Five years after exiting a welfare spell, college graduates—as compared to high school graduates—had higher rates of employment (86% versus 81%), lower rates of return to welfare (20% versus 50%), and lower rates of family poverty (43% versus 68%). Finally, Wallace (2007) used SIPP data from the 1990s to examine probabilities of enrollment in welfare (Aid to Families with Dependent Children [AFDC] or Temporary Assistance for Needy Families [TANF]) for females. College attendance had a strong effect on entry onto AFDC or TANF rolls, but no effect on exit rates from AFDC or TANF.

In addition, unadjusted administrative data show lower rates of welfare receipt. Based on Washington state administrative data in 1993-1994, Grubb (2002b) reported the impact—three years out—of community college attendance on receipt of unemployment insurance (falling from 8.3% to 5.7%), AFDC (4.2% to 3.6%), and food stamps (11.3% to 8.9%). Based on state administrative data from Florida in 1995, Grubb also reported welfare receipt rates for high school graduates at 7.4% and for community college associate's degree holders at 1.7% (unadjusted for covariates).

Criminal Involvement

It is plausible to assume that community college enrollment will reduce criminal activity. There is a substantial evidence base on the negative association between education and crime and between income and crime (Farrington, 2003). For example, Lochner and Moretti (2004) identified the impact of education on rates of arrest (for murder, rape, violent crime, property crime, and drugs offenses) and on the probability of incarceration. Using NLSY79 data, the identification strategy employed by Lochner and Moretti included a full set of background control variables, but results were reported either for years of schooling or for high school graduation versus dropping out. In addition, Lochner and Moretti used pooled 1960-1980 Census and FBI data to examine the relationship between change in compulsory schooling laws and criminal involvement; these results, too, are salient for persons graduating from high school (as opposed to college attendance). Moreover, the data are (mostly) over 20 years old (when incarceration rates were lower), and there was no adjustment for underreporting of crimes. However, Lochner and Moretti drew on Census data to report incarceration rates over the period 1960-1980 by years of schooling (with a limited set of residence and cohort controls). Both White and Black males with 13 to 14 years of education had lower rates of incarceration relative to high school graduates, which is suggestive of an effect from community college enrollment.

Other administrative and survey data show lower rates of criminal activity among those who attend community college. But these data are not adjusted for covariates. Based on state administrative data from Florida in 1995, Grubb (2002b) reported rates of involvement with the Department of Corrections for high school graduates at 1.8% and for community college associate's degree holders at 0.5%. Using 1997 data from the Survey of Inmates in State and Federal Correctional Facilities, Harlow (2003) reported basic cross-tabulations by education level. Only 9% of the state prison populations and 16% of the federal prison populations had "some college," significantly below their representation in the general population (approximately 25% to 30%).

Conclusion

This review reaffirms that there are strong positive earnings gains from community college attendance and completion, as well as from progression to a 4-year college. This evidence is based on more than 20 studies, many of which control for observable personal characteristics that might also be associated with higher earnings. (One note of caution is the reliance on only a few data sets from earlier decades). Moreover, in general these gains appear to be increasing over time. Equally important, these earnings gains underestimate the full returns to community college. They do not account for the significantly higher rates of employer-provided health insurance and pension plans that are associated with more education. (Also, many studies do not fully adjust for differences in labor market participation.)

The earnings literature provides some guidance on which subgroups obtain the biggest advantages, although there are important omissions, notably on the gains across socioeconomic status, for immigrants, for part-time versus full-time enrollment, and for most subject areas (beyond a simple distinction between vocational and academic programs). In addition, there is no literature on the advantages to online degrees or those provided by for-profit institutions. Yet it is also important to generate research that allows for a better interpretation of differences in earnings gaps. Controlling for ability, the returns should be equivalent across students of all characteristics (Hirsch, 2008). Where some groups obtain larger advantages, this might reflect reduced labor market discrimination at the community college level relative to high school graduates; or it may reflect enrollment decisions or college offerings. Without a better understanding of what the earnings gaps mean, it is hard to prescribe policy.

Perhaps most important, there is limited research on the *ex ante* net present value or internal rate of return (IRR) to community college enrollment. Yet these are the appropriate metrics for evaluating whether community college attendance is a worthwhile investment from the private and public perspective. The earnings gains discussed above would have to be predicted over the student's lifetime, and the tuition costs of college would have to be subtracted. As reported in the study by Jacobson et al. (2005a) for Washington state, the IRR is likely to vary across student characteristics and by choice of program at community college.

Finally, this review has examined the literature on the many other possible benefits—improved health status, enhanced economic independence—from community college attendance, many of which may be inferred from the evidence on earnings gains. However, this evidence is far from conclusive. First, these benefits are typically correlated with years of education, not community college attendance, and are thus not informative as to the specific contribution of a community college education. Second, the research evidence concerning these broader benefits does not include systematic investigations of potential biases in the returns to education (in the way that the literature on earnings returns does). Nevertheless, the research literature has not yet enumerated all the potential implications of community college attendance on such benefits as subjective well-being,

TABLE A1

Annual Earnings Gains Over High School, by Gender and by Credential Earned or Years Enrolled Without Earning a Credential

	Annual earnings gains (%)	
	Males	Females
Bachelor's degree	46	92
Associate's degree	17	40
Certificate	8	20
Any number of years enrolled, no credential earned	6	9
2 or more years enrolled, no credential earned	17	25
15 years enrolled, no credential earned	13	17
1 year enrolled, no credential	8	9
0.5 years enrolled, no credential	0	7

Source: Marcotte et al. (2005, pp. 164-165, 170-171).

TABLE A2

Annual Earnings Gains Over High School, by Gender and by Credential Earned or Years Enrolled Without Earning a Credential, 1984, 1987, and 1990

	Annual earnings gains (%) for males			Annual earnings gains (%) for females		
	1984	1987	1990	1984	1987	1990
Bachelor's degree	51	48	55	43	37	53
Associate's degree	20	24	18	36	26	23
Vocational certificate	2	16	7	18	18	24
4 years of college, no credential	35	29	39	46	−2	51
3 years of college, no credential	24	27	22	28	27	9
2 years college, no credential	14	13	7	2	6	22
1 year college. no credential	13	17	10	11	9	6
Less than 1 year of college, no credential	13	4	7	3	7	3

Source: Grubb (1997, p. 240).

Note: Grubb's analysis was based on SIPP data and apply to individuals aged 25 to 64.

TABLE A3

Annual Earnings Gains Over High School for Community College Noncompleters, by Credits Earned and by Gender

	Annual earnings gains (%)	
Credits earned	Males	Females
1-5	−10	−1
6-10	−4	−2
11-20	0	3
21-35	5	9
36-50	0	10
51 or more	−1	16

Source: Jepsen et al. (2009, pp. 44).

asset management, intergenerational well-being, or marital success. A full accounting of these implications would appear to be a promising area for research.

Appendix

Acknowledgments

The authors appreciate comments from Judy Scott-Clayton and Nikki Edgecombe (Teachers College, Columbia University), and from Ann Person (Gates Foundation). The authors also thank John Heywood (University of Wisconsin–Milwaukee) for his detailed comments, particularly on sheepskin effects.

Declaration of Conflicting Interests

The author(s) declared no potential conflicts of interests with respect to the authorship and/or publication of this article.

Funding

This review was funded by the Bill & Melinda Gates Foundation through the Community College Research Center, Teachers College, Columbia University.

Notes

1. Using North Carolina data, Bowen et al. (2009) found that of all students who were "presumptively eligible" to attend a selective college (i.e., their grade point averages or Scholastic Aptitude Test scores were high enough), 40% did not (p. 102). Moreover, these "under-matched" students had lower graduation rates.

2. Some of the studies report wages and earnings. Only the latter are included in this review, although we note that there is some ambiguity in the use of these terms.

3. Some studies use the term *returns* to refer to the gross wage or earnings advantages. Except where the studies explicitly address at least some of the costs of enrollment, the term *returns to college* is not used here.

4. Therefore, including this literature would require us to model the expected probability of completing a bachelor's degree, conditional on enrolling at community college, and adjust for the quality of college degrees that community college students obtain. We do not perform this modeling or adjustment here but recognize that the first would almost certainly reduce the wage returns to community college and the second would likely do so also. There is a growing literature on general college quality indicating that higher quality institutions are associated with higher returns (see Black & Smith, 2006; and Dale & Krueger, 2002; Long, 2008).

5. The term *Mincerian* refers to the pioneering research of Professor Jacob Mincer, who set out models of earnings, including a formulation that earnings increase with work experience but at a declining rate.

6. Other studies have also found positive wage returns to community college education. Using national data on registered nurses, Septz (2002) found that wage returns to associate's degrees in nursing were equivalent to, and in some years exceed, wage returns to a bachelor's degree in nursing. Based on state administrative data from California and North Carolina, Grubb (2002b) reported unadjusted salaries by certificate. Raw salaries for associate's degrees were higher than for certificates, which in turn were significantly higher than those for persons with at least 12 units but no credential. Based on state administrative data from Washington, Grubb (2002b) also reported pre- and postcollege wage gains by credits accumulated (but unadjusted for covariates). In addition, using the public-use microdata samples from the U.S. Census Bureau for 2000, Albrecht and Albrecht (2009) reported significant earnings advantages for persons with some college over those with a high school diploma or below (unadjusted for covariates). Finally, Jacobson and Mokher (2009) analyzed data on young adults in 2005 in Florida. Unadjusted salary advantages over those who leave college without a credential were 8% for those who obtained associate's degrees and 27% for those with certificates.

7. For Canada, Ferrer and Riddell (2008a) estimated that the returns for immigrants appear to be higher than for the native born.

8. Looking across the entire college population, Arcidiacono (2004) found higher returns to natural sciences and business.

9. We are aware of only one study that has looked at the returns to a double major over a single major across all college graduates. Del Rossi and Hersch (2008) used data from the 2003 National Survey of College Graduates, which sampled individuals who declared having a bachelor's degree or higher on the 2000 Census (and which therefore included some community college graduates). Overall, there appeared to be statistically significant returns to earning a double major. The average earnings gain was 2.3% over a single major, although the gains depended dramatically on the particular subjects in which the student earned double majors.

10. For Canadian community colleges, Ferrer and Riddell (2002) estimated a sheepskin effect of approximately 5% for completion of a community college degree. However, at least 20% of this sheepskin effect may be attributable to the higher skills levels of completers (Ferrer & Riddell, 2008b).

11. In all other years of the CPS, no distinction is made between years of education and credentials.

12. Attainment effects are the main focus of chapter 7 in Bowen et al. (2009), although the authors also consider the equity implications of the diversion argument.

13. As well, Bowen et al. (2009) found that these transfer students graduated at comparable rates to students who started as freshman at 4-year colleges (albeit at slightly lower rates than the 4-year colleges' "homegrown" juniors). That said, the fact that these transfer students do so well suggests that a high proportion could have started out at the 4-year college.

14. This literature is salient for identifying institutional characteristics associated with higher earnings. However, there are no studies that link earnings with the specific characteristics of community colleges (such as size or the proportion of the faculty employed full time). Some studies have examined how completion rates vary with these characteristics (e.g., Calcagno, Bailey, Jenkins, Kienzl, & Leinbach, 2008).

15. The economic perspective emphasizes opportunity costs and resource use, not nominal dollar amounts. The latter is simply a metric by which to compare resource usage.

16. A study by Dee (2004) used proximity to a community college to identify the impacts of education on voter participation and found very strong benefits.

References

Abraham, K. G., & Spletzer, J. R. (2009, January). *New evidence on the returns to job skills.* Paper presented at the 2009 conference of the American Economic Association, San Francisco, CA.

Albrecht, D. E., & Albrecht, S. G. (2009). Economic restructuring, the educational income gap, and overall income inequality. *Sociological Spectrum, 29,* 519–547.

Alfonso, M. (2006). The impact of community college attendance on baccalaureate attainment. *Research in Higher Education, 47,* 873–903.

Arcidiacono, P. (2004). Ability sorting and the returns to college major. *Journal of Econometrics, 121,* 343–375.

Attewell, P., & Lavin, D. E. (with Domina, T., & Levey, T.). (2007). *Passing the torch: Does higher education for the disadvantaged pay off across the generations?* New York, NY: Russell Sage.

Averett, S., & Dalessandro, S. (2001). Racial and gender differences in the returns to 2-year and 4-year degrees. *Education Economics, 9,* 281–292.

Backlund, E., Sorlie, P. D., & Johnson, N. J. (1999). A comparison of the relationships of education and income with mortality: The National Longitudinal Mortality Study. *Social Science and Medicine, 49,* 1373–1384.

Bailey, T., Kienzl, G. S., & Marcotte, D. E. (2004). *The return to a sub-baccalaureate education: The effects of schooling, credentials, and program of study on economic outcomes.* New York, NY: Columbia University, Teachers College, Community College Research Center. Retrieved from http://www2.ed.gov/rschstat/eval/sectech/nave/subbac-ed.pdf

Belfield, C. R., & Levin, H. M. (Eds.). (2007). *The price we pay: Economic and social consequences of inadequate education.* Washington, DC: Brookings Institution Press.

Black, D. A., Kolesnikova, N., & Taylor, L. (2009). Earnings functions when wages and prices vary by location. *Journal of Labor Economics, 27,* 21–47.

Black, D. A., & Smith, J. A. (2006). Estimating the returns to college quality with multiple proxies for quality. *Journal of Labor Economics, 24,* 701–728.

Bollinger, C. R., & Hirsch, B. T. (2006). Match bias from earnings imputation in the Current Population Survey: The case of imperfect matching. *Journal of Labor Economics, 24,* 483–520.

Bowen, W. G., Chingos, M. M., & McPherson, M. S. (2009). *Crossing the finish line: Completing college at America's public universities.* Princeton, NJ: Princeton University Press.

Calcagno, J. C., Bailey, T., Jenkins, D., Kienzl, G. S., & Leinbach, D. T. (2008). Community college student success: What institutional characteristics make a difference? *Economics of Education Review, 27,* 632–645.

Card, D. (1999). The causal effect of education on earnings. In O. Ashenfelter & D. Card (Eds.), *Handbook of labor economics* (Vol. 3, pp. 1801–1863). Amsterdam, The Netherlands: North-Holland.

Card, D., & Lemieux, T. (2001). Can falling supply explain the rising return to college for younger men? A cohort-based analysis. *Quarterly Journal of Economics, 116,* 705–746.

Cheng, T. (2006). Children's access to four medical services: Impact of welfare policies, social structural factors, and family resources. *Children and Youth Services Review, 28,* 595–609.

Cutler, D. M., & Lleras-Muney, A. (2010). Understanding differences in health behaviors by education. *Journal of Health Economics, 29,* 1–28. doi:10.1016/j.jhealeco.2009.10.003

Dahl, G. B. (2002). Mobility and the return to education: Testing a Roy model with multiple markets. *Econometrica, 70*, 2367–2420.

Dale, S. B., & Krueger, A. B. (2002). Estimating the payoff to attending a more selective college: An application of selection on observables and unobservables. *Quarterly Journal of Economics, 117*, 1491–1527.

Dee, T. S. (2004). Are there civic returns to education? *Journal of Public Economics, 88*, 1697–1720.

Del Rossi, A. F., & Hersch, J. (2008). Double your major, double your return? *Economics of Education Review, 27*, 375–386.

Farrington, D. P. (2003). Developmental and life-course criminology: Key theoretical and empirical issues. *Criminology, 41*, 221–255.

Ferrer, A. M., & Riddell, W. C. (2002). The role of credentials in the Canadian labour market. *Canadian Journal of Economics 35*, 879–905.

Ferrer, A. M., & Riddell, W. C. (2008a). Education, credentials and immigrant earnings. *Canadian Journal of Economics, 41*, 186–216.

Ferrer, A. M., & Riddell, W. C. (2008b, November). *Understanding "sheepskin effects" in returns to education: The role of cognitive skills.* Paper presented at the Canadian Labour Market and Skills Researcher Network Workshop, University of Toronto, Toronto, Ontario, Canada.

Fortin, N. M. (2006). Higher education policies and the college wage premium: Cross-state evidence from the 1990s. *American Economic Review, 96*, 959–987.

Gill, A. M., & Leigh, D. E. (2000). Community college enrollment, college major, and the gender wage gap. *Industrial and Labor Relations Review, 54*, 163–181.

Gill, A. M., & Leigh, D. E. (2003). Do the returns to community colleges differ between academic and vocational programs? *Journal of Human Resources, 38*, 134–155.

Grogger, J. T. (2004). Welfare transitions in the 1990s: The economy, welfare policy, and the EITC. *Journal of Policy Analysis and Management, 23*, 671–695.

Grubb, W. N. (1993). The varied economic returns to postsecondary education: New evidence from the class of 1972. *Journal of Human Resources, 28*, 365–382.

Grubb, W. N. (1995). Response to comment. *Journal of Human Resources, 30*, 222–228.

Grubb, W. N. (1997). The returns to education in the sub-baccalaureate labor market, 1984–1990. *Economics of Education Review, 16*, 231–245.

Grubb, W. N. (2002a). Learning and earning in the middle, Part I: National studies of pre-baccalaureate education. *Economics of Education Review, 21*, 299–321.

Grubb, W. N. (2002b). Learning and earning in the middle, Part II: State and local studies of pre-baccalaureate education. *Economics of Education Review, 21*, 401–414.

Hamermesh, D. S., & Donald, S. G. (2008). The effect of college curriculum on earnings: An affinity identifier for non-ignorable response bias. *Journal of Econometrics, 144*, 479–491.

Harlow, C. W. (2003). *Education and correctional populations* (NCJ No. 195670). Washington, DC: U.S. Department of Justice, Bureau of Justice Statistics. Retrieved from http://bjs.ojp.usdoj.gov/content/pub/pdf/ecp.pdf

Heckman, J. J., & LaFontaine, P. A. (2006). Bias-corrected estimates of GED returns. *Journal of Labor Economics, 24*, 661–700.

Heckman, J. J., Lochner, L. J., & Todd, P. E. (2008). Earnings functions and rates of return. *Journal of Human Capital, 2*, 1–31.

Hilmer, M. J. (2002). Human capital attainment, university quality, and entry-level wages for college transfer students. *Southern Economic Journal, 69*, 457–469.

Hirsch, B. T. (2008). Wage gaps large and small. *Southern Economic Journal, 74*, 915–933.

Hollenbeck, K. (1993). Postsecondary education as triage: Returns to academic and technical programs. *Economics of Education Review, 12*, 213–232.

Ishikawa, M., & Ryan, D. (2002). Schooling, basic skills and economic outcomes. *Economics of Education Review, 21*, 231–243.

Jacobson, L. S., LaLonde, R. J., & Sullivan, D. G. (2005a). The impact of community college retraining on older displaced workers: Should we teach old dogs new tricks? *Industrial and Labor Relations Review, 58*, 398–416.

Jacobson, L. S., LaLonde, R. J., & Sullivan, D. G. (2005b). Estimating the returns to community college schooling for displaced workers. *Journal of Econometrics, 125*, 271–304.

Jacobson, L. S., & Mokher, C. (2009). *Pathways to boosting the earnings of low-income students by increasing their educational attainment.* Washington, DC: Hudson Institute Center for Employment Policy. Retrieved from http://www.hudson.org/files/publications/Pathways%20 to%20Boosting.pdf

Jaeger, D. A., & Page, M. E. (1996). Degrees matter: New evidence on sheepskin effects in the returns to education. *Review of Economics and Statistics, 78*, 733–40.

Jepsen, C., Troske, K., & Coomes, P. (2009). *The labor market returns to community college degrees, diplomas and certificates* (Discussion Paper Series 2009–08). Lexington, KY: University of Kentucky Center for Poverty Research. Retrieved from http://www.ukcpr.org/ Publications/DP2009-08.pdf

Kane, T. J., & Rouse, C. E. (1995a). Labor-market returns to two-and four-year college. *American Economic Review, 85*, 600–614.

Kane, T. J., & Rouse, C. E. (1995b). Comment on W. Norton Grubb: "The varied economic returns to postsecondary education: New evidence from the class of 1972." *Journal of Human Resources, 30*, 205–221.

Leigh, D. E., & Gill, A. M. (1997). Labor market returns to community colleges: Evidence for returning adults. *Journal of Human Resources, 32*, 334–353.

Light, A. (1995). The effects of interrupted schooling on wages. *Journal of Human Resources, 30*, 472–502.

Light, A., & Strayer, W. (2004). Who receives the college wage premium? Assessing the labor market returns to degrees and college transfer patterns. *Journal of Human Resources, 39*, 746–773.

Lleras-Muney, A. (2005). The relationship between education and adult mortality in the United States. *Review of Economic Studies, 72*, 189–221.

Lochner, L., & Moretti, E. (2004). The effect of education on crime: Evidence from prison inmates, arrests, and self-reports. *American Economic Review, 94*, 155–189.

London, R. A. (2006). The role of postsecondary education in welfare recipients' paths to self-sufficiency. *Journal of Higher Education, 77*, 472–496.

Long, B. T., & Kurlaender, M. (2008). *Do community colleges provide a viable pathway to a baccalaureate degree?* (NBER Working Paper No. 14367). Cambridge, MA: National Bureau of Economic Research.

Long, M. C. (2008). College quality and early adult outcomes. *Economics of Education Review, 27*, 588–602.

Marcotte, D. E., Bailey, T., Borkoski, C., & Kienzl, G. S. (2005). The returns of a community college education: Evidence from the National Education Longitudinal Survey. *Educational Evaluation and Policy Analysis, 27*, 157–175.

Rank, M. R., & Hirschl, T. A. (2005). Likelihood of using food stamps during the adulthood years. *Journal of Nutrition Education and Behavior, 37*, 137–146.

Reynolds, C. L. (2006). *Where to attend? Estimates of the effects of beginning at a two-year college* (Working Paper). Ann Arbor: University of Michigan.

Rouse, C. E. (1995). Democratization or diversion? The effect of community colleges on educational attainment. *Journal of Business and Economic Statistics, 13*, 217–224.

Rouse, C. E. (2007). Consequences for the labor market. In C. R. Belfield & H. M. Levin (Eds.), *The price we pay: Economic and social consequences of inadequate education* (pp. 99–124). Washington, DC: Brookings Institution Press.

Sandy, J., Gonzalez, A., & Hilmer, M. J. (2006). Alternative paths to college completion: Effect of attending a two-year school on the probability of completing a four-year degree. *Economics of Education Review, 25*, 463–471.

Schmitt, J., & Baker, D. (2006). *The impact of undercounting in the Current Population Survey.* Washington, DC: Center for Economic Policy and Research.

Spetz, J. (2002). The value of education in a licensed profession: The choice of associate or baccalaureate degrees in nursing. *Economics of Education Review, 21*, 73–85.

Steinberg, J. (2010, May 15). Plan B: Skip college. *New York Times.* Retrieved from http:// www.nytimes.com/2010/05/16/weekinreview/16steinberg.html

Surette, B. J. (2001). Transfer from two-year to four-year college: An analysis of gender differences. *Economics of Education Review, 20*, 151–163.

Waldfogel, J., Garfinkel, I., & Kelly, B. (2007). Welfare and the costs of public assistance. In

C. R. Belfield & H. M. Levin (Eds.), *The price we pay. Economic and social consequences of inadequate education* (pp. 160–174). Washington, DC: Brookings Institution Press. Wallace, G. L. (2007). Welfare flows and caseload dynamics. *Journal of Applied Economics, 10,* 415–442.

Wolfe, B., & Zuvekas, S. (1997). Nonmarket outcomes of schooling. *International Journal of Education Research, 27,* 491–502.

Clive R. Belfield is an associate professor in the Department of Economics, Queens College, City University of New York, Flushing, New York.

Thomas Bailey is the George and Abby O'Neill professor of economics and education in the Department of International and Transcultural Studies at Teachers College, Columbia University, New York, New York. He is also the director of the Community College Research Center at Teachers College, Columbia University.

CHAPTER 11

INSTITUTIONAL AMBIGUITY: CONTINUED STRUGGLES OF THE CONTRADICTORY COLLEGE

J. M. BEACH

In the wake of the civil rights movement in America, many radical thinkers sought to critically analyze the rhetoric and policy of early junior college leaders to ascertain the true mission of this institution in light of America's professed ideals of democracy and equality. A band of New Left critics exposed the hypocrisy of junior college leaders and pointed out the many educational failures of a beleaguered, second-rate institution of higher education. The community college was once assumed to be the people's college, but critics pointed out that this institution rarely served the interests of the people. It especially did not serve nonwhite minorities and the poor who more often than not earned second-class educations in underfunded and underresourced urban institutions. The New Left critics of the 1970s and 1980s exposed the underside of the community college and opened up a new critical discourse that focused on the failures of this newly legitimated institution, and thereby put the community college and its leaders on the defensive. In the wake of this critical development, community college leaders, scholars, and the policy community have tried to understand the predicament of the community college in more empirical detail to reengineer a renewed vision of the open-door community college for the 21st century. Consensus over a revised orthodoxy for the community college has not yet been reached. Criticisms still abound. The prospects of the community college and its mission remain clouded by contention and doubt. To be sure, this institution has earned a permanent place in state systems of higher education and regional labor markets, but whether this institution serves the ends of democratic opportunity, social efficiency, or capitalist accommodation (or some measure of all three) is still widely debated and will continue to be debated for the foreseeable future.

A Critique of Orthodoxy: The New Left Evaluates Community Colleges, 1970s–1980s

Many political critics and social scientists were animated by the civil rights and countercultural movements of the 1960s. An ethos of romanticism, critical bravado, and utopianism pervaded not only popular social movements, but also scholarly circles—especially those of historians and social scientists. The New Left became the political moniker of a diverse group of neoprogressive and quasi-Marxist political activists who were antagonistic toward the sociopolitical status quo and who were seeking to foment social change however possible. Many participants in the New Left during the 1960s used the New Left ideological frame of reference during the 1970s to critique education and schooling in the United States, often pointing out how education was nothing more than the social reproduction of an inequitable, class-based society.

Burton R. Clark's cooling-out thesis was famously extended by leftist critics many times over during the 1970s and 1980s. The basic argument, as Fred L. Pincus explained, was that community colleges "did more to reproduce class and race inequality than to provide meaningful avenues of upward mobility." Community colleges were the lowest track in a hierarchically arranged system of higher education, and lower-class students were structurally herded into subpar institutions of not-so-higher education. New Left critics also pointed to the capitalist environment surrounding community colleges, which structured an inequitable and competitive labor market that forced lower-class students into vocational programs and poorly paid jobs. Critics have argued that community colleges should challenge inequitable capitalist relations in several ways. They wanted this institution to empower lower-class students by teaching a broad set of technical skills and laying a critical foundation in the liberal arts, as well as establish relationships with unions and politically progressive community groups to promote democratic participation and social equality. In many ways the New Left critique expanded the democratic-oriented rhetoric of Bouge and Gleazer because it focused more on the underprivileged classes that had been excluded from American society and educational institutions.

L. Steven Zwerling wrote one of the first extended New Left monographs criticizing the community college in 1976. He argued that the "people's colleges do not serve the people" because they were embedded in an inequitable class structure, and they had the "hidden social function" of reproducing a hierarchical social order. He also argued that community colleges were second-best institutions of higher education that systematically denied working-class students a quality education while they also lowered student aspirations through a cooling-out process that encouraged students to take their place in the "lower ranks of the industrial and commercial hierarchy." Zwerling also made more deterministic arguments, somewhat in contradiction to earlier claims, by stating that all schools in the United States were "instruments of social and political control" that consciously socialize students into a particular class. He also argued that high rates of student attrition at community colleges were "one of the two-year colleges' primary social functions." Zwerling wanted his book to expose the "deceitful, manipulated reality" of the community college that was "rigged" in many ways against lower-class students. He thought that community college students could be taught the truth about their situation, which might empower them to demand community colleges be reformed. Ultimately Zwerling wanted to foment change in the community college so that it could be remade as a more progressive institution and, thereby, help to "provoke a reformation of society."

Howard B. London conducted the first ethnographic study of the culture of community colleges in the mid-1970s. His account delivered a veiled yet trenchant critique of community college students and faculty as half-conscious and limited agents. In the constraining environment of the community college, students and faculty structured self-defeating rituals of defensive resistance: absenteeism, limited effort, and cheating on the part of students, lowered academic standards and demoralized resignation on the part of faculty. Through subtle hostility and resignation, students and faculty "ensur[ed] the very defeat they wished to avoid." As one student described it:

In a way it's puzzling, because we're here to get a better job, to make something of ourselves, but we put down the school and stay away from it. This teacher gives you a lot of reading and writing to do and immediately you're pissed off. . . . It's biting the hand that can feed you. You'd think people would try harder, but they don't and that's bad for them, me, for anybody.

London's study revealed antagonistic relationships that defined the interactions of students and faculty and thereby limited any possibility of true education from taking place. As one student explained, "I think it's because people have a need to pull other[s] down to their level. Working-class people are notorious for this. . . . the students may resent the teachers because the teachers represent education and intellect."

London critiqued Clark's cooling-out thesis as superficial and "distorted" because Clark did not actually observe firsthand how the students internalized their scholastic failure. Quoting German sociologist Max Weber, London argued that the process was much more an "inarticulate half-consciousness" on the part of students and faculty. Both parties were trapped in a struggle over identity, aspirations, and social class, and both parties were constrained and defeated by the institutional parameters of the community college. London took his conception of educational struggle from Willard Waller's classic 1932 study *The Sociology of Teaching*. In this famous work Waller argued that American schools were "despotic political structures" where students were "subordinated" to "autocratic" authority figures, such as teachers and administrators. Waller argued that schooling was in a constant state of "perilous equilibrium" wherein "conflict groups" played out their roles of authority and resistance to authority in an uneasy yet ritualized politics of "ever-fickle equilibrium." London used Waller's conceptual insight to expose the conflicted terrain inside community colleges, which undercut and defeated the lofty rhetoric surrounding this institution.

In 1985 Lois Weis reiterated what had become the standard complaint of New Left critics of the community college: These colleges were institutions of social reproduction in a racist and sexist society. But community colleges were not completely determined by the oppressive social structure of U.S. society, as they also sought to embody a democratic ethos that offered increased opportunities for social mobility. Weis's contribution to the critical literature on community colleges was to differentiate the experiences of working-class African Americans who occupied a "caste" distinct from the travails of working-class whites. Weis's ethnographic study of the African American cultural experience of community colleges explored how racialized and class-bound students could "embrace and reject schooling at one and the same time." Weis also pointed out that while community colleges might help individuals escape the chains of underclass life, "the group can never follow," thus, "the college cannot possibly work for blacks as a collectivity." Therefore, Weis looked beyond the myth of an enlightened faculty, and she argued for a modest program of teaching students and faculty about their position in a racialized and classed society.

Fred L. Pincus took community colleges to task for their growing emphasis on vocational education. He saw the vocationalization of community colleges as part of an institutionalized tracking system that was being erected to divert community college students to lower-status occupations in an inequitably stratified and class-bound society. He also criticized institutional collusion with corporations in the form of customized contract training. This training included community colleges offering tailored employee training to local businesses. Pincus did not believe the notion that everybody benefits when community colleges serve local industries, and he argued that not all parties necessarily gained from contract training. Corporations were able to get cost-effective training services, and community colleges were able to bring in new sources of revenue and enrollments, but the benefits to students and to the society at large were more ambiguous. Contract training represented a larger "drift toward narrow vocationalism at the expense of critical thinking and broad-based knowledge," which gave students employable skills in the short term but put them at a disadvantage in the long term by reducing the chance of further economic mobility through higher levels of degree attainment. Pincus argued that institutions of higher education should have broader goals than simply putting students to work with "just enough technical skills and 'positive' attitudes so that the corporation can operate at a profit." For Pincus, contract training represented the abdication of educational ideals and the renunciation of liberal curricular principles. Community colleges were already not helping many students attain bachelor's degrees. About 15 to 25 percent of community college students transferred to a 4-year school, but overall only 10 to 15 percent of these students would earn bachelor's degrees. Pincus argued that the new trend toward increased contract training would only further reduce the chances of students' push for upward economic mobility.

The most acclaimed and sophisticated work of New Left criticism came in 1989. Steven Brint and Jerome Karabel wrote *The Diverted Dream: Community Colleges and the Promise of Educational Opportunity in America, 1900–1985*. In this book they argued that the educational system in the United States had always been "hierarchically differentiated" because it was "closely linked" to the capitalist labor market and to the inequitable class structure of American society. But they also stressed the fact that the American educational system was a relatively open and democratic structure, especially in the 20th century. Most Americans viewed education in America as a ladder of opportunity for upward economic mobility. Thus the institution of community colleges was defined paradoxically in relation to the broader contradictions of American society. The community college embodied an egalitarian promise, but at the same time it also reflected the constraints of the capitalist economic system in which it was embedded. The United States was an optimistic society that generated more ambition than it could structurally satisfy, which created a need for elaborate and often hidden tracking systems to channel students into occupationally appropriate avenues, largely based on their socioeconomic origins.

From its beginnings the community college had the contradictory function of opening higher education to larger numbers of students from all socioeconomic backgrounds, while supporting a highly stratified economic and educational system that created a need to select and sort students. This cooling-out function, or *the diversion effect,* caused ever-increasing numbers of lower-socioeconomic-status students in higher education to be diverted into more modest positions at the lower end of the labor market. Burton Clark once admitted that "for large numbers failure is inevitable and *structured* [italics in original]." Brint and Karabel argued that not only do community colleges help "transmit inequalities" through their sorting function, but they also "contribute to the legitimization of these inequalities." This institution helps legitimize inequality by uncritically parroting meritocratic rhetoric that often blames the victim for failing to succeed in a structurally rigged class system. Brint and Karabel forcefully argued,

> The very real contribution that the community college has made to the expansion of opportunities for some individuals does not, however, mean that its *aggregate* [italics in original] effect has been a democratizing one. On the contrary, the two-year institution has accentuated rather than reduced existing patterns of social inequality.

Brint and Karabel focused specifically on the increased vocationalization of the community college as it developed over the course of the 20th century, which often disproportionately affected the poor, the working class, immigrants, and ethnic/racialized minorities. The secondary school curriculum became more vocationally oriented in the early 20th century, and early junior college leaders sought to carve out a distinct educational niche for their institution by providing postsecondary occupational certification for regional labor markets. However, it is unclear if early vocational programs were able to place their students into skilled work because of the lack of any type of evidence to prove such a claim. Many scholars have pointed out that the majority of junior college students during the first half of the 20th century resisted terminal programs and sought instead an undergraduate academic curriculum that would allow them to transfer to a 4-year university. Part of this resistance was because the majority of students who enrolled in junior colleges were high school graduates who wanted to earn a bachelor's degree, while the more occupationally inclined either dropped out of high school early to get a job or waited until earning their high school diploma to enter the workforce. Yet the point of Brint and Karabel and others remains substantial. Junior college leaders in conjunction with community business leaders did actively try to manipulate student aspirations by engineering more and more terminal programs. They also encouraged this route more passively by neglecting a pedagogically appropriate curriculum and adequate student support services geared toward less academically prepared students who tended to either drop out or would settle for a terminal occupational certificate. During the 1970s, up to 75 percent of low-achieving students dropped out during their 1st year in urban community colleges. Critics also pointed out that it was not an accident that the lowest-achieving students in secondary and postsecondary schools have historically been, and continue to be, the economically disadvantaged, ethnic/racialized minorities, immigrants, the disabled, and dislocated low-skilled workers.

At the beginning of the 1990s, several mainstream academics justified the basic outline of the New Left critique of community colleges. In their comprehensive review of the literature on how college affects students, Ernest T. Pascarella and Patrick T. Terenzini argued, "There is reasonably strong evidence in support of Clark's argument that community colleges can also function to 'cool out' students' educational aspirations." David F. Labaree concurred. He stated that over the course of the 20th century, the community college had developed a safe, "narrowly defined vocational" niche at the "bottom rung of the status hierarchy in higher education." Community colleges were denied the ability to grant the coveted credential of social mobility, the bachelor's degree, and thus this institution was damned to a "permanently junior status," acting more the role of an "agent of social reproduction rather than a pathway to opportunity." In his analysis, Labaree argued that a close reading of history seemed to support the views of New Left critics such as Brint, Karabel, Pincus, and Zwerling. According to Labaree, the community college was caught in a bind between conflicting democratic and capitalist goals, and "in spite of 'false promises' to provide equal opportunity, the primary function of this institution is to promote the reproduction of social inequality."

Revised but Confused Orthodoxy: The Contradictory Community College's New Missions, 1990s–2000s

From the 1970s into the 21st century the debate over the purposes of the American community college became more diverse and more heated, largely because of the charges of New Left critics. Traditionalist defenders of the community college had a strong reaction. They argued that this institution kept the door open to deserving 2-year graduates so they could transfer to 4-year universities, while offering other less-talented students a route to occupational training and some measure of economic rewards. In the middle of this debate, and at the front lines of the battle for efficiency and equity, marginalized and undertrained community college education professionals have struggled over the last century to find a professional identity. They are caught in the midst of the uncertainty surrounding shifting community college missions. Compounding the confusion further, the parameters of the debate began to perceptively shift by the 1990s as the community college noticeably began to change in response to a postindustrial, globalized U.S. economy. The debate over the diverse mission and coherence of the community college continues unresolved into the 21st century. In fact, the ambiguity of and the conflict over the diverse community college mission seems to have itself become institutionalized, subtly enshrining the institution with a new moniker: the contradictory college.

In the 1990s Arthur M. Cohen and Florence B. Brawer, authors of the most widely read textbook on community colleges, defended this institution against its critics. Cohen and Brawer argued that New Left critics were blinded by ideology. They said these critics were overly focused on the "American social-class system" and "the fanciful dream of class leveling." Cohen and Brawer argued that hierarchical class systems were inevitable, and that educational institutions cannot "break down class distinctions." Thus, they implied, such critics miss the real work that community colleges do in providing equal access to what Cohen and Brawer assumed to be a meritocratic higher educational system. Cohen and Brawer wanted a narrower research focus that would closely appraise the complex work community colleges actually did in the effort to serve a diverse array of individuals who had nowhere else to turn. As Arthur Cohen famously argued, "For most of the community college students, *the choice is not between the community college and a senior residential institution; it is between the local college and nothing* [italics added]." But as one historian of the community college has argued, defenders of the community college status quo have always rationalized the good intentions of the institution by "pointing to the degree of access" it provides students, while ignoring the larger structural constraints that work at counterpurposes to those of the institution and that limit the ability of individuals to gain a measure of educational, social, or economic success. W. Norton Grubb and Marvin Lazerson have argued that community colleges are *both* "egalitarian institutions extending schooling upward for greater numbers of students" as well as "inegalitarian institutions keeping the masses away from the university."

In 1994 Kevin J. Dougherty reexamined the critical debate over the origins, functions, and purposes of the community college to try to resolve scholarly disagreement by focusing on the actual work that community colleges did and the larger social, political, and economic constraints that affected the institution. Dougherty critiqued the three dominant critical schools of thought: functionalist, Marxist, and institutionalist. Functionalist scholars advocated the community college as a democratic educational initiative focused on increased opportunity, meeting the needs of society, and protecting the academic quality of universities. Instrumentalist Marxists have criticized the community college as a capitalist tool that reproduces social and economic inequalities. Institutionalists have also criticized the community college, but instead of focusing on the capitalistic structure of society these scholars focused on the institutional dynamics of the system of higher education and how community colleges serve as a diversion to preserve the academic integrity of universities. Dougherty did not disagree with any of these theories, but he argued that each was limited and flawed in some respects; thus, each offered only a partial explanation of the origins and purposes of the community college.

Dougherty said the community college has been and continues to be a hybrid institution full of contradictory purposes. The community college was constrained by its sociopolitical environment but also exercised some relative autonomy in terms of institutional missions and practice. Dougherty demonstrated that community colleges, while responsive to a wide variety of external influences, were only loosely coupled with social and economic pressures because educational administrators and state officials direct this institution according to their own interests, such as gaining votes, increasing their prestige, or engineering social and educational efficiency. Thus, the performance of community colleges has been only loosely linked to the cultural, political, and economic structure of society, that is, there has been no deliberate conspiracy to keep students from succeeding in higher education and attaining bachelor's degrees. However, Dougherty did make clear that community colleges, as institutions of higher education, were not very good at their job of demonstrating positive student outcomes, especially in helping students earn bachelor's degrees through transferring to 4-year colleges and universities. According to Dougherty, community colleges were not structurally determined institutions designed to cool out students, they were just inefficient, nonencouraging, antiacademic, low-performing, and overly vocationalized institutions with contradictory goals. This stark judgment moved community college discourse worlds away from the heady optimism of the mid-20th century.

The organizational and pedagogical inefficiency of community colleges was further documented by several scholars in the 1990s. Joanne Cooper and Ken Kempner demonstrated how fragile and dysfunctional the organizational cultures of community colleges could be, especially with transient leadership at the top. Cooper and Kempner painted a portrait of bullying senior faculty, out-of-date curricula, and factional power struggles between newer and older faculty and between faculty and administrators. In more than a few community colleges, faculty and administrators were a primary part of the problem of poor student academic achievement. W. Norton Grubb and associates conducted a nationwide study specifically focused on the conditions of teaching in community colleges. Until the late 1990s almost no empirical investigation of teaching in what was assumed to be a teaching institution was conducted, let alone empirically based evaluations of teaching effectiveness. Grubb argued that while teaching was the central organizational purpose of community colleges, it was often "an isolated and idiosyncratic activity" that was largely ignored by the institutional culture. Community colleges, according to Grubb, "have failed to assume much institutional responsibility for the quality of instruction," and therefore good teaching in community colleges was "essentially random." In effect community colleges had institutionalized mediocre teaching. Community college administrators needed to redesign institutional commitments to teaching, including funding priorities, to create the conditions for more collaborative and student-centered pedagogies in a reimagined teacher's college, otherwise the community college's commitment to open access would be reduced to empty rhetoric.

Of course Grubb's judgment of mediocre teaching was nothing new to insightful community college instructors. Robert M. Pirsig reminisced about his experience as an instructor in a teacher's college in the 1950s:

> At a teaching college you teach and you reach and you teach with no time for research, no time for contemplation, no time of participation in outside affairs. Just teach and teach and teach until your mind grows dull and your creativity vanishes and you become an automaton saying the same dull things over and over to endless waves of innocent students who cannot understand why you are so dull, lose respect, and fan this disrespect into the community. The reason you teach and you teach and you teach is that this is a very clever way of running a college on the cheap while giving the false appearance of genuine education.

But missing from Grubb's critique on teaching, and from most critical exposés on community colleges, was a hard look at the community college student. As any community college faculty member can tell you, many students are simply not up to the task of higher education, and these students can frustrate even the best educational intentions and methods. A significant percentage of students in every class refuse to do much at all to better themselves: They regularly miss more than 10 percent of required seat time, they don't read course textbooks, they don't complete homework, they don't participate in class, and they don't ask instructors for help, all the while expecting their lackluster performance will earn them a passing grade by the end of the term. Many faculty, as critics have amply demonstrated, simply lower their standards out of despair, pity, or fear of student evaluations. Students who would fail under the most basic higher education standards are routinely allowed to pass watered-down courses in the community college. Some faculty try to keep some semblance of standards, and they do their best to inspire the unmotivated, but in the end these faculty more often than not are forced to lower the hammer on upward of 50 to 75 percent of students in any given college-level class. One anonymous adjunct faculty described this precarious predicament in *The Atlantic*:

> For I, who reach these low-level, must-pass, no-multiple-choice-test classes, am the one who ultimately delivers the news to those unfit for college: that they lack the most basic skills and have no sense of the volume of work required; that they are in some cases barely literate; that they are so bereft of schemata, so dispossessed of contexts in which to place newly acquired knowledge, that every bit of information simply raises more questions. They are not ready for high school, some of them, much less for college.
>
> I am the man who has to lower the hammer.

The perpetual challenge of the community college instructor is trying to deliver some semblance of higher education to a student population whose members can barely read, refuse to do homework, and do not understand the value of learning. It is an almost impossible task under the best of circumstances.

But there is also substantial evidence that community colleges, independent of student characteristics, reduce the ability of students to earn a baccalaureate degree by about 15 to 20 percent. According to data gathered in the 1990s, community college students who were able to attain a baccalaureate degree were more than twice as likely as 4-year students to take more than 6 years to degree. But there was positive news: Students who were able to successfully transfer to a 4-year institution seemed to be at no disadvantage and were just as likely as 4-year students to graduate, aspire to graduate school, and attend graduate school. However, successful transfer students were more likely to be young, white, male; academically prepared in high school; continuously enrolled; to have high degree expectations; and to come from families in high socioeconomic brackets. These "traditional" students represented 56 percent of successful transfers who obtained a bachelor's degree in the 1990s, but very few community college students in the United States have many of these characteristics. There was also evidence that community colleges did cool out and lower the educational aspirations of students when compared to students in 4-year institutions. However, when community college students were compared to students with no postsecondary education, it seemed that community colleges did in fact have a positive warming effect, which raised the educational aspirations of students with no previous postsecondary futures.

Other voices in the 1990s were much less critical of the community college. Some focused less on the academic shortcomings of this institution and more on its idealistic goal of being open to the needs of the community. Marlene Griffith and Ann Connor reiterated Gleazer's call for a more community-oriented college. Griffith and Connor claimed, "The public comprehensive community college is committed to serving *all* segments of its community [italics added]." These defenders of the community college were worried that the open door was beginning to close. They saw the comprehensive missions of the community college as competing with each other. They saw new restrictions on enrollment through tests and tuition increases. And they saw a diminishing of the educational opportunities available to the community. Griffith and Connor wanted a renewed commitment to the community college as a teacher's college focused on the learning and diverse needs of its unique students. They wanted a renewed commitment to the community college as an institution responsive to the "economic and social realities of their communities." Above all Griffith and Connor wanted community colleges to strive after "lofty and idealistic" missions, such as upholding the tradition of democracy's college, while also keeping flexible and in tune with the real needs of the local community. But the central claims of Griffith and Connor sink beneath their idealistic rhetoric as a testament to the ebullient optimism and naive myths of traditional community college boosterism that has been constant since the mid-20th century.

John E. Roueche, Lynn Sullivan Taber, and Suanne D. Roueche also argued for a more community-oriented college. Roueche et al. interviewed the CEOs of 14 community colleges across the United States and Canada to survey how specific colleges were trying to become more responsive to local, regional, national, and even international communities. Taber argued that while the idea of a community-based college has been widely discussed, there had been no "consistent vocabulary," nor had there been any empirical reports on specific community outreach programs or successful practices. Taber also explained how many community colleges in the 1980s and 1990s were balancing the trade-offs of trying to find funding for community outreach programs and trying to cut back on resources without losing community support. There were no easy answers as the community-oriented college tried to be all things to all people, but Roueche et al. did put forth a plan whereby community colleges could strike a balance between multiple partnerships. They reframed the community college mission in terms of multiple, overlapping fields of development: economic development, community development, people development, organizational development, and resource development. And they stressed that in an environment of reduced state resources, solidifying multiple, mutual relationships within the community could help foster a foundation for renewed legitimacy and collaborative funding. But other scholars, such as John S. Levin and John D. Dennison, warned that community colleges might be more concerned with institutional legitimacy and political stability, thereby using a community orientation to become "less for the community" and more for the "social organizations in the community." Levin and Dennison noted that the new social functions of the community college were less concerned with community needs than with institutional survival.

Part of the inherent contradiction of the community college has been the fact that this institution has never known organizational stability because of its high degree of community and labor market responsiveness. According to John S. Levin, the community college continually revises its "ever-expanding" mission in an attempt to "be all things to all people." Economic and political developments in the 1980s and 1990s pushed many community colleges away from comprehensiveness and back toward the terminal vocational emphasis of the early junior college leaders. A new era of constrained resources, combined with legislative calls for economic development and institutional accountability, helped move the community college to reduce its long emphasis on liberal arts education and community services to develop a new vocationalism, which supposedly would integrate the various goals of regional economic development, workforce training, and semiprofessional education. Thomas R. Bailey and Irina E. Averianova argued that the comprehensive mission of the community college had been downgraded as career education and the "entrepreneurial college" became the "only viable core function for most community colleges."

But John S. Levin went further. He argued that the community college acquired yet another new institutional mission, even though many administrators and faculty were not yet fully conscious of this change. Despite the transfer mission's remaining a primary emphasis for most community colleges throughout the 20th century, the constant management and change of institutional purposes by community college leaders, the business community, and state officials have remained intense. Over the last couple of decades community colleges in the United States and Canada, with the support of government and corporate policies, have taken a more corporate and businesslike approach to education. Community colleges have become focused more on money and less on educational objectives. As a result these institutions have shifted the curricular focus toward competitive, workplace skills (learning for the sole purpose of earning) to meet what business leaders and eager-to-please administrators considered to be workforce needs. John S. Levin and D. Franklin Ayers, among others, have demonstrated how many community colleges have "altered their role from a social to an economic agency," and have evolved into a new vocational institution: the *nouveau* college.

Community college administrators have increasingly adopted an ideological stance of neoliberal corporatism over the past couple of decades, which has directed them to focus on efficiency, productivity, marketplace needs, and economic ends, making educational institutions homogenized and education programs commodified and vocationalized. Education has been reduced to occupational training and marketable skills. John Levin argued that by the end of the 20th century community colleges had become different institutions with an altered identity and mission. The educational endeavor of community colleges has become primarily a capitalistic enterprise. "A globally competitive environment, economic in nature and capitalistic in ideology" has "opened the doors to more business-oriented practices and a corporate style of management." Levin concluded, "The former mission of community colleges, while vibrant in rhetoric, was becoming obsolete."

One specific indicator of the re-visioning of community colleges in terms of economic development was the growth in contract training as an important resource-generating community college function. Contract training developed as a priority during the 1990s as many business enterprises incorporated new technology into the marketplace and demanded an increasing level of skills from employees. By the early 1990s over 90 percent of community colleges in the United States were offering contract training. The increase in this particular workforce development activity was driven partly by a growing need for alternative sources of funding and increased student enrollments, partly by a desire to raise the responsiveness of colleges to community needs, partly because of attempts to strengthen local prestige and political support for community colleges, and partly by new demands from government agents, community college associations, and businesses for state-sponsored human capital development. The long-term impact of increased contract training remains unclear, but community colleges have been able to raise revenues and student enrollments while gaining more support from the community, businesses, and the state. Contract training, however, may have some unintended consequences: There seems to be a growing divide between credit and noncredit courses, which makes it difficult for students to continue their education and apply contract training courses toward degree programs. Additionally, a general eroding of institutional commitment to the traditional curriculum seems to be occurring, as new monies are increasingly being used to invest in resource-generating programs rather than buttress established but resource-starved areas such as liberal arts.

Global responsiveness and the new vocationalism have been perhaps the most dramatic new trends among community colleges, but they have not been the only new institutional missions developed during the 1990s. In the two decades following the dramatic events of the late 1960s, several sociopolitical grassroots mobilizations for minority civil rights, immigration reform, and cultural diversity coalesced by the mid-1980s into a broad social and academic movement for political pluralism, equal rights for all people, and multiculturalism. This movement sparked a wide debate over national identity in the late 1980s and throughout the 1990s, which many came to call a "cultural war." In 1993 James Valadez argued that many community college students, especially nonwhite minorities, first-generation students, and immigrants, lacked the "cultural capital" to succeed in institutions of higher education in the United States. Valadez explained that there were many unstated "linguistic codes" and "cultural competencies" that helped facilitate student success in college. Many students also brought cultural resources and competencies that were not always "recognized or valued by the institution," and these cultural resources became a liability that impeded students from succeeding in the institution. Valadez argued that the accepted and taken-for-granted institutional functions often acted as barriers to many students who needed "a system of emotional as well as academic support," not only to help them succeed in the institution but also to help mediate and overcome the educational failures they experienced from previous schooling.

In the 1990s many scholars employed the theory and politics of multiculturalism to investigate current educational practices and the future possibilities of community colleges. Multiculturalists argued that this institution had come to serve a very diverse student population, thus, it must not only respect but also celebrate the cultural differences of its students and the local community. Community colleges needed to engage students holistically in a learning process that empowers students to become "full participants in both education and social life." This included a broader view of vocational education that would combine technical training and an education in democracy that could be used to help workers barter for better wages and working conditions. Some critical multiculturalists carried this project further by arguing that community colleges should also teach students to criticize the inequitable power relations and social hierarchies that control knowledge production, cultural transmission, and social identities. This critical pedagogy, developing political and social insights by writers of the New Left, sought to teach students to develop a critical consciousness to raise self-esteem, encourage motivation, and ultimately empower students to take charge of their own future.

Perhaps the most exciting trend, but very frightening to many traditionalists, has been the move toward making community colleges baccalaureate-degree-granting institutions. This movement could potentially redefine the whole identity of the institution. Discussions of community colleges' granting bachelor's degrees began in the 1980s, but only a few states had actually developed these degree programs by the 1990s. The rhetoric surrounding this new programming articulated a move not to change the previous missions of the open-door comprehensive community college but to add an additional mission that had the potential to alleviate some of the continued inequality in community college students' ability to successfully transfer to 4-year institutions to earn a bachelor's degree. Theoretically, with baccalaureate degree programs on the community college campus, many of the roadblocks to transferring would be removed because students could stay at a local low-cost institution near supportive networks of family, friends, and employers. This would naturally increase the chances of many students who would otherwise never attain a bachelor's degree. Some have also framed this new mission in neoliberal rhetoric, arguing that better-educated local workforces can meet the specific needs of regional labor markets.

Some critics, however, have warned that developing baccalaureate degree programs might overshadow the established missions of the comprehensive community college and threaten open-door policies. These critics have pointed to a few former community colleges that used baccalaureate degree programs as a vehicle to transform into 4-year state colleges. But this debate is still young and has more questions than answers at this point. As of 2000 only 57 community colleges in the United States had developed these degree programs, prompting the Carnegie Foundation for the Advancement of Teaching to brand these institutions as baccalaureate/associate's colleges. Offering bachelor's degrees at community colleges will potentially increase community college students' access to these degrees; however, these degrees have been so far offered primarily in vocational/technical fields such as nursing, which is a high-demand field with currency in local labor markets. Extending the baccalaureate to arcs and sciences would take a restructuring of the faculty and curricular apparatus to hire more highly trained PhDs to create 4-year academic programs. This would most likely create a greater rift between remedial and college-level faculty and programs. And awarding liberal arts bachelor's degrees could potentially flood local markets with devalued credentials from already stigmatized second-class institutions at the bottom rung of the higher education hierarchy. Holding a community college bachelor's degree might turn out to be nothing more than a second-class credential, much like the associate's degree, which would invariably be downgraded in the public's eye to a third-rate credential or worse.

By the late 1990s and early 21st century, it became increasingly clear that community colleges had comprehensive missions, multiple organizational ideologies, divisive organizational cultures, and an extremely diverse student population. The 21st-century community college is not an easy institution to define, let alone govern. Over the past decade many scholars have argued that community colleges needed to embrace organizational multiplicity. In coming to terms with the conflicting nature of such a comprehensive institutional structure, scholars have fruitfully applied the insights of postmodernism. Many have conceptualized the community college as a cultural text with a multiplicity of interpretations. Kathleen Shaw has not only researched the complex and fluid multiple identities of community college students, but she has also studied political and organizational ideologies, in particular organizational cultures and their effects on specific academic programs. In one study, Shaw investigated remedial education programs as an " ideological battleground," whereby larger political debates over the nature and purpose of higher education interacted with district-level policy and organizational cultures. She explored how larger political ideologies and district policies have been mediated by the local organizational culture and were either reinforced or resisted through formal and informal educational practices. In another study, Shaw and Howard B. London argued, "Ideology and culture are seldom monolithic. It is far more likely for an institution to have internal factions that emphasize or contest different aspects of its culture." Thus, community college policy institutional missions, and educational programming should be seen as pluralistic and divisive political processes in which different parties struggle over the definition and control of organizational identities, purposes, and practices. Community college administrators are not really leaders who plan and initiate change, rather they are mediators (often with their own interests) caught between warring factions, trying to negotiate institutional policy and disciplinary practice.

In taking stock of the conflicted diversity of the community college in the 21st century, Thomas Bailey and Vanessa Smith Morest were able to briefly summarize the predicament of this contradictory public institution of higher education:

> Community colleges face an especially difficult task. They enroll those students who have the most daunting educational, economic, and social barriers to their education, yet they have the fewest resources per student to serve those students . . . . At the same time, as public institutions, they are asked to carry out a variety of different functions, some of which conflict with their access and equity missions.

Smith Morest argued that the public community college was so overloaded with diverse missions that "it is impossible to do any of them well." While Bailey and Smith Morest noted the rise in vocational enrollments and the increase of contract training and continuing education programs, Smith Morest argued that community colleges were still committed to traditional academic and vocational programs.

Increasingly, however, these traditional programs have taken on new hybrid forms. One example is vocational-transfer programs in traditional vocational areas that used to result in terminal certificates or an associate's degree, such as nursing or electrical engineering. Now these programs are geared toward creating pathways to baccalaureate attainment at 4-year institutions. But Smith Morest noted that a serious conflict may be arising between credit programs, academic and vocational, and noncredit programs, mainly vocational. This potential conflict, she explained, could create "a new schism" between credit and noncredit programming by segregating working adult students into noncredit training programs. Many scholars, including Bailey, Bragg, Smith Morest, Grubb, and Lazerson, have all argued that community colleges need to somehow find ways to integrate their diverse institutional missions into a coherent vision for education. But to do this successfully, community colleges would need broad financial support from state policy makers who would need to create a comprehensive policy to promote educational equity and give community colleges the resources to create a coherent, comprehensive mission that can fully meet the plethora of state and local needs. While money is not a sufficient cause of institutional integration and efficiency, it is a necessary component.

But state support has been steadily waning over the past several decades, and it has dramatically decreased because of the Great Recession of 2007–2009. Amid recent calls for increased institutional efficiency of community colleges, many believe the older rhetoric of democracy and educational opportunity may be eroding. The tuition costs of community colleges have increased considerably over the past 20 years while state government funding of higher education has decreased. Thus, students bear much more of the financial burden to finance their education. In 2001 the average cost of tuition and fees for a full-time community college student was $1,705 per year, plus books, transportation, living expenses, and the opportunity costs of forgone wages, which can make a community college education prohibitively expensive to many low-income students. The financial burden is even greater for low-income students who need remedial education because it takes these students more time to obtain a certificate or degree. About 42 percent of first-year students need at least one remedial education course, and 60 percent of students in remedial courses are African American and Latino/Latina students. A recent study of Los Angeles community college students found that students who needed the most remediation spent up to 5 years in the community college, and those who successfully transferred to a 4-year institution spent up to 3 more years earning their bachelor's degree.

So those students with the most need have to pay the greatest personal cost. For underprivileged students, the cost in time, tuition, and foregone earnings is greater than it is for the more academically prepared and socioeconomically privileged. Lower-class students have also lately been penalized with less financial aid, meaning they have to take on more student loans, which will take a significant and often crippling percentage of their future income. Also, the evidence continues to show that upper-middle-class community college students are much more likely to successfully transfer to 4-year institutions. Because of a growing influx of middle-, upper-middle-, and upper-class students to community colleges because of the lack of space at overcrowded universities, this trend could have the potential to displace current resources that support lower-class and at-risk students.

However, in the face of fiscal constraints, state policy makers have lately ignored issues of decreased opportunity and educational inequality. Instead, a national discourse of institutional effectiveness has swept the nation. Alicia C. Dowd has argued for a broad coalition of community college professionals, activists, and academic researchers to resist the totalizing logic of this new effectiveness discourse to engage in a political dialogue. Dowd argues the effectiveness discourse can oversimplify the complexity and diversity of the community college, and it can also displace larger sociopolitical issues. Dowd argues that previous policies focused on the democratization of higher education and increased educational access should not be displaced by new institutional efficiency concerns. While institutional efficiency measures can strengthen pedagogical practice, Dowd wants policy makers to also align the community college with the larger issues of "reducing social and economic inequality and strengthening democratic processes."

But beyond the more idealistic claims for equal access to higher education and the strengthening of democracy, many practical issues are still unresolved. The whole notion of increased efficiency becomes a problem because this particular institution may have a serious design flaw. What happens to the majority of community college students who never transfer to a 4-year institution and obtain a bachelor's degree? Is the terminal, vocational mission of the community college of any benefit to those students who will only graduate with an associate's degree or vocational certificate, or does the 21st century community college remain a holding pen for the masses of "young idle youth" who cannot find adequate employment in the constricted labor market, and who are being subtly encouraged in the open-door college to take whatever jobs might be readily available? Does the community college actually help students gain well-paid employment, or are community college credentials merely devalued commodities in a discriminatory labor market?

Are There Economic Returns to Community College Credentials? An Economic Assessment, 1990-2010

Wrapped in the broader debate over the competing missions of the community college is the assumption that any amount of certified education increases an individual's social mobility and economic welfare. But does a community college credential actually produce solid economic returns for students? At the core of recent calls for institutional assessments of the community college is the unquestioned assumption that community colleges adequately serve the majority of students who do not transfer to 4-year institutions and earn bachelor's degrees. But what if community colleges, as Brint and Karabel argued two decades ago, structure the failure of even successful community college students because of the degraded value of subbaccalaureate degrees in a highly inequitable and discriminatory labor market?

Reviewing 20 years of research from the 1970s and 1980s, Ernest T. Pascarella and Patrick T. Terenzini revealed that not much was known about this issue. In the 1980s W. Norton Grubb noted that based on the available research, subbaccalaureate vocational programs "do not confer on students the labor market advantage that is their principle reason for being," although "there is some evidence of successful programs." He also noted that secondary-level vocational programs are "uniformly negative" in their effects, while the outcomes of community colleges, based on the very limited available evidence, are decidedly mixed. Grubb also pointed out that vocational guidance in secondary and postsecondary schooling is also "not particularly effective" in helping students train for and make the transition into midskilled jobs because vocational guidance involves the impossible feat of "occupational forecasting." Grubb's conclusion: Vocational programs are highly overrated, are ideologically motivated, have few positive effects, and they are "successful only under special circumstances." Despite the lack of efficiency or success, vocational education programs and vocationalism has gained enormous influence because of the institutional and political power of its defenders.

By the 1990s Pascarella and Terenzini reported an increase in research on the economic returns to subbaccalaureate education. Several important research papers and literature reviews in the mid-1990s were more optimistic than Grubb but certainly revealed decidedly mixed results for economic returns to subbaccalaureate education. Kevin J. Dougherty reviewed the limited research on subbaccalaureate degrees and credentials and found the evidence troubling. He argued that the evidence on whether a community college education delivers increased earnings compared to a high school diploma was "quite mixed," and at best subbaccalaureate education gave graduates a "very slight edge." But in some studies there was contrary evidence that community college students actually did worse economically than workers with only a high school diploma. Whitaker and Pascarella found that subbaccalaureate education led to a "significantly lower occupational status" and lower earnings than a bachelor's degree, and these authors recommended community colleges only as a stepping-stone to a 4-year baccalaureate-granting institution. Stern et al. found some evidence of increased earnings for those with an associate's degree, but the earnings seemed to decline over the course of a worker's lifetime, and the value of the associate's degree might be more of a reflection of personal characteristics than the degree itself since associate's degree earners tended to come from "more educated or affluent families than those who completed high school only." Overall the results were "divergent," and Stern et al. warned that one could not make any generalizations about the monetary effects of subbaccalaureate education. But based on the evidence, and controlling for personal characteristics, Stern et al. estimated the value of an associate's degree was between $1,000 and $2,000 a year more than a high school diploma for people between the ages of 24 and 32, and that the earnings differential was greatest for women with a vocational degree while almost nil for males.

Grubb conducted the first comprehensive scholarly attempt to find solid evidence on the midskilled or subbaccalaureate labor market to evaluate the claims about education's economic returns, especially for midskilled workers who in the early 1990s constituted the majority of the workforce, 60 percent of all employed workers. Grubb researched specific occupations in four midskilled labor markets at the local level. He found that the subbaccalaureate labor market is mostly a "local phenomenon" with the parameters of the market determined by the vagaries of the business cycle. A subbaccalaureate worker is not very mobile in job searching, most likely tied to a specific locality, and any vocational credentials earned will have their highest currency in the local labor market where the community college or technical school is known.

A few important characteristics of the subbaccalaureate labor market affect student transitions from school to work, one being the large number of small businesses and firms in this market. These firms hire few workers and offer smaller salaries and less opportunity for advancement than larger firms. These small firms are not well informed about educated labor supplies; they are not often tied to or communicate with local educational institutions; and they usually have informal hiring practices; which makes it difficult to prepare students for interviews or specific job related skills. Smaller firms also tend to be more dependent on flexible and multiskilled employees because short-handed firms often blur occupational boundaries to get the job done cheaply and with fewer resources. Another characteristic of the midskilled labor market is the highly cyclical nature of market demand. This creates unstable employment opportunities, which in turn increases informal hiring policies, which then makes it difficult for job seekers and administrators of vocational programs to determine exactly what local employers want and when they want it. Because of the inefficiency of the subbaccalaureate market, it is very difficult for educational institutions to know, let alone teach, the skills employers want. And further, Grubb pointed out that because of the blurring of occupational boundaries and the flexible nature of smaller firms, "most of the competencies required by employers in the sub-baccalaureate labor market *cannot* readily be taught in schools and colleges."

Based on the available evidence, Grubb was very clear in pointing out that community colleges can "*under the right conditions* [italics in original] provide students with substantial benefits." But under suboptimal conditions community colleges "may benefit not at all." Specifically Grubb pointed out that the benefits of a community college are maximized if students can enroll in economically viable occupations and find related employment in the local labor market, but this is rarely the case because community colleges tend to be isolated islands disconnected from other educational institutions and the labor market.

Grubb also investigated the value of short-term job training programs often offered by community colleges through federal and state contracts, although they are also offered by a host of other ad hoc institutions supported by government contracts. Since the 1960s short-term job training programs have increased in size and purpose. Grubb sought to evaluate the outcomes of these programs to determine if they were successes or failures in their goals of employment gains, increased annual earnings, and reduction of welfare payments. Overall Grubb found these programs lead to "small but statistically significant increases in employment and earnings and (for welfare recipients) small decreases in welfare payments." Grubb pointed out that "the social benefits usually (but not always) outweigh the costs" (meaning that programs make financial sense in terms of cost-benefit analysis). However, he argued that the personal benefit to individuals is "quite small from a practical standpoint," and any gains are not only "insufficient to move individuals out of poverty or off welfare," but gains also disappear over time. Grubb argued that the modest and trivial gains of job training are not impressive and, further, populations of enrollees such as youths and welfare recipients see negative results, calling into question the overall effectiveness of job training programs for everyone. Grubb also criticized these programs as "too short, too focused on immediate employment rather than on the enhancement of skills, unaware of pedagogical issues, and independent of related efforts." Grubb argued that short-term job training disconnected from mainstream educational institutions and programs seem to be " push[ing] individuals into the labor force without increasing their skills substantially," which can hurt individuals in the long run in access to future education or in finding good careers with the possibility of advancement. He argued that more "*sustained* [italics in original] interventions are necessary to improve the life chances of low-income individuals." Here was Grubb's conclusion:

> The results from nearly thirty years of evaluating job training programs are remarkably consistent—surprisingly so, given the variation in the programs supported and the differences in the methods used to evaluate them. Many job training programs lead to increased earnings, and the benefits to society generally outweigh the costs. However, the increases in earnings, moderate by almost any standards, are insufficient to lift those enrolled in such programs our of poverty. Welfare-to-work programs also increase employment and reduce the amount of welfare payments received, but they rarely allow individuals to leave welfare. Furthermore, any benefits probably fade after four or five years: job training programs do not seem to put many individuals on career trajectories with continued earnings increases, as formal schooling does.

Grubb's recommendation was not to abandon second-chance job training programs but to better coordinate and integrate these programs with mainstream educational institutions, like community colleges, that offer degree programs. Thus, short-term job training programs could be used as a vehicle to attract a significant source of government funds and as the first stage in a coordinated pipeline to longer-term educational goals. However, this idealized educational pipeline rarely becomes reality for most students in these types of programs.

A couple of publications from 1998 to 2001 reached some positive conclusions about the economic returns of subbaccalaureate education in the form of associate's degrees and community college vocational certificates. A collection of studies by Sanchez and Laanan and another study by Grubb revealed some evidence of significant returns for the associate's degree and the vocational certificate. But several studies in the anthology by Sanchez and Laanan seemed to overstate these returns by not properly filtering out several key variables, such as the personal characteristics of students (which can skew actual worth of the credential) and using students' last year in college as the baseline for income comparisons (which can skew actual earnings data because many students are not working full-time while in college). Also, the positive earnings data presented by Sanchez and Laanan seem to be highly dependent on different regional and state economies, which makes national generalizations on earnings potential for subbaccalaureate credentials a problem, but this issue is not adequately discussed.

In the late 1990s Michael B. Paulsen reviewed the literature on the returns of investment in subbaccalaureate credentials, and he found the student populations of subbaccalaureate institutions, largely community colleges and 2-year technical institutes, skewed the labor market value of this type of education and make estimates very "problematic." According to Paulsen, the average community college student who has never attended a 4-year institution and who doesn't even earn a degree sees earnings of about 9 percent to 13 percent greater than a high school graduate with similar background characteristics and no college. One year of community college credit, independent of earning a degree, can lead to an average in increased earnings between 5 percent and 8 percent, and 2 years of credit can lead to 10 percent to 16 percent increased earnings. The effect of a subbaccalaureate education, either a credential or an associate's degree, can lead to earnings increases between 15 percent and 27 percent. The average earning potential is greatest for women and low-income students, but there is evidence to suggest that the average earnings increases for subbaccalaureate credentials may be greatly affected by the significant earning potentials from an associate's degree in nursing.

Other recent analyses of subbaccalaureare credentials are less optimistic than Paulsen's. Kienzl echoed Grubb's conclusions and found that "the economic benefits to a sub-baccalaureate education are unclear or ambiguous" and that a bachelor's degree "remains the most economically beneficial" educational credential. Economic data further corroborate these general, more pessimistic, findings. From 1973 to 2005 in constant 2005 U.S. dollars the real hourly wage for an average worker with only a high school education has decreased from \$14.39 to \$14.14 an hour, while the real hourly wage for an average worker with some college but less than a bachelor's degree increased slightly (less than 0.1 percent) from \$15.50 to \$15.89 an hour. Mishel, Bernstein, and Allegretto argued that the policy of educating low-skilled workers and making them midskilled workers "does not make sense" because "we have too many middle-skilled workers already." Further, they said,

> Given that the wages of entry-level college workers and those of all college graduates have declined or been flat over this business cycle, a strategy of vastly increasing the number of college graduates seems certain to drive down the wages of current and future college graduates. The possibility of increased off-shoring of white-collar work may make such a strategy even more untenable in the future.

Altogether, the economic outlook for the current and future value of subbaccalaureate credentials appears bleak.

In spite of a rhetoric of optimism, the consensus of many scholars on the positive outcomes of vocational education appears to be bleak. Student preparation for and placement in careers have been lauded by all as a noble idea, but there is little evidence over the past century that American schools, especially subbaccalaureate institutions, are particularly successful with these tasks. Indeed, few community colleges have clear and well-developed connections to the labor market, nor do they have a formal understanding of what skills students need, how these skills are measured, and how they should be promoted to future employers. As a result, many subbaccalaureate vocational curricula and short-term job training programs, such as welfare-to-work initiatives, have shown little success in increasing students' employment or earnings. Some scholars have even argued that short-term job training programs can be harmful to certain types of students, decreasing their earnings or welfare support. In sum, little evidence exists to show how well occupational programs prepare students for employment and place them in careers, primarily because few community colleges are able to reliably track students' job placements or advancements. Furthermore, colleges do not yet have a good way of assessing whether vocational programs are teaching students the skills employers want, let alone the lifetime learning skills students need to navigate a rapidly changing American economy.

The subbaccalaureate labor market poses several challenges to developing vocational education and career pathway programs. Employers in this market are frequently small businesses that hire few workers and offer lower salaries and fewer opportunities for advancement than larger organizations. Furthermore, these small businesses are often not well informed about the supply of educated labor; few are in continuous communication with local community colleges or other educational institutions, and they usually have informal hiring practices, which makes it difficult to prepare students for interviews or specific job-hunting skills. Smaller businesses also tend to be more dependent on flexible and multiskilled employees who can cross occupational boundaries to accomplish a job cheaply and with fewer resources. As such, many "of the competencies required by employers in the sub-baccalaureate labor market cannot readily be taught in schools and colleges."

In addition, the subbaccalaureate labor market is dependent upon the highly cyclical nature of demand. This creates unstable employment opportunities, which in turn increases informal hiring policies, which then makes it difficult for job seekers and vocational programs to determine exactly what local employers want and when they want it. These features of the subbaccalaureate labor market make it difficult for community colleges to determine—let alone teach—the skills employers want and need.

Available data are mixed on how well students make the transition into well-paying jobs in the subbaccalaureate labor market. The benefits of vocational education can be maximized if students can enroll in economically viable occupations related to their credentialing, but even then the benefits of vocational credentials are mediated by socioeconomic status, race, gender, and even academic markers such as grades and test scores. And the economic benefits of a vocational degree or certificate decrease the more disconnected community colleges are from regional labor markets and job placement agencies. Overall, the benefits of some college or an associate's degree continue to be unpromising in the United States and may further decrease in value as the number of bachelor's degree holders continues to increase and as the effects of the Great Recession of 2007–2009 run their course.

By the end of 2009 national unemployment rates already exceeded 10 percent, although this number hides recurrent racial disparities, as 16 percent of African Americans were out of work (with over 18% of black men unemployed). The total number of unemployed and underemployed Americans was around 17.5 percent. These numbers also mask the many state and regional variations in the U.S. labor market. By August 2009 California had already exceeded 12 percent unemployment, with certain regions in the state exceeding 15 percent. The labor market reflects long-term inequalities in American society and there are still deeply entrenched differential employment rates according to race, gender, and age. Earnings differentials were noted in the U.S. Census report "Income, Poverty, and Health Insurance Coverage in the United States: 2008," but few news organizations bothered to pass much of this information to the American public. One variation that did receive treatment was age. The national unemployment rate for teenagers reached 25.5 percent in September 2009, the highest rate it had ever been since collection of this data began in 1948. Inflation-adjusted median household income in 2008 had fallen around 3.6 percent, reducing middle-class households to income levels not seen since 1997, and these income levels are expected to drop further by 2010. Latinos saw the greatest reduction in income at 5.6 percent (to $37,913), then Asians at 4.4 percent (to $65,637), African Americans at 2.8 percent (to $34,218), and whites only lost 2.6 percent (to $55,530). Clearly widespread inequality in incomes remains a problem, with the average African American family earning 38 percent less than the average white family. An additional 2.6 million people also fell into poverty in 2008, with Latinos (23.2 percent in poverty) and African Americans (24.7 percent) still disproportionately impoverished. Most likely these numbers will only get worse in 2010 before they get better.

With the massive economic downturn of the past 2 years, even college graduates have been affected. The hiring of new graduates with a bachelor's degree or higher is expected to fall by 22 percent in 2009. Even students with law degrees from top universities are finding it difficult to find jobs because top law firms are cutting new positions by about 50 percent. With jobs so scarce for new graduates, a new avenue of inequality has come to light. College graduates from wealthy families have begun to pay thousands of dollars to buy their way into unpaid internships via private placement firms.

Human capital in the United States has been greatly devalued because of the growing economic inequality of the past 30 years and the current recessionary period. In these tough economic times, community college credentials and certificates may become almost worthless commodities as the economy has greatly contracted. However, thousands of new students and laid-off workers are seeking refuge in this institution. But budgets of community colleges are being slashed, faculty and staff laid off, new hires frozen, and course offerings trimmed. Miami Dade Community College, to take but one example, has lost 18 percent of its funding from 2006 to 2009, about 11 percent just in 2009, and administrators expect about 30,000 students will not be able to enroll in the classes they need or will be turned away completely because enrollment capacities will be exceeded. The paradoxical predicament of the community college has never been greater than now and its future never more uncertain.

President Obama has pledged $12 billion over the next decade to increase community college graduation rates in order to meet the needs of the midskilled labor market, but questions remain. Will this money really be allocated by an overextended federal government dealing with a lingering recession, an astronomical federal deficit, and major health care reform? How will this money be allocated? And with the cutbacks of the last few years, do community colleges have the capacity and resources to meet the growing numbers of students they are expected to serve? And when the president pledges to increase the number of Americans with college degrees, does this generalized pledge simply mean more community college associate's degrees and certificates in a labor market flooded with underemployed and underpaid Americans with bachelor's and advanced degrees?

The uncertainty clouding the American economy has again revealed the contradictions at the heart of the community college and its place in American society. There are no easy answers to any of these questions, and the time has come to admit this hard fundamental truth. If this institution is going to live up to its promise as a gateway to opportunity then its missions will need to be *clarified* through some sort of national consensus of policy makers and practitioners, *unified* through local and regional organizational planning, and *resourced* through increased federal and state fiscal commitments. However, the institutionalized stickiness of the comprehensive and contradictory community college has made it extremely resistant to change. Educational reformers, policy makers, and even administrators often appear as no more than ceremonial figures presiding over a loosely coupled educational institution that seems locked into an incoherent future. Still, faith in the "politics of agency" may yet work wonders, as educators and administrators act on the conviction that the community college can be refashioned into a more equitable and efficient institution of higher education. Modern humanity is defined by such faith: that we can better rationalize and organize social institutions to achieve our ideals. Thus, in the words of a preeminent political philosopher, "We can only do what we can: but that we must do, against difficulties."

CHAPTER 12

STATEWIDE GOVERNANCE STRUCTURES AND TWO-YEAR COLLEGES

RICHARD C. RICHARDSON, JR. AND GERARDO E. DE LOS SANTOS

Most of the literature on the statewide governance and coordination of higher education has historically focused on four-year colleges and universities.[1] Since the 1970s, state governance and coordination of community colleges has been the focus of only a small number of community college specialists.[2] Yet during the past decade, as the 20th century drew to a close, writers looked increasingly at community college issues as part of the larger question of achieving integrated designs that respond in cost-effective ways to the entire range of a state's needs and priorities for higher education. This new focus is overdue. Campus-based and state-level community college practitioners have received little guidance in their efforts to achieve an appropriate balance between growing state accountability concerns and their continuing commitments to the communities they serve. The tension has been aggravated by the failures of both state and local governments to provide adequate funding for enrollment increases, threatening the community college access mission by making users responsible for an ever-increasing share of operating costs.[3]

Adequate state financing is far from the only policy issue confronting community college leaders, and it may not even be the most important. For example, referendums in California and Washington have eliminated affirmative action practices that operate on the basis of race or ethnicity, and courts have challenged such practices in Texas and Michigan. Two of the three largest higher education systems in the country have eliminated remedial education in four-year institutions. One of the early proposals advanced for the City University of New York (CUNY) would have eliminated remedial education in the university's community colleges as well. Some 14 states have initiated or taken under consideration plans similar to the Georgia Hope Scholarships, which award public financial assistance on the basis of merit rather than need. Distance education, credit by examination, greater emphasis on competency-based and proficiency-based learning, and limits on the number of state-subsidized credits that are applicable to degrees not only threaten traditional learning practices, but also call into question the formulas that have been used to allocate resources to community colleges. In every state, legislators call for better K-12 linkages to higher education, improved articulation between two- and four-year institutions, and stronger school-to-work connections. Additionally, the mushrooming costs and capabilities of technology raise questions about service boundaries and interinstitutional collaboration.

While these few examples only begin to identify the complex issues that surround the statewide governance and coordination of higher education, they serve to remind us that state community college governance is laden with ever-changing dynamics and competing interests. Since the inception of public, two-year colleges nearly 100 years ago, administrators have been challenged to walk the "tightrope" of coordination with four-year colleges and universities. Elected state leaders have expected that all publicly funded institutions will work cooperatively instead of competing to admit freshman and sophomore students. More often than not, however, the reality has been competition and protectionism, as manifested in student transfer difficulties and increased costs. Now, under the influence of constrained resources and with the aid of new information technologies, states are moving to address long-standing issues of coordination and collaboration through renewed attention to the linkages between state government and all forms of higher education.

We begin this chapter by tracing the evolution of statewide governance and coordination for community colleges. Next, we propose a way of thinking about statewide structures that takes into account the various approaches states have adopted for coordinating and governing the public two- and four-year institutions they support. We developed the State Community College Governance Structures Typology to compare the strengths and weaknesses of arrangements currently in use across the nation's 50 states in the context of recent developments. In addition, we suggest that some arrangements are better designed than others to respond to the demands of the 21st century. In this regard, we differ from some of our predecessors who have suggested that success or failure in state-level coordination depends more on the philosophy and approach of the state director and staff than on the structure or range of powers of the organization.[4] Finally, we summarize current arrangements and suggest a number of issues that must be considered in the 21st century as states give renewed attention to the chronic problem of how to create integrated and collaborative systems out of the disjointed institutional arrangements that they inherited from the growth era of the 1950s and 1960s.

Historical Perspective

The explosive growth of community colleges during the 1960s, combined with the movement to separate these institutions from the public school districts, under whose auspices many had been founded, led to the establishment, not only of local community college governing boards, but also of new, state-level boards charged with the responsibility for coordinating new systems of community colleges. Examples include Arizona, Illinois, Colorado, Washington, Maryland, North Carolina, and Florida. Other states chose not to establish a specific coordinating board focused exclusively on community colleges, but instead strengthened coordinating arrangements for new or developing community college systems, either through a division within a coordinating board responsible for all educational services (Pennsylvania) or, more commonly, through a board with coordinating responsibilities for all postsecondary education institutions (Missouri, New Jersey, and Texas). Some states (generally the less populated) addressed coordination issues by placing all public institutions under a single governing board (Hawaii, North Dakota, South Dakota, Rhode Island, and Utah).

Prior to the mid-1970s, the activities of state coordinating boards focused primarily on the management of growth. During this era the literature suggests little, if any, criticism of their operations. Beginning in the mid- to late 1970s, however, coordinating boards were called on increasingly to administer legislative interventions and budget cuts, resulting in a marked deterioration of relationships with institutional boards and administrators (Glenny, 1979).

The list of external influences impinging on both local and state boards is a lengthy one. Both local and state boards were increasingly caught in a multifaceted decision-making process, in which ultimate accountability was distorted by the many agencies and interests that intervened. Executive orders, lapsing and allocation procedures, accounting requirements, informational demands, contract controls, legal opinions, audits, and program and budget controls were only some of the influences identified as emanating from a variety of state agencies (Mundt, 1978). During the 1970s and early 1980s, some events that added to these influences include equal access/equal opportunity legislation and regulations, collective bargaining, and proviso language restricting the use of appropriated funds (Owen, 1978). Thus, it is apparent that state coordinating boards were only one part of the web of increasing state regulation about which institutions complained. Furthermore, actions taken by a wide range of state and federal agencies were commonly channeled through state coordinating or governing boards, making them, from an institutional perspective, the most visible constraint on autonomy.

The reasons for the increase in state interest in regulation and accountability during the 1980s and early 1990s were not difficult to discover. Chief among them was the growing importance of community colleges as major users of state revenues. When community colleges derived most of their resources from a local property tax, it was a simple matter for the legislature to control state expenditures by using formula-driven appropriations that changed more slowly than the rate of inflation. In that era, community college leaders complained about being ignored in the legislative process. By the 1980s, with state appropriations running from 75 to 90 percent of the total expenditures for community colleges in many states, these institutions had become major competitors for tax dollars. The stage was set for the accountability movement that came to fruition in many states during the current decade and threatens to become the norm in the 21st century.

Given the nature of community colleges as resource-dependent organizations, the ideal of local autonomy will always be something to be pursued rather than an attainable end. Hence, community college presidents will never have all the autonomy they would like. Many of the regulations adopted by state coordinating boards have their genesis in the requirements of other state and federal agencies. Beyond agency intervention, the magnitude of state tax dollars required to maintain the enterprise guarantees continuing close scrutiny from legislators and governors. Most community college leaders accept the reality of state-level coordination and governance, particularly as it applies to budgeting and allocating resources fairly; being accountable for state appropriated funds; planning for statewide access to an appropriate range of programs, including the use of technology to deliver distance education; assuring barrier-free articulation and transfer; and providing credible information to elected state leaders and the general public about services and performance. Less accepted realities are actions that cap enrollments, require high-stakes tests of student competencies, specify admission eligibility, mandate responsibility for remedial education, limit program or course availability, mandate faculty governance arrangements, or base allocations on state-specified performance criteria.

Given the movement toward increased state coordination during the past two decades, it is not surprising that a considerable amount has been written on how to minimize conflict between state and local boards. The delineation of functions, the approach chosen by California when the board of governors was created in 1969, is particularly appealing because it holds out the promise of preserving the highest degree of local control and autonomy by defining responsibilities so that they appear mutually exclusive and by assigning them to either one board or the other (Clark, 1980). Of course, in real life there is a high degree of interdependence, both between functions and between boards. As a result, the delineation of functions approach worked in California only as long as the board of governors chose not to exercise its prerogatives and the funding arrangements for community colleges placed the major burden on the local property tax. By 1980, however, it was apparent that board functions, as they pertained to issues of mutual responsibility, were paramount. Therefore, the more important question to ask was no longer, "Who did what?" but, rather, "What can we do together that otherwise cannot be done?" (Callan, 1981; Clark, 1980).

Despite calls for state and local boards to work closely together, most writers who have examined the interface between local and state-level boards have not been sanguine about their findings. Tillery and Wattenbarger (1985) described local state relationships as characterized by an inadequate delineation of authority and by the appearance that the state always wins the arguments. A decade later, Tschechtelin (1994) asserted that dualistic advocacy remained a major challenge. State governments expected community colleges to appreciate state priorities and to be accountable, while community college leaders resisted intrusion and valued autonomy while expecting strong financial support.

The functions of governing institutions cannot be defined so as to make them exclusively a local or a state responsibility. Autonomy, rather than an unqualified virtue, is desirable to the extent that those to whom it is granted can demonstrate superior performance. Local boards function to ensure responsiveness to local needs, while state boards ensure accountability for state funds. Communication between state and local boards, as well as among other community college participants, is indispensable to achieving effective results under conditions of interdependency.

Toward a New Typology of State Community College Governance Structures

A recent study of higher-education coordinating and governance arrangements in seven large states developed a new approach to classifying systems based on the answers to two key questions:

- Does the state system have a coordinating board/agency with at least some statutory authority for serving as the interface between higher-education institutions and state government for the four central work processes: budgeting, program planning and approval, information management and dissemination, and articulation and collaboration? (Coordinating boards do not have authority over such decisions as the appointment and removal of presidents or day-to-day management and operation of the institution.)

- Does the state system have more than a single governing board for all of its degree-granting, postsecondary institutions, including community colleges and technical institutes? (Governing boards have legal authority to operate the institution, including appointment and removal of presidents and all other decisions not specifically reserved by the state for purposes of coordination and accountability) (Richardson, Bracco, Callan, & Finney, 1998).

If the answer to the first question is "yes," then the state higher-education system is classified as "federal" because policy makers have chosen to separate the powers of institutional governance and advocacy from responsibility for representing the public interest in a way that reflects the influences of federalism in the U.S. Constitution.[5]

If the answer to the first question is "no," then we move to the second question. If the answer to the second question is "no," then the system is unified. If the answer to the second question is "yes," then the system is classified as segmented. Institutions in segmented systems are divided into two or more sectors, each with its own governing arrangements. There is considerable variation among states in the degree of segmentation, ranging from Michigan, where almost every institution has its own governing board, to states such as Florida and Arizona, where there may be only a single governing board for all public four-year institutions.

We can summarize the three basic designs that the answers to these questions yield:

- Segmented systems have two or more governing boards that supervise single institutions or groupings of institutions. No single statewide agency has statutory authority over all four of the key coordinating work processes: budgeting; program planning and approval; articulation; and providing information to elected policy officials and the general public.

- Unified systems place all degree-granting, public higher-education institutions under a single governing board, which works directly with the governor and the legislature on budgeting; program planning and approval; articulation; and determining the available information about capacity and performance.

- Federal systems organize degree-granting, public institutions under some range of governing boards that are required to work directly with a statewide coordinating board with legislatively delegated authority for representing the public interest in such key areas as budgeting, program planning and approval, articulation and collaboration, and information collection and reporting.

So far, our classification system has considerable overlap with the most widely used taxonomy, which was published by the Education Commission of the States (1997). While the most recent version of this sourcebook gives expanded treatment, over earlier versions, to associate degree institutions, the publication still provides less clarity about state governance of community colleges than is desirable for our purposes. The typology developed in this chapter draws sharper distinctions among state governing and coordinating arrangements for community colleges by asking the same two questions for community colleges that we earlier asked about the entire state system:

- Do community colleges and technical institutes have a coordinating board/agency with some statutory authority for serving as the interface between these institutions and state government in such key areas as budgeting, program planning and approval, articulation and collaboration, and information collection and reporting? If the answer is "yes," then the community college system is classified as federal. If the answer is "no," then we move to the next question.

- Does the state system of community colleges and technical institutes have more than one governing board? If the answer is "no," then the system is unified. If the answer is "yes," then the system is segmented.

TABLE 1

Conceptual Model of State Structures for Community Colleges

	State Governance and Coordinating Arrangements for All Higher Education		
	FEDERAL	**UNIFIED**	**SEGMENTED**
	FEDERAL 1 [2]	FEDERAL N/A	FEDERAL 5 [10]
	UNIFIED 2 [7]	UNIFIED 4 [9]	UNIFIED 6 [7]
	SEGMENTED 3 [11]	SEGMENTED N/A	SEGMENTED 7 [5]

(Row label, left vertical: State Governance and Coordinating Arrangements for Community Colleges)

The answers to these two sets of questions create a 3 × 3 table that permits grouping all 50 state systems into seven categories. Since state systems are not as neat as our taxonomy, we have had to make a number of "judgment calls" about where to place specific states that exhibit characteristics of more than one category. Our reasons for these judgments are explained more fully in the comments on strengths and weaknesses.

The table above shows the seven possible conceptual categories. Unified state systems, by definition, cannot have federal or segmented arrangements for community colleges. The numbers in brackets in each cell indicate the number of states using that arrangement. The bracketed numbers total to 51 because New York appears in both the segmented federal and the segmented unified cells.

Applying the Typology

In this section of the chapter, we discuss groupings in the order in which they appear in Table 1.

Federal/Federal States. Only two states, Illinois and Washington, have a coordinating board for all higher education, a separate statewide coordinating structure for community colleges, and local governing boards. In Washington, the governor appoints local boards, the community college coordinating board, and the coordinating board for all higher education. This arrangement seems to produce fewer jurisdictional problems than in Illinois, where local board members are elected. Significantly, however, the governor's 2020 Commission recently recommended narrowing the authority and responsibilities of the Washington Higher Education Coordinating Board (governor's 2020 Commission, 1998). In 1995, the coordinating board for all higher education in Illinois (IBHE) rearranged the priorities for capital projects submitted to it by the state community college board. This action precipitated an effort by some community college leaders and legislators to remove the community college board from the jurisdiction of the IBHE. The legislation passed both chambers by wide margins but was vetoed by the governor. Nonetheless, it was widely interpreted as a wake-up call for the IBHE to exercise greater sensitivity to the concerns and priorities of community colleges.

Two state-level coordinating boards, one reporting to the other, represent a considerable amount of state oversight for institutions that have, in addition, their own local governing boards. Illinois adopted this arrangement in 1965, and Washington, in 1967. Maryland had a comparable arrangement between 1988 and 1992, when it abolished a state board for community colleges that had been established in 1969. While state higher-education systems seem likely to receive more, rather than less, planning and collaboration in the 21st century, there are clearly limits on the amount of state bureaucracy that can be expected to add enough value to offset its costs and complexity. While current arrangements seem to work reasonably well in both Illinois and Washington, these states are probably at the outer limits of cost-effective state governance and coordination.

Federal/Unified States. Seven states, Alabama, Colorado, Connecticut, Kentucky, Massachusetts, Tennessee, and Virginia, have statewide coordinating boards for all higher education and a single statewide governing board for community colleges and technical institutes. In Massachusetts and Tennessee, the statewide governing board for community colleges also oversees a system of four-year colleges and universities, excluding the state's flagship university. The Massachusetts Board of Higher Education, which governs community and state colleges, also serves as a coordinating board for the University of Massachusetts system. In Colorado, three small community colleges still retain their locally elected governing boards, but most of the state's community colleges are governed by the statewide board, which is appointed by the governor. The trend in Colorado seems to be in the direction of having all community colleges governed by a single board.

Kentucky established its statewide governing board for community colleges only within the past year. Previously, community colleges were part of the University of Kentucky system. None of these states (with the exception of Colorado) has any tradition of local governing boards. In states where community colleges have been governed by the same board that governs some four year institutions (Kentucky, Massachusetts, and Tennessee), there is evidence that community colleges have been held back in their development or less well utilized than in states where they have their own governing arrangements. Certainly this was a factor in the changes that were made in Kentucky, and it was a part of the recent discussions by a special higher-education study committee in Tennessee ("Sunquist Targets Higher Education Reform," 1998). The advantages of statewide governance in an age of technology can be clearly seen in the Colorado Electronic Community College, an imaginative organization that would not have been feasible in the absence of structural arrangements that permitted the pooling of resources across a state system of collaborating institutions.

Federal/Segmented States. Eleven states, Arkansas, Indiana, Louisiana, Maryland, Missouri, Nebraska, New Jersey, Ohio, Oklahoma, South Carolina, and Texas, have both a statewide board that coordinates all higher education and more than one community college or technical institute with its own governance arrangement; this is, by a slim margin, the arrangement most frequently observed. States using this approach are highly diverse, ranging from such relatively well-developed and orderly systems as those in Maryland, Missouri, New Jersey, and Texas to the mixed models in Arkansas, Louisiana, Ohio, and South Carolina, where evolutionary combinations of two-year branch campuses, community colleges, technical institutes, and their diverse state and local governing arrangements often defy description.

Indiana really deserves its own category. In the 1960s, an influential president of the University of Indiana succeeded in blocking the development of Indiana community colleges. One corollary has been the state's consistently poor college-going rates, a performance that numerous grants awarded by the Lilly Endowment have done little to change. Very recently, the governor proposed that the state's sole community college (Vincennes University Junior College) should collaborate with the state's system of technical colleges (Ivy Tech) to offer comprehensive community college services across the state.

The consequences of high levels of segmentation in the absence of a coherent state plan for comprehensive, two-year, postsecondary services can be observed even in some of the more orderly systems. Oklahoma, Texas, and Louisiana have a history of legislatively converting two-year colleges into four-year institutions. Oklahoma provides the most recent example in the conversion of Rogers University to four-year status. Louisiana may finally overcome some of the legacy of its dual system as it moves to implement the statewide community college system adopted in 1998. If federal/federal models provide too much of a good thing, then the more chaotic federal/segmented systems may well provide too little.

Unified States. Nine states, Alaska, Hawaii, Idaho, Montana, Nevada, North Dakota, Rhode Island, South Dakota, and Utah have a single board that governs all degree-granting institutions of higher education. These states tend to be less populated and to have fewer institutions and less complex systems.

There is considerable diversity in unified systems, and even some anomalies. For example, the community college in Valdez retained independent status when other Alaskan community colleges were swept into the University of Alaska system in the mid-1980s. In Idaho, a single board governs both K-12 and higher education. Some elected leaders in Idaho argue that this arrangement has contributed to the state's failure to a develop coherent system of community colleges. In Montana, a 1994 reorganization merged former vocational technical centers into two of the state's universities and strengthened the powers of the board of regents, which functions as the governing board for all four-year public institutions. However, the board exercises primarily coordinating authority over the state's community colleges, which continue to be governed by locally elected boards. Although South Dakota does have several technical institutes that operate under local boards, there are no public community colleges in the state. In Rhode Island, a single community college operates a number of campuses statewide. Many of the Western states in this category have tribally controlled community colleges that are primarily funded by the federal government. Typically, such institutions are not involved in state coordination activities.

Unified systems seem to serve the needs of their respective states effectively. No state using this arrangement has chosen to modify it other than by providing greater authority to the central governing authority. Some states encourage greater responsiveness to local needs by providing for appointed boards at each institution to which the unified board delegates specified authority. As was the case in the federal/unified structure, boards with the responsibility for governing both two- and four-year institutions may be tempted to neglect the needs and development of the former in order to have more resources available for baccalaureate and graduate programs.

Segmented/Federal States. Ten states, Arizona, California, Florida, Georgia, Kansas, Mississippi, New York (State University of New York), North Carolina, Wisconsin, and Wyoming have two or more governing boards for higher-education institutions, along with a coordinating or governing board for community or technical colleges. Nine of the states in this category and all of those in the two that follow have no single statewide agency, either governing or coordinating, with delegated authority for all higher-education institutions in the key decision areas of budgeting, program planning and approval, articulation and collaboration, and information collection and dissemination. Only Kansas, with its 1999 legislatively mandated system redesign, has designated the board that governs four-year institutions as a coordinating board for community colleges and technical institutes, which also retain their own local governing boards. This arrangement is similar to one used by New York, which we have listed both here and in the segmented/unified category because all public institutions in that state are divided into two heterogeneous systems, each with its own governing board. Both two-and-four-year institutions outside the city of New Your make up the State University of New York (SUNY). In SUNY, each community college is governed by an appointed local board, and the board of trustees of SUNY serves as a coordinating board for all SUNY community colleges. The City University of New York (CUNY) is a unified system in which community colleges, baccalaureate and master's degree–granting institutions, and a graduate center are all governed by the same appointed board.

The degree of segmentation in these nine states varies considerably. Arizona, Florida, Georgia, Mississippi. North Carolina, Wisconsin, and Wyoming have only two statewide boards, with one governing all public four-year institutions and the other coordinating or governing a system of community or technical colleges. Kansas has a single statewide board that governs both systems. Georgia operates a postsecondary vocational education system under the auspices of the state board of technical and adult education, as well as 15 public two-year degree-granting colleges that are governed by the Board of Regents of the University System of Georgia. A similar arrangement in Wisconsin assigns responsibility for governing all four-year institutions and most campuses offering the first two years of a baccalaureate program to the Board of Regents of the University of Wisconsin system. Technical colleges, including the three that offer college transfer programs, have their own governing boards and receive statewide coordination in selected areas from the Wisconsin Board of Vocational, Technical and Adult Education.

California divides its four-year institutions into two segments, each with its own governing board. Community colleges have elected governing boards, and the community college segment is coordinated by a board of governors. Both California and Florida have weak statewide coordinating agencies, which have some advisory responsibilities for all higher education, including community colleges. States with this governing arrangement have experienced a variety of problems that seem related both to the nature of their local governance arrangements and to the absence of a statewide structure with enough authority to accomplish meaningful coordination for all higher education. Articulation between two- and four-year institutions remains an issue for most of these states, although less so in states like Georgia, New York, and Washington, where a single board has at least some responsibility for both two- and four-year institutions. The hope for improved articulation was certainly a factor in the approach to system redesign chosen by Kansas.

Community college governance is perhaps most controversial in California, where a board with essentially coordinating powers (Board of Governors of the California Community Colleges) thinks, and sometimes acts, like a governing board and locally elected boards of trustees have the responsibility for negotiating collective bargaining agreements with employee unions, which are largely responsible for their election. Since the passage of Proposition 13, however, these same boards no longer have responsibility for raising local tax rates to pay for the generous agreements they negotiate. A legislative attempt to fix the problems in 1988 by mandating "shared governance" simply made matters worse in the opinion of most community college leaders. By the late 1990s, knowledgeable observers were questioning whether some California community college districts had become ungovernable. A recent citizen's commission has recommended extensive changes, including the elimination of locally elected boards and the negotiation of collective bargaining agreements on a statewide basis (California Citizens Commission on Higher Education in the Twenty-First Century, 1998).

Florida is often cited as one of the states most subject to legislative micromanagement. Long noted for its CLAST (rising junior) exam, the state recently implemented one of the first performance funding plans for community colleges. Florida also has more legislation applying to student transfer between community colleges and universities than any other state, although California runs a close second. Higher-education leaders in New York have questioned the wisdom of having the same board that governs one of the nation's largest higher education systems also serve as a coordinating board for a very large system of locally governed community colleges.

The combination of locally elected boards and a statewide community college coordinating board is clearly one of the most volatile arrangements for community college governance. States with appointed local boards (Florida, New York, Mississippi, Georgia, and North Carolina) seem to report fewer jurisdictional problems and appear to provide more examples of interinstitutional collaboration than combination states like Arizona, California, and Wyoming.

Segmented/Unified States. Seven states, Delaware, Maine, Minnesota, New Hampshire, New York (CUNY), Vermont, and West Virginia have two or more statewide governing boards for higher education, one of which has responsibility for community colleges or technical institutions. Only Delaware, Maine, and New Hampshire have separate governing boards for community colleges or technical institutes. In the remaining four states, community colleges are governed by a board that also has responsibility for baccalaureate and graduate degree–granting institutions. This arrangement is very recent in Minnesota, which merged separate state college and community college systems in 1995, and relatively new in West Virginia, which adopted similar arrangements in 1989.

In none of these states is there any tradition of local governance for community colleges. Delaware, like Rhode Island, is served by a single community college that operates multiple campuses. The Community College of Vermont operates statewide, but in a noncampus format. Vermont also has a two-year residential technical college. The extremes in population, demographics, rural/urban character, and geographic size characterizing these states suggest that they have adopted relatively centralized forms of state governance to address unique population needs under conditions of resource constraint. Recent adoptions of this structural arrangement suggest the continuing search in many states for designs that promise the most services for the least cost.

Segmented/Segmented States. Five states, Iowa, Michigam, New Mexico, Oregon, and Pennsylvania, have two or more governing boards for higher education, local governing boards for community colleges, and no statewide colleges and technical institutes. All of these states except New Mexico assign some coordinating or regulatory responsibilities for community colleges to state hoards that also have responsibility for coordinating and regulating K-12 education. Judging from recent efforts in Kansas and Iowa to create specific boards charged with the sole responsibility for overseeing community colleges and technical institutes, state governance arrangements that call for the same board to oversee both K-12 and postsecondary institutions work no better now than they did in the 1950s and 1960s, when many junior colleges were governed by the same boards that were responsible for public schools.

Of all the states, New Mexico has one of the least systematic approaches to providing postsecondary services. Three of the state's universities operate their own systems of state-funded two-year branch campuses. There is a unique residential two-year college with its own board, appointed by the governor. The cities of Hobbs and Farmington operate comprehensive community colleges with locally elected boards that levy property taxes to pay for the same types of services the state funds in other communities. The same pattern is followed by the former vocational technical institutes in Albuquerque and Luna, which now have the status of locally controlled community colleges. Santa Fe, thanks to a special legislative dispensation, seems to have the best of both possible worlds, with state funding and a locally elected board. This description scarcely does justice to the full range of institutional arrangements to which the state's weak coordinating agency, the commission on higher education, is charged with bringing coherence. Not the least of the problems caused by this approach involves the criteria for deciding where services are to be provided. Institutions compete to provide services where revenues exceed costs and seek to avoid areas where costs exceed revenues. Many people in New Mexico believe this arrangement gives excessive weight to market forces.

States in the segmented/segmented category give the appearance of a work in progress. Community colleges in Pennsylvania receive little leadership, guidance, or advocacy from the state board. Those colleges that have the misfortune of operating under school district sponsorship must devote large amounts of time and energy to securing approval from their members for budgets that include no more than 15 to 20 percent of local tax dollars. In Michigan, all two-year, and most four-year, institutions have their own governing boards. All four-year institutions have constitutional status; only voluntary arrangements exist for coordination and collaboration. Statewide articulation policies are spelled out in a voluntary 1978 agreement developed by the Michigan Association of Collegiate Registrars and Admission Officers, which has never been signed by the University of Michigan. In the absence of any effective mechanism for encouraging institutional responsiveness to state priorities, legislators and citizens must be satisfied with whatever programs and services institutions decide to deliver.

Segmented/segmented systems are at the opposite extreme from their federal/federal counterparts. Boards of Education preoccupied with K-12 problems seem able to devote only regulatory attention to the postsecondary institutions that they have been assigned, almost by default. Only the governor and the legislature have ongoing, statewide responsibilities for making certain that state resources in aggregate are wisely used and for ensuring that the sum of what institutions deliver is equal to what citizens need. If federal/federal designs provide more coordination than absolutely essential, it seems likely that segmented/segmented systems provide considerably less.

Summing Up

As this chapter shows, state-level higher education coordination and governance arrangements can vary significantly from state to state, and the issues that surround such coordination are often complex and dynamic. Here we summarize arrangements and suggest a number of important issues that states must address in the 21st century.

Almost half the nation's states (23) have chosen to have community colleges and technical institutes governed by a single statewide board to which all higher-education institutions report. In 15 of these states, two-year institutions are part of consolidated systems that also include at least some of the state's four-year institutions. While these states seem well positioned to respond to the requirements for articulation and collaboration that will confront all systems in the 21st century, boards with combined responsibilities for two- and four-year institutions often fail to make optimum use of the two-year sector, thus leading to problems in both coherence and efficiency. Community colleges and technical institutes provide access and school-to-work solutions that their more traditional four-year counterparts rarely develop. Community colleges and technical institutes also provide these functions at lower cost than four-year institutions, and with greater flexibility and shorter lead times. Boards that supervise both two- and four-year institutions sometimes spend more time refereeing disputes over students, programs, and fiscal resources than worrying about how to best serve the public interest.

Eleven states have created coordinating boards that focus exclusively on community colleges. An additional 19 states assign responsibility for coordinating community colleges to a statewide board that also has responsibility for all public higher education. These 30 states include most of the largest and most complex higher education systems in the country.

As they confront the challenges of the 21st century, states that have used federal principles in the design of their governance systems for community colleges will enjoy three inherent advantages. First, federal systems are dynamic. Through frequent, smaller adjustments, they avoid the major restructuring that segmented and unified systems must occasionally undergo as the price for their capacity to resist change. Second, federal systems divide responsibility for representing the public interest from institutional advocacy, leaving the latter to governing boards and assigning the former to the coordinating board. This arrangement is more realistic than expecting the same board to do both. Finally, federal systems have empowered a statewide agency with the capacity to provide leadership on such key 21st-century issues as collaboration in the use of technology and in achieving barrier-free access and mobility for increasingly diverse student populations.

However, states with federal systems do not face the millennium free from the need to address some very pressing problems. A number of states with federal systems, either for community colleges or for all institutions, confront problems of coherence and system development. Some have strange combinations of technical institutes, community colleges, and branch campuses that suggest more attention was paid to political compromise than to planning or the public interest. Some states, like Indiana, are simply cases of arrested development. Others have elected local governing boards that worry more about defending their turf from state incursions than about finding ways to collaborate with other colleges to effectively and efficiently serve the needs of their constituencies. Also, states where collective bargaining legislation or taxpayer initiatives have drastically altered the environment for higher education often lack ways of making complementary changes in the way colleges are governed.

Now that Kansas has moved into the segmented/federal category, only five states have segmented community college systems operating in segmented structures involving all of higher education. On the basis of their own assessments, as well as ours, this group of states seems the least well positioned to respond to the challenges of a new century. Their arrangements incorporate many of the problems and few of the advantages we reported for other designs. With the exception of Michigan, where legislators talk about higher education as the fourth branch of state government and seem resigned to accepting whatever the institutions choose to deliver, these states seem likely candidates for change.

All states will face complex issues in the 21st century, but some will have to do so with the disjointed, underdeveloped, and inefficient community college systems inherited from the 20th century. Predictably, such states will have more difficulty in producing relevant and efficient responses than states that bring with them from the past quarter-century more coherent and responsive systems. In the 21st century, all states will need better integrated, more synergistic, and less bureaucratic state governance arrangements to meet the issues already visible on the horizon. Those that have not yet developed coherent and efficient systems will need to do so quickly or fall even further behind in the global competition that they are already experiencing. The recent attention devoted to restructuring in such states as Indiana, Iowa, Kansas, Kentucky, and Louisiana offers evidence that at least some policy makers in these and other states share this assessment. We hope the conceptual perspectives offered in this chapter will he helpful to elected and appointed higher education leaders in all states as they confront the increasingly important tasks of assessing and modifying their systems of higher education to keep them both competitive and responsive to the public interest.

Notes

1. See, as examples, the following: L Glenny (1971), *Coordinating higher education for the '70's* (Berkeley: University of California at Berkeley, Berkeley Center for Research and Development in Higher Education); R. O, Berdahl (1971), *Statewide coordination of higher education* (Washington, DC: American Council on Education); J. D. Millett (1984), *Conflict in higher education: State government coordination and versus institutional independence* (San Francisco, CA: Jossey-Bass); E. B. Shick, R. I Novak, J. A. Norton, and H. G. Elam (1992), *Shared visions of public higher education: Structures and leadership styles that work* (Washington, DC: American Association of State Colleges and Universities); T. J. MacTaggert et al. (1998). *Seeking excellence through independence: Liberating colleges and universities from excessive regulation* (San Francisco, CA: Jossey-Bass).
2. The best known include L. W. Bender, S. V. Martorana, and J. L. Wattenbarger.
3. D. Campbell, L. Leverty, and K. Sayles (1996), "Funding for community colleges: Changing patterns of support," Chapter 8 in *A Struggle to Survive: Funding Higher Education in the Next Century*, edited by D. S. Honeyman, J. L. Wattenbarger, and K. C. Westbrook (Thousand Oaks, CA: Corwin Press) document these trends and point out the degree to which available data is skewed by the California experience.
4. See, for example, L. W. Bender's (1975) *The states, communities, and control of the community college* (Washington, DC: American Association of Community Colleges). The more contemporary study by Schick et al. (1992), *Shared vision of public education*, reached a similar conclusion.
5. See C. Handy's (1992, November/December) 1992 "Balancing corporate power: A new Federalist Paper," *Harvard Business Review, 70*(6), pp. 59–72, for an extended discussion of concepts underlying the idea of the federal model.

References

California Citizens Commission on Higher Education in the Twenty-first Century. (1998). *A state of learning.* Los Angeles. Center for Governmental Studies.

Callan, P. M. (1981). Declaring interdependence. *AGB Reports, 23*(1), 30–31.

Clark, G. W. (1980). *The essentials of local autonomy: A contemporary focus on control and responsibility.* Sacramento: California Community and Junior College Association.

Education Commission of the States. (1997). *State postsecondary education structures sourcebook: State coordinating and governing boards.* Denver, CO: Education Commission of the States.

Glenny, L. (1979). The state budget process: Roles and responsibilities. In F. F. Hlarcleroad (Ed.), *Financing postsecondary education in the 1980s* (pp. 35–45). Tucson, AZ: Center for the Study of Higher Education.

Governor's 2020 Commission on the Future of Post-Secondary Edcuation. (October 1998). *Learning for life.* Olympia, WA: Governor's Executive Policy Office.

Mundt, J. C. (1978). State vs. local control: Reality and myth over concern for local autonomy. In C. F. Searle (Ed.), *Balancing state and local control* (New Directions for Community Colleges, No. 23, pp. 49–61). San Francisco: Jossey-Bass.

Owen, H. J. (1978). Balancing state and local control in Florida's community colleges. In C. F. Searle (Ed.), *Balancing state and control* (New Directions for Community Colleges. No. 23, pp. 25–31), San Francisco: Jossey-Bass

Richardson. R. C. Bracco, K. R., Callan, P. M., & Finney, J. E. (1998), *Designing state higher education systems for a new century.* Phoenix, AZ: Oryx Press.

Sundquist targets higher education reform as showpiece for second term, (1998). *The Tennessee Journal, 24*(23), 1–2.

Tillery. D., & Wattenbarger. J. L. (1985). State power in a new era: Threats to local authority. In W. L. Deegan & J. F. Gollattscheck, (Eds.), *Ensuring effective governance* (New Directions for Community Colleges, 49, 13, pp. 5–23). San Francisco: Jossey-Sass.

Tschechtelin. J. D. (1994). The community college and the state. In A. M. Cohen & F. B. Brawer (Eds.), *Managing community colleges* (pp. 101–122). San Francisco, CA: Jossey-Bass.

SECTION III

ORGANIZATION, ADMINISTRATIVE LEADERSHIP, AND FINANCE

SECTION III: ORGANIZATION, ADMINISTRATIVE LEADERSHIP, AND FINANCE

Community colleges, like their four-year counterparts, are complex and diverse organizations. As now recognized by the updated Carnegie Classifications, community colleges are geographically diverse (urban, suburban, and rural), are of varying sizes (from very large to very small), and have a variety of undergraduate programs beyond associate degrees that range from certificates to baccalaureate programs. There are also multi-campus community colleges, those that serve over 100,000 students per year, those with residential status which indicate that students live on campus, and those with a few buildings and a handful of academic programs. The diversity is relevant to how community colleges are organized, led, and financed through federal and state systems.

Who will lead America's community colleges in the future is of great concern given that the majority of current community college presidents are reaching retirement age. This is particularly significant given that community colleges are under increased pressure to enroll larger numbers of students while improving transfer and graduation rates to support a more educated workforce. The climate for state and federal funding adds another layer to the complexity as funding has yet to provide the support needed to educate current students and fulfill federal, state, and philanthropic efforts to increase the number of Americans with a college education or experience. Community colleges are being called on to do more without the financial support necessary to support larger numbers of students.

In this section, we present six chapters that address conceptualizations, qualifications, and definitions of leadership that apply to community college presidents and trustees who have a responsibility for the success of the institutions. We also present articles that explain and critique the complex nature of funding. Each of these chapters provides evidence and arguments that illustrate the connections between leadership, organization, and funding.

Chapter Thirteen, "Emerging definitions of leadership in higher education: New visions of leadership or same old 'hero' leader?," by Eddy and VanDerLinden begins the discussion of leadership in community colleges with a review of the leadership literature with attention to the notions of "heroic" leadership. The authors question if more contemporary, alternative notions of leadership impact if leaders define and describe their leadership philosophy and practices. The focus of their study is the discourse community colleges leaders use to describe their own leadership philosophies and style.

Chapter Fourteen, "Revisioning leadership in community colleges" by Amey and Twombly continues the discussion of community college leadership by Eddy and VanDerLinden in Chapter Thirteen. Amey and Twombly focus on the images and rhetoric of leadership found in published and unpublished conference materials provided by national associations and conclude that leadership continues to be aligned with "great men" theories; the examples of exemplary leadership focus on just a few great leaders that shaped community colleges early on. Their study has implications for perceptions of leadership behavior, desired leadership characteristics, and notions of leader competencies as well as constructions of gender and leadership. For those interested in gender and leadership, this is a must read.

Plinske and Packard, authors of Chapter Fifteen, "Trustees' perceptions of the desired qualifications for the next generation of community college presidents," focus on community college trustees who have the authority for hiring community college presidents. They use a Delphi process to examine what characteristics, competencies, and experiences trustees seek in presidential candidates. Comparing data from 1969 to 2008, they found that expectations remain largely unchanged with trustees seeking presidents who are experienced, energetic, well respected, and married. The chapter concludes with recommendations for current and aspiring presidents, boards of trustees, and national associations and professional organizations.

In Chapter Sixteen, Dowd and Grant, "Equity and efficiency of community college appropriations: The role of local financing," turn our attention to how community colleges are funded to provide a national perspective of community college funding patterns. Their intention is to identify the role of local finance in creating inequity across the community college sector. They examine local and state appropriations, tuition, and fees, which are the largest sources of revenues for community colleges to document disparities across states. While their focus is on high funding states, their analysis has implications for all community colleges.

Chapter Seventeen, "The moving target: Student financial aid and community college student retention," authored by Kennamer, Katsinas, and Schumacker make the connection among student enrollment, retention, and financial aid. Their analysis of changes in state and local funding from 2000 to 2006 uses national data and refutes the thesis that student financial aid alone is a retention tool. The modest increases in federal direct grant aid, for example, lessen the ability for financial aid to influence student retention due to the high tuition increases and large enrollment increases at community colleges. This analysis identifies the interconnectedness of federal policy decisions on individual institutions and student success.

Chris Mullin, "Doing more with less: The inequitable funding of community colleges," in Chapter Seventeen has a similar purpose to that of Dowd and Grant in Chapter Sixteen. Mullin argues that increasing the role of community college in the postsecondary educational attainment of Americans must be accompanied with increased resources for community colleges. He outlines funding inequity across different community college types and the consequences of those inequities. Recommendations for policy conclude this chapter.

Section III of this volume complicates notions of leadership and presents compelling evidence of the impact of and inequity in funding structures for community colleges. Many of the chapters also challenge public perception that community colleges are simple and small organizations with little diversity among the colleges. This section is an important read for those who work in, research, and seek to understand this sector of higher education.

CHAPTER 13

EMERGING DEFINITIONS OF LEADERSHIP IN HIGHER EDUCATION: NEW VISIONS OF LEADERSHIP OR SAME OLD "HERO" LEADER?

PAMELA L. EDDY
CENTRAL MICHIGAN UNIVERSITY, MOUNT PLEASANT

KIM E. VANDERLINDEN
STUDENTVOICE, BUFFALO, NEW YORK

The higher education literature suggests that alternative leadership styles are replacing the traditionally held definitions of leadership and provide new and different (and possibly superior) ways to understand leadership. This article looks for parallels within the current leadership literature to see if community college administrators use the alternative language or emerging definitions of leadership to self-describe their own leadership or if their self-descriptions fit the more traditional hierarchical ideal of the positional or "hero" leader.

Keywords: leadership styles, positional leader, leadership development, administrators

Challenges and opportunities exist simultaneously in the administrative and leadership ranks of our colleges and universities. The current context of higher education is shaped by the decline of institutional resources (Johnstone, 1999), changing student demographics (Hurtado & Dey, 1997), shifts in teaching to student-centered learning (Barr & Tagg, 1995), the impact of technology on faculty roles (Baldwin, 1998), and the paradigm shift from an industrial age to an information age (Dolence & Norris, 1995). The historical demand-response nature of community colleges pushes for strategic responses on the part of leaders (Gumport, 2003). Although the calls for leadership to address challenges and take advantage of opportunities are not new, the emerging definitions of what it means to be an institutional leader or practice leadership are changing.

Throughout the last half of the 20th century, scholars spent considerable time postulating the requirements for and definitions of leadership. A scan of recent books published in higher education literature suggests that an interest in leadership continues to prevail (see, for example, Astin & Astin, 2000; Bowen & Shapiro, 1998; Chliwniak, 1997; Davis, 2003; Nidiffer, 2001). In addition to investing much time and energy studying leadership in the academy, colleges and universities, as well as local, state, and national associations and organizations, have devoted valuable resources to fund and send campus members to leadership training workshops and programs. In 2003, for example, the American Association of Community Colleges offered a Future Leaders Institute. The Institute targeted senior administrators and had the stated objectives of instilling the skills, knowledge, and attitudes necessary for successful leaders. Yet with all these expended resources and pursuits, a question remains: Have the traditionally held definitions of leaders and leadership changed substantially within the ranks of administrative leaders?

The literature suggests that alternative leadership styles are replacing the traditionally held definitions of leadership and provide new and different (and possibly superior) ways to understand leadership. According to Davis (2003), leadership has been recognized as an activity that can "bubble up" in various places within institutions and no longer is only focused on formal leadership roles. Discussions of leadership throughout the organization (Peterson, 1997), team leadership (Bensimon & Neumann, 1993), servant leadership (Greenleaf, 1977; Spears & Lawrence, 2003), transformative leadership (Burns, 1978), inclusive leadership (Helgesen, 1995), and the role of followership (Kelley, 1998) have replaced the traditional discussions of the "great man" or "hero" leader.

Alternative definitions of leadership demand rethinking the traditional images and the traditional relationships associated with leaders and followers (Green, 1997). Central to this rethinking is the transition from theoretical discussions of appropriate leadership to the actual practice of leadership at colleges and universities. To that end, this article looks for parallels within current leadership literature to see if community college administrators use the alternative language or emerging definitions of leadership to self-describe their own leadership or if their self-descriptions fit the more traditional hierarchical ideal of the positional or "hero" leader. The following research questions are addressed:

1. How do community college administrators self-report their leadership role at their institutions?

2. Do female and male administrators use similar language and categories when describing themselves as leaders?

3. Do administrators have varying views of their leadership based on administrative position?

Addressing these questions will illuminate the challenge of applying the leadership rhetoric advanced in higher education discourses to the actual institutional settings in which leaders find themselves.

Literature Review

The literature on leadership is as plentiful as it is diverse. Several definitions of leadership as well as theories of leadership exist. Some authors strive for a concise definition and understanding of leadership. For example, according to Davis (2003), the term *leadership* implies movement, taking the organization or some part of it in a new direction, solving problems, being creative, initiating new programs, building organizational structures, and improving quality (p. 4). Others, however, struggle with the complexity of leadership. Bass and Stogdill (1990) reported on more than 3,000 empirical investigations of leadership, which provided varied conceptions of what leadership means. In light of the lack of precision regarding leadership definitions, Birnbaum (1992) said, "Any comprehensive consideration of academic leadership must be able to accommodate both the strong leader and the weak leader views, because evidence suggests that while both may be incomplete, both are in some measure correct" (p. 8).

Rost (1991) noted that traditional leadership scholars and the theories they developed were concerned with the peripheries of leadership, such as traits, personality characteristics, and whether leaders are born or made. Rost went on to explain that leadership scholars are interested in the components of leadership and what leaders need to know to be influential in an organization. Less research has been "aimed at understanding the essential nature of what leadership is, and the processes whereby leaders and followers relate to one another to achieve a purpose" (p. 4). In the postindustrial era, Rost argued, change would be undergirded by values such as collaboration, common good, global concern, diversity and pluralism in structures and participation, client orientation, civic virtues, freedom of expression in all organizations, critical dialogue, qualitative language and methodologies, substantive justice, and consensus-oriented policy-making processes. An understanding of leadership within the realm of higher education relies upon the spectrum of various leadership theories purported over time and across disciplines. In early discussions of leadership, definitions and understandings coalesced around the 19th-century notion of the "great men" and their impact on society (Heifetz, 1994). Bensimon, Neumann, and Birnbaum (1989) completed a comprehensive exploration of the theories and models of leadership within higher education. These authors classified the theories into the following six categories: trait theories, power and influence theories, behavioral theories, contingency theories, cultural and symbolic theories, and cognitive theories. Several aspects of these theories are relevant to community college leadership discussions.

Leadership Within Community Colleges

Community colleges, perhaps more so than 4-year institutions, are facing what some call a leadership crisis, as some 79% of 2-year college presidents plan to retire in the next 8 years (Evelyn, 2001; Schults, 2001; Weisman & Vaughan, 2002). This projected rapid turnover in administrative positions, however, presents an opportunity to "bring in fresh blood at a time when two-year colleges face increasingly complex demands" (Evelyn, 2001, p. A36) and may present an opportunity to embrace new and emerging definitions and enactments of leadership.

The historical development of public junior colleges, from the establishment of the first public junior college in Jolliet, Illinois, in 1901 (Cohen & Brawer, 2003) to the birth of the modern-day community college in the 1960s, provides a relatively short history and limited research literature from which to draw information. Twombly (1995) reviewed four eras of community college leadership, including the period from 1900 to the 1930s, in which the "great man" theory dominated; the 1940s to 1950s, in which leaders sought to become independent from secondary schools and forge an identity of their own; the 1960s to 1970s, in which the present-day version of the community college was born with the strong, dominant leadership that was necessary during those pioneering days; and the 1980s to 2000, when attention to resource issues was more necessary, and models from business began to be used that emphasized efficiency and strategic planning (Rowley & Sherman, 2001).

Vaughan's (1986) book *The Community College Presidency* provided a profile of leaders of 2-year institutions. This portrait of the presidency stressed qualities of community college presidents including integrity, judgment, courage, and concern for others (p. 4). At the time of Vaughan's writing in the late 1980s, community college presidents and other constituents were just beginning to discuss the roles of subordinates and the importance of relationships. By 1989, Vaughan was writing about leadership in transition at community colleges. His work began to move beyond the personal descriptions of presidential traits to acknowledge the change from the "builder" presidents at community colleges to leaders with a broader range of duties. In his 1989 book *Leadership in Transition* (Vaughan, 1989b), women and minority presidents were acknowledged for having a role in community college leadership, thus marking and acknowledging a change in the demographic profile of community college presidents. In 1991, for example, 89% of community college presidents were males and 11% were minorities. A decade later, this percentage had shifted, as 28% of presidents were women and 14% were people of color (Weisman & Vaughan, 2002).

Building on the research by Bass (1985) and Burns (1978) that argued that transformational leaders sought to heighten followers' awareness about issues of consequence and subsequently change followers' goals and beliefs, Roueche, Baker, and Rose (1989) examined and categorized exemplary community college leaders using transformational behavioral attributes. Roueche et al. used five themes for analysis: Transformative leaders (a) believe in teamwork and shared decision making, (b) value people both as members of the team and as individuals, (c) understand motivation, (d) have a strong personal value system and, finally, (e) have a vision of what their college can become (p. 12). Roueche et al. concluded that leaders are most effective when they empower others.

During the 1990s, community colleges faced a decline in economic resources, a change in student composition with more adults turning to the community college for their educational needs, and a push to offer more community development programming. These forces necessitated a different kind of community college leader. Baker and Associates (1992) argued for cultural leadership, recognizing the interdependence of organizational culture and leadership. Their research draws from leadership theory based on culture and symbolic management of meaning by college presidents. How leaders help create meaning for others in a given cultural context is at the heart of cultural leadership.

In the late 1990s, many community colleges embraced the concept of the learning college (O'Banion, 1997). Conceptions of leadership under this organizational paradigm call for shared leadership: "It means embracing organizational learning so leadership will be a responsibility shared by all members based on understanding, competence, and creativity" (Gratton, 1993, p. 103). One manifestation of shared leadership involves conceptions of shared governance. Lucey (2002) argued that in shared governance institutional members have specific roles, that faculty are responsible for academic and curricula issues and decisions, and that administrators are accountable for institutional strategy and decisions regarding resource allocation. Shared leadership calls for followers to be active and accountable

The recognition of the role of followers and shared leadership argues for new conceptualizations of what it means to be a community college leader. The shift from early founder to multitask manager requires an emphasis on communication, restructuring of organizational reporting and responsibilities, and a call for accountability (Lewis, 1989). Shifts in decision making over time, from within the exclusive domain of the president to a more participatory process involving shared governance, reflect changes in community college leadership.

Gender and Leadership

At community colleges, women currently occupy approximately 28% of all presidencies. Women also represent 21% of deans of instruction positions (or similarly titled positions such as vice president for academic affairs or chief academic officer) at community colleges (Weisman & Vaughan, 2002). Because the prime pathway to the community college presidency remains through the provost or the senior academic affairs administrator, it is likely that the future will show more women heading community colleges.

As noted above, conceptualizations of college presidents' approach to leadership has changed from the "take charge," "great man" approach to approaches emphasizing participatory and shared decision making—approaches that are more often associated with women leaders (Chliwniak, 1997). Several authors (DiCroce, 1995; Getskow, 1996; Vaughan 1989a) have suggested ways in which women leaders can influence the culture of the community college and improve future opportunities for women: (a) Encourage the elimination of institutional gender stereotypes, (b) redefine power and the power structure of the institution, (c) enact gender-related policies and procedures, (d) raise collegial consciousness and initiate collegial dialogue on gender and related issues, and (e) take a proactive stance on public policy and debate beyond the local campus. As more women hold the top position on community college campuses, norms regarding the presidency and leadership will begin to change.

Literature on women's leadership suggests more sharing of power and a participatory orientation to leading (Chliwniak, 1997; Townsend & Twombly, 1998). Townsend and Twombly (1998) argued, however, that a feminist orientation toward leadership at the community college must be centered on attention to women's issues and needs versus general campus issues. And Glazer-Raymo (2003) contended that, in analyses, gender needs to be considered as an analytic category versus merely a demographic variable in order to formulate policy that adequately addresses the needs of women.

Leadership Throughout the Organization

New conceptions of "leadership look at leadership as a process in which leaders are not seen as individuals in charge of followers, but as members of a community of practice" (Horner, 1997, p. 277). One model for this type of leadership is distributed leadership (Gronn, 2000). Rather than leadership formed on a dualistic premise, the responsibility for leading the college is shared throughout the organization. Instead of a focus on the sole positional leader of the president, the interdependencies of the relationship are emphasized, in which roles change over time. The modification of strict roles over time makes the differentiation between leader and follower increasingly arbitrary (Birnbaum, 1992).

Multidimensional leadership is "likely to be the result of a team effort or of participation at differing levels, rather than the capacity of a single individual" (Peterson, 1997, p. 154). Similarly, Helgesen (1995) conceptualized leadership as a web in which there is structure but also an ever-evolving shape. The leader at the center of the web works on building consensus and valuing the parts of the web—parts that are built on relationships.

The emphasis on the learning organization (O'Banion, 1997) also supports new conceptions of leadership in which "presidents and senior administrative staff need to be comfortable with fluid organizational dynamics that promote continuous learning, rigorous analysis and creative responses at all levels of the organization" (Dever, 1997, p. 62). Learning organization tenets suggest that involvement of and feedback from followers within the organization are critical for organizational success

Although different authors use a variety of terms in describing leadership throughout the organization (e.g., shared leadership, distributed leadership, multidimensional leadership, web of inclusion, and such), each author and corresponding theory chooses not to focus on the hierarchical leader in the organization. Instead, leadership is described more in terms of relationships. In addition to the roles of leaders, the roles of followers are also highlighted as essential to organizational success. This study examines whether these new conceptualizations of leadership are present in the community college administrative ranks.

Method

The data reported here come from a national survey of community college administrators. The survey instrument consisted of 34 questions and was pilot tested with community college administrators, two peer reviewers, and a panel of three experts from the American Association of Community Colleges (AACC). A stratified random sample of 1,700 community college administrators across 14 position codes was drawn from the AACC databank, providing representation by geographic location, urban and rural locales, and single campus and multicampus sites. During early 2000, letters of introduction and survey packets were mailed, extensive electronic and phone follow-ups were conducted, and a second mailing was distributed, yielding a response rate of 54% ($n = 910$) usable surveys.

For this study, the question of interest was an open-ended question that asked administrators if they considered themselves to be leaders at their institutions and, if so, why. Of the survey respondents, 682 responded to this question. Content analysis was used to analyze the responses. Content analysis is a research method that allows for the counting and tallying of categorized themes within data. Content analysis has been described as a systematic and replicable technique for compressing many words of text into fewer content categories based on explicit rules of coding (Stemler, 2001).

Emergent coding of the responses was used. Categories were established after some preliminary examination of the data. Following the steps outlined by Haney, Russell, Gulek, and Fierros (1998), the two researchers independently reviewed the responses and developed a set of categories that formed a checklist. The researchers then compared checklists to reconcile any differences between lists. After extensive discussion, the two checklists were consolidated, and both researchers coded the responses independently. Interrater reliability was high (85% agreement between the two reviewers).

Limitations of content analysis are that it is inherently reductive, especially when dealing with complex topics, and leads to some simplistic choices that may limit analysis. For example, many of the responses reviewed had more than one code, but for analysis purposes, we chose only the primary code.

Findings

Research Question 1:
Self-Reporting of Leadership Role on Campus

Content analysis of the 682 responses resulted in 11 primary classifications of responses regarding categorization of leadership (see Table 1). Each category is discussed in more detail below with the corresponding percentages of responses that fell into that category.

The first category of responses exemplified the traditionally held definitions of leadership and related to positional leadership. Respondents in this category stated that the position required them

TABLE 1

Coding Scheme

Code	Content
1	Positional, responsibilities, committees, decision making, related to job function, experience, leader within area
2	Change agent, initiate change, create environment for change
3	Provide vision, shape direction
4	Knowledge, personal mastery, expertise, frequently asked or consulted because of expertise, other personal traits
5	Others see me as a leader, people trust me and/or respect me
6	Fulfilling mission of the college, working for the good of the organization
7	Empower others, advocate for others, provide support, mentor, motivate others, role model, set example
8	Me-centered, I am successful, I have the ability to make things happen
9	Teamwork, inclusiveness, collaboration, building consensus
10	Influence, power, authority, control financial resources
11	Not a leader, experiencing barriers to being a leader, or too new in the position to be a leader

to be leaders. Other respondents discussed making decisions within functional areas and fulfilling job responsibilities such as serving on important institutional committees. Respondents also discussed their years of experience in the position. Responses that typified this category included: "I am part of the Executive Committee of the college and I have major institutional responsibility," and "[I am a leader] by virtue of my position and my history of leadership here." Approximately 47% of responses fell within this classification.

A second category of responses related to initiating change, taking on the change agent role, or making the environment conducive for change. Some responses that illustrate this category are: "I am a transformational change agent," and "I have taken on numerous new projects and am considered an innovator." Nine percent of responses were classified in the change category.

Providing vision and direction were the defining phrases in the third category of responses. Seven percent of responses spoke of vision, including the following: "I set the tone, shape and communicate the visions, and position the college on critical issues" and "I am responsible for developing, cultivating, and implementing the institutional vision."

A similar percentage of respondents (6.6%) indicated that they were leaders at their institutions because of the knowledge and expertise they possessed. Many of the responses that fell into this category spoke about personal mastery. Examples of such responses included the following: "I am recognized statewide for expertise in my field," and "I am called upon often for insight and recommendations."

Some respondents (4.5%) believed that they were leaders because others saw them in that light and because they were trusted and respected on their campuses. As one respondent wrote, "My views and suggestions are received with respect." Another administrator wrote, "I have the trust and confidence of faculty and administrator."

Rather than indicating personal characteristics when asked if they were leaders on campus, approximately 3% of the administrators discussed fulfilling the mission of the college. For example, one administrator wrote, "I play a key role in advancing the mission of the institution through my work." In a similar sentiment, another administrator wrote, "[I have the] ability to understand the mission and focus people and community towards the mission."

Although writings on empowerment abound in the literature, few administrators (3.1%) discussed empowering others, mentoring, advocating for others, role modeling, or motivating others as reasons why they were leaders at their institutions. One administrator explained, "I have been able to motivate and support faculty and colleagues to accomplish their goals." Another wrote, "I try to pull together the resources necessary for others to do their job."

A surprisingly small percentage of administrators (1.9%) talked of team leadership. Examples of statements from those who did are: "I am viewed as a leader who values participative decision-making and team approaches" and "I consider myself a team player who leads when appropriate."

Approximately 2% of respondents spoke of their influence, power, and authority as being reasons why they were leaders at their institutions. For example, one administrator said, "I have power, influence, and respect." Similarly, another administrator explained, "I seem to be able to successfully influence faculty/staff."

Two percent of administrators focused solely on their success and their ability to get the job done as the reasons why they were leaders at their institution. As one administrator explained, "I get things done for the college when I see a need—job description or not." Another administrator stated, "People look to me to make things happen. I do."

And finally, close to 6% of the respondents did not believe that they were leaders at their institutions. Many stated that they faced barriers to leadership or that they were too new in their positions at their institutions to be leaders. One administrator wrote, "[It is] difficult if not impossible to be a leader at this institution unless you are a faculty member or came from faculty ranks." Another indicated, "My area of responsibility is secondary to the primary mission of the institution," whereas yet another stated, "I consider myself a colleague more than a leader."

Research Question 2:
Women's and Men's Descriptions of Leadership

In dividing the coded data set based on gender, the categorizations of responses showed no significant difference based on sex. Some qualitative differences, however, are worth noting (see Table 2).

Although not statistically significant, a slightly higher percentage of men than women were likely to describe their leadership based on their position and responsibilities (49.2% of men compared to 45.1% of women). As one male stated, "My title says I am supposed to be a leader." Likewise, women referred to their positional location but often did so in terms of their experience and roles of responsibilities: "Yes. I have a position with a great deal of responsibility and continue to be put into leadership positions on task forces and committees."

Another area with a slightly higher percentage of male responses was within the category of "me-centered." Men were more likely than women to describe their leadership with themselves as the focal point (3.3% of men compared to 1.7% of women). One male respondent said, "Yes, [I am a leader] because I have the ability to make things happen." On the other hand, a woman respondent in this category noted, "Yes, I get things done." Whereas both of these responses are coded for "me-centered," the orientation of the male respondent is to his ability to influence others to make things happen, versus the woman respondent, who sees herself as the person actually doing things.

In the category related to knowledge and personal mastery, a slightly higher percentage of women were more likely than men to consider themselves a leader given their expertise (8.0% of women compared to 6.1% of men), although, again, this difference was not statistically significant. One female respondent commented, "My advice is often sought, as are my skills." A male respondent in this area said, "I am considered an expert on technical education by upper administration and my peers in this institution and throughout the state." The adage of "knowledge is power" provides the backdrop for this leadership definition. In the examples cited, the female leader focused on her skills, whereas the male response focused on his expertise.

Finally, although not representing a large portion of the sample, a slightly larger percentage of women defined their leadership as based on their ability to collaborate and build teamwork (2.8% of women versus 1.3% of men). A female commented, "I try to bring consensus in our decisions—try to include people in the decision-making process. I'm not afraid, however, to make an unpopular decision based on what is right." Similarly, one male leader wrote, "I am viewed as being a leader who values participative decision-making and team approaches."

TABLE 2

Gender Differences in Primary Themes

Coding Theme	Percentage Male ($n = 396$)	Percentage Female ($n = 286$)
Positional, responsibilities, committees, decision making related to job function, experience, leader within area	49.2	45.1
Change agent, initiate change, create environment for change	7.8	8.7
Provide vision, shape direction	7.1	7.0
Knowledge, personal mastery, expertise, frequently asked or consulted because of expertise, other personal traits	6.1	8.0
Others see me as a leader, people trust me and/or respect me	5.1	4.5
Fulfilling mission of the college, working for the good of the organization	2.8	3.8
Empower others, advocate for others, provide support, mentor, motivate others, role model, set example	3.1	3.1
Me-centered, I am successful, I have the ability to make things happen	3.3	1.7
Teamwork, inclusiveness, collaboration, building consensus	1.3	2.8
Influence, power, authority, control financial resources	1.8	2.1
Yes, but no explanation	6.8	7.0
Not a leader, experiencing barriers to being a leader, or too new in the position to be a leader	5.8	5.9

Note: There were no significant gender differences.

Research Question 3: Varying Views of Leadership Based on Administrative Position

Differences in responses were measured among six different position categorizations: presidents and provosts, academic affairs, student affairs, occupational and continuing education, administrative areas (e.g., business affairs, institutional research, human resources, and development), and learning resources and distance education (see Table 3). The significant differences in positional categorizations of responses are reported below, along with notable qualitative differences.

Presidents/Provosts

A historical trait of leadership is the ability to provide vision (Roueche et al., 1989). Presidents and provosts were more likely than administrators in the other positions to indicate that they provided vision and shaped the direction of the college, as close to 20% of presidential responses referenced vision. As one president stated, "I provide a focused vision for the future." Another president commented, "I have an overall vision of the college as integral to the community and have moved it successfully toward being recognized as such."

TABLE 3

Position Differences in Primary Themes (in percentages)

	Presidents, Provosts (n = 86)	Academic Affairs (n = 131)	Student Affairs (n = 98)	Occupational and Continuing Education (n = 151)	Administrative Areas, Business Affairs, Institutional Research, Human Resources, and Development (n = 162)	Learning Resources/ Distance Education (n = 54)
Positional, responsibilities, committees, decision making related to job function, experience, leader within area	43.0	46.6	49.0	48.3	52.5[a]	37.0[a]
Change agent, initiate change, create environment for change	4.7	10.7	11.2	9.3	5.6	7.4
Provide vision, shape direction	19.8[b]	8.4	4.1	3.3	6.8	0.0
Knowledge, personal mastery, expertise, frequently asked or consulted because of expertise, other personal traits	1.2[c]	6.9	9.2[c]	6.6	8.6	7.4
Others see me as a leader, people trust me and/or respect me	1.2[d]	8.4[d]	4.1	6.7	2.5[d]	5.6
Fulfilling mission of the college, working for the good of the organization	3.5	1.5	5.1	3.3	2.5	5.6
Empower others, advocate for others, provide support, mentor, motivate others, role model, set example	1.2	3.8	2.0	3.3	3.7	3.7
Me-centered, I am successful, I have the ability to make things happen	4.7	0.8	2.0	2.6	3.1	3.7
Teamwork, inclusiveness, collaboration, building consensus	2.3	3.1	1.0	0.7	1.9	3.7
Influence, power, authority, control financial resources	3.5	1.5	1.0	4.0	0.6	0.0

(continued)

TABLE 3 (cont.)

Position Differences in Primary Themes (in percentages)

	Presidents, Provosts (n = 86)	Academic Affairs (n = 131)	Student Affairs (n = 98)	Occupational and Continuing Education (n = 151)	Administrative Areas, Business Affairs, Institutional Research, Human Resources, and Development (n = 162)	Learning Resources/ Distance Education (n = 54)
Yes, but no explanation	14.0	6.9	6.1	3.3	7.4	5.6
Not a leader experiencing barriers to being a leader, or too new in the position to be a leader	1.2[e]	1.5[e]	5.1	8.6[e]	4.9	20.4[e]

a. Administrative areas were significantly more likely than learning resources/distance education to indicate positional, responsibilities, etc. ($p = .041$).

b. Presidents were significantly more likely to indicate provide vision, shape direction ($p < .05$ for each position category).

c. Student affairs administrators were more likely than presidents/provosts to indicate knowledge, personal mastery, expertise, etc.($p = .021$).

d. Academic affairs administrators were more likely than presidents/provosts ($p = .03$) and more likely than those in administrative areas ($p = .03$) to indicate that others see them as leaders.

e. In all instances, learning resources/distance education administrators were more likely to indicate that they were not leaders at their institutions. Those in administrative areas were also more likely than presidents/provosts ($p = .021$) or academic affairs administrators ($p = .008$) to indicate that they were not leaders.

Academic Affairs Administrators

Academic affairs administrators were more likely than presidents and provosts or those in administrative areas (business affairs, institutional research, human resources, and development) to indicate in their responses that others saw them as leaders. As one vice president of academic affairs answered, "People react to me as if I am a leader." Some academic administrators referred both to their position in the administrative hierarchy as well as to expectations placed on them by colleagues, "As [the] #2 person at the college, a lot of people look to me for guidance and expect me to provide leadership."

Although not statistically significant, other identifying factors showed up differently for those responding from positions in academic affairs. Those administrators working in academic affairs indicated more often than presidents that they were a change agent (10.7% of academic affairs administrators compared to 4.7% of presidents). As one academic dean stated, "By nature I am a strategic planner and motivator. Both skills have resulted in change." Another director commented, "I have spearheaded several initiatives with success," capturing the immediate connection between plans and actions.

Those in academic affairs also identified themselves as a leader due to their knowledge or mastery more often than presidents or provosts (6.9% of academic affairs administrators compared to 1.2% of presidents). As midlevel administrators, these employees' job function is tied more directly to particular tasks or functions, making mastery of an area a sought-after leadership quality for those in charge. One director's comment—"I have led in my area of specialty"—illustrates the idea that knowledge and mastery convey leadership for these administrators. Finally, academic affairs respondents indicated that they were a leader because others see them as a leader (8.4% of academic affairs administrators compared to 1.2% for presidents and provosts).

Student Affairs Administrators

A relatively high percentage (11.2%) of student affairs administrators indicated that they were change agents at their colleges. The day-to-day interaction that student affairs personnel have with students may be a contributing factor for this high percentage. Being a change agent may be expected within student affairs as it is constantly necessary to make adjustments to meet student needs. As one dean of students commented, "I am a problem-solver and integrator." The bridge between student affairs and academic affairs highlights collaboration for student learning (Kezar, 2003), and this collaboration was reflected in some of the responses. According to a dean of students, "I am regularly involved in building momentum and clearing the path for new initiatives." The ability to adapt quickly to changing cultural norms and student development issues is key for student affairs employees. According to one vice president of student affairs, "I have the opportunity to go as far with new ideas/programs as I want. I'm encouraged to be innovative."

Occupational and Continuing Education Administrators

Occupational and continuing education administrators, as compared to the other positional categories, were very similar in their responses to the question, "Do you consider yourself a leader at your institution?" This group of administrators was more likely than presidents and academic affairs administrators to indicate that they were not leaders at their institutions, however. One vice president of occupational education stated, "Ours is a very autocratic institution where second level administrators do not have a voice in the administration of the institution." And one director of continuing education noted, "President's actions indicate he desires to be the only leader; others have difficulty asserting leadership."

Administrative Areas (Business Affairs, Institutional Research, Human Resources, and Development)

This group of administrative personnel had the highest percentage that indicated they were leaders because of their positions (although it was not statistically significant across most positions). Perhaps due to the nature of their work, this group of administrators readily referred to their positional duties: "I manage several key operations on campus"; "I am in a high profile position which requires me to plan and oversee events"; and "I direct institutional assessment planning; overall coordination of Title III grant, and am responsible for federal and state enrollment reporting."

Learning Resources/Distance Education Administrators

Those in charge of learning resources and distance education programs were more likely than the other position categories to indicate that they were not leaders at their institutions or that they were experiencing leadership barriers. Administratively, those located in this category are seemingly among the lower ranks of the hierarchy. One director of learning resources noted, "It is difficult if not impossible to be a leader at this institution unless you are a faculty member or came from faculty ranks." One director of distance education commented, "My area receives low priority." Individuals in this category perceived their positions as marginalized in the organization. Quite telling was the lack of respondents in this category using the self-descriptors of setting the vision for the campus or of having influence or power. None of the administrators in these positions identified themselves by using either of these descriptors.

Discussion and Conclusion

The findings from this research indicate that despite calls for new forms of leadership, the survey respondents still largely viewed themselves as leaders primarily due to their position. What is encouraging, however, is that although no other single definition of leadership ranked as high as position, cumulatively, the nonposition responses account for half of the descriptors. Thus, administrators are now conceiving of themselves as leaders using expanded ideals beyond just position.

Few differences existed in how men or women defined their leadership. Where there were slight percentage differences based on gender, the male and female responses were captured in stereotypical ways: namely, the view of male leadership as more directive and autocratic (based on position; me-centered) and female leadership as more participatory and valuing meritocracy as measured by value of knowledge (create environment for change; knowledge mastery; working for the good of the college). These findings suggest a need to think differently about gender and leadership. The weak differences found in defining leadership by gender underscores that gender is not always the defining variable of difference in how one chooses to lead. Rather, colleges may need to concentrate instead on institutional structures that may act as barriers or impediments for the advancement of women (VanDerLinden, 2003).

Those in the position of president or provost were more likely to see themselves as shaping the direction of the college. Although being a visionary is often typically ascribed to these positional leaders, it is not without a cost. Pfeffer (1991) reported that presidents, as the positional leaders on campus, were limited in the amount of power and control at their disposal. The findings reported here continue to bear out this claim. Administrators in academic affairs and those located at different levels in the administrative hierarchy perceive themselves as having more ability to enact change. Part of the reason for this finding may be that midlevel administrators have fewer areas of control in their domain and therefore can exert more influence on those areas actually within their control. Also, the president and provost roles are more publicly visible, both on campus and to the larger community. Actions taken by these positional leaders are more scrutinized and involve more political negotiation among competing parties.

Presidents and provosts were not likely to say they were leaders because others see them as such. Instead, the perception others have of these campus leaders was implicit based on their organizational chart positions at the top of the hierarchy. In general, presidents and provosts did not define their leadership using concepts of teams or empowering others. And it was student affairs personnel and those in learning resources who saw themselves most often as working to fulfill the mission of the college. These personnel perceived direct ties between their leadership and the work of the college. As visionary leaders, presidents and provosts again may have made assumptions about their leadership roles, assuming that their work inherently fulfills the mission of the college.

The findings related to positional differences indicate more variation amongst positions, as compared to gender differences. These findings raise interesting questions regarding the route to the presidency. Because fewer leadership differences were accounted for by gender and more by position, the question becomes, Is it a person's position that elicits different conceptions of leadership? Viewing the findings by position indicated that along with additional influence as one moves up the administrative hierarchy, one also assumes additional limitations. Barriers were also perceived by those located further down the organizational hierarchy in learning resources or distance education. Barriers faced by these lower level administrators may be due to the marginalization of these organizational units in the college.

Implications

If community colleges want to embrace the ideal of participatory leadership and leadership throughout the organization, organizational structures and the mindsets of leaders may need to change. Currently there is still a reliance on the bureaucratic and reporting hierarchy in how administrators see themselves as leaders. Given that more women are ascending to positions of power on campus, community colleges may witness a change. New definitions and models of what it means to lead a community college campus may become more apparent and move in the direction of increased emphasis on participation and team leadership.

Community colleges have been previously described as bureaucratic in orientation—meaning that "structures are established to efficiently relate organizational programs to the achievement of specified goals" (Birnbaum, 1992, p. 107). Historically, this organizational orientation reifies and values positional leadership over other types. The question remains: Have the structures of community colleges evolved to allow for and support other conceptions of leadership? The findings from this research indicate a qualified yes.

Many of the responses provided more than one definition of leadership. The administrators' primary responses formed the basis of the findings reported here. The multiple coding of the responses, however, indicates that individuals are thinking more complexly about leadership, rather than merely attributing it to position or one characteristic. Providing ways to support expanded definitions of leadership is critical. Leadership development and training opportunities are an opportune time to nurture expanded conceptions of what it means to be a leader. The expected leadership turnover in community colleges during the next decade provides such an opportunity for change.

References

Astin, A., & Astin, H. (2000). *Leadership reconsidered*. Battle Creek, MI: Kellogg Foundation. (ED 444437)

Baker, G. A., & Associates. (1992). *Cultural leadership: Inside America's community colleges*. Washington, DC: American Association of Community and Junior Colleges.

Baldwin, R. G. (1998). Technology's impact on faculty life and work. In K. H. Gillespie (Ed.), *The impact on technology on faculty development, life, and work* (pp. 7–21). San Francisco: Jossey-Bass.

Barr, R. B., & Tagg, J. (1995). From teaching to learning: A new paradigm for undergraduate education. *Change, 27*(5), 12–25.

Bass, B. M. (1985). *Leadership and performance beyond expectations*. New York: Free Press.

Bass, B. M., & Stogdill, R. M. (1990). *Bass and Stogdill's handbook of leadership* (3rd ed.). New York: Free Press.

Bensimon, E. M., & Neumann, A. (1993). *Redesigning collegiate leadership: Teams and teamwork in higher education*. Baltimore: Johns Hopkins University Press.

Bensimon, E. M., Neumann, A., & Birnbaum, R. (1989). *Making sense of administrative leadership: The "L" word in higher education* (ASHE-ERIC Higher Education Report No. 1, ED 316 074 MF-01). Washington DC: George Washington University.

Birnbaum, R. (1992). *How academic leadership works: Understanding success and failure in the college presidency*. San Francisco: Jossey-Bass.

Bowen, W. & Shapiro, H. (1998). *Universities and their leadership*. Princeton, NJ: Princeton University Press.

Burns, J. M. (1978). *Leadership*. New York: Harper & Row.

Chliwniak, L. (1997). *Higher education leadership: Analyzing the gender gap* (ASHE-ERIC Higher Education Report [Vol. 25, No. 4]). Washington, DC: ASHE.

Cohen, A. M., & Brawer, F. B. (2003). *The American community college* (4th ed.). San Francisco: Jossey-Bass.

Davis, J. (2003). *Learning to lead*. Westport, CT: American Council on Education/Praeger.

Dever, J. T. (1997). Reconciling educational leadership and the learning organization. *Community College Review, 25*(2), 57–63.

DiCroce, D. (1995). Women and the community college presidency: Challenges and possibilities. In B. K. Townsend (Ed.), *Gender and power in the community college. New directions for community colleges* (No. 89). San Francisco: Jossey-Bass.

Dolence, M. G., & Norris, D. M. (1995). *Transforming higher education: A vision for learning in the 21st century*. Ann Arbor, MI: Society for College and University Planning.

Evelyn, J. (2001). Community colleges face a crisis of leadership. *Chronicle of Higher Education, 36*(31), A36.

Getskow, V. (1996). *Women in community college leadership roles. ERIC digest* (ED400025). Los Angeles: ERIC Clearinghouse for Community Colleges.

Glazer-Raymo, J. (2003). Women faculty and part-time employment: The impact of public policy. In B. Ropers-Huilman (Ed.), *Gendered futures in higher education: Critical perspectives for change* (pp. 97–110). Albany: State University of New York Press.

Gratton, M. (1993). Leadership in the learning organization. *New Directions for Community Colleges, 84*, 93–103.

Green, M. (1997). No time for heroes. *Trusteeship, 5*(2), 6–11.

Greenleaf, R. K. (1977). *Servant leadership: A journey into the nature of legitimate power and greatness*. New York: Paulist Press.

Gronn, P. (2000). Distributed properties: A new architecture for leadership. *Educational Management & Administration, 28*(3), 317–338.

Gumport, P. J. (2003). The demand-response scenario: Perspectives of community college presidents. *Annals of the American Academy of Political and Social Science, 586*, 38–61.

Haney, W., Russell, M., Gulek, C., & Fierros, E. (1998). Drawing on education: Using student drawings to promote middle school improvement. *Schools in the Middle, 7*(3), 38–43.

Heifetz, R. A. (1994). *Leadership without easy answers*. Cambridge, MA: Belknap.

Helgesen, S. (1995). *The web of inclusion: A new architecture for building great organizations*. New York: Currency/Doubleday

Horner, M. (1997). Leadership theory: Past, present, & future. *Team Performance Management, 3*(4), 270–287.

Hurtado, S., & Dey, E. L. (1997). Achieving the goals of multiculturalism and diversity. In M. Peterson, D. D. Dill, L. Mets, & Associates (Eds.), *Planning and management for a changing environment* (pp. 405–431). San Francisco: Jossey-Bass.

Johnstone, D. B. (1999). The challenge of planning in public. *Planning for Higher Education, 28*(2), 57–64.

Kelley, R. E. (1998). In praise of followers. In W. Rosenbach & R. L. Taylor (Eds.), *Contemporary issues in leadership* (4th ed., pp. 96–106). Boulder, CO: Westview.

Kezar, A. (2003). Achieving student success: Strategies for creating partnerships between academic and student affairs. *NASPA Journal, 41*(1), 1–22.

Lewis, M. D. (1989). *Effective leadership strategies for the community college president*. Long Beach, CA: Long Beach City College. (ED307948)

Lucey, C. A. (2002). Civic engagement, shared governance, and community colleges. *Academe, 88*(4), 27–31.

Nidiffer, J. (2001). New leadership for a new century. In J. Nidiffer & C. Bashaw (Eds.). *Women administrators in higher education* (pp. 101–131). Albany: State University of New York Press.

O'Banion, T. (1997). *A learning college for the 21st century*. Phoenix, AZ: American Council on Education Oryx Press Series on Higher Education.

Peterson, M. (1997). Using contextual planning to transform institutions. In M. Peterson, D. Dill, L. A. Mets, & Associates (Eds.), *Planning and management for a changing environment* (pp. 127–157). San Francisco: Jossey-Bass.

Pfeffer, J. (1991). The ambiguity of leadership. In M. Peterson (Ed.), *Organization and governance in higher education* (4th ed., pp. 345–354). Needham Heights, MA: Simon & Schuster Custom Publishing.

Rost, J. C. (1991). *Leadership for the twenty-first century*. New York: Praeger.

Roueche, J. E., Baker, G. A., III, & Rose, R. R. (1989). *Shared vision: Transformational leadership in American community colleges*. Washington, DC: Community College Press.

Rowley, D. J., & Sherman, H. (2001). *From strategy to change: Implementing the plan in higher education*. San Francisco: Jossey-Bass.

Schults, C. (2001). *The critical impact of impending retirements on community college leadership*. Washington, DC: American Association of Community Colleges Press.

Spears, L. C., & Lawrence, M. (Eds.). (2003). *Focus on leadership: Servant-leadership for the twenty-first century*. San Francisco: Jossey Bass.

Stemler, S. (2001). *An introduction to content analysis*. College Park, MD: ERIC Clearinghouse on Assessment and Evaluation.

Townsend, B. K., & Twombly, S. B. (1998). A feminist critique of organizational change in the community college. In. J. S. Levin (Ed.), *Organizational change in the community college: A ripple or a sea change?* (pp. 77–85). San Francisco: Jossey-Bass.

Twombly, S. B. (1995). Gendered images of community college leadership: What messages they send. *New Directions for Community Colleges, 23*(1), 67–77.

VanDerLinden, K. (2003, April). *Career advancement and leadership development of community college administrators*. Paper presented at the annual meeting of the American Educational Research Association, Chicago.

Vaughan, G. B. (1986). *The community college presidency*. New York: Macmillan.

Vaughan, G. B. (1989a). Female community college presidents. *Community College Review, 17*(2), 20–24.

Vaughan, G. B. (1989b). *Leadership in transition: The community college presidency*. Washington, DC: American Council on Education/Oryx Press Series on Higher Education.

Weisman, I. M., & Vaughan, G. B. (2002). *The community college presidency, 2001. AACC Research Brief*. Washington, DC: American Association of Community Colleges.

Pamela L. Eddy is an assistant professor and doctoral program coordinator at Central Michigan University.

Kim E. VanDerLinden is the director of assessment services at Student Voice.

CHAPTER 14

RE-VISIONING LEADERSHIP
IN COMMUNITY COLLEGES

MARILYN J. AMEY AND SUSAN B. TWOMBLY

From their modest beginnings as small junior colleges has emerged a system of community colleges that enrolls millions of credit/noncredit, non-traditional/traditional students from all racial, ethnic, gender, and social class groups. This system has been labeled the success story of twentieth-century U.S. education (Breneman and Nelson, 1981). However, the generation of leaders who oversaw two decades of tremendous growth during the 1960s and 1970s is approaching retirement, and the system faces an inevitable transition in leadership.

This transition has not gone unheralded. Jess Parrish, president of Midland Community College in Midland, Texas, summarized: "The alarm has been sounded in speeches, articles, reports, and conversations among colleagues: the first generation of great community college leadership is passing from the scene, and its replacement is uncertain" (1988, [1]). The changing of the guard is understandably a concern for community colleges because, as Dale Tillery and William Deegan observed, "No other educational institution has been so shaped and promoted by so few leaders as has the community college" (1985, 14). The importance of leadership is heightened because most community colleges are entering stages in their organizational life cycles at which they are on the verge of renewal or decline. Appropriate leadership may be the key variable in determining whether the community college movement as a whole and individual colleges are able to engage in effective renewal or whether they will enter a period of decline.

The type of leadership behavior and qualities sought in new leaders in community colleges, as in all organizations, is influenced by context and the particular demands of a social situation (Selznick 1984). We argue, drawing on insights from discourse analysis and organizational life cycle theory, that ideas about leadership are also shaped and constrained by beliefs and images about the kind of leadership called for and the characteristics required in those who assume leadership positions. The language in which these images are communicated serves both symbolic and political purposes—defining legitimate leadership regardless of contextual demands for leadership. Obviously, the consequences of images that no longer fit can hamper the effectiveness of an institution.

A striking element about the language of community college leadership literature is the vivid descriptors and images that have been used over time. Although critical, conceptual, or theoretical discussions of institutional leadership may be rare, the scholarship is so replete with heroic images of leaders, triumphantly constructing this unique sector of higher education, that the literature on four-year college leaders seems pale by comparison. The reader may question the "what" of community college leadership but the "who" of leadership is never in doubt. The certainty, perpetuated through vivid imagery, about the desired and even necessary style of community college leaders invited a more critical analysis of that language from the early 1900s to the present. We feel certain that those images will, in the absence of purposeful intervention, shape future community college leadership.

Our purposes in this study were to (1) identify the images and rhetoric of leadership in junior/community colleges; (2) observe the sociohistorical and organizational context of these images; and (3) examine the effect of images and rhetoric on leadership behavior—specifically on the types of individuals who could be considered leaders and on the future of leadership in community colleges. Jess Parrish noted, "A generation of community college lore is available to current and up-and-coming leaders, and the smart ones are using it" (1988, [1]). It is that lore, as evidenced in published materials, which we are going to critically examine. In short, we are going to engage in what author Adrienne Rich calls re-visioning: "the act of looking back, of seeing with fresh eyes, of entering an old text from a new critical direction" (Kolodny 1985, 59). By engaging in the process of re-visioning, we hope to provide the basis for developing new models of effective leadership that reflect not only changes in the organizational life cycle but changes in the rhetoric and images of leadership.

Discourse Analysis

Our purpose is to analyze and question the dominant ideology that has permeated the community college leadership literature from two perspectives: (1) to question the relevance of the images of leadership for the different stages in the organizational life cycle through which community colleges have developed, and, more importantly, (2) to question how the ideologies behind these images of leadership have maintained a particular type of leader and have excluded or severely limited access to leadership positions by those who do not fit that specific image. This critical perspective allows us to move away from assumptions so fundamental that they have been taken as objective truths and instead focus on the literature as social constructions of leadership, where social and historical contexts are important considerations.

Our approach to the research tasks was grounded generally in critical theory and more specifically in discourse analysis. F. Michal Connelly and D. Jean Clandinin (1990) argue that narrative inquiry—the study of texts—is both a phenomenon and method. And so, we argue, is discourse analysis both a framework for looking at the community college literature and a way of analyzing what we found. Richard Terdiman defines discourse as "the complexes of signs and practices which organize social existence and social reproduction" (Giroux 1988, 219). Discourse encompasses such "signs and practices" as language and narrative or stories.

Critical theorists whose work is based in an analysis of discourse believe that discourse serves very important social functions, giving "differential substance to membership of a social group or class or formation, which mediate[s] an internal sense of belonging, and outward sense of otherness" (Terdiman in Giroux 1988, 219). Sociologists and social psychologists point out how discourse becomes an instrument for consolidating and manipulating concepts and relationships in areas of power and control as well as other areas of ideological/social structure (e.g., Gergen 1988; Potter and Wetherell 1987; Shotter and Logan 1988). Language is used to enforce existing positions of authority, exploit privilege, give a sense of belonging, or communicate a sense of otherness in both obvious and subtle ways. The intentional use of language reinforces the status and roles on which people base their claims to exercise power and, in turn, those which perpetuate subservience (Fowler 1985).

Because the dominant class has the power to make and perpetuate meaning through its control of language and its dissemination through such outlets as scholarly journals, we can see that language is not only a reflection of inequality but that it, in effect, fosters inequality and operates as censorship, exclusion, blockage, and repression (Michel Foucault in Cherryholmes 1988, 34-36). In the United States, the dominant class consists largely of white, middle- or upper-class men. By constructing and reiterating certain selected images, phrases, and stories the dominant class can insist that a selected set of concepts make up social reality. In our case, we found that a relatively few writers have created, used, and perpetuated persuasive images of leadership in community colleges.

For those who match these images, it obviously benefits them to maintain, reinforce, and legitimize that particular understanding of the world, "regardless of how incomplete it may be" (Nielson 1990, 11). But obviously some groups are excluded. Dale Spender (1980) argues that as white men have constituted the dominant class, women (and by implication, blacks and other nondominant groups) have largely been excluded from formulations of cultural meanings, including their production of forms of thought, images, and symbols. She points out that women are forced to use language which they had no role in creating but which has become so ingrained in organizational culture that changing the language or accepting new images is very difficult.

Discourse often refers to spoken language, but Emile Benveniste emphasizes that the written word (texts)—for our purposes, scholarly books and articles—are also legitimate discourse and part of the social world (Cherryholmes 1988). As an active shaper of administrative culture and practice, scholarly discourse should be open to critical scrutiny from all sectors. Cleo Cherryholmes (1988) asserts that constructs and discourses, particularly of professional life, are often accepted with little analysis or criticism. In not being critical in our analysis of the language used in scholarship, we continue to replicate text, talk, and images as though they were natural, required, or predestined descriptions of reality; the present social order is legitimated.

Our analysis of community college leadership literature builds from these perspectives. We use discourse analysis as a means of focusing "reflexively" on "the rhetorical structure" of knowledge (Warren 1988, 48). To determine what a word means, one looks to the discourse and not just to the word. To determine what a discourse means, we need to examine its history, culture, politics, economics, conventions, and institutions to account for how it operates to produce "truth" and what is said. Rules of inclusion and exclusion are sometimes explicit, sometimes implicit; they govern what is said, what remains unsaid, who can speak with authority, and who must listen. The rules of discourse are based on ideas, concepts, values, and power arrangements that both transcend and ground what is said and done (Cherryholmes 1988, 33; Lather 1991, 86-92).

Through the use of discourse analysis, we begin to grasp how such features of the social context as gender, status, power, and roles impact on the style, thematic structure, or cognitive interpretation of text and talk (van Dijk 1985, 4-5). Using this analytic approach allows the researcher to do more than just say that there are differences; it illuminates how the participants in a given social interaction enact social roles, show power, and exert control through language. Discourse analysis also reminds the researcher of the part that literature and research (discourse) play in reproducing larger societal problems, "in social and political decision procedures, and in institutional management and representation of such issues" (van Dijk 1985, 7).

In short, an approach to a body of literature rooted in discourse analysis brings to the fore a different set of conceptual questions about knowledge and meaning than those typically asked. Whose knowledge is represented in the literature? What is the context of this knowledge? Whose meaning is perpetuated by word and action? In looking at leadership issues, whose issues do we focus on? Whose definitions of leadership are perpetuated as real? The focus of our discourse analysis moves to the different meanings that images and expectations of leadership can have, according to the ideological position of those images' creators. We can also determine the effects of the sociohistorical conditions in which these symbols have been produced.

Organizational Life Cycle Theory

The organizational life cycle of the junior/community college provides an appropriate sociohistoric context within which to analyze leadership. Kim Cameron (1984) suggests that organizations progress through at least four sequential, though recyclable, stages with recognizable characteristics and general problems to overcome. He emphasizes the important role managers play in facilitating or impeding progress through the organizational adaptations. More specifically, an organizational structure or leadership style effective at one stage of development may be inappropriate or even dysfunctional at another (Greiner 1972; Cameron and Zammuto 1983). Therefore we would expect to observe different leadership images, expectations, and styles associated with organizational structure and mission at various stages in community college development.

Although there are many life cycle schema from which to chose, we have selected John Gardner's (1986) four-stage organizational life cycle, in conjunction with Deegan and Tillery's (1985) description of generations of community college development to provide a sociohistoric context for our analysis. Gardner's stages are (1) birth, corresponding roughly to Deegan and Tillery's first generation, (2) growth, corresponding to Deegan and Tillery's second and third generations, (3) maturity, corresponding to Deegan and Tillery's fourth generation, and (4) renewal or decline, corresponding to Deegan and Tillery's fifth generation. The community college movement and most individual community colleges have experienced the first three of these stages and now face the challenges of renewing mature colleges (Hudgins 1990). If Larry Greiner's (1972) description of stage-style match is correct, then we would expect analysts and scholars to advocate different leadership expectations and styles for this new period in organizational development. In the discourse on leadership in each new organizational life stage and context, we would also expect to find different images of leadership with different meanings ascribed to those images as stages change.

Data Analysis

We undertook a comprehensive examination of the community college leadership literature from the early 1900s to the present. This literature base included published articles and books as well as unpublished materials found in *Resources in Education*, conference and workshop materials provided by the American Association of Community and Junior Colleges, and *Leadership Abstracts* published by the League for Innovation in the Community College. We conducted this review of the literature, or scholarly discourse, according to the stages of the community college life cycle identified by Gardner (1986) and Tillery and Deegan (1985), following existing guidelines for engaging in discourse analysis. Within this broad framework, we were interested in identifying the organizational context and structure, expectations of leadership, and most importantly, the images and language used to describe and reinforce leadership.

Tillery and Deegan segment the evolution of two-year colleges into five generations based on institutional characteristics. We discuss each of these periods according to tasks of leadership associated with organizational growth and development:

1. Tillery and Deegan's High School Extension, 1900-30. We call this period Birth and Youth.

2. Tillery and Deegan's period of the Junior College, approximately 1930-50. We discuss this period under the heading, "Changing Expectations."

3. Tillery and Deegan's generation of the Community College, 1950-70. We discuss this metamorphosis of junior colleges into larger, more comprehensive schools under the heading "Growth and Maturation" along with their fourth category.

4. Tillery and Deegan's generation of the Comprehensive Community College, mid-1970s to mid-1980s. We discuss this development under "Growth and Maturation."

5. Tillery and Deegan did not have an appropriate label in 1985 for contemporary times. We discuss what seems to be an emerging fifth generation under the heading, "Alternative Images."

Clearly, the years associated with each period are somewhat arbitrary; and while many junior colleges may have become comprehensive by the mid-1970s, surely not all had. The years associated with the Tillery and Deegan schemata should be used as guidelines rather than as definitive "watershed" dates. Likewise, many others wrote both retrospectively and about the present, making it inaccurate to associate particular authors and sources with specific periods. Many of the most telling images of leadership emerged out of attempts to characterize the past in a way that made sense to contemporary scholars. Indeed, it is partially the point of this paper that Jesse Bogue, for example, writing in 1950, or Steven Brint and Jerome Karabel in 1989, chose to characterize early leaders as they did.

As with other forms of meta-analysis, there are several viable approaches to discourse analysis. We relied on Cherryholmes's approach to post-structural criticism; it involves a five-step, interdependent process of reading, interpretation, criticism, communication, and evaluation and judgment (1988, 153-77). As we read, we looked for stories within the texts, stories which are connected to and by "codes in language, culture, and society." These stories are subject to multiple readings and submit to different tellings. The overlapping meanings which result connect reading with the next step in the process—interpretation—as a means of "getting from the said and read, to the unsaid" (Robert Scholes in Cherryholmes 1988, 155-56). In this way, we, the researchers, engage in interpretation, which will eventually become a new story or text.

It is important to emphasize at this point the role of the reader and the complex of perspectives and biases she or he brings to the task of reading and interpreting the text. This phenomenon has been emphasized by feminist literary critics. (See, for example, Annette Kolodny, 1985.) Readers of this article, for example, may not agree with our interpretation of the literature; however, we assume that multiple interpretations of any text are possible. Interpretation of texts allows for the identification of binary distinctions/oppositions, metaphors, models, modes of argumentation, inferences, and repetitions within a larger context. We move from noting the cultural codes to understanding the attitudes taken toward the codes by the makers of the text.

During the third step, criticism, variant readings of the literature emerge, some of them different from the traditional and dominant interpretations of the text. These variant interpretations are especially important when texts present themselves as "objective" descriptions of the way things really are. In this step of the process, the reader evaluates, discusses, examines, and questions the categories, orientations, and metaphors distinguished during the identification step of the process. "Reading produces stories," says Cherryholmes. ". . . Interpretation provides context. Criticism brings to light and evaluates that which narrative and interpretation has omitted, suppressed, devalued, silenced, and opposed as well as what has been claimed, asserted, and argued" (1988, 159).

Criticism, like interpretation, depends on the perspectives and background of the critiquing individual. The results of moving through these first three stages of discourse analysis do not necessarily lead to some "new truth." But the process has brought us to a place where we may enter the fourth stage—communicating to others the criticisms of the literature which we discovered during our reading and interpretation. Those who use or respond to our work will continue the discourse on community college leadership.

Our analysis of the community college leadership literature produced two major findings. First, the discourse used to recount the organizational development of the community college sector continuously reinforces the ideology of both a particular institution—the community college—and a specific dominant class—a relatively small group of white male scholars and practitioners. The discourse has crystallized into relevancy a set of concepts about community colleges such as constant change, democratic ideals concerning their role society, and powerful autocratic leaders. By continually speaking and writing in heavily value-laden images, community college scholars and practitioners (and even their critics) have been able to maintain a strong sense of cohesion, organizational definition, and professional boundaries over time. From an organizational development perspective, this pattern may have been critical in the early stages of birth and growth; however, it may be ineffective as a means of addressing organizational renewal if ideas about effective leadership are inappropriate to critical organizational tasks.

Second, the effect of such writing has been the systematic exclusion of, or failure to include, those who do not use the same language, exhibit the characteristic behaviors, or fit the symbolic image of leadership perpetuated by "mainstream" authors who have been almost exclusively white men. The community college literature rings with pervasive and persuasive nouns, verbs, and phrases which create and reinforce a particular image of leadership—the "great man" (both literally and figuratively). This image, we argue, precludes others from being seen as legitimate leaders and shapers of the community college future.

Birth and Youth: Images of the 1900-1930s

Jesse Bogue, former president of the American Association of Junior Colleges (AAJC) said, "The community college is not an institution. It is a movement" (1950, 239). A strong case can be made that, during the first half-century of junior college existence, the "movement" had leaders and individual institutions had administrators. Prominent university leaders like Alexis Lange of the University of California, William Rainey Harper of the University of Chicago, Henry Tappan of the University of Michigan, and David Starr Jordan of Stanford, and successive generations of national junior/community college leaders generally are credited with conceptualizing the idea of the junior college and solidifying the junior college's position in the structure of the U.S. educational system by developing, rationalizing, and communicating a mission and organizational form. In short, these few men are widely credited with creating and molding the paradigm for the contemporary comprehensive community college. Although it is doubtful that university leaders like Harper were actually involved in the development of individual junior colleges (Ratcliff 1987), the junior college literature almost universally cites their instrumental role in developing the junior/community college movement.

The paradigm offered by these "great men" was often at odds with the views of faculty, students, and parents, further reinforcing their influence (Brint and Karabel 1989). The "great man" theory of leadership dominated during this early period (Ratcliff 1987). These few early leaders actually wrote very little about leadership *per se*; however, they modeled a style of leadership about which others wrote admiringly; and as models, they continue to define normative leadership even in the 1990s. Consequently, it is from those who wrote about these "great men" and their role in the junior college movement that we get our ideas about leadership during the birth and youth periods.

The founding of the American Association of Junior Colleges in 1920 and the rising influence of Leonard Koos, Walter Eells, and Doak Campbell had more long-term impact on the identity and mission of these fledgling institutions than did their university benefactors. Koos, Eells, and Campbell are universally regarded as the movement's first real leaders—leaders it could call its own, leaders committed totally to the development of the junior college for its own sake. Koos and Eells were both university professors; and Campbell, a former college president, was the first president of AAJC. These men have been described as missionaries of middle class, small-town, religious backgrounds who were education small colleges (Brint and Karabel 1989; Goodwin 1971). The motives ascribed to these men, like those of their Progressive contemporaries, were those of searching for a means of uplifting society; junior colleges, they believed, would help channel students to their proper station in an orderly and efficient society (Brint and Karabel 1989; Goodwin 1971).

Even more interesting for this study is how authors have described junior colleges and their leaders in frontier, pioneer, and military images. George Zook, a higher education specialist for the U.S. Department of Education and a contributing author of the influential President's Commission on Higher Education Report (1947), described the junior college movement in 1940 "as an army of 'struggling frontiersmen' put together by 'General Koos and Colonels Eells and Campbell,' who then led them into all parts of the country, even storm(ing) the New England citadel" (Brint and Karabel 1989, 35). Steven Brint and Jerome Karabel then comment: "The analogy is apt in many ways. These intellectual commanders did undertake a massive job of organization. They did lead their recruits to fight many battles before their institutions were accepted, and many more before their vision of the junior colleges became widely adopted" (1989, 35).

Brint and Karabel further reinforce the vivid images portrayed by Zook, as other contemporary community college writers repeatedly do, by describing Koos, Eells, and Campbell as the "vanguard" (also a military term) of the community college movement. They not only created and established a paradigm for two-year postsecondary education, which they helped to institutionalize, but also, according to Brint and Karabel's thesis, they and their successors successfully refocused the junior/community college's focus from transfer to vocational mission, despite the wishes of students, faculty, and parents. Although one may disagree with the motives Brint and Karabel attribute to these men, Koos, Eells, and Campbell were transformational leaders in the truest meaning of the term. Furthermore, Koos, Eells, and Campbell groomed a generation of junior/community college men to take their places—including Jesse Bogue, Joseph Cosand, Leland Medsker, S. V. Martorana, Raymond Schultz, and Edmund Gleazer, to name but a few. More recently still, Arthur Cohen, John Roueche, George Vaughan, and Dale Parnell, among others, have assumed prominence on the national level while a group of college presidents has also gained attention, among them, William Priest, Judith Eaton, Robert McCabe, and Larry Tyree.

In this early period, presidents of AAJC were identified as important leaders of the movement. Through its annual meeting and journal, the AAJC served as a forum for the discussion and spread of ideas. Early AAJC presidents like Doak Campbell and Jesse Bogue are portrayed as having particular influence on the institutionalization and rationalization of a paradigm for the modern comprehensive community college. We argue that as the movement itself and individual institutions have matured, the influence of campus leaders has increased, while the direct influence of the AACJC (formerly AAJC) presidents has decreased—although they each made an attempt at transforming the overall mission of the community college in some way. For example, Edmund Gleazer (1980) advocated that community colleges become the "nexus" of community activity— perhaps even dropping the designation "college." More recently, Dale Parnell pressed for a reemphasis on the vocational mission through a 2 (high school) + 2 (community college) plan for the "neglected majority" (1985, 14). Although his book sold thousands of copies, the concept of tracking students into a community college vocational program in the tenth grade has not been widely embraced.

Several factors affected expectations and actions of early *institutional* leaders, notably the newness of the two-year college as an educational form and its relationship to the public school. Heads of private junior colleges, of which there were many in this early period, held the title of president, while early public junior college leaders held the title of dean and typically reported to district school superintendents or principals, reflecting organizational relationships with public school districts (Brothers, 1928; and Green in Eells 1931; Lee and Rosenstengel 1938). Interestingly, the second most important administrative position in these early colleges was the dean of women (Eells 1931; Foster 1933; Hill 1927). Unfortunately, little is written about this position or the women who held it after these early treatises on the junior college.

Early authors were not satisfied with the status, duties, or roles of these early college deans. A post-structuralist classification of objects would find a binary opposition in leadership discourse between the active images of "pioneer," "commander," and "builder" and the passive image of the "errand boy," who has few significant responsibilities and little power. Proctor (1927) noted that the dean of the junior college should be a general advisor to students. Fifteen years later, J. R. Johnson, president of the Nebraska Association of Junior Colleges, and W. W. Carpenter, professor of education at the University of Missouri doubted that "deans actually have the position of educational leader." Do they not "merely carry out the instructions of the board of education and superintendent of schools?", they asked, and quoted an unnamed dean as asking, "I wonder if the dean of the public junior college isn't, after all, primarily an errand boy?" (1942, 381). They concluded, based on a survey, that deans were not over-burdened with responsibilities and were not given much latitude in critical areas of policy making.

Eells, looking toward the future, said: "It is plainly evident that many of the deans were denied, in whole or in part, important administrative functions" and quoted Green, who agreed but also argued that the rapidly developing junior college presented unlimited opportunities for leadership ability and that deans must be prepared and willing to assume such functions (1931, 372).

Changing Expectations: Images of the 1930s-50s

In the 1940s and 1950s, a change in the imagery describing desirable and actual leadership practices began to emerge in the writings about junior colleges. Tillery and Deegan (1985) describe these two decades as the period during which leaders began to seek college identity and to gain independence from the secondary schools.

In 1951, Pierce described a line-staff relationship between presidents and deans of junior colleges. He saw the president as the leader in policy making, the liaison between the board of control and the college, and the chief public relations and chief business officer. Pierce concluded, "It appears, then, that junior colleges are coming more and more to have two general administrative officers, a chief administrator most often called 'president' and a second in command called 'dean'; and with the line-and-staff administrative organization, the other administrative officers are usually co-ordinates of equal rank serving under the leadership of the president and the dean" (1951, 366).

Recognizing the importance of the board of control to leadership of the college, Bogue insisted that "standards and practices should be revised to include definite provisions for preparation, functions and limitations of the *supreme* elected officers" (1950, 282; italics ours). Use of *supreme* leaves little doubt of his feeling that junior colleges should be governed by their own boards and that these boards should take charge. The chief executive officer, he stated, must be directly responsible to the board of control. Furthermore, this chief executive officer was expected to delegate authority as well as assume it. "Be in command, if that is your assignment," he approvingly quoted James C. Miller, president of Christian College. "Never be autocratic, but always be in command. No one feels secure with an administrator who is vacillating and weak. Always be fair, but be positive and constructive in performing your administrative duties" (1950, 287). Bogue then describes the ideal junior/community college leader:

> Especially for the community college, one needs an element of inspiration, the spirit of the pioneer and a sense of thrilling adventure. The quality referred to is sometimes called inspiring leadership ability. While it must have a foundation in character that creates confidence, sound judgement that enlists respect, intellectual honesty and scholarship that men trust, it nevertheless reaches beyond these characteristics. It is almost indefinable: one applauds the star when he appears on stage; the colorful gamey athlete when he runs onto the playing field; the rugged, courageous sea captain when he takes command of his ship. Just as one knows the difference between a day of sunshine and one of shadows so one knows the difference between a leader and a follower. It might be represented by the sharp line between the batter who "steps into it" when the balls come over the plate and the other who hesitates. (1950, 299)

On the same page, he adds yet another image: "The kingpin is the chief executive. His acumen in financial affairs, his ability to recognize and select the right kind of associates and delegate authority to them, his character, attitudes, and personality that create confidence in all the publics of the college naturally give him the leading role. If he plays his part well, he will have the whole-hearted support of his entire cast and the applause of the audience" (1950, 299). There was no question in Bogue's mind or images about the centrality of the president in the junior college.

Bartky spoke directly about the preferred leadership style of presidents in the post-war period. Drawing on his experience in the U.S. Navy, Bartky likened the junior college to a battleship. Because society's objectives for the junior college

> . . . are value judgements approaching absolutes when applied to junior colleges . . . a junior college should approach its objectives in the manner of a well-trained battleship. Society has set its objectives and expects them to be attained. There is no place for debate that frustrates society's designated purposes. It is undemocratic to act in ways that hamper society's designated leadership. The junior college organization has a job to perform and must not dissipate its efforts with too much consideration of the whims of the faculty and with tolerance toward those who would dilly dally with its socially define purposes. In this way only it can become a truly democratic organization. (1957, 7)

It says much about the character of the times that such openly advocated disregard for faculty opinion can be held up as a "truly, democratic" ideal. And commanding this "well-trained battleship," naturally, is the president.

The studies reported here seem to represent the sum total of the published material on leaders and leadership before 1950. Thus, an unanswered historical question is when and how the "errand boy image disappeared from the consciousness of junior/community college leadership to be replaced by the "commander." Nevertheless, it seems clear that World War II reinforced some of the changes in leadership rhetoric. Lee and Rosenstengel, writing as the conflict in Europe began, observed: "War emphasizes the responsibility of the administrative officer usually called the dean. To him is delegated the grave responsibility of keeping the machinery of the college rolling and in good order and contributing to the total defense of America" (1938, 21). Thus, not only did junior colleges contribute to the orderly assignment of people to their places in life but they also played a part in defending America (Brint and Karabel 1989; Bartky 1957).

The change in title from dean to president occurred between 1930 and 1950, coinciding with the separation of junior colleges from the public schools. Oddly enough, the reasons and conditions surrounding the separation are not discussed in the literature. The imagery of commanders and kingpins coincides with the stage in the history and organizational life cycle of community colleges when the struggle for independence dominated other considerations. Junior college authors seem to have seen this extremely active, even domineering, "great man" leadership style as necessary before the junior college could break away from the public schools and fulfill its "manifest destiny," a phrase George Vaughan applies to the development of community colleges.

By 1972, Richardson, Blocker, and Bender described community colleges as having "autocratic leaders making all the major decisions in the context of rigid bureaucracy, secrecy and attitude, 'if you don't like it, you can leave'" (p. v). The once-positive image of the "commander" leading the ship had given way to the image of the autocrat, which under specific organizational conditions, was not viewed as acceptable by at least some writers. The idea of shared decision making that Richardson et al. advocated provided a brief interlude in the pursuit of the "great man" ideal of leadership. The contrasts between the "errand boy" of the junior college under control of the public school, and the supreme elected officer, kingpin, gamey athlete, and the commander of the post-war years, and the autocratic leader of the 1960s suggest that the attribution of autocratic leadership styles to community college leaders is, more appropriately, a function of history and organizational life cycle—partially a result of the community college struggle for independence from the public schools, rather than a result of its origins there.

Growth and Maturation: Imagery of the 1960s to mid-1980s

As community colleges continued to develop and more clearly define their educational roles during the 1960s, they entered a period of growth and maturation. Leadership images are still predominantly those of the "commander" and "great man," probably because the explosive growth in the number of community colleges meant that many institutions were individually replicating the earlier historical patterns of the 1940s and 1950s. Many of the characteristics—particularly "inspiration" and a "pioneering" spirit—once attributed to the national leaders in the community college movement became part of the rhetoric used to describe institutional leaders as well. Many new college presidents approached their office in the tradition of those prominent national figures.

John Roueche, George Baker, and Robert Rose, describing the 1960s, characterized them as "times [that] demanded builders, political persuaders, organizers and master plan developers" (1989, 40). The "builders" were great pioneers with great visions who translated their ideas and dreams into programs and buildings. Presidents were (and, as importantly, were expected to be) competitive, innovative, fast-moving, flexible, calculated risk takers, tough, dominating, and ones who played to win (Brint and Karabel 1989; Deegan and Tillery 1985). Even as the administrative infrastructure of the developing community college became more differentiated, most community college presidents continued to adopt the strong authoritarian and power figure role of the early national leaders (Alfred and Smydra 1985, 204).

Institutional growth, increased organizational complexity, and expanded involvement by a wide range of constituents characterized community colleges during the late 1960s and early 1970s. It had been critical that the founding presidents be visionaries, able to engage the community in the concept of community colleges as a viable educational sector, and that they have the quality of inspiring leadership (Bogue 1950). During the period of organizational growth and maturation, community colleges needed presidents who were efficient managers, rather than visionaries. The emphasis of the manager-leader president was on efficiency and increased productivity during the late 1960s and 1970s, coupled with the internal and external environmental changes related to organizational maturity. This inward focus belies a subtle shift in the presidential role from provider of a global community college vision to individual institutional vision, although not all presidents effectively communicated local visions. In many cases, college presidents were unwilling, unable, or at least very hesitant to clearly interpret and articulate their institutional missions to relevant constituency groups (Hall and Alfred 1985; Vaughan 1988). Sometimes this silence resulted in constituent confusion and disenchantment; but, in fact, during this period when community colleges truly attempted to be "all things to all people," there may have been benefits in not attempting to clarify mission.

Community colleges as educational organizations approaching maturity during the late 1970s no longer faced rapid expansion or abundant funding. Roueche et al. suggest that this slowed growth "resulted in myopic vision" (1989, 116) in community college leaders which, in turn, eventually led to constituent demands for reinforcing a broader, comprehensive sense of institutional identity. In looking to the 1990s and beyond, James Hudgins, president of Midlands Technical

College, captures the growth of community college organizations in these life cycle images: "Most [community colleges] experienced the excitement of birth in the 1960s, the headiness of growth in the 1970s, and the trials and difficulties of adolescence and young adulthood in the 1980s" (1990, [1]). Maturity is characterized by stabilization of growth (Lorenzo 1989), after which the organization faces the inevitable choice of renewal or decline. Both Hudgins and Lorenzo agree that the primary leadership task for community college presidents during the maturity phase is to establish a basis upon which organizational renewal can occur. Inevitably, this foundation involves the reclarification and/or reinterpretation of the institutional mission.

One of the conflicts in resolving the organizational positioning of community colleges for the future seems to stem, in part, from the sense that this reclarified mission should be a dramatic and sweeping vision, something radically new that fundamentally alters the nature of the community college. For example, Roueche et al. urge leaders "to create something new out of something old"— a major change, not just "incremental adjustments of transactional leadership" (1989, 32). The traditional perspective on transformational leadership, as described by J. MacGregor Burns (1978), is an emphasis on change, usually an all-consuming overhauling of mission, goals, and values concerned with ideals such as liberty, justice, and equality. This definition, however, also implies that leadership originates from a "single, highly visible individual" who then communicates it persuasively and powerfully, down to the faculty and out to the community (Bensimon, Neumann, and Birnbaum 1989, 74). The logical candidate for this position is the dynamic community college "commander."

Transformational leadership, in its traditional form, has usually been associated with national or social movements, which makes it natural to see great-man leadership in the community college movement as well. At an institutional level, however, transformational leadership is most relevant for an institution in crisis where an autocratic, charismatic leader is not only needed but welcomed. Although they certainly face important choices at this stage of organizational maturity, most community colleges are no longer in crisis nor are they likely to accept willingly a dominating "great man" president again.

On the one hand, this emphasis on transforming leadership, the "great man," and dynamic change should come as no surprise. These images have been consistent in community college literature over time and are currently popular in trade publications. Given the stage in the organizational life cycle of most community colleges, we question the appropriateness of this popularity, however. A closer examination of the research which provided the substance of the Roueche et al. (1989) book, *Shared Vision: Transformational Leadership in American Community Colleges*, emphasizes elements of effective leadership (for example, cultural awareness and continuity with change) that resemble those Estela Bensimon (1989) describes as "trans-vigorational" and that John Gardner (1986) describes as renewal. Yet, as "mainstream" community college authors, Roueche et al. chose to call their leadership behaviors "transformational" and their leaders, "blue chippers," both terms continuing the traditional, elite imagery. There is an apparent recognition of the kind of leadership required for community colleges in the maturity life cycle stage, yet there is an equally strong reluctance to relinquish the heroic images ingrained in the literature and in the minds of scholars and critics. It is as though choosing to use alternative language somehow makes the leadership images less real, less valid.

Roueche et al. (1989) are not alone in their inability to re-vision leadership for the future of community colleges by finding persuasive images of participative or renewing leaders. Several authors describe the activities community college leaders must undertake to move their institutions into renewal and away from decline, indicating a certain understanding about this stage of the organizational life cycle. In some cases, these activities are outlined in "image neutral" phrases. For instance, George Vaughan (1986), a scholar of the community college in addition to being a former community college president, defines the four primary roles of community college presidents for the 1990s as interpreting and communicating the institutional mission, managing the institution, creating the campus climate, and serving as educational leader. John Keyser (1988), president of Clackamas Community College, advocates collaborative decision making for the future, as does the report *Building Communities: A Vision for a New Century* (Commission 1988).

In other cases, some authors reinforce the imagery of command when describing appropriate leadership behaviors for renewal, which continues to legitimate "great man" leadership. John Jacob (1989), president and chief executive officer of the National Urban League, invokes military images when he talks of leaders who need to "marshall" community support and "join forces" with community organizations. An editor's note in *Leadership Abstracts* quotes certain leadership traits that *U.S. News & World Report* advocated for the executive of the twenty-first century as applicable to community college leaders of the future. Among them were "Master of Technology" and the "Leader/Motivator" who would be "less a commander than a coach" (Doucette 1988 [1-2]). Again, while the leadership behaviors (for example, technological innovation and motivation) seem appropriate for an institution moving toward renewal, the repeated use of male pronouns, male nouns (Doucette uses only male examples), and military and athletic metaphors project into the twenty-first century a community college executive image that continues to be exclusionary.

Jess Parrish (1988) also uses athletic imagery in discussing future leaders of community colleges: "Leaders, like athletes, are bigger, stronger, quicker, and better coached than ever. A generation of community college lore is available to current and upcoming leaders, and the smart ones are using it. . . . Somewhere out there is another Priest, another Cosand, and another Fordyce" (1988, [1]). Parrish's new leader is simply a new version of the old hero who should be relying on the lore (stories, myths, legends, etc.) to understand his or her role. We would argue that the use of such language has become so ingrained in the community college literature and the leadership images created by this language so normative that the authors may not realize the limitations of the message they are reinforcing.

Alternative Voices

There have been and continue to be alternative voices and images of leadership. Writing in 1972, Richard Richardson, Clyde Blocker, and Louis Bender provided the earliest, most obvious alternative when they disapprovingly described the "autocratic" style of community college leaders (p. v). They proposed instead a model of shared governance, with ideals of participation. Although some scholars picked up the concept, our review suggests that major community college authors have only recently adopted it.

Alternative voices and images of leadership, while not exclusively those of women, have most frequently emerged from the feminist movement. Alternative images have allowed women to be included where traditional images exclude them. At least two widely read books on the community college presidency have attempted, more or less successfully, to address past inattention to women presidents often by devoting a chapter specifically to women presidents. For example, Roueche, Baker, and Rose include such a chapter, written by a woman graduate student who was listed as chapter author but was not accorded a place as one of the book's authors (1989, 235-63). Only four of the fifty elite "blue chippers," who are the focus of the entire volume, are women.

George Vaughan (1989) also reserves a chapter for women presidents, but much of its attention goes to the problems women have in becoming and being presidents rather than the opportunities for creative leadership that they offer. The overall message is thus a discouraging one for women, even though Vaughan reports that the presidency is described as "asexual" by those women who make it, which in itself may not be an encouraging note. Former community college president Judith Eaton makes a serious contribution toward a new image by asking whether leadership, as traditionally defined, is important to enhancing individual capacity, whether educational institutions can make a difference in individuals, and even whether presidents, by themselves, can make a difference in modern society (Eaton 1988). She seems to be calling for a more involving form of leadership, a sharing of leadership roles.

The most significant of the current alternative voices emanates from the National Institute for Leadership Development. Supported by the American Association of Women in Community and Junior Colleges, the Maricopa Community College District, and now also by the League for Innovation in the Community College, the National Institute seeks to promote "leadership in a different voice": leadership based on connectedness and collaboration rather than hierarchy, authority, and power. Rooted in the work of Carol Gilligan (1982), the National Institute assumes that women's leadership styles and preferences are different from men's, and thus provides a new model of leadership based on the many threads in the web of campus life rather than on the all-powerful leader. Carol Cross and John Ravekes praise Mildred Bulpit and Carolyn Desjardins as

> . . . leaders for their work in running the National Institute for Leadership Development. These women have been a major influence on the way that a significant number (over 1,100) of the women in community colleges view themselves and their jobs. They are also central to the growing national women's network among community college personnel. Few presidents have such direct impact on the people they direct as these women do on the colleagues they nurture. (1990, 12)

The fact that Bulpit and Desjardins are praised for nurturing rather than commanding is significant. At least in the work of the National Institute, nurturing is an alternative image to be encouraged.

The *AAWCJC Journal* is another example of an alternative voice, where the image of leadership reflected in various articles printed in the 1988, 1989, and 1990 issues conveys connectedness, cooperation, and "webs and nets" rather than pyramids and hierarchical ladders. These alternative voices, however, are frequently marginalized. The *AAWWCJC Journal* is received only by members, is indexed on ERIC only by entire issue, not by author or title, and is not received by most libraries. In work that is more widely disseminated, alternative models and voices are relegated to a chapter typically toward the end of the book, if they are included at all (for example, Vaughan 1989). On the occasion of the National Institute for Leadership Development's tenth anniversary, it was formally honored for its work by the League for Innovation at the league's Summer Institute. Once recognized by the "mainstream," perhaps this group will acquire more legitimacy.

Conclusion

In this paper we have attempted to show, through an examination of the literature, that the leadership behaviors exemplified by "General Koos and Colonels Eells and Campbell" have become immortalized in the community college lore about leadership. These strong, often militaristic, descriptors have perpetuated the "great man" style of leadership, even when the writers sometimes recognize a need for a different type of leadership (e.g., Roueche et al. 1989). Contemporary writers (e.g., Deegan and Tillery 1985; Parrish 1988; Brint and Karabel 1989), like those of the past (e.g., Bogue 1950), reinforce the "great man" view of leadership by repeatedly referring to the few great leaders who have shaped the movement. They tell us that community colleges, more so than any other segment of postsecondary education, have been shaped and promoted by a handful of influential leaders. Furthermore, we are reminded of the critical need of replacing these specific leaders when they retire from active duty. (For example, Parrish referred to Priest, Cosand, Fordyce, Colvert, Martorana, and others [1988, (1)]). Perhaps we should expect no less from institutions that are considered part of a larger movement. The very use of this term implies some great force at work that demands great leadership from a select few.

One consequence of this approach to leadership is its unspoken but effective removal of leader candidates who do not fit the images and the marginalization of writers who do not use the same language in their writing.

Two aspects of this finding merit discussion. The first relates to the creation and control of knowledge itself. A relatively few scholars or writers have been stamped as the spokespersons for the community college movement and have retained control of knowledge and the discourse by which it is disseminated. These scholars, with a few exceptions, have been relatively closed to research done by individuals outside of the circle and defensive in the face of criticism or change. The research of the core writers on community college leadership, such as that of Vaughan, Roueche et al., has been criticized for sacrificing objectivity for message.[1] Gaining access to the inner circle of accepted writers in the field is also difficult, especially for those promoting alternative images. Consequently one of the concerns for leadership in community colleges, particularly since they are so reliant on the "lore," is who is writing and will write on the topic in the future.

This concern is directly related to the second point: Can women and minorities possibly fit the images of leadership portrayed in the literature? As Rosemary Gillett-Karam (1989) concluded, effective leadership is "a concept relating attributes of community college presidents without reference to their sex" (1989, 255). In other words, she found few differences between women and men on major dimensions of leadership behavior. This is consistent with Cynthia Epstein's (1988) review of much of the gender research of the last two decades. Epstein concludes that gender differences are not empirically "real." Rather, because of how gender and gender relations are socially constructed, we persist in believing that there are differences. We perpetuate these differences in our language, writing, symbols, and images. For instance, it is not easy to imagine women or minorities as pioneers[2], commanders, builders, athletes, and even blue-chippers.

Even as women slowly gain access to community college presidencies, their accomplishments are marginalized or discussed in terms of "problems" rather than potential. For example, Vaughan observes: "Although women encounter certain difficulties that men do not when seeking the presidency, to assume that being female caused failure to be selected for a given presidency is to greatly oversimplify the presidential selection process . . . . Trustees are obligated to determine the right fit, or chemistry for a college at a particular time and location. There are some cases when the right fit requires a white male president and other cases when it requires a female president (1989, 76). Such a statement dramatically reinforces our point: Images of leadership, in this case, gender images, whether appropriate or not, determine who gains access to positions of power.

Yet can community colleges, serving such diverse constituencies, afford to maintain images of leadership that are narrow and exclusionary? Organizationally, can they afford to perpetuate the great-man model of leadership when many writers agree that different behaviors are called for?

Linda Alcoff (1988) commented that post-structuralism deconstructs but offers no alternative construction in its wake. The challenge facing community college scholars and practitioners is to create alternative construction(s) of leadership that reflect and convey the rich tradition, history, and spirit of the community college movement, that meet the demands of leadership for organizational renewal, and do not recreate the binary oppositions (commander/subordinate) which have permeated the discourse in the past. Using terms like *great man, pioneer, builder, commander, visionary* (and their opposites) in effect excludes groups of people who do not fit the image and perpetuates the view that the success or failure of any community college rests in the hands of one or a few "great leaders."

More promising images of leaders are also found in John Gardner's pathfinder (1990, 128) and Harland Cleveland's (1985) knowledge executive. Although more inclusive than military or sports images and more reflective of behaviors necessary for organizational renewal in the twenty-first century, these images still focus on *the* leader in positions of influence. However, if leadership is viewed as a process rather than a position one might adopt verbs such as *empower, facilitate, collaborate,* and *educate,* and metaphors such as *weaver, cultivator, networker,* and *connector* to capture the essences of effective leadership.

Attempting to conceptualize alternative images of leadership has demonstrated the difficult challenge confronting community colleges, as well as other organizations. Our study underscores how strongly Western conceptions of leadership are grounded in the ideology of the philosopher-king and military hero even when behaviors associated with such leadership are viewed as inappropriate. It might be fruitful to search other cultures for alternative images. The Chinese philosopher Lao Tzu instructs leaders: "Imagine that you are a midwife. . . . You are assisting at someone else's birth. . . . The leader is helping others to find their own success. There is plenty to go around. Sharing success with others is very successful" (in Heider 1989, 162-63). How different might community colleges (and the world) be if these were the images of leadership to which we ascribed and to which we aspired? And where are these more appropriate than for institutions called *community* colleges?

Notes

1. We do not intend to imply that this situation is different from or worse than writing on leadership in four-year colleges and universities. We argue that bias In that sector is thinly veiled as science and results from theoretical and methodological choices.

2. Much has recently been written about women pioneers in western history. These accounts tell of the activities of the women who went west rather than ignoring women based on an a priori definition of *pioneer* that would exclude the activities of women.

Bibliography

Alcoff, Linda. "Cultural Feminism Versus Post-structuralism: The Identity Crisis in Feminist Theory." In *Reconstructing the Academy*, edited by Elizabeth Minnich, Jean O'Barr, and Rachel Rosenfeld, 257–88. Chicago: University of Chicago Press, 1988.

Alfred, Richard L., and David F. Smydra. "Reforming Governance: Resolving Challenges to Institutional Authority." In *Renewing the American Community College*, edited by William L. Deegan, Dale Tillery, and Associates, 199–228. San Francisco: Jossey-Bass, Inc., 1985.

Bartky, John. "The Nature of Junior College Administration." *Junior College Journal* 28 (1957): 3–7.

Bensimon, Estela M. "Transactional, Transformational and 'Trans-vigorational' Leaders." *Leadership Abstracts* 2, no. 6 (April 1989), not paginated. Newsletter of the League for Innovation in the Community College.

Bensimon, Estela M., Anna Neumann, and Robert Birnbaum. *Making Sense of Administrative Leadership: The 'L' Word in Higher Education*. ASHE-ERIC Higher Education Report No. 1. Washington, D.C.: School of Education and Human Development, George Washington University, 1989.

Bogue, Jesse P. *The Community College*. New York: McGraw-Hill, 1950.

Brint, Steven, and Jerome Karabel. *The Diverted Dream: Community Colleges and the Promise of Educational Opportunity in America, 1900-1985*. New York: Oxford University Press, 1989.

Brothers, E. Q. "Present Day Practices and Tendencies in the Administration and Organization of Public Junior Colleges." *School Review* 36 (1928): 665–74.

Burns, J. MacGregor. *Leadership*. New York: Harper and Row, 1978.

Cameron, Kim. "Organizational Adaptation and Higher Education." *The Journal of Higher Education* 55 (April/May 1984): 122–44.

Cameron, Kim, and Ray Zammuto. "Matching Managerial Strategies to Conditions of Decline." *Human Resource Management* 22, no. 4 (Winter 1983): 359–75.

Carpenter, W. W., and J. R. Johnson. "The Junior College Dean." *Junior College Journal* 13 (1942): 19–21.

Cherryholmes, Cleo. *Power and Criticism: Poststructural Investigations in Education*. New York: Teachers College Press, 1988.

Cleveland, Harlan. *The Knowledge Executive: Leadership in an Information Society*. New York: E. P. Dutton, 1985.

Commission on the Future of Community Colleges. "Building Communities: A Vision for a New Century." *Leadership Abstracts* 1, no. 12 (July 1988), not paginated. Newsletter of the League for Innovation in the Community College.

Connelly, F. Michal, and D. Jean Clandinin. "Stories of Experience and Narrative Inquiry." *Educational Researcher* 19 (June/July 1990): 2–14.

Cross, Carol, and John E. Ravekes. "Leadership in a Different Voice." *AAWCJC Journal* 1990, 7–14.

Doucette, Don, ed. "The 21st Century Executive." *Leadership Abstracts* 1, no. 8 (April 1988), not paginated. Newsletter of the League for Innovation in the Community College.

Eaton, Judith S. "Love Me, Lead Me, and Leave Me Alone." In *Leaders on Leadership: The College Presidency*, edited by James L. Fisher and Martha W. Tack, 75–80. New Directions for Higher Education No. 61. San Francisco: Jossey-Bass, Inc., 1988.

Eells, William C. *The Junior College*. Boston: Houghton Mifflin Co., 1931.

Epstem, Cynthia. *Deceptive Distinctions: Sex, Gender, and the Social Structure*. New Haven: Yale University Press and New York: Russell Sage Foundation, 1988.

Foster, F. M. "Uniformity in Administrative Nomenclature *Junior College Journal* 3 (1933): 362–64.

Fowler, Roger. "Power." In *Handbook of Discourse Analysis, Volume* 4, edited by Teun A. van Dijk, 61–82. London: Academic Press, 1985.

Gardner, John W. *On Leadership.* New York: Free Press, 1990.

_____. *Tasks of Leadership.* Leadership Papers No.2. Washington, D.C.: Independent Sector, 1986.

Gergen Mary McCanney. "Feminist Critique of Science and the Challenge of Epistemology." In *Feminist Thought and the Structure of Knowledge,* edited by Mary McCanney Gergen, 87–104. New York: New York University Press, 1988.

Gillett-Karam, Rosemary. "Women in Leadership Roles." In *Shared Vision: Transformational Leadership in American Community Colleges,* edited by John E. Roueche, George A. Baker III, and Robert R. Rose, 235–63. Washington, D.C.: The Community College Press and the American Association of Community and Junior Colleges, 1989.

Gilligan, Carol. *In a Different Voice: Psychological Theory and Women's Development.* Cambridge, Mass.: Harvard University Press, 1982.

Giroux, Henry A. *Schooling and the Struggle for Public Life: Critical Pedagogy in the Modern Age.* Minneapolis: University of Minnesota Press, 1988.

Greiner, Larry. "Evolution and Revolution as Organizations Grow." *Harvard Business Review* 50 (July-August 1972): 37–46.

Hall, Robert A., and Richard L. Alfred. "Applied Research on Leadership in Community Colleges." *Community College Review* 12 (1985): 36–41.

Heider, John. "The Leader Who Knows How Things Happen." In *Contemporary Issues in Leadership,* edited by William E. Rosenbach and Robert L. Taylor, 161–67. Boulder, Colo.: Westview Press, 1989.

Hill, Morton. "Steps in the Organization of the Junior College." In *The Junior College: Its Organization and Administration,* edited by W. M. Proctor, 26–40. Palo Alto, Calif.: Stanford University Press, 1927.

Hudgins, J. L. "Renewing a Mature Community College." *Leadership Abstracts* 3, no. 4 (February 1990), not paginated. Newsletter of the League for Innovation in the Community College.

Jacob, John E. "Education and the Revitalization of Urban America." *Leadership Abstracts* 2, no. 19 (1989), not paginated. Newsletter of the League for Innovation in the Community College.

Johnson, J. R, and W. W. Carpenter. "Dean or Errand Boy?" *Junior College Journal* 13 (1943): 381–83.

Keyser, John S. "Collaborative Decision-making." *Leadership Abstracts* 1, no. 17 (October 1988), not paginated. Newsletter of the League for Innovation in the Community College.

Kolodny, Annette. "A Map for Rereading: Gender and the Interpretation of Literary Texts." In *Feminist Criticism: Essays on Women, Literature and Theory,* edited by E. Showalter, 46–62. New York: Pantheon Books, 1985.

Lather, Patti. *Getting Smart: Feminist Research and Pedagogy with/in the Postmodern.* New York: Routledge, 1991.

Lee, Charles, and W. E. Rosenstengel. "Philosophy of Junior College Administration." *Junior College Journal* 8 (1938): 227–30.

Lorenzo, Albert L. "A Foundation for Renewal." *Leadership Abstracts* 2, no. 12 (July 1989), not paginated. Newsletter of the League for Innovation in the Community College.

Nielsen, Joyce McCarl. Introduction. In *Feminist Research Methods: Exemplary Readings in the Social Sciences,* edited by Joyce McCarl Nielsen, 1–37. Boulder: Westview Press, 1990.

Parrish, Jess H. "Individual and Croup Responsibility for Leadership Development." *Leadership Abstracts* 1, no. 7 (April 1988), not paginated. Newsletter of the League for Innovation in the Community College.

Pierce, A. C. "Deans in the Organization and Administration of Junior Colleges." *Junior College Journal* 21 (1951): 364–66.

Potter, Jonathan, and Margaret Wetherell. *Discourse and Social Psychology: Beyond Attitudes and Behavior.* London: Sage Publications, 1987.

President's Commission on Higher Education. *Higher Education for American Democracy.* Washington, D.C.: U.S. Government Printing Office, 1947.

Proctor, W. M. *The Junior College: Its Organization and Administration.* Palo Alto, Calif.: Stanford University Press, 1927.

Ratcliff, James L. "'First' Public Junior Colleges in an Age of Reform." *Journal of Higher Education* 58 (1987): 151–80.

Richardson, Richard C., Clyde E. Blocker, and Louis W. Bender. *Governance for the Two-Year College.* Englewood Cliffs, N.J.: Prentice-Hall, 1972.

Roueche, John E., George A. Baker III, and Robert R. Rose. *Shared Vision: Transformational Leadership in American Community Colleges*. Washington, D.C.: The Community College Press and the American Association of Community and Junior Colleges, 1989.

Selznick, Philip. *Leadership in Administration*. 1957; reprint ed., Berkeley and Los Angeles: University of California Press, 1984.

Shotter, John, and Josephine Logan. 'The Pervasiveness of Patriarchy: On Finding a Different Voice." In *Feminist Thought and the Structure of Knowledge*, edited by Mary McCanney Gergen, 69–86. New York: New York University Press, 1988.

Spender, Dale. *Man Made Language*. London: Routledge & Kegan Publishers, 1980.

Tillery, Dale, and William L. Deegan. "The Evolution of Two-Year Colleges through Four Generations." In *Renewing the American Community College: Priorities and Strategies for Effective Leadership*, edited by William L. Deegan and Dale Tillery, 3–33. San Francisco: Jossey-Bass, Inc., 1985.

van Dijk, Teun A. "Introduction: The Role of Discourse Analysis in Society." In *Handbook of Discourse Analysis, Volume 4*, edited by Teun A. van Dijk, 1-8. London: Academic Press, 1985.

Vaughan, George B. *The Community College Presidency*. New York: ACE/Macmillan, 1986.

_____. Bringing Focus to the Presidency. *Leadership Abstracts* 1, no. 6 (March 1988), not paginated. Newsletter of the League for Innovation in the Community College.

_____. Leadership in Transition: The Community College Presidency. New York: ACE/Macmillan, 1989.

Warren, Carol A. B. *Gender Issues in Field Research*. Newbury Park, Calif.: Sage Publications, 1988.

Marilyn J. Amey is assistant professor and Susan B. Twombly is associate professor in the Department of Educational Policy and Administration at the University of Kansas in Lawrence. The authors thank numerous community college administrators, reviewers, and members of the Review *staff for their helpful comments and criticisms.*

CHAPTER 15

TRUSTEES' PERCEPTIONS OF THE DESIRED QUALIFICATIONS FOR THE NEXT GENERATION OF COMMUNITY COLLEGE PRESIDENTS

KATHLEEN PLINSKE[1] AND WALTER J. PACKARD[1]

Abstract. Although the authority for hiring a community college president resides with the board of trustees, few studies have directly explored trustees' perceptions of the desired qualifications for presidents. Using a Delphi process, this study identified the characteristics, competencies, and professional experiences that Illinois community college trustees value in presidential candidates.

Keywords: trustees, presidents, Delphi technique, Illinois

Community colleges have become centers of educational opportunity, responding to the unique needs of the local areas they serve. Committed to accessibility and affordability, community colleges have open-admission policies and relatively low tuition costs, and they serve students of diverse ages, academic preparation levels, ethnic and cultural heritages, and socioeconomic backgrounds. Although community colleges have become vital components in support of the health and economic well-being of the communities they serve, it is well known that community colleges are facing a sea change in presidential leadership (Schults, 2001; Weisman & Vaughan, 2007).

As a result, it is critical that trustees and those interested in becoming community college presidents approach this time of significant institutional transition thoughtfully, examining the criteria boards use to make presidential selections. As illustrated in Figure 1, a great deal of research has been conducted on the selection of community college presidents. The items in Figure 1 represent studies (drawn from a ProQuest search covering the years 1990 through 2006) of what key community college stakeholders perceive to be the requisite competencies and characteristics of successful presidents. However, rather than exploring trustees' perceptions directly, many of these studies examine the characteristics and professional experiences of current presidents or explore current presidents' perceptions about what factors led a board of trustees to select them as presidents. Although the results of these studies could potentially be used to extrapolate the criteria that board members have used when selecting a president, it would be more effective to directly explore board members' perceptions about hiring criteria. As one president responded in a study of presidents' perceptions of factors affecting the selection process, "Who cares what the president thinks. It's the board that counts; I want to know what they think" (Bumpas, 1998, p. 177). Furthermore, the roles of community college presidents are changing, and the expectations placed on them are growing more complex (Hockaday & Puyear, 2000). Therefore, it is possible that the characteristics of current presidents may not necessarily mirror the ideal characteristics that boards of trustees will identify for future presidential candidates.

---

[1]McHenry County College, Crystal Lake, IL

	Hammons & Keller (1990)	Hood (1997)	Townsend & Bassoppo-Moyo (1997)	Pierce & Pedersen (1997)	Hockaday and Puyear (2000)	Desjardins & Huff (2001)	Brown, Martinez, & Daniel (2002)	Wallin (2002)	Powell (2004)	Olson-Nikunen (2004)	Cook (2004)	Turner (2005)
Communication skills	•	•				•	•		•	•		•
Leadership		•			•	•				•	•	•
Sound judgment	•	•		•	•							•
Budgetary skills			•			•		•		•	•	
Vision					•	•	•			•	•	
Ability to make sound decisions	•	•									•	•
Ability to build relationships					•	•		•	•			
Integrity and ability to build trust	•				•							•
Ability to influence strategically						•				•		•
Delegates effectively and empowers others	•					•						•
Creates cohesiveness/teambuilding						•				•		•
Interpersonal skills	•						•					
Knowledge of and commitment to mission	•						•					
Embraces cultural diversity			•			•						
Flexibility			•	•								
Champions change						•				•		
Creates student-centered learning environment						•						•
Maintains high standards						•				•		
Accepts personal responsibility											•	•
Able to control personal conduct											•	•
Commitment to students											•	•
Persistence and commitment	•				•							
Mediation, negotiation, & consensus-building skills							•					•
Personnel selection	•											
Motivation	•											
Literate in technology			•									
Openness			•									
Patience			•									
Personal adaptability				•								
Confidence					•							
Courage					•							
Technical knowledge of community colleges					•							
Maintains perspective						•						
Maintains equilibrium						•						
Prevents crises						•						
Fosters creativity and innovation						•						
Recognizes and rewards excellence						•						
Invests in professional development						•						
Strengthens infrastructure						•						
Enhances productivity						•						
Corrects performance problems						•						
Conflict resolution skills							•					
Ability to assess institutional effectiveness							•					
Knowledge of curriculum development							•					
Organization and time management skills							•					
Personal code of ethics												•
Maintains core values												•

Figure 1 Summary of competencies and characteristics recommended for community college presidents

It has been widely documented that community colleges are facing an "impending leadership crisis" (Schults, 2001, p. 1). Many current presidents began their careers in community colleges during the time of rapid growth in the 1960s and 1970s (Schults, 2001); therefore, large numbers of presidents are approaching retirement age. In fact, a 2006 study revealed that 84% of community college presidents anticipated retiring within 10 years (Weisman & Vaughan, 2007). These anticipated retirements are significant because "inestimable experience and history, as well as an intimate understanding of the community college mission, values, and culture, will disappear, leaving an enormous gap in the collective memory and the leadership of community colleges" (Schults, 2001, p. 2). To preserve their vitality, community colleges must be prepared to effectively select candidates to fill a large number of presidential openings. Accordingly, this study explores the characteristics, competencies, and professional experiences that trustees believe are critical for future community college presidents to possess.

Selection of Community College Presidents

The ultimate authority for selecting a community college president resides with the board of trustees (Association of Community College Trustees, 2009). Community colleges are governed by a board, and, depending on the state where the college is located, trustees are either locally elected, locally appointed, state elected, or state appointed (Vaughan, 2006). Regardless of its structure, one of the most important roles of a community college board of trustees is to recruit, select, and hire a new president (Boggs, 2006). In this role, trustees are responsible for appointing a search committee, determining the characteristics and qualifications of an ideal candidate, overseeing advertisement of the position and recruitment of candidates, reviewing applicants, interviewing finalists, and, finally, appointing a new president (Association of Community College Trustees, 2007).

Although the responsibilities of boards of trustees in the presidential search process are clearly outlined, the criteria that trustees use to make hiring decisions are not as apparent. Higher education, in principle, has long recognized the importance of identifying position and candidate requirements in presidential searches. Giles (1969) reported that developing criteria for the position was one of the key roles of the presidential selection committee. Likewise, Bromert (1984) found that successful presidential searches depend in part on a clear articulation of the qualifications expected of candidates. Furthermore, the Association of Community College Trustees (2007) has indicated that the determination of qualifications and ideal characteristics of a presidential candidate is one of the key roles that a board of trustees plays in the presidential selection process.

Despite the fact that presidential openings are often advertised with a published position statement that includes desired characteristics and minimum qualifications of applicants, these statements often include generic descriptions that are broad and ambiguous and that are subject to a number of different interpretations by the members of the board of trustees. Examples of these ideal characteristics include being "a strong advocate on behalf of students" (Chippewa Valley Technical College, 2007), having the ability to "understand and commit passionately to the mission of a comprehensive community college" (North Idaho College, 2007), possessing "excellent communication skills" (Durham Technical Community College, 2007), and being able "to plan strategically" (Eastern Wyoming College, 2007). These advertised qualifications are often quite broad and seem to merely enumerate the minimum expectations of a chief executive. In addition, "institutional fit" is often cited as a factor influencing the selection of community college presidents (Bumpas, 1998), but it is unclear what factors the term *fit* encompasses or how it is recognized or interpreted by board members. Accordingly, board members themselves admit to using criteria beyond the qualifications listed in presidential position statements in hiring decisions (Nasworthy, 2002).

Research Design

This study used a Delphi process to explore the beliefs of experienced community college trustees in the state of Illinois regarding characteristics, competencies, and professional experiences considered essential for future community college presidents. The Delphi process was first developed by the RAND Corporation to assist in forecasting and decision making by surveying experts who would be difficult to bring together in a face-to-face group. A Delphi study "may be characterized as a method for structuring a group communication process so that the process is effective in allowing a group of individuals, as a whole, to deal with a complex problem" (Linstone & Turoff, 1975, p. 3).

Procedural Steps in the Delphi Process

The Delphi process begins by soliciting input individually from a panel of experts, followed by the researcher's review and compilation of the responses. The compiled responses are then sent back to panel members for their review and ranking. The researcher then reviews and compiles the rankings and sends the results back to the panel for reconsideration, taking into account the collective opinion of the group.

Phase 1. The first phase of a classical Delphi study includes soliciting input about a topic from the panel of experts through a series of open-ended questions that allow participants complete freedom in their responses. The list of items generated during the analysis of data collected in the first phase of a Delphi study is the basis of the questionnaire instrument used in Phase 2 of the study.

Phase 2. The second phase of a Delphi study consists of "reaching an understanding of how the group views the issue (i.e., where the members agree or disagree and what they mean by relative terms such as importance, desirability, or feasibility)" (Linstone & Turoff, 1975, p. 6). Each member of the expert panel is sent a copy of the list of items generated in Phase 1 and asked to individually rate or rank each item. This is frequently achieved through the use of a 5- or 7-point Likert-type scale (Clayton, 1997; Jenkins & Smith, 1994).

The data collected in this second phase are analyzed, and a statistical summary, including a measure of central tendency and level of dispersion, is calculated for each item. (Participants in this study were asked to rate the importance of each item on a scale of 1 to 7, with 1 representing the lowest rating and 7 representing the highest rating.) Commonly, this includes a calculation of the median and interquartile range (Jenkins & Smith, 1994) to identify items for which consensus was reached on their relative importance.

Phase 3. In the third phase, panel members are sent a questionnaire that includes each of the items for which consensus was not achieved along with its corresponding statistical summary, which was calculated in the second phase of the study. Participants also receive a Likert-type scale to reevaluate the items. The items on the questionnaire should be "ordered randomly . . . to minimize formation of response sets" (McBride, Pates, Ramadan, & McGowan, 2003, p. 491). Each member of the panel is asked to individually "examine the data and, in effect, to reassess his own position based on the group's responses" (Brooks, 1979, p. 378).

Identifying consensus and stability. The primary purpose for using the Delphi process "is to gain consensus or judgment among a group of perceived experts on a topic" (Keeney, Hasson, & McKenna, 2006, pp. 209-210). Accordingly, the data collected in the second and third phases are analyzed to determine if consensus has been reached among the experts. The literature, however, does not provide clear criteria for selecting measures of consensus (Keeney et al., 2006), and levels of consensus vary from study to study (Rayens & Hahn, 2000).

One common method for determining consensus is to examine the interquartile range (IQR) of the ratings of each of the items (Rayens & Hahn, 2000; Rojewski & Meers, 1991). As Rayens and Hahn (2000) explain, "the interquartile range is the absolute value of the difference between the 75th and 25th percentiles, with smaller values indicating higher consensus" (p. 311). Based on the literature, an IQR that is 20% of the rating scale appears to be a conservative but acceptable criterion for determining consensus.

While IQR values can be used to determine if consensus has been achieved for each item, the literature provides little guidance as to the percentage of items for which consensus should be achieved before concluding the study. Furthermore, it is possible that consensus will not be achieved on the relative importance of particular items, even after multiple rounds. It is therefore also useful to analyze responses for stability as well as consensus. Stability has been defined as less than a 15% change in responses between rounds (Scheibe, Skutsch, & Shofer, 1975).

Procedures and Analysis

Selection of Experts

The selection process for the panel of experts for this Delphi study began by considering all 312 community college trustees in the state of Illinois. The sampling frame included only those trustees who are locally elected, excluding the 39 student trustees in the state and the seven members of the Board of Trustees of the City Colleges of Chicago who are appointed, for a total of

266 trustees. According to Delbecq, Van de Ven, and Gustafson (1975), panel members "must have a deep interest in the problem and important knowledge or experience to share" (p. 88). Therefore, criteria for inclusion in the panel were at least 5 years of service on a community college board and participation in at least one presidential search process.

Sixty trustees responded to the original request for participation; 41 of those respondents were eligible to participate. Of the 41 eligible trustees, 22 indicated that they were planning to attend the Association of Community College Trustees (ACCT) National Legislative Summit, the intended site for initial interviews. It was determined that the 19 trustees who indicated that they were not planning to attend the Legislative Summit would add richness to the study in terms of diversity of community college districts represented as well as in terms of years of experience serving on a board and number of presidential searches in which they participated. Therefore, while 17 trustees participated in an interview as part of Phase 1 of the study, all 41 eligible trustees were included in Phases 2 and 3 of the study, representing 23 of the 39 community college districts in the state of Illinois (59%).

Three research questions were addressed through this study:

1. What characteristics are critical for future community college presidents to exhibit?

2. What competencies are critical for future community college presidents to demonstrate?

3. What professional experiences are critical for future community college presidents to possess?

Results

Characteristics Important for Future Community College Presidents

Participants in the study identified 15 personal attributes that they considered to be important for future community college presidents to possess. These personal attributes are listed below in order of importance as ranked by the participants:

1. Passionate about education—is a champion of community colleges (Mdn = 7.0; IQR = 0.0);

2. Dependable—follows through on commitments; arrives on time or early for appointments and meetings (Mdn = 7.0; IQR = 1.0);

3. Energetic—has a high energy level and is in good health (Mdn = 6.0; IQR = 0.0);

4. Calm under pressure—ability to juggle multiple challenges (Mdn = 6.0; IQR = 1.0);

5. Charismatic—is well liked and respected (Mdn = 6.0; IQR = 1.0);

6. Community involvement—membership in Rotary Club or Kiwanis (Mdn = 6.0; IQR = 1.0);

7. Organized—ability to manage time and resources effectively (Mdn = 6.0; IQR = 1.0);

8. Presence—looks the part of a president, is the image of the institution (Mdn = 6.0; IQR = 1.0);

9. Renaissance person—well rounded and well versed in multiple areas (Mdn = 6.0; IQR = 1.0);

10. Self-aware—has a sense of who he or she is as a person (Mdn = 6.0; IQR = 1.0);

11. Self-motivated—willing to take on challenges (Mdn = 6.0; IQR = 1.0);

12. Tactful—can provide constructive criticism diplomatically (Mdn = 6.0; IQR = 1.0);

13. Well balanced—has a balanced personal and professional life; pursues hobbies and diversions (Mdn = 6.0; IQR = 1.0);

14. Friendly—good sense of humor (Mdn = 5.5; IQR = 1.0);

15. Family person—is married (Mdn = 4.0; IQR = 1.0).

Several of these items have previously been identified in the literature as important characteristics for community college presidents. For example, previous studies have comparable items indicating that it is important for a president to be passionate about education, charismatic, and organized (Cook, 2004; Hammons & Keller, 1990; Hood, 1997; Turner, 2005). However, several characteristics and competencies have not been thoroughly discussed in the recent literature. These include looking "like a president" and being dependable, calm under pressure, self-aware, well balanced, energetic, married, and involved in the community. It appears that other studies have focused more on recommended competencies for presidents rather than on personal attributes.

Competencies Important for Future Community College Presidents

Participants in the study identified 13 general competencies, 8 communication skills, and 12 leadership skills that they considered to be important for future community college presidents to demonstrate. The identified general competencies are listed below in order of importance as ranked by the participants:

1. Has the ability to establish trust (Mdn = 7.0; IQR = 1.0);
2. Has an understanding of accounting and finance—possesses financial acumen, is able to read a financial statement, is able to understand a budget (Mdn = 6.5; IQR = 1.0);
3. Has an understanding of community college funding—including state and local funds, tuition, grants, federal programs, and fundraising (Mdn = 6.5; IQR = 1.0);
4. Has an understanding of the different communities in the college district and their respective needs (Mdn = 6.0; IQR = 0.0);
5. Has an understanding of legal issues facing community colleges (Mdn = 6.0; IQR = 1.0);
6. Has an understanding of marketing—how to attract customers (Mdn = 6.0; IQR = 1.0);
7. Has an understanding of multiculturalism—is comfortable working with people from diverse cultures (Mdn = 6.0; IQR = 1.0);
8. Has an understanding of negotiations and contracts (Mdn = 6.0; IQR = 1.0);
9. Has an understanding of technology—possesses technological literacy (Mdn = 6.0; IQR = 1.0);
10. Has an understanding of the challenges and opportunities of the specific college at which he or she is applying; has done "homework" by reviewing minutes of past board meetings (Mdn = 6.0; IQR = 1.0);
11. Has an understanding of the community college system in general (Mdn = 6.0; IQR = 1.0);
12. Has an understanding of the mission of community colleges (Mdn = 6.0; IQR = 1.0);
13. Has an understanding of unions and labor laws (Mdn = 5.0; IQR = 1.0).

The majority of these competencies have been previously identified in the literature as important skills for community college presidents. In particular, broad and general competencies such as budgetary skills, technical skills, and the ability the build trust are prevalent in the literature related to the community college presidency (Cook, 2004; Desjardins & Huff, 2001; Hammons & Keller, 1990; Hockaday & Puyear, 2000; Townsend & Bassoppo-Moyo, 1997; Turner, 2005; Wallin, 2002). Nevertheless, several narrowly defined competencies emerged from this study that have not been specifically identified in the literature, including an understanding of the different communities in the college's district and their respective needs, an understanding of legal issues facing community colleges, an understanding of marketing, an understanding of the specific college at which a presidential candidate applies, and an understanding of unions and labor laws. The identification of these additional specific competencies may potentially assist aspiring presidents prepare professionally for the position as well as aid boards of trustees as they define the skills they expect their future presidents to possess.

The eight communication skills identified in this study as important for future community college presidents to exhibit are listed below in order of importance as ranked by the participants:

1. Articulate—ability to communicate in written and oral form clearly and professionally (Mdn = 7.0; IQR = 0.0);
2. Good listener—makes people feel like what they are saying is important; is able to read body language effectively (Mdn = 7.0; IQR = 1.0);
3. Media savvy—comfortable working with the media and familiar with media issues (Mdn = 6.0; IQR = 0.0);

4. Networking—skilled at building partnerships and coalitions (Mdn = 6.0; IQR = 1.0);

5. People-person—ability to talk with almost anyone, including different employee groups and constituencies (Mdn = 6.0; IQR = 1.0);

6. Politically savvy—understands the importance of building relationships with legislators and is comfortable with lobbying efforts (Mdn = 6.0; IQR = 1.0);

7. Public speaking—comfortable speaking extemporaneously in front of a large group (Mdn = 6.0; IQR = 1.0);

8. Student-focused—ability to relate to a diverse student body and understand their needs (Mdn = 6.0; IQR = 1.0).

In the review of the literature (see Figure 1), the most frequently occurring recommendation for community college presidents was to possess strong communication skills (Brown, Martinez, & Daniel, 2002; Desjardins & Huff, 2001; Hammons & Keller, 1990; Hood, 1997; Olson-Nikunen, 2004; Powell, 2004; Turner, 2005). The items that emerged in this study help to further clarify and refine the specific competencies that are contained within the overall theme of communication skills. Trustees in this study reached consensus on the importance of eight communication skills, and they agreed that it is critically important for future community college presidents to be articulate and good listeners, as defined by achieving the highest possible median score (7.0).

The 12 leadership skills considered important for future community college presidents to exhibit are listed below in order of importance as ranked by the participants:

1. Good moral character—honest, has integrity, is trustworthy (Mdn = 7.0; IQR = 0.0);

2. Team-player—understands the value of a team, able to recruit and assemble an effective team (Mdn = 7.0; IQR = 1.0);

3. Vision—recognizes where the college is today, articulates where the college should be in the future, and generates buy-in for that vision (*Mdn* = 7.0; IQR = 1.0);

4. Leads by example—is able to motivate employees and bring out the best in them (Mdn = 6.5; IQR = 1.0);

5. Innovative—flexible and open to change (Mdn = 6.0; IQR = 0.0);

6. Persuasive—generates buy-in for decisions, particularly by using facts and data (Mdn = 6.0; IQR = 0.0);

7. Risk-taker—is comfortable taking measured risks (Mdn = 6.0; IQR = 0.0);

8. Sense of confidence and humility—leads without always having to be in the limelight (Mdn = 6.0; IQR = 0.0);

9. Thick-skinned—have a personality that can withstand not always being liked for the decisions he or she makes (Mdn = 6.0; IQR = 0.75);

10. Ability to build consensus—knows how to listen to all sides and help people collate different ideas and reach a good conclusion (Mdn = 6.0; IQR = 1.0);

11. Confronts challenges—faces issues head on and does not pretend they do not exist (Mdn = 6.0; IQR = 1.0);

12. Structured and logical—can outline the steps necessary to realize a vision; able to delegate effectively (Mdn = 6.0; IQR = 1.0).

Just as the importance of strong communication skills for community college presidents is mentioned frequently in the literature, many studies also discuss the importance of possessing strong leadership skills (Cook, 2004; Desjardins & Huff, 2001; Hockaday & Puyear, 2000; Hood, 1997; Olson-Nikunen, 2004; Turner, 2005). The items that emerged in this study help to further define the specific skills contained within the overall theme of leadership. Trustees in this study reached consensus on the importance of 12 leadership competencies, and they agreed that it is critically important for future community college presidents to have good moral character, to be a team-player, and to have the ability to articulate a vision.

Professional Experiences Important for Future Community College Presidents

Participants in the study identified 17 professional experiences and 3 educational backgrounds that they considered to be important for future community college presidents to possess. These professional experiences are listed below in order of importance as ranked by the participants:

1. Experience in senior management/administration in any field (Mdn = 6.0; IQR = 0.5);
2. Demonstrates professional commitment—has not simply spent a year or two in previous positions (Mdn = 6.0; IQR = 1.0);
3. Experience working in a political environment—experience working with representatives and regulators (Mdn = 6.0; IQR = 1.0);
4. Employment at institutions with a good reputation (Mdn = 6.0; IQR = 2.0);
5. Experience as a senior administrator specifically at a community college (Mdn = 5.5; IQR = 1.0);
6. Experience at a community college (Mdn = 5.5; IQR = 1.0);
7. Experience with outcome-based accountability initiatives (i.e., Academic Quality Improvement Program; Mdn = 5.5; IQR = 1.0);
8. Having been mentored by or having experience working for a well-respected leader (Mdn = 5.0; IQR = 0.75);
9. Experience at any higher education institution (Mdn = 5.0; IQR = 1.0);
10. Experience serving on a board (Mdn = 5.0; IQR = 1.0);
11. Experience teaching at the community college level (full-time or part-time; Mdn = 5.0; IQR = 1.0);
12. Fundraising experience (Mdn = 5.0; IQR = 1.0);
13. Is well respected in the community college professional community— participates in national organizations, has published papers (Mdn = 5.0; IQR = 1.5);
14. Experience at an organization that is unionized (Mdn = 5.0; IQR = 2.0);
15. Experience teaching (at any level; full-time or part-time; Mdn = 5.0; IQR = 2.0);
16. Employment in the state or region (Mdn = 4.0; IQR = 2.0);
17. Experience in a senior management position specifically in the business/private sector (Mdn = 4.0; IQR = 2.0).

Many of the professional experiences that emerged from this study as important for future community college presidents are supported in the literature. Specifically, the majority of competencies on which consensus was reached regarding their degree of importance have been previously identified in other studies. However, trustees in this study agreed on the importance of two additional professional experiences that were not specifically identified in the literature review (see Figure 1): professional commitment, and experience at organizations with a good reputation. Furthermore, trustees in this study identified as important three other professional experiences that had not emerged as important factors in previous studies: employment in the state or region, administrative experience specifically in the business/private sector, or experience at an organization that is unionized. However, the trustees in this study did not reach consensus on the degree to which these experiences were important.

The educational backgrounds identified in this study are listed below in order of importance, as ranked by the participants:

1. Master's degree required (Mdn = 7.0; IQR = 0.0);
2. Doctorate required (Mdn = 6.0; IQR = 1.25);
3. Has a liberal arts background (Mdn = 4.0; IQR = 1.0).[1]

Trustees reached consensus that a master's degree is critically important for a community college president. Although a doctorate was not considered critically important, its median importance rating of 6.0 indicates that many trustees still highly value a doctoral degree. This finding is supported by the literature in that 88% of current community college presidents in 2006 held an earned doctorate (Weisman & Vaughan, 2007). Although a doctorate is not an absolute requirement, it still is extremely common among community college presidents.

Items of Critical Importance

Of the 68 total characteristics, competencies, and professional experiences identified as important for community college presidents to possess in the future, nine emerged as critically important in that they achieved the highest possible median score of 7.0:

1. Passionate about education—is a champion of community colleges;
2. Good moral character—honest, has integrity, trustworthy;
3. Articulate—ability to communicate in written and oral form clearly and professionally;
4. Master's degree required;
5. Dependable—follows through on commitments; arrives on time or early for appointments and meetings;
6. Good listener—makes people feel like what they are saying is important; is able to read body language effectively;
7. Has the ability to establish trust;
8. Team-player—understands the value of a team, able to recruit and assemble an effective team; and
9. Vision—recognizes where the college is today, articulates where the college should be in the future, and generates buy-in for that vision.

Findings of Interest

Items of Critical Importance With Greatest Consensus

Four of the items that emerged as critically important for future community college presidents also achieved the greatest possible degree of consensus among participants, as indicated by an IQR = 0.0.

   Good moral character. Importance ratings for this item ranged from 5 to 7, and 26 of 35 trustees rated the importance of this item as a 7, indicating critical importance. During the interviews in the first phase of the study, many trustees offered "integrity" as their first response to the question, "What characteristics are critical for future community college presidents to exhibit?" Trustees provided a number of descriptions of "good moral character." As one trustee plainly stated, "I want someone who is fair and honest" (Anonymous, personal communication, January 28, 2008). Another described good moral character as "When you can look them straight in the eye and just feel that you're getting the pure, unvarnished truth, whatever the issue might be" (Anonymous, personal communication, February 1, 2008). In addition, several trustees commented on why they believed good moral character was critically important, particularly as it related to building trust. As one trustee explained, "If one has the integrity, the honesty, and really the heart and soul of the community college interest at the top of what you are trying to do, the majority of people will believe in that person" (Anonymous, personal communication, February 11, 2008).

   Passionate about education. Importance ratings for this item ranged from 5 to 7; 27 of the 35 trustees rated the importance of this item as a 7, indicating critical importance. A number of trustees indicated that "a deep commitment to education" is critical for future community college presidents and that the "person must be a champion of the community college." One trustee elaborated that "they have to be the spokesperson, they have to be the cheerleader . . . a real champion of the community college is what we want to see, not someone who just takes it as a bureaucratic job" (Anonymous, personal communication, February 11, 2008). Another trustee explained, "I don't care how much you know until I know how much you care," and further clarified that "how much you know will help you get the job; how much you care will help you keep the job" (Anonymous, personal communication, March 10, 2008).

Articulate. Importance ratings for this item ranged from 6 to 7; 26 of the 35 trustees rated the importance of this item as a 7, indicating critical importance. During the interviews in the first phase of the study, many trustees offered "communication skills" as their first response to the question, "What competencies are critical for future community college presidents to demonstrate?" One trustee explained that "being a good communicator is the most important thing" (Anonymous, personal communication, February 8, 2008), and another clarified that a critical competency for a president is the "ability to communicate, both written and verbal" (Anonymous, personal communication, February 9, 2008).

Master's degree required. Although many trustees specifically mentioned that they do not believe a doctorate is critically important for future community college presidents, the majority of trustees believed that a master's degree is critically important. Importance ratings for this item ranged from 3 to 7; 26 of the 35 trustees rated the importance of this item as a 7, indicating critical importance. One trustee who specifically commented that a president does not need a doctorate to "run an institution" clarified her belief by adding, "I do feel that the person has to have a minimum of a master's degree" (Anonymous, personal communication, January 30, 2008).

Items on Which Consensus Was Not Reached

After the third phase of the Delphi process, there were six items on which consensus (an IQR equal to or less than 1.4) was not reached. However, stability (a change in median value equal to or less than 1.05 between rounds) was reached on all six items.

Employment at institutions with a good reputation. During the interviews in the first phase of the study, one trustee commented on the importance of future community college presidents having been employed at institutions with good reputations. He commented, "Generally I think the track record of what they've done before is an indicator . . . I think having gone to good colleges and seeing good modeling is usually a good predictor" (Anonymous, personal communication, February 9, 2008). Nevertheless, importance ratings for this item ranged from 2 to 7, and only one trustee out of 33 rated the item as a 7, indicating critical importance. Although consensus was not achieved on the item (IQR = 2.0), stability was achieved after the third phase with a median importance rating of 6.0.

Is well respected in the community college professional community. During the interviews in the first phase of the study, several trustees mentioned the importance for future community college presidents to be active in national organizations and to understand the "pulse" of community colleges. Another trustee specifically mentioned, "I think it would be interesting to know if they have written papers, if they have been published" (Anonymous, personal communication, February 9, 2008).

Nevertheless, other trustees expressed concern that national community college organizations were creating a "good-old-boys" network, and explained that they did not value presidential participation in national associations. Accordingly, ratings of importance for this item ranged from 1 to 7, and 3 trustees out of 35 rated the item as a 7, indicating critical importance. Although consensus was not achieved on the item (IQR = 1.5), stability was achieved after the third phase with a median importance rating of 5.0.

Experience teaching (at any level; full-time or part-time). Many trustees indicated during the interviews in the first phase of the study that they believed it was critically important for future presidents to have some teaching experience, regardless of the grade level. As one trustee indicated, "I think everyone who heads a college should have taught in a classroom somewhere along the line" (Anonymous, personal communication, January 28, 2008). Another trustee commented, "I don't necessarily think that it has to come from the traditional background of where we've sought other community college presidents," but added that "it may be helpful for that person to have taught somewhere in their career, to have been in a classroom, maybe as an adjunct faculty member" (Anonymous, personal communication, February 11, 2008).

However, other trustees indicated that they did not believe teaching experience was a critical factor. As one trustee mentioned, "I'm not married to the prejudice of it has to be a traditional individual that has come through the educational system to become a president" (Anonymous, personal communication, February 9, 2008). Others cautioned that requiring a president to have teaching experience potentially eliminates strong candidates unnecessarily. One trustee remarked, "The emphasis to have candidates with a strong academic background, to the detriment of other background factors, I think gets you in trouble" (Anonymous, personal communication, February 11, 2008). Another added, "If you limit the pool of potential applicants, you don't know what you might be missing" (Anonymous, personal communication, February 10, 2008). Accordingly, importance ratings for this item ranged from 2 to 7, and 3 trustees out of 35 rated the item as a 7, indicating critical importance. Although consensus was not achieved on the item (IQR = 2.0), stability was achieved after the third phase with a median importance rating of 5.0.

Nevertheless, it is important to note that consensus was achieved on the importance of teaching experience specifically at the community college level, with a median importance rating of 5.0. Therefore, although trustees did not agree on the importance of teaching experience at any level, they did agree on the importance of teaching experience specifically at the community college level. Furthermore, it is interesting that full-time teaching experience did not emerge as a professional experience important for future community college presidents. The literature often refers to full-time teaching experience as part of the "traditional" career path for community college presidents (Kubala & Bailey, 2001), and in 2006, 48% of community college presidents had full-time teaching experience at the community college level (Weisman & Vaughan, 2007). Nevertheless, trustees in this study did not identify full-time teaching experience as an important professional experience for future community college presidents.

Experience at an organization that is unionized. Several trustees mentioned the importance of experience at an organization that is unionized during the interviews in the first phase of the study. As one trustee noted, "Probably the most important thing, at least in the Illinois system, is an ability to be able to surf the troubled waters of the unionized organization" (Anonymous, personal communication, February 11, 2008). Other trustees commented, "There's nothing like a union experience" (Anonymous, personal communication, February 9, 2008), "It would be better if they had worked someplace that had a union because they'd see how it would function" (Anonymous, personal communication, January 28, 2008), and one added, "It might be a make or break" (Anonymous, personal communication, February 10, 2008).

However, not all trustees believed that experience at an institution that is unionized is critically important for future community college presidents. This disagreement among trustees is not unexpected; it is likely that trustees' perception of the importance of this item depends in part on the number and strength of the unions in their community college district. Accordingly, importance ratings for this item ranged from 2 to 7, and only 1 out of 35 trustees rated the item as a 7, indicating critical importance. Although consensus was not achieved on the item (IQR = 2.0), stability was achieved after the third phase with a median importance rating of 5.0.

Experience in a senior management position specifically in the business/private sector. During the interviews in the first phase of the study, several trustees mentioned that they believed that administrative experience specifically in the business or private sector was of critical importance for future community college presidents. One trustee explained that he was looking for future presidents to have "a background in good business skills rather than education skills because a good leader can hire sergeants and captains and related staff to back him or her up" (Anonymous, personal communication, February 10, 2008).

Several trustees expressed concern that the "traditional" practice of hiring presidents with an academic background excludes candidates who could potentially bring a different perspective to community colleges. As one trustee remarked,

> I think we need that cross-pollination . . . I've told [our president] and his vice presidents . . . look at yourselves, you all have exactly the same education experience, the same background experience, what different things do any one of you bring to the table? (Anonymous, personal communication, February 11, 2008)

Another trustee added, "I think it's helpful to have some experience in the private sector . . . hopefully that's a high-level administrative type position. I think it's helpful to have outside of higher education experience, maybe bring a different perspective, that's helpful" (Anonymous, personal communication, February 11, 2008).

Trustees also cited the multidimensional nature of the mission of community colleges as a rationale for considering experience in the business or private sector critically important for future presidents. As one trustee explained,

> I believe that we've got to start looking outside the academia world, we've got to look in the business world, and bring those people in because in a community college . . . we're working constantly with businesses to do their training, so we need somebody that knows something about that. (Anonymous, personal communication, February 12, 2008)

Nevertheless, not all trustees agreed that experience in the business or private sector is critically important for future community college presidents. One trustee cautioned, "Community college people . . . have a different outlook than do people in business" (Anonymous, personal communication, February 2, 2008). Another trustee added, "It would have to be a special person not to have a community college background" (Anonymous, personal communication, February 12, 2008). Accordingly, importance ratings for this item ranged from 1 to 7, and 2 out of 35 trustees rated the item as a 7, indicating critical importance. Although consensus was not achieved on the item (IQR = 2.0), stability was achieved after the third phase with a median importance rating of 4.0.

Employment in the state or region. During the interviews in the first phase of the study, several trustees mentioned that they believed that it was important for future community college presidents to have professional experience in the state or region. As one trustee explained,

> I look for talent, local talent . . . somebody that's familiar with the system, familiar with the needs of the community, familiar with the economy demands of the area, and the possibilities of the area, and the history is very important too. (Anonymous, personal communication, February 12, 2008)

However, another trustee cautioned against limiting a search to local applicants, explaining, "I think it's really critical that you go through the national search process because you've got to have that feeling that you gave it your best shot and that you got your best candidate" (Anonymous, personal communication, February 10, 2008). Ratings of importance for this item ranged from 1 to 6, and although consensus was not achieved on the item (IQR = 2.0), stability was achieved after the third phase with a median importance rating of 4.0.

Expectations for Presidents Remain Virtually Unchanged

During the interviews in the first phase of the study, several trustees made comments that closely mirror observations recorded in the literature more than 40 years ago. First, it was common for trustees to comment on the unreasonable expectations placed on community college presidents. As one trustee observed, "the expectations for a president are just short of walking on water" (Anonymous, personal communication, February 10, 2008). Another summarized her requirements for a president by commenting that she and her fellow trustees typically look for "super people" (Anonymous, personal communication, February 9, 2008). These observations mirror the commentary of Henry Wriston (1959), a former college president, who quipped that boards tend to outline such grandiose qualifications and desired attributes for presidents that "no less than the Archangel Gabriel could meet the bill of particulars—and he is not available" (p. 50). After nearly 50 years, trustees clearly continue to hold extremely high expectations for aspiring presidents. One of the participants in this study wrote on the second questionnaire, "it appears many trustees are 'unrealistic' to think one person can possess all these criteria" (Anonymous, personal communication, March 19, 2008).

Just as the level of expectations for college presidents remains extremely high, the specific desired qualifications have changed little in four decades. In 1969, Rauh observed that typical criteria for college presidents included "unquestioned character, a religious attitude, good health, youth, maturity, scholarly interest, administrative experience, advanced degrees, imagination, judicial ability, democratic spirit, platform presence, thrift, children, and a wife with social grace" (Rauh, 1969, p. 13). As illustrated in Table 1, although the specific vocabulary used to identify these criteria has changed, many of the underlying assumptions regarding the desired qualifications for college

TABLE 1

Similarity in Perceptions of Desired Qualifications of College Presidents in 1969 and 2008

Desired Qualifications—1969[a]	Desired Qualifications—2008[b]
Unquestioned character, a religious attitude	Good moral character
Good health, youth	Energetic
Maturity, platform presence	Presence—looks the part of a president, is the image of the institution
Scholarly interest	Well respected in community college professional community—participates in national organizations, has published papers
Administrative experience	Experience in senior management/administration in any field
Advanced degrees	Master's degree required
Imagination	Innovation—flexible and open to change
Judicial ability, democratic spirit	Ability to build consensus—knows how to listen all sides and help collate different ideas and reach a good conclusion
Thrift	Understanding of accounting and finance—possesses financial acumen, is able to read a financial statement, is able to understand a budget; has an understanding of community college funding—including state and local funds, tuition, grants, federal programs, and fundraising
Children, wife with social grace	Family person—is married

a. From Rauh (1969).

b. From the study reported in this article.

presidents remain unchanged. Although much of the recent literature does not address issues such as the marital status or physical appearance of aspiring presidents, the results of this study reveal that these "unspoken" characteristics may indeed play a role in the presidential selection process.

It does, however, appear that many trustees are now more willing to consider presidential candidates from outside the traditional "academic pipeline." Many trustees mentioned that they would be willing to consider an applicant from business and industry or that they would be willing to consider an applicant who did not hold a doctoral degree. Several expressed concerns that the "pool" of traditional applicants has been declining in size and explained that it would be necessary to consider candidates from outside of academia. Nevertheless, most concurred that the individual would have to "be a special person" or "have unique competencies" to compensate for a nontraditional background.

Recommendations for Utilization of Findings

Given that the participants of this study reached consensus on a series of characteristics, competencies, and professional experiences that are important for future community college presidents to possess, findings from this study can be used by aspiring community college presidents, current community college presidents, boards of trustees, national associations, and professional organizations.

Current and Aspiring Presidents

Both aspiring and current community college presidents alike can use the findings of this study for self-assessment purposes and to guide the selection of professional development opportunities. Current and aspiring presidents can consider their own personal characteristics, competencies, and professional experiences, comparing them with the items that were identified in this study. Furthermore, current presidents who serve as mentors for aspiring presidents can use these findings to help guide future leaders and ensure that they have opportunities to develop the competencies and skills that were identified as critically important by trustees.

Boards of Trustees

One of the first phases of the presidential selection process is the identification of desired qualifications of an ideal candidate. Accordingly, the findings from this research can be used by boards of trustees as a catalyst for the discussion of desired characteristics, competencies, and professional experiences of an ideal presidential candidate. Furthermore, it is possible that boards of trustees could use the findings of this study to identify the potential weaknesses of a new president. The board and new president could use this analysis to identify potential professional development opportunities that may increase the likelihood of a successful presidential tenure.

National Associations and Professional Organizations

There are a number of national associations and professional organizations that offer training for aspiring community college leaders, and the results of this study could be used to help shape professional development opportunities for future presidents. For example, workshops are frequently offered that aim to prepare presidential candidates for the interview process; the findings of this study could be used to help applicants identify what trustees might be looking for in a future president. Furthermore, many state and national organizations exist to support the professional development of trustees; the results of this study could be used to help inexperienced trustees understand the critical characteristics, competencies, and professional experiences of ideal presidential candidates.

Conclusions

Given the number of students they serve and their broad mission and scope, community colleges are clearly a critical component of the higher education system and are vital to the nation's economic development. Community colleges currently face a myriad of challenges, including the anticipated retirement of a significant number of presidents. To preserve their vitality, community colleges must be prepared to effectively fill a large number of presidential vacancies in the next decade.

One of the most important roles of a board of trustees has been and will continue to be the recruitment, selection, and hiring of a new president. Although the ultimate authority for hiring a community college president resides with the board of trustees, few studies have been conducted to explore the perceptions of trustees regarding the desired characteristics and qualifications of an ideal presidential candidate. The results of this study provide important insight into the characteristics, competencies, and professional experiences that community college trustees from the state of Illinois perceive to be critically important for future presidents to possess. Many opportunities for future research exist to further explore trustees' expectations for future community college presidents, including replicating the study in other states. Given the enthusiasm exhibited by the trustees who participated in this study, future researchers should have no difficulty in recruiting trustees who are willing to share their wisdom and expertise.

Declaration of Conflicting Interests

The authors declared no potential conflicts of interests with respect to the authorship and/or publication of this article.

Funding

The authors declared no financial support for the research and/or authorship of this article.

Note

1. Although consensus was achieved on this item, the median importance rating was 4.0, indicating that in general trustees do not perceive this to be critically important. As one trustee commented, "I prefer a person with a liberal arts background, you know somebody who understands all phases of the curricula" (Anonymous, personal communication, February 10, 2008).

References

Association of Community College Trustees. (2007). *The search process*. Retrieved June 21, 2007, from http://web.archive.org/web/20061005044418/http://www.acct.org/Acct/files/ccLibraryFiles/FILENAME/000000000045/NewPresidentialprocesschart.pdf

Association of Community College Trustees. (2009). *Guide to trustee roles and responsibilities*. Retrieved July 19, 2009, from http://www.acct.org/resources/center/roles-responsibilities.php

Boggs, G. R. (2006). *Handbook on CEO-board relations and responsibilities*. Washington, DC: Community College Press.

Bromert, J. D. (1984). *College search committees* (ERIC Digest 84-2). Washington, DC: American Association of University Administrators and the ERIC Clearinghouse on Higher Education. (ERIC Document Reproduction Service No. ED284511)

Brooks, K. W. (1979). Delphi technique: Expanding applications. *North Central Association Quarterly, 53*, 377–385.

Brown, L., Martinez, M., & Daniel, D. (2002). Community college leadership preparation: Needs, perceptions, and recommendations. *Community College Review, 30*(1), 45–74.

Bumpas, R. K. (1998). *Factors that affect the selection of community college presidents*. Unpublished doctoral dissertation, Texas A&M University, Commerce.

Chippewa Valley Technical College. (2007). *CVTC's 2008 presidential search*.

Clayton, M. J. (1997). Delphi: A technique to harness expert opinion for critical decision-making tasks in education. *Educational Psychology, 17*, 373–386.

Cook, V. S. (2004). *Exploration of leadership competencies needed by future Illinois community college presidents: A Delphi study*. Unpublished doctoral dissertation, Capella University, Minneapolis, MN.

Delbecq, A. L., Van de Ven, A. H., & Gustafson, D. H. (1975). *Group techniques for program planning: A guide to nominal group and Delphi processes*. Glenview, IL: Scott Foresman.

Desjardins, C., & Huff, S. (2001). *The leading edge: Competencies for community college leadership in the new millennium*. Mission Viejo, CA: The League for Innovation in the Community College.

Durham Technical Community College. (2007). *Durham Tech president search*. Retrieved June 12, 2007, from http://web.archive.org/web/20071019024151/http://durhamtech.edu/president/ profile.htm

Eastern Wyoming College. (2007). *Presidential search*. Retrieved June 12, 2007, from http:// web.archive.org/web/20070711005540/ http://ewc.wy.edu/administration/search/search brochure.pdf

Giles, F. T. (1969). Selecting and securing a junior college president. In B. L. Johnson (Ed.), *The junior college president* (pp. 33–41). Los Angeles: UCLA Graduate School of Education.

Hammons, J. O., & Keller, L. (1990). Competencies and personal characteristics of future community college presidents. *Community College Review, 18*(3), 34–41.

Hockaday, J., & Puyear, D. E. (2000). *Community college leadership in the new millennium*. Washington, DC: Community College Press.

Hood, J. A. (1997). *An analysis of selection criteria, roles, skills, challenges, and strategies of 2-year college presidents*. Unpublished doctoral dissertation, The University of Alabama, Tuscaloosa, AL.

Jenkins, D. A., & Smith, T. E. (1994). Applying Delphi methodology in family therapy research. *Contemporary Family Therapy, 16*, 411–430.

Keeney, S., Hasson, F., & McKenna, H. (2006). Consulting the oracle: Ten lessons from using the Delphi technique in nursing research. *Journal of Advanced Nursing, 53*, 205–212.

Kubala, T., & Bailey, G. M. (2001). A new perspective on community college presidents: Results of a national study. *Community College Journal of Research and Practice, 25*, 793–804.

Linstone, H. A., & Turoff, M. (1975). *The Delphi method: Techniques and applications*. Reading, MA: Addison-Wesley.

McBride, A. J., Pates, R., Ramadan, R., & McGowan, C. (2003). Delphi survey of experts' opinions on strategies used by community pharmacists to reduce over-the-counter drug misuse. *Addiction, 98*, 487–497.

Nasworthy, C. (2002). Selecting community college presidents for the 21st century: A trustee's perspective. In D. F. Campbell (Ed.), *The leadership gap: Model strategies for leadership development* (pp. 67–78). Washington, DC: Community College Press.

North Idaho College. (2007). *North Idaho College presidential position profile.*

Olson-Nikunen, S. L. (2004). *Community college presidents in the new millennium: Competencies for leadership as identified by position announcements and relationship to board type.* Unpublished doctoral dissertation, University of North Dakota, Grand Forks, ND.

Pierce, D. R., & Pedersen, R. P. (1997). The community college presidency: Qualities for success. In I. M. Weisman & G. B. Vaughan (Eds.), *Presidents and trustees in partnership: New roles and leadership challenges* (New Directions for Community Colleges, No. 98, pp. 13–20). San Francisco: Jossey-Bass.

Powell, C. R. (2004). *Community college leadership in the new millennium: Traits and characteristics of presidents of effective community colleges.* Unpublished doctoral dissertation, Cleveland State University, Cleveland, OH.

Rauh, M. A. (1969). *The trusteeship of colleges and universities.* San Francisco: McGraw-Hill.

Rayens, M. K., & Hahn, E. J. (2000). Building consensus using the policy Delphi method. *Policy, Politics, and Nursing Practice, 1*, 308–315.

Rojewski, J. W., & Meers, G. D. (1991). *Directions for future research in vocational special needs education.* Urbana-Champaign: University of Illinois. (ERIC Document Reproduction Service No. ED339837)

Scheibe, M., Skutsch, M., & Shofer, J. (1975). Evaluation: Delphi methodology. In H. A. Linstone & M. Turoff (Eds.), *The Delphi method: Techniques and applications* (pp. 257–281). Reading, MA: Addison-Wesley.

Schults, C. (2001). *The critical impact of impending retirements on community college leadership.* Washington, DC: American Association of Community Colleges.

Townsend, B. K., & Bassoppo-Moyo, S. (1997). The effective community college academic administrator: Necessary competencies and attitudes. *Community College Review, 25*(2), 41–57.

Turner, R. A. (2005). *The perceptions of Texas community college chancellors, trustees, and presidents of the desired competencies of college presidents.* Unpublished doctoral dissertation, The University of Texas at Austin, Austin.

Vaughan, G. B. (2006). *The community college story* (3rd ed.). Washington, DC: Community College Press.

Wallin, D. L. (2002). Professional development for presidents: A study of community and technical college presidents in three states. *Community College Review, 30*(2), 27–42.

Weisman, I. M., & Vaughan, G. B. (2007). *The community college presidency 2006* (Report No. AACC-RB-07-1). Washington, DC: American Association of Community Colleges.

Wriston, H. M. (1959). *Academic procession: Reflections of a college president.* New York: Columbia University Press.

Kathleen Plinske is the interim president of McHenry County College, Crystal Lake, Illinois.

Walter J. Packard is president emeritus of McHenry County College, Crystal Lake, Illinois.

CHAPTER 16

EQUITY AND EFFICIENCY OF COMMUNITY COLLEGE APPROPRIATIONS: THE ROLE OF LOCAL FINANCING

ALICIA C. DOWD AND JOHN L. GRANT

More than two decades ago, David Breneman and Susan Nelson posed the question, "Should Serrano Go to College?" (1981). The authors of *Financing Community Colleges* were referring to the landmark case of *Serrano v. Priest*, which was decided in the California State Supreme Court in 1971. The *Serrano* decision found the California school financing system unconstitutional under the equal protection provision of the state constitution. The educational resources provided to students depended on the wealth of the neighborhoods in which they lived, a fundamentally unjust arrangement stemming from the tradition of local control and local financing. Breneman and Nelson concluded that, similarly, the local finance role for community college systems likely creates resource disparities that disadvantage students in less affluent communities (p. 126).

As in primary and secondary school (K–12) finance, approximately half the states in the United States have a local government finance role for funding community colleges. Colleges serving areas with a weak economic base that rely on local property or other taxes for a share of their revenues will receive lower revenues than peer colleges located in wealthier areas of their state, creating an inequitable finance system.

Three decades after *Serrano*, which set off waves of school finance litigation and reform across the United States (Verstegen, 1998), the effect of local control on school finance equity is still a matter of contentious debate and legal action. (The Web site of the Campaign for Fiscal Equity http://www.schoolfunding.info/ summarizes recent legal actions and court decisions.) In contrast, since Breneman and Nelson's consideration of community college finance equity, and a similar study at that time by Walter Garms (1981), the role of local control in community college finance systems and its effect on equity have received comparatively little attention.

This comparative inattention may result from the authors' conclusion that community college finance equity is a less pressing issue than school finance equity because a college education is not compulsory, nor "essential for functioning or succeeding in life" (p. 124). In addition, Breneman and Nelson (1980, p. 174) argued the efficiency benefits of local control: Those who are most likely to take advantage of a community college have the opportunity to express their educational preferences through the local governance and tax system. Furthermore, the task of disentangling geographic and program cost differentials across colleges in a state, economies of scale on large and small campuses, and the impact of student college choice and their effects on measures of resource equity presents a daunting challenge that may have inhibited study of this topic. With funding coming from state, local, and federal governments and from the private sector in the form of tuition, fees, and philanthropic donations, community college finance systems are relatively more complex than K–12 finance systems.

Nevertheless, even in an era when efficiency rhetoric dominates the politics of public finance (Alexander, 2000; Dowd, 2003), the issue of community college finance equity has not entirely faded. Several state-level reports provide evidence that wide variations do exist in the level of resources allocated to community colleges and that finance equity is a concern of state policy analysts (*Budget Development*, 2000; *Community Colleges and SUNY*, 1999; *Iowa Community College*, 1998). The Education Commission of the States (*State Funding*, 2000) issued a comprehensive state-by-state portrait of community college finance systems and highlighted policy questions that arise from the local finance role, including the issue of equal access to postsecondary education within states (p. 10). In a paper updating the application of the economic tenets of equity and efficiency to an analysis of community college finance, Richard Romano (2003) highlights local taxes as more regressive than state and federal taxes, because they rely on property taxes, rather than more progressive income taxes. Flores (2003) analyzed state community college finance data from Texas and found inequities in the funding of Hispanic-serving institutions (HSIs) located on the U.S.-Mexican border. Most recently, in a case with arguments echoing K–12 finance litigation, three community colleges in Oregon challenged the state's equalization formula, arguing that it was unfair to penalize colleges that received relatively high, local property-tax revenues. In November 2003, a circuit court judge ruled against the plaintiffs, upholding the right of the Board of Education to determine the funding formula. The decision did not directly rule on the equity of the finance system (Gomstyn, 2003).

In a trend perceived as equity enhancing, the local share of income for community colleges has declined over time (Breneman & Nelson, 1981; *State Funding*, 2000). From 1950 to 1997, it decreased on average from 49% to 19%, while the average share of state revenue increased from 26% to a high of 60% in 1980, before declining to 44% in 1997 (Romano, 2003, Table 3). The view that financing systems are more equitable under state control is consistent with the direction of court-ordered school finance reforms, which have often mandated "power-equalizing" roles for state governments to redistribute resources among school districts of disparate wealth.

While a community college education is not compulsory and states do not have a legal obligation to provide equitable postsecondary schooling resources, as they do for primary and secondary schooling, there is, perhaps, a growing sense that an associate's degree is today the minimal credential necessary to attain social and economic security. This view is reflected in the rhetoric that surrounded Bill Clinton's initial proposal for the federal "Hope Scholarship." In his acceptance speech at the Democratic National Convention in 1996, Clinton proposed a tax credit for the first two years of college to "make at least two years of college as universal as four years of a high school education is today" (Bill Clinton, 1996).

That the implementation of the "scholarship" as a tax credit provided a boon for the middle class more than it helped low-income students enter college (*Study*, 2003) demonstrates the tension between the rhetoric of access and the politics of resource distribution. The growing importance of a college education and heightened conflicts over financial resources suggest that the equity of community college financing systems deserves greater national consideration. This study contributes to that goal by analyzing the local role, which is generally viewed as an equity-reducing component of finance systems, in resource distribution to community colleges within state systems.

Conceptual Framework

Based on national data, this study characterizes current intrastate variation in revenues from state and local sources to community colleges and analyzes differences and similarities in distribution patterns in states with and without local-share financing. We consider the fairness of these funding variations from the perspective of equity and efficiency. The conceptualization of equitable and efficient funding strategies is based on the scholarship of school finance (Monk, 1990; Odden & Picus, 2004; Verstegen, 1998; Wong, 1994) and community college finance (Breneman & Nelson, 1981; DesJardins, 2002; Garms, 1981). Equal funding for students with equal needs is understood as creating "horizontal equity," while the provision of greater resources for students with greater need contributes to "vertical equity."

Under the principles of horizontal and vertical equity, equal funding does not necessarily represent equitable funding. Equal funding is considered just when students have equal needs but unjust when students have disparate needs. Providing more public resources to less affluent communities is understood as promoting vertical equity, while providing more resources to affluent communities undermines it.

Disparities in funding can be created by rational and political factors. Rational funding strategies such as cost adjustments for urbanization, economies of scale, and program type may create funding disparities as a matter of efficiency. These factors generate disparities in per capita student funding that are not viewed as inequitable, as, for example, when a state provides greater resources to colleges to rent facilities in high-cost urban areas. A plan to locate high-cost facilities for technical programs at just one campus in a system may be argued from the perspective of investment efficiency, even though it would provide greater resources to one college in comparison to the others. The investment benefits of initiating such a program might well be outweighed by the costs if the state undertook to build the necessary facilities on each campus. A college's capacity to convert resources to outputs presents another efficiency consideration, that of productive or "technical" efficiency. For example, some states award funding premiums to rural schools and colleges to offset inefficiencies in the "production" of educated students due to smaller class sizes in comparison to more populated urban areas.

However, these rational systems may be undermined by "politically mobilized and well-connected groups," who garner a greater share of resources through political means (Timar, 1994, p. 144). These political forces can have equitable effects (as when their efforts result in creating categorical aid for students with high educational needs) or inequitable effects (as in the flow of funds to wealthy suburbs). Recent research by Caroline Hoxby (2001), Jeffrey Metzler (2003), and Thomas Timar (2003) shows that court-ordered finance reform is often an ineffective tool to counter finance inequities. Their studies indicate that rational resource allocation systems are undermined by political lobbying and individual choices in educational markets. Therefore, rational policies can be counteracted by political systems operating at both the local and state levels.

Within this conceptual framework, we addressed the following questions:

1. How much do college revenues per student vary within state systems?
2. Is local-share funding associated with higher or lower revenues per student?
3. Is local-share funding associated with higher intrastate variation in tuition and fees?
4. Is local-share funding associated with higher intrastate variation in revenues per student?

To establish the context of revenue disparities, Questions 1 and 2 provide descriptive information. Question 3 evaluates the relationship between local funding and variation in tuition and fees to test a conclusion presented in the Education Commission of the States community college financing report, where the authors observed, "Dramatic differences in property tax valuations across a state can lead to large disparities in tuition rates between wealthier communities and poorer districts, because poorer districts may be forced to raise tuition and fees to meet their basic budgets" (*State Funding*, 2000, p. 10). We would therefore expect greater variation in tuition and fees in states with local financing.

Question 4 builds on the assumption that states relying strictly on state funding will have lower variation in revenues than states with local shares, due to the equalizing effects of the state role. As high variation in state-funded states may be created by power-equalizing formulas, which are intended to direct greater than average funds to colleges with high-need students, we also examine the relationship between funding disparities and community wealth.

This study focuses on local and state appropriations and tuition and fees, which are the largest sources of revenues for community colleges. Other sources of funding may well have an impact on finance equity, but we do not address these effects here. Our purpose is to document revenue disparities and present descriptive statistics and graphs that facilitate comparisons of revenue distribution patterns in local-share and state-funded states. The study serves as a starting point for future state-level analyses by supporting purposeful sampling of states with similar and dissimilar funding patterns. It fills a gap in the literature by providing a systematic national analysis of contemporary community college funding patterns with a focus on the role of local financing.

Data and Methods

We analyzed a subsample of data from the national 2000–2001 Integrated Postsecondary Education Data System (IPEDS) Finance survey. IPEDS is a census survey of higher education institutions in the United States. Because IPEDS is a census and the analyses are descriptive, we treat the data as population rather than sample data and do not present tests of statistical significance for observed differences in values. We limit the sample to institutions that IPEDS classifies as two-year public colleges in U.S. states (not territories) and that did not contain the word "technical" in their names. Our reason for omitting technical colleges was that technical programs often carry greater costs for equipment and materials. While this step restricts the institutional type, it does not completely omit technical programs, which are also offered in community colleges.

Since we focused on variation in revenues to colleges within a state, we excluded those reporting financial data on fewer than five community colleges. This step excluded 15 states: Alaska (2), Delaware (3), Idaho (3), Indiana (13 of 14 technical colleges), Kentucky (which reported financial data for Lexington Community College only), Maine (7 of 7 technical colleges), Montana (5 of 8 technical colleges), Nevada (3), New Hampshire (5 of 7 technical colleges), Rhode Island (1), South Dakota (4), Utah (3), Vermont (1), West Virginia (3) and Wisconsin (16 of 17 technical colleges). The remaining sample includes 705 community colleges with nonmissing data in 35 states.

Our primary focus is on appropriations from state and local governments. To compare revenue across colleges with different enrollments, we analyzed appropriations per full-time equivalent student (FTE).[1] We group colleges in five local funding-share categories based on the ratio of local appropriations to state appropriations. Based on the distribution of colleges in these five categories, we designate states as primarily local-share funded or as state-funded.

Our measure of variation in local and state appropriations is the deviation from the median value for each state. We used median values as the measure of central tendency because the means are affected by outliers that may be colleges with a special mission or unusual funding. Similarly, we measure dispersion by statistics that are not affected by extreme values, including the interquartile range (*IQR*) and the ratio of 90th to 10th percentile values. The mean of absolute revenue deviations for each state provides a summary statistic of variation for comparison across states. A college's position above or below the median of state and local appropriations within the state is also represented by an index of the college's revenue divided by the state median. The index is an expression of revenue deviations that is not sensitive to the differing magnitudes of spending in states. To test the direction of revenue deviations as flowing toward relatively wealthy or poor communities, we used the proportion of full-time students at each college who receive federal grant aid as a measure of community wealth. A college's geographic locale is indicated with an ordinal variable with seven categories ranging from "large city" to "rural."

Limitations

The research design has several important limitations. First, the study does not directly account for state-level differences in community college history, mission, status, governance, and finance structure. We treat local funding as evidence of a local political role but do not investigate the nature of state and local political structures. For this reason, we measure revenue disparities at the state level and present descriptive statistics summarizing revenue deviations by state. This step facilitates the review of the findings by knowledgeable analysts at the state level.

Second, while all surveys are subject to measurement error, with hundreds of institutional researchers and administrators across the country entering complex financial data, IPEDS may suffer from this problem even more greatly than usual. We acknowledge this limitation but emphasize that IPEDS is the primary national collection of college financial data. Analyses of the type reported here that may reveal significant measurement error may strengthen this major data source.

We use the percentage of full-time students receiving federal financial aid as a proxy for community wealth for each community college. Variation in tuition and fees, which occurs both across and within states, partially determines who qualifies for financial aid. Both financially needy students and students attending more expensive colleges are more likely to be eligible for aid. Therefore, we restrict our analysis to intrastate differences in the proportion of students receiving grant aid and to states where the correlation between tuition and aid is weak.

We evaluated the accuracy of using this financial aid variable as a measure of community wealth by using census data from New York State and Massachusetts, matching colleges to the county or counties in which they are located. Using logarithmic transformations to correct for skewed distributions, we found that the Pearson correlation between aid and the percentage of children in poverty was moderately strong at $r = .766$ and $r = .614$ in New York State ($n = 32$) and Massachusetts ($n = 15$), respectively.

Finally, the study uses the NCES's FTE measure, in which three part-time students are treated as equivalent to one full-time student, to compare per capita funding. This measure is not sensitive to potential differences in the resource needs of campuses with high and low proportions of part-time students and may not be equally appropriate to campuses serving different populations of students. Alternative measures of student enrollment may produce different results concerning resource disparities among campuses.

Results

In this sample of U.S. community colleges, state appropriations are the largest source of all revenues with a mean share of 38%. Tuition and fees contribute 20% and federal grants and contracts add another 13%. Including colleges with zero local share, local appropriations average 13%. The local share contingent on non-zero local funding increases to 20%, reducing the state share to 34%. Auxiliary revenues contribute 6%, and state grants contribute 5%. Other sources of revenue such as private gifts and local grants contribute 3% or less, on average.

The mean value of total revenues from all sources except tuition and fees per FTE is $8,230, with a standard deviation (SD) of $3,800. The mean value of state and local appropriations per FTE is $5,180 ($SD = $2,440). The median of this skewed variable is $4,740. Average tuition and fees are $1,400 ($SD = $717). Table 1, which presents the median and interquartile range of state and local appropriations per FTE by state, reveals a great deal of variation both within and across states. In 16 states in the sample, the median value is zero local appropriations. A review of the full range of values indicates that in ten states no colleges received local funding.

We created five categories of local funding share based on the ratio of local appropriations to state appropriations. These categories, which were created based on the overall distribution of ratios as shown by a histogram, encompass local-share funding ratios of 0.0–0.01 ($n = 268$), 0.02–0.50 ($n = 199$), 0.51–1.0 ($n = 121$), 1.01–2.0 ($n = 70$), 2.1 and above ($n = 47$). Colleges within the same state may appear in different local funding share categories, because the ratios differ by college. Table 2 shows the distribution of colleges within the local-share categories by state, divided into 17 "local-share" and 17 "state-funded" states (n = 256 and 368 colleges respectively). We designated states as funded by local share when at least 75% of the colleges reported ratios greater than 0.02. All local-share states also have state funding.

In some states, such as Connecticut, Florida, and Georgia, colleges consistently report no local funding. Five states—Alabama, Arkansas, Colorado, Ohio, and Oklahoma—are dominantly state funded, but have two or more cases reporting local funding. In two of these states, Arkansas and Ohio, local taxes may be raised and used to fund community colleges in 2000. In Colorado, two junior colleges previously funded by their local districts were recently incorporated into the state system and uniquely continued to receive local funding (*State Funding*, 2000, pp. 12–13).

TABLE 1

State and Local Appropriations ($s) per FTE

State	n	State		Local	
		MDN	IQR	MDN	IQR
AL	21	4187	1669	0	27
AR	15	5361	2368	0	416
AZ	19	1396	1344	3188	1243
CA	77	3044	1073	1824	1046
CO	15	3243	1771	0	0
CT	12	7197	1109	0	0
FL	28	4617	1513	0	0
GA	14	6211	2203	0	0
HI	7	4609	886	0	0
IA	14	3439	853	675	355
IL	45	1560	869	2302	1388
KS	19	1856	664	3773	2927
LA	6	3363	757	0	0
MA	14	5840	1554	0	0
MD	15	2307	988	2844	1307
MI	28	3129	1058	2484	3505
MN	12	4618	2237	0	0
MO	10	2727	1169	940	1335
MS	15	4348	955	722	377
NC	49	6142	1561	1008	426
ND	5	5057	1882	0	0
NE	5	4000	182	1147	117
NJ	19	1662	350	2037	712
NM	15	4693	1714	658	990
NY	33	2359	229	1786	914
OH	28	3750	743	0	0
OK	14	3569	1003	0	0
OR	13	4222	1148	2209	688
PA	14	2495	312	1462	885
SC	5	5401	737	0	0
TN	10	3691	316	0	0
TX	58	3432	1103	1194	1569
VA	24	4055	850	23	22
WA	27	3928	657	0	0
WY	7	4414	897	1365	1964

Source: NCES IPEDS 2000-2001

Number of colleges in state based on n reporting fi nancial data.

We apply the "local-share" designation to states where local funding is a regular component of the funding system. In states with a local funding role, such as Illinois, Kansas, and Maryland, colleges are distributed across the funding share categories. California colleges report local funding share across the five categories. However, we analyze California separately due to the large number of colleges and the state's unique funding system in the state. Here "districts receive a portion of the 1% countywide property tax based on their proportional share of property tax revenue received from their county prior to tax control (Prop. 13, 1978)" (*State Funding*, 2000, p. 12).

TABLE 2

Distribution of Colleges by Funding Type by State

State	State-Funded State					Local-Share State				
	0.0-	0.02-	0.51-	1.1-	>2.0	0-	0.02-	0.51-	1.1-	>2.0
AL	19	2								
AR	11	4								
AZ							1	1	5	12
CO	13			1	1					
CT	12									
FL	28									
GA	14									
HI	7									
IA						1	13			
IL							6	9	13	13
KS							2	5	4	8
LA	6									
MA	14									
MD						1		5	8	1
MI						6	5	5	9	3
MN	12									
MO						1	6	3		
MS							15			
NC							46			
ND	5									
NE							5			
NJ								7	11	1
NM						2	9	4		
NY							4	20	8	1
OH	22	3	2	1						
OK	12	1	1							
OR						7	5	1		
PA							7	7		
SC	5									
TN	10									
TX						7	34	13	3	1
VA	24									
WA	27									
WY							5	1	1	
*CA						9	24	33	5	6
Total	241	10	3	2	1	18	165	85	63	40

Source: NCES IPEDS 2000-2001

Number of colleges in state based on n reporting financial data. Local-share categories represent a ratio of local-to-state appropriations of 0.0-0.01, 0.02-0.50, .51-1.0, 1.1-2.0, > 2.0.

Local-share states include those with at least 75% of colleges reporting a ratio of local-to-state appropriations > = 0.02

*California colleges report local shares; but we examine that state, which includes a large proportion of U.S. community colleges, separately.

Table 3 presents the mean and standard deviation of tuition and fees and the percentage of students receiving federal grant aid, by local funding category and by state. The tuition burden placed on students varies considerably, from a low of $314 in California to a high of $2,650 in Ohio. As the standard deviations indicate, tuition and fee charges vary considerably within states.[2] State-funded states have higher mean tuition, $1,700 ($SD$ = $555), than local-funded states, which have a mean tuition of $1,479 and higher variation (SD = $638). Whether assessed by the range or IQR of the distribution,

TABLE 3

Tuition/Fees and Federal Grant Aid by Funding Type and State

State-Funded	Tuition/Fees($s)		Grant Aid(%)	
	M	SD	M	SD
AL	1681	158	48	17
AR	1042	218	48	17
CO	1739	284	34	15
CT	1870	34	26	12
FL	1438	149	30	11
GA	1646	505	40	14
HI	1061	19	30	8
LA	1178	338	39	10
MA	1822	190	30	15
MN	2621	155	34	14
ND	1948	88	56	19
OH	2650	568	32	15
OK	1296	451	34	17
SC	2200	0	36	12
TN	1437	6	27	22
VA	1181	167	42	16
WA	1725	56	23	10

Local-Funded	Tuition/Fees($s)		Grant Aid(%)	
	M	SD	M	SD
AZ	910	105	38	19
IA	2208	220	36	14
IL	1522	190	29	19
KS	1387	119	34	10
MD	2165	436	33	19
MI	1754	378	32	15
MO	1504	271	38	15
MS	1144	358	54	12
NC	897	64	42	18
NE	1429	95	42	27
NJ	2284	448	36	18
NM	808	392	52	16
NY	2560	248	49	14
OR	1726	230	36	18
PA	2156	294	26	12
TX	874	275	37	21
WY	1469	109	34	11
CA	314	61	28	17

Source: NCES IPEDS 2000–2001

local-share states have greater variation in tuition and fees. The median range and IQR in local-share states are $1,412 and $300, both more than double the respective values of $713 and $138 in state-funded states.

The mean proportion of students receiving grant aid ranges from a quarter to half, with the lowest standard deviation at 8% and typical values ranging between 10 to 19%. This indicates that in all states the dispersion of the grant aid variable is sufficient to distinguish the relative wealth of the college's local community. The mean and standard deviation of grant aid receipt is similar in state- and local-funded states, at 35% (*SD* = 16%) and 38% (*SD* = 18%), respectively. The value in California where tuition is low is also relatively low at a mean of 29% (*SD* = 15%).

The upper panels of Table 4 and Figure 1 illustrate that colleges in the zero local-share category have the lowest median appropriations, which at $4,259 is roughly $400 to $1,000 less per FTE than the median value of any of the local-share categories. With an inter-quartile range only slightly higher or less than the other categories, the 75th percentile value for zero local-share colleges is always less than the 75th percentile in the other categories and, in some comparisons, is closer to the median value for colleges receiving local appropriations. Only one college with local funding has per FTE appropriations less than the lowest values in the zero-share category. Typically, then, colleges that receive local funding have higher levels of appropriations per FTE from state and local sources than colleges that receive state-level appropriations only.

The lower panel of Table 4 and Figure 1 illustrate these analyses using a measure of revenues per FTE from all sources, excluding tuition and fees. Colleges in the zero local-share category no longer have the lowest median value. At a median of $7,454 and *IQR* of $3,132, the distribution is very similar to that for colleges in the local-to-state appropriations ratio categories of 0.51–1.0 and 1.1–2.0. Colleges reporting a local-share ratio of 0.02–0.50 have the highest distribution of revenues from all sources per FTE, with a median value $1000 greater than that for colleges with no local share. The colleges with a local share greater than 2.0 have a high median, but also have a high *IQR*, which makes the overall distribution similar to the zero-share category. Typically, then, colleges with no local appropriations have levels of total revenue similar to those of colleges with local appropriations, with the exception of colleges in the smallest local-share category.

Table 5 reports, by state within the local- and state-share funding categories, the extent to which the FTE funding received by colleges from local and state appropriations varies within states. Five

TABLE 4

Variation in Revenue per FTE ($s) by Local-Share Categories

Local and State Appropriations

Local-Share Funding Ratio	*n*	Min	Mdn	IQR	Max
0.0–.01	259	2007	4259	1984	32373
0.02–0.50	175	2574	5207	2656	34652
0.51–1.0	88	2586	4636	2036	9677
1.1–2.0	65	3175	4979	2290	10853
>2.00	41	1283	5389	1954	11208
Total	628	1283	4676	2276	34652

Total Revenues, Minus Tuition and Fees ($s)

Local-Share Funding Ratio	*n*	Min	Mdn	IQR	Max
0.0–0.01	259	3182	7454	3132	58690
0.02–0.50	175	3840	8459	2839	47286
0.51–1.0	88	4444	7390	2791	14054
1.1–2.0	65	4720	7347	3181	13931
>2.00	41	3373	8059	3246	15550
Total	628	3182	7715	3121	58690

Source: NCES IPEDS 2000-2001

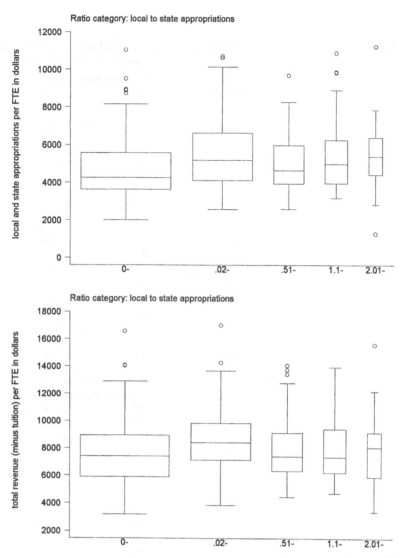

Figure 1 *Local and state appropriations (top panel) and revenues from all sources excluding tuition (lower panel) per FTE by college ratio of local appropriations to state appropriations. The width of the boxes corresponds to the proportion of cases in each category. The lower and upper bounds of the box represent the 25th and 75th percentile, the center line is the median, and the circles beyond the whiskers are outliers. Five extreme values are omitted, excluding one case in 0.0-0.01 and 4 in 0.02-0.50 categories.*

states each have one case reporting revenues more than double the 95th percentile value in the state. These have been treated as extreme, unique values and omitted from the estimates of average revenue deviations.[3] The mean (absolute value) deviation of revenues from the state median is $973 (*SD* = $314) per FTE, excluding California, which has a mean deviation of $1,330. The ratio of appropriations at the 90th percentile to the 10th percentile is equal to or greater than 2.0 in 13 of the 26 states. The majority of states exceed an *IQR* of $1,000 per FTE and 15 states have an *IQR* greater than $1,500.

Local-share funding is associated with a slightly higher intrastate variation of local and state appropriations per FTE. The upper panel of Table 6 and Figure 3 compare the distribution of average absolute deviations per FTE measured in dollars by local-share and state-funded states.[4] At $904, the median deviation in local-share states is $100 more than the median value of $807 in state-funded states. The 25th percentile in local-share states ($846) is also higher than the median value in state-funded states. One hundred dollars is 2% of the mean value of $5,000 of state and local appro-

TABLE 5

Variation in Local and State Appropriations per FTE by Funding Type and State

State Funded	n	Mean Deviation ($s)	90P/10P	Deviations from Median		
				IQR ($s)	min ($s)	90P ($s)
AL	21	763	1.6	1713	-1045	1543
AR	15	1334	2.5	2368	-2778	3764
CO	15	1052	2.4	1945	-1814	2242
CT	12	757	1.5	1109	-1478	1524
FL	28	1081	2.0	1513	-1551	2987
GA	14	1139	1.8	2203	-3804	1070
HI	7	929	2.4	886	-942	4313
LA	6	590	2.0	757	-885	1569
MA	14	815	1.5	1554	-1217	1288
MN	12	1097	1.9	2237	-1674	1487
ND	5	780	1.6	1882	-1878	142
OH	28	807	1.9	1223	-1025	1898
OK	14	817	1.8	1431	-767	1997
SC	5	651	1.7	737	-1679	841
TN	10	454	1.8	316	-1504	665
VA	24	690	2.0	840	-1014	2248
WA	27	533	1.8	657	-1142	1163

State Funded	n	Mean Deviation ($s)	90P/10P	Deviations from Median		
				IQR ($s)	min ($s)	90P ($s)
AZ	19	846	2.0	1796	-1441	1749
IA	14	792	1.8	769	-1026	2866
IL	45	904	1.9	1303	-2781	1925
KS	19	1266	2.1	2549	-2025	2003
MD	15	1128	2.2	1425	-1485	4077
MI	28	1467	2.8	2788	-3558	2555
MO	10	334	1.4	705	-523	671
MS	15	517	1.4	1052	-1503	1327
NC	49	1472	2.0	1827	-2598	2381
NE	5	753	1.8	299	-686	2778
NJ	19	633	1.6	755	-1270	1571
NM	15	1360	2.1	1800	-3623	1955
NY	33	872	1.7	1103	-1435	1471
OR	13	856	1.4	1132	-1564	970
PA	14	551	1.6	1088	-733	1250
TX	58	1350	2.4	2341	-2241	2792
WY	7	697	1.4	1912	-603	1698
CA	77	1330	2.5	1488	-4748	2036

Source: NCES IPEDS 2000–2001

Mean deviation equals the sum of the absolute value of deviations from the state median divided by the number of colleges with non-missing data in the state. 90P/10P is the 90th percentile/10th percentile ratio.

priations per FTE. Thus, while variation is typically larger in local- than in state-funded states, the revenue disparities at the center of the distribution are not great. Above the median, local-funded states cluster near a 75th percentile value of $1,350, while state-funded states fall around a lower 75th percentile value of $1,081. This difference in variation, nearing $300, is greater, but still a relatively small proportion of typical state and local appropriations.

Variation in Revenue Deviations by Funding Type

In Dollars	n	Min	25P	Mdn	75P	90P	Max
State funded	256	454	690	807	1081	1139	1334
Local funded	368	334	846	904	1350	1472	1472
Total	624	334	763	872	1334	1467	1472
Revenue Index	**n**	**Min**	**25P**	**Mdn**	**75P**	**90P**	**Max**
State funded	256.00	0.39	0.86	1.00	1.14	1.37	2.15
Local funded	368.00	0.32	0.89	1.00	1.19	1.38	2.60
Total	624.00	0.32	0.74	1.00	1.16	1.38	2.60

Source: NCES IPEDS 2000–2001

n is based on sample with non-missing data, excluding California.

The revenue index is the absolute value of college revenue deviations as a proportion of the state median.

The larger variation in revenues in local-share states is in part due to higher levels of spending in those states. When revenue deviations are indexed by college as a proportion of the state median (Table 6, lower panel), the distribution is quite similar under both funding types, with the exception that the index for local-share states has a higher maximum value. In addition, as shown in Figure 2, the local-share category includes 6 of 17 states with an average deviation lower than the median in the state-funded category, which indicates that variation in local-share states is not uniformly high. Similarly, six states without a local role have an average deviation greater than $900, the midpoint of deviations in local-share states, which indicates that high-revenue deviations are found in states with no local role.

To assess the hypothesis that revenue deviations in state-funded states promote vertical equity by providing higher levels of funding to communities with greater need, while deviations in local-funded states are regressive, we selected an average funding deviation of $1,000 as a threshold for designating high-disparity states. This designation encompasses five state-funded states (Arkansas, Colorado, Florida, Georgia, and Minnesota) and six local-funded states (Kansas, Maryland, Michigan, North Carolina, New Mexico, and Texas). The use of an IQR exceeding $1,500 as a selection criterion would add Alabama, Massachusetts, and North Dakota as state-funded, high-disparity states and Arizona, Illinois, New Mexico, and Wyoming as high-disparity local-funded states. We graphed revenue deviations against the proportion of full-time, first-time students at each college receiving federal grant aid. Since the grant aid proportion serves as a proxy for community wealth, we first obtained the Pearson's correlation between tuition/fees and grant aid. The correlation between

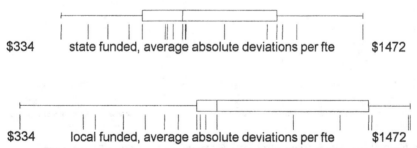

Figure 2 *Average absolute deviations per FTE by state and local funding. The lower and upper bounds of the box represent the 25th and 75th percentiles and the center line is the median. Each vertical line under the boxes represents the location of a state in the distribution of values.*

these two variables was relatively weak, ranging from $r = .11$ to $r = .23$, with the exception of Arkansas and Colorado, where the values were $r = .28$ and $r = .47$, respectively. We excluded Colorado from the analysis to eliminate variation in tuition as a strong alternative explanation for differences in the proportion of students receiving financial aid.

Scatterplots graphing revenue deviations by the proportion of students receiving grant aid are presented for state-funded states in Figure 3 and local-share states in Figures 4 and 5. The case markers indicate the geographic locale of the college to assess simultaneously if revenue deviations may be attributed to geographic cost differences or economies of scale. Revenue deviations in Minnesota are strongly correlated with grant aid receipt ($r = .80$). In addition, all colleges with positive revenue deviations are located in small towns, while most with negative deviations are located on the fringe of large cities, suggesting economies of scale for larger campuses. Deviations are more weakly, but positively, correlated in Florida ($r = .35$) and Arkansas ($r = .12$), where, in the latter case, the low value does not provide a good summary. The graph for Arkansas shows a stronger linear relationship with the exception of an unusual case with high positive revenue deviations and a relatively small proportion of grant recipients. In both these states, small towns tend to have positive deviations. In contrast, the correlation in Georgia is negative ($r = -.26$). Colleges with lower proportions of grant recipients have positive revenue deviations. Small towns appear both above and below the median line.

In local-share states, Michigan and North Carolina (Figure 4) have positive correlations with grant receipt ($r = .31$ and $.19$, respectively). Rural and small towns appear both above and below the median line in both states. Maryland (Fig. 5) has a positive correlation of $r = .39$, but this high value is strongly affected by one rural college with high positive deviations and high grant receipt. The association between funding and need in Maryland is much weaker among the remaining cases.

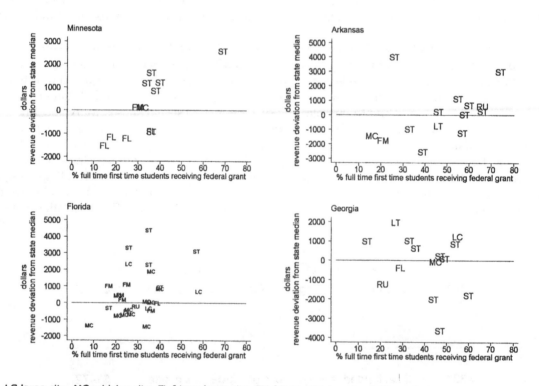

LC large city, MC midsize city, FL fringe large city, FM fringe midsize city, LT large town, ST small town, R rural

Figure 3 *Revenue deviations by grant receipt in state-funded states, with geographic locale as case marker. The y-axis scale differs by state.*

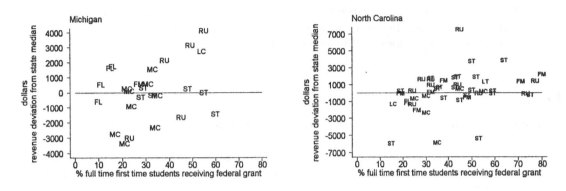

LC large city, MC midsize city, FL fringe large city, FM fringe midsize city, LT large town,
ST small town, R rural

Figure 4 *Revenue deviations by grant receipt in local-share states, with positive associations. Geographic locale is the case marker. The y-axis scale differs by state.*

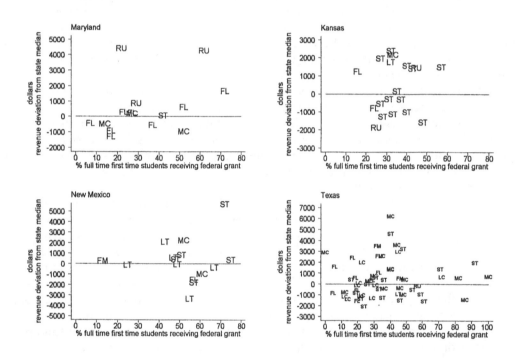

LC large city, MC midsize city, FL fringe large city, FM fringe midsize city, LT large town,
ST small town, R rural

Figure 5 *Revenue deviations by grant receipt in local-share states, with no association. Geographic locale is the case marker. The y-axis scale differs by state.*

Similarly, Kansas, New Mexico, and Texas have weak correlations, at $r = .13$, $.10$, and $.08$, respectively. In Texas, all but one of six colleges with more than 70% of students receiving grant aid have positive revenue deviations, but many colleges with lower proportions of grant recipients show equivalent or higher positive deviations. In California (not shown), where the average absolute revenue deviation is $1,330, there is no correlation between revenue deviations and grant receipt ($r = .01$). In summary, while deviations in three of four state-funded colleges are positively associated with grant aid, this relationship is found in only two of six local-share colleges. Positive revenue deviations in state-funded states are also more consistently associated with smaller geographic locales, suggesting that economies of scale are at play in these states.

Discussion

This study examines several questions about the impact of local funding on community college finance equity. Community college systems in half of the United States have a structure similar to K–12 finance systems in that they rely on local governments for funding. By analogy between community college and K–12 finance structures, we hypothesized that local funding in community colleges creates revenue disparities that disadvantage the least affluent communities in a state.

Analyzing the federal IPEDS 2000–2001 finance data in 35 states, the study demonstrates that significant intrastate revenue disparities do exist. The average amount of appropriations from local and state governments for community colleges is $5,000 per FTE. The average of the absolute value of college revenue deviations from the state median is close to $1,000, approximately 20% of typical appropriations. The majority of the 35 states analyzed have an inter-quartile range of revenue disparities greater than $1,500 per FTE. In half of the states analyzed, the ratio of appropriations at the 90th and 10th percentiles falls in the range of 2.0 to 2.8. In comparison, Kenneth Wong (1994) characterizes spending disparities between high and low revenue K–12 districts of 2.6 in New York, 3.1 in Illinois, and 2.8 in Texas as among the "most severe" (p. 277), based on a 1990 report by the Congressional Research Service.

Though not as pronounced as these K–12 disparities, the size of community college revenue disparities in many states may nevertheless be considered quite substantial. Further analysis is required to determine where these disparities may be attributed to different combinations of general education, vocational, remedial, and other programs across campuses in a state. Several states employ weighting schemes in their funding formulas, based on cost studies of different fields of instruction, in which technical and remedial courses receive 1.5 to 2.0 times the funding of general education courses (*State Funding*, 2000).

Revenue variations tend to be larger in states with a local finance role, but the difference is a small proportion of total funding and is due in part to higher levels of appropriations in those states. Taking into account this broader context, state- and local-funded states have quite similar levels of revenue variation. However, some resource disparities are progressive, or equity enhancing, while others are regressive. To assess the equity of resource differences, we examined a subsample of 10 states with average absolute deviations exceeding $1,000 per FTE. We observed revenue deviations in these high-disparity states as equity enhancing in three of four state-funded states and in two of six local-share states, suggesting that local funding is more often, though not always, regressive. Since all local-share states also have state funding, these differences in funding patterns cannot be attributed exclusively to the local role but may be understood as resulting when local funding is commingled with state funding. Thus, the direction of revenue disparities, not the overall level, presents a cause for concern.

The results support theoretically based equity and efficiency arguments about the effects of a local role on community college finance. The local finance role appears to create revenue disparities that do not promote vertical equity. On the other hand, local-share states tend to have lower tuition and higher levels of funding from within-state sources, which may reflect the "efficient" nature of local voters supporting their local colleges. Colleges with a ratio of local appropriations to state appropriations of less than one-half also have the highest levels of revenues from all sources, excluding tuition and fees. This correlation suggests that, when local governments have responsibility for funding community colleges in collaboration with state governments, students benefit from a broader revenue stream. With government officials at both the state and local level having a stake in the success of the local college, lobbying on behalf of the college and support for entrepreneurial activities may well increase.

These findings have implications for community college finance systems. States with a local finance share subordinate to the state share appear to receive higher revenues. It appears that intrastate variation in the resources available to a college in these states is also less likely to be determined by "rational" planning objectives, such as budget adjustments for low-income students or economies of scale. This situation may be socially beneficial if local financing contributes to a "leveling up" of resources, where all colleges benefit from higher public funding than they would in the absence of the local contribution. If this is the case, states with an existing local finance role should maintain them, while adopting policies that tax relatively high local revenue districts to provide additional funds to low-revenue districts. As Hoxby (2001) has shown in her analysis of the "leveling up" and "leveling down" effects of K–12 finance reforms, the tax price on high wealth districts should not be so high that it provides a disincentive for local funding in those districts; otherwise, the equalization policy may depress funding.

As state funding decreases, even states without a traditional local-finance role are placing greater expectations on individual colleges to generate additional funds, whether through academic entrepreneurship, auxiliary business activities, or fund raising (Burke & Serban, 1998). These efficiency initiatives have the potential of raising additional revenues but also create equity concerns as the state role in allocating resources diminishes. These states should also incorporate resource-sharing policies into incentive plans.

It is important to note that several factors for which controls have not been included due to data limitations may affect the interpretation of the findings. Most important, the observed correlation between positive revenue deviations and the proportion of students receiving grant aid may have meanings other than the equity-enhancing effect ascribed to it in this analysis. The proportion of students receiving grant aid may be affected by access to information and counseling regarding financial aid or by clarity of purpose among first-time students. If such factors are decisive in determining the proportion of grant recipients at a college, the positive correlation between higher levels of local and state appropriation and grant receipt may indicate revenue disparities in favor of more affluent communities with higher levels of college-related information and networking, or "social capital" (Coleman, 1988). In future analyses, the use of the IPEDS federal grant receipt variable should be supplemented with census income and poverty data to provide a better control for community wealth.

The higher levels of funding going to small-town colleges in some states have been interpreted here as compensating for diseconomies of scale. However, determining whether observed revenue disparities are appropriate for that purpose requires more information about fixed and variable costs and controls for geographic price differences among urban, suburban, and rural areas. Higher costs in urban areas are likely to diminish the purchasing power of each dollar in revenue. This means that, for more accurate comparison revenue, differences must be adjusted by a cost index similar to those developed for studies of K–12 finance equity. Generally, we would expect that the use of a geographic index will shift state funding from rural to urban areas (Carey, 2003; Odden & Picus, 2004). With significantly greater appropriations per FTE awarded to rural and small colleges in several of the high-disparity states, it is important to evaluate whether the appropriation premiums for small size are based on actual cost differences. Such estimates are clearly politically sensitive, as they have the potential to significantly shift funding among institutions. In states where white residents are disproportionately located in small towns and students of color in urban areas, the higher funding for small towns may be due to racial group politics and disparities in legislative power. Complex interactions may also be at play. Stella Flores (2003) shows that Texas's funding formula and reliance on local-share funding results in both higher and lower funding for Hispanic Serving Institutions (HSIs) in communities providing a threshold tax rate. The majority of the HSIs receiving the short end of the deal are located on the U.S.-Mexican border.

As discussed above, some portion of the revenue disparities may be due to the location of high-cost programs, but there may also be differences in the geographic accessibility of students to those programs. States may locate specialized programs requiring technical facilities at a small number of campuses and expect mobile adults to travel to them, but this may not be a realistic option for students constrained by work and family commitments. Thus, while high-cost programs may explain some portion of the funding disparities, their location may also raise equity issues in regard to program access.

K–12 finance equity cases initially focused on inputs, but over time the judicial focus has shifted to promoting equitable student outcomes. This approach is termed "adequacy," and it holds states accountable for providing resources to schools sufficient to enable students to meet educational standards and become successful competitors in a global economy (Verstegen, 1998). The incorporation of adequacy standards into community college finance analyses would be consistent with the recent policy focus on higher education performance accountability (Dowd, 2003). An adequacy, or "outcome equity," approach shifts the question from "Is equitable funding being provided to colleges in the state?" to "Are equitable program completion rates being achieved?" The answer to the latter question implies disparate funding because students with greater educational needs will require greater resources. For example, a college enrolling a relatively high proportion of immigrants in a nursing degree program may well require resources to provide language tutoring to attain graduation rates equal to those of a program enrolling native English speakers. This example underscores the significance of such funding decisions when we consider the shortage of bilingual and ethnically diverse nurses in the United States (Butters, 2003). Similarly, as community colleges take on an increasing role in remedial education, it is important to ask what levels of resources are needed to successfully educate students to desired standards of achievement.

This study has focused on states with high-revenue deviations. However, it should also be noted that states with low funding disparities may have inequitable systems if students with unequal needs are being treated as equals by the financing system. In addition, without state-by-state information about unique programs and institutional missions, the analysis has focused on conservative measures of variation that were not determined by extreme values. This approach may have minimized the characterization of funding inequities in some states.

Half of the states in the sample have 90th percentile revenue deviation values greater than $1,900, which may deserve greater attention. Does the high funding for these institutions stem from unique institutional histories, unusual levels of political clout, data-reporting error, or rational planning decisions to efficiently locate high-costs programs? This study provides a foundation for future multivariate analyses and purposeful sampling for case studies. State analysts and institutional researchers may wish to replicate the results for their state using IPEDS and state data. The following factors should be considered when evaluating the equity of revenue disparities: economies and diseconomies of scale, geographic price differences, mix of program types, community and student racial and demographic characteristics, and program completion rates.

Notwithstanding the recent community college finance litigation in Oregon (Gomstyn, 2003), determination of what constitutes "fair" intrastate community college resource allocations will most likely depend on political processes, rather than on legal decisions like those that have so significantly shaped K–12 financing. While primary and secondary schooling are a constitutional right mandated by state law, postsecondary education is not. Today, however, many would argue that a community college education now sets the contemporary standard for full participation in the economic and democratic institutions of our country. If this rhetorical claim gains political support, then it could also be argued that states have a responsibility to fund community colleges according to adequacy or "outcome equity" standards. Many community college students have limited options about where they attend college, constrained as they often are by family responsibilities, employment obligations, and financial hardship. In these conditions, the funding disparities documented in this paper certainly deserve greater understanding through academic analysis, action research by community college practitioners, and political debate within states.

Notes

1. The FTE calculation is based on the same ratio used to publish enrollment statistics in the annual *Digest of Education Statistics*. For the public two-year sector, the FTE equals full-time enrollment plus part-time enrollment multiplied by one-third.

2. To some extent, such variations in tuition and fees are due to mismeasurement at the college level. A review of reported tuition charges in Massachusetts, where the Board of Higher Education sets a uniform tuition, showed that individual colleges reported different tuition rates, in some cases due to different approaches to calculating full-time enrollment status. In Massachusetts, fees are set by the individual colleges and therefore create valid variation in the total of tuition and fees.

3. The cases and values are Mid-South Community College, Arizona ($26,648 per FTE above the state median of local and state appropriations), South Piedmont Community College, North Carolina ($27,547), Coahoma Community College, Minnesota (($15,516), Illinois Eastern Community Colleges—Olney Central College, ($13,491), and Foothill College, California ($9,114).

4. The five extreme cases are excluded from the calculation of average deviations.

References

Alexander, F. K. (2000). The changing face of accountability. *Journal of Higher Education, 71*(4), 411.

Bill Clinton's view on education: From acceptance speech. *Chronicle of Higher Education* (1996, September 16). Retrieved December 19, 2003, from http:// www.chronicle.com.

Breneman, D. W., & Nelson, S. C. (1981). *Financing community colleges: An economic perspective.* Washington, DC: Brookings Institution.

Budget development approach/options and impact of formula/fair share funding. (2000). (Budget Request Framework Proposal). Boston: Board of Higher Education.

Burke, J. C., & Serban, A. M. (Eds.). (1998). *Performance funding for public higher education: Fad or trend?* San Francisco: Jossey-Bass.

Butters, C. (2003). *Associate degree nursing students: A study of retention in the nursing education program.* Unpublished dissertation, University of Massachusetts Boston.

Carey, K. (2003). *The funding gap: Low-income and minority students still receive fewer dollars in many states.* Retrieved December 15, 2003, from http://www2. edtrust.org/EdTrust/Product+Catalog/special+reports.htm#2003.

Coleman, J. S. (1988). Social capital in the creation of human capital. *American Journal of Sociology, 94* (Supplement), S95–S120.

Community colleges and the State University of New York. (1999). Boulder, CO: National Center for Higher Education Management Systems.

DesJardins, S. L. (2003). Understanding and using efficiency and equity criteria in the study of higher education policy. In J. C. Smart & W. G. Tierney (Eds.), *Higher education: Handbook of theory and research* (pp. 173–219). New York: Agathon Press.

Dowd, A. C. (2003, March). From access to outcome equity: Revitalizing the democratic mission of the community college. *Annals of the American Academy of Political and Social Science, 586,* 92–119.

Flores, S. (2003, November). *Disproportionate policies: Latino access to community colleges in Texas.* Paper presented at the Association for the Study of Higher Education, Portland, Oregon.

Garms, W. I. (1981). On measuring the equity of community college finance. *Educational Administration Quarterly, 17*(2), 1–20.

Gomstyn, A. (2003). Oregon judge rejects community-colleges' lawsuit seeking more state money. *Chronicle of Higher Education.* Retrieved November 17, 2003, from http://chronicle.com.

Hoxby, C. M. (2001, November). All school finance equalizations are not created equal. *Quarterly Journal of Economics,* 1189–1231.

Iowa Community College funding formula task force report. (1998). N.p.: Iowa Department of Education.

Metzler, J. (2003, Spring). Inequitable equilibrium: School finance in the United States. *Indiana Law Review, 36,* 561–608.

Monk, D. H. (1990). *Educational finance: An economic approach.* New York: Mc-Graw Hill.

Odden, A. R., & Picus, L. O. (2004). *School finance: A policy perspective* (3rd ed.). Boston: McGraw-Hill.

Romano, R. M. (2003, October). *Financing community colleges across the states: An economic perspective.* Paper presented at the "Complex Community College" Conference, Cornell Higher Education Research Institute, Cornell University, Ithaca, NY.

State funding for community colleges: A fi fty-state survey. (2000). Denver, CO: Center for Community College Policy, Education Commission of the States.

Study: Hope and Lifetime Learning are middle-class tax benefits, not fi nancial aid. (2003, March 14, 2003). Retrieved December 19, 2003, from www.NASFAA. org.

Timar, T. B. (1994). Politics, policy, and categorical aid: New inequities in California school finance. *Educational Evaluation and Policy Analysis, 16*(2), 143–160.

Timar, T. B. (2003). *School governance in California: You can't always get what you want.* Retrieved April 30, 2003, from www.ucla-idea.org.

Verstegen, D. A. (1998, Summer). Judicial analysis during the new wave of school finance litigation: The new adequacy in education. *Journal of Education Finance, 24,* 51–68.

Wong, K. K. (1994). Governance structure, resource allocation, and equity policy. *Review of Research in Education, 20,* 257–289.

ALICIA C. DOWD is Assistant Professor, Department of Leadership in Education, University of Massachusetts Boston. JOHN L. GRANT is Director, Office of Institutional Research and Development, Cape Cod Community College. Sections of this paper were presented in earlier drafts at the Cornell Higher Education Research Institute's (CHERI) "Complex Community College" Conference (October 2003) and at the Association for Institutional Research's Annual Forum (May 2003). The authors thank Jeff Groen and Jane Wellman for their review of the CHERI draft. Address queries to Alicia C. Dowd, Assistant Professor, Graduate College of Education, University of Massachusetts Boston, 100 Morrissey Blvd., Boston, MA 02125; telephone: (617) 287-7593; fax: (617) 287-7664; email: alicia.dowd@umb.edu.

CHAPTER 17

DOING MORE WITH LESS: THE INEQUITABLE FUNDING OF COMMUNITY COLLEGES

CHRISTOPHER M. MULLIN

Introduction

Increasing the proportion of Americans whose levels of educational attainment extend beyond a high school diploma is a broad national priority. Attaining the ambitious goals that have been articulated will require the additional education of traditional-age students entering college directly from the K–12 system, as well as reengaging millions of young adults and experienced workers. Community colleges, which educate nearly half of all undergraduates, are committed to being a part of the solution.

The role of community colleges in helping people and the government respond to the current economic crisis and meeting widely articulated goals for college completion has resulted in an unprecedented amount of attention on the colleges, accompanied by heightened expectations. However, the thesis of this brief is that significantly increasing outputs from community colleges can be achieved only with increased resources. Compared to other sectors, community colleges have not received a fair share of funding in light of their role in the country's higher education system. Improvements in the delivery of community college education cannot overcome the stark reality of inadequate funding.

In this brief, I compare the funding of community colleges to that of other sectors of higher education, to set into context the challenges community colleges face as well as to highlight the policy priorities implicit in addressing funding inequities. To that end, I describe

- The magnitude of inequities between institution types.
- Some consequences of the inequities.

The Magnitude of Funding Inequities by Sector

To consider one dramatic statistic, community colleges received just 27% of total federal, state, and local revenues (operating and nonoperating) for public degree–granting institutions in 2007–2008 while serving 43% of undergraduate students. This imbalance in funding public institutions results from a number of state and federal funding priorities. For example,

- Community colleges have historically received just 20% of the state tax appropriations for higher education.
- Judged through a variety of metrics, community colleges received considerably fewer federal funds than do other sectors of higher education.

Consequences of Inequitable Funding

Community colleges educated 43% of all undergraduate students in 2007, including the greatest proportion of underrepresented students: 53% of Hispanic, 45% of Black, 45% of Asian/Pacific Islander, and 52% of Native American undergraduates. Given that projected shifts in the U.S. population indicate that increasing numbers of college students will come from these backgrounds, community colleges are critical doorways to true educational equality.

Community colleges have concentrated what money they do receive on instruction. They spent 44.5% of education and general funds on instruction compared to 39.6% at private research institutions and 36.1% at public research institutions. Their faculty earn less and teach more than colleagues in other sectors of higher education. In part because of the fiscal free-fall that state treasuries took beginning in 2008, community colleges are now having to turn away students from needed programs. This is an extremely troubling development.

Moving Forward

In July, 2009, the Obama administration announced its American Graduation Initiative (AGI), a plan to place community colleges at the forefront of the country's effort to regain global prominence in higher education attainment, with funding to help accomplish the task. Some argued that such an action placed, for the first time in federal policy, one sector of higher education ahead of others. But AGI has to be considered in the context of the broader funding of community colleges.

The ability of community colleges to serve their students and communities is due in large part to the investment of federal, state, and local governments and federal agencies; however, increasing productivity by 50%, as envisioned by the Obama administration's call for five million more community college graduates, will be possible only if resources are significantly increased. The $2 billion available to higher education as a result of the Health Care and Education Reconciliation Act of 2010 via the Community College and Career Training grant program is a strong start, but those funds can be viewed only as a down payment on needed federal investments that must be accompanied by a resolution of structural funding inequities.

Introduction

Increasing the proportion of Americans whose levels of educational attainment extend beyond a high school diploma is a broad national priority. Attaining the ambitious goals that have been articulated will require the additional education of traditional-age students entering college directly from the K–12 system, as well as reengaging millions of young adults and experienced workers. Community colleges, which educate nearly half of all undergraduates, are committed to being a part of the solution. Six organizations have partnered in their commitment to increase college completion by 50%: the American Association of Community Colleges (AACC), the Association of Community College Trustees, the Center for Community College Student Engagement, the League for Innovation in the Community College, the National Organization for Staff and Organizational Development, and Phi Theta Kappa (AACC, 2010b).

The role of community colleges in helping people and the government respond to the current economic crisis and meeting widely articulated goals for college completion has resulted in an unprecedented amount of attention on the colleges, accompanied by heightened expectations. However, the thesis of this brief is that significantly increasing outputs from community colleges can be achieved only with increased resources. Compared to other sectors, community colleges have not received a fair share of funding in light of their role in the country's higher education system. Improvements in the delivery of community college education cannot overcome the stark reality of inadequate funding.

Surging enrollments at community colleges over the past two years have not been met with proportional increases in fiscal support,[1] placing community colleges across the country in the position of doing more with less, or, in some cases, simply doing less. Increasingly, these cuts are hitting core institutional activities; for example, many students are being denied access through course reductions and enrollment caps (see, e.g., Killough, 2009; Moltz, 2009, 2010). Asking community colleges to graduate more students with less money will likely result in stunting the growth of the U.S. workforce at a time when projections indicate that 26.7 million new jobs need to be filled with college-educated workers by 2018—an outcome the nation can ill afford (Carnevale, Smith, & Strohl, 2010).

In this brief, I compare the funding of community colleges to that of other sectors of higher education, to set into context the challenges community colleges face as well as to highlight the policy priorities implicit in addressing funding inequities. To that end, I describe

- The magnitude of inequities between institution types.
- Some consequences of the inequities.

The Magnitude of Funding Inequities by Sector

Institutional diversity makes the U.S. higher education system unique and dynamic, enabling students to engage in learning tailored to their individual interests and abilities. However, while the diversity of institutional missions is fundamental to the vitality of higher education, the asymmetrical way institutions are funded is not. To consider one dramatic statistic, community colleges received just 27% of total federal, state, and local revenues (operating and nonoperating) for public degree–granting institutions in 2007–2008 (NCES, 2009) while serving 43% of undergraduate students (AACC, 2010a).

State Funding

Regrettably, overall state fiscal support for public higher education has been on a long-term downward slope. State disinvestment in public higher education decreased most sharply in the early 1990s, when the percentage of state revenues devoted to higher education decreased from 7.0% in 1989 to 5.4% in 1993 to 4.5% in 2008 (see Figure 1).[2] Unfortunately for community colleges, in

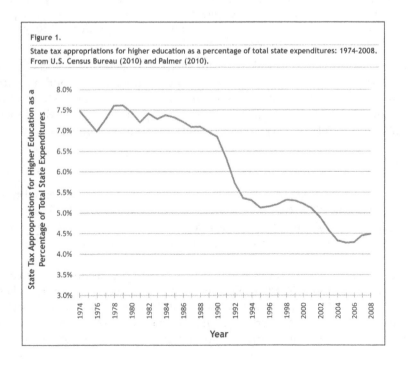

Figure 1.

State tax appropriations for higher education as a percentage of total state expenditures: 1974-2008. From U.S. Census Bureau (2010) and Palmer (2010).

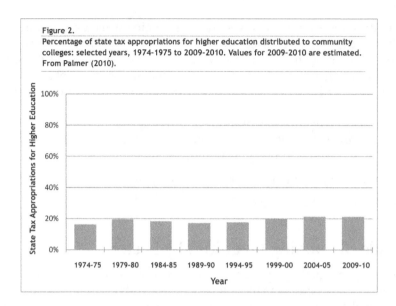

Figure 2.
Percentage of state tax appropriations for higher education distributed to community colleges: selected years, 1974-1975 to 2009-2010. Values for 2009-2010 are estimated. From Palmer (2010).

comparison to public 4-year institutions, historically they have received approximately 20% of state tax appropriations for higher education (see Figure 2).

Furthermore, despite the recent strong public emphasis on the contributions of community colleges, states continue to allocate to the colleges a relatively small share of higher education funds. For example, public funds in Maryland are allocated to community colleges via the Cade formula, which stipulated that, for FY 2010, community colleges shall receive "not less than an amount equal to 23.6% of the State's general fund appropriation per full-time-equivalent student to the *4-year public institutions of higher education in the State* [emphasis added]" (Annotated Code, 2009). When New York was developing the State University of New York (SUNY) system, it decided to adopt the perspective of John E. Burton, then director of budget for New York State and member of the commission that developed the SUNY system. He stated:

> While recognizing that there was a place in our system for community colleges, I could not quite see why community colleges should be placed, as proposed, at the very core of our system of higher education. The community college would thus become the major recipient of the state's higher education funds . . . we should strengthen the state's private universities and colleges through an expanded scholarship program. (cited in Cármichael, 1955, p. 170)

The mounting pressure on states to budget for Medicaid, corrections, and elementary and secondary education has contributed to the disinvestment in public postsecondary education in general and especially in community colleges. Not surprisingly, research has shown that educational attainment rates improve with increases in state fiscal support (Zhang, 2008). If increasing educational attainment is a true state priority, commensurate fiscal support must follow.

Federal Funding

Inequities in state fiscal policy extend to federal funding streams as well, albeit within very different mechanisms of support. In 2008, the federal government invested $36.4 billion directly in higher education, of which $28.8 billion was administered by the U.S. Department of Education (ED). Aid in the form of federal student assistance constituted $28.4 billion—or 98.4%—of ED's higher education spending.[3]

The Pell Grant program is the hallmark of federal access to postsecondary education and critical for community college students: 32.8% of Pell recipients attended community colleges, and these students were awarded 36.5% of all funds in 2009–2010 (Federal Student Aid, 2010). Only 10% of community college students take out federal loans, in contrast to 42% of public 4-year, 55% of private 4-year, and 88% of students at for-profit institutions (College Board, 2009, Figure 4). But, aside from programs directly aiding students, community colleges received considerably fewer federal funds from ED when compared to other sectors of higher education (see Table 1). The resulting inverse distribution pattern is inequitable and inadequate to meet our national goal of increasing educational attainment (see Figure 3).

The preceding discussion briefly outlines some of the current fiscal inequities between sectors of postsecondary education. These inequities are troubling because of their implications for access, quality, and success in higher education.

Table 1.

Federal Funds Allocated by the U.S. Department of Education For Postsecondary Aid, by Program and Sector: 2009–2010

Program	Sector					Total Amount
	Community college	Public	Private nonprofit	For-profit	Other	
Office of Federal Student Aid						
Pell Grant	32.8%	29.0%	13.2%	25.0%	–	$29,360,615,964
Academic Competitiveness Grant	18.3%	52.9%	25.2%	3.8%	–	$467,860,428
SMART Grant	0.0%	67.1%	25.2%	7.6%	–	$343,502,405
TEACH Grant	0.3%	48.1%	45.2%	6.4%	–	$90,917,464
Federal Work-Study	15.8%	34.7%	43.2%	6.4%	–	$1,118,930,076
Federal SEOG	17.6%	30.1%	35.5%	16.8%	–	$756,863,567
Office of Postsecondary Education (new and continuing grants as of August 9, 2010)						
Minority-Serving Institutions: SIP (Title III-A)	65.9%	14.1%	20.0%	–	–	$61,683,811
TRIO: Talent Search	36.8%	35.6%	10.7%	–	16.9%	$112,057,298
TRIO: Upward Bound (UB)	37.1%	35.2%	16.0%	0.4%	11.3%	$226,471,275
TRIO: UB Math & Science Comp.	24.1%	56.0%	14.8%	–	5.1%	$29,611,309
TRIO: Ed. Opportunity Centers	40.8%	43.2%	5.7%	–	10.3%	$21,073,888
Minority Science Improvement	23.7%	47.0%	29.4%	–	–	$5,432,393
Other programs	3.0%	15.3%	76.5%	–	5.1%	$225,070,353
Office of Vocational and Adult Education						
Grants to states	–	–	–	–	–	$1,877,781,771

Note. Additional programs were funded by the U.S. Department of Education, but data were not available at the time of writing. The "Other" column includes K-12, community-based organizations, among others. Data are adapted from Federal Student Aid (2010) and U.S. Department of Education (2010).

Figure 3.

Total education and general (E&G) spending per FTE student, by enrollment and institution type: 2008. From Desrochers et al. (2010).

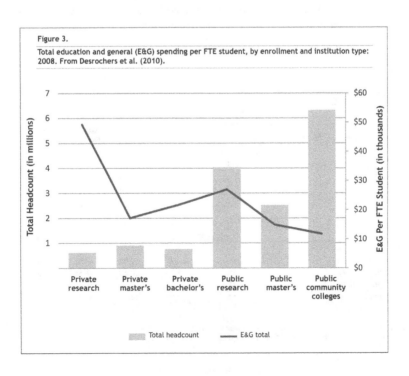

Consequences of Inequitable Funding

Community colleges educated 43% of all undergraduate students in 2007 (AACC, 2010a), including the greatest proportion of underrepresented students: 53% of Hispanic, 45% of Black, 45% of Asian/Pacific Islander, and 52% of Native American undergraduates (AACC, 2010a). Given that projected shifts in the U.S. population indicate that increasing numbers of college students will come from these backgrounds, community colleges are critical doorways to true educational equality.

Limited Services

With relatively limited fiscal resources, community colleges have to make difficult decisions about where to target their resources. Community colleges have concentrated that money on instruction, spending a greater percentage on that function than do other sectors (see Table 2). Full-time faculty at community colleges are paid less than their peers at public and private institutions: The average salary of full-time faculty at a community college in 2008–2009 was $60,587, compared to $74,209 at public 4-year institutions and $78,316 at private 4-year institutions (Snyder & Dillow, 2010, Table 257). At the same time, community college faculty spend comparably more time teaching than their peers at other types of institutions (see Figure 4). In 2003, community colleges employed 43% of all part-time faculty, 11.3% of whom where Black or Hispanic, compared to between 5.6% and 7.8% at public and private research, doctoral, and comprehensive institutions (Snyder & Dillow, 2010, Table 253).

College adminstrators also receive less pay for the same work. For example, in 2008–2009, the median salary for a chief executive was $380,293 at doctoral institutions, $242,050 at master's institutions, $225,000 at baccalaureate institutions, and $164,947 at community colleges (College and University Professional Association, 2009). Across all executive categories, similar differentials apply.

The focus on instruction has been a community college constant. However, due to limited funds, community colleges generally have not been able to allocate more money to other activities that promote student success and increase educational attainment, including academic support and student services. As was recently highlighted in a 2010 College Board report, counseling can play a significant role in making college more affordable through demystifying the student aid process. This is a major issue: Only 58% of Pell-eligible students at community colleges applied for financial aid, compared to 77% of Pell-eligible students at public 4-year institutions and 84% of Pell-eligible students at private 4-year institutions (Kantrowitz, 2009). Furthermore, early alert systems and "intrusive academic counseling"—a proactive approach whereby the college initiates the need to

Table 2.
Total Postsecondary Education and General (E&G) Expenditures Per FTE Student, by Institution Type: 2008

| Institution Type | Instruction-Related E&G | | | | |
	Instruction	Academic support	Student services	Other E&G	Total E&G
Expenditure per FTE student					
Public community colleges	$5,216	$367	$982	$5,167	$11,732
Public master's	$6,209	$629	$1,490	$6,577	$14,905
Public research	$9,732	$1,912	$2,775	$12,553	$26,972
Private bachelor's	$8,172	$628	$2,017	$10,859	$21,676
Private master's	$7,056	$467	$1,711	$7,949	$17,183
Private research	$19,520	$1,293	$5,471	$23,014	$49,298
Percentage distribution					
Public community colleges	44.5%	3.1%	8.4%	44.0%	100%
Public master's	41.7%	4.2%	10.0%	44.1%	100%
Public research	36.1%	7.1%	10.3%	46.5%	100%
Private bachelor's	37.7%	2.9%	9.3%	50.1%	100%
Private master's	41.1%	2.7%	10.0%	46.3%	100%
Private research	39.6%	2.6%	11.1%	46.7%	100%

Note. The "Other E&G" column includes research, public service, institutional support, operations and maintenance, and net scholarships and fellowships. From Desrochers et al. (2010).

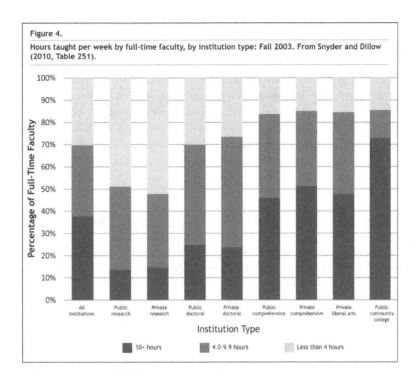

Figure 4.

Hours taught per week by full-time faculty, by institution type: Fall 2003. From Snyder and Dillow (2010, Table 251).

meet with the student—have increasingly been recognized as ways to increase academic achievement, especially for disadvantaged students (see, e.g., Grubb, 2006; Wojciehowska, 2010).

Idle Assets

Each student denied the opportunity to engage in higher education who might benefit from it constitutes an idle asset. Given that the state budget cuts that commenced in 2008 show only faint signs of abating, community colleges have now been forced to explicitly or implicitly deny access to students. To look at just one sector of the economy, community colleges are the leading producers of graduates in nursing and allied health. Among the various sectors of higher education, community colleges educate more than 50% of all new nurses (National Commission on Community Colleges, 2008).

Nurses who graduate from associate degree programs do as well as those graduating from bachelor's degree programs on the national licensing exam (National Council on State Boards of Nursing, 2009). Despite their productivity, community colleges could still provide much more opportunity: In 2004–2005, associate degree registered nurse programs turned away more than three times more students than did bachelor's degree programs (AACC 2010c). Furthermore, 58% of all sub-baccalaureate completers in health professions and related clinical sciences earned their credentials at community colleges in 2007–2008 (National Center for Education Statistics [NCES], 2010).[4]

The role of community colleges in educating health-care professionals is critical: A projected 2.7 million jobs will be open by 2018 in the field (Carnevale et al., 2010). More funding could assist in meeting the demand for nurses, allied health professionals, and other critical occupations.

Moving Forward

In July, 2009, the Obama administration announced its American Graduation Initiative (AGI), a plan to place community colleges at the forefront of the country's effort to regain global prominence in higher education attainment, with funding to help accomplish the task. Some argued that such an action placed, for the first time in federal policy, one sector of higher education ahead of others. The analysis of fiscal inequities, contained in this brief, shows why the basic policy thrust of AGI was so appropriate—and overdue. But AGI was not enacted and, even if it had been enacted, it would have left stark funding disparities between community colleges and other sectors.

Community colleges are heavily dependent on the investment of federal, state, and local governments; however, increasing productivity by 50%, as envisioned by the Obama administration's call for five million more community college graduates, will be possible only if resources are significantly increased. The $2 billion available to higher education as a result of the Health Care and Education Reconciliation Act of 2010 (Pub. Law 111-152) via the Community College and Career Training grant program is a strong start, but those funds can be viewed only as a down payment on needed federal investments that must be accompanied by a resolution of structural funding inequities.

Notes

1. Although data for the most recent fiscal year has yet to be released, in some cases allocations to institutions from state governments have been held at FY 2006 levels because of maintenance-of-effort (MOE) provisions in federal policy while there have been double-digit increases in enrollments at community colleges, which I estimate has resulted in a decrease in dollars per full-time-equivalent student. For a discussion of MOE provisions see, Alexander, Harnisch, Hurley, and Moran (2010). For a discussion of enrollment increases, see Mullin and Phillippe (2009).

2. Percentages were derived using methodology from Thomas and Orzag (2002); however, due to revisions in the Grapevine database (Palmer, 2010), derived values vary slightly from those reported by Kane and Orzag.

3. Data for the other $7.6 billion were not available at the sector level and come from numerous federal departments and agencies. For more information, see Snyder and Dillow (2010, Table 375).

4. This percentage was derived from analysis of data from the Integrated Postsecondary Education Data System's Completions Survey (NCES, 2010).

References

Alexander, F. K., Harnisch, T., Hurley, D., & Moran, R. (2010, April). *"Maintenance of effort:" An evolving federal–state policy approach to ensuring college affordability* [Policy brief]. Washington, DC: American Association of State Colleges and Universities.

American Association of Community Colleges. (2010a). *2010 AACC fact sheet.* Available from http://www.aacc.nche.edu/aboutcc/documents/factsheet2010.pdf

American Association of Community Colleges. (2010b, April 20). *National organizations sign student completion call to action.* Available from http://www.aacc.nche.edu/newsevents/News/articles/Pages/042020101.aspx

American Association of Community Colleges. (2010c). *Nursing education and practice.* Available from the AACC Web site: http://www.aacc.nche.edu/Resources/aaccprograms/health

Annotated Code of Maryland, sec. 16-305. (2009). Available from http://mlis.state.md.us/asp/web_statutes .asp?ged&16-305

Carmichael, O. C., Jr. (1955). *New York establishes a state university: A case study in the processes of policy formation.* Nashville, TN: Vanderbilt University Press.

Carnevale, A., Smith, N., & Strohl, J. (2010, June). *Help wanted: Projections of jobs and education requirements through 2018.* Washington, DC: Center on Education and the Workforce. Available from http://cew.georgetown.edu/

College Board. (2009, October). *Trends in student aid: 2009.* Washington, DC: Author.

College Board. (2010, May). *The financial aid challenge: Successful practices that address the underutilization of financial aid in community colleges.* Washington, DC: Author.

College and University Professional Association for Human Resources. (2009, February 27). Median salaries of college administrators by job category and type of institution, 2008-9. *Chronicle of Higher Education.*

Desrochers, D. M., Lenihan, C. M., & Wellman, J. V. (2010). *Trends in college spending: 1998–2008. Where does the money come from? Where does it go? What does it buy?* Washington, DC: Delta Project on Postsecondary Education Costs, Productivity, and Accountability.

Federal Student Aid, U.S. Department of Education. (2010). Data Center [Data files]. Available from the Federal Student Aid Web site: http://federalstudentaid.ed.gov/datacenter/programmatic.html

Grubb, W. N. (2006). Like, what do I do now? The dilemmas of guidance counseling. In T. Bailey & V. S. Morest (Eds.), *Defending the community college equity agenda* (pp. 195–222). Baltimore: The Johns Hopkins University Press.

Kane, T. J., & Orzag, P. R. (2002, October 14). *Use of state general revenue for higher education declines* Washington, DC: Tax Policy Center.

Kantrowitz, M. (2009, October 14). *FAFSA completion by level and control of institution.* Available from the FinAid Web site: http://www.finaid.org/ search/htdig/htsearch.cgi?words=institutions

Killough, A. (2009, May 29). Largest community college in U.S. will cap enrollment. *The Chronicle of Higher Education.* Available from http:// chronicle.com/article/Largest-Community-College-in/47663

Moltz, D. (2009, July 21). No vacancy. *Inside Higher Ed.* Available from http://www.insidehighered.com/news/2009/07/21/california

Moltz, D. (2010, July 29). Adding classes while others cut. *Inside Higher Ed.* Available from http://www.insidehighered.com/news/2010/07/29/sdccd

Mullin, C. M., & Phillippe, K. (2009). *Community college enrollment Surge: An analysis of estimated fall 2009 headcount enrollments at community colleges* (AACC Policy Brief 2009-01PBL). Washington, DC: American Association of Community Colleges.

National Center for Education Statistics, Data Analysis System. (2009). *IPEDS 2009 spring compendium tables* (Table 21). Washington, DC: U.S. Department of Education. Available from http://nces.ed.gov/das/library/tables_listings/ipeds_comp_spring09.asp

National Center for Education Statistics. (2010). IPEDS data center [Data files]. Washington, DC: U.S. Department of Education.

National Commission on Community Colleges. (2008, January). *Winning the skills race and strengthening America's middle class: An action agenda for community colleges.* New York, NY: The College Board. Available from http://professionals.collegeboard.com/profdownload/winning_the_ skills_race.pdf

National Council of State Boards of Nursing. (2009, October). *2010: Number of candidates taking NCLEX examination and percent passing, by type of candidate* [data table]. Chicago, IL: Author.

Obama, B. (2009, July 14). *Remarks by the president on the American Graduation Initiative.* Washington, DC: The White House, Office of the Press Secretary. Available from http://www.whitehouse.gov/the_press_office/Remarks-by-the-President-on-the-American-Graduation-Initiative-inWarren-MI/

Palmer, J. C. (2010). Grapevine [Database]. Normal, IL: Illinois State University, Center for the Study of Education Policy. Available from http://www. grapevine.ilstu.edu/index.shtml

Snyder, T. D., & Dillow, S. A. (2010, April). *Digest of education statistics: 2009* (NCES 2010-013). Washington, DC: U.S. Department of Education, National Center for Education Statistics.

U.S. Census Bureau. (2010). *2008 annual survey of state government finances* [Database]. Washington, DC: Author. Available from the U.S. Census Bureau Web site: http://www.census.gov/govs/state/

U.S. Department of Education (2010). ED Discretionary and Formula Grant Award Database. Available from the U.S. Department of Education Web site: http://www2.ed.gov/fund/data/award/grntawd.html

Wojciechowska, I. (2010, August 6). A major push on advising. *Inside Higher Ed.*

Zhang, L. (2008). Does state funding affect graduation rates at public four-year colleges and universities? *Educational Policy, 23*(5), 714–731.

CHAPTER 18

THE MOVING TARGET: STUDENT FINANCIAL AID AND COMMUNITY COLLEGE STUDENT RETENTION

MICHAEL A. KENNAMER
NORTHEAST ALABAMA COMMUNITY COLLEGE, RAINSVILLE

STEPHEN G. KATSINAS

RANDALL E. SCHUMACKER
THE UNIVERSITY OF ALABAMA, TUSCALOOSA

Abstract. This article reviews recent literature on student financial aid as a retention tool at community colleges. Enrollment and tuition data from the National Center for Education Statistics (NCES) Integrated Postsecondary Education Data System (IPEDS), and federal direct grant student aid data from the IPEDS Student Financial Aid Surey are used to analyze changes from 2000-01 to 2005-06. The new 2005 Carnegie Basic Classification of Associate's Colleges is used to reveal differences among rural, suburban, and urban community college types, and the Grapevine definition is used to reveal differences among states with local funding and those without significant local funding. A key finding is that the 40% increase in tuition and the 2.2 million new students enrolled in the past five years overwhelmed the very modest increases in federal direct grant student aid (Pell and Supplemental Education Opportunity Grant) over the same period, lessening the ability of student aid to positively Impact retention at America's community colleges.

Introduction

Community colleges in the United States are facing challenging times. Even before the current recession, state appropriations for higher education in general and community colleges in particular, were in long-term decline (Roessler, 2006), as Medicaid and corrections have commanded an ever increasing percentage of state tax funds (Katsinas, 2005; Macallair, 2002; National Association of State Budget Officers [NASBO], 2002; Zeidenberg & Schiraldi, 2002). According to Roessler, Katsinas, and Hardy (2006), in Fiscal Year 1980-81, state appropriations accounted for 60% or more of total revenues for community colleges in 16 states. By FY2000-01 no state could boast of that level of revenue. In FY1980-81, 55% of U.S. community college students were enrolled in one of the 22 states where state appropriations accounted for 50% or more of total revenue: by FY2000-01, just 8% attended one of only seven small states with similar revenue conditions. With a severe recession simultaneously producing a dramatic decline in slate tax revenues and equally dramatic increases in demands on Medicaid, state budgets have been stressed as never before (Katsinas & Tollefson,

2009). Since public colleges, unlike other state priority areas such as elementary and secondary education, corrections, and healthcare, can generate revenue through tuition, state governments typically turn first to compel tuition increases at public community colleges and public regional and flagship universities to fill the breach created by decreasing state appropriations and increased demand for services (Macallair, 2002; Katsinas & Tollefson, 2009), The 2008 Delta Report revealed that recent tuition increases were seen as substitutes for declining state investments, effectively shifting the burden from the states to students and their parents (Wellman, Desrochers, Lenihan, et al. 2008).

This article reviews recent literature on student financial aid as a tool for community college retention. It draws heavily from Kennamer's 2009 study, which investigated changes in enrollment, tuition, and federal direct student aid (pell Grants and Supplemental Opportunity Grants), to offer key discussion points regarding the effects of student financial aid on retention in America's community colleges.

Literature Review

A 2004 study jointly conducted by The Institute for Higher Education Policy and Scholarship America reported that in the mid-1970s, the maximum federal Pell Grant covered 84% of the average cost of attendance at a public 4-year collage. By the mid-1990s, however, the maximum Pell Grant only covered about 34% of the cost of attending college. Loans, which have overtaken grants as the primary form of financial aid for postsecondary students, now account for more than half of all federal dollars paid directly to students to facilitate enrollment and retention in college (Baum & Payea, 2004).

Kipp, Price, and Wohlford (2002) found that public 2-year colleges are consistently the most affordable higher education choice in every state. However, for low-income independent students—those who do not depend on their parents for support—at least half of these institutions in 38 states became affordable *only* if they are willing (and able) to incur loan debt. Hardy (2005) found that students at rural community colleges are more dependent on loans than students at urban and suburban colleges. College is becoming less affordable for low-income students, and more than half of American undergraduates now incur debt to pay for college (Kipp et al., 2002).

The federal government and many of the states have focused their student financial aid investments on serving middle-income students. While this strategy provides middle-income students more choices about where they might attend college, it may in fact fail to help low-income students to whom access is vitally more important than choice (Baum, 2003a). While few Americans would deny that America faces a health care crisis, one should note that over the past 25 years leading up to 2006, average tuition and fees at U.S. public colleges and universities has increased faster than inflation, consumer prices, personal income, prescription drugs, or health insurance (Wellman, 2006). At a time when President Obama is calling for all Americans to commit themselves to at least one year of college (Obama, 2009), the respected higher education researcher Tom Mortensen has found that the college participation rate for 18 to 24 year olds peaked and has remained at a plateau since 1992 (Postsecondary Education Opportunity, 2007b).

The Kennamer Study

Kennamer found that from 2000-01 to 2005-06, an additional 2.2 million students enrolled at our nation's community colleges while tuition increased by an average of 40%. Federal investments in student aid also increased in those same years. From 2000-01 to 2005-06, federal investments in the Pell Grant program increased by 76%, from $2.1 billion to $3.8 billion (Kennamer, 2009). Yet this increased commitment by Congress and then-President George W. Bush to send and keep economically disadvantaged students in college was not enough to offset the great growth in enrollments and tuition increases. The Kennamer study included only public Associate's Colleges that submitted enrollment and tuition data for both years to the Integrated Postsecondary Education System.

While the maximum Pell Grant increased from $3,300 in 2000-01 to $4,050 in 2005-06 (Kantrowitz, 2009). Kennamer found the impact of 2.2 million new students and significant tuition increases overshadowed the ability of increased expenditures in federal direct grant aid—Pell

Grants and Supplemental Education Opportunity Grants to cover the higher cost charges. According to the American Association of Community Colleges (2005), 66% of students at America's community colleges attend part-time, and consequently do not receive the maximum Pell Grant award. It is important to note that not all students who attend college full-time receive the maximum Pell Grant award (Kennamer, 2009).

Table 1 indicates both enrollments and the percentage of tuition and fees covered by the maximum Pell Grant award In both 2000-01 and 2005-06 for each state. In most states, any gains in Pell Grant maximums were offset if not overwhelmed by increased tuition and fees. Of course, tuition and fees are not the only costs to be considered when calculating the real cost of college (Baum & Payca, 2006). Other expenses, including room, board, books, and transportation must also be considered. And for many students in America's community colleges, the cost of childcare is a significant college-related expense (Baum & Payea, 2006). Only eight states saw Pell Grants covering an increasing percentage of tuition and fees in 2005-06 compared to 2000-01: Alaska, Illinois, Maine, New Jersey, Nevada, New York, South Dakota, and Wyoming.

Table 2 displays the enrollment and average tuition and fees data by percentage grouping for each state from 2000-01 to 2005-06. Three states did not report data. Just 17 states reported enrollment increases less than 30%, 15 states reported enrollment increases of between 31 and 100%, and 15 states reported enrollment increases greater than 100%. These are percentage increases of enrollment not seen since the baby-boom of 1965 to 1973, the years in which the modem community college system first developed in America.

Table 2 also shows that just one state, Alaska, reported a decline in tuition during this five year period, and only two states, Illinois and Nevada, reported tuition increases less than 10%, In contrast, 13 states reported tuition increases of between 11 and 30%, 15 states raised tuition between 31 and 50%, and 18 states saw tuition increases greater than 51%. It is highly likely that at no period since publication of the Truman Commission report in 1947 have community colleges seen such dramatic increases in tuition.

State Differences

While Tables 1 and 2 highlight the general trends of dramatic growth in enrollments and high levels of increasing, if not skyrocketing, tuition between 2000-01 and 2005-06, one may learn more by drilling down into the data to see how students in individual states are impacted. While a thorough analysis of all the state-by-state descriptive data mined in the Kennamer study is beyond the scope of this article, a few examples can begin to give the reader a sense of the extant stale-by-state diversity. As but one example, data from the states of Alabama and Georgia are presented to paint the picture.

In 2000-01, five of the 25 public community colleges in the State of Alabama reported that they offered federal student loans. These five institutions reported 282 loans incurred with an annual average debt incurred of $2,067. By 2005-06, three additional public community colleges in addition to the five reporting in 2000-01 reported, for a total of eight institutions reporting 1,314 student loans incurred, with an annual average debt incurred of $2,452 (sec Table 3). Incredibly, Alabama's community colleges saw a 366% increase in the number of federal student loans offered in just five years. A likely factor that might account for this increase in loans is the dramatic reported average tuition increase from $1,535 in 2000-01 to $2,649 in 2005-06, a 72% jump.

In neighboring Georgia, 14 community and technical colleges reported offering federal student loans in 2000-01 and again in 2005-06. However. the number of students taking loans in 2005-06 was 2,347—up from 1,207 in 2000-01. That increase of 1,320, or 129% suggests that many more students had to incur debt to continue attending a Georgia Associate's College in 2005-06 than in 2000-01.

Not surprisingly, the amount of debt incurred per year also increased substantially. In 2000-01, the average student loan debt per year was $1,717, By 2005-06, it had increased by 39%, to $2,387. During this same time period, Georgia's average tuition increased from $1,095 to $1,460, for an increase of 33%, while enrollment increased during this same five year period by a whopping 184%.

The rapid rise in college costs and the relative decline in investment in federal direct student aid (Pell Grants and SEOG) come at a time of surging enrollments. America's public community

TABLE 1

Enrollment, Average Tuition and Fees, and Percentage of Average Tuition and Fees Covered by the Maximum Pell Grant, 2000-1 and 2005-6

| State | Enrollment | | | | Average Tuition and Fees | | | | % of Tuition and fees Covered by Maximum Pell | |
| | | | Change, 2000-1 to 2005-6 in | | | | Change, 2000-1 to 2005-6 in | | | |
	2000-1	2005-6	Numbers	%	2000-1	2005-6	Dollars	%	2000-1	2005-6
Alabama	101,968	117,181	15,213	15%	$1,537	$2,649	$1,112	2%	215%	153%
Alaska	3,919	3,919	18	0	1,909	1,854	−55	−3	173	218
Arizona	318,483	365,489	47,006	15	842	2,239	1,397	166	392	181
Arkansas	30,687	49,054	18,367	60	1,284	1,987	703	55	257	204
California	2,363,699	2,169,976	−193,723	−8	328	723	394	120	1006	560
Colorado	87,335	128,622	41,287	47	1,792	2,221	429	24	184	182
Connecticut	24,810	65,801	40,991	165	1,856	2,519	664	36	178	161
Delaware	18,452	19,583	1,131	6	1,678	2,240	562	33	197	181
Florida	370,822	422,018	51,196	14	1,360	1,876	516	38	243	216
Georgia	81,389	230,795	149,406,	184	1,095	1,460	365	33	301	277
Idaho	11,025	18,347	7,322	66	1,973	2,548	575	29	167	159
Illinois	625,020	680,622	55,602	9	4,968	5,458	491	10	66	74
Indiana	No data	104,708	—		1,986	2,589	603	30	166	156
Iowa	87,996	123,782	35,786	41	2,197	3,212	1,016	46	150	126
Kansas	88,285	125,150	36,865	42	1,379	2,124	745	54	239	191
Kentucky	57,820	116,065	58,245	101	1,371	2,355	983	72	241	172
Louisiana	69,066	66,422	−2,644	−4	751	1,285	534	71	439	315
Massachusetts	38,727	123,122	84,395	218	1,808	2,845	1,037	57	183	142
Maryland	73,648	173,103	99,455	135	3,547	4,542	994	28	93	89
Maine	9,240	17,334	8,094	88	2,730	3,083	353	13	121	131
Michigan	69,799	346,565	276,766	397	2,374	3,016	642	27	139	134
Minnesota	148,837	158,638	9,801	7	2,491	3,994	1,503	60	132	101
Missouri	37,776	130,926	93,150	247	2,139	3,309	1,169	55	154	122
Mississippi	40,108	102,966	62,858	157	1,087	1,694	607	56	304	239
Montana	3,712	6,465	2,753	74	2,161	3,372	1,211	56	153	120
North Carolina	181,256	283,216	101,960	56	888	1,280	392	44	372	316
North Dakota	No data	10,853	—		1,954	3,117	1,163	60	169	130
Nebraska	47,742	81,666	33,924	71	1,404	1,848	444	32	235	219

(continued)

TABLE 1(cont.)

Enrollment, Average Tuition and Fees, and Percentage of Average Tuition and Fees Covered by the Maximum Pell Grant, 2000-1 and 2005-6

State	Enrollment				Average tuition and fees				% of Tuition and fees Covered by Maximum Pell	
			Change, 2000-1 to 2005-6 in				Change, 2000-1 to 2005-6 in			
	2000-1	2005-6	Numbers	%	2000-1	2005-6	Dollars	%	2000-1	2005-6
New Hampshire	2,400	11,554	9,154	381	3,851	5,689	1,838	48	86	71
New Jersey	105,589	217,625	112,036	106	3,866	4,428	563	15	85	91
North Mexico	57,831	70,683	12,852	22	890	1,264	374	42	371	320
Nevada	23,775	24,950	1,175	5	1,395	1,471	76	5	237	275
New York	330,768	393,672	62,904	19	2,712	3,253	541	20	122	125
Ohio	153,875	242,198	106,323	78	2,321	3,268	947	41	142	124
Oklahoma	11,085	87,203	76,118	687	1,376	2,112	737	54	240	192
Oregon	135,293	144,542	9,249	7	1,584	2,762	1,178	74	208	147
Pennsylvania	101,404	188,021	86,617	85	4,317	5,520	1,203	28	76	73
Rhode Island	No data	22,407	—		1,806	2,470	664	37	183	164
South Carolina	93,250	106,875	13,625	15	1,647	3,194	1,551	94	200	127
South Dakota	2,411	5,875	3,464	144	2,523	3,034	511	20	131	133
Tennessee	72,167	104,903	32,736	45	1,438	2,392	954	66	229	169
Texas	610,190	837,077	226,887	37	1,272	1,979	707	56	259	205
Utah	22,215	62,908	40,693	183	1,523	2,150	627	41	217	188
Virginia	224,232	233,465	9,233	4	1,162	2,116	954	82	284	191
Vermont	4,571	9,310	4,739	104	3,004	4,012	1,008	34	110	101
Washington	316,939	330,408	13,469	4	1,763	2,576	813	46	187	157
Wisconsin	87,274	159,064	71,790	82	2,161	2,720	559	26	153	149
West Virginia	3,351	18,042	14,691	438	1,753	2,254	501	29	188	180
Wyoming	24,745	30,524	5,779	23	1,522	1,795	274	18	217	226

Source: Integrated Postsecondary Education Data System

Notes:: (1) Includes only data reported to IPEOS; some colleges/states did not report. (2) States that are italicized have community colleges that receive in excess of 10% of total revenues from local sources. (3) States in bold are megastates.

TABLE 2

Percentage Change in Enrollment and Average Tuition and Fees, 2000-1 to 2005-6, and Percentage of Average Tuition and Fees Covered by Maximum Pell Grant, 2005-6

	Enrollment Change, 2000-1 to 2005-6	Average Tuition and Fees, 2000-1 to 2005-6
Decline	*California*, Louisiana	Alaska (–3%)
0-10%	Alaska, Delaware, *illinois*, Minnesota, Nevada, *Oregon*, Virginia, Washington	*Illinois*, Nevada
11-20%	Alabama, Arizona, **Florida**, **New York**, South Carolina	Maine, *New Jersey*, **New York**, South Dakota, *Wyoming*
21-30%	*New Mexico, Wyoming*	*Colorado, Idaho*, Indiana *Maryland, Michigan, Oregon*, Wisconsin, West Virginia
31-40%	**Texas**	Connecticut, Delaware, **Florida**, Georgia, *Nebraska*, Rhode Island, Vermont
41-50%	*Colorado, Iowa, Kansas*, Tennessee	*Iowa, Mississippi, New Hampshire*, **North Carolina**, *Ohio*, Utah, Washington
51-75%	Arkansas, *Idaho*, Kentucky, *Montana, Nebraska*, **North Carolina**	Arkansas, *Kansas*, Louisiana, Minnesota, *Missouri, Montana*, North Dakota, *Oklahoma*, *Oregon*, Tennessee, **Texas**
76-100%	Maine, **Ohio, Pennsylvania**, *Wisconsin*	Alabama, *South Carolina*, Virginia
101-150%	Kentucky, *Maryland*, *New Jersey*, South Dakota, Vermont	**California**, Vermont
151-200%	Connecticut, Georgia, *Mississippi*, Utah	*Arizona*
Over 200%	Massachusetts, *Michigan*, *Missouri*, New Hampshire, *Oklahoma*, West Virginia	

TABLE 3

Changes in Student Loans at Public Associate's Colleges in Two Southern States (Alabama and Georgia) from 2000-1 and 2005-6

	2000-1			2005-6			Change, 2000-1 to 2005-6		
	Associate's Colleges Offering Loans	Number of Loans Incurred	Average Annual Student Debt	Associate's Colleges Offering Loans	Number of Loans Incurred	Average Annual Student Debt	Colleges Offering Loans	Average Number of Loans Incurred	Annual Student Debt
Alabama	5	282	$2,067	8	1,314	$2,452	3 (60%)	366%	84%
Georgia	14	1,207	$1,717	14	2,347	$2,387	—	94%	39%

TABLE 4

Summary of Changes in Tuition, Federal, State, and Institutional Direct Student Aid from 2000-1 and 2005-6 in the State of Minnesota

Carnegie 2005 Basic Classification of Associate College by Type	Tuition Change	Federal (FDS) Change	State (SDS) Change	Institutional (IDS) Change
Rural	$1,620	$408	$5	$251
Suburban	$1,449	$610	$ 118	$294
Urban	$1,290	$278	– $262	– $1,030

colleges recently experienced what Hardy, Katsinas, and Bush (2007) called "the most dramatic enrollment surge since the middle of the 1960s Baby Boom" (p. 23). Annual unduplicated headcount In U.S. community colleges increased by 2.2 million students, or 30%, from 2000-01 to 2005-06 (Kennamer, 2009). In 1994, Clark Kerr predicted a surge in enrollment that would last until 2010. However, it is likely that this surge will continue well beyond 2010, as those who are unemployed as a result of the 2009 recession return to college to seek the skills necessary to survive the current economic crisis (Kennamer, 2009). Those workers who are employed, but find themselves in need of retraining or skills upgrades will also look to their local community colleges to keep them relevant in today's global economy (Kennamer, 2009).

In his 2009 study, Kennamer told the story of public rural. suburban. and urban community colleges in Minnesota (see Table 4). Tuition in Minnesota jumped from $2,491 in 2000-01 to $3,994 in 2005-06, an increase of $1,503, or 60%. Table 4 shows that while federal direct student aid grew at all types of Associate's Colleges (rural, suburban, and urban) in the State of Minnesota, that growth in no way came close to approaching the tuition and fees growth during the same period. State direct student aid grew modestly in rural and suburban colleges, and decreased in urban colleges. Institutional direct student aid followed a similar pattern, with increases in rural and suburban colleges, and a significant decrease in urban colleges.

Kennamer (2009) defined the unmet needs as tuition and fees minus the direct student grant aid dollar amount, which produces a remaining dollar value that a student and/or the family will need to finance through either work or loans. This was computed for both the 2000-01 and 2005-06 academic years. The unmet needs change (UNC) is the difference in unmet needs obtained from subtracting the 2005-06 remaining dollar value from the 2000-01 remainder. A higher UNC value indicates that more students needed to take out higher loan amounts or work more hours in 2005-06 than in 2000-01. As Table 4 shows, the UNC for rural Associate's Colleges in Minnesota was $408. This means that students in 2005-06 had to finance $408 more than they did in 2000-01 just to cover the required tuition and fees. The change in the amount of unmet needs for students attending Minnesota's suburban colleges was $610, and $278 for urban colleges in 2005-06. It is worth noting that the UNC does not include costs for books, transportation, or other required college expenses, costs that are likely higher in rural than in urban areas, a proposition that can at least be inferred from these data. Again, the UNC only deals with tuition and required fees. One conclusion is abundantly clear from this analysis: students in Minnesota paid more for the privilege of attending supposedly "low cost" community colleges in 2005-06 than in 2000-01 (Kennamer, 2009).

Implications for Retention

While enrollment and persistence in college are the result of a number of factors, studies have shown for many decades that low income and minority students are strongly influenced by the availability of financial aid (Student-retention.org, 2005). Singell (2001) found that the provision of need-based aid improves both enrollment and retention, and that while non-economic factors are important in retention, those who cannot afford college are very likely to drop out.

MacCallum (2008) studied the relationship between enrollment rate, retention, and success of students who received financial aid with financial aid policies and procedures at California's community colleges. He found that student outcomes are contingent upon the financial aid support services they receive. The quicker that financial aid was processed, the more likely the student was to persist, and not surprisingly, the need to upgrade financial aid staff was negatively related to student retention.

Dowd and Coury (2006) revealed that students who take a student loan in their first year are less likely to persist to the second year than those who do not take a loan in the first year. Hardy and Katsinas (2006) found that students in smaller colleges are more reliant on federal grant aid than students in any other college sector. Tinto (1997) found that students who are engaged are more likely to stay in college, and Zhao and Kuh (2004) stated that participation in a learning community of some form is related to student success. But participation in learning communities and student engagement is tremendously difficult when students are struggling to pay for college. For these students, the college becomes one of the stops that they make during their busy day rather than being the primary focus of their day.

Studies show that most community colleges students work while attending college (American Association of Community Colleges, 2008; Postsecondary Education Opportunity, 2007a). According to the American Association of Community Colleges (Phillippe, 2000), 30% of public community college students who work full time also attend college full time. A full time student who also works 40 hours per week at the current minimum wage ($7.25 per hour) will earn an annual pre-tax income of $15,080 in a year. According to the National Center for Education Statistics (2007), the average annual undergraduate tuition, fees, room, and board at a 2-year institution in 2005-06 was $6,492. (The federal minimum wage in 2005, consequently, was $5.15, which netted full time employees an annual wage of $10,712.) Is it possible for a student to be fully engaged in college life and studies while working full time to pay for the very thing that will help to improve his or her life? Is it likely that a full-time employee making minimum wage can support him/herself while simultaneously investing a portion of income on future hopes and dreams? Can the community college student who works full time devote adequate time to study, much less engagement in campus life?

A large body of research has found that on-campus, part-time employment of 10-19 hours per week tends to have a positive influence on academic performance (Astin, 1975, Dundes & Marx, 2006). However, studies have shown that working long hours (more than 20/week) off-campus adversely impacts academic success, retention, and a student's ability to become involved with campus activities and engaged with faculty and peers (Ehrenberg & Sherman, 2008; Furr & Elling, 2000). Most would agree that it is monumentally difficult to be successful as a full-time student while working full-time, especially if enrolled in a very demanding program of study.

Unfortunately, many students who do not want to go into debt for college may have no other option than to work long hours. According to Dundes and Marx (2006), 38% of students in their study worked 20 or more hours per week in an effort just to pay tuition. Of the students who worked 20 or more hours per week, 82% did so just to meet basic living expenses.

Data from the Kennamer study (2009) clearly shows that students were taking more debt in 2005-06 than in 2000-01. How difficult is it to succeed as a full-time college student while struggling to pay for an opportunity to make a better living, and a better life? And what is the likely direction of loans incurred by students who, in a time of double-digit unemployment, borrow because the prospects of part-time employment are so poor?

Some argue the American federal financial aid system assures no one who wants to attend college is denied that opportunity. After all, for more than 40 years, the Pell Grant program and its precursor Educational Opportunity Grant Program created by the Higher Education Act of 1965, and Basic Educational Opportunity Grant created by the Higher Education Amendments of 1972, have provided increased opportunities and financial assistance to the poor and middle class (Center for Higher Education Support Services, 2003). However, the ability of the federal financial aid programs to keep pace with rapidly rising tuition is questioned by both experts and the lay public, and not without good reason.

The Minnesota illustration presented earlier is only one of many that tell the same story. Simply put, a combination of tuition increases averaging 40% and the addition of 2.2 million students into rural, suburban, and urban Associate's Colleges made it considerably more difficult go to college in 2005-06 than it was in 2000-01. Some may argue that cost is not really an issue as evidenced by all-time record enrollments at community colleges. We therefore expect some to advance the simplistic conclusion that price has no impact on enrollment. Yet Kennamer predicted that "if increases in tuition continue and grant aid increases continue to be flat, there will be a point at which low-income and some middle-income students will no longer be able to attend college" (2009, p. 123).

Trying to assess the twin impacts of record enrollment and higher tuition will be difficult when the federal government cannot tell how many community colleges even exist (Katsinas & Tollefson, 2009) and financial data are only collected on first-time, full-time students at community colleges, in an era when many institutions find part-time enrollments exceeding 60 and even 70%. One might consider California as an example of what can happen when fees at community colleges are significantly increased. In a move that went against the state's 1960 Master Plan for Higher Education, California Governor George Deukmejian in 1982 placed significant fees on the backs of all California public college students. This increase in fees resulted in a decrease of 50,000 students the following year (Lindsey, 1982; Reinhold, 1991). This example of price sensitivity indicates that *price is important* to community college students, and that a tipping point exists in which price will cause students to stop attending college.

President Barack Ohama has called on every American to commit to at least one year of higher education or advanced training in an effort to help the United States to secure the highest proportion of college graduates in the world (Obama, 2009). Workers displaced by the current economic recession are flocking to community colleges at unprecedented rates, and many colleges are increasing tuition and cutting services in an effort to survive the current economic crisis (Jaschik, 2009). If community colleges across the United States are to help President Obama achieve his goal, they must be able to admit and retain students. Working one's way through college is difficult enough without adding an unnecessary financial strain. But the foundation that has allowed millions access to America's public community colleges is crumbling due to a domino effect of declining state appropriations, increasing tuition, increased demand, and subsequent cuts in services.

Many communities across the United States stand today at an economic crossroads. High skills and high technology are required to compete in the world economy, making access to higher education more important than ever before. The United States cannot meet its workforce goals while continuing a pattern of dramatically increasing tuition without equivalent increases in direct student aid. To do so establishes an insurmountable barrier for low-income students.

While some would argue that tuition revenues should help colleges cover the costs of a accommodating additional students, it is impractical to expect colleges to be able to build the additional facilities, hire more instructors, and equip classrooms and labs to accommodate this growth, all while trying to maintain and upgrade existing facilities as state investments in higher education continue to shrink. It is reasonably expected that some colleges—especially those already in good financial condition—been able to do so. However, it is very likely that many colleges are still struggling to accommodate the increased enrollment and declining state funding experienced between 2000-01 and 2005-06. Of course, not all colleges and states saw enrollment increases, but most did (Kennamer, 2009).

When large increases in enrollment are not accompanied by increased state appropriations to offset these increases, some aspect of the student's educational experience is apt to suffer. Consider the case of Jefferson State Community College, an urban multi-campus community college in Birmingham. Alabama, where enrollment increased from 9,297 in 2000-01 to 11,425 in 2005-06, an increase of 2,128 students, or 23%. When put in perspective, that would be akin to adding the entire student body of a small rural community college like Lurleen B. Wallace Community College in Andalusia, Alabama, to the enrollment at Jefferson State. One might expect this scenario to occur during a merger or consolidation, but mergers usually bring facilities, personnel, and resources, along with students, to the college. Yet Jefferson State Community College's growth was accomplished without additional state funding and no local funding for classroom facilities, lab equipment, or instructional and support staff.

A similar situation occurred at Weatherford College, a suburban single campus public Associate's college in Weatherford, Texas. Enrollment at Weatherford increased from 4,084 in 2000-01 to 6,331 in 2005-06. This addition of 2,247 students, which represents a 55% increase, is roughly akin to adding the entire student body of Frank Phillips College in Borger, Texas *and* half the students at Ranger College in Ranger, Texas to enrollment at Weatherford. Again, these enrollment increases are occurring at a time of declining state appropriations in Texas.

While employees at America's public community colleges are accustomed to doing more with less, there is a limit to how much can be done with limited personnel and funds. Will the services that are cut impact retention? At San Joaquin Delta College in Stockton, California, president Raul Rodriguez recently announced that budget cuts would result in the elimination of entire programs in an effort to minimize additional cuts to others (Jaschik, 2009). Developmental education for those functioning at the lowest levels and English as a Second Language (ESL) will be among the first to be cut (Jaschik, 2009). Will these cuts impact retention? Are these programs likely to benefit the neediest low income students?

According to Katsinas and Tollefsen (2009), community colleges in 34 states took mid-year budget cuts in fiscal year 2008-09, with average cuts of 5.9% Thirty-nine state directors of community colleges reported that they agree or strongly agree that they are concerned about a potential budget shortfall in the 2011 base budget for community colleges in their state when the one-time infusion of American Recovery and Reinvestment Act (ARRA) funds are gone (Katsinas & Tollefsen, 2009).

If the United States is serious about helping more low-income students realize the dream that may be accessed at America's community colleges, federal and state grant aid should be dramatically increased to levels *above* recent tuition increases. The federal government, which seems to emphasize loans and tax credits as primary means of student financial aid, should focus on the provision of grants to benefit low-income students. Though loans and tax credits have their place in helping improve access and college choice for middle-income students, they may be of limited value to low-income students (Dowd & Grant. 2006b). Kennamer (2009) argues that Pell Grant maximums should be increased to keep pace with recent and expected tuition increases and to provide funds for books and other expenses, including transportation and housing. In the mid-1970s, the maximum federal Pell Grant covered 84% of the average cost of attendance at a public 4-year college, but by the mid-1990s, the maximum Pell Grant covered about 34% of costs (Scholarship America, 2004). *To bring the buying power of the Pell Gram back to its mid-1970s level, the maximum Pell Grant would have to be increased to $10,877.* This figure represents 85% of the average annual published tuition, fees, and room and board charges at public 4-year colleges in 2006-2007, as reported by The College Board (Baum & Payea, 2006). Some may argue that a jump to $10,877 is excessive. However, an increase of this magnitude is necessary to offset the seeming indifference of federal policy over the past several years, which has ignored the issue and has not kept up with the rising costs of tuition and other expenses. If the United States is to compete in a global economy, federal policy must place higher priority on access to higher education and job skills training, and this will require additional investments.

According to the American Association of Community Colleges (2008), more than 5 million college students receive Pell Grants each year, of whom 87% are from families with annual incomes of $40,000 or less (AACC, 2008). Thus, the Pell Grant is the best mechanism for low-income students to receive the training and/or education that they need. In fact, for some, the Pell Grant is the *only* path to the middle class. An appropriate increase in the maximum Pell Grant would help keep the dream alive for millions of Americans, both now and for years to come. But Pell Grants must be accessible and adequately funded so that students can afford the cost of college without being forced to work excessive hours or go into debt.

More study is certainly needed to understand the impact or the fast moving target of increasing tuition on persistence rates of America's community college students. We especially note here the paucity of empirical research on the impact of (the presence or lack of) local funding on student retention in the 25 states that have local funding. For that reason, a national study examining retention as well as transfer rates is recommended, using the new 2005 Basic Classification of the Carnegie Foundation for the Advancement of Teaching, which for the first time classifies the Associate's

College sector geographically. Such a study could also capture and differentiate states with and without significant local funding, to help policy makers better understand the return on investment (ROI) of federal and state dollars in direct student aid. We also believe that further research conducted in this manner would likely underscore the importance of the Obama Administration's efforts to increase Pell Grant funding, to help the nation again regain its top rank of baccalaureate degree attainment. For these reasons, we believe further investment in the federal Pell Grant program and state need-based aid programs could provide the best long-term benefit of any federal stimulus program.

References

American Association of Community Colleges (AACC). (2005). *Achieving the dream: Community colleges count.* Fact sheet. Washington. DC: Author.

American Association of Community Colleges. (2008). *AACC-ACCT Joint legislative agenda for the 110th Congress.* Washington, DC: Author.

Astin, A. W. (1975). *Preventing students from dropping out.* San Francisco, CA: Jossey-Bass.

Author. (2005). *Retention 101—Why students leave.* Downloaded November 13, 2009 from http://www .studentretention.org

Baum, S. (2003a). *The financial aid partnership: Strengthening the federal government's leadership role.* National Dialogue on Student Financial Aid. Washington, DC: The College Board.

Baum, S. (2003b). *The role of student loans in college access.* National Dialogue on Student Financial Aid. Washington, DC: The College Board.

Baum, S., & Payea, K. (2004). *Trends in student aid.* Washington, DC: The College Board.

Baum, S., & Payea, K. (2006). *Trends in college pricing.* Washington, DC: The College Board.

Center for Higher Education Support Services. (2003). *History of financial aid.* Retrieved January 11, 2008, from www.chessconsulting.org

Dowd, A. C., & Coury, T. (2006a). The effect of loans on the persistence and attainment of community colleges students. *Research in Higher Education, 47*(1), 33–62.

Dowd, A. C., & Grant, J. L. (2006b). Equity and efficiency of community college appropriations: The role or local financing. *The Review of Higher Education, 29*(2), 167–194.

Dundes, L., & Marx, J. (2006). Balancing work and academics in college: Why do students working 10 to 19 hours per week excel? *Journal of College Student Retention: Research, Theory & Practice, 8*(1), 107–120.

Ehrenberg, R. G., & Sherman, D. R. (1987). Employment while in college, academic achievement, and post-college outcomes: A summary of results. *The Journal of Human Resources, 22*(1), 1–23.

Furr, S. R., & Elling, T. W. (2000). The influence of work on college student development. *NASPA Journal, 37*(2), 454–470.

Hardy, D. E. (2005). *A two-year college typology for the 21st century: Updating and utilizing the Katsinas-Lacey classification system.* Unpublished doctoral dissertation, University or North Texas, Denton, Texas.

Hardy, D. E., & Katsinas, S. K. (2006). *The critical rule of financial aid for first-time/full-time students enrolling at rural-serving community colleges.* Partnership Brief. Meridian, MS: The MidSouth partnership for Rural Community Colleges.

Hardy, D. E.. Katsinas, S. K., & Bush, V. B. (2007). Tidal wave II, community colleges, and student financial aid. *Enrollment Management Journal, 1*(1), 23–48.

Jaschik, S. (2009, October 5). *Sophie's choice for 2-year colleges.* Inside Higher Education. Retrieved October 8, 2009 from http://www.insidehighered.com

Kantrowitz, M. (2009). *Pell Grant historical figures.* Retrieved November 21, 2009 from http://www.finaid.org/ educators/pellgrant.phtml

Katsinas, S. G. (2005). Increased competition for scarce state dollars. In S. G. Katsinas & J. C. Palmer (Eds.), *Sustaining financial support for community colleges.* New Directions for Community Colleges, Number 132. San Francisco, CA: Jossey-Bass.

Katsinas, S. G., & Tollefson, T. A. (2009). *Funding and access issues in public higher education: A community college perspective.* Tuscaloosa, AL: Education Policy Center at the University of Alabama.

Kennamer, M. A. (2009). *Associate's college Carnegie classification and funding type differences in enrollment, student aid, and unmet need from 2000-2001 to 2005-2006.* Doctoral dissertation, University of Alabama, Tuscaloosa. Proquest Digital Dissertations, UMI 3385385.

Kipp III, S. M., Price, D. V., & Wohlford, J. K. (2002). *Unequal opportunity: Disparities in college access among the 50 states.* Washington, DC: Lumina Foundation.

Lindsey, R. (1982, December 28). California weighs end of free college education. *The New York Times.* Retrieved February 10, 2009, from www.nytimes.com

Macallair, D. (2002). *From classrooms to cell blocks: A national perspective.* San Francisco, CA: Center on Juvenile and Criminal Justice.

MacCallum, M. (2008)· Effect of financial aid processing policies on student enrollment, retention and success. *NASFAA Journal of Student Financial Aid,* 37(2), 17–32.

Mortenson, T. (2007a). Labor force status of college students ages 16 to 24 years 1970 to 2006. *Postsecondary Education Opportunity, 180,* 11-16.

Mortenson, T. (2007b). Duh: An editorial. *Postsecondary Education Opportunity, 185,* 1–3.

National Associallon of State Budget Officers (NASBO). (2002). *NASBO Analysis: Medicaid to stress state budgets severely into fiscal 2003.* Washington, DC: National Association of State Budget Officers.

National Center for Educational Statistics. (2007). FAST FACTS. Retrieved April 22, 2010, from: http://NCES.ED.GOV/FASTFACTS/display.asp?id=76

Obama, B. H. (2009, January 24). *Remarks to joint session of Congress.* Retrieved February 27, 2009 from http://www.whitehouse.gov

Phillippe, K. A. (Ed.). (2000). *National profile of community colleges: Trends and statistics* (3rd ed.). Washington. DC: Community College Press.

Reinhold, R. (1991, November 10). Amid cuts, California is curtailing college dreams. *The New York Times.* Retrieved February 10, 2009, from www.nytimes.com

Roessler, B. C. (2006). *A quantitative study of revenue and expenditures at U.S. public community colleges, 1980-2001.* Unpublished doctoral dissertation, University of North Texas, Denton, Texas.

Roessler, B. C. Katsinas, S. G., & Hardy, D. E. (2006). *The downward spiral of state funding for community colleges, and its impact on rural community colleges.* A policy brief of the University of Alabama Education Policy Center for the MidSouth Partnership for Rural Community Colleges. Mississippi State, MS: MidSouth Partnership for Rural Community Colleges.

Scholarship America. (2004). *Investing in America's future: Why student aid pays off for society and individuals.* Washington. DC: The Institute for Higher Education Policy.

Singell, Jr., L. D. (2001, August). *Come and stay a while: Does financial aid effect enrollment and retention at a large public university?* New York: Cornell Higher Education Research Institute.

Tinto, V. (1997). Classrooms as communities: Exploring the educational character of student persistence. *Journal of Higher Education,*68(6), 599–623.

Wellman, J, V. (2006). *Costs, prices and affordability: A background paper for the Secretary's Commission on the Future of Higher Education.* Washington, DC: U.S. Department of Education.

Wellman, J. V., Desrochers, D. M., Lenihan, C. M., Kirshstein, R. J., Hurlburt, S., Honegger, S., et al. (2008). *Trends in college spending.* A Report of the Delta Cost Project. Washington, DC: Lumina Foundation for Education.

Zhao, C. M., & Kuh, G. D. (2004). Adding value: Learning communities and student engagement. *Research in Higher Education, 45*(2), 115–138.

Zeidenberg, J., & Schiraldi, V. (2002). *Cellblocks or classrooms?: The funding of higher education and corrections and its impact on African American men.* Washington, DC: Justice Policy Institute.

SECTION IV

THE INSTRUCTIONAL CORE – COMMUNITY COLLEGE FACULTY

SECTION IV: THE INSTRUCTIONAL CORE – COMMUNITY COLLEGE FACULTY

The basic function of the community college is teaching and learning, thus making faculty the core of the institution. Faculty at community colleges are focused primarily, and oftentimes exclusively, on teaching and institutional service to include faculty governance and curricular development and management. They play a significant role in the success of community college students who, more often than not, live off campus, attend college part-time, and spend little time engaged in on-campus activities. Faculty serves as academic advisors, counselors, advocates, instructors, and help to establish student engagement and success.

While the original intent was to have faculty from business and industry maintain a focus on local workforce as well as full-time faculty with disciplinary expertise, the composition of community college faculty evolved over time to represent a majority of contingent faculty—those faculty who are classified as part-time, adjunct, or non-tenured. Contingent faculty often do not have access to or voting rights in campus-based governance or curricular decisions and may not have office space or other institutional supports. The changes in the composition of faculty place undue burden on those that are full-time who participate in faculty governance and are often responsible for curricular development and management. Additionally, the impact of contingent faculty on student success is inconclusive. Several national studies have identified a negative impact on student success when enrolled in courses taught by contingent faculty.

Another concern of community college faculty is the large number of faculty members who are women. Community colleges, unlike four-year universities, have approximately 50% female faculty. The success of achieving gender parity raises a host of questions around representation versus equity. Have female faculty achieved equity with representation? Are there differences in salary, rank, and tenure among faculty? Have cultural norms changed alongside numerical parity?

This section presents seven chapters that address the issues and concerns of community college faculty. Each chapter presents a nuanced picture of the demographic composition, lived-experience, and significance of community college faculty on the success of community colleges from student engagement to organizational culture.

Chapter Nineteen by Twombly and Townsend, "Community college faculty: What we know and need to know," reviews the existing literature on community college faculty. Their analysis thoroughly and comprehensively summarizes the nature of research and topics related to community college faculty. This chapter gives context to the research on community college faculty included throughout this section. In addition, Twombly and Townsend suggest topics for future research, providing many ideas for those interested in this area of inquiry.

Chapter Twenty, authored by Lester, "Performing gender in the workplace: Gender socialization, power, and identity among women members," specifically calls attention to gender among community college faculty with a focus on gender norms, socialization, and identity. In her unique study, Lester presents the narrative of a female welding instructor to show how experiences related to gender inside and outside the college shape faculty perceptions of gender norms that impacts their individual identity. This chapter extends the work on gender and community college faculty with attention to organizational culture, socialization, and identity. Those readers interested in gender and identity are encouraged to read this chapter.

Cejda and Hoover, "Strategies for faculty-student engagement: How community college faculty engage Latino students," in Chapter Twenty-One, turn our attention to the relationship between faculty and student engagement and student success. Identified as a predictor for student success, the authors explore the strategies that community college faculty use to engage Latino students, in particular. The strategies discussed in this chapter establish the role of cultural sensitivity and learning styles in the classroom as a mechanism to engage Latino students and increase retention and persistence.

Chapter Twenty-Two, "New rural community college faculty members and job satisfaction," focuses on rural community college faculty. Murray looks at a specific group of community college faculty—those that work in rural institutions. Murray argues that rural community colleges are at a disadvantage when hiring faculty because of a lack of financial, cultural, and social advantages. The chapter has many specific recommendations for community college leaders to consider when recruiting and hiring rural community college faculty.

In Chapter Twenty-Three, "Unintended consequences: Examining the effect of part-time faculty members on associate degree completion," Jaeger and Eagan begin to build the empirical record on the impact of the growing number of part-time community college faculty on student success. Part-time faculty members are the majority of community college faculty outpacing hiring trends for full-time faculty. Using data from the California community college system, the largest single community college system in the country, they outline modest, but significant, declines in associate degree completion for students who are exposed to part-time faculty. The findings have policy implications for all community colleges that are continuing to fill faculty positions with a part-time majority.

Chapter Twenty-Four by Akroyd, Bracken, and Chambers, "A comparison of factors that predict the satisfaction of community college faculty by gender," present a comparison of job satisfaction among male and female community college faculty. Their analysis examines multiple factors, such as motivating and human capital variables, to predict job satisfaction using the National Study of Postsecondary Faculty data. Their findings address the differences across gender, academic disciplines, and occupational fields. They also include race as a variable for comparison.

Jain and Turner, "Purple is to lavender: Womanism, resistance, and the politics of naming," in Chapter Twenty-Five complete this section with a study that explores the politics of identity and paradoxes of feminism in perpetuating women of color being an afterthought in feminist theory and often "othered" in the academy. The authors give a rich description of the lived experiences of an untenured female faculty of color and a female senior scholar of color. This chapter is a case in point for self as part of the instrumentation, demonstrating reflexivity, offering constructive criticism of feminism, and acknowledging racialized and gendered realities that align with womanism in naming self as reflected in their counter-storytelling.

CHAPTER 19

COMMUNITY COLLEGE FACULTY: WHAT WE KNOW AND NEED TO KNOW

SUSAN TWOMBLY
UNIVERSITY OF KANSAS, LAWRENCE

BARBARA K. TOWNSEND
UNIVERSITY OF MISSOURI, COLUMBIA

This review of existing literature about community college faculty members speculates about why they have received so little scholarly attention, summarizes the nature of existing research, including its methodology and topics, and suggests what else needs to be known about them.

Keywords: student outcomes assessment, curriculum and instruction, quantitative methods, research methods

"Community college faculty receive scant attention from postsecondary researchers—or worse, are simply dismissed as a separate, and by implication lesser, class of college professors" (National Center for Postsecondary Improvement, 1998, p. 43). Although this statement is almost 10 years old, it still holds true today, with few exceptions. What is intriguing about the neglect of community college faculty members in the research literature and the lack of respect they often receive is that their numbers alone suggest they should at least merit attention. As of fall 2003, 43% of all full- and part-time faculty members in public, nonprofit higher education institutions were in public community colleges ("Almanac," 2005). In addition, community college faculty members teach around 37% of all undergraduates, including about half of all freshmen and sophomores. Among these students are more than half of all Hispanic and American Indian students and approximately 40% of African American and Asian students ("Almanac," 2005).

In addition to teaching students whose first higher education experience is in the community college, community college faculty members also teach many students who start at four-year colleges or students who are still in high school. Increasingly, high school students are exposed to community college faculty through dual-credit or dual-enrollment courses. In other cases, four-year college and university students either return to the community college to gain a skill or complete a program after accumulating a considerable number of credits at the four-year school, or they take a community college course while enrolled at a four-year institution to meet a baccalaureate graduation requirement. Thus, an increasing number of four-year college graduates include community college course taking as part of their baccalaureate education (Townsend, 2001).

Considering only the traditional transfer function, community college faculty members teach thousands of students each year who enter four-year colleges by transferring from two-year colleges. Although transfer rates from two-year to four-year colleges have remained around 25% for several decades (Townsend & Wilson, 2006), in the 21st century a variety of factors are converging that will likely push up the rate of transfer. As the societal press on individuals to earn a bachelor's degree increases, a number of very populous states are turning to community colleges to absorb the first two years of a college education. States such as California and Florida have long done this, but other states have been slower to rely on their community colleges in this way. For example, New Jersey recently passed a law that requires that "an associate degree awarded by a county [community] college must be fully transferable and count as the first two years toward a baccalaureate degree at any of the state's public institutions" (Redden, 2007). Although most state universities have had articulation agreements with community colleges in their states for at least two decades (Ignash & Townsend, 2000), these agreements can be very complicated. The intent of the New Jersey law is to simplify transfer. Laws such as New Jersey's emphasize even more strongly that community colleges are no longer an isolated sector in the U.S. higher education "system." Consequently, as instructors of the first two years of the baccalaureate curriculum, community college faculty members are increasingly "our" faculty.

Further acknowledging the important role of community college faculty members in higher education, the American Psychological Association (APA) recently "[established] an affiliate membership category for psychology teachers at community colleges and the APA Committee of Psychology Teachers at Community Colleges (PT@CC) to address their needs" (Hailstorks & Boenau, 2007, p. 6). This decision was prompted by the reality that "about 50% of the undergraduate students enrolled in psychology courses are matriculating at community colleges" (p. 6), and many undergraduate psychology majors start their postsecondary education in the community college. APA is now acknowledging the importance of a partnership between two-year and four-year faculties in educating undergraduates who take psychology courses and major in psychology.

Knowing about the faculty members who instruct community college courses is important because a lack of knowledge about them often results in the reluctance of four-year college faculty members to accept community college courses and in their disinterest in admitting two-year college transfer students. Not only do some four-year college and university faculty members typically question the quality of community college courses and therefore the faculty members who teach them, they also tend to hold a general sense of arrogance about the status of two-year college faculties relative to the status of university faculties. The comments posted in response to *Inside Higher Education*'s September 14, 2007, story about New Jersey's law mandating the acceptance of the associate's degree as the first two years of a four-year degree (Redden, 2007) provide vivid evidence of this bias (http://www.insidehighered.com/news/2007/09/14/newjersey). In the comments, community colleges and thus implicitly (and sometimes explicitly) their faculty members are denigrated for their "easy courses," low grading standards (e.g., "one of the community colleges in the Detroit area passed out A and B grades like plastic beads at Mardi Gras"), and academically weak students (e.g., "probably half of the students in them should not be in them in the first place").

Because we believe that community college faculty members merit attention *and* respect, in this article we first suggest why so little attention has been paid to them in the scholarly literature. Then we briefly describe what is known about community college faculty members and conclude with what needs to be known about them. To do this, we sought literature about the community college faculty, with particular emphasis on peer-reviewed articles, chapters, and books published in the past two decades. To find the peer-reviewed articles, we examined the table of contents of the two major journals about community colleges (*Community College Journal of Research and Practice* and *Community College Review*) and the three major general higher education journals (*Journal of Higher Education, Research in Higher Education*, and *Review of Higher Education*). We set the time period of January 1990 through September 2007 as our parameters so as to examine relatively current articles. Believing a historical perspective is important, we also searched the tables of contents of all the issues of the *Community College Journal*, published since 1930 by the American Association of Community Colleges. A review of this journal's tables of contents provides a glimpse into some of the concerns of two-year college leaders and faculty members over many decades. We also drew heavily on three recent books about various aspects of community college faculty members' lives (Grubb & Associates, 1999; Levin, Kater, & Wagoner, 2006; Outcalt, 2002) as well as chapters from older texts.

Why so Little is Known About Community College Faculty Members

There are several possible reasons for the relative lack of attention to community college faculty members. One may be that research designed for publication is primarily conducted by individuals at research universities as part of their quest for tenure, promotion, or merit pay. Those who write about higher education issues and constituents tend to focus on the world they know—the research university—and not on the world they may never have experienced—the community college. As partial evidence, an examination of articles published from 1990 through 2003 in five major higher education journals (*Journal of College Student Development, Journal of Higher Education, NASPA Journal, Research in Higher Education*, and *Review of Higher Education*) revealed that only 8% of the articles focused on community colleges (Townsend, Donaldson, & Wilson, 2005). In addition, although research faculty members can study themselves and get rewarded for doing so, the same is not true for community college faculty members. They are not required to do research, and if they do choose to do so they are encouraged to engage in the scholarship of teaching and focus on ways to improve the teaching–learning process (Palmer, 1992; Vaughan, 1986, 1988).

Sometimes research about the community college faculty appears as part of a general study of the U.S. professoriate. Works such as *The New Academic Generation: A Profession in Transformation* (Finkelstein, Seal, & Schuster, 1998) and *The American Faculty: The Restructuring of Academic Work and Careers* (Schuster & Finkelstein, 2006) address community college faculty members but typically do so by comparing them to four-year faculty members, as when national survey data are used to illustrate points about faculty work and careers. These comparisons are important, even necessary, to put the community college professoriate in perspective. Given higher education's tendency to privilege status, however, such comparisons often render the community college, its students, and its instructors as deficient. Even when these books do not engage in specific comparisons but provide baseline data on the community college faculty, their authors seldom delve into the nature of faculty work lives at community colleges in any great depth.

This situation is beginning to change. Within the past decade, three books have helped provide a portrait of specific aspects of faculty work at community colleges. These books include *Honored But Invisible: An Inside Look at Teaching in Community Colleges*, by Grubb and Associates (1999); *A Profile of the Community College Professorate, 1975-2000*, by Outcalt (2002); and *Community College Faculty: At Work in the New Economy*, by Levin et al. (2006). These works build on earlier studies by Earl Seidman (1985; *In the Words of the Faculty*) and Howard London (1978; *The Culture of a Community College*). The 1999 work by Norton Grubb and Associates took a qualitative look at arts and science and occupational technical faculty members in several community colleges across the nation, providing critical insights into how they approach teaching. Issues of professionalization in the community college professoriate were explored by Charles Outcalt (2002), who used descriptive data from a national survey for his findings. Through both quantitative and qualitative means, Levin et al. (2006) examined the roles of community college faculty members as managed professionals in the globalized economy. Each of these books portrays specific aspects of the lives of community college faculty members, but none offers a comprehensive synthesis of what is known about these individuals and the conditions of their work.

Other than books about community college faculty members, research about them most often appears in community college journals, those periodicals that publish only articles on community colleges. For example, an examination of articles published in six selected journals from 1990 through 2000 (Townsend, Bragg, & Kinnick, 2001) revealed that the three journals focusing on community colleges (*Community College Journal of Research and Practice, Community College Review*, and *Journal of Applied Research in Community Colleges*) published a total of 86 articles about the community college faculty (11% of all 777 articles in these three journals during the specified period). In

TABLE 1

Articles on Community College Topics in Selected Journals, 1990 to 2000

Topic	JHE		RHE		RevHE		CCJRP		CCR		JARCC		Total	
	n	%	n	%	n	%	n	%	n	%	n	%	n	%
General resources	1	12	0	0	0	0	65	14	9	4	1	1	76	9
Students	1	12	6	40	1	14	77	17	49	21	23	28	157	19
Faculty	1	12	0	0	2	29	49	11	32	14	5	06	89	11
Governance, administration, and planning	1	12	2	13	2	29	79	17	44	19	17	21	145	18
Financing and budgeting	0	0	0	0	0	0	21	5	7	3	5	6	33	4
Instruction, instructional support, and student services	0	0	0	0	0	0	76	16	27	11	8	10	111	14
Occupational education	0	0	1	7	0	0	34	7	6	3	3	4	44	5
Remediation, developmental education	0	0	2	13	0	0	10	2	4	2	3	4	19	2
Continuing education and community service	0	0	0	0	0	0	5	1	13	6	0	0	18	2
Collegiate function	1	12	4	27	1	14	22	5	24	10	7	8	59	7
Educational opportunity and social mobility	2	25	0	0	1	14	1	0	7	3	2	2	13	2
Miscellaneous	1	12	0	0	0	0	22	5	12	5	8	10	43	5
Total articles	8		15		7		461		234		82		807	

Source: Townsend, Bragg, and Kinnick (2001).

Note: JHE = Journal of Higher Education; RHE = Research in Higher Education; RevHE = Review of Higher Education; CCJRP = Community College Journal of Research and Practice; CCR = Community College Review; JARCC = Journal of Applied Research in the Community College. Percentages should be read downward.

comparison, the three higher education journals that were examined—those that are commonly considered to have a general focus on higher education rather than on a specific higher education sector (*Journal of Higher Education*, *Research in Higher Education*, and *Review of Higher Education*)—published a total of 30 articles about some aspect of the community college, and only three (14%) of these articles were about community college faculty members (see Table 1). Although the community college journals publish the vast majority of work on the community college faculty, it is important to note that even in these journals research on the faculty composes a relatively small portion of the research published on community colleges.

Also, faculty members and administrators in four-year institutions are unlikely to read the community college journals because their focus would not appear relevant to the professional world of the four-year college faculty. Research about community college faculty members also appears in other venues with limited distribution, such as dissertations and institutional reports. Some of this research may eventually appear in journal format, but it is likely to be in the community college journals.

What we Know About Community College Faculty

Although research about community college faculty members is less extensive than research about university faculty members, some research nonetheless exists. It is not possible to recount in this article the full extent of what is known about the community college faculty. Therefore, we briefly describe some of the topics most frequently represented in the literature, after first noting some methodological characteristics of these writings.

Methodological Characteristics

Much of what we know about the community college faculty results from small-scale quantitative or qualitative studies conducted at the institutional or state level. Given the tremendous variation among institutions in terms of size, population served, and geographic location, this approach makes sense. On the other hand, the localized nature of the research makes it difficult to generalize findings across institutions and states or to assume the transferability of findings in the case of qualitative research.

Because most research on the community college faculty is based on local- or state-level studies, it can be inferred that there is (or has been) little interest on the part of external agencies to fund large-scale studies of community college faculty members. For example, the National Science Foundation invests substantial funds in research on various aspects of the faculty in science, mathematics, and engineering. This research has yet to substantially contribute to knowledge of community college faculty members in these fields.

However, in the past decade or so, there has been an increasing use of national data sets to derive faculty profiles and perceptions. In particular, the electronic availability of data from the National Study of Postsecondary Faculty (NSOPF) surveys, which have been conducted since 1988, has resulted in a spate of studies about community college faculty members, examining such topics as their intent to leave (Rosser & Townsend, 2006), their job satisfaction in general (Issac & Boyer, 2007) and their satisfaction with their autonomy in particular (Kim, Wolf-Wendel, & Twombly, 2008), their perceptions of gender and racial status in the institution (Perna, 2003), the changing nature of their work (Levin et al., 2006), and community college labor market characteristics (Gahn & Twombly, 2001). Although the results of these studies have greater generalizability than the results of small-scale studies, studies based on national data sets have their own weaknesses, namely that the already-existing data shape the questions that can be asked. Outcalt (2002) and his colleagues at the Center for the Study of Community Colleges in Los Angeles have developed their own national surveys for the specific purpose of looking at the community college faculty. As a result, their research may more accurately reflect the community college world than do some of the studies that are based on NSOPF data. Local or single-institution studies also presumably address questions of importance to individual colleges, whereas national studies based on NSOPF or other national databases are more likely to address general policy-oriented questions that may or may not be relevant at the local level.

Topics

Whether studied locally or nationally, quantitatively or qualitatively, community college faculty members have primarily been examined in terms of the following topics: characteristics of the community college professoriate, both full-time and part-time; faculty work in the context of the community college; dimensions of the faculty career and labor market; the influence of various institutional factors, such as unions, on faculty work; and community college teaching as a profession.

Characteristics. First, it is important to note that approximately two thirds of community college faculty members are employed on a part-time basis. This percentage has held fairly steady for at least a decade. Although part-timers outnumber their full-time counterparts, nationally they teach only about one third of community college courses (Roueche, Roueche, & Milliron, 1995). Given this fact, it is important to be careful about painting the community college professoriate as mostly consisting of part-time faculty members. Although technically accurate, such a statement misrepresents who actually does the bulk of the teaching.

A fairly clear demographic picture of community college faculty members, both full- and part-time, emerges from the literature. The data consistently indicate that 80% of the community college faculty is white, a higher percentage than might be expected, given the demographics of the student body. (We note here as an aside that there is almost no research about being a minority faculty member in the community college, whereas numerous books and articles have been published about being a minority faculty member in universities [e.g., Berry & Mizelle, 2006; Cooper, 2006; Li & Beckett, 2005]). The community college professoriate is evenly split between men and women, thus making this group of faculty members more gender balanced than the faculty members in any other higher education sector (Townsend & Twombly, 2007a). It is somewhat more difficult to determine the average age of community college faculty members. Some studies have shown the average age of full-time faculty members to be 50 (e.g., Rosser & Townsend, 2006). Looking at age in another way, the U.S. Department of Education (2005) determined that approximately 36% were younger than 44, whereas 32% were between the ages of 45 and 54 and 22% were between the ages of 55 and 64; only 8% were older than 65. In terms of teaching area, Levin et al. (2006) found that the largest single group of full- and part-time faculty members (47%) teaches in the liberal arts. Approximately 40% teach in professional areas (e.g., business and nursing), 8% in vocational areas, and 4% in developmental education (Levin et al., 2006). Although we know the approximate percentage of the faculty who teach in each of these disciplinary areas, demographic profiles for each of these subgroups of the community college faculty have not been ascertained. The average salary for full-time community college faculty members on 9- or 10-month contracts in 2005-2006 was $55,380, as compared to $67,909 for full-time faculty members in four-year public institutions (Clery & Topper, 2007, p. 20). With the exception of salary, the differences within the part-time group by teaching field are likely to be greater than differences between full- and part-time faculty members.

Faculty work. Faculty work in community colleges is shaped by the institution's mission: its commitment to provide access to higher education to everyone who can benefit from some sort of postsecondary education; to offer transfer, vocational, remedial, and academic programs; and to do so at the two-year level. Thus the institution's students come with varying levels of academic ability, English-language ability, and economic resources. Faculty members teach predominantly lower-level courses. It is not surprising that the literature is very clear that the major work of community college faculty members is teaching; their average teaching load was five three-hr courses per semester in 2004 (Townsend & Rosser, 2007). Community colleges provide little support for research, and it is not surprising that their faculty members do little of it. NSOPF 2004 data indicate that, as a group, two-year college faculty members published—on average—0.25 juried and 0.41 nonjuried articles and made fewer than two presentations between 2002 and 2004 (Townsend & Rosser, 2007).

Two other topics fall under the broader category of faculty work: faculty development and faculty satisfaction. Although scholars have written a lot about faculty development, much of the literature merely catalogs what colleges do. The literature that does exist is quite critical of faculty-development programs for being ad hoc, lacking in institutional support, and having powerless coordinators (Grant & Keim, 2002; Murray, 2001). In terms of job satisfaction, community college faculty members, including minority faculty members, are the most satisfied faculty group in academe. Consistently, national studies of faculty job satisfaction show this (e.g., Antony & Valadez, 2002; Flowers, 2005; Kim et al., 2008). In addition, studies that compare the satisfaction of full- and part-time community college faculty members show few, if any, statistically significant differences (Valadez & Antony, 2001). Perhaps some of this job satisfaction, at least for full-time faculty members, occurs because community college faculty members have the shortest work week among the professoriate. An analysis of NSOPF data revealed that the community college faculty members surveyed in 1993 reported an average work week of not quite 47 hours, as compared to an average work week of at least 50 hours for faculty members employed at the various kinds of four-year public institutions. Similarly, community college faculty members surveyed in 2004 had an average work week of slightly more than 49 hours, as compared to an average work week at four-year colleges that ranged from a low of approximately 52 hours for those in liberal arts colleges to a high of almost 55 hours for faculty members in research institutions (Townsend & Rosser, 2007).

Dimensions of the faculty career and labor market. The qualifications of two-year college faculty members have been a topic of research interest throughout the history of the community college. A number of conclusions about the faculty career and labor market emerge from the available research. Becoming a community college faculty member may not be a person's initial career goal but may emerge as a positive choice compared to work in other settings (Townsend & Twombly, 2007b). Although K-12 public schools have diminished as a source of community college faculty members, a substantial proportion of the faculty has held previous positions in other settings before moving to the community college (Gahn & Twombly, 2001). No formal preparation for a teaching position is required other than the desired academic credential, which is typically a master's degree with 18 graduate hours in the teaching field. The master's degree is seen as less narrow than a doctorate yet still providing the depth needed to teach associate's degree students (Townsend & Twombly, 2007b). Vocational and technical fields may require the baccalaureate degree or less, when combined with work experience in the teaching field. Community colleges typically prefer some teaching experience or demonstrated potential to be a good teacher as well as fit with the mission of the community college.

Relatively little else is known about the labor market for community college faculty members, which is a bit surprising given the fact that community colleges, like most postsecondary institutions, are facing a wave of baby boomer faculty retirements. The literature suggests that although community colleges may advertise positions nationally, particularly in certain fields such as the sciences, they often hire locally or, at best, regionally (Twombly, 2005). Unlike their four-year college counterparts who follow a fairly typical path from graduate school to teaching, community college faculty members come from a variety of sources (e.g., business and industry, K-12 public schools, four-year institutions), which allows the institution a hiring flexibility not found in other postsecondary sectors. In sharp contrast to market forces that drive faculty salaries in national markets, faculty salaries in community colleges are typically set by unions or are determined by matching a candidate's qualifications to the appropriate step on the set salary ladder. Because institutions tend to hire locally or regionally, community college salaries are not as subject to market forces as those in research universities (Rhoades, 1998; Twombly, 2005). The exception here may be faculty members in vocational areas, although there is very little research on this topic. There is some evidence to indicate that vocational faculty members are subject to the same salary scales as faculty members in transfer areas (Twombly, 2005), thereby prohibiting colleges from paying more for faculty members in fields such as computer networking than for faculty members who teach English. It is likely that the market forces at work are very different ones from those governing national faculty markets because many vocational or occupational faculty members are employed locally while teaching. Much more needs to be learned about how this market works.

In sum, the faculty labor market in community college works very differently from that of four-year colleges and universities, a conclusion that has significant implications for graduate students who might consider the community college as a place to teach as well as for community colleges as they seek to fill positions.

Influence of various institutional factors on faculty work. Unions and faculty governance are the two institutional factors about which the most has been written, but that is not to say that much has been written about either. Community colleges in both their current and earlier junior college forms have been described as bureaucratic institutions in which administrators had (and have) more power and faculty members less power than administrators and faculty members in four-year colleges and universities (Alfred, 1994). It is not entirely clear how many community colleges are unionized and what percentage of the faculty is part of collective bargaining units. Rhoades (1998) provided the most in-depth examination of union contracts, although his work is somewhat dated now. According to his data, most unionized community colleges have a set salary schedule primarily based on seniority and the academic degree held rather than on merit, market, or any sort of equity. These institutions are less likely than four-year colleges to have specific rules guiding layoffs but are more likely to cover part-time faculty members. It is interesting that Rhoades found that two-year college contracts protect the intellectual property of the faculty more so than do contracts in unionized four-year institutions. Although scholars such as Rhoades and Levin et al. (2006) tended to see unions as an indication of an increasingly managed professoriate, few studies of unions look at how faculty performance is affected. Salaries do not appear to improve over the long haul as a result of unionization, and unionized faculty members do not appear to be more satisfied than are nonunionized ones (Townsend & Twombly, 2007b).

Although most colleges have some form of shared governance (as distinct from unionization), little is known about the role shared governance plays in the work lives of community college faculty members and its importance to them. Studies of shared governance suggest that community college faculty members view their college administrations as more autocratic than democratic (Thaxter & Graham, 1999). Levin et al. (2006) also suggested that although community college administrators increasingly involve faculty members in governance activities, doing so serves the institution's managerial and administrative interests, but not the faculty's.

It is clear that other institutional factors, such as the academic department and connections with the professional field, are likely to affect community college faculty work, but these connections have not been widely studied. External factors, such as state and national policies surrounding issues such as accountability and the addition of baccalaureate degrees, will also affect faculty work but are rarely studied.

Community college teaching as a profession. Being a faculty member in the community college has many positives, as is clear from the high degree of satisfaction evident in the national studies that have examined job satisfaction. However, there are also negatives. The down side of being a community college faculty member is articulated both in opinion pieces and in research studies. The down side includes feelings of being disrespected by those in four-year institutions (e.g., Townsend, 1995; Townsend & LaPaglia, 2000). As well, some community college faculty members are disrespected or held in lower esteem by some of their own colleagues. For example, those who teach students in developmental education and English as a second language are sometimes considered by other community college faculty members as lesser in status (Grubb, Badway, & Bell, 2003; Perin, 2002). Status tensions also occur between "academic" faculty members, those who teach in the general education or transfer programs, versus those who teach in the career and technical nontransfer programs (Grubb, 2005; McGrath & Spear, 1991). We do note, however, that internal divisions or pecking orders are not unique to community colleges. Within research universities, certain disciplines have more status than others, as education faculty members quickly learn.

Perhaps because of status concerns, the question of whether community college teaching is a profession is a longstanding one within the literature about community college faculty. The scholars who have tackled the subject have used various definitions of a profession (e.g., Cohen & Brawer, 1987, 2003; Garrison, 1967; Levin et al., 2006; Outcalt, 2002; Palmer, 1992). As a consequence, the evidence about the extent to which community college teaching is a profession is mixed, dependent on which characteristics are used in defining a profession. In addition, authors who write about community college teaching as a profession tend to focus on professionalism with an explicit or implicit comparative in mind—typically the research university (e.g., Clark, 1987; Outcalt, 2002).

Some scholars of professions have argued that specific professions conform to the characteristics of the ideal profession to a greater or lesser extent (Sarfati-Larson, 1977). In this view, there is no perfect or ideal profession; each meets characteristics of the ideal to a greater or lesser extent. Thus, the question is not whether community college teaching is a profession but whether community college teaching is so significantly different from teaching in other types of educational institutions that it constitutes a unique profession. In addition, where does community college teaching fall on a continuum of professionalization? As to the first question, there seems to be little evidence that community college teaching is unique and different from teaching in other sectors. Community college teaching does not employ different methods, require different pedagogical training, or have substantially different norms than teaching in any other sector. With respect to the second question, the results seem equally clear: Community college teaching exists between high school teaching and university teaching in terms of the extent to which it exhibits the characteristics of ideal professions.

Emerging curricular trends in the community college, such as the development of baccalaureate degrees awarded by community colleges and the push to count associate in applied science courses and degrees as transfer-level courses and credentials, are events likely to raise the required entry credential for career education faculty members and to increase the number of community college faculty members with doctorates. Given that a prolonged preparation time is one hallmark of a profession (Townsend & Twombly, 2007b), these developments may lead to perceptions of greater professionalization of the community college faculty.

What is not clear is whether perceptions of greater professionalization would really make a substantive difference in community college faculty members' work lives, their relationships with students, and the teaching–learning process. It is possible that if four-year faculty members begin to accept community college teaching as a profession, they may develop greater respect for community college faculty members and thus for their students who transfer to four-year institutions. However, we simply do not know if this would occur, partly because these issues have not been researched, which leads to the next topic: what needs to be known about the community college faculty.

What Needs to be Known About the Community College Faculty

Does it really make any difference in the work lives of community college faculty members or in the learning of the students they teach if these faculty members remain under the radar screen of higher education researchers seeking to understand the professoriate? We argue that it can. Beyond the obvious use of research by individuals to earn tenure, promotion, and merit pay, research can influence policy and practice. Research on the community college faculty can do this only if it goes beyond the received, and often unquestioned, story that community colleges are teaching institutions and that therefore, by definition, their faculty members are good teachers who produce learning. In this concluding section, we not only suggest that community college faculty members *should* receive greater attention because of the increasingly important role they play but also suggest some topics, based on our review, that merit greater attention.

Before identifying specific topics for study, we offer two general conclusions. One has to do with the nature of research conducted, and the second gets to the heart of what should be studied. Based on our review of the literature, we argue that research on the community college faculty has a horizontal nature. That is, an institutional or statewide descriptive study is conducted on some aspect of the community college faculty, such as professional development; this study is then replicated in other individual states, with an article published on each state. Again, given the local nature of community colleges, this approach makes some sense. The disadvantage is that the same knowledge tends to be replicated. Rather than deepening knowledge of a phenomenon, the research tends to generalize it. Unquestionably, both breadth and depth are needed. The use of national databases helps to provide the generalization, and we would hope that studies using other methods could help deepen that knowledge.

Second, we argue that research on community college faculty members needs to be tied more to their roles in the teaching and learning process. Much of the existing literature on the community college faculty accepts the construction of community colleges as teaching institutions and the assumptions about faculty members that accompany such a construction. The resulting research examines an aspect of faculty work as an end in and of itself. This trend exists regardless of topic, whether it is professional development, faculty satisfaction, participation in governance, or faculty careers. As an example, one can read the literature and come away with a pretty good idea of the characteristics of faculty-development programs. What the literature does not indicate is whether or how any of them improve teaching and learning. Nor is it known, for example, whether community college faculty members with master's degrees are better teachers or, in the current economic model of teaching, produce more learning than do university faculty members with PhDs.

Thus, we need more research that, like the work of Grubb and Associates (1999), seeks to get beyond the rhetoric that community colleges care for the success of their students and that individuals who teach in community colleges are excellent teachers simply because they teach in teaching colleges. As Bailey and Morest (2006) pointed out all too clearly, little is known about the success of students in community colleges and what might be done to improve rates of success. Although many factors may contribute to enhanced "productivity" of community colleges (used here to mean successful graduation, students' attainment of career goals, institutional transfer rates, and achievement of the myriad purposes community colleges serve), the quality, preparation, and pedagogical skills of the faculty have to be central. We know something about their preparation, institutional efforts at professional development, the role of unions in determining work responsibilities, and the influence of globalization in the work of community colleges. But we know almost nothing about the relationship of these factors (and others) to the teaching and learning process. For example, do unions promote or discourage improved teaching practices?

The same can be argued for the study of faculty job satisfaction. Researchers may seek to ascertain what variables affect job satisfaction with the hope that relevant variables can be manipulated in the actual workplace so as to produce greater job satisfaction. If research demonstrates that community college faculty job satisfaction is less high among faculty members who previously worked at a four-year college (Rosser & Townsend, 2006), this finding may suggest to community college administrators that they should not hire individuals with this background, if having satisfied faculty members is an administrative goal or concern. Satisfaction is an important case in point because the national surveys of faculty members collect data on satisfaction, thus making it a relatively easy topic to study. Although satisfaction is a useful and important end, we might also ask whether increased satisfaction improves student learning.

There is no question that, to produce good learning outcomes, community colleges must employ effective faculty members. How effective faculty members are recruited and selected is unknown. Other faculty-oriented research that might influence policy and practice would be research that examines the labor market for community college faculty, both from the faculty member's perspective and from the institutional perspective. Although the research provides a description of community college faculty careers that is pretty clear and consistent, we know little about the relationship between labor market characteristics and hiring practices, for example, and about learning outcomes.

For those seeking to work in the community college and for those who already do, research could also strengthen their understanding of how the promotion and tenure process works in the 72% of community colleges that have tenure (Parsad & Glover, 2002). In the four-year sector, the bar for achieving tenure seems to be increasingly raised (Townsend & Rosser, 2007). Does the same hold true for the two-year college sector? Also, institutional leaders (and thus faculty members) might benefit from a greater understanding of the promotion and tenure process in other two-year institutions and of ways to support faculty members in their efforts to achieve promotion and tenure. As part of this research, there should be an examination of possible differences by race or ethnicity, gender, teaching field, and unionization status.

Using these variables in examinations of other aspects of faculty work lives at community colleges would also be productive. For example, there is some research to indicate that faculty members in career and technical education, developmental education, and continuing education have lower status within the community college than do faculty members who teach transfer-level courses. First of all, is this an accurate reflection of relationships in the majority of community colleges? If so, does the status differentiation affect the performance of the faculty members who are perceived to have lower status? Do their students suffer in any way from the negative status perceptions of their faculty members? Institutional leaders need to be concerned about the possibility of this issue affecting not only individual faculty members' job satisfaction but also their performance and thus the education of their students.

The ultimate justification for knowing more about community college faculty members is their impact on the higher education system through the teaching of so many students. The community college's educational mission is solely to transmit knowledge, in contrast to the university's mission, which is to generate knowledge. From this perspective, conducting research about how community college faculty members teach and what student outcomes occur because of their teaching approaches would seem critical. Ascertaining the effectiveness of particular pedagogical approaches in the general transmission of knowledge and also more specifically examining which pedagogies work best in certain teaching areas (e.g., developmental education, vocational education, and transfer education) is critical in improving student learning outcomes in these areas. It seems highly fitting that the institution that most prides itself on being a teaching institution should be the institution whose faculty members are most studied for their teaching approaches and student learning outcomes.

References

Alfred, R. (1994). Research and practice on shared governance and participatory decision-making. In G. A. Baker III (Ed.), *A handbook on the community college in America* (pp. 245–258). Westport, CT: Greenwood.

Almanac. (2005, August 26). *Chronicle of Higher Education, 52*(1).

Antony, J. S., & Valadez, J. R. (2002). Exploring the satisfaction of part-time college faculty in the U.S. *Review of Higher Education, 26,* 41–56.

Bailey, T., & Morest, V. (Eds.). (2006). *Defending the community college equity agenda.* Baltimore: Johns Hopkins University Press.

Berry, T. R., & Mizelle, N. (Eds.). (2006). *From oppression to grace: Women of color and their dilemmas within the academy.* Sterling, VA: Stylus.

Clark, B. (1987). *The academic life: Small worlds, different worlds.* Lawrenceville, NJ: Carnegie Foundation for the Advancement of Teaching.

Clery, S. B., & Topper, A. M. (2007). Faculty salaries: 2005-2006. In *The NEA almanac of higher education* (pp. 7–26). Washington, DC: National Education Association.

Cohen, A. M., & Brawer, F. B. (1987). *The collegiate function of community colleges.* San Francisco: Jossey-Bass.

Cohen, A. M., & Brawer, F. B. (2003). *The American community college* (4th ed.). San Francisco: Jossey-Bass.

Cooper, T. L. (2006). *The sista' network: African American women faculty successfully negotiating the road to tenure.* Boulton, MA: Anker.

Finkelstein, M., Seal, R., & Schuster, J. (1998). *The new academic generation: A profession in transformation.* Baltimore: Johns Hopkins University Press.

Flowers, L. (2005). Job satisfaction differentials among African American faculty at 2-year and 4-year institutions. *Community College Journal of Research and Practice, 29,* 317–328.

Gahn, S., & Twombly, S. B. (2001). Dimensions of the community college labor market. *Review of Higher Education, 24,* 259–282.

Garrison, R. (1967). *Junior college faculty: Issues and problems. A preliminary national appraisal.* Washington, DC: American Association of Junior Colleges.

Grant, M. R., & Keim, M. (2002). Faculty development in publicly supported two-year colleges. *Community College Journal of Research and Practice, 26,* 793–807.

Grubb, W. N. (2005, June 6). Is the tech vs. liberal arts debate out-of-date? Two views. *Community College Week,* pp. 4–5.

Grubb, W. N., & Associates. (1999). *Honored but invisible: An inside look at teaching in community colleges.* New York: Routledge.

Grubb, W. N., Badway, N., & Bell, D. (2003). Community colleges and the equity agenda: The potential of noncredit education. *Annals of the American Academy of Political and Social Science, 586,* 218–240.

Hailstorks, R., & Boenau, M. (2007, October 12). APA aims to broaden network of two-year instructors. *Community College Times,* p. 6.

Ignash, J., & Townsend, B. K. (2000). Evaluating state-level articulation agreements according to good practice. *Community College Review, 28*(3), 1–21.

Issac, E. P., & Boyer, P. G. (2007). Voices of urban and rural community college minority faculty: Satisfaction and opinions. *Community College Journal of Research and Practice, 31*, 359–369.

Kim, D.,Wolf-Wendel, L., & Twombly, S. (2008). Factors predicting community college faculty satisfaction with institutional autonomy. *Community College Review, 35*, 159–180.

Levin, J. S., Kater, S., & Wagoner, R. L. (2006). *Community college faculty: At work in the new economy.* New York: Palgrave Macmillan.

Li, G., & Beckett, G. (2005). *"Strangers" of the academy: Asian women scholars in higher education.* Sterling, VA: Stylus.

London, H. B. (1978). *The culture of a community college.* New York: Praeger.

McGrath, D., & Spear, M. B. (1991). *The academic crisis of the community college.* Albany: State University of New York Press.

Murray, J. P. (2001). Faculty development in publicly supported 2-year colleges. *Community College Journal of Research and Practice, 25*, 487–502.

National Center for Postsecondary Improvement. (1998). A changing understanding of community college faculty. *Change, 30*(6), 43–46.

Outcalt, C. L. (2002). *A profile of the community college professorate, 1975-2000.* New York: Routledge Falmer.

Palmer, J. (1992). Faculty professionalism reconsidered. In K. Kroll (Ed.), *Maintaining faculty excellence. New directions for community colleges* (No. 79; pp. 29–38). San Francisco: Jossey-Bass.

Parsad, B., & Glover, D. (2002). *Tenure status of postsecondary instructional faculty and staff: 1992-98* (NCES 2002210). Retrieved April 9, 2008, from http://nces.ed.gov/pubsearch/pubsinfo.asp?pubid =2002210

Perin, D. (2002). The location of developmental education in community colleges: A discussion of the merits of mainstreaming vs. centralization. *Community College Review, 30*, 27–44.

Perna, L. (2003). The status of women and minorities among community college faculty. *Research in Higher Education, 44*, 205–240.

Redden, E. (2007, September 14). Un-complicating community college transfer. *Inside Higher Education.* Retrieved October 19, 2007, from http://www.insidehighered.com/news/2007/09/14/newjersey

Rhoades, G. (1998). *Managed professionals: Unionized faculty and restructuring academic labor.* Albany: State University of New York Press.

Rosser, V. J., & Townsend, B. K. (2006). Determining public 2-year college faculty's intent to leave: An empirical model. *Journal of Higher Education, 77*, 124–147.

Roueche, J. E., Roueche, S. D., & Milliron, M. D. (1995). *Strangers in their own land: Part-time faculty in American community colleges.* Washington, DC: Community College Press.

Sarfati-Larson, M. (1977). *The rise of professionalism.* Berkeley: University of California Press.

Schuster, J. H., & Finkelstein, M. J. (2006). *The American faculty: The restructuring of academic work and careers.* Baltimore: Johns Hopkins University Press.

Seidman, E. (1985). *In the words of the faculty.* San Francisco: Jossey-Bass.

Thaxter, L., & Graham, S. (1999). Community college faculty involvement in decision-making. *Community College Journal of Research and Practice, 23*, 655–674.

Townsend, B. K. (1995). Women community college faculty. On the margins or in the mainstream? In B. K. Townsend (Ed.), *Gender and power in the community college. New directions for community colleges* (No. 89; pp. 39–46). San Francisco: Jossey-Bass.

Townsend, B. K. (2001). Redefining the community college transfer mission. *Community College Review, 29*(2), 29–42.

Townsend, B. K., Bragg, D., & Kinnick, M. (2001, April). *Taking stock of the literature on community colleges.* Presentation at the annual meeting of Council for the Study of Community Colleges, Washington, DC.

Townsend, B. K., Donaldson, J., & Wilson, T. (2005). Marginal or monumental? Visibility of community colleges in selected higher education journals. *Community College Journal of Research and Practice, 29*, 123–135.

Townsend, B. K., & LaPaglia, N. (2000). Are we marginalized within academe? Perceptions of two-year college faculty. *Community College Review, 28*(1), 41–48.

Townsend, B. K., & Rosser, V. (2007). Workload issues and measures of faculty productivity. *Thought & Action, 23*, 1–14.

Townsend, B. K., & Twombly, S. (2007a). Accidental equity: The status of women in the community college. *Equity & Excellence in Education, 40,* 208–217.

Townsend, B. K., & Twombly, S. (2007b). *Community college faculty: Overlooked and undervalued.* (ASHE higher education report. Vol. 32, No. 6). San Francisco: Jossey-Bass.

Townsend, B. K., & Wilson, K. B. (2006). The transfer mission: Tried and true buttroubled? In B. K. Townsend & K. Dougherty (Eds.), *Community college missions in the 21st century.* (New directions for community colleges. No. 136; pp. 33–41). San Francisco: Jossey-Bass.

Twombly, S. B. (2005). Values, policies and practices affecting the hiring process for full-time arts and sciences faculty in community colleges. *Journal of Higher Education, 76,* 423–447.

U.S. Department of Education. (2005). *Digest of education statistics: 2005. Table 230: Full-time and part-time instructional faculty and staff in degree-granting institutions, by type and control of institution and selected characteristics: Fall 1992, fall 1998, and fall 2003.* Retrieved April 9, 2008, from http://nces.ed.gov/programs/digest/d05/tables/dt05_230.asp

Valadez, J. R., & Antony, J. S. (2001). Job satisfaction and commitment of two-year college part-time faculty. *Community College Journal of Research and Practice, 25,* 97–108.

Vaughan, G. B. (1986). In pursuit of scholarship. *Community, Technical, and Junior College Journal, 56*(4), 12–16.

Vaughan, G. B. (1988). Scholarship in community colleges: The path to respect. *Educational Record, 69*(2), 26–31.

Susan Twombly is the chairperson of and a professor in the Department of Educational Leadership and Policy Studies at the University of Kansas, Lawrence.

Barbara K. Townsend is a professor in the Department of Educational Leadership and Policy Analysis at the University of Missouri, Columbia.

CHAPTER 20

PERFORMING GENDER IN THE WORKPLACE: GENDER SOCIALIZATION, POWER, AND IDENTITY AMONG WOMEN FACULTY MEMBERS

JAIME LESTER
OLD DOMINION UNIVERSITY

Organizational cultures shape and reinforce socially appropriate roles for men and women. Drawing on a performativity framework, which assumes that gender is socially constructed through gendered "performances," this study employs interviews with and observations of six women faculty members to examine how dominant discourses define and maintain the formation of gender roles within a community college context. The experiences of one of these faculty members, a welding instructor, are highlighted. Results indicate that the women faculty members performed a variety of stereotypical feminine gender roles based on (a) socialization experiences external to the college, (b) socialization within the college's organizational culture, and (c) the individual's construction and negotiation of gender identity.

Keywords: performance theory, gender, women faculty, identity

Yes, I get a lot of people from industry, and they need to understand that I take my job seriously. It is unfortunate, but automatically when they see you are a woman, they don't take you seriously. There's a certain seriousness and distance that you need to keep, but that is not me. So you just have to do that to be effective, but I try not to be, you know. The essence is the same, but the delivery is the difference. I can be more compassionate and loving at home.

Rosa, Architecture professor

In this job there are dress issues. Most guys, like this one guy who has a ponytail and is attractive, he wears jeans and he looks great. I came in this summer a couple of times dressed like that, in a jeans and t-shirt, people say, "Hey '60s throwback." Dress is clearly an issue. There's gender stuff operating. It pisses me off that I feel like I have to. I guess that I don't *have* to. Some women come in dressed how they want. I guess I don't want to go through not being respected. I just don't want to undercut being respected. I don't want to make it an issue.

Susan, English professor

Over the last several decades, organizational scholars have noted the prevalence of organizational discourses and social practices that characterize appropriate roles for men and women. These roles include nurturing, caretaking, and exhibiting additional interest in the emotional health of students and fellow faculty members (Blackwell, 1996; Boice, 1993; Dallimore, 2003; Stein, 1994; Tierney & Bensimon, 1996). Tierney and Bensimon (1996) found in a study of promotion and tenure practices that women faculty members perceive that they are expected to perform "mom" and "smile" work, maintaining a caring and nurturing demeanor while also avoiding confrontation. Women faculty members also perform the "glue work" of the academic department by participating at greater rates then their male counterparts in service activities that often keep departments and universities functioning (Eveline, 2004; Tierney & Bensimon, 1996). Furthermore, women in leadership roles are expected to fit the leadership images of "philosopher-kings and military heroes that render women invisible" (Amey & Twombly, 1992, p. 476). Women are often signaled early in their careers that traditional male traits are expected in senior administrative roles and that promotion depends on their ability to act like men (Tedrow & Rhoades, 1999).

Similarly, several researchers have noted that women faculty members feel obligated to advise a disproportionate share of students, conduct research that addresses gender relations, and perform "emotional work" that provides emotional support to colleagues and students, thus reinforcing traditional feminine roles (Acker & Feuerverger, 1996; Bird, Litt, & Wang, 2004; Knights & Richards, 2003; Tierney & Bensimon, 1996). Although the emotional work "is necessary and beneficial to educational institutions" (Knights & Richards, 2003, p. 223), women do not find it beneficial to their careers. In fact, when women satisfy all the various responsibilities expected of them, including caring for others and being "good" faculty citizens, they acknowledge that the reward system does not value all of the caring and citizenship roles they carry out, leaving them to feel unfulfilled (Acker & Feuerverger, 1996).

The literature on gender roles and faculty work paints a complex picture of the various ways that women are constrained into traditionally feminine roles. However, we know less about how these roles affect individual identity. The few studies that address identity issues among women and minority faculty members describe significant cultural conflicts that arise as individuals attempt to negotiate their own identity in an ethnically homogenous and male-dominated academic culture (Johnsrud & Sadao, 1998; Turner, 2002; Turner, Myers, & Creswell, 1999). To expand our understanding of women faculty members and identity, I focus on gendered performances (or "doing gender") and on how social practices define gendered behaviors in the context of a community college. Specifically, this study addresses the following research questions:

1. What do female community college faculty members believe are appropriate gender roles?

2. What social practices and discourses communicate and reify appropriate gendered performances as defined by roles?

3. What is the relationship between gender roles, performances, and individual gender identity?

Gendered performances, a concept derived from performativity theory, are an expression of the social norms and gender roles within an organization and help us understand how particular performances are favored within organizations and how, in turn, individual gender identity is constructed and complicated by performances. The quotes at the beginning of this article illustrate gendered performance. The architecture instructor, Rosa, describes how she hides her feminine identity and maintains a tough persona to gain respect among her colleagues and students. Susan describes how she dresses in a manner that she perceives as appropriate and respectful. These women and their experiences describe how female faculty members perceive gender roles, behaviors, and expectations in the context of a community college and the discourses and social practices that communicate gender roles and behaviors. By identifying the social norms and roles that define the expected gendered behaviors that faculty members perform or resist, the subtle organizational cultural practices that discriminate against women and prevent gender equity will be uncovered.

In what follows, I provide a review of the literature on organizational discourses and practices concerning gender. This literature provides the framework for understanding how individuals come to know gender roles within an organization. This is followed by a discussion of the theory of performativity and how this theory serves as a major conceptual and methodological lens for this study. After a review of the research design, a detailed narrative of one of the study participants is provided to highlight how women faculty members are socialized into, perform, and negotiate gender roles in a higher education institution.

Review of the Literature

For the last few decades, feminists have examined the various ways in which gender roles (and ideologies) are communicated and embedded in organizational practices (Acker, 1990; Bailyn, 1993,

2003; Ely, 1994, 1995; Ely & Meyerson, 2000; Kanter, 1977; Martin, 1996, 2003). Gender is partially constructed and reinforced by organizational processes, including social interactions between workers, salary differentials, and the ways in which work is segregated and divided by paid and unpaid labor (Acker, 1990). The construction of gender in organizations occurs via four social phenomena: (a) the construction of divisions along lines of gender, (b) symbols and cultural images, (c) informal social interactions, and (d) organizational narratives (Acker, 1990; Ely & Meyerson, 2000). The first category, the construction of divisions along lines of gender, includes the way in which labor is divided, the physical space of offices or laboratory space, and access to decision making. Each of these constructs determines who has power and privilege within the organization. In addition, the imbalance between men and women in organizations has been found to significantly affect the gender identity of female workers, influence the structures and norms that informally create barriers to the advancement of women, impact the adoption and use of family leave policies, lead to fewer women seeking advancement, and create more salary inequity (Bellas, 1997; Chliwniak, 1997; Ely, 1994, 1995; Kanter, 1977). Furthermore, the proportion of women in an academic department is related to the extent to which women feel welcomed in the department. Having fewer women in a department is associated with increased perceptions of an organizational climate that is hostile toward women (Riger, Stokes, Raja, & Sullivan, 1997).

The second category of social practices includes symbols and cultural images of idealized heroic workers that are aligned with masculine traits. *Heroic workers* are defined as always-available workers who have the ability to prioritize work over other responsibilities. The heroic worker ideology is reinforced by images and norms of individualistic heroes who are fully committed to all activities that are associated with the organization (Rapoport et al., 1996). Women who traditionally hold more household responsibilities are disadvantaged by evaluations that are based on time spent on the job or on the willingness to be flexible with extra work hours (Ely & Meyerson, 2000; Halford & Leonard, 2001). In faculty jobs, the image of an ideal worker is no different. With evaluations rooted in productivity, women faculty members in all disciplines face evaluation criteria that favor men and women who do not have children or extensive family responsibilities (Armenti, 2004; Bailyn, 2003; Benschop & Brouns, 2003; Rosser, 2002; Wolf-Wendel & Ward, 2003). Women faculty members consistently cite pressure to postpone pregnancy or relent on their aspirations for childbearing to acquire tenure, or they limit job searches to specific geographic regions because of their parental responsibilities (Aisenberg & Harrington, 1988; Armenti, 2004; Bronstein, Black, Pfenning, & White, 1986, 1987; Elliott, 2003).

The third category includes informal social interactions that create and reinforce patterns of dominance and submission, thereby reinforcing the organizational norms of femininity and masculinity. These interactions legitimize the differences between men and women and "reduce the scope for action of others not only through influencing overt behavior, but also by ideological, symbolic and disciplinary means" (Alvesson & Due Billing, 1997, p. 73). The way in which men present themselves and embody masculinity reinforces an idealized monolithic category of male and female (Ely & Meyerson, 2000). Style of dress, use of language, and expression of emotions reinforce representations of what is masculine and feminine, widening further the divisions of gender within the organization. Social interactions are both subtle and blatant. Subtle interactions include expectations to perform both masculine and feminine qualities. As a result, women may feel excluded by colleagues, experience intimidating behaviors by students, and receive unfair treatment in the tenure and promotion evaluations (Bronstein & Farnsworth, 1998; Pini, 2005;[1] Winkler, 2000). Blatant interactions are exemplified in the prevalence of sexual harassment. Women faculty members are found to experience inappropriate sexual attention at rates far greater than men regardless of the length of time they have been employed at their institutions (Bronstein & Farnsworth, 1998; Dey, Korn, & Sax, 1996; Sandler & Shoop, 1997).

Finally, organizational narratives disguise and perpetuate the gendered nature of social practices (Ely & Meyerson, 2000; Olsson, 2002). Narratives about gender and gendered traits support distinctions between masculinity and femininity and create a sense of an "objective" reality. The narratives are not just the opinions of the storyteller, but also an indication of reality or "the way things are" in the organization. As Clark (1972) states, "An organizational saga is a powerful means of unity in the formal workplace. It makes links across internal divisions and organizational boundaries as internal and external groups share their common beliefs" (p. 183). Gender roles and norms are communicated and perpetuated in organizational sagas that create an appearance of gender neutrality; gendered practices and ideologies are just "the ways things are" and function as exemplars of gendered practices and behaviors (Kaye, 1995). They are the organizational reality that is devoid of discriminatory practices.

The description of the four ways in which gender operates within organizations provides the framework for understanding how individuals come to know gender roles within an organization. For example, the way in which labor is divided, the physical space of offices or laboratory space, access to decision making, and the proportion of men to women in a department serve to divide work along lines of gender and construct gender roles within the organization. Each of these categories is not discrete, but operates simultaneously and creates a system that continuously defines and reinforces gender alongside power within organizations. However, the four-part gender and organizations framework discussed above does not explain how and why women choose to participate in these gendered social practices or how these practices are reinforced within the organizational context. To describe how social practices are replicated, represented, and reinforced, I turn to performativity. The performances serve as representations of the gendered social practices and roles that simultaneously reinforce social arrangements based on gender.

Theoretical Framework

In her groundbreaking book *Gender Trouble*, Butler (1990) theorizes that gender is a socially constructed category created during gendered "performances." Refuting previous claims of the existence of gender norms, Butler argues that feminine or masculine performances create the ideology of gender. Gender emerges as a reality only to the extent that it is performed. Butler claims that individuals do not entirely act out a set of predetermined gender roles; rather, the roles are established, recreated, and reinforced within the performances. Butler (1990) explains that by agreeing to "perform, produce, and sustain discrete and polar genders as cultural fictions . . . the construction 'compels' our belief in its necessity and naturalness" (p. 178). It is within the act of performing that gender norms are defined and seen as natural. In this regard, gender does not exist outside of the performance; there is no preconceived notion of gender that is based on biological fact or other functionalist conceptions. Rather, gender and how it is perceived are constituted within the performances. In addition, gender identity is created through the performances. An individual's gender identity is discursively constituted as the effect rather than the cause—an individual's identity does not exist behind the performance, but is created by the performance itself. To further explain the theory of performativity, I now turn to an explanation of its main tenets: identity, agency, and power.

The first tenet of performativity is identity, which refers to the conscious and unconscious thoughts or ways in which an individual understands herself in relation to the world. Within performativity, an individual's identity is created and recreated through discourse. Identity is thus precarious and unstable. By decentering the subject and presupposing that individual identity is created through discourse, identity can be changed at any given moment. Therefore, identity is not a fixed state of being, but a fluid process that is able to change. Multiple and competing identities exist simultaneously with individuals choosing to perform each identity based on the contexts in which they find themselves.

Choosing to perform one's gender means navigating gender norms and individual agency. One's gender identity (and performances) are determined to the extent that social norms support and enable the performances. The content of the performances is determined by social convention, thus limiting individual agency. Butler (2004) acknowledges that "the physical body is that which can occupy the norm in myriad ways, exceed the norm, rework the norm, and expose realities to which we thought we were confined" (p. 215). Agency is not entirely limited, and by overperforming or resisting the norm, the norm is exposed and has the potential for social transformation. Importantly, agency and resistance are not without consequences. As will become clear in the following discussion of power, agency is further limited by hegemony.

For Butler (2004), gender identity stands at a paradox where gender regulations (e.g., power) work to paralyze agency. Put simply, certain identities are aligned with power and considered more contextually appropriate, thus limiting the scope of agency and identity. Individuals may choose to represent and perform a gendered identity, but they must consider the implications of resistance or assimilation. Interpreting Foucault, Butler (2004) states, "regulatory power not only acts upon a pre-existing subject but also shapes and forms that subject" (p. 41). Regulatory power operates on gender and has its own disciplinary regime, which primarily functions as a norm. "A norm operates within social practice as the implicit standard of normalization" and "is a measurement and a means of producing a common standard, to become an instance of the norm is not fully to exhaust the norm" (p. 50). Certain cultural configurations (or norms) of gender have seized a hegemonic hold. For, "to veer from the gender norm is to produce the aberrant example that regulatory powers (medical, psychiatric, and legal, to name a few) may quickly exploit to shore up the rational for their continuing regulatory zeal" (Butler, 2004, p. 52). When one resists hegemonic gender norms, regulatory powers, such as the law and medical diagnosis, work to identify those actions as inappropriate and problematic.

Butler's performativity is thus essential in this study, because it establishes the socially constructed nature of gender as well as how social practices and roles are replicated, represented, and reinforced. First, the ways in which gender is performed embody those social practices that are contextually defined. Watching how individuals represent gender by dress, mannerism, and social interactions, for example, provides clues as to how the culture and context define gender roles. Second, the way in which an individual performs in relation to those contextually and culturally performed roles indicates forms of acceptance or resistance. Forms of power are made evident by understanding the nature of resistance. Third, by virtue of performing gender, one reinforces and replicates social norms and roles, legitimizing their existence. As Butler (2004) states, "What this means is that through the practice of gender performativity, we not only see how the norms that govern reality are cited but grasp one of the mechanisms by which reality is reproduced and altered in the course of that reproduction" (p. 218). Finally, performativity conceptualizes a connection between performing gender and gender identity. Individuals do not just perform gender roles as a character fictitiously adopts roles for a play; rather, individuals perform roles in relation to their identity and often recreate and reinforce their gender identity through the act of performing. Performing gender is a site for the deconstruction of how and why individuals interpret and maintain dominant organizational gender roles and how these roles affect individual identity.

Research Design

To explore gendered performances among faculty members, I conducted an ethnographic case study (Merriam, 1988; Spradley, 1979) relying on the perspectives of critical ethnography. Critical ethnography disrupts the status quo by bringing forth underlying operations of power and control. Going beyond descriptions of social life, it refines social theory (Carspecken, 1996). A case study is "chosen precisely because researchers are interested in insight, discovery, and interpretation rather than hypothesis testing" (Merriam, 1988, p. 10). An ethnographic case study provides in-depth descriptions of the culture being studied and allows members to tell their stories (Van Maanen, 1988). Because the definitions and identification of gender roles are culturally specific, this research design assisted in uncovering the individual ways in which socializing experiences and organizational practices are characterized. It also allowed the researcher to observe individual faculty members and their performances of gender in many different contexts (e.g., meetings, classrooms, etc.).

Study Sample and Data Collection

This study relies on interviews with and observations of six full-time women faculty members at an urban community college. A community college was chosen because of the historically large representation of women on the faculty and the varying proportions of men to women across departments (i.e., subcultures). To understand the importance of departmental culture on gendered

TABLE 1

Study Participants

	Department and Field	Race	Marital Status	Number of Children	Number of Years at College
Arlene	Construction technologies/welding	African American	Divorced	1	10
Mary	Culinary arts/breakfast cookery	Caucasian	Single	0	14
Rosa	Construction technologies/architecture	Latina	Married	3	15
Susan	Language arts/English	Caucasian	Married	0	5
Sara	Language arts/honors English	Caucasian	Married	0	4
Diane	Language arts/English as a second language and theater arts	Latina	Married	0	16

performances, two departments were selected based on the number and availability of women faculty members and on the academic or vocational status of the departments. Selection criteria for the study participants included full-time status and employment at the institution for more than two years; the goal was to include three women in an academic department with high female representation and three women in a vocational department with low female representation. The resulting sample is detailed in Table 1. The selection criteria allowed for a comparison across departmental type (academic versus vocational) and across departments with variable gender representation.

The interviews and observations were conducted over a four-month time frame. All participants were interviewed five times, and each interview lasted approximately one hour. In addition, each participant was observed on six occasions. Altogether, there were 30 interviews and 36 observations, constituting approximately 170 hours of interaction with the participants. The interviews focused on perceptions of cultural norms of gender, how women are socialized into cultural norms of gender, and gender identity. All observations were conducted either while the participant was teaching or attending meetings. The observations gave visibility to women's experiences (Reinharz, 1992) and allowed the researcher to witness performances of gender and question the participants about those performances in subsequent interviews. Extensive field and observation notes were taken with attention to the ways in which women faculty members interacted with students and colleagues, understood the symbols and sagas encountered throughout the college, perceived the exercise of power in the organization, and performed their gender through a variety of means, including attention to dress, mannerisms, and language.

Data Analysis

All interviews were transcribed and analyzed inductively and deductively for common themes related to gender roles and behaviors, socialization into gender roles, and gender identity. Because much of the data was in a narrative or story format, narrative analysis was also conducted. Narrative analysis examines a participant's story (or a series of stories), analyzing the structure, words and phrases, and language used to describe the culture. To analyze the interview data, I used two techniques: data reduction and interpretation. Data reduction is the process of reducing the text into short phrases and organizing the narrative into a core narrative that described how the women faculty members understood gender roles in the college (Riessman, 1993). To choose the pertinent stories from the transcripts that related to gender, I first selected those pieces of text that addressed gender broadly. I then began the process of retranscribing the narratives into the narrative core of abstract, orientation, complicating action, and resolution.

The second technique used is interpretation that situates the narratives in social, cultural, and institutional discourses (Riessman, 1993). Using the retranscribed narratives derived from the data reduction process, I situated and compared the narratives with the observation data. This analysis helped call attention to the organization of responses and to the subtleties of social discourses that reveal and shape individual interpretations of gender. For example, the participants' choice of stories, their characterization of gender, and the ways they resolved gender conflicts experienced within the organization revealed their understanding of gender, their gender identity, and how gender is understood within the context of the college.

To validate the study findings, I relied on the assumptions of triangulation articulated by Stake (1995), who describes triangulation as a process of understanding the possibility of nuances and individual experiences that situate human experience without relying on congruency between multiple sources of data. The veracity of the data in this study does not fall under the positivistic paradigm of establishing a "true" reality. The authenticity of this study is found in the comparison of multiple sources of data. Authenticity of the data, therefore, was established by conducting thorough observations and by questioning the behaviors and beliefs of the participants during the interviews. Furthermore, the perspective of performativity theory did not preclude openness to other perspectives. The author looked for counter narratives that would potentially reject the framework and conducted member checks—the process of sharing written interpretations of the data with research participants—to verify interpretations. Member checks allowed for a dialogue with the participants to provide more accurate research results.

Interpretations

In this section, I review the major research findings of this study. Because the analysis is based on the individual narratives, I first present and describe the overarching themes and then use the narrative of one of the participants, Arlene, to provide a rich description of the study findings. There are three main themes that emerged from the interviews and observations and that are related to organizational construction of gender roles and gender performances. Each of these themes is organized in three acts similar to those in a play.[2] First, the study participants were found to construct gender roles prior to becoming faculty members. These gender socialization experiences external to the college were often compared and contrasted with the college's gender roles. Influences of external gender socialization included societal images and symbols, family influence, and vocational culture. For example, Arlene, the welding faculty member, was strongly influenced by societal images of a welder. She was often discriminated against for her chosen profession. External influences were strongest among those faculty members who were in vocational programs that are male dominated.

The next theme is organizational culture socialization that identifies how individuals come to understand gender within the context of the college. Social interactions with colleagues often resulted in workplace bullying, classroom dynamics, tokenism, and other experiences within the college that influenced how the participants perceived and performed gender in the workplace. Memorable negative interactions with male colleagues defined the appropriate behaviors.

Finally, one of the goals of this study was to understand the intersection of gender roles, performances, and individual identity. Specifically, I sought to determine how and if performing gender influenced identity. The last theme of construction and negotiation of identity describes how the participants negotiated their individual identity with gender role expectations. In some cases, the participants actively managed their gender performance to suit the gender roles while maintaining and hiding their gender identity. At other times, the participants adopted those roles as identities, thus constructing new, complex gender identities.

To illustrate the individual differences and complexities of each of the themes, Arlene's narrative is described below. A summary of these themes as revealed in the experiences of the other research participants is included in the appendix.

Arlene: The Welder

Act 1: Gender Socialization External to the Faculty Work Environment

One of the major themes that emerged from the narratives of the women faculty members is the prominence of gender socialization external to faculty work. Because Arlene worked primarily in the welding industry before entering faculty work, she had very prominent socializing experiences related to her gender and to her chosen career as a welder. These experiences are related both to her token status as a woman welder and to the masculinity of the construction profession.

The majority of commercial welding is completed on construction sites. Heavy machinery, cranes, building materials, and large groups of men populate the sites. On these construction sites, masculinity is the norm. Arlene explained that sexually explicit jokes, toughness, and physical prowess were common traits that the men expressed. To survive in this masculine culture, Arlene initially conformed. She adopted a tough and unemotional persona.

> In nontraditional, you can't show your weaknesses. If some guy said something to me at work and he knows I went to my car and cried that would be the end of it, I would get it twice as bad. I have to say, "That is all you have, can't you come up with something better than that. My Mama tells better jokes." I have to jump in their face, but then I would go to my car and call my mom and cry. I would act tough. I always had that wall. I have to be so tough. When I was younger, I definitely played the role. I was very physical.

While Arlene was working on the construction sites, she put on a performance of toughness. She felt as if she had to maintain that role or "I would get it twice as bad." What is troubling is the expectation of abuse that Arlene felt she would encounter if she did not act tough. Crying in front of the men was not an option. She had to form a wall, despite the emotional strain that these encounters caused.

Arlene, however, found that acting tough and performing masculinity was not the long-term solution to working in the masculine culture. Arlene explained that the other male workers began to reject her when she intruded on the masculine sphere. They would criticize her for "showing off" if she welded too well. Arlene explained, "There was a lot of pressure to act like everyone else. The men would sometimes get angry that I would weld better. Arlene is showing off." In addition, the men were verbally abusive to the women who acted masculine, calling them gay or butch. Arlene began to intentionally adopt a new persona that acknowledged her femininity and allowed her male colleagues to view her as submissive.

> When I worked on the job, I would sometimes act feminine. One day I cut my finger. It was a little cut. I started screaming and men came to help. They said look at Arlene, she is acting like a girl. I would tell my mom about how the men would treat me. She said, "Let the work speak for itself." I would let the men carry the big pipes.

Arlene also altered her appearance to appear as more feminine. "I would go to the job with my hair done and at that time it was $25 a shot. I would go three days a week, that was $75 a week and that's just to keep my hair groomed."

From the moment that Arlene began working in the welding profession, she encountered the masculine culture of the industry and had to contend with navigating gender dynamics. To appease her male colleagues and to prevent further backlash, Arlene adopted an intentional work persona that combined the qualities of femininity and masculinity. She continued to work on the construction sites successfully by overperforming femininity in an all-male sphere. These experiences of learning her position in relation to societal expectations of a welder and her experiences in the construction sites are precursors to her life as a faculty member. Arlene takes these experiences and strategies into her faculty work.

Act 2: Organizational Culture Socialization

In contrast to the gender role and norm socialization that occurred outside of the college, Arlene experienced socialization into new gender roles and norms within the college. At times, the nature of the gender roles mirrored stereotypical societal expectations of the women's role, such as the role of women as departmental caretakers. And at times, the gender roles mirrored stereotypical masculine roles as reflected in how the hypermasculinity of the welding industry overlapped into the welding classroom. Arlene also experienced challenges by students and discrimination in a hypermasculine classroom culture.

Arlene works in the construction technologies (CT) department within Vocational Community College. The CT department is one of the largest on campus, with nine different disciplines, yet Arlene is one of the two women in the department. Arlene's office and classroom space serve as a metaphor for the masculinity of the department. Her office is located within the larger welding shop behind a caged door that slides back to reveal several old, metal desks and file cabinets. The space is antiquated, lacking any technology or semblance of an era dominated by computers. The smell of burning metal pervades the space, and the machines roar loudly while sparks fly, dancing in the air. The only feminine symbols in the office and shop are the little metal hearts that are scattered across Arlene's desk. As the only woman in this masculine space, Arlene often finds that her male colleagues expect her to play the typical women's role. Arlene explains, "I will be at a meeting and be forced to take notes. I tell them, not me. I am a welder. I don't know how to write. It is the idea of why would you just pick me. Because they see me, you know [as the only woman]." She continues:

> So, "Arlene why don't you make the coffee?" Once in a while that is just the way it happens, and I don't know if they were trying to be malicious. It is just for so long that this was the women's role. You take the notes, you make the coffee. If the offices are dirty, you clean off my desk. What does this have to do with me teaching? They will expect you to teach the classroom work. And they will do the hands-on. You are teaching blueprints because, quote unquote, females could always read books. It happens.

During the few meetings that Arlene attends each year, she is often the only woman. She finds that she is expected to play the typical woman's secretarial role. Because Arlene learned on the construction sites how to manipulate a scene in which she is expected to perform the woman's role, she has developed strategies to counteract those expectations. Arlene uses humor to resist the expectation that she should be the meeting secretary. Despite the resistance, this experience also shapes Arlene's perception of the departmental culture. Faculty culture is not too dissimilar from the construction sites; she is still expected to perform the woman's role.

The culture of the classroom is another site where Arlene became socialized into the gender dynamics of faculty work. The student population is primarily male and often mimics many male-dominated cultures. In any given semester, Arlene will have only one or two women students in her class, and these women students are often marginalized by the dominating male majority. During her first day of teaching, Arlene encountered a startling and memorable experience that shaped her perception of the difference between teaching generally and teaching welding specifically:

> The first day I went to teach a class I had on some good 3-inch heels, pumps with a suit, Ann Taylor or something. A silk blouse and it was a light silver. My nails were done. It was my first day of class, and I was 21, and the students came in saying, "Where is the instructor?" I said I was the instructor and they said, "You. It is not bad enough that they gave us a lady but you have on heels." There was this one guy I will never forget. I was at Urban College. He was Hispanic and said, "I know this is . . . [name of college] so they just gave us anybody, but it is bad enough that they go and give us a lady and she has the nerve to have on a skirt." The whole class, 30 something students, just laughed and I was about to cry. I was thinking this was not in the book of techniques of teaching. The teacher did not tell me they were going to act like this. I was talking, and they were still laughing. I was writing my name and passing out papers, they were still laughing. My voice was going down; it is cracking and in my head I'm thinking God please help me through this. I never came in a skirt again.

This is one of the most startling and blatant narratives in this study, because it illustrates how one experience within the context of the college can alter behavior. Despite Arlene's experience on the construction sites and her understanding of gender dynamics within the welding industry, she believed that the teaching profession would not have the same dynamics. She was clearly mistaken and quickly corrected. The impact of this experience cannot be overstated. It was this one experience that led to Arlene permanently altering her performance. Arlene has a particular uniform in the welding shop at Vocational Community College. She wears a black, long-sleeve shirt to cover her arms from the dancing sparks that fall just to the right of her as she sculpts and bonds two pieces of hard steel. Looking closely, there are small holes in her shirt where sparks have landed. Her pants and shoes are black and look comfortable on her six-foot-two frame. Arlene often shuffles around the shop with a strong, determined, and unforgettable presence. Arlene's appearance is masculine and understated to prevent her gender from being a distraction as she teaches highly masculine male students.

In the context of the classroom, students often question Arlene and challenge her authority and credibility. To maintain respect and repress challenges from the students, Arlene feels that she has to be tough and stern. When asked if she acts differently at work than at home, she explains, "Yes, when I work I tend to be more stern because of what I do. At home, I tend to play the clown and I think that I am more myself there than at work. I am playful and easygoing." Arlene has often had students challenge her abilities as a welder and her authority as an instructor. She states, "You have to be good because the students will challenge you." In the classroom, Arlene speaks in a strong tone, demands that students be on time and rejects late homework. She performs in a tough and stern manner by dominating the classroom, and she demonstrates her superior welding abilities during the laboratory portion of the course. The possibility of being challenged by her students has resulted in Arlene altering her work persona. Similar to acting tough on the construction sites, Arlene feels the need to be sterner in the classroom.

Arlene's gendered performance is not as simple as a stern persona. She creatively uses the gender norms of the classroom to motivate the students. Simply, Arlene has adapted her knowledge and experience to create a positive classroom environment. Arlene explains, "When I do a demo the students will say, 'He let a girl beat you.' Those guys will get over there and be determined to weld better than me. It does motivate them." Furthermore, Arlene has a board in her office that marks the progress of each student. When the male students see that a female student has exceeded them in skill and performance, the male students tend to work additional hours in the welding laboratory to exceed the progress of a female student. After all, the male students "can't be beat by a girl." Arlene purposefully uses these demonstrations to motivate the students, and, as she claims, the male students feel the need to do better than a girl to assert their masculinity.

Each of the two acts presented thus far illustrates how Arlene has come to understand the gender dynamics of the welding industry, the organization, the department, and the classroom. Her experiences with discrimination in the welding industry socialized her to understand her role as a female welder and to understand the expectations of women faculty members in a male-dominated department. In addition, the gender dynamics within each of these cultures often overlapped. The masculine culture of the welding trade, for example, was represented in the classroom. Arlene's perceptions have led to an intentional gender performance that combines many of the qualities of masculinity and femininity. The process of constructing a performance is not linear. An experience alone, for example, does not directly result in a new or altered gendered performance. Rather, it is the process of coming to understand gender dynamics and norms and how each of these subjectivities is valued within the specific context. This process is constantly occurring as gender norms are reconstructed from each experience. Arlene's hybrid performance was constructed from her initial experiences in the welding profession, but also by those experiences within the context of the college. Her performances, however, did not just occur as the temporary adoption of a persona. As Act 3 illustrates, her performances were constantly negotiated with identity.

Act 3: Negotiation and Construction of Identity

Within the theory of performativity, gender does not exist outside of the performance; rather, gender identities are constituted within the performances. Individuals are continuously refining and recreating their gender identity by performing gender. Arlene intentionally constructs her performance. She uses techniques such as crying on the job site when she gets a cut to manipulate the gender dynamics of the culture. Often, these techniques are meant to prevent backlash, but each time she makes the decision to perform, she reflects on the relationship between the performance and her identity.

> Sometimes, I have to be a little more tough because I can't betray that role. I am not going to say that I like teddy bears. They already know that I am kinda girly. I have the nails, but I would not tell them that I cry at Disney movies, no way. I am in a role where if I was to actually always be me, I would not get any respect. Of course, I think that women have to play the role.

Arlene makes it a point to mention that she considers herself feminine. As she states, the students already know that she is "kinda girly." However, she believes that she has to play a tough role, and that role must be upheld. Importantly, the tough performance is not congruent with Arlene's identity as a woman. To negotiate those conflicting identities, she uses symbols to represent her femininity; her desk is cluttered with pictures of roses and hearts. She proudly displays a metal heart with a welding line down the middle and has pasted Mickey Mouse stickers on her black welding mask. Yet, Arlene relinquishes her true self and hides her emotions from the students.

When Arlene was beginning her welding career, she often faced the difficult negotiation of her identity as a woman and the expectations of the masculine industry.

> Welding, I knew that I had to prove that I was a lady, a girl. I realize it had nothing to do with my femininity. I was always a lady. I could go home and take those clothes off and put those other clothes on and still be a lady. It was not about me proving my womanhood, my femininity. It was about me being good at what I do. My mother would tell me that I did not have to prove myself, my work would speak for itself. As a person, you know who and what you are. That is what's important. Whether or not they think you are masculine or feminine, my mother said you have to be a confident woman and confident in your femininity.

To negotiate her hybrid gender performance with her identity, Arlene decided that she had two spheres of life. She had the job site and home. She separated her performance on the job site and her identity as a woman.

> I always tell my female students that you don't have to lose your femininity. If you lose it, it was going to go anyways. Don't blame it on the trade. You decided not to have it. In class someone may perceive that I am not very feminine because my mind is not on my femininity. It is on doing the job. Outside I am a female. I am a woman. I like my trade, but I want to look pretty and I should not lose that when I go home. You're still a feminine woman, I tell my students.

Her masculine performance became a reflection of the culture and not a reflection of her internal feelings as a woman. After all, she could come home and put those feminine clothes on. However, there are long-term implications to maintaining two identities and a hybrid performance.

In a few of the individual cases, the participants would reflect on how their performance has altered their identities. Arlene has been intentionally performing multiple genders throughout her career. She was once the welder who had her hair and nails groomed. Arlene intentionally separated her work identity from her internal gender identity. After 25 years of separating her identities, they have begun to overlap, constructing a new identity.

> When I would go to work I would be very well groomed. I think that happens consciously sometimes. We do it, and I think unconsciously we do it. Here I am more relaxed and lazy with my legs all over, with no posture, with my belly sticking out. I become the couch potato. But in church, even if I wore sweats, I would have matching tennis shoes and socks. Here my nails look bad, but on Friday I am going to the shop. Here the masculine part of me comes out. Now that you say it, I think that subconsciously, you just carry yourself differently in different places.

For most of Arlene's career, her masculine identity was just a performance, a mask that she intentionally put on while working. Yet, she has realized that masculinity has become a part of her identity and that it just comes out more when she is at work. Agreeing with Butler's concepts of performativity, Arlene's performance is constructing her identity. The construction of a new identity is evident when observing Arlene in the context of her role as an instructor. She dresses masculine, physically moves in a masculine manner, and communicates with the students using a serious tone and dominating demeanor. Arlene's gender identity has changed in such a manner that she has unintentionally constructed an identity that reflects a hybrid gender performance.

Over the span of 25 years, Arlene has learned to actively alter her front-stage performances to reflect the requirements of the context. Arlene often uses a combination of masculine and feminine qualities to prevent confrontation and backlash. She began to construct a hybrid performance in the welding industry to subvert criticism and discrimination while maintaining the physical requirements of the job. In her roles as a faculty member, Arlene quickly learned that similar gender dynamics apply to the welding classroom. Arlene became the token woman expected to perform the stereotypical women's role and often faced challenges from her male students. Again, Arlene used her hybrid performance to succeed and ultimately motivate her students. Performing gender and negotiating identity alongside that performance led to the construction of a work persona that transcended the backstage and actively became a part of Arlene's gender identity. Arlene's experience may appear to rely heavily on her role as a vocational instructor in a community college setting. However, all of the participants in this study, including those in more traditional academic disciplines, experienced similar gender performances. The specific nature of the organizational socialization and the specific gender roles differed, but the need to negotiate gender roles and norms with identity was consistent.

Discussion

Arlene's story and the narratives of the other participants illustrate several aspects of gender roles and norms within a community college setting. First, the roles and norms that women faculty members perform in the college are similar to those identified in the literature. The women faculty members in this study said that they are expected to perform the "mom" roles by maintaining an emotional and supportive connection to the students. Students often expected them to adhere to the traditional caretaker roles by listening to their problems and helping them succeed. Sara, an English instructor, attempted to reject the caretaker role by noting on her syllabi that she does not listen to stories by students. She explained that this addendum prevents students from automatically perceiving her as a maternal figure—a role that she did not see as part of her identity. In addition, faculty colleagues expected the women faculty to perform the "glue work"—taking meeting notes and organizing social activities—of the department. Diane, a theater arts and English instructor, noted that the women faculty members in her department were consistently called on to manage committees and organize social events. The definition of roles and norms, however, was highly dependent on the specific subculture, and the roles were often complex performances that incorporated a variety of gender stereotypes. The gender role expectations changed from the classroom, for example, to the department meetings. Whereas Arlene used humor to mitigate the expectations that she should perform the secretarial role in department meetings, she created a hybrid masculine and feminine persona in the classroom. In this regard, the women faculty members had to develop sophisticated performances that they are able to change from one moment to the next.

Second, organizational discourses and social practices diffuse throughout the college to define gender roles and norms via social interactions with colleagues and students. Arlene interacted with colleagues who expected her to carry out the role as the departmental secretary and caretaker. In the classroom, the students challenged her to maintain a masculine and authoritarian welding style while paradoxically expecting her to remain a caring and compassionate female teacher. Challenges to credibility by students and colleagues were often experienced by many of the research participants. Rosa, an architecture faculty member, was physically reprimanded by a colleague when she attempted to question his authority. Sara and Susan found that their credibility was often challenged by colleagues who assumed that they were "catty" and jealous women. The social interactions with colleagues and students served as a form of regulatory power that defined and limited the performances of the women faculty members. For when they veered from the expected gender roles, regulatory power in the form of challenges to their credibility and negative reactions from colleagues limited the agency of the women to choose other gender roles. It is important to note, however, that this study also illustrated the importance of external influences in interpreting gender roles within the college. For example, Susan, like Arlene, used her experience in the airline trade unions as a point of comparison with her college environment and as a source of strategies she could use to succeed in her department. The participants' previous experiences and their perceptions of faculty work served as points of reference that helped them interpret gender roles in the context of the college.

Third, adhering to the gender roles and norms goes beyond simply performing a role that is external to identity. To continue performing her gender in relationship to culturally defined gender roles, Arlene actively negotiated her identity with her performances. Using both characteristics of femininity and masculinity, Arlene created a hybrid performance that created a positive classroom environment and an identity that helped her negotiate the hypermasculine culture of the classroom and department. This hybrid performance, also practiced by many of the study participants, was an intentional act, yet the constant repetition, as predicted in performativity theory, recreated her gender identity to include those masculine qualities. To use a Goffman (1959) term, Arlene's front stage performances blurred with her backstage performance; her intentionally constructed performances became a part of her identity. In addition, the unintentional adoption of these masculine qualities legitimated the gender roles regardless of the fact that they were initially incongruent to Arlene's expectation of faculty work and her gender identity. The construction of gender roles that adopt culturally and contextually defined identities has the potential to hide and naturalize inequitable practices.

Contribution and Implications

This study makes several contributions to research on gender roles and women faculty members. The first contribution of this study is the identification of power. Several studies have examined identity issues among women and minority faculty members, concluding that they often face internal identity conflicts as they attempt to negotiate the hegemonic culture with their "minority" race and gender status (Johnsrud & Sadao, 1998; Turner et al., 1999). However, these studies are limited in their identification of more intangible power structures that continue to reinforce traditional gender roles. By focusing on how individual faculty members perform gender, rather then conceptualizing gender as a fixed and marked (or embodied) identity, new forms of power that are contextually specific and that function internally are made evident. For example, the ways in which regulatory power changes in each context and in each culture (i.e., department versus classroom cultures) are made evident using a performativity conceptualization of identity.

The second contribution made by this line of research lies in its capacity to uncover the importance of the impact of gender roles on individual identity. Individuals do not just perform gender roles, such as performing in a maternal and caretaking manner as suggested in the research. Rather, women faculty members, by virtue of the existence of these gender roles, adopt, negotiate, and often construct new gender identities. This finding has implications for current research on work and family balance, on the matriculation of women and minority-group members into faculty work, and on how women and minority faculty members experience the academic culture. By providing alternative explanations of how gender roles create identity conflicts, we may better understand how and why women faculty members continue to experience conflicts with academic culture and why work and family conflicts remain a prevalent issue in higher education institutions. In addition, the adoption of gender roles was found to hide potential inequities. The participants conformed to and thus accepted oftentimes discriminatory gender roles by constructing new hybrid identities. Understanding how gender roles become normalized has the potential to alter examinations of inequitable organizational practices via organizational informants.

Third, this study conceptualizes gender roles as performances that express the social norms within an organization. This new conceptualization of gender roles helps deconstruct how gender identity is altered by culturally specific gender roles. Performativity helps make evident the relationship between identity and gender roles, regulatory power, and the ways in which gender roles are made legitimate in an organizational setting. Exposing the ways in which gender roles are reproduced in gender performances has implications for postsecondary institutions, and acknowledging that women faculty members continuously perform many traditional gender roles has implications for the ways in which faculty work is distributed. If women faculty members are expected to continue to perform the role of maternal and emotional worker, they are relegated into more service-oriented work that distracts from their primary roles as teachers. Although causal linkages are not possible, one of the reasons that we continue to see an underrepresentation of women at the full-professor rank may be the presence of these traditional gender roles. Institutions of higher education need to examine and deconstruct faculty work and the possibility of work being aligned with gender and gender roles.

The implications of this study are most evident in the specific discourses and practices that diffuse throughout the institution to define gender roles and norms. For example, in social interactions with colleagues and students, women community college faculty members may be placed in traditional women's roles and may often face discriminatory practices. Institutions need to consider the impact of those social interactions as well as how they can address biases that lead to these interactions. What are the implications for job satisfaction, the retention of women faculty members, and their productivity? Similarly, why do colleagues and students continue this behavior, and how does the institution tolerate these actions and biases? Finally, gender performances and the construction of new identities hide and naturalize inequitable practices in higher education. For many decades, institutions and scholars of higher education have documented inequitable practices (i.e., sexual harassment, salary inequities, etc.) in an attempt to create more equitable educational institutions. Yet, inequities along the lines of gender perpetuate.

Institutions of higher education and scholars need to look beyond specific practices to understand how these inequities are perpetuated by the very people who experience the discrimination. This is not to suggest that we should "blame the victim," but, rather, that community colleges need to consider and deconstruct how they perpetuate strict notions of gender through discourses and social practices and how these gender roles become an inextricable part of academe and the identities of faculty members.

APPENDIX

Research Participants and Themes

	Gender Socialization Experiences External to the College	Organizational Cultural Socialization	Construction and Negotiation of Identity
Arlene	Arlene's experiences on construction sites led to the adoption of a hybrid gender performance that combines the qualities of femininity and masculinity. Her success on the construction sites was determined by her ability to perform femininity in an all-male sphere.	Arlene was expected to play the typical woman's secretarial role in the context of the department. She experienced challenges to her credibility by students.	Arlene negotiated her identity by using symbols to represent her femininity while acting masculine. She developed two separate gender identities—her performance on the job site and her identity as a woman. Her constructed work persona eventually became a part of her gender identity.
Mary	Mary's experiences in the food industry, a physical and challenging profession that demands toughness, led to a masculine performance. She believes that success is determined by a need to be tough and strong and that women must conform to the male norm. Success in the food industry is primarily an outcome of her willingness to conform to the masculine culture of the food industry.	Mary expected to continue the same masculine roles in the college kitchen. Her behavior was reinforced by two male colleagues who mentored her.	Mary readily adopted masculine behaviors. She negotiated her sexuality contrary to the cultural norm. Masculinity became a part of Mary's identity.
Rosa	Rosa experienced a gender-inequitable architecture culture. She was advised to not have children, and she experienced gender and race discrimination at a national conference. She decided that her femininity is an integral part of her identity and made a conscious decision to perform gender in a feminine manner.	Rosa experienced blatant discrimination and challenges to her credibility by male faculty and students. Gender and race were used to subvert her activism and assertiveness in changing the architecture program and the department. She also experienced isolation, both physically and symbolically, as a woman in a male-dominated department.	Rosa negotiated the masculine norms by resisting the traditional role of women and embracing her femininity by making it an important part of her teaching style. She constructed a hybrid performance that she used to establish credibility among students and colleagues. Rosa did not find that her serious and distant persona conflicted with her gender identity.

APPENDIX (cont.)

Research Participants and Themes

	Gender Socialization Experiences External to the College	Organizational Cultural Socialization	Construction and Negotiation of Identity
Susan	Susan's experience in a highly masculine trade led to a hybrid performance that combines both masculine and feminine qualities. She acted in submissive (a stereotypically feminine trait) and masculine ways, using crass language and masculine mannerisms.	Susan was expected to perform in typical feminine roles, such as providing the "emotional work," and her dress became delineated along gender lines. Women were expected to dress professionally, and if they chose to dress more casually, they jeopardized the respect in which they were held.	Susan did not actively negotiate her identity, but involuntarily developed a work persona that used the techniques she learned in the trades. Her constructed identity occurred earlier in her experiences in the trades.
Sara	Sara experienced strong influences from family gender socialization. She constructed a hybrid gender that combined assertiveness—she is known as the dictator—with a demeanor and physical appearance that is feminine.	Sara felt expected to maintain a feminine appearance. Her lack of experience in other work cultures led her to view many gendered practices as "normal." She practiced impression management to prevent being perceived as a jealous woman.	Sara did not actively negotiate identity; she found that her identity was congruent with cultural expectations. She acknowledged a hybrid performance that was shaped by reactions both in and out of the workplace.
Diane	Diane's experiences in previous instructor positions led to an understanding of the importance of dress and the power of male students. She emphasized her focus on appearance.	Diane felt expected to perform the "glue work" of the department. She viewed gender inequities as a subcultural (departmental) issue. Student infatuations resulted in altering her gendered performance.	Diane constructed two gender identities that existed separately. She separated her gender identity from her gender performances and refused to acknowledge that she may act masculine.

Notes

1. In a study of agricultural female leaders, Pini (2005) found that these women perform a "third sex"—one that encompasses both masculine and feminine characteristics. The female managers amplified normative traits of femininity, which include being communicative, encouraging relationship building, and being people-oriented. They also had to maintain the proper masculine traits associated with agriculture—being objective, desexualized, and rational, all in addition to being unencumbered by household duties.

2. The structure of a play is intentional. Acts in a play assume a temporality; the second act follows the first, and so on. Many of the stories do have linearity. Often, experiences external to the work environment occur before the participants enter faculty work. Other external experiences occur while working as a faculty member, particularly for those faculty members who have strong external ties, such as consulting work. Also, a play is conducted on a stage in front of an audience. Many actors are involved in the crucial socializing scenes that serve as a true and metaphoric audience policing the gender performances. Finally, a play has both a front stage and a backstage. The front stage is where the performance is conducted in front of the audience, whereas the backstage is behind the curtain where performances are practiced and prepared. It is in the realm of the backstage that performances are reflected on, intentionally constructed, and negotiated with identity.

References

Acker, J. (1990). Hierarchies, jobs, bodies: A theory of gendered organizations. *Gender & Society, 4,* 139-158.

Acker, S., & Feuerverger, G. (1996). Doing good and feeling bad: The work of women university teachers. *Cambridge Journal of Education, 26,* 401–422.

Aisenberg, N., & Harrington, M. (1988). *Women of academe: Outsiders in the sacred grove.* Amherst, MA: University of Massachusetts Press.

Alvesson, M., & Due Billing,Y. (1997). *Understanding gender and organisation.* London: Sage.

Amey, M., & Twombly, S. (1992). Re-visioning leadership in community colleges. *Review of Higher Education, 15,* 125–150.

Armenti, C. (2004). May babies and posttenure babies: Maternal decisions of women professors. *Review of Higher Education, 27,* 211–231.

Bailyn, L. (1993). *Breaking the mold: Women, men, and time in the new corporate world.* New York: Free Press.

Bailyn, L. (2003). Academic careers and gender equity: Lessons learned from MIT. *Gender, Work, and Organization, 10*(2), 137–153.

Bellas, M. L. (1997). Disciplinary differences in faculty salaries: Does gender bias play a role? *Journal of Higher Education, 68,* 299–321.

Benschop, Y., & Brouns, M. (2003). Crumbling ivory towers: Academic organizing and its gender effects. *Gender, Work, and Organization, 10,* 194–212.

Bird, S., Litt, J., & Wang, Y. (2004). Creating status of women reports: Institutional housekeeping as "women's work." *NWSA Journal, 16,* 194–206.

Blackwell, J. E. (1996). Faculty issues: The impact on minorities. In C. Turner, M. Garcia, A. Nora, & L. I. Rendon (Eds.), *Racial and ethnic diversity in higher education* (pp. 315–326). Needham Heights, MA: Simon & Schuster Custom Publishing.

Boice, R. (1993). New faculty involvement for women and minorities. *Research in Higher Education, 34,* 291–333.

Bronstein, P., Black, L., Pfenning, J. L., & White, A. (1986). Getting academic jobs. *American Psychologist, 41,* 318–322.

Bronstein, P., Black, L., Pfenning, J. L., & White, A. (1987). Stepping onto the academic career ladder: How are women doing? In B. A. Gutek & L. Larwood. (Eds.), *Women's career development* (pp. 110–128). Newbury Park, CA: Sage.

Bronstein, P., & Farnsworth, L. (1998). Gender differences in faculty experiences of interpersonal climate and processes for advancement. *Research in Higher Education, 39,* 557–585.

Butler, J. (1990). *Gender trouble: Feminism and the subversion of identity.* New York, NY: Routledge.

Butler, J. (2004). *Undoing gender.* New York: Routledge.

Carspecken, P. F. (1996). *Critical ethnography in educational research.* New York: Routledge.

Chliwniak, L. (1997). *Higher education leadership: Analyzing the gender gap* (ASHE-ERIC Higher Education Report, Vol. 25, No. 4). Washington, D.C.: The George Washington University, Graduate School of Education and Human Development.

Clark, B. R. (1972). The organizational saga in higher education. *Administrative Science Quarterly, 17*, 178–184.

Dallimore, E. J. (2003). Memorable messages as discursive formations: The gendered socialization of new university faculty. *Women's Studies in Communication, 26*, 214–265.

Dey, E. L., Korn, J., & Sax, L. J. (1996). Betrayed by the academy: The sexual harassment of women college faculty. *Journal of Higher Education, 67*, 149–173.

Elliott, M. (2003). Work and family role strain among university employees. *Journal of Family and Economic Issues, 24*(2), 157–187.

Ely, R. (1994). The effects of organizational demographics and social identity on relationships among professional women. *Administrative Science Quarterly, 39*, 203–238.

Ely, R. J. (1995). The power in demography: Women's social constructions of gender identity at work. *Academy of Management Journal, 38*, 589–634.

Ely, R. J., & Meyerson, D. E. (2000). *Theories of gender in organizations: A new approach to organizational analysis and change* (CGO working paper, No. 8). Boston, MA: Center for Gender in Organizations, Simmons Graduate School of Management.

Eveline, J. (2004). *Ivory basement leadership: Power and invisibility in the changing university.* Crawley, Western Australia: University of Western Australia Press.

Goffman, E. (1959). *The presentation of self in everyday life.* Garden City, NY: Doubleday.

Halford, S., & Leonard, P. (2001). *Gender, power and organizations.* New York: Palgrave.

Johnsrud, L. K., & Sadao, K. C. (1998). The common experience of "Otherness": Ethnic and racial minority faculty. *Review of Higher Education, 21*, 315–342.

Kanter, R. M. (1977). *Men and women of the corporation.* New York: Basic Books.

Kaye, M. (1995). Organizational myths and storytelling as communication management. *Journal of Australian and New Zealand Academy of Management, 1*, 1–13.

Knights, D., & Richards. W. (2003). Sex discrimination in UK academia. *Gender, Work and Organization, 10*, 213–238.

Martin, P. Y. (1996). Gendering and evaluating dynamics: Men, masculinities, and managements. In D. Collinson & J. Hearn (Eds.), *Men as managers, managers as men: Critical perspectives on men, masculinities, and managements* (pp. 186–209). London: Sage Publications.

Martin, P. Y. (2003). "Said and done" versus "saying and doing": Gendering practices, practicing gender at work. *Gender & Society, 17*, 343–366.

Merriam, S. B. (1988) *Case study research in education: A qualitative approach.* San Francisco: Jossey-Bass, Inc.

Olsson, S. (2002). Gendered heroes: Male and female self-representations of executive identity. *Women in Management Review, 17*, 142–150.

Pini, B. (2005). The third sex: Women leaders in Australian agriculture. *Gender, Work, and Organization, 12*, 73–88.

Rapoport, R., Bailyn, L., Kolb, D., Fletcher, J., Friedman, D., Eaton. S., et al. (1996). *Rethinking life and work: Toward a better future. Report to the Ford Foundation based on a collaborative research project with three corporations.* New York: Ford Foundation.

Reinharz, S. (1992). *Feminist methods in social research.* New York: Oxford University Press.

Riessman, C. (1993). *Narrative analysis.* Newbury Park, CA: Sage Publications.

Riger, S., Stokes, J., Raja, S., & Sullivan, M. (1997). Measuring perceptions of the work environment for female faculty. *Review of Higher Education, 21*, 63–78.

Rosser, S. (2002). Institutional barriers for women scientists and engineers: What four years of survey data of National Science Foundation POWRE awardees reveal. In J. DiGeorgio-Lutz (Ed.), *Women in higher education: Empowering change* (pp. 145–160). Westpost, CT: Praeger.

Sandler, B. R., & Shoop, R. J. (1997). *Sexual harassment on campus: A guide for administrators, faculty, and students.* Needham Heights, MA: Allyn & Bacon.

Spradley, J. (1979). *The ethnographic interview.* New York: Holt, Rinehart and Winston.

Stake, R. E. (1995). *The art of case study research.* Thousand Oaks, CA: Sage.

Stein, W. (1994). The survival of American Indian faculty. *Thought and Action: The National Education Association Higher Education Journal, 10*, 101–114.

Tedrow, B., & Rhoades, R. A. (1999). A qualitative study of women's experiences in community college leadership positions. *Community College Review, 27*(3), 1–18.

Tierney, W. G., & Bensimon, E. M. (1996). *Promotion and tenure: Community and socialization in academe.* Albany, NY: State University of New York Press.

Turner, C. S. V. (2002). Women of color in academe: Living with multiple marginality. *Journal of Higher Education, 73,* 74–93.

Turner, C. S. V., Myers, S. L., & Creswell, J. W. (1999). Exploring underrepresentation: The case of faculty of color in the Midwest. *Journal of Higher Education, 70,* 27–59.

Van Maanen, J. (1988). *Tales of the field: On writing ethnography.* Chicago: University of Chicago Press.

Winkler, J. (2000). Faculty reappointment, tenure, and promotion: Barriers for women. *Professional Geographer, 52,* 737–750.

Wolf-Wendel, L. & Ward, K. (2003). Future prospects for women faculty: Negotiating work and family. In B. Ropers-Huilman (Ed.), *Gendered futures in higher education: Critical perspectives for change* (pp. 111–134). Albany, NY: State University of New York Press.

Jaime Lester is an assistant professor in the Darden College of Education at Old Dominion University, Norfolk, Virginia.

CHAPTER 21

STRATEGIES FOR FACULTY-STUDENT ENGAGEMENT: HOW COMMUNITY COLLEGE FACULTY ENGAGE LATINO[1] STUDENTS*

BRENT D. CEJDA

RICHARD E. HOOVER
UNIVERSITY OF NEBRASKA–LINCOLN

Abstract. Student-faculty engagement has been identified as the best predictor of Latino student persistence (Hurtado & Carter, 1997). This study explores the strategies that community college faculty employ to engage Latino students. Findings indicate that knowledge, appreciation, and sensitivity to Hispanic cultures and an understanding of the preferred learning styles of Latino students are important considerations to establishing classroom environments that engage Latino students and, thus, facilitate their retention and academic success.

Introduction

The community college has been described as the pipeline for Latinos in higher education (Laden, 1992, 2001; Rendon & Nora, 1989). In Fall 2004, 59% of Hispanic undergraduate enrollment in the United States was at two-year institutions (Cook & Cordova, 2007). Community colleges, however, have struggled to improve overall retention, degree or certificate completion, and transfer rates (Bailey, Crosta, & Jenkins, 2006) and Latino community college students have historically had the lowest retention rates and highest transfer losses (Harvey, 2002; Rendon & Garza, 1996).

Student-faculty engagement has been identified as the best predictor of Latino student persistence (Hurtado & Carter, 1997). The Quality Education for Minorities Network (1997) found that among the institutions graduating the greatest numbers of minority students in mathematics, engineering, and science, most were able to identify a number of faculty members who were engaged with minority students outside of class and beyond their regular office hours. Other studies have found that faculty-student interaction positively influenced Latino students' degree aspirations and academic success (Colorado State Advisory Committee, 1995) or played an important role in the decision to transfer to a four-year institution (Brawer, 1995; Britt & Hirt, 1999).

---

[1]We use the terms Latino and Hispanic interchangeably in this article. Participants in this study also used the terms Chicano and Mexican-American.

*The TG Public Benefit Grant Program provided funding for this study. The opinions expressed in this report are those of the authors and do not necessarily represent the views of TG, its officers or employees. A previous version of this article was presented at the annual conference of the Association for the Study of Higher Education, Vancouver, British Columbia, Canada, November, 7, 2009.

Ewell (1997) argued for additional research on institutional and faculty practices that promote student learning in order to improve student learning. From this call, a number of studies have focused on self-reported student engagement behaviors. This line of inquiry has drawn from previous models of student persistence (Astin, 1993; Tinto, 1993), principles of good practice (Chickering & Gamson, 1987; Education Commission of the States, 1995), and studies of predictors of student retention (Pascarella & Terenzini, 1991; Stage & Hossler, 2000). From these efforts, two related initiatives have emerged. The National Survey of Student Engagement (NSSE) was established in 1998 and focuses on four-year colleges and universities. Recognizing the unique mission and student populations of two-year institutions, the Community College Survey of Student Engagement (CCSSE) was launched in 2001. Each of these initiatives has also begun to measure faculty expectations for student engagement, NSSE conducted a faculty survey in 2003 and CCSSE launched a faculty survey in 2008. From the initial NSSE faculty survey, Umbach and Wawrzynski (2005) found that the educational contexts that faculty created resulted in a positive effect on student learning and engagement and proposed five classroom practices that promote student success. These practices are briefly described in the following paragraph.

The first identified practice involves course-related interactions, faculty and students interacting in the classroom about matters and content related to the course. A positive relationship was also found between student learning and active and collaborative learning techniques. Involving students in their learning has contributed to their success in the classroom. The third practice, academic challenge, means more than simply requiring a significant amount of homework. Rather, the term refers to establishing standards for achievement that are, in part, consistent with prior academic preparation, but also provide a gentle push for students to achieve more than they think they can accomplish. Emphasizing higher-order cognitive activities also contributes to student success. Examples of higher-order activities include the use of course content, the application of theories or concepts, or a synthesis of materials from different courses to address issues directly related to students' interests and lives. The fifth practice, enriching educational activities, includes co-curricular involvement such as community service or service learning as well as practica, internships, and other culminating experiences.

As mentioned above, NSSE focuses on four-year institutions. Thus, there is a gap in the existing knowledge concerning the educational context established by community college faculty. The initial faculty survey conducted in conjunction with CCSSE (CCFSSE) included questions that provided the faculty perspective on student engagement. This perspective, however, is based on *what* occurs in the class. One of the CCFSSE questions is, "How often do students in your selected course section ask questions or contribute to class discussions?" A different perspective is *how* faculty draws students into active participation in the class. This different perspective asks, "What strategies do you use to elicit questions from students or to encourage their contributions to class discussions?" Given the importance of student-faculty engagement on the persistence of Latino students, our primary purpose in this study was to explore the strategies that community college faculty employ to engage Latino students in the classroom. A corollary purpose was to examine whether community college faculty use the same strategies identified by Umbach and Wawrzynski (2005) to create an educational context that promotes student engagement.

Methodology

This study was developed around two guiding questions:

1. What strategies do community college faculty use to engage Latino students in the classroom and thus facilitate their academic success?

2. Do community college faculty use the same strategies as four-year faculty to create classroom environments that promote student engagement?

We incorporated a multiple case study design to examine how community college faculty members created an educational context that facilitated the academic success of Latino students. Creswell (2008) indicated that although qualitative researchers usually are reluctant to generalize their results to other cases, multiple cases do allow for the researchers to make modest claims of generalizable results when they "... identify findings that are common to all cases using cross-case analysis" (p. 490).

To gain a broader perspective, we sought participating institutions on the basis of the three primary categories of community colleges: rural, suburban, and urban. In addition, the participating institutions have differing levels of Latino enrollments. These institutions are profiled below.

Rural Community College

Rural Community College (RCC) is a multi-campus community college serving 25 counties—an area of approximately 14,000 square miles with a population of more than 300,000. RCC describes itself as having three full-service campuses, three limited-service educational centers, and providing additional credit and non-credit educational opportunities throughout its service area through a variety of distance learning technologies. In the last decade, the Hispanic population in the RCC region has more than doubled. This fall, the kindergarten class in the public school system of the largest city with a full-service campus is almost 50% Hispanic. RCC is also beginning to see increased Latino enrollment. In the fall of 2006, 7% of the credit student population identified themselves as Hispanic representing a 100% increase over the past five years.

RCC offers 33 career and technical education programs requiring two years or less to complete. In 2005-06 RCC awarded 1,516 degrees, diplomas, and certificates in these career and technical programs. RCC also offers an academic transfer program, granting slightly more than 100 transfer degrees in 2005-06. In 2005-06, a non-duplicated headcount of slightly more than 13,500 students enrolled in credit courses, resulting in an FTE (based on 30 semester hours) of slightly more than 3,750.

Suburban Community College

Suburban Community College (SCC) is one of five comprehensive community colleges in a community college district that serves 1,400 square miles in two suburban counties of a major metropolitan statistical area. The main campus of SCC is in an unincorporated suburban area, the college has two additional educational centers and also provides online and hybrid distance education offerings. The vast majority of students at SCC are from a county that between the years 2000 and 2005 experienced an 11% increase in the Hispanic population. SCC is designated as a Hispanic-Serving Institution (HSI). In the fall of 2006, 31% of the student population at SCC was Hispanic, slightly less than the 37.5% Hispanic population in the primary county the institution serves.

SCC offers 23 career and technical education programs leading to 26 AAS degrees and 79 certificates and a university transfer program. In 2005-06, SCC awarded 610 associates degrees and 444 certificates. Based on a non-duplicated headcount of slightly more than 10,000, the FTE (based on 30 semester hours) in 2006-07 was slightly less than 4,900. The majority (60%) of SCC students are traditional aged (18-24) and more than two-thirds (68%) attend classes during the day.

Urban Community College

Urban Community College (UCC) is located in one of the largest metropolitan statistical areas in the United States, the fastest growing MSA in its state. UCC describes itself as having a main campus, three education centers, and also offers courses via the Internet. Between 1990 and 2004, the Hispanic population of the MSA has increased by approximately 80%. UCC is designated as a Hispanic Serving Institution (HSI). Currently the student population at UCC is 42% Hispanic, which is representative of the Hispanic population in the MSA.

The overwhelming majority (90%) of UCC students enter the institution with the intent to transfer to a baccalaureate institution. Transcripts reveal, however, that almost 60% of the degree recipients have completed some vocational courses. In 2006-07, UCC awarded 1,371 degrees and 643 certificates. Based on a non-duplicated headcount of slightly more than 19,850, the FTE (based on 30 semester hours) in 2006-07 was slightly more than 14,000. As the locations on the campus and centers are in close proximity to each other, students often attend multiple locations of UCC. Among the 2006-07 student population, 87.8% enrolled on the main campus, 29.3% enrolled at one of the three centers, and 12.5% completed courses via the Internet.

To assist in the logistical aspects of the study, we established a relationship with an institutional contact, an instructional administrator, at each of the three community colleges. We described the research project to the institutional contact, assuring the anonymity of the faculty who would participate in interviews and the steps we would take to also protect the identity of the institution. These institutional contacts helped us communicate with the college president to determine if the college was willing to participate in the study. We approached four community colleges, with three agreeing to participate. After the institution agreed to participate, we asked the institutional contacts to identify and provide contact information for 15 faculty members who were considered "effective" in engaging Latino students in the classroom, thus facilitating their academic success; but we allowed each institution to establish their definition of effective. We asked the institutional contact to seek nominations from a variety of constituencies: students, staff members, faculty, and administrators at the college. After receiving the nominations, we sent each possible participant a letter asking if he/she was willing to be interviewed as part of this project and providing the necessary information to RSVP to the researchers. Individuals who agreed to be interviewed received a packet of information concerning this project that included: an introductory letter, a consent form that fully informed them of the purpose and the process of the research, and sample questions similar to those used during the interview. Our goal was to conduct a minimum of 12 interviews at each respective community college. We completed a total of 41 interviews, 14 at RCC and UCC respectively and 13 at SCC.

At the beginning of each interview, the interviewees were asked to provide some basic information concerning their involvement on their college campus. As shown in Table 1, 37 of the 41 (90%) individuals we interviewed held faculty positions and one person held a combined faculty/professional staff position. Each of the three administrators we interviewed previously held faculty positions and was nominated based on experiences. In terms of faculty status, the individuals we interviewed overwhelmingly held or had held a full-time faculty appointment (35 out of 41, 88%) but four current full-time faculty indicated that their initial employment had been as an adjunct

TABLE 1

Interviewee Demographics

	Rural College	Suburban College	Urban College	Total
Position				
Faculty/Instructor	13	10	14	37
Administrator/Staff	1	2		3
Faculty/Staff		1		1
Faculty Status				
Full-time	13	10	13	36
Part-time	1	3	1	5
Length of Service				
1-5	7	2	4	13
6-10	3	3	6	12
11-15	2	3	0	5
16-20	1	1		2
21-25	1	1	1	3
26+		3	3	6

TABLE 2

Instructional Areas of Interviewees

Discipline	RCC	SCC	UCC
Math/Science	4	3	—
Social Science	4	1	5
Career/Vocational	5	1	3
Fine Arts/Humanities	2	5	8
Developmental	5	7	3

with subsequent full-time employment. The length of service presented in the table represents the years of service at the participating colleges. In many cases, the participants had additional years of experience at other educational institutions.

We also asked faculty to identify the number of sections in the respective disciplines they were teaching during the semester of the interview. As shown in Table 2, a breadth in courses and disciplines was represented among the participants. While many of the faculty members taught multiple sections of the same class, others taught three to five different courses.

We were also interested in determining if the respondents had opportunities to interact with students outside of the classroom by serving as an advisor or the sponsor of a club or organization. Three of the respondents at RCC, eight of the respondents at SCC, and five of the respondents at UCC indicated that they were currently serving as sponsors of clubs or organizations. Eight of these individuals were sponsoring organizations related to cultural identity and five individuals were sponsoring organizations related to academic disciplines.

Prior to the scheduled campus visits, the participants were contacted via e-mail to arrange a time to conduct the interview. The interviews were conducted one-on-one in an office or conference room provided by the institution or in the interviewees' offices. At the beginning of the interviews the participants were asked if they had read the consent form, offered the opportunity to ask questions about the study, and then were asked to sign the consent form. The interviews were conducted over a span of seven months during the 2007-2008 academic year. All interviews were audio recorded and coupled with field notes as supplementary information.

The interviews were conducted using a structured interview guide as well as probes for each of the questions. Interview questions were developed from the NSSE and CCSSE faculty surveys and followed the guiding questions of the study. The probes could either be a further explanation of the question asked or a request for further explanation. To protect the anonymity of participants, we assigned each interviewee a code and identified them only by that code. We conducted one focus group session with 11 individuals to pilot the interview questions and made slight modifications to questions that were not clear or did not illicit the information the question was intended to gather.

A professional transcriptionist converted the audio recordings to written transcripts. We started the analysis process by independently coding eight transcripts and then met to compare our findings. We coded the remaining transcripts independently and held subsequent sessions to discuss and reach consensus regarding the analyses. Creswell (2008) explained the coding process as the step where researchers:

> . . . make sense out of text data, divide it into text or image segments, label the segments with codes, examine the codes for overlap and redundancy, and collapse these codes into broad themes. Also in this process you will select specific data to use and disregard other data that do not specifically provide evidence for your themes. (p. 251)

The researchers used both *in vivo* codes as well as lean coding. *In vivo* coding uses words or phrases directly taken from the transcripts. For lean coding, the researcher only assigns a few codes to large amounts of material (p. 252).

According to Creswell (2008) "describing and developing themes from the data consists of answering the major research questions and forming an in-depth understanding of the central phenomena through description and thematic development" (p. 254). We first describe cultural aspects of Latino students and their preferred learning styles. Common themes regarding the classroom environment that emerged from our analyses are provided and we conclude with consideration of whether the community college setting is similar to the activities described by Umbach and Wawrzynski (2005).

Culture Matters

The three participating community colleges are in geographic areas that have experienced significant growth in Hispanic populations. Although each respective community college indicated attempts to increase Latino representation among the administration, faculty, and staff, the majority of faculty are white non-Hispanic. The community college faculty we interviewed stressed that "culture matters," and pointed to knowledge, appreciation, and sensitivity to Hispanic culture as the key component to successfully engaging Latino students. As Torres (2006) pointed out, "students do not leave their cultural values at the door" (p. 316).

Family commitment is a characteristic common to most Hispanic cultures (Griggs & Dunn, 1996) and the responsibility to both immediate and extended family was evident in the stories that were shared with us. In explaining the importance of the family in Latino culture, Rendon and Valadez (1993) illustrated that financial support is a primary aspect of commitment to family. In analyzing the transcripts of interviews, we found an "order of importance" with the family considered as most important, employment as next important, and participating in post-secondary education a distant third. In other words, the majority of faculty indicated that Latino students are reluctant to place education over family and work. We were struck by the number of comments about Latino males who had demonstrated the ability to be successful in college, but left because of the need to provide financial support for their extended family. In addition, males at RCC and UCC tended to pursue vocational programs, based on the need for employment and income. The examples we heard matched previous research regarding the selection of fields of study (McGlynn, 2004; Rendon & Valadez, 1993) and challenges to persistence and transfer to four-year institutions (Pew Hispanic Center/Kaiser Family Foundation, 2004; Rendon, Justiz, & Resta, 1988).

A second cultural aspect that emerged from the transcripts was that of community—helpfulness, cooperation, and collaboration. Faculty participants explained that they often found Latino students would turn to each other for help rather than approach the instructor. Agencies that work with immigrant Hispanic populations have found that prior negative experiences in the country of origin often leave Hispanics wary of authority figures (McMahon, 2002). A number of faculty members at RCC and SCC, areas with higher numbers of immigrant Latino families, spoke of the importance of earning the trust of Latino students as a prerequisite before students would take the step of asking for assistance.

These two cultural aspects lead to an important point—in order to successfully engage the Latino student population, community college faculty reported that they must often move outside of the classroom and, possibly, even off the campus. A previous study (Mina et al., 2004) supports this contention, contending that the successful Latino collegiate experience must also include the family and community. At RCC and UCC, faculty shared individual and institutional efforts to extend the college into the community. At both institutions, field trips and course assignments are commonly used to take students into the greater Latino community. RCC is engaged with the community through its commitment to provide learning centers that focus language skills in a major workplace in one community and in public libraries in two additional communities. UCC faculty are actively involved in off-campus student recruitment activities in the Latino community and administrators and faculty have taken leadership roles with community agencies such as food banks and Habit for Humanity. Participation in the broader Latino community was described as "expected" and "part of what we do" by the faculty at UCC.

SCC had developed a series of activities (e.g., speakers, art exhibits, cultural celebrations) to occur on their campus, but the palticipants indicated that the events had not drawn large numbers and very few non-students came to the campus for these events. There were a number of SCC faculty who pointed to the philosophy of an "if you offer it they will come" attitude, and these individuals expressed the opinion that this was one reason why the institution had not had greater academic success with Latino students. One faculty member stressed, "I think that if we call ourselves a community college we need to be actively engaged in helping the community address pertinent issues . . . and as a whole, the college is not involved with the Hispanic community."

The Hispanic Student as a Learner

There is consensus that a relationship exists between the culture a student lives in and preferred ways of learning (Guild, 1994). Intertwined with the statements of cultural importance were descriptions of how the culture impacted learning styles. Sanchez (1996) incorporated Curry's Theoretical Model of Learning Style Components and Effects (1991) to analyze the learning preferences of adult Hispanic learners at three levels: motivational maintenance, task engagement, and cognitive strategies. We used the levels of this model to describe the observations of community college faculty regarding the learning preferences of the Latino students they had experienced.

The motivational maintenance level of Curry's model (1991) considers the preferred method of interacting with faculty members and peers, the willingness to work on a task and persist through completion of the task, and the level of need that the student brings to the classroom. The task engagement level of Curry's model involves the interaction between the motivation of the learner and the processing work required by the learning task. The cognitive strategies level of Curry's model involves the processes by which students receive and retain information.

Motivational Maintenance

The faculty we interviewed described Latino students as social learners. One faculty member indicated, "What I see particularly before and after class in those critical 10 to 15 minutes (is a) high level of interaction (among Hispanic students). And what they're doing is build(ing) relationships and a support network. A teacher can either encourage that by being flexible with time, or destroy it by forcing students to (start) right on time."

The faculty have observed that Latino students prefer to sit together in class and to work in small groups rather than as individuals. On field trips they often prefer to travel in groups so that they can share the experience. If they have a class assignment that requires them to interact with individuals or organizations, they prefer to do so in twos or threes rather than by themselves. In short, Latino students have demonstrated a preference for cooperation and collaboration rather than individualism and competition.

Latino students have appreciated a high level of formative feedback and appreciate receiving feedback in a manner that is constructive and encouraging. The manner in which they receive feedback is also important, as a number of faculty have had Latino students explain that they prefer not to receive individual feedback from a professor in front of their classmates. In terms of summative evaluation, Latino students have valued professors who find reasons to recognize the accomplishments of the class as a whole. Even small celebrations are reported as highly effective motivational tools.

Task Engagement

Latino students show a greater interest in learning when they are able to connect the class materials to their personal experiences. A number of faculty indicated that they used journals as a way to encourage students to relate course material to their personal lives. Journaling activities have been well received by Latino students and sharing information from their journals with each other serves as a mechanism to encourage active participation in the class.

The faculty observed that Latino students prefer a building block approach to processing material. Many of the faculty members shared that they begin the class by reviewing concepts and materials from the previous class session before they introduce new material. Others have observed that Hispanic students may need time to reflect on information before they are ready to ask questions. They have often used a "reflection assignment" approach—"Your assignment is to come to the next class with two questions about the material we covered today." Others indicated that Latino students prefer to process abstract concepts or theories in a step-by-step rather than holistic approach.

Cognitive Strategies

When discussing higher-order cognitive processing, faculty stressed the preference of Latino students to active approaches to learning. In this regard, developing the means to demonstrate that information had been received and retained was the most common instructional technique. The interviewees were quick to point out that while Latino students, in general, do not respond well to competition, they have thrived in classes where active learning techniques are followed by active evaluation strategies.

A second active learning strategy employed is assignments requiring students to find additional information on a topic and to share that information with the class. This strategy requires the student to make judgments. The faculty also observed that Latino students prefer application in a "real world" setting. A number of faculty incorporate simulations, a capstone assignment, or field trips so that students can either demonstrate or view the application of the classroom to work or life situations.

It is important that we point out that none of the individuals we interviewed specifically design instruction or assignments to meet the preferred learning styles of Latino students and that they pointed to the wide variations in preferences among the Hispanic population. A number of faculty stressed that Latino students can and have adapted to different instructional approaches.

The Classroom Environment

In their investigation of faculty in four-year institutions, Umbach and Wawrzynski (2005) concluded that "The educational context created by faculty behaviors and attitudes has a dramatic effect on student learning and engagement" (p. 180). Sanchez (2000) found that creating a classroom environment that considers the learning preferences of Latino students is crucial to improving student learning and, thus, persistence. As with learning style preferences, the community college faculty we interviewed emphasized that they did not tailor the classroom environment specifically for Latino students. We identified three themes that illustrate how these faculty members create an environment that incorporates the preferences of Latino students while providing the opportunity for all students to be academically successful.

Develop Relationships with Students

In order to engage students in the classroom, some community college faculty have developed a student-faculty relationship to overcome the fact that some Latinos are wary of authority. One faculty member indicated, "I try to learn one thing about the life of each student and I find that if I share something from my life with them, they are more willing to share with me." Another commented, "It is important to earn the trust of Latino students. To do that I try to establish a learning community within my classroom and adopt a role as a member of the community rather than as the authority figure."

Others spoke of engaging the student outside of the classroom in casual conversation or developing relationships by attending social or cultural activities and then extending that relationship into the classroom and academic matters. Latino students have responded positively to personal attention and, once a relationship is developed, value one-on-one time with faculty.

Classroom Learning Communities

Tinto (1997) described the classroom as the crossroads of academic and social integration. He argued that, for commuter students or those with additional obligations, it may be the only place where students interact with faculty or with each other. The faculty we spoke with, in large part, agreed with that statement, again stressing that creating a learning community facilitates the academic success of all students. How have the individuals we interviewed created such environments? They have been patient, used humor, and let the students know that mistakes were okay. As many community college students have a low level of self-esteem, they have worked to build their confidence through frequent feedback and encouragement.

Creating a supportive learning community does not mean that faculty must lower standards or expectations. Rather, many of the faculty related that they have initiated learning communities through frank discussions that emphasize standards and expectations. Through this initial discussion, faculty were able to provide information on available academic support services, to outline their willingness and availability to work with students outside of class, and often allowed time so that study groups could be organized. "It is important for the class to understand that the goal is for everyone to accomplish the desired outcomes at a level that is acceptable for a college class and to realize that I won't lower my standards or expectations just so everyone receives a passing grade," explained one faculty member. At the same time, the interviewees also indicated the importance of maintaining standards without discouraging students. A number of faculty pointed to using the step-by-step approach described in the previous section as a strategy to promote success by evaluating progress in much smaller segments. Most have used multiple formative evaluations to prepare the student for a summative evaluation and often allow a student to submit work for the formative evaluation stage numerous times.

In terms of Latino students, a number of faculty members emphasized the importance of being flexible with time in order to create learning communities. As quoted earlier in the article, one faculty member pointed to flexibility at the beginning and end of class periods. Other interviews also indicated that faculty provide opportunities for students to interact with each other at the beginning, during, or at the end of the class session. These individuals indicate that such practice provides for the Latino cultural aspect of turning to each other for help, but also provides the opportunity for a group to ask the faculty member a question. Once the "ice is broken" and one group begins to engage the faculty member, others soon follow and then individuals become more willing to be active participants in the class. Another opportunity of allowing for informal group interaction is for the faculty member to "float" throughout the room and listen in on the topics of conversation, often pointing to potential difficulties that some are encountering. The faculty member can then bring the entire class together with a statement such as, "It seems that a number of you have questions about. . . . Let's go back and make sure that everyone understands before we move on." A few faculty spoke of extending the class time by starting earlier or staying later—allowing students to attend the time segment that best fits their schedules and needs.

Faculty also expressed a great deal of attention to creating learning communities that focus on success. They have been careful to not call on Latino students in class if they have perceived that doing so makes them uncomfortable. They have been nonconfrontational in evaluating student work, focusing on suggestions for improvement rather than elaborating on shortcomings. If language is a problem, they have utilized interpreters. Several reported exhaustively searching for texts and other learning resources in the native language of the student and allowing them to speak or write in their primary language. Many have incorporated peer tutoring or study groups to provide supplementary instruction.

SCC has developed learning communities by enrolling the same group of students in two courses. Student feedback at SCC revealed frustration with the applicability of assignments in developmental courses. To address this concern, a number of SCC faculty have developed "paired" courses, one developmental and the other for college credit. For example, a developmental writing course may be paired with an academic course that focuses on written assignments. Preliminary results indicate that this strategy has increased both retention and success and resulted in greater levels of student satisfaction.

Developing an Appreciation of Culture

Community college faculty who have facilitated the academic success of Latino students point to the importance of gaining some knowledge and sensitivity to Hispanic cultures. Some faculty sponsored student clubs or organizations or attended and celebrated Hispanic events with the students. Many encouraged students to share their culture in classroom assignments and discussion. When warranted, they stressed cultural relevance to the course content. Recognizing that Latinos value the community rather than the individual, a significant number of faculty have also incorporated community issues or focus on matters of social justice to apply abstract theory and classroom learning to practical real-life and work applications.

A point emphasized by the faculty at each location was that there was not a single Latino culture in existence on their respective campuses. One faculty member recounted,

> The first semester I taught here I had three Latino males in my class. I put them together for a group project, thinking that they would have commonalities. What a mistake I made . . . . One had immigrated from Mexico the year before with family, one was of Brazilian descent, and the other was the third generation of his family to be born in the U.S.—in fact he didn't even speak a word of Spanish. I learned that it is important for me to learn about the individual cultures of Latinos and not to make assumptions.

A common strategy is to have students compare their culture to others, as a way to engage students in class discussion and to promote questioning. A number of faculty use popular media to explore other cultures: newspapers and magazines, television, movies, and popular music were referenced as ways to expand cultural awareness.

Equally important is introducing the student to the culture of college. Faculty relayed that many Latino students do not understand the academy. Stanton-Salazar (1997) has used the concept of social capital to illustrate that Latinos are often the first in their families to attend college, and thus lack a network of family and other individuals to provide guidance about the college-going process. Faculty indicated the importance of having information on academic support programs, financial aid, and other common student needs (child care, transportation) in order to fill this gap.

We experienced groups of faculty committed to student success at each of the respective institutions we visited. One institution, however, stood out for an organizational approach to welcoming students and instilling a sense of belonging. UCC can be described as an institution that practices celebratory socialization (Tierney, 1997) by valuing and recognizing the distinctiveness of the students' culture and building on their socialization into the college culture through a variety of academic and student support programs.

Concluding Comments

We found faculty members participating in formal and informal groups, striving to understand the cultures of underrepresented populations on their respective campuses, working to improve their instruction and to create environments that facilitate student success. While some of the commitment can be attributed to administrative leadership, it evident that faculty leadership has greatly contributed to developing and sustaining efforts to facilitate student success.

Virtually all of the faculty we spoke with share the perception that new faculty hires need to be aware of the nature of the community college, the students that attend the institution, and Hispanic culture. At UCC we found a model, year-long faculty orientation program that includes information on the student population, instruction on learning styles, and exposure to the various resources available to faculty and to the students on their campus. In addition, there were continuing professional development activities for returning faculty that also focused on student success. At RCC and SCC, smaller groups of faculty were beginning to meet to discuss ways to improve the academic success of first generation Hispanics. At each respective institution, the faculty we interviewed displayed a keen interest in "what was working" for other faculty members at their institution and for faculty at the other institutions in our study.

Although faculty leadership is important, faculty working alone will not be able to sustain an ongoing professional development agenda. Community colleges that have an interest in student engagement and success need to develop a culture of caring and support on their campus. It is important for the administration to work with faculty to develop a series of structured professional development seminars that help faculty and student affairs professionals better understand the cultures of historically underrepresented students and how culture impacts preferred learning styles. In addition, seminars can be conducted that help faculty improve their classroom process, pedagogy, and approach to students. For campuses with multiple sites, communication becomes even more important. Encouraging faculty and student affairs professionals to learn new approaches and to share "what works" and "lessons learned" lays the groundwork to develop a broader culture of student learning and success.

A genuine passion and philosophy of the community college as an "opportunity college"was prevalent among the faculty we interviewed. It is important to note that the overwhelming majority of individuals we interviewed were full-time faculty, and that each of these institutions employs significant numbers of adjunct faculty. Our field notes and debriefings after each visit focused on the amount of time these individuals dedicate to crafting quality educational environments for such a diverse student population. The faculty we interviewed were united in announcing that, for the Latino population, developing a personal relationship with the students was the initial step to effectively engaging students in the classroom. Additional research is needed to explore the question of how adjunct faculty members are able to develop relationships and handle the time commitment necessary to "take the classroom" to the community and to develop classroom environments that engage Latino learners.

As this study bears out, culture matters when working with Latino students. The greater the amount of time and effort faculty dedicate to learning and appreciating Latino culture, the better able they will be to help Latino students adapt and progress through the academic rigors of their campus. Part of this cultural aspect is the need for the college to be seen as an active agent in the community. Two of the three institutions we visited had obviously made institutional commitments toward this goal. Many faculty, however, spoke of much smaller, initial steps—shopping at local Latino businesses, attending cultural events, and so on—always with the mindset of representing the community college. One faculty member stressed, "We aren't recruiting individual Latino students, we are recruiting the entire Latino community." In one word, we describe the faculty we interviewed as passionate as not one complained about the necessary time commitment or the responsibility of community outreach. Most certainly, institutions that developed appropriate support and reward mechanisms would seem more likely to be able to develop faculty "buy-in" for such actions.

Do Community College Faculty Use the Same Strategies as Four-Year Faculty?

A corollary purpose of this study was to examine whether community college faculty use the same strategies as four-year college and university faculty to create an educational context that promotes student engagement. Community college faculty who were identified as facilitating the academic success of Latino students reported that they do not do anything "different," specifically for Latino students. They have, however, recognized that students enrolled in their classes will have a variety of cultural experiences and learning style preferences. Moreover, they have worked hard to incorporate these experiences and preferences into the classroom. Community college faculty do incorporate course-related interactions, active and collaborative learning techniques, academic challenges, higher-order cognitive activities, and academic enrichment activities as strategies that promote student engagement. As one faculty member stressed, "If I am able to engage a student in the class, to move them from being a passive to an active learner, then I feel that I have contributed to their academic success. At the community college engagement is the key to success."

Based on the responses from the interviews, and drawing from the work of Umbach and Wawrzynski (2005), we propose 10 strategies to promote greater engagement between community college faculty and Latino students .

- Learn about, and become involved with the Latino community(ies) served by your community college.
- Develop personal relationships with students—learn something personal about each student and share something personal about yourself.
- Encourage small group interaction focusing on course content at the beginning and end of each class or during class as "check points" before moving to new material.
- Create a learning community within the class that emphasizes success.
- Emphasize active learning strategies and incorporate cooperative learning.
- Connect class materials to personal, work, or real-life experiences and encourage students to share their experiences in class presentations and discussion.
- Present material in a step-by-step or building block approach, connecting new learning to previous material.
- Establish and maintain high standards and discuss expectations in your class.
- Provide frequent formative feedback in a constructive and encouraging manner.
- Recognize the accomplishments of the class as a whole.

References

Astin, A. (1993). *What matters in college: Four critical years revisited.* San Francisco, CA: Jossey Bass.

Bailey, T., Crosta, P. M., & Jenkins, D. (2006). *What can student right-to-know graduation rates tell us about community college performance?* New York: Community College Research Center, Teachers College, Columbia University, Working Paper No. 6. Retrieved February 4, 2008 from http://ccrc.tccolumbia.edu/

Brawer, F. B. (1995). *Policies and programs that affect transfer.* Los Angeles, CA: Center for the Study of Community Colleges. (ERIC Document Reproduction Service No. ED 385336.)

Britt, L. W., & Hirt, J. B. (1999). Student experiences and institutional practices affecting spring semester transfer students. *NASP A Journal, 36,* 198–209.

Chickering, A. W., & Gamson, Z. F. (1987). Seven principles for good practice in undergraduate education. *AAHE Bulletin, 39*(7), 3–7.

Colorado State Advisory Committee to the U.S. Commission on Civil Rights. (1995). *The retention of minorities in Colorado public institutions of higher education: Fort Lewis and Adams State Colleges.* Denver, CO: Author. (ERIC Document Reproduction Service No. ED 409134.)

Cook, B. J., & Cordova, D. I. (2007). *Minorities in higher education, twenty-second annual status report: 2007 supplement.* Washington, DC: American Council on Education.

Creswell, J. W. (2008). *Educational research: Planning. conducting, and evaluating quantitative and qualitative research* (3rd ed.). Columbus, OH: Pearson-Merrill Prentice-Hall.

Curry, L. (1991). Patterns of learning styles across medical specialities. *Educational Psychology, 11,* 247–277.

Education Commission of the States. (1995). *Making quality count in undergraduate education.* Denver, CO: Education Commission of the States.

Ewell, P. (1997). Organizing for learning: A new imperative. *AAHE Bulletin, 50,* 3–6.

Griggs, S., & Dunn, R. (1996). *Hispanic-American students and learning slyle.* ERIC digest. Urbana, IL: ERIC Clearinghouse on Elementary and Early Childhood Education. (ERIC Document Reproduction Service No. ED 393607.)

Guild, P. (1994, May). The culture/learning style connection. *Educational Leadership, 51,* 16–21.

Harvey, W. (2002). *Minorities in higher education 2000-2001: Nineteenth annual status report.* Washington, DC: American Council on Education.

Hurtado, S., & Carter, D. F. (1997). Effects of college transition and perceptions of the campus racial climate on Latino college students' sense of belonging. *Sociology of Education, 70,* 324–345.

Laden, B. V. (1992, October). *An exploratory examination of organizational factors leading to transfer of Hispanic students: A case study.* Paper presented at the annual meeting of the Association for the Study of Higher Education, Minneapolis, MN. (ERIC Document Reproduction Service No. ED 352922.)

Laden, B. V. (2001). Hispanic-serving institutions: Myths and realities. *Peabody Journal of Education, 76,* 73–92.

McGlynn, A. P. (2004). Nurturing Hispanics to four-year degrees. *Education Digest, 69(5),* 51–56.

McMahon, J. (Ed.). (2002). Working with first generation Latino families. *Children's Services Practice Notes, 7*(3), 6–8. Retrieved February 4, 2008 from http://ssw.unc. edu/fcrp/Cspn/cspn.htm

Mina, L., Cabrales, J. A., Juarez, C. M., & Rodriguez-Vasquez, F. (2004). Support programs that work. In A. M. Ortiz (Ed.), *Addressing the unique needs of Latino American students, New directions for student services, 105* (pp. 17–27). San Francisco, CA: Jossey-Bass.

Pascarella, E., & Terenzini, P. (1991). *How college affects students: Findings and insights from twenty years of research.* San Francisco, CA: Jossey Bass.

Pew Hispanic Center/Kaiser Family Foundation. (2004). *National survey of Latinos: Education. Summwy and chartpack.* Washington, DC: Pew Hispanic Center and the Henry J. Kaiser Family Foundation.

Quality Education for Minorities Network. (1977). *Weaving the web of MSE success for minorities: Top ten colleges and universities report.* Washington, DC: Author. (ERIC Document Service Reproduction No. ED 432209.)

Rendon, L. I., & Garza, H. (1996). Closing the gap between two- and four-year institutions. In L. I. Rendon & R. O. Hope (Eds.), *Educating a new majority: Transforming America's educational system for diversity* (pp. 289–308). San Francisco, CA: Jossey-Bass.

Rendon, L. I., Justiz, M. J., & Resta, P. (1988). *Transfer education on southwest border community colleges.* New York: The Ford Foundation.

Rendon, L. I., & Nora, A. (1989). A synthesis and application of research on Hispanic students in community colleges. *Community College Review, 17*(1), 17–24.

Rendon, L. I., & Valadez, J. R. (1993). Qualitative indicators of Hispanic student transfer. *Community College Review, 20*(4), 27–37.

Sanchez, I. M. (1996). *An analysis of learning style constructs and the development of a profile of Hispanic adult learners.* Unpublished doctoral dissertation, Department of Education, University of New Mexico.

Sanchez, I. M. (2000). Motivating and maximizing learning in minority classrooms. In S. R. Aragon (Ed.), *Beyond access: Methods and models jor increasing retention and learning among minority students, New directions for community colleges, 112* (pp. 35–44). San Francisco, CA: Jossey-Bass.

Stage, F. K., & Hossler, D. (2000). Where is the student? Linking student behaviors, college choice, and college persistence. In J. M. Braxton (Ed.), *Reworking the student departure puzzle* (pp. 170–195). Nashville, TN: Vanderbilt University Press.

Stanton-Salazar, R. D. (1997). A social capital framework for understanding the socialization of racial minority children and youth. *Harvard Educational Review, 67,* 1–39.

Tierney, W. G. (1997). Organizational socialization in higher education. *Journal of Higher Education, 68,* 1–16.

Tinto, V. (1993). *Rethinking the causes and cures of student attrition* (2nd ed.), Chicago, IL: University of Chicago Press.

Tinto, V. (1997). Classrooms as communities: Exploring the educational character of student persistence. *Journal of Higher Education, 68,* 599–623.

Torres, V. (2006). A mixed method study testing data-model fit of a retention model for Latino/a students at urban universities. *Journal of College Student Development, 47,* 299–318.

Umbach, P. D., & Wawrzynski, M. R. (2005). Faculty do matter: The role of college faculty in student learning and engagement. *Research in Higher Education, 46,* 153–184.

CHAPTER 22

RECRUITING AND RETAINING RURAL COMMUNITY COLLEGE FACULTY

JOHN P. MURRAY

Much is being written about a potential shortage of qualified community college faculty. Rural community colleges may be at the greatest disadvantage in attracting and retaining new faculty because they cannot offer the financial, cultural, and social advantages that more urban institutions can. This chapter describes the factors rural community college leaders must consider when recruiting and hiring new professors.

Many educators believe that because of unprecedented faculty attrition (Berry, Hammons, and Denny, 2001), rural community colleges will have difficulty recruiting and retaining qualified faculty (Leist, 2005). Nonetheless, there is a paucity of literature that specifically addresses faculty job satisfaction at community colleges, much less at rural community colleges. This chapter begins by describing the challenges presented by rural settings to those who might wish to teach at a rural community college and offers suggestions for recruiting and retaining faculty in a rural setting.

Challenges of the Rural Environment

Faculty members face a number of challenges when they accept a position at a rural community college. Prospective community college faculty members need to understand that individuals living in rural areas suffer from a number of social and economic ills. Rural areas often have high levels of illiteracy, low levels of educational attainment, high unemployment, and extreme poverty. Although not all rural communities are impoverished, many are. "Of the almost four hundred counties with poverty rates of 20 percent or greater in every decade since 1959, 95 percent are rural" (Mosley and Miller, 2004, p. 2).

The poverty of rural areas is exacerbated by the loss of industry and the consequent loss of employment opportunities. America's traditional rural job base is rapidly disappearing. Agricultural and extractive industries, such as mining, fishing, and lumbering, are declining, and those that remain are frequently low-paying and subject to the whims of global and national economic downswings, causing frequent shutdowns and layoffs (Mosley and Miller, 2004). The manufacturing base of rural America has traditionally been low-paying and labor-intensive. However, many of these industries have automated and now require a highly skilled labor force. Unfortunately, because educational attainment in rural America is low, many of these industries have relocated to urban areas, seeking a better-educated workforce. Others have outsourced their jobs overseas in search of cheaper labor. The steady attrition of employment opportunities leaves rural communities "with relatively unskilled workforces, and without the necessary infrastructure to rebuild" (McNutt, 1994, p. 196).

The steady erosion of unskilled jobs negatively affects the educational environment of rural communities, and thus creates greater poverty. Many young people become discouraged over the lack of opportunities in their community and drop out of school. Those who graduate from high school or college often leave home in search of better jobs. Indeed, far fewer rural citizens hold college degrees than their metropolitan counterparts. "As of 2001, more than 26 percent of metropolitan residents possessed at least a college degree, compared to only 15 percent of those in nonmetropolitan areas" (Mosley and Miller, 2004, p. 5).

Rural community colleges represent hope for a better future for rural citizens. In *Worlds Apart: Why Poverty Persists in Rural America,* Duncan (1999) wrote: "A good education is the key that unlocks and expands the cultural toolkits of the have-nots, and thus gives them the potential to bring about lasting social change in their persistently poor communities" (p. 208). Although education may be seen as a way to reduce poverty, some researchers (Mosley and Miller, 2004) have found that education has less of an effect on rural Americans than on metropolitan residents. This may be partially explained by the relocation of educated youths; although a college education may be seen as a ticket out of poverty, it is also too often a ticket out of the rural community (McNutt, 1994). This exportation of many individuals who could assist in the revitalization of rural communities only intensifies the poverty and leaves behind the elderly, the unskilled, and the undereducated. An overlooked outcome of this outmigration of educated citizens is the effect on the tax base. The loss of educated individuals places the tax burden on those least able to pay additional taxes to support a community college or any educational institution.

The impoverished tax base and lower levels of educational attainment in rural communities present several challenges for those developing curricula at rural community colleges. When it comes to funding, rural community colleges suffer a double bind. States expect the local community to contribute to the funding of the local community college. They also expect the individuals who will benefit from the education to pay their fair share through tuition and fees. However, because many rural communities are poverty-stricken and have a low tax base, they are hard-pressed to support a community college, and the residents have little disposable income to spend on tuition (Higgins and Katsinas, 1999; McNutt, 1994). This means that there is not much money for high-cost curricula, adjunct or full-time faculty salaries, or faculty development. Often rural community colleges cannot afford to provide high-cost technical programs. Furthermore, even if they have the resources, they may be unable to find qualified faculty who will relocate for the salary they can pay. This often forces rural community colleges to offer less costly transfer curricula. Students who transfer are less likely to return to the rural community, which further drains the educated individuals from rural communities.

Recruiting Faculty

Although many believe that a severe shortage of faculty is not yet upon us, several commentators have noted that in highly specialized disciplines the crisis is already here (Burnett, 2004; Evelyn, 2001; Leist, 2005). "Already, colleges have seen shortages in qualified faculty in areas like math, science, nursing, technology, special education, and English as a Second Language" (Burnett, 2004, p. 7). Moreover, for rural community colleges the state of affairs is a bit more complicated than just recruiting faculty to teach highly specialized courses. Increasingly, it is also difficult to find faculty in less specialized areas, including some that once produced an abundance of applicants. An administrator at one rural community college complained that "while fifteen years ago, an English faculty opening would bring in about 150 applicants, today the number is closer to 30 applicants. And if there are 10 of those who are qualified, it's unusual" (Burnett, 2004, p. 8). Because there are usually few local citizens who are qualified to teach at a community college, college leaders often must try to convince individuals to move to their communities. Despite what may be a bucolic setting, the lack of cultural, social, shopping, and recreational amenities in rural areas makes for a tough sell in recruiting new faculty (Leist, 2005). Daniel P. Doherty, the dean of instruction at Western Nebraska Community College, put it this way: "We have a lot of trouble just getting them in the door, just to see the campuses. . . . [S]omeone has to know this country and want to come here" (Burnett, 2004, p. 7).

Rural community colleges are also hard-pressed to recruit a racially and ethnically diverse faculty. It is often very hard to recruit minorities to move to rural communities. Also problematic is the recruitment of an intellectually diverse faculty. For rural community colleges it is often easiest to recruit from nearby universities, which can lead to an intellectually insular faculty.

Retaining Faculty

Even when faculty are successfully recruited to a rural community college, it can be difficult to retain them. Many community colleges are experiencing an unprecedented turnover in early and midcareer faculty: "Many of the faculty who leave early go back to earn their doctorates. . . . Others go to work at larger community colleges" (Burnett, 2004, p. 8). This is a serious problem for rural community colleges, given the difficulty they face recruiting full-time faculty.

Organizational theorists, including those who study higher education, stress that the way in which an employee is socialized into a profession is often critical to the willingness of novice employees to remain with the institution and the career (Aryee, Chay, and Chew, 1994). Moreover, the literature suggests that new faculty members are much more likely to be successfully socialized into the profession when they have realistic expectations of what it will entail (Feldman, 1981; Gaff and Lambert, 1996). This also seems to be the case at rural community colleges (Murray, 2005; Murray and Cunningham, 2004).

Some organizational theorists note that met expectations theory best explains career commitment, voluntary job turnover, and job satisfaction (Aryee, Chay, and Chew, 1994; Aryee and Tan, 1992). Individuals whose expectations of the job are more closely aligned with the reality of the job are more likely to experience job satisfaction, and therefore, more likely to find a career fit. Organizational researchers have concluded that person-environment fit best accounts for job satisfaction (Bertz and Judge, 1994). Individuals whose expectations are met tend to have higher job satisfaction, and those with higher job satisfaction are judged by superiors as being better performers, are more committed to the organization, and have longer tenures.

What should new rural community college faculty members expect? As the saying goes, there is good news and bad news. The bad news is not always unique to rural colleges. All community colleges share some features that can cause a new faculty member discomfort if he or she is unaware of them. Although new faculty members are aware that community colleges are open admissions institutions, the uninitiated are often shocked when they realize the range of student abilities they will face in the classroom. Sax, Astin, Korn, and Gilmartin (1999) found that 80 percent of community college faculty members believe that their students are less academically prepared than they should be for the rigors of college-level work.

Another potential shock for those not familiar with the community college environment is the heavy workload. At most community colleges, faculty teach five to six courses an academic term and spend between 15 and 28 hours a week in instructional settings. In addition, they are often expected to advise students, serve on committees, and do community service. Yet another surprise for the unaware is the repetitive nature of the work. Community college faculty usually teach the same three or four introductory courses year after year, with little opportunity to teach advanced courses in their discipline.

The innocent often fail to realize that they will have little time to pursue more specialized academic interests, and this can lead to a kind of intellectual estrangement from the discipline. There is little or no time to pursue research or even to read professional journals. For faculty at rural community colleges, this sense of professional isolation is further exacerbated by the fact that an instructor may be the sole faculty teaching in a discipline. In addition to being cut off from colleagues who share their academic interests, these one-person "departments" increase these faculty members' workload. The instructor must carry the entire burden of advising majors, developing and keeping the curriculum up to date, coordinating articulation agreements or job placement programs, and recruiting new students.

Rural community colleges face at least one more unique concern when trying to recruit and retain faculty: location. The faculty members who express the most satisfaction with teaching at a rural community college are those who are comfortable living and working in a rural community. It can be very difficult to recruit individuals to a rural area for the many quality-of-life reasons discussed earlier in this chapter. Moreover, once faculty are recruited, it can be difficult to retain those who have no previous experience living in a rural area. This can be a serious concern for minorities when there are few other minorities in the community. Moreover, for dual-career couples, there is often little opportunity for employment for the spouse.

If we are to help prospective rural faculty members develop realistic expectations that might lead them to stay, we should also explain the joys rural community college faculty find in their work. Study after study has found that the majority of community college faculty members find teaching to be a satisfying career; overwhelmingly, faculty report that their greatest satisfaction comes from teaching. Ironically, they also often tell researchers that it is the teaching of the unprepared or underachieving student that is most satisfying (Wolfe and Strange, 2003).

Suggestions for Recruiting and Retaining Faculty

Given what has been said about the rural environment, how should community colleges go about recruiting and retaining faculty? The following suggestions are drawn from my own previous research as well as my experience at a rural community college.

Recruitment. The following may be helpful in recruiting faculty to rural community colleges.

Look Carefully in Your Own Backyard. Community college leaders looking for new faculty might start by involving current faculty in the recruitment process. One study (Murray and Cunningham, 2004) found that many new faculty said they had been recruited by other faculty. A number of participants also mentioned that they had been adjuncts before becoming full-time.

Think Family. Often dual-career couples settle in metropolitan areas because there are employment opportunities for both individuals. Many times an individual can be recruited if there is also a possibility of employment for a trailing spouse. The position can be a staff position, or if the spouse is qualified, a faculty position. Employing two members of a household also increases the likelihood of retaining both.

Look Far and Wide. Many individuals like the idea of living in rural settings. Contact universities with graduate programs (especially those with large master's programs) and discuss the advantages of your community. These may be access to national or state parks, lakes, or historic sites; the low cost of living; good school systems; and so forth. Offer to sponsor a weekend visit to the community for interested candidates. This is also a good time to make prospective candidates aware of opportunities for their significant others.

Take a Risk. Creative rural community colleges' leaders might consider creating a teaching fellows program. Such a program would recruit recent graduates or students finishing their dissertations and provide them with a mentor, a title, and a promise of gaining experience. It would also give the college an opportunity to convince the best graduates to stay at the college.

Grow Your Own. Keep track of community college students who have transferred to four-year colleges. Some of them will go on to obtain an advanced degree and may welcome the opportunity to return and teach in the community they grew up in.

Retention. Once a faculty member is recruited, the next challenge is to retain that individual. If rural community colleges wish to retain faculty, they will need to be innovative. For so long, community college leaders have not had to concern themselves with the needs of the faculty. Until recently, there has been a plentiful supply of candidates and a shortage of openings. In a tight job market, retention becomes a minor issue because those with jobs are much less likely to have opportunities to leave. However, with the potential of a large turnover at both four-year colleges and community colleges, administrators will find it necessary to be more concerned with meeting the needs of faculty.

Individuals tend to leave positions for a variety of reasons; some we can control and some we cannot. Among the main reasons for leaving a position are burnout, the feeling that the compensation is inadequate, the lack of job security, and the perception that the quality of life is poor. Although institutional leaders cannot always control these factors, they can ameliorate them to some extent.

The most difficult of these factors for administrators to deal with are job security and compensation issues. Leaders can work hard to devise a fair compensation package. For many prospective employees the fringe benefits package is often extremely important. Employers who offer a generous package will have an advantage.

Although not all the factors contributing to burnout can be addressed by administrators, some common causes can be addressed. Burnout is often caused by the repetitious nature of teaching the same courses year after year. Consider providing faculty with avenues for professional growth such as funds for travel to professional conferences, the latest technology, seed money for small research projects, assistance in preparing manuscripts, and release time to develop new curricula. Also consider moving faculty out of the classroom for periods of time by assigning them to special projects or having them temporarily take an administrative role when an employee suddenly leaves or takes an extended leave of absence.

For many faculty and staff, balancing work and family obligations is a great stressor (Luce and Murray, 1998). Young families have to balance child rearing, and older families are often faced with helping aging parents. Community colleges can help reduce the stress by providing flexible work hours, assistance with day care, and flexible family leave plans.

Among the reasons for leaving that community college leaders can control is the perception that one's contribution to the college is not being appreciated. Recognition of excellence need not be costly. When faculty are recognized for their accomplishments, they develop professional pride, and professional pride can be a powerful motivator. Faculty recognized for excellence might be given a teaching award with or without a modest stipend, a title such as faculty associate or teaching mentor, a plaque, a framed certificate, a gift certificate from a bookstore or restaurant, a close-by parking space, or lunch with the president.

Conclusion

Rural community colleges can do a better job of recruiting and retaining faculty if they take the time and effort to develop orientation programs that introduce prospective faculty to the realities of teaching and living in a rural community college. Those realities include a heavy workload, life in a rural community, and teaching a socially and economically diverse student body that may be underprepared for college-level work. When researchers examine the reasons for staying or leaving a college, several things stand out. Those wishing to stay are also those who find it satisfying to work with a diverse student body. They want to teach individuals, not just a subject matter. They believe that what they are doing is important and valued by others. In other words, faculty who have realistic expectations about their jobs will find it satisfying when those expectations are met. Recruiting and retaining good employees do not just happen. In a tight market, wise community college leaders need to carefully plan for and work at maintaining an excellent faculty.

References

Aryee, S., Chay, Y. W., and Chew, J. "An Investigation of the Predictors and Outcomes of Career Commitment in Three Career Stages." *Journal of Vocational Behavior*, 1994, *44*, 1–16.

Aryee, S., and Tan, K. "Antecedents and Outcomes of Career Commitment." *Journal of Vocational Behavior*, 1992, *40*, 288–305.

Berry, L. H., Hammons, J. O., and Denny, G. S. "Faculty Retirement Turnover in Community Colleges: A Real or Imagined Problem?" *Community College Journal of Research and Practice*, 2001, *25*, 123–136.

Bertz, R. D., and Judge, T. A. "Person-Organization Fit and the Theory of Work Adjustment: Implications for Satisfaction, Tenure, and Career Success." *Journal of Vocational Behavior*, 1994, *44*, 32–52.

Burnett, S. "Using Our Imagination." *Community College Week*, 2004, *17*(4), 6–8.

Duncan, C. (1999). *Worlds Apart: Why Poverty Persists in Rural America*. New Haven, Conn.: Yale University Press, 1999.

Evelyn, J. "The Hiring Boom at Two-Year Colleges." *Chronicle of Higher Education*, 2001, *47*(40), A8–A9.

Feldman, D. C. "The Multiple Socialization of Organization Members." *Academy of Management Review*, 1981, *6*, 301–318.

Gaff, J. G., and Lambert, L. M. "Socializing Future Faculty to the Values of Undergraduate Education." *Change*, 1996, *4*, 39–45.

Higgins, S. C., and Katsinas, S. G. "The Relationship Between Environmental Conditions and Transfer Rates of Selected Rural Community Colleges: A Pilot Study." *Community College Review*, 1999, *2*(27), 1–25.

Leist, J. E. "Exemplary Rural Community College Presidents: A Case Study of How Well Their Professional Qualities Mirror Job Advertisements." Unpublished doctoral dissertation, Texas Tech University, 2005.

Luce, J., and Murray, J. P. "New Faculty's Perceptions of Academic Work Life." *Journal of Staff, Program, & Organizational Development*, 1998, *15*(3), 103–110.

McNutt, A. S. "Rural Community Colleges: Meeting the Challenges of the 1990s." In G. A. Baker III, J. Dudziak, and P. Tyler (eds.), *A Handbook on the Community College in America: Its History, Mission, and Management.* Westport, Conn.: Greenwood, 1994.

Mosley, J. M., and Miller, K. K. *What the Research Says About Spatial Variations in Factors Affecting Poverty.* Research Brief 2004–1. Corvallis: Oregon State University, Rural Poverty Research Center, 2004.

Murray, J. P. "Meeting the Needs of New Faculty at Rural Community Colleges." *Community College Journal of Research and Practice*, 2005, *29*(3), 215–232.

Murray, J. P., and Cunningham, S. "New Community College Faculty Members and Job Satisfaction." *Community College Review*, 2004, *32*(2), 19–32.

Sax, L. J., Astin, A. W., Korn, W. S., and Gilmartin, S. K. *The American College Teacher: National Norms for the 1998–1999 HERI Faculty Survey.* Los Angeles: University of California, Higher Education Research Institute, 1999.

Wolfe, J. R., and Strange, C. C. "Academic Life at the Franchise: Faculty Culture in a Rural Two-Year Branch Campus." *Review of Higher Education*, 2003, *26*(3), 343–362.

JOHN P. MURRAY is professor of higher education at Texas Tech University and program director for the higher education administration program.

CHAPTER 23

UNINTENDED CONSEQUENCES: EXAMINING THE EFFECT OF PART-TIME FACULTY MEMBERS ON ASSOCIATE'S DEGREE COMPLETION

AUDREY J. JAEGER
NORTH CAROLINA STATE UNIVERSITY, RALEIGH

M. KEVIN EAGAN, JR.
UNIVERSITY OF CALIFORNIA, LOS ANGELES

Employment of part-time faculty members by community colleges has become an increasingly common approach to reducing institutional costs, which may have unintended consequences for student outcomes. This study examines the relationship between part-time faculty members and the associate's degree completion of community college students. The authors use hierarchical generalized linear modeling to analyze student- and institution-level data from the California community college system to determine how student exposure to part-time faculty members affected the likelihood of earning an associate's degree. Findings indicate that students experienced a significant yet modest negative effect from exposure to part-time faculty members on the probability of completing an associate's degree.

Keywords: associate's degrees, part-time faculty members, hierarchical generalized linear modeling, student outcomes, California

Examining the effects of the part-time faculty on student outcomes in community colleges is critical given that these institutions educate almost 45% of the country's undergraduates (American Association of Community Colleges, 2006) and employ more part-time faculty members than any other type of institution of higher education. Across 1,052 associate's degree-granting institutions, 65.6% of faculty members were employed in part-time appointments in the fall of 2005, considerably higher than any other category within the Carnegie Classification of Higher Education Institutions (American Association of University Professors, 2006). Community colleges have also been the primary institutions of higher education to provide postsecondary education to underserved populations (Levin, 2001; Shaw & London, 2001; Shaw, Rhoads, & Valadez, 1999). The defining elements of community colleges, such as open access, low tuition, a multitude of services, and convenient

Authors' Note: This research is supported by the California Community College Collaborative (C4) at the University of California, Riverside. This material is based on work supported by the Association for Institutional Research, the Institute of Education Sciences and National Center for Education Statistics, and the National Science Foundation under Association for Institutional Research Grant Number 07-213. Any opinions, findings, and conclusions or recommendations expressed in this material are those of the authors and do not necessarily reflect the views of the Association for Institutional Research, the Institute of Education Sciences and National Center for Education Statistics, or the National Science Foundation.

locations, are especially pertinent to students with low socioeconomic status, to women with children, to minorities, and to those who are underemployed, who are academically unprepared, who are physically and mentally disabled, or who are adults looking for a second chance in education (Cohen & Brawer, 2003; Dougherty, 1994; Phillippe, 2000). Investigating how these students can be successful in their academic pursuits is important for the student and the institution.

Recent research has begun to address the effects of exposure to instruction from part-time faculty members at both four-year institutions and community colleges. Although part-time faculty members provide institutions some financial flexibility (Gappa, 1984; Schuster & Finkelstein, 2006), their increased use has raised concerns for constituents inside and outside of higher education. Part-time faculty members spend a greater proportion of their overall time teaching, but the initial evidence suggests that these appointees are less accessible to students, have less-frequent interactions with students, are more transient, bring less scholarly authority to their jobs, and are less integrated into the campus culture (Schuster, 2003; Umbach, 2007).

This article examines the relationship between the part-time faculty and student outcomes, focusing on associate's degree completion. Although the conferral of degrees is only one function of community colleges, the completion of an associate's degree often serves as a springboard to further education at four-year institutions (Quigley & Bailey, 2003). By investing in additional years of education, students have the ability to obtain a more holistic education while simultaneously increasing their earning potential in the labor market (Kane & Rouse, 1999). Considering that higher education is seen as a flexible and convenient avenue for social mobility, particularly for disadvantaged individuals (Bowen, 1996), identifying facilitators of and barriers to completing an associate's degree has important implications.

This study draws from two conceptual frameworks—faculty-student interaction and social capital—to examine the effects of exposure to part-time faculty on associate's degree completion. We use hierarchical generalized linear modeling (HGLM) to analyze student- and institution-level data from 107 community colleges across the state of California. This study seeks to determine whether increased exposure to instruction from part-time faculty members significantly affects the likelihood that community college students will complete an associate's degree.

Literature Review

We draw from several key areas of research to inform this study. We begin by discussing community colleges and their students. Second, given the reliance on part-time faculty members at community colleges, we provide an overview of part-time faculty members in the United States. We then examine studies addressing the effects of part-time faculty members on student outcomes. Although this research is limited and typically focuses on four-year institutions, several key studies provide insight for our research, which adds an important dimension by focusing on community colleges. Finally, the review concludes with a critique of literature related to the associate's degree completion of community college students.

Community College Context

Community colleges maintain complex missions that include preparing students for degree programs, offering degree programs, preparing students to transfer to four-year institutions, and providing a host of other educational and vocational opportunities (Cohen & Brawer, 2003). Characterized by low tuition, flexible scheduling, convenient locations, and comprehensive missions (Cohen & Brawer, 2003; Phillippe, 2000), community colleges offer students a possible vehicle for pursuing postsecondary education, particularly for first-generation students, single parents, economically and educationally disadvantaged students, and individuals with full-time employment (Choy, 2002; Cohen & Brawer, 2003; Grubb, Badway, & Bell, 2003). Community college faculty members have garnered some attention by scholars recently (Levin, Kater, & Wagoner, 2006; Townsend & Twombly, 2007; Twombly & Townsend, 2008; Wagoner, 2007), although Twombly and Townsend point out that this attention is relatively insignificant given the critical role these faculty members play. Important to this research is the uniqueness of part-time faculty members and their role with students.

Part-Time Faculty Members at Community Colleges

Fiscal constraints at the college and state levels create an increased demand for part-time faculty members (Gappa, 1984; Schuster & Finkelstein, 2006). Across public community colleges, nearly 67% of all faculty appointments made in 2003 were part-timers (American Association of University Professors, 2006). This is a dramatic increase from the late 1960s when just 27% of faculty members held part-time appointments (Cataldi, Fahimi, Bradburn, & Zimbler, 2005; Schuster & Finkelstein, 2006).

As employment of part-time faculty members has increased at community colleges, researchers have examined more closely the characteristics associated with these individuals. Demographically speaking, part-time faculty members closely resemble their full-time colleagues (Eagan, 2007). In fact, educational attainment represents the only substantial difference between part-time and full-time faculty members, as a higher proportion of full-timers hold master's, professional, and doctoral degrees than do part-time faculty members (Eagan, 2007).

In addition to demographic differences, Levin (2007) noted differences in job satisfaction, showing that part-time instructors in the humanities and social sciences are less satisfied with their work environment than those in occupational and vocational areas. Levin added that compensation alone does not explain this difference. As community colleges adapt to economic globalization, the organizational context tends to be more favorable for part-time faculty members who offer specific expertise in career or technical fields than for part-time faculty members in academic fields (Levin, 2001, 2007; Levin et al., 2006). Levin (2007) asserted that liberal arts faculty members are hired not for their expertise but, rather, for their labor as substitutes for full-time instructors. In contrast, occupational and professional program faculty members are more often sought for their specialized knowledge. As we consider the role part-time faculty members play with students, it is important to consider this distinction. Part-time faculty members from the vocational and professional areas gain their professional identity outside of academia through nonacademic employment (Wagoner, 2007) and thus may be less invested in the overall institution.

Although the reliance of community colleges on part-time instructional labor has continued to rise, a recent analysis of part-time faculty members in California's community college system concluded that there is a lack of stability in the part-time faculty workforce. Yoshioka (2007) wrote the following:

> To recap, economic uncertainty, little or no job security, low pay, inadequate health benefits, and minimal paid office hours all contribute to the shocking 20 to 25 percent annual turnover of part-time faculty. . . . Just stabilizing the part-time workforce would be a major achievement, yet administrators treat part-time faculty as an endlessly renewable resource. (p. 43)

Community college part-time faculty members face a challenging role as they attempt to meet the institution's growing demands for access to education and a trained workforce while at the same time working within an organization that may not adequately meet their needs.

Part-time Faculty Members and Student Outcomes

The part-time faculty represents a critical component of the success of community colleges, which must remain responsive to market and student demands. Part-time faculty members often teach larger, lower-level courses or specialized advanced courses at times that are often more convenient for part-time students. In addition to serving an important niche in relation to types and times of courses offered, part-time faculty members who bring real-world experiences and community connections to the classroom are helpful to community college students (Green, 2007).

The increased employment of part-time faculty members continues to draw criticisms from scholars who see part-timers as threats to the development of quality academic programs (Haeger, 1998). In discussions regarding the connection between student learning outcomes and the employment of part-time faculty members, scholars, including us, are diligent in noting that blame for any negative impact on outcomes does not rest solely on the part-time faculty member. At the same time, we need to be much more cognizant of how increased levels of part-time faculty instruction affect students and how institutions of higher education can address any negative consequences. Recent research (Ehrenberg & Zhang, 2004; Harrington & Schibik, 2004; Jaeger & Hinz, 2008; Jaeger, Thornton, & Eagan, 2007; Ronco & Cahill, 2004) has begun to examine this issue but has focused primarily on four-year institutions. In addition, most of this research has looked at the institution as the unit of analysis rather than at an entire state system of higher education. Yet, in each of these studies, researchers have found some type of negative relationship between increased levels of part-time instruction and student academic success (e.g., persistence).

Fewer studies have focused on the relationship between student exposure to part-time faculty members and student outcomes at community colleges. One of the first research efforts was conducted by Burgess and Samuels (1999), who examined the impact of full-time versus part-time faculty instruction on student performance and persistence in selected sequential courses. Drawing on analyses of data from a large, urban multicampus community college district, the results indicated that students whose first course was taught by a full-time instructor were better prepared for their second, subsequent course than were students whose first course was taught by a part-time instructor. Yet, because full-time instructors did not significantly outperform part-time instructors, and because the sample was limited to one college district, Burgess and Samuels provided only a starting point to examine the effects of part-time instruction on student outcomes.

More recently, Calcagno, Bailey, Jenkins, Kienzl, and Leinbach (in press) used data from the National Education Longitudinal Study of 1988 (NELS: 88) and the Integrated Postsecondary Education Data System (IPEDS) to examine the effect that institutional dependence on part-time faculty members has on the graduation rates of students at community colleges. The researchers found a significant and negative relationship between the level of part-time faculty employment and student degree completion (i.e., certificate, associate's degree, or bachelor's degree) or student success in transferring to a four-year institution. Because of the broad definition of degree completion used by Calcagno et al., the results from this study did not provide evidence that specifically addressed the relationship between part-time faculty members and associate's degree completion rates at community colleges.

Also using IPEDS data, Jacoby (2006) examined whether graduation rates at public community colleges nationwide differed as institutions increased their use of part-time faculty members. Jacoby's study focused on institutional data, and, although his analyses included state-level controls, he did not account for student-level variables. Jacoby concluded that increased employment of part-time faculty members at community colleges negatively affected institutional associate's-degree completion rates. Although the focus on institutional factors provided insight into the effects of part-time faculty employment on community college graduation rates from a macroperspective, Jacoby's study did not advance the literature on how the exposure of individual students to part-time faculty members affects their likelihood of earning an associate's degree.

Associate's Degree Completion at Community Colleges

Students seeking associate's degrees represent just one category of students attending community colleges. Although comprising a distinct group, associate's-degree seeking students represent great diversity, as some of these students enter community colleges with strong academic preparation (e.g., those entering science and technology fields), whereas others begin their coursework by registering for remedial classes (Cohen & Brawer, 2003). Those students needing significant remedial work will require more time and resources to complete their degree and often have low social and cultural capital.

Scholars increasingly have focused on factors affecting the likelihood that students will transfer from community colleges to four-year institutions; however, many of the students entering community colleges have no intention of transferring and instead aspire to a subbaccalaureate credential or associate's degree (Grubb, 1996; Rendon & Nora, 1989). Despite this fact, no study has considered explicitly how exposure to part-time faculty members affects the likelihood that community college students will complete an associate's degree. However, a number of studies have examined other factors affecting associate's degree completion.

Dowd and Coury (2006) studied the effect of subsidized loans on the associate's degree attainment of community college students. They concluded that neither the receipt of financial aid (dichotomously coded) nor the actual amount of aid (continuously coded) had a significant effect on whether students earned an associate's degree within 5 years of initial enrollment in a community college. Students with higher community college grade point averages (GPAs) and those who identified themselves as being financially dependent on their parents had significantly higher odds of earning an associate's degree. Conversely, older students, single parents, and individuals who had either not declared a major or who had enrolled in vocational programs had significantly reduced odds of attaining an associate's degree. The study by Dowd and Coury added to the literature examining community college degree attainment, but their research is limited in terms of sample size, variables included in the analyses, and the types of analyses conducted. Although Dowd and Coury used appropriate weights for their sample, the actual analytic sample had just 694 students from the Beginning Postsecondary Students Longitudinal Survey covering the years 1990-1994. The authors did not include any experiential factors, such as interactions with faculty members, in their analyses. In addition, the single-level analyses did not account for the multilevel, clustered nature of the data that reflect the grouping of students within individual community colleges. By ignoring the clustering effect of students within institutions, the authors may have underestimated standard errors of the estimated parameters in their model, which may have resulted in Type I statistical errors (Wang & Fan, 1997).

In a qualitative study, Cejda and Rhodes (2004) examined how the connections Hispanic community college students had with faculty members affected their retention and program completion. They discovered that frequent and intentional interactions with faculty members inside and outside the classroom significantly contributed to the students' success in completing a subbaccalaureate credential, earning an associate's degree, or transferring to a four-year institution. The faculty members in the study emphasized that becoming role models and mentors for these Hispanic students played an important role in encouraging and fostering their success in community colleges (Cejda & Rhodes, 2004).

Associate's degree completion within the state of California has its own set of unique challenges. For example, students who obtain an associate's degree at one of the California community colleges take two courses over the number transferable to a University of California institution (J. S. Levin, personal communication, September 7, 2008). Taking two additional courses, which would not transfer to a four-year institution, to obtain an associate's degree may not be an economically feasible choice for the many low-income community college students. Obtaining an associate's degree versus obtaining two years of equivalency work is an important decision for community college students in California.

Our study addresses the limitations of prior research related to associate's degree completion across community colleges. By drawing on student- and institution-level data from California's community college system, and by utilizing advanced statistical analyses, our study aims to identify how student traits and behaviors interact with institutional contexts in relation to completing an associate's degree. Furthermore, this study specifically examines how exposure to part-time faculty members at the student level, as well as the proportion of part-time faculty members employed at the institutional level, affect associate's degree completion for community college students.

Conceptual Framework

Drawing on a conceptual model from previous work (Eagan & Jaeger, in press), this study assumes that students exposed to greater levels of instruction from part-time faculty members experience fewer meaningful interactions with those faculty members than they would with full-time instructors. As a consequence, students may become less integrated into the campus academic culture, an outcome supported by studies indicating the importance of faculty-student interactions to student success (Cotten & Wilson, 2006; Endo & Harpel, 1982; Gaff & Gaff, 1981; Nora,

Barlow, & Crisp, 2005; Pascarella & Terenzini, 1977, 2005). In addition, Baldwin and Chronister (2001) noted that students may view part-time faculty members as less stable or less secure. To the extent that this occurs—something that should be assessed in future research—students may be less likely to connect with these faculty members and see them as potential mentors or role models. Research has suggested that faculty-student interaction, particularly outside of the classroom, serves as a positive predictor of cognitive and affective development, academic achievement, and overall satisfaction with the college experience (Cotten & Wilson, 2006; Endo & Harpel, 1982; Milem & Berger, 1997).

It is plausible that students who have few interactions with part-time faculty members or who have few meaningful connections to these faculty members may become dissatisfied with their experience and thus more inclined to leave their college or university (Eagan & Jaeger, in press). Students who are more satisfied with their experience indicate that their instructors are more accessible and involved (Jaasma & Koper, 2002). A 2007 national report released by the Community College Survey of Student Engagement (CCSSE) analyzed 5 years of engagement data, revealing that the accessibility of faculty is critical. Almost half (47%) of the students responding to the CCSSE indicated they had never discussed course readings with a faculty member outside of class. In addition, as few as 8% reported they had often or very often worked with instructors on activities outside of class (Community College Survey of Student Engagement, 2006). McClenney (2007) added to the concern for the lack of student engagement by highlighting the differences between part-time and full-time students. She noted that part-time students are significantly less likely to work with other students on projects either inside or outside of class; to interact with instructors via email or have conversations about grades, assignments, or career plans; and to make a class presentation. Thus, CCSSE data illustrate that the experience of part-time students appears to be systematically less engaging than the experience of full-time students.

Another perspective that informs this work is social capital and students' ability to generate and utilize social capital during their time at a community college (Jaeger & Eagan, 2008). Social capital corresponds to the production function of social connections (Coleman, 1988). By engaging in closed network systems, individual actors can tap into information channels and engender a sense of trust and reciprocity with others in the social network (Coleman, 1988). Developing relationships with and connections to other actors within a social system enables individuals to generate social capital for themselves (Portes, 1998).

This study utilizes the idea of social capital to help understand how community college students may be disadvantaged by increased exposure to part-time faculty members. The disadvantaged backgrounds from which many community college students originate, as well as a tendency for these students to be less academically prepared than their peers in four-year institutions, may place community college students at a deficit when considering their levels of both cultural and social capital. To counteract this potential deficit, community college students may need additional nurturing and guidance from mentors and faculty members.

Although social capital involves trust and reciprocity, information and knowledge, and norms and sanctions, we focus on how social capital facilitates networks of information and knowledge. This study builds on other research (Cejda & Rhodes, 2004; Stanton-Salazar & Dornbusch, 1995) that considers how students can generate social capital through their connections with institutional agents. Community college students can build social capital by connecting with various institutional agents including faculty members, advisors, and administrators. These relationships help students navigate the institution and make progress in their courses or toward degree completion. Yet, students who are unable to connect with these institutional agents or who are exposed to greater numbers of part-time faculty members who themselves are less integrated into the campus culture (Schuster, 2003) may be at a disadvantage. If part-time faculty members are less accessible to students (Umbach, 2007), their ability to help students successfully navigate the academic processes within a community college may be curtailed. Research (Cotten & Wilson, 2006; Milem & Berger, 1997) has demonstrated the importance of having an engaged and available faculty on campus, showing positive links between student–faculty interactions and student development while in college.

Method

Research Question

Drawing from social capital theory and previous research examining part-time faculty members, this study seeks to address the following research question: Controlling for background characteristics, does exposure to part-time faculty members in community colleges significantly affect students' likelihood of completing an associate's degree? It is hypothesized that as students' exposure to part-time faculty members increases, their likelihood of completing the associate's degree decreases. A secondary research question asks the following question: Controlling for student-level characteristics, does the percentage of part-time faculty members employed by an institution significantly affect the average likelihood of associate's degree completion at community colleges?

Data and Sample

This study draws on student transcript, faculty employment, and institutional data from the California community college system. Utilizing two cohorts of first-time, credit-seeking students in 2000 and 2001, this study tracks the college-going behavior of California community college students over 5 years. The initial sample of students included more than 700,000 cases within each cohort, which translated into an initial overall sample of nearly 1.5 million students in 107 community colleges.

Because this study focuses on associate's degree completion, we reduced the sample to reflect those students whose initial aspirations as well as 1st-year course-taking behavior demonstrated a serious intention of completing an associate's degree. We delimited the sample to those students who initially indicated when they first enrolled in this system that they intended to complete an associate's degree and who had completed at least nine credit hours by the end of their 1st year of enrollment. Although scholars have suggested that initial aspirations provide a poor measure of actual intention and future behavior (Adelman, 2005; Cohen, 1991), we wanted to analyze a sample of students who had at least indicated an initial inclination toward an associate's degree rather than a sample that included all students, such as lifelong learners and individuals from four-year institutions taking classes at their local community college. In addition, by further delimiting the sample to students who had completed at least nine units by the end of the 1st year, we attempted to eliminate individuals who may have used their time in the community college system as a single-term placeholder before moving into a four-year institution. With these constraints imposed, the final analytic sample for this study included 178,985 students in 107 community colleges.

In addition to the student-level data provided by the California community college system office, we merged institutional data from IPEDS into our institution-level dataset. Variables we retrieved from IPEDS for each of the 107 California community colleges included the proportion of the faculty employed on a part-time basis, institutional size, and total revenues generated by each community college. Data from IPEDS provided a more complete picture of community colleges in the state of California.

Variables

In addition to the students' first-year and cumulative GPAs, the student dataset provided by the system office included variables related to students' background characteristics, enrollment traits, and course-taking behaviors. The dependent variable, associate's degree completion, represented a dichotomous variable reflecting whether or not a student completed an associate's degree within 5 years of initially enrolling in the system of community colleges. We included gender, ethnicity, age, and citizenship as demographic controls in the model. We created dummy variables for gender (male as the reference group), each race (White as the reference group), and citizenship (noncitizen as the reference group). We kept students' age as a continuous variable.

Variables relating to students' enrollment characteristics included controls for enrollment status (full-time student as the reference group), academic program, and financial aid. We controlled for students in vocational studies and those with undeclared majors, with students studying in traditional academic programs as the reference group. We had two variables related to financial aid. First, we controlled for whether students applied for and received aid. Second, we included the average amount of financial aid a student received across all terms of his or her enrollment at a particular community college.

We used student transcript data to create variables representing the extent of exposure students had to part-time faculty members. We defined part-time faculty members as those instructors hired at or below 98% of a full-time appointment. To examine possible differences between exposure to part-time faculty members in the students' first-year of enrollment and overall exposure to part-time faculty members at community colleges over the 5-year period covered by the study, we created two separate yet related variables. We added the number of credits a student completed with part-time faculty members in the first year and divided that total by the number of credits the student completed during his or her first year. We used an identical procedure to create a variable for the overall exposure to part-time faculty members across all years in which a student enrolled at a community college. These quotients, representing students' exposure to part-time faculty members in the first year and overall, provided the percentage of credits students took with part-timers. We recoded these variables so that a one-unit increase corresponded to an increase of 10% in students' time with part-time faculty members.

In addition to student-level variables, we included several institutional variables in our analyses. We controlled separately for the proportion of instruction offered by part-time faculty members as well as the proportion of faculty members employed in part-time appointments at each community college. We also included in our models the percentage of students identified as racial minorities, state and local revenues, institutional size as measured by the number of full-time equivalent students, and the urbanicity of the institution. For urbanicity, we used dummy variables for urban and rural campuses, with suburban campuses as the reference group.

Analyses

The multilevel, clustered design of the data necessitated the use of advanced statistical techniques (Raudenbush & Bryk, 2002). With this design and a dichotomous outcome variable, we utilized HGLM to understand the unique effects of student- and institution-level variables on students' likelihood of earning an associate's degree. HGLM enables analysts to distinguish between institutional and individual effects on the dependent variable. The use of single-level statistical techniques, such as logistic regression, for complex, multilevel data structures, may underestimate the standard errors of the estimated parameters in the model. Underestimated standard errors may lead to a Type I statistical error, which occurs when a researcher erroneously concludes that a parameter is statistically significant. (Raudenbush & Bryk, 2002).

Generally, to warrant the use of hierarchical linear modeling, the outcome variable must significantly vary across institutions (Raudenbush & Bryk, 2002). With continuous outcome variables, researchers can calculate the intraclass correlation (ICC) to determine whether the dependent variable varies significantly across groups. The heteroskedasticity of the variance of the dichotomous outcome variable in this study makes an ICC calculation non-instructive; instead, we relied on graphs of Empirical-Bayes (EB) residuals to determine whether the average associate's degree completion rates varied across institutions. Inspection of these graphs suggested that institutional graduation rates significantly differed; thus, we proceeded with the use of HGLM. Finally, in constructing our models, we centered all continuous variables around their grand mean.

Limitations

This study has at least three limitations. First, an important limitation to this study exists in the potential lack of consistency in data collection methods across the institutions in the sample. Despite the system office's efforts to standardize data collection methods, definitions and methods may continue to vary slightly across institutions. Second, because we analyze secondary data, we are restricted by the variables and definitions available in the community college system and

IPEDS datasets. For example, the system dataset did not provide information about students' prior academic performance because community colleges generally do not have any selection criteria in admitting students (Cohen & Brawer, 2003); thus, they rarely collect or report this information for students who enroll. Finally, the identification of the students included in the analytic sample has a certain level of subjectivity. The method used to identify the analytic sample may lead to a certain bias in the analyses by excluding some students who decided to pursue an associate's degree long after their initial enrollment in the community college system. Although we recognize this as a limitation, we believe that having an exclusion bias provides more realistic results than having an inclusion bias, which would occur had we included all of the students in the initial population.

Results

Descriptive Statistics

Table 1 presents descriptive statistics for the student- and institution-level variables included in the analyses. Even after reducing our analytic sample to include students who completed at least nine credits in their first year and who initially indicated an intent to earn an associate's degree, just 19% of students in our sample actually earned the degree. Such a low percentage of associate's degree completers among a cohort of students who initially aspired to earn the degree underscores the importance of investigating the facilitators of and barriers to successfully completing an associate's degree.

On average, students earned 48% of their credit hours in courses taught by part-time faculty members during their 1st-year of enrollment. This figure increased slightly to 49% when considering all years of enrollment. Disaggregating the sample by enrollment status showed that exposure to part-time faculty members was slightly higher for part-time students than it was for their full-time counterparts. Considering another variable related to academics, students had an average first-year GPA of 2.74. Students' GPAs tended to decline slightly with time, as their final cumulative GPAs averaged 2.45.

Women comprised 55% of the analytic sample, which resembled their representation (54%) in the larger population of California community college students. Asian American and Pacific Islander students accounted for 14% and 5% of the analytic sample, respectively. These percentages indicated a slight overrepresentation of Asian Americans and Pacific Islanders in the analytic sample; students in both groups combined constitute 13% of the entire community college population in California. White students constituted 41% of the sample, which was slightly less than the percentage of White students enrolled in the state's community college system (46%). Comparatively, Latino and Black students made up 25% and 7% of the analytic sample, respectively. In the California community college system, Latino students represent 25.3% of the overall population, and Black students represent approximately 8% of the total student population.

The average age of students in the analytic sample was 21.6, which was significantly lower than the average age (28 years old) of students enrolled throughout the system. This statistic suggests that younger students may be more likely than older students to enroll in community colleges with an intent to pursue an associate's degree. Older individuals may have other goals in mind, such as vocational retraining or lifelong learning, when they first enroll. Less than half (44%) of the students in the sample applied for and received financial aid, and the average amount of financial aid received per year was just under US$400. Nearly two thirds of students enrolled on a part-time basis. Approximately 29% of students in our sample did not declare a major, and 5% of the students majored in vocational studies programs. The balance of students studied a variety of fields, ranging from liberal arts and humanities to science and technology.

Among the institutional variables, part-timers constituted 65% of all faculty members across all the institutions in the system in 2002. The mean total state revenue for institutions was just more than US$23 million but ranged widely across institutions from US$1.14 million to US$87.06 million. Similarly, local revenues averaged US$18 million but ranged across institutions from US$1.04 million to US$74.04 million. About 44% of the campuses were located in urban areas, whereas 31% were in suburban locations and 25% were in rural areas.

TABLE 1

Descriptive Statistics for Variables in the Model

Variable	M	SD	Min.	Max.
Dependent variable (n = 178,985)				
Earned an associate's degree	0.19	0.39	0.00	1.00
Independent student-level variables (n = 178,985)				
Female	0.55	0.50	0.00	1.00
Asian	0.14	0.34	0.00	1.00
Black	0.07	0.25	0.00	1.00
Pacific Islander	0.05	0.22	0.00	1.00
Latino	0.25	0.43	0.00	1.00
Other race or ethnicity	0.07	0.15	0.00	1.00
White	0.41	0.49	0.00	1.00
Citizenship	0.79	0.41	0.00	1.00
Age	21.64	6.92	17.00	70.00
Received financial aid	0.44	0.48	0.00	1.00
Average financial aid per year (in US$)	377.81	647.08	0.00	10,356.67
Enrolled part-time	0.63	0.48	0.00	1.00
Undeclared major	0.29	0.46	0.00	1.00
Vocational studies major	0.05	0.21	0.00	1.00
1st-year grade point average	2.74	0.76	0.00	4.00
1st-year percent exposure to part-time faculty members ($\times10$)	4.80	0.14	0.00	10.00
Cumulative grade point average	2.45	0.75	0.00	4.00
Overall percentage exposure to part-time faculty members ($\times10$)	4.90	0.23	0.00	10.00
Independent institution-level variables (n = 107)				
Percentage of faculty members in part-time appointments	0.65	0.09	0.08	0.86
Full-time equivalent (FTE) student enrollment (in 100s)	65.48	37.55	5.63	177.41
State revenues (in US$1,000,000s)	23.20	16.45	1.14	87.06
Local revenues (in US$1,000,000s)	18.09	12.57	1.04	74.04
Urban campus	0.44	0.50	0.00	1.00
Rural campus	0.25	0.44	0.00	1.00
Suburban campus	0.31	0.46	0.00	1.00
% of students identified as racial minorities ($\times10$)	5.42	2.01	1.29	9.92

Note: Min. = Minimum; Max. = Maximum.

HGLM Analyses

Table 2 presents the results from the HGLM analyses and details the log-odds, the odds ratios, and the delta-p statistics. Petersen's (1985) formula was used to calculate delta-p statistics, and we show these statistics only for those variables that were significant at $p < .05$. Table 2 shows the results for two models; however, the models differ only slightly. Model 1 includes first-year GPA and first-year percentage exposure to part-time faculty (i.e., the proportion of credits completed during the 1st year that were earned in classes taught by part-time faculty members.) In contrast, Model 2 includes total cumulative GPA and overall percentage of exposure to part-time faculty members across all years in which a student was enrolled. The control variables did not differ significantly between the two models, thus we only discuss the results of the control variables from Model 1.

TABLE 2

Hierarchical Generalized Linear Modeling (HGLM) Results

Variables	Model 1				Model 2			
	Log Odds	SE	Sig.	Delta-P	Log Odds	SE	Sig.	Delta-P
Student-level variables								
Female	0.36	0.02	***	6.2%	0.36	0.01	***	6.2%
Asian American	0.01	0.02		0.03	0.02			
Black	−0.08	0.03	**	−1.2%	−0.07	0.03	**	−1.1%
Pacific Islander	0.04	0.03		0.14	0.03***			2.2%
Latino	−0.06	0.01	***	−0.9%	0.06	0.01	***	0.9%
Other	−0.12	0.06	*	−1.8%	−0.08	0.06		
Citizenship	0.03	0.01	**	0.5%	0.09	0.01	***	1.4%
Age	0.01	0.00	***	0.2%	0.01	0.00	***	0.2%
Financial aid status	−0.20	0.05	***	−2.9%	−0.15	0.05	***	−2.2%
Average financial aid per year	0.02	0.00	***	0.3%	0.02	0.00	***	0.3%
Undeclared major	−0.22	0.01	***	−3.2%	0.21	0.01	***	3.4%
Vocational studies major	−0.34	0.04	***	−4.7%	−0.33	0.04	***	−4.6%
Part-time student	−1.68	0.01	***	−14.8%	−1.46	0.01	***	−13.8%
1st-year grade point average	0.39	0.01	***	6.7%				
1st-year percent exposure to part-time faculty	−.03	.00	***	−1.0%				
Total cumulative grade point average					0.81	0.01	***	15.5%
Total percent exposure to part-time faculty					−0.04	0.00	***	−1.1%
Institutional variables								
Intercept	−0.73	0.09	***		−1.06	0.10	***	
Percent of faculty in part-time appointments	−0.57	0.40		−0.52	0.44		*	−6.8%
State revenues	0.01	0.00	*	0.2%	0.01	0.00		
Local revenues	0.01	0.01		0.01	0.01	0.01		
Institutional size (FTE students)	−0.01	0.00	*	−0.2%	−0.01	0.00	*	−0.2%
Urban campus	0.05	0.11		0.05	0.05	0.11		
Rural campus	−0.01	0.13		−0.01	−0.01	0.14		
% of students identified as racial minorities	−0.05	0.02	*	−0.8%	−0.05	0.03		

Model Statistics	Model 1		Model 2	
Level-2 variance	0.19		0.19	
Intercept reliability	0.94		0.94	
Chi-square	2694.96	***	2737.94	***

Note: SE = standard error; FTE = full-time equivalent.

*$p < .05$. **$p < .01$. ***$p < .001$.

The key variable of interest in this study was the percentage of credits students completed with part-time instructors. Model 1 tested the significance of students' exposure to part-time faculty members during their first year of enrollment. The results suggest that an increase of 10% in the first-year proportion of credits earned in courses taught by part-time faculty members resulted in students becoming 1% less likely to earn an associate's degree. In Model 2, we included a measure of exposure to part-time faculty members across all years of enrollment, and the effect was quite similar. Although the log-odds coefficient in Model 2 associated with exposure to part-time faculty members had a slightly greater magnitude than the coefficient in Model 1, the delta-p statistic remained stable. Indeed, a 10% increase in the overall proportion of credits earned in courses taught by part-time faculty members reduced the students' likelihood of earning an associate's degree by 1%. This effect may seem quite small; however, considering that the average student earned approximately 50% of all of his or her credit hours in courses taught by part-time faculty members, the average student became 5% less likely to graduate with an associate's degree compared to his or her peers whose courses were taught by full-time faculty only. About 5,000 students, or just less than 3% of the analytic sample, had no exposure to part-time faculty members. In contrast, approximately 90,000 students earned between 40% and 60% of their credits in classes taught by part-timers. Similarly, more than 7,800 students (4.4% of the analytic sample) in this study earned all of their academic credits in courses taught by part-time faculty members, which translated into their being 10% less likely to earn an associate's degree than their peers who took courses taught only by full-time faculty members.

In contrast to exposure to part-time faculty members, first-year GPA had a significant and positive effect on students' likelihood to complete an associate's degree completion. For every one-unit increase in first-year GPA, students became about 7% more likely to earn an associate's degree. This trend held for Model 2 as well, although the effect of GPA became much more substantial when considering students' cumulative, rather than 1st-year GPA. For every one-unit increase in cumulative GPA, students became almost 16% more likely to earn an associate's degree.

Among the demographic characteristics, gender emerged as a significant variable in that women appeared to be 6% more likely to earn an associate's degree than their male peers. Several controls for race were significant, though the effect was marginal at best. Black and Latino students were approximately 1% less likely than their White counterparts to earn an associate's degree. Similarly, students classified as Other in terms of ethnicity were just 2% less likely to earn an associate's degree.

Financial aid seemed to have a significant and substantial effect on students' likelihood to earn an associate's degree. Students who received financial aid because of demonstrated financial need were about 3% less likely to earn an associate's degree than their peers who did not receive financial aid. Because of the poor quality of the parental and student income variables, we were unable to accurately control for students' socioeconomic status or actual financial need; therefore, the variable related to receipt of financial aid served in some ways as a proxy for socioeconomic status. The amount of financial aid that students received also had a significant albeit modest effect on associate's degree completion. For every US$100 increase in average aid per year, students became less than 1% more likely to earn an associate's degree.

Several student entry characteristics emerged as significant predictors of associate's degree completion in the models. Part-time students were 15% less likely than their full-time counterparts to earn an associate's degree. Similarly, students with undeclared majors or those majoring in vocational studies were 3% and 5%, respectively, less likely to earn an associate's degree than students majoring in all other fields, such as science, mathematics, humanities, and liberal arts. Students were only assigned an undeclared status if they never declared a major during their enrollment or if they left before declaring a major.

In addition to the student-level variables, a few institution-level variables emerged as significant in both models. For simplicity purposes, we describe only the results from Model 1 because both models produced similar results in regard to institution-level predictors. Students attending community colleges that enrolled higher proportions of racial minority students were significantly less likely to earn an associate's degree. Specifically, a 10% increase in the proportion of minorities enrolled at a community college resulted in an average decrease of approximately 1% in a student's probability of earning an associate's degree. Similarly, institutional size had a statistically significant yet practically negligible negative effect on completion rates; indeed, the effect of a 100-student increase resulted in a 0.2% decrease in a student's likelihood of earning an associate's degree. State revenues had a significant positive effect on associate's degree completion, but the effect was negligible. The proportion of faculty members employed in part-time appointments had no significant effect on individuals' likelihood to earn an associate's degree, which is an important finding that we will discuss further in the next section. In other models (not shown), we included the proportion of instruction offered by part-time faculty members in lieu of the proportion of faculty members employed on a part-time basis. This variable did not emerge as significant and actually appeared to add error to our model.

Both models had a modest fit for the data. Table 2 includes the chi-square statistics for each model. Each model accounted for approximately 19% of the variance in degree completion rates across institutions. Level-one variance was heteroskedastic; therefore, HGLM cannot estimate explained variance for level one.

Discussion

This study sought to determine whether exposure to part-time faculty members affected students' likelihood of completing an associate's degree at a community college. Findings from the HGLM analyses suggest that exposure to part-time faculty members had a significant yet modest negative effect on completing an associate's degree. Although we recognize that degree completion represents a limited outcome variable for use with community colleges, the completion of an associate's degree often serves as a catalyst to advanced educational training at four-year institutions (Quigley & Bailey, 2003). Yet, as students' exposure to part-time faculty members increased, their likelihood of completing an associate's degree significantly decreased. This effect remained stable across time as students advanced through their academic programs.

As previously noted, a 10% increase in overall exposure to part-time faculty members resulted in a 1% reduction in the students' likelihood of earning an associate's degree. Although this effect appears small, administrators and policymakers should consider that the average California community college student spends nearly 50% of his or her classroom time in courses with part-time instructors. According to estimates from our models, this level of exposure translates into the average student being at least 5% less likely to graduate with an associate's degree compared to his or her peers who only have full-time instructors in the classroom, holding constant all other variables in the model. In general, these findings are similar to the results of prior research on the negative effects of exposure to part-time faculty members on student retention and degree completion at four-year institutions (Ehrenberg & Zhang, 2004; Harrington & Schibik, 2004; Jaeger & Hinz, 2008; Ronco & Cahill, 2004).

Although the effect of exposure to part-time faculty members was smaller compared to other variables in the model, community college administrators and policy makers actually have some control in addressing this issue. As prior research has demonstrated, a more available and fully engaged faculty positively contributes to a number of student outcomes, including transfer and associate's degree completion (Cejda & Rhodes, 2004). Inferring from prior research (Eagan, 2007; Haeger, 1998; Umbach, 2007), the dissatisfaction of part-time faculty members with employment benefits, along with their lack of integration into the campus culture, may contribute to their inaccessibility and limited availability to students. With increased incentives, part-time faculty members may make a more concerted effort to be more available to students and work harder to engage students in the classroom.

By becoming more engaged with students, part-time faculty members have an opportunity to contribute to the development of community college students' social capital. As demonstrated by Milem and Berger (1997) and Cotten and Wilson (2006), connecting with faculty members inside and outside the classroom positively affects students in a number of ways. The negative correlation between exposure to part-time faculty members and associate's degree completion may indeed be related to the students' sense that they receive little support and guidance from part-time faculty members, who may lack the time and perhaps the necessary knowledge needed to assist their students in navigating the academic terrain at their respective institutions. At the same time, these students may need additional encouragement from the faculty to help them realize the potential benefits of completing their associate's degrees. Students arriving at the community colleges often need greater nurturing from the faculty, yet with high levels of exposure to part-time faculty members, they may not find the academic support necessary to work toward the completion of an associate's degree program.

In addition, this study suggests that it is important to consider how colleges might better meet the needs of part-time students. Part-time students in this study were approximately 15% less likely than their full-time peers to earn an associate's degree. Students attend college on a part-time basis for a variety of reasons, such as family commitments, work obligations, and general preferences (Cohen & Brawer, 2003). Because of their more limited time on campus, part-time students may experience greater challenges than full-time students in making connections to faculty members and peers. Because these connections may enhance students' social capital by providing additional information and support that help sustain progress toward an associate's degree, part-time students appear to have a substantial disadvantage compared to their full-time peers.

The authors of the 2007 national report released by the CCSSE noted that rethinking part-time faculty work will likely have the greatest effect on part-time students, because part-time faculty members are more likely to teach at night and on weekends when part-time students are more likely to take classes. This suggests that decisions regarding what courses part-time faculty members teach and when those courses are offered have important consequences. Unfortunately, this study was unable to specifically examine factors that contribute to part-time students' reduced likelihood of completing an associate's degree. Additional research should examine how administrators might better reach out to part-time students and encourage their continued academic success.

One finding from this study was inconsistent with prior research. The results from this study suggest that neither the proportion of faculty members employed in part-time appointments at community colleges nor the proportion of instruction offered by part-time faculty members had a significant effect on associate's degree completion rates. Jacoby (2006) analyzed only institutional-level data and found that part-time faculty members negatively affected graduation rates at community colleges. By analyzing both student and institution-level variables, this study appropriately separated multilevel variance and suggested that the reduced likelihood in graduation rates likely has more to do with individual student exposure to part-time faculty members than it does with the overall proportion of part-timers employed by a community college. Other institution-level results provide little practical insight for administrators and policymakers in community colleges.

In addition to highlighting the need to assist part-time students, this study suggests that campus administrators should provide additional encouragement and support to students who have not declared a major or who enroll in vocational studies programs. Undeclared and vocational studies majors were 3% and 5%, respectively, less likely to complete an associate's degree compared to their peers in other fields. In addition, it is likely that students who have not declared a major may also be attending on a part-time basis, which presents an even greater challenge to completing a degree.

Future Research

This study lays the foundation for future research that can be undertaken in a number of directions. First, future studies should consider sensitivity analyses to determine how the selection of the analytic sample affects the results of the regression analyses. This study relied on students' initial degree aspirations at the outset of their enrollment as well as on the students' first-year course-taking behavior to select cases for inclusion in the analyses. Rather than relying on degree aspirations to reduce the sample, future researchers might consider only eliminating individuals who enroll for lifelong learning purposes as well as students from four-year institutions who enroll to take a course that is related to their baccalaureate degree.

Second, future research should include more controls for students' socioeconomic status, family obligations, and employment commitments. The initial dataset for this study included limited information on students' socioeconomic status, and the variables to which we had access had a substantial number of missing cases. Similarly, limited information related to students' family obligations and employment existed in the data. Given the diversity of the population of students who enroll in community colleges, it is important for future research to consider these additional nuances when predicting degree completion.

Third, including variables that provide a more comprehensive picture of the climate at individual institutions would enhance the analyses and potentially explain more variance in institutional completion rates. For this study, IPEDS data had limited information that could be included in the analyses. However, in future analyses, we intend to aggregate student-level predictors to generate a more complete picture of the institutional context in which students enroll. Some of these aggregated variables may include the percentage of students who transfer to four-year institutions as well as the percentage of students who major in or graduate from programs devoted to vocational studies. Within this particular state system of community colleges, institutions vary significantly in their purposes; some institutions specialize in vocational studies whereas others are more committed to encouraging transfer to four-year institutions and baccalaureate degree completion among students studying more traditional academic disciplines.

Future research might also consider using other advanced analyses. For example, students in the present study may have enrolled simultaneously in multiple community colleges. HGLM is limited in that it accounts for the effect of one institution at a time even though a student's likelihood of degree completion may be affected by multiple institutional contexts. Cross-classified hierarchical linear modeling would more accurately account for the varying contexts students experience when they simultaneously enroll at more than one community college. Finally, we have undertaken a new project to consider specific factors that lead to increased cost and production efficiencies in the California community colleges. Using an advanced econometric technique known as stochastic frontier analysis, we will estimate the extent to which California's community colleges can simultaneously improve both their efficiency at constraining costs while increasing their production of associate's degree earners, certificate holders, and transfer students.

Implications and Conclusion

As higher education enrollments continue to expand (Martinez, 2004), policy makers will look to public community colleges and four-year institutions to accommodate the increased demand for postsecondary degrees. Following recent growth patterns, community colleges likely will accommodate the bulk of this expansion (Martinez, 2004). With more students entering community colleges across the United States, administrators and policy makers need to develop a better understanding of how students navigate the community college system, particularly those who have an interest in earning an associate's degree. In addition, as enrollments in community colleges increase, community colleges may continue their efforts to maintain economic efficiency by relying more heavily on part-time faculty members, which could have unintended consequences on student outcomes. Policy makers, faculty members, and administrators should consider various curricular decisions, such as what time of day and what courses part-time faculty members teach. Some of these decisions may be negotiable and have a significant effect on student outcomes, particularly for part-time students. Administrators and faculty members should also provide additional support to undeclared students, who often enroll on a part-time basis, because, according to this study, they have an increased chance of not achieving their aspirations for an associate's degree. Because the study results suggest that students with a clearer educational plan have a significantly increased likelihood of earning an associate's degree, administrators and faculty members need to offer special attention to undeclared students to help them identify a clearer academic path.

It is clear that part-time faculty members serve an important role across all institutions of higher education, and this research does not rest blame with the part-time faculty. It is financially and administratively impractical for community colleges to begin reducing the proportion of part-time faculty members they employ; thus, community college administrators and policy makers should consider how they can improve the environment in which these part-timers work. If administrators and full-time faculty members worked to increase the integration of part-time faculty members into campus and departmental cultures, and if attempts were made to address the concerns part-timers have about employment benefits, a greater sense of commitment and enthusiasm from part-time faculty members might be generated. Improving the work environment for part-time faculty members at community colleges has the potential to increase their sense of commitment, which may have positive implications for a variety of student outcomes, including associate's degree completion.

References

Adelman, C. (2005). *Moving into town—and moving on: The community college in the lives of traditional-age students.* Washington, DC: U.S. Department of Education.

American Association of Community Colleges (2006). *Achieving the dream: Success is what counts.* Retrieved May 7, 2008, from http://www.achievingthedream.org/docs/SUCCESS-counts-FINAL-11.6.pdf

American Association of University Professors. (2006). *AAUP contingent faculty index.* Washington, DC: Author. Retrieved December 14, 2006, from http://www.aaup.org/NR/ rdonlyres/F05FF88E-B2A8-4052-8373-AF0FDAE060AC/0/ConsequencesAnIncreasingly ContingentFaculty.pdf

Baldwin, R. G., & Chronister, J. L. (2001). *Teaching without tenure: Policies and practices for a new era.* Baltimore: Johns Hopkins University Press.

Bowen, H. R. (1996). *Investment in learning: The individual and social value of American higher education.* Edison, NJ: Transaction.

Burgess, L. A., & Samuels, C. (1999). Impact of full-time versus part-time instructor status on college student retention and academic performance in sequential courses. *Community College Journal of Research and Practice, 23,* 487–498.

Calcagno, J. C., Bailey, T., Jenkins, D., Kienzl, G., & Leinbach, T. (in press). Community college student success: What institutional characteristics make a difference? *Economics of Education Review.*

Cataldi, E. F., Fahimi, M., Bradburn, E. M., & Zimbler, L. (2005). *2004 National study of postsecondary faculty (NSOPF:04) report on faculty and instructional staff in fall 2003* (NCES Report No. 2005–172). Washington, DC: U.S. Department of Education, Institute of Educational Sciences.

Cejda, B. D., & Rhodes, J. H. (2004). Through the pipeline: The role of faculty in promoting associate degree completion among Hispanic students. *Community College Journal of Research and Practice, 28,* 249–262.

Choy, S. P. (2002). Nontraditional undergraduates. In *The condition of education 2002* (NCES 2002-025, pp. 25–39). Washington, DC: U.S. Department of Education, National Center for Education Statistics.

Cohen, A. M. (1991). Deriving a valid transfer rate. In E. B. Jones (Ed.), *A model for deriving the transfer rate: Report of the transfer assembly project* (pp. 115). Washington, DC: Community College Press.

Cohen, A. M., & Brawer, F. B. (2003). *The American community college* (4th ed.). San Francisco: Jossey-Bass.

Coleman, J. S. (1988). Social capital in the creation of human capital. *American Journal of Sociology, 94,* S95–S120.

Community College Survey of Student Engagement. (n.d.). *Key findings: Student-faculty interaction.* Retrieved June 29, 2008, from Community College Survey of Student Engagement Web site, http://www.ccsse.org/survey/bench_sfi.cfm.

Community College Survey of Student Engagement. (2007). *Committing to student engagement: Reflections on CCSSE's first five years.* Retrieved June 29, 2008, from Community College Survey of Student Engagement Web site, http://www.ccsse.org/publications/ 2007NatlRpt-final.pdf.

Cotten, S. R., & Wilson, B. (2006). Student-faculty interactions: Dynamics and determinants. *Higher Education, 51,* 487–519.

Dougherty, K. J. (1994). *The contradictory college: Conflicting origins, impacts, and futures of the community college.* Albany, NY: State University of New York Press.

Dowd, A. C., & Coury, T. (2006). The effect of loans on the persistence and attainment of community college students. *Research in Higher Education, 47,* 33–62.

Eagan, K. (2007). A national picture of part-time community college faculty: Trends and demographics in employment characteristics. In R. L. Wagoner (Ed.), *The current landscape and changing perspectives of part-time faculty* (New Directions for Community Colleges, No. 140, pp. 5–14). San Francisco: Jossey-Bass.

Eagan, M. K., & Jaeger, A. J. (in press). Closing the gate: Contingent faculty in gatekeeper courses. In J. M. Braxton (Ed.), *The role of the classroom in college student persistence.* (New Directions for Teaching and Learning, No. 115). San Francisco: Jossey-Bass.

Ehrenberg, R. G., & Zhang, L. (2004). *Do tenured and tenure track faculty matter?* (NBER Working Paper No. W10695). Cambridge, MA: National Bureau of Economic Research.

Endo, J. J., & Harpel, R. L. (1982). The effect of student-faculty interaction on students' educational outcomes. *Research in Higher Education, 16,* 115–138.

Gaff, J. G., & Gaff, S. (1981). Student-faculty relationships. In A. W. Chickering & Associates (Eds.), *The modern American college* (pp. 642–656). San Francisco: Jossey-Bass.

Gappa, J. M. (1984). *Part-time faculty: Higher education at a crossroads* (ASHE Report No. 3). Washington, DC: Association for the Study of Higher Education.

Green, D. W. (2007). Adjunct faculty and the continuing quest for quality. In R. L. Wagoner (Ed.), *The current landscape and changing perspectives of part-time faculty* (New Directions for Community Colleges, No. 140, pp. 29–40). San Francisco: Jossey-Bass.

Grubb, W. N. (1996). *Working in the middle: Strengthening education and training for the mids-killed labor force.* San Francisco: Jossey-Bass.

Grubb, W. N., Badway, N., & Bell, D. (2003, March). Community colleges and the equity agenda: The potential of noncredit education. *The Annals of the American Academy of Political and Social Science, 586,* 218–240.

Haeger, J. D. (1998). Part-time faculty, quality programs, and economic realities. In D. W. Leslie (Ed.), *The growing use of part-time faculty: Understanding causes and effects* (New Directions for Higher Education, No. 104, pp. 81–88). San Francisco: Jossey-Bass.

Harrington, C., & Schibik, T. (2004, Spring). *Caveat emptor: Is there a relationship between part-time faculty utilization and student learning outcomes and retention?* AIR Professional File, No. 91, 1-6. Retrieved August 5, 2008, from http://airweb3.org/ airpubs/91.pdf

Jaasma, M., & Koper, R. (2002). Out-of-class communication between female and male students and faculty: The relationship to student perceptions of instructor immediacy. *Women's Studies in Communication, 25,* 119–137.

Jacoby, D. (2006). Effects of part-time faculty employment on community college graduation rates. *Journal of Higher Education, 77,* 1081–1103.

Jaeger, A. J., & Eagan, K. (2008, May). *Part-time faculty at community colleges: Implications for student persistence and transfer.* Paper presented at the meeting of the Association for Institutional Research, Seattle, WA.

Jaeger, A. J., & Hinz, D. (2008). The effects of part-time faculty on first-year freshman retention: A predictive model using logistic regression. *Journal of College Student Retention, 10(3),* 33–53.

Jaeger, A. J., Thornton, C. H., & Eagan, K. (2007, November). *Effects of faculty type on first year student retention and performance.* Paper presented at the meeting of the Association for the Study of Higher Education, Louisville, KY.

Kane, T. J., & Rouse, C. E. (1999). The community college: Educating students at the margin between college and work. *Journal of Economic Perspectives, 13,* 63–84.

Levin, J. S. (2001). *Globalizing the community college: Strategies for change in the twenty-first century.* New York: Palgrave.

Levin, J. S. (2007). Multiple judgements: Institutional context and part-time faculty. In R. L. Wagoner (Ed.), *The current landscape and changing perspectives of part-time faculty* (New Directions for Community Colleges, No. 140, pp. 15--20). San Francisco: Jossey-Bass.

Levin, J. S., Kater, S., & Wagoner, R. L. (2006). *Community college faculty: At work in the new economy.* New York: Palgrave Macmillan.

Martinez, M. C. (2004). *Postsecondary participation and state policy: Meeting the future demand.* Sterling, VA: Stylus.

McClenney, K. M. (2007). Engagement research update: The community college survey of student engagement. *Community College Review, 35,* 137–146.

Milem, J., & Berger, J. (1997). A modified model of college student persistence: Exploring the relationship between Astin's theory of involvement and Tinto's theory of student departure. *Journal of College Student Development, 38,* 387–400.

Nora, A., Barlow, E., & Crisp, G. (2005). Student persistence and degree attainment beyond the first year in college. In A. Seidman (Ed.), *College student retention* (pp. 129–153). Westport, CT: Praeger.

Pascarella, E. T., & Terenzini, P. (1977). Patterns of student-faculty informal interaction beyond the classroom and voluntary freshman attrition. *Journal of Higher Education, 48,* 540–552.

Pascarella, E. T., & Terenzini, P. T. (2005). *How college affects students: Vol. 2. A third decade of research.* San Francisco: Jossey-Bass.

Petersen, T. (1985). A comment on presenting results from logit and probit models. *American Sociological Review, 50,* 130–131.

Phillippe, K. A. (Ed.). (2000). *National profile of community colleges: Trends and statistics* (3rd ed.). Washington, DC: American Association of Community Colleges.

Portes, A. (1998). Social capital: Its origins and applications in modern sociology. *Annual Review of Sociology, 24,* 1–24.

Quigley, M., & Bailey, T. W. (2003). *Community college movement in perspective: Teachers college responds to the Truman Commission.* Lanham, MD: Scarecrow Press.

Raudenbush, S. W., & Bryk, A. S. (2002). *Hierarchical linear models: Applications and data analysis methods* (2nd ed.). Thousand Oaks, CA: Sage.

Rendon, L. I., & Nora, A. (1989). A synthesis and application of research on Hispanic students in community colleges. *Community College Review, 17*(1), 17–24.

Ronco, S. L., & Cahill, J. (2004, June). *Does it matter who's in the classroom? Effect of instructor type on student retention, achievement, and satisfaction.* Paper presented at the 44th Annual Forum of the Association for Institutional Research, Boston, MA.

Schuster, J. H. (2003). The faculty makeover: What does it mean for students? In E. Benjamin (Ed.), *Exploring the role of contingent instructional staff in undergraduate learning* (New Directions for Higher Education, No. 123, pp. 15–22). San Francisco: Jossey-Bass.

Schuster, J. H., & Finkelstein, M. J. (2006). *The American faculty: The restructuring of academic work and careers.* Baltimore: Johns Hopkins University Press.

Shaw, K. M., & London, H. B. (2001). Culture and ideology in keeping transfer commitment: Three community colleges. *Review of Higher Education, 25,* 91–114.

Shaw, K. M., Rhoads, R. A., & Valadez, J. R. (1999). Community colleges as cultural texts: A conceptual overview. In K. M. Shaw, J. R. Valadez, & R. A. Rhoads (Eds.), *Community colleges as cultural texts: Qualitative explorations of organizational and student culture* (pp. 1–14). Albany, NY: State University of New York Press.

Stanton-Salazar, R. D., & Dornbusch, S. M. (1995). Social capital and the reproduction of inequality: Information networks among Mexican-origin high school students. *Sociology of Education, 68,* 116–135.

Townsend, B. K., & Twombly, S. B. (2007). *Community college faculty: Overlooked and undervalued* (ASHE Higher Education Report, Vol. 32, No. 6). San Francisco: Jossey-Bass.

Twombly, S., & Townsend, B. K. (2008). Community college faculty: What we know and need to know. *Community College Review, 36,* 5–24.

Umbach, P. D. (2007). How effective are they? Exploring the impact of contingent faculty on undergraduate education. *Review of Higher Education, 30,* 91–124.

Wagoner, R. L. (Ed.). (2007). *The current landscape and changing perspectives of part-time faculty* (New Directions for Community Colleges, No. 140). San Francisco: Jossey-Bass.

Wang, L., & Fan, X. (1997, March). *The effect of cluster sampling design in survey research on the standard error statistic.* Paper presented at the annual meeting of the American Education Research Association, Chicago, IL.

Yoshioka, R. B. (2007). Part-time faculty in California: Success, challenges, and future issues. In R. L. Wagoner (Ed.), *The current landscape and changing perspectives of part-time faculty* (New Directions for Community Colleges, No. 140, pp. 41–47). San Francisco: Jossey-Bass.

Audrey J. Jaeger is an associate professor at North Carolina State University.

M. Kevin Eagan, Jr., is a doctoral student at the University of California, Los Angeles.

CHAPTER 24

A COMPARISON OF FACTORS THAT PREDICT THE SATISFACTION OF COMMUNITY COLLEGE FACULTY BY GENDER

DUANE AKROYD
NORTH CAROLINA STATE UNIVERSITY

SUSAN BRACKEN
NORTH CAROLINA STATE UNIVERSITY

CRYSTAL CHAMBERS
EAST CAROLINA UNIVERSITY

Abstract. Using data from the 1999 National Study of Postsecondary Faculty, this study examines selected structural factors, intrinsic/extrinsic motivating factors and human capital factors that predict the job satisfaction of community college faculty by gender. We found that instructional autonomy and time spent on disciplinary activities were significant and positive predictors of faculty satisfaction for both women and men. Findings also suggest that women in general education disciplines are more satisfied than women who taught in occupational areas and white men tended to be generally less satisfied than men of color.

Male and female faculty in two- and four-year schools and in comprehensive universities experience different work environments and different reward systems, and thus can have different perceptions of their satisfaction with their work. This study focuses on the perceptions and satisfaction of faculty in two-year colleges and includes data on both male and female faculty members. Much of the literature on faculty job satisfaction, stress, productivity, turnover, and retention is conducted using samples from four-year institutions (Perna, 2003). For example, a recent similar study investigated how the intersections of gender, race, and marital status may influence faculty salary, but the study was limited to four-year institutions (Toutkoushian, Bellas & Moore, 2007). Analyses of work conditions and their association with job satisfaction outcomes for faculty in four-year institutions may not neatly translate for faculty in community colleges. Even with the knowledge, for instance, that gender gaps in salary and status exist in both the two- and four-year sectors (Townsend, 1995), we do not have enough information that focuses solely on the two-year environment (Harper, Baldwin, Gansneder, & Chronister, 2001; Nettles, Perna, & Bradburn, 2000; Perna, 2001a). Therefore, this study addresses the call of Truell, Price, and Joyner (1998); McBride, Munday, and Tunnell (1992); and Townsend and Twombly (2007) for ongoing, consistent research on job satisfaction of community college faculty as a critical topic with broad implications for practice. Additionally, this study provides an opportunity to examine the status and experience of community college women faculty, a population often overlooked in higher education literature (Townsend, 1995; Clark, 1998; Perna, 2003).

Job satisfaction for faculty is more than a matter of work rewards to an individual, but a matter of unit cohesiveness and productivity as well as overall institutional function and turnover. Dissatisfied faculty members who do not choose to leave tend to not only drain department morale (Norman, Ambrose, & Houston, 2006), but can also ultimately result in poorer teaching and other interactions with students (Bedeian, 2007). Yet during an era where scores of faculty are retiring, lapses in the supply of qualified community college teachers exist, and there is nonacademic competition for quality faculty, letting non-tenured faculty go is not an easy decision (Berry, Hammons, & Denny, 2001; Fugate & Amey, 2000; Wild, Ebbers, Shelly, & Gmelch, 2003). Turnover is costly financially given recruitment and faculty search efforts, especially with regard to faculty hiring administrative processes. In regards to tenured faculty, administrative processes are limited in their ability to influence the behavior of disgruntled, disengaging, uncivil faculty who stay (Huston, Norman, & Ambrose, 2007). In this vein, dissatisfied faculty, regardless of tenure status, are difficult to weed out and remove from the organization.

Literature Review

The mission, structure, and work of two-year institutions are distinctive and unique (Clark, 1987), with tenure awards less predictable at the two-year institutions (Perna, 2001b). Community college faculty warrant independent study as their members comprise over one-quarter of all faculty nationally (Gahn & Twombly, 2001; Perna, 2003). If part-time faculty are included in the figures, then the proportion of faculty members at community colleges grows to 43 percent (Townsend & Twombly, 2007). As in other work contexts, job satisfaction for faculty is directly associated with outcomes at the level of the individual, department or unit, and the overall institution. When job satisfaction is positive, faculty as workers reap intrinsic rewards from their work in addition to salary and benefits; departmental units gain productive colleagues; and an institution is more likely to successfully retain the employee. In contrast, negative job satisfaction is associated with individual faculty stress, contentious departmental units, and institutional turnover.

Community colleges are facing a situation where they will experience significant faculty retirements in the coming years and retention and lowered faculty turnover rates will become even more important (Rosser & Townsend, 2006). Community college faculty members are sometimes conceptualized in the literature as a temporary or underclass workforce due to a perceived pecking order among higher education institutional types. Levin's (2006) work argues convincingly that community colleges, and their faculty, are environments that serve a valuable purpose and ought to be studied with a lens that honors the legitimate and unique mission and working environment that exists in its own right. He further argues that the over-emphasis of understanding faculty and administrative tensions (such as those about job satisfaction) are not simply issues of faculty-management, nor of individual institutional climate alone. In his work, he broadens discussions of community college faculty experiences to one that is part of a larger, complex, neoliberal social and economic system. In Townsend and Twombly's (2007) book, they focus on providing a comprehensive overview of the worklives of community college faculty, to both balance out information on the community college setting and provide a stronger and more complete baseline for those who wish to compare community college faculty with faculty at other types of institutions.

There is also a fair amount of literature dedicated to exploring the ways that male and female faculty may experience their environments differently. Previous work has pointed to women community college faculty being more satisfied 'overall' than male faculty counterparts, yet women report issues of dissatisfaction concerning benefits, and juggling family issues and work (Rosser & Townsend, 2006). Previous work by Toutkoushian and Bellas (2003) establishes that proportionally more part-time faculty are women and take a position that women faculty members' may prefer part-time positions and that this has a positive relationship with their job satisfaction. One interpretation of this working condition is that, indeed, women may prefer and desire part-time job opportunities as faculty members. An alternative approach is to question how some of the systemic devaluing of part-time faculty members are disproportionately experienced by women workers. More general studies on female faculty members across institutional types consider pipeline access and advancement issues; perception and experiences of climate; managing work and family roles;

policy analyses; and mechanisms for women faculty to seek institutional change (Bracken, Allen, & Dean, 2006). Specific to community colleges, there is still concern, similar to stated above, that the higher concentration of women faculty in community college settings is a reflection of systemic marginalization and needs to be investigated and discussed further (Townsend, 1995).

Previous job satisfaction studies on community college faculty have focused primarily on full-time faculty. An exception is work by Outcalt (as cited in Townsend & Twombly, 2007), whose work reported that community college faculty with doctorates are slightly less satisfied than those without doctorates and that liberal arts faculty tend to be slightly less satisfied than their community college counterparts in other disciplines. The authors also reported a study by Flowers (as cited in Townsend & Twombly, 2007) that found faculty of color were more likely to report job satisfaction at community colleges than at four-year schools. Rosser and Townsend (2006) used the 1999 National Study of Post-secondary Faculty to analyze the influence of demographic factors in addition to personal and professional pressures on faculty intent to leave. The intent of this study was to identify where deans and department heads could target to support faculty job satisfaction and thereby improve institutional retention of faculty. They found that overall, community college faculty are satisfied with their work (Rosser & Townsend, 2006), confirming findings on job satisfaction synthesized in Cohen and Brawer (2003). In terms of areas where administrators can seek to improve satisfaction levels, community college faculty are even more satisfied with their work when there is an overall perception of quality work life and facilities, especially with regard to libraries and technology (Rosser & Townsend, 2006).

While gender was included among the demographic characteristics tested in the Rosser and Townsend (2006) structural equation models, no statistically significant gender differences in perceptions of work life quality or intent to leave were found. However, when considered in conjunction with other literature comparing the job satisfaction of faculty by gender, these findings seem an anomaly. In their analysis of the satisfaction of financial returns to faculty work among Ph.D. scientists, Bender and Heywood (2006) found monetary rewards to function differently by faculty gender. In that study, women faculty discounted financial rewards in favor of intrinsic rewards to work. Looking at other satisfaction measures by gender in an urban institution, Fraser and Hodge (2000) found the profiles of satisfied male and female faculty distinct. Male faculty (mostly white) who embraced gender and racial diversity were more satisfied, perceived organizational processes to be fair, and gained greater intrinsic rewards from faculty work. For women, however, perceptions of fairness were not significant as the original expectation of working conditions was unfairness. Instead, interpersonal relations with other women, such as opportunities for networking and mentoring were found to be key to job satisfaction for women (Fraser & Hodge, 2000). Note that these latter two studies were not conducted in the specific context of community colleges. The present analysis is centered on the community college context, examining the interactions among salary and status factors, organizational structure, and differences in job satisfaction for each gender.

Theoretical Framework

Using data from the 1999 National Study of Postsecondary Faculty, this paper examines community college faculty perceptions of job satisfaction factors to analyze gender differences in faculty satisfaction. The purpose of this study is to examine the predictive value of human capital variables (educational attainment and years of experience), structural variables (presence of tenure system, presence of union, and enrollment), productivity variables (number of courses taught and time in non-instructional activities), market variables (discipline), satisfaction with instructional autonomy, satisfaction with time spent on disciplinary activities, and satisfaction with salary and benefits on the overall job satisfaction for community college faculty by gender.

To examine gender differences in job satisfaction among community college faculty, this study draws upon three theoretical perspectives. The theoretical frames employed are human capital theory, work rewards to the individual theory and global job satisfaction theory. First, human capital theory holds that education, whether formal or on-the-job is an investment for both the individual and society (Becker, 1975, 1993; Langelett, 2001). Additionally, productivity and marketability relate to classical labor market employment outcomes such as retention and turnover. Factors related to human capital used in this study are educational attainment and job experience. In addition, a variable indicating discipline is included as research literature on community colleges suggests there is wide variation among faculty expertise and the market returns to those various areas (Brint, 2003; Becher, 1989; Gahn & Twombly, 2001; Palmer, 2002). This latter factor can be considered marketability. As teaching is the primary focus of community college faculty work (Bayer & Braxton, 1998; Grubb & Associates, 1999; Zimbler, 2001), the number of courses taught and time spent on non-instructional duties will be used as a measure of productivity. With respect to the latter, the idea is that the more time spent on non-instructional duties, the less time devoted to teaching.

Human capital theory assumes a perfect market; yet, organizational structures don't always fit this notion. Therefore, researchers such as Youn (1988) contend that it is important to examine human capital productivity within the structures of organizations. Structural approaches emphasize the attributes of the organizations where people work. For this study structural factors are defined as the presence of tenure system, presence of faculty union, and total institutional enrollment. The former two factors are expectant proxies of faculty support and empowerment, the latter a function of power dilution. Thus we predict that faculty will feel more empowered and supported on community college campuses where tenure and union membership is available, and where institutional enrollment is smaller (Altbach, 1995; Rhoades, 1998). Under these conditions, we expect that faculty members are more likely to reach their human capital potential and thereby be more satisfied.

Beyond human capital, a second framework centers on a basic conceptualization of work. Research by Katz and Van Maanen (1977) contend that the various aspects of work form three conceptually and empirically distinct clusters or dimensions of work rewards. These clusters include task, social and organizational rewards and roughly correspond to the distinction commonly made between intrinsic and extrinsic rewards in the earlier work of Herzberg (1966), and Wernimont (1966). For this study, survey responses related to satisfaction with instructional autonomy and time spent on disciplinary activities were considered two different types of intrinsic rewards that relate to the teaching and the disciplinary function of community college faculty. Respondent's perceptions of the financial aspects of their job and their rating of the institutional treatment of women and minorities were operationalized as two extrinsic organizational rewards. Given the importance of race in understanding returns to work, it is included in both models as a covariate.

Finally, the third theoretical frame uses a social psychological approach to viewing work satisfaction (job satisfaction). From this perspective, job satisfaction is a positive orientation toward work based upon the congruency between ones perception of the work situation and their values regarding those dimensions. In this study the outcome or dependant variable is conceptualized as an overall measure of how respondent's felt about their job. Such a conceptualization is consistent with Gruneburg's (1979) notion of global job satisfaction. Global satisfaction takes into consideration all aspects or facets of a position when evaluating the job.

The three theoretical frames of human capital theory, work rewards to the individual and global job satisfaction are used in this study to examine the predictive value of selected factors on the job satisfaction of community college faculty by gender. The question guiding research is: What is the predictive value of human capital variables (educational attainment and years of experience), structural variables (presence of tenure system, presence of union, and enrollment), productivity variables (number of courses taught and time in non-instructional activities), market variables (discipline), satisfaction with instructional autonomy, satisfaction with time spent on disciplinary activities, and satisfaction with the financial aspects of community college employment on the overall job satisfaction of community college faculty by gender?

Methodology

Sample and Data

Data for this study are from the 1999 National Study of Postsecondary Faculty (NSOPF:99), a survey project funded by the National Center for Educational Statistics (NCES, 1999). It uses a two-stage stratified clustered probability design to select the sample. The first stage consisted of sampling postsecondary institutions and the second stage consisted of sampling faculty from first stage institutions. The final data set consisted of responses from a representative sample of 17,600 faculty working full-time or part-time at a variety of postsecondary educational institutions (n=960). In order to account for this complex design and sample stratification, we used the PROC SURVEYLOGISTIC procedure in SAS with the STRATUM, CLUSTER and WEIGHT statements. In total, there were 4,392 public two-year college faculty respondents from 298 public, two-year colleges. For analysis in this study, only two-year faculty at public institutions that met the following criteria was included: had faculty status, had instructional duties for credit courses, teaching was their primary responsibility, and faculty were full-time. Applying the criteria resulted in 1,779 respondents. Some totals will not be 1,779 since some respondents did not respond to all questions or they were not applicable.

Note that on some community college campuses, part-time faculty comprise the majority of the faculty body. The engagement of part-time faculty is by definition limited; therefore satisfaction with their part-time employer may not be indicative of the total employment atmosphere at community colleges. As such, the authors chose to focus on full time faculty as their workload, teaching and non-teaching, comprise the backbone of community college operations. However, as part-time faculty are a significant part of community college campus, they are of independent research import, worthy of future study.

Independent Variables

The human capital variables included are educational attainment and years of experience. Educational attainment is measured by coding education as 1=masters or higher and 0=less than masters and years of experience, measured by a statement in the questionnaire, "how many years of experience do you have in higher education". The structural variables were presence of a tenure system (1=institution has tenure system and 0=no tenure system), presence of union (1=institution has union, and 0=institution has no union), enrollment (number of FTE undergraduate students). The productivity variables were number of courses taught (list number of course taught in one semester), time in non-instructional activities (measured by combining questions on committee membership). The market variable was discipline, and for this study faculty were divided into two groups (1=occupational or 0=general education). Satisfaction with instructional autonomy consisted of the summed score of 3 questions related to instructional autonomy (alpha=0.72). Satisfaction with time spent on disciplinary activity was measured by the summed score of four questions related to the topic (alpha=0.84). Satisfaction with financial aspects of the job consisted on the summed score of four questions related to the topic (alpha=0.81).

Dependant Variable

The dependant variable was overall job satisfaction and it was measured by modifying a four point liker-type question (1=very unsatisfied, 2=unsatisfied, 3=satisfied, 4=very satisfied) into a categorical variable with 1= unsatisfied and 0=satisfied.

Analysis

Logistic regression is used to provide the information to answer the research question. It is the optimal method for the regression analysis when the dependant variable is dichotomous (Allison, 2001). Logistic models estimate the log-odds of one outcome occurring relative to the baseline category, which in this case is satisfaction with the job, since the dependent variable was operationalized as 0=satisfied and 1=not satisfied. Separate logit models were examined for men and women to determine the predictive power of each model, identify factors that were significance in each model, and compare the magnitude of contribution of statistically significant variables in each model using odds ratios. The odds ratio represents the change in the odds of an outcome relative to the reference outcomes that is associated with a unit change in the specific independent variable of interest.

Limitations

While NSOPF:99 is a large nationally representative data set with high response rates, one limitation is availability of appropriate proxies. The NSOPF:99 data did not attempt to directly access human capital, and market variables and we attempted to use those variables in the data set that seemed to best represent those constructs. Additionally when adding race as a covariate to the logit models, we used only majority / minority. We did not break out the minority groups into separate areas due to the possible low cell counts and possible problems with coefficient estimates and standard errors.

Results

Table 1 displays selected demographics for the sample used in this study. Males constituted a slight majority of the sample (52%) and they tended to hold a higher percentage of doctoral degrees than women and had slightly more years of teaching experience than women. The single largest discipline group for both men (34.5%) and women (39.9%) was the occupational area.

The logit models for women and men were both significant and approximately the same predictive power (See Table 2). As would be expected, both men and women were more likely to be satisfied with their job as their perceptions of the financial aspects of their job increased, about 60 percent more likely. Instructional autonomy and time spent on disciplinary activities were also significant and positive predictors of faculty satisfaction in both female and male models.

The magnitude of the contribution to both groups' satisfaction was very similar. For example both men and women were about 30-49% more likely to be satisfied with their jobs with increases in instructional autonomy and time to spend on disciplinary activities.

TABLE 1

Selected Sample Demographics (all numbers are percentages)

	All Faculty (n=1779)		Females (n=943)		Males (n=836)	
Highest Degree						
Doctoral	20.5		16.4		25.2	
Masters	60.9		65.8		55.6	
Bachelors	12.7		13.5		11.6	
≤Associate	5.9		4.6		7.3	
Gender			48.0		52.0	
Discipline						
Humanities	19.6		19.6		19.4	
Occupational	36.9		39.9		34.5	
Natural Science	17.9		12.8		23.5	
Social Science	25.7		28.5		22.6	
Race						
American Indian	.8		.3		1.3	
Asian	3.3		3.3		3.2	
Black	7.9		8.6		7.2	
Hispanic	6.6		5.4		8.0	
White	81.3		82.3		80.3	
	Mean	**SD**	**Mean**	**SD**	**Mean**	**SD**
Age	48.4	9.0	47.1	8.6	49.9	9.3
Years Teaching Exp	15.7	9.5	14.6	8.8	16.4	10.0
Years Current Position	12.5	9.5	11.4	8.8	13.8	10.2

TABLE 2

Predictors of Job Satisfaction for Community College Faculty by Gender

Independent Variable	Women			Men		
	B	Std. Error	Exp(B)	B	Std. Error	Exp(B)
Human Capital						
Ed Attainment	-0.022	0.246	0.957	0.234	0.274	1.159
Yrs Experience	-0.042*	0.017	0.959	-0.055*	0.019	0.946
Structural						
Presence of Tenure System	0.013	0.156	1.026	0.249	0.231	1.645
Presence of Union	-0.197	0.142	0.674	-0.085	0.215	0.844
Enrollment	-0.000	0.000	1.000	-0.000	0.000	1.000
Market						
Discipline	0.443*	0.143	2.427	-0.125	0.182	0.779
Faculty Intrinsic Reward						
Instructional Autonomy	.351*	0.074	1.421	0.398*	0.080	1.488
Time On Disciplinary Activity	0.261*	0.064	1.299	0.311*	0.114	1.365
Faculty Extrinsic Rewards						
Financial aspects of job	0.470*	0.075	1.599	0.480*	0.086	1.616
Treatment of Women and Minorities	0.213*	0.103	1.237	-0.010	0.139	0.990
Productivity						
# Courses Taught	-0.006	0.054	0.994	0.047	0.057	1.048
Time on Instructional Activities	0.582	0.064	0.935	0.442	0.087	1.045
Covariate						
Race	-0.047	0.204	0.910	-0.435**	0.223	0.419
Number of Cases in Analysis	943			836		
Wald Chi Sq (p) for model	187.47		(p <.0001)	142.04		(p<.0001)
% classified correctly	91.7			92.1		

Notes: B = regression coefficients, * indicates p < .01, ** p = .059, Odds ratios (Exp{B}) are relative to faculty being satisfied with their job.

Of the human capital factors, only years of experience registered a statistically significant correlation with job satisfaction. This relationship, however, is negative and may reflect a need for future research in the area of burnout among community college faculty. Furthermore, neither structural nor productivity factors were significantly predictive of satisfaction for either group.

Perhaps the two most interesting findings were the effect of discipline on women's satisfaction and race on job satisfaction for men. Women who were in general education disciplines were 2.4 times more likely to be satisfied with their jobs than women who taught in occupational areas. White males, however, were 58% more likely to be dissatisfied than minority males.

Discussion

Women faculty in general education more satisfied. Why are community college women who teach general education subjects more satisfied than women who teach in occupational areas? Previous studies on job satisfaction of occupational community college faculty (Truell et al., 1998) found that part-time faculty were generally more satisfied than full-time faculty, but did not examine differences between the occupational and general education faculty members' satisfaction. Fugate and Amey (2000) conducted a qualitative study examining the early career paths of both vocational/occupational and liberal arts or general education community college faculty and found that there was relatively little difference among the two faculty groups in terms of career path, view of their roles as teachers, or in terms of professional development, which are indirect connections to factors which can lead to satisfaction or dissatisfaction with work roles. Ropers-Huilman (2000) suggest that women faculty members are more satisfied with their work when the work contributes to positive social change or has other meaningful content and also value teaching and learning relationships. The differences in satisfaction by discipline found in this research are also consistent with anthropological/ethnographic work in the area of faculty organization and governance (Beecher, 1989; Palmer, 2002).

It may be the case that women working in occupational areas are more subject to internal and external institutional pressures to respond to market demands (Duderstadt, 1999; Duderstadt & Womack, 2003). While some research exploring the chilly climate for women community college faculty members is inconclusive (Hagedorn & Laden, 2002) other research has consistently asserted that women faculty in the sciences across institutional types, including applied sciences, report chilly climates (Hagedorn, Nora & Pascarella, 1996). Jena (1999) finds that women are more likely to report job stress or perception of the presence of discrimination in environments where gender stereotyping is more prevalent, similar to what one might expect in certain occupational or vocational areas of study. The notion that occupational and science environments may enhance the perception and reality of a chilly climate may well account for the lower satisfaction of women faculty in occupational disciplines at the community college. Additionally, as women in the general education disciplines are more likely to have come to the community college from four-year or other institutions, it may be the case that women in general education find a better "fit" between themselves and the community college institutional type (Gahn & Twombly, 2001). Given the significant occupational focus in many community colleges, the disparity in the satisfaction of women faculty from the two disciplinary groups warrants further exploration.

Race, Gender and Job Satisfaction

Also of significance, white males were 58% more likely to be dissatisfied than men of color with their work in the community college. This finding is definitely perplexing given that most studies on race related job stress or dissatisfaction among faculty indicate that faculty of color are more likely than white faculty members to report job-related stress, frustration and therefore by inference, less job satisfaction. Faculty of color generally report feelings of lower social or environmental support and increased perception of isolation; studies indicate they report higher perceptions of tokenism and that they feel they have to work harder than their white counterparts to be considered at an equal level (Niemann & Dovidio, 1998; Vigil Laden & Hagedorn, 2000). Bower's (2002) reports similar findings, writing that minority faculty at community colleges are more likely to be involved with interdisciplinary or team teaching; to be teaching either honors or remedial special sections; to express concern about racial and ethnicity issues on campus; and to describe a heightened sense of isolation, separation, or alienation. Given the findings in this study contradict our general understandings of faculty of color experience, we believe they indicate a strong need for continued in-depth research to enhance and more fully develop our understanding of racial and ethnic issues in all college environments, and in this case the community college environment.

While this study finds male faculty of color are clearly more satisfied with their environment, we do not have explanatory data. However, there are several areas ripe for future research. A place to start the quest to understand race/ethnicity and gender interactions in the satisfaction of community college faculty are the pathways to community college teaching. Faculty who choose to work in support of community college missions are generally more satisfied and motivated toward good work in this context than faculty who do not buy into this mission (Cohen & Brawer, 2003). As faculty of color and women both tend to place a higher value on community service and uplift through higher education, there may be frustration between the community college mission and work rewards for white males (Gahn & Twombly, 2001; Townsend, 1998). Another area for further inquiry is the interaction between the institution's embrace of diversity and the job satisfaction of white men. Fraser and Hodge (2000) directly attribute threats to white male privilege as fodder for dissatisfaction among white male faculty in an urban four-year institution. Given that the proportion of white male faculty in community colleges is less than their proportion at four-year institutions (Cohen & Brawer, 2003), the phenomena Fraser and Hodge (2000) document may be of an even greater magnitude.

Conclusion

Community colleges are important institutions in the overall study of postsecondary education. As the labor force continues to grow and become more diverse, it is vital that we understand how to create working environments that are satisfactory to women and to men of all racial or ethnic backgrounds. From this work the authors find that community college faculty place a high value on disciplinary and job autonomy as well as perceptions of fair and equitable pay. The findings also indicate that female and male faculty members experience community college environments differently based upon their disciplinary affiliations and their racial backgrounds. As such, there is a demonstrated need for continued in-depth research exploring the complex dynamics that affect faculty job satisfaction.

This study is limited by the focus on full-time faculty, as well as broad overarching questions posed in national surveys, the data source upon which this research is based. While this study deliberately focuses on full-time faculty as core faculty on community college campuses, part-time faculty are an integral part of community college faculty, often comprising a majority of the faculty labor force. The satisfaction of part-time faculty as well as the interactions between full-and part-time status with job satisfaction are of independent import, but beyond the constructs of the present study. In addition, while this work provides a broad stroke over the job satisfaction of community college faculty by gender, more specific qualitative designs are better able to tease out the intricacies of race and gender variations in community college faculty job satisfaction.

Nevertheless, this work adds to our general understandings of community college faculty job satisfaction. In terms guiding future practice, this study affirms community college faculty's valuation of disciplinary and job autonomy and perceptions of fair and equitable pay. Towards that end continued efforts to support professional development, faculty participation in regional and national disciplinary organizations, as well as salary and status equalization should be pursued. However, in pursing this course in equity, not all faculty will perceive these changes as beneficial. As such, special efforts may be necessary to address the role of privilege and job satisfaction among white men.

References

Allison, P. (2001). *Logistic regression using the SAS system: Theory and application*. Cary, NC: SAS Institute.

Altbach, P.G. (1995). Problems and possibilities: The US academic profession. *Studies in Higher Education, 20*(1), 27–45.

Bayer, A. & Braxton, J. (1998). The normative structure of community college teaching -A marker of professionalism. *Journal of Higher Education, 69*(2), 187–205.

Becher, T. (1989). *Academic tribes and territories: Intellectual inquiry and the cultures of disciplines*. Bristol, PA: Society for Research into Higher Education/Open University.

Becker, G.S. (1975). *Human capital: A theoretical and empirical analysis, with special reference to education*. New York, NY: Columbia University Press.

_____. (1993). *Human capital: A theoretical and empirical analysis, with special reference to education*. New York, NY: Columbia University Press.

Bedeian, A.G. (2007). Even if the tower is "ivory," it isn't "white:" Understanding the consequences of faculty cynicism. *Academy of Management Learning & Education, (6)*1, 9–32.

Bender, K.A. & Heywood, J.S. (2006). Job satisfaction of the highly educated: The role of gender, academic tenure, and earnings. *Scottish Journal of Political Economy, 53*, 253–279.

Berry, L.H., Hammons, J.O., & Denny, G.S. (2001). Faculty retirement turnover in community colleges: A real or imagined problem? *Community College Journal of Research and Practice, 4*, 263–276.

Bower, B.L. (2002). Campus life for faculty of color: Still strangers after all these years? In C. Outcalt (Ed.), *New directions for community colleges, No. 118, Community college faculty: Characteristics, practices, and challenges* (pp. 79–87). San Francisco, CA: Jossey-Bass.

Bracken, S.J., Allen, J.K., & Dean, D.R. (Eds.) (2006). *The balancing act: Gendered perspectives in faculty roles and work lives*. Sterling, VA: Stylus.

Brint, S. (2003). Few remaining dreams: Community colleges since 1985. *Annals of the American Academy of Political and Social Science, 586*, 16–37.

Clark, B. (1987). *The academic life: Small worlds, different worlds*. Princeton, NJ: Carnegie Foundation for the Advancement of Teaching.

Clark, S. (1998). Women faculty in community colleges: Investigating the mystery. *Community College Review, 26*, 77–88.

Cohen, A. & Brawer, F.B. (2003). *The American community college, 4th ed*. San Francisco, CA: Jossey-Bass.

Duderstadt, J.J. (1999). New roles for the 21st-century university. *Issues in Science and Technology, 16*(2), 37–44.

Duderstadt, J.J., & Womack, F. (2003). *The future of the public university in America: Beyond the crossroads*. Baltimore, MD: Johns Hopkins University.

Fraser, J. & Hodge, M. (2000). Job satisfaction in higher education: Examining gender in professional work settings. *Sociological Inquiry, 70*, 172–187.

Fugate, A.L., & Amey, M.J. (2000). Career stages of community college faculty: A qualitative analysis of their career paths, roles, and development. *Community College Review, 28*(1), 1–22.

Gahn, S., & Twombly, S. (2001). Dimensions on the community college labor market. *Review of Higher Education, 24*, 259–282.

Grubb, W.N., & Associates. (1999). *Honored but invisible: An inside look at teaching in community colleges*. New York, NY: Routledge.

Gruenburg, M. (1979). *Understanding job satisfaction*. New York, NY: Wiley.

Hagedorn, L.S., Nora A, & Pascarella. E.T. (1996). Pre-occupational segregation among first-year college students: An application of the Duncan dissimilarity index. *Journal of College Student Development, 37*(4), 425–437.

Hagedorn, L.S. & Laden, B.V. (2002). Exploring the climate for women as community college faculty. In C. Outcalt (Ed.), *New directions for community colleges, No. 118, Community college faculty: Characteristics, practices, and challenges* (pp. 69–78). San Francisco, CA: Jossey-Bass.

Harper, E., Baldwin, R., Gansneder, B. & Chronister, J. (2001). Full-time women faculty off the tenure track: Profile and practice. *The Review of Higher Education, 24*(3), 237–257.

Hertzburg, F. (1966). *Work and the Nature of Man*. Cleveland, OH: World Publishing.

Huston, T.A., Norman, M., & Ambrose, S.A. (2007). Expanding the discussion of faculty vitality to include productive but disengaged senior faculty. *Journal of Higher Education, 78*, 493–522.

Jena, S.P.K. (1999). Job, life satisfaction, and occupational stress of women. *Social Science International, 15*(1), 75–80.

Katz, R. & Van Maanen, J. (1977). The loci of work satisfaction: Job interaction and policy. *Human Relations, 30*, 469–486.

Langelett, G. (2001). Human capital: A summary of the 20th century research. *Journal of Educational Finance, 28*, 1–24.

Levin, J.S. (2006). Faculty work: Tensions between educational and economic values. *The Journal of Higher Education, 77*(1), 62–88.

McBride, S.A., Munday, R.G., & Tunnell, J. (1992). Community college job satisfaction and propensity to leave. *Community/Junior College Quarterly, 16*, 157–165.

Niemann, Y.F. & Dovidio, J.F. (1998). Relationship of solo status, academic rank and perceived distinctiveness to job satisfaction of racial/ethnic minorities. *Journal of Applied Psychology, 83*(1), 55–71.

Nettles, M., Perna, L., & Bradburn, E. (2000). Salary, promotion, and tenure status of minority and women faculty in U.S. colleges and universities. *Education Statistics Quarterly, 2*(2), 94–96.

Norman, M., Ambrose, S.A., & Huston, T.A. (2006). Assessing and addressing faculty morale: Cultivating consciousness, empathy, and empowerment. *Review of Higher Education, 29*, 347–381.

Palmer, J.C. (2002). Disciplinary variations in the work of full-time faculty members. In C. Outcalt (Ed.), *New directions for community colleges, No. 118, Community college faculty: Characteristics, practices, and challenges,* (pp. 9–20). San Francisco, CA: Jossey-Bass.

Perna, L. (2003). The status of women and minorities among community college faculty. *Research in Higher Education, 44*, 205–240.

_____. (2001a). Sex differences in faculty salaries: A cohort analysis. *Review of Higher Education, 24*, 283–307.

_____. (2001b). Sex and race differences in faculty tenure and promotion. *Research in Higher Education, 42*, 541–567.

Rhoades, G. (1998). *Managed professionals: Unionized faculty and restructuring academic labor.* Albany, NY: State University of New York.

Ropers-Huilman, B. (2000). Aren't you satisfied yet? Women faculty members' interpretations of their academic work. In L. Hagedorn (Ed.), *New directions for institutional research, No. 105* (pp. 21–32). San Francisco, CA: Jossey-Bass.

Rosser, V. & Townsend, B. (2006). Determining public 2-year college faculty's intent to leave: An empirical model. *The Journal of Higher Education, 77*, 124–147.

Toutkoushian, R.K. & Bellas, M.L. (2003). The effects of part-time employment and gender on faculty earnings and satisfaction: Evidence from NSOPF:93. *The Journal of Higher Education, 74*(2), 172–195.

Toutkoushian, R.K., Bellas, M.L., & Moore, J.V. (2007). The interaction effects of gender, race, and marital status on faculty salaries. *Journal of Higher Education, 78*(5), 572–601.

Townsend, B. (1995). Women community college faculty: On the margins or in the mainstream? In B. Townsend (Ed.), *New directions for community colleges: No. 89, Gender and power in the community college,* (pp. 39–46). San Francisco, CA: Jossey-Bass.

Townsend, B. (1998). Women faculty: Satisfaction with employment in the community college. *Community College Journal, 22*(7), 655–662.

Townsend, B.K. & Twombly, S.B. (2007). Community college faculty: Overlooked and undervalued. ASHE Higher Education Report: 32(6). San Francisco, CA: Jossey-Bass.

Truell, A.D., Price, W.T., & Joyner, R.L. (1998). Job satisfaction among community college occupational-technical faculty. *Community College Journal of Research & Practice, 22*(2), 111–123.

Vigil Laden, B. & Hagedorn, L. (2000). Job satisfaction among faculty of color in academe: Individual survivors or institutional transformation? In L. Hagedorn (Ed), *New directions for institutional research, No. 105* (pp. 57-66) San Francisco, CA: Jossey-Bass.

Wernimont, P. (1966). Intrinsic and extrinsic factors in job satisfaction. *Journal of Applied Psychology, 50*, 41–50.

Wild, L.L., Ebbers, L.H., Shelley, M.C., & Gmelch, W.H. (2003). Stress factors and community college deans: The stresses of their role identified. *Community College Review, 31*, 1–23.

Youn, T. (1992). The sociology of academic careers and academic labor markets. *Research in Labor Economics, 13*, 101–130.

Youn, T. (1988). Studies of academic markets and careers: An historical review. In D. Breneman and T. Youn (eds.), *Academic Labor Markets and Careers* (pp. 8–27). New York, NY: Falmer.

Zimbler, L.J. (2001). *1999 National Study of Postsecondary Faculty: Background characteristics, work activities, and compensation of faculty and instructional staff in postsecondary institution.* (NCES 2001-152). Washington, DC: U.S. Department of Education/Institute of Education Sciences, National Center for Education Statistics.

Duane Akroyd is a Professor in the Department of Leadership, Policy and Adult and Higher Education at North Carolina State University.

Susan Bracken is an Associate Professor in the Department of Leadership, Policy and Adult and Higher Education at North Carolina State University.

Crystal Chambers is an Assistant Professor in the Educational Leadership Department at East Carolina University.

CHAPTER 25

PURPLE IS TO LAVENDER: WOMANISM, RESISTANCE, AND THE POLITICS OF NAMING

DIMPAL JAIN[1]
UNIVERSITY OF THE PACIFIC

CAROLINE TURNER
CALIFORNIA STATE UNIVERSITY SACRAMENTO

Abstract. We explore the politics of naming for non-White women faculty in higher education as it relates to womanist theory. A discussion of these faculty experiences in general, and women faculty in particular are provided to illuminate the many challenges we face in the academy. One such challenge is how we come to identify our scholarship and align ourselves epistemologically. By not identifying as feminists or labeling our raced and gendered work as part of feminist theory, we are engaging in the politics of naming. Jain examines this issue of naming by interviewing eleven non-White women community college student leaders and exploring their relationships with feminism. This exploration provides context to how these women in the United States have critiqued the term feminist and the etymology of both feminism and womanism. At each of our career stages, Jain as junior faculty and Turner as senior faculty, we offer narrative and empirical examples of how we were introduced to womanism and the mentoring that took place while writing this article.

Introductory Narratives

Dimpal

As the only non-White woman in the class I was baffled by the students' head nods and looks of affirmation as the topic of feminism was being discussed. It was my first year in graduate school and I had limited prior exposure to women's studies and/or ethnic studies. As a first generation college student I was grappling with a new city, a new school, and a new lexicon to keep pace with other doctoral students and faculty. However, I knew that the term feminism was contested and that I did not like how it fit in my mouth. It was uncomfortable and scratchy, almost like a foreign substance that I was being forced to consume as the White women continued to smile with comforting looks of familiarity and pride.

A year after this experience I was introduced to womanist theory (Walker, 1983) through a multicultural pedagogy course. The course, an elective seminar, was my first graduate school experience of being taught by a non-White woman faculty member. While examining alternative pedagogies such as critical and feminist pedagogy, I was struck by how limiting feminism was and could not ignore its contentious past with racism. The term still made me uncomfortable. My

---

[1]Address correspondence to Dimpal Jain, University of the Pacific, Gladys L. Benerd School of Education, Educational Administration and Leadership, 3601 Pacific Avenue, Stockton, CA 95211 or djain@pacific.edu.

professor allowed me to examine the literature more in depth until I stumbled upon womanist thought. After doing a thorough examination of the scholarship my final assignment was a literature review of womanist pedagogy from a third world immigrant woman's faculty perspective. The instructor proposed to the class that we submit our papers for a major conference in our field and to our surprise, we were accepted. It was through this supportive scholarship structure, from an adjunct woman professor, that I was allowed to explore womanism through subsequent courses and my dissertation fieldwork.

As I graduated with my doctoral degree and transitioned to a faculty position in the academy, I was anxious about not identifying with feminism in my application materials or teaching demonstration. I was unsure of how I was going to be received by potential employers, in addition, as a South Asian woman I knew that I did not resemble my faculty peers and that being in the social sciences, rather than the physical sciences, was enough to cause confusion by those who still believed in the model minority stereotype (Suzuki, 1977; 2002). Currently, as the only junior tenure-track non-White woman faculty in my college of education, I continue to struggle with issues of representation and validation. As one of the few faculty members who examine race and gender through a critical lens, it is easy to find my work and myself at the margins. Concomitantly, not associating with the term feminist continues to raise questions and doubt amongst my peers.

Caroline

> Picking tomatoes and cutting apricots with my family in California, I played games and scenarios in my mind to keep me otherwise occupied. I never dreamed of becoming a professor or even going to college. I grew up doing field work and now, as a qualitative researcher, I find it amusing that I still find myself doing field work (Turner, 2008a, p.97).

Working on papers can be considered field work, especially when I have interviewed non-White women, and when editors at times note that these women do not call themselves feminists; then they asked me why? This question made me feel that this work could not be viewed as accurate if women did not identify as feminist. I would answer that this was not a term that they applied to themselves and realized that I did not consider myself under the label of feminist either, never feeling an affinity for the term. It is not that I do not use labels as I refer to myself as a non-White woman from a "no collar" class, a Latina/Filipina from a large immigrant family. No collar because my roots are as a California farm laborer and this work, in my view, cannot even be labeled blue collar.

I have written about how multiple social identities shaped my opportunities in higher education. For example, I described a time when I first explored graduate school options and was discouraged from applying to a program in business by an admissions officer:

> The admissions officer stated that I would not fit. I was a woman, a minority, a single parent, I had a background in the public sector, and I had some but not enough math background. This would make it nearly impossible for me to succeed as others in the program fit another and opposite profile. . . I remember being struck by the many ways I could be defined as not "fitting" and, therefore, not encouraged and, more than likely, not admitted. I was so easily "defined out" rather than "defined in" (Turner, 2002b, p.74).

Today, I find myself a full professor and a scholar-advocate who conducts research to illuminate access and equity issues for women and men who are underrepresented as well as marginalized in higher education. In my research, the dynamics of defining out diversity is found not only to exist at the point of student admissions but also at the points of hiring and promotion of faculty and administrators. As I work to improve the quality of life for people in higher education institutions, I combine research with service. For example, as I see myself and others like me reflected in my research and writing, I realize that I must extend this work and act to increase the numbers of racial and ethnic minorities in the professoriate. Toward that end, I conduct workshops and deliver lectures nation-wide to faculty and administrators who want to increase the numbers of non-White faculty on their campuses. These presentations are based primarily on a book length synthesis of published research and resources for use by practitioners (Turner, 2002a). Selling over 17,000 copies and making an impact on the field, *Diversifying the Faculty: A Guidebook for Search Committees* is written for a practitioner audience. Categorized as faculty service, this work is not as valued in the tenure and promotion process as are publications written for a researcher audience. As a non-White woman, I cannot help but reflect on how these types of merit biases have affected the evaluation of my work as well as the work of others who examine the lives of those occupying marginalized spaces in academe, and who also spend time communicating our research for use in practice. Some of these reflections have recently been published in on-line essays focused on the status of non-White women, specifically Latinas, in academe (Turner, 2011a & 2011b). However, this is the type of work that I feel is making a difference and gives me energy to persist in higher education.

Direct mentoring of non-White faculty is also very important to me. While mentorship is not the only factor contributing to successful graduate and faculty careers, it is cited as one of the most important by academics who are interested in how students and faculty advance and succeed in academia. For example, in a meta-synthesis of 252 research studies on faculty diversity published over a twenty year period, the importance of positive mentoring experiences was a dominant theme (Turner, González, & Wood, 2008). Recently I taught at a National Faculty Mentoring Institute, it was here that I met my coauthor. Dimpal challenges me to think further about how identity shapes my experience. Writing this article together, I have a chance to explore with her perspective, an emerging womanist framework. In my view, this article itself provides an example of how tenured faculty can also be mentored by pre-tenured faculty. As noted above, I do not use the term feminist to categorize myself, but neither do the non-White women I have interviewed nor do I use the term womanist when describing our social identities. Woman, Latina, and Filipina are terms I am comfortable using, however I do see the utility of naming as we represent marginalized women in the academy.

Overview

As underrepresented women academics there are many obstacles we face as we progress through the academy. Aiming to explore this further, we begin with an examination of non-White faculty in the academy, particularly the experiences of these women faculty. How we orient our scholarship and the methodological approaches we employ act as labels to our research and our identity as scholars. As we are surrounded by faculty who do not share the same backgrounds as us, the choice to align or not align ourselves with frameworks such as feminism comes with consequences—both positive and negative.

To examine this more closely, we introduce the politics of naming and how these women in the United States have critiqued the term feminism and the importance this has in the practice of higher education. Next, a discussion of the origins of feminism and its applicability to higher education will be explored. We then introduce the term womanism and the reasoning behind aligning ourselves with this framework. Lastly, based on our personal experiences and empirical research, we offer techniques and strategies for survival in academe from two different career stages.

Non-White Faculty

Much has been written regarding our experience as non-White women faculty in academe with common themes such as feelings of isolation, dismissal, marginalization, and encountering resistance to our presence by predominantly White faculty and White students (Hebbani, 2007; Thomas & Hollenshead, 2001; Turner, 2002b; Wong, 2007). Allen, Epps, Guillory, Suh, Bonus-Hammarth, and Stassen (1991) note that "women from underrepresented populations face barriers due to historical, cultural, and social factors that have shaped their experience and development in American society. . . . Pervasive racist and sexist attitudes continue to limit educational opportunities for [non-White] women" (p. 190). In addition to how our presence often negatively impacts others, our teaching, research, and service; it also becomes politicized as we are under constant scrutiny by peers and students (Stanley, 2006; Turner, 2008c).

Turner and Myers (2000) examined challenges associated with being non-White faculty in a mixed-method study including interviews with non-WhiteThe study conducted by Turner and Myers (2000) concluded that these faculty often experienced racial or ethnic bias, an isolating and unsupportive work environment, a lack of information about tenure and promotion, gender bias, discrimination based on their language or accent, a lack of mentors, and a lack of support from superiors. For example, one woman professor stated:

> I'm the department chair in the [science] department and I meet with a lot of people who don't know me—you know, prospective students and their parents...their first reaction to me is that I'm an Asian American woman, not that I'm a scientist or that I'm competent (Turner & Myers, 2000, p. 91).

Gender bias manifested itself in several ways in this study as well, including role conflict between career and family responsibilities and being challenged by students. Such factors compound workplace stress for these women faculty. For example, one tenured social science professor stated:

> I know that there are lots of values...that sometimes get in the way of the careerist profile. Family for example...My family is more important to me than my career. That is not the position that will...get one to the top in the conventional academic setting (Turner & Myers, 2000, p. 109).

In addition, a tenure track Black woman shared:

> Let's put it like this, if a White male professor says something that's wrong in class, my observation is that even if the students perceive that it's wrong, they may say something outside of class, but they hesitate to challenge a 50+ White male professor. They feel quite comfortable challenging a [Black] African American woman. . . .I just think it's society and the way that they're brought up and the way that they perceive people (Turner & Myers, 2000, p. 110).

Recent publications by Turner (2002b; 2008b) indicate that these issues remain critical to non-White faculty and, in particular, for women faculty, as they continue to describe similar biases in their workplace. When reviewing recent numbers of these faculty in higher education the image becomes increasingly bleak. According to The Chronicle of Higher Education Almanac (2009) there were 703,643 faculty members at the rank of full professor, associate professor, assistant professor, instructor, and lecturer teaching in American higher education. Fifty-eight percent were men, 42% were women, and 77% of the total identified as White faculty. This leaves 23% or less than half, remaining for non-White faculty employed in higher education institutions (The Chronicle of Higher Education [CHE] Almanac, 2009).

For non-White women the numbers are even more disconcerting, in that for each racial and ethnic group, with the exception of Blacks, men outnumbered their women counterparts. In fact, their representation decreases significantly at the level of full professor (CHE Almanac, 2009). Thus, it is safe to say as non-White women faculty in higher education, we are outnumbered.

As we are outnumbered in faculty ranks and our potential to succeed becomes threatened by a lack of senior faculty mentoring, unclear promotion and tenure guidelines, student teaching evaluations that do not take into account the role of race and racism, and a general negative campus climate we realize how serious it is for us not to align ourselves with mainstream theoretical paradigms in our field of study. As we both do work related to race and gender, yet do not call ourselves feminists or even non-White feminists, we realize this makes us vulnerable in terms of scholarship and colleagueship. We are often questioned by our peers, students, mentors, journal editors, and family members about the reasons we do not use the term feminism as they see it as a mistake or deficiency in our work. Yet, we do not make apologies for our stance, nor aggressively defend it, as we subscribe to the politics of naming.

The Politics of Naming

We view the politics of naming through multiple academic lenses, i.e., sociology, gender studies, and ethnic studies (Bhatia, 2005; Richardson & Robinson, 1994). The crux of the politics of naming is that names serve as identifiers and are not neutral when attached to social movements, ideas, and groups of people. Naming and labeling become politicized acts when they serve to determine any type of membership at a group level. Bhatia (2005) defines the politics of naming as "examining how names are made, assigned and disputed, and how this contest is affected by a series of global dynamics and events" (p.7). Specifically, Bhatia examines the term *terrorist* and how the labeling of certain social movements as *terrorism* has become contested, especially in a post 9-11 era of media sensationalism (Faludi, 2007). He states:

> Once assigned, the power of a name is such that the process by which the name was selected generally disappears and a series of normative associations, motives and characteristics are attached to the named subject. By naming, this subject becomes known in a manner which may permit certain forms of inquiry and engagement, while forbidding or excluding others (Bhatia, p. 8).

When names are attached to social movements, they have the power to determine outsiders and insiders. To name a movement can be to name it with the express intent of recruiting supporters and serve as a way to disseminate a discourse of belonging and opposition. In addition, naming serves as a way to justify the movement's actions (Bhatia). Feminism, as a movement, espouses a particular set of ideals that denotes membership and subscribed ideology (hooks, 1984).

In addition to the naming of social movements, another area where naming becomes contentious is race and ethnicity. For example, the decision to identify as Hispanic, or Latina, or Chicana represents a host of political choices for the individual and may differ based on audience and locale (Mindiola, Niemann, & Rodriguez, 2002). Mihesuah (2003) continues this discussion by reviewing the politics of naming for Native American students in the classroom. He states that "students must know the controversies over the term *Indian* and that 'names can be empowering or insulting to Natives, and teachers must attempt to be respectful'" (p. 467). The intersection between the politics of naming and pedagogy is just one example of how differing terminology impacts education discourse.

According to Joireman (2004) the fundamental questions related to the politics of naming are "who is it who decides what group a person is a member of, or who is included and excluded from a group? Is it the individual themselves, or someone else?"(p. 2). Joireman argues that naming is a politicized action and that naming ethnicity at the group level is much more radical than at the individual level. She posits that naming becomes significant when "individuals choose their own ethnic identification and in other instances it is forced upon them" (p. 13).

In terms of higher education, one way the politics of naming surfaces is how we classify our colleges and universities, in particular the historical and contemporary terms associated with minority serving institutions. Hutcheson (2008) reflects on naming and power as he coined the term "essentially White universities" when discussing the differences between historically Black colleges and universities and predominantly White institutions. Hutcheson (2008) states:

> Indeed I rejoice at the occasional use of the term. In a scholarly world where many argue that the naming of the subject is a creation of subjugation, it seems obvious that the more likely usage of the White wording, the predominantly White institution (PWI), elicits knowledge that confirms not only racial and ethnic differences but also power relations. In simple terms, historically Black colleges and universities are historically minority, carrying a tradition that is simultaneously proud and named as lesser (p. 43).

Here Hutcheson (2008) demonstrates how we often blindly accept hierarchies and taxonomies in higher education and do not question the power dynamics of how we have come to identify our different institutions. The politics of naming shows that names do matter and to identify with a label, whether it is attached to a social movement or an identity, is a political act. We argue that the personal becomes political through the act of naming and for a non-White woman scholar. What is more personal than calling oneself a feminist? When discussing the terms feminist and feminism we see how prominent the politics of naming becomes, how contested this label is, particularly in the United States of America and in the practice of higher education. To call oneself a feminist is not a neutral, passive declaration; to associate with this label signifies that one subscribes to its dominant tenets, whatever those may be.

Feminism

The term feminism can trace its origins to the French term *féminisme* which began to be used widely in France in the early 1890's (Offen, 1988). Historically the term became synonymous with women's emancipation, particularly in the United States as the feminist movement grew out of the suffragist and abolitionist movements fighting to secure basic rights for women—e.g., the right to vote, own and inherit property, and to be citizens. (Cott, 1986).

The label of feminist was used not only by proponents and challengers of women's emancipation, but also by the observers of their struggles in the media. Offen (1988) states that "then, as now, many parties used the terms polemically, as epithets, rather than analytically; then, as now, the words were not used by everyone to mean the same thing" (p. 128). Not until the 1960s and 1970s did the term come into popular usage in the United States. Offen (1988) continues to define what it means to label oneself as a feminist:

> We owe it to the public and to one another to. . . address the fear that induces would-be supporters to disclaim the label of feminism even when they support what we would consider feminist goals. To allow so many to get away with saying, 'I'm not a feminist, but. . .' seems highly problematic in the light of current political necessities (p. 120).

hooks (1984) also shares similar concerns as Offen (1988), she states: "women often acknowledge that they have benefited from feminist-generated reform measures which have improved the social status of specific groups of women, [however] they do not wish to be seen as participants in [the] feminist movement" (p. 22-23). When we look at the term feminist through the lens of the politics of naming we see that it is not an impartial label and that there are multiple reasons why women are reluctant to identify with it. According to hooks, some of these reasons could be: they do not know what feminism means; they are from oppressed ethnic groups and do not want to be seen as supporting a racist White women's rights efforts; they see it as synonymous with lesbianism and their homophobia leads them to reject the label; some fear the label because it is attached to a political movement; and lastly there are those women who do not want to be associated with women's rights at all and oppose feminism in any form.

The argument for disassociating oneself with the term feminist, even though it can be ambiguous at times, assumes that women and men subscribe to its ideals but are lacking knowledge to properly label themselves as feminists. To say "I'm not a feminist, but. . ." does not help the feminist cause of gaining recognition and significance among other political movements and ideologies. Yet hooks (1994) continues to say "it is this term's positive and political significance and power that we must now struggle to recover and reclaim" (p.23). Although we empathize with this argument, we are not wholly convinced by it. Feminism is too fraught with contradictory histories and misaligned allegiances for us to associate with the term. Not only has it been challenged by non-White women for not being inclusive of their lived experiences, it has also been disputed within the gay community (Lorde, 1984; Taylor & Whittier, 1999), and those who work in the area of disability studies (Garland-Thomson, 2002; Morris, 1995) for dismissing their particular identity politics. It is still not something we feel comfortable identifying with, and we are not alone.

In alliance with the politics of naming we choose not to identify with this term. We are making the personal political (Lorde). Why subscribe to a label that we have to continuously defend? Why feel forced to say "I'm a feminist, but not that kind of a feminist?" As women faculty we are aware that we are under constant scrutiny for our raced and gendered work yet we choose not to identify with this dominant paradigm. To fully understand our reluctance to disassociate with feminism is to first recognize the struggle of women who came before us as they attempted to gain recognition in a racist, sexist, homophobic feminist movement in the United States.

Feminism versus Womanism

In the United States non-White women first examined the role of feminism by calling into question the racism within the 1960's and 1970's women's movement (Collins, 2000; Lorde, 1984; Moraga &

Anzaldúa, 1981). A majority of these women who were active in the feminist movement felt that feminism did not explicitly examine the intersections of race, class, sexuality, and gender (hooks, 1981; Moraga & Anzaldúa, 1981). Soon the term itself was contested and a new term emerged that honored the Black feminist woman in the United States women's movement—womanism (Collins, 1999; Walker, 1983). Womanism can be defined as an epistemological perspective based on the collective experiences of Black women or other non-White women (Phillips, 2006). Womanists (especially womanist educators) often demonstrate the following three characteristics: an embrace of the maternal, an ethic of risk, and political clarity (Beauboeuf-Lafontant, 2002).

Moraga and Anzaldúa (1981), Lorde (1984), and hooks (1981) are all key authors that articulate feelings of isolation and exclusion for women who practice feminism. Their writings could be classified under the heading of womanism because they espouse "a consciousness that incorporates racial, cultural, sexual, national, economic, and political considerations" (Brown, 1989, p. 613). Alice Walker (1983) coined the term womanism in the opening pages of *In Search of Our Mothers' Gardens*. There are four definitions put forth of womanism with sub-definitions: (a) the first being a Black feminist or other non-White feminist, (b) the second as someone who is committed to the survival and wholeness of males and females, (c) the third as someone who loves herself, and (d) the fourth as an analogy of womanism being to feminism as purple is to lavender (Walker, 1983). As Walker (1994) explained her rationale for using the term womanist:

> I don't choose womanism because it is "better" than feminism. . .I choose it because I prefer the sound, the feel, the fit of it; because I cherish the spirit of the women (like Sojourner) the word calls to mind, and because I share the old ethnic-American habit of offering society a new word when the old word it is using fails to describe behavior and change that only a new word can help it more fully see (p.94).

Phillips (2006), in her comprehensive volume *The Womanist Reader*, collects and cements various strands of womanist thought related to theology, literature, history, theatre, media, psychology, anthropology, education, social work, medicine, sexuality, and urban studies. She argues that although Walker (1983) had previously defined womanism in a seminal manner, the definition has the potential to often become misappropriated as it is in poetic form. More than twenty years after Walker's (1983) influential definition, Phillips (2006) attempts to solidify a single definition of womanism as:

> a social change perspective rooted in Black women's and other [non-White] women's everyday experiences and everyday methods of problem solving in everyday spaces, extended to the problem of ending all forms of oppression for all people, restoring the balance between people and the environment/ nature, and reconciling human life with the spiritual dimension. I take the perspective that womanism is not feminism. . . .Unlike feminism, and despite its name, womanism does not emphasize or privilege gender or sexism, rather, it elevates all sites and forms of oppression (Phillips, 2006, p. xx).

Phillips (2006) goes on to state that womanism can not be identified as a version of feminism and has five overarching characteristics; it is (a) antiopressionist, (b) vernacular, (c) nonideological, (d) communitarian, and (e) spiritualized. In addition she states that it has not been limited to an American context, having been explored by women and men in international settings such as Asia, Europe, Africa, and Latin America.

Although the term womanism was created, especially as a counterlabel to feminist, it still does not carry the familiarity and weight of feminism. As Offen (1988) states "there seems to be no satisfactory substitute. The term 'feminism' can be endlessly qualified, but it seems impossible to eliminate it from our vocabulary" (p. 134). As researchers and faculty we understand that feminist thought will continue to persist in the academy and that there are multiple versions of feminism that have come through scholarship in different "waves" (Bailey, 1997. With that said, however, we continue with our womanist agenda and subscribe to the politics of naming by associating ourselves with this school of thought.

Womanism as Experienced and Practiced in the Academy

As mentioned earlier, I (Dimpal) was introduced to womanism as I completed a class assignment in the early stages of my academic career. Although I (Caroline) have not explicitly done work in this area of scholarship previously, I too have rejected the framework of feminism as I conduct scholarly work on women and race. For both of us, womanism has impacted the way we conduct our scholarship by emphasizing the importance of lived experience and voice (Sheared, 1994).

I, Dimpal, used womanism as an intersectional framework along with critical race theory (Delgado & Stefancic, 2001) within my dissertation study (Jain, 2009) that explored concepts of leadership and transfer readiness among community college students who were non-White women. Over the course of an academic year, my study used semi-structured interviews, a focus group interview, and participant observation of eleven women who were leaders within their racial and ethnic student organizations. The interviews and observations centered on their experiences of extracurricular involvement and transfer preparation at Coastal Community College (CCC) (a pseudonym), one of the largest diverse, most transfer-intensive community colleges in the state of California.

The four student organizations that these women led (all pseudonyms) included the Black Student Union (BSU), Native American Student Union (NASU), Pilipino Student Union (PSU), and the United Latino Students (ULS). Through reputational sampling (Neuman, 2000), three women who held formal and/or informal leadership positions were selected from each organization, however I was only able to secure two leaders from NASU due to the severe underrepresentation of Native students at CCC.

Reputational sampling (Neuman, 2000) is a purposeful sampling strategy that allows one to ask experts in a field to provide recommendations for data collection. In my case I asked the positional leaders of the student clubs, who hypothetically would have been experts of their organizations, who they believed the women leaders were within their organization. By using reputational sampling I hoped to further ensure that those who did not display typical, positional qualities of leadership, would also be part of the sample. This was important to me as in concordance with womanism I knew that not all women, in particular non-White women, displayed leadership in a traditional manner and at times considered the word leader to be problematic (Arminio et al, 2000; Bernal, 1998).

By using a womanist framework I was able to center the intersectional identities of these women who grappled with dominant definitions of leadership and feminism. They often felt discriminated against based on their appearance, attitude, and dating status. The women shared the contradictions that they experienced when demonstrating strong leadership skills such as being labeled with the term "bitch." This derogatory term not only became gendered, but also raced when directed towards them (Kleinman, Ezzell, & Frost, 2009). In addition, when interacting with male leaders the women were at times put into compromising situations such as having other women brought into leadership roles so the men could increase their chances of dating them. Further, when attempting to outreach with other clubs off campus, some women felt that these partnerships were being forged so that men from other organizations could date women within their organization.

These various experiences impacted (a) the way the women thought about themselves, (b) how they viewed other women, (c) their views on topics such as motherhood and feminism, and (d) how these factors would impact them in the future as they continued their educational journeys. Only a few of the women would identify themselves as feminists and generally felt uncomfortable in admitting this to others. By sharing with them that I too was uncomfortable with being labeled as a feminist, we were able to dialogue in a much more meaningful, authentic way. One specific conversation was with Paola, a Dominican student who was the Vice President of the Black Student Union and majoring in industrial engineering. The following is her response to how she felt about the feminist movement and what it meant to her as a woman engaged in leadership:

> The whole let's burn our bras and not shave our armpits because of it, I like my armpits shaven. Within every movement, there's always the mainstream image that gets put out there, and I stay away from the feminist movement sometimes because I find that there's a lot of that. Especially, these White women get involved, and they have this whole different idea of what's important, and again it has nothing to do with the world view and I'm like: "pfft, I'm not going to sit here and waste time on burning my bra because there [are] more important things going on, there [are] people starving." So, you do that.

Here Paola shares a mature understanding of feminism for her young age. At the time of the interview she was 21 and was already familiar with the antiquated stereotypical connotations associated with feminism such as bra burning and unshaven armpits (Houvouras & Carter, 2008). Although one could argue that feminism is more than this and its contemporary version has moved from its stereotypical past (Mohanty, 2003), Paola still does not agree with it. What is more important here is that she recognizes that she does not subscribe to feminism because of the "world view" of White women and how she believes there are more important things to consider.

While conducting this study with Paola and the other ten women, multiple conversations arose where they were questioning the intersections between their race and gender, of how they were treated by men in their group, how they balanced the multiple demands of family, and how they were struggling to transfer despite their prominent leadership roles (Jain, 2010). By using womanism as a frame of analysis I was able to honor their experiences, to be fully committed to their survival as women, and to share the practice of self love (Walker, 1983) as some of them broke down in tears questioning their intellectual and leadership abilities.

Womanism has allowed me to support their alternate definitions of leadership, family, mothering, community, and success. To do these same things through feminism would not have been possible for me and would not have yielded the type of relationships that I continue to have with these women. In our conclusion, we offer additional insight to our womanist identities and provide a narrative to how we continue to persist within the academy from two stages of our professional careers, on one end as a pre-tenure faculty member, and on the other end of the spectrum, as a full professor.

Conclusion

Dimpal

As someone who identifies as a womanist I realize I am disrupting the Black/White binary that is commonly associated with this term. Often womanism becomes synonymous with Black feminism and has been contested as a divisive term in Black feminist scholarship for those who do not see the utility of the label (charles, 1997). Although we recognize the historical significance and necessity for Black women being able to name their own experiences (hooks, 1981), we adhere to the multiple definitions of womanism that include Black women specifically, and other non-White women in general.

As women from India and other parts of the global south have also renounced feminism (Kishwar, 1990; Mitra, 2011; Mohanty, 1991), I know that it means something different for me as a South Asian woman who is employed by the U.S. higher education system. Often, I am first challenged on the term as if I had mispronounced it, committed an error that my colleagues are generally more than happy to correct. Perhaps this response reflects their preconceived notion that English is my second language. I then explain that it was not an accident of the tongue, and that I do not subscribe to feminism. As the listener either begins with an inquisition or a look of confusion and then moves on, I am left with an odd mix of pride and sadness as I claim the term womanism with confidence.

This confidence however has come with time. As a recent graduate student I recall doing a presentation on womanism as part of my dissertation framework at large scale national conferences and hesitating as I approached the podium, unsure of who was in the audience and what their politics were. To my surprise, I learned to become familiar with the look of White women smiling at me as I presented content that described feminism as a historically racist, sexist, and homophobic movement. These same women would then approach me and applaud my work—some in a patronizing way, others attempting to connect as true allies. As I transitioned to the professoriate, I realized that some of these women are now my colleagues and may present additional challenges and benefits as I continue with my scholarship.

By being untenured faculty I constantly negotiate my space and remember that both the personal *and* professional are political. The key to my persistence in this work is to recall that I was hired using these same theoretical frameworks that I used in my dissertation; there is no need to censor myself. I did not stray from my womanist and critical race theory agenda at the onset of my entrance into the academy; that was essential to my survival throughout my first year. To identify with womanism in the academy means that I understand the possible consequences that can accompany my choice. I have been prepared by mentors like Caroline to brace myself for whatever may come next.

Caroline

At this point in my career, I have worked on many projects (some of which are cited in this paper) in collaboration with women who embrace a feminist perspective, a womanist perspective, or neither of these perspectives. I hope to continue to do so. Professionally, not using the term feminist may have lessened my ability to publish some of my work. Being questioned by publishers about the lack of this terminology in my research findings and approaches, especially those related to the examination of lived experiences of non-White women, causes me to have this perception. In addition, some scholars may not see the value of my work on non-White women as I do not employ a feminist perspective or lens in my writing. At least I do not name it so.

While working with Dimpal, I came to the realization that a womanist approach is likely what I have used without naming it. Certainly I agree with several of the womanist tenets noted in this article, such as a commitment to the survival and wholeness of males and females as well as ending all forms of oppression for all people. While I know that gender is important in shaping my life, I react negatively to those who would focus only on this trait without recognizing how my mixed race, ethnicity, and class have also shaped reality for me (Turner, 2003). This drives me more in line with a womanist rather than a feminist orientation. However, this is my first direct experience with these ideas and I have much more to learn. I am glad to have shared this journey with my colleague. Although further along in my academic career, I am young in this endeavor. As with all my work to date, I learn much about my own experience as well as how others view their lived experience.

References

Allen, W., Epps, E., Guillory, E., Suh, S., Bonus-Hammarth, M., & Stassen, M. (1991). Outsiders within: Race, gender, and faculty status in U.S. higher education. In P. Altbach & K. Lomotey (Eds.), *The racial crisis in American higher education* (pp. 189–220). Albany: State University of New York Press.

Arminio, J.L., Carter, S., Jones, S.E., Kruger, K., Lucas, N., Washington, J., Young, N, & Scott, A. (2000). Leadership experiences of students of color. *NASPA Journal, 37,* 496–510.

Bailey, C. (1997). Making waves and drawing lines: The politics of defining the vicissitudes of feminism. *Hypatia, 12,* 17–28.

Beauboeuf-Lafontant, T. (2002). A Womanist experience of caring: Understanding the pedagogy of exemplary Black women teachers. *The Urban Review, 34,* 71–86.

Bernal, D.D. (1998a). Grassroots leadership reconceptualized: Chicana oral histories and the 1968 East Los Angeles school blowouts. Frontiers, 19, 113–138.

Bhatia, M.V. (2005). Fighting words: Naming terrorists, bandits, rebels and other violent actors. Third World Quarterly, 26, 5–22.

Brown, E.B. (1989). Womanist consciousness: Maggie Lena Walker and the Independent Order of Saint Luke, Signs, 14, 610–633.

(charles). H. (1997). The language of womanism: Re-thinking difference. In H. S. Mirza (Ed). *Black British feminism* (pp. 278–297). New York: Routledge.

Chronicle of Higher Education Alamanac (2009). Number of full-time faculty members by sex, rank, and racial and ethnic group, fall 2007. Retrieved from: http://chronicle.com/article/Number-of-Full-Time-Faculty/47992/

Collins, P.H. (1993). What's in a name? Womanism, Black femnism, and beyond. In R.D.Torres, L.F. Mirón, & J.X. Inda (Eds.), *Race, identity, and citizenship: A reader* (pp. 126–137). Malden, MA: Blackwell Publishing.

Collins, P.H. (2000). Black feminist thought: Knowledge, consciousness and the politics of empowerment (2nd ed.). New York: Routledge.

Cott, N. (1986). Feminist theory and feminist movements: The past before us. In J. Mitchell & A. Oakley (Eds.), *What is feminism?* New York: Pantheon Books.

Delgado, R. & Stefancic, J. (2001). *Critical race theory: An introduction.* New York: University Press.

Falludi, S. (2007). *The terror dream.* New York: Metropolitan Books. Garland-Thomson, R. (2002). Integrating disability, transforming feminist theory. *Feminist Formations, 14,* 1–32.

Hebbani, A.G. (2007). You can't "de-race" and "de-womanize" me: Experiences when you go global. *New Directions for Teaching and Learning,* 110, 45–53.

hooks, b. (1981). *Ain't I a woman: Black women and feminism.* Cambridge, MA: South End Press.

hooks, b. (1984). *Feminist theory: From margin to center.* Cambridge, MA: South End Press.

Houvouras, S., & Carter, J.S. (2008). The f word: College students' definitions of a feminist. *Sociological Forum, 23,* 234–256.

Hutcheson, P.A. (2008). Shall I compare thee? Reflections on naming and power. In M. Gasman, B. Baez, & C.S. Turner (Eds.). *Understanding minority servings institutions* (pp. 43–54). Albany, NY: State University of New York Press.

Jain, D. (2009). *Women of color student leaders: The role of race and gender in community college transfer readiness.* Unpublished dissertation. University of California, Los Angeles.

Jain, D. (2010). Critical race theory and community colleges: Through the eyes of women student leaders of color. *Community College Journal of Research and Practice, 34,* 78–91.

Joireman, S.F. (2004, December). *Multiculturalism and the Politics of Naming.* Paper presented at the International Conference on Political Challenges and Democratic Institutions, Taipei, Taiwan.

Kishwar, M. (1990, November–December). Why I do not call myself a feminist. *Manushi, 61,* 2–8.

Kleinman, S., Ezzell, M.B., & Frost, C. (2009). Reclaiming critical analysis: The social harms of "bitch". *Sociological Analysis, 3,* 47–68.

Lorde, A. (1984). *Sister Outsider.* Freedom, CA: The Crossing Press.

Mitra, A. (2011). To be or not to be a feminist in India. *Affilia, 26,* 182–200.

Mohanty, C.T (1991). Under Western eyes: Feminist scholarship and colonial discourses. In C.T. Mohanty, A. Russo, & L. Torres (Eds.), Third World women and the politics of feminism (pp. 51–80). Bloomington, IN: University of Indiana Press.

Mohanty, C. T. (2003). *Feminism without borders: Decolonizing theory, practicing solidarity.* Durham, NC: Duke University Press.

Moraga, C. & Anzaldúa (Eds). (1981). *This bridge called my back: Writings by radical women of color.* Latham, NY: Kitchen Table: Women of Color Press.

Morris, J. (1995). Personal and political: A feminist perspective on researching physical disability. In P. Potts, F. Armstrong, & M. Masterton (Eds) *Equality and diversity in education: National and international contexts* (2nd ed., pp. 208–219). New York: Routledge.

Mindiola, T., Niemann, Y.F., & Rodriguez, N. (2002). *Black-brown relations and stereotypes.* Austin, TX: University of Texas Press.

Neuman, W.L. (2000). *Social research methods: qualitative and quantitative research approaches.* Needham Heights, MA: Allyn & Bacon.

Offen, K. (1988). Defining feminism: A comparative historical approach. *Signs, 14,* 119–157.

Phillips, L. (Ed) (2006). *The womanist reader.* New York: Taylor & Francis.

Richardson, D., & Robinson, V. (1994). Theorizing women's studies and masculinity: The politics of naming. *European Journal of Women's Studies, 1,* 11–27.

Sheared, V. (1994). Giving voice: An inclusive model of instruction—a womanist perspective. *New Directions for Adult and Continuing Education, 1994,* 27–37.

Stanley, C. A. (Ed.). (2006). Faculty of color: Teaching in predominantly White colleges and universities. Bolton, MA: Anker Publishing Company Inc.

Suzuki, B.H. (1977). Education and the socialization of Asian Americans: A revisionist analysis of the "model minority" thesis. *Amerasia, 4,* 23–51.

Suzuki, B.H. (2002). Revisiting the model minority stereotype: Implications for student affairs practice and higher education. *New Directions for Student Services, 97,* 21–32.

Spann, J. (1990). *Retaining and promoting minority faculty members: Problems and possibilities.* Madison, WI: The University of Wisconsin System.

Taylor, V., & Wittier, N.E. (1999). Collective identity in social movement communities: Lesbian feminist mobilization. In J. Freeman, & V. Johhnson, (Eds). Waves of protest: Social movements since the sixties (pp. 169–194). Lanham, MD: Rowman and Littefield Publishers.

Thomas, G.D., & Hollenshead, C. (2001). Resisting from the margins: The coping strategies of Black women and other women of color faculty members at a research university. *The Journal of Negro Education, 70,* 166–175.

Turner, C.S. (2002a). *Diversifying the faculty: A guidebook for search committees.* Washington, D.C.: Association of American Colleges and Universities (AAC&U).

Turner, C.S. (2002b). Women of color in academe: Living with multiple marginality. *The Journal of Higher Education, 73,* 74–93.

Turner, C.S. (2003). Incorporation and marginalization in the academy: From border toward center for faculty of color? *Journal of Black Studies 34,* 112–125.

Turner, C.S. (2008a). Toward public education as a public good: Reflections from the field. In K. P. González and R. V. Padilla (Eds.). *Doing the public good: Latina/o scholars engage civic participation* (pp. 97–112 Sterling, Va.: Stylus Publishing, LLC.

Turner, C.S. (2008b). Women of color in academe: Experiences of the often invisible. In J. Glazer-Raymo (Ed.). *Unfinished agendas: New and continuing gender challenges in higher education* (pp. 230–252). Baltimore, MD: The Johns Hopkins University Press.

Turner, C.S. (2011a). Latinas in higher education: A presence that remains tenuous. *On Campus with Women: Forty Years of the Program on the Status and Education of Women,* 39(3). Retrieved from: http://www.aacu.org/ocww/volume39_3/feature.cfm?section=3

Turner, C.S. (2011b). An Update on Challenges to Diversity in Higher Education Today. Retrieved from: http://www.pearsonlearningsolutions.com/blog/2011/03/08/an-update-on-challenges-to-diversity-in-higher-education-today/

Turner, C.S., González, J.C., & Wood, J.L. (2008). Faculty of color in academe: What 20 years of literature tells us. *Journal of Diversity in Higher Education, 1,* 139–168.

Turner, C.S., & Myers, S.L., Jr. (2000). *Faculty of color in academe: Bittersweet success.* Needham Heights, MA: Allyn & Bacon.

Walker, A. (1983). *In search of our mothers' gardens.* New York: Harcourt Brace Jovanovich.

Walker, A. (1984, February 12). The Black woman's story. *New York Times Sunday Magazine,* p. 94.

Wong, K. (2007). *Emotional labor of diversity work: Women of color faculty in predominantly White institutions.* Unpublished dissertation. Arizona State University.

Section V

Diverse Students at Two-Year Institutions of Higher Learning

SECTION V: DIVERSE STUDENTS AT TWO-YEAR INSTITUTIONS OF HIGHER LEARNING

Community colleges are among the most diverse institutions in the United States. According to the American Association of Community Colleges (2012)[i], women comprise 57% of community college attendees while students of color make up 37% of two-year collegians. Community college demographics have become gradually more diverse as the two-year context has been the postsecondary segment responsive to meeting the needs of students that are first-generation, older, part-time, single parents, displaced workers, and/or individuals with disabilities. This section of the *Reader* seeks to reveal a modicum of the spectrum of diversity community college learners encompass.

Chapter Twenty-Six, "Research on race and ethnic relations among community college students," authored by Maxwell and Shammas, provides a commentary on prior research and presents a call to action for future research that focuses on race/ethnic relations among community college students. More specifically, Maxwell and Shammas discuss how the extant literature on cross-racial relations with regard to perceptions of campus climate, experiencing discrimination, and overall benefits of institutional diversity primarily focused on four-year colleges and universities. The authors assert that this oversight has produced critical gaps in the knowledge base on student diversity and race relations. The article is a primer for additional inquiry that illustrates the heuristic value of theoretical frameworks such as contact theory, structural assimilation, and acculturation theories. Additionally, a discussion of conflict theory and critical race theory provide conceptual underpinnings for empirical studies examining the racialized context of student relations within the two-year context.

In Chapter Twenty-Seven, J. Luke Wood, "Leaving the 2-year college: Predictors of black male collegian departure," provides the reader with a quantitative analysis of Black male attrition at community colleges. Through *ex post facto* secondary data analysis, the author examined Black male students with their male counterparts to find that little overlap exists between Black male collegians with non-Black collegians. Wood found that Black males had a greater likelihood of institutional departure for reasons other than financial concerns, program dissatisfaction, military deployment, course scheduling, etc. Based on the findings from the "Beginning Postsecondary Students Longitudinal Study (BPS)," there were greater odds of Black male departure when dissatisfied with their programs as opposed to financial or academic reasons in contrast to other male counterparts.

Chapter Twenty-Eight by Crisp and Nora, "Hispanic student success: Factors influencing the persistence and transfer decisions of Latino community college students enrolled in developmental education," investigated factors affecting persistence and decisions to transfer among Latino(a) community college students in developmental courses. The authors consider the underpreparedness of many community college students with particular attention paid to the mismatch in student aspirations, transfer, and subsequent degree completion as high numbers of Latino/a students are concentrated in two-year institutions with especially little successful transfer activity. Crisp and Nora draw on Tinto's model of student integration and cultural capital theory as useful frameworks to examine the "Beginning Postsecondary Students Longitudinal Study (BPS)." This article illustrates the importance of college readiness and shows that various environmental factors along with academic ill-preparedness negatively affecting Hispanic students from matriculating and successful transfer.

---

[i]American Association of Community Colleges (2012). *2012 Community college fast fact sheet*. Retrieved from http://www.aacc.nche.edu/AboutCC/Pages/fastfacts.aspx

In Chapter Twenty-Nine, "Following their every move: An investigation of social-class differences in college pathways," Goldrick-Rab returns us to a discussion of students who enter community colleges and attempt to navigate the collegiate experience offered by these institutions. She describes students' attendance patterns by social class to determine if differences in postsecondary attendance are related to the extent to which students are advantaged or disadvantaged by their family background, including economic background, and prior high school preparation. Using national longitudinal data from postsecondary transcripts, Goldrick-Rab shows that, after controlling for prior academic preparation, students from lower socioeconomic backgrounds are less likely than economically advantaged students to enroll continuously in college once they enter, adding another "layer of stratification in higher education."

With over two-fifths of undergraduates studying at America's community colleges, the intersectionality of identities is present on community college campuses. However, limited literature exists that examines issues facing LGBT students at two-year institutions of higher learning. Kiekel, in Chapter Thirty, "Perceptions of campus climate and engagement for lesbian, gay, bisexual, and transgender community college students," explores the campus climate for LGBT community college students. Drawing from the theoretical underpinnings of the student engagement and campus climate literature, to understand how LGBT students describe the community college environment. The author shares while students expressed the campus climate was positive, LGBT students reported positive and negative classroom exchanges and microaggressions. However, engagement in LGBT student organizations/clubs aided in feeling a sense of belonging and safety at this particular urban community college.

Mamiseishvili and Koch, authors of Chapter Thirty-One, "Students with disabilities at 2-year institutions in the United States: Factors related to success," discuss diverse students in community colleges. The "Beginning Postsecondary Students (BPS) Longitudinal Study" is examined and the authors present the relationship of students with disability characteristics, educational services received, and college persistence at two-year institutions. With this sample, roughly one-quarter of students with disabilities did not persist beyond their first year and over half left college by the end of their third year. The findings revealed physical or orthopedic conditions, depression, and other factors that were associated with attrition while academic advising, high GPAs, full-time attendance, and high degree aspirations positively related to the persistence of students with disabilities at two-year institutions.

CHAPTER 26

RESEARCH ON RACE AND ETHNIC RELATIONS AMONG COMMUNITY COLLEGE STUDENTS

WILLIAM MAXWELL

DIANE SHAMMAS
UNIVERSITY OF SOUTHERN CALIFORNIA

Considerable research has been conducted in the past two decades on race and ethnic relations among community college students. The atheoretical underpinnings of this research have led to vague and conflicting findings regarding such concepts as campus climate, discrimination, and the benefits of campus diversity. This article briefly reviews potentially relevant theories and research methods and offers many specific suggestions for future research on student diversity.

Keywords: race relations, ethnic relations, intergroup relations, interracial contact, social interaction, campus surveys, campus climate, discrimination, community college students, two-year colleges

Despite dramatic demographic, political, and cultural changes in North American society, there is a remarkable absence of scholarly research on student race relations and campus climates in community colleges. Political forces have struggled over immigration and affirmative action policies, including the landmark court case *University of California v. Bakke* (1978) and the more recent *Grutter v. Bollinger* (2003). Demographic trends show that the proportion of racial and ethnic minority students doubled in the colleges from 15.7% to 30.3% between 1976 and 1996 and will continue to increase in the next 25 years (Kee, 1999). Yet a recent review of the burgeoning scholarship on this issue refers almost entirely to four-year university settings (Hurtado, Dey, Gurin, & Gurin, 2003).

Given this significant gap in the literature, this review addresses two central questions:

Research Question 1: How have scholars previously examined relations among community college students from diverse racial and ethnic groups?

Research Question 2: What are promising future theoretical topics and research methods for studying relations among community college students from diverse racial and ethnic groups?

For the purposes of this review, the students of interest are those who attend community colleges with considerable structural diversity (i.e., those who attend two-year colleges other than tribal colleges, historically Black colleges, overwhelmingly White colleges, and others populated almost entirely by one cultural group). This article begins with a brief description of several theories of race relations among diverse racial and ethnic students. These theories are borrowed mainly from the social sciences and four-year college literature. The remainder of the review examines empirical studies of diversity and campus climate in community colleges. We do not conclude this review with a list of findings or future research suggestions because few well-established conclusions can be drawn from the literature. Rather, we focus the discussion in each section on future research opportunities instead of deferring them to the conclusion.

In addition to student race and ethnic relations, which is the subject of this review, community college scholarship has also considered race and ethnicity as discrete categories. These studies are outside the scope of this review but have included, for example, analyses of success rates among student groups, instructional and programmatic efforts designed for diverse students, and relations between diverse students, faculty, and staff (see, e.g., Cejda & Rhodes, 2004; Nora, 2004; Rendon, Hope, & Associates, 1996; Townsend, 2000).

Theories About Student Race Relations

The preeminent theories of student race relations rarely comment on community colleges. As such, the theories discussed in this section depend heavily on the four-year college literature. Note that although the most cited theories emphasize the psychological features of diversity efforts, this analysis will also address the social factors of diversity and, where the limited literature permits, the cultural dimensions of diversity.

Functional Theories

The prevailing perspective on campus diversity is drawn from Allport's (1954) contact theory. This theory proposes that intergroup interaction can reduce prejudice among college students, given four conditions: (a) equal status of the groups in the college setting, (b) common goals, (c) intergroup cooperation, and (d) support of authorities, law, or custom. Contact theory has successfully reached across scholarly disciplines to address psychological, social, and cultural features of race relations and has received wide acceptance among behavioral and social scientists and higher education researchers (e.g., Brown & Hewstone, 2005; Pettigrew, 1998). The contact hypothesis has been used to imply that equality within the college, communication, and common values readily occur within American colleges to foster prejudice reduction. Scholars have applied this theory frequently in research on four-year campuses but not often to community colleges.

Gurin, Dey, Hurtado, and Gurin (2002) have advanced a similar theory, which they posited the potential benefits of diversity efforts in four-year colleges. A central thesis of this perspective is that efforts to increase diversity on American campuses have led to democracy outcomes, which include knowledge and awareness about other cultures, civic cooperation, and integration in settings such as classrooms, voluntary organizations, and the workforce. Like contact theory, this functional perspective also assumes open communication and relatively equal status among students in American colleges. This line of analysis has rarely been applied to research on community college students.

Acculturation and Assimilation Theories

The preceding psychological approaches are paralleled by long-standing functional perspectives in sociology in theories of immigration, ethnic stratification, and inevitable assimilation. These lenses are quite relevant to community colleges because these institutions are on the front lines in the education of recent immigrants. Gordon (1964) defined *structural assimilation* as consisting of several kinds of social relations subsumed under two categories: secondary relationships in colleges and workplaces and primary relationships such as friendships and cliques. The emphasis on communication and assimilation in these sociological perspectives is very similar to the emphasis on cultural and social involvement in higher education theories of integration and engagement (Pike & Kuh, 2005; Tinto, 1997). In general, these theories focus on communication and cooperation instead of power differentials and the social exclusion and competition experienced by some students at culturally diverse colleges. Although they do not emphasize campus conflict, Bean and Metzner (1985) have adapted a functional approach to pay special attention to the cultural groups off campus from which students may draw social support (see, e.g., Person & Rosenbaum, 2006).

Conflict Theories

Various conflict theories focus on the tension and struggle among racial and ethnic groups. A central implication from conflict perspectives is that campus intergroup processes are closely linked to structures of domination and reproduction in the societal context of the college (Omi & Winant, 1994). These theories implicitly suggest that disadvantaged students tend to respond to discrimination with resistance or alienation. However, these theories tend to underemphasize how students from marginal cultures willfully cooperate with and accept the practices and beliefs of the dominant culture.

A few recent innovations in conflict theory have attempted to refine the conceptions of intergroup struggle and to incorporate the insights of assimilation perspectives. Integrated threat theory (Stephan & Stephan, 2000) and social dominance theory (Sidanius & Pratto, 1993) both suggest that conflicts emerge between those who are trying to acquire material resources and those who are trying to retain them. Assimilation processes have been acknowledged by recent conflict theories in new conceptions of dissonant, consonant, and selective acculturation that tend to discount the notion of full assimilation (Portes & Rumbaut, 2001).

A very different theoretical approach concerns such conflicts as the subtle racial insults experienced by African American students at primarily White universities. These conflicts have been analyzed through the lens of critical race theory (Solorzano, Ceja, & Yosso, 2000). Critical race theory advocates a method for developing personal insight and understanding the organizational structure that leads to covert discrimination in U.S. institutional settings. This is a potentially useful method in community colleges, where racism is less overt and where an ideology of a welcoming and open door is prevalent. For a time, particularly in the 1980s, scholars frequently reported overt racial conflicts on four-year campuses but they did not often monitor these struggles in the community colleges (Farrell & Jones, 1988).

Glaring racial and cultural divides found in the de facto ethnic and racial tracking of students into remedial and college-level courses have attracted little research from a conflict perspective. Although the classroom is the only place on campus where many community college students are engaged, enrollments by race and ethnicity vary extremely among classrooms (Maxwell et al., 2003). Conflict theories could explore whether there are processes by which minority racial and ethnic groups are marginalized from more rigorous college courses.

Although theories about race relations on two-year college campuses are few, there have been empirical studies of intergroup race relations at community colleges. We discuss these studies in the following section.

Empirical Studies of Student Race and Ethnic Relations in Community Colleges

In the paragraphs that follow, we examine ethnically diverse student relations along a few dimensions of assimilation—acculturation, and secondary and primary structural assimilation—as well as two student conflict variables: discrimination and prejudice. Most of the available research comes not from academic and scholarly periodicals but from the practical and action-oriented publications of college institutional research offices, government administrative centers, and education associations. Most of the studies available in national databases were conducted in the blue (Democratic) states, particularly on the West Coast, some in the Midwest and Northeastern region, and very few in other regions.

Studies of Campus Racial Climate

Several researchers have examined racial climates at community colleges. There are several dimensions of campus climate, including social relations among diverse groups of students, friendliness, comfort, belonging, college support of diversity, safety, and equitable treatment by staff, faculty, and students. Despite the fair number of campus climate studies conducted within individual community colleges, there has been only one national study. In 1997, the American Association of Community

Colleges (AACC) surveyed 1,450 community college presidents and administrators, of whom 360 replied (Kee, 1999). The central measure on the questionnaire asked administrators and presidents to rate campus climate on a 5-point scale: *contentious* to *harmonious*. None rated their colleges with a score of 1 at the contentious pole of the scale; 21% of participants rated their colleges as harmonious with a score of 5; and 39% rated their colleges as 4, somewhat harmonious. Almost one third, 31%, selected the midpoint score of 3, a mix of conflict and harmony. Seven percent indicated the score of 2, for somewhat contentious campus climates.

Given the low response rate, the limited theoretical depth of the analysis, and the reliance on only one unvalidated measure of racial climate, these national data must be used with caution. However, the study does suggest that a majority of community college presidents perceive their campus climates as harmonious and that a substantial proportion of the nation's colleges are also perceived as less than harmonious.

Research at Individual Community Colleges

With the exception of the AACC study, the majority of data on individual community college campus climate is found in 17 studies in the 1990s of one or more community colleges. The samples have typically not been randomly selected and have only modest indications of being representative. However, many of these samples do not appear to be unrepresentative and many are large, with more than 600 students. For example, one of the studies surveyed approximately 13,000 students at 25 different college campuses (Washington State Board, 1997).

However, without any theoretical uniformity or solid conceptual base for these studies, the particular measures used varied considerably in content. For example, London (1978) and Weis (1985) conducted ethnographies, Person and Rosenbaum (2006) both conducted interviews and surveyed respondents, and three studies explored a few student focus groups (Clements, 1997; Weissman, Bulakowski, & Jumisko, 1998; Willett, 2002). This lack of uniformity dilutes the comparability of the studies and likely accounts for much of the variation in findings.

In broad terms, the research findings from individual colleges portray many campuses—particularly those on the West Coast—as welcoming and supportive social zones. Questionnaire surveys were administered at 39 campuses: 32 colleges were described as positive by 85% or more of the students, although it must be cautioned that the estimates for the 25 Washington colleges were statewide averages that may obscure group differences at individual campuses (Arnold, 1995; Hart, Lutkemeier, & Gustafson, 2002; Milwaukee Area Technical College, 1988; San Diego Community College District, 1994; Washington State Board, 1997; Willett, 2002). Four of the college climates were rated by 70% to 84% of the students as positive (Clements, 1997; Howard Community College, 1998; Mattice, 1994), and three campuses were rated as positive by 48% to 58% of the students (Boughan, 1992; Lee, 1994; Luan, 1995).

To some extent, positive campus climate ratings can be attributed to the predominance of White students who typically rate the racial and ethnic climate as higher than do non-White students. For example, in a focus group conducted by Weissman et al. (1998) at a 75% White suburban Chicago campus, a White student ironically remarked, "It is so diverse here. I think it's great" (p. 33).

Minority students do not always rate campus diversity climates lower than do White students. For example, for the 13,000 students at the 25 colleges surveyed by the Washington State Board (1997), on average, 96% of Asian American, Latino, and White students and 87% of African Americans rated their campus climate as positive.

The positive description of campus racial climates at many individual colleges is largely consistent with the AACC study cited earlier. Furthermore, these positive studies do not show the strident kinds of White racism reported in two ethnographies conducted in northeastern states in the 1970s and 1980s: verbal intimidations, physical threats, antagonistic group depictions of other groups, covert hostility, and an absence of informal contact outside the campus (London, 1978; Weis, 1985). Perhaps this is evidence that the racism perceived by many as prevalent on community college campuses in decades past has dissipated or changed forms. We might also attribute differences in findings to variations in geographic region or methods of research.

These individual campus climate studies have established important foundations for the future study of racial and ethnic climates in community colleges. The samples are large, and although they are not random, they are not easily discounted. In general, many of the studies used technically proficient measures often borrowed from a common item pool such as those provided in the California Postsecondary Education Commission (1992) publications.

The most basic limitation of these studies has already been mentioned: the absence of explicit and consistent theoretical foundations, although Person and Rosenbaum (2006) is an important exception. For example, theoretical development is needed to expand the concept of climate to include prejudice, tension, exclusion, struggle, and discrimination.

Various methodological advances are warranted as well. Very few studies have relied on interviews, focus groups, or observation. These methods of exploration could be used to develop initial conceptual frameworks for understanding current campus race relations. Several specific technical questionnaire issues may also be raised: response-set bias from stating almost all the survey items in a positive tone and halo effect bias from grouping all of the ethnicity items together. Standard survey procedures for randomly varying item valence and mixing various topics in the sequence of items would resolve these problems in future research. Most studies have not attempted to reconcile item divergences or develop an overall measure of the climate. Thus, for example, in a very diverse San Francisco East Bay suburban college (Arnold, 1995), where 84% of the students agreed with the single item "there is respect for differences in race/ethnicity" and 90% agreed with the item "I feel welcome," 32% also agreed that "tension between different cultural groups that leads to verbal abuse or physical violence is a problem" and 31% reported that they did not feel "physically safe and secure on campus." Finally, none of the studies described above reported efforts to ascertain the reliability or validity estimates for the survey items. Future research must thus address the development of multi-item scales and ascertain the reliability and validity of the meaning of the measures.

Another uncertain feature of the research methods is the unusually large percentage of students who selected the neutral response category or did not respond to questionnaire items concerning race relations on campus. The number of neutral responses and nonresponses comprises as much as two thirds of otherwise large samples. Although some reports discard all neutral and missing responses, these data are in fact related to important student perceptions including uncertainty, fears, and tensions (Howard Community College, 1998; San Diego Community College District, 1994). Future research can deal with these issues by incorporating neutral and missing responses as an important form of response, by developing other measures that elicit a more direct form of negative or positive response, and by directly examining the nature of related fears and uncertainties.

Discrimination and Racism at Community Colleges

Conflict theories posit that intergroup racial competition, struggle, and discrimination are likely present at diverse colleges. However, only about one third of the studies examined discrimination on campus. On most of the campuses where racism was studied, less than one fifth of the students reported that they were the targets of discrimination. For example, in the San Diego Community College District (1994), where Whites comprise slightly more than half of the student population, 13% of students indicated that they had frequently or occasionally "been discriminated against because of my race/ethnicity," and a clear majority of each ethnic category indicated that they had "never" been discriminated against. Similarly, at a suburban Chicago campus where three quarters of the students are classified as White, a Latino student in Weissman et al.'s (1998) focus group commented,

> I felt better when I came to CLC because I don't look at people as a color. When you are in the outside world, people look at you and judge you. Here at CLC, it doesn't matter if you are young, old, what color, and that is what the great part about it is. (p. 34)

To a substantial extent, these findings parallel earlier evidence of relatively harmonious campus climates. Yet in the Chicago focus group, a Latina recounted, "When I first started in class when I was walking in, they said, 'All those Hispanics are stupid and all are in gangs. All they do is drink.' Automatically, they all thought bad of me" (p. 34). Racism and discrimination are not far away from many classrooms and campus networks. Although the resilient Latina quoted above went on to say, "By the end of the class I had my good points. . . . They finally respected me" (p. 34), the threat of rejection and inequity lurks for many under the amiable surface of academe. It may be the uncertainty of the threat that leads so many of the students to be reluctant to answer some survey questions about race relations and that leads many other respondents to select the neutral or unsure response categories.

Although in these studies some students from each ethnic background reported that they had encountered discrimination, people of color were about 10% more likely to report discrimination than were White people. For example, at the four colleges studied in San Diego, only 10% of Whites indicated that they had experienced discrimination, compared to 18% of African Americans, 22% of Asian Americans, and 12% of Latinos (San Diego Community College District, 1994). Black and White students at Milwaukee Area Technical College (1988) reported corresponding discrimination levels.

Future research needs to explore the nature and the frequency of prejudice, racism, and discrimination on community college campuses. The limitations of the past decade's survey research methods—the high rates of neutral responses and nonresponses and conceptually vague measures that underestimate discrimination rates—indicate that future research must investigate whether the rates of subtle discrimination, racism, and neglect are considerably more accurate than the relatively optimistic reports in the current literature. For example, in an exception to prevailing questionnaire methods, a Maryland campus survey included a detailed list of 18 different types of racial bias, and 38% of the students indicated that they were the recipients of at least one of the 18 types of discrimination, about twice the discrimination rate usually reported (Boughan, 1992). The implication should be obvious: Researchers need to develop detailed theories of discrimination and corresponding measures so that the targets of racism can fully report their college experiences.

Racial Relations in the Classroom

Classrooms are the focus of student campus activity and are the most likely spaces of intergroup contact among students, many of whom are part-time students and leave the college immediately after class. Despite the focus of the colleges on classroom learning, there has been almost no research about the interpersonal racial processes occurring in diverse classrooms.

Participation rates in classroom activities may vary among races. In a Washington State Board (1997) study of 25 community colleges, about half of African American students reported that they frequently asked questions in class, which is more than any other ethnic group. Asian American and Latino students participated the least in class discussions; only about one third said that they frequently asked questions.

Some minority students expressed uncomfortable classroom experiences of loneliness or tokenism. Weissman et al. (1998) reported that these students wished for more minority students in their classes and that many did not want the teacher to ask them to explain the attitudes or behavior of their ethnic group. Mattice (1994) cited students who wrote, "Of all the classes I have taken at COC [College of the Canyons], I have been the only African American enrolled. Sometimes I ask myself what I am doing at COC. This has nothing to do with me sensing any prejudice or discrimination at all" (p. 38).

Future research could address the extent and nature of these tensions in classrooms, including loneliness and racial and ethnic tokenism. In addition, studies could examine whether the loneliness of isolated minority community college students as compared to residential students in four-year colleges is partially alleviated by the opportunity community college students have to return daily to their homes and familiar social networks. Researchers might also examine whether the threat of unalleviated racial isolation at a residential college leads many to enroll at a local two-year or four-year commuter campus.

College teaching could also benefit from research on race relations in the classroom. For example, contact theory could be explored for the development of strategies for building equal classroom status positions among racially and ethnically diverse students. Research using theories of structural diversity may consider its application to intergroup relations and cross-group and same-group formations; dominance theories can help inform the emergence of competition for scarce resources and rewards; and critical race theory can be applied to identify practices of unconscious group privilege and discrimination in the classroom.

Studies of Race Relations in Students' Social Lives

Previous research suggests that few community college students are socially integrated in extracurricular campus networks (Dougherty, 1992). Similarly, the Washington State Board (1997) study found that 70% to 80% of students spent fewer than seven hours outside class on campus per week. Correspondingly low levels of social interaction were reported at colleges in rural California (Willett, 2002), in Maryland (Boughan, 1992), and in New York's Westchester County (Lee, 1994). In Weis' (1985) study of social interaction, one East Coast urban college instructor reported, "While there is no overt hostility between black and white students in classes, at the end of classes, they don't see each other at all" (p. 57).

Despite the skepticism of many observers over whether there is social life at community colleges, several studies indicate that some students feel they have friends at the colleges. Of the students at the four relatively diverse colleges in the San Diego Community College District (1994), 61% agreed with the statement "I have many friends at this campus." Similarly, Person and Rosenbaum (2006) reported findings on same-group versus cross-group friendships in Latino campus enclaves. However, few other community college scholars have paid attention to the current debate about the benefits of same-group versus cross-group friendships in research on schools, four-year colleges, and other institutions (Antonio, 2004). Although previous studies of community college student relations have shown some student interest in contact across cultural divides, there has been little examination of cross-group friendships. In several different California colleges, approximately 70% to 90% of the students reported that "students of similar racial/ethnic backgrounds tend to 'hang out' on campus together" (San Diego Community College District, 1994) or "stick with their own clique" (Arnold, 1995). A student at a Los Angeles suburban college said,

> I think that the different ethnic groups do everything they can to separate themselves. In the cafeteria the blacks, the whites, the brown, and the what have you, seem to have their own tables. But then again, I only see it sometimes because I am a part-time student. I do know that in the classroom every ethnic group gets along and helps each other out when it comes to study groups. (Mattice, 1994, p. 54)

A basic premise of functional theories is that large groups such as community colleges are founded on communication. Questionnaire survey responses about intergroup relations have produced various findings. When asked about communication among students on campus, students of all racial and ethnic categories generally report that "diverse groups communicate well," and substantial numbers from all races report a desire to interact with other students outside their cultural group (Mattice, 1994). Similarly, about 70% to 90% of the students at three different colleges in California agreed with various survey items such as "I value making friends with students of other cultural and ethnic backgrounds" (Arnold, 1995; Mattice, 1994; Willett, 2002). When survey questionnaire items are framed differently, however, a shift in results appears. Fewer Whites, as compared to other ethnic groups, expressed a desire for more intergroup communication (Mattice, 1994; Washington State Board, 1997). In a northern California suburban college, 55% of students surveyed agreed that "there is a lack of communication among students of different ethnic/cultural groups at [this college]" (Arnold, 1995). Future research on functional theories of community colleges needs to examine additional evidence and interpret this tension with the theories' basic assumptions about communication.

Some of the studies mentioned previously also explored questions about cultural dominance on college campuses and struggles for resources across racial and ethnic groups. At the few colleges where these matters have been researched, the majority of community college students are not concerned about or familiar with such issues. For example, Arnold (1995) reported that fewer than half of the students at a diverse San Francisco East Bay college responded to the item "Some ethnic groups here dominate or have an unfair influence on the decision-making process in student clubs, organizations, and government." Of those who did respond, 54% agreed that some ethnic groups dominated or held an unfair advantage on campus (Arnold, 1995). Similarly, at a southern California campus only 35% of White students agreed with the statement, "There is not enough interaction among different racial/ethnic organizations at [the college]" (Mattice, 1994), considerably less than the 51% of Latinos and 61% of Asians and Pacific Islanders who agreed with the item (Mattice, 1994). Student comments from this latter survey illustrate several different points of view:

> To strengthen diversity, have more clubs for students . . . more social things. While I think the clubs and organizations for separate ethnic backgrounds are helpful in educating those who belong, it also helps to separate and exclude others who may be interested in learning about different cultural backgrounds. The more ethnic clubs [the college] has, the greater the segregation will become among students. (Mattice, 1994, p. 52-53)

A basic necessity in future research on intergroup relations is the use of both conflict and functional theories, and negative as well as positive measures. In the survey items cited above, approximately 70% of the White students expressed interest in friendships and contact with persons of other racial and ethnic groups. But the limited validity of single survey items, which are positively phrased, must be considered in future research. Our analysis suggests that when surveys include a mix of positive- and negative-worded items, more comprehensive findings can be revealed. For example, when students rated the variable survey item "The amount of interaction. . . between individual students of different racial/ethnic groups" as "too much, about. . .right, [or] not enough," differences in responses were striking (Mattice, 1994). Only 29% of Whites reported not enough interaction, compared with 36% of Native Americans, 45% of Latinos, 50% of Asians and Pacific Islanders, and 69% of African Americans surveyed (Mattice, 1994).

Although many White students are interested in more intergroup contact, future research might inquire whether White students are the most isolated from intergroup activity and, if so, why? Past research has not significantly addressed fears, threats, prejudice, discrimination, and the dynamics of intergroup struggles in the colleges. It is time that these theoretical topics become central elements in our research. Future research can also ask why several studies have demonstrated that African American students have been the most active and interested in expanding their contacts with other races and how these interests can be leveraged in developing more civil attitudes and relationships among all groups.

Outcomes and Benefits of Intergroup Relations

There has not been definitive research on the impact of race and ethnic relations, although the limited evidence is consistent with the interpretation that the outcomes are positive. In the Washington State Board (1997) survey, approximately one half of the 13,000 students reported substantial progress in response to a question about how much progress they experienced in "getting along with diverse people," with minority students about 5% to 10% more likely than White students were to report this level of progress. About half of these students reported that they were "clearer about. . . their own values" with little variation among ethnic groups on this survey item. Open-ended student survey responses regarding the diversity impact of two Massachusetts colleges included the following:

> I have developed a respect for every human being. . . learned to take others into consideration, I have grown mostly in my relations with other ethnic people, and I enjoy it. . . .I also have a lot more respect for people of different races. . . although I have always been active in anti-racism, I found that I am more sensitive to this and more receptive to people's feelings." (Clements, 1997, pp. 9-10)

A basic shift needed in community college outcomes research methods is a movement away from these one-shot surveys and case studies toward both qualitative and quantitative longitudinal designs. Simply asking people if the college has had an impact on them offers thin research grounds for confidence in the estimates of impact or the assurance that the outcomes are any different from what the student might have experienced if not at the college.

Future research on outcomes has many promising topics. Will opportunities for supportive and equitable participation for minorities provide the opportunities needed for academic success? Although community colleges are lauded as democratic colleges, research is needed on the consequences of community college diversity relationships for intergroup civility in workplaces and neighborhoods and for the responsibilities of citizenship. Threat and fear are likely to accompany periods of demographic change in the colleges. White flight has been a consequence in the past. Research is needed for strategies that allay fears and prejudice and nourish cooperation.

Conclusion

This review of student ethnic and race relationships has not generated a list of theoretical findings. Other than depicting some campuses as having a positive diversity climate, the research has been too atheoretical, diffuse, exploratory, and based on weak methodological designs to establish any set of conclusions. Furthermore, relatively few relevant publications can be found in scholarly journals because most of the research has been recorded in institutional reports. The evidence in these latter reports has raised many fascinating questions. Therefore, instead of empirical conclusions, we have included suggestions for future research in each section of this review.

We cannot overemphasize the point that this entire field of study requires a new generation of community college theorists and debate to lay the groundwork for future research. For example, there is some evidence that students perceive racial and ethnic cooperation and tolerance on college campuses. Yet there is no community college race relations model that adequately explains why there is so little overt struggle over resources and status among cultural groups. There are fruitful analyses of the relative absence of class conflict in the colleges (Brint & Karabel, 1989; Dougherty, 1994) but not of the muted racial competition and tensions over intergroup domination. Exploratory ethnographies, such as the groundbreaking work by Weis (1985), are very rare in community college research and would be a useful source of theoretical insights on such a topic.

We call for a new wave of studies in the coming decade of shifting demographics and increased immigration to understand relations among diverse racial and ethnic groups and ethnoreligious groups, including Arab and Muslim Americans. Research and action are needed to counter the recent climate of international terrorism and fear that has permitted hostility toward and even vicious oppression of some minorities and international students. This concerted effort needs to take place across all regions of the United States.

We look forward to the ideas that scholars will develop to understand the kinds of relationships that emerge among students in culturally diverse classrooms and campuses. This research can move beyond the description of campus climates to analyzing the determinants and consequences of various diversity climates. The first step in advancing this line of research is having a fundamental commitment to expanding current theoretical frameworks and to applying more rigorous methods to the studies. Longitudinal studies will be particularly useful. We look forward to a lively debate on these issues.

References

Allport, G. (1954). *The nature of prejudice*. Cambridge, MA: Perseus.

Antonio, A. (2004). The influence of friendship groups on intellectual self confidence and educational aspirations in college. *Journal of Higher Education, 75,* 446–471.

Arnold, C. L. (1995). *Chabot College campus climate survey results: Fall 1994*. Hayward, CA: Chabot College Office of Institutional Research.

Bean, J. P., & Metzner, B. S. (1985). A conceptual model of nontraditional undergraduate student attrition. *Review of Educational Research, 55,* 485–540.

Boughan, K. (1992). *Student perceptions of the racial climate at Prince George's Community College, Spring 1992: A preliminary report*. Largo, MD: Prince George's Community College, Office of Institutional Research. (ERIC Document Reproduction Service No. ED346925)

Brint, S., & Karabel, J. (1989). *The diverted dream: Community colleges and the promise of educational opportunity in America, 1900-1985.* New York: Oxford University Press.

Brown, R., & Hewstone, M. (2005). An integrative theory of intergroup contact: The effects of group membership salience. *Advances in Experimental Social Psychology, 37,* 255–343.

California Postsecondary Education Commission. (1992). *Resource guide for assessing campus climate* (Commission reports 92-24). Sacramento, CA: Author.

Cejda, B. D., & Rhodes, J. H. (2004). Through the pipeline: The role of faculty in promoting associate degree completion among Hispanic students. *Community College Journal of Research and Practice, 28,* 249–262.

Clements, E. (1997). *Creating a campus climate that truly values diversity.* Bedford, MA: Middlesex Community College.

Dougherty, K. J. (1992). Community colleges and baccalaureate attainment. *Journal of Higher Education, 63,* 188–214.

Dougherty, K. J. (1994). *The contradictory college: The conflicting origins, impacts, and futures of the community college.* Albany: State University of New York Press.

Farrell, W. C., Jr., & Jones, C. K. (1988). Recent racial incidents in higher education: A preliminary perspective. *Urban Review, 29,* 211–233.

Gordon, M. (1964). *Assimilation in American life: The role of race, religion, and national origins.* New York: Oxford University Press.

Grutter v. Bollinger, 539 U.S. 306, 123 S. Ct. 2325 (2003).

Gurin, P., Dey, E. L., Hurtado, S., & Gurin, G. (2002). Diversity and higher education: Theory and impact on educational outcomes. *Harvard Educational Review, 72,* 330–366.

Hart, K., Lutkemeier, J., & Gustafson, C. (2002). *Analysis of Shasta College student survey results, Fall 2002.* Redding, CA: Shasta College Planning and Research Office.

Howard Community College. (1998). *Student satisfaction: The 1998 YESS survey results* (Report 101). Columbia, MD: Author.

Hurtado, S., Dey, E., Gurin, P. Y., & Gurin, G. (2003). College environments, diversity, and student learning. *Higher Education Handbook of Theory and Research, 18,* 145–190.

Kee, A. (1999). *Campus climate: Perceptions, policies, and programs in community colleges* (Research Brief AACC-RB-992). Washington, DC: American Association of Community Colleges.

Lee, M. M. (1994). *SUNY student opinion survey, 1994, sections I-IVB: Student characteristics, why students select Westchester Community College, college services & facilities, faculty & classroom, and college climate.* Valhalla, NY: Westchester Community College, Office of Institutional Research.

London, H. B. (1978). *The culture of a community college.* New York: Praeger.

Luan, J. (1995). *Cabrillo students' campus climate survey.* Aptos, CA: Cabrillo College.

Mattice, N. J. (1994). *Campus climate survey.* Santa Clarita, CA: College of the Canyons. (ERIC Document Reproduction Service No. ED374854)

Maxwell, W., Hagedorn, L. S., Cypers, S., Moon, H. S., Brocato, P., Wahl, K., et al. (2003). Community and diversity in urban community colleges: Coursetaking among entering students. *Community College Review, 30,* 21–46.

Milwaukee Area Technical College. (1988). *MATC student opinions regarding discrimination and MATC institutional attitudes toward women and minorities.* Milwaukee, WI: Author. (ERIC Document Reproduction Service No. ED300064)

Nora, A. (2004). The role of habitus and cultural capital in choosing a college, transitioning from high school to higher education, and persisting in college among minority and non-minority students. *Journal of Hispanic Higher Education, 3,* 180–208.

Omi, M., & Winant, H. (1994). *Racial formation in the United States.* New York: Routledge.

Pettigrew, T. F. (1998). Intergroup contact theory. *Annual Review of Psychology, 49,* 65–85.

Person, A. E., & Rosenbaum, J. E. (2006). Chain enrollment and college enclaves: Benefits and drawbacks of Latino college students' enrollment decisions. In C. L. Horn, S. M. Flores, & G. Orfield (Eds.), *Latino educational opportunity. New directions for community colleges no. 133* (pp. 51–60). San Francisco: Jossey-Bass.

Pike, G., & Kuh, G. (2005). First- and second-generation college students: A comparison of their engagement and intellectual development. *Journal of Higher Education, 76,* 276–300.

Portes, A., & Rumbaut, R. G. (2001). *Legacies: The story of the immigrant second generation.* Berkeley: University of California Press.

Rendon, L. I., Hope, R. O., & Associates. (1996). *Educating a new majority.* San Francisco: Jossey-Bass.

San Diego Community College District. (1994). *Campus climate student survey, spring 1994.* San Diego, CA: Author.

Sidanius, J., & Pratto, F. (1993). The inevitability of oppression and the dynamics of social dominance. In P. M. Sniderman & P. E. Tetlock (Eds.), *Prejudice, politics, and the American dilemma* (pp. 173–211). Palo Alto, CA: Stanford University Press.

Solorzano, D., Ceja, M., & Yosso, T. (2000). Critical race theory, racial microaggressions, and campus racial climate: The experiences of African American college students. *Journal of Negro Education, 69,* 60–73.

Stephan, W. G., & Stephan, C. W. (2000). An integrated threat theory of prejudice. In S. Oskamp (Ed.), *Reducing prejudice and discrimination* (pp. 225–246). Mahwah, NJ: Lawrence Erlbaum.

Tinto, V. (1997). Classrooms as communities: Exploring the educational character of the undergraduate population. *Journal of Higher Education, 68,* 375–391.

Townsend, B. K. (2000). Integrating nonminority instructors into the minority environment. In S. R. Aragon (Ed.), *Beyond access: Methods and models for increasing retention and learning among minority students. New directions for community colleges, no. 112* (pp. 85–93). San Francisco: Jossey-Bass.

University of California v. Bakke, 438 U.S. 265, 98 S. Ct. 2733 (1978).

Washington State Board for Community and Technical Colleges, Education Division. (1997). *The effect of race and ethnic background on students' community and technical college experience* (Research Report 97-5). Olympia, WA: Author.

Weis, L. (1985). *Between two worlds: Black students in an urban community college.* Boston: Routledge & Kegan Paul.

Weissman, J., Bulakowski, C., & Jumisko, M. (1998). A study of White, Black, and Hispanic students' transition to a community college. *Community College Review, 26*(2), 19–42.

Willett, T. (2002). *Gavilan College campus diversity climate survey, 2002.* Sacramento, CA: California Community Colleges, Office of the Chancellor. Retrieved June 1, 2006, from http://www.gavilan.edu/research/reports/cc02.pdf

William Maxwell is an associate professor at the University of Southern California.

Diane Shammas is a doctoral candidate in educational policy at the University of Southern California.

CHAPTER 27

LEAVING THE 2-YEAR COLLEGE: PREDICTORS OF BLACK MALE COLLEGIAN DEPARTURE

J. LUKE WOOD[1]

Abstract. The purpose of this study was to investigate Black male collegians' reported reasons for leaving college. This study examined students in public two-year colleges, comparing Black male collegians with all other male collegians. Data examined were derived from the first two waves (2003-2004 and 2005-2006) of the Beginning Postsecondary Students Longitudinal Study. Data were analyzed using logistic regression. Findings from descriptive data indicated that Blacks and non-Blacks had few similarities in the areas they reported as their reasons for leaving. Logistic regression analyses revealed little differences in patterns across the two waves in leaving college for academic problems. However, they illustrated that Black males were less likely to leave college for program dissatisfaction, financial reasons, military reasons, or scheduling issues. In contrast, patterns indicated that Black males were more likely to leave for other reasons not included in the response categories. Two variables examined in this study illustrated differences across the waves. In the first wave, the odds of Black male departure due to family responsibilities were greater for Black males, while they were lower in the second wave. This suggested that Black men who will leave college due to family responsibilities will do so early on. Furthermore, the odds of Black male departure were lower for other reasons in the first wave and greater in the second wave.

Keywords: Black, male, persistence, community college

The two-year college often represents Black men's first experience with postsecondary education, and for many, their last opportunity for obtaining a degree beyond a high-school diploma. (Bush & Bush, 2005, para. 1)

The community college's open-access mission embraces nearly every individual with the intent to pursue postsecondary education.[1] As a result, the community college is perceived as a door of opportunity for students who desire to engage in higher education. This door has been increasingly sought out by a growing body of diverse students. As a result, a large portion of com-college enrollees are composed of nontraditional students (e.g., students of color, part-timers, adult returnees, exceptional or special needs, veterans; [Nevarez & Wood, 2010]).

As noted by the quote above from Bush and Bush (2005), Black males are among those who seek out the benefits of enhanced educational attainment at the community college.[2] However, while the majority of Black males enter higher education through two-year colleges (Wood & Turner, 2011), few succeed in this endeavor. Thus, although success stories are evident, researchers and practitioners should recognize that access is not always synonymous with success. For many, the perceived open door to opportunity is not a door at all but merely an entrance to another set of doors that lead to very divergent outcomes. Whereas some doors lead students to their certificate, degree, job skills, personal interest, and transfer goals, many do not lead anywhere at all. Sometimes, students find themselves returning time and time again to the entrance, where they hope to select a better door

---

[1]San Diego State University, San Diego, CA, USA

the next time around (the stop-out phenomenon; [Burley, Butner, & Cejda, 2001; Grosset, 1993]); and other times, students simply relinquish their pursuit of a better door, leaving the community college altogether and never returning (the dropout phenomenon; [Herzog, 2005; Stratton, O'Toole, & Wetzel, 2005]).

Chiefly, this manuscript is concerned with the latter, the student who does not continue at the community college. Many words are used to describe this phenomenon: *persistence* and *retention* (terms used for positive continuation) as well as *attrition, departure,* and *dropping out* (references to negative continuation). While many groups face persistence challenges, Black males are among some of the most likely to depart from the community college (Glenn, 2003-2004; H. P. Mason, 1994, 1998; Wood & Turner, 2011). This problem is exponential over time, as 11.5% of Black males will leave the community college without degree attainment after Year 1, 48.9% by Year 3, and 83% by Year 5 (U.S. Department of Education, 2009).

While it is clear that departure occurs, what is difficult to understand is why it occurs. Thus, the purpose of this study was to investigate Black male collegians' reasons for leaving college. Specifically, this study examined student departure in public two-year colleges, comparing Black male collegians with all other male collegians. This research takes a unique view of factors affecting students' continuation in college. Typically, studies have employed a persistence lens, focusing on background academic, environmental, psychological, and institutional variables associated with or predictive of student persistence. This study differs in that it examined the perspectives of students who did not continue, as reported by the students themselves. Thus, instead of reporting on factors positively related to continuation, this study reports on factors positively related to departure, as made in comparison with other male students. The next section will discuss relevant literature, which provides context to the topic of departure.

Relevant Literature

Poor success among community college students (e.g., persistence, graduation, achievement, transfer) has led to criticism of the institution (Cohen & Brawer, 2003; Richardson, 1987). This issue is of particular importance, given that Nevarez and Wood (2010) have noted that student success is a core mission component of the community college. As noted by Bush (2004), Black male students have placed their confidence in this mission and have been let down, as the community college has failed to facilitate their upward mobility and enhanced livelihood.

While the topic of college persistence and departure has been written about extensively, fewer studies have examined persistence among Black male students in two-year colleges. Among the studies that have, some congruent findings have emerged. Several metathemes have emerged from literature on Black male success (i.e., persistence, academic success) in the community college. Hagedorn, Maxwell, and Hampton (2001-2002) and Hampton (2002) have indicated that in general, younger students are more likely to persist than older students. Youthfulness also seems to be associated with achievement, as findings from Perrakis (2008) found that age was an important indicator of academic success. Parents' education has also been identified as a variable effecting persistence. For example, Freeman (2003) found that *some* education by students' mothers was a negative factor to student success. With this in mind, Freeman noted that "some education" meant that students' mothers had not completed college and that this influence seemed to have a negative relationship with Black males' college completion.

Another variable relevant to students' families, family support, has been discussed as well. Both Mosby (2009) and Stevens (2006) have suggested this as a factor for student success. Stevens found that Black males were supported by strong families, specifically, by strong mothers who aided students in achieving success. Although high school grade point average was not found by H. P. Mason (1994, 1998) as relevant to persistence, it was found to have a positive relationship by several other researchers, including Hagedorn et al. (2001-2002), Hampton (2002), Perrakis (2008), Rideaux (2004), and Riley (2007). Having strong educational goals was identified by Mosby (2009) as a strong positive to student success. In essence, students who had goals were more likely to achieve academically than students who had no goals or had goals that were transitory in nature.

Similar findings were identified by Dorsey (1996), Freeman (2003), Ihekwaba (2001), Perrakis (2008), and Riley (2007).

Motivation to succeed based on family responsibilities was identified by Beckles (2008), Freeman (2003), Ihekwaba (2001), and H. P. Mason (1994, 1998) as important to student success. Family responsibilities include those related to ancestors, children, immediate family, and non-biological family. Thus, a student's desire to make family members proud (even those who were deceased) served as a motivational factor for success. In general, the literature has suggested that an affirming campus climate is a positive factor toward persistence by Beckles (2008), Ihekwaba (2001), and Roberts (2009). Conversely, an unwelcoming climate was identified as a negative factor for persistence (Harrison, 1999; Wilkins, 2005). Lack of diversity among campus personnel has also been found by Riley (2007) and Travis (1994) to be negatively related to student success.

Several authors, including Bush (2004), Freeman (2003), Ikehwaba (2001), Poole (2006), Riley (2007), and Stevens (2006), have connected students' relationship with faculty to persistence. They concurred that students who talk with faculty outside of class, have ongoing interactions with them, and seek their assistance are more likely to persist than students who do not. In a similar vein, mentorship by campus faculty, staff, and administration was identified as important to student success by Brown (2007), Glenn (2003-2004), Ikehwaba (2001), Jordan (2008), Mosby (2009) and Pope (2006). For instance, Poole indicated that campus friendships were vital to student success, since friendships and institutional commitment may improve students' academic and social integration.

The vast majority of research on Black male persistence in the two-year college is influenced by Tinto's (1975, 1987, 1988, 1993) theory on student retention and departure. This theory has been utilized by a number of scholars (Bates, 2007; Dabney-Smith, 2009; Dorsey, 1996; Flowers, 2006; Hagedorn et al., 2001-2002; Hampton, 2002; Ihekwaba, 2001; Jordan, 2008; Miller, 2006; Mosby, 2009; Ray, Carly, & Brown, 2009; Riley, 2007; Scaggs, 2004; Shannon, 2006). Tinto's (1975) theory suggested that student attrition should be viewed from a longitudinal perspective as a process in which social and academic systems are interacting with the individual. These interactions result in constant modifications of academic objectives and dedication to the institution.

Tinto's work was informed by the work of Spady (1970), who perceived the phenomenon of dropping out of college as analogous to suicide. Guided by Durkheim's (1951) theory of suicide, Spady conceived that few interactions with individuals within an institution and commitment to congruent values presumably leads to higher risk of attrition (in college) or suicide (in society). Thus, Tinto (1975) proffered the notion that the persistence process is impacted by the degree of students' academic and social integration into institutions of higher education. Integration is the degree to which students become committed to and imbedded within the campus academic and social systems. Greater integration is associated with greater commitment to the institution, which in turn leads to a higher likelihood of completion.

While Tinto placed emphasis on the importance of social and academic factors in the process of student persistence, other work has suggested the importance of other considerations. Chief among these is the work of Bean and Metzner (1985) in the model of nontraditional student attrition, which has guided several studies of persistence and academic success both directly (H. P. Mason, 1994, 1998; Riley, 2007) and indirectly (Wood, 2010; Wood & Turner, 2011). Bean and Metzner's model of nontraditional student attrifocused on the role of four factors in the attrition of students who commute to school, work part-time, and are older than traditional-age students. As with previous research, Bean and Metzner recognized the importance of (a) background variables (e.g., age, race-ethnicity, gender, educational goals, high school success), (b) academic variables (e.g., course availability, study habits, attendance), and (c) social integration variables (extracurricular activities, on-campus peer relationships). They noted that these serve as important drivers for student persistence.

Bean and Metzner (1985) extended that environmental variables were of chief consideration to the persistence of nontraditional collegians. They suggested that environmental variables are factors over which colleges have minimal influence but that serve to directly detract from nontraditional students' continuation. The environmental variables in their model included (a) finances, with inadequate income viewed as a primary cause for dropping out; (b) employment, where excessive work commitments, especially those off campus, were viewed as negatively associated with persistence; (c) outside encouragement, in which a dearth of positive encouragement and influence toward success in college and the utility of academic endeavors facilitate attrition; (d) family responsibilities, where commitments to rearing children, family obligations, and supporting dependents superseded one's commitment to, and subsequent engagement in, college; and (e) opportunities to transfer, where the perceived likelihood of transfer to another institution was negatively associated with attrition.

Informed by the work of Bean (1980) and Bean and Metzner, H. P. Mason's (1994, 1998) model of urban Black male persistence in the community college is, to date, the only published persistence model specific to Black males in this institutional type. His work examined Black males who (a) dropped out in their first semester, (b) completed the first semester and did not enroll in the second semester, (c) finished the first semester and began the second, and (d) completed two consecutive semesters. Mason's findings suggested that 14 factors were relevant to student persistence. One background or defining variable, referred to as educational goals, was identified as an important factor for persistence. Three variables relevant to students' academics were also identified, including study habits, absenteeism, and major certainty.

Given the relevance to Bean and Metzner's (1985) model, H. P. Mason (1994, 1998) emphasized the importance of environmental variables, including finances, hopelessness, outside encouragement, and family responsibilities.[3] He also identified five psychological outcomes resultant from background, academic, and environmental variables, including utility (the perceived worthiness of one's academic endeavors), satisfaction, goal commitment (one's level of commitment to their academic goals), stress, and goal internalization (the degree to which one has internalized one's academic goals). As a result, Mason's model's specificity to Black male students in community colleges, this study used Mason's model as a conceptual guide into the phenomenon of student persistence. The next section will discuss methods used in this investigation.

Method

In order to examine respondents' reported reasons for leaving college, African American male collegians in two-year colleges were compared to their non-Black counterparts. This study employed data derived from the 2004-2009 Beginning Postsecondary Students Longitudinal Study (BPS). BPS is a national data set conducted through the National Center for Education Statistics (NCES). This data set is designed to investigate factors relevant to student success in college (e.g., enrollment, persistent, attainment). BPS was first conducted in 2003-2004, and two follow-up surveys collected additional data in three-year interviews, 2006 and 2009, referred to as the first, second, and third waves. BPS is a spinoff survey from the National Postsecondary Student Aid Survey (NPSAS; Cominole, Wheeless, Dudley, Franklin, & Wine, 2007). Data from this study focus on responses from the first wave and second wave.

NPSAS is representative of respondents who were enrolled in federally designated Title IV institutions. Title IV refers to degree-granting institutions approved by the U.S. government to participate in federal financial aid programs. NPSAS was first conducted in the mid-1980s and has been disseminated every few years since that time. The primary focus on this data set is to investigate how collegians finance their postsecondary endeavors. The survey serves as a base study for both the BPS and the Baccalaureate and Beyond longitudinal study. BPS and NPSAS produce reliable estimates of student characteristics (Cominole, Riccobono, Siegel, Caves, & Rosen, 2008; Cominole, Riccobono, Siegel, & Caves, 2010). To participate in the study, students must have been enrolled in at least one course as part of an academic program. Data collected employ cross-sectional weights, which enable researchers to engage in individual student-level analyses (Cominole et al., 2010). BPS reports on data from approximately 16,100 students. Data from this study included 2,235 respondents; all participants included in this examination were two-year collegians during the first wave of data collection in 2003-2004. The next section will examine the variables employed from this data set.

Variables

Participants were examined as representative of two dichotomous groups, Black males and non-Black males. As such, racial-ethnic affiliation served as the dependent variable (Y) in this study. Non-Black males was an inclusive category that combined data reported from students of all racial-ethnic categories other than Black, including White, Hispanic or Latino, Asian, American Indian or Alaskan Native, Native Hawaiian or other Pacific Islander, Other, and more than one race. The primary co-variates (X) examined in this study were variables that indicated why students left college. They are referred to interchangeably throughout the findings section as reasons for leaving and departure. These variables reported on data from students who left college (a) before their academic term ended, (b) without transferring to another institution, (c) without any plans to transfer, and (d) without any plans to be enrolled in the next academic year. Response types for covariates were coded 0 for no and 1 for yes. A description of each covariate used in this study is listed below.

- Academic problems: A dichotomous variable, reflecting whether a student reported academic problems or concerns as a reason for leaving the two-year college.

- Dissatisfied with program: A dichotomous variable, indicating whether the collegian left college as a result of his dissatisfaction with his academic or degree program, the college, campus, or faculty members.

- Family responsibilities: A dichotomous variable, illustrating if the respondent left the two-year college as a result of family responsibilities or concerns.

- Financial reasons: A dichotomous variable, reflecting if a student's reason for leaving is a result of financial reasons or challenges.

- Other reasons: A dichotomous variable, indicating whether respondents left college for reasons not specified in the other response categories (e.g., academic problems, dissatisfaction with program, family responsibilities).

- Personal reasons: A dichotomous variable, illustrating whether students reported leaving college for personal reasons.

- Scheduling reasons: A dichotomous variable, reflecting if a student's reasons for leaving the two-year college were a result of scheduling concerns or issues due to unavailable classes or inconvenient course offerings.

- Called for military duty: A dichotomous variable, indicating that the student left college on account of being called for active military service.

In addition to these covariates, one variable for leaving college was omitted from this study. This variable allowed respondents to indicate that they left college as a result of finishing their desired courses. However, there was an insufficient sample size of affirmative responses to include for analysis. Several control variables (Z) were employed in this study. Control variables were identified based upon their linkage to student departure in prior research. Respondents' age was included as a control in this study. This variable was continuous, reflecting the respondent's age as of December 2003 (the initial survey year). Age was included as a control in this study given prior research from Hagedorn et al. (2001-2002), Hampton (2002), and Perrakis (2008), who identified age as an important indicator of persistence and academic success among Black male students in two-year colleges. Their findings indicated that younger students persist longer and outperform older students. Income percentile rank, a continuous variable, indicating students' income percentile, was also used. This variable was calculated separately for independents and dependents and then merged into one scale ranging from 1 to 100. Finances were included as a control given its treatment in the literature on Black males in two-year colleges as a predictor of persistence and identified barrier among students (see Hampton, 2002; Mosby, 2009).

In addition to age and income percentile rank, student collegiate grade point average (GPA) was also employed as a control. GPA was a continuous variable, reflecting students' self-reported GPA while in college. This variable calculated on a scale from 4 to 400, with a 400 representing a

4.0 GPA. GPA is often used as a measure of academic success (Perrakis, 2008; Wood, 2010; Wood & Turner, 2011) and is used as an outcome variable in persistence studies among Black male students in community colleges (e.g., H. P. Mason, 1994, 1998). The final control used in this study was time status, a continuous variable indicating whether students were enrolled full-time or part-time during the academic year. This variable is based on the number of months enrolled full-time; thus it mitigates differences between semester and quarter systems. This variable is included as a control given prior research that found part-time students and students with lower course loads to have lower persistence and success rates (Freeman, 2003; Hagedorn et al., 2001-2002; Hampton, 2002; Miller, 2006). The next section will discuss the procedure used to analyze the variables identified in this section.

Analytical Procedure

Data were analyzed using logit analysis, also referred to as logistic regression. This procedure was selected given the dichotomous nature of the independent variable and the combination of dichotomous and continuous variables included in the models (Menard, 2002). Peng, So, Stage and St. John (2002) cite two generally acceptable rules for sufficient sample size as articulated by Lawley and Maxwell (1971) and Long (1997). Lawley and Maxwell (1971) required 51 participants beyond the number of variables examined. Long (1997) suggested that at least 10 observations are needed for each variable in the analysis. All analyses conducted in this study well exceeded both criteria.

This study employed a two-stage design with two models developed in each stage. In Stage 1, data from the 2003-2004 BPS were used for students' reasons for leaving college. Two models were examined in this stage. The first model examined the effect of the covariates, reasons for leaving college (X), on the dependent variable, Black versus non-Black respondents (Y). In the second model, data were analyzed using the same approach; however, Model 2 included the control variables (Z). This approach allowed for analysis of departure variables with and without relevant controls, enabling the researcher to determine the effect (if any) of the controls on the analyses. In Stage 2, a similar two-model design was employed; however, Stage 2 examined data from the 2005-2006 BPS to determine differences, by racial-ethnic affiliation, among respondents in reference to their reasons for leaving college. In the third model, the effect of the covariates (Y), student's reasons for leaving college, was examined on the dependent variable (X). This final model computed included data examined in the third model as well as the study control variables (Z). One covariate examined in Stage 2, called for military service, was not included in Stage 1 due to the inclusion of this variable in the second wave of BPS and not in the initial wave.

Data in this study were analyzed using PowerStats, a statistical software accessible through the NCES data lab. In reality, leaving college is likely a confluence of factors. This notion was recognized by NCES; thus it should be noted that respondents in BPS could indicate more than one reason for leaving college. As a result, the researcher examined both variance inflation factor levels and correlations between covariates (Hair, Anderson, Tatham, & Black, 1995; R. L. Mason, Gunst, & Hess, 1989; Neter, Wasserman, & Kutner, 1983; O'Brien, 2007). Data are reported in the form of odds ratio, a ratio depicting the probability of the occurrence of a particular event (Rudas, 1998). Given that BPS data are a result of a complex design and are not adjusted for nonresponses, p values greater than $p < .01$ should be interpreted with caution (Broene & Rust, 2000; Flowers, 2006). The next section of this manuscript will discuss the limitation of this study.

Limitations

Data collected from BPS present a limited number of potential reasons for respondents' departure. Thus, it is unlikely that the findings from this study represent the totality of factors impacting student departure. Furthermore, given that the data were collected from student perspectives, students may not be able to fully articulate the full range of factors affecting their persistence. For example, it may be more difficult for a student to discuss how cognitive variables (e.g., high school GPA, assessment test scores, SAT or ACT scores) could be related to their persistence. Thus, given the limited number of variables examined, findings from this study should be viewed as an extension of H. P. Mason's (1994, 1998) work rather than a comprehensive model of Black male persistence in two-year colleges. Additionally, this article presents analyses from the first and second waves of BPS. Participant responses are included in each wave, regardless of their previous responses. Thus, if a student left after the 2003-2004 academic year and returned and left again in 2005-2006, they were likely included in both the 2004 and 2006 variables. However, if they did not return after 2004, then they were omitted. Given the existence of the stop-out phenomenon in the community college, where students leave the institution and then return, it is possible that findings could present data for the same student. However, this is not to assume that the student left college for the same reason(s); thus, this is not a limitation, per se. Finally, the variable "other reasons," which reflected whether respondents left college for reasons not specified, does not provide information beyond excluding those in the general response categories (e.g., academic problems, dissatisfaction with program, family responsibilities). Thus, the rationale for students indicating this as a departure reason is unknown. The next section will present findings derived from the analyses described.

Findings

As evident in Table 1, Black males are most likely to leave due to family responsibilities (26.9%), program dissatisfaction (23.2%), and other reasons (21.8%), while non-Black students are most likely to leave due to personal reasons (21.2%). In 2005-2006, Blacks' top reasons for leaving were other reasons (26.0%) and personal reasons (22.1%). As evident in this table, there are few areas where more than 15% of Blacks and non-Blacks reported as their reason for leaving. The only exception to this is other reasons in 2005-2006, which 26.0% and 17.2% of Blacks and non-Blacks cited as rationales for leaving. Thus, a cursory review of these data indicates that Blacks and non-Blacks seem to leave college for differing reasons. This is an important consideration, given that the focus of this analysis is on differences between these groups.

The first stage of analysis examined students' reported reasons for departure, examining students who enrolled in college for the first time in 2003-2004 and left before the 2004-2005 academic year. The first model examined student departure without controls, in order to investigate general findings from the sample. Two nonsignificant findings emerged from this initial analysis: The odds of Black males' leaving college were 37% lower for academic problems and 44% lower for financial reasons. However, several variables indicated significant results; see Table 2. The odds of Black males' leaving college due to dissatisfaction with their programs of study were 127% greater in comparison to other male students, $p < .05$.

TABLE 1

Percentage Distribution of Reasons for Leaving

Variable	2003-2004		2005-2006	
	Black	Non-Black	Black	Non-Black
Academic problems	13.2	16.3	9.8	19.7
Dissatisfied with program	23.2	14.4	4.2	21.3
Family responsibilities	26.9	12.9	10.5	19.9
Financial reasons	12.3	18.4	14.0	20.0
Other reasons	21.8	13.5	26.0	17.2
Personal reasons	10.1	21.2	22.1	13.8
Scheduling reasons	0.9	17.4	12.1	19.5
Called for military service	—	—	0.9	19.4

TABLE 2

Model 1: Departure for Black Males Without Controls, 2003-2004

Variable	OR	95% CI
Academic problems	0.630	[0.15, 2.62]
Dissatisfied with program	2.279*	[1.19, 4.36]
Family responsibilities	4.941***	[2.32, 10.50]
Financial reasons	0.566	[0.27, 1.18]
Other reasons	2.543***	[1.56, 4.13]
Personal reasons	0.254***	[0.12, 0.50]
Scheduling reasons	—	—

Note: OR = odds ratio; CI = confidence interval.

*$p < .05$. **$p < .01$. ***$p < .001$.

Family responsibilities were also presented as an important rationale for departure. The odds of Black male collegians' attributing departure to family responsibilities were 394% greater than those of their male counterparts. This finding was significant at $p < .001$. Black male respondents were also more likely, by odds of 154%, to characterize their rationale for departure as being for other reasons (those not included in the other response categories), $p < .001$. In contrast to their male counterparts, the odds of Black male collegians' departing from college as a result to personal reasons were 75% lower than those of their male peers, $p < .001$. Although not reported in Table 2 due to instability of the relative standard errors and estimates, Black males were certainly less likely to leave college for scheduling reasons.

In the second model, data from the initial analysis were subjected to several controls (e.g., age, income percentile rank, college GPA, and full-time status). As noted earlier, according to the literature on Black men in two-year community colleges, these variables are related to student performance. Even with these controls in place, minimal differences in significant findings were evident between the first and second models in this study. One difference identified is that the controls mitigated for student dissatisfaction. In the first model, the odds of Black males' departure for dissatisfaction with their program were 127% greater than those of their counterparts; however, controls reduced the odds to 58%. As such, this variable was not significant in the second model, $p = ns$. In contrast, while the financial reasons variable was not significant in the first model, significant differences were detected in the second, $p < .05$. Findings from the second model revealed that the odds of Black male collegians' leaving college for financial reasons were 51% less than those of other male students. In terms of nonsignificant findings, as with the first model, there were no significant differences in leaving college for academic problems between Black males and their counterparts (see Table 3).

Several items that were significant in the first model remained significant in the second. For instance, the odds of Black males' departure for family responsibilities were 453% greater than those of their male counterparts, an increase in odds size from the first analysis, $p < .001$. Further, the odds of leaving college for other reasons remained significant, with departure for other reasons being 137% greater for Black males, $p < .001$. Further, the odds of Black males' departure remained lower, by 80%, for personal reasons. This finding was significant at $p < .001$. Further, as with the first model, Black males were certainly less likely to cite schedule issues as a rationale for departure.

In the second analytic stage, departure data were examined for Black males who entered college in 2003-2004 and left college either after their first year of study or during the 2006 data collection year. Thus the second stage includes responses not for students examined in the first stage but for those who persisted for a longer period of time. As with the first analytic stage, data were compared with and without controls. Findings from data with controls (the third model) indicated two nonsignificant and six significant findings. With respect to nonsignificant findings, the odds of Black males' departure for academic problems and financial reasons were lower than those of their male counterparts ($p = ns$), by 25% and 5%, respectively (see Table 4).

TABLE 3

Model 2: Departure for Black Males With Controls, 2003-2004

Variable	OR	95% CI
Academic problems	0.546	[0.13, 2.18]
Dissatisfied with program	1.580	[0.82, 3.04]
Family responsibilities	5.539***	[2.36, 12.95]
Financial reasons	0.494*	[0.24, 1.01]
Other reasons	2.371***	[1.40, 4.01]
Personal reasons	0.206***	[0.09, 0.43]
Scheduling reasons	—	—

Note: Controls included age, income percentile rank, grade point average, and time status.
OR = odds ratio; CI = confidence interval.

TABLE 4

Model 3: Departure for Black Males Without Controls, 2005-2006

Variable	OR	95% CI
Academic problems	0.754	[0.27, 2.07]
Dissatisfied with program	0.161***	[0.02, 0.99]
Family responsibilities	0.374**	[0.15, 0.92]
Financial reasons	0.958	[0.48, 1.90]
Other reasons	3.743***	[2.13, 6.55]
Personal reasons	2.299***	[1.58, 3.33]
Scheduling reasons	0.295*	[0.09, 0.95]
Called for military service	0.092***	[0.00, 66.357]

Note: OR = odds ratio; CI = confidence interval.

As with previous models, program dissatisfaction was a significant finding. The odds of Black males' departure for dissatisfaction with their program were 84% lower than those of their male counterparts, $p < .001$. In terms of family responsibilities, the odds of Black males' departure for family responsibilities were 63% lower than those of other males in public two-year colleges, $p < .01$. Further, the odds of departure were also lower for scheduling reasons, as Black males were 71% less likely to report scheduling as a rationale for leaving the two-year college, $p < .05$. In addition, the odds of departure due to being called for military service were 91% lower than those of their male counterparts, $p < .001$. Two variables illustrated that Black males were more likely than their peers to depart from college. The odds of Black males' departure for other reasons were 274% greater than those of other male collegians. Also, Black males' odds of departure for personal reasons were 128% greater than those of their male counterparts. Both of these findings were significant at $p < .001$.

Even with controls added, the fourth model presented (see Table 5) illustrated similar findings to the third model. Two variables were found to have nonsignificant findings, indicating that the odds of Black males' departure for academic problems and financial reasons were 6% and 18% lower than those of other male collegians in the two-year college, $p = ns$. Findings from Model 4 indicated that the odds of Black males' departure were lower on four significant variables. The odds of leaving were 86% lower for Black males in comparison to their peers for dissatisfaction with their programs. This finding was significant at $p < .001$. Also, departure odds were lower for family responsibilities. The analysis revealed that the odds of Black males' leaving college as a result of family responsibilities were 68% lower than those of their peers, $p < .01$. The odds of leaving college,

TABLE 5

Model 4: Departure for Black Males With Controls, 2005-2006

Variable	OR	95% CI
Academic problems	0.944	[0.34, 2.62]
Dissatisfied with program	0.140***	[0.02, 0.86]
Family responsibilities	0.327**	[0.13, 0.79]
Financial reasons	0.826	[0.42, 1.62]
Other reasons	3.208***	[1.80, 5.71]
Personal reasons	1.846**	[1.22, 2.78]
Scheduling reasons	0.347*	[0.10, 1.14]
Called for military service	0.088***	[0.00, 61.78]

Note: Controls included age, income percentile rank, grade point average, and time status.
OR = odds ratio; CI = confidence interval.

among Black males, were 66% lower than those of their peers for scheduling reasons, $p < .05$. Further, the odds of leaving college were 92% lower for Black males in comparison to other males at two-year colleges, $p < .001$. However, as with the third model, Black males were more likely to report leaving college for other reasons and personal reasons. The odds of Black males' departure for other reasons were 220% greater than those of their peers, $p < .001$. In addition, departure odds for personal reasons were 84% greater for Black males in comparison to other male students in two-year colleges, $p < .01$.

Discussion

Comparing findings across 2003-2004 and 2005-2006 data provides for interesting insights and generalities across 1- and 3-year departure reasons (see Table 6). The analyses in this study revealed that there were no real differences between Black males and their non-Black counterparts in leaving

TABLE 6

Comparison of Findings From 2003-2004 and 2005-2006

Variable	2003-2004	2005-2006
Without controls		
Academic problems	Less (*ns*)	Less (*ns*)
Dissatisfied with program	Greater (*)	Less (***)
Family responsibilities	Greater (***)	Less (**)
Financial reasons	Less (*ns*)	Less (*ns*)
Other reasons	Greater (***)	Greater (***)
Personal reasons	Less (***)	Greater (***)
Scheduling reasons	—	Less (*)
With controls		
Academic problems	Less (*ns*)	Less (*ns*)
Dissatisfied with program	Less (*ns*)	Less (***)
Family responsibilities	Greater (***)	Less (**)
Financial reasons	Less (*)	Less (*ns*)
Other reasons	Greater (***)	Greater (***)
Personal reasons	Less (***)	Greater (**)
Scheduling reasons	—	Less (*)
Called for military service	—	Less (***)

college for academic problems. However, in general, Black males were less likely to leave college for program dissatisfaction, financial reasons, military reasons, or scheduling issues. In contrast, they were more likely to leave for personal reasons not included in the response categories.

Two variables examined in this study illustrated how differences occurred over time. In the 2003-2004 sample, the odds of Black males' departure due to family responsibilities were greater; however, in the 2005-2006 sample, Black males were less likely to leave for family reasons. Possibly, family responsibilities serve to have a greater influence on Black males' departure within their first year of college; however, those persisting past the first year may not be as challenged by family responsibilities. In essence, those who will leave college as a result of family responsibilities will do so early. Either way, this finding is consistent with findings from H. P. Mason's (1994, 1998) model that identified family responsibilities as a factor effecting Black male students' persistence in the community college.

Further, the odds of Black males' departure in the 2003-2004 sample was lower for other reasons while greater in the 2005-2006 sample. Possibly, respondents selected this category due to issues with campus personnel (e.g., faculty, administration), goal modification, inadequate understanding of campus policies, or a lack of perceived utility (the worthiness of their academic endeavors). All of these issues have been addressed in prior research as directly relating to student persistence (Brown, 2007; Dorsey, 1996; Freeman, 2003; Glenn, 2003-2004; Ikehwaba, 2001; Jordan, 2008; H. P. Mason, 1994, 1998; Mosby, 2009; Perrakis, 2008; Pope, 2006; Poole, 2006; Riley, 2007; Travis, 1994; Wilkins, 2005). Unfortunately, given that the reasons are not necessarily specified, it is difficult to deduce why this may have occurred.

In all, findings from this study did indicate higher reported rates of departure for Black males, in comparison to other college males, who were challenged by personal reasons, finances, and other reasons. These findings seem to reinforce the notion proffered by Bean and Metzner (1985) and extended by H. P. Mason (1994, 1998) that environmental variables are an important persistence consideration for nontraditional students, in this case, African American male students. This is not to disaffirm the role of social and academic considerations in Black male persistence. Rather, findings suggest that there is a need to consider the role of factors external to an institution, understanding with the objective of better understanding how these factors impact outcomes within an institution.

It should be noted that Bean and Metzner (1985) believed that environmental variables were "factors over which the institution has little control" (p. 502), thereby displacing the role of the institution in providing an environment conducive to success for collegians. As noted by Bush (2004), Glenn (2003-2004), and Wood and Turner (2011), the institution is of central importance to the success of students and can serve to mitigate external factors. As noted by Bush and Bush (2010), "both in practice and in the body of the literature the institution as a focus is likened to the elephant in the room that no one desires to engage" (p. 57). The next section will address the "elephant" by providing recommendations for institutions to address the issues identified in this study.

Implications for Practice and Research

Recommendations for practice are offered that emphasize the role of the institution in supporting student persistence. Suggestions include the implementation of a mandatory orientation, pre-entry counseling, formal and informal mentorships, and an early warning system. A description of each recommendation follows.

Mandatory orientation. Community colleges should have mandatory in-person orientation sessions that discuss the time commitment needed for success in college. As part of this orientation, students can complete real or mock weekly schedules that include (at a minimum) their class time and time needed to study for each course. This will better allow students to prepare for and determine how to best balance their personal and family responsibilities with their collegiate obligations.

Pre-entry counseling. To reinforce the time commitment required for success in college, students should engage in mandatory first-semester counseling. This counseling should not be limited solely to academic course work but should include issues of school-life balance. Counselors should encourage students to consider the timeliness of their academic enterprises in relationship to their familial obligations. Further, students should be required to engage discussions that require them to consider how they will avoid conflicting obligations. This will necessitate that students consider academic programs, degree intensity (part- or full-time), and flexible offerings (evening, weekend, online, hybrid) that will allow them to balance personal and family responsibilities.

Formal and informal mentoring or role models. Once a student enters the community college, the institution should establish formal or informal mentoring or role-modeling relationships. This necessitates that faculty and staff members as well as administrators establish personal relationships with students that go beyond social niceties. Institutional personnel must know their students' nonverbal and verbal communication patterns. Bonds must be established that allow mentors and role models to ask questions of students specific to school-life balance, to provide meaningful encouragement, and to refer students to resources as necessary. Once institutional affiliates (e.g., faculty members, administrators, staff members, students) become aware of personal, family, and other issues impacting students, a reporting mechanism should be in place to encourage the student to seek counseling services.

Early warning system. As part of after entry monitoring, colleges should establish early warning systems. An early warning system is a tracking system that provides an early warning to college staff and administration when a student is not making adequate progress. An early warning policy would require institutional personnel (e.g., counselors, staff, faculty, administrators) to file a report when students' performance (primarily measured by grades, attendance, completion of homework, and/or classroom engagement) becomes a concern. Once a student has been reported for one or more of these issues, counselors, faculty, and administrators can meet with the student and enact immediate interventions, provide referral and guidance, and support the student with all reasonable means of the institution to prevent attrition and/or poor academic success.

This study has illustrated the importance of environmental factors in Black male departure in the community college. While this study made comparisons between Black males collegians and all other males in two-year colleges, future research should disaggregate the other male students by racial-ethnic affiliation. This will allow for more intricate comparisons (e.g., Black vs. White, Black vs. Hispanic or Latino, Black vs. Asian), thereby providing more insight into issues of student departure. Further, if sample size permits, various subgroups (e.g., older, low income, biracial, immigrant, married) among Black males should be examined. These intricacies could be examined within group (among Black males) and between groups, as this study has done. Most importantly, future research should seek to better understand what the categories "other reasons" and "personal reasons" mean to Black males. Determining why these categories were selected and what factors these students identified that affect their persistence, which was not addressed in the questionnaire, would add an important element to the departure puzzle.

Declaration of Conflicting Interests

The author declared no potential conflicts of interest with respect to the research, authorship, and/or publication of this article.

Funding

The author received no financial support for the research, authorship, and/or publication of this article.

Notes

1. This study uses the terms *two-year college* and *community college* interchangeably, as the overwhelming majority of community colleges are two-year degree-granting institutions.
2. This study uses the terms *Black* and *African American* interchangeably.
3. H. P. Mason (1994, 1998) classified hopelessness as an environmental variable. He defined hopelessness as "the perception that whatever is attempted, or however much effort is devoted to that attempt, it will

not be successful because of the societal forces that tend to work against the subjects" (p. 123). This variable seems to be misclassified, as it is almost undoubtedly a psychological outcome variable rather than an environmental variable.

References

Bates, V. M. (2007). *The impact of preparedness, self efficacy, and math anxiety on the success of African American males in developmental mathematics at a community college* (Doctoral dissertation). Available from ProQuest Dissertations and Theses database. (UMI No. 3258440)

Bean, J. P. (1980). Dropouts and turnover: The synthesis and test of a causal model of student attrition. *Research in Higher Education, 12,* 155–187.

Bean, J. P., & Metzner, B. S. (1985). A conceptual model of nontraditional undergraduate student attrition. *Review of Educational Research, 55*(4), 485–540.

Beckles, W. A. (2008). *Redefining the dream: African American male voices on academic success* (Doctoral dissertation). Available from ProQuest Dissertations and Theses database. (UMI No. 3314150)

Broene, P., & Rust, K. (2000). *Strengths and limitations of using SUDAAN, Stata, and WesVar PC for computing variances from NCES data set* (NCES 2000-03). Washington, DC: U.S. Department of Education.

Brown, T. D. (2007). *Keeping the brothers focused: A study of the impact of male mentoring on the community college level* (Doctoral dissertation). Available from ProQuest Dissertations and Theses database. (UMI No. 3274692)

Burley, H., Butner, B., & Cejda, B. (2001). Dropout and stopout patterns among developmental education students in Texas community colleges. *Community College Journal of Research and Practice, 25,* 767–782.

Bush, E. C. (2004). *Dying on the vine: A look at African American student achievement in California community colleges* (Doctoral dissertation). Available from ProQuest Dissertations and Theses database. (UMI No. 3115606)

Bush, E. C., & Bush, L. (2005). Black male achievement and the community college. *Black Issues in Higher Education, 22*(2), 44.

Bush, E. C., & Bush, L. (2010). Calling out the elephant: An examination of African American male achievement in community colleges. *Journal of African American Males in Education, 1*(1), 40–62.

Cohen, A. M., & Brawer, F. B. (2003). *The American community college* (4th ed.). San Francisco, CA: Jossey-Bass.

Cominole, M., Riccobono, J., Siegel, P., & Caves, L. (2010). *2007-2008 National Postsecondary Student Aid Study (NPSAS:08) full-scale methodology report* (NCES 2011–188). Washington, DC: U.S. Department of Education, National Center for Education Statistics. Retrieved from http://nces.ed.gov/pubsearch

Cominole, M., Riccobono, J., Siegel, P., Caves, L., & Rosen, J. (2008). 2008 *National Postsecondary Student Aid Study (NPSAS:08) field test methodology report* (NCES) 2008-01). Washington, DC: U.S. Department of Education, National Center for Education Statistics, Institute of Education Sciences.

Cominole, M., Wheeless, S., Dudley, K., Franklin, J., & Wine, J. (2007). 2004/06 *Beginning Postsecondary Students Longitudinal Study (BPS:04/06) methodology report* (NCES 2008-184). Washington, DC: U.S. Department of Education, National Center for Education Statistics, Institute of Education Sciences.

Dabney-Smith, V. L. (2009). *A multi-level case study analysis of campus-based male initiatives programs and practices and the impact of participation on the perceptions of first-year African American male community college students* (Doctoral dissertation). Available from ProQuest Dissertations and Theses database. (UMI No. 3378673)

Dorsey, M. E. (1996). *An investigation of variables affecting persistence of African-American males at a Maryland community college* (Doctoral dissertation). Available from ProQuest Dissertations and Theses database. (UMI No. 9633148)

Durkheim, E. (1951). *Suicide.* Glencoe, IL: Free Press.

Flowers, L. A. (2006). Effects of attending a 2-year institution on African American males' academic and social integration in the first year of college. *Teachers College Record, 108*(2), 267–286.

Freeman, T. L. (2003). *Theoretical model for studying year-to-year persistence of two year college students by ethnicity using the beginning Postsecondary Students Longitudinal Study 1996-98* (Doctoral dissertation). Available from ProQuest Dissertations and Theses database. (UMI No. 3094695)

Glenn, F. S. (2003-2004). The retention of Black male students in Texas public community colleges. *Journal of College Student Retention, 5*(2), 115–133.

Grosset, J. M. (1993). A profile of community college stop-outs. *Community College Review, 20*(4), 51–58.

Hagedorn, S. L., Maxwell, W., & Hampton, P. (2001-2002). Correlates of retention for African- American males in the community college. *Journal of College Student Retention, 3*(3), 243–263.

Hair, J. F., Jr., Anderson, R. E., Tatham, R. L., & Black, W. C. (1995). *Multivariate data analysis* (3rd ed.). New York, NY: Macmillan.

Hampton, P. (2002). *Academic success for African-American male community college students* (Doctoral dissertation). Available from ProQuest Dissertations and Theses database. (UMI No. 3073786)

Harrison, C. K. (1999). *Perceptions of African American male student-athletes in higher education* (Doctoral dissertation). Available from ProQuest Dissertations and Theses database. (UMI No. 9987606).

Herzog, S. (2005). Measuring determinants of student return vs. dropout/stopout vs. transfer: A first-to-second year analysis of new freshmen. *Research in Higher Education, 46*(6), 883–928. doi: 10.1007/s11162-005-6933-7

Ihekwaba, R. H. (2001). A comparative analysis of African American male and female students' perceptions of factors related to their persistence at a Texas community college. Unpublished manuscript, University of Texas, Austin.

Jordan, P. G. (2008). *African American male students' success in an urban community college: A case study* (Doctoral dissertation). Available from ProQuest Dissertations and Theses database. (UMI No. 3311541)

Lawley, D. N., & Maxwell, A. E. (1971). *Factor analysis as a statistical method*. London, UK: Butterworth.

Long, J. S. (1997). *Regression models for categorical and limited dependent variables*. Thousand Oaks, CA: SAGE.

Mason, H. P. (1994). *The relationships of academic, background, and environmental variables in the persistence of adult African American male students in an urban community college* (Doctoral dissertation). Available from ProQuest Dissertations and Theses database. (UMI No. 9430242)

Mason, H. P. (1998). A persistence model for African American male urban community college students. *Community College Journal of Research and Practice, 22*(8), 751–760.

Mason, R. L., Gunst, R. F., & Hess, J. L. (1989). *Statistical design and analysis of experiments: Applications to engineering and science*. New York, NY: Wiley.

Menard, S. (2002). *Applied logistic regression analysis*. Sage University Series on Quantitative Applications in the Social Sciences. Thousand Oaks, CA: SAGE.

Miller, K. K. (2006). *The impact of remedial mathematics on the success of African American and Latino male community college students* (Doctoral dissertation). Available from ProQuest Dissertations and Theses database. (UMI No. 3257667)

Mosby, J. R. (2009). *From strain to success: A phenomenological study of the personal and academic pressures on African American male community college students* (Doctoral dissertation). Available from ProQuest Dissertations and Theses database. (UMI No. 3368203)

Neter, J., Wasserman, W., & Kutner, M. H. (1983). *Applied linear regression models*. Homewood, IL: Richard D. Irwin.

Nevarez, C., & Wood, J. L. (2010). *Community college leadership and administration: Theory, practice, and change*. New York, NY: Peter Lang.

O'Brien, R. M. (2007). A caution regarding rules of thumb for variance inflation factors. *Quality and Quantity, 41,* 673–690.

Peng, C. Y. J., So, T. S. H., Stage, F. K., & St. John, E. P. (2002). The use of interpretation of logistic regression in higher education journals: 1988-1999. *Research in Higher Education, 43*(3), 259–293.

Perrakis, A. I. (2008). Factor promoting academic success among African American and White male community college students. *New Directions for Community Colleges, 142,* 15–23.

Pope, M. L. (2006). Meeting the challenges to African American men at community colleges. In M. J. Cuyjet (Ed.), *African American men in college* (pp. 210–236). San Francisco, CA: Jossey-Bass.

Poole, J. S. (2006). *Predictors of persistent Black male students' commitment to rural Mississippi two-year public institutions* (Doctoral dissertation). Available from ProQuest Dissertations and Theses database. (UMI No. 3211245)

Ray, K., Carly, S. M., & Brown, D. (2009). Power of mentoring African American males in community colleges. In H. T. Frierson, W. Pearson Jr., & J. H. Wyche (Eds.), *Black American males in higher education: Diminishing proportions* (pp. 271–297). Bingley, UK: Emerald Group.

Richardson, R. C. (1987). The presence of access and the pursuit of achievement. In J. S. Eaton (Ed.), *Colleges of choice: The enabling impact of the community college* (pp. 25–46). New York, NY: Macmillan.

Rideaux, L. (2004). *African American male participation at Tomball College: Barriers, outreach, and retention* (Doctoral dissertation). Available from ProQuest Dissertations and Theses database. (UMI No. 3150598)

Riley, N. M. (2007). *A steady drop will wear a hole in the rock: Feminism, the John Henry myth and the Black male experience in higher education: A persistence case study* (Doctoral dissertation). Available from ProQuest Dissertations and Theses database. (UMI No. 3291817)

Roberts, A. A. (2009). *Institutional factors supporting the enrollment and persistence of African-American males in Virginia community colleges* (Doctoral dissertation). Available from ProQuest Dissertations and Theses database. (UMI No. 3354265)

Rudas, T. (1998). *Odds ratios in the analysis of contingency tables: Quantitative applications in the social sciences.* Thousand Oaks, CA: SAGE.

Scaggs, S. L. (2004). *The retention of Black male students at Mississippi public community and junior colleges: Identifying best practices in rural Mississippi community colleges* (Doctoral dissertation). Available from ProQuest Dissertations and Theses database. (UMI No. 3120822)

Shannon, V. (2006). *A case study: Higher education and parenting- African American female and male persistence and the community college experience* (Doctoral dissertation). Available from ProQuest Dissertations and Theses database. (UMI No. 3205348)

Spady, W. G. (1970). Dropouts from higher education: An interdisciplinary review and synthesis. *Interchange, 1,* 64–85.

Stevens, C. D. (2006). *Skating the zones: African-American male students at a predominantly White community college* (Doctoral dissertation). Available from Pro-Quest Dissertations and Theses database. (UMI No. 3247770)

Stratton, L. S., O'Toole, D. M., & Wetzel, J. N. (2005). *A multinominal logit model of college stopout and dropout behavior.* Richmond, VA: Department of Economics.

Tinto, V. (1975). Dropouts from higher education: A theoretical synthesis of recent research. *Review of Educational Research, 45*(1), 89–125.

Tinto, V. (1987). *Leaving college: Rethinking the causes and cures of student attrition* (1st ed.). Chicago, IL: University of Chicago Press.

Tinto, V. (1988). Stages of student departure: Reflections on the longitudinal character of student leaving. *Journal of Higher Education, 59*(4), 438–455.

Tinto, V. (1993). *Leaving college: Rethinking the causes and cures of student attrition* (2nd ed.). Chicago, IL: University of Chicago Press.

Travis, R. L. (1994). *Noncognitive predictors of academic success for nontraditional students at a large, southeastern, urban community college* (Doctoral dissertation). Available from ProQuest Dissertations and Theses database. (UMI No. 9420383)

Wilkins, R. D. (2005). *Swimming upstream: A study of Black males and the academic pipeline* (Doctoral dissertation). Available from ProQuest Dissertations and Theses database. (UMI No. 3244696)

Wood, J. L. (2010). *African American males in the community college: Towards a model of academic success* (Doctoral dissertation). Available from ProQuest Dissertations and Theses database. (UMI No. 3410569)

Wood, J. L., & Turner, C. S. V. (2011). Black males and the community college: Student perspectives on faculty and academic success. *Community College Journal of Research and Practice, 35,* 1–17.

U.S. Department of Education. (2009). *NPSAS: 2008 undergraduate students.* National Center for Education Statistics. Washington, DC: Author.

J. Luke Wood, PhD is an Assistant Professor of Administration, Rehabilitation, and Postsecondary Education (ARPE)/Interwork Institute at San Diego State University. Dr. Wood is Chair of the Multicultural & Multiethnic Education (MME) special interest group of the American Educational Research Association (AERA). His research focuses on community colleges, specifically in the areas of ethical leadership and decision-making, Black male achievement, and leadership development.

CHAPTER 28

HISPANIC STUDENT SUCCESS: FACTORS INFLUENCING THE PERSISTENCE AND TRANSFER DECISIONS OF LATINO COMMUNITY COLLEGE STUDENTS ENROLLED IN DEVELOPMENTAL EDUCATION

GLORIA CRISP

AMAURY NORA

Abstract. This study examined the impact of a set of theoretically-derived predictor variables on the persistence and transfer of Hispanic community college students. Early models of student persistence have been validated primarily among four-year college students. While the constructs have been well-established, the relationships of those relevant factors remain unexamined among community college transfer students, and specifically, among Hispanic students enrolled in developmental coursework and planning to transfer from a community college to a four-year institution. Logistic regression analysis was used to test the hypothesized conceptual framework on an existing set of quantitative persistence data drawn from a national sample of Hispanic students.

Keywords: Hispanic students, Persistence, Success, Developmental education, Community college

Recent estimates suggest that nearly 30% of the population in the United States will be Hispanic by the year 2050 (Aizenman 2008). Such large numbers of Hispanic individuals suggest the need to prepare for their higher education. Not surprisingly, the majority of these students will begin their postsecondary education in community colleges (Chronicle of Higher Education 2001; Fry 2004; Nora et al. 1999), as recent reports indicate that 58% of Hispanic students are currently enrolled at two-year colleges, compared to 42% of White students (Snyder et al. 2006). While two-year institutions serve many functions, a very important one is the transfer of students seeking an undergraduate degree from a four-year institution. Among the general population, 90% of students who enroll at a community college intend to obtain a degree or certificate or to transfer to a four-year institution (Hoachlander et al. 2003). As for Latino/a students, findings from the National Center for Urban Partnerships database indicate that 85% of Hispanic students who attend community colleges view the community college as a first step to obtaining a baccalaureate degree (Rendon and

This study is based upon work supported by the Association for Institutional Research, the National Center for Education Statistics, National Science Foundation and National Postsecondary Education Cooperative under an Association for Institutional Research Grant for 2007–2008.

Nora 1997). In other words, not only are the majority of Latino/a students attending community colleges, but their intended goal is to successfully transfer to a four-year university and to earn an undergraduate degree or higher.

While the intent to transfer is evident among Hispanic students, less than a quarter of all Latino/a students who begin their educational experience at a community college actually transfer to a four-year institution and/or earn a bachelor's degree (Fry 2004). In fact, Alexander et al. (2007) found that Hispanic community college students are "less likely than their White counterparts. . . to complete an associate's degree, transfer to a four-year institution, and—among those who do transfer—obtain a bachelor's degree" (Bailey and Weininger 2002; Fry 2004; Swail et al. 2005; Wilds and Wilson 1998; Woodlief and Chavez 2002, pp. 174–175). Because so many Latino/a students are intensely concentrated in community colleges, the exceedingly low transfer rate for those whose original intent is to transfer makes the issue quite disturbing (Dougherty 2002).

Contributing to the issues of low transfer and high student attrition rates for Latino students is another disturbing figure—the number of Hispanics who enter higher education academically unprepared or underprepared to engage in college level coursework. An examination of postsecondary transcripts of students who were in 12th grade in 1992 and enrolled in postsecondary education between 1992 and 2000 indicated that 61% of students who first enrolled in a public two-year institution completed at least one developmental course (Parsad et al. 2003). Moreover, Hoyt (1999) found that roughly 21% of all entering community college students required remedial education in two subject areas while 11% were required to enroll in developmental work in three subject areas.

Although numerous studies documenting the impact of enrolling in developmental coursework on community college student outcomes exist (e.g., Burley et al. 2001; Crews and Aragon 2007; Melguizo et al. 2008), the majority of studies have failed to control for important selection biases, such as high school curriculum or parental education (Attewell et al. 2006). Moreover, the longitudinal impact of enrolling in developmental coursework among Hispanic community college students has not been properly evaluated. As such, research is needed to track Hispanic students who enroll in developmental coursework and then persist and/or transfer to a four-year institution (Higbee et al. 2005). According to Hurtado and Kamimura (2003), we must understand that a student's withdrawal decision is contingent on a variety of institutional support structures and college experiences in order to more fully realize why Hispanic students may not persist to graduation. Although many of these factors influencing the success of Hispanic students have been previously identified (e.g., encouragement and support, financial assistance), with the exception of Nora and Garcia (2001), the effects of developmental coursework within a comprehensive theoretical model of student success has not been previously examined. In turn, the purpose of this study was to examine the demographic, pre-college, socio-cultural, environmental, and academic experiences that impact the "success" (i.e., persisting, transferring, or earning a two-year degree) of Hispanic students through the second and third years of college. The following research questions were examined:

1. For Hispanic community college students who intend to transfer to a four-year institution, what factors are related to the probability of being successful in the second and third years of college?

2. How do the variables that are related to success vary among developmental and non-developmental students?

Conceptual Framework

Research specific to Hispanic students attending community colleges has been described as being in its infancy stages, and there is no one comprehensive theory to explain the specific factors influencing the success of this unique group of students. As such, the conceptual model guiding the present study was framed using Tinto's (1993) Model of Student Integration, Nora's (2003) Student/Institution Engagement Model, and Bourdieu's (1973) Cultural Capital Theory, conceptual models specific to Latino students (e.g., Nora and Garcia 2001; Torres 2006), and empirical evidence around developmental students. The following paragraphs provide context to the variables used in the logistic models which posit that the persistence and transfer decisions of Hispanic students attending community colleges were related to demographic and pre-college variables, socio/cultural capital, environmental

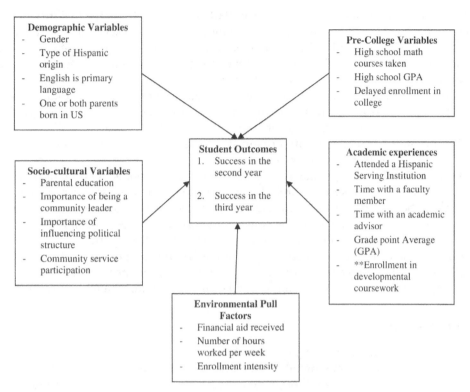

Figure 1 A theoretical model of persistence and transfer among Hispanic community college students who intend to transfer to a four-year institution

pull-factors, and academic experiences (including enrolling in developmental coursework). A graphical depiction of the conceptual framework is presented in Fig. 1.

Pre-college Variables

Tinto's (1993) Model of Student Integration demonstrates that pre-college academic preparation, such as high school coursework and grades, influences persistence among traditional college students. The impact of pre-college academic preparation has also been found to be related to persistence and/or successful transfer among community college students (e.g., Wassmer et al. 2004) as well as for Hispanic students enrolled at the community college level (e.g., Arbona and Nora 2007; Suarez 2003). For instance, Arbona and Nora (2007) found that the academic preparation of Hispanic students in high school in the area of mathematics increased the likelihood of community college students transferring to a major institution or earning some form of credential. In addition, research findings indicated a relationship between college success among minority students and the type and quality of education that students received prior to college (Castellanos and Jones 2004). In addition, findings by Rendon and Hope (1996) tell us that cultural factors such as limited English proficiency or irregular attendance patterns may impinge on the retention of minority students. Similarly, research has consistently shown that not immediately enrolling in college after high school (i.e., delayed enrollment) is negatively related to community college students' decisions to persist in college or earn a degree (e.g., Adelman 1999, 2006).

Socio-cultural Capital

Tinto's (1993) framework also emphasizes the importance of social integration (i.e., participation in campus activities, interaction with peers) in solidifying students' commitment to the institution and to earning a college degree. However, Tinto's (1993) work has long been criticized for not being relevant for minority students (e.g., Rendon et al. 2001; Tierney 1992), as the majority of research on Latino/a students has failed to identify a direct relationship between social integration and persistence (e.g., Nora 1987; Nora and Cabrera 1996; Nora et al. 1996). As such, researchers focused on Latino/a success have also considered the impact of more culturally relevant social experiences, including participation or leadership in community service. For example, borrowing from Putnam's (2000) notion that participation in civic activities represents a form of social capital, recent findings by Nunez (2009) demonstrate a direct relationship between students' obligations to give back to the community and Latino/a students' sense of belonging. Similarly, Hurtado and Carter (1997) found that membership in a social-community organization was significantly related to Latino students' sense of belonging in the third year of college.

Bourdieu's (1973) Cultural Capital Theory contributes to our understanding of how social class may impact Latino/a student success through parental education. More specifically, parental education is thought to be important to students' success in college as first generation students often lack the cultural capital needed to navigate the college environment (Berger 2000). Evidence to support this notion has been found for both Latino/a and community college populations (e.g., Logerbeam et al. 2004; Pascarella et al. 2003). Moreover, qualitative findings by Rendon and Valdez (1993) suggest that Hispanic community college students who have immigrant parents or families with limited understanding of college may face substantial barriers in transferring to a four-year institution.

Environmental Pull Factors

Nora's (2003) Student/Institution Engagement Model posits that a set of environmental factors exert a "pulling away" or a "drawing in" of students into the academic and social campus environments. Subsequently, these pulls are thought to impact a student's tenacity to continue a college education and center on variables external to university life such as having to work off-campus, family responsibilities, financial concerns, attending campus part-time, or having to commute to campus. Numerous studies have documented the negative influence of environmental pull factors on Hispanic success, including early research by Nora and Rendon (1990) who found Hispanic community college students were less likely to transfer to a four-year institution due to a lack of financial resources and the need to work. However, Nora and Wedham (1991) found that working on-campus may exert a positive pull to college by providing the opportunity to interact with faculty and peers. As another pull factor, a lack of financial support has been shown to pull Hispanic students away from campus (Cabrera et al. 1993; Cabrera et al. 1990; Logerbeam et al. 2004; Stampen and Cabrera 1988). For instance, Nora (1990) found that Hispanic community college students who did not receive campus-based or off-campus-based financial aid (i.e., Pell grants) were significantly less likely to persist, earn more credit hours, or receive a certificate or degree.

Academic Experiences

Another variable that has been shown to contribute to student persistence for Latino/a students is college climate. Findings by Nora and associates (i.e., Cabrera and Nora 1994; Cabrera et al. 1993; Nora and Cabrera 1996) established the negative impact that discriminatory behavior, both in and outside of the classroom, has on the persistence decisions of Hispanic students. Moreover, Logerbeam et al. (2004) found that Latino/a students who perceived their campus as ethnically diverse (such as a Hispanic Serving Institution) were more likely to persist in college.

In addition, Tinto's (1993) Model of Student Integration further specifies that academic integration (i.e., interactions with faculty and staff, time spent on homework) positively influences students' persistence decisions. Academic experiences also have been shown to play an important role in Hispanic students' decisions to persist, transfer, or earn a degree. For instance, Hurtado et al. (1996) found that a large concentration of Hispanic students and positive interactions between students and faculty were two major reasons contributing to the persistence decisions of four-year Hispanic students. Similarly, a causal model recently tested by Torres (2006) specific to Latino/a students identified a direct effect between academic integration, (defined as using the library and meeting with faculty outside of class) and students' commitment to the institution. Qualitative findings by Cejda and Rhodes (2004) revealed faculty interaction to be a key factor in facilitating Hispanic students' movement from a Hispanic Serving community college to a four-year institution. In addition, research by Suarez (2003) suggested that support from staff members was important to the success of Hispanic community college students.

Furthermore, research has found that one of the most influential factors on Hispanic students' decisions to persist in college is the student's academic performance (e.g., Nora and Cabrera 1996; Nora et al. 1996; Hu and St. John 2001). Findings also demonstrate that Hispanic students are more likely to persist as college grade point average (GPA) increases. Nora et al. (1997) and Hu and St. John (2001) substantiated the importance of academic performance on the persistence decisions of Hispanic students, finding that the GPA of these students had a significant and positive direct influence on their decisions to remain in college. Moreover, Nora and Cabrera (1996) found that not only did the academic achievement of Hispanic students have a positive impact on persistence, but that even the perceptions that they had made cognitive gains during their first year in college were influential in Hispanic students' decisions to remain enrolled in college.

Enrollment in Developmental Coursework

Many empirical studies have examined the impact of remediation on community college students. For instance, Hoyt (1999) concluded that as the number of areas needing remediation increased for students, dropout rates also consistently increased. The effect of developmental education was noted not only in terms of student persistence but in other student outcomes, such as the student's GPA during his or her first-term in college. In contrast, Bettinger and Long (2005) examined the impact of English and math remediation on student persistence. The sample consisted of first-time community college students from 1998 to 2003. The researchers found that students placed into developmental courses persisted just as well as similar individuals who were not enrolled in developmental courses, although math remediation appeared to improve some student outcomes.

Bettinger and Long's (2005) findings substantiated those of Jepsen (2006), who had analyzed the impact of taking developmental courses on persistence to the second year of college for a similar sample of community college students in the state of California. Jepsen also found that enrolling in developmental courses was associated with returning to college for the second year as well as completing transfer-level classes. However, Jepsen found differences in grouping the students by age. For the more traditional college-age students, developmental courses were negatively associated with transfer; for older students, the association was positive for returning and attaining a degree or certificate.

In other studies, the focus of the investigation has not been on the total developmental program but, rather, on individual remedial courses and the impact they may have on student outcomes. For example, Crews and Aragon (2004) examined the relationship between first semester enrollment in a developmental writing course at a community college and student persistence and goal attainment. Their analysis revealed that students who had been enrolled in a developmental writing course had completed more of the hours they had attempted compared to those students who were not required to enroll in a developmental writing course. At the end of a three-year period, participants and non-participants were examined for differences in degree/certificate completion. Findings indicated similar completion rates among students enrolled and not enrolled in the writing course.

Although not specific to community colleges or Hispanic student populations, Kreysa's (2007) study advances the developmental literature by focusing on the explanatory predictors of student persistence among developmental and non-developmental students attending a large private four-year institution. Factors that were found to most strongly predict whether non-developmental students would persist included declaring a major upon entering college (positive influence), changing majors (negative influence), and the students' cumulative GPAs (positive influence). Similarly, factors that influenced developmental students' decisions to re-enroll in college included students' SAT verbal scores (positive influence), changing majors after declaring one (negative influence), and cumulative GPA (positive influence).

Finally, as previously mentioned, Nora and Garcia (2001) is the only study to date that has examined the impact of Hispanic students enrolling in developmental coursework within a comprehensive theoretical model. In this study, the researchers examined the attitudes and perceptions held by students enrolled in developmental courses. Results indicated that seven factors were found to be related to remedial attitudes among Hispanic students including: (1) whether the students perceived themselves as needing remediation, (2) the perceived value of developmental coursework, (3) pre-college academic preparation and curriculum, (4) personal attributes and skills, (5) feelings of discrimination related to being enrolled in remedial courses, (6) validation from faculty, staff, and peers, and (7) plans for degree attainment.

Method

Database and Sample

The Beginning Postsecondary Students Longitudinal Study tracks students longitudinally in an attempt to collect data specific to transfer patterns, co-enrollment, persistence, and degree attainment. Students sampled in the BPS Longitudinal Study (n = 23,090) were classified as first-time beginners (FTBs) during the base-year survey of the National Postsecondary Student Aid Study (NPSAS:04). FTBs were operationally defined as students who first enrolled at a post-secondary institution during the 2003–2004 academic year. Participants were initially interviewed in 2004 at the end of their first year in college, and then interviewed again several years later in the first follow-up study (BPS: 04/06).

Data sources included in the BPS:04/06 were derived from institutional records, federal and Pell grant records, federal financial aid applications, National Student Clearinghouse enrollment records, college admissions test agencies, and student interviews. Approximately 15,000 students completed an interview in 2006, resulting in a 77% weighted response rate. The sample utilized in the present study included Hispanic students who first enrolled at a two-year public community college in 2003–2004 and who planned to transfer to a four-year institution (n = 570).[1]

Outcome Variables

Community college researchers are increasingly seeking alternative outcome measures for community college students that are thought to be more valid and/or comprehensive measures of success such as enrolling at multiple institutions, earning an associates' degree, and transferring to a four-year institution (e.g., Calcagno et al. 2008). As such, the present study examined two dichotomous outcomes considered to accurately represent a "successful" outcome for Hispanic students attending a community college: (a) successful, coded as 1 and defined as persisting, transferring to a different educational institution, or earning a degree at the end of their second year of college *versus* unsuccessful, coded as 0 and defined as not continuing to enroll at a two- or four-year institution or earning a degree or certificate, and (b) success in the third year, coded as 1 and defined as persisting, transferring to a different educational institution, or earning a degree *versus* unsuccessful, coded as 0 and defined as not continuously enrolled at a two or four-year institution or earning some form of a college degree or certificate.

Predictor Variables

Five blocks of variables were hypothesized to predict the above mentioned outcomes from the BPS:04/06 data files. Four *demographic variables* were included in the first block of the model including students' gender, type of Hispanic origin, whether English was the students' primary language, and whether one or both of the students' parents were born in the United States. Next, several *pre-college variables* were added to the model. Pre-college variables were assessed using the rigor of high school math courses taken by students, high school grade point average, and whether or not the student had delayed his or her entry into college. Third, four items designed to measure *socio-cultural capital* were used including: parental education level, whether the student felt it was important to be a community leader or to influence the political structure, and whether or not the student participated in community service in the year preceding college. The fourth set of predictor variables centered on *environmental pull factors* including enrollment intensity through 2006, the number of hours worked per week, and the amount of financial aid that the student received. Several *academic experiences* were then added to the final block. This group of variables included whether the student attended a Hispanic Serving Institution (HSI), frequency of spending time with a faculty member outside of class, time spent with an academic advisor, GPA in the first year, and whether the student enrolled in a developmental course. Table 1 presents the model specifications.

Data Analysis

Descriptive statistics were computed to explore the relationship among the variables and to compare the demographic characteristics of participants. Next, chi-square and *t*-tests were computed for all relevant characteristics (such as gender, GPA) in order to identify significant differences/relationships. Using block sequential modeling, six logistic regression analyses were run to predict the likelihood of occurrence of the outcome variables based on the predictor variables (Garson 2008). Dichotomous logistic regression (DLR) was chosen over an ordinary least squares (OLS) analysis because the measurement of the outcome variables (i.e., successful or not successful). Moreover, data were not all normally distributed and the probability of the outcome variable could not be assumed to be linearly related to the predictor variables (Lottes et al. 1996).

All regression analyses were run using SPSS 17.0 with the exception of missing data, which were handled using multiple imputations (MI) with LISREL 8.80 (Enders 2008). All categorical predictors were recoded into dummy variables before they were entered into the logistic regression models. The variance inflation factor (VIF) was examined for each of the predictor variables, as a test of multicollinearity within the model. Variables with a VIF greater than 2.5 were not included in the final models. As recommended by Peng et al. (2002), the logistic regression models were evaluated through an examination and interpretation of the overall fit of the regression models and diagnostic statistics. Evaluation of the logistic regression models involved an examination of the chi square goodness of fit and predicted probabilities (PCP). Next, beta weights, standard errors, the Wald chi-square statistic, associated p-values, and odds ratios were examined and interpreted for significant relationships (Garson 2008).

Logic of Regression Models

Four logistic regression equations were used in addressing the research questions. The first model tested the predictive nature of the set of variables underlying the five blocks in the conceptual framework *(demographic variables, pre-college variables, socio-cultural variables, environmental variables,* and *academic experiences)* for Hispanic students at the end of year two. The second equation tested the same set of variables in the conceptual framework for Hispanics students at the end of year three. Included in the fifth block— *academic experiences*—was the variable that indicated whether the student had enrolled in a developmental course or not in each academic year with the intent of establishing if enrollment in a remedial class played a role in student success.

Because enrollment in a developmental course was found to be significant in year two but not in year three, it was decided to split the students into two groups, those categorized as developmental students and those categorized as non-developmental students to ascertain differences in the significance, magnitudes, and directions in the hypothesized sets of variables between the two groups for each academic year. The third and fourth regression equations were used to examine those differences.

TABLE 1

Logistic Model Specifications

Variables	Coding
Demographic variables	
Gender	*Male = 0, Female = 1
Type of Hispanic origin	*Mexican or Chicano descent = 0, Other or mixed Hispanic origin = 1
English is primary language	No = 0, *Yes = 1
One or both parents born in US	No = 0, *Yes = 1
Pre-college variables	
High school math courses taken	5 category variable representing highest level of math class taken: None of these = 1, Calculus = 5
High school grade point average	7 category variable representing GPA range:.5 to .9 = 1, 3.5 to 4.0 = 7
Delayed enrollment in college	Yes, delayed enrollment = 0, *No, entered college immediately following high school = 1
Socio-cultural variables	
Parental education	10 category variable representing highest level of parental education: Did not complete high school = 1, Doctoral degree or equivalent = 10
Importance of being a community leader	In 2004, whether the student indicated it was or was not important to be a community leader: No = 0, *Yes = 1
Importance of influencing political structure	In 2004, whether the student indicated it was or was not important to influence the political structure: No = 0, *Yes = 1
Community service participation	In 2004, whether or not the student participated in any community service: No = 0, *Yes = 1
Environmental pull factors	
Amount of financial aid received	5 category variable representing the total amount of financial aid received in 2003–2004: Did not receive financial aid = 0, 1 to 1000 dollars = 1, 1001–2000 = 2, 2001–3000 = 3, 3001–4000 = 4, 4001 to highest value = 5
Number of hours worked per week	Continuous variable representing the average number of hours worked per week (range 0 to 60)
Enrollment intensity	2 category variable representing the students enrollment intensity through 2006: *Part-time = 1, Mixed or Full-time = 2
Academic experiences	
Attended a Hispanic serving institution	Attended a HSI = 0, *Did not attend a HSI = 1
Time with a faculty member	3 category variable representing in 2004, the frequency of talking with faculty outside of class: Never = 1, Sometimes = 2, Often = 3
Time with academic advisor	3 category variable representing in 2004, the frequency of meeting with an academic advisor: Never = 1, Sometimes = 2, Often = 3
Grade point average (GPA)	Continuous variable representing students' grade point average in 2003–2004 (mean = 2.77, standard deviation = .822)
Developmental course enrollment	*Student took any remedial course in 2003–2004: Yes = 0, *No = 1
Outcome variables	
Student success in second year of college	Persistence, transfer or attainment anywhere 2004–2005: No = 0, *Yes = 1
Student success in third year of college	Persistence, transfer or attainment anywhere 2005–2006: No = 0, *Yes = 1

* Reference category

Results

Descriptive Findings

Of the 570 Hispanic students who first attended a community college in 2003–2004 with the intention of transferring to a four-year institution, 57% were female and nearly half were of Mexican or Chicano descent (48%). A little more than 10% (12%) of the sample was of Puerto Rican decent, 3% were Cuban, 6% indicated that they were of mixed decent and the remaining 31% classified themselves as "other" Hispanic origin. Nearly half (48%) of the students took Algebra 2 as the highest math course in high school, while 15% took trigonometry and only 12% completed calculus prior to attending college. Moreover, 54% of the sample completed high school with less than a "B" grade point average (i.e., less than 3.0). Nearly half (42%) of the students delayed entering college, 40% indicated that English was not their primary language, and less than half attended college full-time (47%). In addition, 52% of the sample took one or more developmental courses during their first year of college and 41% attended a community college classified as an HSI. Furthermore, half of the respondents indicated that their parents did not attend college. Slightly more than a third (35%) of the students were not successful in persisting or transferring to another institution in the second year of college and 41% did not persist or transfer in the third year.

Findings of chi-square and t-tests revealed several significant differences among developmental and non-developmental students. Delayed enrollment in college was found to be significantly related to taking developmental courses $\chi^2(1, n = 570) = 4.568$, $p < .05$, with a higher percentage of students who required remediation not delaying college enrollment. Similarly, student success in the second year was not found to be independent of enrolling in developmental coursework $\chi^2(1, n = 570) = 6.500$, $p < .05$, with developmental students more likely to be successful in the second year. Finally, non-developmental students were found to have a significantly higher GPA in the first year of college $t (570) = 2.563$, $p < .05$.

Logistic Regression Analyses

Predicting Success in the Second Year of College

The first analysis examined the influence of demographic, pre-college, socio-cultural capital, environmental pull factors, and academic experiences on whether Hispanic students persisted, transferred, and/or earned an associates' degree in the second year of college. Table 2 displays the parameter estimates, significance values, standard errors, odds ratios, and fit statistics for the final regression models. Results indicated each block significantly improved the fit of the model. Moreover, the overall model was found to be significant $\chi^2(19, n = 570) = 98.555$, $p < .001$ and yielded correct predictions for 73% of the sample. A review of the parameter estimates and associated probabilities identified that the likelihood of being successful in the second year of college was uniquely influenced by the level of math courses taken in high school, delaying enrollment in college, parental education levels, the amount of financial aid received, enrollment intensity, the number of hours students worked per week, and enrolling in developmental courses.

An examination of the direction of the odds ratios indicated that enrolling in higher math courses during high school, having parents with higher levels of education, and receiving more financial aid increased the odds of being successful. Conversely, delaying enrollment in college and working more hours were both found to decrease the odds that a student would persist, transfer or earn an associate's degree in two years. In addition, the odds of being successful were found to be 2.75 times as large for students who enrolled in college full time and 1.61 times as large for students who enrolled in developmental courses.

Predicting Success in the Third Year of College

The second regression examined the influence of the above mentioned variables on whether a student was still enrolled, transferred to another institution, and/or earned an associate's degree in the third year of college. Results indicated pre-college variables, socio-cultural capital, environmental pull factors, and academic experiences significantly improved the fit of the model, which was found

TABLE 2

Logistic Regression Models: Parameter Estimates and Model Evaluation—Analysis Split by Year

	b	S.E.	Odds Ratio[a]
Student success in year 2 (n = 570)			
Demographic variables			
Gender	−.332	.198	
Type of Hispanic origin	−.351	.206	
English is primary language	.052	.253	
One or both parents born in US	.349	.251	
Pre-college variables			
High school math courses taken	.224*	.096	1.252
High school grade point average	.004	.102	
Delayed enrollment in college	−.408*	.204	.665
Socio-cultural variables			
Parental education	.131**	.043	1.140
Importance of being a community leader	.012	.207	
Importance of influencing political structure	−.398	.230	
Community service participation	.292	.217	
Environmental pull factors			
Amount of financial aid received	.118*	.049	1.125
Number of hours worked per week	−.022***	.006	.978
Enrollment intensity	1.010***	.222	2.745
Academic experiences			
Attended a Hispanic serving institution	.391	.211	
Time with a faculty member	.014	.165	
Time with academic advisor	.080	.158	
Grade point average	.173	.122	
Developmental course enrollment	.475*	.197	1.608
Model evaluation			
−2 Log likelihood for final model	638.76		
χ^2	98.56***		
Cox and Snell R^2	.160		
Nagelkerke R^2	.219		
P.C.P	72.5%		
Student success in year 3 (n = 570)			
Demographic variables			
Gender	−.320	.188	
Type of Hispanic origin	−.197	.196	
English is primary language	−.024	.238	
One or both parents born in US	.315	.236	
Pre-college variables			
High school math courses taken	.209*	.089	1.232
High school grade point average	−.041	.097	
Delayed enrollment in college	−.408*	.194	.665
Socio-cultural variables			
Parental education	.140**	.041	1.151
Importance of being a community leader	.010	.196	
Importance of influencing political structure	−.182	.221	
Community service participation	.141	.206	
Environmental pull factors			
Amount of financial aid received	.049	.046	
Number of hours worked per week	−.022***	.006	.978
Enrollment intensity	.456*	.202	1.577

(continued)

TABLE 2 (cont.)

Logistic Regression Models: Parameter Estimates and Model Evaluation—Analysis Split by Year

	b	S.E.	Odds Ratio[a]
Academic experiences			
Attended a Hispanic serving institution	.406*	.201	1.500
Time with a faculty member	.068	.155	
Time with academic advisor	−.020	.149	
Grade point average	.267*	.116	1.306
Developmental course enrollment	.306	.187	
Model evaluation			
−2 log likelihood for final model	693.58		
χ^2	72.89***		
Cox and Snell R^2	.121		
Nagelkerke R^2	.163		
P.C.P	66.1%		

[a] Odds ratios only reported for statistically significant coefficients

* p < .05; ** p < .01; *** p < .001

to be significant $\chi^2(19, n = 570) = 72.888$, $p < .001$ and yielded correct predictions for 66% of the sample. Similar to the second year, high school math courses, delaying enrollment in college, parental education, the number of hours worked, and enrollment intensity uniquely influenced success in the third year of college. In addition, attending a HSI and students' GPAs in the first year of college were found to be significantly related to success in the third year of college. More specifically, odds of being successful were found to be 1.50 times as large for students who chose to attend an HSI and a one-unit increase in GPA increased the odds of success in the third year by a factor of 1.31.

Predicting Success among Non-Developmental Students
The third and fourth regressions examined the influence of the variables that were found to be significantly related to second and third year success for Hispanic students who were not required to take developmental courses. The models were found to be significant for both the second $\chi^2(8, n = 280) = 51.607$, $p < .001$ and third $\chi^2(8, n = 280) = 53.328$, p < .001 years. The model for the second year correctly predicted 71% of the sample while the third year model correctly predicted 68% of the sample. The likelihood of being successful in the second year of college for non-developmental students was found to be uniquely influenced by the level of math courses taken in high school and environmental pull factors (i.e., number of hours worked, financial aid, enrollment intensity). It is notable that the odds of being successful were 3.69 times as large for non-developmental students who enrolled in college full-time. Similarly, success in the third year of college was found to be significantly related to high school math courses, the number of hours worked per week, and enrollment intensity. Parental education, as a form of social-cultural capital, was also found to uniquely predict student success among non-developmental students in the third year (see Table 3).

Predicting Success Among Developmental Students
The last two regressions examined the influence of the variables that were found to be related to second and third year success for students who enrolled in developmental courses. Once again, both models were found to be significant for both the second $\chi^2(8, n = 300) = 34.599$, p < .001 and third $\chi^2(8, n = 300) = 16.622$, p < .05 years. The model for the second year correctly predicted 72% of the sample while the third year model correctly predicted only 65% of the sample. Similar to non-developmental students, all three environmental pull variables (number of hours worked, financial

TABLE 3

Logistic Regression Models: Parameter Estimates and Model Evaluation—Analysis Split by Developmental Status (year 2)

	Developmental Students (n = 300)			Non-developmental Students (n = 280)		
	b	S.E.	Odds Ratio[a]	b	S.E.	Odds Ratio[a]
Student success in year 2						
Pre-college variables						
High school math courses taken	−.001	.135		.420**	.132	1.523
Delayed enrollment in college	−.486	.280		−.289	.276	
Socio-cultural variable						
Parental education	.164**	.059	1.178	.067	.058	
Environmental pull factors						
Number of hours worked per week	−.018*	.009	.983	−.029**	.009	.971
Amount of financial aid received	.153*	.069	1.165	.131*	.065	1.141
Enrollment intensity	.698*	.295	2.009	1.306***	.325	3.692
College variables						
Attended a Hispanic Serving Institution	.402	.285		.147	.290	
Grade point average	.297	.169		.012	.166	
Model evaluation						
−2 Log likelihood for final model	324.49			320.11		
χ^2	34.60***			51.61***		
Cox and Snell R^2	.112			.171		
Nagelkerke R^2	.158			.231		
P.C.P	71.9%			70.5%		

[a] Odds ratios only reported for statistically significant coefficients

* $p < .05$; ** $p < .01$; *** $p < .001$

aid, enrollment intensity) were found to uniquely influence the success of developmental students in the second year of college. In addition, parental education levels were found to be significantly related to success in the second year for developmental students. In contrast, none of the variables found to be related to the overall sample were found to be significantly related to student success for developmental students in the third year (see Table 4).

Limitations

The results should be considered in light of several data limitations. First, the BPS 04:06 does not include additional variables that previously have been found to impact the success of Latino students such as educational hopes and aspirations (Cabrera et al. 1993; Nora et al. 1992; Zurita 2004), perceiving prejudice or discrimination on campus (Cabrera and Nora 1994; Nora et al. 1992; Nora and Cabrera 1996), or support from *la familia* (Castellanos and Jones 2004; Hurtado et al. 1996). As such, these variables could not be considered in the conceptual model. Second, the dataset limited our ability to consider students' perceptions of developmental coursework or institutional policies or programs that may have been related to student success. Although a more longitudinal measure of student success was desired, the BPS: 04/06 data currently has data available for students through the third year of college. Finally, the operational definition of student "success" did not allow for an examination how the predictor variables may have a different impact on student outcomes that are more narrowly defined (e.g., students who persisted but did not transfer, students who persisted and earned a two-year degree).

TABLE 4

Logistic Regression Models: Parameter Estimates and Model Evaluation—Analysis Split by Developmental Status (year 3)

	Developmental Students ($n = 300$)			Non-Developmental Students ($n = 280$)		
	b	S.E.	Odds Ratio[a]	b	S.E.	Odds Ratio[a]
Student success in year 3						
Pre-college variables						
High school math courses taken	.024	.124		.340**	.128	1.405
Delayed enrollment in college	−.333	.259		−.460	.273	
Socio-cultural variable						
Parental education	.101	.052		.170**	.059	1.185
Environmental pull factors						
Number of hours worked per week	−.014	.008		−.035***	.009	.965
Amount of financial aid received	.059	.063		.073	.065	
Enrollment intensity	.257	.264		.694*	.305	2.002
Academic experiences						
Attended a Hispanic Serving Institution	.395	.262		.268	.286	
Grade point average	.233	.157		.276	.168	
Model evaluation						
−2 Log likelihood for final model	369.22			324.40		
χ^2	16.62*			53.33***		
Cox and Snell R^2	.055			.176		
Nagelkerke R^2	.075			.236		
P.C.P	65.1%			67.6%		

[a] Odds ratios only reported for statistically significant coefficients

* $p < .05$; ** $p < .01$; *** $p < .001$

Discussion

Four major comparisons are the focus of this section, each comparison centered on the similarities and differences in student success among the groups being compared. The first comparison considers factors that were found to significantly impact a more global definition of student success for years two and three. Consistent with previous research on Hispanic community college students (e.g., Arbona and Nora 2007), the academic preparation of students in high school mathematics courses was found to be associated with student success in both years two and three. Similarly, results from the present study parallel previous research (e.g., Adelman 2006, 1999) that indicates delaying enrollment into a postsecondary institution immediately after graduating from high school negatively impacts the likelihood of transferring or earning a credential.

Parental education levels, as a form of social capital, were also found to be positively related to success for Hispanic community college students. Moreover, community college students who are financially fortunate enough to enroll full-time were significantly more likely to be successful at the end of years two and three. Related to the inability to enroll full-time is the need to work at the same time that the student is attending college. Unfortunately, this circumstance was found to negatively impact the likelihood of student success.

Some Hispanic students enter community colleges with the social and cultural capital to keep them enrolled in college and influence their educational aspirations to transfer, earn a college credential, or both. However, consistent with early research on Hispanic students (e.g., Nora and Rendon 1990; Nora and Wedham 1991), findings of this study indicate that even stronger socioeconomic conditions and financial circumstances may delay the student's entrance into higher education, forcing the student to work a substantial number of hours, and to engage the academic and social environment of the college which they are attending merely as part-time students. In turn, these environmental factors collectively were found to "pull" Hispanic students away from successfully transferring or persisting.

In past studies, the receipt of financial support has been consistently shown to have a positive effect on student persistence (e.g., Cabrera et al. 1993; Cabrera et al. 1990; Logerbeam et al. 2004), and was substantiated by success in the second year in the present study. There are many plausible reasons why financial assistance was not found to be significant in the third year. One such speculation, for example, is that students come to rely on financial packages upon entering college. However, those grants that are available to students oftentimes do not come close to covering college costs. In those cases, students may be forced to apply for loans that can add up rather quickly (leading to debt aversion) and forcing students to seek employment off-campus. Students come to depend more on work if those costs cannot be met more effectively through financial aid. The sad fact is that as students work more and more hours to meet their educational expenses, the increase in the number of hours that they work pulls them away from accomplishing their educational goals.

Another factor that exerted its influence in only the second year was enrollment in developmental coursework. Adding to the literature on developmental education, the current study establishes enrollment in at least one developmental course as having a positive impact on student success. Students who required remediation in at least one area and were placed in a developmental course were found to benefit from that experience up until the end of their second year in college. In addition, the likelihood of transferring or earning a credential was increased for those that needed some form of remediation.

For the third year, Latino community college students were positively affected by two factors that did not make a difference in prior years, including attending an HSI and their academic performance in college (i.e., GPA). It could be speculated that attending a more culturally-sensitive institution where the campus climate fosters a sense of belonging (Hurtado and Ponjuan 2005) directly or indirectly impacted Latino/a student success. Previous research tells us that when students feel that they are welcomed and that they belong on a campus, their academic achievement is evident in the form of their GPAs (Nora and Cabrera 1996; Nora et al. 1996).

These findings are not particularly startling and serve to further substantiate previous findings in the literature that have primarily utilized students attending public four-year institutions. What is more interesting in the current study are the findings related specifically to Hispanic students attending two-year institutions and enrolled in developmental education. Currently, there is very little that is known regarding the academic performance, student adjustment, and persistence of Latino students who are required to take developmental courses upon entering college.

In an effort to tease out the differences between developmental and non-developmental students, the analysis was conducted separately for each group by each year. Similar to the analysis for the entire sample, environmental pull-factors (i.e., working too many hours, not receiving enough financial aid to pay for college, and enrolling part-time in college) negatively affected the success of both developmental and non-developmental students, thereby affirming the importance of including this construct in theoretical models for different groups of traditionally underserved students. The differences were found for two other factors—previous high school preparation in mathematics and parental education (a proxy for social capital). For development students, the lack of impact from high school math courses may represent a lack of access to advanced math courses in high school or a lack of encouragement and support to engage in a stronger academic curriculum while in high school.

The second factor, parental education, is a different story. This variable was found to be significant for developmental students but not for non-developmental students. If one considers the educational attainment of parents as a proxy for social capital, the finding makes sense. For those students requiring developmental coursework, if their parents reported higher levels of educational attainment, that form of social capital may have influenced developmental students in the form of support and encouragement to succeed (in spite of the challenges associated with enrolling in developmental coursework).

It is also important to examine the differences between years two and three for Hispanic developmental students, as variables in the model were useful in predicting the likelihood of success only for the second year. The amount of time spent at work, the amount of financial assistance received, full-time enrollment status, and the level of social capital with regard to parental education were all found to impact the persistence, transfer, or degree attainment of Hispanic community college students during their second year of college. However, none of those influences carried over to the following year. As such, additional research is needed to investigate the factors influencing the success of Hispanic community college students enrolled in developmental coursework beyond the second year in college (e.g., family support, mentoring).

Turning to non-developmental Hispanic students, the positive influences exerted by academic preparation in high school, the ability to enroll as a full-time student, and non-dependence on a job to meet the costs of an education were felt during both the second and third years. The only differences among non-developmental students in years two and three was the educational attainment of parents (significant only in year three) and the amount of financial aid received (significant only in year two). It is believed that a higher level of educational attainment on the part of the parents exerts positive pressure on non-developmental students to remain committed to the goal of degree attainment, be it through transferring to a baccalaureate degree-granting institution or through the attainment of an associate's degree. These commitments to that goal may be so strong that even when financial assistance may not be available, the desire to earn a college degree or credential overcomes the negative influence of financial circumstances.

Concluding Remarks

The present study is intended to inform policy and intervention efforts aimed at achieving equity in higher education among Hispanic students by providing empirically and theoretically-based evidence regarding the academic preparation, experiences, and success of Latino/a community college students. More specifically, the findings reveal three major conclusions regarding Latino/a success. The first centers on the variables represented in the theoretical framework. There are a common set of factors that previously have been found to impact different measures of success for students enrolled at four-year institutions that are substantiated for Hispanic developmental and non-developmental community college students. As such, the findings contribute to the existing theory on Latino students.

Second, the findings support the influence of environmental pull-factors as important for both developmental and non-developmental students, substantiating the need for additional financial support for Latino students entering higher education. Finally, while there were a common set of variables that impacted student success for developmental and non-developmental students, factors included in the present study were more influential early on for developmental students. This third conclusion implies some identified set of variables might be impacting developmental students' success beyond the first two years, such as institutional policy surrounding developmental students.

Note

1. Unweighted sample sizes are rounded to the nearest ten, per IES Data Security guidelines.

References

Adelman, C. (1999). Answers in the tool box: *Academic intensity, attendance patterns, and bachelor's degree attainment*. Washington, DC: National Center for Education Statistics.

Adelman, C. (2006). *The toolbox revisited: Paths to degree completion from high school through college*. Washington, DC: U.S. Department of Education, 2006.

Aizenman, N. C. (2008, February 12). *U.S. Latino population projected to soar*. Washingtonpost.com (p. A03). Retrieved on February 2, 2009, from http://www.washingtonpost.com/wp-dyn/content/article/2008/02/11/AR2008021101294.html.

Alexander, B. C., García, V., González, L., Grimes, G., & O'Brien, D. (2007). Barriers in the transfer process for Hispanic and Hispanic immigrant students. *Journal of Hispanic Higher Education, 6*(2), 174–184.

Arbona, C., & Nora, A. (2007). Predicting college attainment of Hispanic students: Individual, institutional, and environmental factors. *The Review of Higher Education, 30*(3), 247–270.

Attewell, P., Lavin, D., Domina, T., & Levey, T. (2006). New evidence on college remediation. *The Journal of Higher Education, 77*(5), 886–924.

Bailey, T., & Weininger, E. B. (2002). Performance, graduation, and transfer of immigrants and natives in City University of New York community colleges. *Educational Evaluation and Policy Analysis, 24*(4), 359–377.

Berger, J. B. (2000). Optimizing capital, social reproduction, and undergraduate persistence: A sociological perspective. In J. M. Braxton (Ed.), *Reworking the student departure puzzle* (pp. 95–126). Nashville, TN: Vanderbilt University Press.

Bettinger, E., & Long, B. T. (2005). Remediation at the community college: Student participation and outcomes. *New Directions for Community Colleges, 129*, 17–26.

Bourdieu, P. (1973). Cultural reproduction and social reproduction. In R. Brown (Ed.), *Knowledge, education, and cultural change* (pp. 71–112). London: Travistock.

Burley, H., Butner, B., & Cejda, B. (2001). Dropout and stopout patterns among developmental education students in Texas community colleges. *Community College Journal of Research and Practice, 25*, 767–782.

Cabrera, A. F., & Nora, A. (1994). College students' perceptions of prejudice and discrimination and their feelings of alienation: A construct validation approach. *The Review of Education/Pedagogy/Cultural Studies, 16*(3–4), 387–409.

Cabrera, A. F., Nora, A., & Castaneda, M. B. (1993). College persistence: Structural equation modeling test of an integrated model of student retention. *Journal of Higher Education, 64*(2), 123–137.

Cabrera, A. F., Stampen, J. O., & Hansen, W. L. (1990). Exploring the effects of ability to pay on persistence in college. *Review of Higher Education, 13*(3), 303–336.

Calcagno, J. C., Bailey, T., Jenkins, D., Kienzl, G., & Leinbach, T. (2008). Community college student success: What institutional characteristics make a difference? *Economics of Education Review, 27*(2008), 632–645.

Castellanos, J., & Jones, L. (2004). Latino/a undergraduate experiences in American higher education. In J. Castellanos & L. Jones (Eds.), *The majority in the minority*. Sterling, VA: Stylus.

Cejda, B. D., & Rhodes, J. H. (2004). Through the pipeline: The role of faculty in promoting associated degree completion among Hispanic students. *Community College Journal of Research and Practice, 28*, 249–262.

Chronicle of Higher Education. (2001, Aug 21). *The Chronicle of Higher Education: Almanac Issue, 48*(1), Washington, DC.

Crews, D. M., & Aragon, S. R. (2004). Influence of a community college developmental education writing course on academic performance. *Community College Review, 23*, 1–18.

Dougherty, K. J. (2002). The evolving role of the community college: Policy issues and research questions. In J. C. Smart & W. G. Tierney (Eds.), *Higher education: Handbook of theory and research* (Vol. XVII, pp. 295–348). New York: Agathon Press.

Enders, C. K. (2008, March 25). *Analysis of missing data*. Paper presented at the annual meeting of the American educational research association, New York, NY.

Fry, R. (2004). *Latino youth finishing college: The role of selective pathways*. Pew Hispanic Center. Retrieved June 24, 2004, from www.pewhispanic.org.

Garson, D. (2008). *Logistic regression*. Retrieved December 3, 2008, from http://faculty.chass.ncsu.edu/ garson/ PA765/logistic.htm.

Higbee, J. L., Arendale, D. R., & Lundell, D. B. (2005). Using theory and research to improve access and retention in developmental education. *New Directions for Community Colleges, 129*, 5–15.

Hoachlander, G., Sikora, A. C., & Horn, L. (2003). *Community college students: Goals, academic preparation, and outcomes*. Washington, DC: U.S. Department of Education, National Center for Education Statistics.

Hoyt, J. E. (1999). Remedial education and student attrition. *Community College Review, 27*, 51–73.

Hu, S., & St. John, E. P. (2001). Student persistence in a public higher education system: Understanding racial and ethnic differences. *Journal of Higher Education, 72*(3), 265–286.

Hurtado, S., & Carter, D. F. (1997). Effects of college transition and perceptions of the campus racial climate on Latino college student's sense of belonging. *Sociology of Education, 70*, 324–435.

Hurtado, S., Carter, D. F., & Spuler, A. (1996). Latino student transition to college: Assessing difficulties and factors in successful college adjustment. *Research in Higher Education, 37*, 135–157.

Hurtado, S., & Kamimura, M. (2003). Latina/o retention in four-year institutions. In J. Castellanos & L. Jones (Eds.), *The majority in the minority: Expanding the representation of Latina/o faculty, administrators, and students in higher education* (pp. 139–150). Sterling, VA: Stylus.

Hurtado, S., & Ponjuan, L. (2005). Latino educational outcomes and the campus climate. *Journal of Hispanic Higher Education, 4*(3), 235–251.

Jepsen, C. (2006, April). *Basic skills in California's community colleges: Evidence from staff and self referrals.* Paper presented at the American education research association (AERA) meeting, San Francisco.

Kreysa, P. G. (2007). The impact of remediation on persistence of under-prepared college students. *Journal of College Student Retention: Research, Theory, and Practice, 8*(2), 251–270.

Logerbeam, S. D., Sedlacek, W. E., & Alatorre, H. M. (2004). In their own voices: Latino student retention. *NASPA Journal, 41*(3), 538–550.

Lottes, I. L., DeMaris, A., & Adler, M. A. (1996). Using and interpreting logistic regression: A guide for teachers and students. *Teaching Sociology, 24*(3), 284–298.

Melguizo, T., Hagedorn, L. S., & Cypers, S. (2008). Remedial/developmental education and the cost of community college transfer: A Lost Angeles county sample. *The Review of Higher Education, 31*(4), 401–431.

Nora, A. (1987). Determinants of retention among Chicano college students: A structural model. *Research in Higher Education, 26*(1), 31–59.

Nora, A. (1990). Campus-based aid programs as determinates of retention among Hispanic community college students. *Journal of Higher Education, 61*(3), 312–327.

Nora, A., & Wedham, E. (April, 1991). *Off-campus experiences: The pull factors affecting freshman-year attrition on a commuter campus.* Paper presented at the annual meeting of the American educational research association, Chicago: IL.

Nora, A., & Garcia, V. (November, 2001). *The role of perceptions of remediation on the persistence of developmental students in higher education.* Paper presented at the annual meeting of the association for the study of higher education.

Nora, A. (2003). Access to higher education for Hispanic students: Real or illusory? In J. Castellanos & L. Jones' (Eds.), *The majority in the minority: Expanding the representation of Latina/o faculty, administrators and students in higher education* (pp. 47–68). Sterling, VA: Stylus.

Nora, A., & Cabrera, A. F. (1996). The role of perceptions of prejudice and discrimination on the adjustment of minority students to college. *Journal of Higher Education, 67*(2), 120–148.

Nora, A., Cabrera, A. F., Hagedorn, L. S., & Pascarella, E. T. (1996). Differential impacts of academic and social experiences on college-related behavioral outcomes across different ethnic and gender groups at four-year institutions. *Research in Higher Education, 37*(4), 427–451.

Nora, A., Castaneda, M. B., & Cabrera, A. F. (1992). *Student persistence: The testing of a comprehensive structural model of retention.* Paper presented at the annual conference of the association for the study of higher education, Minneapolis, MN.

Nora, A., Kraemer, B., & Hagedorn, L. (November, 1997). *Persistence among non-traditional Hispanic college students: A causal model.* Paper presented at the annual meeting of the association for the study of higher education, Albuquerque, New Mexico.

Nora, A., & Rendon, L. I. (1990). Determinants of predisposition to transfer among community college students: A structural model. *Research in Higher Education, 31*(3), 235–255.

Nora, A., Rendon, L. I., & Cuadraz, G. (1999). Access, choice, and outcomes: A profile of Hispanic students in higher education. In A. Tashakkori & H. S. Ochoa's (Eds.), *Readings on equal education: Education of Hispanics in the U.S.: Policies, policies and outcomes* (Vol. 16). New York: AMS Press Inc.

Nunez, A. (2009). Latino students' transitions to college: A social and intercultural capital perspective. *Harvard Educational Review, 79*(1), 22–48.

Parsad, B., Lewis, L., & Greene, B. (2003). *Remedial education at degree-granting postsecondary institutions in fall 2000 (NCES 2004-010).* Washington, DC: National Center for Education Statistics.

Pascarella, E. T., Wolniak, G. C., Pierson, C. T., & Terenzini, P. T. (2003). Experiences and outcomes of first-generation students in community colleges. *Journal of College Student Development, 44*(3), 420–429.

Peng, C. J., So, T. H., Stage, F. K., & St. John, E. P. (2002). The use and interpretation of logistic regression in higher education journals: 1988–1999. *Research in Higher Education, 43*(3), 259–293.

Putnam, R. (2000). *Bowling alone: The collapse and revival of American community.* New York: Simon & Schuster.

Rendon, L. I., & Hope, R. O. (1996). *Educating a new majority: Transforming America's educational system for diversity*. San Francisco, CA: Jossey-Bass.

Rendon, L. I., Jalomo, R., & Nora, A. (2001). Minority student persistence. In J. Braxton's (Ed.), *Rethinking the departure puzzle: New theory and research on college student retention*. Nashville: Vanderbilt University Press.

Rendon, L., & Nora, A. (1997). *Student academic progress: Key trends*. Report prepared for the national center for urban partnerships. New York: Ford Foundation.

Rendon, L. I., & Valdez, J. R. (1993). Qualitative indicators of Hispanic student transfer. *Community College Review, 20*(4), 27–37.

Snyder, T. D., Tan, A. G., & Hoffman, C. M. (2006). *Digest of education statistics 2005 (NCES 2006–030). U.S. Department of Education, National Center for Education Statistics*. Washington, DC: U.S. Government Printing Office.

Stampen, J. O., & Cabrera, A. F. (1988). Is the student aid system achieving its objectives? Evidence on targeting and attrition. *Economics of Education Review, 7*, 29–46.

Suarez, A. L. (2003). Forward transfer: Strengthening the educational pipeline for Latino community college students. *Community College Journal of Research and Practice, 27*, 95–117.

Swail, W. S., Cabrera, A. F., Lee, C., & Williams, A. (2005). *Pathways to the bachelor's degree for Latino students*. Washington, DC: The Educational Policy Institute.

Tierney, W. (1992). An anthropological analysis of student participation in college. *Journal of Higher Education, 63*(6), 603–618.

Tinto, V. (1993). *Leaving college: Rethinking the causes and cures of student attrition* (2nd ed.). Chicago: University of Chicago Press.

Torres, V. (2006). A mixed method study testing data-model fit of a retention model for Latino/a students at urban universities. *Journal of College Student Development, 47*(3), 299–318.

Wassmer, R., Moore, C., & Shulock, N. (2004). The effect of racial/ethnic composition on transfer rates in community colleges: Implications for policy and practice. *Research in Higher Education, 45*(6), 651–672.

Wilds, D. J., & Wilson, R. (1998). *Minorities in higher education: Sixteenth annual status report*. Washington, DC: American Council on Education.

Woodlief, L., & Chavez, L. (2002). *California tomorrow fact sheet: Outcomes for students in California community colleges*. Oakland: California Tomorrow.

Zurita, M. (2004). Stopping out and persisting: Experiences of Latino undergraduates. *Journal of College Student Retention, 6*(3), 301–324.

CHAPTER 29

FOLLOWING THEIR EVERY MOVE: AN INVESTIGATION OF SOCIAL-CLASS DIFFERENCES IN COLLEGE PATHWAYS

SARA GOLDRICK-RAB
UNIVERSITY OF WISCONSIN–MADISON

As more Americans enter college than ever before, their pathways through the broadly differentiated higher education system are changing. Movement in, out, and among institutions now characterizes students' attendance patterns—half of all undergraduates who begin at a four-year institution go on to attend at least one other college, and over one-third take some time off from college after their initial enrollment. This study investigated whether there is social-class variation in these patterns, with advantaged and disadvantaged students responding to new postsecondary choices by engaging in different pathways. National longitudinal data from postsecondary transcripts were used to follow students across schools and to examine the importance of family background and high school preparation in predicting forms of college attendance. The results demonstrate that students from lower socioeconomic backgrounds are more likely than are economically advantaged students (net of prior academic preparation) to follow pathways that are characterized by interrupted movement. Such pathways appear to be less effective routes to the timely completion of degrees. Thus, differences in how students attend college represent an additional layer of stratification in higher education.

The contemporary American higher education system is composed of more disparate institutions offering a larger number of choices and opportunities to students than ever before. Today's 15 million undergraduates have over 4,000 institutions from which to choose when pursuing a college degree, ranging from two-year open-door community colleges to four-year private selective universities (U.S. Department of Education 2003). At the same time, the doors to higher education have opened, and institutions are enrolling and serving a larger and more diverse population of students. Women, minority, low-income, and first-generation students are entering four-year colleges at higher rates than previously, altering the profile of the "American undergraduate" and diminishing the meaning of the label "nontraditional student" (Baker and Velez 1996). In 1995–96, nearly half (48.5%) of all beginning postsecondary students whose parents did not attend college started at four-year institutions. Moreover, according to the same survey, over half of all beginning students who attend four-year institutions were women, nearly 30 percent were minorities, and nearly one-fifth had family incomes of less than $25,000 (Kojaku and Nuñez 1998).

Growth in both the number of postsecondary institutions and the number and types of college students has resulted in an expansive higher education marketplace where students act as consumers and colleges act as vendors (McDonough 1994; Newman and Couturier 2001; Newman, Couturier, and Scurry 2004; O'Meara 2001; Winter 2003). Furthermore, increased competition among institutions and the rapid expansion of program options have changed the way students attend college, and transitions into college have expanded beyond the normative transition from high school directly into postsecondary education (Newman et al. 2004). In other words, the field of college admissions has widened; in addition to high school seniors, students who are already enrolled in college and those who entered higher education and subsequently departed ("dropouts" or "stopouts") may also be enticed to attend other institutions (Newman and Couturier 2004; Newman et al. 2004). In this new environment, it is not uncommon to see advertisements, such as one run by New School University in the *New York Times*, which read: "Start. Stop. Start. Stop. Start. Finish Your BA at the New School." Past research has indicated that when educational institutions treat students as consumers, students respond in kind by attending multiple institutions to meet their specific needs (Newman and Couturier 2001). Previously, students tended to change colleges only if they began at a two-year institution and the desire to earn a bachelor's degree necessitated their move to a four-year institution. Today, 47 percent to 50 percent of undergraduates who begin at a four-year college attend more than one institution within six years, and 15 percent to 19 percent attend more than two (McCormick 2003). National studies have also revealed that 25 percent to 30 percent of undergraduates take some time off from college and subsequently return (Berkner 2002; Carroll 1989).

These new forms of postsecondary attendance raise issues that have been set aside by most research on students' persistence. Popular higher education theories of institutional retention (e.g., Tinto 1993), while useful in identifying factors that keep students attached to a single school, do not address concerns about students' mobility patterns in the wider system of higher education. Furthermore, they focus on the choices that students make when they begin the transition to college, setting aside the options that students encounter following their entry into college. But given that such choices are made in the context of both significant constraints and opportunities, one may expect that some students are more likely and able to make effective decisions, and thus that this new marketplace environment may present opportunities for increased stratification in educational outcomes. Prior research has uncovered social-class differences in where students begin college, whether they enroll full time, and their chances for completing a degree. Students from lower socioeconomic backgrounds are disproportionately less likely, relative to more advantaged students, to start at a four-year institution (Alexander, Holupa, and Pallas 1987; Karen 2002), engage in a full credit load (Cabrera, Burkum, and La Nasa 2003), and complete a bachelor's degree (Cabrera et al., 2003). Whether they are more likely or less likely to attend multiple institutions and to interrupt their schooling to do so is unknown. But as Newman et al. (2001:13) noted, "students who have a clear sense of their own needs, a growing interest in convenience and price, and a readiness to attend multiple institutions on the way to a degree have more choices." It is therefore plausible that specific multi-institutional pathways are more often followed by students from certain family backgrounds—in other words, they may be further evidence of tertiary-level differentiation.

The study presented here addressed that concern by examining the intersection of two dimensions of students' movement that are occurring within contemporary college pathways: multi-institutional attendance and discontinuous enrollment. These two forms of attendance were chosen as the focus because they constitute students' mobility—movement in, out, and among the higher education institutions. They are conceptualized in tandem in recognition that for some groups of students, movement among institutions may collide with movement in and out of them, and I empirically tested this hypothesis. I also examined a second hypothesis that students who follow more complex pathways may differ in socioeconomic characteristics and high school background from those who follow more traditional pathways. Thus, the following specific questions are addressed in this article: (1) What is the relationship of a student's social-class background to the probability of engaging in specific nontraditional postsecondary pathways, rather than a more traditional pathway? and (2) Does a student's high school preparation mediate the effects of social class on the probability of following a nontraditional pathway? Are better-prepared students—regardless of their class background—more likely to stay continuously enrolled in one school, perhaps because their academic prowess allows them to do so? The emphasis in this analysis is therefore on how family background and preparation for college affect the choices that students make once they are in college. Certainly, students' experiences after they enter college (including, for example, how they perform in their courses and whether they make friends) affect their decision making as well, but I leave an empirical analysis of these relationships for future research.

It is important to recognize that this study focused on the mobility patterns of students who begin at four-year institutions. As I noted earlier, one of the most significant (and most often studied) forms of stratification in higher education is the disproportionate entry of less-advantaged students into two-year institutions, which do not grant bachelor's degrees. Students who begin at a two-year school must, by necessity, move to a four year institution to obtain a bachelor's degree. Thus, the implications of their movement for later educational attainment are much more likely to be positive. Yet a significant proportion of students who start at a four-year institution eventually move on to another school, and not all earn a bachelor's degree. There is a great deal of heterogeneity that merits attention in both the composition and outcomes of students who begin at four-year institutions. Moreover, there are many salient differences among four-year institutions that can affect students' pathways, related to a school's selectivity and control. Thus, this study's sample was limited to students who began at a four-year institution to examine whether there are significantly different pathways among students who manage to gain initial entrance to bachelor's degree-granting institutions.[1] These students are perhaps the most "marketable" in the system and represent the consumers that institutions are most trying to attract.

The Complex Educational Pipeline

Students who follow the traditional route to a bachelor's degree are now in the minority of college students, by one estimate constituting only one-fourth of the undergraduate population (Choy 2002).[2] From the 1970s to the 1990s, there was a significant shift in the number of schools that undergraduates attended, from one to three or more schools, rather than from one to two (Adelman 1999; Adelman et al. 2003). It is interesting that while the most recognized form of multi-institutional attendance is an upward transfer from a two-year to a four-year school, today's multi-institutional attendance patterns do not always involve a permanent transfer; of the 1982 high school graduates who attended two schools, 60 percent eventually returned to their first institution (McCormick 2003). Adelman (2003) and McCormick (2003) identified nearly a dozen different educational pathways involving multi-institutional attendance. These pathways range from "excursions," in which attendance at the second or third institution is temporary and includes only a small number of credits, to "migration," which involves a permanent transition from one school to another across the two-year and four-year sectors. In some cases, students alternate attendance among multiple institutions (known as "fragmentation," "discovery," or "rebounding"), while in others, they attend schools in sequence (called "serial transfer"). Some observers of higher education have called these new forms of movement the "transfer swirl," but that term has never been operationalized (Bach et al. 2000; de los Santos and Wright 1990; Townsend and Dever 1999). As Townsend and Dever described the phenomenon, students may "swirl upward from a two-year to a four-year school, float laterally from one two-year school to another two-year school, or spin downward from a four-year to a two-year school" (p. 5).

A small body of research has examined the characteristics of students who have followed non-traditional postsecondary pathways. Carroll's (1989) descriptive analysis of data from High School and Beyond (HS&B) indicated that students from lower socioeconomic backgrounds are more likely than are advantaged students to depart from the "persistence track" by moving from a four-year school to a two-year school, interrupting their schooling, or dropping out. In contrast, Kearney, Townsend and Kearney's (1995) study, focused on a single institution, examined students who changed schools multiple times and found that these students were from high socioeconomic backgrounds and had high degree ambitions and good academic preparation. But there was substantial selection bias in that study, since the sample was drawn from one school—in other words, all the students eventually transferred to a large, urban public university. Furthermore, in a recent analysis of data from the national Beginning Postsecondary Students Longitudinal Study, researchers again did not find statistically significant differences in income among students who attended multiple schools and those who did not (Peter and Forrest Cataldi 2005). However, that study did not examine other aspects of family background, and the measure of multi-institutional attendance was based on self-reports, rather than transcripts, and was therefore flawed.

In research that examined multiple components of college attendance simultaneously, Hearn (1992) used data from HS&B to assess the characteristics of students who delayed enrollment between high school and college; attended part time, rather than full time; and enrolled in non-degree-granting programs. Hearn found that rather than engage in clustered forms of nontraditional attendance, students with different types of nontraditional characteristics made different enrollment decisions. But students of low socioeconomic status (SES) were consistently nontraditional in their attendance choices; they were more likely to start college later, enroll part time, and enroll in noncredit programs. However, Hearn did not follow students across schools or examine socioeconomic variation in students' mobility patterns.

Thus, although there is growing evidence that educational trajectories, much like contemporary life-course trajectories (Rindfuss, Swicegood, and Rosenfeld 1987; Shanahan 2000), are increasingly nonlinear and disrupted, there is limited knowledge about who engages in which patterns and why. Previous research has been imperfect partly because of the failure to track students across schools, to assess the relative importance of ascriptive characteristics versus high school preparation in predicting college behavior, and to examine the full range of students' movement.

"Choice" in Postsecondary Pathways

There is reason to believe that the way in which one engages in higher education matters. As students' movement in, out, and among institutions increases, it is likely that where one attends college, when, and for how long will be increasingly significant for educational outcomes (Eckland 1964; Hearn 1992). As an article in the *New York Times* (Leonhardt 2005) observed, there are enormous social-class differences in college completion. Among 1992 high school seniors who began college at four-year institutions, 84 percent of those in the top fifth of the socioeconomic distribution finished their bachelor's degrees by age 26, compared to barely 39 percent of the students from families in the bottom fifth (author's calculations using data from the National Education Longitudinal Study, NELS). Variation in facets of postsecondary pathways may contribute to some of these differences. Research has demonstrated that engaging in nontraditional pathways has a negative effect on students' chances for completing bachelor's degrees. Cabrera et al. (2003) found that students who engaged in continuous enrollment while in college were 23 percent more likely to complete their bachelor's degrees than were those who took time off from school. Continuity of enrollment was a particularly strong predictor of the completion of degrees among lower-SES students—students in the second-lowest SES quartile increased their chances for completion by 38 percent, and students in the lowest quartile increased their chances by 27 percent, by maintaining continuous enrollment. Adelman's (1999) "toolbox" study of the completion of bachelor's degrees also found a positive impact of continuous enrollment. Thus, research has indicated that pathways involving discontinuities are less likely to lead to bachelor's degrees.

Furthermore, attending multiple institutions has a negative association with the completion of bachelor's degrees (Adelman 1999; Peter and Forrest Cataldi 2005). Adelman (1999) identified a negative impact of the number of institutions attended on a student's chances for completion if the student did not return to the first school that she or he attended. The odds of receiving a bachelor's degree were reduced by nearly half if a student attended multiple institutions (leaving the first school that she or he attended and not returning).[3] This effect was notably more evident among students with the same levels of college performance. Furthermore, a study of beginning postsecondary students who began at four-year institutions found a negative relationship between multi-institutional attendance and the completion of a bachelor's degree within six years if that form of attendance was not entirely comprised of coenrollment (Peter and Forrest Cataldi 2005).[4] Therefore, postsecondary pathways that are characterized by interruptions and movement appear to have negative effects on educational attainment, largely by reducing students' chances for the timely completion of their degrees.[5] Given strong evidence that the early completion of postsecondary degrees yields higher economic returns to those degrees (Elman and O'Rand, 2004), individuals who follow college pathways leading to the later completion of degrees are less likely to reap the benefits of college attendance.

Family background may shape how a student attends college by introducing both opportunities and constraints into the attendance process. A large body of research has demonstrated that family background is associated with the social, cultural, and economic resources (or capital) that are needed to further educational attainment (Bourdieu and Passeron 1977; Coleman 1974, 1988; DiMaggio 1982). In the case of higher education, students from families with higher incomes and those whose parents attended college are more likely to have access to critical information and financial resources that enable them to follow more "traditional" college pathways. The quantity and quality of information that students have at their disposal when entering and proceeding through college is essential to their decision-making processes. To make effective decisions in an environment with a plethora of choices, actors need both more and better information (Rosenbaum 2001). Although the ideal model of a free market assumes that individuals have all the information they need to make rational choices and complete access to that information, many students only have partial information. For example, if students of college-educated parents with financial resources fail a course or decide that they dislike their major, they are likely to be able to negotiate the complex advising and registration system to make a change within that institution or at another institution. Students from lower- class backgrounds who lack such support may obtain initial access to college, aided by policies, such as financial aid and affirmative action, but have difficulty remaining in college. These students, when faced with academic failure or increasing tuition, may be forced to change schools or leave college for a time.

What is important is that the lack of adequate information about what college requires, what options it offers, and what it costs does not deter low-income students from aspiring to earn a bachelor's degree. Indeed, nearly all high school students (90 percent) indicate that they expect to attend college and earn a degree, even if their career choice does not require it (Schneider and Stevenson 1999). A mismatch between information and expectations may result in what Schneider and Stevenson called an "ambition paradox." Although Schneider and Stevenson used the term to describe the behavior of students with high ambitions for a bachelor's degree who choose to begin college at a two-year school (where they are unlikely to complete a bachelor's degree), it can also be applied to students who enter a four-year college with the goal of earning a bachelor's degree but subsequently follow a pathway that is unlikely to result in the timely completion of the degree.

Overall, then, one should expect to find different shapes and trajectories in students' attendance patterns. Some students may indeed "shop" their way through college and thus engage in concerted and intentional moves among institutions, while others may be shuttled or pushed throughout the system by various constraints. If such variation occurs along the dividing lines of social class, it certainly merits attention.

Data and Measures

An accurate understanding of complex postsecondary attendance patterns and the students who follow them requires that students be followed across all the schools they attend, not simply the ones where they begin college. This study accomplished that task by using national longitudinal data from postsecondary transcripts. The data were drawn from the last three waves of the NELS, which was conducted by the National Center for Education Statistics (NCES) of the U.S. Department of Education. NELS is a longitudinal educational study of a national probability sample of 25,000 eighth graders who were first surveyed in 1988 and reinterviewed during four additional follow-ups. The fifth and final wave occurred in 2000, when the students were 26 or 27 years old; at that time, 12,144 individuals were interviewed, and requests for the postsecondary transcripts of the 9,602 students who had attended college by 2000 were submitted to the relevant institutions. As a result, 15,562 transcripts were received for 8,889 students. Thus, these students were followed for eight years after high school graduation, which provides a substantial window within which to observe their postsecondary pathways.

The sample of students came from the 2000 wave of NELS and included only those who participated in the second (1992), third (1994), and fourth (2000) follow-ups,[6] attended at least one postsecondary institution, and had a complete transcript record (N = 8,285).[7] Students whose only college attendance occurred during the summer were also excluded, since attendance during the traditional academic year is generally required to progress toward a bachelor's degree. In addition, owing to the small sample sizes, American Indian students were excluded. Finally, only students who began at a four year institution were included, making the sample size 4,628.[8] After weighting, the sample was representative of the approximately 1.5 million high school seniors who enroll in four-year colleges and universities each year following graduation from high school.

Measuring Attendance Patterns

The dependent variable in the analysis was a measure of a student's attendance pattern. As I noted earlier, I hypothesized that multi-institutional attendance and discontinuous enrollment intersect in meaningful ways, and thus the two were combined into four categories (described later). This dependent variable was constructed from data from postsecondary transcripts in NELS. Self-reported data on attendance patterns are somewhat unreliable, and it is therefore preferable to use postsecondary transcripts, rather than student-provided information in constructing these measures.[9] In an analysis of HS&B transcript and self-report data, Adelman (1999) found discrepancies between student's reports of degrees claimed versus data on degrees earned in transcripts, as well as discrepancies in students' reports of grades and course work. Especially relevant to this study, he also found that during computer-assisted telephone interviews, the students tended to underreport the number of postsecondary institutions they attended; for example, in the NELS survey, 9.6 percent of the postsecondary attendees did not report at least one institution that they attended (Adelman 2003). In gathering transcript data for the NELS, survey officials first requested transcripts for all the institutions a student reported attending. They then requested transcripts for schools that appeared on a student's transcripts but were not reported by the student (i.e., attendance at an additional school was evidenced by transfer credits). In this way, the officials ensured a more complete postsecondary history of students than if they had relied on students' reports.

Multi-institutional attendance (attending more than one school)[10] was based on the number of undergraduate institutions attended, as evidenced by a student's postsecondary transcripts, subtracting the institutions that the student attended only during the summer.[11] Discontinuous enrollment was also defined using the transcript data. The public-use data available in NELS, based on students' self-reports, simply indicates whether a student reported ever taking more than six months off from college. In contrast, the threshold of discontinuous enrollment (or stopout) in the restricted-use transcript file is one academic year within the boundaries of a student's enrolled terms (not including summer terms), as determined by two judges who did a hand-and-eye reading of the students' complete records. A student who registered but later dropped all courses for that term was not considered to be enrolled. It is important to note that forms of enrollment, such as distance learning, which do not fit neatly into a continuity framework, are classified as enrollment in this data set. In other words, if the distance learning course resulted in credits posted to a student's transcript for that semester, then a student was considered enrolled during that term. If a student used distance learning for all his or her attendance at a given institution, that institution was still included in the number of schools attended. NELS students attended a variety of institutions, including those on semester, trimester, and quarter calendars, and thus it is difficult to introduce a measure of discontinuity that is based on a semester out of school. In addition, a student may miss part or all of a semester because of illness or a family emergency, which may not accurately reflect a true interruption; thus, defining discontinuous enrollment (sometimes called "stopout") as missing an entire academic year is a more conservative estimate. It is also worth noting that since data collection ceased in 2000, students who were out of school at that time (following a period of enrollment) were counted as stopouts; hence, all potential dropouts from college are stopouts according to this classification.

The four categories of attendance patterns are depicted in Figure 1. Category A is the "traditional" pattern, consisting of students who attended one school and did not take any time off. In this sample, 52 percent (2,400 students) engaged in the traditional pattern. Students who took time off from college but attended only one school were included in Category B, "interruption," which

Number of Schools Attended

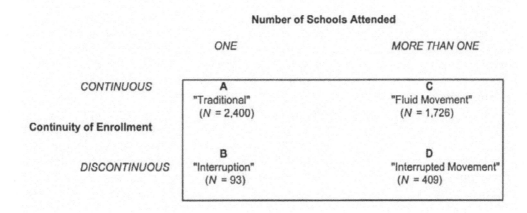

Figure 1   Postsecondary Pathways: Two Dimensions of the Students' Movement

had 93 students (2% of the sample).[12] Category C, termed "fluid movement," includes students who attended more than one institution without interruption. In this sample, 37 percent of the students (N = 1,726) engaged in that pattern. Finally, Category D includes students who attended multiple institutions discontinuously, a pattern that is termed "interrupted movement." This category included 9 percent of the sample (N = 409). These categories were intentionally given descriptive, rather than analytical, labels, to leave open questions about composition and impact and to avoid any value judgments or negative connotations, such as those contained in terms like "swirling."

Students' Characteristics

The selection of the independent variables was driven by the work of contemporary educational researchers, including Adelman (1999, 2003) and Hearn (1992). The main components of interest were students' demographic characteristics and high school preparation. Students' ascriptive characteristics were measured in terms of gender (female = 1), race (black or Hispanic = 1, white or Asian = 0)[13] and SES—a composite measure that was derived from parental education, occupation, and income in 1992; coded into quintiles; and then collapsed into three categories: low (the lowest quintile), middle (the middle three quintiles), and high (the highest quintile).[14] In this sample, all low-SES students' parents lacked bachelor's degrees, only 51 percent had high school diplomas, and 80 percent earned less than $25,000 each year. Students in the middle-SES category came from families in which nearly every parent (99%) had a high school diploma, 19 percent had at least a bachelor's degree, and 71 percent earned more than $35,000 each year. High-SES students came from families in which 94 percent of the parents had at least a bachelor's degree and 79 percent earned more than $50,000 a year.

High school preparation was indicated by tested ability, using a standardized test administered to NELS seniors (percentiles were collapsed into quintiles and then into three groups);[15] grade point average (GPA) (on a four-point scale, collapsed into quintiles and then into three groups);[16] curricular intensity of the courses taken (collapsed into quintiles and then into three groups);[17] and educational expectations as of 1992 (coded 1 = expected to earn a BA or higher, 0 = less than a BA). Tested ability was included as a measure of aptitude. GPA was used to assess both the student's achievement and the student's commitment to school. The curricular intensity measure was included as a way to assess the meaning of the student's high school GPA in terms of college preparation; in other words, including this measure indicates whether a student's high school GPA or the content of the courses the student took mattered more in shaping whether the student remained in college. Educational expectations were included in models to test the hypothesis that high-SES students attend college differently because they have higher aspirations and therefore work harder. For individual cases for which data on the independent variables were missing (there were no missing data for the dependent variable), conditional mean imputation was used (Allison 2002).[18]

Method of Analysis

As was described earlier, this study modeled college outcomes by using a systemwide, rather than an institutional, definition of persistence and by examining the role of ascriptive characteristics relative to ability and achievement measures. Students' ascriptive characteristics and measures of high school preparation were added in blocked fashion to examine whether the effects of the former persisted after the latter were controlled for.

Multinomial logistic regression was used to predict the overall type of attendance pattern that a student followed (a categorical variable). This type of modeling more accurately reflects the rubric of students' decision making; rather than simply choosing between staying enrolled or leaving a school (which could be modeled using logistic regression), this method considers the likelihood that a student will maintain continuous enrollment at one school versus other options, such as discontinuous enrollment at one school or at multiple schools. All analyses were weighted to adjust for oversampling, nonresponse, and survey attrition, and the multivariate analyses were adjusted to account for the complex survey design of the data set, namely, stratification and clustering.[19] Survey estimators that calculate correct standard errors for all coefficients using a Taylor series approximation are reported in all the analyses, as is consistent with the recommendations of statisticians at the U.S. Department of Education and the survey's creators (Broene and Rust 2000). The statistical software package STATA was used because of the advantages provided by its survey (svy) commands, which easily adjust for stratification, clustering, and individual weighting (Broene and Rust 2000).

Results

This article asks the questions, After transitioning into four-year colleges and universities, which students are most likely to follow nontraditional pathways? Are students who are engaged in patterns of "interrupted movement" different from students who follow "traditional" routes, and if so, in any significant ways? These questions are important because they provide a window into processes of within-system, or "horizontal," stratification (Gerber and Schaefer 2004). If students are following different pathways in college, based, in part, on their families' socioeconomic background, then one may conclude that separate, potentially inequitable, tracks exist within the higher education system, beyond the two-year/four-year track division.

Table 1 presents the average characteristics of the sample, which was comprised of 1992 12th graders who attended college before 2000, beginning at four-year institutions. There were more women (54%) than men (46%) and more whites and Asians (84%) than blacks and Hispanics (16%) in this group, reflecting national trends in college attendance. The socioeconomic composition of this sample is especially notable. The measure of social class was created for the 12th-grade NELS student cohort and coded into quintiles, meaning that 20 percent of the students fell into each category (thus, in the collapsed three-category structure, there should be one-fifth in the lowest category, three-fifths in the middle category, and one fifth at the top). However, in this sample of students who started at four-year colleges, only 5 percent were from the lowest fifth of the SES distribution, whereas 41 percent were from the top fifth. This is a clear reflection of the socioeconomic disparities in access to college that have been noted by previous studies (Bowen, Kurzweil, and Tobin 2005; Karen 2002).

In addition, students with low test scores, students with low GPAs in high school, and those who engaged in less rigorous high school curricula are underrepresented in this group. Most (90%) students indicated as high school seniors that they aspired to attain a bachelor's degree, and nearly all (93%) began college within a year of high school graduation.[20]

Table 1 also describes the students according to the type of attendance pattern that they followed. With respect to gender differences, women were especially likely to engage in "fluid movement," while men were overrepresented among students experiencing an "interruption." Black and Hispanic students were more likely than were white and Asian students to have had an interrupted pathway. The tendencies among students from different socioeconomic backgrounds varied. Students from low and middle socioeconomic backgrounds were overrepresented in pathways involving interruption,

TABLE 1

Descriptive Means of the Sample, by Attendance Pattern[a]

		Attendance Pattern[c]			
		A	**B**	**C**	**D**
Independent Variables[b]	**All**	**Traditional**	**Interruption**	**Fluid Movement**	**Interrupted Movement**
Gender					
Men	46	47	53	43	51
Women	54	53	47	57	49
Race					
Black or Hispanic	16	16	18	15	20
White or Asian	84	84	82	85	80
Socioeconomic Status					
1st–20th percentile (low)	5	4	11	4	13
21st–80th percentile (middle)	54	55	60	52	55
81st–100th percentile (high)	41	41	29	44	32
High School Background					
NELS Senior Test Score Percentile					
0–25th percentile	5	4	10	4	7
26th–50th percentile	15	13	18	15	18
51st–75th percentile	34	32	46	35	37
76th–100th percentile	46	51	26	46	38
GPA Quintile					
Quintile 1 (low)	6	6	14	6	11
Quintiles 2–4 (middle)	66	63	65	69	78
Quintile 5 (high)	28	31	21	25	11
Curriculum Intensity Quintile					
Quintile 1 (low)	3	3	7	3	4
Quintiles 2–4 (middle)	62	58	70	63	77
Quintile 5 (high)	35	39	23	31	19
Expected to Earn BA, as of 1992	90	90	82	92	84
Number of Schools Attended	1.69	1	1	2.44	2.51
Total %	100	52	2	37	9
N (Unweighted Sample Size)	4,628	2,400	93	1,726	409

[a] The sample is limited to 1992 12th graders who attended college, beginning at a four-year institution.

[b] Means are weighted.

[c] Two-way analyses of variance were conducted to assess differences between all the measures; the compositions of all groups are significantly different from each other with one exception: In this sample, the composition of attendance pattern B does not differ signficantly from the composition of attendance pattern D.

while high-SES students were slightly overrepresented among students who were engaged in fluid movement among schools. With regard to high school background, students with low test scores, those with low GPAs in high school, and those who had weaker high school preparation were more likely to have experienced an interrupted pathway, particularly one involving interrupted movement. It is not surprising that students who had anticipated as high school seniors that they would earn a college degree were more likely to remain continuously enrolled in one or more institutions.

All the mean differences between the four categories of attendance patterns in Table 1 are significant, with one exception. In this sample, the composition of Category D (interrupted movement) does not appear to differ significantly from that of Category B (interruption). However, these two categories are significantly different from the other two categories (A: traditional and C: fluid movement), even when they are combined into one. Thus, although the students in this sample who

TABLE 2

Multinomial Logistic Regression of Engaging in a Traditional Attendance Pattern (one school, no stopout) (Odds Ratios Shown)

Independent Variable	Interruption versus Traditional		Fluid Movement versus Traditional		Interrupted Movement versus Traditional	
	Model 1	Model 2	Model 1	Model 2	Model 1	Model 2
Ascriptive Characteristics[a]						
Female	0.64*	0.66	1.18*	1.20*	0.81	0.91
	(.16)	(.17)	(.12)	(.12)	(.13)	(.15)
Black/Hispanic	0.89	0.71	0.94	0.88	0.97	0.88
	(.26)	(.23)	(.15)	(.15)	(.23)	(.21)
Socioeconomic Status Quintile (Reference: 81st–100th percentile; high)						
1st–20th percentile (low)	4.18***	2.99***	0.92	0.85	4.11***	3.36***
	(1.69)	(1.22)	(.18)	(.17)	(1.46)	(1.08)
21st–80th percentile (middle)	1.59*	1.25	0.87	0.82*	1.32	1.16
	(.43)	(.33)	(.09)	(.09)	(.25)	(.22)
High School Background NELS Senior Test Score Percentile (Reference: 76th–100th percentile) 0–25th percentile	—	2.90**	—	1.09	—	0.85
		(1.56)		(.26)		(.29)
26th–50th percentile	—	1.99	—	1.31*	—	0.86
		(.95)		(.20)		(.20)
51st–75th percentile	—	2.58***	—	1.13	—	0.94
		(.83)		(.13)		(.18)
GPA Quintile (Reference: Quintile 5, highest)						
Quintile 1 (lowest)	—	1.51	—	1.12	—	4.18***
		(.69)		(.25)		(1.39)
Quintiles 2–4 (middle)	—	0.89	—	1.28*	—	2.82***
		(.28)		(.16)		(.67)
Curriculum Intensity Quintile (Reference: Quintile 5, highest)						
Quintile 1 (lowest)	—	1.64	—	1.00	—	1.40
		(.87)		(.24)		(.55)
Quintiles 2–4 (middle)	—	1.35	—	1.13	—	1.93***
		(.45)		(.13)		(.33)
Expected to Earn BA or Higher (as of 1992)	—	0.75	—	1.36*	—	0.78
		(.28)		(.23)		(.18)
F Statistic	3.32	3.37	3.32	3.37	3.32	3.37
Prob > F	0.00	0.00	0.00	0.00	0.00	0.00

Notes: Numbers in parentheses are standard errors. The reference category for all models is one school, no stopout.

Regressions are weighted, and standard errors are adjusted for sampling design effects.

$N = 4,628$.

[a] Gender, race, and SES interactions were tested and were not significant in these models.

* $p < =.10$, ** $p < =.05$, *** $p < =.01$.

moved across schools differed in their background characteristics from students who moved in and out of schools, it is uncertain whether students who moved across schools with interruption actually differed from students who simply interrupted their enrollment at one school. The small number of students in this sample who interrupted their enrollment at one school (Category B) is likely a contributing factor here and is an important limitation of this study.

To examine the impact of family background and high school preparation on attendance patterns comprehensively, I used multinomial logistic regression techniques to predict the probability of engaging in one of three nontraditional attendance patterns (interruption, fluid movement, or interrupted movement), rather than a traditional pattern of continuous enrollment at a single school. Nested regressions are presented in Table 2, so that the effects of ascriptive characteristics can be assessed, along with the mediating impact of high school preparation.

It is immediately apparent upon examining Table 2 that among students' ascriptive characteristics, social-class background plays the strongest role in predicting whether a student engages in nontraditional postsecondary attendance patterns. In the first model, which takes into account only a student's gender, race, and SES, students from families with fewer resources have over four times (4.18) the odds of experiencing an interrupted pathway and over four times (4.11) the odds of engaging in interrupted movement than do students from upper socioeconomic backgrounds. In addition, there is an association of gender with both interrupted enrollment and with fluid movement—women experience higher odds than do men of moving among schools continuously (compared to engaging in a traditional pattern), whereas men have greater odds of interrupting their enrollment at a single institution.

Model 2 in Table 2 reveals that the relationship between family background and college attendance patterns is partly attributable to differences in high school preparation and degree expectations. After these factors are taken into account, the association of gender with the "interruption" attendance patterns weakens and becomes nonsignificant in this sample. It appears that the greater propensity of men to take time off from college is attributable to their lower levels of tested ability. On the other hand, even after differences in high school preparation are controlled for, women are significantly more likely than are men to attend multiple colleges continuously.

It is notable that within this sample of students who were beginning their college education at a four-year college or university, there do not appear to be racial differences in how students attend college. Neither Model 1 nor Model 2 provide any evidence to support the idea that white and Asian undergraduates engage in different attendance patterns than black and Hispanic undergraduates, after socioeconomic background is taken into account.

Disparities in tested ability, high school GPA, and the rigor of high school course work account for some, but not all, of the relationship between social class and nontraditional attendance. Even after these factors were controlled for, students in the bottom 20 percent of the SES distribution had nearly three times the odds (2.99) of stopping out from one school, and over three times the odds (3.36) of moving among schools with interruption, relative to students in the top fifth of the SES distribution. It is important to note, however, that high school GPA is a stronger predictor of interrupted movement (but not interruption) than is social class. Specifically, the odds that students with the lowest high school GPAs will engage in interrupted movement are four times higher than for students with the highest GPAs, and even students with average GPAs have nearly three times the odds of engaging in this nontraditional pattern, compared to students with the highest GPAs. The association of high school GPA with fluid movement (in comparison to traditional enrollment) is much weaker than it is with interrupted movement.

Last, it appears that students from higher socioeconomic backgrounds, relative to students from middle-class backgrounds, are *more likely* to attend multiple schools without stopping out. In other words, this analysis reveals that lower-class students have a higher propensity for *interrupted* movement, while upper-class students have a higher propensity for *fluid* movement among schools.

Discussion

This analysis investigated whether postsecondary pathways within the higher education system are differentiated by family back-ground. The results support the contention that socioeconomically disadvantaged students attend college differently from advantaged students. While movement across schools is relatively common among today's undergraduates, the ability to change schools while maintaining enrollment appears to depend partly on whether one's parents went to college and have high incomes. Given that interruptions in enrollment are more likely than is movement across schools to delay (or prevent) the completion of a bachelor's degree (Adelman 1999; Cabrera et al. 2003), which, in turn, is associated with smaller returns to the degree (Elman and O'Rand 2004), these differences in *how students attend college* represent an additional layer of stratification in higher education. Thus, while extant research has revealed significant class disparities in who attends college and where they start, this study has provided evidence that there are substantial differences in the attendance patterns that students follow *after* they enter college.

Social-class differences in college enrollment patterns may be attributable to several opportunities and constraints that are introduced both prior to and during college enrollment. As I noted earlier, whereas higher education was once dominated by white men who attended college shortly after they completed high school, focused solely on schooling while in college, and subsequently transitioned from university to work, today's college students lead more complex lives. The transition to college is no longer marked by a significant transition to adulthood, nor is the college experience itself fully differentiated from work or familial experiences. College students have many choices to make after they enter college. But the numerous enrollment options that are presented by contemporary colleges and universities appear to be embraced by students differently, depending on their social background, and interruptions in contemporary postsecondary schooling are likely to be both involuntary and voluntary. This study has revealed that interruptions seem to be more common among students with fewer financial resources and those with lower grades. Thus, students from disadvantaged family backgrounds and those with poorer high school preparation are following pathways in college that are unlikely to lead to the successful completion of degrees. Students from advantaged backgrounds are able to move among schools while maintaining their enrollment, while disadvantaged students who change schools also take some time off. It is only the advantaged students who are successfully "comparison shopping," that is, moving among schools with smooth transitions.

These findings imply that students with greater access to financial resources are better able to take advantage of the new higher education marketplace. Given the significant link between social class and interrupted schooling, it seems reasonable to conjecture that low-SES students who change schools interrupt their schooling not because they are shopping, partying, or choosing to take time off to "find themselves," but because they have suffered academically or financially in school.[21] Thus, while some analysts have suggested that competition among institutions will benefit disadvantaged students, who theoretically should enjoy greater opportunities to assess and compare their multiple options (Levine 2001; Newman and Couturier 2001), these results indicate otherwise.

The findings of this study also suggest that financial resources may matter more than access to information in shaping postsecondary pathways. Interinstitutional movement appears to be relatively common among both poor and rich students. As I noted earlier, the difference is in the students' ability to remain enrolled while changing schools. One potential explanation for these differences is that financial aid and students' work is affecting students' decision making—students with greater unmet needs tend to work longer hours, which interferes with the time they spend on schoolwork (King 2002; Walpole 2003). If a decline in academic performance results, the students may leave school for a period to save money and later return to a more affordable institution. Students who are unaware of the ways in which working affects their financial aid package tend to be surprised when the package decreases (either because of new income earned or a shift to part-time enrollment as the result of longer working hours), and their new income does not always compensate for their need. Prior research has supported these hypotheses; students who receive adequate levels of financial aid have been found to be less likely to stopout from school (DesJardins, Ahlburg, and McCall 2002). Clearly, disadvantaged students, who are less likely to receive informed financial aid counseling while in high school, are more susceptible to these changes while in college (Paulsen and St. John 1997; St. John, Kirshstein, and Noell 1991; St. John et al. 1994). However, these hypotheses were not tested in this study because the NELS data set lacks measures of the quality of financial aid offers and packages. Future research ought to investigate these possibilities, and new data sets should be created to facilitate such analyses.

Furthermore, a preliminary examination of the institutions that these students move into and out of suggests that the places that they move to differ on the basis of the students' social class (Goldrick-Rab 2004). Students from low-SES backgrounds are disproportionately likely to leave their first four-year institution for a community college, whereas more advantaged students move from one four year institution to another four-year institution. Given that most community colleges do not grant bachelor's degrees, there are clear implications for the educational attainment of low-income students who move to these schools. Thus, students' mobility among specific types of institutions is highly associated with social class, even after students' ability and test scores are controlled for.

These findings also support Hearn's (1992) contention that low-SES students are consistently nontraditional in their enrollment patterns. Moreover, these students are more likely not only to delay enrollment in college and enroll part time and in noncredit programs (Hearn 1992), but to take time off from college once they have enrolled and to change schools with interruption. It is important to note, however, that more of the variation in students' enrollment patterns is attributable to differences in high school preparation and tested ability than to socioeconomic background. Clearly, well-prepared academically able students are more likely to get good grades in college and to move smoothly toward attaining a degree. But it is also clear that differences in preparation do not entirely account for class differences in postsecondary pathways. Moreover, this study did not find significant differences in college attendance patterns by racial background, suggesting that racial differences in college completion rates stem from factors other than how students attend college. At the same time, men appear more likely than women to interrupt their schooling, and this is likely a factor in the lower degree-completion rates of today's male undergraduates.

Students who engaged in attendance patterns involving movement and/or interruption accounted for 48 percent of NELS postsecondary attendees who began at four-year institutions, representing 700,000 students who enter four-year colleges each year nationwide. This number may well grow as private institutions consider joining together to offer students admission to multiple institutions for one price (O'Meara 2001). The important role of family background in predicting students' movement in, out, and among schools merits the attention of both sociologists who are interested in gaining a better understanding of new forms of educational stratification and policy makers and educational administrators who are concerned with educating, and graduating the students who enter their institutions. Certain forms of nontraditional attendance, particularly the "interrupted movement" pattern identified here, appear to represent disadvantageous tracks that are most often followed by poor students. This does not imply, however, that mobility and discontinuity in enrollment must always have negative consequences for these students. It only means that in our current system, they do.

U.S. postsecondary institutions and policies are designed with traditional students, engaged in traditional attendance patterns, in mind. The structures and incentives that are present in the American higher education system must be redesigned, with a new understanding that students follow complex, rather than linear, pathways through college. Such efforts ought to challenge outdated views of college retention that may work further to disadvantage already-disadvantaged high school students who manage to make it to college. Given the stagnant social- class gap in college completion, it is clear that policy makers, educators, and researchers need to work harder to facilitate the success, not only the access, of students from lower-class backgrounds in higher education.

Notes

1. Some of these students attend two-year colleges, subsequent to their attendance at a four-year institution. In other words, many types of multi-institutional attendance are still included in the attendance patterns of these students, such as reverse transfer (4 to 2), upward transfer (2 to 4), and lateral transfer (2 to 2, 4 to 4). Thus, students in the sample may have had the following patterns for the first three schools they attended: 4-2-4, 4-4-4, 4-2-2, and 4-4-2.

2. Choy (2002) defined the traditional route as enrolling in a four-year college immediately following high school, attending that institution continuously and full time, and completing a degree in four years.

3. It should be noted that Adelman did not find a significant effect of the number of institutions attended on completion when the measure was simply "more than one school" versus one. When he distinguished between two patterns of movement—upward transfer from a two- to a four-year institution and movement with no return—he found a positive effect of the former and a negative effect of the latter. Since my study focused on students who started at four-year institutions, the second finding is more relevant here.

4. Co-enrollment alone appeared to have a positive impact on the completion of a degree and was positively correlated with students' income (Peter and Forrest Cataldi 2005).

5. Of course, it is worth noting that the completion of bachelor's degrees has never been a truly "timely" process taking place within the intended four-year time frame. As early as 1964, Eckland noted that barely 40 percent of students completed a bachelor's degree within four years of starting at a "four year" institution. Today, that percentage is 37, with another 26 percent taking either five or six years (Carey 2004).

6. The sample was not further limited to students who participated in the first survey, since information from the eighth-grade year is not central to this study's questions. I will study the elementary and middle school experiences of students following complicated college pathways in future research.

7. Restricting the sample in this way was deemed appropriate, given that attempting to impute for the dependent variable in this analysis (postsecondary pathways) would be unadvisable. Limiting the sample to students with complete records meant excluding 14 percent of the cases. Students who enrolled in only general equivalency diploma programs or basic skills programs and those who took only a single course or fewer than five credits were excluded. The number of institutions attended, a component of the dependent variable, is highly correlated with having a complete transcript record; thus, all means and regressions that are presented in this article are weighted. Patterning by SES was not found among the excluded cases.

8. The transcript data identify the "true" first institution attended, excluding any institution that a student attended only during the summer between high school and college; there were no cases of students starting at a two- and four-year institution at the same time.

9. Several previous studies of multi-institutional attendance, such as the one by Peter and Forrest Cataldi (2005), used data from the Beginning Postsecondary Students Longitudinal Study, which contains only selfreported data on attendance patterns.

10. It should be noted that credit thresholds were not used to assess the number of institutions attended. Research has demonstrated that there is socioeconomic variation in credit enrollment (McCormick 1999). Whereas some researchers (most notably Adelman 1999) used such thresholds in analyses predicting the completion of degrees or transfers, in my study, in which the primary interest was in the enrollment patterns of different socioeconomic groups, such restrictions were deemed inappropriate, since they would likely exclude part of the attendance pattern of low-SES students.

11. Although students take courses during the summer for a variety of reasons, attendance during the academic year remains central to postsecondary schooling, and thus differences in how students attend college during the academic year are the focus of this analysis. It would be worthwhile to investigate the role of summer schooling during college in future research.

12. The number of students in this category and the number in Category D are particularly small, and thus multivariate findings regarding comparisons made to these categories should be considered fragile. The small number of students from this sample in these categories should not be interpreted to mean that the interruption patterns are especially rare. The reader should keep in mind that the NELS survey was constructed to sample eighth-grade students, not beginning postsecondary students, and thus estimates of nontraditionality are likely to be underestimates in this sample. Unfortunately, national studies of beginning postsecondary students that have been conducted so far have not included data from college transcripts, which is central to this analysis.

13. Racial categories were combined in this manner because of the relatively small samples of black and Hispanic college goers. Whites and Asians have higher college participation rates than do blacks and Hispanics owing to a variety of factors, including lower levels of socioeconomic disadvantage and higher levels of high school academic preparation. In addition, Hispanics are disproportionately likely to begin college at a two-year institution (Baker and Velez 1996) and thus represent an especially small proportion of this sample, and those who were included were more advantaged than the average Hispanic student. Thus, this measure of race assesses the average differences between overrepresented (and therefore advantaged) groups and underrepresented groups. The racial categories, other than Hispanic, exclude Hispanic origin.

14. The purpose of coding many of the independent variables in quintiles was to assess any nonlinear effects, particularly SES, on attendance patterns. Indeed, many such nonlinear effects were found, as the results demonstrate. Differently coded independent variables did not suggest significantly different findings.

15. This standardized test was a special test of general learned abilities that was administered to the participants in the 12th grade.

16. GPA was derived by the NCES staff from college transcripts (Adelman et al. 2003). The dividing lines for the GPA quintiles are low (less than 2.0), middle (2.0–3.32), and high (greater than 3.32).

17. On the basis of a student's high school transcript, this variable assesses the rigor of the curriculum that the student engaged in across several components (math, Advanced Placement courses, English, foreign language, science, social sciences, and computer sciences) by assessing both the quality of the courses taken and the number of "hard" courses taken. For example, students with the highest scores on this measure took at least 3.75 Carnegie units of math, with the highest level at trigonometry or higher, along with at least 3.75 units of English, 2 units of a foreign language, 2 units of laboratory science, 2 units of history, and one Advanced Placement course. For more on the construction of this variable, see Adelman (1999).

18. Although there were data on 4,628 students, the initial regression analysis was performed on only 3,284 students; thus 29 percent of the observations were unused because of missing data. Three variables accounted for the majority of the missing values—high school GPA (29 percent missing), test scores (7 percent missing), and curricular intensity (11 percent missing). There was no patterning by a student's SES in any of the missing data. To make full use of all the student observations, I imputed independent variables with missing data on the basis of the means of the other independent variables in the analysis. Although there is no perfect method for imputation and all methods involve some inherent "guessing" as to true values, a comparison of the regression results before and after imputation indicated no significant underestimation of standard errors or overestimation of test statistics and therefore no suspected bias.

19. On the basis of the sample restrictions discussed earlier, the F4F2P3WT weight (the participation weight for members of the 12th-grade freshened panel with complete postsecondary transcript records) was used. This weight works to preserve the representativeness of the sample on the basis of the level of certainty of postsecondary participation and the completeness of the transcript record; incomplete and single-case records, which would distort or bias analyses, were excluded.

20. Thus, 7 percent of the students technically experienced an interruption between high school graduation and college entry. However, since this represents a precollege interruption (prior to enrollment), it is not classified as an "interruption" for the purposes of categorization in Table 1.

21. Therefore, the findings of this study dispute Vedder's (2004) assertion that the time to the completion of a degree can be reduced by requiring students who do not finish quickly to repay their financial aid. The finding that low-SES students are disproportionately likely to follow pathways that inhibit the completion of their degrees suggests that rather than wasting time by partying, these students are working because of economic necessity.

References

Adelman, Clifford. 1999. *Answers in the Tool Box: Academic Intensity, Attendance Patterns, and Bachelor's Degree Attainment.* Washington, DC: U.S. Department of Education.

———. 2003. "The Story-Lines of Multi-Institutional Attendance." Paper presented at the Association for Institutional Research, Tampa, FL.

Adelman, Clifford, Bruce Daniel, Ilona Berkovitz, and Jeffrey Owings. 2003. *Postsecondary Attainment, Attendance, Curriculum, and Performance.* Washington, DC: National Center for Education Statistics.

Alexander, Karl L., Scott Holupka, and Aaron M. Pallas. 1987. "Social Background and Academic Determinants of Two-Year versus Four-Year College Attendance: Evidence from Two Cohorts a Decade Apart." *American Journal of Education* 96(1): 56–80.

Allison, Paul. 2002. *Missing Data.* Thousand Oaks, CA: Sage.

Bach, Susan K., Melissa T. Banks, Mary K. Kinnick, Mary F. Ricks, Juliette M. Stoering, and R. Dan Walleri. 2000. "Student Attendance Patterns and Performance in an Urban Postsecondary Environment." *Research in Higher Education* 41:315–30.

Baker, Teresa L., and William Velez. 1996. "Access to and Opportunity in Postsecondary Education in the United States: A Review." *Sociology of Education* 69:82–101.

Berkner, Lutz. 2002. *Descriptive Summary of 1995–1996 Beginning Postsecondary Students: Six Years Later.* Washington, DC: National Center for Education Statistics.

Bourdieu, Pierre, and Jean-Claude Passeron. 1977. *Reproduction in Education, Society and Culture.* London: Sage.

Bowen, William G., Martin A. Kurzweil, and Eugene M. Tobin. 2005. *Equity and Excellence in American Higher Education.* Charlottesville: University of Virginia Press.

Broene, Pam, and Keith Rust. 2000. *Strengths and Limitations of Using SUDAAN, Stata, and WesVarPC for Computing Variances from NCES Data Sets.* Washington, DC: National Center for Education Statistics.

Cabrera, Alberto F., Kurt R. Burkum, and Steven M. La Nasa. 2003. "Pathways to a Four-Year Degree: Determinants of Degree Completion among Socioeconomically Disadvantaged Students." Paper presented at the Association for the Study of Higher Education, Portland, OR.

Cabrera, Alberto F., and Steven M. La Nasa. 2000. Three Critical Tasks America's Disadvantaged Face on Their Path to College. *New Directions for Institutional Research* 27(3):23–29.

Carey, Kevin. 2004. *A Matter of Degrees: Improving Graduation Rates in Four-Year Colleges.* Washington, DC: The Education Trust.

Carroll, C. Dennis. 1989. *College Persistence and Degree Attainment for 1980 High School Graduates: Hazards for Transfers, Stopouts and Part-Timers.* Washington, DC: National Center for Education Statistics.

Choy, Susan P. 2002. *Nontraditional Undergraduates: A Special Analysis.* Washington, DC: National Center for Education Statistics.

Coleman, James. 1974. *Youths: Transition to Adulthood.* Chicago: University of Chicago Press.

_____. 1988. "Social Capital in the Creation of Human Capital." *American Journal of Sociology* 94:S95–S120.

de los Santos, Jr., Alfredo, and Irene Wright. 1990. "Maricopa's Swirling Students: Earning One-Third of Arizona State's Bachelor's Degrees." *Community, Technical, and Junior College Journal* 60(6):32–34.

DesJardins, Stephen L., Dennis A. Ahlburg, and Brian P. McCall. 2002. "Simulating the Longitudinal Effects of Changes in Financial Aid on Student Departure from College." *Journal of Human Resources* 37:653–79.

DiMaggio, Paul. 1982. "Cultural Capital and School Success." *American Sociological Review* 47:189–201.

Eckland, Bruce. 1964. "Social Class and College Graduation: Some Misconceptions Corrected." *American Journal of Sociology* 70:36–50.

Elman, Cheryl, and Angela M. O'Rand. 2004. "The Race Is to the Swift: Socioeconomic Origins, Adult Education, and Wage Attainment." *American Journal of Sociology* 110:123–60.

Gerber, Theodore P., and David R. Schaefer. 2004. "Horizontal Stratification of Higher Education in Russia: Trends, Gender Differences, and Labor Market Outcomes." *Sociology of Education* 77: 32–59.

Goldrick-Rab, Sara. 2004. "Swirling Among Schools: Social Class, Institutional Type, and Postsecondary Pathways." Paper presented at the annual meetings of the Association for the Study of Higher Education, Kansas City, MO.

Hearn, James C. 1992. "Emerging Variations in Postsecondary Attendance Patterns: An Investigation of Part-Time, Delayed, and Nondegree Enrollment." *Research in Higher Education* 33:657–87.

Karen, David. 2002. "Changes in Access to Higher Education in the United States: 1980–1992." *Sociology of Education* 75:191–210.

Kearney, Gretchen, Barbara Townsend, and Terrance Kearney. 1995. "Multiple Transfer Students in a Public Urban University: Background Characteristics And Interinstitutional Movements." *Research in Higher Education* 36:323–44.

King, Jacqueline. 2002. *Crucial Choices: How Student's Financial Decisions Affect Their Academic Success.* Washington, DC: American Council on Education.

Kojaku, Lawrence K., and Anne-Marie Nuñez. 1998. *Descriptive Summary of 1995–1996 Beginning Postsecondary Students.* Washington, DC: National Center for Education Statistics.

Levine, Arthur. 2001. "Privatization in Higher Education." Pp. 133–50 in *Privatizing Education: Can the Marketplace Deliver Choice, Efficiency, Equity, and Social Cohesion?* edited by Henry Levin. Boulder, CO: Westview Press.

Leonhardt, David. 2005, May 24. "Class Matters: The College Dropout Boom." *New York Times,* p. A1.

McCormick, Alexander C. 1999. *Credit Production and Progress Toward the Bachelor's Degree: An Analysis of Postsecondary Transcripts for Beginning Students at 4-Year Institutions.* Washington, DC: National Center for Education Statistics.

_____. 2003. "Swirling and Double-Dipping: New Patterns of Student Attendance and Their Implications for Higher Education." *New Directions for Higher Education* 121:13–24.

McDonough, Patricia. M. 1994. "Buying and Selling Higher Education: The Social Construction of the College Applicant." *Journal of Higher Education* 65:427–46.

Newman, Frank, and Lara K. Couturier. 2001, September–October. "The New Competitive Arena: Market Forces Invade the Academy." *Change* 33(5):10–17.

_____. 2004. "Rhetoric, Reality, and the Risks." *American Academic* 1(1):61–75.

Newman, Frank, Lara K. Couturier, and Jamie Scurry. 2004. *The Future of Higher Education: Rhetoric, Reality, and the Risks of the Market.* San Francisco: John Wiley & Sons.

O'Meara, Kerry Ann. 2001. "The Impact of Consumerism, Capitalism, and For-profit Competition on American Higher Education." *International Higher Education* (Vol. 22). Boston: Boston College Center for International Higher Education.

Paulson, Michael B., and Edward P. St. John. 1997. "The Financial Nexus Between College Choice and Persistence." *New Directions for Institutional Research* (Vol. 1997, Issue 95), pp. 65–82. San Francisco: Jossey-Bass.

Peter, Katharin, and Emily Forrest Cataldi. 2005. *The Road Less Traveled? Students Who Enroll in Multiple Institutions.* Washington, DC: National Center for Education Statistics.

Rindfuss, Ronald, C. Gray Swicegood, and Rachel A. Rosenfeld. 1987. "Disorder in the Life Course: How Common and Does It Matter?" *American Sociological Review* 52:785–801.

Rosenbaum, James. 2001. *Beyond College for All: Career Paths for the Forgotten Half.* New York: Russell Sage Foundation.

Schneider, Barbara, and David Stevenson. 1999. *The Ambitious Generation: America's Teenagers, Motivated but Directionless.* New Haven, CT: Yale University Press.

Shanahan, Michael J. 2000. "Pathways to Adulthood in Changing Societies: Variability and Mechanisms in Life Course Perspective." *Annual Review of Sociology* 26:667–92.

St. John, Edward P., Sandra C. Andrieu, Jeffrey Oescher, and Johhny B. Starkey. 1994. "The Influence of Student Aid on Within-Year Persistence by Traditional College-Age Students in Four-Year Colleges." *Research in Higher Education* 35:455–80.

St. John, Edward P., Rita J. Kirshstein, and Jay Noell. 1991. "The Effects of Student Financial Aid on Persistence: A Sequential Analysis." *Review of Higher Education* 14:383–406.

Tinto, Vincent. 1993. *Leaving College: Rethinking the Causes and Cures of Student* Attrition (2nd ed.). Chicago: University of Chicago Press.

Townsend, Barbara K., and John T. Dever. 1999. "What Do We Know About Reverse Transfer Students?" *New Directions for Community Colleges* 106:5–13.

U.S. Department of Education. 2003. *Digest of Education Statistics*, Table 172. Washington, DC: National Center for Education Statistics.

Vedder, Richard. 2004. *Going Broke By Degree: Why College Costs Too Much.* Washington, DC: American Enterprise Institute.

Walpole, Marybeth. 2003. "Socioeconomic Status and College: How SES Affects College Experiences and Outcomes." *Review of Higher Education* 27(1):45–73.

Winter, Greg. 2003, October 5. "Jacuzzi U.? A Battle of Perks to Lure Students." *New York Times*, p. A1.

Sara Goldrick-Rab, Ph.D., is Assistant Professor of Educational Policy Studies and Sociology at the University of Wisconsin–Madison. Her research focuses on identifying inequalities in higher education and improving both college access and success among low-income and first-generation students. Currently, she is engaged in a project on "Postsecondary Educational Transitions," funded by the American Educational Research Association and the Association for Institutional Research. Dr. Goldrick-Rab was named a 2004 Rising Scholar by the National Forum on Higher Education for the Public Good.

This research was supported by dissertation grants from the Spencer Foundation and the American Educational Research Association, which receives funds for its AERA Grants Program from the National Science Foundation, and the U.S. Department of Education's National Center for Education Statistics and the Institute of Education Sciences under NSF Grant REC-9980573. The author would like to thank James Hearn, Michael Olneck, Josipa Roksa, Scott Thomas, and Elizabeth Vaquera for their helpful comments and guidance in developing this article. Of course, all opinions and conclusions belong solely to the author. Address correspondence to Sara Goldrick-Rab, Department of Educational Policy Studies, University of Wisconsin–Madison, 210 Education Building, 1000 Bascom Mall, Madison WI 53706; e-mail: srab@education.wisc.edu.

CHAPTER 30

PERCEPTIONS OF CAMPUS CLIMATE AND ENGAGEMENT FOR LESBIAN, GAY, BISEXUAL, AND TRANSGENDER COMMUNITY COLLEGE STUDENTS

CRYSTAL KIEKEL

Over the last four years, a group of Senate leaders has worked to raise awareness about the special needs of lesbian, gay, bisexual, and transgender (LGBT) students in our colleges. This group has conducted breakout sessions at various conferences and formed the LGBT Caucus. The following article, which will be followed by another in the winter, is part of this effort. It describes a case study that was conducted in 2011 to explore community college campus climate as It relates to LGBT students. This article will provide an overview of the study and its findings, while the next one will explore the major findings in more detail.

Applying current research and theory on student engagement, campus climate, and LGBT student characteristics and experiences, the study explores the extent to which the campus climate at one community college engages and supports LGBT students. It focuses on community colleges as a unique destination for LGBT students, one which has the opportunity to provide a safe space where students can learn to engage, take risks, and thrive.

Student perceptions of campus climate have a significant impact on student engagement; engagement, in turn, is the single greatest predictor of college persistence and success (Kuh, 2001, 2003). Underrepresented groups, like people of color, women, and LGBT students, tend to express more negative views of campus climate than their majority counterparts (Rankin & Reason, 2005; Worthington, 2008). The literature that examines the role of campus climate on LGBT student engagement, persistence, and success in higher education demonstrates that LGBT students experience marginalization and discrimination at higher rates than their heterosexual peers and even other unrepresented groups. However, although structures that begin to address the unique needs and strengths for many underrepresented groups have been created, the voices and needs of LGBT students remain largely unrecognized on community college campuses (Rankin & Reason, 2005; Worthington, 2008).

There is substantial literature to support the fact that LGBT students experience discrimination and marginalization that puts them at risk for academic failure. In high school, these students are at higher risk for depression, suicide, truancy, and homelessness (D'Augelli, 2002; Espelage, Aragon, Birkett, & Koenig, 2008). They are about half as likely to have plans to go to college (Fisher, Matthews, & Selvidge, 2008). They are more likely to disengage from the educational process and fail coursework, are less socially integrated, and less likely to complete college-preparation courses. Despite these added academic risk factors, in 2010, fewer than 7% of institutions of higher education offered institutional support for LGBT students, demonstrating a severe lack of systemic response to the needs of this underrepresented group (Rankin, Weber, Blumenfeld, & Frazer, 2010).

The framework for this study draws from two theories for understanding student success: student engagement and campus climate (Astin, 1999; Hurtado, 1992; Kuh, 2001). Student engagement is the extent to which students engage in educationally purposeful activities; evidence suggests that engagement in these activities is associated with academic persistence. Campus climate theory demonstrates that a supportive campus climate plays a substantial role in helping students feel valued and comfortable in an institution, which increases engagement and persistence. Campus climate literature suggests that an institution's commitment to diversity can have a significant impact on underrepresented students' perceptions of climate (Hurtado, 1992; Kuh, 2001). Using these theoretical models to provide a framework for understanding the LGBT community college experience, two research questions were explored:

1. How do self-identified LGBT community college students describe their community college campus climate?

2. What are the experiences of self-identified LGBT students who engage in college-related activities?

The site of this study was a large, urban community college. Primary data were collected through ten LGBT student and five faculty member interviews and one focus group comprised of nine students. The theoretical framework provided a lens through which these perceptions and experiences were examined and interpreted. These findings were triangulated with a document analysis. Data were analyzed for themes around climate and engagement.

The first theme that emerged was that there was a complex relationship between how students viewed the climate overall and the descriptions of the individual "microaggressions" students reported. Overall, students had positive perceptions of campus climate. Faculty and students agreed that the campus was a relatively safe, accepting, and inclusive place for LGBT students. On the other hand, students encountered multiple microaggressions on campus. Microaggressions are subtle, non-verbal, or even preconscious daily actions that marginalize members of underrepresented groups. As single events, these acts may go unnoticed or may be forgotten. However, over time, persistence of microaggressions contributes to a constant subtext of threat and stress for members of underrepresented groups. The pervasive presence of these behaviors belled an undercurrent at the college that was difficult to pinpoint, and therefore difficult to address. These actions were sometimes overt, like seemingly innocuous gay jokes told by instructors or students. Some were subtle or unconscious behaviors, like a barely perceptible glance or even a general sense or feeling of otherness.

The second theme that emerged was that classroom experiences can have a powerful impact, positive or negative, on how students engage with their learning environments. Faculty behaviors and attitudes about the LGBT community influenced classroom engagement for these LGBT students. Seemingly subtle behaviors, like making passing jokes or even lack of behaviors, like failing to intervene when microaggressions occur in the classroom, left these LGBT students feeling alienated from their learning environments. On the other hand, affirming behaviors, like intervening when microaggressions occur in the classroom or incorporating LGBT topics into the curriculum, had a substantial positive impact. These small gestures of inclusion allowed these LGBT students to feel like they could engage more fully in the classroom.

These students derived a strong sense of belonging and identity through their affiliation with the LGBT club. The significance of this club supports literature that underscores the importance of social groups as predictors of college success. Peer association is particularly important for underrepresented students, who often perceive campus climate as more hostile or less inclusive. Similar to the sanctuaries or counterspaces that Grier-Reed (2010) described, this club provides a safe space for students to feel welcome and normal. The fact that students identified this club as their primary, and sometimes their only, social network underscores its importance. Students saw the club as an opportunity to learn about their community, teach others on campus about the community, and find vital peer support and acceptance.

This research supports three conclusions that make a significant contribution to our understanding of how LGBT students experience community college: (1) these students do not experience campus climate in the same way that heterosexual students do; (2) their social and classroom experiences had a major impact on their perceptions and levels of engagement; and (3) while this community college has made significant progress in helping them feel safe and respected on campus, the pervasiveness of microaggressions continues to leave them feeling stigmatized on campus.

We recommend providing ongoing, accessible, and comprehensive professional development for faculty, increasing campus dialogue across faculty, staff, and student constituencies, and fostering leadership around LGBT student engagement and support. By creating a culture of inclusivity and respect for all students, leaders can create an environment where students feel safe enough to take academic risks and engage in meaningful academic activities that lead to success.

References

Astin, A. W. (1999). Student involvement: A developmental theory for higher education. *Journal of College Student Development, 40(5)*, 518–529.

Bloomberg, L D., & Volpe, M. F. (2008).

D'Augelli, A. R. (2002). Mental health problems among lesbian, gay and bisexual youths ages 14 to 21. *Clinical Child Psychology and Psychiatry, 7(3)*, 433–456.

Espelage, D.L, Aragon, S.R., Birkett, M, & Koenig, B.W. (2008). Homophobic teasing, psychological outcomes, and sexual orientation among high school students: What influence do parents and schools have? *School Psychology Review, 37,* 2002–216.

Fisher, K., Matthews, C.R., Selvidge, M.D. (2008). Addictions counselors' attitudes and behaviors toward gay, lesbian, and bisexual clients. *Journal of Counseling and Development 83*(1).

Grier-Reed, T. (2010). The African American student network: Creating sanctuaries and counterspaces for coping with racial microaggressions in higher education settings. *The American Counseling Association, 49,* 181–188.

Hurtado, S. (1992).The campus racial climate: Context of conflict. *Journal of Higher Education, 63,* 539–569.

Hurtado, S., Griffin, K.A., Arellano, L & Cuellar, M. (2008). Assessing the value of climate assessments: Progress and future directions. *Journal of Diversity in Higher Education. 1*(4), 204–221.

Hurtado, S., Milem, J., Clayton-Pedersen, A.R., and Allen, W. R. (1998) Enhancing campus climates for racial/ethnic diversity: Educational policy and practice. *The Review of Higher Education, 21*(3) 279-302.

Kuh, G.D. (2001). Organizational culture and student persistence: Prospects and puzzles. *Journal of College Student Retention, 3,* 23–39.

Kuh, G. D. (2003). What we're learning about student engagement from NSSE: Benchmarks for effective educational practices. *Change, 35(2),* 24–32.

Kuh, G. D. (2009). The national survey of student engagement: Conceptual and empirical foundations. New *Directions for Institutional Research, 141,* 5–20.

Lock, J., Steiner, H. (1999) Gay, lesbian and bisexual youth risks for emotional, physical and social problems: results from community-based survey. *Journal of the American Academy of Child and Adolescent Psychiatry, 38,* 297–304.

Pearson, J., Muller, C., Wilkinson, L. (2007). Adolescent same-sex attraction and academic outcomes: The role of school attachment and engagement. *Social Problems, 54*(4), 523–542.

Rankin, S.R., Reason, R.D. (2005). Differing perceptions: How students of color and white students perceive campus climate for underrepresented groups. *Journal of College Student Development, 46*(1), 43–61.

Rankin, S., Weber, G., Blumenfeld, W., Frazer, S. (2010). State of Higher Education for lesbian Gay, Bisexual, and Transgender People: 2010 National College climate Survey. Charlotte: campus Pride.

Renn, K.A. (2010). LGBT and queer research in higher education: The state and status of the field. *Educational Researcher, 39*(2), 132–141.

Sheets, R.L, Mohr, J.J. (2009). Perceived social support from friends and family and psychosocial functioning in bisexual young adult college students. *Journal of Counseling Psychology, 56*(1), 152–163.

Solórzano, D., Ceja, M., Yosso, T. (2000). Critical race theory, racial microaggressions, and campus racial climate: The experiences of African American college students. *Journal of Negro Education. 69*(1/2).

Worthington, R. L. (Guest Ed.) (2008). Special Issue: Measurement and Assessment in campus Climate Research. *Journal of Diversity In Higher Education, 1,* 201–274.

CHAPTER 31

STUDENTS WITH DISABILITIES AT 2-YEAR INSTITUTIONS IN THE UNITED STATES: FACTORS RELATED TO SUCCESS

KETEVAN MAMISEISHVILI[1] AND LYNN C. KOCH[1]

Abstract. This study used data from the Beginning Postsecondary Students Longitudinal Study to examine the demographic and in-college characteristics of students with disabilities at two-year institutions, identify the types of educational services available to them, and determine how students' disability conditions and their selected demographic and in-college characteristics related to their persistence. Nearly 25% of the students with disabilities in the sample did not persist beyond their first year, and almost 51% left without return by the end of their third year. The results from chi-square tests revealed that nonpersistence was associated with depression, physical or orthopedic conditions, and other conditions not specified in the survey. Delayed enrollment decreased the likelihood of both first-to-second and three-year persistence. Conversely, full-time enrollment, high grade point averages (GPAs), high degree aspirations, and meetings with academic advisors were positively related to persistence. Recommendations for faculty members, administrators, and disability services staff members at two-year institutions are provided.

Keywords: students with disabilities, academic persistence, academic advisors, study groups, orthopedic disabilities, learning disabilities, dyslexia, mental health

The relationship between completion of a college degree or certificate and improved employment outcomes has been well established in the higher education and rehabilitation literature. However, individuals with disabilities enter postsecondary education at lower rates than their peers without disabilities and are less likely to persist until completion of their educational programming (Ponticelli & Russ-Eft, 2009; Quick, Lehmann, & Deniston, 2003). Although students with disabilities are still underrepresented in higher education, they are entering postsecondary institutions in growing numbers (Garrison-Wade & Lehmann, 2009; Hawke, 2004). Data on the enrollment of students with disabilities in postsecondary institutions have not been systematically collected, but estimates indicate that the percentage of postsecondary students who reported a disability increased from 2.6% in 1978 to 10.5% in 1998 (Getzel, Stodden, & Briel, 2001). More recently, national data collected from degree-granting postsecondary institutions about students with disabilities revealed that in the 2008-2009 academic year, 707,000 students with disabilities were enrolled in postsecondary institutions, with about half of these students attending public two-year institutions (Raue & Lewis, 2011). The growth in the number of students with disabilities can be attributed to factors such as enhanced assistive and instructional technology, expanded disability support service programs, greater self-determination among individuals with disabilities, and increased public awareness regarding the capabilities of individuals with disabilities (Prentice, 2002). Continued

---

[1]University of Arkansas, Fayetteville, AR, USA

enrollment increases are also anticipated because of the passage of recent legislation (e.g., the Americans with Disabilities Act Amendments Act of 2008, the Higher Education Opportunity Act, and the Post-9/11 Veterans Education Act) that expands civil rights protections and educational benefits to individuals with disabilities (Mamiseishvili & Koch, 2011).

Research has documented that community colleges are the primary avenue for participating in higher education for individuals with disabilities. A study sponsored by the U.S. Department of Education found that nearly 60% of college students with disabilities attended institutions with two-year programs or programs of less than 2 years in duration (Horn, Peter, & Rooney, 2002). More recently, Mamiseishvili and Koch (2011) found that approximately two thirds of a total national sample of college students with disabilities in the 2004-2006 Beginning Postsecondary Students Longitudinal Study data set attended two-year or less-than-two-year institutions. Johnson, Zascavage, and Gerber (2008) speculated that two-year institutions may provide more intensive support services for students with disabilities and that these supports foster a greater sense of self-efficacy for college success. For those individuals who do not plan to transfer to four-year institutions, two-year institutions also provide opportunities to acquire marketable job skills and occupationally specific training within a relatively short period of time (Lindstrom, Flannery, Benz, Olszewski, & Slovic, 2009). They are often more affordable than four-year institutions, have open enrollment, and offer developmental or remedial classes to those who need them (Ankeny & Lehmann, 2010). As such, they serve students with varying degrees of academic preparedness and provide educational options that are not available at four-year colleges and universities.

With continuing growth in the enrollment of students with disabilities at two-year institutions, it is essential that these institutions are prepared to serve the needs of this population by providing the necessary educational accommodations and academic supports for their success. However, our extensive review of the higher education and rehabilitation literature revealed that only limited research has identified the factors that influence the persistence of two-year college students with disabilities until completion of their programs of study or transfer to four-year institutions. Much of the existing research on persistence and college success has focused on students with disabilities at four-year colleges and universities (e.g., DaDeppo, 2009; Vogel & Adelman, 1992; Wessel, Jones, Markle, & Westfall, 2009). The limited research that exists on students with disabilities at two-year institutions has utilized local or regional samples instead of nationally representative samples. For example, Lindstrom et al. (2009) examined factors associated with program completion in a sample of students with disabilities at four community colleges. These community colleges partnered with a state vocational rehabilitation office to provide short-term skills training to participants in the study. The researchers found that women, older participants, and individuals who received financial support were more likely to persist until certificate completion, obtain employment, and maintain employment for 90 days; individuals with psychiatric disabilities were less likely to obtain positive outcomes. In another study, Ponticelli and Russ-Eft (2009) examined the transfer outcomes of students with disabilities attending California community colleges between 1995-1996 and 2006-2007. They found that the average number of years for a transfer to a four-year college for these students was 5.83. Furthermore, the study revealed that the proportion of transfer courses students took and the proportion of units they completed were the two strongest predictors of transfer.

The purpose of our study was to examine the persistence outcomes of a nationally representative sample of students with disabilities enrolled in two-year postsecondary institutions in the United States. More specifically, we examined first-to-second and three-year cumulative persistence rates of two-year college students with disabilities and investigated how their persistence varied by disability condition and other selected demographic and in-college characteristics. The following questions guided our investigation:

Research Question 1: What are the demographic and in-college characteristics of students with disabilities enrolled in two-year institutions?

Research Question 2: What types of educational services and accommodations are available to them?

Research Question 3: How do students' disability conditions and their selected demographic and in-college characteristics relate to their first-to-second-year and three-year cumulative persistence?

Conceptual Framework

A substantial theoretical basis has been established to guide the study of student persistence. One of the earliest theoretical models developed by Tinto (1975, 1993) argued that students' interactions with the social and academic systems of the institution affect their decisions to persist or depart from college. Tinto's (1975, 1993) model has had considerable influence on community college research (Bailey & Alfonso, 2005); however, Braxton, Hirschy, and McClendon (2004) noted that the utility of Tinto's model in explaining two-year college student departure has remained "undetermined and open to empirical treatment" (p. 18). In particular, researchers have questioned the relevance of Tinto's social integration concept for students at two-year institutions, many of whom are older, more likely to enroll part-time, and have family and other personal commitments. Bean and Metzner (1985) suggested that "academic variables represent the primary way in which nontraditional students interact with the institution" (p. 492). Braxton and Hirschy (2005) also argued that in the absence of social communities, "the academic realm of the institution holds the primary status" (p. 78). In their theory of student departure in commuter institutions, Braxton et al. described three elements (student entry characteristics, academic integration, and environments on and off campus) that influence students' institutional commitment and, subsequently, their decision to persist. It should be noted that none of these aforementioned theoretical perspectives has been developed specifically for two-year institutions. For example, Bean and Metzner's model of nontraditional student persistence does not differentiate between nontraditional students at two- and four-year institutions. Similarly, the model developed by Braxton et al. focuses on commuter colleges and universities overall, and not on two-year commuter institutions in particular. Despite these constraints, these models provide a good theoretical foundation to explain student persistence behaviors in two-year college settings.

In addition to the existence of a strong theoretical basis, there also exists a substantial empirical basis to guide the study of student persistence at two-year colleges. Researchers have extensively explored the effects of students' demographic and in-college characteristics on two-year college persistence. For example, past research has identified delayed enrollment in postsecondary institutions as a potential risk factor for nonpersistence. Studying a sample of first-time, full-time students at a community college in New England, Craig and Ward (2007-2008) found that the length of time between high school graduation and college enrollment was the only demographic predictor that was significantly related to student retention.

Among in-college characteristics, the effects of academic integration and academic performance on two-year college student success have been thoroughly researched (e.g., Bers & Smith, 1991; Deil-Amen, 2011; Hagedorn, Maxwell, Rodriguez, Hocevar, & Fillpot, 2000; Karp, Hughes, & O'Gara, 2010-2011; Mutter, 1992; Nippert, 2000-2001). Past research has revealed that students with low first-semester grade point averages (GPAs) or in need of remediation are at a higher risk of attrition (Bailey, 2009; Barbatis, 2010; Crews & Aragon, 2004; Fike & Fike, 2008; Hoyt, 1999). Hoyt's study, conducted at a large urban community college, found that students' first-semester academic performance had the strongest influence on retention. Furthermore, students who took two or more remedial courses were significantly more likely to leave than their peers who did not need remedial education. In addition, Nippert, in a study of two-year college students using the data from the Cooperative Institutional Research Program's 1986 and 1990 surveys, found that involvement in academic activities significantly influenced persistence and degree attainment. Two recent studies have also highlighted the importance of academic interactions with faculty members, staff members, and peers for students at two-year institutions. Deil-Amen conducted interviews with 125 students from 14 public and private two-year institutions and concluded that students' in-classroom interactions facilitated both academic and social integration. Karp et al., based on interviews with students at two Northeastern urban community colleges, also found that many academic relationships that developed as part of the academic process, such as study groups, encompassed social elements and extended to social interactions as well (p. 83).

Over the past several decades, interest in studying student persistence has remained strong because "it is an outcome that mediates other outcomes: attainment, graduate school attendance, income, and career status" (Walpole, 2007, p. 48). Despite this substantial research base on persistence in two-year college settings, there is still a need to examine educational outcomes of disadvantaged student groups such as students with disabilities. Although they are attending community colleges in growing numbers, research on their persistence outcomes is still underdeveloped.

Method

The study utilized a nonexperimental research design combining survey and explanatory correlational research (Creswell, 2008) to examine trends in the sample of students with disabilities attending two-year institutions, including their demographic and in-college characteristics, disability conditions, and types of accommodations available to them. The study also sought to investigate the association between these variables and the likelihood of first-to-second and three-year cumulative persistence.

Data Source and Sample

Our investigation utilized data from the Beginning Postsecondary Students Longitudinal Study (BPS:04/06) data set. The BPS:04/06 data set includes a nationally representative sample of college students who started their postsecondary education for the first time in the fall of 2003. The 2003-2004 base-year sample of 23,090 students was drawn from 1,360 postsecondary institutions (Cominole et al., 2007). The students were first surveyed at the end of the 2003-2004 academic year and then surveyed again in the first follow-up study conducted in 2006. Survey interviews were administered in three modes: web-based, self-administered interviews; computer-assisted telephone interviews; and computer-assisted personal interviews. Approximately, 18,640 of the 23,090 base-year sample members were determined to be eligible for inclusion in the first follow-up study (Cominole et al., 2007). The overall unweighted response rate for eligible sample members was 80%, with a weighted response rate of 77%.

For the purposes of this study, we selected the sample of students with disabilities who enrolled at two-year postsecondary institutions in the fall of 2003. Within this sample, there were 890 individuals who reported having some type of disability or condition that had lasted 6 months or more, including any sensory impairment, such as blindness, deafness, or a severe vision or hearing impairment; any mobility impairment that substantially restricted students' basic physical activities; or any other mental, emotional, or learning condition limiting students' ability to learn, remember, and concentrate. Because the BPS:04/06 data set relied on a complex sampling design, which included stratified multistage sampling with unequal probabilities of sample selection, we utilized relative weights to correct for oversampling and make the data representative of the target population (Thomas & Heck, 2001). Relative weights were computed by dividing the raw weights provided in the data set by their mean and applied to data analysis by using WEIGHT BY command in SPSS.

Variables

Persistence. Two success measures served as outcome variables in our study: first-to-second-year persistence and three-year cumulative persistence. The first outcome variable indicated students' persistence and attainment anywhere in the system at the end of the first academic year. Students who had attained an associate's degree or a certificate by the end of the first year, or who had enrolled for at least 1 month during the 2003-2004 academic year and reenrolled at any institution of higher education in a later year, were considered to be persisters; those who left without return by the end of the first year and who had not earned a degree or certificate were coded as nonpersisters. On the second outcome measure, students who had attained any certificate or degree, or who were still enrolled at any postsecondary institution by the end of the third year in June 2006, were coded as persisters; those who were no longer enrolled and who had not attained any degree or certificate were considered to be nonpersisters. In other words, the three-year persistence variable indicated the cumulative outcome of enrollment by the end of the third year, regardless of any breaks or stops.

As evident from the description of the outcome variables provided above, measures of system or individual persistence, rather than institutional persistence, were used in this study. System persistence focuses on the individual student and takes into account whether the student remains enrolled in the higher education system as a whole (Hagedorn, 2005). Therefore, according to this approach, students who transferred to another institution but remained enrolled anywhere in the system were also coded as persisters.

Disability-related variables. Disability-related variables included both students' disability conditions and the types of educational services provided to them. The variable indicating students' main disability type or condition included the following categories: sensory condition (i.e., hearing impairment, blindness, or visual impairment), orthopedic or mobility impairment, specific learning disability or dyslexia, attention-deficit disorder (ADD), health impairment or problem, emotional or psychiatric condition, depression, and other (e.g., speech or language impairment, developmental disability, brain injury, or other conditions not included in any other category). Disability-related services or accommodations included adaptive equipment and technology (e.g., assistive or listening devices, talking computers), alternative examination format or additional time, course substitution or waiver, readers, classroom notetakers or scribes, registration assistance or priority class registration, sign language or oral interpreters, tutors to assist with ongoing homework, and other services. The respondents were asked to report which of these services they needed but did not receive and which of these services they received during 2003-2004 academic year.

Demographic and in-college characteristics. We examined the following demographic and in-college characteristics of students with disabilities at two-year institutions: gender, race and ethnicity, delayed enrollment, first-year GPA, attendance intensity, remediation, degree aspirations, and academic integration variables. The variable of gender was represented by two categories: male and female. The variable of race and ethnicity included four categories: Whites, Blacks/African Americans, Hispanics or Latino/as, and Other (i.e., individuals who were in other race categories or who were in more than one race category). The delayed enrollment variable was dichotomous, indicating whether or not students delayed their enrollment in postsecondary education after high school graduation. The first-year GPA variable represented students' cumulative GPA in academic year 2003-2004. It was standardized to a 4-point scale and included four categories: 1 = 0.1 to 1.0 (D- to D), 2 = 1.1 to 2.0 (C- to C), 3 = 2.1 to 3.0 (B- to B), and 4 = 3.1 to 4.0 (A- to A). The attendance intensity variable was collapsed into a dichotomy based on the students' enrollment patterns during the 2003-2004 academic year: 1 = full-time, and 0 = part-time or mixed (i.e., both part-time and full-time at differing points during the academic year). The remediation variable included two categories: 1 = students enrolled in at least one remedial course in their first year, and 0 = students did not take any remedial course. The degree aspirations variable indicated the highest level of education that the students ever expected to complete: 1 = no degree or certificate, 2 = associate's degree, 3 = bachelor's degree, 4 = postbachelor's certificate or master's degree, and 5 = doctoral or first-professional degrees. Academic integration included four variables that indicated how often students participated in study groups, had social contact with faculty members, met with an academic advisor, or talked with faculty members about academic matters outside of class. On each of these academic integration variables, respondents were asked to report the frequency of their participation (i.e., 0 = *never*, 1 = *sometimes*, and 2 = *often*) in each of these activities during the 2003-2004 academic year.

Data Analysis

Descriptive statistics were used to observe the characteristics of students with disabilities at two-year institutions, including their disability conditions, types of disability services available to them, persistence rates, and their selected demographic and in-college characteristics. After the descriptive analysis, Pearson's chi-square tests were conducted to examine whether there was any significant association between persistence of students with disabilities and their disability conditions, as well as with selected demographic and in-college characteristics. The data met the assumptions for the chi-square test: Each item in the data contributed to only one cell in the contingency table, and all expected frequencies were greater than five (Field, 2005). Phi and Cramer's V statistics were examined for each chi-square test to indicate the strength of the association between the variables (Field, 2005). The phi statistic was used when both variables have only two categories. Cramer's V statistic was reported when variables have more than two categories.

Results

Demographic, In-College, and Disability-Related Characteristics

Of the total sample of 890 students with disabilities at two-year institutions, the most frequently reported disability types were orthopedic or mobility impairment (22.1%), followed by health impairment or problem (16.1%), and attention-deficit disorder (16.0%). Other disability conditions reported by the students were emotional or psychiatric condition (11.6%), sensory impairment (9.4%), depression (8.9%), learning disability or dyslexia (7.9%), and other unspecified conditions (8.0%). These data are summarized in Table 1, along with the data on the persistence rates of students with disabilities by the end of the first and third years.

Table 2 provides data on the background and in-college characteristics of students with disabilities, in the aggregate as well as for the persister and nonpersister groups. The sample comprised 66.9% Whites, 12.4% Hispanics, 9.4% Blacks or African Americans, and 11.4% individuals in other race and ethnicity categories or in more than one race category. More than half (54.3%) were female, and 45.7% were male. Nearly 54.0% of the students delayed their enrollment in college after high school and a slight more than half of the sample (51.0%) attended part-time or had a mixed enrollment pattern (i.e., both part-time and full-time). Of the total sample, 26.5% took one or more remedial courses during the 2003-2004 academic year. The majority of the students' GPAs were above 2.0 (79.7%). The students also revealed high degree aspirations, with 32.0% aspiring to complete a bachelor's degree and 30.6% aspiring to complete a postbaccalaureate certificate or a masters degree. In terms of their

TABLE 1

First-to-Second-Year and Three-Year Cumulative Persistence of Students With Disabilities at Two-Year Institutions by Their Disability Type

Disability Types	Total $N = 890$ (%)	First-to-Second-year Persistence			Three-year Cumulative Persistence		
		Persisters $n = 670$ (%)	Leavers $n = 220$ (%)	χ^2	Persisters, $n = 440$ (%)	Leavers, $n = 450$ (%)	χ^2
Sensory condition	9.4	9.6	8.7	0.145	10.4	8.4	0.959
Orthopedic or physical condition	22.1	21.3	24.6	1.073	19.0	25.1	4.917*
Learning disability, dyslexia	7.9	9.8	1.9	14.617***	9.8	6.1	4.620*
Attention-deficit disorder (ADD)	16.0	15.0	19.1	2.250	13.7	18.2	3.424
Health impairment or problem	16.1	17.3	12.4	3.011	18.3	14.0	3.192
Emotional or Psychiatric condition	11.6	12.6	8.8	2.383	14.0	9.4	4.775*
Depression	8.9	7.5	13.1	6.844**	7.3	10.4	2.563
Other condition not specified	8.0	6.9	11.5	4.677*	7.6	8.4	0.203

Note: *$p < .05$. **$p < .01$. ***$p < .001$.

TABLE 2

Background and In-College Characteristics of Students With Disabilities at Two-Year Institutions

	Total $N = 890$ (%)	First-to-Second-year Persistence			Three-year Cumulative Persistence		
		Persisters, $n = 670$ (%)	Leavers, $n = 220$ (%)	χ^2	Persisters, $n = 440$, (%)	Leavers, $n = 450$ (%)	χ^2
Gender							
Female	54.3	57.0	46.1	7.776**	56.3	52.4	1.344
Male	45.7	43.0	53.9	—	43.7	47.6	—
Race							
White	66.9	66.4	68.5	1.352	69.5	64.4	7.249
Black	9.4	9.7	8.5	—	8.6	10.1	—
Hispanic	12.4	12.9	10.7	—	9.7	14.9	—
Other	11.4	11.0	12.3	—	12.2	10.5	—
Delayed enrollment							
Yes	53.7	49.3	67.4	22.127***	44.4	62.8	29.959***
No	46.3	50.7	32.6	—	55.6	37.2	—
Remediation							
Remedial course	26.5	25.4	30.1	1.954	27.4	25.5	0.444
No remedial course	73.5	74.6	69.9	—	72.4	74.5	—
Attendance intensity							
Full–time	49.0	53.7	34.5	23.722***	51.5	53.5	2.145
Part-time or mixed	51.0	46.3	65.5	—	48.5	46.5	—
GPA							
0.01-1.00	5.5	5.1	7.0	2.132	3.1	7.9	11.557**
1.01-2.00	14.8	15.6	12.3	—	14.1	15.4	—
2.01-3.00	35.3	35.2	35.6	—	35.0	35.6	—
3.01-4.00	44.4	44.2	45.1	—	47.9	41.0	—
Degree aspirations							
No degree or certificate	6.4	5.5	9.3	10.816*	5.0	7.8	16.711**
Associate's degree	17.2	16.3	19.9	—	17.6	16.8	—
Bachelor's degree	32.0	31.3	34.3	—	33.3	30.8	—
Master's degree	30.6	31.6	27.4	—	26.5	34.5%	—
Doctoral or professional	13.8	15.3	9.2	—	17.7	10.1	—

Note: *$p < .05$. **$p < .01$. ***$p < .001$.

academic involvement, as illustrated in Table 3, 73.0% of the students never had any informal meet-ings with faculty members, and 59.9% never participated in study groups during their first year in col-lege. Overall, the number of students who reported that they were often involved in any of the academic activities examined in the study ranged from 6.1% to 13.5%.

Data on the availability of disability-related accommodations during the first year in college are summarized in Table 4. Of the total sample of 890 students, 12.6% received assistance with alternative examination formats or additional time on examinations, 10.7% worked with tutors who assisted with homework, 7.6% were provided with registration assistance, 4.3% were provided with readers or class-room notetakers, 4.0% received adaptive equipment and technology assistance (e.g., assistive listening devices, talking computers, etc.), 1.1% individuals received course substitutions or waivers, .5% were assigned sign language or oral interpreters, and 4.8% received other accommodations that were not specified in the survey. When asked about accommodations that were needed but not provided, 10.6% of the students indicated tutors to assist with homework, 8.3% indicated alternative examina-tion formats, 3.5% indicated readers or classroom notetakers, 3.2% indicated registration assistance,

Table 3

Persistence and Academic Integration of Students With Disabilities at Two-Year Institutions

		First-to-Second-year Persistence			Three-year Cumulative Persistence		
	Total $N = 890$	Persisters, $n = 670$	Leavers, $n = 220$	χ^2	Persisters, $n = 440$	Leavers, $n = 450$	χ^2
Faculty informal meetings							
Never	73.0	72.7	73.9	4.500	71.9	74.1	2.341
Sometimes	20.9	20.3	22.7	—	22.7	19.2	—
Often	6.1	6.9	3.4	—	5.4	6.8	—
Faculty contact outside of class							
Never	35.6	34.8	38.3	2.165	35.7	35.6	0.584
Sometimes	53.2	53.2	53.2	—	52.3	54.1	—
Often	11.1	12.0	8.5	—	12.0	10.3	—
Meetings with academic advisors							
Never	44.3	42.4	50.1	5.271	40.5	47.9	6.571*
Sometimes	42.2	43.0	39.8	—	43.7	40.7	—
Often	13.5	14.6	10.1	—	15.7	11.4	—
Study groups							
Never	59.9	59.0	62.5	0.867	57.3	62.4	2.923
Sometimes	33.5	34.2	31.2	—	35.2	31.8	—
Often	6.7	6.8	6.3	—	7.5	5.8	—

Note: *$p < .05$.

Table 4

Percentages of Students Who Received Services and Who Needed but Did Not Receive Disability Accommodations During Their First-Year at Two-Year Institutions

Disability-related Services	Percentage of Students Who Received the Service, $N = 890$ (%)	Percentage of Students Who Needed and did not Receive the service, $N = 890$ (%)
Adaptive equipment and technology	4.0	1.6
Alternative examination format	12.6	8.3
Course substitution or waiver	1.1	2.6
Readers or classroom notetakers	4.3	3.5
Registration assistance	7.6	3.2
Sign language or oral interpreters	0.5	0.8
Tutors to assist with homework	10.7	10.6
Other accommodation	4.8	5.6

2.6% indicated course substitution waivers, 1.6% indicated adaptive equipment and technology, and .8% indicated sign language or oral interpreters; 5.6% indicated other services not listed in the survey.

Factors Related to Persistence of Two-Year College Students With Disabilities

The data revealed that of the total sample of 890 two-year-college students with disabilities, 220 (24.7%) left without return by the end of the first year and 450 (50.6%) left by the end of the third year. Pearson's chi-square tests were conducted to determine if the type of disability had any significant association with students' first-to-second-year and three-year cumulative persistence outcomes. As indicated by chi-square values reported in Table 1, students with depression were more likely to leave than persist through the second year, $\chi^2(1) = 6.844$, $p < .01$. In addition, students with other conditions were also at a higher risk of leaving by the end of the first year, $\chi^2(1) = 4.677$, $p < .05$. Furthermore, students with orthopedic or physical conditions were at an increased likelihood of dropping out sometime within the first 3 years, $\chi^2(1) = 4.917$, $p < .05$. On the other hand, significant positive associations were observed between emotional or psychiatric condition and three-year persistence and between dyslexia and both measures of persistence.

Chi-square tests were also conducted to see whether there was any significant association between any of the students' demographic and in-college characteristics and their likelihood of persistence. Results from these chi-square tests, provided in Table 2, reveal that delayed enrollment decreased the likelihood of both first-to-second-year persistence, $\chi^2(1) = 22.127$, $p < .001$, and three-year persistence, $\chi^2(1) = 29.959$, $p < .001$, with phi statistics of $-.16$ and $-.18$, respectively ($p < .001$). More specifically, 67.4% of the students who delayed their enrollment for 1 year or more after finishing high school did not persist through the second year, as opposed to 32.6% who enrolled in college right after high school. Similarly, in terms of their three-year persistence, 62.8% of the nonpersisters had delayed enrollment, and 37.2% did not have a gap between high school and college. Higher degree aspirations were also significantly and positively associated with both persistence outcomes, $\chi^2(4) = 10.816$, $p < .05$, and $\chi^2(4) = 16.711$, $p < .01$, with Cramer's values of .11 and .14, respectively.

As illustrated in Table 2, full-time enrollment during the first year in college was not significantly related to three-year cumulative persistence; however, it had a positive effect on the first-to-second-year persistence, $\chi^2(1) = 23.722$, $p < .001$, with the phi value of .16. More specifically, among the first-to-second-year nonpersisters, 65.5% were enrolled part-time or mixed (i.e., both part-time and full-time at differing points during the academic year) compared to only 34.5% who were enrolled fulltime. GPA was not significantly related to the likelihood of first-to-second-year persistence. On the other hand, higher first-year GPAs increased the likelihood of persistence over the three-year period, $\chi^2(3) = 11.557$, $p < .01$, with a significant Cramer's V of .11 ($p < .01$). Finally, chi-square tests were also conducted to observe any significant association between academic involvement and persistence. As indicated by chi-square values in Table 3, among academic integration variables, meetings with academic advisors had a significant positive association with students' long-term persistence outcome, $\chi^2(2) = 6.571$, $p < .05$, with a Cramer's V statistic of .09 ($p < .05$). More frequent academic advisor meetings decreased the likelihood of a student leaving without return over a three-year period.

Discussion

Two-year colleges serve the largest segment of the population of postsecondary students with disabilities and offer educational options and academic supports that may not be available at four-year institutions, yet half of the two-year college students with disabilities in our nationally representative sample failed to persist, transfer, or complete a degree or a certificate by the end of their third year. This finding represents a pressing problem for administrators and disability support staff members at two-year institutions, and failure to seriously examine what these institutions can do to increase the persistence rates of students with disabilities disadvantages a large segment of the student population. Also of concern is our finding that having an orthopedic or physical condition was negatively associated with three-year cumulative persistence because students with these conditions represented the largest portion of the total sample of students with disabilities. It is also noteworthy that depression decreased the likelihood of first-to-second-year persistence. The onset of depression typically occurs during adolescence or young adulthood, and the symptoms associated with depression (e.g., insomnia, fatigue, diminished ability to concentrate) can substantially interfere with one's ability to fulfill the requirements of postsecondary education (Collins & Mowbray, 2005). Consequently, the stress of transitioning into postsecondary education is often compounded by the simultaneous onset of disruptive symptoms.

On the other hand, emotional or psychiatric conditions were positively associated with three-year cumulative persistence. This finding is promising in light of prior research indicating that approximately 86% of individuals with psychiatric disabilities withdraw from college prior to completion of their program of study (Collins & Mowbray, 2005). Greater stigma is often associated with psychiatric disabilities, in comparison to physical disabilities, because of the ambiguous nature of these conditions (Smart, 2009), and prior research has indicated that students with psychiatric disabilities are often hesitant to request the academic supports necessary for their success out of fear that the responses they will receive will be negative (Brokelman, Chadsey, & Loeb, 2006; Collins & Mowbray, 2005). Perhaps our finding reflects a positive change in attitudes toward psychiatric disability as well as improvements in the capacity of two-year institutions to academically support and retain these students. The same could hold true for students with learning disabilities, specifically with dyslexia, whose disability type was positively associated with persistence. It appears that two-year institutions are doing an adequate job of accommodating students with learning disabilities in a way that facilitates their persistence, and research has, in fact, documented that two-year institutions possess many characteristics that facilitate the persistence of students with learning disabilities to completion of their programs of study (McCleary-Jones, 2008). Finally, in interpreting the findings regarding the association of disability type to persistence, it must be taken into consideration that responses were derived from the question, "What is the main type of condition or impairment you have?" and survey respondents were instructed to choose only one disability type. This imposes limitations on our ability to truly understand the impact of disability type on persistence and necessitates further research.

Assistance with examinations and the provision of tutors to assist with homework were among the most frequently received accommodations by students with disabilities in this study. These were also the services that were most frequently mentioned as those that were needed but not received. Access to appropriate accommodations may play a critical role in the success of students with disabilities; however, based on our study, it was difficult to determine the reasons why students did not receive these accommodations. In the postsecondary education context, it is the student's responsibility to request the services and present the necessary documentation to receive the supports (Getzel, 2008). Students with disabilities may not be aware of what the process is for obtaining and utilizing these accommodations, or they may not be ready to disclose their disability and ask for specific services. Getzel indicated that "understanding how to access and use accommodations is a critical self-determination skill" (p. 210) for college students with disabilities and institutions need to assist these students with the development of these skills.

More than half of the students with disabilities in this study (53.7%) delayed their enrollment in postsecondary education after finishing high school. In addition, 51.0% maintained only part-time or mixed enrollments during their first year in college. The study showed that both of these non-traditional student indicators put students with disabilities at a higher risk of dropping out and decreased their likelihood of persistence. These findings are consistent with much of the previous research on students without disabilities as well (e.g., Craig & Ward, 2007-2008; Summers, 2003). However, delaying enrollment in college and navigating full-time enrollment during their first year may create additional challenges that are unique to students with disabilities. Getzel (2008) stated that adjusting to college life is difficult for all students, but managing accommodations together with the demands of postsecondary education may have greater effects on the persistence of students with disabilities.

Our study also revealed that having higher GPAs and degree aspirations during the first year in college were associated with an increased likelihood of persistence. It is also noteworthy that the majority of students with disabilities in this study entered two-year institutions with high degree expectations. Almost 77.0% of the students aspired to earn a bachelor's degree or higher, yet half of the students with disabilities in this study (50.6%) left without returning at some point over a three-year period. These findings suggest that there is a mismatch between what these students aspire to and what actually happens once they start navigating postsecondary education.

Previous research has consistently demonstrated that students greatly benefit from in- or out-of-classroom interactions with their peers, faculty members, and staff members. For students with disabilities, these interactions create a sense of inclusiveness and belonging that become essential elements for their success in college (Belch, 2004-2005; Johnson, 2000). A mixed-methods study by McCleary-Jones (2008) examining the experiences of students with learning disabilities at two community colleges indicated that faculty members play an important role in the success of these students. McCleary-Jones concluded that in the context of similar resources and accommodations, the students with disabilities were retained longer and had higher GPAs at the community college that had a better rapport between faculty members and these students. Given the significance of involvement with peers and faculty members, it is concerning to find that majority of students with disabilities attending two-year institutions in our study never had informal meetings with faculty members and never participated in study groups (73.0% and 59.9%, respectively).

In addition, 44.3% of students in this study reported that they never met with their academic advisors during their first year in college. This latter finding is particularly significant because the analyses revealed that more frequent academic advisor meetings during the first year in college were positively and significantly associated with three-year persistence of students with disabilities. Previous research shows that meetings with academic advisors facilitate students' short- and long-term academic planning and assist them with choosing the right course of study to complete an associate's degree or transfer to a four-year institution (Purnell, Blank, Scrivener, & Seupersad, 2004). Academic advisors may play a critical role in the process of educational planning that leads to successful college outcomes. For example, after examining transfer patterns of 31,590 students with disabilities in the California community college system over a 12-year period, Ponticelli and Russ-Eft (2009) found that course enrollment patterns (e.g., the proportion of transferable courses or credit completed, the number of degree-applicable courses completed) were among the strongest predictors of transfer.

Implications for Policy and Future Research

The findings of our study have important implications for policy and future research. The focus should not just be on improving access to college for students with disabilities but also on helping these students persist to degree completion once they are in college. The focus on improving successful outcomes of college must start at the secondary school level. School counselors and special educators should encourage students with disabilities to enter postsecondary education soon after finishing high school and educate them on the process of requesting and utilizing accommodations in college. Once in college, academic advisors and disability services staff members should assist these students with academic planning and choosing a program of study that is realistic and fits their goals. Full-time enrollment should be encouraged when the abilities and circumstances of the student make full-time study possible. New student orientation programs should be used to lay the foundation for students' academic integration through encouraging frequent interactions with faculty and academic advisors (Nippert, 2000-2001). In addition, our findings seem to suggest that two-year institutions need to further improve the persistence of students with disabilities, especially those with depression and physical or orthopedic conditions, by (a) removing environmental barriers that impede persistence in addition to providing classroom accommodations, and (b) coupling supports such as health management and campus-based mental health services with the academic supports that are offered by campus disability services offices (Collins & Mowbray, 2005).

The study revealed that students with disabilities enroll in two-year institutions with high degree aspirations. But our study also showed that having high aspirations may not be sufficient without proper academic planning and realistic action plans. Faculty and staff members working with students with disabilities need to foster high goals and aspirations in these students, but, at the same time, they need to provide proper supports to help them persevere and achieve their goals. Yuen and Shaughnessy (2001) have recommended helping students with disabilities develop life plans based on their goals, objectives, and available resources. They suggested the use of reflective journals and discussions to help students become more self-aware, develop options, and find resources to fulfill their goals.

Academic integration through faculty and peer interactions should continuously be encouraged. Faculty members can play a critical role in creating a learning environment that encourages collaboration with peers within and outside of the classroom. Recent studies (e.g., Deil-Amen, 2011; Karp et al., 2010-2011) have shown that for community college students, relationships that begin in the classroom extend beyond academics to the social spheres of their lives. Student-centered, collaborative learning opportunities, such as study groups, can be one way to foster these relationships and a sense of connectedness with the institution for students with disabilities.

The study has several limitations that must be acknowledged. We examined the availability of disability-related accommodations (i.e., whether the student received a service or whether the student needed a service but did not receive it); however, it should be noted that having access to specific services does not mean that the services are necessarily appropriate or effective. For example, Kurth and Mellard (2006) examined community college students' perceptions of the accommodation process and found that participants rated many accommodations typically found on college campuses as ineffective "at least 25% of the time" (p. 81). Future study needs to further examine the effectiveness of the accommodations provided to students with disabilities at two-year institutions.

Our study examined persistence of students with disabilities through the second year in college and by the end of their third year in college. Previous research has indicated that students with disabilities generally take longer to complete their course of study and graduate (e.g., Murray, Goldstein, Nourse, & Edgar, 2000). On the basis of our findings, we were not able to determine whether the students who were on the persistence track but who had not yet transferred to a four-year institution or completed any degree or certificate by the end of the third year would eventually be achieving these outcomes. Future study needs to examine persistence pathways and educational outcomes of students with disabilities at two-year institutions over a longer time frame than 3 years. It is through "program completion that students realize the greatest economic benefits of higher education" (Corrigan, 2003, p. 25). A college degree leads to better employment outcomes, greater earning power, and overall improved quality of life. Therefore, it is important to know whether the students with disabilities who stayed on the persistence track for the first 3 years would eventually earn their degrees.

Declaration of Conflicting Interests

The authors declared no potential conflicts of interest with respect to the research, authorship, and/or publication of this article.

Funding

The authors received no financial support for the research, authorship, and/or publication of this article.

References

Ankeny, E. M., & Lehmann, J. P. (2010). The transition lynchpin: The voices of individuals with disabilities who attended a community college transition program. *Community College Journal of Research and Practice, 34,* 477–496.

Bailey, T. (2009). Challenge and opportunity: Rethinking the role and function of developmental education in community college. In A. C. Bueschel & A. Venezia (Eds.), *Policies and practices to improve student preparation and success* (New Directions for Community Colleges, No. 145, pp. 11–30). San Francisco, CA: Jossey-Bass.

Bailey, T. R., & Alfonso, M. (2005). *Paths to persistence: An analysis of research on program effectiveness at community college* (New Agenda Series, Vol. 6, No. 1) Indianapolis, IN: Lumina Foundation for Education. (ERIC Document Reproduction Service No. ED484239)

Barbatis, P. (2010). Underprepared, ethnically diverse community college students: Factors contributing to persistence. *Journal of Developmental Education, 33*(3), 14–24.

Bean, J. P., & Metzner, B. S. (1985). A conceptual model of nontraditional undergraduate student attrition. *Review of Educational Research, 55*(4), 485–540.

Belch, H. A. (2004-2005). Retention and students with disabilities. *Journal of College Student Retention, 6*(1), 3–22.

Bers, T. H., & Smith, K. E. (1991). Persistence of community college students: The influence of student intent and academic and social integration. *Research in Higher Education, 32,* 539–556.

Braxton, J. M., & Hirschy, A. S. (2005). Theoretical developments in the study of college student departure. In A. Seidman (Ed.), *College student retention: Formula for student success* (pp. 61–87). Westport, CT: Praeger.

Braxton, J. M., Hirschy, A. S., & McClendon, S. A. (2004). *Understanding and reducing college student departure* (ASHE-ERIC Higher Education Research Report Series, Vol. 30, No. 3). San Francisco, CA: Jossey-Bass.

Brokelman, K. F., Chadsey, J. G., & Loeb, J. W. (2006). Faculty perceptions of university students with psychiatric disabilities. *Psychiatric Rehabilitation Journal, 30,* 23–30.

Collins, M. E., & Mowbray, C. T. (2005). Higher education and psychiatric disabilities: National survey of campus disability services. *American Journal of Orthopsychiatry, 75,* 304–315.

Cominole, M., Wheeless, S., Dudley, K., Franklin, J., Wine, J., & Hunt-White, T. (2007). *2004/06 Beginning Postsecondary Students Longitudinal Study (BPS:04/06) methodology report* (NCES 2008-184). Washington, DC: National Center for Education Statistics.

Corrigan, M. E. (2003). Beyond access: Persistence challenges and the diversity of low-income students. In J. E. King, E. L. Anderson, & M. E. Corrigan (Eds.), *Changing student attendance patterns: Challenges for policy and practice* (New Directions for Higher Education, No. 121, pp. 25–34). San Francisco, CA: Jossey-Bass.

Craig, A. J., & Ward, C. V. L. (2007-2008). Retention of community college students: Related student and institutional characteristics. *Journal of College Student Retention, 9*(4), 505–517.

Creswell, J. W. (2008). *Educational research: Planning, conducting, and evaluating quantitative and qualitative research* (3rd ed.). Upper Saddle River, NJ: Pearson.

Crews, D. M., & Aragon, S. R. (2004). Influence of a community college developmental education writing course on academic performance. *Community College Review, 32*(2), 1–18.

DaDeppo, L. M. W. (2009). Integration factors related to the academic success and intent to persist of college students with learning disabilities. *Learning Disabilities Research & Practice, 24,* 122–131.

Deil-Amen, R. (2011). Socio-academic integrative moments: Rethinking academic and social integration among two-year college students in career-related programs. *The Journal of Higher Education, 82,* 54–91.

Field, A. (2005). *Discovering statistics using SPSS* (2nd ed.). Thousand Oaks, CA: Sage.

Fike, D. S., & Fike, R. (2008). Predictors of first-year student retention in the community college. *Community College Review, 36*(2), 68–88.

Garrison-Wade, D. F., & Lehmann, J. P. (2009). A conceptual framework for understanding students' with disabilities transition to community college. *Community College Journal of Research and Practice, 33,* 417–445.

Getzel, E. E. (2008). Addressing the persistence and retention of students in higher education: Incorporating key strategies and supports on campus. *Exceptionality, 16,* 207–219.

Getzel, E. E., Stodden, R. A., & Briel, L. W. (2001). Pursuing postsecondary education opportunities for individuals with disabilities. In P. Wehman (Ed.), *Life beyond the classroom: Transition strategies for young people with disabilities* (3rd ed., pp. 247–259). Baltimore, MD: Paul H. Brookes.

Hagedorn, L. S. (2005). How to define retention: A new look at an old problem. In A. Seidman (Ed.), *College student retention: Formula for student success* (pp. 89-106). Westport, CT: Praeger.

Hagedorn, L. S., Maxwell, W., Rodriguez, P., Hocevar, D., & Fillpot, J. (2000). Peer and student-faculty relations in community colleges. *Community College Journal of Research and Practice, 24,* 587–598.

Hawke, C. S. (2004). Accommodating students with disabilities. In R. C. Cloud (Ed.), *Legal issues in the community college* (New Directions for Community Colleges, No. 127, pp. 17–27). San Francisco, CA: Jossey-Bass.

Horn, L., Peter, K., & Rooney, K. (2002). *Profiles of undergraduates in U.S. postsecondary institutions: 1999-2000* (NCES 2002-168). Washington, DC: National Center for Education Statistics.

Hoyt, J. E. (1999). Remedial education and student attrition. *Community College Review, 27*(2), 51–71.

Johnson, D. (2000). Enhancing out-of-class opportunities for students with disabilities. In H. A. Belch (Ed.), *Serving students with disabilities* (New Directions for Student Services, No. 91, pp. 41–53). San Francisco, CA: Jossey-Bass.

Johnson, G., Zascavage, V., & Gerber, S. (2008). Junior college experience and students with learning disabilities: Implications for success at the four-year university. *College Student Journal, 42,* 1162–1168.

Karp, M. M., Hughes, K. L., & O'Gara, L. (2010-2011). An exploration of Tinto's integration framework for community college students. *Journal of College Student Retention, 12*(1), 69–86.

Kurth, N., & Mellard, D. (2006). Student perceptions of the accommodation process in postsecondary education. *Journal of Postsecondary Education and Disability, 19*(1), 71–84.

Lindstrom, L. E., Flannery, K. B., Benz, M. R., Olszewski, B., & Slovic, R. (2009). Building employment training partnerships between vocational rehabilitation and community colleges. *Rehabilitation Counseling Bulletin, 52*, 189–201.

Mamiseishvili, K., & Koch, L. C. (2011). First-to-second-year persistence of students with disabilities in postsecondary institutions in the United States. *Rehabilitation Counseling Bulletin, 54*(2), 93-105. doi:10.1177/0034355210382580

McCleary-Jones, V. (2008). Students with learning disabilities in the community college: Their goals, issues, challenges and successes. *ABNF Journal, 19*, 14–21.

Murray, C., Goldstein, D. E., Nourse, S., & Edgar, E. (2000). The postsecondary school attendance and completion rates of high school graduates with learning disabilities. *Learning Disabilities Research and Practice, 15*, 119–127.

Mutter, P. (1992). Tinto's theory of departure and community college student persistence. *Journal of College Student Development, 33*, 310–317.

Nippert, K. (2000-2001). Influences on the educational degree attainment of two-year college students. *Journal of College Student Retention, 2*(1), 29–40.

Ponticelli, J. E., & Russ-Eft, D. (2009). Community college students with disabilities and transfer to a four-year college. *Exceptionality, 17*, 164–176.

Prentice, M. (2002). *Serving students with disabilities at the community college* (Report No. EDO-JC-0202). Los Angeles, CA: ERIC Clearinghouse for Community Colleges. (ERIC Document Reproduction Service No. ED467984)

Purnell, R., Blank, S., Scrivener, S., & Seupersad, R. (2004). *Opening doors: Support success services that may help low-income students succeed in community college*. Retrieved from http://www.mdrc.org/publications/399/full.pdf

Quick, D., Lehmann, J., & Deniston, T. (2003). Opening doors for students with disabilities on community college campuses: What have we learned? What do we still need to know? *Community College Journal of Research and Practice, 27*, 815–827.

Raue, K., & Lewis, L. (2011). *Students with disabilities at degree-granting postsecondary institutions* (NCES 2011-018). Washington, DC: National Center for Education Statistics.

Smart, J. (2009). *Disability, society, and the individual* (2nd ed.). Austin, TX: Pro-Ed.

Summers, M. D. (2003). ERIC review: Attrition research at community colleges. *Community College Review, 30*(4), 64–84.

Thomas, S. L., & Heck, R. H. (2001). Analysis of large-scale secondary data in higher education research: Potential perils associated with complex sampling designs. *Research in Higher Education, 42*, 517–540.

Tinto, V. (1975). Dropout from higher education: A theoretical synthesis of recent research. *Review of Educational Research, 45*, 89–125.

Tinto, V. (1993). *Leaving college: Rethinking the causes and cures of student attrition* (2nd ed.). Chicago, IL: University of Chicago Press.

Vogel, S. A., & Adelman, P. B. (1992). The success of college students with learning disabilities: Factors related to educational attainment. *Journal of Learning Disabilities, 25*, 430–441.

Walpole, M. (2007). *Economically and educationally challenged students in higher education: Access to outcomes* (ASHE Higher Education Report, Vol. 33, No. 3) San Francisco, CA: Jossey-Bass.

Wessel, R. D., Jones, J. A., Markle, L., & Westfall, C. (2009). Retention and graduation of students with disabilities: Facilitating student success. *Journal of Postsecondary Education and Disability, 21*, 116–125.

Yuen, J. W. L., & Shaughnessy, B. (2001). Cultural empowerment: Tools to engage and retain postsecondary students with disabilities. *Journal of Vocational Rehabilitation, 16*, 199–207.

Ketevan Mamiseishvili is assistant professor of higher education in the Department of Rehabilitation, Human Resources and Communication Disorders at the University of Arkansas, Fayetteville.

Lynn C. Koch is professor of rehabilitation education and research in the Department of Rehabilitation, Human Resources and Communication Disorders at the University of Arkansas, Fayetteville.

SECTION VI

CAREER-TECHNICAL AND WORKFORCE EDUCATION

SECTION VI: CAREER-TECHNICAL AND WORKFORCE EDUCATION

Whereas career and technical education (CTE) and workforce education are strongly related, these concepts have different meanings within the community college environment. With CTE having its genesis as vocational education at the high school level in the early 1990s, the notion of workforce education was not formulated until later in the 20th century when the labor force required postsecondary education of a more specialized and technical nature. Generally accepted today, CTE and workforce education are vital components of a comprehensive community college curriculum that is needed to prepare youth and adults for family-wage employment.

Predominant theories associated with CTE and workforce education include human capital, globalization, signaling theory, and sheepskin theory. Specifically, CTE is seen as important to building a competent workforce through human capital investment. Related to human capital theory is signaling theory, which suggests that an individual's ability to perform in the workplace is largely obscured from employers who need cues or signals to inform them when a person possesses the ability to perform productively in a job. Signaling theory provides rationale for why employers advocate for credentials and stridently encourage the education system to adopt them. Sheepskin effects extend from signaling theory, suggesting individuals who receive credentials experience benefits over and above students with comparable education but no credentials. In an age where credentialing has assumed a top priority on the nation's college completion agenda, an examination of the role of CTE and workforce education in awarding credentials to diverse students is important.

Chapter Thirty-Two, "The community college: Educating students at the margin between college and work," authored by Kane and Rouse, examines a number of issues pertaining to the benefits of a community college education, including the labor market payoffs to community college education. Their article considers this important question from the standpoint of panel study data, census data, and experimental studies. Their research is important because it considers the effects of college credits as well as the sheepskin effects attributable to an associate's degree. Kane and Rouse conclude that labor market returns to community college attendance are comparable to four-year college attendance, they are higher for women than men, and they are higher for students enrolled in quantitatively or technically-oriented courses, such as health, technical/professional, technical trade, science and math courses. The authors point out experimental studies have not produced as promising results as panel studies; however, problems with measurement explains to some degree why the studies differed from panel study research. Their research also suggests that there are sheepskin effects for white men and especially for white women, with much of this effect attributable to women's completion of nursing degrees.

Chapter Thirty-Three by Bragg, "Career and technical education," discusses the philosophical and theoretical debates that were present at the origins of vocational education in the early 1900s, and traces these debates through to the present when vocational education became known as career and technical education (CTE) and the application of work-oriented education became integral to the secondary and postsecondary education systems. This chapter points out how the debate over essentialism versus pragmatism framed the understanding of differentiated instruction and tracking, including detrimental effects, and the evolution of new vocational reforms that have emerged over the past two decades. Whereas the human capital rationale looms large as a rationale for CTE, evidence of economic benefits remains surprisingly limited, particularly for under-represented students. Whereas critics have complained about this limited evidence, some educators have argued for CTE to be a response to social issues by having a democratizing effect on the educational system. This argument suggests that CTE is not so much about preparing people for work as about whetting their appetite for learning and providing them with opportunities to navigate through education and into the labor market, and contributing to quality of life.

Chapter Thirty-Four, "Socio-academic integrative moments: Rethinking academic and social integration among two-year college students in career-related programs," by Regina Deil-Amen notes that little research has focused on community college or private two-year college students, despite the fact that about half of first-time postsecondary students enroll in a two-year college. Deil-Amen's study used qualitative data to examine Tinto's Theory of Student Departure to understand persistence for two-year college commuting students whom she identified as one among many nontraditional student groups, the preponderance of whom never obtain any postsecondary credentials. To reflect how students successfully cultivate feelings of belonging and competence, reinforce goal commitment, and access valuable social capital, a new conceptual fusion of the formerly distinct processes of academic integration and social integration is considered. Her description of proactive guidance and procedural agency provide a useful means of understanding how two-year college students experience academic and social integration in career-related programs. She cautions researchers to not dismiss past theories but rather suggests that there may be value in integrating them with current research on the experiences of marginalized and minority students.

In Chapter Thirty-Five, "Teaching by choice: Community colleges expand K-12 STEM pathways and practices," Patton shares concerns regarding the United States maintaining a competitive edge in the global knowledge economy in lieu of changing demographics as well as the supply and demand for highly qualified K-12 teachers in science, technology, engineering, and mathematics (STEM). The shortage of competent STEM teachers in elementary and secondary schools mirrors the shortage of workers in the U.S. labor market with STEM skill gaps. Patton asserts community colleges are key players in narrowing the STEM skills gap through teacher education programs at two-year institutions. Patton's work highlights collaboration of the American Association of Community Colleges with the National Association of Community College Teacher Education Programs to further K-12 professional development opportunities in STEM education and enhance STEM pathways via transfer and post-baccalaureate programming at community colleges.

Chapter Thirty-Six, "The community college baccalaureate in the U.S.: Models, programs, and issues," by Floyd documents the emergence of the community college baccalaureate in the United States. The author describes various models for increasing access to baccalaureate programming at community colleges, identifying concerns and issues raised by a modern trend that is considered controversial across various stakeholder groups. Floyd offers a typology of community colleges and baccalaureate degrees, sharing the rationale for delivery of this model of four-year degree programs particularly in areas such as business, computer science, criminal justice, elementary education, and nursing.

The demand for four-year degrees is high in some states and the ability of four-year institutions to meet the demand is limited, which can produce overcrowding of four-year colleges. However, the community college is arguably poised to extend applied baccalaureates in technical areas of expertise that subsequently would meet local, state, and regional workforce needs. Chapter Thirty-Seven in this section, "Update on the community college baccalaureate: Evolving trends and issues," authored by Russell discloses that the community college baccalaureate is not a new trend as there has been substantial growth, yet there is variation state by state in the number of community college baccalaureate degree options. Russell discusses how the multiple missions of the community college are juggled as an institution shifts from a two-year into a baccalaureate institution. This chapter frames the arguments for and against community colleges offering baccalaureate degrees with this route to a four-year degree still being more of the exception than the rule.

CHAPTER 32

THE COMMUNITY COLLEGE: EDUCATING STUDENTS AT THE MARGIN BETWEEN COLLEGE AND WORK

THOMAS J. KANE AND CECILIA ELENA ROUSE

Community colleges have assumed an increasingly central role in the nation's education and training system. Between 1980 and 1994, the proportion of 18- to 24-year-olds enrolled in college grew by more than one third, from 26 to 36 percent. Nearly half of this increase in enrollment was absorbed at community colleges (U.S. Department of Education, 1997, Tables 178 and 186, p. 188, 196). Yet despite the increasing interest in community colleges among both students and policymakers as a potential source of education for workers seeking to upgrade their skills, relatively little is known about them.

We have four goals in this paper. The first is to provide background on the history and development of community colleges in the United States in the last half century. Second, we survey the available evidence on the impacts of community colleges on educational attainment and earnings. Third, we weigh the evidence on the impact of public subsidies on enrollment at community colleges and explore some weaknesses in the current higher education financing structure. Finally, we reflect on how the students who have been responding to the rise in the payoff to education are to be absorbed by our postsecondary training institutions.

The History and Development of Community Colleges

In the late 19th century, when William Rainey Harper, founding president of the University of Chicago, developed a plan to separate the first two years of college from the second two years, he started a movement that would revolutionize higher education. The plan, modeled after the German "Gymnasium," was to create university-affiliated six-year high schools and two-year colleges, called "junior colleges," that would teach students the lower-division "preparatory" material. Although their evolution differed across the country, junior colleges were generally designed to increase access to higher education without compromising and burdening the existing four-year colleges. These colleges are generally defined as "any institution accredited to award the associate's in arts or science as its highest degree" (Cohen and Brawer, 1982, pp. 5–6). This definition includes comprehensive two-year colleges and many technical institutes (both public and private), but it excludes publicly funded vocational schools, adult education centers, and most proprietary schools. In this article, we use the terms "community college," "junior college," and "two-year college" interchangeably.[1]

429

The first phase in the expansion of junior colleges began after World War II when millions of former military personnel were given a tuition voucher under the GI Bill to attend college. Between 1944 and 1947, enrollments in junior colleges nearly doubled. The end of the Korean War brought another similar increase in junior college enrollments (Witt et al., 1994). The final phase in the expansion occurred in the 1960s, when the first baby boomers began to reach college age, Vietnam War veterans began to return home, and Americans enrolled in college to avoid the military draft. Over the 1960s, the number of junior colleges more than doubled and enrollments quadrupled (Witt et al., 1994). This immense expansion led Clark Kerr, an architect of the California higher education system, to term the junior college the great innovation in American higher education in the 20th century (Brint and Karabel, 1989, p. v).

Originally, junior colleges focused on what is termed the "transfer function": students would complete two years of a general undergraduate education and earn an associate's degree (AA) at the two-year college, and those who wanted to and were capable would transfer to a four-year college to complete a bachelor's degree. Since then, two-year colleges have broadened their mission to include vocational degree programs, continuing adult education programs, and workforce, economic and community development programs. In addition, community colleges have traditionally striven to increase access to higher education through an open admissions policy—often not even requiring a high school diploma—and low, or no, tuition. In 1996–97, full-time students paid, on average, $1,283 for annual tuition and required fees at public two-year colleges compared to $2,986 at public four-year colleges (U.S. Department of Education, 1997).

Although private junior colleges were common at the turn of the century—at that time, only 26 percent of two-year colleges were public—96 percent of the 5.5 million students enrolled in two-year colleges in 1995 were enrolled in public institutions (U.S. Department of Education, 1997). These 5.5 million students represent 38 percent of enrollments in all postsecondary institutions and 48 percent of enrollments in public institutions (U.S. Department of Education, 1997). Figure 1 shows the importance of community colleges by graphing the proportion of first-time first-year students enrolled in public two-year colleges from 1955 through 1995. In 1955, only 17 percent of all such students were enrolled in a public two-year college; today, that percentage has grown to 44 percent.

This explosion in enrollment in community colleges was powered primarily by the growth in part-time students. Part-time enrollments in public two-year colleges increased 222 percent between 1970 and 1995, compared to an increase of 63 percent in full-time enrollments. Today, roughly 65 percent of community college students attend part-time.

Although community colleges exist nationwide, they are not equally represented in all states. In California, which enrolls one-fifth of all students enrolled in public two-year colleges, 47 percent of all college enrollments are in public two-year colleges—compared to Louisiana and Montana which each have less than 7 percent. States with more developed four-year college systems tend to have less developed two-year college systems, and vice versa, suggesting that states choose to invest in one system or the other (Rouse, 1998).

The faculty at two-year colleges also differs from that at four-year colleges. The master's degree is the highest degree of 64 percent of full-time faculty in public community colleges, while

Source: *Digest of Education Statistics* (1997).

Figure 1   Proportion of First-time First-year Students in Public Two-year Colleges

68 percent of four-year comprehensive college faculty have doctorates. Almost two-thirds (60 percent) of the faculty at public two-year colleges teach part-time, compared to one-third of comprehensive four-year college faculty. Only 32 percent of the full-time faculty at public two-year colleges hold a rank of either associate or full professor, compared to over 60 percent at public four-year universities. Instead, community colleges rely more heavily on non-tenure track faculty; 40 percent of community college faculty hold a rank of instructor or lecturer and 11 percent have no rank; for comparison, 11 percent of faculty at comprehensive and 8 percent at public research universities hold the rank of instructor or lecturer, and fewer than 1 percent have no rank (U.S. Department of Education, 1997). Of course, the heavy reliance on part-time and adjunct faculty help maintain community colleges' flexibility to respond to changing educational needs in the community.

Community college faculty also spend far more time on teaching than their four-year college counterparts. Two-year college faculty spend 69 percent of their time teaching and 4 percent of their time conducting research or scholarship (the bulk of the rest of their time is spent on administration, non-teaching service, and professional development), while faculty at comprehensive public four-year colleges spend 60 percent of their time teaching, and faculty at public research universities spend 40 percent of their time teaching. Similarly, 58 percent of faculty at community colleges teach more than 15 hours per week, compared to 18 percent of faculty at comprehensive four-year colleges and 7 percent of faculty at public research universities (U.S. Department of Education, 1997). The focus on teaching both lowers the educational costs and is hailed by many students as an advantage of attending a community college, particularly for those who seek more personal attention in the classroom.

Who Goes to Community College?

About one-third of all high school graduates will attend a community college at some point in their lives (Rouse, 1994). Compared to students who first enroll in a four-year college, community college students are more likely to be the first in their family to attend college and are much less likely to have parents who have graduated from a four-year college. The combined student body of community colleges is 70 percent white, 11 percent black, and 11 percent Hispanic. Almost 36 percent of community college students are at least 30 years old, compared to only 22 percent of public four-year college students. As noted above, most community college students attend part-time.

A community college education appeals to many students because of the lower costs of attendance. The average tuition is less than one-half that at public four year colleges, and because community colleges are located in most towns and cities, many students can live at home while attending college.[2] Community colleges have also lowered other costs of attendance. Courses are not only offered during the "traditional" daytime hours, but also at night and on weekends. Many community colleges offer courses at work sites, or via audio, video, or computer technologies. As a result, 84 percent of community college students work while also attending college compared to 78 percent of students attending public comprehensive four year colleges. Although the proportion of students reporting some employment is comparable at two-year and comprehensive four-year colleges, roughly one-half of those attending a community college who are employed report work as their primary activity, compared to only one-quarter of those attending public comprehensive four-year colleges (Horn, Becktold and Malizio, 1998).

Do the attractively low tuition and neighborhood convenience of community colleges divert students from four-year colleges? Or do they provide a place in higher education for those who would not have otherwise attended college? Of course, the social importance of this issue ultimately depends on the extent to which the type of institution one attends affects one's educational attainment, as we discuss below. The few studies that attempt to address such issues tend to find that community colleges draw both types of students, although it appears that slightly more than half of community college students are non-traditional students who probably would not have attended four-year institutions (Grubb, 1989; Rouse, 1995, 1998). This suggests that community colleges have increased overall educational attainment, and that a major role of community colleges is to provide a place in higher education for those not traditionally served by the four-year college system.

The Changing Shape of a Community College Education

Originally, students at community colleges completed courses that mimicked the first two years of a university curriculum before transferring to a four-year college. As a result, most students followed an academic curriculum delivered in a traditional manner. Today, however, community college courses have taken a variety of other approaches.

A significant fraction of community college students enroll in terminal (usually vocational) degree programs. Community colleges also serve an important remediating function within our higher education system. In 1995, almost all public two year colleges provided remedial courses, compared to 81 percent of public four year institutions (Lewis, Farris and Greene, 1996). About 41 percent of community college students took at least one remedial course compared to only 22 percent of public four-year college students. There seems to be an increased interest in limiting the amount of remediation done at four-year colleges; for example, the trustees of the City University of New York (CUNY) voted in May 1998 to deny admission to students who cannot pass reading, writing, and mathematics proficiency tests (Arenson, 1998). If educational offerings of four-year colleges are limited in this way, the remediation role of community colleges is likely to increase.

As another example of their flexibility in adapting to labor market conditions, a growing number of community colleges are providing contract training—that is, classes offered to employees of a business, industry, labor union, or public agency—often at a site designated by the contracting agency. As of the late 1980s, 94 percent of community colleges provided at least one course by contract. The most common form of contract training was teaching the job-specific skills needed to perform a job, to improve current performance, or to prepare for advancement on a contract basis with firms; 93 percent of community colleges provided such courses (Lynch, Palmer and Grubb, 1991). Sixty percent of community colleges provided contract courses in basic reading, writing, or math skills. The median ratio of contract enrollment (in 1988-89) to regular credit enrollment was 0.22, indicating that at one half of colleges there was one or fewer contract students for every five or so regularly enrolled students (Lynch, Palmer and Grubb, 1991). Krueger and Rouse (1998) evaluated one such workplace education program in which a community college provided basic literacy education to employees at a manufacturing company and a service company. They reported positive and significant effects of the training on the wage growth and job progression of employees at the manufacturing company, but no such effects at the service company.

The Net Effect of Community Colleges on Educational Attainment

One concern among observers of community colleges is that as they provide education services in non-traditional ways, the quality of such services may suffer. Critics point to the fact that community college students typically do not complete many college credits. Figure 2 shows the distribution of credits completed at two-year colleges.[3] The credits have been divided by 30 so as to represent years of enrollment on the horizontal axis. The figure shows that a majority of students who ever enroll in a two-year college complete one year or less; 35 percent of students complete only one semester or less.

Similarly, Table 1 shows degree attainment, 10 years after high school, by whether students first attended a two- or four-year college.[4] Of all students who enroll in a two-year college, over one-half do not complete any degrees. About 15 percent complete a certificate, another 16 percent attain an associate's degree and about 16 percent complete at least a bachelor's degree. In contrast, nearly 60 percent of four-year college entrants complete at least a bachelor's degree. The remaining columns of the table refer to opinions that the students expressed about their own future while seniors in high school. While the percentages of students who complete a degree increases among two-year college students who would either be "disappointed if they do not complete college," or feel they are "'definitely' able to complete college," or for whom "a bachelor's degree is the lowest level of education with which they would be satisfied," degree completion still lags considerably behind that of four-year college students.

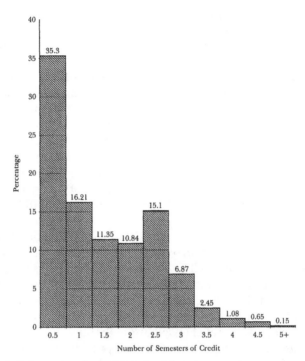

Source: Authors' calculations using the *High School and Beyond.*

Figure 2   Distribution of Two-year College Credits *(among those with positive two year college credits).*

TABLE 1

Degree Attainment by Type of First College Attended and by Degree Aspirations in the 12th Grade
(among high school seniors in 1982/degree attainment as of 1992)

Highest Degree Attained	All	Disappointed if Do Not Complete College	"Definitely" Able to Complete College	BA+ is Lowest Level of Education With Which Would be Satisfied
		Two-year College Students		
None	53.7	47.8	60.1	44.9
Certificate	14.6	12.8	12.9	8.5
Associate's Degree	16.1	18.7	14.8	12.8
Bachelor's Degree	14.8	19.5	11.3	31.0
Graduate Degree	0.8	1.1	0.8	2.9
All		68.0	73.4	17.9
		Four-year College Students		
None	29.4	26.7	39.4	22.5
Certificate	5.3	3.8	6.1	2.5
Associate's Degree	6.4	6.1	7.7	2.8
Bachelor's Degree	48.5	52.2	41.8	56.8
Graduate Degree	10.4	11.3	5.0	15.5
All		87.1	83.5	56.0

Note: Authors' calculations using the High School and Beyond sophomore cohort (self-reported postsecondary attendance and degree attainment). The cells represent percentages of the column. All percentages are weighted using the fifth follow-up panel weight. "Two-year Students" are those who started at a two-year college; "Four-year Students" are those who started at a four-year college.

The skewed distribution of completed credits and the relatively small proportion of students who complete degrees raises an important question: Do two-year college students simply maintain modest educational objectives or is there some aspect of two-year colleges that discourages students from completing more courses? Policymakers in certain states, such as California and New York, are considering limiting enrollment at four-year colleges and encouraging students to begin at a two-year college (Trombley, 1991; Kelley, 1998, p. 2). A key question is whether such a policy will affect the educational attainment of those students denied admission to a four-year college. If educational outcomes of students who begin in a community college only differ from those who begin in a four-year college because the two-year college students desire less education, then students who begin at a two-year college with a certain level of desire for schooling should fare as well as those who begin at a four-year college. However, if it appears that some aspect of community college discourages otherwise equally motivated and prepared students from completing more courses, which is one possible interpretation of Table 1, policymakers might ask why.

One could argue that two-year college students attain less education than four-year college students because, although two-year and four-year college students have the same aspiration levels while seniors in high school, their desired level of schooling changes over time and this change is unrelated to the type of institution that the individuals attend. Of course, if this is the case, policymakers need not be concerned about differences in educational attainment between the two types of institutions. However, it is also possible that the difference is due to some effect of community colleges. Clark (1960) and Brint and Karabel (1989) argue that the vocational education and terminal degree programs of community colleges are not conducive to completing four years of college, even for those who aspire to a four-year college degree. Their thesis is that two-year colleges are not appropriate institutions for students interested in completing a four-year degree because transferring can be costly and burdensome; conversely, they argue, the four-year college environment helps to keep students focused on the bachelor's degree. Essentially these authors argue that many students lack the necessary information to make an informed decision between two- and four-year colleges, and so they do not fully realize in attending a two-year college that they are reducing their chances of completing a four-year degree.

The potential importance of starting at a two-year or four-year college on eventual educational attainment is an empirical issue. But the effect is difficult to estimate, because desired levels of schooling and academic preparation are difficult to measure. Some authors have concluded that students who begin at a two-year college complete less education, on average, than similar students who begin at a four-year college (Alba and Lavin, 1981; Anderson, 1981; Breneman and Nelson, 1981; Dougherty, 1987; Velez, 1985). However, these studies limit their analysis to students who have already started at a college. As a result, they not only miss an important component of the mission of community colleges—to include students who ordinarily would not attend college—but they also bias their estimates of the effect of having been diverted from a four-year college on educational attainment. Rouse (1995) accounts for all students, not just those who have started college, and also uses college proximity as an instrumental variable that is correlated with the type of college first attended, but hypothetically uncorrelated with educational attainment (conditional on the type of college attended). As with other authors, she finds that students who begin at a two-year college (and who otherwise would have attended a four-year college) complete less schooling—about three-quarters of a year—than those who begin at a four-year college. However, unlike the previous literature, she also finds that starting at a two-year college does not appear to affect the likelihood of attaining a bachelor's degree for those diverted from a four-year college. Therefore, it appears there is some negative effect of starting at a two-year college on years of education completed for an individual who would otherwise have attended a four-year college, perhaps because with so few students living on campus, peer effects are not as strong as on four-year campuses and because transferring from a two-year to a four-year college can be difficult and burdensome.

Labor Market Payoffs to Community College

Despite the fact that community colleges enroll a large share of those starting college—and an even larger share of those persuaded by public subsidies to enter college—we know relatively little about the relationship between community college coursework and future earnings. The standard educational attainment question used by the U.S. Bureau of the Census inquires about years of schooling completed (or, more recently, degrees received)—not about the type of institution one attended. The resulting lack of data has been a serious limitation for research on community colleges.

Evidence from Panel Survey Data

The handful of available analyses of the labor market payoffs to community colleges has relied on panel surveys beginning with high school-age youth, which follow respondents through college and beyond, eventually observing sample members' earnings in the years after college. Table 2 summarizes the results from six papers estimating the relationship between community college attendance and earnings.[5] Five of the papers attempt to control for prior differences in academic preparation between college entrants by using either a standardized test score or high school class rank (or both) as regressors. The paper by Jacobson, LaLonde and Sullivan (1997) uses information on earnings prior to college entry to "control for" such differences.

One could draw two primary generalizations from the results reported in Table 2. First, as reported by Leigh and Gill (1997) and Kane and Rouse (1995), the average community college entrant (who never attended a four-year college), who enrolls but does not complete a degree, earns 9 to 13 percent more than the average high school graduate with similar high school grades and/or test scores between the age of 29 and 38. Second, Kane and Rouse (1995), Grubb (1995), and MonkTurner (1994) estimate that each year of credit at a community college is associated with a 5-8 percent increase in annual earnings—which happens to be the same as the estimated value of a year's worth of credit at a four-year college.

Most of the above results are based on the labor market experiences of those who entered community college soon after high school. However, given the recent policy interest in retraining for older workers, the earnings impacts for older adults is of particular interest. The papers by Leigh and Gill (1997) and by Jacobson, LaLonde and Sullivan (1997) provide what evidence we have on this issue. Leigh and Gill test for differences in the educational wage differentials for those entering college at different ages, and do not find evidence that the earnings differentials associated with associate degrees or with community college coursework are any different for the one-third of those who attend community college after age 25. Jacobson, LaLonde and Sullivan's analysis of samples of displaced workers suggests that the earnings differential associated with a year of community college coursework is approximately 2-5 percent. However, the authors estimate substantially larger returns (on the order of 15 percent per year) for courses in more quantitatively or technically-oriented courses such as vocational health, technical/professional, and technical trade courses, and science and math academic courses, but find negligible returns to non-quantitative courses like sales/service, non-technical vocational, social science/humanities, health/physical education/consumer oriented, and basic education. Despite these gains, the average earnings of displaced workers did not return to pre-displacement levels.

Evidence from Differentials by State and Over Time

An alternative approach to analyzing the labor market effects of community colleges is to use evidence on historical differences in the prevalence of community and four-year colleges between states and over time. We used the micro-data from the 1990 census to estimate the difference in each state in the log of annual earnings between high school graduates (with no postsecondary training) and those with "some college, no degree," for 25-34 year-old males.[6] (In an attempt to categorize the men by the states in which they were trained, the income differentials were measured by the state in which men

TABLE 2

Summarizing Research on Labor Market Effects of Community College Education

			Annual Earnings Differential: (relative to high school graduates)	
Authors	Data Sources:	Covariates:	A.A. Degree Holders:	Some College: No Degree
Leigh and Gill (1997)	NLSY (1993)	*Ability Measure:* AFQT Score *Other Covariates:* Race, ethnicity, age, gender, work exp., region, part-time emp.	.235 (.040) (No sig. diff. over age 25)	2-Yr Coll .118 (.031) 4-Yr Coll .093 (.035)
Kane and Rouse (1995)	NLSY(1990)	*Ability Measure:* AFQT Score *Other Covariates:* Race, ethnicity, age, gender, work exp., region, part-time emp., parents' education.	.271 (.038)	2-Yr Coll .100 (.030) 4-Yr Coll .125 (.036)
	NLS-72 (1986)	*Ability Measure:* H.S. Class Rank, NLS-72 Test Score *Other Covariates:* Race, ethnicity, gender, work exp., region, part-time employment, parental income.	.159 (.034) (Differential larger for women)	*Per Year:* 2-Yr Coll .061 (.016) 4-Yr Coll .061 (.012)
Grubb (1995)	NLS-72 (1986)	*Ability Measure:* NLS-72 Test Scores, H.S. Grades *Other Covariates:* Race, ethnicity, parental income, an index of parental socio-economic status, work experience, tenure on current job, indicators for firm-provided training.	Voc. .106 AA (.033) Acad −.021 AA (.044)	*Per Year:* Voc .046 2-Yr (.042) Voc .120 4-Yr (.025) Acad .047 2-Yr (.025) Acad −.012 4-Yr (.014)
Jacobson, LaLonde and Sullivan (1997)	Displaced workers in PA and WA.	*Ability Measure:* Person Fixed Effects *Other Covariates:* Prior industry, age	—	2-Yr, PA .015 (.004) 4-Yr, WA .052 (.005)
Monk-Turner (1994)	Parnes NLS	*Ability Measure:* IQ Score (on H.S. Transcript) *Other Covariates:* Race, gender, parental educ., region, work exp. marital status, educational plans.		*Per Year:* 2-Yr Coll .054 (.02) 4-Yr Coll .079 (.01)
Heineman and Sussna (1977)	HS Graduates (Class of 1964 and 1967)	*Ability Measure:* H.S. Class Rank *Other Covariates:* Race, age, gender, work exp., parental family income, parental education, religion, military service.	.150	—

Note: In the studies which report impacts by year or by gender, the above estimates represent weighted averages using sample sizes as weights. Standard errors for the pooled estimates were calculated under the assumption of independence. Where impacts were reported in dollars, we divided by the relevant average annual earnings to convert to percentages. Where impacts were reported in units of log earnings, we reported log earnings differentials, which approximate percentage differences.

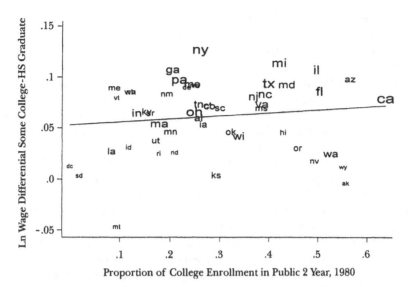

Note: Ln wage differentials for 25-34 year-old males estimated by state using the 1990 5% PUMS. The wage differentials were estimated with separate log wage equations for each state, including regressors for age (10 categories), race/ethnicity, and category of educational attainment. The size of the symbol for each state reflects the reciprocal of the standard error on the estimated coefficient.

Source: Kane and Rouse (1995).

Figure 3   The "Some College" Wage Differential and Community College Enrollment by State

were living five years earlier.) In Figure 3, we then plot these state average earnings differentials by the proportion of enrollment in each state in community colleges. If those attending community colleges were receiving lower earnings differentials from college attendance than those attending four-year colleges, we might expect to see a downward sloping graph. As is apparent from Figure 3, there is no strong relationship between the "some college" earnings differential and the proportion of enrollment in community colleges.[7] In fact, the "some college/high school graduate" earnings difference in California—with relatively large community college enrollments—is higher than the national average. Moreover, as we reported in Kane and Rouse (1995), there is no evidence that the "some college" earnings differential has fallen over time as community college enrollments have risen.

Experimental Evidence

The non-experimental evidence summarized to this point suggests substantial effects of community college training on annual earnings. However, experimental evaluations of training programs have offered a much less optimistic appraisal of the impacts of classroom training for the unemployed and out-of-school youth.[8] For instance, in 1986, the U.S. Department of Labor commissioned an experimental evaluation of training provided to adults and out-of-school youth under the Job Training Partnership Act. Because many of the training providers under the Job Training Partnership Act JTPA) were community colleges—indeed, over one-half of community colleges receive JTPA funds (Lynch, Palmer and Grubb, 1991)—the results of the JTPA evaluation provide another indirect assessment of the labor market value of a community college education.

The primary difference between the non-experimental results summarized above and the results of the typical randomized controlled experiment lies in the fact that the experiments can only estimate the incremental impact of a new opportunity for training—not the value of the training itself. For instance, many members of the control group in the JTPA experiment received classroom training at the very same institutions where the treatment group members received their training—they just paid for the training themselves or took advantage of other government programs, such as the federal Pell Grant program, to help pay the cost. Thus, the experimental evidence provides no direct evidence on the value of training vs. no training, but rather estimates only the difference between the training opportunities provided to the treatment group and the training opportunities available elsewhere. The more similar JTPA training was to training available elsewhere, the more likely one would find a zero incremental impact of the JTPA program.

Indeed, this may explain the divergence between the results of the JTPA evaluation and the non-experimental estimates cited above. The impacts of the JTPA program on earnings were not statistically distinguishable from zero for several subgroups—leading some observers to conclude that classroom training had little impact. However, the differences in the amount of classroom training received by the treatment and control groups were also quite small.

In fact, if one translates the point estimates of the educational wage differentials arising out of the JTPA experiment into the framework we have been using, the results are quite comparable in magnitude. For example, during the final year of the JTPA evaluation follow-up, the average adult woman assigned to classroom training earned $282 (5.1 percent) more than those in the control group (Orr et aI., 1994). They also received 147 hours more training than those in the control group. If there are 420 hours of classroom training in a typical academic year (that is, 14 weeks per semester, 15 classroom hours per week, and two semesters a year), then our point estimate would be that receiving an academic year's worth of training would have been associated with an annual earnings differential per year of 14.6 percent. Similar results hold for the adult male and female youth groups, although the impacts for male youth were smaller than the 5 to 8 percent differential implied by the non-experimental estimates. In other words, even though the JTPA experimental estimates were generally not statistically distinguishable from zero, because alternative training opportunities were so readily available to the control group, the implied estimates of the differential per year of training received were generally on the high end of the non-experimental estimates above. Heckman, Hohmann, Khoo and Smith (1997) have used the JIPA data to generate non-experimental estimates of the value of classroom training. Their results also suggest substantial private internal rates of return to classroom training, albeit with more ambiguous social returns.

The Payoff to Completing an Associate's Degree

With only about 16 percent of community college entrants completing an associate's degree, the incremental value of degree completion itself has been central to the policy debate over community colleges. While the evidence presented in the last section suggests there are returns to completing community college credits, some argue that the main return to attending a community college comes with completing an associate's degree.

The evidence in Table 2 reports the total earnings differential between associate's degree recipients and high school graduates, inclusive of any credits completed. (One exception: the associate's degree effects reported for Grubb (1995) should be interpreted as incremental to the number of credits completed.) Completing an associate's degree appears to be associated with a 15 to 27 percent increase in annual earnings. Since estimates suggest that two years of community college credit is associated with a 10 to 16 percent increase in earnings (that is, the 5 to 8 percent annual gain times two), there appears to be some additional gain to the associate's degree itself. The evidence also suggests that this differential is larger for women, largely reflecting the value of nursing degrees where the earnings gain is especially pronounced (Kane and Rouse, 1995; Grubb, 1995).[9]

Discontinuities in the relationship between average log earnings and years of schooling completed at 14 and 16 years of schooling have traditionally been interpreted as reflecting the value of completing an associate's or bachelor's degree (Hungerford and Solon, 1987).[10] However, before 1992, the standard Census Bureau question on educational attainment did not allow one to distinguish between those who had completed an associate's or bachelor's degree and those who had completed 14 or 16 years of schooling without degrees. To assess whether the return to the associate's degree reflects a "sheepskin effect" or the effect of having completed two years of college, Jaeger and Page (1996) exploit a 1992 change in the Census Bureau educational attainment question; the earlier question focused solely on years of schooling completed, while the new one inquires about degree completion. After matching responses in the March 1991 *Current Population Survey* (including the question regarding years of schooling completed) and March 1992 survey (with data on degree completion), they found that white men with associate's degrees earn 8-19 percent more than men reporting similar years of schooling completed, but no degrees, and white women with associate's degrees earn 24-31 percent more than women reporting similar years of schooling completed, but no degrees. Again, it seems that nursing degrees account for much of the importance of associate's degrees for women (Kane and Rouse, 1995).

However, such estimates likely overstate the direct effect of degree completion for two reasons. First, the estimates are not adjusted for prior differences in family background and ability between degree completers and dropouts—because such information is not available on the *Current Population Survey*. It appears that those completing degrees not only have higher earnings than others with similar years of schooling, but they also seem to have higher prior test scores and more advantaged family backgrounds as well, and so controlling for these other factors would shrink the effect of degree completion.

Second, the magnitude of sheepskin effects may partially reflect the nature of measurement error in self-reported measures of educational attainment. Kane, Rouse and Staiger (1997) develop a technique for estimating the amount of measurement error in both self-reported and transcript-reported schooling in the NLS72. Their findings suggest that respondents are more likely to misreport the number of years of college they have completed than they are to misreport degrees completed. While more than 95 percent of those who report a bachelor's degree 7 years after graduating from high school are estimated to be reporting accurately, one third of those who report 3 years of college credit are estimated to have completed only 0, 1 or 2 years of college. Similarly, among those who report 1 year of college, 30 percent are estimated to actually have 0, 2 or 3 years of college. As a result, estimates based on self-reported schooling are likely to provide an accurate estimate of the earnings of those with a bachelor's degree and underestimate the differences in earnings per year of college for those without a bachelor's degree. Any discontinuity of earnings between those reporting 3 years of college and those reporting a bachelor's degree is likely to be exaggerated. In other words, the "sheepskin" effects reported in the literature may well be due in part to the nature of the reporting error in educational attainment.

Finally, even what remains of the "sheepskin" effect, after controlling for individual heterogeneity and measurement error, overstates the relative value of degrees and understates the anticipated value of postsecondary entry for those who do not complete degrees. There may be an option value to college entry for those uncertain of their prospects for finishing (Manski, 1989; Altonji, 1991; Comay et al., 1973). If the returns to education are uncertain or if youth are uncertain as to whether they are "college material," youth may gain some information in the first few months of college which helps to resolve the uncertainty. The wage differentials only reflect later monetary payoffs to college attendance. However, to the extent that the decision to enroll in college is an experiment for many, the anticipated outcome of that experiment may be sufficient to justify the public and private investments required, even if, after running the experiment, students do not finish the degree. This argument also suggests that we might wish to avoid proposals which seek to limit aid to those who complete degrees, as is occasionally suggested as a policy response to the high non-completion rates at community colleges (for example, Fischer, 1987).

A Rough Approximation of the Private and Social Rates of Return

How do the earnings differentials associated with a year at a community college compare to the costs of attendance? Using the average annual earnings of current 25–64 year-old workers (employed full-time, full-year) to estimate future earnings and employing a discount rate of 6 percent, the present value of expected lifetime earnings for the average male high school graduate in 1992 would have been $480,500 (in 1997 dollars).[11] The present value of a 5 to 8 percent increase in lifetime earnings for someone with career income of $480,500 would be $24,000 to $38,400 before taxes or $15,600 to $25,000 after taxes (assuming a combined federal and state tax rate of 35 percent).

The full cost to a family of a year at a community college includes both the earnings foregone by students as well as the cost of tuition. (We have left out room and board, since individuals would have to eat even if they were not in school). In 1992, the average income of a male 18-24 year-old high school graduate working full-time, full-year was $19,400 (in 1997 dollars). Foregoing nine months at that salary would imply costs of $14,600 before taxes or $9,500 after taxes. As mentioned above, a minority of students actually seem to forego nine months of full-time earnings, since a majority of both two-year and four-year college students work while they are in school. Nevertheless, such calculations provide a rough approximation of the "unit price" of a year of full-time schooling, even if relatively few students decide to "purchase" a full nine months away from work.

Adding in the private cost of tuition at the average public two-year college, the rise in after-tax lifetime income of $15,600 to $25,000 would be larger, but not dramatically larger, than the estimated private cost of $10,800 ($9,500 in foregone after-tax earnings plus $1,300 per year for tuition).

Calculations along these lines also reveal why it may not be surprising that the earnings differential associated with a year at a community college is similar in magnitude to that associated with a year at a four-year college. Although the tuition charges at community colleges are typically lower ($1,300 per year compared to $3,000 at the average public four-year institution), the vast majority of the private cost of attendance is foregone earnings, not tuition. To the extent that students are choosing on the margin between two-year and four-year colleges, we might expect students to attend each type of college to the point where the payoffs were similar.

Given the size of the public subsidies directed at community colleges, the average tuition families face ($1,300) is considerably less than the actual cost of a year of full-time education. Rouse (1998) estimates that average variable cost of a year in community college is $6,300 (in 1997 dollars).[12] However, this figure does not include capital costs, which Winston and Lewis (1997) estimate to be an additional $1,700 per student (27 percent of expenditures per student). To the extent that the private cost families face is considerably lower than the actual cost of the resources required to produce a year at a community college, we might fear students would over-invest in post-secondary education. However, even if we were to count only the earnings increases associated with community colleges (and ignore any of the other hard-to-measure benefits, such as civic participation or greater social mobility), the estimated 5 to 8 percent earnings differential would imply gains roughly the same as the full cost of the resources used: the combined cost of pre-tax earnings and expenditures per pupil of $22,600 is comparable in magnitude to the $24,000 to $38,400 estimate of the present value of future earnings differentials.

Although these back-of-the-envelope calculations can of course be subjected to criticism on many dimensions, it thus appears possible that a year of community college increases earnings by an amount roughly equal to the value of the resources used to produce that year.

Student Financing Issues

Community colleges are heavily dependent upon public subsidies for their operations; 62 percent of current-fund revenues are appropriated by state and local governments (U.S. Department of Education, 1997, Table 328, p. 344). Because students must be enrolled at least half-time to qualify for many federal aid programs such as the guaranteed student loan programs, only a quarter of community college students report receiving state or federal grant aid to help cover the cost of tuition and fees (U.S. Department of Education, 1992–93, Table 3-1a, p. 62).

Future demographic trends are likely to strain the ability of states to maintain this commitment in coming years. The size of the traditional college-age population (that is, 15 to 24 year-olds) has declined by 15 percent since 1980, partially relieving the cost pressure produced by rising college enrollment rates. However, this college-age population is now projected to rise by one-fifth over the next 15 years (Campbell, 1994). The rise is projected to be particularly dramatic in California, where the number of 15 to 24 year-olds is projected to increase at roughly twice the national rate. If the labor market wage premiums favoring college entry persist, and college enrollment rates remain high, states are likely to be forced to choose between raising tuition and increasing public expenditures on higher education.

Should states decide to increase tuition, it is likely to have an unusually large impact on community college enrollments. The demand elasticities with respect to upfront costs of college entry are quite high. After reviewing 25 estimates of tuition price responses, Leslie and Brinkman (1988) reported a median estimate of a 4.4 percentage point difference in postsecondary entry for every $1,000 difference in tuition costs (in 1997 dollars).[13] A number of others have found similar results, including Cameron and Heckman (1998b), Rouse (1994), Kane (1995), Kane (1994) and McPherson and Schapiro (1991). Enrollment at two-year colleges appears to be particularly sensitive to tuition changes (Kane, 1995; Rouse, 1994; Manski and Wise, 1983).

In addition, students seem to be more sensitive to tuition changes than to changes in future wage differentials. While the payoff to college was rising dramatically during the 1980s, the proportion of high school graduates entering college within two years of high school rose by only 7 percentage points, from 65 to 72 percent (U.S. Department of Education, *Condition of Education*, 1997, p. 64). Using the estimates of tuition sensitivity described above, a tuition increase of $1500 would have been enough to have wiped out that rise in college entrance rates—even though the present value of the college earnings differential rose by far more than $1500 during the 1980s.

One potential explanation for the sensitivity of students to the tuition costs at community colleges is that they face borrowing constraints in the private capital market. Indirect evidence on this point is provided by Card (forthcoming), who summarizes evidence suggesting higher marginal returns to schooling for disadvantaged groups than for the population as a whole. Such findings may result from the fact that lower-income families have more difficulty arranging financing for college. In a similar vein, most studies find that large differences in college entry by family income remain, even among those with similar test scores and academic performance in high school.[14]

The most obvious constraints which limit family borrowing for community college are the explicit limits on student borrowing in the federal student loan programs. Since 1992, the most a dependent student could borrow under the Stafford loan program has been $2,625 during the freshman year, $3,500 during the sophomore year and $5,500 per year thereafter. Independent students who are married, have dependents, are veterans or are over age 24 can borrow an additional $4,000 per year during their first two years and an additional $5,000 per year thereafter. However, such amounts may not be sufficient to pay living expenses on top of tuition bills. Some states and institutions have their own loan programs, but in 1992-93, less than 1 percent of undergraduates received either a state loan (0.5 percent) or an institutional loan (0.4 percent); in contrast, 20 percent of undergraduates received federal loans. A third source of borrowing constraints may be the confusing nature of the application process. Several studies cited in Orfield (1992) suggest that low-income families are often unaware of eligibility rules and procedures.

An important challenge will be to create a financing structure that will allow community colleges to expand in the next few years to meet the training needs of the population—and then eventually to contract as the relevant population declines. The current system of "backward-looking" means-testing, which looks back at the parents' income to determine student eligibility for financial aid, is more appropriate for the student of traditional college age and is less well-suited to the population of community college entrants. If community colleges are to remain an engine of innovation in postsecondary education, we will require similarly creative and flexible financing strategies to match. As an alternative to the current form of financing with several advantages would be greater reliance on income-contingent loans—that is, loans where the amount of repayment depends to some extent on future income earned—as discussed in this journal in Krueger and Bowen (1993). The expected subsidy implicit in an income-contingent loan is lower than the cost of a dollar in appropriations to public institutions, which in turn means that families and youth would have a stronger incentive to allocate society's educational resources in a prudent manner. Moreover, the means-test implicit in income-contingent loans does not involve the same difficulty in distinguishing students who are "dependent" on parents' resources from those who are "independent."

Conclusion

For the past five decades, the debate over access to higher education and the role of higher education in economic development has implicitly been a debate about community colleges. In any discussion involving marginal incentives, community colleges have been the margin. They have been the gateway for those on the verge of enrolling in college: older students, those who cannot afford to attend full-time, and those who need to develop their basic skills. Ironically, though, we know less about community colleges than about other sectors of higher education. The evidence we do have, as summarized above, suggests that community colleges increase aggregate educational attainment, and are associated with higher wages, even for those not completing degrees.

If current labor market conditions persist, we can expect significant increases in demand for postsecondary training slots in the future, due to the projected growth in college-age cohorts. Historically, community colleges have been the buffer, absorbing much of the increase in enrollment when veterans returned from war or when demand for skilled labor outpaced supply. Enrollment at community colleges also has swelled much more dramatically than at other institutions during economic downturns, when opportunity costs of such investments in training are lowest (Betts and McFarland, 1996).

Recent technological developments in distance learning will likely allow colleges to be even more responsive to changes in demand for higher education and have raised hopes of improving productivity in instruction.[15] Community colleges are participating in this growing trend. In 1995, 58 percent of public two-year colleges were offering distance learning courses serving over 400,000 students (or about 7 percent of their total enrollment).[16] However, community colleges are not the only institutions turning to distance learning: two-thirds of public four-year colleges offered such courses in 1995 and an additional 25 percent were planning to offer such courses by 1998. To the extent that geographic accessibility and flexible scheduling have been a traditional source of community colleges' market niche, the technological revolution may allow other institutions, such as four-year colleges and private for-profit institutions, to compete more effectively in the markets traditionally served by community colleges.[17] The net result of these technological changes—whether they lead to an increasing or decreasing role for community colleges in the future—remains to be seen.

We thank Lauren Brown for expert research assistance, Mark Lopez far help with some calculations, and Brad De Long, Alan Krueger, John Siegfried, Timothy Taylor, and participants at the JEP Symposium on Higher Education held at Macalester College on June 26, 1998 for helpful comments. Kane acknowledges the generous support of the Andrew W. Mellon Foundation.

Notes

1. Although we use the terms interchangeably, we know of no private "community" colleges while "junior" and "two-year" colleges are both public and private.
2. Rouse (1994) shows that college proximity is an important determinant of college attendance. We discuss the literature on the effects of tuition below.
3. Figure 2 is based on authors' calculations from the *High School and Beyond Post-secondary Transcript file*, which is for students who were sophomores in 1980 (the "sophomore cohort"). The figure includes only students who had a complete set of (cumulative) transcripts and who had earned any credits at a two-year college as of 1992; the distributions are weighted by the post-secondary transcript weight. If the sample is limited to those who have no four-year credits, the distribution looks quite similar.
4. Proprietary schools were not counted as college for this exercise; therefore, if a student first attended a proprietary school and then attended either a two-or four-year college, we count the two-or four-year college as the "first" school attended.
5. Hollenbeck (1993) and Surette (1997) also report results consistent with those in Table 2 using the National Longitudinal Study of the Class of 1972 (NLS-72) and the National Longitudinal Survey of Youth (NLSy) respectively.
6. To match as closely as possible the state where the person was educated, sample members were categorized by their state of residence in 1985, when they would have been 20 to 29. The regressions also adjusted for race/ethnicity and year of age.

7. Weighting by the reciprocal of the standard error of each estimate, the slope coefficient in Figure 3 was .038 with a standard error of .029, meaning that for every 10 percentage point increase in the proportion of students in the state enrolled in community colleges, the estimated wage differential is estimated to rise by a statistically insignificant third of a percentage point.

8. For instance, in a recent summary in this journal, LaLonde (1995) concluded: "Finally, the National JTPA Study found that ... those men assigned to a strategy that offered classroom training did not appear to benefit from JTPA services."

9. The estimated earnings differential for associate's degree completion for women falls by one-third when one includes a dummy variable for nurses.

10. In contrast, studies of the relationship between log earnings and the number of years of schooling suggest that the percentage increase in earnings between the 13th and 14th years of schooling is similar to that between the 12th and 13th years of schooling; there is no discontinuity (for example, Park, 1994).

11. This may be a conservative estimate since we are implicitly assuming no real wage growth. However, it may also be overly optimistic, since the continuing increases in college enrollment may eventually lead to a decline in earnings differentials.

12. Excluding "fixed costs" such as research, administration, student services and admissions. her estimate would be $4,200.

13. Leslie and Brinkman's (1988, appendix table 6) actual estimate was that a $100 increase in tuition in 1982-83 dollars was associated with a .7 percentage point decline in enrollment among 18-24year-olds. We have converted to 1997 dollars in the text.

14. Kane (1998), Manski and Wise (1983) and Hauser and Sweeney (1997) report differences in postsecondary entry by family income, conditioning on both parental education and student test scores. Using the NLSY, Cameron and Heckman (1998a) find differences in college entry by family income to be greatly reduced, but not eliminated, after including controls for AFQT scores.

15. The Department of Education defines distance learning as "... education or training courses delivered to remote (off-campus) locations via audio, video, or computer technologies" (Lewis et al., 1997).

16. The most common form of the distance learning is one-way pre-recorded video classes (67 percent), although half of public two-year colleges also offer two-way interactive video.

17. We thank Michael Rothschild for pointing out the potential vulnerability of community colleges as the technology for distance learning improves.

References

Alba, Richard D. and David E. Lavin. 1981. "Community Colleges and Tracking in Higher Education." *Sociology of Educatiun.* 54, pp. 223–37.

Altonji, Joseph. 1991. "The Demand for and Return to Education When Education Outcomes are Uncertain." National Bureau of Economic Research. Working Paper No. 3714, May.

Anderson, Kristine L. 1981. "Post-High School Experiences and College Attrition." *Sociology of Education.* 54, pp. 1–15.

Arenson, Karen W. 1998. "CUNY To Tighten Admissions Policy at Four-Year Schools." *New Yom Times.* May 27, Section A, Page 1.

Barbett, Samuel F., Roslyn Korb and MacKnight Black. 1988. *State Higher Education Profiles: 1988 Edition.* Washington, D.C.: National Center for Education Statistics.

Betts, Julian and Laurel McFarland. 1996. "Safe Port in a Storm: The Impact of Labor Market Conditions on Community College Enrollments." *Journal of Human Resources.* 30:4, pp. 742–65.

Bloom, Howard S. et a1. 1994. *National JTPA Study Overview: Impacts, Benefits and Costs of Title II-A: A Report to the U.S. Department of Labor.* Bethesda: Abt Associates, January.

Breneman, David W. and Susan C. Nelson. 1981. *Financing Community Colleges: An Economic Perspective.* Washington, D.C.: The Brookings Institution.

Brint, Steven and Jerome Karabel. 1989. *The Diverted Dream: Community Colleges and the Promise of Educational opportunity in America, 1900–1985.* New York: Oxford University Press.

Bruno, Rosalind R. and Andrea Cuny. 1996. *School Enrollment—Social and Economic Characteristics of Students: October 1994.* U.S. Bureau of the Census, Current Population Reports, P20–487. Washington, D.C.: U.S. Government Printing Office.

Cameron, Stephen V. and James J. Heckman. 1998a. "Life Cycle Schooling and Dynamic Selection Bias: Models and Evidence for Five Cohorts of American Males." *Journal of Political Economy.* 106:2, pp. 262–333.

Cameron, Stephen V. and James J. Heckman. 1998b. "The Dynamics of Educational Attainment for Blacks, Hispanics, and Whites." Working Paper, Columbia University Department of Economics, September.

Campbell, Paul R. 1994. *Population Projections Jar States, by Age, Race and Sex: 1993–2020.* U.S. Bureau of the Census, Current Population Reports, P25–1111. Washington, D.C.: U.S. Government Printing Office.

Card, David E. Forthcoming. "The Causal Effect of Education on Earnings," in *Handbook of Labor Economics, Volume* 3. Orley Ashenfelter and David E. Card, eds. New York, NY: North Holland.

Clark, Burton R. 1960. "The 'Cooling-Out' Function in Higher Education." *American Journal of Sociology.* 65, pp. 569–76.

Cohen, Arthur M. and Florence B. Brawer. *1982. The American Community College.* San Francisco: Jossey-Bass Publishers.

Comay, Y., A. Melnick and M. Pollatschek. 1973. "The Option Value of Education and the Optimal Path for Investment in Human Capital." *International Economic Review.* 14, pp. 421–35.

Dougherty, Kevin. 1987. "The Effects of Community Colleges: Aid or Hindrance to Socioeconomic Attainment?" *Sociology of Education.* 60, pp. 86–103.

Fischer, Frederick. 1987. "Graduation-Contingent Student Aid." *Change.* November/December, pp. 40–47.

Griliches, Zvi. 1977. "Estimating the Returns to Schooling: Some Econometric Problems." *Econometrica.* 45, pp. 1–22.

Grubb, W. Norton. 1993. "The Varied Economic Returns to Postsecondary Education: New Evidence from the Class of 1972." *Journal of Human Resources.* 28:3, pp. 365–82.

Grubb, W. Norton. 1995. "Postsecondary Education and the Sub-Baccalaureate Labor Market: Corrections and Extensions." *Economics of Education Review.* 14:3, pp. 285–99.

Grubb, W. Norton. 1988. "Vocationalizing Higher Education: The Causes of Enrollment and Completion in Public Two-year Colleges, *1970-1980." Economics of Education Review.* 7, pp. 301–19.

Grubb, W. Norton. 1989. "The Effects of Differentiation on Educational Attainment: The Case of Community Colleges." *Review of Higher Education,* 12, pp. 349–74.

Hauser, Robert M. and Megan Sweeney. 1997. "Does Poverty in Adolescence Affect the Life Chances of High School Graduates?" In *Consequences of Growing Up Poor.* Greg J. Duncan and Jeanne Brooks-Gunn, eds. New York: Russell Sage.

Heckman, James J. et al. 1997. "Substitution and Drop Out Bias in Social Experiments: A Study of an Influential Social Experiment." University of Chicago Working Paper, August.

Heineman, Harry N. and Edward Sussna. 1977. "The Economic Benefits of a Community College." *Industrial Relations.* 16:3, pp. 345–54.

Hollenbeck, Kevin. 1993. "Postsecondary Education as Triage: Returns to Academic and Technical Programs." *Economics of Education Review.* September, 12:3, pp. 213–32.

Horn, Laura J., Jennifer Berktold and Andrew G. Malizio. 1998. *Profile of Undergraduates in U.S. Postsecondary Education Institutions: 1995–96.* Washington, D.C.: National Center for Education Statistics.

Hungerford, Thomas and Gary Solon. 1987. "Sheepskin Effects in the Returns to Education." *Review of Economics and Statistics.* 69:1, pp. 175–77.

Jaeger, David A. and Marianne E. Page. 1996. "Degrees Matter: New Evidence on Sheepskin Effects in the Returns to Education." *Review of Economics and Statistics.* 78:4, pp. 733–40.

Jacobson, Louis S., Robert J. LaLonde and Daniel G. Sullivan. 1997. "The Returns from Community College Schooling for Displaced Workers." Federal Reserve Bank of Chicago, WP-97–16, June.

Kane, Thomas J. October 1994. "College Attendance By Blacks Since 1970: The Role of College Cost, Family Background and the Returns to Education." *Journal of Political Economy.* 102:5, pp. 878–911.

Kane, Thomas J. 1995. "Rising Public College Tuition and College Entry: How Well Do Public Subsidies Promote Access to College?" National Bureau of Economic Research Working Paper No. 5164, April.

Kane, Thomas J. 1998. "Are College Students Credit Constrained?" Working Paper, Kennedy School of Government, Harvard University, May.

Kane, Thomas J. and Cecilia Elena Rouse. 1995. "Comment on W. Norton Grubb, 'The Varied Economic Returns to Postsecondary Education: New Evidence from the Class of 1972'."*Journal of Human Resources.* Winter, 30:1, pp. 205–21.

Kane, Thomas J. and Cecilia Elena Rouse. 1995. "Labor-Market Returns to Two-and Four Year College." *American Economic Review.* June, 85:3, pp. 600–14.

Kane, Thomas J., Cecilia Elena Rouse and Douglas Staiger. December 1997. "Estimating Returns to Schooling When Schooling is Misreported." Unpublished paper, Kennedy School of Government, Harvard University.

Kelley, Pam. 1998. "Free K-14 Could Become the Standard in North Carolina." *Community College Week.* June, 10:22, p. 6.

Krueger, Alan B. and William G. Bowen. 1993. "Policy Watch: Income Contingent Loans." *Journal of Economic Perspectives.* 7:3, pp. 193–201.

Krueger, Alan B. and Cecilia Elena Rouse. 1998. "The Effect of Workplace Education on Earnings, Turnover, and Job Performance." *Journal of Labor Economics.* January, 16:1, pp. 61–94.

LaLonde, Robert J. 1995. "The Promise of Public Sector-Sponsored Training Programs." *Journal of Economic Perspectives.* Spring, 9:2, pp. 149–68.

Leigh, Duane E. and Andrew M. Gill. 1997. "Labor Market Returns to Community Colleges: Evidence for Returning Adults." *Journal of Human Resources.* Spring, 32:2, pp. 334–53.

Leslie, Larry and Paul Brinkman. 1988. *Economic Value of Higher Education.* New York: Macmillan.

Lewis, Laurie, Elizabeth Farris and Bernie Greene. 1996. *Remedial Education at Higher Education Institutions in Fall 1995.* Washington, D.C.: U.S. Department of Education, National Center for Education.

Lewis, Laurie et aI. 1997. *Distance Learning in Higher Education Institutions.* Washington, D.C.: U.S. Department of Education, National Center for Education.

Lynch, Robert, James C. Palmer, and W. Norton Grubb. 1991. *Community College Involvement in Contract Training and Other Economic Development Activities.* Berkeley, CA: National Center for Research in Vocational Education, October.

Manski, Charles F. 1989. "Schooling as Experimentation: A Reappraisal of the Postsecondary Dropout Phenomenon." *Economics of Education Review.* 4, pp. 305–12.

Manski, Charles F. and David A. Wise. 1993. *College Choice in America.* Cambridge, MA: Harvard University Press.

McPherson, Michael S. and Morton Owen Schapiro. 1991. "Does Student Aid Affect College Enrollment? New Evidence on a Persistent Controversy." *Amelican Economic Review.* 81, pp. 309–18.

Monk-Turner, Elizabeth. 1994. "Economic Returns to Community and Four-Year College Education." *Journal of Socio-Economics.* 23:4, pp. 441–47.

Orfield, Gary. 1992. "Money, Equity and College Access." *Harvard Educational Review.* Fall, 72:3, pp. 337–72.

Orr, Larry L. et aI. 1994. *National JTPA Study: Impacts, Benefits and Costs of Title II-A.* Draft report to the U.S. Department of Labor, March.

Orr, Larry L. et aI. 1996. *Does Training for the Disadvantaged Work?* Washington, D.C.: Urban Institute.

Park, Jin Heum. 1994. "Returns to Schooling: A Peculiar Deviation from Linearity." Princeton University Industrial Relations Section Working Paper No. 335, October.

Pincus, Fred L. 1980. "The False Promises of Community Colleges: Class Conflict and Vocational Education." *Harvard Educational Review.* 1980,50, pp. 332–61.

Rouse, Cecilia Elena. 1994. "What To Do After High School? The Two-year vs. Four-year College Enrollment Decision." In *Contemporary Policy Issues in Education.* Ronald Ehrenberg, editor. Ithaca, NY: ILR Press, pp. 59–88.

Rouse, Cecilia Elena. 1995. "Democratization or Diversion? The Effect of Community Colleges on Educational Attainment." *Journal of Business Economics and Statistics.* April, 13:2, pp. 217–24.

Rouse, Cecilia Elena. 1998. "Do Two-year Colleges Increase Overall Educational Attainment? Evidence from the States." *Journal of Policy Analysis and Management.* Fall, 17:4, pp. 595–620.

Surette, Brian J. 1997. "The Effects of Two Year College on the Labor Market and Schooling Experiences of Young Men." Working paper, Finance and Economics Series, Washington, D.C.: Federal Reserve Board, June.

Tinto, Vincent. 1985. "College Proximity and Rates of College Attendance." *American Educational Research Journal.* 10, pp. 277–93.

Trombley, William. 1993. "College Running Out of Space, Money." *Los Angeles Times.* October 18, 3A

U.S. Department of Education. 1997. *Condition of Education 1997.* Washington, D.C.: National Center for Education Statistics.

U.S. Department of Education. 1997. *Digest of Education Statistics 1997*. Washington, D.C.: National Center for Education Statistics.

U.S. Department of Education. *Student Financing of Undergraduate Education, 1992–93*. U.S. Government Printing Office: National Center for Education Statistics.

Velez, William. 1985. "Finishing College: The Effects of College Type." *Sociology of Education*. 58, pp. 191–200.

Winston, Gordon C. and Ethan G. Lewis. 1997. "Physical Capital and Capital Service Costs in U.S. Colleges and Universities: 1993." *Eastern Economic Journal*. Spring, 23:2, pp. 165–89.

Witt, Allen A. et aI. 1994. *America's Community Colleges: The First Century*. Washington, D.C.: The Community College Press.

Thomas J Kane is Associate Professor of Public Policy, John F. Kennedy School of Government, Cambridge, Massachusetts. Cecilia Elena Rouse is Associate Professor of Economics and Public Affairs, Princeton University, Princeton, New Jersey. Their e-mail addresses are (tom_kane@haroard.edu) and (rouse@princeton.edu), respectively.

CHAPTER 33

CAREER AND TECHNICAL EDUCATION: OLD DEBATES, PERSISTENT CHALLENGES IN COMMUNITY COLLEGES

DEBRA D. BRAGG

Introduction

Career and technical education is rooted in federal legislation first passed in 1917 to fund secondary vocational education. In spite of staunch support from early junior college advocates, the federal government did not fund career and technical education (then labeled vocational education) beyond high school until the 1960s, and even then appropriations were modest. However, vocational education has expanded and diversified considerably since mid-20th century, leading scholars to question whether the access agenda of community colleges is threatened by an increasing preoccupation with economic development (Levin, 2001). Critics have claimed the vocational mission of community colleges overshadows individual benefits (Brint & Karabel, 1989), but politicians, business representatives, and college leaders continue to seek an intensified connection to the labor market (Harmon & MacAllum, 2003). Situated in the middle of this long-standing debate is the student who seeks a college education for many reasons, one of which is to secure a good job.

Since 1963, federal legislation has authorized funding for postsecondary vocational education to increase enrollments through strengthened connections to business and industry, with community and technical colleges at the heart of this workforce development strategy (Bragg, 2001a). Integral to implementation of vocational education at the postsecondary level were articulation agreements with high schools to create academic pathways that enable traditional-age students to transition to college. Skill-specific training programs were offered to assist unemployed and incumbent adult workers to obtain credentials and re-enter or advance in the labor market. These diverse trajectories represent the outer boundaries for what has become a broad set of curricular offerings that represent contemporary career and technical education (CTE).

This chapter begins with an analysis of federal support for secondary vocational education that began in 1917. It continues by examining vocational education at mid-20th century when dramatic social and economic change occurred nationwide, prompting federal funding for vocational education by community, junior, and technical colleges. At the end of the 20th century and beginning of the new millennium, postsecondary vocational education evolved into an even more complex, multidimensional enterprise, and the terminology shifted from vocational education to CTE, which was codified in the Carl D. Perkins Career and Technical Education Improvement Act in 2006. Increasingly, CTE has been positioned as an instrumental tool to prepare workers for the global economy, extending the long-standing debate about whether vocational education should be integrated into the general curriculum or kept distinct to facilitate economic development.

From Vocational Education to Career and Technical Education

Since the early 20th century, the nation has debated the fundamental role of public education. At one extreme, the core purpose of public education is to provide liberal education to develop the whole person and, at the other extreme, the key goal is to develop specific skills for work. This intention to distinguish education for employment from education for life's fuller endeavors represents one of the most important yet contentious debates over public education in the U.S. (see, for example, Labaree, 2010). Over much of the 20th century, this debate played out in public high schools where students prepared to attend college or enter the workplace.

The comprehensive high school took shape at about the turn of the 20th century when educators, politicians, and business leaders actively debated how best to educate the nation's growing and increasingly diverse student population. The nation was seeing an increasing number of young people leave the farms for urban areas, and immigration was bringing non-native speakers into the population (Wirth, 1992). To address these trends, high schools were thought most efficient if they replicated the social and economic order of the day, helping students find a place in the school curriculum that would prepare them to matriculate to college or prepare them for employment. This focus on efficiency contributed to the replication of structural inequalities that separated students by income, ethnicity and race, gender, and other defining characteristics. Hence, high school education for the wealthy and elite class focused on preparation for college, and preparation for the rest, especially the working class, concentrated on preparation for employment. Males were the primary recipients of high school technical instruction, with domestic life as the focus for the education of females (Wirth, 1992).

The Smith Hughes Act

Vocational education began to be offered as part of public schooling when the federal Smith Hughes Act was passed in 1917, through vocational agriculture and manual training programs for males and domestic science (or home economics) for females. Vocational curriculum was especially useful to educate students who were likely to drop out (Lazerson & Grubb, 1974), and was therefore heralded as a democratizing mission of public education, according to the U.S. government (Benavot, 1983; Lazerson & Grubb, 1974). Simultaneously, employers praised the benefits that vocational education provided by offering specific skill training to students who would otherwise fail to find work that would sustain a living wage. Similar to policy-makers, employers foresaw benefits of vocational education for both the economy and students by motivating students to stay in school and enter employment (Wirth, 1992).

Championing vocational education as a democratizing form of public education, Prosser (1913) observed, "The American school will truly become democratic when we learn to train all kinds of men [sic], in all kinds of ways, for all kinds of things" (p. 406). Through vocational education, students were expected to experience a more practical form of education that was presumed to be directly applicable to their future as laborers and line workers in factories that were needed to grow the U.S. industrial economy. Vocational education would heighten students' abilities to secure skilled jobs (rather than fill unskilled jobs that predominated the labor market at that time). For the working class, education for citizenship and for life was presumed to be fulfilled if they were prepared for work (Wonacott, 2003).

Separate and Unequal

The Smith Hughes Act established vocational education as a separate system of education administered by state boards to perpetuate distinct curricula. Because the administration of federal funds required an independent administrative system, state boards that propagated separate curriculum (what eventually became known as tracks) were also perpetuated through separate teacher preparation programs and reinforced by professional and student organizations that complimented practical classroom instruction (Rojewski, 2002). However, critics of the separate system for vocational education, such as John Dewey, claimed that vocational education missed opportunities to connect pedagogical approaches to broader aspects of education, work, and the community that were necessary to move marginalized populations into the mainstream of society (Wirth, 1992). Dewey and others argued that a separate system of vocational education weakened the entire educational system, and these perspectives laid the groundwork for debates about the goals of public education that have lasted for decades (Wirth, 1992).

In an historical account prepared for the U.S. Department of Education, Hayward and Benson (1993) described the "isolation of vocational education from other parts of the comprehensive high school curriculum" as "a division between practical and theoretical instruction" (p. 3) that would have detrimental effects on U.S. public schools. Educating students to perform job specific skills to the exclusion of academic education limited students' options to transition to college and advance into professional employment. Isolation was not only evident between vocational and academic education but within vocational education because fields of study associated with agriculture, manual training (eventually industrial arts and then technology education), home economics, business, and other areas were funded and delivered separately (Rojewski, 2002). Even within vocational education, different fields of study were separate and unequal, depending on their alignment with larger social and economic strata. This separation of curriculum between vocational and academic education, as well as further differentiation within vocational education, prevailed into the mid-20th century when federal legislation expanded to the postsecondary education level.

At the time the Smith Hughes Act was passed, Charles Prosser and David Snedden, prominent spokespersons, advocated for "an *essentialist* approach toward vocational education—firmly grounded in meeting the needs of business and industry" (Rojewski, 2002, p. 7, emphasis in original). Citing historical accounts authored by Sarkees-Wircenski and Scott (1995), Rojewski observed that essentialism emphasizes instruction in basic academics (reading, writing, and arithmetic), respect for the prevailing power structure, and appreciation of middle-class values. As noted previously, this philosophy was countered by John Dewey, who warned that "too specific a mode of efficiency defeats its own purpose," and he called for education that would be neither too labor-market specific nor too distinct from the rest of schooling so that there was not a diminution of its benefits to the individual or to the community (Dewey, 1916, p. 119). The perspectives of Prosser and Snedden, in contrast to Dewey, which continued to be associated with vocational education to the present, contribute to an uneven playing field for historically marginalized populations who seek opportunities to benefit from public education directed at college and career preparation.

Extension of Vocational Education to the Postsecondary Level

Expansion of vocational education to the postsecondary level occurred in the 1960s, launching vocational programs that would continue to evolve throughout the rest of the 20th century. However, the increase in vocation education programs was not without controversy due to the continued delivery of programming that was accessed by and accessible to some but not all student groups. Efforts to diversify the student population that participated in vocational education were acknowledged by new federal legislation in the 1970s, but limitations of these laws contributed to inequities for ethnic and racial student groups.

The Vocational Education Act of 1963

Until the 1960s, federal monies for vocational education were devoted entirely to secondary education. Numerous leaders of junior colleges advanced the idea of terminal vocational education for several decades, including national commissions advocating for applied associate degree programs in the health sciences, manufacturing, and other fields. However, none of these efforts produced support for dedicated federal funding for vocational education beyond high school until the mid-1960s when the nation launched a comprehensive higher education agenda. Intellectual leaders of the junior college were adamant supporters of an alternative curriculum to transfer education for working-class students, and they articulated widely the importance of a strong vocational function in junior colleges (Meier, 2008). Walter Crosby Eells, Leonard V. Koos, and other early scholars of the community college considered vocational education to be a proper alternative to transfer for students who were unlikely to be successful pursuing baccalaureate degrees. They advocated for a diversified curriculum that paralleled the stratified labor market, believing that vocational education was essential to the long-term survival of junior colleges. State higher education systems lent their support, creating separate institutional types to support the administration of two-year college and four-year university education to address a range of student abilities (Brint & Karabel, 1989; Dougherty, 2004). This argument, including the rhetoric of democratizing education, is hauntingly similar to the perspectives of early vocational education advocates who believed a vocational curriculum that replicated the social and economic hierarchy was necessary to sustain high schools.

With passage of the Vocational Education Act of 1963, the door opened to federal funding for vocational education in junior, community, and technical colleges (Calhoun & Finch, 1976), resulting in a more visible and integral role for vocational education at the postsecondary level. Federal policymakers recognized that occupations required higher levels of technical instruction, using the label of "semi-professional" to describe the preferred tier of employment for junior college graduates. Whereas federal funds had been non-existent for vocational education beyond high school prior to the 1960s, the 1963 legislation recommended 20% of federal funding be awarded to programs enrolling students between 20 and 25 years old, 15% to programs enrolling students between 25 and 65, and 5% to programs enrolling students of any age, and the remaining funds appropriated to secondary education (Calhoun & Finch, 1976). To this day, the U.S. Department of Education, Office of Vocational and Adult Education does not prescribe the precise allocation to the secondary and postsecondary level (Bragg, 2001a). Although there are some exceptions, it is common for states to allocate a higher proportion of funds to the secondary than postsecondary level, in spite of strong rationale for most occupational instruction to be delivered by community colleges due to workforce requirements necessary in the modern labor market (Carnevale, Smith, & Strohl, 2010). Looking at funding from all levels of government, Silverberg, Warner, Fong and Goodwin (2004) estimated federal Perkins funds made up approximately 2% of local community college budgets that support vocational education.

Expanding Access

The 1963 Vocational Education Act also signaled the importance of preparing college-age citizens and adults for employment. Technological advancements prompted by the Kennedy presidency and social commitments supported by the Johnson administration encouraged community colleges to develop vocational programs to prepare students for technical and semi-professional occupations (Rojewski, 2002). Also important during this period, the civil rights movement raised the nation's awareness of discrimination in the workplace, in education, and in public life by expanding voting rights, abolishing national-origin quotas in immigration laws, and banning discrimination in housing. These larger social forces provided an important context for expanding vocational education at the same time that many community colleges were first opening their doors (Cohen & Brawer, 2008). Although there is no evidence to point to the expansion of vocational education as a direct response to the civil rights movement, there is no doubt that the nation's efforts to rectify historical discrimination laid the foundation for scrutiny of all forms of education, including vocational education. The timing was right to encourage community colleges to adopt a comprehensive and inclusive mission, as foreshadowed by the Truman Commission immediately after World War II.

It is not surprising, then, that community colleges established in the late 1960s and 1970s articulated vocational education as integral to their core mission. In an important book defining the emergence of vocational education as a legitimate component of compulsory education, Grubb and Lazerson (1974, p. 1) introduced the notion of "vocationalism" that had swept public education in the 20th century (and before). This book showed how the vocational purpose of schooling had expanded significantly, noting that vocational education had not strayed far from the vision of federal policy-makers in the early 1900s. Over 30 years later, Grubb and Lazerson (2005) projected this same observation onto community colleges and eventually to all of higher education, arguing that vocationalism is at the heart of the entire educational enterprise in the U.S.

The notion of extending vocational education beyond high school to include two years of college, culminating in an associate's degree, was solidified in policy in the 1960s, but in fact, not executed fully until the 1970s (Evans & Herr, 1978). Articulation processes were important to the growth of postsecondary vocational education because community colleges needed a way to help students who had participated in high school level vocational classes to matriculate to college to participate in more advanced vocational training. An action discouraged for vocational education students at the beginning of the early 20th century, transition from secondary to postsecondary education was encouraged by the late 1960s and thereafter. Articulation agreements between local high schools and community colleges began to be forged in the late 1960s in some states, with support from state administrative agencies that authorized vocational course sequences thought appropriate to articulate with advanced vocational training (Bragg, Layton, & Hammons, 1994). Articulated curriculum offered the potential for students to access college, but it also had the disadvantage of extending tracking, with many tracks ending with a two-year applied and terminal degree, primarily the associate of applied science (AAS). These developments created the potential to extend the essentialist approach (Rojewski, 2002) begun in K-12 curriculum to the postsecondary level.

Who's In and Who's Out?

An important factor in the evolution of vocational education was the targeting of programs to special populations, which began to take place in the late 1960s and 1970s. Associated with the enrollment of students thought unable to attend or disinterested in attending college, the Vocational Education Act of 1963 recognized students with special needs as learner populations that could benefit from vocational education (Rojewski, 2002). However, federal legislation passed in 1968 and 1976 established categorical funding for students with disabilities and students identified as economically disadvantaged, along with students with limited English proficiency, teen parents, displaced homemakers, and students in programs considered non-traditional for their gender. The Education of All Handicapped Children Act of 1975 reinforced the importance of vocational education serving special population students, and it aligned vocational education with special education in ways supportive of the enrollment of students with intellectual, emotional, and physical disabilities (Meers, 1987; Sarkees-Wircenski & Scott, 1995).

Racial and ethnic minorities were not identified as a special population group for vocational education. According to LaFollette (2011), the omission of persons of color from the federal vocational education legislation was no mistake. The late Senator Carl Perkins, long-time congressional leader of the federal vocational education agenda, believed strongly that vocational education was necessary to address the poverty he saw in his home state of Kentucky, and he advanced a federal agenda for the nation that was favorable to his constituency. Why other Congressional leaders did not push for equitable access to federally funded vocational education is uncertain. The lack of explicit identification of ethnic and racial minority students as beneficiaries of vocational education raised questions about the commitment of vocational education to enroll racial and ethnic minority students (Oakes & Saunders, 2008) and address historic inequities made evident in the passage of the Civil Rights Act of 1964.

Lauded for democratizing K-12 schools by helping at-risk students graduate from high school and find employment, advocates for aligning vocational education with special education did not anticipate the extent to which this decision would stigmatize vocational programs and their students (Rojewski, 2002). Although well intended, linking vocational education to special education deepened schisms between the curricular tracks: college prep, general education, and vocational education. Although not completely duplicative, students enrolling in vocational programs were many of the same students who were marginalized from mainstream curriculum, especially the college-bound track (Lucas, 1999; Oakes, 1985). Tracking reinforced that college prep was for the most academically and economically privileged; general education was for the middle ability, middle income student; and, vocational education was for those having inadequate academic preparation, low income status, or other characteristics making them unqualified for or unworthy of a college education. Inequitable curriculum structure created by tracking diverse groups constrained students' abilities to access the academic curriculum and prepare for college (Oakes, 1985). Later, in a national study of vocational education mandated by Congress, Boesel, and McFarland (1994), it was suggested that, due to years of implementation in secondary schools, vocational education had become "a backwater, a dumping ground" (p. 11) for economically disadvantaged and disabled students. This research reinforced claims made by Oakes (1985) and others about the ways vocational education contributed to inequitable outcomes. Although this critique was directed at K-12 education, the push for articulation of secondary vocational education with postsecondary curriculum created the potential to replicate patterns of inequitable outcomes at the collegiate level unless drastic changes were made.

The New Vocationalism

Recognizing the inherent problems in tracking that limits students' educational options, a dialogue about a new form of vocationalism emerged among educators and scholars in the latter part of the 20th century. Reflecting on changes to federal legislation associated with reauthorization of the federal vocational education law in 1990, Benson (1997) provided an argument for "new vocationalism" (p. 201) that encouraged the movement of vocational education from the margins to the mainstream of the U.S. curriculum. According to Benson, new vocationalism had three distinct components that distinguished it from vocational education of the past. First, it integrated academic and vocational education by blending theory with practical skills. Second, it aligned secondary with postsecondary education to provide opportunities for more high school students to matriculate to college. Third, it established a "closer relationship between education and work, such that these two main components of human activity should each enhance and elevate the other" (Benson, 1997, p. 201). Various policies governing vocational education from the early 1990s to the present have advanced these tenets of reform, echoing ideas advanced by early 20th century philosophers such as John Dewey (1916). However, in spite of the promise to revisit the progressive education philosophy of education and the excitement that these reform tenets created (Wirth, 1992), implementation of vocational education reforms has been uneven across the nation, creating a mixed picture of program quality and student outcomes (Lewis, 2008).

Vocational Education Reform

Numerous models emerged in the 1990s that attempted to strengthen the relationship between academic education and vocational education, including tech prep, career academies, youth apprenticeships (Lewis, 2008), and other school reforms of which High Schools that Work (HSTW) is most widely recognized and researched (see, for example, Kaufman, Bradby, & Teitelbaum, 2000). These reforms emphasized better integration between academic education and vocational education. Concerns about tracking were on the minds of educators at all levels by this time, thus reformers associated with new vocationalism were cognizant of the need to increase academic education participation as part of an integrated academic and CTE program of study (Lynch, 2000). Technical preparation (or tech prep) conceived by Parnell (1985) is an example of a model that attempted to execute the tenets of reform associated with new vocationalism as proposed by Benson (1997).

In *The Neglected Majority,* Parnell (1985) criticized the compulsory education system for failing to recognize that individual differences should be attributed to students' unique learning styles and not just to their intellectual abilities. He remarked that "despite our rhetoric about the uniqueness of each individual, many people still advocate that 'academic' means advanced and is for the 'smart' students and that career education is for the 'dumb' students" (p. 55). Building on this image of students locked into distinct tracks that stigmatize them according to their innate intelligence, Parnell advanced the notion of careers education that is both "information-rich and experience-rich" (1985, p. 69), and he advocated for a plurality of pedagogical strategies leading to career opportunities that students could pursue over their lifetimes. The specific proposal that emerged from Parnell's vision was for technical preparation (tech prep) designed to provide the programmatic structure and substance to transition students in the middle two quartiles of the high school student body to a community college where they would study the "mid-range of oc-cupations requiring some beyond-highschool education and training but not necessarily a baccalaureate degree" (1985, p. 140). Enthusiastically adopted by federal policy-makers, the Carl D. Perkins vocational education legislation of 1990 and 1998 provided states and local enti-ties with the authority and funding to implement tech prep as part of the federal Tech Prep Education Act. Accordingly, these programs were expected to offer an integrated academic and CTE curriculum that started by at least the junior year of high school and continued through two years of postsecondary education to the associate degree, a two-year certification or a formal apprenticeship. Articulation agreements providing high school students with college credit (referred to as articulated credit and later dual credit) and applied pedagogical instruction formed the backbone of the tech prep model (Hull, 2005).

In tech prep and other models that emerged as part of new vocationalism, CTE lessened its focus on specific occupations associated with historical federal policy and paid more attention to career development and preparation at the high school level, recognizing that job-specific train-ing may yield immediate pay-offs but limit long-term economic benefits to students (Lewis & Cheng, 2006). Thus, while agriculture, consumer and family studies (formerly home economics), business and marketing, and industrial/technology education continued to exist, CTE began to be conceptualized as part of a progression of educational experiences for students, beginning at the middle school or high school level, extending through the postsecondary level, and into the labor market (Meeder, 2008). Collaborative efforts between the U.S. Department of Education and the U.S. Department of Labor to map the nation's labor force resulted in the States Career Cluster Framework in 1999, which encouraged rethinking of the way students prepare for em-ployment, recognizing that more than one career trajectory had become commonplace in the labor market (Ruffing, n.d.). This framework had a dual purpose: It intended to create more co-herency in education for employment for learners at all levels of the lifespan, youth to adults; and it intended to show students how they could progress through the education and training systems, moving in and out of school and college enrollment as they advanced in a career or moved from one career to another.

The States Career Cluster Framework identified 16 clusters of occupations and broad indus-tries, with each cluster further delineated into career pathways and programs of study. This frame-work has been applied broadly to the nation's entire labor market, and it has guided the development of curriculum and instruction intended to prepare students for the lifelong learning associated with college and career preparation. Curriculum developed to accompany this frame-work necessitated an integrated approach to academic and CTE, as envisioned by Benson (1997), particularly to nullify the separation of CTE from academic education. The ultimate goal was to provide students with an interdisciplinary approach to education that connects and reinforces theory and practice in ways that enable students to pursue their academic goals and simultaneously prepare for employment. Although the States Career Cluster Framework has not paid substantial attention to citizenship education, this framework has attempted to engage a broad constituency in conversations about the fundamental purpose of schooling. Scholars such as Oakes and Saunders (2008) have pointed out that civic education is a natural ally to CTE in that students need "multiple pathways" that include civic education to prepare them to better serve their communities, the na-tion, and global interests (p. 6).

Reforms associated with new vocationalism have expected secondary and postsecondary edu-cators to work together collaboratively to develop and align curriculum that prepares students to pursue their college and career goals and aspirations (Taylor et al., 2009). This approach has asked stakeholders to rethink educational goals that have impeded access to and success in college and ca-reer preparation (Bragg & Bennett, 2011). Curriculum that helps students pursue a wide range of goals and outcomes, including ensuring that students have access to associate and baccalaureate degrees, represents a pathway unthinkable for vocational education programs in earlier times. Pro-grams of study that extend to the baccalaureate represent an expansion of new vocationalism to the rest of higher education (Grubb & Lazerson, 2005), and a vivid commitment to rectifying social in-equities associated with tracking in K-12 (Bragg & Ruud, 2011).

Mixed Results

Research on the new vocationalism is limited, but a few empirical studies address the question of whether CTE programs are working. For example, results of a study of eight tech prep consortia in four states that attempted to implement comprehensive reforms consistent with new vocationalism showed academic course requirements mattered to students' choices of high school courses (academic and CTE). Students who were encouraged to take more academic courses as part of their tech prep programs did so, and this action was positively associated with matriculation to college (Bragg et al., 2003). When student participation in core academic courses was linked to rigorous course requirements, the students took a greater number of academic courses and they advanced to higher levels in the academic curriculum, which offered them better preparation for college. In a secondary analysis of this same dataset, Bragg, Zamani, Yoo, Jung-sup, and Hill, (2001) found tech prep participants took at least as many advanced academic courses as the comparison group of students who graduated with similar academic performance, and in some cases more. These tech prep students were less likely to need remediation when they entered the community college relative to the comparison group.

Albeit promising, Bragg et al.'s (2001) work also showed results on student outcomes that raised questions about whether tech prep had ameliorated inequities associated with historical tracking policies in high schools. Bragg et al. showed students' preparation for college differed by ethnic and racial group membership, favoring white students. Although not evident in all eight sites, in the two sites offering some of the most intensive academic course requirements, there was a significant difference between white and African American students on college readiness, controlling for other student characteristics. In both sites, African American students were more likely to require remediation at the community college than white students. Based on their increased likelihood of having to enter college taking remedial courses, African American students were also disadvantaged on other transition outcomes such as progress to degree and college completion relative to white students. This pattern of secondary education that is linked to differential preparation for college by ethnic and racial group and income status represents a troubling pattern of inequity that continues to persist (Schmid, 2010).

In a study of CTE transition programs similar to tech prep, Lekes et al. (2007) studied students in two regions of the country. Findings revealed CTE transition students in both sites scored significantly higher than their matched non-CTE transition student counterparts on the Reading for Information subtest items of ACT WorkKeys. A significant difference was noted between the two groups on dual credit course-taking, with CTE transition students taking more dual credit than non-CTE students. Such positive findings would be encouraging of new vocationalism were it not for the troubling pattern of differential benefits that emerged, similar to the Bragg et al. (2007) study. Lewis (2008) concluded that various new vocationalism reforms had revealed mixed results due to the questions they raised about equitable outcomes for minority students. His synthesis revealed modest evidence of the advantage of tech prep, career academies, and youth apprenticeships over traditional education, speculating that new vocationalism reforms had not been implemented thoroughly enough to test their effects. He suggested, "POS [Programs of Study] are unlikely to produce marked improvements in achievement and transition to postsecondary education" (p. 180) unless they are implemented sufficiently to overcome patterns associated with the past. He concluded that incremental change, admittedly less complex to implement, had resulted in partial reform and, as a consequence, new vocationalism had not achieved the major effects it had hoped to realize.

The Community College Role

Much of the conversation about new vocationalism has been directed at the K-12 level, particularly at high schools, except to the extent community colleges have been seen as partners to receive CTE students who are advancing to the postsecondary level (Grubb & Lazerson, 2005). For some community colleges, tech prep, career pathways, and programs of study represented useful avenues to student recruitment to maintain or grow postsecondary CTE program enrollments. However, since many students who enroll in postsecondary CTE classes are beyond traditional college age, community college practitioners have not always embraced models and approaches that transition high school students to college as eagerly as they have adopted workforce development strategies for adults (Alssid & Goldberg, 2011; Grubb, Badway, Bell, Bragg, & Russman, 1997). Whereas concern about access to postsecondary CTE programs for matriculating high school graduates is recognized as important to keeping enrollments healthy, postsecondary CTE programs often enroll substantial numbers of adults who already have labor market experience (with some also having prior college enrollment) and who seek to retrain or upgrade their skills to attain a better job. For many students, the postsecondary CTE curriculum provides a way to fulfill their employment goals, with college and industry-related credentials being the reward for program completion (Alssid & Goldberg, 2011).

In an extensive report on CTE for the National Center for Education Statistics (NCES), Levesque et al. (2008) reported that over 5,000 public, not-for-profit, and for-profit postsecondary institutions offered CTE (called "career education" in the report), suggesting that over 90% of Title IV eligible postsecondary institutions offered these courses. Over 1,100 public community colleges offered CTE courses, accounting for almost 20% of all two-, four-year, and less-than-two year, and public, not-for-profit, or for profit postsecondary education providers. This summary report claimed that U.S. postsecondary institutions had approximately 4.4 million associate degree seekers and 1 million certificate seekers among all CTE students, with business and marketing, health care, education, and computer science majors as the predominant fields of study among associate degree seeking students. Personal and consumer services and trade and industry were common CTE majors among students seeking certificates.

Students who enroll in postsecondary CTE programs are more diverse than the overall community college postsecondary student population. Compared to their counterparts enrolled in the general or transfer curriculum, a higher proportion of CTE students represent ethnic and racial minority groups, non-traditional college age students, individuals who are financially independent from their families and married with financial dependents, students who attend college while also working part- or full-time, and low income students. Hence, at this level, the diversity of student enrollment is extensive (Bragg, 2001b). This demographic diversity is especially evident among postsecondary CTE students who pursue college credentials at less-than-degree level (Levesque et al., 2008). Thus, whereas students enrolled in postsecondary CTE are demographically diverse relative to the rest of the college enrollment, stratification within CTE is apparent in that more minority and low income students are present in the student group that pursues certificates rather than degrees. Specific skill training that prepares students for immediate employment is an important goal of many of these students—albeit an "en route" goal to the associate degree (Bragg, Cullen, Bennett, & Ruud, 2011, p. 9), which explains why a career pathway and program of study approach is important to achieving greater equity in student access and completion among underserved student populations (Foster, Strawn, & Duke-Benefield, 2011).

Predominant theories undergirding the skills-training agenda reinforce the essentialist approach (Rojewski, 2002) mentioned earlier in this chapter, along with human capital, globalization, signaling theory, and sheepskin theory, all prevalent in the CTE and higher education literature (see, for example, Levin, 2001). Gray and Herr (1995) pointed to the importance of CTE curriculum to build a competent workforce, arguing that skill-related training is predicated on human capital investment. Human capital theory (Becker, 1993) suggests that individuals and, by extension, the firms that employ them are most productive when high quality goods and services are produced at a relatively low cost because individuals can apply the knowledge and skills they have acquired through education. Related to human capital theory is signaling theory (Spence, 2002), which suggests that an individual's ability to perform in the workplace is largely obscured from employers who need cues or signals to inform them when a person possesses the ability to perform productively in a job. Signaling theory provides rationale for why employers advocate for credentials and stridently encourage the education system to adopt them. Sheepskin effects extend from signaling theory, suggesting individuals who receive credentials experience benefits over and above students with comparable education but no credentials (Bailey, Kienzl, & Marcotte, 2004). In an age where credentialing has assumed a top priority on the nation's higher education agenda (Matthew, 2011), an examination of CTE's role in awarding credentials to all students, especially underserved populations, is important.

Furthermore, arguments concerning globalization of the economy suggest CTE reflects the influence of technology and increased commodification of the curriculum, resulting in increased centering of CTE as the primary mission of community colleges (Levin, 2000, 2001). Jacobs (2001) and Jacobs and Dougherty (2006) pointed to the importance of CTE programs that are tightly coupled to the economy to prepare students for technology-rich, globalized work environments. They argued that postsecondary CTE is not only critical to employment in the first job, but to ensuring that students and graduates keep pace with evolving technologies so that they are prepared for career advancement. In this respect, the form of CTE envisioned by Dougherty and Jacobs is consistent with the career pathways and programs of study that award a series of increasingly valuable credentials in the marketplace. Indeed, multiple pathways (Oakes & Saunders, 2008) that provide options for students, including certificates and degrees, represent a potentially democratizing form of curriculum. Questions remain, however, about whether these career pathways and programs of study are fulfilling this democratization goal and whether the credentials and other benefits associated with them are distributed equitably to all.

Promising Results

Research conducted for the national assessment of vocational education (Bailey et al., 2004; Silverberg, Warner, Fong, & Goodwin, 2004) using three national longitudinal datasets showed, overall, students who completed postsecondary CTE programs did at least as well as, and in some cases significantly better, than students who enrolled in academic programs at comparable levels of postsecondary education. In a comprehensive synthesis of over 20 studies of the benefits of attending and completing a community college education, Belfield and Bailey (2011) reported "strong positive earnings from community college attendance and completion, as well as from progression to a four-year college" (p. 60), and they reported that these gains increase over time. Certificate and associate degree holders had higher returns than individuals with similar years of postsecondary education but no credential, giving credence to the presence of the sheepskin effect, particularly for female students. Inadequate evidence of effects was available for ethnic, minority, and low income groups, leaving the question of equity in student outcomes unanswered and suggesting the importance of research that disaggregates results by sub-groups to understand the role postsecondary CTE plays in addressing historic inequities faced by underserved populations.

Referencing again the democratization function of community colleges, recent experimentation with new vocationalism at the postsecondary level includes the offering of bridge programs, career pathways, and programs of study that are extended to underserved populations, including ethnic minority and low income students, particularly adult learners. Prince and Jenkins (2005) observed that adult students are less likely to be retained in college and receive any type of certificate or degree than younger students. Evaluating the effects of bridge and career pathway programs for adults in Washington state, Prince and Jenkins applied the notion of a "tipping point" to the college enrollment and credentialing phenomenon, suggesting the importance of low income adult learners attending at least one year of college, typically CTE, and earning a credential to boost their labor market outcomes in terms of employment and earnings. Taking remedial courses concurrently with CTE produced significant average rates of employment and quarterly earnings, and these results held true for adults and low income learners. Again, drawing on data from Washington state, Jenkins and Weiss (2011) recommended that younger learners would benefit from programs of study that link academic and CTE course work systematically with support services that encourage persistence. These results offer modest support for new vocationalism reforms that engage diverse learners and support their completion of certificates and degrees.

Old Debates, Persistent Challenges

Philosophical and theoretical debates have been used to support vocational education policy and practice since its beginning nearly a century ago. As vocational education evolved into CTE, the debate over essentialism versus pragmatism has provided a useful frame for understanding the evolution of differentiated instruction and tracking, including detrimental effects, and the potential for new vocationalism reforms that have emerged slowly over the past two decades and continue to struggle to find a viable place in curriculum. Whereas the human capital rationale looms large as a rationale for CTE on several levels, Rojewski (2002) observed that some educators have consistently argued for CTE to be a response to economic and social issues, having a democratizing effect on the educational system because of its ability to reach and serve underrepresented learners. From this perspective, CTE programs recognize that students are complex, malleable, and receptive to learning when the teaching and learning process is reflective of the multiple dimensions of life (Sarkees-Wircenski & Scott, 1995). This aim suggests that CTE is not so much about preparing people for work as about whetting their appetite for learning and providing them with relevant options and opportunities to help them navigate through education, into the labor market, and, most importantly, on with all of the facets of their lives (Oakes & Saunders, 2008).

In spite of the century-long experience with CTE, there remains relatively limited knowledge of educational and economic benefits, particularly for ethnic and racial minorities, low income students, and other underrepresented learners. Limitations to research designs that attempt to examine outcomes for students who participate in CTE relative to students with comparable characteristics who have not participated have been a perennial problem, going so far as to threaten future federal support for CTE (Duncan, 2011). Calls for improvements to CTE and better research to report empirical evidence of program quality and student outcomes are frequent (see, for example, Lewis, 2008), but mostly addressed insufficiently to satisfy the critics. Similar to the debate that gave birth to vocational education in the U.S. in 1917, the merits of CTE continue to be contested. Although CTE is unlikely to go away entirely, given the rise of new vocationalism, more scrutiny and better research are needed to understand how CTE benefits the increasingly diverse student populations that seek to access and complete community college credentials and degrees. The promise of a more democratic form of education and a better future for all the nation's learners may be at stake.

Questions for Discussion

1. In what ways does the concept of "new vocationalism" pertain to the community college?

2. How do we address questions of CTE program quality in a period of declining resources combined with increased interest in CTE programs?

3. When education is increasingly looked upon as a private good, and the community college's access mission threatened by an economic development agenda, is CTE appropriately placed within the community college? Why or why not?

References

Alssid, J., & Goldberg, M. (2011). Workforce strategies for America's future: Community college contributions. In American Association of Community Colleges, *21st-Century Commission on the Future Community Colleges, Working Briefs* (pp. 72–81). Washington, DC: Author.

Bailey, T., Kienzl, G., & Marcotte, D. (2004, August). Who benefits from postsecondary occupational education? Findings from the 1980s and 1990s, No. 23. New York, NY: Teachers College, Columbia University.

Becker, G. (1993). *Human capital: A theoretical and empirical analysis, with special reference to education* (3rd ed.). Chicago: University of Chicago Press.

Belfield, C., & Bailey, T. (2011). The benefits of attending community college: A review of the evidence. *Community College Review, 39*(1), 46–68.

Benavot, A. (1983). The rise and decline of vocational education. *Sociology of Education, 56,* 63–76.

Benson, C. S. (1997). New vocationalism in the United States: Potential problems and outlook. *Economics of Education Review, 16*(3), 201–212.

Boesel, D., & McFarland, L. (1994, July). *National assessment of vocational education: Final report to Congress* (Vol. I). Washington, DC: U.S. Department of Education, Office of Educational Research and Improvement.

Bragg, D. (2001a). Community college access, mission, and outcomes: Considering intriguing intersections and opportunities. *Peabody Journal of Education, 76*(1), 93–116.

Bragg, D. (2001b). The past, present and future role of federal vocational legislation in the United States. *Journal of Applied Research in Community Colleges, 9*(1), 57–67.

Bragg, D., & Bennett, S. (2011). *Introduction to pathways to results*. Champaign, IL: Office of Community College Research and Leadership, University of Illinois at Urbana-Champaign. Retrieved from http://occrl .illinois.edu/files/Projects/ptr/Modules/PTR%20Intro%20Module.pdf

Bragg, D., Cullen, D., Bennett, S., & Ruud, C. (2011). *All or nothing? Midpoint credentials for college students who stop short of credential requirements* (Working paper). Champaign, IL: Office of Community College Research and Leadership, University of Illinois at Urbana-Champaign.

Bragg, D., Layton, J., & Hammons, F. (1994, September). *Tech prep implementation in the United States: Promising trends and lingering challenges*. Berkeley, CA: National Center for Research in Vocational Education, University of California at Berkeley.

Bragg, D., Loeb, J., Gong, Y., Deng, P., Hill, J., & Yoo, J. (2003). *Transition from high school to college and work for tech prep participants in eight local consortia*. St. Paul, MN: National Research Center for Career and Technical Education, University of Minnesota.

Bragg, D., & Ruud, C. (2011). *The adult learner and the applied baccalaureate: Lessons from six states*. Champaign, IL: Office of Community College Research and Leadership, University of Illinois at Urbana-Champaign. Retrieved from http://occrl.illinois.edu/files/Projects/lumina/Report/LuminaABFinalReport.pdf

Bragg, D., Zamani, E., Yoo, Jung-sup, & Hill, J. (2001, April). *The impact of tech prep on college readiness and retention in two disparate consortia*. Paper presentation at the annual meeting of the American Educational Research Association, Division, J, Seattle, WA.

Brint, S., & Karabel, J. (1989). *Diverted dream: Community colleges and the promise of educational opportunity in America 1900–1985*. London: Oxford University Press.

Calhoun, C., & Finch, A. (1976). *Vocational education: Concepts and operations* (2nd ed.). Belmont, CA: Wadsworth Publishing Company.

Carnevale, A. P., Smith, N., & Strohl, J. (2010). *Help wanted: Projections of jobs and education requirements through 2018*. Washington, DC: Georgetown University, Center on Education and the Workforce. Retrieved from http://cew.georgetown.edu/jobs2018/

Cohen, A. M, & Brawer, F. B. (2008). *The American community college* (5th ed.). San Francisco: Jossey-Bass.

Dewey, J. (1916, March 11). Vocational education. *New Republic, 6*, 159–160.

Dougherty, K. (2004). *The contradictory college: Th e conflicting origins, impacts, and futures of the community college*. Albany, NY: State University of New York Press.

Duncan, A. (2011, February 2). The new CTE: Secretary Duncan's remarks on career and technical education. (Press release.) Retrieved from http://www.ed.gov/news/speeches/new-cte-secretaryduncans-remarks-career-and-technical-education

Evans, R., & Herr, E. (1978). *Foundations of vocational education* (2nd ed). Columbus, OH: Charles E. Merrill Publishing Company.

Foster, M., Strawn, J., & Duke-Benefield, A. (2011). *Beyond basic skills: State strategies to connect low-skilled adults to an employer-valued postsecondary education*. Center for Law and Social Policy, (2010). Retrieved from http://www.clasp.org/admin/site/publications/files/Beyond-Basic-Skills-March-2011.pdf

Gray, K. & Herr, E. (1995). *Other ways to win: Creating alternatives for high school graduates*. Th ousand Oakes, CA: Corwin Press, Inc.

Grubb, N., Badway, N., Bell, D., Bragg, D., & Russman, M. (1997, October). *Workforce, economic, and community development: The changing landscape of the entrepreneurial community college*. Mission Viejo, CA: League for Innovation in the Community College, National Center for Research in Vocational Education

Grubb, W. N., & Lazerson, M. (1974). *American education and vocationalism: A documentary history, 1870 – 1970*. New York, NY: Teachers College Press.

Grubb, W. N., & Lazerson, M. (2005). *The education gospel: The economic power of schooling*. Cambridge, MA: Harvard University Press, and National Council for Occupational Education.

Harmon, R., & MacAllum, K. (2003). *Documented characteristics of labor market-responsive community colleges and a review of supporting literature*. Washington, DC: Academy for Educational Development. ED 479 041

Hayward, G. C., & Benson, C. S. (1993). *Vocational-technical education: Major reforms and debates 1917–present*. Washington, DC: Office of Vocational and Adult Education, U.S. Department of Education. (ERIC Document Reproduction Service No. ED 369 959)

Hull, D. (Ed.) (2005). *Career pathways: Education with a purpose*. Waco, TX: Center for Occupational Research and Development.

Jacobs, J. (2001). What is the future of post-secondary occupational education? *Journal of Vocational Education Research, 26*(2), 172–205.

Jacobs, J., & Dougherty, K. (2006). The uncertain future of the community college workforce development mission. *New Directions for Community Colleges, no. 136* (pp. 53–62). San Francisco: Jossey-Bass.

Jenkins, D., & Weiss, M. (2011, September). *Charting pathways to completion for low-income community college students.* CCR Working Paper No. 34. New York, NY: Teachers College, Columbia University.

Kaufman, P., Bradby, D., & Teitelbaum, P. (2000). *High Schools That Work and whole school reform: Raising academic achievement of vocational completers through the reform of school practice.* Columbus, OH: National Center for Dissemination of Career and Technical Education, The Ohio State University. (ERIC Document Reproduction Service No. ED 438498)

Labaree, D. (2010). *The thinning mission of public mission of the American public school.* Paper presentation for the Educational Theory Summer Institute, College of Education, University of Illinois at Urbana-Champaign.

LaFollette, A. (2011). *An historical policy analysis of the Carl D. Perkins legislation: Examining the history, creation, implementation and reauthorization of the law.* (Doctoral dissertation). Retrieved from IDEALS http://hdl.handle.net/2142/26060

Lazerson, M., & Grubb, W. N. (1974). *American education and vocationalism: A documentary history 1870–1970.* New York, NY: Teachers College Press.

Lekes, N., Bragg, D., Loeb, J., Oleksew, C., Mazsalek, J., Laraviere, M., & Hood, L. (2007). *The impact of career-technical education transition program practices on student outcomes.* St. Paul, MN: National Research Center for Career and Technical Education, University of Minnesota.

Levesque, K., Laird, J., Hensley, E., Choy, S. P., Cataldi, E. F., and Hudson, L. (2008). *Career and technical education in the United States: 1990 to 2005* (NCES 2008–035). Washington, DC: National Center for Education Statistics, Institute of Education Sciences, U.S. Department of Education.

Levin, J. (2000). The revised institution: The community college mission at the end of the twentieth century. *Community College Review, 28*(2), 1–25.

Levin, J. (2001). *Globalizing the community college: Strategies for change in the twenty-first Century.* New York, NY: Palgrave.

Lewis, M. (2008). Effectiveness of previous initiatives similar to programs of study: Tech prep, career pathways, and youth apprenticeships. *Career and Technical Education Research, 33*(3), 165–188.

Lewis, T., & Cheng, S. (2006). Tracking, expectations, and the transformation of vocational education. *American Journal of Education, 113*(1), 67–99.

Lucas, S. (1999). *Tracking inequality: Stratification and mobility in the American high school.* New York, NY: Teachers College Press.

Lynch, R. L. (2000). *New directions for high school career and technical education in the 21st century* (Information Series No. 384). Columbus, OH: The Ohio State University, ERIC Clearinghouse on Adult, Career, and Vocational Education. (ERIC Document Reproduction Service No. ED 444 037)

Matthew, D. (2011). The case for college completion. In American Association of Community Colleges, *21st-Century Commission on the Future Community Colleges, Working Briefs* (pp. 22–30). Washington, DC: Author.

Meeder, H. (2008). *The Perkins Act of 2006: Connection career and technical education with the college and career readiness agenda.* Washington, DC: Achieve, Inc. Retrieved from http://www.achieve.org/files/AchieveCTEPolicyBrief-02-07-08.pdf

Meers, G. D. (1987). *Handbook for vocational special needs education* (2nd ed.). Rockville, MD: Aspen.

Meier, K. (2008). *The community college mission: History and theory, 1930–2000* (Unpublished doctoral dissertation). University of Arizona, Tucson, AZ.

Oakes, J. (1985). *Keeping track: How schools structure inequality.* New Haven, CT: Yale University Press.

Oakes, J., & Saunders, M. (2008). *Beyond tracking: Multiple pathways to college, career, and civic participation.* Cambridge, MA: Harvard University Press.

Parnell, D. (1985). *The neglected majority.* Washington, DC: Community College Press. (ERIC Document Reproduction Service No. ED 262 843)

Prince, D., & Jenkins, D. (2005, April). Building pathways to success for low-skill adult students: Lessons for community college policy and practice from a statewide longitudinal tracking study. *Community College Research Center Brief, no. 25.* New York, NY: Teachers College, Columbia University.

Prosser, C. A. (1913, May). The meaning of industrial education. *Vocational Education, 406.* 401–410.

Rojewski, J. (2002). *Preparing the workforce of tomorrow: A conceptual framework for career and technical education.* Columbus, OH: National Dissemination Center for Career and Technical Education, The Ohio State University.

Ruffing, K. (n.d.). *The history of career clusters*. Retrieved from http://www.google.com/search?q=Ruffing%2C+Career+Clusters%2C+history&ie=utf-8&oe=utf-8&aq=t&rls=org.mozilla:en-US:offi cial&client=firefox-a

Sarkees-Wircenski, M., & Scott, J. L. (1995). *Vocational special needs* (3rd ed.). Homewood, IL: American Technical.

Schmid, C. (2010). Challenges and opportunities of community colleges. In F. Lazin, M. Evans, & N. Jayaram (Eds.), *Higher education and equality of opportunities: Cross-national perspectives* (pp. 25–40). Lanham, MD: Lexington Books.

Silverberg, M., Warner, E., Fong, M., & Goodwin, D. (2004). *National assessment of vocational education*. Washington, DC: United States Department of Education.

Spence, M. (2002, June). Signaling in retrospect and the informational structure of markets. *The American Economic Review, 92*(3), 434–459.

Taylor, J., Kirby, C., Bragg, D., Oertle, K., Jankowski, N., & Khan, S. (2009, July). *Illinois program of study guide*. Champaign, IL: Office of Community College Research and Leadership, University of Illinois at Urbana-Champaign.

Wirth, A. (1992). *Education and work for the year 2000: Choices we face*. San Francisco: Jossey-Bass.

Wonacott, M. (2003). *History and evolution of vocational and career and technical education*. Columbus, OH: Center for Education and Training for Employment, Ohio State University.

CHAPTER 34

SOCIO-ACADEMIC INTEGRATIVE MOMENTS: RETHINKING ACADEMIC AND SOCIAL INTEGRATION AMONG TWO-YEAR COLLEGE STUDENTS IN CAREER-RELATED PROGRAMS

REGINA DEIL-AMEN

College student persistence and dropout have been studied for decades, but little inquiry has focused on community college or private two-year college students. Although about half of first-time postsecondary students enroll in a two-year college, researchers understand little about why only approximately a quarter of these degree-seekers complete any degree five years after entrance (Rosenbaum, Deil-Amen, & Person, 2006). Models that exist to aid our understanding have been generated primarily from research on residential, four-year college students. The present analysis uses rich qualitative data to excavate the potential of Tinto's Theory of Student Departure for understanding the dynamics of persistence for a more nontraditional group—two-year college commuting students. To better reflect how these students successfully cultivate feelings of belonging and competence, reinforce goal commitment, and access valuable social capital, a new conceptual fusion of the formerly distinct processes of academic integration and social integration is considered

This study was funded in part by grants from the NAEd/Spencer Foundation and the Sloan Foundation, and the author would like to thank James E. Rosenbaum and Ann E. Person, who were instrumental in development and execution of the study.

Theoretical Framework and Research Literature

The Appeal and Relevance of Tinto's Model

The major models of persistence include Tinto's Theory of Student Departure (1975, 1987, 1993), Astin's Theory of Involvement (1984), and Pascarella's model (1985). All the models were developed based on traditional students in traditional residential institutions. However, Tinto's theory, despite its origins, leaves room for an examination of students' institutional experiences in a way that does not necessarily need to be dependent on the traditional college-student lifestyle.[1] Building on Durkheim (1951), a conceptual cornerstone of the theory is that a *subjective* sense of belonging and membership is a fundamental component of student decisions and outcomes. Students choose to persist when they perceive intellectual and social congruence, or a normative fit between the student and the values, social rules, and academic quality of the college community. This congruence with the academic and social systems of the college reinforces a student's commitment to their institution and educational goals. Tinto referred to this as "academic integration" and "social

461

integration," and described lack of integration as isolation, or incongruence between a student and the intellectual and social communities in the college, which hinders commitment and leads to withdrawal. This sociology grounds the model, now the "most studied, tested, revised, and critiqued in the literature" (Braxton & Hirschy, 2005). Over 700 studies have cited the model, creating a Tintonian Dynasty (Bensimon, 2007).

Most studies find social and academic integration matter, to some extent, for persistence among four-year students (Pascarella & Terenzini, 1991, 2005) but the relative importance of each form of integration is contested. Some research highlights the importance of in-class academic experiences (e.g., Braxton, Milem, & Sullivan, 2000; Hurtado & Carter, 1997; Nora, Cabrera, Hagedorn, & Pascarella, 1996), but Braxton, Hirschy, and McClendon (2004) found a lack of empirical backing for the influence of academic integration in residential universities. They suggest serious revisions to Tinto's model, including dropping academic integration from the model and conceptually expanding toward six factors that influence social integration for residential students. Nevertheless, several studies find the two forms of integration to be interconnected (Tinto, 1998). When both forms occur, students are even more likely to persist (Stage, 1989), and one form of integration can act as a vehicle for the other form of integration, with high levels of social integration compensating for weaker academic integration (Pascarella & Terenzini, 1983; Stage, 1989; Tinto, 1975).

Applying the model to two-year and other commuting students has generated even more mixed, and less solid, results. On the one hand, some research suggests the model is not relevant. Voorhees (1987) found no association between persistence and integration in one community college. For commuting students, Bean and Metzner (1985), Tinto himself (1993), and Braxton, Sullivan, and Johnson (1997) contend background characteristics and external circumstances have a greater impact on persistence than on-campus factors. This aligns with research on the pivotal influence of significant others who encourage college goals in students' personal lives (Cabrera, Nora, & Castaneda, 1993; Nora, 1987; Nora, Attinasi, & Matonak, 1990). On the other hand, studies using national two-year samples (Deil-Amen, 2002; Pascarella & Terenzini, 1991, 2005) and a meta-analysis of six studies (Wortman & Napoli, 1996) show academic and social integration do influence attainment, but the findings of most studies are mixed regarding which form of integration is most important. Halpin (1990), Mutter (1992), and Pascarella and Chapman (1983) found community college persistence was influenced by academic integration, not social, and Tinto, Russo, and Kadel (1994), and later Tinto (1997) found classroom involvement not only facilitates academic integration, but also promotes integration beyond the classroom. In contrast, other scholars find community college students, similar to racial/ethnic minority students in other settings, experience "validation" *outside* the classroom, which influences persistence (Attinasi, 1989; Rendon, 1994; Terenzini et al., 1994). Also, several qualitative studies find the social dimensions of two-year colleges play a role in persistence, with intellectual and social contact with faculty, staff, and other students outside of class of particular salience (Deil-Amen & Rosenbaum, 2003; London, 1978; Neuman & Riesman, 1980; Rosenbaum et al., 2006; Weis, 1985).

In light of this multiplicity of findings, it is important to realize most attempts to validate Tinto's model more generally (Braxton et al., 1997; Braxton et al., 2004), do not specifically address the validity of social and academic integration as valuable concepts. In fact, few studies examine the direct relationship between integration and persistence, since the model theorizes an indirect relationship via goal commitment or institutional commitment. Therefore, further exploring the concepts upon which Tinto's interactionalist framework rests is a useful task. Garnering insight from past and current research that qualitatively explores students' direct experience with these processes can be especially valuable. Taking cues from accumulated prior quantitative research is prudent as well. Braxton and colleagues (2004) reviewed the relatively few attempts to test Tinto's theory on two-year and other commuting students, and they propose a theory of student departure to apply to commuter institutions. In contrast to residential universities, they expect academic integration, or "academic communities" (p. 48) play an important role in enhancing student commitment, in addition to the major influences of student entry characteristics, family, work, and finances.

The Challenges and Value of Applying Tinto to Marginalized and Non-Traditional Students

Social and academic integration may be valuable concepts to be retained, but scholars should rethink how to better conceptualize and measure the concepts for two-year college students. In fact, Braxton et al. (1997) suggested strengthening Tinto's model by identifying new sources of academic and social integration. The present study considers how these concepts should be altered to apply more appropriately to two-year students and the relevance of class, race and ethnicity for their integrative experiences.

Critics fault Tinto's model as inadequate for minority students because it assumes disconnection from a home community must occur before integration into a college community can happen (e.g Guiffrida, 2006; Hurtado & Carter, 1997; Tierney, 1992, 1999). Such critiques reinforce the need to understand the experiences of marginalized students of another type—two-year college students—whose institutional environments have not been thoroughly incorporated into prior retention models (Reason, 2003; Rendon, Jaloma, & Nora, 2000).[2] The vast majority of two-year students enroll in community colleges while remaining in their communities of origin, so the issue of separating from a culture of origin is less salient. After all, the name of the institution implies students can attend "college" while remaining in the "community." Such circumstances differ markedly from the residential contexts on which the above critiques were based, and the work of Torres (2006) on commuting university students suggests key differences do exist. The dynamics of race, class, and culture have not yet been adequately explored in *two-year* contexts while utilizing Tinto's concept of integration to frame the discussion.

It is important to explore two-year students' own perspective on their experience of integration because this subjective process is central to Tinto's model. Research has not carefully explored how they perceive a normative congruence between their own expectations and what their college offers.[3] This subjective component was present in Spady (1971) and Tinto (1993), but it is complex and difficult to measure, leaving researchers to concentrate on *behaviors* while neglecting students' *psychological experience* of identification and affiliation within campus communities. This distinction between behavior (participation, involvement) and a psychological sense of integration was highlighted over a decade ago by Hurtado and Carter (1997) who suggested that "integration can mean something completely different to student groups who have been historically marginalized in higher education" (p. 326–332). These and other critics of Tinto's model have attended to this subjective framework as it applies to racial and ethnic minority students in four-year residential institutions, but they have not considered how the psychological components of integration might differ for two-year college commuting students. Torres (2006) noted that commuting students do frame their expectations of what they need from their institution differently than residential students. They are "not as concerned with whether they fit with the environment as much as whether they understood how to navigate the system" (p. 311). They also confront the unique psychological challenges of continually negotiating between their college demands and their family and work obligations, and they are affected by how closely the actions of faculty, staff, and administrators reflect a commitment to the welfare of students (Braxton, Hirschy, & McClendon, 2004).

Other critics claim Tinto's model wrongly depicts the student as author of his or her success, while the advocacy of practitioners and "institutional agents" (Stanton-Salazaar, 1997, 2001) in facilitating the success of minority and two-year students is overlooked (Bensimon, 2007). This critique foregrounds the possibility that institutional agents, rather than just the characteristics or behaviors of students, play a pivotal role in providing social capital and other benefits to enable student persistence. Research on student diversity on traditional campuses, for instance, emphasizes the importance of faculty-student interactions on African American and Latino student academic performance and persistence (Allen, 1992; Anaya & Cole, 2001; Davis, 1991; Nettles, 1991) and the importance of peer interaction about academic matters, course-related faculty contact, and mentor relationships for minority students' intellectual self-concept (Cole, 2007). These studies, combined with the critiques of Guiffrida (2006), Tierney (1992, 1999), and Bensimon (2007), inform a need to focus on the role of the institutionally-located *people* who make success possible for students often thought to be at-risk of non-persistence and on the institutional spaces where such support and integrative processes take place. The prior research noted above suggests marginalized students are more successful at navigating the cultural, psychosocial, and intellectual college terrain when they benefit from key forms of assistance from institutional agents. Thus far, such processes have been little explored within community colleges.

Attention to the Where and How Integration Happens Among Two-Year Students

Given the prominence of Tinto's model, the potential of its sociological underpinnings, and evidence that applicability of the model varies by institutional level and type, the present study qualitatively explores how the concept of integration resonates for a sample of non-traditional, commuting, two-year college students. Research has not fully conceptualized, measured, or operationalized integration effectively for students who commute, and few studies identify how or where the process of integration occurs in non-residential colleges. Although many studies have *quantified* social[4] and academic[5] integration into measurable behaviors and assessed their impact on student outcomes, researchers still understand little about the quality and nature of integrative processes—especially how and why certain actions enhance belonging, commitment, and persistence for *two-year* commuting students, who are among the most marginalized in higher education. As noted by Estella Bensimon in her ASHE presidential address:

> The reality is that underperformance, dropping out, and low degree-attainment is a problem that affects the "marginal" student disproportionately, yet student success, with few exceptions, is treated as a generic phenomenon and many of the measurement instruments and analytical models do not account for the unique circumstances of "students at the margins." (Bensimon, 2007, p. 449)

No other study has qualitatively analyzed students' perceptions of the integration process across several different two-year institutions, whose students are among those most likely to forego on-campus activities traditionally associated with integration and most likely to possess tenuous goals (Manski, 1989). Relevant questions remain unanswered. Do integrative behaviors of two-year college students differ substantially from those we've traditionally measured among four-year students? What are the qualitative dimensions of this integrative process, particularly when opportunities for traditional forms of integration are limited and the norms and expectations of college life are different? The present study explores how a variety of two-year college students describe their experiences of belonging and congruence in an attempt to identify how and where integration occurs for them and the experiences that engender such feelings and motivate their behavior. It is hypothesized that their experiences may differ from traditional measures of such processes, which have been generated from studies of more traditional contexts.

Methods

Data were collected as part of a multi-method, multi-site study that employed triangulation, utilizing surveys, interviews, and observations. A total of 238 semi-structured interviews were conducted with students, staff, and faculty at seven public community and seven private two-year colleges in and near a large Midwestern city.[6] Of the 238 interviews, 125 were students selected to ensure variability in race, SES, gender, age, and program of study. Nearly all students were selected within comparable business/secretarial, computer/electronics, and medical/health programs across public and private institutions. Thirty-seven percent of the students were Latino, 35% African-American, 19% White, and 9% of Asian, Indian, or Middle-Eastern decent. Two-thirds attended an "urban" college, and 76% were first-generation college students. Eighty-one percent self-reported coming from low (below $30K) to middle income ($30K–$60K) families, and their ages ranged from 18 to 46 with an average age of 24.

Interviews were an hour long and were recorded and transcribed verbatim. A team of three researchers content analyzed the interviews by first developing initial codes.[7] Then, based on both the intersection and partitioning of those initial codes, themes and sub-themes were identified. The initial codes of commitment, belonging, and integration were content analyzed and subdivided into themes and coded as academic, social, fitting-in, comfort/discomfort, connection/disconnection, college or program size, SES, motivation, teachers, advisors, in-class, out-of-class, friends, help/support, discouragement, clubs/groups, cohorts, and self-perception. These codes were then scanned for content that intersected with the first set of initial codes and sub themes and checked for patterns across program of enrollment, age, and race/ethnicity.

To enhance reliability of data collection and coding (Babbie, 2004), three researchers conducted the interviews and were similarly trained with a standardized interview format (Kirk & Miller, 1986; LeCompte & Goetz, 1982).[8] To validate the data, informant feedback was provided.[9] To further enhance validity, as relationships and themes in the data emerged, new interviews were conducted at different institutions to replicate the themes to confirm patterns (Strauss & Corbin, 1990).

Findings and Discussion

Students described experiences of social and academic integration in each two-year college context. Several colleges were small, located in urban ethnic enclaves, and offered limited programs. Some were huge downtown public and non-profit private campuses with students who arrived by bus and train to enroll not only in the occupational programs in this study, but also in a wide range of transfer, basic, and continuing education classes seeking everything from one class to workforce certificates to post-baccalaureate degrees. Other colleges, including two of the community colleges and one for-profit, were located in inner-suburbs, where nearly everyone drove to campus. Student stories told of struggle and determination—from the young Puerto Rican single parent who juggled work, school, and childcare to earn a degree to assist an accountant, to the African American man in his late 20s trying to gain a foothold in the primary labor market after years of low-wage jobs by studying computer-aided drafting, to the returning forty-something White mom learning about electronics engineering, to the Indian immigrant hoping to be a radiography assistant, to the Mexican American man wanting to trade in his hard hat for a job designing websites. Remarkably, distinguishable patterns emerged across this diverse sample in how they described feelings of belonging within their college environments and the behaviors that led to their making connections and navigating their institution.

Student perceptions of what helped them integrate were closely linked to institutional actors, or agents, that facilitated the process for them. Given this consistency across institutional type and students' race, class, and SES background, findings lend support to the notion that institutional agents (Stanton-Salazaar, 1997, 2001) and practitioners (Bensimon, 2007) in the form of instructors/faculty, other staff, and students as well, were instrumental in how the two-year students integrated. Although many students noted family support, 92% highlighted a college-specific "agent" or "agents" who were instrumental to their sense of adjustment, comfort, belonging, and competence as college students. A focus on students' subjective perceptions regarding what facilitated their integration process contributes to a better understanding of how their experiences and their perceptions of their experiences may differ substantially from traditional students.

Some sub-group patterns did appear. African Americans were much more likely to explicitly articulate a desire for a cultural or personal connection with an individual or group on campus. Other racial subgroups discussed such connections, but tended to refrain from defining a desire or need for such interpersonal connections. Nearly all students commented equally on their limited time to engage while on-campus, challenging the presumption that younger students have more time to seek traditional forms of campus interaction. Many of these younger students had families of their own, were working to support themselves or "help out" their families of origin, or were spending quite a bit of time commuting to and from college and maintaining close relationships with and obligations to family members of all kinds.

Patterns that emerged in the data are detailed below and illustrate the potency of social and academic integration processes and how and why they enhance feelings of congruence, even among non-traditional aged, remedial, part-time, working students who may also be parents. Given Manski's (1989) consideration of the tenuousness of community college students' goals, it is not surprising that interviews reveal a link between students' integrative experiences and a reinforcement, strengthening, or refinement of their goals.

Integration During Class Time

Although quantitative measures of integration emphasize frequency of contact with faculty, advisors, and fellow students *outside* of class, feelings of belonging and connection often happen in arenas other than purely out-of-class social interactions. In fact, for the students studied, connections tended to happen during *in-class* interactions. Deanna is a good example of the many students who identified teacher-student and student-student interactions *in the classroom* as important contributors to their sense of comfort in the college environment. Deanna is a traditional-aged Latina attending a private two-year college full-time while working up to 35 hours per week as a receptionist at a real estate office and caring for her young niece for several days each week. While Deanna dismissed college "friends" as unrealistic in her busy life, she identified teacher and student support and approachability *in the classroom* as fundamental to her feelings of social comfort. She pointed to the importance of individual faculty members taking an interest in her academic success as a fundamental reason for why she feels comfortable as a college student.

> I really feel comfortable in this school because . . . I realized it was small . . . The teachers . . . pay more attention to . . . your needs, and ask questions . . . I feel comfortable. I really do. I never thought I would, but I feel comfortable. I feel like I could . . . walk in and it's my home, you know? I do feel comfortable. I like it.

Cheryl, a 33 year-old African American housewife, mother and full-time worker from the south side of Chicago enrolled at one of the community colleges part-time, feels similarly.

> Cheryl: The classes that I've taken, I feel real comfortable there, and I want to finish . . . It's a real warm feeling . . . I'm very determined to get through . . . Completion is really important for me.
>
> Interviewer: You said there's a warm feeling there. What do you think makes it a warm feeling?
>
> Cheryl: In my experience, the teachers, and the students, 'cause I've been going there for four years and it's a lot of students that's in the same predicament that I'm in—working part time. So, you know, it's like a family thing; encouragement.
>
> Interviewer: Can you explain to me what it is about [your instructor] that you like?
>
> Cheryl: Her encouragement. She's just truly an inspiration. You know, an African American woman that's made it—that's encouraging. The way she teaches, she allows . . . students to really express themselves. . . . I was able to express myself. It was a safe place for me. . . . I was just determined and I didn't give up. It was truly a safe and a warm place for me. . . . Truly great.

Approximately three-quarters of the students identified such support and approachability of teachers or other students within the classrooms as fundamental to their feelings of comfort in college. For them, a fear of displaying their inadequacy fed the initial discomfort they experienced in each new college classroom they entered. Many thought instructors or classmates would get frustrated about having to repeat the information or embarrass them publicly for their lack of knowledge. So they tended to act cautiously. As Yared, an African immigrant at a community college put it, "Students are afraid to answer because they don't want to appear stupid." This fear was prominent among native born African American and Latino students of all ages. Attempts by instructors to welcome and solicit student questions in the classroom tended to mitigate such fears and engender feelings of comfort, an important precursor to student commitment to persistence. Maria is a Puerto Rican, divorced, single-parent who dropped out of high school and returned to community college in her early thirties. Although she ended up with mainly As and a member of the college's honor society, her confidence was low upon enrollment. She described the pivotal role played by her instructors' approaches to her during class time, detailing her experience with her English professor:

> He took the time to take me aside when I wrote my first paper, which was the first paper I had ever written in my whole life. I had never done it in high school. . . . I was really nervous about handing it in. . . . He started telling everybody their grades . . . calling them out into the hallway. I was really nervous. He grabbed my paper and I went out there. "Oh God, he's going to tell me . . . that it doesn't make sense . . ." and I was really nervous. He just held my hand and said, "You made it real difficult for me to grade your paper. I didn't know what to do with this. I've never gotten a paper like this and

it was an A+." He wrote really totally positive comments. He said, "Don't be afraid of writing just because you're going to make a mistake. You obviously like writing. Keep writing and if you make mistakes, so what?" He took the time. From then on we were pretty close.

However, instructors making the effort to help students overcome their fear without a systematic and effective plan for doing so unfortunately didn't guarantee success. Some students continued to suffer despite the opportunity to get help during class time because they were too timid to exploit the opportunity. Adriana, a Latina who works part-time and cares for her younger sister, is an example:

Interviewer: So now you're finding out the classes are getting a little harder?

Adriana: Yeah . . . actually, there's just one, in what I'm majoring in, Accounting 2. It's getting harder. I really don't understand . . . what's the deal . . . but I try to handle it.

Interviewer: Now what do you do to try? Do you try to get any help, or . . . what do you do?

Adriana: I've never tried getting help from here. I, actually, when I'm at home, when I get my days off, I actually study, those days. It's kind of hard, too, because I have a little sister that I'm taking care of, and it's really noisy, so . . . I feel like if I ask a question . . . and he goes over it, and, like, people already know it, they get frustrated, y'know? It's not their fault that I don't understand. Sometimes that's how I feel. So really I don't ask questions, I try to understand on my own.

Interviewer: Does your teacher ever say it's okay to ask questions?

Adriana: Yeah. He's always, y'know, "Does anybody have questions?" But sometimes I still feel like he's gonna get frustrated or other students are gonna get frustrated, and it's like, I don't want that to happen, y'know, so I really don't ask questions.

In contrast to most quantitative measures of integration that emphasize interactions outside of class, the pronounced importance of in-class experiences makes sense for commuting students. Unfortunately, our lenses for viewing student persistence have not prioritized the classroom, perhaps because most research has focused on large residential universities populated by students with the privilege of living on campus. However, the consistency of the present findings with findings regarding the relevance of classroom dynamics for four-year students supports the notion that such a classroom-centered focus may be more broadly applicable (Braxton et al., 2000; Hurtado & Carter, 1997; Nora et al., 1996). Regarding two-year college students, Tinto (1997) contributes consistent findings. In a coordinated studies program at one community college, he found classrooms can serve as smaller communities of learning that provide "a mechanism through which both academic and social involvement arises and student effort is engaged" (p. 615). His findings reveal students' supportive relationships with peers in class and the learning and engagement that result from the program's unique approach. However, Tinto is similar to other scholars of persistence, the classroom-centered studies noted above, and to his prior research with two-year college samples (Tinto, Russo, & Kadel, 1994) in his preoccupation with social relationships *outside of the classroom* as the linchpin of integration. Although he does acknowledge that for commuting students, "if academic and social integration is to occur, it must occur in the classroom" (Tinto, 1997, p. 559), he nevertheless chooses to center his discussion of his findings on the potential of the classroom to serve as a bridge, or gateway to subsequent academic and social involvement in college communities *external to* the classroom.

In the present study, students enrolled in "regular" classes (not part of any special learning communities) spoke of the approachability of instructors during class time and the feelings of comfort, belonging, and intellectual welcome to learning that it generated. Most students neither expected nor desired that these in-class relationships with instructors and students extend to social communities beyond the classroom. For them, feeling that they could ask questions and ask for assistance in class without being looked upon negatively by their instructor or classmates was enough to combat their fear of not belonging and inspire their drive to persist. For students with limited time, resources, and inclination to seek assistance and support outside of class, a framework that truly centers on the academic experience as the central vehicle of integration is critical. Likely the same time and resource constraints that lead students to choose the two-year college option in the first place also color their integration strategy.

Beyond the Classroom: The Interplay Between the Classroom and the Organizational Context

Organizational structures that limited the accessibility of faculty and instructors had consequences for students who chose particular in-class behaviors. Adriana's attempt to do it on her own rather than seeking help after class was in line with her college's lack of capacity to meet her needs due to the high number of adjunct faculty who were not available for office hours at convenient times. However, this in combination with her ineffective in-class strategies, fueled her subjective feelings about how her academic needs had become incongruent with her ability to gain help with her work, thereby diminishing her confidence in her own persistence. She described her confidence about her ability to finish when she first enrolled as a 7 or 8 on a scale of 10. However she explained that her rating had become low because "it's getting harder," yet she hesitated to seek additional help either in or outside of class and planned to keep to her strategy of studying on her own despite feeling unsure she was "gonna make it":

> Adriana: Everything I can do on my own. Like, I, I don't mind asking teachers, but, like I said, I don't want to annoy them either so, I do it more on my own.
>
> Interviewer: Now, are teachers also available, like, after school time, outside of class?
>
> Adriana: They're really more here, like, in the mornings . . . when I'm in class. So it's kinda harder to meet up with their schedule, so. . . . It's really hard, because as soon as I get out of here, there's times when I have to go straight to work. . . . And I get home around 8:00, like, 9:00, and it's like, I gotta eat, and go back to sleep 'cause then I gotta wake up early the next morning.

Given these circumstances, understandings of persistence should center on the particular characteristics of the two-year college student experience, with all of its limitations and potential strengths, including the lack of availability of out-of-classroom opportunities for assistance due to the combination of students' lives and organizational structures. In the two-year college setting, the diversity of potential interactions within the classroom, the intersection of in-class and out-of-class interactions, and students' subjective interpretation of those interactions should all be considered as central to a commuting students' integration process. Further, a one-size-fits-all curricular approach may not be appropriate since both faculty and students vary in their teaching and learning strategies. For instance, Christine, a 20-year-old community college student and child of Korean immigrants feels intimidated "talking out in class" like Adriana, but she has encountered instructors who structure in time inside and outside of class for individual help:

> The classes are really small. It's even smaller than high school. You get more attention and can ask a lot of questions. You can have more private time with professors in class and they're really open and if I don't understand stuff I can just go off to them and ask. They'll be nice to you.

When asked if she visits faculty during their office hours, Christine explained, "It was kind of hard for me to match those times, so I just go up to them after class or before class or leave a note and they usually call me." Jason is a 22-year-old, African American student who holds three jobs and reverse transferred from a four-year university and is now at a community college enrolled in remedial English. He was also motivated by the personal access that his English professor gives to her students:

> The other schools . . . gave you a syllabus, "These are my office hours. This is my office phone . . . Catch me if you can. If you do catch me, 'Oh I'm busy for the next two weeks.'" Here, it's a thing where teachers don't mind. Miss McVeigh, I love the lady for it. You can stay 5 or 10 minutes after class . . . that's *her* free time. Go down to her office, she's on the way out, she says, "Yes, what you need, Hon? OK . . . let me explain that to you." That's a good response because it makes me want to learn more. It makes me want to go to the teacher more. . . . She gives you her home phone number. Wonderful! I applaud that. . . . If I can't catch her, she says "Call me." She's a late night person, 10 or 11:00 pm. . . . I'm out all day. I'm in school. I may go straight to work. I don't get home until 8, or 9 or 10. . . . That's perfect for me.

Samantha is a White, former military, thirty-year-old divorced mother of several kids enrolled at a for-profit college in an electronics and computer technology program. Although similarly lacking in initial academic confidence, Samantha's in-your-face strategy presents a sharp contrast to Adriana and Christine:

> Interviewer: Do you feel like your confidence level has changed since you've started here?
>
> Samantha: Yeah, 'cause . . . actually, you know, with me like, goin' to these other colleges, I was like flunkin' . . . not doin' well or whatever, and I'm just like, "maybe I just don't know this stuff." And then I came here and I'm like passin' and doin' good, I'm just like, "I *am* smart." You know, like, "hey, I have it," you know? It's just, I guess the way it's taught to me. My confidence has really been boosted since I started here . . . 'cause if I have a question, I'll ask [the instructor] fifty questions, you know, and he'll be like, "(sighs) . . . you again?" (jokingly) you know, "Yeah, it's me." But I mean, he'll still answer it, you know, he'll take the time.

Given this diversity in students' approaches, it is optimal to identify how two-year students subjectively define and interpret their opportunities for integration *in the classroom* and how access to instructors is defined and organized in formal and informal ways both in class and *as an extension beyond the formal structure of class*. In his study of full-time, four-year college students, Cole (2007) finds "accessibility cues" are enacted within classrooms to signal faculty and students' desire for contact outside of class, and several components of the classroom environment enhance faculty-student interaction and students' intellectual self-concept (p. 276). Although Cole does not employ Tinto's framework, these components—overtly engaging students and valuing their comments, linking out-of-class events with class content, and allowing students to constructively challenge the professor—can guide further exploration of the value of in-class experiences for the social and academic integration of two-year students as well. The findings of the present study layer onto such in-class experiences, the unique structural constraints of a commuting institution as well as the challenge of students with extremely low academic self-confidence and limited time. The present findings are also consistent with and demonstrate in more detail, how the interconnectedness of social and academic integration (Pascarella & Terenzini, 1983; Stage, 1989; Tinto et al., 1994) become manifest in two-year college settings. Furthermore, they show that in-classroom dynamics can be a vehicle not just for social, but also academic integration beyond the classroom as well.

The Nature of Meaningful but Limited Social Integration with Other Students

Although students did not prioritize relationships with other students, they did describe dimensions along which such relationships were meaningful. Deanna and Cheryl (above) are good examples of how students developed relationships that did not extend very far beyond the classroom but were meaningful indicators of a positive peer climate for them. Each noted personal and work-related time constraints as an impediment to cultivating friendships with classmates and interacting with other students outside of class. Yet, Cheryl did explain that feelings of "warmth" between students that occur "at school" were important to her. These relationships appear limited in their resemblance to the more social activity-driven nature of friendships more typical among four-year students, particularly given the heavy time investment of such relationships. Quantitative measures of social integration emphasize *purely social* relationships with other students, but the two-year students highlighted the academic dimensions and instrumental quality of these relationships and interactions (in and out of the classroom, but not beyond). Students described limited, yet purposeful interactions with other students. For instance, Deanna relied quite heavily on other students' answering of her questions "just in class time; not out of class, like when I have a question to ask, and they know, and tell me." With regard to friendships or social interactions outside of class, she explains:

> I really don't . . . have any friends [at this college]. I do talk to some people, but I don't consider them friends, like, close friends. That's not what I'm here for. I'm not here to meet friends. I mean I don't mind, I like having friends, but I believe it takes time. So, I really . . . I mean, they're nice . . . some people are really nice, and I do talk to them, but I don't consider that really true friends.

Julia, a GED recipient and single parent in her mid-twenties with a seven-year-old, began at a private two-year college part-time in remedial classes while working part-time. She resembles

Deanna in her description of how working together with other students was extremely helpful academically and contributed to her positive feelings about the college social climate, despite the fact that these interactions did not extend into the arena of friendship. She was being interviewed in her college's student lounge when she explained the frequent tendency for her and her fellow collegemates to form spontaneous informal study groups:

> If I'm in the lounge . . . like right now, and I was studying and someone will be, "Oh, you know what, can you help me?" You know, we'll get together. It's like people see, "Oh you're in that class? What do you do here and what do you do there?" It's pretty much everybody helps each other out. That's what I like. Nobody's like, "Well, you figure it out yourself." Nobody's really mean like that.

Smaller colleges, smaller majors, and programs that clustered students into cohorts that progressed through their program together enhanced students' opportunities for such meaningful contact to occur. The consistency of scheduling and the repetition of students gathering in similar spaces that are often part of smaller, cohort based education provided these additional "social" opportunities for students to interact regarding coursework and larger goals. This was more common among students at the private for-profit and non-profit colleges and among community college students in more cohort-oriented programs in medical and electronics fields. Samantha extolled the benefits of taking classes with the same students from one term to the next: "Yeah, because you kinda know who really knows the stuff and you can get help from them, you know, instead of goin' to somebody new every time." Similarly, however faculty in various departments at community colleges that encouraged students to work together in formal or informal study groups during class time or for short periods outside of class time also encouraged the development of such limited but valuable interactions. For instance, several English instructors at one community college organized students into long term working groups and this facilitated ongoing communication. Jamille, a traditional college-aged, part-time, African American student stated, "I get along with people in the groups, and we help each other out . . . exchange phone numbers. If you have a problem, just call one of them and they can help you out."

Research on Latino university students finds that discussions of course content with other students outside class contributes to a sense of belonging in residential colleges, which is a central component of the social cohesion necessary to engender identification with the college community and combat marginalization (Hurtado & Carter, 1997). In the present study, students across the racial/ethnic groups studied found this to be helpful. Jamille is one example of the many African American students who communicated about academic matters with other students outside of class. Students of all other ethnic backgrounds did the same.

That this communication with other students was limited to mostly academic matters was normative, while more involved social relationships were reserved for the neighborhood/community based activities to which students remained attached. When students were asked about groups in which they participated, many described these community-based involvements more prominently than campus social involvements. Natalie is a traditional college-aged African-American enrolled in a non-profit private college graphic design program. When she was asked if she was "involved in any clubs or student groups" she responded by describing her role as a "youth leader" in her church "every other Wednesday, like . . . seven o'clock, eight o'clock." Lou is a single father of a nine-year-old daughter from the Philippines who is a full-time student and part-time worker. He echoed this norm in which a students' primary social/cultural life is off-campus while social interactions on campus revolve around academics:

Interviewer: Do you socialize with other students from school?

Lou: Yeah, a lot.

Interviewer: What kinds of things do you do?

Lou: Mostly school work . . . Sometimes I invite them, like . . . my daughter's birthday . . . all my friends were invited, not only Filipinos, different, cause I have friends from different parts. Whites, everybody.

Interviewer: Do you think you will continue to see these people after you leave school?

Lou: (Nodding) I think I will be seeing the Filipinos more 'cause most of the Filipino friends I have live near our place so we usually see each other a lot. (Shaking his head) My other friends are living (gesturing with his hands) . . . I am here, they are here, and [the for-profit college] is here.

Lou's discussion also highlights a situation common for 70% of the students interviewed. Given the geographic racial segregation of the area, their off-campus cultural/social life was embedded in same-race social groups, whereas their on-campus peer interactions tended to be more racially/ethnically diverse.

Carolyn exemplifies a pattern of networking with "similar" students that occurred for almost 40% of the sample. Carolyn, a White woman, returned to community college part time after 30 years of working and raising her kids. Carolyn's description of her challenges and associated strategies highlights the infrastructure of supports she relied on when her commitment wavered and she, like so many other students in the sample, doubted her competence. She passionately recalled how important networks among older students were for providing social support along with academic information and strategizing. Her sentiments were similar to students who discussed the benefits of taking part in the formal and informal study groups encouraged by some of their professors:

It's easy to talk to those students who have the same goals in mind as I do . . . to express our concerns and fears, how hard subjects are. . . . As adult students . . . when you come back into school your study habits may have gone, if you ever had them to begin with. . . . Unless you're lucky to have support at home . . . it is hard. . . . You can talk to another student and find out you're not alone and how do they overcome the simple things? . . . How do you cram for a test? What's the best way to study? What works for you? . . . ideas . . . and support, basically understanding when you doubt yourself, your intelligence. . . . You feel as though you can't make it, you're not going to make it . . . it's a horrible feeling. Your husband . . . doesn't understand or your children can't understand it as much . . . then there's no one here . . . there's no one. It's a tough feeling. You feel alone. . . . When you find a student that says, "I know what you're talking about . . . yes I have that same problem," even if she's never solved it and you're still experiencing it, you're not alone any more.

Carolyn's experience reveals the multiple struggles students confronted in their attempts to strategize academically, overcome self-doubt, and become stable and grounded in their college student identity. Her interactions with similar students provided the disruption of alienation she needed to persist. Her discussion also revealed the importance of a vital interpersonal element of social integration that is not centered in what we would traditionally think of as involvement in a college "social life" (participating in clubs and organizations, going out with friends, becoming politically active on campus).

Arnold's interview reveals an aspect of integration that supported goal commitment in a different way. Arnold is a Latino student who delayed his college enrollment for four years, was initially placed in remedial math, and attends college part-time while also working 12-hour shifts three days a week at a construction job. Arnold is much closer to a traditional age student than is Carolyn and does not suffer from doubts about his competence. However, he stressed the importance of being able to turn to fellow students for support while he was on campus. Similar to 41% of the students interviewed, his home environment did not provide the same quality of support. His college peers kept him focused on his goals because they shared his goals and his logic for pursuing them, unlike his family, who did not share his logic or commitment to his postsecondary plans. Although supportive, they had trouble understanding what he was trying to accomplish by going to college when he had already acquired a "good" construction job after high school:

My family and friends are just like, "Arnold is crazy, doing everything. He's doing this, he's doing that, he's busy." . . . When I need support, they're there, but they don't *encourage* me to do this . . . They really haven't had that exposure, so I'm kind of the lone one out there. . . . They would tell me, "You need to go to school," but they weren't really encouraging it too much. It was, "You did OK. You did good," and that was basically it. "Oh, you got a job? OK. You're doing OK."

These findings are consistent with prior research on the importance of social interactions beyond the classroom for marginal and two-year students (Attinasi, 1989; Rendon, 1994; Terenzini et al., 1994), yet they reveal two differences. First, the on-campus interactions defined by students as most important take on a distinctly academic rather than social flavor. Second, off-campus interactions provide an alternative source of same-race social interaction that may mitigate the absence of such interactions on campus. Third, limited interactions with networks of students facing similar challenges can be extremely affirming.

Socio-Academic Integrative Moments and Social Capital

In his attempt to more fully include classrooms as sites of both academic and social integration, Tinto (1997) critiques his own model of persistence, which depicts social and academic systems of colleges as two separate boxes. Instead, he acknowledges "a fuller relationship between these two spheres of activity" more accurately represented as "nested spheres" to better depict the ways "in which social and academic life are interwoven" (p. 619). In fact, such a conceptual distinction between the "academic" and the "social" creates a false dichotomy that obscures the nature of the fused socio-academic encounters that dominate the integration experiences of commuting two-year college students and their subjective understandings of the student-institution interaction. The concept of a "socio-academic integrative moments" can be used to describe opportunities for specific instances of interaction in which components of social and academic integration are simultaneously combined. The word "moment" is used to indicate that such an opportunity can, but does not necessarily have to, involve formally structured, in-depth, routine, or even frequent interactions. All the students above offer examples of typical socio-academic integrative moments in which the *academic* influence is coupled with elements of *social* integration to provide needed support and enhance feelings of college belonging, college identity, and college competence. Such processes revolve around events, activities, interactions, and relationships reflecting "moments" that combine academically and socially integrative elements.

In addition to providing feelings of attachment and belonging, relationships forged with other students, as well as faculty or counselors, enhanced students' acquisition of the knowledge to make more effective choices and better strategize their college careers, both academically and procedurally. Embedded within socio-academic integrative moments were components that facilitated information gathering and the construction of specific strategies in a way that resembled both strands of scholarship on the concept of social capital. Bourdieu defines social capital as a set of durable, deliberate, institutionalized relationships and the benefits that accrue to individuals as a result of the existence of such social bonds (Bourdieu, 2001), while Coleman emphasizes the benefits and function of these relationships, particular that of information access and exchange (Coleman, 1988). In other words, in addition to socio-academic integrative moments having *social* benefits (greater feelings of college competence and sense of belonging to the institution, the overcoming initial doubts, and a more solidified sense of their college student identity), these moments also had *informational* benefits.

This suggests an additional social capital dimension to Tinto's emphasis on integration and normative fit. Socio-academic ties, or relationships, can also be crucial points of information-exchange where students' strategies for attaining goals are improved. This information access enhances feelings of congruence and a focus on shared goals, especially for students who often begin college with relatively high goals but too little information or support to see those goals to fruition. Relationships and meetings with faculty, counselors, advisors, or other students provide the social capital to strengthen academic knowledge and lend encouragement and needed information about cognitive, behavioral, and procedural strategies for success in class, college, and career. First-generation two-year college students are otherwise not likely to have ready access to this information through their family or peer networks.

Among the two-year college students studied, socio-academic integrative moments occurred both within and outside the classroom as evidenced in the examples above. Interestingly, the fusion of social and academic elements in such relationships was emphasized as being of critical value, as described in the sections that follow. In contrast, purely social relationships were devalued and even described as unwanted obstacles or distractions. For example, Jennifer, a White 18-year-old in a court reporting program in a private non-profit, works full-time and finds herself enrolled part-time in evening classes with older students where "everyone pretty much lives their own lives." She sees this as a positive because when she comes to class there are no distractions. "No one is talking about their weekends or about their social lives." On the other hand, the students welcomed interactions with classmates that were not purely social and tended to define friendliness as students' willingness to be academically functional for one another. In fact, a majority of those interviewed either expected or were pleasantly surprised by such interactions, defining the absence of them as an unfriendly climate. Samantha, who had been enrolled in two community colleges before persisting at her current for-profit, describes her disdain for an "unfriendly" climate in contrast to a classroom climate in which students help each other out academically.

> Other colleges . . . I walk into class, sit down, don't say nothin' to nobody, nobody says nothin' to me, and I'm gone. I used to be like, "gosh, you guys are so unfriendly." . . . They were more independent. They didn't really like, depend on someone for help. Even if they had no clue what they were doin', they would sit there . . . until it was time to go . . . without askin' for help from your fellow classmates . . . which . . . I believe that's what we're here for, to help each other . . . because I might have a way of learning something that would be very easy for you and you might have the same thing.

Note that Samantha's definition of friendly student relationships did not extend to the expectation that students would socialize outside of class, participate in other campus events or activities together, or develop long-term friendships. These more traditional measures of social integration were not within the realm of expectations for 87% of the students' interviewed. As described in the section above, limited but meaningful socio-academic interactions comprised the norm of expectations among these students across institutional type. Student-faculty or student-staff socio-academic moments were somewhat similar in that they revolved around the informational benefits, but they also tended to involve the institutional agent taking a proactive personal interest in helping the student in some way.

Pro-Active Guidance and Procedural Agency

Seemingly simple bureaucratic hurdles often confronted students as overwhelming and opaque obstacles. The proactive guidance of faculty and counselors in overcoming these obstacles cannot be overstated. *Proactive* faculty and counselors/advisors provide strategic guidance and support for students' adjustment and information access in ways that counteract the alienation that may precede dropout. Greg is a good illustration of the impact of this pro-active guidance noted by more than half the sample.

Greg, a White student, was fearful based on his prior academic nonsuccess as a high school dropout. When asked if he thought he was "college material" prior to his decision to attend college, he responded, "I didn't even know what college material was. I couldn't even imagine." Greg, who started taking community college classes one at a time at the remedial level when he was 19 while working full-time, noted the importance of faculty support as critical to his adjustment: He lacked college knowledge and had miserable experiences with the financial aid office. Feeling procedurally overwhelmed and uninformed, it was mentor relationships with faculty that provided information, inspiration, and "procedural agency." In fact, the proactive assistance of one of his professors was the key factor in Greg's ability to continue full-time toward his associate's degree and transfer plans. Greg uses the words "drew me in" to describe how the actions of a particular faculty member and his growing relationship with that professor not only helped him practically, but also inspired him to become more committed to his educational goals:

> Luckily, I had Professor Homewood for an English class. At that time I was trying to secure financial aid. . . . I had gone to the library and looked at the college blue book for scholarships, and I just found the whole thing kind of overwhelming. . . . I had gone to the financial aid department here at the school. . . . It was just such a miserable experience. They couldn't help me at all . . . when I asked the woman about scholarships, she told me that I could apply but I probably wouldn't get them anyway, so why bother . . . I was completely discouraged I thought I was just going to quit school and leave. I went into Professor Homewood's class. He was announcing this . . . scholarship to everybody. I figured, "what the heck, I'll try it." I filled it out, and I got the scholarship! That just gave me a rebirth,

so to speak. . . . Once you get it, as long as you maintain at least a 3.0, you will continue to get the scholarship for each semester you're here. . . . So he just did such an amazing thing. . . . That is what really drew me in, his ability to help me find those avenues to get to where I wanted to go.

In the community college context, with its organizational and bureaucratic complexity, the experience of students receiving conflicting or incomplete information is not uncommon (Rosenbaum et al., 2006). Having a faculty or other staff member willing to take a proactive role in enhancing students procedural agency can counteract such misinformation and provide role models for negotiating career and future educational goals. When asked if he had developed any mentor relationships with professors, it became clear just how central such relationships were to Greg's progress in college as he explained the value of the four or more mentor relationships he had developed during his time at the community college:

> Definitely, there have been certain professors that I've met here that I've just clicked with and have shared interests with. So that usually leads to conversations of a more personal nature than just academics. That kind of opened a door for me. . . . It starts off in class . . . a professor just recognizes something in you, and you get into a conversation and before you know it. . . . I just truly enjoy that. . . . So I definitely view Professor Homewood as a mentor, among other teachers that do that.

Greg's example includes features of traditional measures of academic integration while also highlighting the pivotal role played by in-class communication in overcoming bureaucratic, procedural hurdles and influencing his college/career identity. For 28% of the students interviewed the social capital role of institutional agents in negotiating procedural obstacles was described as fundamental to their decision to continue because it had implications for their identity. It empowered students to redefine their position from powerless victim to a competent player worthy of attention from "important" faculty and staff. These elements are not highlighted in traditional accounts of academic integration.

Julia shared experiences similar to Greg's financial aid dilemma. Appearing in nearly all the interviews, having to overcome procedural hurdles was quite common. Julia admits, "In the beginning of this whole college process, I didn't know anything." She started out doing "college prep" remedial classes at a private non-profit two-year college and then had some trouble with her financial aid and her course scheduling, "They just really messed up my paperwork." She was placed into all late evening classes, which would have been impossible for her to attend given the fact that she is raising a seven-year old son. She explained, "It was really, really, just. . . . It was a bad experience," and elaborated on her frame of mind: "I wasn't in a good place. I was like, 'I wanna go to college but I don't think I can afford it. . . . I might as well just give it up.' . . . But Marisela . . . she cleared things up for me." Marisela was an admissions counselor at a for-profit two-year college. Julia's younger sister had enrolled there and convinced Julia to come to talk with Marisela. So Julia went with her sister and friend:

> My sister actually came here for the paralegal program and she told me they also had a business program and I came and talked to one of the counselors and she just told me everything I needed to hear and just made me feel really comfortable.

Marisela quickly figured out how to process Julia's financial aid and enroll her in a sequence of day classes. Julia's description of her experience stands in sharp contrast to the bureaucratic tangle that many students encounter in their attempts to negotiate their college strategies. In our interviews, it was quite often vital that students access the proactive assistance of a counselor or faculty member in order to provide a way out of the dilemma. This is an example of the kind of integrative "moment" that allowed students to persevere in the face of menacing organizational structures:

> I came in and I saw Marisela in Admissions. . . . My sister and myself and Crystal . . . came together. . . . She told us about . . . all kind of different business programs, what we really wanted, what type of classes we were thinking about taking, and she talked to us about the financial part and the loans and the grants and all that kind of stuff. . . . I had already applied for everything at [the other college], so my grant money was just sitting there and all she had to do was transfer it over. So I was just ready to go.

Before slipping through the cracks and simply dropping out of college, Julia got the one on one time with a counselor that she needed to gain crucial information about financial aid and scheduling options in order for her to continue her college enrollment with a full package of financial aid.

Like Greg, Julia is an example of the one-half of all students interviewed who received personalized procedural help and the one-quarter of all students for whom this help was linked to a relationship or set of relationships that bolstered their identity as college students. Ready to lose hope for her college goals after feeling victimized by the financial aid/scheduling snag at the other college, Julia's brief encounter with an admissions counselor who leveraged her knowledge of the system to intervene, put Julia back on a college pathway and procedurally coached her through her first year transition. It was through their relationship that Julia's confidence to make it on her own through college developed. Marisela was the one institutional agent with whom Julia connected and sought assistance:

> I know in my second quarter I was like, "I don't even know how to pick classes," and they said "Go see your advisor." Well, I was like, "I don't know what I'm doing. I don't even know who my advisor is!" And [Marisela], . . . she really helped me a lot . . . she was just an admissions counselor and that really wasn't her job, but . . . she talked to me like I was her good friend . . . so, she was a real good help. . . . Now that I'm totally confident, I know what classes I need and what I should take now. . . . I've totally learned the process, so, I don't really have any problems.

The crucial aspect of these relationships—procedural assistance—is not highlighted in traditional measures of academic or social integration. Many two-year students are marginal in that they are so tenuous in their college student role that seemingly minor setbacks are not interpreted as such and could easily throw them off course and back into a re-adoption of a non-college student identity. Greg was "just going to quit school and leave." Julia was ready "just give it up." Maria, in her first semester, constantly thought, "What the hell am I doing here?" It was the help offered to procedurally navigate the institution that emerged as a centerpiece of relationships that solidified their confidence in and commitment to their college student role. Greg described his transformation as a "rebirth." Rating her confidence on a scale of 1 to 10 Julia said, "When I started, I'd say about a five, but now I'm . . . I'd say about a nine." Maria, toward the end of her second year as a part-time student, confidently stated, "Now I'm completely turned around and I'm not stopping."

"Tenuous" students in the sample who did *not* access this assistance chose to depart college.[10] Although the vast majority of African American students interviewed said they experienced no negative treatment in college based on their race, Nikita represents some whose struggles included what they felt was an instructor's racist bias against them. Nikita is from a low-income single-parent family and enrolled in community college after high school. She faced procedural hurdles with financial aid, with accessing tutoring, with a part-time math instructor whose foreign accent caused difficulty, and with this English professor that gave her what she considered an unwarranted failing grade. Despite Nikita's attempts to seek help with these problems from a counselor and others, no one in the institution took a pro-active role in helping. When asked if she had talked to or received any help or encouragement from other faculty, she scoffed, "Oh, no. They didn't really talk about school. They didn't talk about classes. They talked about the lessons they were supposed to teach and that was it." Failing to access any proactive guidance, she failed math and English and dropped out.

The notions of both social capital and procedural agency resemble the process through which Torres (2006) finds urban commuting students access assistance from mentors, faculty, and other sources who "show them the way" to maneuver through the college environment. Similarly, in these two-year settings such mentorship, proactive guidance, and information-giving transmit the tools students needed to exert their agency and direct their trajectory.

Close Interpersonal Contact with Faculty

Contact with faculty over academic matters not only can provide needed academic support, it can also enhance feelings of belonging for marginalized students. Hector, a 29 year-old Latino painter who continued to paint part-time while in college full-time, provides a clear illustration of this dynamic. He represents the third of the students interviewed who struggled with a sense of competence and confidence in their college student identity in addition to any informational and procedural hurdles:

> Hector: I had no idea of what college was like, except for high school, and that was a joke.
>
> Interviewer: Were you worried about whether you'd be able to perform?
>
> Hector: Definitely . . . I thought the teachers were so smart, and if they didn't think I was college material, they wouldn't pay attention to me. . . . I was afraid to raise my hand in front of everybody. . . . I was insecure. Are they going to pay attention to me if I'm not living up to their standards and my ability? Do they think I'm worth it? . . . Everything was just overwhelming. I got some help though. The teachers have been very helpful. It wasn't all that serious as I made it up to be in my head. I did well in the classes. What I didn't understand came to me with a little bit of work, of course. I was just more overwhelmed because of the amount of work . . . the papers due and all the tests.
>
> Interviewer: How did you get help?
>
> Hector: When I didn't understand something, the teachers took the time to explain it. They were helpful.
>
> Interviewer: Did you use their office hours?
>
> Hector: Yes or ask them in class.

Hector benefited from the kind of faculty attention and proactive assistance in and out of class that disrupted his alienation, allowed him to overcome doubts about whether or not he belonged, and helped him manage his academic struggles and increase his self-confidence. His description reveals contact with faculty over academic matters can have important value beyond the academic—it can enhance feelings of belonging for marginalized students who are vulnerable to such insecurities. Unlike traditional views of integration that emphasize frequency of behaviors, attention to the subjective component of students' experiences highlights the complex and nuanced identity-related psychological processes that occur. This imbues faculty-student contact—an objective behavior—with a rich subjective meaning that extends beyond a mere measure of frequency of contact. It provides a relevant contribution to Spady's (1971) neglected psychological dimension of perceived integration. Hector, with the help of instructors, was able to get to a place where he was able to perceive his ability and worthiness to be more in congruence with his experiences.

Shared personal knowledge and "closeness" with instructors also provided integrative elements. Stacey, a White, nearly 30-year-old wife and mother who also started out in remedial classes, runs an at-home daycare with a neighbor while attending night classes. She explained how her networks of support were grounded in the close personal interactions she was able to have with her instructors both in and out of the classroom at the for-profit college she attends. In this respect, she is representative of students who valued the personalized attention of instructors that nurtured their feelings of belonging. In fact, students who were similar to Stacey in this respect often used the language of "friendship":

> My husband started at [another college]. He hated it. There were just so many kids in a lab. There were so many students in a classroom, and it was just so hard to get personalized treatment. Here, my instructors, I love them. They know you by name, they know your family situation, they know where you're coming from, they know what kind of job you have, they tease you about it! They're more like a friend. It's fantastic, I can't imagine going to a school where you're one of hundreds sitting in a lecture hall, and you don't get the personalized treatment. I just, I love it.

This sense of friendship and surrogate family located in instructor-student interactions differs from traditional models in which social, rather than academic, spaces are arenas for cultivating new communities of involvement and long-term friendships. For nearly half of the students, the key component of their relationship with faculty moved beyond the academic to engender feelings of closeness resembling elements of family and friend relationships. Natalie had casual personal relationships with instructors outside of class:

> We have pretty good relationships . . . as far as not . . . talking about school, but life in general. So you have that relationship with your professor that'll make you know that they really care whether you succeed or not, and . . . how you're doing personally.

Maria's described her faculty as both friends and family. Of her professors in general, she explained, "they're something else":

> Oh yes, they're my friends, like my English teacher I took for 101 and 102. . . . They've been really really supportive. . . . I have just as many faculty friends as I do students. . . .

> I never thought you could really become friends with teachers . . . and seek their advice and actually get on a personal level besides the classes. I like that.

Of one particular professor, she claims a more familial connection:

> Sometimes I need advice from him . . . even on a personal level, and he's there. . . . I come from a family of eight and I'm not close at all. . . . So it's important that I have some kind of a family. Wherever I go that I develop a sense of some kind of foundation, and I got it here . . . thank God.

These findings add a layer of qualitative texture to prior research noting the positive influence of establishing mentor relationships with faculty on the intellectual self-concept of students (Cole, 2007). The personal, family-like elements of mentor relationships fed feelings of caring and comfort for some students and relate closely to what prior research suggests regarding how important it is that commuter students perceive an institution's commitment to the welfare of students (Braxton, Hirschy, & McClendon, 2004).

Vehicles for Socio-Academic Integrative Moments

Socio-academic integrative experiences were the predominant vehicles for cultivating the type of integration Tinto (1993) defines as a sense of "competent membership." The most common mechanisms were (a) a range of *in-class* interactions and dynamics, (b) formal or "spontaneous" study groups, (c) social-capital relevant interactions and mentor relationships with trusted faculty or other staff, (d) consistent access to communication with "similar" students (usually facilitated by some form of cohort scheduling that created consistency in the students that interacted with each other from one term to the next, and, to a lesser extent, (e) academically-relevant clubs and activities. These mechanisms helped students strategize academic success by incorporating college into their social identity, planning better, scheduling their time more effectively, and placing limits on their demands outside of school.

Purely social interactions—going places with friends, attending social events, participating in sports—did not emerge as primary mechanisms of social integration. Unlike four-year residential students, such relationships were neither expected nor desired for most of the students interviewed, given the family, work, and other demands facing them as they struggled to prioritize college. However, structures such as cohort based programming and scheduling enhanced opportunities for students to interact with other students who were facing similar challenges. Such structures were more common in the smaller, private for-profit and nonprofit colleges and in community college programs in medical and electronics fields.

Conclusions

The findings of the present study are consistent with previous research showing academic integration to be more significant than social for community college students, with traditional forms of social integration unrelated to persistence (Braxton et al., 2004; Halpin, 1990; Mutter, 1992; Pascarella & Chapman, 1983). Academic integration appears more salient in this study, rising to prominence amid limited opportunities for social integration, and consistent with recently proposed theories of departure for commuting students (Braxton et al., 2004). However, compartmentalizing two-year college student experiences into distinct social and academic realms may not be useful. Not only did academic integration take a slightly more social form than one would expect based on previous measures, but also, social integration was often characterized by academic utility, and the tight interconnectedness of the two forms of integration often make them indistinguishable in these two-year settings. *Socio-academic* integrative moments were cited most frequently by students across all 14 two-year colleges as precursors to their persistence.

Faculty-student involvement was nuanced and served multiple functions. In-classroom interactions were dominant mechanisms of socioacademic integration, which confirms and extends Tinto's (1997) acknowledgement of the classroom as a site of integration. During class, instructors allowed time for one-on-one communication and assistance and confirmed students' ability, which not only boosted students' academic performance, but also validated their self-worth, sense of competence and belonging, and belief in their ability to succeed. In interactions outside of class, contact with faculty served the same academic support and identity-boosting function, particularly for nontraditional and underserved students. Furthermore, findings identify faculty/instructors as primary sources of social capital both in and out of the classroom, transmitting valuable information to students. Interactions with faculty were discussed by students as more pivotal for social capital transmission than their exchanges with advisors or counselors. The guidance of proactive faculty who extended themselves in an effort to help or inform students afforded students a degree of agency within the organization that allowed them to surmount procedural obstacles.

"Institutional agents" of various sorts were pro-active in supporting these two-year students, and the nature of this support should continue to be explored. Rendon (1994) explains how nontraditional students interpret someone taking an active role in reaching out to them and assisting them as an important precursor to involvement and feeling "validated." The present study confirms the importance of this process, particularly for the Latino and Korean students, and reveals how such validation can occur through in-class as well as out-of-class interactions and how this process extends beyond academic, personal, and cultural validation to also include an element of procedural assistance as well. Although Rendon (1994) and Rendon et al. (2000) present validation as a more useful and appropriate concept than integration, the two can in fact be viewed as compatible, in that validation can act as a strong integrating force. Maria, Greg, and Hector provide excellent examples of these validating interactions and relationships.

The social capital element of students' integration experiences emerged as quite important in the study. Students emphasized the valuable informational benefits and enhanced *procedural agency* of socioacademic interactions. These findings are useful for expanding Milem and Berger's (1997) cycle in which initial student involvement behaviors affect their perceptions, which in turn affect subsequent behavior. Early connections with faculty and others could enhance students' sense of congruency and make them more likely to seek ways to remain enrolled and successful.

Limited contact between students provided meaningful integrative moments valued not for the depth or length of contact, but for their contribution to a sense of connection from shared experiences and challenges. This finding is similar to what Tinto found in a more formalized learning community—building supportive peer groups is instrumental in helping commuting students integrate into a networked community of peers to ease their transition into college (Tinto, 1997). However, unlike Tinto's study, being part of a learning community was not necessary for the commuting students in the present study to accomplish this integration. Both formal and spontaneous informal study groups as well as "friendly" casual and limited interactions between students were sufficient to create a sense of comfort, belonging, and information-sharing. Long-term friendships were not expected. These findings also suggest the importance of understanding what students expect from the institution and how they perceive their experiences based on those expectations. In contrast to four-year residential students, two-year students may have very different initial expectations and perceptions of college interactions and relationships that do not fit neatly into the traditional categories.

Overall, this study is consistent with research that finds the interracial interactions of minority students with faculty in and out of class and with other students over academic matters to have a positive relationship with intellectual self-concept (Cole, 2007), grades (Anaya & Cole, 2001), and persistence (Davis, 1991) at predominantly-White four-year institutions. Recognizing the pivotal role of such academically-focused contact in vastly different institutions highlights the opportunity to identify commonalities for marginalized students across different institutional levels with differing compositions of student and faculty diversity. It also supports the challenge to resist desires to dismiss more traditional frameworks for understanding persistence (i.e. Tinto) based on their weaknesses. Rather, integrating the strength of such frameworks with current research on the experiences of marginalized and minority students in different types of postsecondary institutions can be of great value.

Recommendations for Research and Practice

Traditional quantitative measures of social and academic integration may be inadequate to capture the precise means through which two-year students develop feelings of congruence within their institution for several reasons. First, how students experience the subjective aspect of the integration process has been underdeveloped. For example, whether or not an interaction with an instructor occurs within or outside of the classroom or is about academic or non-academic matters may be less important than the meaning that interaction has for a student's academic identity development and the role it plays in their feelings of connection to the institution, their confidence about their college pursuits, or motivation to stay. Attempting to quantify socio-academic moments will force researchers to think more carefully about the link between behaviors and the more subjective components of the integration process—reinforcement of intellectual self concept, or academic identity, and facilitation of feelings of belonging. These elements have not traditionally been incorporated into studies of persistence using Tinto's framework, although the work of Torres (2006) represents a useful attempt to include such subjective measures outside of the Tinto model.

Second, efforts should be made to identify measures (i.e. the vehicles noted above) that reflect fused socio-academic integration experiences and to consider their distinct impact. Operationalizing the two forms of integration separately reinforces a false dichotomy and could be understating the true importance of socio-academic integrative experiences by recognizing only half of their socio-academic function. Traditional ways of conceptualizing and quantifying integration may be attributing too much importance to purely social or academic interactions if, in fact, *socio-academic* interactions are driving commitment and persistence.

Third, in traditional models, interactions that occur within the classroom (such as those detailed by Cole, 2007) still represent a black box. The meaning of those interactions for enhancing students' procedural agency, engendering feelings of belonging, and inviting connections with faculty and other students outside of class have yet to be quantitatively explored as they relate to integration processes. More detailed studies of exactly how two-year students experience and respond to in-class cues and interactions with faculty and other students should be conducted so that more useful measures can be either developed or effectively borrowed from other frameworks. The same can be said of the often limited but meaningful, validating, and sometimes social-capital rich interactions that occur beyond the formal structure of the classroom.

Recommendations for practice include efforts on the part of two-year institutions to proactively connect students early on with faculty and advisors who can mentor students, affirm their sense of academic competence, and provide procedural agency to help students navigate the institution. Tinto (1998) advocates the construction of learning communities, and the findings of the present study lend support for such efforts. Placing the responsibility with the institutional actors (faculty, counselors, staff, administrators) rather than students, for *proactively* initiating various forms of contact would be more effective, as the present findings and those of Rendon (1994) suggest. Some of the colleges in the study had created systems in which instructors and advisors worked together to monitor student progress—both to identify high achieving students who might need encouragement and to connect with students who missed a certain number of classes or whose grades were dropping. Also, group advising routinely brought counselors in contact with multiple students to increase contact beyond what could be accomplished in one-on-one meetings. These group advisories were vital in facilitating procedural agency, providing topics of discussion along with open ended question-and-answer to reduce the obstacle of students often not knowing what to ask or not aware of what they don't know. In other colleges, key faculty members, advisors, and staff reached out to mentor, advise, and encourage students—to serve as "institutional agents." Institutions should reduce teaching loads, create incentives, and provide other professional rewards or "credit" to encourage more of such behavior—again, in the classroom as well as beyond the classroom.

Similarly, structuring opportunities for students to interact with each other could enhance integration on that front. Modified cohort models can create more sustained contact over time, and the use of in-class time to let students get to know each other and work together could also be productive in this regard, even if these opportunities are limited. Online networking might also be considered as a tool to allow students to similar others with shared experiences based on such things as parenting and single parenting, racial/ethnic background, gender, immigrant status, intended major or program of study, etc. Students could join listservs, chat groups, and information-based sites based on these commonalities.

Scholars have also previously recommended ways institutions might try to enhance support from the spouses, life partners, and parents of students (e.g. Braxton et al., 2004, Tinto, 1998). These efforts are important, particularly as the experiences of Carolyn and Arnold reveal in their lack of sufficient support at home, but both students were able to persist due to their ability to recreate supportive relationships on campus with faculty and peers. More investment should be directed to developing institutionally-based "significant others" for students. Torres (2006) explains how commuting students already tend to develop personal support networks that include encouragement from their family and community, but the present findings reveal the importance of those within the institution providing the personal attention needed to help students to both feel competent and confident in their intellectual identity and also learn how to navigate within institution. Ultimately, the success of two-year students is contingent upon how they manage the complex negotiation of their daily lives in and out of college. Prior work has highlighted the importance of the encouragement of significant others in students' personal lives to enhance persistence (Cabrera, Nora, & Castaneda, 1993; Nora, 1987; Nora et al., 1990). The present findings highlight the importance of significant others located *within the institution* to fulfill that function in a way that extends well beyond encouragement.

Notes

1. It is important to note that the work of Milem and Berger (1997) and Berger and Milem (1999) acknowledges the broader application of Astin's model and argues for a modified model of persistence that incorporates conceptual elements from both Tinto and Astin. Such work, however, remains limited to the four-year residential institutions.

2. Two-year commuting students can be considered marginalized for several reasons. They attend college at the margins of the traditional college experience, historically constructed as selective and residential and framed by most prior research in this way. They disproportionately include populations historically excluded from higher education and at greatest risk of departing—non-traditional aged, underserved racial minorities, low-income, and first-generation college students.

3. Research has also not directly addressed the extent to which community colleges reflect specific campus cultures to which students are expected to assimilate in order to be academically successful. This may be an important area for future research, especially since, despite the premise that community colleges are more responsive and accommodating to the diverse populations that enroll, they also demand a degree of social know-how to navigating their complex bureaucratic structure.

4. Social integration is generally measured using variables to capture: participation in school clubs and fine arts activities; sports participation; frequency with which students go places with friends from school; peer group interactions; and informal out-of-class interactions and conversations with college faculty and personnel. For descriptions of social integration and its operationalization see Bers & Smith, 1991; Braxton, Milem & Sullivan, 2000; Christie & Dinham, 1991; Flowers, 2006; Mutter, 1992; Pascarella & Terenzini, 1991, 2005; Sullivan, 1997; Wortman & Napoli, 1996.

5. Academic integration is generally measured using the following variables: actual or predicted first-year grades; students' sense of their intellectual/academic development; students' perception of faculty concern; frequency of social contact or conversations with faculty and/or advisors about academic or career matters outside of class time; participation in out-of-class study groups; time spent on homework; and enrollment in freshman seminars. For descriptions of academic integration and its operationalization see Braxton, 2000; Braxton & Brier, 1989; Cabrera, Castaneda, Nora, & Hengstler, 1992; Flowers, 2006; Maisto & Tammi, 1991; Pascarella, Duby, & Iverson, 1983; Pascarella & Terenzini, 1980, 1983; Stage, 1989; Sullivan,1997; Terenzini, Pascarella, Theophilides, & Lorang, 1985; Wortman & Napoli, 1996; Zea, Reisen, Beil, & Caplan, 1997.

6. Questions were open-ended, giving respondents to the opportunity to elaborate at will. Interviewers probed for details.

7. Codes included: enrollment choice, enrollment process, difficulties/meeting challenges, program choice, academic performance, curriculum, soft-skills, commitment, belonging, integration, external obligations, time management, decision-making, changes in plans, future education and career plans, job search knowledge, transfer.

8. For eight interviews, the researchers "check-coded" by first coding alone and then coming together to compare codes (Miles & Huberman, 1994), followed by collective meetings to create a more standardized coding process.

9. This feedback came in the form of reports to each college studied, and more informally, after interviews, students listened to brief summaries of what the interviewer understood the student to be saying. Students had an opportunity to elaborate or correct the interviewer's interpretation (Creswell, 1998; Miles & Huberman, 1994).

10. These students were captured in the sample because they had re-enrolled into a college in the study years later.

References

Allen, W. R. (1992). The color of success: African American college student outcomes at predominantly white and historically black public colleges and universities. *Harvard Educational Review, 62*(1), 26–44.

Anaya, G., & Cole, D. (2001). Latina/o student achievement: Exploring the influence of student-faculty interaction on college grades. *Journal of College Student Development, 42*(1), 3–14.

Astin, A. (1984). Student involvement: A developmental theory for higher education. *Journal of College Student Personnel, 25*, 297–308.

Attinasi, L. (1989). Getting in: Mexican Americans' perceptions of university attendance and the implications for freshman year persistence. *The Journal of Higher Education, 60*, 247–277.

Babbie, E. (2004). *The practice of social research* (10th ed). Belmont, CA: Wadsworth Publishing Company.

Bean, J., & Metzner, B. (1985). A conceptual model of nontraditional undergraduate student attrition. *Review of Educational Research, 55*, 485–540.

Bensimon, E. M. (2007). The underestimated significance of practitioner knowledge in the scholarship on student success. *The Review of Higher Education, 30*(4), 441–469.

Berger, J. B., & Milem, J. F. (1999). The role of student involvement and perceptions of integration in a causal model of student persistence. *Research in Higher Education, 39*, 103–119.

Bers, T. H., & Smith, K. E. (1991). Persistence of community college students: The influence of student intent and academic and social integration. *Research in Higher Education, 32*, 539–556.

Bourdieu, P. (2001). The forms of capital. In M. Granovetter & R. Swedberg (Eds.), *The sociology of economic life.* Boulder, CO: Westview Press.

Braxton, J. M. (Ed.). (2000). *Reworking the student departure puzzle.* Nashville, TN: Vanderbilt University Press.

Braxton, J. M., & Brier, J. M. (1989). Melding organizational and interactional theories of student attrition: A path analytic study. *Review of Higher Education, 13*(1), 47–61.

Braxton, J. M., & Hirschy, A. S. (2005). Theoretical developments in the study of college student departure. In A. Seidman (Ed.), *College student retention: Formula for student success* (pp. 61–87). Westport, CT: Praeger.

Braxton, J. M., Hirschy, A. S., & McClendon, S. A. (2004). *Understanding and reducing college student departure.* San Francisco: Jossey-Bass.

Braxton, J. M., Milem, J. F., & Sullivan, A. S. (2000). The influence of active learning on the college student departure process: Toward a revision of Tinto's theory. *The Journal of Higher Education, 71*, 569–590.

Braxton, J. M., Sullivan, A. S., & Johnson, R. M. (1997). Appraising Tinto's theory of college student departure. In J. C. Smart (Ed.), *Higher education: Handbook of theory and research*, (Vol. 12, pp. 107–164). New York: Agathon.

Cabrera, A. F., Castaneda, M. B., Nora, A., & Hengstler, D. (1992). The convergent and discriminant validity between two theories of college persistence. *The Journal of Higher Education, 63*, 143–164.

Cabrera, A. F., Nora, A., & Castaneda, M. B. (1992). The role of finances in the persistence process: A structural model. *Research in Higher Education, 33*(5), 571–593.

Cabrera, A. F., Nora, A., & Castaneda, M. B. (1993). College persistence: Structural equations modeling test of an integrated model of student retention. *The Journal of Higher Education, 64*, 123–139.

Christie, N., & Dinham, S. (1991). Institutional and external influences on social integration in the freshman year. *The Journal of Higher Education, 62*, 412–436.

Cole, D. (2007). Do interracial interactions matter?: An examination of student faculty contact and intellectual self-concept. *The Journal of Higher Education, 78,* 248–272.

Coleman, J. (1988). Social capital in the creation of human capital. *American Journal of Sociology, 94,* S95–S120.

Creswell, J. W. (1998). *Qualitative inquiry and research design: Choosing among five traditions.* Thousand Oaks, CA: Sage Publications.

Davis, R. B. (1991). Social support networks and undergraduate student academic-success-related outcomes: A comparison of Black students on Black and White campuses. In W. R. Allen, E. G. Epps, & N. Z. Haniff (Eds.), *College in Black and White: African American students in predominantly White and in historically Black public universities* (pp.147–153). Albany: State University Press of New York Press.

Deil-Amen, R. (2002). *From dreams to degrees: Social processes of opportunity and blocked opportunity in community colleges.* Unpublished doctoral dissertation, Northwestern University, Evanston, IL.

Deil-Amen, R. J., & Rosenbaum, J. E. (2003). The social prerequisites of success: Can college structure reduce the need for social know-how? In J. Jacobs & K. Shaw (Eds.)., *Annals of the American Academy of Political and Social Science,* (Vol. 586, pp. 120–143). Newbury Park, CA: Sage Publications.

Durkheim, E. (1951). *Suicide* (John A. Spaulding & George Simpson, Trans.). Glencoe, IL: Free Press

Flowers, L. A. (2006). Effects of attending a 2-year institution on African American males' academic and social integration in the first year of college. *Teachers College Record, 108*(2), 267–286.

Guiffrida, D. A .(2006). Toward a cultural advancement of Tinto's theory. *The Review of Higher Education, 29*(4), 451–472.

Halpin, R. L. (1990). An application of the Tinto model to the analysis of freshman persistence in a community college. *Community College Review, 17*(4), 22–32.

Hurtado, S., & Carter, D. F. (1997). Effects of college transition and perceptions of the campus racial climate on Latino college students' sense of belonging. *Sociology of Education, 70*(4), 324–345.

Kirk, J., & Miller, M. L. (1986). *Reliability and validity in qualitative research.* Beverly Hills, CA: Sage Publications.

LeCompte, M. D., & Goetz, J. P. (1982). Problems of reliability and validity in educational research. *Review of Educational Research, 52*(2), 31–60.

London, H. B. (1978). *The culture of a community college.* New York: Praeger.

Maisto, A., & Tammi, M. (1991). The effect of content-based freshman seminar on academic and social integration. *Journal of the Freshman Year Experience, 3,* 29–47.

Manski, C. F. (1989). Schooling as experimentation: A reappraisal of the postsecondary dropout phenomenon. *Economics of Education Review, 8*(4), 305–312.

Milem, J. F., & Berger, J. B. (1997). A modified model of college student persistence: The relationship between Astin's theory of involvement and Tinto's theory of student departure. *Journal of College Student Development, 38*(4), 387–400.

Miles, M. B., & Huberman, A. M. (1994). *Qualitative data analysis: A sourcebook of new methods.* Thousand Oaks, CA: Sage Publications.

Mutter, P. (1992). Tinto's theory of departure and community college student persistence. *Journal of College Student Development, 33,* 310–317.

Nettles, M. T. (1991). Racial similarities and differences in the predictors of college student achievement. In W. R. Allen, E. G. Epps, & N. Z. Haniff (Eds.), *College in Black and White: African American students in predominantly White and in historically Black public universities* (pp. 49–63). Albany: State University of New York Press.

Neumann, R. W., & Riesman, D. (1980). The community college elite. In G. Vaughan (Ed.), *New directions in community colleges: Questioning the community college role* (Vol. 32, pp. 53–71) San Francisco: Jossey-Bass.

Nora, A. (1987). Determinants of retention among Chicano college students: A structural model. *Research in Higher Education, 26,* 31–59.

Nora, A., Attinasi, L. C., & Matonak, A. (1990). Testing qualitative indicators of precollege factors in Tinto's attrition model: A community college perspective. *Review of Higher Education, 13,* 337–356.

Nora, A., Cabrera, A., Hagedorn, L., & Pascarella, E. (1996). Differential impacts of academic and social experiences of college-related behavioral outcomes across different ethnic and gender groups at four-year institutions. *Research in Higher Education, 34,* 243–262.

Pascarella, E. T. (1985). College environmental influences on learning and cognitive development: A critical review and synthesis. In J. Smart (Ed), *Higher education: Handbook of theory and research* (Vol. 1, pp. 1–64). New York:Agathon.

Pascarella, E. T., & Chapman, D. W. (1983). A multi-institutional, path analytic validation of Tinto's model of college withdrawal. *American Educational Research Journal, 20*, 87–102.

Pascarella, E. T., Duby, P. B., & Iverson, B. K. (1983). A test and reconceptualization of a theoretical model of college withdrawal in a commuter institution setting. *Sociology of Education, 56*, 88–100.

Pascarella, E. T., & Terenzini, P. T. (1980). Predicting freshmen persistence and voluntary dropout decisions from a theoretical model. *The Journal of Higher Education, 51*, 60–75.

Pascarella, E. T., & Terenzini, P. T. (1983). Predicting voluntary freshman year persistence/withdrawal behavior in a residential university: A path analytic validation of Tinto's model. *Journal of Educational Psychology, 75*(2), 215–226.

Pascarella, E. T., & Terenzini, P. T. (1991). *How college affects students: Findings and insights from twenty years of research.* San Francisco: Jossey-Bass.

Pascarella, E. T., & Terenzini, P. T. (2005). *How college affects students: A third decade of Research.* San Francisco: Jossey-Bass.

Reason, R. D. (2003). Student variables that predict retention: Recent research and new developments. *NASPA Journal, 40*(4), 172–191.

Rendon, L. (1994). Validating culturally diverse students: Toward a new model of learning and student development. *Innovative Higher Education, 19*, 33–51.

Rendon, L. I., Jalomo, R. E., & Nora, A. (2000). Theoretical considerations in the study of minority student retention in higher education. In J. M. Braxton (Ed.), *Reworking the student departure puzzle* (pp. 127–156). Nashville, TN: Vanderbilt University Press.

Rosenbaum, J. E., Deil-Amen, R., & Person, A. E. (2006). *After admission: From college access to college success.* New York: Russell Sage Foundation.

Spady, W. (1971). Dropouts from higher education: Toward an empirical model. *Interchange, 2*, 38–62.

Stage, F. (1989). Reciprocal effects between the academic and social integration of college students. *Research in Higher Education, 30*, 517–530.

Stanton-Salazar, R. D. (1997). A social capital framework for understanding the socialization of racial minority children and youths. *Harvard Educational Review, 67*(1), 1–40.

Stanton-Salazar, R. D. (2001). *Manufacturing hope and despair: The school and kin support networks of U.S.-Mexican youth.* New York: Teachers College Press.

Strauss, A., & Corbin, J. (1990). *Basics of qualitative research: Grounded theory procedures and techniques.* Newbury Park, CA: Sage Publications.

Sullivan, A. (1997). Rites and passages: Students' views of academic and social integration. *College Student Affairs Journal, 16*(2), 4–14.

Terenzini, P. T., Pascarella, E. T., Theophilides, C., & Lorang, W. G. (1985). A replication of a path analytic validation of Tinto's theory of college student attrition. *Review of Higher Education, 8*(4), 319–340.

Terenzini, P. T., Rendon, L. I., Upcraft, M. L., Millar, S. B., Allison, K. W., Gregg, P. L., & Jalomo, R. (1994). The transition to college: Diverse students, diverse stories. *Research in Higher Education, 35*(1), 57–73.

Tierney, W. G. (1992). An anthropological analysis of student participation in college. *The Journal of Higher Education, 63*, 603–618.

Tierney, W. G. (1999). Models of minority college-going and retention: Cultural integrity versus cultural suicide. *Journal of Negro Education, 68*(1), 80–91.

Tinto, V. (1975). Dropout from higher education: A theoretical synthesis of recent research. *Review of Educational Research, 45*, 89–125.

Tinto, V. (1987). *Leaving college: Rethinking the causes and cures of student attrition.* Chicago: University of Chicago Press.

Tinto, V. (1993). *Leaving college: Rethinking the causes and cures of student attrition.* (2nd ed.). Chicago: University of Chicago Press.

Tinto, V. (1997). Classrooms as communities: Exploring the educational character of student persistence. *The Journal of Higher Education, 68*, 599–623.

Tinto, V. (1998). Colleges as communities: Taking research on student persistence seriously. *Review of Higher Education, 21*, 167–177.

Tinto, V., Russo, P., & Kadel, S. (1994). Constructing educational communities: Increasing retention in challenging circumstances. *Community College Journal, 64*, 26–30.

Torres, V. (2006). A mixed method study testing data-model fit of a retention model for Latino/a students at urban universities. *Journal of College Student Development, 47*(3), 299–318.

Voorhees, R. A. (1987). Toward building models of community college persistence: A logit analysis. *Research in Higher Education, 26,* 115–129.

Weis, L. (1985). *Between two worlds: Black students in an urban community college.* Boston: Routledge & Kegan Paul.

Wortman, P. M,. & Napoli, A. R. (1996). A meta-analysis of the impact of academic and social integration of persistence of community college students. *Journal of Applied Research in the Community College, 4*(1), 5–21.

Zea, M., Reisen, C., Beil, C., & Caplan, R. (1997). Predicting intention to remain in college among ethnic minority and nonminority students. *Journal of Social Psychology, 137,* 149–160.

Regina Deil-Amen is a professor in The Center for the Study of Higher Education at the University of Arizona.

CHAPTER 35

TEACHING BY CHOICE: COMMUNITY COLLEGES EXPAND K-12 STEM PATHWAYS AND PRACTICES

MADELINE PATTON

The American Association of Community Colleges (AACC) convened "Teaching by Choice: Beyond 2 + 2" (TBC), a conference to focus on community colleges' growing role as providers of teacher education and as sources of professional development for elementary, middle, and secondary teachers of science, technology, and mathematics. The conference, held in February 2008 in Denver, was supported by the National Science Foundation (NSF), and was held in partnership with the National Association of Community College Teacher Education Programs (NACCTEP).

This report, based on the discussions of the forty conference participants, includes recommendations for community colleges to expand post-baccalaureate teacher education programs and to enhance professional development in science, mathematics, and technology for teachers in kindergarten through twelfth grade (K–12). Some community colleges already offer these services to their communities. For most community colleges, providing post-baccalaureate and professional development programs is an extension of their traditional role as transfer institutions. Most public community colleges provide the first two years of baccalaureate studies in a wide array of fields, including education, for students who transfer to other colleges and universities to complete four-year degrees. Researchers estimate that 20–40 percent of the nation's teachers began their post-secondary educations at community colleges (Recruiting New Teachers, Inc. 2002; Shkodriani 2004; Tsapogas 2004). NSF was among the first organizations to recognize that a significant number of elementary teachers in the United States take most of their science and mathematics courses at community colleges.

Consequently, since the 1990s, NSF has supported efforts to improve science, technology, engineering, and mathematics (STEM) programs at community colleges as a way of improving elementary, middle, and secondary school instruction.

The trend in community colleges to move beyond more traditional transfer, or 2 + 2, teacher education programs responds to the nation's critical need for K–12 teachers in STEM subjects. It also responds to the professional needs of teachers who must keep current in their fields as they vie for the attention of students who have grown up immersed in fast-paced digital media. Technological advances not only add to the competition for students' attention, they also raise the stakes for students and educators by adding to the list of complex skills that students need in order to succeed. In an era of heightened calls for accountability, teachers also face the increasing demand for schools to adopt curricula that integrate assessment with the latest research-based teaching and learning strategies.

This report addresses key issues for recruiting and retaining K–12 mathematics and science teachers, for designing and delivering programs that will place well-prepared instructors in the nation's K–12 classrooms, and for developing appropriate assessment and evaluation strategies for community college post-baccalaureate teacher education and professional development programs. Its recommendations encourage community college educators to build on their colleges' strengths as teaching-focused institutions that are committed to lifelong learning and continuing education for professionals and as access points to new skills for career changers.

Insights from K–12 Classroom Teachers

The presence and participation of eight elementary, middle, and secondary public school teachers grounded the Teaching by Choice conference discussions in real-world classroom experiences. The K–12 attendees were either graduates of community college postbaccalaureate teacher education programs or participants in community college professional development programs. Their candor and willingness to discuss their teaching experiences during an opening facilitated dialog set a positive, productive tone for the conference. The K–12 teachers shared their thoughts and opinions on

- opportunities and challenges that national trends generate for K–12 teachers of science, technology, and mathematics;
- opportunities and challenges that state and local issues create for K–12 teachers of science, technology, and mathematics; and
- the impact of community college teacher education programs and professional development experiences on classroom practices.

The teachers expressed appreciation for new technologies that make a wide array of materials available for use in their classrooms, including virtual labs in science courses and the multimedia resources that come with many new textbooks. However, not all K–12 teachers have access to, or knowledge of, these new educational technologies. The teachers noted the importance of community college faculty knowing what technology is (or is not) available in local schools when designing programs for current and future teachers. By opening their labs and classrooms to local school districts, community colleges can offer K–12 teachers and their students access to more advanced technologies. In fact, some of the teachers indicated that they attended community college-sponsored professional development programs to refresh their technology skills and to learn how to assess when and where it is most effective to use technology as a teaching tool.

Although the teachers came from different parts of the United States, they experienced common demands to meet detailed curricula requirements and simultaneously prepare students for high-stakes standardized tests. Despite the depth of curricula, classroom lessons do not always match the material covered in state and federal tests. The K–12 teachers identified a particularly compelling challenge: the hands-on and inquiry-based instruction that researchers find most efficacious for learning math and science simply takes more time due to its emphasis on student-driven exploration and investigation.

Praising their community college experiences, the teachers reported that their best preparation for teaching came from courses where the learning outcomes were clearly identified. They also appreciated post-baccalaureate and professional development program instructors who modeled the same effective pedagogies they advised teachers to use in K–12 classrooms. After the opening dialog, conference participants reflected on the ways in which the remarks of the K–12 teachers might inform their own post-baccalaureate teacher education or professional development programs.

The conference participants reached consensus on several issues and recommended that community colleges

- begin teacher education and professional development programs with student outcomes clearly stated in order to build the skills of current and future teachers in creating lesson plans and activities that focus on outcomes for their students;

- model hands-on, inquiry-based teaching methods in professional development and post-baccalaureate programs;

- offer professional development workshops in multiple venues, at various times, and in a sequence that grants continuing education units, academic credits, or stipends based on attendance or completion of specific activities such as the development of lesson plans;

- offer content-specific professional development in ways that blend classroom management, pedagogy, and strategies for motivating students;

- develop online professional development programs that incorporate some face-to-face instruction and teamwork; and,

- know which technologies local school districts have available and prepare teachers to use them.

Using the K–12 teachers' remarks as a starting point, the TBC participants worked in small groups to brainstorm recommendations for community college post-baccalaureate teacher education and professional development programs, specifically addressing recruitment and participation, program design and delivery, and assessment and improvement. A series of questions, developed by the conference coordinating committee, guided the discussions and helped the conferees reach consensus across all topic areas.

Community College Post-Baccalaureate Teacher Education Programs

Framework for Discussion

How can community college post-baccalaureate programs increase recruitment of a diverse cadre of future K–12 teachers with degrees and work experience in STEM fields? What are the critical program design components of an effective post-baccalaureate STEM teacher education program? What are the critical program delivery components of an effective post-baccalaureate STEM teacher education program? What are the outcomes of a successful post-baccalaureate program for future K–12 STEM teachers? How do post-baccalaureate programs systematically assess these outcomes? How are assessment results used to improve post-baccalaureate programs?

Community college post-baccalaureate programs are an effective approach for boosting the nation's teaching ranks with mid-career professionals and retirees whose first careers in STEM fields enrich their teaching of elementary, middle, and high school students. The cost-effectiveness of community college tuition and the colleges' geography provide particular incentives for career switchers. These features can be strong assets in a post-baccalaureate teacher education program recruitment plan. Community colleges can capitalize on their proximity to diverse neighborhoods and rural communities, which are often most in need of teachers, to recruit retirees or career switchers from downsizing industries, as well as from community organizations with which faculty and staff already interact. The TBC conference participants suggested that community colleges partner with local school districts to recruit future teachers from among the parents of school children. As one participant pointed out, parents who have stayed at home to rear young children often are looking for new and different career challenges when their youngsters begin attending school full time.

Structuring post-baccalaureate programs to meet the scheduling needs of various groups of mid-career professionals can make a huge difference in whether an individual decides to pursue a career in teaching. Stay-at-home parents looking for a new career may need courses that coincide with their children's school schedule. Business people may want compressed programs offered in the evenings or on weekends, while those transitioning from military and government work may prefer full-day, full-week courses.

As institutions that have long served both older adult students and traditional college-age students, community colleges have the flexibility to adjust their teacher education programs to meet the needs of mid-career professionals. Adults with years of career experience are accustomed to multitasking, digesting complex information quickly, and getting things done in competitive mar-

---

Recommendations for Increasing Diverse Applicant Pools

- Utilize community organizations and activities that serve diverse cultures in outreach efforts.
- Create opportunities for peer-to-peer recruiting where career switchers can meet mid-career professionals who are considering a new career in teaching.
- Develop partnerships with professional organizations and STEM discipline societies.
- Recruit prospective teachers from business, community organizations, and parents of local K–12 school students.

Recommendations for Program Design and Delivery

- Model collaborative, hands-on, and inquiry-based teaching practices in all teacher education courses.
- Offer early, structured, and extensive field experiences in local K–12 schools.
- Build content-specific resources such as "toolkits" for teachers to use in classrooms.
- Focus on pedagogy, particularly strategies that help STEM professionals translate their deep content knowledge into lessons for K–12 students.
- Inform mid-career professionals about the nuances of school cultures and provide them with strategies for dealing with multiple management layers and school procedures.
- Add in-person instruction to online courses to foster communities of practice and peer support networks.

Recommendations for Assessment and Improvement of Post-Baccalaureate Programs

- Survey post-baccalaureate program completers, their mentors, and employers periodically.
- Track the licensure exam passage rate of post-baccalaureate program completers.
- Monitor retention rates of post-baccalaureate teacher education program completers.
- Modify the post-baccalaureate program curriculum and completion requirements based on assessment results.

---

kets. Typically, once mid-career professionals or retirees have made the decision to teach, they are eager to get the credentials and experience they need to work in classrooms. Post-baccalaureate programs that include early, extensive field experiences capitalize on this enthusiasm and give the novice teachers the opportunity to test their teaching skills with the support of mentors from the community college and K–12 arenas. The proximity of community colleges to where novice teachers live and work makes ongoing mentoring feasible.

Helping career switchers move successfully from retirement, business, military, or government careers requires extra attention from community college faculty who lead post-baccalaureate programs. Explicit information about school cultures and how they differ from business environments should be woven into programs. While teachers have some autonomy in their classrooms, some career switchers will need to be prepared to deal with the challenges of navigating multiple layers of authority—the school board, principal, department chair, and taxpayers—and multiple constituencies—the students and their parents and guardians.

Post-baccalaureate programs must also provide their future teachers with practical tactics for motivating students and managing a classroom. From their work in teaching-centered institutions, community college faculty members possess classroom management skills and know how to break complex concepts into segments that students can absorb and understand. Content-specific toolkits

New Pathways to Teaching in New Jersey (NPTNJ)

Mid-career professionals enrolled in the NPTNJ post-baccalaureate teacher education program have the benefit of an experienced community college educator observing their teaching and providing constructive advice. The in-class observation is an important extension of the courses that the novice teachers attend as a cohort once or twice each week during their first year of teaching.

Fifteen New Jersey community colleges participate in the NPTNJ partnership with New Jersey City University, the New Jersey Department of Education, and the local school districts. New Pathways students have the option of taking the program for graduate credit that several New Jersey universities accept toward master's degrees.

An attentive approach to the practical aspects of teaching begins even before the NPTNJ students—who all have bachelor's degrees and passing scores on the Praxis II exam for content knowledge—begin teaching.The first stage of the program requires that students complete a 60-hour pre-service component to help them gain insights about teaching as they learn classroom management and pedagogical skills.

As many as 400 NPTNJ students will embark on their first year of teaching in 2008. Since the program began in 2003, more than 3,000 individuals have completed the pre-service component, and more than 2,000 people have completed the one-year teaching experience.

For more information, see http://web.njcu.edu/sites/nptnj/Content/default.asp.

Virginia Community College System Career Switchers Program

The Virginia Community College System's Career Switchers post-baccalaureate teacher education program delivers instruction statewide using compressed video for real-time teleconferences at six campuses, online assignments, interactive student dialogs, a 30-hour field placement, and one daylong meeting during which the students work in large and small groups.

This blending of distance and face-to-face instruction with in-school experience makes for an intense 16 weeks of teacher education.The prospective middle school and high school teachers, whose average age is 43, also must pass a Praxis II exam for the content areas in which they hope to teach. All the Career Switcher program participants already have bachelor's degrees and at least five years of full-time experience in another career; many previously worked as engineers or served in the military.

Experienced K–12 teachers are mentors as well as colleagues for the Career Switchers during their first year of teaching with a provisional license. They also stay in contact with their Career Switcher cohort and instructors by attending five seminars and sharing assignments monthly. More than 80 percent of the 202 Career Switchers who completed their first year of teaching obtained a five-year teaching license by 2007. During the 2007–2008 academic year, 135 students completed the 16-week semester.

For more information see http://www.educateva.com.

filled with best practices that meet national standards are essential resources that community colleges can provide to help their newly certified teachers start well.

Obtaining accurate data about the teaching experiences of post-baccalaureate teacher education program graduates and their K–12 students' performance is essential for continuous improvement of these programs. Students can be key players in this improvement process. Conference participants urged community colleges to track the career switcher students to determine the effectiveness of their programs and analyze the results. Post-baccalaureate programs establish strong relationships with their students and can capitalize on these relationships to track their students' success. Ongoing contact with program graduates and their employers can help assess the program and respond to school and community needs.

Community College Professional Development Programs in K-12 STEM Education

Framework for Discussion

How can community colleges recruit current K–12 teachers to participate in professional development opportunities in STEM disciplines? What are the critical program design components of an effective professional development program in K–12 STEM education? What are the critical program delivery components of an effective professional development program in K–12 STEM education? What are the outcomes of a successful professional development program in K–12 STEM education? How do community colleges systematically assess STEM teacher professional development outcomes? How are assessment results used to improve professional development programs?

Professional development programs offer opportunities for K–12 teachers to reflect on their current teaching methods and acquire new knowledge and strategies that they can apply in their classrooms.

Conference participants encouraged community colleges to create professional development programs that integrate STEM content with pedagogy. It is one thing to understand a concept theoretically and quite another to be able to teach it to a young child or teenager. Teachers want practical applications; they need them to engage students and to teach them to understand and apply new concepts. As one community college faculty participant explained, when he was a high school teacher he considered professional development workshops and conferences successful "if I [had] one new thing to take and put in my classroom on Monday."

Conference participants urged community colleges to create their professional development programs with state standards in mind. They also recommended that community colleges systematically follow up with their program attendees to assess the impact of the teachers' learning on student performance. When structuring professional development programs, the conference participants urged community colleges to design standards-based programs that incorporate promising practices identified by national organizations such as the American Mathematical Association of Two-Year Colleges, National Council of Teachers of Mathematics, the National Science Teachers Association, and the Association for Supervision and Curriculum Development. National Science Foundation-supported programs, like those the agency funds through the Advanced Technological Education program, are also valuable resources for innovative curricula and teaching materials that are available to U.S. educators free of charge. (See http://www.nsf.gov/ate and http://www.aacc.nche.edu/ateprogram.)

Close collaboration between community colleges and local school systems generates substantial benefits for students, parents, teachers, and the community. Broadening these partnerships to include state education departments, four-year colleges and universities, and area businesses can provide additional resources as school districts identify gaps in student learning that teachers can address with the aid of targeted professional development provided by community colleges. By offering content-specific professional development programs, community colleges can truly help districts that need to enhance student performance in particular subjects. The proximity of community colleges to local schools in most communities makes it easy for them to deliver programming when and where school districts need it to fit teachers' busy schedules. This geographic accessibility of

Recommendations to Encourage Participation in K–12 STEM Professional Development Programs at Community Colleges

- Create programs rich in mathematics and science content and classroom applications.
- Partner with local school districts to use local and federal funds to support programs.
- Establish professional development networks with school districts, community colleges, and four-year colleges and universities to design, implement, and advertise opportunities.
- Provide stipends, academic credits, continuing education units, and other incentives to teachers.

Recommendations for Program Design and Delivery

- Align programs with state and national curriculum standards for math and science.
- Supply classroom materials and demonstrate strategies for teachers to use immediately with students.
- Include cross-curricular activities that integrate mathematics skills and concepts into science courses, and science topics into mathematics instruction.
- Deliver programs in formats and at times and locations that are convenient for teachers.

Recommendations for Assessment and Improvement of Professional Development Programs

- Assess pedagogy and content needs of K–12 teachers regularly.
- Follow up with participants to determine the usefulness and applicability of their new knowledge and teaching strategies.
- Design collaborative assessments with local school districts to collect and analyze student performance data before and after their teachers participated in the professional development program.
- Establish advisory committees to evaluate assessment results and make recommendations for future programming.

Communication in Science Inquiry Project (CISIP)

CISIP cultivates the development of "science discourse communities" in middle and high school English and science courses. This professional development program offered by the Maricopa Community Colleges in Arizona introduces its cross-discipline methods to teams of K–12 teachers during a three-week summer institute. CISIP reinforces ways to use inquiry-based lessons effectively to boost student science knowledge and writing skills with Saturday programs during the school year.

With support from the National Science Foundation, CISIP designs and delivers its research-based curriculum using a team of master teachers from secondary schools, community colleges, and universities. The project aims to partner with math and science organizations in other states to broaden dissemination efforts to begin in 2009.

For more information see http://www.maricopa.edu/academic/teachered/ CISIP.html.

community colleges also favors online, hybrid delivery of professional development programs. This blending of asynchronous and in-person instruction helps teachers who prefer the flexibility of online courses to gain the added benefit of periodic meetings with faculty instructors and teacher colleagues who are pursuing similar professional goals. Such face-to-face meetings help build a community of practice among teachers who can stay connected online even after their courses end.

Whether community colleges offer professional development on their campuses or take their programs to teachers in their schools, these programs are opportunities for community college faculty to share their expertise in STEM disciplines and to make the campus facilities and academic resources, such as lab equipment and other educational materials, available to the K–12 teachers. With standardized tests built into the accountability measures of the No Child Left Behind Act of 2001 and state benchmarks, community colleges can provide a service to local school districts simply by offering professional development programs that educate teachers about strategies that can assist their students in taking standardized tests.

The TBC conference participants saw these K–12 professional development programs as a venue for community colleges to share from their strengths to meet the national need for exemplary STEM instruction.

Conclusion

Community colleges across the United States are reinventing and redefining pathways for K-12 teacher education and professional development. The recommendations that emerged from the "Teaching by Choice: Beyond 2+2" conference encouraged community colleges to maintain this trend toward innovation. Participants renewed the call for community colleges to take the lead in providing STEM experiences for current and future K–12 teachers and to demonstrate research-based teaching methodologies. To strengthen such experiences, the conference participants encouraged community colleges to partner with K–12 schools, four-year colleges and universities, and local STEM businesses and industries to share resources as well as ideas.

Conferees also emphasized the need for greater acceptance of systematic formative assessment to improve and expand community college post-baccalaureate teacher education and professional development programs. By integrating assessment measures into program design, community colleges can demonstrate their commitment to offering high-quality programs that address the needs of their students, the local K–12 schools, and the larger community.

References

National Science Foundation. 1998. *Investing in Tomorrow's Teachers: The Integral Role of Two-Year Colleges in the Science and Mathematics Preparation of Prospective Teachers*. Report from a National Science Foundation Workshop. NSF-9949. Arlington, VA: National Science Foundation.

Patton, Madeline. 2005. *Teaching by Choice: Community College Science and Mathematics Preparation of K–12 Teachers*. Ed. Lynn Barnett and Faith San Felice. Washington, DC: American Association of Community Colleges.

Patton Madeline. 2006. *Teaching by Choice: Cultivating Exemplary Community College STEM Faculty*. Ed. Lynn Barnett and Faith San Felice. Washington, DC: American Association of Community Colleges.

Recruiting New Teachers, Inc. 2002. *Tapping Potential: Community College Students and America's Recruitment Challenge*. Belmont, MA: Recruiting New Teachers, Inc.

Shkodriani, Gina. 2004. Seamless pipeline from two-year to four-year institutions for teacher training. In *PT3 Policy Brief*. Denver, CO: Education Commission of the States.

Tsapogas, John. 2004. The role of community colleges in the education of recent science and engineering graduates. In *InfoBrief 04-315*. Arlington, VA: Division of Science Resources Statistics, National Science Foundation.

CHAPTER 36

THE COMMUNITY COLLEGE BACCALAUREATE IN THE U.S.: MODELS, PROGRAMS, AND ISSUES

DEBORAH L. FLOYD

This chapter has three purposes. First and foremost, it aims to identify and describe community college models for expanding access to the baccalaureate. Among these models are community colleges that confer these degrees and partner with others to provide the "net effect" of a baccalaureate degree experience for community college graduates. Much like the 1960s, this is an era of innovation: Community colleges are changing rapidly as an increasing number of them strive to "make good" on their promise of access by implementing diverse (and sometimes controversial) models of baccalaureate programming.

Second, this chapter seeks to encourage constructive dialogue on this topic, using pragmatic descriptors of current U.S. programming models. Third, it raises questions and issues that invite further exploration, especially in ways that will assist policy makers at the national, state, and local levels.

By way of fulfilling these three purposes, this chapter offers first a four-part typology of community colleges and baccalaureate degrees and then a look at how this emerging megatrend is shaping research, policy, and practice vis-à-vis community colleges.

To help illustrate these models consider the case of a fictitious student who embodies many of the characteristics of community college students that are relevant to the rationale for these baccalaureate models. Martha Jane Smith is a 32-year-old first-generation college student enrolled in Rolling Hills Community College, a small rural college in the southeastern United States.[1] Her husband, Bill, is a union laborer who has worked construction all his life, like his father. They had the first of their three children when Martha Jane was only 16, and she dropped out of high school to take care of her family, as did her husband. Now, 16 years later, Martha Jane is taking time to pick up where she left off educationally, and she is a sophomore at the local community college.

Monday through Friday her three children ride the bus to rural public schools while she drops her husband off at his construction site and drives herself to classes at the community college, 22 miles away. When not in class, she spends most of her time in the college library using the computer and studying. Her goal is to earn an associate degree at the community college and eventually finish a bachelor's degree so that she can teach high school science and math classes in her hometown. "I want to be a teacher because I want to help kids learn," she said, "but I also know that a teaching job will bring me security and a good income." She is well on her way towards that goal and lacks only 15 semester hours to complete her associate of science degree.

Martha Jane is a determined woman who doesn't want to end up like her mother, who is completely dependent on her husband. So, three years ago, Martha Jane (who knew instinctively that an education would be a key to her independence) decided to earn her high school diploma by enrolling for GED classes at night in a local elementary school. Her oldest daughter babysat for the younger two children when her husband was busy with bowling or spent the evening "with the boys" at the union hall. As she continued her GED classes, Martha Jane's confidence in herself grew in tandem with her rising competence in math, science, communications, and other basic fields. In less than a year, she completed her GED and was on her way to fulfilling her dream of earning a college degree and becoming a high school teacher.

Thanks to advice and encouragement from her community college's GED professor, Martha Jane successfully maneuvered the bureaucracy of financial aid and received enough money to pay for her tuition and books. While she tested into a "pre college" English class, she enrolled for a full load of college-level general-education courses each term, and her grades have earned her a place on the college dean's list. Last semester she accepted an invitation to join the college's Phi Theta Kappa honor society, which has connected her with a network of new friends.

After completing courses next semester, Martha Jane Smith will be the first in her family to graduate from a college. But she knows that this associate degree is only one step towards the baccalaureate, another major hurdle before she will qualify to work in her chosen field. Private and public state universities have offered her scholarships, but she cannot accept those offers because the institutions are too far away from her home, and commuting would be prohibitively expensive and time-consuming. Rolling Hills Community College has several articulation agreements with area universities, and a few of them offer courses on its campus, but only occasionally and without consistency. For the first time in her college career, Martha jane knows that the toughest step of her journey towards becoming a high school teacher lies ahead of her: How will she get access to the courses that she needs to complete a bachelor's degree?

Martha Jane, like so many place-bound community college students, is likely to become a victim of a system that promises access to a college degree but simply fails to deliver the necessary programs.[2] Fortunately, the GED program worked well for her as a seamless entry to college. Like so many community college students, Martha Jane feels comfortable at the community college and would like to conclude her education locally, without having to leave her family and travel to a university. But unless the barriers that are now restricting her continued enrollment are removed, Martha Jane will be become a sad statistic, a would-be-teacher denied access to the necessary credentials for the teaching profession.

U.S. community colleges are noted for being responsive to community needs and addressing issues of access. They are "people's colleges" and the "last chance" for many individuals. These "open-door" institutions rarely turn away students as a demonstration of their commitment to access, at least until transition at the baccalaureate level becomes restrictive. States such as Florida led the way in mandating transfer of all community college credits and their counting towards state universities baccalaureate requirements. Most state universities and community colleges have articulation agreements that govern transfer into entire programs, but access may necessitate major and unexpected sacrifices. As some universities aspire to become more selective and research oriented, their emphasis on undergraduate education, especially off campus, often diminishes. Where does that leave Martha Jane, and many like her, who want to matriculate at a four-year college or university, but simply may not do so, given the transfer models currently available?

The topic of the community college baccalaureate has become extremely controversial, partly because of the lack of clarity in defining models and the use of an inconsistent, even confusing terminology. For example, the term "community college baccalaureate" has been used interchangeably to describe delivery models in which community colleges and universities collaboratively offer programs leading to the baccalaureate, with the university conferring the actual degree. Elsewhere, university branch and extension campuses conferring only associate degrees have recently added community college baccalaureates. Some community colleges that have added the baccalaureate to their degree offerings (without having a university partner) also use this term. Clearly, community colleges are trying to address increased need for access to the baccalaureate. Simultaneously, they are seeking a terminology to accurately represent a fundamental expansion in community colleges' mission.

Without question, community college educators would strongly agree that Martha Jane should have access to a bachelor's degree so that she might fulfill her dream. But, as the old adage goes, "The devil is in the details." Who will offer the upper-level courses? Who should confer the degrees? Where will courses be offered? Who will accredit these programs? And how will these programs be funded? Such devilish details complicate any well-intended desire to expand access to the baccalaureate for the place-bound.

A Four-Part Typology: Community Colleges and Baccalaureate Programs

Historical Context

Providing access to the baccalaureate was an early and central role of the two year college. The first transfer agreement, adopted in 1903 by the University of Chicago and the new public junior college in Gary, Indiana, permitted Gary's, young people to remain in their community for an additional two years before relocating to Chicago's south side (Pedersen 2000).

The transfer function is a key role of community colleges with deep historical roots. Some commentators have argued that early junior colleges were established to permit universities to focus on upper-division instruction (Cohen & Brawer, 2003; Zwerling, 1976); others have asserted that they allowed place-bound students to remain at home for an additional one or two years of study before relocating to a university campus, law school, or medical college (Pedersen, 2000). Yet junior colleges never secured a monopoly over lower-division college instruction. Four-year colleges and universities never relinquished this role (Cohen & Brawer, 2003). Having retained a sense of control over the entire undergraduate curriculum, four-year colleges and universities became the "gate-keepers" of American higher education and used their power to approve (or deny) credits for "junior college" transfer courses.

Perhaps part of the underlying reason for the contemporary friction about the community college baccalaureate is that U.S. universities have had the authority to control the baccalaureate and this role has not been effectively challenged, until now. Those community colleges now proposing broad access to the baccalaureate may seem to threaten the power of universities to determine the baccalaureate curriculum and to award these degrees. While many argue that community college baccalaureate programs are "all about bumping up access for non-traditional students and helping to meet shortages like those in nursing and teaching fields," others fear that this movement could be counter-productive and mark the end of traditional community colleges (Troumpoucis, 2004, p. 6).

According to Cohen and Brawer (2003), "the community colleges have suffered less from goal displacement than have most other higher education institutions. They had less to displace; their goals were to serve the people with whatever the people wanted. Standing outside the tradition [of universities], they offered access" (p. 29). Today, community colleges are implementing numerous programmatic models and governance structures to deliver "whatever the people want." Increasingly, what people want includes proximate access to the baccalaureate, regardless of who confers the degree.

The typology offered here posits four models—articulation, the university center, university extension, and the community college baccalaureate—and reflects the author's best efforts to assimilate information from various sources. This list of institutions and models is not comprehensive, but is offered as a schema, with examples, to help shape the debate over the proper mission of community colleges. This typology may be useful to practitioners, researchers, and policy makers to study, compare, and contrast "like" programs. A comparison of key features that differentiate these models from one another is described in Table 3.1.

Articulation Model

Articulation agreements that ensure acceptance of freshman and sophomore credits by senior colleges and universities are vital to community colleges' transfer mission. In some states, such as Florida, associate degree graduates who complete a prescribed general-education core are

TABLE 1

Comparison of Different Baccalaureate Models

	Articulation Model	University Center Model	University Extension Model	Community College Baccalaureate Model
Sequential attendance at community college followed by university	YES	YES	NO	NO
University uses community college facilities	NO	YES	NO	NO
Students complete baccalaureate degree at a campus other than the conventional university campus	NO	YES	YES	YES
University controls baccalaureate degree requirements	YES	YES	YES	NO
Community college controls baccalaureate degree requirements	NO	NO	NO	YES

guaranteed acceptance of credits and junior status at their state university. States such as California, Illinois, New York, Oklahoma, Tennessee, Texas, and Washington have transfer rates well above the norm because most of their community colleges participate in a collaborative project with a nearby four-year college or university, with procedures governing student transfer spelled out in an intrastate agreement applicable to both institutions. In fact, according to a recent study of state policies and the success of community college transfer students, "effective state policies are at the heart of baccalaureate success for students transferring from two-year to four-year institutions with the goal of achieving their degrees" (Wellman, 2004 p. 1). Cohen and Brawer (2003) assert the articulation agreements become more effective when community colleges and universities collaboratively develop two-plus-two agreements in such specific program areas as teacher education, health, engineering, and agriculture and farm management.

With respect to teacher education, for example, recent studies report that almost 80 percent of U.S. community colleges (approximately 900 institutions) are implementing articulation agreements that encourage students to earn the first two years of a four-year degree at their local community college and also guarantee the full transfer of credits to a state university (Floyd & Walker, 2003; Hudson, 2000).

The dynamics of a community college student's transfer to a university, including the programmatic pathways and matriculation outcomes, have been the focus of numerous studies. Arthur M. Cohen (2003) describes the many roles that community colleges assume in assisting students with transfer transitions. He recognizes that there are models other than traditional transfer, which require community colleges' students to travel to an often-distant university for upper-division course work. New models, beyond the traditional two-plus-two models whereby students complete two years of study at the community college and transfer to a four-year college or university to finalize baccalaureate studies, are emerging. Some of these models include universities' offering upper-division courses on community college campuses. It is important to note that within the framework of the articulation model, creative three-plus-one models are becoming more popular (especially with propriety and private colleges) whereby students complete 90 hours with a community college and the four-year college provides the final year leading to a baccalaureate.

For many students, articulation models work well, but for others like Martha Jane Smith, a traditional articulation model is not feasible because she is unable to leave her family and travel to a university to' continue her studies in a traditional on-campus format. While the community college and university may have perfectly articulated transfer agreements, she is "place-bound" and needs relevant junior- and senior-level courses offered locally.

University Center Model and Concurrent-Use Campuses

The university center model is becoming increasingly popular. Often these centers are located close to or on community college campuses. The university confers the degree in partnership with others, including community colleges and sometimes other universities.

Implementation of this model often involves consortia of colleges and universities that jointly use facilities for the delivery of upper-division courses and programs. In Michigan, for instance, the Northwestern Michigan College University Center includes 11 four-year universities with programming that allows seamless entry to junior- and senior-level course work from the community college. In Texas, North Harris Montgomery Community College's university center includes six public universities that offer over 21 unduplicated bachelor's degree programs and 24 master's degree programs (Windham, Perkins, & Rogers, 2001). In south Florida, Broward Community College's central campus is the home of the 4,500-student Florida Atlantic University campus that is part of a much larger higher-education complex. The Edison University Center, on Florida's Edison College[3] campus, is an alliance among a number of regionally accredited colleges and universities that houses several baccalaureate programs that articulate with Edison's associate degree programs. Arizona Western College, located in isolated areas of Yuma and La Paz Counties, created a Yuma Educational Consortium with all levels of education providers, and they also house buildings and programs provided by Northern Arizona University.

Private and proprietary colleges and universities are becoming increasingly active partners with community colleges in the delivery of baccalaureate degrees on community college campuses, via distance learning and with university centers. For instance, through their bachelor degree granting partner, Charter Oak State College (COSC) Bridgepoint Education (formerly Charter Learning) accepts 90 hours of transfer credits and offers the final year of upper-division courses on community college campuses in Arizona and Washington State, with plans to expand to California and other states soon (Scott Turner e-mail communication April 27, 2004). COSC is accredited by the New England Association of Schools and Colleges and is a public college in the Connecticut state university system. Bridgepoint Education is a private for-profit organization founded in 1999, and has offered degree completion programs at corporate sites such as Boeing, BF Goodrich, and the National Guard. Their first community college agreement was with the Maricopa County Community College District colleges in 2001, and later with Arizona's Pima Community College and Washington's Skagit Valley College. Another example of the three-plus-one university center partnership is the relationship between Regis University and Colorado's community colleges through online and on-site delivery of courses. Regis University, accredited by the North Central Association (NCA), launched a new initiative called Associate's to Bachelor's ™ and in January 2004, hired Joe D. May, a former community college president, as its executive director of partnerships.

These are just a few of the many examples of the university center approach to delivery of the baccalaureate. These centers often engage private, proprietary, and state institutions as partners and may include online and on-site course delivery.

This model of joint-use facilities has emerged since the 1960s as a popular approach embraced by a number of states. According to the findings of a 1999 survey of State Higher Education Executive Officers (SHEEOs) on joint-use facilities (Windham, Perkins, & Rogers, 2001), 20 states reported the utilization of joint use facilities.[4] The governance models vary and include joint boards, local college governance, private boards, and some that are led by individual directors and presidents.

While the university center and concurrent-use models are not new, they are gaining in momentum and becoming increasingly popular. In Chapter 5, Albert L. Lorenzo describes various university centers and frames the discussion with a typology of six models: co-location, enterprise, virtual, integrated, sponsorship, and hybrid. The hybrid model is just that, a hybrid of other models, with one major addition—the community college is authorized to confer certain baccalaureate degrees.

Various forms of the university center model have been quite effective for expanding access to the baccalaureate and beyond to thousands of students. In fact, for Martha Jane Smith, the university center model may help her to obtain her baccalaureate in teaching. She would be dependent, however, on the university's keeping a promise to offer the courses (even if they had small enrollments) and to do so on a schedule that would allow her to complete her degree requirements locally.

University Extension Model

Universities have long provided baccalaureate education through off-campus and extension centers. Indeed, this was the mandate of the land-grant institutions from their inception. More recently, private and proprietary, as well as public institutions have seen this as a viable means of furthering their mission.

The twenty-first-century definition of the university extension model has various interpretations. Some colleges use their university affiliation in their own name, despite their own independent accreditation. Diverse forms of state governance further blur distinctions. Hawaii, for example, has given three of the University of Hawaii's community colleges (Honolulu, Kapi'olani, and Maui) approval to award the baccalaureate (Patton, 2003). West Virginia's Parkersburg Community College became the University of West Virginia in Parkersburg in 1989 and received legislative authority to grant the baccalaureate four years later. Westark Community College, Arkansas's oldest community college, became the University of Arkansas at Fort Smith in 2002 after a few years of offering four-year degrees. All the above institutions are associated with a university title, but they are independently accredited.

Another example of a university extension model for baccalaureate programming is the Louisiana State University—Alexandra, which was granted legislative authorization to move toward four-year status and by 2003, had reorganized itself. Its plans include officially completing the conversion by fall 2004, along with a tuition increase (www.lsua.edu/community/4year.htm). An interesting plan is the Pennsylvania State University plan that authorizes 14 of its 17 branch campuses to offer baccalaureate degrees to address unmet needs of place-bound students (University Colleges of Technology, 1997).

Oklahoma State University (OSU) is unique among land-grant institutions in possessing two independently accredited campuses that deliver certificate and associate degree education in technical areas. OSU's Okmulgee campus won state approval in 2004 to award baccalaureates in specialized areas that articulate with its associate degree programs.[5] This development seems to be congruent with the traditional focus of land-grant universities and the original federal mandate for "mechanical and practical arts."

The university extension model is similar to the university center model in that baccalaureate courses are offered at a campus other than the main or largest campus of a university, however, in the university extension model, the campus where these courses are offered is formally part of the university.

No doubt, these university extension programs have been very successful in expanding access to the baccalaureate, especially in workforce areas. In theory, for students like Martha Jane, these university extension programs could present seamless opportunities to earn the baccalaureate, if offered in a timely and accessible format in the areas that the student needs. In practice, however, programs such as teacher education are not commonly offered through the university extension model.

Community College Baccalaureate

The term "community college baccalaureate" describes various models of delivery, including those described in the models discussed previously. Most frequently, however, it denotes community colleges that now "confer" the baccalaureate, not just partner with others for baccalaureate programming. A possible definitional problem associated with the term "community college baccalaureate" is that in some classification systems, a community college might be reclassified when it begins to offer baccalaureate degrees—even a single baccalaureate degree. For example, it appears that the practice of some, but not all, accreditation associations is to classify institutions according to the highest degree the institution awards. In such a case, a two-year institution that gains approval to offer a few baccalaureate programs would be reclassified as a four-year institution, even if the institution's intention is to remain effectively a community college, but one that offers a few baccalaureate programs. In reality, what we find in the field is the emergence of a new institutional type that embodies characteristics of different existing institutional types. The choice for classification is somewhere between trying to fit this new institutional type (imperfectly) into existing classification systems and developing a new way of classifying and describing these hybrid institutions.

An example of such a new way of classifying these hybrid institutions is the approach taken by The Southern Regional Education Board (SREB).[6] The SREB identifies those as associate/baccalaureate institutions, community colleges that grant mostly associate degrees but also some baccalaureates; specifically, Dalton State College and Macon State College in Georgia, and West Virginia University at Parkersburg.[7] It also includes University of Arkansas at Fort Smith (formerly Westark College) and will soon add Florida's community colleges that are (or will be) offering four-year degrees: Chipola, Miami Dade, St. Petersburg, and Okloosa Walton.

Similarly, three community colleges in Texas (Brazosport College, Midland College, and South Texas Community College) were granted authorization by the Texas Coordinating Board to offer baccalaureates in certain applied technical and science fields in July 2003 (Larose, 2003; Wertheimer, 2003). In time, they will become SREB "hybrids," even though the Southern Association of Colleges and Schools (SACS), their regional accrediting association, will classify them as four-year institutions, not community colleges.

In 2001, a task force of the North Central Association's (NCA's) Higher Education Commission issued a report with recommendations for dealing with community colleges' requests to offer four-year programs.[8] The report explains the task force's deliberations; in each case, the NCA classifies community colleges offering and conferring four-year degrees as four-year colleges. In fact, according to NCA's executive director, Ron Baker, five colleges have "moved from associate institutions to baccalaureate institutions and received accreditation at the baccalaureate level while retaining accreditation at the associate level" (e-mail communication with Ron Baker, October 1, 2003).

In 1993, Utah Valley Community College's name and status changed to Utah Valley State College, as a part of its initial baccalaureate candidacy; in 1995, it received accreditation at the baccalaureate level in several areas. Similarly, Utah's Dixie College became Dixie State College of Utah in 2000, during the candidacy phase, and obtained final accreditation in 2002. NCA gave Montana's Salish Kootenai College candidacy in 1990 and accreditation for baccalaureate offerings as of 1993. NCA granted Great Basin College in Nevada candidacy in 1999, initial accreditation in 2003 with formal accreditation awarded retroactively to September 1, 2002 (Danny Gonzales, June 23, 2004 personal communications).

The University and Community College System of Nevada's elected Board of Trustees governs all state postsecondary institutions. Great Basin College, in an isolated northern area, received approval in 2002 to confer baccalaureates in elementary education, integrated and professional studies, electronic instrumentation, and management technology; nursing is currently in development (Gonzales, 2003).

Thus a community college that is adding a baccalaureate emphasis, but keeping associate degree programs, may still fit the model of the community college baccalaureate. This "hybrid" institution is the result of a strong push to offer baccalaureate opportunities in communities.

For Martha Jane Smith, the other models—articulation, university center, and university extension—may not meet her needs, since partnerships with four-year colleges do not always result in appropriate courses being taught locally and in a timely manner. It is reasonable to assume that Martha Jane may not achieve her dream of being a high school teacher . . . at least not without a new model that offers relevant upper-division courses locally. If denied access to the baccalaureate, she would be justified in voicing her frustrations to leaders of the local community college (and anyone else who would listen) in hopes that it will take the lead by gaining approval to grant the baccalaureate. If the systems of four-year colleges that control the upper-division course work of the baccalaureate are unresponsive to this woman, who is typical of many place-bound students who deserve a chance to succeed in college, the local institution may have to do the "right thing" and lead the way toward implementing a community college baccalaureate.

A Mega-trend: Research, Policy, and Practice

Keeping current with local and state developments in community colleges and other associate degree—granting institutions that are petitioning for legislative and governance approval to confer baccalaureates is a challenge for even the most competent journalist. For instance, a bill introduced in California in early 2003 (Sturrock, 2003) would allow community colleges to offer upper-division courses jointly with the California State University System, although the model is unclear in terms of which institutions would confer the degrees. Also, in 2003, a failed South Carolina bill (Grimsley, 2003) would have allowed Trident Technical College to add one bachelor's degree to its offerings—culinary arts.[9] In suburban Chicago, Harper College has been exploring four-year degree offerings (*Community College Times*, 2003; Granderson, 2003); an editorial cautioned local leaders to "go slowly on the four-year degree idea" and to look at states with four-year community colleges, such as Arkansas, Florida, Texas, and Utah (*Daily Herald Reports*, 2003). Unquestionably, news sources across the country will continue to cover these evolutionary changes in baccalaureate programming. But, in the absence of clear and consistent terms and concepts to describe these approaches, some reported information may not be accurate, at least to scholars studying technical details.

Recent Research

Surprisingly, there is little research published about the specifics of national and state policies and practices related to the community college baccalaureate. While models and partnerships abound, specific information consists of anecdotal news and stories, opinion-editorial articles, a few journal articles, and a handful of doctoral dissertations. Clearly, these new programming areas are ripe for publications and research. This section looks at two recent related documents.

Floyd and Walker Survey

As an ancillary focus, one recent study of state practices in teacher education programming may be of interest. In 2002-2003, Deborah L. Floyd and David A. Walker (2003) surveyed state directors of community colleges and asked if one or more colleges in their state were awarding bachelor's degrees in teacher education. Thirty-three responded to their survey, for a 64 percent response rate, which yielded a sample representative of U.S. community colleges. Only two states, Florida and Nevada, responded "yes" (community college baccalaureate model). Almost 20 percent responded "yes" but added that these degrees are being awarded through partnerships with universities (university center model). Further, almost 80 percent of U.S. community colleges are implementing articulation agreements for teacher education, suggesting the dominance of the articulation model. Community colleges in Florida and Nevada that may now confer the baccalaureate are four-year colleges to their regional accrediting associations, although clearly the state directors still view them as community colleges.

Community College Baccalaureate Survey

In mid-2003, the Community College Baccalaureate Association (CCBA) commissioned an independent study to ascertain interest among U.S. community college presidents in organizational and programmatic issues related to the delivery of baccalaureate programs, including the community college baccalaureate model.[10] Researchers sent surveys to 500 presidents selected randomly and received 101 responses, a response rate of slightly over 20 percent. Among the key findings, presidents would prefer to partner with a "mission complementary" four-year university in hopes of delivering baccalaureate degrees locally (CCBA, 2003).

Other major findings of this study of presidents are as follows:

- Many presidents indicated that their state legislatures have considered, or are planning to consider, expanding the baccalaureate through community colleges.

- Over half noted that community college-based baccalaureate programming is not completely understood by the state's higher-education community and policy makers.

- Not surprisingly, interest in baccalaureates is greatest in areas where students are place-bound, such as isolated rural communities.

- Colleges that have expanded the baccalaureate through one or more of these models have done so in key academic areas such as business, computer science, criminal justice, education, elementary education, and nursing.

- Almost half of the colleges already offer some form of baccalaureate programming on their own or in partnership.

- Over a third of respondents indicated that four-year institutions in their area are not meeting baccalaureate demand.

- More than one-third affirmed that the majority of their students do not transfer to four-year colleges and universities because of geographical or financial barriers.

- Over two-thirds agreed that there are specific, high-demand career fields that require a baccalaureate and that currently the four-year institutions in their area are not meeting these demands.

- Approximately a fourth had received requests from area employers to offer the baccalaureate in certain fields.

- Over one-third affirmed that their faculty and staff have expressed interest in developing the capacity to offer baccalaureate programming on their campus.

- Approximately half noted that several of their academic programs are well positioned for transition to four-year offerings, including having the necessary faculty, infrastructure, and technology.

- Most have not completed a feasibility study or needs assessment or otherwise researched the impact of, or need for, a community college baccalaureate in their service area.

- Almost half affirmed personal interest in participating in a national association advocating community college-based baccalaureates.

Critics may argue that these findings represented the views of just slightly over 100 people and thus might not be representative of all U.S. community colleges. However, this survey of presidents offers the most current research about this topic and is useful for practitioners and policy makers. Further, and more important, its findings offer much food for thought regarding the need to frame and address issues of policy, research, and practice.

Issues for Policy and Research

The ramifications of what appears to be a mega-trend among community colleges focusing on baccalaureate programming are many and multidimensional. The mere fact that current research is woefully inadequate to addressing these trends is troubling and offers an opportunity well worth embracing. One must wonder why national policy groups and associations have not been placing more emphasis on this trend. Is it because this topic is controversial so people imagine that not talking about it will make it "go away"? Perhaps associations, groups, and individuals have not fully grasped the enormity of this movement and the increasing pressures community college leaders face from students and communities to provide better opportunities for baccalaureate access. Or does the lack of engagement merely reflect normal inertia and uncertainty in the face of new challenges? Do some people look at community colleges' baccalaureate programming negatively and as involving "status creep" (Pedersen, 2001) or "mission creep" (Mills, 2003), or do they believe that colleges should "stick to what they do best" (Wattenbarger, 2002) and not take on baccalaureate programming?

Regardless of the reason, the time is overdue for state, national, and local policy makers, organizations, and leaders to recognize that this trend is very real and is begging for attention and focus. It necessitates articulation of a common language (terminology), such as the typology proposed in this chapter, to facilitate meaningful and useful policy studies and research. Foundations and other funding agencies should encourage the Community College Baccalaureate Association (CCBA) to serve as a convener to discuss relevant issues and as a documenter of this movement. The CCBA has been playing this role with very limited fiscal resources while dealing with an area of enormous interest to community college presidents and leaders.

Policy Issues

This mega-trend poses a number of other questions, such as:

- Is there truly a community college baccalaureate degree, since most regional accrediting associations view community colleges that confer the baccalaureate as four-year colleges?

- Do the regional accrediting associations, the Carnegie classification system, and organizations such as the SREB and AACC need a new scheme that recognizes these "new" colleges that are shifting to baccalaureate programming? What are the projected ramifications of such a move and of doing nothing in this regard?

- Is this movement actually a natural evolution of the community colleges' mission and promise of access to educational opportunities for the masses?

- If four-year colleges and universities do not respond to the underserved, who will, if not community colleges?

- What are the ethical and moral responsibilities of community colleges in terms of access to relevant baccalaureate programs after completion of the associate degree? Should they ensure that students understand fully the ramifications of a baccalaureate from each of the models proposed in this chapter, including the reality that some universities might not accept these baccalaureates as entry for graduate study and beyond?

- What are the specific curricular areas of emphasis and are they primarily workforce related or "new baccalaureates" rather than more traditional programs?

- As more universities are closing their doors to transfer students and cutting back for financial reasons, what will happen to community college students who need and want a baccalaureate but are not served by universities? Will community colleges seek new ways of providing access to baccalaureate programs without depending on universities?

- When universities shift focus and emphasize research while downplaying undergraduate education, should community colleges alter their missions and concentrate on the baccalaureate?

- How will these programs be funded? If community colleges are taking on baccalaureate programming, will universities relinquish state-appropriated monies for those functions and corresponding curricular control?

- What role do faculty members assume in these models of baccalaureate programming? What policies and practices will best sustain morale, fairness, support for their work, and other factors?

Research Issues

- One must ask who is responsible for this research agenda? Who will ensure that a timely, relevant research agenda is implemented for the benefit of practitioners, policy makers, researchers, and students? Will policy decisions rely solely on emotion and political factors, or will a research agenda help drive policy decisions? One hopes that this movement will catch the eye of influential leaders and organizations so that meaningful research can become part of this history in the making.

- There is a critical need for research about this mega-trend. But useful research requires a common language. The models of articulation and two-plus-two programming, university center, university extension, and community college baccalaureate must serve as discrete models. Not all baccalaureate programming that involves community colleges comprises a community college baccalaureate. There are many effective models whereby community colleges are providing access to the baccalaureate, in meaningful ways, without conferring the degree.

Conclusion: A Pressing Need

For Martha Jane Smith, and thousands like her in the United States, the issue of *who* confers the baccalaureate is not as important as having the accessible and affordable courses leading to that degree. Like the place-bound community college student who recently won the CCBA essay Contest (McKinney, 2003), Martha Jane also wants access to the baccalaureate immediately after graduation from the community college.

Community college leaders are justified in their concern about providing access for graduates, such as Martha Jane, when better and more secure jobs require a baccalaureate. When times are toughest, universities and other four-year colleges are likely to close doors of opportunity to people like Martha Jane Smith, and community colleges will once again be struggling to keep the name of "people's college" by demonstrating their commitment to access in creative and new ways that make good on the promise of the "open door."

Notes

1. This story is representative of many situations the author observed while serving as a president of a community college. Individual names, including people and the college, are fictitious.
2. The Education Commission of the States (ECS) released a study, October 1, 2003, entitled "Getting Ready to Pay for College," part of a larger study by ECS to assist policy makers with efforts to increase attendance rates in higher education. According to ECS's president, Ted Sanders, "America is at risk for losing a vital ingredient for success—an educated populace" (Gomstyn, October 2, 2003 [online]). Sandra Rupert, director of the report and study, stated that the United States once was first in the world in baccalaureate-degree participation rates but now ranks eleventh because its rates did not grow while other nations invested in higher education and training (Mollison, 2003). The Lumina Foundation for Education has funded college-access projects, including one with the American Association of Community Colleges to address ways to increase access to the baccalaureate degree. While the United States once led the world in attainment of higher degrees, recent reports indicate that it is "losing ground."
3. Edison College was formerly Edison Community College. The College's name was changed by the Florida legislature in late April 2004, House Bill 1867.
4. States reporting joint-use facilities include Arizona, Colorado, Florida, Hawaii, Idaho, Illinois, Kentucky, Mississippi, Nebraska, New Jersey, Ohio, Oklahoma, Oregon, South Carolina, South Dakota, Tennessee, Texas, Utah, Virginia, and Wisconsin. The Windham, Perkins, and Rogers (2001) article in the *Community College Review* includes a more thorough analysis.
5. OSU's Okmulgee technical campus proposal to offer specific baccalaureate programs was approved by the OSU Board late in 2003. The Oklahoma Board of Regents unanimously approved the plan February 13, 2004.
6. SREB comprises Alabama, Arkansas, Delaware, Florida, Georgia, Kentucky, Louisiana, Maryland, Mississippi, North Carolina, Oklahoma, South Carolina, Tennessee, Texas, Virginia, and West Virginia.
7. Dalton State College began offering the baccalaureate in 1998 in three types of management studies: industrial operations, information systems, and technology. Macon State College began offering these programs in 1997 in communications and information technology, health information, human services, health services administration, and BSN nursing. Parkersburg Community College (West Virginia University at Parkersburg) began offering these programs in 1993. The classifications listed are as of 2002.
8. The North Central Association (NCA) includes Arizona, Arkansas, Colorado, Illinois, Indiana, Iowa, Kansas, Michigan, Mississippi, Nebraska, New Mexico, North Dakota, Ohio, Oklahoma, West Virginia, Wisconsin, and Wyoming.
9. According to a March 17, 2004 press release posted to the college's Web site (http://www.tridenttech.edu/ttcnews/3-17-04-bill-dh.html), legislation was passed by the 2004 South Carolina Legislature (after overriding the governor's veto). Prior to offering this degree, approvals must be gained from the South Carolina State Board for Technical and Comprehensive Education and the Commission on Higher Education. According to May 3, 2004 electronic mail communications from Kaye Koonce, general counsel for Trident Technical College, the College plans to submit the program proposal paperwork to the State Tech Board and the Council for Higher Education by mid-Summer, 2004.
10. The contractor for this study was The Education Alliance from Farmington, Massachusetts and the Community College Baccalaureate Association owns these unpublished data.

References

Cohen, A. M. (2003). *The community colleges and the path to the baccalaureate.* University of California–Berkley: Center for Studies of Higher Education. www.repositories/edlib/cshe/CSH4-03.

Cohen, A. M., & Brawer, F. B. (2003). *The American community college* (4th ed.) San Francisco: Jossey Bass.

Community College Baccalaureate Association (CCBA). (2003). *Baccalaureate Needs Assessment Survey.* Unpublished survey results available from the CCBA offices at Edison College, Ft. Myers, FL.

Daily Herald Reports. Go slowly on four-year degree idea. *Daily Herald.* Retrieved September 8, 2003 from www.dailyherald.com/search/main_story.asp?intID= 37872128.

Floyd, D. L., & Walker, D. A. (2003). Community college teacher education: A typology, challenging issues, and state views. *Community College Journal of Research and Practice, 27*(8), 643-663.

Gomstyn, A. (October 2, 2003). Nation faces a college-access crisis, education policy group warns. *Chronicle of Higher Education.* Retrieved October 2, 2003 from www.chronicle.com/prm/daily/2003/10.

Gonzales, D. A. (2003). *Great Basin College.* Presentation delivered March 14–16, 2003, to the Community College Baccalaureate Association Conference, Phoenix, Arizona. Available from the author at dgon1@gw-mail.gbcnv.

Granderson, K. (September 7, 2003). Four years at Harper? *Daily Herald.* Retrieved September 18, 2003, from www.dailyherald.com.

Grimsley, J. A. (January 20, 2003). Letters to the editor: Culinary arts program. *Post and Courier.* Retrieved October 13, 2003, from www.charleston.net/stories/013003/let_30letters.shtml.

Hudson, M. (2000). *National study of community college career corridors for K–12 teacher recruitment.* Belmont, MA: Recruiting New Teachers, Inc.

Illinois College Considers Offering Baccalaureate. (September 29, 2003). *Community College Times, 16*(4), 10.

Larose, M. (July 8, 2003). Three Texas community colleges to offer bachelors. *Community College Times, 15*(15), 5.

McKinney, D. T. (April 14, 2003). We need a baccalaureate now. *Community College Week, 15*(18), 4.

Mills, K. (2003). Community college baccalaureates: Some critics decry the trends as "mission creep." *National CrossTalk.* Published by the National Center for Public Policy and Higher Education. www/highereducation.org/crosstalk/ct0103/news0103-community.html.

Mollison, A. (October 2, 2003). Too few go to college, reports say. *Atlanta Journal Constitution.* Retrieved October 2, 2003, from www.ajc.com/paper/editions/Thursday/news_f3b71da411be913D00.

Patton, M. (May 27, 2003). University of Hawaii reorganizes community colleges. *Community College Times, 15*(11), 10.

Pedersen, R. P. (2000). *The Early Public Junior College: 1900–1940.* Unpublished dissertation, Columbia University.

Pedersen. R. P. (July 23, 2001). You say you want an evolution? Read the fine print first. *Community College Week,* 4–5.

Sturrock, C. (February 10, 2003). Bill alters community college role. *Contra Costa Times.* www.bayarea.com/mlp.cctimes/5146642.htm.

Troumpoucis, P. (April 12, 2004). The best of both worlds? *Community College Week, 16*(16), 6–8.

University Colleges of Technology Alfred-Canton-Cobleskill-Delhi-Morrisville.(1997). *Report on the applied baccalaureate: A new option in higher education in the United States. May 1997.* Available from the United States ERIC Clearinghouse. Document number JC 970-340.

Walker, K. P. (2001). *An open door to the bachelor's degree.* www.league.org/publication/abstracts/leadership/labs 0401.html.

Wattenbarger. J. (2002). Colleges should stick to what,they do best. *Community College Week, 13*(18), 4–5.

Wellman, J. V. (2004). *Policy Alert.* Summary of *State Policy and Community College Baccalaureate Transfer.* San Jose, CA: The National Center of Public Policy and Higher Education. Available on line at www.highereducation.org.

Wertheimer, L. K. (July 19, 2003). Three Texas community colleges to grant bachelor's degrees. *Dallas Morning News,* B1 & B5.

Windham, P., Perkins, G., & Rogers, J. (2001). Concurrent use: Part of the new definition of access. *Community College Review, 29*(3), 39–55.

Zwerling, L. S. (1976). *Second best: The crisis of the community college.* New York: McGraw Hill.

CHAPTER 37

UPDATE ON THE COMMUNITY COLLEGE BACCALAUREATE: EVOLVING TRENDS AND ISSUES

ALENE BYCER RUSSELL

Over the past two decades, the number of community colleges independently offering baccalaureate degree programs has steadily risen. Though still confined to a very small number of institutions and limited degree programs, this phenomenon continues to generate widespread attention and controversy. This occurs because the trend challenges fundamental assumptions about the mission of two-year colleges and threatens to upset the existing balance between the two- and four-year sectors in the U.S. higher-education system.

To place this development in context, there are several more common policy approaches that involve community colleges in baccalaureate degree production. Such methods—which this chapter intentionally does not focus on—typically involve collaboration between the two- and four-year sectors, where the four-year institution (not the community college) confers the baccalaureate degree. First, many states, systems, and collaborating institutions have developed transfer and articulation agreements, 2 +2 arrangements, and other cooperative means to facilitate baccalaureate attainment by students who complete their general education requirements at community colleges. A second approach is partnerships between two- and four-year institutions that bring four-year degree programs on-site to community colleges and other convenient locations where university access is limited—university centers, shared facilities, joint programs, and other arrangements. Finally, online degree programs, enhanced by partnership and transfer agreements, are increasingly available to community college students who seek a bachelor's degree without leaving home. All of these policy options are well established and less controversial. They are continuing to expand nationwide, even in states that have begun to approve independent community college baccalaureate programs.

The focus of our attention is on a specific phenomenon that has arisen largely in response to increased demands for baccalaureate degrees in particular geographic areas and fields of study—often rural locations and high–demand fields, such as education, nursing, and technical subjects. It generally occurs where there is limited access to a four-year institution or where demand exceeds the existing capacity of the four-year sector. This phenomenon is also fueled by the upgraded educational credentials now needed for certain applied and technical fields, occupations in which associate's degrees once sufficed, but where employers now prefer or require workers to possess a four-year degree.

This chapter is based on an earlier publication: Russell, A. (2010, October). "Update on the community college baccalaureate: Evolving trends and issues." *Policy Matters: A Higher Education Policy Brief.* Washington, DC: American Association of State Colleges and Universities.

The independently offered community college baccalaureate has virtually never been the first response to meeting these needs. Generally, the community college baccalaureate requires legislative approval, or, at minimum, the approval of a systemwide governing body. Normally, there is a thorough review process through which workforce and student demand must be documented, alternatives explored and exhausted, costs estimated, and community college capacity determined. Following approval, two-year institutions must undergo regional accreditation in order to offer a four-year degree program. Faculty must then be hired, libraries and facilities brought up to speed, and so on. In sum, it is not a trivial endeavor, nor one that can be carried out quickly.

But times are changing, and it is unclear whether past trends will predict the future. The Obama administration has called for the nation to have the highest proportion of college graduates in the world by 2020, despite the tremendous challenges of access, cost, and capacity. As new ideas to meet this goal are being examined, this is a good time to take stock of what is happening with the community college baccalaureate. This chapter presents recent trends in the community college baccalaureate, describes variations among the states and pending issues, summarizes arguments for and against the community college baccalaureate, and presents implications for policy makers considering this option.

Steady Growth of the Community College Baccalaureate

The number of states that have approved at least one community college to offer a baccalaureate program has grown steadily over the past decade, as have the numbers of institutions and degree programs approved. Currently, there are 18 states in which a community college has been approved to offer four-year degrees, compared with 11 states in 2004 (Russell, 2004). There are now 57 institutions that have received such approval, compared with 21 institutions 7 years ago. These institutions now offer—or have been approved to offer—a total of 468 four-year degree programs, compared with 12.8 programs in 2004. Taken together, these data illustrate the considerable growth in the community college baccalaureate that has taken place in less than a decade (table 6.1).

TABLE 1

Summary of Approved Community College Baccalaureate Programs by State

State	Year of First Approval	Number of Approved Institutions	Total # of Approved Programs	# Offering Teacher Education Programs	# Offering Nursing (BSN) Programs
Arkansas	1998	1	1	1	44
Colorado	2010	1	0	0	0
Florida	2001	18	12	11	113
Georgia	1997	7	6	3	71
Hawaii	2004	1	0	0	2
Indiana	2004	1	1	1	6
Louisiana	2001	1	1	1	12
Minnesota	2003	1	1	0	2
Nevada	1998	3	1	1	15
New Mexico	2004	1	1	1	11
New York	1996	5	0	3	84
North Dakota	2006	1	0	0	1
Oklahoma	2004	2	0	0	4
Texas	2003	3	0	0	4
Utah	1992	2	2	2	69
Vermont	1993	1	0	0	11
Washington	2005	7	0	1	8
West Virginia	1989	1	1	0	11
Total		57	27	25	468

As part of this trend, there has been substantial growth in baccalaureate-level teacher education programs available at community colleges. Today, 10 states have approved a total of 27 community colleges to offer at least one such program. In 2004, 6 states had approved just 9 two-year institutions to offer a baccalaureate in this field. This growth has been stimulated by teacher shortages in specific geographic locations.

Similarly, there has been parallel growth in baccalaureate-level nursing programs available at community colleges. Today, 10 states have approved a total of 25 institutions to offer a bachelor of science in nursing (BSN) at a community college. In 2004, 5 states had approved only 6 community colleges to offer such a program. This tremendous growth is a result of both nursing shortages as well as efforts by the nursing profession to create a more highly educated nursing workforce (i.e., upgrading from the RN to BSN degree).

Identifying and counting these institutions is not an exact science, however, and these totals could be a conservative estimate of this phenomenon. In cases where institutions underwent transformation into baccalaureate institutions some years ago, it was not possible to include them in the count, This accounting is generally consistent with the literature on this topic, which has tracked observable developments since the late 1990s.

As the most recent example of this trend, the Colorado legislature authorized its first community college baccalaureate in 2010. Recognizing the priority of improving access to higher education for citizens in rural areas of the state, Senate Bill (SB) 10-101 authorized Colorado Mountain College, a comprehensive community college with seven, physical campuses and distance learning, to offer no more than five baccalaureate degree programs, to be approved by the Colorado Commission on Higher Education. The college must first demonstrate workforce and student demand, comply with all accreditation requirements, demonstrate that its provision of the program "is the most cost-effective method of providing the baccalaureate degree program in the service area," and that the additional program "will not create a negative impact for the college or require additional state appropriated moneys to operate." Surveys to date have shown high demand for programs in resort-related business, teacher education, and environmental science.

Continued Controversy and Opposition

Despite substantial growth, the community college baccalaureate remains a very limited phenomenon, and considerable controversy and opposition remain. Not all states are jumping onto the community college baccalaureate bandwagon. Two states in particular, after years of discussion and debate, rejected proposals to allow their community colleges to offer four-year degrees. In 2005, Arizona came close to taking this step, when the House passed a bill that would have allowed 10 community colleges to offer four-year degrees in teacher education, health professions, law enforcement, fire services, and other workforce-related disciplines not currently offered by state universities. This bill, opposed by the state's three universities, was defeated in the Senate appropriations committee, and subsequent versions df the bill were also defeated. These actions followed debates going back to 1997, with supporters citing population growth, critical shortages in the health professions and other fields, rising university tuition, and the need to inprove access for rural students. Opponents cited high start-up costs, likely increases in tuition and taxes, and threats to the traditional community college mission.

In 2009, Illinois adopted an alternative approach that favors collaboration between two- and four-year institutions. SB 1883 requires the Board of Higher Education to implement a Collaborative Baccalaureate Degree Development Grant Program "to help deliver upper-division courses and bachelor's degree programs offered by bachelor's degree-granting colleges and universities at a location geographically convenient to student populations currently being served by existing public community colleges." As background, in 2005, after years of debate, the Illinois, Board of Higher Education rejected a proposal from Harper College, a two-year institution, to pilot a four-year degree program. This proposal had raised broad statewide questions and led to the creation of a Baccalaureate Access Task Force that eventually recommended against giving community colleges authority to offer baccalaureate degrees. Harper College continued to fight this battle for several years, leading to the introduction of competing bills in 2009. It was SB 1883, supported by both the Community College Board and the Board of Higher Education, which was eventually passed into law.

Substantial Variation Among States

Among states that have adopted the community college baccalaureate, approaches have varied widely. There is variation in the number and types of institutions and programs approved, and in the extent to which approved institutions retain their community college mission and culture.

Morphing Into Baccalaureate Institutions

Several states have authorized just one or two isolated community colleges to offer baccalaureate degrees, with no intention of expanding this practice to other two-year colleges in the state. Over time, such colleges have typically added more baccalaureate programs—including arts and sciences—and subsequently evolved into baccalaureate colleges, often as part of a state university system. For example:

Arkansas
Westark Community College, approved to offer its first four-year degree in 1998, became the University of Arkansas-Fort Smith in 2002. It now offers 44 baccalaureate programs, representing nearly half of all degrees conferred.

Louisiana
Louisiana State University–Alexandria, approved to offer four-year degrees in 2001, now offers 12 baccalaureate degrees, including degrees in arts and sciences, making up more than half of all degrees conferred.

Utah
Utah Valley Community College, first approved to offer a baccalaureate in 1992, became Utah Valley State College in 1993 and Utah Valley University in 2008. It now offers 53 baccalaureate programs, making up just more than half of all degrees conferred, as well as master's degrees in education, nursing, and business administration. Dixie State College of Utah, formerly Dixie Junior College (which was approved to offer four-year programs in 1999), now offers 16 four-year programs, making up a fifth of all degrees conferred annually.

West Virginia
The former Parkersburg Community College became West Virginia University at Parkersburg in 1989. It now offers 11 baccalaureate programs that make up more than a third of all degrees conferred.

New Mexico
Though not as far along in its development into a four-year institution, Northern New Mexico College, formerly Northern New Mexico Community College, is on this same pathway. Once a "normal school" that was first authorized to offer a four-year elementary education degree in 2004, it has since been approved to offer four-year degrees in all subjects, and now offers 11 such programs, making up about 150% of all degrees.

In each of the foregoing cases, the institution was allowed to grow its baccalaureate offerings. Now, these six institutions collectively account for more than 30% of such programs nationwide. Some observers would argue, in fact, that owing to their transformation, such institutions no longer belong in the discussion of the community college baccalaureate.

Multiple Institutions Maintaining Traditional Functions

A second pattern is to expand, more generally, the mission of a state's community colleges, albeit with a commitment that these institutions must maintain their traditional functions. Typically, these states view the community college as critical in meeting the state's baccalaureate needs, especially in high-demand workforce fields; the move is designed to aid place-bound adults who would otherwise have limited access to the baccalaureate. Frequently, states proceed in stages, beginning with a small number of institutions and programs, reviewing progress after some period of time, and making a further determination about continuation and expansion at a later date.

Following a comprehensive review of Washington State's educational system, convened by the governor, the state approved a pilot project in 2005 in which four community colleges were chosen to offer specialized four-year degree programs. The programs were designed to fill community needs not met by other colleges and to meet the needs of place-bound workers. In 2007, South Seattle Community College launched a bachelor of applied science (BAS) in hospitality management, Olympic College a BSN in nursing, Bellevue College a BAS in radiation and imaging sciences, and Peninsula College a BAS in applied management. Based on the success of these pilot programs, the state has since approved additional institutions and baccalaureate degree programs.

Florida stands alone in the extent to which its policy makers have recognized a direct role for community colleges in meeting the state's baccalaureate needs. This arose from concerns about critical workforce shortages in the state, especially in teacher education and nursing, and awareness that the state ranked near the bottom in baccalaureate degree production. This new role for community colleges has evolved and expanded for more than a decade, built on the explicit requirement that these colleges were not to become baccalaureate institutions. Key steps included:

- To avoid having to build new campuses to meet educational needs, a 1999 law encouraged joint baccalaureate programs between two-year colleges and universities. The law also allowed community colleges to seek approval to grant four-year degrees in areas of high demand—only as a last resort where no university was willing to establish a partnership.

- A 2001 law defined criteria for approval of community college baccalaureate programs. St. Petersburg Junior College was the first to receive such approval, and other colleges followed over the decade.

- The 2008 creation of the Florida College System made it possible that all community colleges might eventually offer the baccalaureate degree. Today, 18 of the state's 28 community colleges have been approved to offer at least one four-year degree.

- A 2009 law revised the primary mission of these colleges to include upper-level instruction and the awarding of baccalaureate degrees. It further set forth that beginning in 2010, colleges that have been offering baccalaureate programs for three years may apply to be exempt from the state board of education's approval for subsequent degree programs, the first time any state has made such a move.

Florida's progression thus far has generated significant concerns, especially about competition with universities and duplication of efforts. However, these misgivings have been declining to some degree as universities have faced tough budget constraints and have been unable to meet workforce demands.

The University System of Georgia classifies public institutions in the state as research universities, regional universities, state universities, state colleges, and two-year colleges. Similar to those in the Florida College System, the state colleges in Georgia are a type of hybrid institution designed to serve as associate-level access institutions and to offer limited baccalaureate programs targeted to the economic needs of their region. Macon State College, the first institution to be granted state college status (1997), now offers more than 30 four-year degree programs. Dalton State College, the second state college (1999), now offers 20 four-year degree programs. Five other associate-level institutions were approved to offer four-year degrees within the past five years, and each currently offers just a few four-year programs.

Limited Technical Degrees

A third pattern is to limit approval to applied and technical baccalaureate degrees, such as the bachelor of applied science (BAS), bachelor of applied technology (BAT), and bachelor of technology (BT) degrees. The rationale is that these represent an extension of technical programs already offered at community colleges and are designed to allow associate of applied science (AAS) graduates to further their education; four-year institutions have a shorter (or no) history with such programs.

For example, in 2002, several community colleges in Texas indicated an interest in offering the BAS and BAT degrees, arguing that the few programs of this type offered at four-year institutions were not enough to meet the needs of adult workers. In response, the legislature approved a pilot project in 2003, through which a limited number of community colleges could offer up to five BAS or BAT degrees that would correspond to the needs of local industry. The Texas Higher Education Coordinating Board (THECB) approved three colleges. A 2007 law removed the pilot status of the program, granting permanent approval to offer these programs. Further, a 2009 law directed THECB to prepare a study to examine the feasibility of expanding this to other two-year institutions. THECB issued a report to the legislature in 2010 that recommended using a variety of methods to address specific areas of need, including online education and partnerships between two and four-year institutions (Texas Higher Education Coordinating Board, 2010). It asserted that community colleges' expansion into baccalaureate degrees should be considered only when other options have been exhausted. To date, there are only four community college baccalaureate programs established at the three institutions.

Other examples include:

Oklahoma
Oklahoma State University–Oklahoma City and Oklahoma State University Institute of Technology–Okmulgee, both associate-level colleges, offer a total of four specialized BT programs.

North Dakota
Bismarck State College offers a single four-year program, a BAS in energy management.

Others
Some states do not fit into any of the foregoing models. For example:

Nevada
Great Basin College was approved to offer four–year degrees in 1999 and now offers 13 baccalaureate programs in a variety of workforce subjects. One additional college was approved in 2004 to offer a BS in dental hygiene, and another in 2007 to offer a BT in construction management.

New York
Five of the technical colleges in the SUNY system were authorized to offer four-year degrees in 1996. They now offer a total of 84 baccalaureate programs, up from 37 programs in 2004. Though no additional colleges have been approved since then, three of these colleges have added baccalaureate level nursing programs in recent years, a change from their traditional program offerings.

Ongoing Activity and Debate

As states grapple with ways to increase baccalaureate attainment with limited resources, there is continued interest in and controversy surrounding the community college baccalaureate. At the time of this writing, the University of Wisconsin System Board of Regents was considering action on a five-year pilot project through which six of the system's 13 two-year colleges will be able to develop limited bachelor's of applied arts and science (BAAS) degree programs. Proposed as a way to increase access to the baccalaureate for rural, place-bound adults, this concept had been in the works for several years. Though there has been some internal disagreement about potential "mission creep," no legislative approval is required, and the University of Wisconsin System has not experienced a major backlash by its four-year institutions. In fact, the programs will be developed in collaboration with partnering comprehensive universities, and the proposal was currently being vetted through faculty governance at the partner institutions. These universities will provide both on-site and online instruction, but the two-year colleges will be granting the degree, thus necessitating a mission change. The BAAS is a relatively new degree type that addresses workforce development, but in a manner that is less technical in nature than other applied baccalaureate degrees, as it emphasizes the liberal arts and their application to the work setting. Note that regents more recently approved this proposal (spring 2011).

The State of Michigan is currently embroiled in a heated debate about the community college baccalaureate. For several years, a number of community colleges have been lobbying for legislation allowing them to offer the bachelor's degree in certain technical fields, as well as the bachelor of science in nursing. Their primary arguments concern affordability and accessibility. On the other side of the debate, the Presidents Council, representing the state's four-year universities, has lobbied hard against this proposal and instead supports the expansion of existing collaborations as the most efficient way to address workforce needs. In a letter to state representatives, the Presidents Council states: "Michigan's 15 public universities hereby pledge to collaborate with our community college colleagues to provide locally any new baccalaureate or degree completion program for which there is a demonstrated and sustainable need within that community college district . . . . This pledge by the public universities avoids duplication and waste, can be implemented immediately, and is far less costly." In September 2010, the Michigan House of Representatives passed a bill authorizing limited community college baccalaureate degrees, but the bill never received a hearing in the Senate. A bill was reintroduced during the 2011-2012 legislative session, and once again, the bill passed in the House but continues to languish in the Senate Education Committee.

A bill to authorize the Virginia Community College System to establish baccalaureate programs in nursing, education, applied technology, and other high-need areas was introduced in 2010, but was later tabled. Proponents cited this as a means to promote the governor's goal of producing 100,000 more college graduates in the state, but members of the Higher Education Subcommittee felt the legislation was premature. It was expected that the proposal would receive further consideration as part of the Governor's Commission on Higher Education: Reform, Innovation and Investment, established in 2010.

Arguments in Favor of the Community College Baccalaureate

There are a variety of compelling arguments in favor of the community college baccalaureate.

Improved Access to the Baccalaureate

Supporters argue that baccalaureate programs offered by community colleges increase educational opportunities for place-bound, adult workers, particularly in rural areas where there is no access to four-year institutions. Some argue that for first-generation college-goers and underserved groups, the opportunity to continue one's education in the familiar community college environment makes it more likely that these students will persist in college and earn a four-year degree.

Greater Affordability for Students

Though more expensive than lower-division courses, tuition for upper-division classes at community colleges is typically lower than tuition for similar courses at four-year institutions. Also, the absence of a public four year option might lead some workers seeking baccalaureate degrees to turn to the for-profit sector, which is significantly more expensive.

Reduced Taxpayer Costs

Supporters argue that it is cheaper to offer upper-division classes at community colleges than at four-year institutions, largely because faculty are paid less and teach more, resulting in limited state dollars going farther.

Ability to Meet Local Workforce Demands

Community colleges traditionally work with local employers and develop degree and certificate programs that respond to specified workforce needs. Offering specific baccalaureate degrees in certain high-demand fields is a logical extension of this practice.

Expertise in Applied and Technical Degrees

Traditionally, applied associate degrees offered by community colleges, such as associate of applied science degrees, have been the industry standard for employment in certain technical fields. However, some high-skill occupations increasingly require a baccalaureate for job entry or promotion. Supporters argue that it makes sense to develop these degree programs where two-year programs already exist, because many four-year institutions have no history or expertise in these areas.

Overcrowding at Four-Year Colleges

In some states, demand currently exceeds capacity at four-year institutions. Offering selected baccalaureate programs at two-year colleges can help reduce overcrowding and meet regional and state workforce needs.

Arguments Against the Community College Baccalaureate

There are equally compelling arguments opposing the community college baccalaureate. As a general rule, opponents share the underlying contention that adding one more mission to community colleges is unnecessary, time-onsuming, expensive, and fraught with unintended negative consequences.

Instead, they support expansion of the various models of collaboration between two-year and four-year institutions to address baccalaureate needs of the state (including university centers, shared facilities, joint programs, online education, and articulation agreements).

Mission Creep

Opponents express concern that offering baccalaureate programs at community colleges weakens the traditional community college mission and leaves behind those students it is designed to serve; this option could shift resources, raise tuition for all students, challenge open-door policies, and divert attention away from developmental education. *As* a worst-case scenario, the community college might morph into a four-year institution and, as a result, totally abandon the access mission.

Program Duplication

Many believe this approach produces a less-efficient state system overall, with duplication of programs offered at four-year institutions and creation of competition instead of cooperation. For example, owing to limited availability of nursing faculty and clinical sites, increasing the number of institutions with baccalaureate nursing programs could exacerbate problems rather than solve them.

Accreditation Obstacles

Attaining regional accreditation for four-year programs is both expensive and time consuming. It is far more efficient, many argue, to develop partnerships with four-year institutions that bring programs to the community college campus, thus not necessitating new accreditation.

High Costs/Need for Additional State Dollars

In order to add upper division coursework, community colleges need to upgrade faculty, libraries, and laboratories. In addition to high start-up costs, there are also high ongoing costs in terms of the employment of new categories of faculty.

Faculty Issues

Baccalaureate programs might require faculty with higher degrees who demand more pay. They could be harder to recruit and might be less focused on teaching. Rifts among the different faculty classes could develop.

Too Burdensome on Overtaxed Community Colleges

Community colleges around the nation are increasingly being asked to do more with less. Some are already over capacity and do not have the luxury of taking on more responsibilities. Some community college presidents themselves have expressed these concerns, and not all are seeking mission expansion.

Concerns About Quality

Some critics believe that a baccalaureate degree earned at a community college is inferior to one earned at a four-year institution. The belief is that courses might not be as rigorous, and faculty and resources might be substandard. Some employers share these concerns.

Availability of Online Education

Given the widespread availability of online degree programs, students are no longer limited by where they live. Adding community college baccalaureate programs might be unwarranted, especially for programs that can be effectively delivered online.

Considerations for Policy Makers

Policy makers need to weigh, in context, these pros and cons when considering the approval or expansion of community college baccalaureate programs. The key issue is whether the independently offered community college baccalaureate is the best alternative for meeting student and workforce demands, or whether it is preferable that only four-year institutions confer the baccalaureate degree. In doing so, policy makers should consider the following questions.

Cost and Finance Issues

What are the short-term costs associated with developing new community college baccalaureate degree programs?

What are the long-term costs? How will costs per degree compare with similar costs at four-year institutions?

How will the flow of state funding be affected? If they exist, do state funding formulas need to be altered?

What will the impact be on community college budgets, and how will adequate resources be found?

How will access to federal policy money be affected?

How will tuition rates be affected? Who will bear the increased costs of higher-cost programs?

Mission Issues

What is the long-term purpose of introducing baccalaureate programs into the community college environment? Will the community college be expected to maintain its traditional open access mission? Is the intention for the community college to morph into a baccalaureate institution?

How will the needs of associate-degree students and others currently being served continue to be met?

Will developmental education be protected?

Student Issues

How will chances for baccalaureate completion be affected?

Will it be cheaper or more expensive for students? Will traditionally low tuition rates be maintained for lower-division students?

Will employers accept community college baccalaureates as equal to degrees from four-year institutions?

Faculty/Staff Issues

Will new faculty need to be hired? If so, what qualifications will be sought? How will qualified faculty be attracted and retained?

How will the pay structure be affected?

Will a two-tier faculty result, and how will this affect the institution?

How can faculty and program quality be ensured?

Will additional administrative staff be needed to manage the new programs?

Conclusion

The community college baccalaureate is not a new phenomenon but one that has been growing and evolving for more than two decades. Though there has been tremendous expansion over the past 10 years, such programs are still the exception rather than the rule—often the option of last resort after other alternatives have been exhausted. The current picture is one of great variation among states in how they have implemented this practice, owing to varying demographics, workforce needs, higher education systems, fiscal conditions, and political pushback (from those opposed to the concept). Florida is at the forefront of this movement, but largely stands alone. Other states are making far more limited use of this option, or have rejected it outright.

As pressures mount to reach state and national postsecondary education goals, undoubtedly continued attention will be directed toward this phenomenon. Policy makers and campus leaders are cautioned against viewing the community college baccalaureate as a silver bullet. In considering this option, they should keep in mind the pros and cons outlined here and be alert to unintended consequences. They would be wise to proceed cautiously, following the maxim: "First, do no harm."

References

Russell, A. (2004) Update on the community college baccalaureate. *Policy matters: A higher education policy brief* Washington, DC: American Association of State Colleges and Universities. Retrieved from http://www.congressweb.com/aascu/doc files/vini.pdf.

Russell, A. (2010). Update on the community college baccalaureate: Evolving trends and issues. *Policy Matters: A Higher Education Policy Brief* Washington, DC; American Association of State Colleges and Universities. Retrieved from http://www.congressweb.com/aascu/docfiles/AASCU_Update_Community_College_Baccalaureate. pdf.

Texas Higher Education Coordinating Board. (2010). *The feasibility of expanding Texas' community college baccalaureate programs: A report to the 8Ist legislature (Draft).* Austin, TX: author. Retrieved from http://www.thecb.state.tx.us/index.cfm?ObjectID=388644C9-BI3A-773D-4C38A96BoE769BC2.

SECTION VII

COMMUNITY COLLEGE TRANSFER

SECTION VII: COMMUNITY COLLEGE TRANSFER

The American community college is unique among postsecondary institutions for many reasons; but likely, the feature that sets it most apart is the transfer function. While it is true that many students transfer from one four-year university to another, it is only within the community college that transfer is a planned activity, a student goal, and an indicator of success. It is ironic that while community college transfer is such a positive outcome, those who have benefited from the practice often "sweep it under the rug" after earning the baccalaureate. After all, former community college transfer students earn the same degree as their counterparts who matriculated at the institution as first-year students. Postsecondary history is not displayed on the diploma and the former transfer student is not disadvantaged when applying for graduate study. When asked about their *alma mater*, former transfer students often fail to acknowledge their early college experiences and feel more loyal to the baccalaureate-granting institution. For this reason, the community college transfer function is invisible when it is successful but starkly visible when it dysfunctions.

The transfer function can be viewed as a bridge to the baccalaureate and often to the middle class. The bridge may be crowded with diverse individuals from low socioeconomic backgrounds, people of color, students who are also parents, as well as those older than the age of those traditional students seeking new opportunities. Treading across the bridge are also displaced workers and those young adults direct from high school without strong histories of academic success. Of course, there are also hosts of bright young adults who have chosen to attend the community college for a combination of reasons. Despite the motivation, sadly few of the hopeful students will actually complete the journey to the baccalaureate.

In this section, we present five chapters that delve into the issues of what happens on that bridge from community college to the four-year college or university. Each of the chapters looks at a different aspect of the journey across the bridge to ascertain why so few students make it to the other side. What are the barriers students confront and how can institutions (both community colleges and the transfer destinations) propel them to success?

Chapter Thirty-Eight, "The community college transfer calculator: Identifying the course-taking patterns that predict transfer" introduces a tool that can assist students to plan their transfer journey. Continuing the bridge metaphor, the *Transfer Calculator* can serve as a map that directs students to the transfer destination. The *Calculator* estimates the likelihood of successful transfer based on courses taken, grades earned, and other factors. Authors Hagedorn, Cabrera, and Prather use data that is readily available at all community colleges, and urges institutional research to better utilize transcript-level data to understand the journey that students take and the course-taking patterns that steer them off of the bridge.

Chapter Thirty-Nine, "A hand hold for a little bit: Factoring facilitating the success of community college transfer students to a large research university," concerns the aftermath of transfer, delving into the academic and social experiences at the university; although students may have successfully arrived at the receiving institution, Townsend and Wilson indicate that they may be ill-prepared for what awaits them. The authors aptly indicate that these students would benefit from additional guidance, defined as "a hand hold for a little bit." Using qualitative methods, the researchers recount students' stories of the transfer process and their interpretation of what awaited them. Policy implications for both community colleges and four-year institutions are provided.

In Chapter Forty the authors, Dowd, Cheslock, and Melguizo, investigate a bridge that is less traveled; specifically, transfer from community college to an elite institution. Using two national databases, this work provides estimates of the number of low-income students making the journey from community college to an elite university as compared to less-selective institutions. They also compare the academic preparation for this journey as compared to native students. This study sheds light on why elite institutions do not seek transfers despite what some may interpret as a democratic imperative to do so.

Chapter Forty-One by Laanan, Starobin, and Eggleston, "Adjustment of community college students at a four-year university: Role and relevance of transfer student capital for student retention," introduces the term "transfer capital" as a measure of the accumulated knowledge community college students bring to their transfer process. Although many four-year college administrators and faculty may consider concepts such as credit transfer, admission requirements, and course prerequisites as basic knowledge for all college students, these authors remind us that community college students may enter their transfer destinations without that knowledge and may need, as Townsend and Wilson indicated, "a hand hold for a little bit." These authors incorporate transfer capital as necessary for higher levels of academic and social adjustment.

While transfer rates could be described as suboptimal overall, they are especially low for Latino/Hispanic students. Chapter Forty-Two by Hagedorn et al., "An investigation of critical mass: The role of Latino representation in the success of urban community college students," tests the assumption that Latino students in environments where there is a critical mass of other Latino students may create a supportive and "staying" environment where students are freer to pursue the academic side of their goals and not feel marginalized. Moreover, this chapter also tests the role of Latino faculty and staff who can provide the appropriate role models. This study breaks new ground in establishing that representation matters and students in an ethnically comfortable environment may be more likely to experience higher academic performance.

Taken as a whole, the five chapters presented in this section help us understand the crossing of the bridge from a community college to a four-year university. Indeed, it is a treacherous journey but there are supports that, if enacted, can increase the traffic and the success.

CHAPTER 38

THE COMMUNITY COLLEGE TRANSFER CALCULATOR: IDENTIFYING THE COURSE-TAKING PATTERNS THAT PREDICT TRANSFER*

LINDA SERRA HAGEDORN, PH.D. , IOWA STATE UNIVERSITY, AMES
ALBERTO CABRERA, PH.D., UNIVERSITY OF MARYLAND AND
GEORGE PRATHER, PH.D., LOS ANGELES COMMUNITY
COLLEGE DISTRICT, CALIFORNIA

Using a newly developed software application entitled *The Community College Transfer Calculator©*, this article both quantifies the effect of specific course-taking patterns and stresses the need for an easy to understand tool for community college academic advisors, faculty, and students. The "Calculator" calculates the likelihood of transfer given specific demographic and courses taken and/or scheduled. Moreover, the user can see the difference in the likelihood of transfer that changes in course-taking predict.

Introduction to Issues

Transfer is a necessary component of retention for community college students seeking a baccalaureate. Transfer, therefore, can be viewed as a form of system persistence. The Center for the Study of Community Colleges studied transfer rates from 1984 to 1987 and found a consistent transfer rate of approximately 22% (Cohen & Brawer, 2003), a proportion that has remained relatively static through time (Nora, 2000; Palmer, 2000, 2005; Spicer & Armstrong, 1996). Although transfer rates have been problematically low for most community colleges, the problem may be more crucial in the state of California based on its very large community college student enrollments. California Community Colleges, the subject of this chapter, enroll almost twice as many students as the total sum in the University of California and California State University systems (California State System, 2007; University of California System, 2007). A recent report indicated that California's low graduation and transfer rates that may actually threaten the future of the state (Shulock & Moore, 2007).

In this article we provide information on *The Community College Transfer Calculator©*, a web-based application initially calibrated for the Los Angeles Community College District, but customizable for other colleges, districts, or states. Currently the "Calculator" is an accurate gauge of

*This project was made possible through funding from OVAE. The "Calculator" was first demonstrated at the National Community College Symposium in Washington, DC on June 18, 2008.

characteristics based on a former cohort of students in Los Angeles but may also be instructive to other large urban districts. The "Calculator" is designed to be a tool to assist students to understand the pathway to transfer and thus encourage success.

Transcript Analysis

Throughout this article we use the term "transcript analysis" to include the investigating, coding, and analysis of college records regardless of their type. Transcript analysis consists of a series of planned and systematic analyses of data routinely collected by community colleges including enrollment files, college application data, financial aid records, and other state and federally mandated files. Simply put, records kept at the colleges record demographic information that can be merged with academic data such as the courses in which students enroll, the grades they earn, the courses they drop, the sequence of enrollments they follow, and general course-taking patterns. Unlike information collected via questionnaires, transcript data are not subject to student memory or truthfulness—they are the true records of student accomplishment and actions that can inform policy analyses and enrollment management (Adelman, 1996).

SPECIFIC ISSUES/QUESTIONS EXAMINED

The research questions driving the construction of *The Community College Transfer Calculator*© are:

- What are the key markers of transfer for community college students?
- How is the likelihood of transfer affected by the successful completion of various types of courses?
- How is the likelihood of transfer affected by grades and successful completion of all courses?
- What types of factors or measures can be derived from transcript level data?
- How can transcript level data be transformed into a useful and user-friendly tool?

In response, this article examines the types of measures that can be derived from transcript level data and illustrates how these measures can be constructed and subsequently utilized in a model that predicts the likelihood of transfer of specific students under conditions of common enrollment patterns. We introduce a tool that may not only be useful in its present mode but made more powerful through the application of specific transcript data pertaining to a particular institution or district.

WHAT IS *THE COMMUNITY COLLEGE TRANSFER CALCULATOR*©?

The Community College Transfer Calculator© is a downloadable tool based on transcript analysis of a longitudinal cohort of transfer-aspiring community college students. The tool is calibrated to a logistic regression equation that predicts the impact of key variables on transfer. The tool allows the user to enter student-specific data using pull-down menus and to instantly calculate the result of specific course-taking on the probability of transfer.

The "Calculator" is a tool that can be useful to different audiences. Academic advisors may use the tool to not only understand the effect, powerful in some cases, of taking a specific course pattern, but may also use it to individually advise students to take the courses that may be of most value for the transfer goal. Instructors of college success courses as well as those leading student orientations may find the "Calculator" especially useful in illustrating the power of enrolling in the courses that are more likely to result in student success. Policy makers may benefit from understanding aggregate findings of transcript analysis to create and promote policies that will assist students to achieve their goals. The "Calculator" can also be used to test the extent to which course-taking policies produce the intended results of enhancing transfer. It can also easily assess the impact of simulating course-taking patterns within different levels of academic readiness in English.

Although transcript analysis and *The Community College Calculator*© can be powerful tools, we have not identified a "silver bullet" or answer to students who come to college ill-prepared for the academic rigor necessary to prepare for the four-year university. Indeed, while it may be intuitive to tell a student that "taking transfer level math will increase the likelihood of transfer," in reality many students do not have the math preparation to enroll in the course without several remedial courses. Rather, we contend that the "Calculator" can provide clear evidence of the value of persevering through the necessary developmental math sequence as a step in reaching a transfer goal. The techniques examined and presented will demonstrate the power of courses and academic successes in the likelihood of transfer.

"CALCULATOR" DESIGN AND METHODOLOGY

The design of the "Calculator" stressed specific community college courses known from the literature to be related to student transfer and success. The design stressed mathematics, English, and science courses because previous studies have indicated these specific course types are powerful enablers of transfer to the four-year sector (Adelman, 1999, 2005; Cabrera, Burkum, & LaNasa, 2005). Moreover, the predictive power of these types of courses has been recognized by the national initiative *Achieving the Dream: Community Colleges Count*. The initiative has required each college to identify "gatekeeping courses" and to report data on pass rates.[1]

In the construction of the "Calculator" template, it was necessary to first address the question "what are the key markers of transfer for community college students?" The literature has identified the following items as important predictors of transfer:

- Demographics including age, gender, and ethnicity (Cabrera et al., 2005; Calcagno, Crosta, Bailey, & Jenkins, 2007; Dougherty & Kienzel, 2006; Melguizo, 2006);

- Course completion ratio (Calcagno et al., 2007; Hagedorn, Cypers, & Lester, 2008) or the proportion of courses in which a student enrolls that is successfully completed;

- Remedial/developmental needs (Boylan, 1995; Cabrera et al., 2005; Calcagno et al., 2007; Dougherty, 1994; Townsend, McNerny, & Arnold, 1993);

- Highest level of math completed (Adelman, 1999; Cabrera et al., 2005; Calcagno et al., 2007);

- Number of science courses completed (Cabrera et al., 2005);

- College grades (Adelman, 2006);

- Level of engagement (Calcagno et al., 2007; Driscoll, 2007; Laanan, 2007; McClenney, 2007; Tinto, 1975, 1987, 1993).

Sample

The Los Angeles Community College District is comprised of nine colleges and serves a geographic area covering more than 36 cities across more than 882 square miles (LACCD, 2007). In the fall of 2006, the district recorded a total enrollment of 114,777 students that reflected the diversity of the surrounding communities. The district classified approximately 80% of all students as "minority" while 40% were non-native English speakers (LACCD, 2007). Like all districts in the state of California, the LACCD tuition costs are among the lowest in the country.

We included all first-time transfer-hopeful students enrolling in any one of the nine campuses in the Fall 1997 semester who enrolled in a Mathematics course and followed them longitudinally through their transcript records for 10 years. This selection criterion is consistent with research showing that taking mathematics is a powerful predictor of transfer (Adelman, 1999, 2006; Cabrera et al., 2005; Hagedorn, Maxwell, & Hampton, 2002). Furthermore, transfer hopeful students are advised to take mathematics in the first semester of enrollment. The result was a group of 5,031 individuals, 30% of all entering students who could be followed via transcripts, through the spring 2007 term. The extended time span recognized and acknowledged the transient nature of the students who attend community colleges and at the same time provided adequate time to determine transfer with some certainty. The 10 year span was also chosen based on previous research using these data that revealed the median time for transfer was 11 semesters of active enrollment (Hagedorn, Cypers, & Lester, 2008). However, for many of the students, semesters of enrollment were interspersed with semesters of non-enrollment, meaning that in actuality, the time between first and last enrollments may be chronologically distant. Students were initially placed at a particular level of Mathematics based on their scores on an assessment examination in combination with their high school math record. These initial placements are not infrequently adjusted based on further examination and advice by the instructor of the initial course or by a counselor.

Substantial differences emerged by age, ethnicity and gender in the distribution of the subgroup by their math placement level. Almost 33% of those under 20 were assessed at three courses or more below the Mathematics transfer level, but 69% of those 35 over were so placed. Over 35% of those under 20 were assessed at one course below the transfer level, technically not a basic skills course, or higher. But, only 12% of those 35 plus achieved this placement. Similarly, 6% of Asian, 13% of white, 29% of Latino, and 37% of African-American students were assessed at three levels below transfer or lower. In the same manner, 62% of Asian, 40% of white, 22% of Latino and 15% of African-American students were placed in the highest two levels. By gender, 27% of females but only 20% of males were in the lower grouping, while 25% of females and 36% of males were in the highest categories of placement.

The Data

We began with two data sets from the district. The demographic file consisted of data from college applications such as gender, age, and ethnicity. The second file, called the enrollment or transcript file, consisted of a listing of all enrollments with details on the semester, the grade earned, and the credits accrued. It is important to note how these two files differ. The demographic file uses the student as the unit of analysis (one line per student). On the other hand, the enrollment file structure uses the enrollment or course as the unit of analysis (one line per enrollment creating multiple lines per student). Understanding the difference between records coded for the individual and records coded for courses is a necessary condition for successful transcript analyses. Success in merging individual data with transcript records presumes aggregation of information from the transcript file to form a student measure that can subsequently be merged into the student demographic file.[2]

Types of Measures Derived from Transcripts

The processes of data analysis allow the researcher to create specific measures that can be later utilized in more complex models to study student phenomena. A common example of a measure derived or calculated from transcript data is grade point average (GPA). Whereas the transcript file provides the individual grade earned from a specific course, GPA requires the calculation of an aggregated measure across multiple enrollments and over multiple semesters. To calculate a student GPA each course in which a student enrolls must be coded for the number of credits it provides and the letter grade converted to a numerical value (A = 4; B = 3; C = 2; D = 1, F = 0).[3] GPA is then calculated as:

$$\frac{\sum_{\text{all enrollments}} (\text{Numerical Grade})* (\text{Number of Credits})}{\text{Sum of Credits}}$$

Operationalizing the Variables of Interest

The process we outline requires the careful design and construction of the identified measures through manipulation of the enrollment file. The variables used in the analyses were operationalized as follows:

- *Course completion ratio.* The course completion ratio (CCR) is defined as the proportion of credits successfully completed (grade of A, B, C, D, or Pass) calculated as:

$$CCR = \frac{\Sigma_{\text{credits completed with the grade of A, B, C, D, or P}}}{\Sigma_{\text{of all credits enrolled}}}$$

The CCR compares a student's success against enrollment behavior. In other words, the student acts upon academic plans by enrollment in courses. The CCR then computes the proportion of the goal successfully completed.

- *Developmental needs.* We operationalized remedial or developmental needs by coding the level of the first Math and English courses taken. The LACCD employs a hierarchical structure organized by level and prerequisites first categorizing transfer level (college proficiency) and compares other courses by the number of levels below college proficiency; extending to 4 levels below transfer. Transfer level math courses were initially coded with a "1" while those below transfer level were coded by the number of levels below transfer (-4, -3, -2, -1).

- *Highest math taken.* We used the same coding as described above to record the highest math course in which the student enrolled.

- The number of science courses taken was operationalized through tagging all science courses and subsequently summing the number of courses.[4]

- *Grades* were operationalized by calculating the cumulative GPA.

- Involvement or time on campus was calculated as the average credits per semester.

The Building of the "Calculator"

When calculating a student level variable from the enrollment file, the file was aggregated by student reference number and the item of interest calculated. The aggregated values by student were then merged back into the file that contained demographic information. In this fashion we created a working file that used "the student" as the unit of analysis.

Also merged into the working file was transfer status. Transfer information was secured from the National Student Clearinghouse (NSC). For each of the students in the dataset, a "1" was recorded if the student had enrolled in a four-year institution. Non-transfers were coded with a "0." It may be important to note that enrollment in a four-year college or university does not indicate successful completion of the baccalaureate or in some cases even successful completion of a full semester of courses. The definition of transfer for our calculator is merely enrollment in a four-year institution.

Estimation Method

Since our outcome of interest, transfer, is dichotomous,[5] we employed logistic regression to examine the relationship of personal characteristics and course taking patterns with the probability of transferring (Cabrera, 1994; Hosmer & Lemeshow, 2000). Logistic regression is especially useful for predicting in which of two categories (i.e., transferred or not transferred) a person is likely to fall given certain characteristics or factors (Field, 2005). Logistic regression uses a logarithmic transformation to overcome the assumption of linearity (Field, 2005) and seeks to obtain the best-fitting model to describe the relationship between the dependent variable (in this case, transfer) and the set of independent measures derived from the data.

Data Exploration

Prior to testing a prediction model, we examined the data using several screening criteria. We first paid attention to the distribution of the variables. For some of the variables we noted a high degree of skewness resulting from the low number of cases in some of the categories. In some cases we collapsed values when variability was very low. Next we examined the degree of collinearity among variables. In so doing we first examined the correlations among the selected predictors.[6] We noted a high level of correlation between lowest math course and highest math (.818). A very high level of correlation indicates that these two variables essentially provide the same information and should not be used simultaneously in the estimation of the transfer model. Accordingly, we decided to use the high math variable and to remove the low math from the equation. Subsequently, we examined the variance inflation factor (VIF) and tolerance indices. Both types of indexes fell within the acceptable ranges.[7]

Model Testing

All of the variables were entered into the logistic regression equation using a forced entry (1-block) method. Several measures of goodness of fit were used to appraise the transfer logistic regression model. The χ^2 (chi-squared) signifies the extent to which the variables as a group are associated with transfer. A significant value indicates a good fit. The classification table, or PCC, reports the percentage of cases correctly classified by the model[8] (Aldrich & Nelson, 1984; Hosmer & Lemeshow, 2000). While the -2 log likelihood cannot be interpreted alone, it is useful as a measure of comparing one model to another. In our case, we compare our model to a baseline model using only the calculated constant. The Hosmer and Lemeshow Test compares the models and tests for significant difference between the observed and predicted values of the dependent variable. Thus for this test a non-significant value implies that the model estimates fit the data at an acceptable level. The Cox & Snell and Nagelkerke R^2 values are similar in interpretation to an R^2 in multiple regression. In other words, these R-statistics provide measures of the partial correlation between the dependent variable and each of the predictor variables. The two measures use a different computation and hence the results differ. However, together they provide a "gauge of the significance of the model" (Field, 2005, p. 223). Table 1 provides selected measures of goodness of fit.

We constructed the "Calculator" faceplate using the programming language of C# that could provide an interface with our output and allow a method of inputting the specific values of the template factors.

Use of the "Calculator"

The Community College Transfer Calculator© was made available on the Internet to the Los Angeles Community College District. Figure 1 provides a view of the "Calculator" faceplate.

Table 1. Measures of Goodness of Fit

Measure	Value
χ^2	121.915 (18)*
Classification Table (Percentage Cases Predicted or PCP)	81.7%
–2 Log Likelihood	2571.202
Hosmer and Lemeshow Test (*df*)	9.831 (8)
Cox & Snell *R*-Square	.303
Nagelkerke *R*-Square	.448

*$p < .001$

The Community College Transfer Calculator© is used to calculate the likelihood of transfer for a specific student-type based on specific academic and course variables. The "Calculator" provides several options as well as a helpful description. The Likelihood of Transfer percentage changes as the variable options are altered. By clicking on the link "Description" the user is provided with directions on how to choose the most applicable variable for the student of interest (see Figure 2).

Variable options are changed by clicking on the right hand corner of the options box, and choosing the desired option from the drop-down menu (Figure 3).

The Community College Transfer Calculator© also includes a matrix version that can be viewed by clicking on the tab labeled "Matrix Version" at the top of the "Calculator" window. The variables, options, and descriptions are the same as described earlier. The Matrix version provides a visual display of the likelihood of transfer based on entry level of English and highest level of mathematics completed. The Matrix version (see Figure 4) allows a visual of the different course options and reveals the power of the combination of English and Mathematics.

As indicated, the "Calculator" is currently calibrated for the Los Angeles Community College District but was designed to be customizable to other sites. Once the calculator is installed, the user can customize it by adding institution-specific factors and data. The logistic regression weights or b-values and the constant, calculated via a statistical program such as PASW, SAS, or other software product can be entered by first clicking on the "Update b-Values" button above the "Calculator" tabs (see Figure 5). The results can be transferred to the "Calculator" template by entering the regression b-values and subsequently clicking on the "Update b-Values" button. A window will appear containing a column of variables, options, and values. In order to change values, simply click within the white box next to the desired variable option and enter the derived b-values specific for the institution. When done, simply click "Save" at the bottom of the window. The calculator will be updated and "Likelihood of Transfer" will now be derived based on the newly entered values.

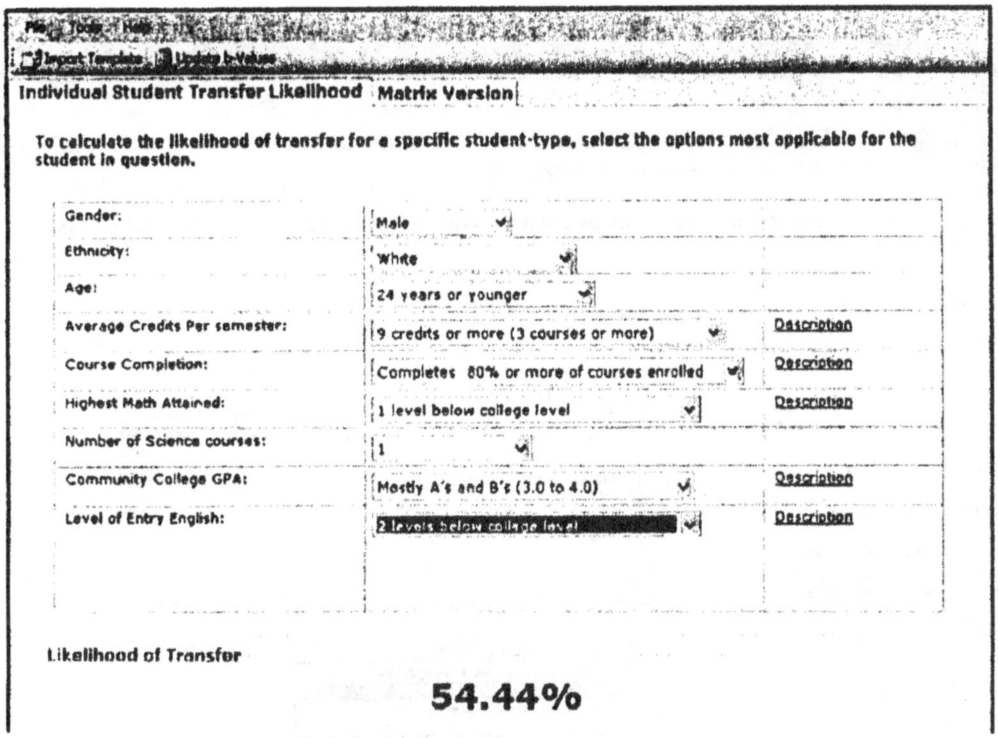

Figure 1. *The Community College Transfer Calculator©.*

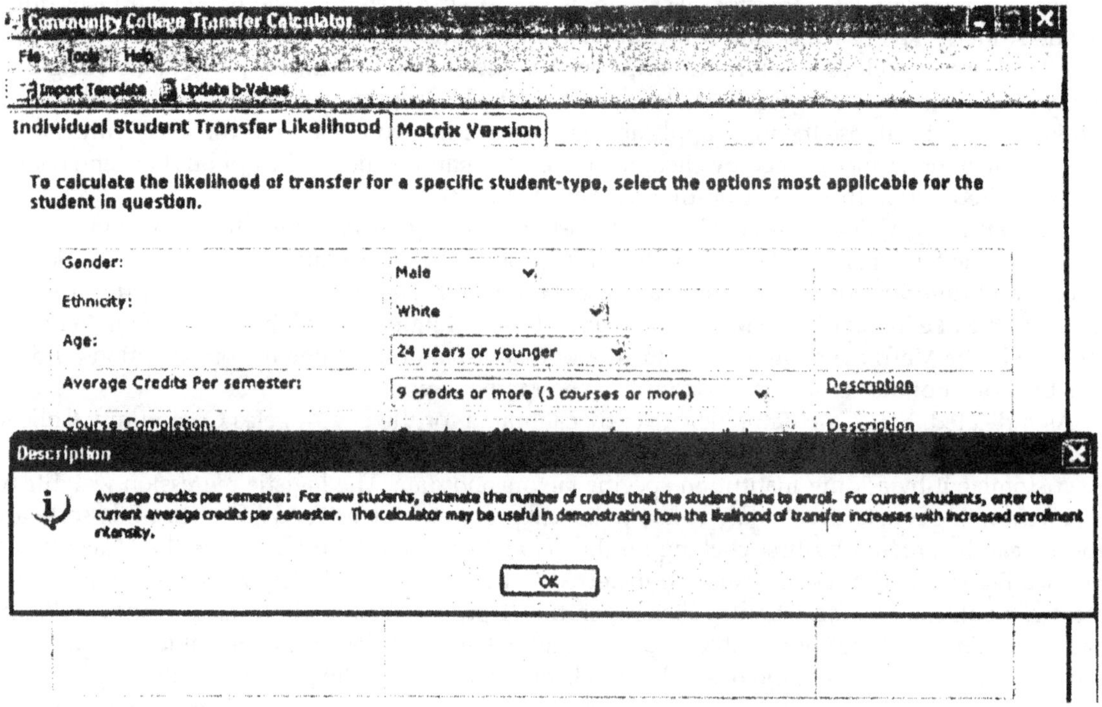

Figure 2. Supplementary descriptions of variables

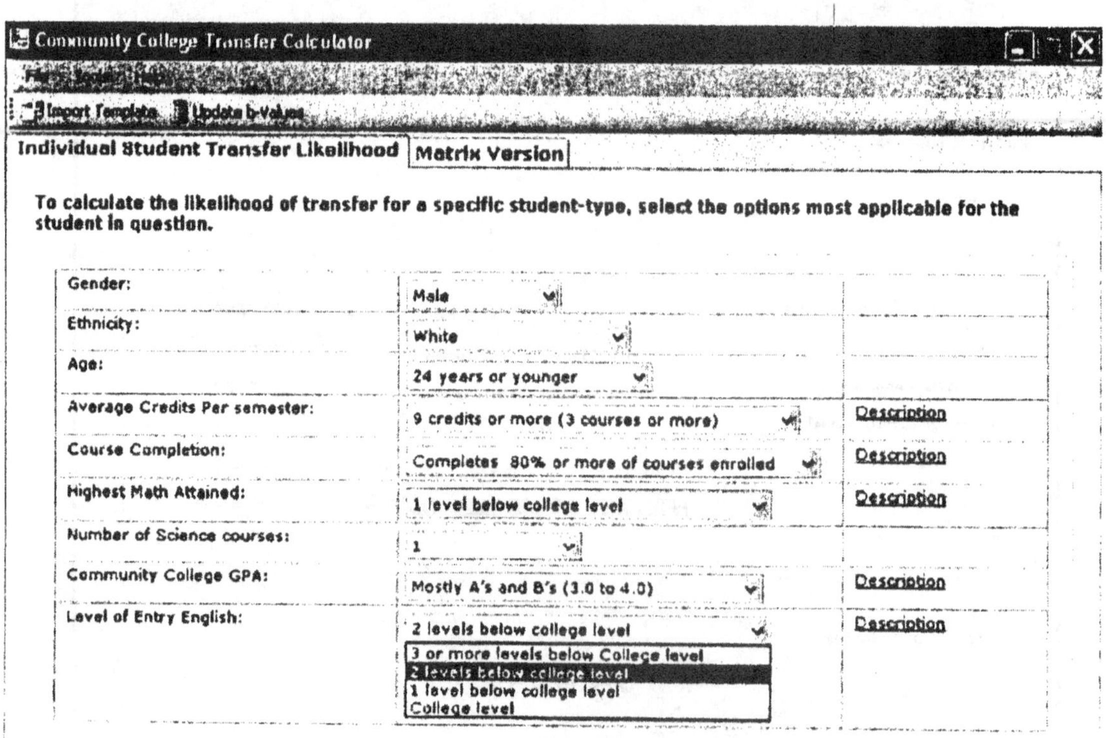

Figure 3. Transfer Calculator dropdown menus.

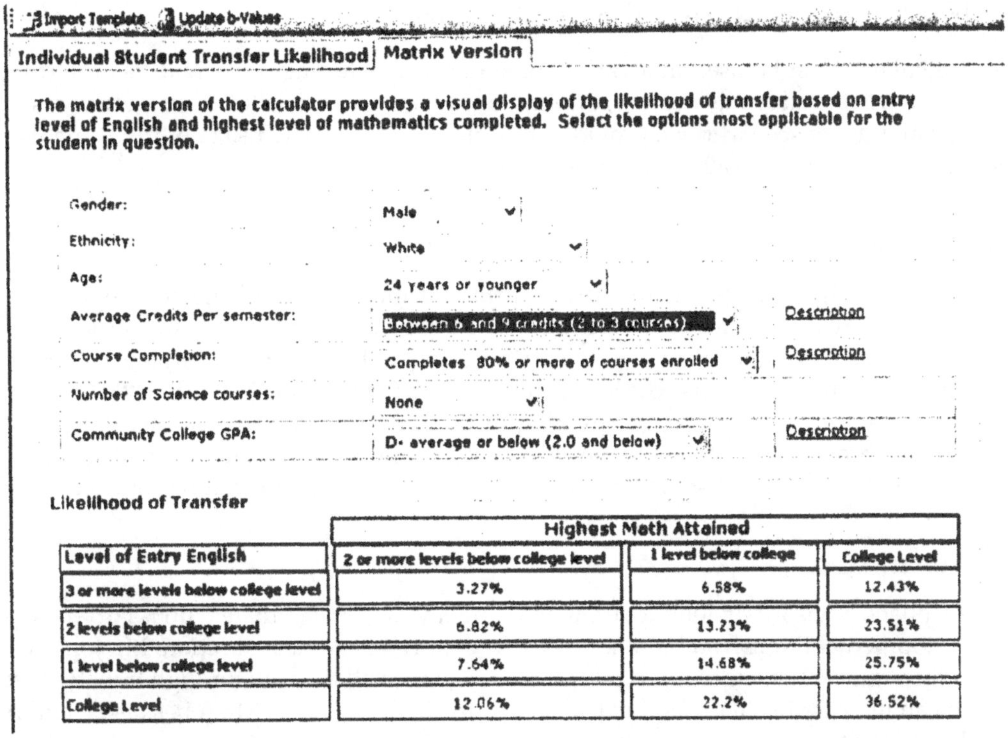

	Highest Math Attained		
Level of Entry English	2 or more levels below college level	1 level below college	College Level
3 or more levels below college level	3.27%	6.58%	12.43%
2 levels below college level	6.82%	13.23%	23.51%
1 level below college level	7.64%	14.68%	25.75%
College Level	12.06%	22.2%	36.52%

Figure 4. Matrix version of *The Community College Transfer Calculator*©.

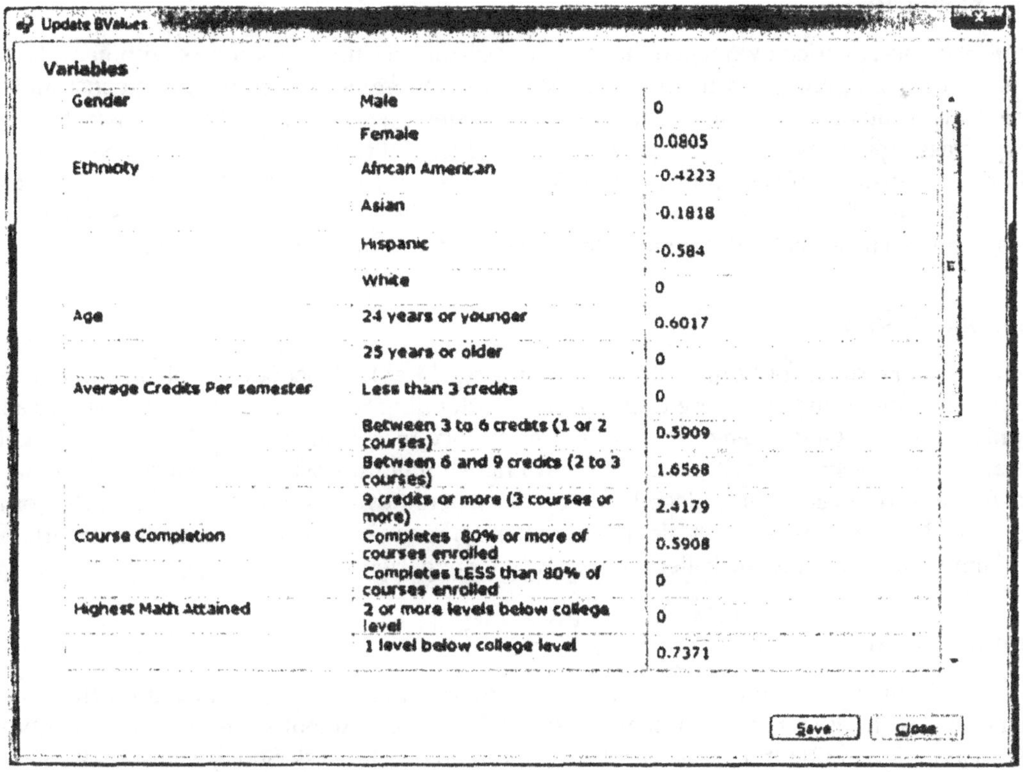

Figure 5. Updating b-values on the downloaded "Calculator."

Policy Implications—Using the "Calculator"

The "Calculator" can be used in a variety of situations including in individual and group settings such as in private advising sessions, orientation sessions or as part of a college success course. Through an "album" of scenarios we provide examples of appropriate usage of the "Calculator" at a hypothetical college; Sunnyvale Community College.

Album Scenario 1

Sunnyvale Community College has recently instituted a mandatory college success course (SCC 100) for all first-time college students. The course is designed to assist students to accrue knowledge about how to be a successful college student. The course is focused on clarifying values, setting goals, and making sound decisions. The instructors use *The Community College Transfer Calculator©* in a lesson on creating program plans, persevering through the curriculum, and avoiding dropping courses. Students are provided access to the "Calculator" and while working in small groups create contingency tables to illustrate the importance of persistence through the math sequence.

Album Scenario 2

Sunnyvale College advisor, Mr. John Jones, is advising a young Asian male who is currently placed in both developmental English and mathematics. In the private advising section, Mr. Jones demonstrates that through perseverance through the math sequence all the way through transfer level, the young man can increase his likelihood of transfer from 28.6% to 62.7%. Mr. Jones also recommends additional courses for the student's program of studies. The "Calculator" is also used to show how in addition to the math sequence, the addition of two science courses can add significantly to the likelihood of success to transfer.

Album Scenario 3

An older African-American woman on a very slow credit-accruing track meets with her advisor to discuss the course offerings for the next semester. Due to family and employment constraints, the mature student can only enroll in one course per semester. The "Calculator" can be used to indicate that by increasing her academic engagement and involvement to a two-course per semester rate, the likelihood of transfer doubles (from 14.6% to 33.0%). The advisor also points out that by increasing the intensity of enrollments, transfer can occur more quickly. The advisor assists the student to find sources of financial aid that will compensate for her reduced employment schedule.

Album Scenario 4

Elaine Green, a recruiter for Sunnyvale, is attending the local high school's "College Night" to talk to groups of students and their parents interested in attending Sunnyvale prior to transfer to a four-year university. Ms. Green demonstrates the importance of enrolling in the high school's college preparatory courses such as college algebra and English literature while in high school so that students will be ready to enroll in college-level courses when they are students at Sunnyvale Community College. Ms. Green uses the "Calculator" in her demonstration to emphasize the importance of early planning for the complete college and university experience.

Album Scenario 5

Sunnyvale's humanities faculty are convinced that their courses prepare students for their university experiences. To attract more students to enroll in the department's offerings, the faculty have begun a campaign entitled "Humanities for All Humans." They ask Sunnyvale's institutional researcher to calculate the increase in likelihood of students transferring by taking 1, 2, or 3 humanities courses. The college's institutional researcher adds the number of humanities courses taken by a past cohort of students and adds the variable to their customized *Community College Transfer Calculator©*. The results of the "Calculator" are used in the campaign to add benefit to enrolling in humanities. The results are discussed not only in faculty meetings of the Humanities faculty, but also among the upper administration at Sunnyvale.

Album Scenario 6

The Board of Trustees of Sunnyvale has asked the College to consider mandatory orientation sessions for all incoming first-time students. Sunnyvale's President has convened a special committee to look into the matter and to suggest a curriculum. The committee first asks the Director of Institutional Research to add a variable to their customized "Calculator" that indicates if students have attended orientation. The Director of Institutional Research notes that for the incoming class of 1998, the academic advisors kept lists of attendees to the then voluntary orientation. Using the directions and templates for *The Community College Transfer Calculator©*, IR creates a custom design that includes not only transfer status but also if the student attended orientation. The "Calculator" is then used to illustrate for the former cohort, the difference in likelihood of transfer depending on attendance at the orientation session. The "Calculator" is further used in the committee's discussions to see the course-taking patterns that also made a difference in likelihood of transfer. This information is made a part of the orientation session's curriculum.

Album Scenario 7

The state university in close proximity to Sunnyvale offers graduate degrees in education. A professor of Counselor Education has designed a new course entitled Seminar in Counselor Education to help doctoral students in the Department of Counselor Education achieve understanding of, insight into, and effective planning for the work, roles, and responsibilities of being a counselor at a community college or university. With permission from Sunnyvale, the professor will be using *The Community College Transfer Calculator©* in her unit on community college transfer.

Interpreting the Community College Transfer Calculator Results— Interpreting Contingency Tables

Using the default data derived from the LACCD (2007), we used *The Community College Transfer Calculator©* to develop a series of contingency tables to illustrate the power of taking specific courses on the probability of transfer. It is interesting to note the "stepping stone" nature of the probabilities. Each step horizontally (to the right) and vertically (down) increases the probability of transfer. Table 2 was derived for a young Asian female enrolling in 9 or more credits taking 1 science course. Note that depending on English entry level and final math the probability of transfer varies from 19.28% to 80.23%. Obviously, student level of initial enrollment makes a difference. Although students must begin in the English level in which they were assessed, persevering through the math sequence is extremely powerful. Tables 2 through 6 are similar but differ by the ethnicity of the student. Although the exact values fluctuate, it is clear that the power of taking college level math holds regardless of ethnicity.

While it may be intuitive to conclude that starting in a higher level of English and/or taking transfer level mathematics is conducive to transfer, *The Community College Transfer Calculator©* provides strong evidence of the power of course-taking and academic success for community college students. Policy makers and others should be aware of these important relationships. In addition to making developmental students aware of the need to take the full math sequence, colleges may consider forming learning communities, mandatory tutoring sessions, and other forms of supplemental instruction for transfer-hopeful students struggling in mathematics.

Tables 7 through 9 display the joint probabilities of math and science. Again, the probabilities step up horizontally and vertically. Using the Asian female (see Table 7) as an example indicates that

Table 2. Highest Level of Math Attained

Level of English upon entry	Two levels below college level	One level below college level	College level
3 or more levels below college level	19.28%	33.2%	50.05%
Two levels below college level	34.07%	51.82%	68.44%
One level below college level	36.84%	54.83%	70.99%
College level	49.18%	66.82%	80.23%

Holding Constant:
Gender = Female
Ethnicity = Asian
Age = 24 years or younger
Average credits per semester = 9 credits or more
Course completion = Completes 80% or more of courses enrolled
Number of science courses = 1
Community College GPA = Mostly As and Bs (3.0 to 4.0)

Table 3. Highest Level of Math Attained

Level of English upon entry	Two levels below college level	One level below college level	College level
3 or more levels below college level	22.3%	37.4%	54.64%
Two levels below college level	38.32%	56.39%	72.27%
One level below college level	41.22%	59.34%	74.63%
College level	53.77%	70.77%	82.99%

Holding Constant:
Gender = Female
Ethnicity = White
Age = 24 years or younger
Average credits per semester = 9 credits or more
Course completion = Completes 80% or more of courses enrolled
Number of science courses = 1
Community College GPA = Mostly As and Bs (3.0 to 4.0)

Table 4. Highest Level of Math Attained

Level of English upon entry	Two levels below college level	One level below college level	College level
3 or more levels below college level	15.84%	28.15%	44.13%
Two levels below college level	28.95%	45.88%	63.09%
One level below college level	31.5%	48.9%	65.86%
College level	43.27%	61.35%	76.19%

Holding Constant:
Gender ≈ Female
Ethnicity ≈ African American
Age = 24 years or younger
Average credits per semester = 9 credits or more
Course completion = Completes 80% or more of courses enrolled
Number of science courses ≈ 1
Community College GPA = Mostly As and Bs (3.0 to 4.0)

Table 5. Highest Level of Math Attained

Level of English upon entry	Two levels below college level	One level below college level	College level
3 or more levels below college level	13.79%	24.97%	40.16%
Two levels below college level	25.71%	41.8%	59.22%
One level below college level	28.09%	44.84%	62.1%
College level	39.32%	57.42%	73.11%

Holding Constant:
Gender ≈ Female
Ethnicity = Hispanic
Age = 24 years or younger
Average credits per semester = 9 credits or more
Course completion = Completes 80% or more of courses enrolled
Number of science courses ≈ 1
Community College GPA = Mostly As and Bs (3.0 to 4.0)

Table 6. Number of Science Courses Taken

Highest level of Math attained	None	One	Two or more
Two or more levels below college level	46.38%	53.77%	62.6%
One level below college level	64.29%	70.77%	77.7%
College level	78.4%	82.99%	87.53%

Holding Constant:

Gender = Female

Ethnicity = White

Age = 24 years or younger

Average credits per semester = 9 credits or more

Course completion = Completes 80% or more of courses enrolled

Community College GPA = Mostly As and Bs (3.0 to 4.0)

Level of English upon entry = College level

the probability of transfer can fluctuate from 41.85% to 85.38%. The contingency tables indicate the importance and value of successfully enrolling in transfer level courses. Although multiple science courses may not be appropriate for all students in all academic disciplines, the use of science in our data indicates reflects the transfer readiness policy in California that includes courses in physical and biological sciences. Thus, as displayed by the "Calculator," students in line with the readiness standards are more likely to transfer.

Like all of the findings, the results of enrolling and completing science courses must be interpreted in conjunction with all of the other findings. It may be argued, for example, that students enrolling in science courses may be more disciplined and/or be more academically able. However, one must be aware that the significance of these courses remains despite the inclusion of math level and GPA in the model (serving as controls). Further, while we do not infer causality, it may be that more disciplined students are more apt to transfer. Or, in reverse it may be that the discipline of science relates to transfer. In other words, we posit that students following a more disciplined path consisting of mathematics and science, may be more successful in transfer. The "Calculator" indicates that enrolling in a disciplined manner may be advisable. Thus, discipline in this sense is not just an attribute internal to the student but also an attribute of the instructional map. Our controls of initial math level and GPA certainly suggest that following the instructional map closely leads to greater student success. We do feel that further research that can distinguish the student's internal discipline from the discipline of the instructional system is needed, not only to provide additional control to our results, but even more significantly to be able to understand how the institution can encourage a more disciplined student approach to course taking.

Table 10 highlights gender and enrollment. This table breaks out the difference in probability between part-time and full-time enrollment for men and women. While many community college students have familial and work-load issues that prevent them from taking a heavier load, the fact remains that casual enrollment threatens the probability of transfer for both genders. Policies to encourage students to enroll more intensely appear appropriate.

Table 7. Number of Science Courses Taken

Highest level of Math attained	None	One	Two or more
Two or more levels below college level	41.85%	49.18%	58.2%
One level below college level	59.96%	66.82%	74.35%
College level	75.12%	80.23%	85.38%

Holding Constant:

Gender = Female

Ethnicity = Asian

Age = 24 years or younger

Average credits per semester = 9 credits or more

Course completion = Completes 80% or more of courses enrolled

Community College GPA = Mostly As and Bs (3.0 to 4.0)

Level of English upon entry = College level

Table 8. Number of Science Courses Taken

Highest level of Math attained	None	One	Two or more
Two or more levels below college level	36.19%	43.27%	52.32%
One level below college level	54.14%	61.35%	69.55%
College level	70.41%	76.19%	82.16%

Holding Constant:

Gender = Female

Ethnicity = African American

Age = 24 years or younger

Average credits per semester = 9 credits or more

Course completion = Completes 80% or more of courses enrolled

Community College GPA = Mostly As and Bs (3.0 to 4.0)

Level of English upon entry = College level

Finally Tables 11 and 12 are included to demonstrate the joint effect of successfully completing courses and enrollment intensity for females and males respectively. While it is intuitive that students who do not complete the majority of their courses are less likely to transfer, the contingency tables provide sound evidence of the drastic consequences of dropping courses.

Table 9. Number of Science Courses Taken

Highest level of Math attained	None	One	Two or more
Two or more levels below college level	32.52%	39.32%	48.25%
One level below college level	50.07%	57.42%	65.99%
College level	66.91%	73.11%	79.64%

Holding Constant:

Gender = Female

Ethnicity = Hispanic

Age = 24 years or younger

Average credits per semester = 9 credits or more

Course completion = Completes 80% or more of courses enrolled

Community College GPA = Mostly As and Bs (3.0 to 4.0)

Level of English upon entry = College level

Table 10. Average Credits per Semester

Gender	Less than 3 credits	Between 3 and 6 credits	Between 6 and 9 credits	9 Credits or more
Male	11.88%	19.29%	40.76%	59.46%
Female	12.73%	20.55%	42.68%	61.35%

Holding Constant:

Ethnicity = African American

Age = 24 years or younger

Course completion ratio = Completes 80% or more of courses enrolled

Highest math attained = One level below college level

Number of science courses = One

Community College GPA = Mostly As and Bs (3.0 to 4.0)

Level of English upon entry = College level

Table 11. Average Credits per Semester

Course completion ratio	Less than 3 credits	Between 3 and 6 credits	Between 6 and 9 credits	9 Credits or more
Completes less than 80% of courses enrolled	9.29%	15.37%	34.32%	52.7%
Completes 80% or more of courses enrolled	15.62%	24.71%	48.58%	66.82%

Holding Constant:

Gender = Female

Ethnicity = Asian

Age = 24 years or younger

Highest math attained = One level below college level

Number of science courses = One

Community College GPA = Mostly As and Bs (3.0 to 4.0)

Level of English upon entry = College level

Table 12. Average Credits per Semester

Course completion ratio	Less than 3 credits	Between 3 and 6 credits	Between 6 and 9 credits	9 Credits or more
Completes less than 80% of courses enrolled	8.64%	14.37%	32.56%	50.72%
Completes 80% or more of courses enrolled	14.6%	23.27%	46.61%	65.04%

Holding Constant:

Gender = Male

Ethnicity = Asian

Age = 24 years or younger

Highest math attained = One level below college level

Number of science courses = One

Community College GPA = Mostly As and Bs (3.0 to 4.0)

Level of English upon entry = College level

Recommendations to Improve Practice for Community College Leaders, Practitioners and Policymakers

Community colleges have been accused of operating without the benefit of enrollment management data. Further, it has been assumed that data-driven decisions require colleges to invest in costly data collections and analyses, most of them involving surveys and questionnaires that are difficult to collect due to the transient nature of the community college student. We contend that the use of transcript analyses allows colleges to make data-driven decisions using data already mandated, collected, and stored. Furthermore, we have demonstrated that it is possible to describe the results of analyzing transcript data in ways that are easily understood by faculty, academic advisors, and others. Our construction of *The Community College Transfer Calculator©* is a tool to make the process a bit easier and more straightforward.

We want to emphasize that colleges should use *their own* data. While we have constructed a working "Calculator" that accurately reports transfer probabilities, the results only truly reflect the population from which the data were derived—the Los Angeles Community College District. Community colleges are all unique in that they reflect their own communities with their distinctive brand of students. To expect that data derived from Los Angeles can accurately predict the likelihood of transfer of a student enrolled in a community college in New York, Montana, or Texas may not be realistic. Further, national data, while informative and useful, can only provide general benchmarks while not taking into consideration the unique community that a college serves. Therefore we emphasize the need for each college to look at its own data and to examine the course taking patterns of the students who enroll for their courses. Each college should isolate the measures of success that are important to their students. Since outcomes such as transfer, graduation, and degree acquisition are dichotomous, the technique we demonstrate is generally appropriate. Further, the "Calculator" Template can accept values for other dichotomous outcomes. Thus, the *Transfer "Calculator"* can become the *AA "Calculator"* or other outcome of interest.

Academic advisors and others should counsel students to design their academic programs and then to adhere to the courses. Unfortunately many students enroll in community colleges ill-prepared for college level work. They must take remedial/developmental coursework prior to transfer and/or degree. Although students in need of deep remediation are less likely than their counterparts who require little or no remediation to transfer, students can be successful if they persevere and climb the developmental ladder. As indicated by our LACCD "Calculator," a full-time student who begins study at one level below transfer level English and two or more levels below transfer level math can increase her likelihood of transfer from 34.3% to 68.6% if she perseveres and climbs the developmental ladder through college level math. Further, this same student can increase her likelihood of transfer by about 12% by taking two science courses.

The transfer "Calculator" can translate student course-taking behaviors into measures of curricular impact. One of those impacts relates to articulation agreements between community colleges and four-year institutions. The "Calculator" could be used to examine the extent to which several course-taking patterns at the community college result in transfer rates consistent with the expectations that guided the original articulation agreements. In other words, the "Calculator" can isolate those course-taking patterns that create obstacles and stumbling blocks and may need revision. Another course-taking impact that can be examined is the extent to which combination of science courses along with different levels of remediation maximize a student's likelihood to transfer. Finally, the course-taking "Calculator" can be used to examine the undocumented impact of students' choices in the timing and kind of courses they take at the community college. The policy maker may be unaware of the combination and patterns of courses and their relative effectiveness in facilitating or even inhibiting transfer across particular student populations (e.g., older students, minorities). In short, we see the "Calculator" as a new means of communication between student actions and student outcomes while informing policy decision making regarding course-taking practices.

Notes

1. At the time of this writing, the Achieving the Dream Initiative is working within 15 states with over 80 campuses.
2. Different districts, colleges, or state structures may employ a different structure. For example, a unit may use a structure where the student's enrollment is recorded by a time structure (such as semester or trimester). In this arrangement, the researcher would need to vector by courses. While the exact extraction of data may differ from our discussion, the final product would need to be merged with demographic data. Although many different structures may exist, in this manuscript we are using a common structure often employed in colleges where the enrollment is the unit of entry.
3. Grades of Withdrawn (W), Incomplete (I), Pass (P), Fail (F), Retake without credit (R) are not included in the GPA calculation.
4. A course was recorded if the student successfully completed it with a grade of A, B, C, D, or P. Science courses that were not successfully completed (grade of W, I, or F) were not included in the count.
5. Dichotomous variables are those that exhibit only two levels—for example gender (M/F). Transfer is dichotomous because students either transfer or they do not.
6. These correlations were estimated using the asymptotic distribution free procedures contained in PRELIS version 8.8 (Joreskog & Sörbom, 2004). PRELIS is suited for estimating correlations among categorical and ordinal variables as is the case in this study (Finney & DiStefano, 2006; Joreskog & Sörbom, 2004).
7. Cohen and Brawer (2003) suggest that VIF values of 10 or higher signify multicollinearity problems. They also indicate that tolerance levels of 0.10 or less are problematic.
8. PCC stands for **P**ercentage of **C**ases **C**orrectly **C**lassified.

References

Adelman, C. (1996). Have you read your college transcript lately? *Change, 28*(1), 48-49.

Adelman, C. (1999). *The new college course map and transcript files: Changes in course-taking and achievement, 1972-1993* (2nd ed.). Washington, DC: U.S. Department of Education.

Adelman, C. (2005). *Moving into town—And moving on: The community college in the lives of traditional-age students.* Washington, DC: U.S. Department of Education.

Adelman, C. (2006). *The toolbox revisited: Paths to degree completion from high school through college.* Washington, DC: U.S. Department of Education.

Aldrich, J. H., & Nelson, F. D. (1984). *Linear probability, logit, & probit models.* Beverly Hills, CA, Sage.

Boylan, H. R. (1995). Making the case for development education in research. *Developmental Education, 12*(2), 1-4.

Cabrera, A. F. (1994). Logistic regression analysis in higher education: An applied perspective. In J. C. Smart (Ed.), *Higher education: Handbook for the study of higher education, 10.* New York: Agathon Press.

Cabrera, A. F., Burkum, K. R., & LaNasa, S. M. (2005). Pathways to a four year degree: Determinants of transfer and degree completion. In A. Seidman (Ed.), *College student retention: A formula for student success* (pp. 155-209). ACE/Praeger Series on Higher Education. Westport, CT: Praeger.

Calcagno, J. C., Crosta, P., Bailey, T., & Jenkins, D. (2007). Stepping stones to a degree: The impact of enrollment pathways and milestones on community college student outcomes. *Research in Higher Education, 48*(7), 775-802.

California State System. (2007). *The California State University System.* Retrieved November 3, 2007, from http://www.calstate.edu

Cohen, A. M., & Brawer, F. B. (2003). *The American community college* (4th ed.). San Francisco, CA: Jossey-Bass.

Dougherty, K. (1994). *The contradictory college.* Albany, NY: State University of New York Press.

Dougherty, K. J., & Kienzel, G. S. (2006). It's not enough to get through the open door: Inequalities by social background in transfer from community colleges to four-year colleges. *Teachers College Record, 108*(3), 452-487.

Driscoll, A. K. (2007). *Beyond access: How the first semester matters for community college students' aspirations and persistence* (Policy Brief 07-2). Berkeley, CA: Policy Analysis for California.

Field, A. (2005). *Discovering statistics using SPSS.* Thousand Oaks, CA: Sage.

Finney, S. J., & DiStefano, C. (2006). Nonnormal and categorical data in structural equation models. In G. R. Hancock & R. O. Mueller (Eds.), *A second course in structural equation modeling* (pp. 269-314). Greenwich, CT: Information Age.

Hagedorn, L. S., Cypers, S., & Lester, J. (2008). Looking in the rearview mirror: A retrospective look at the factors affecting transfer for urban community college students. *Community College Journal of Research and Practice.*

Hagedorn, L. S., Maxwell, W., & Hampton, P. (2002). Correlates of retention for African American males in community colleges. *Journal of College Student Retention: Research, Theory, and Practice, 3*(3), 243-264.

Hosmer, D. W., & Lemeshow, S. (2000). *Applied logistic regression* (2nd ed.). New York: Wiley.

Joreskog, K. G., & Sörbom, D. (2004). *LJSREL 8.5 User's Reference Guide.* Chicago, IL: Scientific Software International.

Laanan, F. S. (2007). Studying transfer students. Part II: Dimensions of transfer students' adjustment. *Community College Journal of Research & Practice, 31*(1), 37-59.

Los Angeles Community College District (LACCD). (2007). Retrieved December 22, 2007 from http://www.laccd.edu/about_us/fast_facts.htm

Melguizo, T. (2006). *Are community colleges an alternative path for Hispanic students to attain a bachelor's degree.* Los Angeles, CA: Rossier School of Education.

McClenney, K. M. (2007). The community college survey of student engagement. *Community College Review, 35*(2), 137-146.

Nora, A. (2000). *Reexamining the community college mission.* Washington, DC: American Association of Community Colleges.

Palmer, J. C. (2000). General education in an age of student mobility. *Peer Review, 2*(2), 8-11.

Palmer, J. C. (2005). What do we know about student transfer? In R. Shoeberg (Ed.), *An overview in general education and student transfer: Fostering intentionality and coherence in state systems.* Washington, DC: Association of American Colleges and Universities.

Shulock, N., & Moore, C. (2007, February). *Rules of the game: How state policy creates barriers to degree completion and impeded student success in the California Community Colleges.* Sacramento, CA: Institute for Higher Education Leadership & Policy.

Spicer, S. L., & Armstrong, W. B. (1996). Transfer: The elusive denominator. *New Directions for Community Colleges, 96,* 45-54. San Francisco, CA: Jossey-Bass.

Tinto, V. (1975). Dropouts from higher education: A theoretical synthesis of the recent literature. *A Review of Educational Research, 45,* 89-125.

Tinto, V. (1987). *Leaving college: Rethinking the causes and cures of student attrition.* Chicago, IL: The University of Chicago Press.

Tinto, V. (1993). *Leaving college: Rethinking the causes and cures of student attrition* (2nd ed.). Chicago, IL: The University of Chicago Press.

Townsend, B. K., McNerny, N., & Arnold, A. (1993). Will this community college transfer student succeed? Factors affecting transfer student performance. *Community College Journal of Research and Practice 17*(5), 433-443.

University of California System. (2007). *University of California StatFinder.* Retrieved November 23, 2007, from http://www.universityofcalifornia.edu/

Direct reprint requests to:
Linda Serra Hagedorn, Ph.D.
Professor and Interim Chair
Department of Educational Leadership and Policy Studies
Iowa State University
N243 Lagomarcino
Ames, IA 50011
e-mail: Lindah@iastate.edu

CHAPTER 39

"A Hand Hold for a Little Bit": Factors Facilitating the Success of Community College Transfer Students to a Large Research University

Barbara K. Townsend and Kristin Wilson

To understand factors affecting the academic and social integration of community college transfer students, we interviewed 19 students who transferred to one state's large research-extensive university. We inquired about the transfer process, efforts of the university to orient and assist them, and perceptions of the university versus the community college. Findings indicate that community college transfer students may need more assistance initially than they are given, partly because of the large size of the university. In addition, transfers from community colleges need to understand how a research institution's institutional mission affects faculty and student behavior. Student affairs staff may need to lead the way in fulfilling four-year institutions' responsibility for integrating community college transfers into the fabric of the institution.

In the past few decades, higher education leaders have become attentive to the importance of academic and social integration in facilitating students' academic success and degree attainment, particularly at institutions whose student body is traditional-age and primarily residential (Astin, 1993; Braxton, Sullivan, & Johnson, 1997; Pascarella & Terenzini, 1991, 2005; Tinto, 1993). Consequently, institutional leaders have supported the development of institutional practices such as learning communities and first-year seminars, practices that enable entering students and faculty to know one another more fully than in large lecture halls. The underlying assumption behind each of these practices is that the more students are involved in or integrated into college life, the greater the likelihood they will stay in college and attain their degree (Pascarella & Terenzini, 2005; Tinto, 1993; 1997).

At the same time that institutional leaders are focusing on the academic and social integration of their first-year students to ensure their retention and academic success, they also have begun to focus on increasing the baccalaureate attainment of community college transfer students. Given current limitations on some four-year colleges' institutional capacity as well as rapidly escalating tuition costs, students entering higher education through the public sector are increasingly likely to begin their college education at two-year colleges. After a year or two at a community college, many students seek to transfer to a four-year school and attain a baccalaureate. While preparing students academically to transfer to four-year colleges or universities and facilitating that transfer has always been a major responsibility of community colleges, four-year institutions are increasingly being viewed as also responsible for students' successful transfer and transition (Berger & Malaney, 2003; Kuh, Kinzie, Schuh, Whitt & Associates, 2005; Weschler, 1989). After helping these students transfer, the receiving institutions are responsible for orienting, advising, and providing support services to them (Kerr, King, & Grites, 2004) as well as ensuring their academic success by providing opportunities for the academic and social integration deemed necessary for their retention (Tinto, 1993). Unfortunately, transfer students are often ignored in retention efforts (Kuh et al.), including activities as basic as orientation to the campus (Herman & Lewis, 2004).

Therefore, the purpose of this study was to ascertain the perceptions of current community college transfer students about institutional factors that influenced their fit within the receiving institution, including the transfer process, orientation to the university, and social and academic experiences there as compared to those in the community college.

Conceptual Framework

Tinto's (1993) theory of factors affecting student retention has greatly influenced retention efforts in the past couple of decades. He posits that undergraduate students' persistence is influenced not only by their own characteristics, goals, and commitments but also by their experiences academically and socially while in college. Academic experiences include interaction with staff and with faculty both inside and outside the classroom as well as engaging classroom learning experiences. Social interactions within the academic system include both formal or institutionally provided co-curricular activities and informal interactions with peers in residential facilities or other institutional settings such as a place to study. These social and academic interactions contribute to a student's sense of belonging to the institution. With sufficient academic and social integration into the educational community, students will likely persist, unless external commitments or changing intentions and goals work against their persistence in a particular institution or even in higher education itself.

Institutional leaders have taken to heart this perspective and, largely through the efforts of student affairs staff, often in partnership with some faculty, have concentrated institutional efforts on retaining first-year students into the next year through such activities as residential learning communities, freshman interest groups, and first-year seminars. Far fewer efforts have been exerted to ensure the retention and success of community college transfer students (Herman & Lewis, 2004; Kuh et al., 2005).

One factor affecting transfer itself is the creation and maintenance of articulation agreements, whether at the state, institutional, or programmatic level. There is abundant literature about the value of these agreements in facilitating what is termed a "seamless transfer," which generally means transfer without loss of credits (Pitter, 1999). Although this phrase alludes to transfer of credits, it could also be viewed as an ideal for the literal transfer and integration of community college students into the receiving institution. Factors affecting or facilitating this kind of seamless transfer include advising by both the sending and receiving institutions, orientation to and availability of support services at the four-year institution, and opportunities for transfer students to become socially and academically integrated into the receiving institution. Tinto's (1993) theory of academic retention suggests factors necessary for academic and social integration and thus a relatively seamless transfer into the fabric of the receiving institution.

Literature Review

Tinto's (1993) theory about student retention has particularly been applied in studies about the academic and social integration of students entering as first-year students into large universities (Braxton et al., 1997). However, little of this research focuses on the actual integration experiences of students. Most is quantitative research using grade point average (GPA) or graduation rates as a proxy for integration. Also, what is striking about this research is that almost none of it has been conducted on students once they transfer to another institution. Instead, research that looks at transfer students' success focuses largely on quantitative measures of their academic performance at the four-year institution: GPA after one semester for evidence of "transfer shock" (Hills, 1965) or a decline in GPA, exit GPA, baccalaureate attainment, and time to degree. Typically the studies include selected student demographic characteristics such as gender and race/ethnicity as well as performance or behavioral characteristics such as number of transferred hours and entering GPA to see if there is a relationship between these characteristics and outcome variables like time to degree (e.g., Carlan & Byxbe, 2000; Glass & Harrington, 2002; Koker & Hendel, 2003; Saupe & Long, 1996). Occasionally studies are conducted at the national level (e.g., Dougherty, 1992) or state level (e.g.,

Arnold, 2001), but more typically researchers conduct institutional-level studies that examine the performance of transfers from a particular community college to a particular four-year college (e.g., Angelin, Davis, & Mooradian, 1995; Townsend, McNerney, & Arnold, 1993), all community college transfers to a particular four-year state institution or system (e.g., Glass & Harrington; Whitfield, 2005), or all two- and four-year college transfers to a particular institution (e.g., Berger & Malaney, 2003; Holahan, Green, & Kelley, 1983; House, 1989). These studies typically document the transfer shock that Hills first identified. Some find that community college transfers attain the baccalaureate at about the same rate or have approximately the same exit GPA as native students (e.g., Washington State Board for Community and Technical Colleges, 1989); others find that community college transfer students are less successful (e.g., House). At the national level "about 70% of students who transfer from two- to four-year colleges after taking at least a semester's worth of credits receive a baccalaureate degree" (Wellman, 2002, p. 8).

While studies have found some demographic differences in student performance after transfer, the behavioral differences that can potentially be rectified through advising and support services merit particular attention by institutional administrators. For example, knowing that two-year college students who transfer with an associate of arts degree are the most likely to complete the baccalaureate and in the shortest time (e.g., Carlan & Byxbe, 2000; Glass & Harrington, 2002) is useful information for community college advisors and four-year college admissions directors and advisors.

Some research has focused on the experiences of students during the transfer process and at the receiving institution. Occasionally researchers look at just one aspect of the transfer student experience such as the transfer process or orientation programs at the receiving institution (e.g., Davies & Casey, 1998; Herman & Lewis, 2004; Jacobs, Busby, & Leath, 1992). Other researchers examine transfer students' perceptions of their experiences at the receiving institution (e.g., Townsend, 1995).

Most of the studies have similar findings. Transfer students perceive both community colleges and the receiving institutions as needing to improve the transfer process by providing more information, which must be accurate, and aiding potential transfer students in understanding which community college courses will transfer (Davies & Casey, 1998). Initial efforts by the receiving institution to orient students are typically limited to a one-day orientation, which not all students attend, and there is little or no effort to provide other assistance in making the initial transition (Jacobs et al., 1992). Students desire more help from the receiving institution after they transfer, e.g., more information about campus resources and outside-of-class opportunities to meet other students. Students also consider community college faculty as more caring, helpful, and interested in their students than are university faculty (Bauer & Bauer, 1994; Townsend, 1995; Vaala, 1991). Perceptions about their academic preparation at the community college are generally positive, with most studies (Bauer & Bauer; Davies & Casey; Jacobs et al.; Vaala) finding students satisfied with their preparation although concerned about heavier academic workloads at their new institution. At large receiving institutions, transfer students often feel anonymous and have difficulty in making social connections with fellow students, as well as academic connections with faculty (Britt & Hirt, 1999; Harbin, 1997; Vaala).

Not only are the findings fairly similar across these studies; so also are the implications for practitioners. Typically, researchers urge two-year college faculty and administrators to do a better job of preparing students for transfer, including making them more aware of what university classes will be as compared to community college classes (e.g., Townsend, 1995) as well as developing transfer centers that will facilitate the process of transfer. Even in recent studies whose authors emphasize the importance of four-year schools facilitating transfer students' adjustment, the recommendations for practice at the four-year level are limited and focus primarily on four-year schools providing community colleges with current information about admissions and institutional expectations; they may also focus upon certain demographic variables such as race and gender that may affect a transfer student's success (Berger & Malaney, 2003). Since these demographic characteristics are inherent to individuals, a focus on them does not seem as productive as would a focus on what four-year colleges could do to facilitate success after transfer.

Many of the above studies were conducted during the 1990s, with some even older. Despite this research indicating what problems community college transfers have experienced in the transfer process and after process, the extent to which either two-year or four-year institutions have worked to rectify these problems is not clear. Given the emerging emphasis on the responsibility of four-year institutions in helping transfer students succeed, as well as the long-standing emphasis on the academic and social integration of students to ensure academic success, it is important to continue studying the experiences of community college transfer students. New studies may indicate whether the transfer process itself has improved for these students and what institutional factors currently contribute to or hinder transfer students' academic and social integration into the receiving institution. Thus, as indicated earlier, this study sought to determine the perceptions of one set of community college transfer students about (a) the transfer process itself, including the level of assistance provided by the sending and receiving institutions; (b) university services, including orientation, for transfer students; and (c) similarities and differences between the institutions in terms of students' academic and social experiences at them.

Method

This was a qualitative study relying upon generic qualitative interview methods to answer our research questions (Merriam, 1998). A qualitative approach is used when "little is known" about a phenomenon, or, as in this study, when there is interest in gaining new perspectives about a phenomenon "about which much is known" already (Stern, 1980, as cited in Strauss & Corbin, 1998, p. 11). While there have been various studies looking at the experiences of community college transfer students, none have focused specifically upon the phenomenon of students transferring from small community colleges to a large university oriented to full-time, traditional-age, residential students, although size of the receiving institution has occasionally been noted as being problematic for transfers. In this study, size of the receiving institution as well as the nature of its student body and its institutional mission provide the institutional context typically ignored in other studies even if identified in the study (e.g., Glass & Harrington, 2002).

To answer our research questions, which were drawn from a study conducted by Townsend (1995), we interviewed students who transferred to a large research university. The university is a selective, research-extensive university in a suburban setting. A public land-grant university, it had a fall 2004 on-campus headcount enrollment of over 25,000 students (20,166 on-campus under-graduates and 5,361 on-campus graduate and professional students). Of its more than 1,300 undergraduate transfers in fall 2004, 33% were from community colleges in the state. The undergraduate student body consists largely of white (84.7% in fall 2003), traditional-age students who attend full-time (93%) and live on or near campus. In contrast, the community colleges in this state had an average of less than 5,000 full-time equivalent credit students during 2003-04. Some of the colleges in rural areas had limited student housing, typically for no more than 200 students.

The students interviewed were solicited from the total population of students who were classified as transfer students (students transferring in at least 24 credit hours) coming from a community college located in the same state as the university, and who attended the university during the 2003-04 academic year. Some transfer students had attended two or more colleges before matriculating at the university, but the last institution attended prior to the university was an in-state two-year college.

Because the university in the study was interested in its transfer students' perceptions, it provided us with a list of all community college transfer students enrolled during summer 2004 and fall 2004. Initially we contacted only those enrolled during the summer to participate in the study, but to increase the number of participants, we also contacted students who enrolled during the fall. One of the researchers sent an e-mail to each student to explain the study and request the student's participation. Students who initially agreed to participate received another e-mail to arrange the interview, intended to last between 30 minutes and 1 hour.

Forty-five students initially agreed to participate, but only 19 set up an interview appointment and also kept it. Among the 19 were 9 women and 10 men. Two self-identified as minority and five as older (mid to late 20s and hereafter referred to as nontraditional age). Ten had completed the associate of arts degree.

After each participant signed a consent form, one of the researchers conducted and taped each interview. The interview consisted of 14 questions, a few of which began with a close-ended question such as, "Did you receive any assistance from the community college when you decided to transfer to the university?" and "Did you attend transfer student orientation at the university?" When participants said yes to any of the close-ended questions, they were asked to elaborate. We chose this approach to save participants' time for responding to questions eliciting a positive response. Time was of concern because several of the people agreeing to be interviewed indicated they did not have an hour but would answer what questions they could in the time they had. The average time for the interviews, not counting the time to secure written consent and answer preliminary questions regarding the study was approximately 40 minutes, with five lasting only 15–20 minutes and five taking well over an hour.

After the tapes were transcribed, each of us tallied responses to the close-ended questions and coded all elaborations to them. We also coded all responses to the open-ended questions in terms of themes emerging from several readings of the interview data (Bogden & Biklen, 2002; Strauss & Corbin, 1998). After developing general categories of codes or themes, each of us, working independently, used axial coding to group related categories or themes to make sense of the data (Creswell, 1994). We then met several times to discuss what were the general categories or themes and how they related to one another. When we differed about particular points, we looked together at the transcript in question and discussed it until consensus was reached (Fraenkel & Wallen, 2003).

As a measure of the trustworthiness of the data, the researchers sought "analyst triangulation" (Patton, 2002, p. 556) through formal presentation of the findings to the university's enrollment management team and its Advisors' Forum. When these individuals heard the student voices through readings of quotations from the transcripts, many said they had heard similar statements from transfer students. Occasionally a staff member would indicate that a response seemed atypical from her/his experience in working with these students, and we kept this perspective in mind when analyzing the data.

Findings

We present students' perceptions about the following areas: (a) extent of assistance received at the community college and at the university in the transfer process, (b) university efforts to orient and assist students after transfer, and (c) comparison of the community college and the university in terms of experiences with faculty and students inside and outside the classroom.

Transfer Process

We defined the transfer process in this study to include students' determining to which institution to transfer, securing its application, completing and submitting it, sending transcripts, and learning which community college credits would be accepted in transfer and how they would fit into the degree requirements for the desired university program.

Assistance From the Community College. Several of the students had similar perceptions about the role of the community college in the transfer process, as these typical quotes illustrate:

> I felt like you were on your own, as far as making a decision to see an advisor, or set up a program of study, and if you go see an advisor, they could give you advice, but the most practical advice they'd give you was to call [the university], or where ever you were looking to transfer to. . . . I recall feeling frustrated they couldn't help me any more than they could. (traditional-age male)

... they didn't want to help me find out what I needed to transfer, what credits would transfer over to [a different university than the one in the study]. . . . They didn't want to work with me . . . it was just very frustrating, and I didn't really know what to do. . . . I don't think she [the community college advisor] was very informed about . . . how she should be advising me. (traditional-age female)

I went . . . to my college and I asked about them about . . . [the transfer scholarship available at the university] and they said there is no such thing. So from then on I didn't trust them with anything because if they didn't know . . . about the scholarship they're not going to know much about the whole transfer process. (traditional-age, minority female)

Thirteen of the 19 students stated they did not receive assistance from the community college; however, only four said they asked for help. As one traditional-age female student said, "I didn't ask for help as to what do I do. . . . I did everything online basically." Over half used the Internet to obtain the university's application or to determine which courses would transfer. Another said, "What was most helpful to me in the transfer process was the [university] course equivalencies website. So I did most of my planning based on that" (traditional-age male).

Assistance From the University. Most of the students perceived they had received assistance from the university in the transfer process. Students indicated they had worked with an advisor in the college they would be entering to determine what would transfer or they had attended one of the formal welcome programs for new students. However, as at the community college, an occasional student did not ask for help partly because as one traditional-age male said, "I didn't really know where to ask, or who to ask."

University's Efforts to Orient and Initially Assist Transfer Students

Once students have been accepted into the university and have decided to transfer, the university provides two kinds of formal efforts to orient them: a Summer or Winter Welcome program for all new undergraduates and a Transfer Student Welcome, an orientation specifically for transfer students. Sixteen of the 19 students attended one of the welcome programs: 4 attended Summer or Winter Welcome and 12 attended Transfer Welcome. Comments about the Transfer Welcome included the following:

I would have liked to have heard from someone that had actually gone through or is going through [being a transfer student] . . . versus someone that is teaching about it. (traditional-age female)

I'd like just more general advice, like, get to know your professors real quick, and what you can do to prepare [for graduate school] . . . as a transfer here, you're closer to graduation than a freshman [is], so you've got to immediately start thinking about graduate school and how to get in there and what to do. (traditional-age male)

Independent of these formal university efforts to orient transfer students, some students had other thoughts about what the university could to assist them:

I would have liked to have seen a course or something to just kind of prepare you as far as class sizes, because the school I came from I was never used to having more than 40 people in a class . . . and it took a while to adjust to the bigger class sizes. (traditional-age female)

Probably the most helpful would have been something to tell you the study habits of community college versus the university are a lot different. It wouldn't have to be very long because we obviously know how to study, but something to kind of show you the difference in how to do that. (traditional-age male)

They could help by letting people know more about the campus, not just the buildings and what goes on, but what types of services are available and also like different hidden fees . . . I didn't know I had to pay for parking. I didn't know I had to park off campus. (nontraditional-age, minority female)

I think what they [university staff members working with transfers] need to do is . . . realize that transfers are a pretty sizable chunk of incoming class each year . . . and we need to extend things out to them. They're going to need as much *of a hand hold for a little bit* [italics added] as the freshman, maybe a little bit less over the course of the year, but especially just getting in . . . like one or two days just going around learning how things work, where the places are, where you go to register, where you go to file a graduation plan, how you drop a class. . . . All this stuff is stuff that freshmen get told, and the transfer students don't know. (nontraditional-age male)

Similarly, another student said:

I had to find everything on my own. I had to find where the shuttle picks people up, where they leave, and that was intimidating. I had a friend who went here and he took me around and he showed me. . . . I think [the university] fails because they think that because we've been through college already, we're more mature and we should find our way around and we don't need any assistance, but really we're pretty much like freshmen when we come up here 'cause we're new, so I think they should be friendlier, maybe like give you your schedule and have somebody show you where these places are and tell you where you can get your parking permit and not just tell you on a piece of paper, but maybe have somebody take you there and kind of *hold your hand through it* [italics added]. (traditional-age, minority female)

Academic Integration

When asked their perceptions of faculty, students had various thoughts about their interaction with faculty at the community college versus those at the university. For example, one student said:

. . . here you kind of feel like you're a number because the professors don't know you. Whereas in the classroom at the junior college . . . you really felt like they knew you . . . if you just really asked a question, it was more like a discussion between you and the professor because you knew the professor, and the professor knew you. (traditional-age male)

Several had similar reactions:

I think the faculty seem really good up here . . . . . .sometimes I think it's harder to get to know a faculty member at a big university like [this one]; at the junior college I had a pretty close relationship with a lot of instructors . . . sometimes even on a first-name basis. Here I don't feel that's as acceptable and I think it's harder to get to know your professors too in that kind of personal way. (traditional-age male)

[The] Community College was nice because there was . . . a little bit more, I guess, one-on-one time if you needed it with the professors. A little laid back atmosphere than [here with] teachers running back and forth from class to class to grad students to TAs, to office hours, their grants, their funding, whatever they're doing. (nontraditional-age male)

. . . as far as just going up to the instructor whenever and talking to them, it seemed like they would be more available at [the community college] than they are here. That's just because [the community college] is a lot smaller place and you know you can run into each other easily. (traditional-age male)

However, not all students had this view. One said:

You always hear these stories . . . that [at the university] you have these huge classes and your professors don't care and they're busy with their research. I didn't have that problem at all. Every professor I've had—even the ones in the big 250-to-300-person lecture halls—it's been obvious to me that they were interested. (nontraditional-age female)

A few described interaction or involvement with faculty in terms of homework assignments:

In the community college we had more [assignments]. . . . we actually turned in our homework or were responsible for having things done where here you can go a whole semester and never have to turn in anything. You just have your test. I think that [the community college approach] got me in the habit of keeping up on my homework. Just because I had to do there to get it checked off or whatever. So I think I did it. It helped me a lot to just keep up on a weekly or daily basis. Where here, sometimes you'll have three or four weeks of lecture with nothing to be accountable for except when you get to the test and it's real easy to let yourself fall behind in that situation. (nontraditional-age female)

It was kind of a shock for me to come up here and find [there are] two papers and a test and that will be your entire basis for your grade . . . it seems to put a lot more stress as far as the work that you put into the class for these assignments and making sure it is absolutely perfect because if you mess up on the paper, it could screw you up for the entire class. (traditional-age female)

A couple others attributed greater interaction with community college faculty partly to differences in attendance policies between the community college and the university:

Here . . . nobody would notice you exist, so, it's just kind of discouraging when you're trying to get ready at 8:00 in the morning and, you're like, well, they're not going to know I'm there, you know, so you have to make yourself come to school here, whereas over there [at the community college], if you don't go, they drop you, so you have to do it here for yourself. (traditional-age minority female)

Similarly, another student said, "Here they don't care if you're there or not [in class], I mean, it's, it's unfortunate but . . . you're just a number" (nontraditional-age female).

However, one student had a somewhat different perspective on faculty's attitude toward attendance:

I guess you can say that here teachers don't care [because they don't take attendance] but that's really true for any college. Once you've paid your money they don't care what you do. If you don't want to come, it's your own thing. That's your issue. (nontraditional-age male)

Some students perceived university faculty as less interested in teaching than were their community college faculty:

You can definitely tell that there are some professors here at [the university] that are here for research, not for teaching. And it comes out the way they teach. In the community college, they're not going to do any research; they're there to help the students. (nontraditional-age female)

It's really one of the first times I've dealt with the concept of the professor doing more research than actually teaching, then being perhaps more concerned with the research of their personal grant than the classes they are teaching. And it's a bit unnerving because you go from a community college where the professors there have one mission and that is to teach and to help you to learn the stuff and they enjoy teaching . . . and you turn around and you come here and there are professors that you can tell would rather be anywhere else than where they are. (nontraditional-age male)

Obviously they [university professors] are here for a reason. A lot of research. I do find that . . . in the introductory classes that I had to take, it's kind of no one wants to teach them, and I found some of the professors just kind of do it because they have to, they're more into research (traditional-age male).

Social Integration

Some students expressed more difficulty in making friends at the university than at the community college. As one student noted, "It's hard if you don't know people here. If you have friends and stuff, but if you don't live in the dorms, you don't know people" (traditional-age female). Similarly, other students said:

There's just so many people [in a class]. You sit down next to one person one day and you start a conversation with them and you feel like you're friends and you want to sit down [next to them] the next time you come to class and you have no idea where they are because you're in a 400-person lecture hall. (traditional-age male)

Coming as a transfer student . . . it just kind of seems like there're already groups, you know, that have been established since like freshman year and there's this kind of bond, and sometimes there doesn't seem to be too much of an interest . . . in adding some more people. (traditional-age female)

I haven't been able to find my niche or really fit in; it just really seems like I go to class and that's it. . . . I feel this campus is very cliquish and that if you aren't a Greek or in the swim team . . . of if you don't belong to something, really you don't have a good opportunity to meet and mingle with people. (nontraditional-age minority female)

In comparison, at the community college "you really get to know everybody in your class . . . and it's kind of personal and you just get to know a person you have fun with. . . . You really get to know more people in that smaller atmosphere" (traditional-age female).

For some of the traditional-age students, social integration was easier at the community college because when they started there, they already had a social network. As one student said,

Most of the kids that went . . . [to her community college] were from neighboring high schools, so it wasn't unusual for you to . . . have 30 people that you knew because you went to school with them, and so it was easy for you to know people and meet new people. (traditional-age female)

In contrast, one traditional-age male felt the university was

a lot more sociable. . . . I think a lot more people work while going to community college, so a lot of people are in a hurry. They don't really want to take the time to socialize, everyone has their own same friends from home too versus when you go away to college, everyone wants to make friends.

Social integration at the community college was also easier for one nontraditional-age female but for different reasons than those expressed by traditional-age students:

In the community college there were a lot more people like myself that were either working and going to school or coming back to school after a long break. I feel very old and out of place here sometimes . . . . I might find one or two other people that have kids or are returning after a break from school, so this is a very different age group.

One form of social integration, albeit with an academic dimension, is the development of study groups. A couple of the transfers wished to form study groups, a practice they were accustomed to in the community college, but could not find native students willing to participate. As one student said,

At the community college in every class you could get a study group together. Here it's a little harder, it's almost like they don't want to do study groups, and I'm hoping that once I go to higher level classes that there will be students who want to get study groups together. . . . It was just a lot easier to study together [at the community college]. (traditional-age female)

Discussion and Implications

As with all qualitative studies, the results of this study are specific to the particular university in the study and can only be suggestive for other institutions. It may also be that the particular group of students who chose to participate in this study had a different perspective than the majority of community college transfers at the institution. However, most of the findings in this study are similar to those in other studies of community college transfers, regardless of the transfer students' country (e.g., Vaala, 1991), state, or receiving institution (e.g., Berger & Malaney, 2003). At the same time, the impact of the receiving university's size upon students' perceptions of faculty and certain institutional practices may be more dramatic than in some institutions because the sending community colleges in this particular state are so small in comparison to the receiving university.

As illustrated by the experiences of students in this study, the process of transfer, at least in terms of transfer of credits, seems to be less problematic than it was for some students in earlier studies. In other words, the ideal of seamless transfer in terms of credit transfer was the reality for the students in this study, although they did not comprehend the institutional efforts necessary to achieve this seamless transfer in terms of developing articulation agreements. Seamless transfer of credit may also have been facilitated because of the ready availability of the results of these agreements through institutional websites detailing what courses would transfer from what institutions and how they would fit into university programs. The development of such websites has helped change the dynamics of the transfer of credits, with students less dependent upon institutional representatives to inform them about what courses will transfer. Additionally the receiving institution's website about how to apply and what form to use contributed to many students saying they had done most or all of the work involved in the transfer process.

Articulation agreements can serve to ensure smooth or seamless transfer of credits, but they do not suffice to ensure the academic success of students after transfer. Advising and orientation programs at the receiving institution are one strategy to assist transfer students in making a good start at their new institution. The students in this study were generally pleased with the university's advising and formal orientation programs, although they had several suggestions for information they would like to receive, whether at the orientation or in some other venue. Satisfaction with advising and institutional orientation programs is likely to vary across institutions, although recent national efforts to focus on them for community college transfer students, efforts such as the recent National Academic Advising Association monograph (Kerr, King, & Grites, 2004), may be helping receiving institutions improve their advising and orientation programs for transfers.

What seems clear from this study, as well as previous studies of community college transfers (e.g., Britt & Hirt, 1999; Davies & Casey, 1998), is that at least some community college transfers, after successfully completing the transfer process, find their new institution an awkward fit, at least initially. For some students the fit might have been easier if they had received "a hand hold for a little bit" during their first few weeks or semester at the university.

One reason some students may have needed a hand hold initially may be because of the difference in size between the university and the community colleges in the state where the study took place. Given the community colleges' small size in comparison to the university, these students' fit within the university may have been particularly problematic. Accustomed to small institutions and small classes and faced, after transfer, with a "huge" university with large lecture courses, these students may have more difficulty in integrating themselves academically and socially than would transfers from larger community colleges. In this study, negative comments about university faculty were usually linked to class size: Students saw the professors in large lecture classrooms as not caring about whether students attended class and disinterested in teaching them.

Two other aspects of the receiving institution likely affected the ability of some of the transfer students to integrate socially within it. The university caters to traditional-age college students who attend full time and live on or near the campus. The first-year to second-year retention rate is over 86%, partly because of major institutional efforts to involve first-year students academically and socially. In this particular study, the nontraditional-age transfer students, finding few like themselves, perceived the lack of older undergraduates as affecting their ability to make social connections. Some of the traditional-age transfer students also had difficulty establishing new friendships because they were entering a community where many friendships had been established during the first year, partly through the university's formal efforts to integrate first-year students into the institution through such activities as residential learning communities and freshman interest groups. University students who bonded together during the first year in school may have little interest in expanding their social groups and making new friends. Also, they may not be accustomed to finding friends in large lecture classes because they have developed friendships elsewhere, e.g., residence halls, participation in co-curricular activities. Thus it may be that the university's efforts to help native students form friendships and connections may render more difficult transfer students' social integration with these students.

Furthermore, the community college transfer students were accustomed to the classroom as a site for social as well as academic engagement. Expecting to find a community of other learners within the classroom, some of the community college transfers were frustrated by their anonymity in large lecture classes and by the unwillingness of other students to form study groups. Perhaps their frustration level with these aspects was higher than if they had been native students because the community college students were used to some academic involvement and integration in the community college, so not finding it quickly and easily at the receiving institution was more problematic for them.

Another important institutional characteristic affecting student perceptions, particularly of academic involvement, is the research mission of the university. Classified in 2000 by the Carnegie Foundation as a research-extensive university, it is also a member of the American Association of Universities. Faculty receive promotion and tenure primarily because of their research publications and presentations and grants, not because of their teaching evaluations. Thus many faculty do indeed concentrate on their research, potentially at the expense of time to talk with students after class. Some students in this study were very aware that their university faculty did research, although how the students knew this is unclear. Regardless of the source of this information, e.g., the professors themselves or promotional material about the university, students did not indicate they saw a value in having faculty who conducted research in what they were teaching. Rather, some saw faculty's time spent on research as time not spent on caring about students or teaching. Thus it is not clear whether these community college transfer students understand the nature of the institution to which they chose to transfer. Not only is it much larger in size than their previous institutions, but its mission and consequent institutional culture are substantially different.

Learning itself was the lost theme in that students did not comment directly about it. Students did not talk about what they were learning or how interesting or boring the material was but rather concentrated on procedures or conditions that hindered their learning, like large class size and teaching assistants instead of professors. Generally, students did not discuss how much they learned or the impact of what they learned on their thinking or behavior. Overall, students were more likely to discuss procedural issues as in test-taking rather than their academic engagement in university-level work.

Implications for Research

Based on the findings from this study, two directions for future research would seem fruitful. One direction would be to focus on aspects of the college choice process when asking transfer students about their fit within the receiving institution. As community college students were deciding where to transfer, were they aware of differences between two-year and four-year institutions besides tuition costs, level of courses offered, and degrees awarded? Did they understand that large research universities would have less of a focus on teaching than did their community colleges, and if so, what effect this different focus might have upon their classroom and faculty interactions? Or did they assume all higher education institutions were similar in teaching orientation? Understanding the institutional perceptions of community college students prior to transfer to particular institutions may provide information useful to four-year institutions during the recruitment process as well as after the students have transferred.

Future research could also pinpoint more precisely students' efforts to integrate themselves socially and academically both before and after transfer. For example, students could be asked if they had participated in co-curricular activities at the community college and whether they wanted to do so at the receiving institution. Similarly, students could be asked if they had tried to talk with faculty after class about non-academic matters and how successful these efforts were. It may be that transfer students are not being proactive in efforts to become integrated into the institution. Also, we need to continue to ask students what the receiving institution can do to facilitate this integration. Many four-year institutions may provide services to assist transfer students but the students do not utilize them. For example, at the university in this study, there are some interest groups for transfer students, but when initially contacted to join these groups, students frequently decline. Students could be asked what can be done to encourage greater use of these services and activities.

Implications for Practice

The increasing development and use of articulation agreements is leading to greater seamless transfer of credits. However, the literal or physical transfer of the student into the receiving institution is more problematic, especially when the sending and receiving institutions are so different in their approaches to and expectations about academic and social integration. To facilitate a more seamless transfer of the student, institutional leaders could improve several aspects, ranging from the transfer process itself to the academic and social integration of community college transfers once at the receiving institution.

Transfer Process. During the late 1980s and into the 1990s, calls for institutional assistance in the transfer process resulted in the creation of community college transfer centers, partly as repositories for information about institutions to which community college students might reasonably be expected to transfer (e.g., Weschler, 1989; Zamani, 2001). According to the students in this study, their community colleges did not seem to have this information. Additionally, a search of these institutions' websites did not indicate any official centers for transfer. Rather, information about transfer was available through academic advising centers, counseling and career services, or student development offices. Why these community colleges do not have actual transfer centers is beyond the scope of this study. At the same time, it may be that having transfer centers with information available in paper format is less necessary in this Internet age. Over half the students in this study used the Internet to download the university's application and to determine on their own which community college courses would transfer, whether as electives or for the university major. Given the importance of the Internet in helping students transfer to another college, it is vital that institutions not only keep their articulation agreements current (Berger & Malaney, 2003), but also post the current ones on the web page in a timely manner.

Orientation of Transfer Students. The university in this study and perhaps other institutions similar in size may need to reexamine and rethink the approach to orienting transfer students. Some transfer students may need more of a hand hold during their initial weeks, particularly those accustomed to small campuses where it is easier to find out what to do and how to do it. More individual attention may be needed for these students, given the large class sizes that seem to work against the academic and social integration so vital to student retention (Tinto, Goodsell, & Russo, 1993). Also, institutions should not assume that transfer students are uninterested in co-curricular activities. Information about co-curricular activities and ways to join them should be available during a formal orientation session, with a list of names and numbers to contact. Those students interested in the information will be appreciative, while those not interested will ignore it, but at least the information will have been made available.

An important step for administrators at research universities to take is to include in the orientation information about the receiving institution's mission as opposed to that of the community college. Community college transfer students are accustomed to small classes where students and professors know one another and where faculty concentrate on their teaching rather than on research. These are hallmarks of the community college. In moving to a research university with a different ethos about teaching and research, community college transfers have to change from one institutional culture to another. As part of the college choice process, community college students should have considered differences in institutional missions when determining to which institution to transfer. Also, community college advisors and faculty should discuss institutional differences in mission. As well, administrators at the research university need to clearly specify their institution's mission, including its implications for students' academic integration into the school. The value of having faculty who conduct research in the subjects they teach should be articulated, perhaps partly by transfer students who have participated in undergraduate research teams. Students should also be reminded that these faculty will teach the smaller classes in their major, bringing cutting-edge information and insights to the subject. Students' lack of understanding of the research university's mission may lessen their commitment to the institution and thus increase the likelihood they will leave, either to attend another school or to leave higher education (Tinto, 1993).

Academic and Social Integration. Professors teaching large classes can do several things to counteract the damaging effect of large classes on academic integration, whether of transfer students or of native students. Professors should be encouraged to use pedagogical techniques to enable students to get to know at least a few students in the class. For example, students could pair off occasionally to discuss a point or answer a conceptual question. The instructor could then randomly ask for reports from a few pairs or small groups (MacGregor, Cooper, Smith, & Robinson, 2000). Instructors could also be encouraged to give more assignments in the class, even if only more Scantron-graded quizzes, to encourage academic involvement throughout the course, rather than at the end in preparation for the final.

Even if university faculty attempt to create small communities within large classes through various pedagogical techniques, these efforts may be marginally successful. Native students may even resist these techniques because they have other means to find a social community, particularly at residential campuses. Native students may have joined a Greek organization or become active in other student organizations during their first year or two in college. They may have developed friendships through their university's efforts to facilitate the retention of first-year student through orientation programs, freshman interest groups, first-year seminars, residential learning communities, and other activities focusing on freshman students. In other words, the very efforts research universities make to integrate new students may work against the integration of transfer students. Four-year institution administrators need to keep this possibility in mind when they work with transfer students.

The major responsibility for facilitating the academic and social integration of transfer students will likely fall to student affairs staff. One strategy for facilitating this integration could include developing some learning communities that are not residentially based and that include transfer students. Student affairs staff could also encourage individual colleges to have transfer student interest groups where students could meet other transfer students as well as a few student affairs staff and faculty in small group settings. These efforts at academic integration will also facilitate social integration, which is more difficult for any student, transfer or native, at large campuses (Pascarella & Terenzini, 2005). Social integration might also be facilitated by formally connecting native upper-division students with incoming transfers or by connecting experienced transfer students with new ones in a peer support system. Formal, active institutional efforts will be required to help community college transfer students develop a sense of belonging to the university community, both within and outside the classroom.

Conclusion

Student fit within an institution is a complex matter that depends on the student's entering characteristics, the nature of the institution, and the student's amount and kinds of interactions within the institution, as well as the student's desired goals and outcomes of college attendance. The findings from this study suggest that the fit of transfer students within the receiving institution may be strongly impacted by cultural differences partly due to differences in the size of sending and receiving institutions and also due to differences in institutional mission. Having experienced one kind of higher education institution—the community college—transfers from this institution are used to a particular kind of institutional culture and may lack sufficient awareness of differences between its culture and those of four-year institutions, and particularly the culture of large research universities. While the phrase "transfer shock" has been used for several decades to describe an initial drop in GPA after a student transfers, the drop in GPA transfer shock may be partly or almost totally a manifestation of the shock experienced in moving from one institutional culture to another, especially when the two cultures are so different. When community college students transfer to institutions so vastly different in culture from the sending school, uneasiness and frustration with the receiving institution is likely to result.

However, four-year college efforts to facilitate the fit of community college transfer students into the receiving institution have been minor in comparison to efforts to assist first-year students. These students typically receive the bulk of an institution's retention efforts through such strategies as first-year seminars, living-learning communities at residential campuses, and learning communities, or a set of related courses, on commuter campuses. Transfer students are more likely to be neglected or ignored in retention efforts (Berger & Malaney, 2003; Kuh et al., 2005) because, as one of the students in this study said, institutions "think that because we've been through college already, we're more mature and we should find our way around and we don't need any assistance." However, as she noted, "We're pretty much like freshmen when we come up here 'cause we're new, so . . . it would be nice to have somebody take you where you need to go and kind of hold your hand through it." Institutional leaders concerned about retention of transfer students should heed these words and develop helping strategies not only during the critical first few weeks for transfer students (Herman & Lewis, 2004; Kuh et al., 2005) but also long-term strategies to ensure their academic and social integration or fit within the institution. Given the importance of the baccalaureate degree to workforce entry into middle-class jobs, it is vital that transfer between community colleges and four-year colleges "works well" (Wellman, 2002, p. 7) and that community college transfers attain the baccalaureate.

Correspondence concerning this article should be addressed to Barbara K. Townsend, Department of Educational Leadership and Policy Analysis, University of Missouri-Columbia, 202 Hill Hall, Columbia, MO 65211; townsendb@missouri.edu

References

Angelin, L. W., Davis, J. W., Mooradian, P. W. (1995). Do transfer students graduate? A comparative study of transfer students and native university students. *Community College Journal of Research and Practice, 19*, 321-330.

Arnold, J. C. (2001). Student transfer between Oregon community colleges and Oregon University System institutions. In F. S. Laanan (Ed.), *Transfer students: Trends and issues* (pp. 45-59). New Directions for Community Colleges, No. 114. San Francisco: Jossey-Bass.

Astin, A. (1993). *What matters in college? Four critical years revisited.* San Francisco: Jossey-Bass.

Bauer, P. F., & Bauer, K. W. (1994). The community college as an academic bridge: Academic and personal concerns of community college students before and after transferring to a four-year institution. *College and University,* 116-122.

Berger, J. B., & Malaney. G. D. (2003). Assessing the transition of transfer students from community colleges to a university. *NASPA Journal, 40*(4), 1-23.

Bogden, R. C., & Biklen, S. K. (2002). *Qualitative research for education: An introduction to theories and methods* (4th ed.). Boston: Allyn & Bacon.

Braxton, J. M., Sullivan, A. V., & Johnson, R. M. (1997). Appraising Tinto's theory of college student departure. In J. C. Smart (Ed.), *Higher education: Handbook of theory and research,* (Vol. XII, pp. 107-164). New York: Agathon Press.

Britt, L. W., & Hirt, J. B. (1999). Student experiences and institutional practices affecting spring semester transfer students. *NASPA Journal, 36*(3), 305-11.

Carlan, P. E., & Byxbe, F. R. (2000). Community colleges under the microscope: An analysis of performance predictors for native and transfer students. *Community College Review, 28*(2), 27-42.

Creswell, J. W. (1994). *Research design: Qualitative and quantitative approaches.* Thousand Oaks, CA: Sage.

Davies, T. G., & Casey, K. L. (1998). Student perceptions of the transfer process: Strengths, weaknesses, and recommendations for improvement. *Journal of Applied Research in the Community College, 5*(2), 101-110.

Dougherty, K. J. (1992). Community colleges and baccalaureate attainment. *Journal of Higher Education, 63*, 188-214.

Fraenkel, J. R., & Wallen, N. E. (2003). *How to design and evaluate research in education* (5th ed.). New York: McGraw Hill.

Glass, J. C., Jr., & Harrington, A. R. (2002). Academic performance of community college transfer student and "native" students at a large state university. *Community College Journal of Research and Practice, 26*(5), 415-430.

Harbin, C. E. (1997). A survey of transfer students at four-year institutions serving a California community college. *Community College Review, 25*(2), 21-39.

Herman, J. P., & Lewis, E. (2004). Transfer transition and orientation programs. In T. J. Kerr, M. C. King, & T. J. Grites (Eds.), *Advising transfer students* (pp. 57-64). Manhattan, KS: NACADA.

Hills, J. R. (1965). Transfer shock: The academic performance of the junior college transfer. *Journal of Experimental Education, 33*, 201-215.

Holahan, C. K., Green, J. L., & Kelley, H. P. (1983). A 6-year longitudinal analysis of transfer student performance and retention. *Journal of College Student Development, 24*, 305-310.

House, J. D. (1989). The effect of time of transfer on academic performance of community college transfer students. *Journal of College Student Development, 30*(2), 144-147.

Jacobs, B. C., Busby, R., & Leath, R. (1992). Assessing the orientation needs of transfer students. *College Student Affairs Journal, 12*(1), 91-98.

Kerr, T. J., King, M. C., & Grites, T. J. (Eds.). (2004). *Advising transfer students: Issues and Strategies.* NACADE Monograph Series No, 12. Manhattan, KS: NACADA.

Koker, M., & Hendel, D. D. (2003). Predicting graduation rates for three groups of new advanced-standing cohorts. *Community College Journal of Research & Practice, 27*, 131-146.

Kuh, G., Kinzie, J., Schuh, J. H., Whitt, E. J., & Associates. (2005). Student success in college: Creating conditions that matter. San Francisco: Jossey-Bass.

MacGregor, J., Cooper, J. L., Smith, K. A., & Robinson, P. (Eds.). (2000). *Strategies for energizing large classes: From small groups to learning communities*. New Directions for Teaching and Learning, No. 81. San Francisco: Jossey-Bass.

Merriam, S. B. (1998). *Qualitative research and case study applications in education*. San Francisco: Jossey-Bass.

Pascarella, E. T., & Terenzini, P. T. (Eds.). (1991). *How college affects students*. San Francisco: Jossey-Bass.

Pascarella, E. T., & Terenzini, P. T. (Eds.). (2005). *How college affects students* (Vol. 2). San Francisco: Jossey-Bass.

Patton, M.Q. (2002). *Qualitative research and evaluation methods* (3rd ed.). Thousand Oaks, CA: Sage Publications.

Pitter, G. W. (1999, June). *Ladders to success: Enhancing transfer from technical associate in science degrees to baccalaureates*. Paper presented at 39th annual forum of the Association for Institutional Research, Seattle.

Saupe, J. & Long, S. (1996, May). *Admissions for undergraduate transfer students: A policy analysis*. Paper presented at the annual meeting of the Association for Institutional Research, Albuquerque, NM.

Strauss, A., & Corbin, J. (1998). *Basics of qualitative research: Techniques and procedures for developing grounded theory* (2nd ed.). Thousand Oaks, CA: Sage.

Tinto, V. (1993). *Leaving college: Rethinking the causes and cures of student attrition* (2nd ed.). Chicago: University of Chicago Press.

Tinto, V. (1997). Classrooms as communities: Exploring the educational character of student persistence. *Journal of Higher Education, 68*, 599-623.

Tinto, V., Goodsell, A., & Russo, P. (1993). Building community among new college students. *Liberal Education, 79*(4), 16-21.

Townsend, B. (1995). Community college transfer students: A case study of survival. *The Review of Higher Education, 18*(2), 175-193.

Townsend, B. K., McNerney, N., & Arnold, A. (1993). Will this community college transfer student succeed? Factors affecting transfer student performance. *Community College Journal of Research and Practice, 17*(5), 433-444.

Vaala, L. D. (1991). Making the transition: Influences on transfer students. *NASPA Journal, 28*(4), 198-209.

Washington State Board for Community and Technical Colleges. (1989). *A study of the role of community colleges in the achievement of the bachelor's degree in Washington State: Results of the spring 1988 bachelor's degree survey*. Olympia, WA: Washington State Board for Community and Technical Colleges. (ED 303 199)

Wellman, J. (2002). *State policy and community college-baccalaureate transfer*. Washington, DC: The Institute for Higher Education Policy.

Weschler, H. (1989). *The transfer challenge: Removing barriers, maintaining commitment*. Washington, DC: Association of American Colleges.

Whitfield, M. (2005). Transfer-student performance in upper-division chemistry course: Implications for curricular reform and alignment. *Community College Journal of Research and Practice, 29*(7), 531-545.

Zamani, E. (2001). Institutional responses to barriers to the transfer process. In F. Laanan (Ed.), *Transfer students: Trends and issues* (pp. 15-24). New Directions for Community Colleges, No. 114. San Francisco: Jossey-Bass.

Barbara K. Townsend is a Professor of Higher and Continuing Education at the University of Missouri-Columbia; Kristin B. Wilson is a Professor of English at Moberly Area Community College.

CHAPTER 40

TRANSFER ACCESS FROM COMMUNITY COLLEGES AND THE DISTRIBUTION OF ELITE HIGHER EDUCATION

ALICIA C. DOWD, JOHN J. CHESLOCK, AND TATIANA MELGUIZO

The admissions practices of the most highly selective colleges and universities of the United States are under scrutiny for their failure to enroll poor and working-class students (Douthat, 2005; Karabel, 2005; Klein, 2005). This negative attention has been spearheaded by findings reported in two important books examining the shortage of low-income students at the pinnacle of American higher education, *Equity and Excellence in Higher Education* by William Bowen, Martin Kurzweil, and Eugene Tobin (2005) and *America's Untapped Resource: Low-Income Students in Higher Education*, edited by Richard Kahlenberg (2004), as well as by research articles (e.g. Winston & Hill, 2005). In a chapter in the Kahlenberg text, for example, Carnevale and Rose reported that only 3% of freshmen entering 146 highly selective institutions in 1992 came from the lowest quartile of a socioeconomic status (SES) index and about 10% came from the entire bottom half of the SES distribution (2004, p. 106). Demonstrating a highly skewed distribution of access, nearly three fourths (74%) of students enrolled at these institutions come from the highest SES quartile.

Contributing further attention to the lack of socioeconomic diversity at elites, Thomas Mortenson of the Pell Institute for the Study of Opportunity in Higher Education began ranking prestigious schools according to their success or failure in enrolling financially needy students, as indicated by the proportion of the student body receiving federal Pell grants (Fischer, 2006a). The findings of these studies have been widely reported (see, for example, Fischer, 2006a; Gose, 2005; Hong, 2005; Selingo & Brainard, 2006), inspiring headlines such as "The chorus grows louder for class-based affirmative action" (Gose, 2005). The controversy raises substantial questions about the way in which valuable educational resources are distributed and the definitions of merit that prevail when elite institutions choose among numerous qualified candidates.

Family affluence clearly affects what type of college a student attends or whether they go to college at all. This is shown, for example, by differences in college participation by high- and low-income students with "medium-high preparedness"—in other words, those who are not at the top of their class but are well qualified for college. Only 3% of well-qualified students from high-income

This work was funded as part of the Study of Economic, Informational, and Cultural Barriers to Community College Access at Selective Institutions by the Jack Kent Cooke Foundation, Lumina Foundation for Education, and the Nellie Mae Education Foundation. We would like to thank Leticia Bustillos, Rhonda Gabovitch, Nancy Ludwig, Lindsey Malcom, Amalia Márquez, Daniel Park, and Edlyn Vallejo Peña for helpful research assistance. In addition, we are grateful to three anonymous reviewers and Guilbert Hentschke who provided helpful recommendations for revisions.

families did not attend college, in comparison to 13% of those from low-income families. Well-qualified students from high-income families were also much more likely to attend a high-priced college than were their low-income peers (52% vs. 20%) (Hoxby, 2000, cited in Bowen et al., 2005, p. 87).

Socioeconomic inequalities in college enrollments raise troubling issues for education in a democratic society. Providing students with the opportunity to enroll at a college appropriate for their level of academic ability, regardless of family circumstances, is a cornerstone of higher education policy (Bowen et al., 2005; Kahlenberg, 2004; St. John, 2003). Maintaining this commitment has become more challenging as per capita government funding for college operating subsidies and low-income student aid has declined (Archibald & Feldman, 2006; *Trends in Student Aid*, 2006; Weerts & Ronca, 2006). As the returns to a college degree have increased, so has demand (*Education Pays*, 2006), particularly for spots at highly selective colleges, whose graduates enjoy an even higher earnings premium than others (Eide, Brewer, & Ehrenberg, 1998). Students at elite colleges enjoy additional benefits as well, including a greater likelihood of degree completion and greater access to graduate and professional study (Carnevale & Rose, 2004). These benefits have spawned intense competition for enrollment at highly selective colleges, and the recent increases in socioeconomic inequities in access (Astin & Oseguera, 2004) suggest that upper-income students have successfully utilized their numerous advantages to win this competition.

Partly because attendance substantially increases one's chances for later success, elite institutions are important symbols of power and prestige. As a result, the representation of lower socioeconomic status and racial-ethnic minority students at all levels of postsecondary education becomes a marker of a fair and just educational system in a multicultural democracy. As Sullivan has observed, the rags-to-riches story of social mobility through hard work and self-improvement is the "archetypal American cultural narrative" (2005, p. 142). Substantial intergenerational mobility becomes more difficult when an important determinant of social position and earnings, attendance at a selective higher education institution, appears to be the near exclusive domain of more affluent groups (Labaree, 1997).

Furthermore, many are concerned that when elite colleges lack sociocultural diversity, society loses the benefits of diverse perspectives among its civic and business leaders (Bowen et al., 2005; Hurtado, 2007; Kahlenberg, 2004). The exclusion of poor, working-class, and racial-ethnic minority students from elite institutions reduces the probability that these students will enter positions of power in society. It also decreases the likelihood that graduates of elite institutions will interact with a diverse set of peers while in college.

The strength of empirical evidence showing the benefits of student body diversity at selective institutions were influential in the recent Supreme Court decisions upholding certain forms of affirmative action in admissions at the University of Michigan (Hurtado, 2007; Joint Statement of Constitutional Law Scholars, 2003). Studies of the effects of interactions in diverse student groups have indicated that, controlling statistically for incoming student predispositions and characteristics, positive interactions are "associated with increases in students' democratic sensibilities including their pluralistic orientation, interest in poverty issues, and concern for the public good" (Hurtado, 2007, p. 191). Such awareness is viewed as necessary for citizenship in a pluralistic democracy and for the production of "leadership with greater social awareness and the complex thinking skills to alleviate social problems related to the complexities of inequality" (p. 193).

Informed by these perspectives, the agenda to reduce socioeconomic inequalities in access to elite institutions supports the larger goals of increasing social mobility, improving democratic participation, and promoting the civic ideals of equal treatment and opportunity.

Responses to the SES Enrollment Gap

The research findings demonstrating a large socioeconomic enrollment gap support the contention that elite colleges must cast their nets wider in recruiting academically capable students of modest family means. Three high-profile responses—one designed to reduce economic barriers to elite college enrollment, another to provide class-based affirmative action, and the last intended to increase transfer access—have emerged in the face of these pressures to increase socioeconomic diversity.

The first, which comes from a relatively small group of affluent institutions that have announced full or significantly increased institutional aid to cover costs for low-income students at their schools (Fischer, 2006a; Wasley, 2006), is not likely to have a broad reach because only the most well-endowed institutions have the financial resources to make such a commitment.

Another limitation of this response stems from the fact that lowering costs without revising admissions practices does not necessarily lead to a significant increase in low-income student enrollment. Changes in enrollment at the University of Virginia after adoption of the "AccessUVa" program illustrate this point. Although the program essentially covers all direct costs for low-income students—removing requirements to work or take loans, as well as providing money for extra expenses— only 6% of the student body was able to take advantage of the offer in the 2005–06 academic year, and university officials reported that they expected incremental annual enrollment growth among low-income students of only 0.5% (Fischer, 2006b).

The small potential impact of "no loans" financial aid policies (and others that provide complete funding for low-income students) results from the strong correlation between income and SAT scores. In comparison to their wealthy counterparts, only a small number of poor students make it into what Bowen et al. (2005) described as the "credible applicant pool" of elite colleges. Well over half (58%) of top SAT exam scorers (i.e., those scoring above 1200) from the high school class of 1992 were students from the highest SES quartile. In comparison, a mere 4% of students from the lowest quartile achieved such high scores (Carnevale & Rose, 2004, p. 130).

In addition, even those low-income students who earn high SAT scores are frequently overlooked by elite colleges. Despite glaring socioeconomic inequities in their enrollments, approximately half of the low-income applicants with SAT scores between 1350 and 1400 in Bowen et al.'s study of 19 highly selective institutions were rejected for admission (2005, p. 181). Under need-blind admissions policies, institutions aim to demonstrate that they do not discriminate against students with financial need, but they do not take affirmative steps to enroll low-income students when applications are reviewed. Consequently, several observers have argued that elite colleges should do more to enroll poor and working-class students through the adoption of class-based affirmative action (Bowen et al., 2005; Carnevale & Rose, 2004; Kahlenberg, 2004).

Bowen et al. (2005) argued that elite colleges should place a "thumb on the scale" in favor of low-income families. They explored the implications of weighting that "thumb" in such a way as to provide an advantage equal to that accorded "legacy" students (children of alumni). They found that by doing so, the colleges in their sample could increase the share of low-income students from 11% to 17% (p. 179). Similarly, Carnevale and Rose (2004) simulated the share of low-income students at the 146 elite colleges in their study who would be enrolled under a number of alternative admissions policies, including those that currently prevail, which are largely neutral in their treatment of income status. Exploring the advantages and disadvantages of class rank plans, selection from among all qualified students by lottery, and economic affirmative action, they argued that the latter provided for the most equitable outcomes and was politically feasible. Through simulation of their plan, which focused on outreach to students with SAT scores between 1000 and 1300, high school GPAs above 3.0, excellent recommendations, and a strong showing in extracurricular activities, they showed that the percentage of students from the lower two SES quartiles can be increased from 10% to 38% (p. 149). While class-based affirmative action policies do show promise, they face several obstacles. Such plans can be perceived as supplanting race-based affirmative action, even when proponents argue for both. Furthermore, institutions may not embrace such policies, fearing that the proposed admissions criteria will have a negative impact on their U.S. News rankings (by lowering SAT scores).

The third response to socioeconomic inequities in elite college enrollment, which is the subject of this study, calls for a fundamental reorientation of admissions policies and practices. Based on the assumption that a pool of academically able low-income students is going untapped, it involves increasing the number of students transferring from community colleges to elite colleges (Burdman, 2003; Capriccioso, 2006; Padgett, 2004; Wyner, 2006). At the institutional level, such efforts have been spearheaded by the Jack Kent Cooke Foundation's Community College Transfer Initiative

(Wyner, 2006), which has stimulated the investment of nearly \$50 million by the foundation and its partner institutions to institute new transfer programs (Kattner, 2006). At the state and federal level, transfer from community to four-year colleges has gained attention as a potentially cost-effective way to increase bachelor's degree attainment, not only for the poor but also for middle-class families feeling squeezed by rising college costs (Keller, 2007; U.S. Department of Education, 2006; Walters, 2006).

A longstanding policy debate, still unsettled, concerns whether community colleges democratize higher education by providing low-cost access or divert students from bachelor's degrees that they would otherwise attain if they began their studies at a four-year college (Brint & Karabel, 1989; Dougherty, 1994; Melguizo & Dowd, in press). As college enrollments become more stratified by socioeconomic status (Astin & Oseguera, 2004), the equity implications of policies that rely on transfer to efficiently provide access to the baccalaureate deserve additional scrutiny (Dowd, 2003). Competition for transfer access is likely to increase as states implement stricter four-year college admission standards (Boswell, 2004; Long, 2005). Theories of social reproduction and class conflict suggest that poor and working-class students are unlikely to prevail in an intensified struggle for educational resources that ensure upward mobility (Bourdieu, 1986; Labaree, 1997).

Purpose of the Study

This study improves our understanding of the potential impact of expanded community college transfer access to elite institutions by examining a variety of key questions using two national databases with complementary strengths. We start by estimating the number of low-income students that transfer to elite institutions from community colleges. This number is the product of answers to three questions: (1) To what extent are elite institutions currently enrolling transfer students? (2) Of those transfers, how many admitted are from community colleges? (3) Of those community college transfers, how many are from low-income family backgrounds? We answer each of these questions for elite institutions and also provide the corresponding estimates for less selective institutions for comparison. We then estimate the total number of two-year transfers at elite institutions to understand the contribution of community college transfer access in reducing the underrepresentation of low-income students at these institutions.

Our findings clearly demonstrate that elite institutions currently enroll very few community college transfers. Consequently, we investigate possible explanations for why these numbers are so low. Our examination centers on two broad questions. First, do community college transfers have the academic preparation required to succeed at highly selective institutions? To answer this question, the academic preparation of community college students is compared with that of students who enrolled directly in highly selective colleges as first-time freshmen. Second, to what extent do highly selective institutions possess characteristics, such as high attrition, that are associated with greater institutional demand for transfer students at four-year institutions? In addition to answering this question, we also investigate whether the effects of these characteristics on transfer enrollment differ between highly selective and less selective colleges.

Prior Research

To our knowledge, this study is unique in its comprehensive investigation of community college student transfer to elite institutions through analysis of two nationally representative databases. Other studies have examined collaborative relationships between elite institutions and community colleges through case study research and qualitative data analysis (Gabbard et al., 2006; Laanan, 1996; Morphew, Twombly, & Wolf-Wendel, 2001) or conducted analyses of transfer to selective and less selective colleges in individual states (Burdman, 2003; Romano, 2005; Townsend & Wilson, 2006; Wassmer, 2003) or from particular community colleges (Bers, 2002). Cheslock (2005; Dowd & Cheslock, 2006) has shown that transfer to elite private colleges and universities is at a historic low point.

By estimating the number of low-income community college students currently transferring to highly selective institutions, this study demonstrates that elite institutions are not currently utilizing the transfer route to substantially increase the representation of low-income students on their campuses. In addition, by examining the influence of student academic preparedness and the effects of institutional characteristics on transfer enrollment rates at elite institutions, this study helps specify the nature of the problem of low transfer access. Although earlier research has described the socioeconomic inequity of the distribution of elite education and the lack of students from poor and working-class backgrounds among the entering freshmen classes of the most prestigious institutions in the United States, this study fills a gap in the literature by examining the socioeconomic distribution of transfer access to elite higher education.

This article is organized into five sections including this introduction. The second section presents the conceptual framework, which draws on three perspectives informing this issue: policy perspectives concerning the equity and efficiency of education; philosophical perspectives considering the legitimate criteria for admissions to elite higher education in a democracy; and institutional fiscal perspectives that influence admissions and enrollment management decisions. The third section describes the data analyzed. The fourth section describes the methods and results of the analyses, and the results are also compared to the findings of prior studies. The final section summarizes the major conclusions of the study and considers their implications.

Conceptual Framework

Policy Perspectives: Equity and Efficiency of Education

Arguments to facilitate transfer from community colleges to elite institutions reflect concerns for educational equity and efficiency and emphasize four points. First, the distribution of quality secondary schooling is highly inequitable. For example, students from the lowest SES quintile are more likely to attend schools that do not offer advanced mathematics courses (Adelman, 2006). Many students from poor families might well have been able to gain acceptance to and succeed at elite institutions if given proper instruction and encouragement during their schooling. That lost opportunity to learn can be provided by community colleges, which focus on teaching to a greater extent than research universities and which pride themselves on being learner-centered institutions (O'Banion, 1997). Second, the number of academically prepared high school graduates who choose to start at community colleges for financial, educational, or family reasons is believed to be getting larger (Adelman, 2005; Bailey, Jenkins, & Leinbach, 2005), increasing the pool of students qualified for successful degree completion at elite institutions. Third, population growth and increased enrollment demand have stressed higher education capacity in many states. As a result, even academically successful high school graduates fail to gain entry to public colleges with competitive admissions. The education of many more students in lower-cost community colleges is efficient and desirable from the standpoint of legislatures facing structural budget deficits. However, the rationing of access to elite institutions undermines educational equity if there is no opportunity for upward mobility through a stratified educational system (Labaree, 1997).

Finally, the number of low-income students concentrated in community colleges is large and provides a ready pool of potential transfers who, by earning a bachelor's degree, would increase their own human capital, contribute to closing the socioeconomic enrollment gap in higher education, and increase overall educational attainment in the United States. Over 6 million students enrolled at community colleges during the fall 2001 semester (Phillippe & González Sullivan, 2005, p. 12). Among them were approximately 1.7 million full-time students 18 to 24 years old (p. 34), the traditional college-age group most often served by elite institutions. Recent estimates indicate that 48% of community college students who were financially dependent on their parents were from the lower half of the income distribution (less than $50,000 in 2003) (p. 54). Together, these statistics suggest the presence of over 800,000 students from the bottom half of the income distribution, the very segment of the population that is absent from elite institutions. While not all of these 800,000 students would be qualified for enrollment at a highly selective college, the estimate gives a sense of the population of students who are the focus of debate regarding transfer access to elite higher education.

The size of the low-income student population in community colleges is very large relative to the number of low-income students missing from elite institutions. Comparative estimates are available. Carnevale and Rose (2004) estimated that for the 170,000 high school graduates who entered their sample of 146 elite institutions in 1992, 17,000 (10%) were from the lower half of the SES distribution. Researchers have sought to give a sense of the magnitude of the underrepresentation of low-SES students by comparing existing enrollments to the SES population distribution. Carnevale and Rose pointed out that if the representation of this group were proportional at 50%, an additional 68,000 low-income students would have enrolled (to reach the proportional number of 85,000). Similarly, Winston and Hill (2005) estimated that at the 28 private institutions that are members of the Consortium on Financing Higher Education (COFHE), the number of low-income students would have to almost double, from 2,750 students matriculated in 2001–2002 (10% of the entering class) to 5,005 students annually, in order to reach a socioeconomic distribution proportional to the national population.

Philosophical Perspectives: Legitimate Admissions Criteria

Nonselective and selective institutions have distinct "primary democratic purposes" (Gutmann, 1987, p. 194). Places at selective institutions, which are responsible for educating political office-holders and professionals, are scarce and valuable social goods. Therefore admissions committees cannot "arbitrarily" exercise "unconstrained preferences" in deciding whom to admit and exclude (Gutmann, 1987, p. 196). In distributing scarce spaces at elite institutions, admissions committees should be held, Gutmann argues, to the principle of nondiscrimination, which creates two main tenets for judging admissions criteria: (a) the desired qualifications must be "relevant to the legitimate purpose" of the institution, and (b) "all applicants who qualify or satisfy those standards should be given equal consideration for admission" (p. 196).

The application of these principles becomes difficult when the legitimate purposes of the university are in conflict in determining admissions criteria. As places of free academic inquiry, universities also have "associational freedom" to select members who share intellectual and educational values (p. 185). This interest in establishing communal standards and a certain type of communal life may place higher value on certain student qualifications than others. The qualifications preferred for associational purposes often appear to conflict with the institution's equal consideration of students' academic qualifications, because some academically qualified students are inevitably excluded on the grounds of associational freedom.

Gutmann argues that admissions standards set to establish the quality of communal life should be subordinate to academic qualifications because elite institutions function as a gatekeeper to important political, civil, and professional offices (1987, p. 202). Therefore, universities "should be constrained to consider academic ability as a necessary or primary qualification for admission, yet free to consider as additional qualifications nonacademic characteristics that are relevant to their social purposes" (p. 202). The tension between the communal goals and the role of gatekeeper, in which institutions serve society, is exacerbated by the difficulty of measuring academic ability or other important qualities, such as "intellectual creativity, honesty, aesthetic sensibility, perseverance, motivation to help others, leadership" (p. 200). Academic ability and a person's "character" are both difficult to judge. (For other philosophical and political-economic discussions concerning the allocation of educational opportunity, see Howe, 1997; Klitgaard, 1985; McPherson & Schapiro, 1990; Rawls, 1993).

These tensions are clearly recognizable in the conflicts an admissions committee faces when evaluating the applications of community college transfer students. Gutmann's principles indicate that the activities and policies that build college communities, student classes, and cohorts within programs and majors—such as residence life requirements, orientation activities, and major field of study prerequisites—are indeed important and in some ways constitute socialization experiences with core educational value. However, a college's general education requirements and cohort-based educational programming do not in themselves trump the right of qualified transfer applicants to receive equal consideration of their academic merits. This follows even if the admission of transfer students, who by definition begin college elsewhere and do not experience the same communal activities as entering freshmen, is perceived as diminishing a strong residential or communal culture.

Fiscal Perspectives: Enrollment Management and Institutional Prestige

The enrollment of low-income transfer students can have several financial implications for an institution. While any low-income student will depress net tuition revenue more than an upper-income student because of the required need-based institutional aid, low-income transfer students may have less of an effect than low-income freshmen if they transfer in a substantial number of credits. The institution may annually allocate less financial aid because transfers will have lower total educational costs as a result of their initial attendance at a lower-priced college. In addition, for "on time" graduates, financial aid need only be offered for two years to transfers as opposed to four years for freshman entrants. Regardless of the student's family income, transfer students can have very different cost implications than students admitted as freshmen. If substantial excess capacity exists in upper-level courses, institutions may actually enroll transfers at a savings, because they are simply filling capacity that would otherwise go unused. In the absence of such capacity, however, transfer students may actually be more costly than freshman admissions, because they spend a larger share of their time in upper-level courses, which are more expensive (Cheslock, 2005).

College and universities are also driven by prestige considerations that affect institutional economics (Garvin, 1980). The impact of transfer enrollment on institutional status is ambiguous. On one hand, some may view admitted transfers as less academically qualified and their admission as a sign of lower status (Gabbard et al., 2006; Manzo, 2004). But transfer enrollment could also serve to improve prestige, due to a "blind spot" in the formulas used in many influential publications, such as the *U.S. News and World Report*, which rank higher education institutions on indicators of selectivity. These rankings are derived from institutional freshman admission rates and on the average standardized test scores of the freshman class. The fact that transfer students are typically omitted from the ranking formulas provides an opportunity for colleges to strategically decrease the size of their freshman class and replace the lost enrollment with transfer students. This would have the effect of decreasing the admissions rate and increasing the average SAT or ACT scores, both of which would lead to higher rankings and signal higher status.

Summary

The three perspectives informing our conceptual framework—policy, philosophical, and fiscal—are interrelated. Given that demand for an elite education outstrips the supply of spaces, the policy perspective argues that moving more students from community colleges to selective institutions makes a lot of sense. The inequities in precollege educational opportunities and the rising costs of college have pushed students with high academic potential to begin at community colleges, even when the two-year sector is not their first choice. As many of these students are from the lower-half of the income distribution, promoting transfer access can help alleviate the severe underrepresentation of low-income students at elite institutions and potentially can do so at a lower cost than through freshman admissions.

Gutmann's (1987) philosophical discussions of the characteristics of a legitimate admissions system in a democratic society provide a framework to argue that these potential community college transfers should, indeed, be given equal consideration for admission. Finally, the fiscal perspective emphasizes the fact that colleges face financial and prestige considerations that will deter them from enrolling community college transfers. However, that will not always be the case, as transfers can fill unused upper-level class space and, by providing increased flexibility in "crafting a class" for freshman admission, even help an institution improve its rankings in popular college guides.

Data

This study takes advantage of the strengths of two national surveys to analyze institutional- and student-level data and presents a comprehensive profile of the prevalence and predictors of transfer admissions to selective institutions in the United States, accompanied by comparative information concerning transfer to less-selective institutions. The 2003 Annual Survey of Colleges and Universities from the College Board, which is an institutional-level census sample of all colleges and universities in the United States, includes the number of transfer students admitted from two-year and four-year colleges at four-year institutions in fall 2002.[1]

Highly selective institutions are defined as those ranked as "most" or "highly" competitive in the *Barron's Profile of American Colleges* 2003 or 2005 editions and are referred to as "selective" or "elite" colleges,[2] where the latter expression is in a generic manner inclusive of both colleges and universities. Taking account of fluidity in the rankings and allowing elite status to be defined by a most or highly competitive ranking in one of these two years creates a larger group of elite institutions—179 cases compared to the 146 examined by Carnevale and Rose (2004)—than those included in previous studies.[3] The estimates of transfer enrollment at institutions of lesser selectivity are based on all the other institutions with valid data for the variables included in the analyses.[4] The final analytic sample includes 892 less selective institutions.

The Department of Education's National Educational Longitudinal Study (NELS:88/2000), which is a nationally representative sample of the graduating high school class of 1992, is analyzed to obtain estimates of the proportion of low-income students among transfers to four-year colleges.[5] In addition, the precollege academic preparedness of community college transfer students is compared to that of four-year college transfers and direct entrants to selective colleges. Following Adelman (2005), community college transfer students are defined as those who (a) begin in a community college, (b) earn more than 10 credits that count toward a degree at the community college before attending a four-year college, and (c) subsequently earn more than 10 credits from four-year colleges.[6] Four-year college transfers are defined in an analogous manner, based on the completion of 10 credits at one four-year college prior to transfer to another. The sample is limited to early or on-time high school graduates and is representative of traditional-age college entrants. The affluence of a student's family is represented by a socioeconomic status (SES) index provided by the National Center for Education Statistics (NCES).[7] Students whose SES index scores fall in the two lowest quintiles of the distribution are referred to as "low-SES" and "low-income" students.

Analyses

Prevalence of Community College Transfers at Elites

The share of transfer students in a four-year college's entering class differs considerably by institutional selectivity and type. As shown in Table 1, typical (median) two-year and four-year combined transfer enrollment shares at selective institutions are 24% in the public sector, 8% among the private non-liberal arts colleges, and 4% at liberal arts colleges. These shares rise by slightly less than half to 33% in the less selective public sector and triple at less selective private universities (26%) and liberal arts colleges (12%), indicating that transfer is much more prevalent at less selective institutions, particularly among private institutions.

In addition to enrolling smaller shares of transfers overall, private selective institutions also have a strong preference for four-year versus two-year transfers. The median share of two-year students among transfers, only 20% at private universities and 12% at private liberal arts colleges, clearly demonstrates that community college students are in the minority among transfers at elite private institutions. The corresponding figures for less selective privates are much higher at 53% and 43%, respectively. This preference for four-year transfers is not discernible among the public elites, where at the median 57% of transfers are from two-year colleges, quite similar to the 61% observed for less selective publics.

TABLE 1
Enrollment Figures, Fall 2002[a,b]

	Public				Private, Non-Liberal Arts				Private, Liberal Arts			
	Mean	25th	Med.	75th	Mean	25th	Med.	75th	Mean	25th	Med.	75th
Selective institutions[c]												
# Freshmen enrolled	3067	1191	3274	4235	1411	751	1104	1685	459	342	454	573
# Transfers enrolled	999	227	891	1603	186	36	84	229	24	10	20	33
# 2-yr transfers enrolled	657	121	371	1209	80	2	14	86	6	0	2	7
# 4-yr transfers enrolled	342	97	213	443	106	24	52	134	19	8	15	23
% Incoming students, transfers	24%	15%	24%	28%	10%	4%	8%	13%	6%	2%	4%	9%
% Transfers, 2-yr	58%	43%	57%	77%	27%	10%	20%	42%	18%	0%	12%	25%
% Incoming students, 2-yr transfers	16%	7%	14%	23%	4%	0%	1%	5%	1%	0%	0%	2%
N	28				48				70			
Less-selective institutions												
# Freshmen enrolled	1658	674	1327	2331	401	186	317	513	319	201	308	440
# Transfers enrolled	887	354	724	1233	149	61	97	170	47	26	44	58
# 2-yr transfers enrolled	564	176	402	761	81	26	49	92	23	8	18	31
# 4-yr transfers enrolled	323	118	243	439	68	27	45	74	24	14	21	31
% Incoming students, transfers	35%	25%	33%	44%	29%	15%	26%	39%	15%	8%	12%	18%
% Transfers, 2-yr	60%	46%	61%	74%	52%	38%	53%	65%	45%	30%	43%	60
% Incoming students, 2-yr transfers	22%	13%	20%	30%	16%	7%	13%	22%	8%	3%	5%	11%
N	267				431				95			

[a]Source: Analysis of the Annual Survey of Colleges of the College Board and Database, 2003–2004. Copyright 2003 College Entrance Examination Board. All rights reserved.
[b]25th denotes the 25th percentile, Med. denotes the 50th percentile (i.e., median), and 75th denotes the 75th percentile.
[c]Selective institutions are those ranked as most or highly competitive in the 2003 or 2005 *Barron's Profiles of American Colleges*.

At private selective institutions, the combination of low overall transfer enrollments and a preference for four-year-college transfers results in an extremely low number of two-year transfers. The median enrollment numbers are two students at elite private liberal arts colleges and 14 students at other elite privates (only 1% or less of new students entering in the fall semester in both cases).[8] The corresponding figures at public selective institutions are higher, a 14% enrollment share and a median two-year transfer enrollment of 371, but they are still small given the emphasis on community colleges as an access point to the baccalaureate.

Prevalence of Low-Income Community College Transfers at Elites

Based on analyses of the NELS data, the disaggregated SES distribution of two-year transfer, four-year transfer, and direct entry students to selective and less selective four-year institutions are shown in Table 2.[9] At selective institutions, approximately 7% of two-year transfers, 5% of four-year transfers, and 8% of direct entrants are from low-SES backgrounds, based on the combined enrollment shares from the two lowest quintiles (i.e., summing the bottom two quintile values in Table 2). The representation of poor and working-class students in the elite college student body is extremely small in all three groups of students. In contrast, the enrollment share of students from the highest SES quintile is 51% among two-year transfers, 71% among four-year transfers, and 65% among direct entrants, a significant overrepresentation in every group beyond the 20% expected for one quintile.

The community college transfer route appears to be a comparatively advantageous pathway to elite institutions for middle-income students. The shares of the second and third SES quintiles are 1.5 times larger (43% vs. 27%) among two-year transfers than direct entrants.[10] In contrast, transfer

TABLE 2

Community college transfers, four-year college transfers and direct attendees at selective and less selective institutions, by socioeconomic status[a, b, c]

	Community college transfer students[d]		Four-year college transfer students[e]		Direct attendees[f]	
	Selective	Less selective	Selective	Less selective	Selective	Less selective
Highest	0.51	0.27	0.71	0.44	0.65	0.33
	(0.10)	(0.03)	(0.04)	(0.03)	(0.04)	(0.02)
Second quintile	0.28	0.29	0.17	0.27	0.18	0.28
	(0.09)	(0.03)	(0.03)	(0.02)	(0.03)	(0.02)
Third quintile	0.15	0.22	0.07	0.15	0.09	0.20
	(0.05)	(0.02)	(0.02)	(0.02)	(0.02)	(0.01)
Fourth quintile	0.05	0.16	0.03	0.10	0.05	0.14
	(0.02)	(0.02)	(0.01)	(0.02)	(0.01)	(0.01)
Lowest quintile	0.02	0.06	0.02	0.04	0.03	0.06
	(0.01)	(0.01)	(0.01)	(0.01)	(0.02)	(0.01)
N	100	780	400	790	670	1,740
Total	29,070	203,200	82,230	174,470	119,170	393,440

[a]Source: Analysis of the National Education Longitudinal Study of 1988/2000 (NCES 2003–402).
[b]Proportions and standard errors (in parentheses) are reported. Weighted Ns reported for all with known first institution of attendance. Flags and weights: For the 1992 senior sample the g12cohrt flag was used with a correction suggested by Adelman. The weight is F4F2P2WT.
[c]Selective institutions are those ranked as most or highly competitive in the 2003 or 2005 *Barron's Profile of American Colleges*.
[d]A community college transfer is defined as a student who first attends a community college, earns more than 10 credits that count towards a degree at the community college before attending a four-year college, and subsequently earns more than 10 credits from the four-year college.
[e]A four-year college transfer is defined as a student who first attends a four-year institution, earns at least 10 credits there, and subsequently transfers to a four-year institution.
[f]A direct attendee is defined as a student who first attends a four-year institution, earns more than 10 credits there, and does not subsequently transfer to either a two-year or a four-year institution by the time of the last follow up.

from four-year colleges to elites does not provide an enrollment boost for middle-income students. Their shares are essentially the same as those for middle-income direct entrants. The distribution of four-year transfers to elites is highly skewed in favor of affluent students in the highest quintile.

At less selective four-year colleges and universities, the low-SES share increases but is still far below proportional representation. For community college transfers, the combined share of the lowest SES quintiles rises from 7% at selective colleges to 22% at less selective institutions. This rise does not indicate that the community college transfer route is substantially more effective than other routes at enhancing socioeconomic diversity at less selective institutions. The share of students from the bottom two SES quintiles is only 2 percentage points lower (20% vs. 22%) for direct entrants than for community college transfers. As is the case for the more selective institutions, the greatest stratification by SES still occurs among four-year transfers, not surprising given the costs associated with transfer among four-year institutions. In total, these results show that low-income students have very poor transfer access to the baccalaureate, especially at the most selective institutions. Transfer serves primarily middle- and high-income students, and the most affluent students have the greatest opportunities for transfer.

Population Estimates of Community College Transfers at Elites

Population estimates based on the College Board data show that the total number of two-year transfers at elites is quite small: 22,691 at the 38 elite public universities, 4,227 at the 65 elite private universities, and 424 at the 76 elite private liberal arts colleges, for a total of 27,343.[11] By multiplying these population estimates by the proportion of low-income two-year transfers at elites (7%, as shown in the previous section), we obtain the following population estimates of low-income two-year transfers entering elite institutions in the fall of 2002: 1588 at public universities, 296 at private universities, and 30 at private colleges, for a total of 1,914.[12] The ratio of these 1,914 low-income two-year transfers and our estimated total of entering freshmen and transfers (293,803) indicates that nationally fewer than 1 in 1,000 (.0065) of the students entering elite institutions each year are low-income community college transfers.

These figures become even more striking when we limit our analysis to the sample of COFHE institutions that were the subject of prior studies of the number of low-income students at elites (e.g., Winston & Hill, 2005). These schools enroll only 287 two-year transfer students in total, and 21 of 31 schools enroll five two-year transfers or fewer. Given the 7% low-income enrollment share presented above, these figures suggest that COFHE institutions enrolled only 20 low-income community college transfers in their fall 2002 entering classes.

The magnitude of 1,914 low-income community college transfers among the entering class of elite institutions can be placed in context by Carnevale and Rose's (2004) finding that, based on the numbers expected under a proportional SES distribution, 68,000 low-income students were missing from elite college campuses. For elite institutions to achieve proportional SES enrollment strictly through community college transfer enrollment, the size of the low-income community college transfer population would need to increase enormously, by a factor of 34. Not even a hundredfold increase in the numbers of low-income community college transfers at COFHE institutions would fill the enrollment gap of 2,255 low-income students estimated by Winston and Hill (2005). These numbers clearly demonstrate the magnitude of the underrepresentation of low-income students at elite institutions and the substantial changes in transfer recruitment and admissions that would be required for those practices to contribute to socioeconomic enrollment equity at elite institutions.

Academic Preparation of Community College Transfer Students

One potential reason why elite institutions prefer transfers from four-year colleges over those from two-year colleges is differences in the academic preparation levels of the two groups. Analysis of NELS data does suggest that four-year transfers are more likely than two-year transfers to have the highest level of academic preparation.[13] Thirty-eight percent of four-year transfers earned high school GPAs in the highest quintile, while only 15% of two-year transfers had GPAs in the highest quintile. Furthermore, 37% of four-year transfers completed calculus or precalculus in high school compared to 13% of two-year transfers.

While the above figures suggest that elite institutions could more easily find academically prepared four-year transfers than academically prepared two-year transfers, they do not imply that an elite institution could not find a pool of prepared two-year transfers if the institution concentrated on this population and recruited nationally. Based on the above figures, about one in seven two-year transfers have strong high school grades and a similar share has high levels of mathematics preparation, a major predictor of college success (Adelman, 2006).[14] Furthermore, some community college students could join the "credible applicant pool" (Bowen et al., 2005) through exceptionally strong performance during their first two years of college.

Elite institutions may not feel compelled to target two-year transfers in general but could be compelled to specifically target low-income community college students in order to improve their socioeconomic diversity. Our analysis of academic preparation using NELS suggests that some academically prepared lower-income students may be available, but students from the lowest income bracket may be few in number. Among those students from the lowest SES quintile who transferred from a community college, only 8% had high school grades in the highest quintile and only 3% completed calculus or precalculus in high school.[15] These figures, however, expand to 19% and 10%, respectively, for students in the fourth quintile (20th to 40th percentiles).

Predictors of Institutional Receptivity to Transfer Enrollment

Cheslock (2005) identified a number of factors that determine the share of an institution's incoming students who are transfers (the transfer enrollment rate), but two factors were found to be the strongest and most consistent predictors: an institution's attrition rate and its share of students living on campus in residence halls. The attrition variable is influential because, through transfer admissions, institutions can replenish upper-level course enrollments and tuition revenues depleted when students drop out. The residential housing variable likely demonstrates the challenge of introducing transfers into cohorts of students who share many academic and social experiences during their first two years of college and develop an identity as a freshman class.

One would expect institutions with higher attrition rates and low campus housing rates to be particularly amenable to increasing the enrollment of transfer students. The most selective schools do not have these characteristics. In our sample of selective institutions from the College Board data, the attrition rate is 11% for public institutions and 9% for private institutions, while the corresponding figures for less selective four-year institutions are 28% and 27%. The mean campus housing rates are 88% and 97% at public and private selective institutions, respectively, compared with considerably lower rates of 62% and 78% for less selective schools.

Furthermore, the attrition rate appears to be an especially influential determinant of transfer enrollment for the selective institutions in our sample. Table 3 contains separate regression analyses for selective and less selective schools.[16] (See Cheslock, 2005, for a complete discussion of the variables, data sources, and analytic model.[17]) The results demonstrate that a 10 percentage point increase in attrition is associated with a 5.8 percentage point increase in the transfer enrollment rate at selective institutions, compared with an increase of only 1.3 percentage points at less selective institutions. The results for campus housing, however, are quite similar for selective and less selective institutions. The larger effect of attrition for elites is not surprising, because selective institutions can more easily adjust their enrollments in response to high attrition. Elite institutions have an ample supply of applicants, including transfers who were turned away as freshmen. Consequently, increasing the enrollment of transfer students only requires the acceptance of applicants who would otherwise have been denied. In contrast, less selective institutions must increase the number of applicants through recruitment and marketing in order to expand enrollment. They may not always be able to meet their enrollment goals for their freshman class and are less likely, faced with attrition, to have a ready supply of upper-class transfer students whose enrollment was deferred because of initial rejection of their application, a less competitive financial aid offer, or placement on an admissions waiting list.

Discussion and Implications of the Findings

The findings of this study make it clear that elite colleges are not using transfer admissions to reduce the inequitable socioeconomic composition of their student bodies, despite the disproportionate enrollment and availability of low-income students in community colleges. In a particularly striking finding, our results show that fully half of all community college transfer students from the high school graduating class of 1992 who enrolled in highly selective colleges were from the very highest SES quintile. In contrast, a mere 7% were from the two lowest quintiles combined. On a national level, the current number of low-income community college transfer students in the entering classes of elite institutions is extremely small—less than 1 in 1,000. Surprisingly, although low-income transfer students increase in numbers at less selective institutions, they are still substantially underrepresented there, with an enrollment share of only 22% for the lowest two SES quintiles. These findings suggest that community colleges do not act as effectively as we might hope as the "people's college" or "democracy's college" (Valadez, 2002) in a higher education system where transfer provides social mobility for poor and working-class students.

Our study also sheds light on why elite institutions do not typically enroll low-income community college transfer students. First, elite colleges and universities admit very few transfer students in general. This is largely because highly selective institutions have very low attrition rates, so, unlike less selective institutions, they have only a minimal need to replenish lost enrollments in upper-

TABLE 3

Determinants of the Fall 2002 Transfer Enrollment Rate, by Selectivity[a,b,d]

Independent variable	Selective[c]	Less selective
First-year attrition rate	0.5780***	0.1270**
	(0.1996)	(0.0567)
% Freshmen in campus housing	−0.3429***	−0.2482***
	(0.0835)	(0.0275)
Number of majors	0.0002	0.0001
	(0.0002)	(0.0002)
Percent of applicants accepted	−0.0296	−0.0289
	(0.0370)	(0.0491)
Undergraduate enrollment (in 1,000s), logged	0.0048	−0.0322***
	(0.0149)	(0.0080)
Tuition & fees (in $1,000s)	−0.0013	−0.0035**
	(0.0012)	(0.0014)
% of state students in two-year institutions	0.0684	0.3036***
	(0.0536)	(0.0519)
Previous cohort size/current cohort size	−0.1005	0.2487
	(0.1905)	(0.1843)
Public institution	0.0734	0.0297
	(0.0487)	(0.0258)
Location: rural or town	−0.0094	−0.0194***
	(0.0130)	(0.0069)
Liberal arts college	−0.0240*	−0.0766***
	(0.0123)	(0.0130)
Intercept	0.4884**	0.1682
	(0.1881)	(0.2067)
N	172	892
R-squared	0.6183	0.4326

[a]Source: Analysis of the Annual Survey of Colleges of the College Board and Database, 2003–2004. Copyright 2003 College Entrance Examination Board. All rights reserved.
[b]Coefficients and standard errors (in parentheses) are reported.
[c]Selective institutions are those ranked as most or highly competitive in the 2003 or 2005 Barron's Profiles of American Colleges.
[d]* $p < 0.10$;   ** $p < 0.05$,   *** $p < 0.01$.

level classes. When elite institutions do admit transfers, the students are far more often arriving from other four-year institutions (and, again, are disproportionately from the highest SES quintile). The pool of students who can present academic credentials that place them in the "credible applicant pool," to use Bowen et al.'s (2005) expression, is much larger among the four-year college transfer population than among community college transfers.

Given these conditions, before elite institutions will begin to recruit and enroll low-income community college transfer students in greater numbers, the case must be made that they have an obligation to do so. Governed by state-level articulation agreements and higher education strategic plans, highly selective public universities in some states, such as California, Florida, Illinois, and Washington, do have a statutory obligation to enroll community college transfers. Compared to their private sector counterparts, they do enroll many more of these students (14% of the entering class versus 1% at private universities) and are clearly playing a role in providing access to the baccalaureate through transfer.[18] This share is somewhat lower than at less selective public universities, where it is 20%, and perhaps also less than what would be necessary to meet the expectations of policies that place considerable emphasis on transfer access to the baccalaureate (Boswell, 2004; Long, 2005; Manzo, 2004; *StateNotes*, 2005). Despite this emphasis, the majority of states do not have efficient and concrete articulation policies (*StateNotes*, 2005) and some agreements become compromised when high-demand colleges or majors do not accept transfer students (Gabbard et al., 2006).

Here we argue that society has a democratic interest in ensuring access to elite higher education for students who were disenfranchised in their precollege schooling and that expanding the community college transfer pathway is an appropriate way to do so. Then we outline a research agenda to deepen understanding of the most effective ways to increase transfer access for low-income students. Because transfer may in fact provide a particularly efficient way to provide such access, we focus on studies that will investigate the costs and effectiveness of transfer policies and programs.

The Democratic Imperative for Community College Transfer Access

A number of objections quickly arise against the notion that elite institutions are obligated to enroll community college transfer students. Given low attrition, for example, there is little room for transfers under current enrollment levels. Further, there is an ample supply of academically prepared low-income high school graduates available to increase the socioeconomic diversity of elite campuses (Carnevale & Rose, 2004). If more low-income students are to be admitted, enrolling them for four-years and exposing them to the full range of curricular and extracurricular benefits of an elite education makes even more sense. Moreover, in their role as gatekeepers and educators of officeholders and professionals, elite institutions have the right to set relevant academic and communal standards for admission.

However, these objections can be countered by the more fundamental point that the system for distributing the benefits of an elite college education is legitimate and nondiscriminatory only when all students meeting the academic standards receive equal consideration. Gutmann (1987) argued that applicants should not be excluded from consideration on the basis of the associational freedom of the elite college or university. According to principles of nondiscrimination, elite institutions have an obligation to evaluate the applications of all qualified applicants, including community college students. In light of the severe underrepresentation of low-income students at elite institutions, the case can also be made for special treatment of low-income community college applicants, who are among those most likely to have been disadvantaged in their precollege schooling.

Although universities are not primarily responsible for the inequities of early schooling, they do have a responsibility not to perpetuate those inequities through their admissions standards and educational practices. This responsibility can be carried out by recognizing that some students had only a "bare opportunity" (Howe, 1997) to gain a high-quality education by the end of high school. Community colleges provide a critical second chance to those students. It is essential that elite institutions accept the educational attainments of community college students as legitimate credentials for application and admission; otherwise educational inequities are perpetuated. This argument is complementary to calls for class-based affirmative action through direct outreach to low-income students in high schools as well as to affirmative action to enroll African American, Latino, and other historically disadvantaged students. The SES gaps in elite college participation are so large that colleges will need to use all strategies at their disposal to achieve an equitable distribution of access.

From a compensatory education perspective, the evaluation of applications of community college students from poor and affluent backgrounds may be subject legitimately to different evaluation criteria. Elite institutions can justify rejecting some qualified applicants to compensate other qualified applicants who were not provided an adequate opportunity to learn during their early schooling (Gutmann, 1987). The admission of lesser qualified students who meet a threshold of academic preparation is justified if the institution can bring educationally disadvantaged students to their standards and graduate them successfully. To some extent, then, the obligation of elite institutions to low-income transfer applicants hinges on their capacity to provide effective compensatory academic programming and student services. Elite colleges need not aim to compensate all who faced educational deprivation in their precollege years. Only those with the ability to benefit deserve special treatment in admissions and the provision of additional resources to ensure they succeed (Gutmann, 1987).

Gutmann (1987) also distinguishes between the academic contributions of the most academically able and the academically able. Restricting admissions to the most academically able does not necessarily enable an institution to generate the greatest academic benefit, because the most academically able are likely capable of learning on their own. In addition, an intellectually, racially and ethnically, and socioeconomically diverse group of academically able learners may well generate a more intellectually stimulating environment by bringing together students who question each others' assumptions, stereotypes, and unconscious cultural perspectives. Supporting this view, the recent Supreme Court decisions in the University of Michigan affirmative action cases (*Grutter v. Bollinger et al.* and *Gratz v. Bollinger et al.*) provide a "ringing endorsement of the value of student body diversity in promoting numerous benefits" (Joint Statement of Constitutional Law Scholars, 2003, p. 5). The Court's decisions established that keeping the paths to positions of leadership open to "all segments of American society" is a compelling democratic interest (cited in Bowen et al., 2005, p. 344, note 54).

A Research Agenda to Support Effective Transfer Access to Elites

This study demonstrates that, despite the democratic imperative to distribute access to elite higher education in an equitable manner, elite institutions are missing an important opportunity to do so. This is surprising, in a way, because expanded recruitment of community college transfer students is one of only a small number of strategies at their disposal to reduce enrollment inequities. Our study reveals several reasons for this underutilization of transfer, such as the low attrition rates at elite institutions and the effort required to identify academically prepared students. We recommend a broad-based research agenda to further improve understanding of the costs and effectiveness of transfer programs and policies.

Our study provides some suggestive evidence regarding the size of the pool of academically prepared low-income community colleges students, but this topic deserves a more extensive examination than allowed here. Such an examination would help identify the extent to which college readiness contributes to the poor transfer rates of low-income students. Researchers also need to examine the interactions between student aspirations, social expectations, and student choice and how these contribute to the number of available community college transfers, a topic not addressed in this study. This choice process is heavily influence by faculty, counselors, and other institutional "transfer" agents (Pak, Bensimon, Malcom, Marquez, & Park, 2006). Additional research into effective outreach, counseling, and academic preparation programs at community and elite colleges is needed.

Elite colleges may have difficulty examining the collegiate academic record of community college transfer applicants, who typically attend institutions with a substantially different mix of missions, pedagogy, and curricular structures than those at selective colleges. This uncertainty may partially explain the preference of elite institutions for four-year transfers over those from community colleges. Studies of those experiences at the community college that are associated with later success at elite institutions will help develop effective transfer admissions standards. Recent research has shown that elite colleges do graduate, at rates similar to direct entrants, community college transfers who had high baccalaureate aspirations at the end of high school (Melguizo & Dowd, in press). Future research should examine the links between successful bachelor's degree attainment and cognitive and noncognitive indicators of ability, such as leadership and community organizing, at the community college level.

Elite colleges may be concerned that transfers will diminish a strong residential or communal culture. Colleges have a legitimate right to define their college culture and communal values through education, residency, and cohort requirements. Program evaluation and interpretive case study research can uncover what is lost and gained in this respect when elite institutions enroll transfers in greater numbers. Elite institutions may also be concerned that increasing transfer students may require an expansion of upper-level courses, which are smaller and consequently more expensive. These costs can be examined empirically, however, to assess transfer capacity in particular courses and majors. Research into these fiscal issues may show that there are areas where transfers can be absorbed with little cost, thereby reducing fiscal barriers to expanded transfer enrollment.

Any elite institution wishing to substantially increase its enrollment of low-income community college transfer students will need to consider new recruitment, admissions, counseling, and curricular structures in order to ensure success. Case studies of successful institutions will be valuable, although relatively few instances appear to exist. A recent national study involving interviews with counselors, administrators, and faculty at highly selective institutions and community colleges demonstrates that a small number of specialized programs currently recruit and graduate community college transfers (Dowd, Bensimon, Gabbard et al., 2006; Gabbard et al., 2006). By and large, however, such efforts are nonexistent or underdeveloped at most elite colleges. Evaluation of the colleges funded by the Jack Kent Cooke Foundation's Community College Transfer Initiative is likely to shed light on the characteristics of effective strategies.

Finally, assessment strategies focused on transfer practices and policies are needed. Researchers have developed a transfer access self-assessment inventory to assist two- and four-year colleges in completing a cultural audit of transfer-oriented practices, programs, and policies (Dowd, Bensimon, & Gabbard, 2006). Assessment instruments should also be developed to conduct cost studies of the human, physical, and material resources allocated to promote transfer and to determine how effectively those resources are used.

Conclusion

Treating transfer to an elite institution as a valuable academic outcome for students who start their postsecondary education at colleges of lesser status, the results of this study demonstrate clear outcome inequities (Dowd, 2003; Howe, 1997) in transfer access for low-income community college students. That the same can be said, based on prior research by others (Bowen et al., 2005; Carnevale & Rose, 2004; Winston & Hill, 2005), about freshmen admission or, based on the results of this study, about transfer to less selective four-year colleges only compounds the problem. These socioeconomic inequities in transfer access severely undermine a higher education system where community colleges are intended to be low-cost engines of social and economic mobility. In a democracy, equitable access to elite institutions is critical to ensure public investments in higher education do not simply reproduce the existing class structure.

Notes

1. Source of Data: the Annual Survey of Colleges of the College Board and Data Base, 2004–2005. Copyright 2003–2004. Copyright 2003. College Entrance Examination Board. All rights reserved.

   Colleges report their total number of transfer students and the proportion of those transfers enrolling from two-year and four-year colleges. The number of two-year and four-year transfers is calculated from the product of these proportions and the total number of transfers.

   The College Board does not provide a precise definition of a transfer student in its survey, so individual institutions determine which students count as transfers. The definitions used by individual institutions will differ slightly from those established by Adelman (2005) and used in our analysis of the NELS data.

   The survey does not distinguish community college transfer students from those transferring from proprietary or private nonprofit two-year colleges. However, given the relative population size of students in these two sectors (Knapp, 2003), it is reasonable to assume that about 95% of these two-year transfers were in fact community college students. In fall 2001, 95% of the more than 6,250,000 students enrolled in degree-granting two-year institutions were at public colleges. About 3.5% were at private for-profit colleges, with the remainder at private not-for-profit colleges (Knapp, 2003).

   To increase sample size, we used the most recently available data from the fall 1999 to fall 2001 period for those schools missing fall 2002 data. This imputation was used for approximately 20% of our sample. Because enrollment figures vary relatively little across corresponding years, this imputation does not introduce substantial measurement error.

2. Institutions in the most competitive bracket had a student body with an average SAT I or ACT score at or above 655 or 29, respectively. Students typically ranked in the top 20% of their class and had an average high school grade point average of B+ or higher. These institutions accept less than a third of their applicants. The equivalent values for institutions ranked as highly competitive are SAT I/ACT scores at or above 620/27, average GPA of B or higher, and an admissions rate less than or equal to 50%.

3. Several unique institutions, such as the military academies, were omitted from the sample. While all 179 institutions are used for the population estimates, smaller subsamples are used in other analyses due to missing data for key variables.

4. The sample does not include proprietary colleges or institutions that were not ranked in one of the following categories of the 2000 Carnegie Classification: Doctoral Research University, Master's College or University, Baccalaureate College, School of Engineering and Technology, or School of Business and Management.

5. The NELS:88/2000 is a complex survey sample with a stratified sampling design and unequal probabilities of selection. The findings are appropriately weighted (using the weight F4F2P2WT) for point and population estimates. Robust methods were similarly employed for variance estimation using the "svy" functions where appropriate in Stata.

6. Many students, including transfer students, attend more than one four-year institution, and often those institutions differ in terms of their institutional selectivity. Therefore, the selectivity of the institution to which a student transfers can be defined by the first, last, or most selective four-year institution attended. In this study, the institutional selectivity of a student's four-year college is represented by the most selective institution attended.

7. The index is based on the father's occupation and education, the mother's education, family income, and material possessions.

8. There are noteworthy exceptions at liberal arts colleges with special programs that serve higher numbers of community college transfers, such as the Ada Comstock Scholars at Smith College, Francis Perkins Scholars at Mt. Holyoke College (both of which are designed for older female students), and Exploring Transfer at Vassar College (Chenoweth, 1998; Geraghty, 1997).

9. While it would be desirable to observe the college readiness of students across the SES distribution and the three comparison groups, the small sample size of community college transfers to selective colleges prohibits a more disaggregated analysis with any reasonable degree of statistical precision.

10. These differences in the middle-class quintiles are not statistically significant due to imprecise estimates for the small sample of two-year transfer students. However, an alternative test using income quartiles in a larger sample of selective institutions yields statistically significant results for differences in the middle-income quartiles with substantively equivalent enrollment shares. In the alternative specification, the sample included institutions coded as selective in the NELS:88/2000 postsecondary transcripts restricted database. The number of cases of community college transfers to selective institutions increases from 99 to 877.

11. By definition, population estimates should be based on the full population of institutions, not only those reporting valid data. For the 33 institutions not included in Table 2 due to missing data in the variable indicating the share of two-year transfers in their entering fall cohort, the number of two-year transfers was calculated by multiplying the institution's reported number of total transfers, which typically was not missing, by the median two-year transfer enrollment share for their institutional type.

12. Four states with a large number of community college students contribute 71% of the total population of two-year college transfer students at elite institutions: Enrollments at selective institutions in California contribute 36% of the elite transfer population, while Texas, Florida, and New York each contribute 11% to 12%.

13. In this analysis, we examine all students who transfer to another four-year institution, regardless of the receiving institution's selectivity. Incorporating students who transfer to less selective institutions allows us to describe the pool of transfer students that may be available to elite institutions.

14. A GPA from the highest quintile or the completion of calculus or precalculus is not sufficient for admission at an elite institution, and some students with these characteristics may lack other credentials necessary for admission. That said, analysis of the high school GPAs and mathematics preparation of direct entrants at elite institutions indicates that a perfect record is not required for admissions at some of these institutions. Thirty-seven percent of direct entrants were admitted with a high school GPA below the top quintile, and 32% had not completed calculus or precalculus.

15. The differences in high school GPAs across SES quintiles should be viewed with caution as they are not statistically significant at conventional levels.

16. We report the results from an ordinary least squares regression (OLS). A curvilinear logistic model was also estimated to test the severity of departure from linearity in the OLS model. The results were similar across the two specifications, indicating the OLS results are robust.

17. Because of the high concentration of a large proportion of community college students in certain states, we use robust standard errors with clustering, which relaxes the assumption that the error terms are identically distributed, as well as the assumption of independence between observations in the data. This technique is an extension of the robust variance estimation developed by Huber (1967) and White (1980) that was first provided in writing by Rogers (1993).

18. Our analyses do not indicate what proportion of these transfers are low-income students. A recent national case study of transfer access at highly selective institutions suggests that highly selective public universities do not typically collect data to analyze transfer enrollment by socioeconomic status and do not typically target their transfer outreach efforts to low-income students (Gabbard et al., 2006). Furthermore, the higher tuition and housing costs (Long, 2005) and the distinct cultural emphasis on competitiveness and prestige (Dowd, Bensimon, Gabbard, et al., 2006) at highly selective research universities may depress the enrollment of low-income transfers.

References

Adelman, C. (2005). *Moving into town-and moving on: The community college in the lives of traditional-age students.* Washington, DC: U.S. Department of Education.

Adelman, C. (2006). *The toolbox revisited: Paths to degree completion from high school through college.* Washington, DC: U.S. Department of Education.

Archibald, R. B., & Feldman, D. H. (2006). State higher education spending and the tax revolt. *Journal of Higher Education, 77*(4), 618–644.

Astin, A. W., & Oseguera, L. (2004). The declining "equity" of American higher education. *Review of Higher Education, 27*(3), 321–341.

Bailey, T., Jenkins, D., & Leinbach, T. (2005). *Community college low-income and minority student completion study: Descriptive statistics from the 1992 high school cohort.* Retrieved February 27, 2006, from http://ccrc.tc.columbia.edu/

Barron's profiles of American colleges. (2003, 2005). Hauppauge, NY: Barron's Educational Series.

Bers, T. (2002). *Tracking Oakton transfers: Students last at Oakton Fall 1997–Spring 2001.* Des Plaines, IL: Oakton Community College.

Boswell, K. (2004). Bridges or barriers? Public policy and the community college transfer function. *Change, 36*(6), 22–30.

Bourdieu, P. (1986). The forms of capital. In J. G. Richardson (Ed.), *Handbook of theory and research for the sociology of education* (pp. 241–258). New York: Greenwood Press.

Bowen, W. G., Kurzweil, M. A., & Tobin, E. M. (2005). *Equity and excellence in American higher education.* Charlottesville: University of Virginia Press.

Brint, S., & Karabel, J. (1989). *The diverted dream: Community colleges and the promise of educational opportunity in America, 1900–1985.* New York: Oxford University Press.

Burdman, P. (2003). Taking an alternate route. *Black Issues in Higher Education,* 32–35.

Capriccioso, R. (2006). *$27 Million for community college pipeline.* Retrieved March 6, 2006, from http://www .insidehighered.com/news/2006/03/06/cooke

Carnevale, A. P., & Rose, S. J. (2004). Socioeconomic status, race/ethnicity, and selective college admissions. In R. D. Kahlenberg (Ed.), *America's untapped resource: Low-income students in higher education* (pp. 101–156). New York: Century Foundation Press.

Chenoweth, K. (1998, February 19). The new faces of Vassar. *Black Issues in Higher Education,* 22–24.

Cheslock, J. J. (2005). Differences between public and private institutions of higher education in the enrollment of transfer students. *Economics of Education Review, 24,* 263–274.

Dougherty, K. J. (1994). *The contradictory college: The conflicting origins, impacts, and futures of the community college.* Albany: State University of New York Press.

Douthat, R. (2005). *Does meritocracy work?* Retrieved December 28, 2005, from http://www .theatlantic.com/doc/prem/200511/college-and-meritocracy

Dowd, A. C. (2003). From access to outcome equity: Revitalizing the democratic mission of the community college. *Annals of the American Academy of Political and Social Science, 586*(March), 92–119.

Dowd, A. C., Bensimon, E. M., & Gabbard, G. (2006). *Transfer access self-assessment inventory* [assessment instrument]. Los Angeles and Boston: University of Southern California and University of Massachusetts Boston.

Dowd, A. C., Bensimon, E. M., Gabbard, G., Singleton, S., Macias, E., Dee, J., Melguizo, T., Cheslock, J., Giles, D. (2006). *Transfer access to elite colleges and universities in the United States: Threading the needle of the American dream.* Retrieved June 28, 2006, from www.jackkentcookefoundation.org

Dowd, A. C., & Cheslock, J. J. (2006). *An estimate of the two-year transfer population at elite institutions and of the effects of institutional characteristics on transfer access.* Retrieved June 28, 2006, from www.jackkentcookefoundation.org

Education pays. (2006). Retrieved February 1, 2007, from www.collegeboard.com/trends

Eide, E., Brewer, D., & Ehrenberg, R. (1998). Does it pay to attend an elite private college? Cross cohort evidence on the effects of college quality on earnings. *Economics of Education Review, 17*(4), 371–376.

Fischer, K. (2006a, May 12). *Elite colleges lag in serving the needy: The institutions with the most money do a poor job of reaching the students with the least.* Retrieved May 12, 2006, from http://chronicle.com/

Fischer, K. (2006b, May 12). Well-heeled U. of Virginia tries to balance access with prestige. *Chronicle of Higher Education,* p. A13.

Gabbard, G., Singleton, S., Macias, E., Dee, J., Bensimon, E. M., Dowd, A. C., Giles, D., Fuller, T., Parker, T., Malcom, L., Marquez, A., Park, D., Fabienke, D. (2006). *Practices supporting transfer of low-income community college transfer students to selective institutions: Case study findings.* Retrieved June 28, 2006, from www.jackkentcookefoundation.org

Garvin, D. A. (1980). *The economics of university behavior.* New York: Academic Press.

Geraghty, M. (1997, May 2). *Smith College clears the way for community college transfers.* Retrieved May 1, 2006, from http://chronicle.com/

Gose, B. (2005, February 25). The chorus grows louder for class-based affirmative action. *Chronicle of Higher Education,* p. B5.

Gratz v. Bollinger, 539 U.S. 244 (2003).

Grutter v. Bollinger, 539 U.S. 306 (2003).

Gutmann, A. (1987). *Democratic education.* Princeton, NJ: Princeton University Press.

Hong, P. (2005, October 23). The rich get smarter: More scholarships for wealthy students cut out the poor kids. *Los Angeles Times,* p. 6.

Howe, K. R. (1997). *Understanding equal opportunity: Social justice, democracy, and schooling.* New York: Teachers College Press.

Hoxby, C. M. (2000). Testimony prepared for U.S. Senate, Committee on Governmental Affairs, hearing on the rising cost of college tuition and the effectiveness of government financial aid. In Senate Committee on

Governmental Affairs, *Rising cost of college tuition and the effectiveness of government financial aid: Hearings,* 106th Cong., 2d sess., 120–128 (2000) (S. Hrg. 106–515, February 9).

Huber, P. (1967). *The behavior of maximum-likelihood estimates under non-standard conditions.* Paper presented at the Proceedings of the Fifth Berkeley Symposium on Mathematical Statistics and Probability, Berkeley, CA.

Hurtado, S. (2007). Linking diversity with the educational and civic missions of higher education. *Review of Higher Education, 30*(2), 185–196.

Joint Statement of Constitutional Law Scholars. (2003). *Reaffirming diversity: A legal analysis of the University of Michigan affirmative action cases.* Cambridge, MA: The Civil Rights Project at Harvard University.

Kahlenberg, R. D. (2004). *America's untapped resource: low-income students in higher education.* New York: Century Foundation Press.

Karabel, J. (2005). *The chosen: The hidden history of admission and exclusion at Harvard, Yale, and Princeton.* Boston: Houghton Mifflin Company.

Kattner, T. (2006, September). Six ways to increase low-income students' transfer to elite institutions. *Recruitment and Retention in Higher Education, 20,* 1–4.

Keller, J. (2007). *Virginia lawmakers consider bill to encourage students to start at a two-year college.* Retrieved January 19, 2007, from www.chronicle.com

Klein, J. M. (2005, November 4). Merit's demerits. *Chronicle of Higher Education,* p. B12.

Klitgaard, R. (1985). *Choosing elites.* New York: Basic Books.

Knapp, L. G. (2003). *Enrollment in postsecondary institutions, Fall 2001 and Financial statistics, fiscal year 2001* (E.D. Tabs No. NCES 2004–155). Washington, DC: U.S. Department of Education, National Center for Education Statistics.

Laanan, F. S. (1996). Making the transition: Understanding the adjustment process of community college transfer students. *Community College Review, 23*(4), 69–84.

Labaree, D. F. (1997). *How to succeed in school without really learning: The credentials race in American education.* New Haven, CT: Yale University Press.

Long, B. T. (2005). *State financial aid policies to enhance articulation and transfer.* Boulder, CO: Western Interstate Commission for Higher Education

Manzo, K. K. (2004). Report: Transfer barriers loom large for two-year students. *Black Issues in Higher Education, 21*(15), 6–7.

McPherson, M., & Schapiro, M. O. (1990). *Selective admission and the public interest.* New York: College Entrance Examination Board.

Melguizo, T., & Dowd, A. C. (in press). *Baccalaureate success of transfers and rising four-year college juniors.* Teachers College Record.

Morphew, C. C., Twombly, S. B., & Wolf-Wendel, L. E. (2001). Innovative linkages: Two urban community colleges and an elite private liberal arts college. *Community College Review, 29*(3), 1–21.

O'Banion, T. (1997). *A learning college for the 21st Century.* Phoenix, AZ: Oryx Press.

Padgett, T. (2004). An Ivy stepladder. *Time,* p. 61.

Pak, J., Bensimon, E. M., Malcom, L., Marquez, A., & Park, D. (2006). *The life histories of ten individuals who crossed the border between community colleges and selective four-year colleges.* Los Angeles: University of Southern California.

Phillippe, K. A., & González Sullivan, L. (2005). *National profile of community colleges: Trends and statistics.* Washington, DC: American Association of Community Colleges.

Rawls, J. (1993). *Political liberalism.* New York: Columbia University Press.

Rogers, W. (1993). Regression standard errors in clustered samples. *Stata Technical Bulletin, 13,* 19–23.

Romano, R. M. (2005). *Tracking community college transfers using National Student Clearinghouse Data.* Tallahassee, FL: Association for Institutional Research.

Selingo, J., & Brainard, J. (2006, April 6). The rich-poor gap widens for colleges and students. *Chronicle of Higher Education,* p. A1.

St. John, E. P. (2003). *Refinancing the college dream: Access, equal opportunity, and justice for taxpayers.* Baltimore: The Johns Hopkins University Press.

StateNotes: Transfer and Articulation. (2005). Retrieved May 1, 2006, from www.ecs.org/clearinghouse /23/75/2375.htm

Sullivan, P. (2005). Cultural narratives about success and the material conditions of class at the community college. *Teaching English in the Two-Year College, 32*(2), 142–160.

Townsend, B. K., & Wilson, K. (2006). "A hand hold for a little bit": Factors facilitating the success of community college transfer students to a large research university. *Journal of College Student Development, 47*(4), 439.

Trends in student aid. (2006). Retrieved February 1, 2007, from www.collegeboard.com/trends

U.S. Department of Education. (2006). *A test of leadership: Charting the future of U.S. higher education.* Washington, DC: Author.

Valadez, J. R. (2002). Transformation of the community colleges for the 21st Century. *Educational Researcher, 31*(2), 33–36.

Walters, A. K. (2006). *U of Virginia offers guarantee of admission to the state's top community-college students.* Retrieved January, 2007, from http:chronicle.com/daily

Wasley, P. (2006, March 17). *Stanford U. increases aid to cover tuition for low-income students.* Retrieved March 17, 2006, from http://chronicle.com/daily

Wassmer, R. (2003). *A quantitative study of California community college transfer rates: Policy implications and a future research agenda.* Sacramento, CA: Institute for Higher Education Leadership and Policy, California State University.

Weerts, D. J., & Ronca, J. M. (2006). Examining differences in state support for higher education: A comparative study of state appropriations for Research I universities. *Journal of Higher Education, 77*(6), 935–967.

White, H. (1980). A heteroskedasticity-consistent covariance matrix estimator and a direct test for heteroskedasticity. *Econometrica, 48,* 817–830.

Winston, G. C., & Hill, C. B. (2005). *Access to the most selective private colleges by high-ability, low-income students: are they out there?* (Discussion Paper No. 69). Williamstown, MA: Williams Project on the Economics of Higher Education.

Wyner, J. (2006, February 10). Educational equity and the transfer student. *Chronicle of Higher Education,* p. B6.

Alicia C. Dowd is Assistant Professor at the Rossier School of Education, University of Southern California. Her area of study is the political economy of higher education, including issues of access, equity, finance, and accountability. John J. Cheslock is Assistant Professor at the Center for the Study of Higher Education at the University of Arizona. His research focuses on the economics of higher education with a special interest in enrollment management, faculty labor markets, and the role of Title IX in intercollegiate athletics. Tatiana Melguizo is Assistant Professor at the Rossier School of Education, University of Southern California. Her research focuses on the differences in educational outcomes and earnings by race/ethnicity and gender. She has substantial experience in social policy and evaluation.

CHAPTER 41

ADJUSTMENT OF COMMUNITY COLLEGE STUDENTS AT A FOUR-YEAR UNIVERSITY: ROLE AND RELEVANCE OF TRANSFER STUDENT CAPITAL FOR STUDENT RETENTION

FRANKIE SANTOS LAANAN, SOKO S. STAROBIN, AND LATRICE E. EGGLESTON, IOWA STATE UNIVERSITY, AMES

Abstract. Community colleges play a critical role in the pathway to a baccalaureate degree for millions of students, especially among women and ethnic minorities. This study investigates the complexity of the transfer experience among students who began their postsecondary education at a two-year college and transferred to a large four-year university. Specifically, the goal of this study was to move beyond the "transfer shock" concept by examining the role and relevance of "transfer student capital" for student retention. Using the L-TSQ instrument, the 133-item online survey reported data from over 900 students regarding their demographic characteristics, community college experiences, and university experiences. Two hypotheticals were employed to understand the factors that influence academic and social transfer adjustment. The findings of this study inform student affairs professionals, admissions officers, retention programs, students, and faculty.

Introduction

For millions of students, especially women and ethnic minorities, the pathway to the baccalaureate degree can be achieved by starting at a community college and transferring to a four-year college or university (Bragg, 2001; Cohen & Brawer, 2003; Hagedorn & Cepeda, 2004; Laanan, 2001; Laanan & Starobin, 2004; Townsend, 1995, 2001; Wolf-Wendel, Twombly, Morphew, & Sopcich, 2004). In particular, it is the transfer function in community colleges that facilitates the movement of students between the two- and four-year sectors. Barriers to successful transfer can be attributed to lack of academic preparation, inaccurate transfer advising, unfamiliarity of academic expectations and rigor of the senior institution, and weak transfer and articulation policies. Taken together, these factors can create challenges for transfer students upon entering the four-year institution.

Because of the numerous opportunities for students to pursue higher education, many individuals choose to start their postsecondary education at the community college. Reasons often cited by students include flexible schedules, low cost, convenient location, smaller class sizes, and emphasis on teaching. In addition, research indicates that community colleges provide larger societal roles by providing access (Bailey & Alfonso, 2005) and social mobility (Roman, 2007). For millions of students, community colleges are the institution of choice because of their open-access philosophy, diverse curricula offerings, and multi-cultural student body.

The transfer function in community colleges can be viewed as a mechanism that allows access and social mobility. In other words, this function provides initial access for students who otherwise would not begin their postsecondary education at a four-year college or university and instead choose to attend the community college to complete the first two years of general education or transfer curriculum. Because community colleges serve a large percentage of ethnic minorities, women, first-generation, economically disadvantaged students and other special populations, these institutions play unique role in serving as a gateway and pathway to the baccalaureate degree (Cohen & Brawer, 2003; Phillippe & Patton, 1999). Economists maintain that there is a positive relationship between education and earnings. Thus, community colleges can be viewed as agents for creating social and economic equity in society for diverse populations. In terms of the transfer function, assuming that effective transfer and articulation policies are in place and formalized between the sectors (i.e., community college and four-year institution), this function is supposed to facilitate access to the baccalaureate for underrepresented populations.

The transfer function has always received attention among policymakers and researchers. In the 1980s and 1990s, the popular questions raised included: What is the transfer rate for an institution or state? What types of transfer and articulation policies exist across states? To what extent are these policies formalized or institutionalized? Recently, the questions posed by researchers and policymakers regarding transfer have been to ask the following: What are the experiences of transfer students (Laanan, 2004, 2007; Laanan & Starobin, 2004; Townsend, 1995; Wolf-Wendel et al., 2004), especially among ethnic minorities and first-generation students (Ornelas & Solorzano, 2004; Rendón, 1993; Shulock & Moore, 2005; Zarkesh & Carducci, 2004)? What is the role of community colleges in increasing women and minorities in science, technology, engineering, and mathematics (STEM) (Starobin & Laanan, 2005, 2008; Tsapogas, 2004)? What is the role of community colleges in preparing students to transfer to highly selective public and private four-year institutions (Wolf-Wendel et al., 2004)? A growing body of knowledge about transfer students is increasing and the questions, methods, and analytic approaches are diverse. Transfer students are complex and the transfer process is multidimensional. As a result, more research is needed to untangle the subtle and complicated elements of the transfer process.

The purpose of this study is to understand the complexity of the transfer experience among students who began their postsecondary education at a two-year college and transferred to a large public four-year university. Specifically, the goal of this study was to move beyond the "transfer shock" concept by examining the role and relevance of transfer student capital for student retention to post-secondary education within a hypothetical transfer adjustment model. Defined by Laanan, the Transfer Student Capital (TSC) refers to the experiences of community college students who transfer to four-year institutions (Pappano, 2006). Specifically, TSC indicates how community college students accumulate knowledge in order to negotiate the transfer process, such as understanding credit-transfer agreements between colleges, grade requirements for admission into a desired major, and course prerequisites. Laanan further argues that the more TSC a student possesses, the greater likelihood of this student to successfully transfer from a community college to a four-year institution (2007). This study is unique because it introduces a new concept of transfer student capital that has not been applied to the empirical study of transfer students or retention studies.

Literature Review

The studies of transfer students date back to the turn of the 20th century with the early study conducted by Showman (1928) in which he compared junior college transfer students and native students at the University of California at Los Angeles. Early studies of transfer students have focused on the concept of "transfer shock" (Hill, 1965). That is, researchers sought to describe transfer students' academic performance as measured by grade point average (GPA) and the extent to which the GPA drops after the first or second semester of attendance at the senior institution. Since then there have been a significant growth of policy reports and empirical studies that have investigated issues related to transfer and articulation policies, transfer student experiences, transfer process, and minority students and transfer.

The approaches to studying transfer students are varied and include different methodologies. According to Kozeracki (2001), the types of researchers who have studied transfer students include institutional researchers at community colleges (Arnold & Ugale, 1996; Boughan, 1995, 1998), university-based researchers (Cejda, 1999; Cejda & Kaylor, 2001; Davies, Safarik, & Banning, 2003; Hagedorn & Cepeda, 2004; Laanan, 1996, 2004, 2007; Laanan & Starobin, 2004; Townsend, 1995, 2000, 2001; Wolf-Wendel et al., 2004), joint efforts between community colleges and four-year institutions (Adams, 1999; Kinnick et al., 1997), graduate students (Laanan, 1996; Minear, 1998), and the federal government (Adelman, 1999; Bradburn & Hurst, 2001; Hoachlander, Sikora, & Horn, 2003; McCormick & Carroll, 1997).

Investigating the complexity of the transfer process has required researchers to employ different methodological approaches. In her review of the literature, Kozeracki (2001) reported that the vast majority of research in the ERIC database was quantitative (Arnold & Ugale, 1996; Boughan, 1998; Minear, 1998) in nature. That is, these studies utilized existing institutional data or collected data using a survey instrument. Examples of such studies include descriptive studies in which research examined the background characteristics of transfer students, enrollment patterns, and academic performance. Other studies have attempted to identify the factors that predict transfer success and transfer adjustment by taking into account students' background characteristics and community college experiences.

Conversely, there is a growing body of research that utilizes qualitative approaches to understanding transfer students (Mittler & Bers, 1994; Townsend, 1995; Wolf-Wendel et al., 2004). These studies attempt to describe the barriers to successful transfer and identify what the community college can do to improve the transfer process.

Given the different methodological approaches to studying transfer students, these studies have focused on understanding students and transfer articulation policies at the institution, state, and national contexts. According to Kozeracki (2001, p. 65), the types of data collected to answer different research questions include the following:

- demographic characteristics such as gender, race, age, socioeconomic status, major or program, and full- or part-time status;
- impact of completing general education requirements or having to take developmental courses;
- effects of special programs, such as honor programs, and choice of major on achievement;
- grades (at the two- and the four-year institution);
- number of credits attempted and received;
- withdrawal, persistence, graduation, and transfer rates;
- time to degree; and
- transfer adjustment or transfer process.

In the last decade the research on transfer has been diverse in terms of questions, methods, and analytic approach. A popular research focus has been to investigate the experiences of minority populations and the transfer process (Hagedorn & Cepeda, 2004; Hagedorn, Moon, Cypers, Maxwell, & Lester, 2006; Rendón, 1993). Researchers have also examined the factors affecting transfer decisions (Monroe & Richtig, 2002) as well as issue related to student involvement, institutional learning, and advising (Swigart, 2000). A growing body of research has been the result of inter-segmental collaboration between two- and four-year institutions (Bers, Filkins, & McLaughlin, 2001). These studies are important because of the need to share data and information about students and the transfer process. The issue of transfer rates has been around for a long time. Specific issues about how to define a transfer rate, who to include and exclude in the definition continue to be argued (Cohen, 1994; Cohen & Sanchez, 1997). More recently, Castañeda (2002) wrote about transfer rates among rural, suburban, and urban institutions. In the last few years, researchers have utilized sophisticated statistical models to examine the determinants of predisposition to transfer among community college students (Laanan, 1998; Nora & Rendón, 1990).

In summary, the research on transfer students has gone from the concept of "transfer shock" to more complex questions about understanding the transfer process using different paradigms. Educational institutions are social organizations and are complex entities. Further, students are complex individuals who bring diverse experiences to the college experience. Transfer and articulation policies are different across institutions and states. Taken together, these factors pose challenges for researchers to accurately account for the factors that explain how and why transfer students are successful, not successful, and what or how the community college experience could facilitate or impede the success among transfer students at the senior institution.

Theoretical Framework

This study takes a tri-fold theoretical framework which includes:

1. the model of student learning and cognitive development by Pascarella (1985);
2. human capital theory (Becker, 1993; Sweetland, 1996); and
3. the notion of transfer as student retention in postsecondary education (Hagedorn et al., 2004, 2006, 2008).

To ascertain the transfer adjustment of students, the model of student learning and cognitive development by Pascarella (1985) was applied. Pascarella suggests that students' learning and cognitive development are a function of the direct and indirect effects of five variables:

1. students' background/precollege traits;
2. structural/organizational characteristics of institutions;
3. institutional environment;
4. students' interactions with agents of socialization; and
5. quality of student effort (1985).

The authors hypothesized a predictive model by identifying social and psychological variables from the model. To measure the role and relevance of transfer student capital, the notion of human capital theory (Becker, 1993; Sweetland, 1996) was applied. The notion of the theory validates the benefits of education, where formal and informal types of education and training have a direct impact on economic returns, health and nutrition, civic engagement, and overall quality of life of individuals (Becker, 1993). The authors contextualized this notion and applied it to examine the benefit of transfer student capital, where cumulative knowledge and experiences of higher education environment promote successful adjustment when students transfer from a community college to a four-year university. Finally, Hagedorn's conceptualization of student retention via transfer was used to guide this study. Her extensive studies of transfer students using transcript analysis (Hagedorn et al., 2004, 2006, 2008) affirm that students' academic success lead to a likelihood of transfer to a four-year institution; thus, retaining them in postsecondary education. The intent of this study was to move beyond the "transfer shock" concept by examining the role and relevance of transfer student capital for student retention in postsecondary education within a hypothetical transfer adjustment model.

Purpose

This study moves beyond the "transfer shock" concept by building on previous studies in an effort to establish new methods, concepts, and frameworks to better understand and characterize the complex transfer process of community college transfer students. Specifically, this study investigates the experiences and performance of community college transfer students at a research university by testing two hypothetical predictive models. The purpose of this study is two-fold:

1. to investigate the experiences and performance of community college transfer students at a research university; and

2. to move beyond the "transfer shock" concept by building on previous studies in an effort to establish new concepts and frameworks to better understand and characterize the complex transfer process of community college transfer students.

Therefore, this study attempted to answer the following research questions:

- What are the community college and university experiences of transfer students?

- To what extent is academic transfer adjustment of students predicted by background information, Community College Experiences, Transfer Capital, and University Experiences?

- To what extent is social transfer adjustment of students predicted by background information, Community College Experiences, Transfer Capital, and University Experiences?

Data Sources and Methods

The target population for this cross-sectional study included more than 900 students who identified as transfer students from public two-year colleges to Midwest University (MU) during 2004 and 2006. Classified as a public institution, MU is a Doctoral/Research University-Extensive. MU is a land-grant university with an undergraduate enrollment over 21,000 students and offers a variety of baccalaureate programs and graduate studies through the doctorate. Located in the Midwest, MU enrolled over 800 transfer students in the state's community colleges in fall 2004 and 2006 semesters. Among undergraduate students in fall 2006, 87.9% were white, followed by 3.5% Asian/Pacific Islander, 3.1% International, 2.7% African Americans, and 2.5% Hispanic. Slightly less than half (43.5%) were female and over 90% were between the 18-24 age group. The population was identified from reports generated by the registrar's office at MU. For this study, the sample was delimited to include former state community college students who transferred to MU in fall 2003, fall 2005, spring 2006, or fall 2006.

Instrumentation

Data were collected using the Laanan-Transfer Students' Questionnaire (L-TSQ). The 133-item L-TSQ was developed by Laanan (1998, 2004) and was modified for this study. For more information about the psychometric properties of the L-TSQ, see Laanan (2004). The L-TSQ is a comprehensive instrument that collects demographic information about transfer students and their academic and social experiences at the two- and four-year environments. The instrument included Likert-type scales that measured students' level of agreement with a statement (e.g., 4 = *strongly agree* to 1 = *disagree strongly*), and frequency of involvement in an activity (e.g., 4 = *very often* to 1 = *never*). Originally a paper-and-pencil instrument, the L-TSQ was converted to a web survey for this study and was administered via online. The L-TSQ is organized in four major areas including:

1. background information;
2. community college experiences;
3. university experiences; and
4. open-ended questions.

An e-mail letter of invitation was sent to students at MU in spring 2004 and spring 2007 informing students about the study and providing directions about how to access the web survey. Each student was assigned a unique log-in name and password to access the web survey. To facilitate a high response rate, two follow-up e-mail messages were sent to students at different intervals (i.e., three weeks after the first e-mail notice and two weeks prior to the deadline).

The background section included items such as place of residence, highest degree aspirations, level of education completed by parents, estimate of parents' total household income, gender, age, and racial/ethnic background. The community college experiences section included items such as general courses, academic counseling services, and transfer process. A sub-section included items that probed students' college activities in course learning, experiences with faculty, learning, and study skills. The university experiences section included items such as employment status and reasons for attending university. A subsection included items about course learning, experiences with faculty, general perceptions of the university, adjustment process, and college satisfaction.

Analytic Methods

To address the research questions, three stages of analysis were conducted. First, student's demographic variables were crosstabulated against gender and survey year to examine the characteristics of the students in the sample. The second stage of the analysis was to measure observed variables by conducting the exploratory factor analysis. The constructs measured by the exploratory factor analysis with alpha reliabilities greater than 0.63 were used to develop hypothetical predictive models based on the human capital theoretical approach to examine the complexity of the transfer process. The final stage of the analysis was to test the regression equations that were applied to the hypothetical predictive models with the sample. The details of the elements and measures in the hypothetical predictive models are described as follows.

Measures and Analyses of Hypothetical Predictive Models

The hypothetical predictive models were developed by four conceptual blocks that are guided by the tri-fold theoretical framework. Each block consists of independent variables that are measured by observed variables and/or composite variables. The hypothetical predictive models for predicting: a) academic transfer adjustment and b) social transfer adjustment are described in Figures 1 and 2. The coding and scaling of the observed variables are included in Appendix A.

In the hypothetical predictive models, three observed variables: (a) mother's education; (b) father's education; and (c) parental income, as well as two composite variables: (a) students' motivations for transfer and (b) reasons for transfer were included in the first block to measure the background characteristics/pre-college traits of the transfer students. The second block, which measures community college experiences, in the hypothetical predictive model consists of two composite variables: (a) experiences with general courses at a community college and (b) course learning at a community college. The third block measures transfer capital includes four composite variables: (a) academic counseling experiences; (b) perceptions of transfer process; (c) experiences with faculty at a community college; and (d) learning and study skills acquired at a community college. The block, which measures MU experiences, consists of six composite variables: (a) general perceptions of university; (b) general perceptions of faculty at a university; (c) course learning at a university; (d) experiences with faculty at a university; (e) satisfaction of the university environment; and (f) stigma as transfer student at a university. The dependent variables of two hypothetical predictive models are measured by two composite variables: (a) academic transfer adjustment and (b) social transfer adjustment.

To analyze two hypothetical predictive models, the prediction equations were developed for predicted value of the dependent variables to compare the predicted value of the dependent variables with obtained value. Thus, the prediction equation can be written as:

$$Y' = A + B_1X_1 + B_1X_1 + B_1X_1 + \cdots + B_kX_k$$

where Y' is the predicted value of Y, A is the value of Y' when all Xs are zero, B_1 to B_k represent regression coefficients, and X_1 to X_k represent the independent variables.

To test for multiple R, the F ratio for mean square regression over mean square residual was used. Further, adjusted multiple R were measured to examine the overall proportion of variance accounted for the prediction. To examine the effects of the independent variables, significance of regression coefficients were tested. The plausibility of the hypothetical predictive models was assessed by using significance level of $p < .05$ or $.01$.

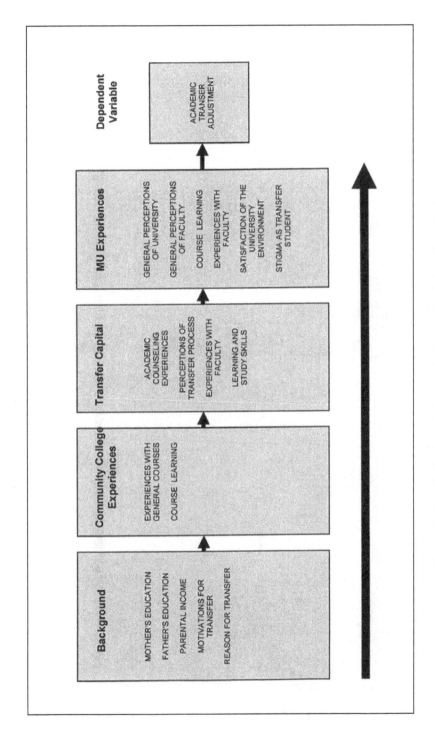

Figure 1. Hypothetical predictive model for academic transfer adjustment.

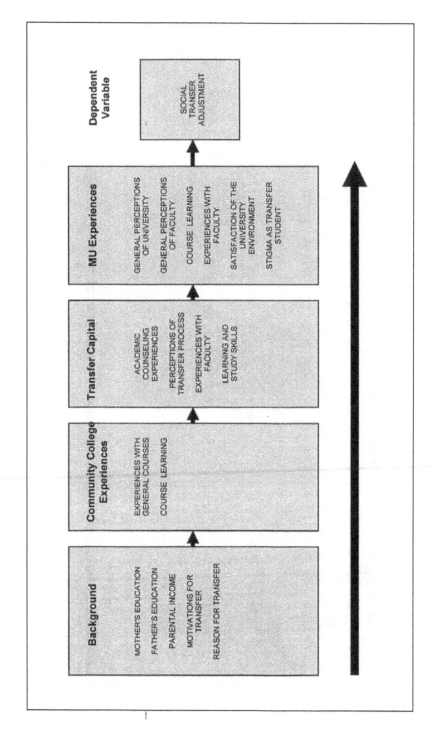

Figure 2. Hypothetical predictive model for social transfer adjustment.

Results

Descriptive Results

The results from the descriptive analysis of the data from the L-TSQ revealed valuable information about transfer students at MU (see Table 1). Demographically, this population was majority traditional-college-age students (more than 87% are 24 years old or younger during 2004 and more than 82% during 2007). Almost 95% in 2004 and 92% in 2007 of the L-TSQ respondents were Caucasians. Regarding the gender distributions, male and female students were equally represented (49% and 51%, respectively). Nearly 80% of the transfer students indicated that their educational aspiration at MU as obtaining a bachelor's degree in 2004 and 2007. When the transfer students were asked to respond their educational aspirations at any four-year institution, almost 80% of both male and female students in 2004 and 2007 indicated that they are planning to obtain a master's degree. The researchers were able to obtain the transfer GPA and the first semester GPA of the 2007 L-TSQ respondents from the Registrar's Office at MU. According to the data provided by the Registrar's Office, 20.6% of females and 14.9% of males had the transfer GPA of A. Approximately equal percentages of male and female students had the transfer GPA of B, 62% and 63% respectively. With regard to their first semester GPA at MU, more female transfer students had A (17%) than male transfer students (11.5%). It is noteworthy that more than 10% of both male and female transfer students had GPA of D, which might indicate their "transfer shock" during the first semester at MU.

Multivariate Results

The hypothetical predictive models were developed by four conceptual blocks that include independent variables that were measured by observed variables and/or composite variables. A complete summary of the factor loadings of each observed variables and alpha coefficient of composite variable are described in Appendix B. Included in the first block of the hypothetical predictive models, the composite independent variable (motivations for transfer) was measured by the responses to a set of four statements regarding student's motivations to transfer from a community college to MU. Another composite variable in the first block (reasons for transfer) was measured by the responses to two statements. Using confirmatory factor analysis, two composite variables: a) motivations and b) reasons were defined. The student's motivations ($\alpha = .77$) were measured by the responses to the statements, which include: "this university has a very good academic reputation," "this university's graduates gain admission to top graduate/professional schools," and "this university's graduates get good jobs." Regarding the student's reasons ($\alpha = .81$) for transfer, students were asked to indicate importance of the statements on a scale of 1 = *not important* to 4 = *very important*. The observed variable, reasons for transfer, was measured by the responses to the followings: "this university has affordable tuition," and "cost." Within our theoretical framework, this first block represents the transfer students' background, which includes their parents' educational attainment, income, and the two composite variables.

The second block in the hypothetical predictive model, community college experiences, was defined by two composite variables: a) experiences with general courses at a community college and b) course learning at a community college. The composite variable, experiences with general courses ($\alpha = .86$) at a community college focus on students' intellectual challenges, development of critical analytical skills, and demands of reading and writing assignment. Students were also asked to report on their course learning experiences ($\alpha = .84$), such as: "participated in class discussion," "thought about practical applications of the material," and "tried to see how different facts and ideas fit together."

Included in the third block of the hypothetical predictive models, transfer capital, was defined by four composite variables: a) academic counseling experiences at a community college; b) perceptions of transfer process; c) experiences with faculty at a community college; and d) learning and study skills acquired at a community college. The composite variable, academic counseling experiences ($\alpha = .93$) at a community college focus on students' experiences with their academic counsel-

Table 1. Descriptive Statistics for Selected L-TSQ Variables (N = 918)

| | 2004 | | | | 2007 | | | |
| | Male | | Female | | Male | | Female | |
	Frequency	Percentage	Frequency	Percentage	Frequency	Percentage	Frequency	Percentage
Racial/Ethnic Background								
Native American/Alaskan Native	3	1.9%	0	0.0%	6	2.0%	2	0.7%
African American/Black	1	0.6%	0	0.0%	7	2.4%	4	1.3%
White (non-Hispanic)	144	92.9%	158	97.5%	265	89.8%	287	93.8%
Asian American/Pacific Islander	3	1.9%	2	1.2%	6	2.0%	3	1.0%
Hispanic or Latino/a	2	1.3%	0	0.0%	2	0.7%	4	1.3%
Other	2	1.3%	2	1.2%	6	2.0%	5	1.6%
Missing					3	1.0%	1	0.3%
n	155	100.0%	162	100.0%	295	100.0%	306	100.0%
Age								
18-19	11	7.1%	5	3.1%	11	3.7%	16	5.2%
20	31	20.0%	49	30.2%	45	15.3%	50	16.3%
21-24	91	58.7%	91	56.2%	193	65.4%	185	60.5%
25-29	15	9.7%	8	4.9%	27	9.2%	29	9.5%
30-39	5	3.2%	8	4.9%	13	4.4%	15	4.9%
40-54	2	1.3%	1	0.6%	5	1.7%	9	2.9%
Missing	0	0.0%	0	0.0%	1	0.3%	2	0.7%
n	155	100.0%	162	100.0%	295	100.0%	306	100.0%

Highest Degree Planned at ISU

	n	%	n	%	n	%	n	%
Bachelor's	128	82.6%	132	81.5%	231	78.3%	248	81.0%
Master's	18	11.6%	16	9.9%	40	13.6%	37	12.1%
Doctorate	2	1.3%	1	0.6%	8	2.7%	4	1.3%
Medical	0	0.0%	7	4.3%	0	0.0%	0	0.0%
Law	0	0.0%	0	0.0%	0	0.0%	0	0.0%
Other	6	3.9%	5	3.1%	9	3.1%	11	3.6%
Missing	1	0.6%	1	0.6%	7	2.4%	6	2.0%
n	155	100.0%	162	100.0%	295	100.0%	306	100.0%

Highest Degree Planned at Any Institution

	n	%	n	%	n	%	n	%
Bachelor's	95	61.3%	91	56.2%	152	51.5%	143	46.7%
Master's	40	25.8%	44	27.2%	87	29.5%	96	31.4%
Doctorate	7	4.5%	9	5.6%	27	9.2%	32	10.5%
Medical	5	3.2%	10	6.2%	9	3.1%	16	5.2%
Law	1	0.6%	3	1.9%	4	1.4%	2	0.7%
Other	6	3.9%	4	2.5%	14	4.7%	15	4.9%
Missing	1	0.6%	1	0.6%	2	0.7%	2	0.7%
n	155	100.0%	162	100.0%	295	100.0%	306	100.0%

ing. Students also responded to questions regarding perceptions of transfer process (α = .77), such as "I spoke to academic counselors at MU about transferring and major requirements" and "I visited the admission office at MU." Regarding the composite variable, the experiences with faculty (α = .91), students responded to six items such as "visited faculty and sought their advise on class," responding to statements on a scale of 1 = *never* to 4 = *very often*. Responses to a set of eight statements defined student's learning and study skills (α = .90). Students were asked to self-report their skills on a scale of 1 = *disagree strongly* to 5 = *agree strongly*. Those learning and study skills include: "note taking skills," "problem solving skills," and "time management skills."

Student's experiences at MU were measured by six composite variables. These six composite variables are: a) general perceptions of university; b) general perceptions of faculty at MU; c) course learning at MU; d) experiences with faculty at MU; e) satisfaction of the university environment; and f) stigma as a transfer student at MU. Responses to three statements, such as "this university is an intellectually stimulating and often exciting place to be" and "I would recommend to other transfer students to come to this university" measured student's general perceptions of university (α = .83). With regard to students' general perceptions of faculty (α = .82), students responded to three items on a scale of 1 = *disagree strongly* to 5 = *agree strongly* to the statements: "university faculty are easy to approach," "university faculty tend to be accessible to students," and "professors are strongly interested in the academic development of undergraduates." Students were also asked to respond to the statements that focus on their course learning experiences (α = .82) at MU. The fourth composite variable was measured by the responses to a set of six statements. The experiences with faculty (α = .91) measured the frequency of students' interactions with faculty at MU. Responses to five statements, such as "overall quality of instruction" and "overall college experience" measured students' satisfaction of the university (α = .86). The last composite variable in this block, stigma as a transfer student (α = .87) was measured by the responses to three statements, which include "there is a stigma at MU among students for having started at a community college," and "Because I was a community college transfer, most faculty tend to underestimate my abilities."

The dependent variable of the hypothetical predictive model for academic transfer adjustment is a composite variable measured by two observed variables. Students were asked to respond on a scale of 1 = *disagree strongly* to 4 = *agree strongly* to four statements focusing on their academic transfer adjustment (α = .63). These statements include: "adjusting to the academic standards or expectations at MU has been easy," and "I experienced a dip in grades (GPA) during my first semester at MU."

The dependent variable of the hypothetical predictive model for social transfer adjustment is a composite variable measured by three observed variables. This composite variable (α = .76) was defined by responses to statements include: "adjusting to the social environment at MU has been easy," "I am meeting as many people and making as many friends as I would like at this university," and "It is easy making friends at this university."

Hierarchical Multiple Regression Results

To examine the factors that affect the successful transfer adjustment among transfer students, this study analyzed the hypothetical predictive models. The validity of the hypothetical predictive models was examined by R squared, F ratio, adjusted R squared values. Further, the significance of regression coefficients were examined at a significance level of p < .05 or .01.

Predictive Model for Academic Transfer Adjustment

The result from the analysis of the predictive model for academic transfer adjustment reveals that R squared change was significantly different at the end of each block. After the fourth block was entered, with all independent variables in the equation, R^2 = .22, $F(17, 665)$ = 11.03, p < .01 were found. The adjusted R^2 value of .20 indicates that 20% of the variability in students' academic transfer adjustment is predicted by students' background, community college experiences, transfer capital, and experiences at MU. To examine the results of the significance of the standardized coefficients for each independent variable, a significance level of p < .05 or .01 was used. From the background block, motivations for transfer was found statistically significant ($\beta = -.14$) at $p < .01$. Within the community college experience block, students' experiences with general courses at a community college was found statistically significant ($\beta = .15$) at $p < .01$. Also found as statistically significant independent variables were in the transfer capital block: a) academic counseling experiences ($\beta = -.09$) at $p < .05$ and b) learning and study skills acquired at a community college ($\beta = .26$) at $p < .01$. From the MU experiences block, three independent variables were found statistically significant predictor of students' academic transfer adjustment: a) general perceptions of university ($\beta = .11$) at $p < .05$; b) course learning at MU ($\beta = .16$) at $p < .01$; and c) stigma as a transfer student ($\beta = -.10$) at $p < .01$ (see Table 2).

Predictive Model for Social Transfer Adjustment

The result from the analysis of the social transfer adjustment predictive model reveals that R squared change was significantly different at the end of each block. After the fourth block was entered, with all independent variables in the equation, $R^2 = .32$, $F(17, 660) = 17.90$, $p < .01$ were found. The adjusted R^2 value of .30 indicates that a third of the variability in students' social transfer adjustment is predicted by students' background, community college experiences, transfer capital, and experiences at MU. To examine the results of the significance of the standardized coefficients for each independent variable, a significance level of $p < .05$ or .01 was used. The results revealed that none of the independent variables from the background block was found statistically significant. Within the community college experience block, students' course learning at a community college was found statistically significant ($\beta = -.12$) at $p < .05$. Unlike the results found from the academic transfer adjustment model, none of the independent variables from the transfer capital block were found statistically significant. Finally, from the MU experiences block, two independent variables were found statistically significant predictor of students' social transfer adjustment: a) experiences with faculty at MU ($\beta = .11$) at $p < .05$; and b) satisfaction of the university environment ($\beta = .46$) at $p < .01$ (see Table 3).

Discussion and Conclusions

The hypothetical predictive models were examined to better understand the complexity of factors that influence academic and social transfer adjustments of transfer students. The following discussion addresses key findings drawn from the results of the study. With regard to students' academic transfer adjustment, students' motivations for transfer and academic counseling experiences at a community college were negatively influencing the academic adjustment. It might be that the transfer students did not receive accurate or adequate information regarding transferring from their community colleges. One of the key findings was the positive influence of learning and study skills at a community college, which is as conceptualized as Transfer Student Capital, on the students' academic transfer adjustment. The examples of the learning and study skills that are found as significant include: "note taking skills," "problem solving skills," and "time management skills." Perhaps, smaller class sizes and intimate class interaction among faculty and students at a community college might contribute to increase students' learning and study skills that resulted in a significant factor in adjusting academically at MU. Another interesting finding was the significant influences of students' positive course learning as well as being stigmatized as transfer students on their academic transfer adjustment. The finding revealed when students recognize their faculty and/or campus environment stigmatize them as transfer students negatively, such experiences would impede students' academic transfer adjustment. It is also assumed that the stigma can negatively influence students' course learning experiences at MU; thus, that would negatively influence on students' academic transfer adjustment.

Although only few independent variables were found statistically significant to predict students' social transfer adjustment, there are some important findings from the analysis. For instance, it was interesting to find that course learning at a community college was not positively influencing students' social transfer adjustment at MU. It might be that students developed their social skills regardless of their course learning experiences at a community college. Further, students' experiences

Table 2. Hierarchical Regression of Background, Community
College Experiences, Transfer Capital, and
MU Experiences on Academic Transfer Adjustment

Variables	B	Std. error	β	t	Sig.	R square	Adjusted R square
Background Block						.003	−.005
Mother's education	.052	.052	.045	1.012	.312		
Father's education	−.024	.048	−.023	−.504	.614		
Parental income	−.028	.045	−.024	−.622	.534		
Motivations for transfer	−.018	.024	−.03	−.733	.464		
Reason for transfer	.022	.041	.023	.544	.587		
With Community College Experiences Block						.069	.059
Mother's education	.044	.05	.038	.874	.382		
Father's education	−.025	.047	−.023	−.53	.597		
Parental income	−.023	.044	−.02	−.516	.606		
Motivations for transfer	−.02	.023	−.034	−.853	.394		
Reason for transfer	.007	.04	.007	.184	.854		
Experiences with general courses	.12	.02	.256**	6.085	0		
Course learning	.001	.021	.003	.066	.947		
With Transfer Capital Block						.127	.113
Mother's education	.05	.049	.043	1.018	.309		
Father's education	−.039	.046	−.036	−.845	.398		
Parental income	−.047	.043	−.041	−1.102	.271		
Motivations for transfer	−.028	.024	−.048	−1.193	.233		
Reason for transfer	−.006	.039	−.006	−.16	.873		
Experiences with general courses	.061	.023	.13**	2.625	.009		
Course learning	−.005	.024	−.009	−.19	.849		
Academic counseling experiences	−.03	.013	−.092*	−2.347	.019		
Perceptions of transfer process	.027	.024	.044	1.136	.256		
Experience with faculty	−.046	.017	−.122**	−2.638	.009		
Learning and study skills	.083	.014	.297**	5.779	0		

Table 2. (Cont'd.)

Variables	B	Std. error	β	t	Sig.	R square	Adjusted R square
With MU Experiences Block						.22	.2
Mother's education	.046	.047	.039	.976	.33		
Father's education	−.035	.044	−.032	−.801	.423		
Parental income	−.046	.042	−.04	−1.098	.273		
Motivations for transfer	−.08	.024	−.137**	−3.357	.001		
Reason for transfer	−.016	.037	−.016	−.421	.674		
Experiences with general courses	.071	.023	.151**	3.154	.002		
Course learning	−.028	.026	−.055	−1.078	.281		
Academic counseling experiences	−.027	.012	−.085*	−2.266	.024		
Perceptions of transfer process	−.017	.023	−.028	−.742	.458		
Experience with faculty	−.025	.017	−.066	−1.443	.149		
Learning and study skills	.073	.014	.261**	5.239	0		
General perceptions of university	.097	.046	.111*	2.087	.037		
General perceptions of faculty	.037	.043	.043	.849	.396		
Course learning	.093	.027	.159**	3.479	.001		
Experiences with faculty	.015	.02	.036	.737	.462		
Satisfaction of the university environment	.043	.036	.067	1.176	.24		
Stigma as transfer student	−.069	.026	−.097**	−2.632	.009		

*p < .05. **p < .01.

Table 3. Hierarchical Regression of Background, Community College Experiences, Transfer Capital, and MU Experiences on Social Transfer Adjustment

Variables	B	Std. error	β	t	Sig.	R square	Adjusted R square
Background Block						.037	.03
Mother's education	.082	.062	.059	1.33	.184		
Father's education	−.032	.058	−.024	−0.55	.581		
Parental income	.05	.054	.036	0.92	.357		
Motivations for transfer	.125	.029	.178**	4.39	0		
Reason for transfer	.018	.049	.015	0.37	.708		
With Community College Experiences Block						.05	.04
Mother's education	.078	.061	.056	1.28	.202		
Father's education	−.02	.057	−.016	−0.35	.724		
Parental income	.032	.054	.023	0.59	.554		
Motivations for transfer	.134	.028	.191**	4.70	0		
Reason for transfer	.023	.049	.019	0.48	.633		
Experiences with general courses	.019	.024	.033	0.78	.437		
Course learning	−.079	.026	.13**	−3.03	.003		
With Transfer Capital Block						.091	.076
Mother's education	.074	.06	.053	1.23	.219		
Father's education	−.011	.056	−.009	−0.20	.843		
Parental income	.027	.053	.019	0.51	.613		
Motivations for transfer	.092	.029	.131**	3.14	.002		
Reason for transfer	.019	.048	.016	0.40	.692		
Experiences with general courses	−.019	.029	−.034	−0.67	.505		
Course learning	−.095	.03	−.156**	−3.14	.002		
Academic counseling experiences	.014	.016	.036	0.90	.367		
Perceptions of transfer process	.141	.029	.192**	4.87	0		
Experience with faculty	−.003	.021	−.006	−0.12	.902		
Learning and study skills	.026	.018	.077	1.47	.143		

Table 3. (Cont'd.)

Variables	B	Std. error	β	t	Sig.	R square	Adjusted R square
With MU Experiences Block						.316	.298
Mother's education	.051	.053	.036	0.96	.338		
Father's education	−.002	.049	−.001	−0.03	.974		
Parental income	−.015	.047	−.011	−0.32	.748		
Motivations for transfer	−.023	.027	−.033	−0.85	.395		
Reason for transfer	−.017	.043	−.014	−0.39	.697		
Experiences with general courses	−.027	.026	−.048	−1.07	.286		
Course learning	−.074	.029	−.122*	−2.54	.011		
Academic counseling experiences	.017	.014	.045	1.27	.205		
Perceptions of transfer process	.046	.026	.063	1.78	.076		
Experience with faculty	.022	.02	.048	1.12	.264		
Learning and study skills	.017	.016	.049	1.06	.29		
General perceptions of university	.005	.052	.005	0.09	.926		
General perceptions of faculty	−.043	.049	−.041	−0.87	.384		
Course learning	.046	.03	.066	1.53	.125		
Experiences with faculty	.051	.023	.105*	2.28	.023		
Satisfaction of the university environment	.354	.041	.464**	8.65	0		
Stigma as transfer student	−.053	.03	−.061	−1.78	.076		

*p < .05. **p < .01.

with faculty at MU were found as a significant factor that could positively influence students' social transfer adjustment. Perhaps, these students expect frequent and deeper interaction with faculty as they might have experienced at a community college in the past. Finally, the satisfaction of the university environment was important factor for students to socially adjust to MU. Again, the transfer students might expect that the university campus environment to be as friendly, welcome, and satisfying as that was at their community college. To make students feel included and comfortable, it is important for MU community to create a welcoming campus environment.

Finally, the results of this study provided insights for future studies. In this study, the measurement of transfer capital was limited to the students' retrospective responses to academic counseling experiences at a community college, their perceptions of transfer process, experiences with faculty and learning and study skills acquired at a community college. Taking the human capital theoretical approach to understand the role and relevance of transfer capital, measurements for student's prior knowledge of: transfer articulation policy and practices between a community college and MU, financial aid to transfer, and other critical knowledge that facilitate seamless transfer can be included in future studies. Further, as Laanan (1998) indicated in his earlier study, the negative impact of stigma as transfer student on students' academic transfer adjustment deserve attention for further investigation. Future research that examines perceptions among faculty, staff, and students at MU toward community college transfer students might provide a better understanding of the influence of stigma on students' academic transfer adjustment.

Implications

The findings of this study are important and can be useful to student affairs professionals, admissions officers, retention programs, students, and faculty. At the two-year colleges, academic counselors need to be aware of the types of information and services prospective transfers need in order to make the successful transition to a four-year university. Faculty can also play an important role. The extent to which the curriculum at the two-year college is rigorous and requires students to do more reading, writing, and researching will improve student preparation for the four-year institution. To enhance transfer student capital, universities can offer new transfer students important information during orientation sessions about the strategies for a successful transition. Workshops offered by the university can also incorporate information gathered from this study. As additional contributor to enhance transfer student capital, various counseling services can provide assistance to transfer students. In working with students individually, counselors will be better informed about transfer students' issues and concerns and will be better prepared to assist students in their social, psychological, and academic adjustment process. Student affairs professionals (e.g., residential life and campus organizations) could also benefit from the findings from this study. Practical implications for this study can be implemented through innovative student services programming. Student-run organizations can provide services to new and current transfer students to foster transfer student capital that they possess. Additionally, the implications from this study could be valuable to campus administrators both at the two- and four-year institutions to foster their partnerships to create seamless transfer experiences for their students. Future research could validate the findings by testing the proposed model with multi-institutional and longitudinal data. Further, institutional characteristics (size, location, selectivity, etc.) can be added to the model to better understand and examine the role and relevance of transfer student capital to predict adjustments of community college transfer students at four-year institutions. As Hagedorn (2006) argues, we contend that transfer has played a role for retaining students in postsecondary education. It is hoped that this exploratory study can play a springboard to address the needs of transfer students, provoke future research inquiries for transfer process as well as transfer capital, and ultimately to increase students retention in postsecondary education.

(Appendixes follow)

APPENDIX A
Coding and Scaling of the Variables

Variables	Coding/Scale
Mother's Education	9-scales: 1 = Elementary school or less; 2 = Some high school; 3 = High school graduate; 4 = Some college; 5 = Associate's degree from 2 year; 6 = Bachelor's degree; 7 = Some graduate school; 8 = Graduate degree; 9 = Don't know
Father's Education	Same as Mother's Education
Parental Income	1 = Less than $20,000; 2 = $20,000-$39,999; 3 = $40,000-$59,999; 4 = $60,000-$79,999; 5 = $80,000 or more

Motivations for Transfer

This university has a very good academic reputation.

This university's graduates gain admission to top graduate/professional schools.

This university's graduates get good jobs.

University's ranking in national magazines.

4-point scale: 1 = not important; 4 = very important

Reason for Transfer

This university has affordable tuition. Cost.

4-point scale: 1 = not important; 4 = very important

Experiences with General Courses

The courses developed my critical and analytical thinking.

The courses demanded intensive writing assignments and projects.

Overall, the courses were intellectually challenging.

The courses prepared me for the academic standards at this university.

The courses prepared me for my major at this university.

The course required extensive reading and writing.

4-point scale: 1 = disagree strongly; 4 = agree strongly

APPENDIX A (Cont'd.)

Variables	Coding/Scale
Course Learning	4-point scale: 1 = never; 4 = very often
Took detailed notes in class.	
Participated in class discussion.	
Tried to see how different facts and ideas fit together.	
Thought about practical applications of the material.	
Worked on a paper or project where I had to integrate ideas from various sources.	
Tried to explain the material to another student or friend.	
Academic Counseling Experiences	4-point scale: 1 = disagree strongly; 4 = agree strongly
I consulted with academic counselors regarding transfer.	
Information received from academic counselor(s) was helpful in the transfer process.	
I met with academic counselors on a regular basis.	
I talked with a counselor/advisor about courses to take, requirements, education plans.	
I discussed my plans for transferring to a 4-year college or university with an academic advisor.	
Counselors/advisors identified courses needed to meet the general education/major requirements of a 4-year college or university I was interested in attending.	
Perceptions of Transfer Process	4-point scale: 1 = disagree strongly; 4 = agree strongly
I researched various aspects of MU to get a better understanding of the environment and academic expectations.	
I knew what to expect at MU in terms of academics.	
I visited the MU campus to learn where offices and departments were located.	
I spoke to academic counselors at MU about transferring and major requirements.	
I visited the admissions office at MU.	
I spoke to former community college transfers to gain an insight about their adjustment experiences.	

APPENDIX A (Cont'd.)

Variables	Coding/Scale
Experiences with Faculty	4-point scale: 1 = never; 4 = very often
Visited faculty and sought their advice on class projects such as writing assignments and research papers.	
Felt comfortable approaching faculty outside class.	
Asked my instructor for information related to a course was taking (grades, make-up work, assignments, etc.).	
Visited informally and briefly with an instructor after class.	
Discussed my career plans and ambitions with a faculty member.	
Asked my instructor for comments and criticisms about my work.	
Learning and Study Skills	5-point scale: 1 = disagree strongly; 5 = agree strongly
Note taking skills.	
Problem-solving skills.	
Reading skills.	
Research skills.	
Test taking skills.	
Time management skills.	
Writing skills.	
General Perceptions of University	4-point scale: 1 = disagree strongly; 4 = agree strongly
This university is an intellectually stimulating and often exciting place to be.	
I would recommend to other transfer students to come to this university.	
If I could start over again, I would go to the same university I am now attending.	
General Perceptions of Faculty	4-point scale: 1 = disagree strongly; 4 = agree strongly
University faculty are easy to approach.	
University faculty tend to be accessible to students.	
Professors are strongly interested in the academic development of undergraduates.	

APPENDIX A (Cont'd.)

Variables	Coding/Scale
Course Learning	4-point scale: 1 = never; 4 = very often
Participated in class discussion.	
Tried to see how different facts and ideas fit together.	
Thought about practical applications of the material.	
Worked on a paper or project where I had to integrate ideas from various sources.	
Tried to explain the material to another student or friend.	
Experiences with Faculty	4-point scale: 1 = never; 4 = very often
Visited faculty and sought their advice on class projects such as writing assignments and research papers.	
Felt comfortable approaching faculty outside class.	
Asked my instructor for information related to a course I was taking (grades, make-up work, assignments, etc.).	
Visited informally and briefly with an instructor after class.	
Discussed my career plans and ambitions with a faculty member.	
Asked my instructor for comments and criticisms about my work.	
Satisfaction of the University Environment	4-point scale: 1 = very dissatisfied; 4 = very satisfied
Decision to transfer to this university.	
Overall quality of instruction.	
Overall College Experience.	
Stigma as Transfer Student	4-point scale: 1 = disagree strongly; 4 = agree strongly
Because I was a "community college transfer," most *students* tend to underestimate my abilities.	
There is a stigma at MU among students for having started at a community college.	
Because I was a "community college transfer," most *faculty* tend to underestimate my abilities.	

APPENDIX A (Cont'd.)

Variables	Coding/Scale
Academic Adjustment	4-point scale: 1 = disagree strongly; 4 = agree strongly
Adjusting to the academic standards or expectations at MU has been easy.	
The large classes intimidate me.	
I experienced a dip in grades (GPA) during my first semester at MU.	
There is a sense of competition between/among students at MU that is not found in community colleges.	
Social Adjustment	4-point scale: 1 = disagree strongly; 4 = agree strongly
Adjusting to the social environment at MU has been easy.	
I often feel (felt) overwhelmed by the size of the student body.	
Upon transferring I felt alienated at MU.	
I am very involved with social activities at this university.	
I am meeting as many people and making as many friends as I would like at MU.	
My level of stress increased when I started MU.	
It is easy making friends at this university.	
I feel comfortable spending time with friends that I made at the 2-year college I attended.	
I feel more comfortable making friends with transfer students than non-transfers.	

APPENDIX B
Factor Loadings and Reliability Coefficients

Variables (alpha coefficients in parentheses)	Factor Loading
Motivations for Transfer (0.77)	
This university has a very good academic reputation.	0.76
This university's graduates gain admission to top graduate/professional schools.	0.76
This university's graduates get good jobs.	0.81
University's ranking in national magazines.	0.76
Reason for Transfer (0.81)	
This university has affordable tuition.	0.92
Cost.	0.92
Experiences with General Courses (0.86)	
The courses developed my critical and analytical thinking.	0.73
The courses demanded intensive writing assignments and projects.	0.76
Overall, the courses were intellectually challenging.	0.82
The courses prepared me for the academic standards at this university.	0.79
The courses prepared me for my major at this university.	0.73
The course required extensive reading and writing.	0.77
Course Learning (0.84)	
Took detailed notes in class.	0.65
Participated in class discussion.	0.74
Tried to see how different facts and ideas fit together.	0.85
Thought about practical applications of the material.	0.81
Worked on a paper or project where I had to integrate ideas from various sources.	0.72
Tried to explain the material to another student or friend.	0.74
Academic Counseling Experiences (0.93)	
I consulted with academic counselors regarding transfer.	0.87
Information received from academic counselor(s) was helpful in the transfer process.	0.85
I met with academic counselors on a regular basis.	0.81
I talked with a counselor/advisor about courses to take, requirements, education plans.	0.87
I discussed my plans for transferring to a 4-year college or university with an academic advisor.	0.88
Counselors/advisors identified courses needed to meet the general education/major requirements of a 4-year college or university I was interested in attending.	0.86

APPENDIX B (Cont'd.)

Variables (alpha coefficients in parentheses)	Factor Loading
Perceptions of Transfer Process (0.77)	
I researched various aspects of MU to get a better understanding of the environment and academic expectations.	0.66
I visited the MU campus to learn where offices and departments were located.	0.83
I spoke to academic counselors at MU about transferring and major requirements.	0.83
I visited the admissions office at MU.	0.77
Experiences with Faculty (0.91)	
Visited faculty and sought their advice on class projects such as writing assignments and research papers.	0.83
Felt comfortable approaching faculty outside class.	0.79
Asked my instructor for information related to a course was taking (grades, make-up work, assignments, etc.).	0.83
Visited informally and briefly with an instructor after class.	0.87
Discussed my career plans and ambitions with a faculty member.	0.84
Asked my instructor for comments and criticisms about my work.	0.85
Learning and Study Skills (0.90)	
Note taking skills.	0.76
Problem-solving skills.	0.82
Reading skills.	0.79
Research skills.	0.73
Test taking skills.	0.79
Time management skills.	0.73
Writing skills.	0.67
General Perceptions of University (0.83)	
This university is an intellectually stimulating and often exciting place to be.	0.83
I would recommend to other transfer students to come to this university.	0.92
If I could start over again, I would go to the same university I am now attending.	0.86
General Perceptions of Faculty (0.82)	
University faculty are easy to approach.	0.87
University faculty tend to be accessible to students.	0.89
Professors are strongly interested in the academic development of undergraduates.	0.80

APPENDIX B (Cont'd.)

Variables (alpha coefficients in parentheses)	Factor Loading
Course Learning (0.82)	
Participated in class discussion.	0.71
Tried to see how different facts and ideas fit together.	0.84
Thought about practical applications of the material.	0.81
Worked on a paper or project where I had to integrate ideas from various sources.	0.70
Tried to explain the material to another student or friend.	0.73
Experiences with Faculty (0.91)	
Visited faculty and sought their advice on class projects such as writing assignments and research papers.	0.85
Felt comfortable approaching faculty outside class.	0.82
Asked my instructor for information related to a course I was taking (grades, make-up work, assignments, etc.).	0.83
Visited informally and briefly with an instructor after class.	0.84
Discussed my career plans and ambitions with a faculty member.	0.80
Asked my instructor for comments and criticisms about my work.	0.83
Satisfaction of the University Environment (0.86)	
Sense of belonging at MU.	0.81
Decision to transfer to this university.	0.84
Overall quality of instruction.	0.74
Sense of community on campus.	0.76
Overall College Experience.	0.86
Stigma as Transfer Student (0.87)	
Because I was a "community college transfer," most *students* tend to underestimate my abilities.	0.91
There is a stigma at MU among students for having started at a community college.	0.88
Because I was a "community college transfer," most *faculty* tend to underestimate my abilities.	0.89
Academic Adjustment (0.63)	
Adjusting to the academic standards or expectations at MU has been easy.	0.82
I experienced a dip in grades (GPA) during my first semester at MU.	0.78
Social Adjustment (0.76)	
Adjusting to the social environment at MU has been easy.	0.77
I am meeting as many people and making as many friends as I would like at MU.	0.85
It is easy making friends at this university.	0.85

References

Adams, J. (1999). Learning from transfer data exchange. *Michigan Community College Journal: Research and Practice, 5*(2), 53-67.

Adelman, C. (1999). Answers in the tool box: Academic intensity, attendance patterns, and bachelor's degree attainment. Washington, DC: Office of Educational Research and Improvement, U.S. Department of Education.

Arnold, C. L., & Ugale, R. (1996). *Student outcomes report: The latest numbers and recent trends in student success, withdrawal, persistence, degrees/certificates, and transfer, Fall 1996.* Hayward, CA: Chabot College (ED 421 196).

Bailey, T. R., & Alfonso, M. (2005). Paths to persistence: An analysis of research on program effectiveness at community colleges. *Lumina Foundation: New Agenda Series, 6*(1), 1-38.

Becker, G. S. (1993). *Human capital: A theoretical and empirical analysis, with special reference to education* (3rd ed.). Chicago, IL: The University of Chicago Press.

Bers, T., Filkins, J. W., & McLaughlin, G. W. (2001). Understanding transfers: A collaborative community college and university research project. *Journal of Applied Research in the Community College, 8*(2), 93-105.

Boughan, K. (1995). Tracking student progress at PGCC: Basic findings of the 1990 entering cohort, four-year academic outcome analysis. Enrollment analysis EA95-7. Largo, MD: Prince George's Community College (ED 382 273).

Boughan, K. (1998). *New approaches to the analysis of academic outcomes: Modeling student performance at a community college.* Paper presented at the annual forum of the Association for Institutional Research. Minneapolis, MN (ED 424 798).

Bradburn, E. M., & Hurst, D. G. (2001). *Community college transfer rates to 4-year institutions using alternative definitions of transfer, NCES 2001-197.* Washington, DC: U.S. Department of Education, National Center for Education Statistics.

Bragg, D. D. (2001). Community college access, mission, and outcomes: Consider ing intriguing intersections and challenges. *Peabody Journal of Education, 76*(1), 93-116.

Castañeda, C. (2002). Transfer rates among students from rural, suburban, and urban community colleges: What we know, don't know, and need to know. *Community College Journal of Research and Practice, 26*(5), 439-449.

Cejda, B. (1999). The role of the community college in baccalaureate attainment at a private liberal arts college. *Community College Review, 27*(1), 1-12.

Cejda, B., & Kaylor, A. J. (2001). Early transfer: A case study of traditional-aged community college students. *Community College Journal of Research and Practice, 25*(8), 621-638.

Cohen, A. M. (1994). Analyzing community college student transfer rates. *New Directions for Community Colleges, 22*(2), 71-79.

Cohen, A. M., & Brawer, F. B. (2003). *The American community college* (4th ed.). San Francisco, CA: Jossey-Bass.

Cohen, A. M., & Sanchez, J. R. (1997). The transfer rate: A model of consistency. *Community College Journal, 68*(2), 24-26.

Davies, T., G., Safarik, L., & Banning, J. H. (2003). The deficit portrayal of underrepresented populations on community college campus: A cross case analysis. *Community College Journal of Research and Practice, 27,* 843-858.

Hagedorn, L. S., & Cepeda, R. (2004). Serving Los Angeles: Urban community colleges and educational success among Latino students. *Community College Journal of Research and Practice, 28,* 199-211.

Hagedorn, L. S., Moon, H. S., Cypers, S., Maxwell, W. E., & Lester, J. (2006). Transfer between community colleges and 4-year colleges: The all-American game. *Community College Journal of Research and Practice, 30*(3), 223-242.

Hagedorn, L. S., Cypers, S., & Lester, J. (2008). Looking in the Rearview Mirror: A retrospective look at the factors affecting transfer for urban community college students. *Community College Journal of Research and Practice, 32*(9), 643-664.

Hill, J. (1965). Transfer shock: The academic performance of the junior college transfer. *Journal of Experimental Education, 33,* 201-216.

Hoachlander, G., Sikora, A. C., & Horn, L. (2003). *Community college students: Goals, academic preparation, and outcomes.* Postsecondary Education Descriptive Analysis Reports, NCES 2003-164. Washington, DC: U.S. Department of Education, National Center for Education Statistics.

Kinnick, M. K., Ricks, M. F., Bach, S., Walleri, D., Stoering, J., & Tapang, B. (1997, May). *Student transfer and outcomes between community colleges and a university in an urban environment.* Paper presented at the annual forum of the Association for Institutional Research, Orlando, FL (ED 410 895).

Kozeracki, C. (2001). Studying transfer students: Designs and methodological challenges. In F. S. Laanan (Ed.), *Transfer students: Trends and issues, No. 114. New Directions for Community College.* San Francisco, CA: Jossey-Bass.

Laanan, F. S. (1996). Making the transition: Understanding the adjustment process of community college transfer students. *Community College Review, 23*(4), 69-84.

Laanan, F. S. (1998). *Beyond transfer shock: A study of students' college experiences and adjustment processes and UCLA.* Unpublished doctoral dissertation, Graduate School of Education and Information Studies, University of California, Los Angeles.

Laanan, F. S. (2001). Transfer student adjustment. In F. S. Laanan (Ed.), *Transfer students: Trends and issues. No. 114. New Directions for Community Colleges.* San Francisco, CA: Jossey-Bass.

Laanan, F. S. (2004). Studying transfer students: Part I: Instrument design and implications. *Community College Journal of Research and Practice, 28,* 331-351.

Laanan, F. S. (2007). Studying transfer students: Part II: Dimensions of transfer students' adjustment. *Community College Journal of Research and Practice, 31*(1), 37-59.

Laanan, F. S., & Starobin, S. S. (2004). Urban community college transfers to a university. *Academic Exchange Quarterly, 8*(2), 139-147.

McCormick, A., C., & Carroll, C. D. (1997). *Transfer behavior among beginning postsecondary students, 1989-94, NCES 97-266.* Washington, DC: U.S. Department of Education, National Center for Education Statistics.

Minear, D. J. (1998). *Models for understanding and predicting the undergraduate educational attainment patterns of public community college students who transfer with the associate in arts degree into a state university system.* Unpublished doctoral dissertation. Florida State University, Tallahassee (ED 427 809).

Mittler, M. L., & Bers, T. H. (1994). Qualitative assessment: An institutional reality check. In T. H. Bers & M. L. Mittler (Eds.), *Assessment and testing: Myths and realities. No. 88. New Directions for Community Colleges.* San Francisco, CA: Jossey-Bass.

Monroe, A., & Richtig, R. (2002). Factors affecting transfer decisions. *Community College Enterprise, 8*(2), 19-40.

Nora, A., & Rendón, L. I. (1990). Determinants of predisposition to transfer among community college students: A structural model. *Research in Higher Education, 31*(3), 235-355.

Ornelas, A., & Solorzano, D. G. (2004). Transfer conditions of Latino/a community college students: A single institution case study. *Community College Journal of Research and Practice, 28,* 233-248.

Pappano, L. (2006). College, my way: Lost, alone and not a freshman. *The New York Times.* New York: The New York Times Company.

Pascarella, E. (1985). College environmental influences on learning and cognitive development: A critical review and synthesis. In J. Smart (Ed.), *Higher education: Handbook of theory and research* (Vol. 1). New York: Agathon.

Phillippe, K., & Patton, M. (1999). *National profile of community colleges: Trends and statistics* (3rd ed.). Washington, DC: Community College Press, American Association of Community Colleges.

Rendón, L. I. (1993). Eyes on the prize: Students of color and the bachelor's degree. *Community College Review, 21*(2), 3-13.

Roman, M. A. (2007). Community college admission and student retention. *Journal of College Admission, 194,* 19-23.

Shulock, N., & Moore, C. (2005). Diminished access to the baccalaureate for lowincome and minority students in California: The impact of budget and capacity constraints on the transfer function. *Educational Policy, 19*(2), 418-442.

Showman, H. M. (1928). Junior college transfers at the University of California at Los Angeles. *California Quarterly of Secondary Education, IV,* 319-322.

Starobin, S. S., & Laanan, F. S. (2005). Influence of precollege experience on self-concept among community college students in science, mathematics, and engineering. *Journal of Women and Minorities in Science and Engineering, 11*(3), 209-230.

Starobin, S. S., & Laanan, F. S. (2008). Broadening female participation in science, technology, engineering, and mathematics: Experiences at community colleges. In J. Lester (Ed.), *Gendered perspectives on community colleges. No. 142. New Directions for Community Colleges* (pp. 37-46). San Francisco, CA: Jossey-Bass.

Sweetland, S. (1996). Human capital theory: Foundations of a field of inquiry. *Review of Educational Research, 66*(3), 341-360.

Swigart, T. E. (2000). Learning and personal growth in community college students who intend to transfer: The role of student involvement, institutional environment, and advising. *Journal of Applied Research in the Community College, 8*(1), 43-55.

Townsend, B. K. (1995). Community college transfer students: A case study of survival. *Review of Higher Education, 18,* 175-193.

Townsend, B. K. (2000). Transfer students' institutional attendance patterns: A case study. *College & University, 76*(1), 21-24.

Townsend, B. K. (2001). Redefining the community college mission. *Community College Review, 29*(2), 29-42.

Tsapogas, J. (2004). *The role of community colleges in the education of recent science and engineering graduates, NSF 04-315.* Washington, DC: National Science Foundation, Directorate for Social, Behavioral, and Economic Sciences.

Wolf-Wendel, L., Twombly, S., Morphew, C., & Sopcich, J. (2004). From the barrio to the bucolic: The student transfer experience from HSIs to Smith College. *Community College Journal of Research and Practice, 28,* 213-231.

Zarkesh, M., & Carducci, R. (2004). Increasing success for Latinos/as in community colleges. UCLA Community College Bibliography. *Community College Journal of Research and Practice, 28,* 705-709.

Direct reprint requests to:
Frankie Santos Laanan
Associate Professor
Educational Leadership and Policy Studies
Iowa State University
N243 Lagomarcino Hall
Ames, IA 50011-3195
e-mail: laanan@iastate.edu

CHAPTER 42

AN INVESTIGATION OF CRITICAL MASS: THE ROLE OF LATINO REPRESENTATION IN THE SUCCESS OF URBAN COMMUNITY COLLEGE STUDENTS

LINDA SERRA HAGEDORN,*,‡ WINNY (YANFANG) CHI,**
RITA M. CEPEDA,*** AND MELISSA McLAIN†

The community college has historically functioned as a primary access point to postsecondary education for Latino students. This study, an investigation conducted through an analysis of the Transfer and Retention of Urban Community College Students (TRUCCS) project, focuses on Latino students enrolled in urban "minority-majority" community colleges, where Latino students have a high representation. The specific interest of this research is the role and effect of the level of representation of Latino community college students on their academic outcomes. The relationship between the level of representation of Latinos, and the levels of academic success are analyzed in concert with other variables, such as, the level of representation of Latino faculty on campus, student age, attitude, academic integration, English ability and aspiration. Findings indicate a relationship between academic success of Latino community college students and the proportion of Latino students and faculty on campus. The findings thus suggest that a critical mass of Latinos may be a positive influence encouraging "minority" students to higher academic performance.

Keywords: community college, Latino students, student success.

INTRODUCTION

Access to education has traditionally been a hallmark of American society. The great democratization of American postsecondary education is due in great part to the community college with its open door access and comprehensive curriculum. Although community colleges have provided access to those who would otherwise be unable to attend college, success has not been consistent

---

*Department of Educational Administration and Policy, College of Education, University of Florida, P.O. Box 117049, Gainesville, FL, USA.

**TRUCCS Program, Rossier School of Education, University of Southern California, Los Angeles, CA, USA.

***San Diego Mesa College, San Diego, CA, USA.

†Rossier School of Education, University of Southern California, Los Angeles, CA, USA.

‡Address correspondence to: Linda Serra Hagedorn, Department of Educational Administration and Policy, College of Education, University of Florida, P.O. Box 117049, Gainesville, FL 32611-7049, USA. E-mail: Hagedorn@coe.ufl.edu

among all groups of students. As a group, Latinos have lagged behind most other groups with respect to college enrollment and graduation (Carey, 2005). Within this context, this study focuses on the academic success of Latino students enrolled in community colleges.

While the dictionary definition for critical mass indicates that it is "the amount of substance necessary for a reaction to begin" (*Longman Dictionary of Contemporary English*, p. 327); within the field of education, the term has been adapted to indicate a level of representation that brings comfort or familiarity within the education environment. Further, critical mass has been hypothesized to foster a "staying environment" for students aligned with a dominant campus culture, in turn promoting retention and persistence (Myers and Caruso, 1992). In a sense, critical mass is expected to help "clear up blockages in the pipeline on the premise that a sufficient number of persons from a previously excluded social category will foster inclusion of others from that background" (Etzkowitz, Kemelgor, Neuschatz, Uzzi, and Alonzo, 1994, p. 53). On the other hand, when critical mass is not achieved, as is oftentimes the case for minority students, marginalization is often the result (Etzkowitz et al., 1994). Without a critical mass of minority students and/or faculty, a lack of sensitivity and understanding may result due to a dearth of comfort and minority role models (Myers and Caruso). Moreover, the lack of a critical mass often fosters feelings of "loneness" and isolation (Laden and Hagedorn, 2000). As a marginalized group approaches critical mass within an educational institution, the dynamics between the minority and majority group changes (Etzkowitz et al., 1994). In the vernacular one often hears that there is power in numbers. This power, be it true or imagined, is the result of a critical mass of individuals.

Latinos are currently the fastest growing ethnic group in terms of both population and proportion (U.S. Census Bureau, 2000). Yet they are also a group with one of the lowest recorded rates of higher education participation and success (Gandara, 1999; Lundquist, 2002). It has been suggested that validation of cultural origin may be central to increasing persistence and transfer among Hispanic community college students (Laden, 1998). This study is focused on the impact of a critical mass of Latinos in community colleges specifically situated within the urban Los Angeles Community College District.

Demographics

Approximately one in every eight people in the United States is of Hispanic origin—more than 32.9 million people representing 12% of the total U.S. population (March 2000). In addition to being the fastest growing ethnic group, Latinos are overrepresented among the young. Currently comprising 14.5% of the total traditional college-age group of 18 to 24 years (more than 3.6 million), it is projected that Latino representation will rise to more than 22% of the age group by the year 2020 (White House Initiative for Educational Excellence for Hispanic Americans, 2000).

When Latinos attend college, they are more often enrolled in a community college (White House Initiative, 2000). Currently, California has the largest proportion of Latino college students in the country. In Los Angeles County, the concentration of Latinos is even higher than the state average. Nearly 29% of *all* Latinos enrolled in higher education in the United States attend one of the 109 California Community Colleges, and almost half (42.9%) of the students enrolled in the Los Angeles Community College District are Latino (Community College League of California). It is clear that describing Latino students in the LACCD as "minorities" is not only misleading from a quantitative viewpoint but also may convey many incorrect assumptions.

The Purpose of the Study

As the proportion of Latino students enrolled in community colleges increases, their relationships and importance within the college environment changes. For this research, the representation level and its effect are of prime interest. While many researchers and scholars have studied the factors contributing to the academic success of Latino community college students, the critical mass, or representation value of Latino students, has been introduced in this paper as a way to understand and study the impact of changing demographics on educational success.

Literature Review

The concept of critical mass has only been applied sparingly to the field of educational research. However, in those instances when it has been used as a framework, definite results have been found.

In a study on critical mass for women in science, researchers looked at 30 academic departments in five disciplines to compare rates of doctoral student graduation for men and women. Results indicated that, without a critical mass of female faculty, women pursuing higher education in the sciences oftentimes felt isolated, stigmatized and excluded. In contrast, modest increases in the number of female faculty resulted in many women feeling increased support and comfort (Etzkowitz et al., 1994). However, results also indicated the creation of a "paradox of critical mass" effect, in which female faculty members divided into competing subgroups as they approached critical mass—one group that shared the values and work-styles of the established male-dominated system, and another group that was working on creating a new model of operation (Etzkowitz et al., 1994). These results indicated that a sheer increase in critical mass may not be sufficient to create lasting change without corresponding changes in the policy and infrastructure of the institution.

Previous research has explored the experience of African American female students on predominantly white college campuses. Results indicated that African American women representing a minority on campus have experienced fear regarding their social and academic competence along with feelings of loneliness, inadequacy and isolation (Johnson-Newman and Exum, 1998). Further, while African American women on predominantly white campuses have been found to be somewhat assertive, they also were suffering from social isolation, competence fears and emotional pain, findings which were not replicated on campuses where African Americans were in the majority (Fleming, 1984). Clearly this research indicates that individuals in the minority on a college campus, regardless of ethnicity may experience academic and personal consequences that are likely to influence both their ability and their desire to persist in higher education.

Within the community college in particular, the increased enrollment of Latino students is rapidly raising questions about the impact of their numbers, especially because this group of students have transfer and persistence rates that are historically quite low (Saenz, 2002). Research has indicated that a lack of a critical mass at educational institutions may result in "culture shock" for incoming students (Fiske, 1988). It has also been suggested that the inherent culture of American institutions may be "alien," or even "discriminatory," in nature for Latino students (Fiske, 1988). While Latinos are rapidly becoming a majority within Los Angeles, they may still remain a minority on college campuses, which, for some, may be their first experience as a member of a subordinate group. However, research has suggested that students in institutions in which they are a distinct minority may exhibit high levels of acculturation, while at the same time may maintain high levels of cultural pride. This finding suggests that cultural values remain important even in environments where majority culture dominates (Torres, 2003; Torres, Winston, and Cooper, 2004). Fiske (1988) has suggested that campuses can improve the climate for minority students by not only investigating ways to increase minority student enrollment, but also to increase the presence of minority faculty thus providing the availability of role models.

Nevarez (2001) has called for educational institutions to create an academic and social climate that fosters the success of specifically Latino students. He suggests that institutions revise curriculum and policy with an awareness of Latino cultural values, create special programs and services to accommodate minority students, provide faculty and administrative role models, and foster a sense of belonging and social integration among students. Nevarez (2001) indicates that "reaching proportional racial/ethnic representation," or approaching critical mass, is one of the best ways that academic institutions can help foster integration and success among their minority students. These findings from previous research reflect the importance of study of the critical mass on the retention and success of Latino students within community colleges.

Research Questions

The current study examines the following research questions:

1. What is the relationship between the level (proportion) of representation of Latino students on campus and their overall academic success?

2. What is the relationship between the level of representation of Latino faculty on campus and Latino student overall academic success?

3. What is the impact of Latino students' age, attitude, English ability, aspiration and academic integration on their overall academic success?

4. Specifically within the Los Angeles Community Colleges, is there evidence of an effect of "critical mass" with respect to Latino students?

To respond to the research questions, we proposed a new measure of student overall success that integrates several measures traditionally used in the previous research on community college students.

Methodology

This study looks at the impact of the level of representation of Latino students and faculty on the academic success of students who identify as Hispanic or Latino. The study also includes a consideration of other factors such as age, English ability, academic integration, aspiration and attitude.

Data collection

Data was collected through the Transfer and Retention of Urban Community College Students (TRUCCS) project. In the fall of 2000, the TRUCCS research team developed a 47-item questionnaire specifically designed for urban community college campuses with diverse student enrollments with large number of students for whom English was not a first language (see Hagedorn, Maxwell and Moon, 2001 for more information on survey design and sampling). The final questionnaire was administered to 5011 students across 241 classrooms in nine colleges within the Los Angeles Community College District.

This study is limited to students who initially self-identified in the first TRUCCS survey as Latino, Chicano, or Hispanic. Information concerning opinions, aspirations, attitudes and other self-reports was derived from the survey responses. In addition, transcript data from the LAC-CD was acquired for all students who signed the requisite consent forms (96% of the sample). Information on course-taking, success ratios and GPA were based on the sample's transcript records. Transcript records date back to the student's first enrollment in the district and extend to Spring of 2005. The students in the sample have participated in the district for various time spans. While some have been students for years (one transcript dates back to 1974), others were first time students in Spring 2001. Some students enroll contiguously, while others may enroll in what can only be described as haphazard in an "on again—off again" fashion.

Measures

Within this study we use a variety of measures to quantify success including the course success ratio, cumulative GPA, Math and English course completion and others. The course success ratio is based on the ratio of the number of courses successfully completed with an A, B, or C grade divided by the total number of courses attempted (Hagedorn et al., 2006). Cumulative GPA is determined by dividing the total number of grade points awarded by the total number of units attempted. The highest level of Math and English courses taken are determined based on an analysis of student transcripts. Consistent with other TRUCCS studies (Hagedorn et al., 2006) Math and English courses were classified using a four-level system consisting of (1) remedial, (2) basic, (3) intermediate and (4) transfer level. Each of these four variables was calculated as described and converted to a standardized measure (Z-score). The next step was the creation of a *meta-success* variable that consisted of the summation of the four success segments for each student. Figure 1 is provided to show the distribution of the total of the four Z-scores. The total Z-score was standardized again and partitioned into five equal groups ranking from 1 (poor), 2 (low), 3 (fair), 4 (good) to 5 (excellent). The resultant measure—hereafter referred to as "metasuccess"— was used to measure students' overall performance. This new variable reflects the changes, variance and trends in all of the four variables while it simplifies the measurement. The rank of overall success is the dependent variable in this study.

Additional variables of exploration include students' age, attitudes, aspirations, academic integration and English abilities. Table 1 shows how these five constructs were derived from the questionnaire items (see Table 1).

To study the effect of Latino representation on campus, we operationalized two separate variables as the representational value (RV) of Latino students or faculty on a per-campus basis. To calculate the RV of Latino students, the number of Latino students per campus was divided by the total campus population (FTE) (Enrollment by ethnicity in Los Angeles Community College District (LACCD), 2004). Based on this proportion, each campus was classified into one of three categories. Three colleges with Latino enrollment of 50% or higher were designated as "high" RV campuses. Three colleges with RV values between 30% and 50% were designated as "moderate" RV campuses; while the three colleges with RV values between 20% and 30% were designated as "low" RV campuses. In the following tables RV levels were represented by 1 for low RV campuses, 2 for moderate and 3 for high.

The RV with respect to Latino faculty was also quantified. Because students encounter both full and part time faculty, the RV faculty values employed a weighting algorithm such that the number of full-time faculty was weighted by a factor of 0.75 while the numbers of part-time faculty was weighted by a factor of 0.25.

Model

Ordinal regression was applied to study the relationship between the ordinal dependant variable, metasuccess, and several predictor variables as described earlier. Based on the methodology of McCullagh (1980), ordinal regression tests the dependence of an ordinal variable, meta-success in this study, on a set of predictors by modeling a function of cumulative probability. In other words, ordinal regression is an appropriate method to predict the probability that a student's success will fall into certain levels based on several predictor variables.

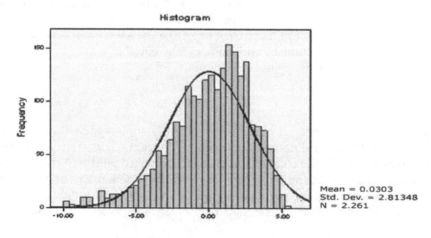

FIG. 1. Distribution of total of Z-score.

TABLE 1. Items and Scales Selected

	Items/Variables Comprising Scale
Background	
Attitude (Alpha = .730)	Strongly Agree to Strongly Disagree (1 to 5)
	Understanding what is taught is important
	I always complete homework assignments
	Success in college large due to effort
	I can learn all skills taught in college
	Enjoy challenging class assignments
	Expect to do well/earn good grades
Aspirations (Alpha = .724)	As things stand, do you think you will
	— Definitely not, probably not, ... definitely
	(1 to 5)
	Transfer to a 4-year college/university
	Get a bachelor's degree
College	
Academic Integration (Alpha = .747)	How often or how many times
	(0 times to 5+ times)
	Talk with instructors before or after class
	Talk with instructors during office hours
	Help another student understand homework
	Study in small groups outside of class
	Speak with an academic counselor
	Telephone/email/student about studies
Student Demographics	
English Ability (Alpha = .923)	Ability in English –Not at all, with
	difficulty, fairly well, very well (1,2,3 and 4)
	Read
	Write
	Understand a college lecture
	Read a college text book
	Write an essay exam
	Write a term paper
	Participate in class discussion
	Communicate with instructor
Age	Actual age when surveyed

Before building the model, data was examined and plotted to visualize the ordinal regression model. Figure 2 is a cumulative percentage plot of the student ranks with separate curves for different student RV levels (1 is for low RV, 2 for middle RV and 3 for high RV). Figure 2 indicates that, while subtle, a larger percentage of students with lower RV fell into the lower success categories while a larger percentage of students with higher RV are in the high rank area.

Figure 3 is a similar plot but delineated by Latino faculty RV levels. Note that a similar pattern of subtle yet higher success in higher RV campuses is evident.

Data Analysis

The methods of analyses included in this study were transcript analysis (Hagedorn, 2005), to calculate grades, level of remediation, and success ratios; descriptive analysis consisting of correlations,

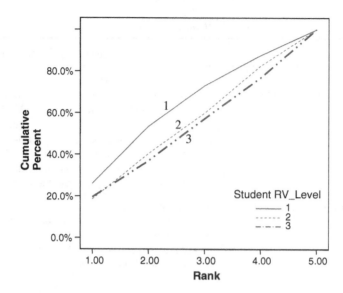

FIG. 2. Cumulative percent plot of meta-success rank by student RV level.

proportions and plots; and ordinal regression analysis to study the relationship between the critical mass of Latino students and faculty (RV) and student success.

Preliminary analysis

Preliminary analysis indicates significant positive correlations between RV and student GPA (coefficient .675, $p<0.01$); as well as between RV and success ratio (coefficient .694, $p<0.01$). Studying on campuses with higher RVs was related to higher GPAs, higher success ratio and more successful patterns of courses completion (with C or better grade) (see Table 2, Charts 1 and 2). The transcript

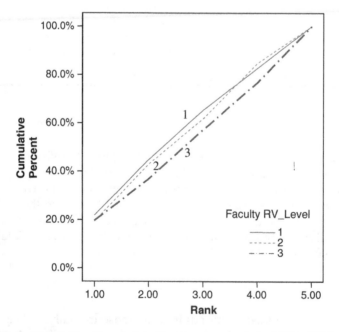

FIG. 3. Cumulative percent plot of meta-success rank by faculty RV level.

TABLE 2. Latino Students' Cumulative GPA and Success Ratio at Different Representational Value Levels as of 2001 Spring Semester in LACCD

Latino Student RV	Campus	Latino students RV (%)	Latino Faculty Weighted RV (%)	Student C. GPA Mean (Std. Deviation)	Success Ratio (% of courses completed with grades of C or better) (Std. Deviation)	Number of courses completed with grades of C or better			
						Minimum	Maximum	Mean	Std. Deviation
HRV (3)	1	76.5	31.2	2.43 (.77)	0.69 (.23)	0	63	12.36	9.67
	2	70.2	17.2						
	3	56.2	15.1						
MRV (2)	4	42.9	8.5	2.34 (.81)	0.67 (.25)	0	54	11.61	8.78
	5	42.1	9.0						
	6	40.0	12.7						
LRV (1)	7	24.1	8.8	2.27 (.85)	0.64 (.28)	0	38	10.15	8.21
	8	23.7	5.0						
	9	19.7	7.8						

analysis also included an evaluation of Math and English course-taking patterns in relation to RV value (see Table 3). Results indicated that the students enrolled at higher RV campuses were more likely to enroll in transfer level courses while lower RV students were more likely to enroll in remedial level courses. As RV decreases, more students tend not to enroll in any English or Math courses.

Ordinal Regression analysis

The Ordinal Regression model was statistically significant, thus allowing us to better understand the relationship of RV to the dependent variable, meta-success, while including controls for the ef-

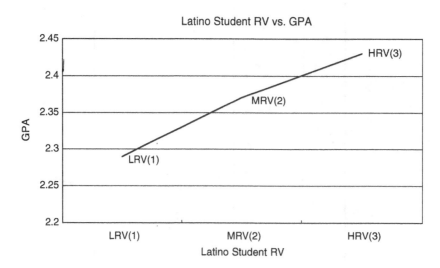

CHART 1. Latino student RV vs. GPA.

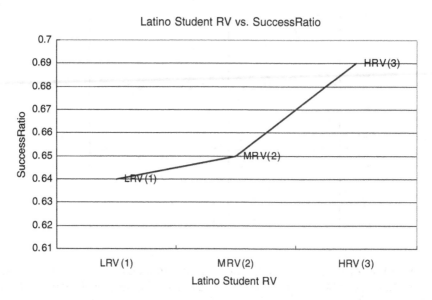

CHART 2. Latino student RV vs. Success ratio.

TABLE 3. Latino Students' Course-Taking Pattern—the Lowest/Highest English and the Lowest/Highest Math Course Completed at Different Representational Value Levels (Percentage)

Latino Student RV Levels	Sample size	English				Math			
		English Lowest			English Highest		Math Lowest		Math Highest
		% not enrolled in any English	% of enrolled in Remedial	% of enrolled in basic and intermediate	% transfer level English	% not enrolled in any Math	% of enrolled in Remedial	% of enrolled in basic and intermediate	% transfer level math
HRV (3)	1,226	8.2	27.6	55	55.4	15.0	44.7	36.2	31.2
MRV(2)	774	5.7	30.2	57.8	61.2	17.2	52.5	26.1	19.0
LRV(1)	281	12.8	35.2	46.6	47.3	21.7	43.8	32.4	13.2

fects of several other predictors (See Table 4 to 9). In these tables meta-success was an ordinal variable coded as 1 to 5 where 1 is poor and 5 is excellent. The fit statistics provided in Tables 4 and 5 indicate that the model fits the data. The model with RV as a predictor provided a significant improvement over the baseline. Note that both the Pearson and deviance values are large. The pseudo R-square values (Cox and Snell .107, Nagelkerke .112) indicate that about 10% of variance in student success is associated with student RV level. The complete model in Table 6 shows that student RV, attitude and aspiration were significant predictors for student success ($p < .05$). Age, English ability and academic integration were not significant predictors of success. It is of note that the esti-

TABLE 4. Model Fitting Information

Model	−2 Log Likelihood	Chi-Square	df	Sig.
Intercept Only	7011.036			
Final	6762.620	248.416	7	.000

TABLE 5. Goodness-of-Fit

	Chi-Square	df	Sig.
Pearson	8671.479	8661	.466
Deviance	6741.590	8661	1.000

Link function: Logit.

TABLE 6. Parameter Estimates

		Estimate	Std. Error	Wald	df	Sig.
Threshold	[RANK = 1.00]	2.931	.401	53.502	1	.000
	[RANK = 2.00]	4.004	.404	98.014	1	.000
	[RANK = 3.00]	4.878	.409	142.451	1	.000
	[RANK = 4.00]	5.931	.414	205.354	1	.000
Location	Age	.010	.005	3.607	1	.058
	Attitude	.430	.061	49.371	1	.000
	Aspirations	.444	.043	106.742	1	.000
	Academic Integration	.015	.050	.088	1	.767
	English Ability	−.037	.070	.274	1	.601
	[Student RV Level = 1]	−.743	.122	37.192	1	.000
	[Student RV Level = 2]	−.143	.084	2.914	1	.088
	[Student RV level = 3]	0[a]			0	

Link function: Logit.
[a]This parameter is set to zero because it is redundant.

TABLE 7. Model Fitting Information

Model	−2 Log Likelihood	Chi-Square	df	Sig.
Intercept Only	7011.036			
Final	6762.620	248.416	7	.000

Link function: Logit.

TABLE 8. Goodness-of-Fit

	Chi-Square	df	Sig.
Pearson	8671.479	8661	.466
Deviance	6741.590	8661	1.000

Link function: Logit.

mated coefficients for rank are clearly at distinctive levels and the ones for student RV low, medium and high are −.743, −.143 and 0 separately; the high RV was set to 0 for the base comparison. The negative coefficients are associated with poorer rank. The lower the coefficient, the more likely the rank is lower as compared to the baseline, high RV. In other words, the ranks for the low RV and moderate RV are statistically lower than that for the high RV students. Overall, a significant and positive relationship was found between the Latino student RV level and their success—as the RV increases, their success increases as well, albeit only moderately.

Similar results were found when Latino faculty RV was substituted in the model (Tables 7 to 9). The relationship between Latino faculty RV and student success is significant, with student attitude and aspirations as additional important predictors. Latino students tend to have higher success rankings as Latino faculty RV level increases on campus.

Conclusions and Implications

This study applied the concept of critical mass to the measurement of success for Latino community college students. Results have indicated that critical mass is indeed an important predictor for student success in urban, Latino community college students.

The level of Latino student critical mass, or RV level, was found to have a positive relationship with student success, enrollment in transfer/non-remedial courses and a negative relationship with enrollment in remedial/precollegiate English and Math courses. Results reveal significantly higher GPAs and success ratios for the High RV and Moderate RV group as compared to the Low RV group. Student aspiration and academic attitude are the significant predictors for success while there is no strong link between age, English ability and academic integration with academic success. While the results of this study do not diminish the importance of acquiring a strong English proficiency, in the case of Latino students in the sample, it appeared not as important as the presence of a critical mass of students.

TABLE 9. Parameter Estimates

		Estimate	Std. Error	Wald	df	Sig.
Threshold	[RANK = 1.00]	2.905	.400	52.704	1	.000
	[RANK = 2.00]	3.970	.404	96.653	1	.000
	[RANK = 3.00]	4.836	.408	140.504	1	.000
	[RANK = 4.00]	5.883	.413	202.812	1	.000
Location	Age	.010	.005	3.456	1	.063
	Attitude	.421	.061	47.550	1	.000
	Aspirations	.443	.043	106.389	1	.000
	Academic Integration	.023	.049	.213	1	.645
	English Ability	−.034	.070	.234	1	.628
	[Faculty RV Level = 1]	−.355	.100	12.737	1	.000
	[Faculty RV Level = 2]	−.255	.092	7.747	1	.005
	[Faculty RV level = 3]	0^a			0	

Link function: Logit.
[a]This parameter is set to zero because it is redundant.

The level of representation of Latino faculty on campus was also found to have a significant impact on Latino student success. Results indicate that the presence of Latino faculty on campus may increase the availability of role models for students and foster a sense of belonging and social integration among students. Therefore availability of, and contact with, Latino faculty may be more important than previously thought. Overall, results from this research indicate that, as the numbers of Latino students and faculty on campus increase to a critical mass, academic success increases as well.

This study has also created a new definition of student success by combining several other established measures (i.e. GPA, course completion ratio, successful course completion ratio, Math and English courses). Because this unified variable comes from several major measures, it has added a degree of parsimony to the otherwise confusing nature of student success.

Although the model exhibited acceptable significance, we acknowledge that the proportions of variance explained were low and the relationship rather weak. However, one would not expect an extremely strong relationship of academic success and critical mass. Rather, we contend that the presence of Latino students and faculty provide a level of comfort for students that encourages success. We acknowledge several limitations of our work.

1. This study focused strongly on the relationship of representational value of Latino community college students on their success. The set of independent variables was purposely parsimonious. Future research may include or control for other variables and factors that may a ect the relationship of RV and success such as gender, goals, financial aid, employment, etc.

2. Ordinal regression analysis has inherent limitations as it cannot accommodate continuous covariates very well. As such variables had to be categorized into a small number of categories thus reducing the variance within the data.

Taken together, this study indicates that critical mass does matter for Latino students in urban community colleges. Students on campuses with higher level of Latino students and faculty experienced greater success. While this relationship was small, it was both positive and significant.

These results suggest interesting policy implications. While it is not suggested that Latino students be directed only to campuses with high Latino representation, it does suggest that districts and campuses take positive steps with respect to local recruitment of both students and faculty. Each of the high RV student campuses in the study was geographically located in a neighborhood with high proportions of Latinos. The designation of "community colleges" over the older term, "junior colleges" is purposeful. Community colleges are to serve the communities in which they reside. Thus, through recruitment of students at local high schools and other neighborhood is one way of serving the community while increasing the proportion of Latinos to a critical mass. Similarly, hiring faculty and staff from the neighborhood may also be beneficial in establishing a critical mass. Ads in local papers, flyers in local establishments, and other local outreach may attract more individuals who are local to the area and thus more likely to reflect the culture of the community.

This paper introduced new terms and new ideas. It is hoped that this study will be a springboard for future inquiries into new areas of critical mass and its effect on various groups of students.

References

Carey, K. (2005). One step from the finish line. Report by the Education Trust. Available http://www.2.edtrust .org/NR/rdonlyres/12656449-03FD-4F3F-A617-920E58F009C0/0/one_step_from.pdf. Accessed December 19, 2005.

Community College League of California (2002). California Community Colleges, Pocket Profile, 2002 [brochure].

Etzkowitz, H., Kemelgor, C., Neuschatz, M., Uzzi, B., and Alonzo, J. (1994). The paradox of critical mass for women in science. *Science New Series* 266(5182): 51–54.

Fiske, E. (1988). The undergraduate Hispanic experience: A case of juggling two cultures. *Change,* May/June: 29–33.

Fleming, J. (1984). *Blacks in college,* Jossey-Bass, San Francisco, CA.

Gandara, P. (1999). Staying in the race: The challenge for Chicanos/as in higher education. In: Moreno, J. (ed.),

The elusive quest for equality: 150 years of Chicano Chicana education, Harvard Educational Review, Cambridge, MA, pp. 169–196.

Hagedorn, L. S. (2005). Transcript analyses as a tool to understand community college student academic behaviors. *Journal of Applied Research in the Community College 13*(1, Fall): 45–57.

Hagedorn, L. S., Maxwell, W. E., and Moon, H. S. (2001). Research on Urban Community College Transfer and Retention: The Los Angeles TRUCCS Project. Available: http://www.usc.edu/dept/education/truccs /Papers/15-truccs%20description.pdf. Accessed December 9, 2005.

Hagedorn, L. S., Moon, H. S., Cypers, S., Maxwell, W. E., and Lester, J. (2006). Transfer between community colleges and four-year colleges: The all American game. *Community College Journal of Research and Practice 30*(3): 223–242.

Johnson-Newman, D., and Exum, H. (1998). Facilitating healthy ego development in African American female college students attending predominantly white universities. *NASPA Journal 36*(1): 70–80.

Laden, B. V. (1998). *Celebratory socialization: Welcoming Hispanic students to college.* Paper presented at the American Educational Research Association (AERA) annual meeting, San Diego, CA. ERIC reproduction Number ED 429 523.

Laden, B. V., and Hagedorn, L. S. (2000). Job satisfaction among faculty of color in academe: Individual survivors or institutional transformers?. In: Hagedorn, L. S. (ed.), *What contributes to job satisfaction among faculty and staff,* Jossey-Bass, San Francisco, pp. 57–66.

Longman Dictionary of Contemporary English. (3rd Ed.), (1995). London: Longman Group Ltd.

Los Angeles Community College District (LACCD). (2004). Enrollment by ethnicity by college, fall 1972–fall 2004. Research and statistics in LACCD. Accessed Oct. 25, 2005 from http://www.research.laccd.edu/student-characteristics/enrollment-by-ethnicity.htm.

Lundquist, S. (2002). *Achieving equity and excellence in 21st century American higher education.* The California Master Plan and Beyond.

McCullagh, P. (1980). Regression model for ordinal data. *Journal of the Royal Statistical Society, Series B 42*: 109–142.

Myers, K. A. and Caruso, R. (1992). The diversity continuum: Enhancing student interest and access, creating a staying environment, and preparing students for transition.

Nevarez, C. (2001). Mexican Americans and their Latinos in postsecondary education: Institutional influences. *ERIC Digest,* ED459038.

Saenz, V. (2002). *Hispanic students and community colleges: A critical point for intervention.* ERIC Clearinghouse for Community Colleges, ED477908.

Torres, V. (2003). A window into the experience of Latino students: Mi casa is not exactly like your house. *About Campus,* May–June.

Torres, V., Winston, R. B., Jr. and Cooper, D. L. (2004). The effect of geographic location, institutional type, and stress on Hispanic students' cultural orientation. *NASPA Journal, 40*(10): 153–172.

U.S. Census Bureau (2000). Population Projections for States by Age, Sex, Race, and Hispanic Origin: 1995 to 2025. Retrieved on October 11, 2005 from http://www.census.gov/population/www/projections/ppl47 .html#tr-race-regional.

White House Initiative (2000). Initiative for educational excellence for Hispanic Americans. Retrieved on October 11, 2005 from http://www.yic.gov/.

Received December 17, 2004.

SECTION VIII

REMEDIATION AND DEVELOPMENTAL EDUCATION

SECTION VIII: REMEDIATION AND DEVELOPMENTAL EDUCATION

The introduction to Section VII used the analogy of the bridge when describing community college transfer. In this section, we extend that metaphor to describe the expanse over which the bridge extends remedial and developmental education. This metaphor is apt because the need for remediation pushes transfer farther away and presents a formidable barrier to the successful crossing of the transfer bridge. Students with goals of transfer are figuratively cast off the bridge and must take a detour on a longer and arguably more treacherous route. Because so many community college students are mired in remediation and developmental education, the topic is the frequent yet controversial subject of research. It is important to note that there are no national definitions or agreements of what level of knowledge constitutes "college ready." Further, there are contentious disagreements about the expenditure of tax dollars, estimated to be over $2 billion dollars per year, spent reteaching material at community colleges that ideally would have been mastered during the K-12 years. Moreover, the students themselves experience costs, both real and opportunity, as well as spend time in "remediation." Others defend the need for developmental education noting its social justice purpose in supplying a second chance to those who experienced less than optimal early education. In addition, denying basic instruction to students serves further disadvantages in a time when most middle-class jobs require some level of postsecondary training.

In this section, we present five chapters that analyze remediation from a multitude of angles and among diverse groups. These chapters pay tribute to the enormity of the problem and the importance of its outcome. It must also be stated that while this section is limited to remediation and developmental education in the community college, the problem is not limited to the nation's two-year institutions. Virtually all postsecondary institutions offer some form of remedial or less than college level education. It is an epidemic without signs of abatement.

Section VIII begins with Chapter Forty-Three, "Does mathematics remediation work? A comparative analysis of academic attainment among community college students," that clearly introduces the topic of mathematics remediation and asks the basic question: Does it work? In terms of numbers of students, math remediation programs are the largest of all needs. Using transcript level data from the full California Community College system cross-referenced with records of all California public universities and colleges as well as National Student Clearinghouse data, Bahr applies a highly sophisticated quantitative model to compare the outcomes of students who have been "remediated" against those who entered the community college with skills at the college level. Finding similar outcomes, the author declares that remedial math programs can be effective.

Chapter Forty-Four, "Referral, enrollment, and completion in developmental education sequences in community colleges," examines the patterns and determinants of student progress through the stages of developmental/remedial education. Although Chapter Forty-Three indicates that remediation can be effective; this chapter reports that few (less than half) students actually complete the remedial sequence all the way to the college level and many never pass even the first course in the sequence. The authors of this chapter, Bailey, Jeong, and Cho, investigate longitudinal records of first time college students within the large national initiative, *Achieving the Dream*. They also compare findings against data from the NELS-88 data. They provide details regarding when students are likely to withdraw from the sequence as well as identifying the demographic groups that are less likely to complete the sequence.

Chapter Forty-Five, "The location of developmental education in community colleges: A discussion of the merits of mainstreaming vs. centralization," by Perin takes a unique look at the practices at community colleges in dealing with students who need developmental or remedial instruction. Perin investigates student placement. More specifically she compares two practices, mainstreaming (or integrating developmental level students into regular departments) and centralizing (housing developmental students in separate organizational units). Comparing the critical educational components of type and quality of received instruction, student services provided, as well as teacher and student reactions to their programs, Perin does not conclude that either mainstreaming or centralization offers the answer. Rather, she provides the advantages and disadvantages of both by offering several recommendations to colleges, administration, and state policy makers.

Chapter Forty-Six, "The social prerequisites of success: Can college structure reduce the need for social know-how," presents a study of seven community colleges and seven private occupational colleges to understand the social or cultural capital (or social know-how) to navigate the colleges' bureaucratic structures. Authors Deil-Amen and Rosenbaum identify the obstacles to the skills and knowledge that students need to be successful. However, they report students enrolled in community colleges are often confronted with more obstacles than those associate-degree seekers enrolled in private occupational colleges (including for-profits) that take a different approach in transforming the implicit to the explicit. By including the private and for-profit sector, this chapter challenges the approaches to non-college ready students that community colleges have taken.

The final chapter by Melguizo, Bos, and Prather, "Is developmental education helping community college students persist?," deals with persistence of remedial students. The authors write a critical review of the extant research. They identify descriptive, quasi-experimental, and experimental as the three main types of summative evaluation. Based on research type, they provide a review of the evidence regarding the relationship between persistence and remediation. Concluding that randomized control trials may not be possible in the context of assigning remediation, the authors explain why regression discontinuity offers the best options for understanding the complex retention outcome of students needing additional "less than college" instruction.

As a whole, this section delves deeply into the community college remedial/developmental set of issues and offers evidence for ways of reducing the problem. Unfortunately, the chapters in this section neither solve the growing issue nor quell current debates, but they do expand the view of the problem and provide structure for the next generation of students who must cross the bridge that hopefully leads to success.

CHAPTER 43

DOES MATHEMATICS REMEDIATION WORK?: A COMPARATIVE ANALYSIS OF ACADEMIC ATTAINMENT AMONG COMMUNITY COLLEGE STUDENTS

PETER RILEY BAHR

Received: 13 March 2007/Published online: 22 February 2008

Abstract. Postsecondary remediation is a controversial topic. On one hand, it fills an important and sizeable niche in higher education. On the other hand, critics argue that it wastes tax dollars, diminishes academic standards, and demoralizes faculty. Yet, despite the ongoing debate, few comprehensive, large-scale, multi-institutional evaluations of remedial programs have been published in recent memory. The study presented here constitutes a step forward in rectifying this deficit in the literature, with particular attention to testing the efficacy of remedial math programs. In this study, I use hierarchical multinomial logistic regression to analyze data that address a population of 85,894 freshmen, enrolled in 107 community colleges, for the purpose of comparing the long-term academic outcomes of students who remediate successfully (achieve college-level math skill) with those of students who achieve college-level math skill without remedial assistance. I find that these two groups of students experience comparable outcomes, which indicates that remedial math programs are highly effective at resolving skill deficiencies.

Keywords: Remediation, Remedial education, Developmental education, Basic skills, Mathematics, Community college, Transfer, Attainment, Achievement, Degree, Certificate

Introduction

Postsecondary remediation is a "hot button" topic on educational policy agendas. On one hand, it fills an important niche in U.S. higher education by providing opportunities to rectify race, class, and gender disparities generated in primary and secondary schooling, to develop the minimum skills deemed necessary for functional participation in the economy and the democracy, and to acquire the prerequisite competencies that are crucial for negotiating college-level coursework. On the other hand, critics argue that taxpayers should not be required to pay twice for the same educational opportunities, that remediation diminishes academic standards and devalues postsecondary credentials, and that the large number of underprepared students who are enrolling in college demoralizes faculty. Following from these critiques, some have argued for a major restructuring of remediation or even the elimination of remedial programs altogether.

In the midst of this debate, surprisingly few methodologically sound, comprehensive, large-scale, multi-institutional evaluations of postsecondary remedial programs have been put forward. While numerous small-scale (or otherwise limited) studies have been published over the last several decades, nearly all of these evidenced important weaknesses and produced findings of questionable value. Thus, despite longstanding controversy and much rhetoric, we have comparatively little dependable information about whether remediation is accomplishing the purpose for which it is intended. This is a critical oversight as decisions are being made about the role that remediation is to play in the future of higher education in the U.S.

The research I present here represents a step forward in rectifying this deficit in the literature, with particular attention to the prevailing area of remedial need, namely mathematics. In this study, I test the efficacy of remedial math programs in community colleges by comparing the long-term academic outcomes (credential attainment and transfer) of students who remediate successfully in mathematics (achieve college-level math skill) with those of students who achieve college-level math skill without the need for remedial assistance. To accomplish this test, I use hierarchical multinomial logistic regression to analyze data that address the entire population of first-time college freshmen who began college attendance in the Fall of 1995 at any of the 107 semester-system community colleges in California. I tracked the mathematics progress of these students for 6 years and their academic attainment for 8 years.

I find that students who remediate successfully experience outcomes that effectively are equivalent to those of students who do not require remediation, indicating that remedial math programs are highly effective at resolving skill deficiencies. However, the majority of remedial math students do not remediate successfully, and the outcomes of these students are not favorable. Thus, while remediation is efficacious for those who remediate successfully, further research is needed to identify the obstacles that hinder the remedial process for so many.

Background

Situating Postsecondary Remediation

Postsecondary remediation—variously referred to as "developmental," "basic skills," "compensatory," or "preparatory" education (Tomlinson 1989)—has been described as "the most important educational problem in America today" (Astin 1998, p. 12). This declaration is not without merit; remediation is as remarkable for its sheer scale as for its unique function. For example, Parsad et al. (2003) estimate that, nationwide, 28% of first-time college freshmen enrolled in remedial coursework during the Fall of 2000. Adelman (2004a), employing a larger window of observation and somewhat different measures, estimates that 41% of students enroll in remedial coursework at some point during attendance. Consistent with these figures, estimates place the national *direct* cost of public postsecondary remedial programs at 1–2 billion dollars annually, and the total *direct* and *indirect* public and private costs at nearly 17 billion dollars annually (Breneman and Haarlow 1998; Greene 2000; Phipps 1998; Saxon and Boylan 2001).

Further supporting Astin's declaration, postsecondary remediation fills a critical niche in U.S. higher education (McCabe 2003). In a democratic society and a free economy, functional participation depends upon minimum levels of reading, writing, and math skill. Remediation embodies a collective societal endeavor to provide these minimum skills (Day and McCabe 1997; McCabe 2003; Phipps 1998; Roueche et al. 2001).

Equally important, remediation is a lifeline in the ascent to economic stability for individuals who lack minimum competencies in fundamental subjects (Day and McCabe 1997). Given that educational attainment is a principal determinant of socioeconomic outcomes (Kerckhoff et al. 2001), remediation opens the door to economic progress by ameliorating deficiencies that obstruct success in acquiring (or, in some cases, even access to) postsecondary credentials (Brothen and Wambach 2004; McCusker 1999; Tomlinson 1989). In light of the self-evident impracticality of sending adults back to high school to acquire necessary skills, remediation is an indispensable bridge to postsecondary credentials over the chasm of inadequate preparation (McCabe 2000; Roberts 1986).

Finally, postsecondary remediation is unique relative to other aspects of the educational system in that it is *not* designed to sort individuals into strata of attainment (Spring 1976). Rather, it is intended ostensibly to equalize attainment, reducing disparities between the disadvantaged and advantaged (Mills 1998; Roueche et al. 2001). This function is made all the more important by the fact that the funding structure of public primary and secondary education (based, in part, on local taxes) ensures substantial inequities in the quality of education provided to students (Cohen and Johnson 2004; Condron and Roscigno 2003; Walters 2001). Thus, remediation is, by definition, a "remedy" intended to restore opportunity to those who otherwise may be relegated to meager wages, poor working conditions, and other consequences of socioeconomic marginalization (Day and McCabe 1997; Roueche and Roueche 1999).

However, postsecondary remediation is a controversial topic (McMillan et al. 1997; Mills 1998). Critics contend that taxpayers should not be required to pay twice for the same learning opportunities, first in high school and then in college (Boylan 1999; Grimes and David 1999; Ignash 1997; Kozeracki 2002; McCabe 2000; Reising 1997; Roueche et al. 2001; Saxon and Boylan 2001). Some argue that providing secondary-level coursework in postsecondary institutions diminishes academic standards and devalues postsecondary credentials (Brothen and Wambach 2004; Costrell 1998; Immerwahr 1999; Oudenhoven 2002; Mazzeo 2002; Roueche and Roueche 1999; Steinberg 1998).[1] Others assert that the large number of underprepared students who are enrolling in college demoralizes faculty (Hadden 2000; Pitts et al. 1999; Trombley 1998). In light of these critiques, some states are shifting the burden of remediation solely to community colleges, while even more drastic proposals have been put forward, including requiring high schools to pay for remediation or the elimination of remediation altogether (Bastedo and Gumport 2003; Bettinger and Long 2005; Boylan et al. 1999; Breneman and Haarlow 1998; Day and McCabe 1997; Jenkins and Boswell 2002; Phipps 1998; Trombley et al. 1998).

Prior Evaluations of Postsecondary Remediation

Given the scale of postsecondary remediation, its core function in higher education, and the mounting controversy surrounding it, empirical evaluations of the relative success or failure of remediation would seem to be a matter of first-order importance. Yet, it is only in the last few years that several methodologically sound, comprehensive, large-scale, multi-institutional evaluations have been published. Prior to this, most evaluative efforts were small in scale, limited in scope, or methodologically weak in other respects. As Phipps (1998, p. 10) observes, "[r]esearch regarding the effectiveness of remedial education programs has been sporadic, typically underfunded, and often inconclusive...the fact remains that there is a dearth of information regarding how well remedial education students perform." Roueche and Roueche (1999, p. 26) echo this assessment, "[p]rogram evaluation has been and remains the weakest component of the remedial effort," as do Koski and Levin (1998, p. 3), "...there is little or no comprehensive and reliable research regarding the efficacy of remedial education...". Even more strongly, Grubb and Gardner (2001, p. 4) state, "...there have been relatively few evaluations of remedial programs, and many existing evaluations are quite useless...".

The numerous small-scale (or otherwise limited) evaluations published over the last several decades paint a varied picture of the efficacy of remediation (Koski and Levin 1998). Some studies indicate that remedial students exhibit academic performance and experience academic outcomes that are comparable to those of students who do not require remediation (Boylan and Saxon 1999a; Crews and Aragon 2004; Kolajo 2004; Kulik et al. 1983; Overby 2003; Purvis and Watkins 1987; Southard and Clay 2004; Waycaster 2001). Other studies suggest the opposite conclusion: remedial students exhibit academic performance and experience academic outcomes that are less favorable than those of their college-prepared counterparts (Bickley et al. 2001; Curtis 2002; Grimes and David 1999; Illich et al. 2004; Tennessee Higher Education Commission 2001; Weissman et al. 1997b; Worley 2003). Still other studies present mixed or inconclusive findings regarding the efficacy of remediation (Gray-Barnett 2001; Seybert and Soltz 1992).

Unfortunately, nearly all of these studies have been plagued with methodological problems of various sorts, resulting in questionable internal validity, external validity, or both (Boylan and Saxon 1999a; Koski and Levin 1998). Among the most common problems evident in prior work are:

reliance on simple bivariate analyses or other analytical methods involving minimal statistical controls (e.g., Crews and Aragon 2004; Overby 2003), reliance on data drawn from a single college (e.g., Bickley et al. 2001; Worley 2003), small sample size (e.g., Purvis and Watkins 1987; Southard and Clay 2004; Weissman et al. 1997b), failure to distinguish remedial students who remediate successfully from those who do not (e.g., Curtis 2002; Tennessee Higher Education Commission 2001), failure to address long-term outcomes in a comprehensive fashion (e.g., Gray-Barnett 2001; Grimes and David 1999), short observation periods (e.g., Illich et al. 2004; Seybert and Soltz 1992), and selection on the dependent variable (e.g., Kolajo 2004; Waycaster 2001). Put simply, *most* prior evaluative research cannot speak clearly concerning the efficacy of remediation.

However, two recent large-scale, comprehensive, multi-institutional studies do offer solid evidence concerning the efficacy of remediation. In the first, Bettinger and Long (2004) found that remedial math students in public four-year colleges in Ohio who remediate successfully are only slightly less likely, on average, to complete a four-year degree than are college-prepared students. In the second, Attewell et al. (2006), using data from the National Educational Longitudinal Study, found that students in community colleges who remediate successfully in English experience an increased likelihood of graduation compared with students who do not require remediation. Attewell and his colleagues otherwise found no differences between underprepared students who remediate successfully and college-prepared students in the likelihood of graduation, in either community or four-year colleges. Taken together, these two studies constitute the beginning of an accumulation of empirical support for the efficacy of postsecondary remediation. It is to this body of work that I seek to contribute with this study.

This Study

The purpose of this study is to evaluate the relative success or failure of one aspect of remediation, namely remedial math in community colleges. Math is of particular interest because more students require remedial assistance with math than with any other subject (Adelman 2004a; Boylan and Saxon 1999b; Parsad et al. 2003). Community colleges are of interest because they constitute the primary venue in which postsecondary remediation is performed (Adelman 2004b; Day and McCabe 1997; Parsad et al. 2003). The question I pose here is, does mathematics remediation work? Said another way, does remediation in math resolve the academic disadvantage faced by mathematically underprepared students? The fundamental principle of remediation is equality of opportunity, and one definitive manner in which this can be demonstrated is equality of outcomes. In other words, students who remediate successfully in math should exhibit academic outcomes that are comparable to those of students who do not require remediation in math, all else being equal.

Among the complexities that have hampered efforts to test the efficacy of remediation is a lack of consensus regarding which "academic outcomes" are the most appropriate to analyze (Bers 1987; Boylan 1997). For example, some studies have examined the rate of success of underprepared students in remedial coursework, and a handful of studies have compared this rate to the rate of successful completion of all students in courses that address a particular subject matter (e.g., Boylan and Saxon 1999a; Curtis 2002; Illich et al. 2004; Waycaster 2001; Weissman et al. 1997a). However, this measure actually does not address the efficacy of remediation because the goal of remediation is to prepare students for success in college-level coursework, and passing a single remedial course is not necessarily indicative of this state.

Another common evaluative measure is persistence or retention (e.g., Grimes and David 1999; Kulik et al. 1983; Purvis and Watkins 1987; Weissman et al. 1997b). These studies ask whether remedial students persist in college at a similar rate to that of college-prepared students. However, this measure also is not informative concerning the efficacy of remediation because simply "sticking around" from semester to semester is not an objective of remediation (Boylan and Bonham 1992; Boylan and Saxon 1999a).

Many studies have compared the mean grade point average of underprepared students with that of college-prepared students, or of underprepared students who enrolled in remedial coursework with that of underprepared students who did not enroll in remedial coursework (e.g., Bickley et al. 2001; Kolajo 2004; Worley 2003). Unfortunately, this method of evaluation is complicated by the fact that not all remedial courses contribute "countable" credits and by the high rate of attrition among poor performing students (Koski and Levin 1998; Shults 2000).

Some studies have compared the pre-test and post-test scores on standardized exams of underprepared students (e.g., Grubb and Gardner 2001; Koski and Levin 1998; Seybert and Soltz 1992). There are problems with this method of evaluation as well. In particular, the goal of remediation is preparation for college-level coursework, and even sizeable gains on standardized exams may not reflect adequate preparation in a given subject matter (depending on the degree to which test scores reflect thresholds of preparation for college-level coursework).

Alternatively, some have compared the rate of success or average performance of college-prepared and underprepared students, or of underprepared students who enrolled in remedial coursework versus those who did not, in the first college-level course for which a given remedial sequence is intended to prepare a student (e.g., Crews and Aragon 2004; McCabe 2000; Southard and Clay 2004). This evaluative measure is among the most widely accepted because, as Boylan and Saxon (1999a, p. 6) argue, "[t]he most essential purpose of remedial courses is to prepare students to be successful in the college curriculum."

Lastly, some studies have compared the long-term academic outcomes (e.g., credential attainment, transfer to four-year institutions) of students who require remediation with those of students who do not require remediation (e.g., Gray-Barnett 2001; Overby 2003; Tennessee Higher Education Commission 2001). This measure arguably is the most robust because, as Grubb and Gardner (2001, p. 23) explain, it is an outcome that has "intrinsic value."

In this study, I focus on the last of these measures: credential attainment and transfer. Given the equalizing aim of remediation, I hypothesize that students who require remediation in math, negotiate successfully the remedial math sequence, and achieve college-level math skill, exhibit patterns of credential attainment and transfer that are comparable to those of students who achieve college-level math skill without the need for remediation. Conversely, although not specifically relevant to testing the efficacy of remediation, I anticipate that students who remediate successfully in math exhibit patterns of credential attainment and transfer that are superior to those of students who do not remediate successfully in math.

Data and Measures

Data

To test this hypothesis, I draw upon data collected by the Chancellor's Office of California Community Colleges. The Chancellor's Office, under mandate by the California Legislature, collects data each term via electronic submission from the 112 community colleges and affiliated adult education centers in California. The data maintained by the Chancellor's Office represent a census of community college students in California and include transcripts, demographics, financial aid awards, matriculation records, degree/certificate awards, etc. Additionally, the database is cross-referenced periodically against the enrollment records of all California public four-year postsecondary institutions and the National Student Clearinghouse database (Boughan 2001) in order to identify students who transferred to public and private four-year institutions, both in-state and out-of-state (Bahr et al. 2005).

I selected for this analysis the Fall 1995 cohort of first-time college freshmen who enrolled in any of California's 107 semester-based community colleges (N = 202,484). Valid course enrollment records were available for 93.9% of these students (N = 190,177). I observed the course enrollments of these students across all semester-based colleges for 6 years, through the Spring of 2001, and retained only those students who enrolled in at least one substantive, nonvocational math course (N = 87,613).[2] I, then, dropped 1,719 students (2.0%) who were missing data on sex, age, or the ID variable used to track student records across colleges, resulting in an analytical cohort of 85,894 students. Finally, in 2003, I refreshed the data with updated information concerning credential awards and transfer to four-year institutions through the Spring of 2003. Thus, the data offer detailed records through the Spring of 2001, while the aspects that address credential awards and transfer encompass an additional 2 years.

Outcome Variable: Academic Attainment

The primary outcome of interest in this study is a given student's long-term academic attainment in the community college system. Within the context of the community college, essentially two expressions of long-term attainment are readily measurable: the award of a credential and transfer to a four-year institution. Two basic categories of credentials are available: associate degrees and certificates. The associate's degree typically requires the completion of a major program of study, general education coursework, and a minimum number of credits. In contrast, the certificate typically requires only the completion of a major program of study. Thus, the associate's degree is considered to be a higher-level credential than the certificate, although not all degree and certificate programs overlap. When these credentials are combined with the possibility of transfer, five mutually exclusive attainment outcomes can be derived, based upon the highest credential earned and whether transfer occurred:

1. *none*—student did not complete a credential and did not transfer;

2. *certificate only*—student completed at least one certificate, but did not complete a degree and did not transfer;

3. *degree with or without certificate*—student completed at least one degree, with or without a certificate, but did not transfer;

4. *transfer without credential*—student transferred, but did not complete a credential prior to transfer; and

5. *transfer with credential*—student completed at least one credential and then transferred.

Explanatory Variable: Math Status

The primary explanatory variable of interest in this study is a student's entry to, and exit from, math coursework. Ideally (methodologically speaking), entry to math would be operationalized using placement exams given at the time of admission. Unfortunately, matriculation processes at the 107 colleges are quite varied, and the only consistent means of classifying students is the skill-level of a given student's first math course. Likewise, exit from math is operationalized using the skill-level of the highest, successfully completed math course.

To categorize math courses, I used course catalogs and course characteristics in the data to determine the skill-level of each math course in which any member of the cohort enrolled at any time during the observation period. In total, I collapsed 2,750 math courses into two categories: remedial and college-level. Remedial math includes basic arithmetic, pre-algebra, beginning algebra, intermediate algebra, and geometry. College-level math includes all courses that address topics of a skill-level equal to, or greater than, college algebra. I ignored nonsubstantive math courses (e.g., math labs) and vocational math, except when a given vocational math course was part of a remedial math sequence or otherwise categorized as college-level.

Using this coding scheme, I classified each student in the cohort as either a remedial math student or a college math student based upon a given student's first math course. As noted earlier, students who enrolled exclusively in vocational math were dropped from the cohort. However, students whose first math course was vocational, but who subsequently initiated the remedial math sequence or enrolled in college-level math, were retained in the cohort and classified based on the skill-level of their first nonvocational math course. The rationale, in this case, is that a sizeable percentage (31.6%) of students whose first math course was vocational subsequently enrolled in remedial or college math. Moreover, whereas a first math enrollment in remedial or college math has value as an indicator of math competency at college entry, a first enrollment in vocational math is not indicative of competency.

My hypothesis predicts that students who negotiate successfully the remedial math sequence and attain college-level math skill exhibit patterns of credential attainment and transfer that are comparable to those of students who attain college-level math skill without the need for remediation. On the other hand, I anticipate that students who do *not* negotiate the remedial math sequence successfully exhibit outcomes that are significantly less favorable. While this suggests a three-category nominal variable, in fact four categories are necessary to account for each of these three conditions *plus* the cases in which students enroll initially in college math but ultimately do *not* complete a college math course successfully. Thus, the primary explanatory variable includes the following four attributes:

1. *college math "completer"* (CC)—student enrolled initially in a college math course and ultimately completed a college math course successfully,

2. *college math "noncompleter"* (CN)—student enrolled initially in a college math course but ultimately did *not* complete a college math course successfully,

3. *remedial math "completer"* (RC)—student enrolled initially in a remedial math course and ultimately completed a college math course successfully, and

4. *remedial math "noncompleter"* (RN)—student enrolled initially in a remedial math course but ultimately did not complete a college math course successfully.

For the purpose of this analysis, a *successful* math course enrollment is one resulting in a grade of A, B, C, D, or Credit.

Student-Level Control Variables

I include a number of student-level control variables found in prior research to be predictors of academic outcomes among remedial students (Bahr 2007, n.d.; Burley et al. 2001; Hagedorn et al. 1999; Hoyt 1999). Among the controls included here are: sex, race/ethnicity, age, three proxies of socioeconomic status (SES), three measures of enrollment patterns, academic goal, grade in first math course, English competency at college entry, and two measures of interaction with academic advising services. Details concerning the operationalization of each of these variables follow. Frequency distributions for each of these variables, as well as long-term academic attainment and math status, are provided in Table 1.

Sex is treated as a dichotomous variable. Race/ethnicity includes nine nominal categories and is treated as a set of dummy variables, with "White" excluded. Age is measured in years, was collected at the time of application for admission, and is treated as continuous.

The three proxies of SES include a dichotomous indicator of receipt of a fee waiver during the first year of attendance, a dichotomous indicator of receipt of any grants during the first year of attendance, and a continuous indicator of the total monetary value of any grants received during the first year of attendance. Students who did not receive any grants were assigned a value of zero for the latter variable.[3]

The three measures of enrollment patterns include: persistence, enrollment inconsistency, and delay of first math course enrollment. Persistence is operationalized as the number of terms (including summer terms, but excluding winter intersessions) in which a given student enrolled in courses from Fall 1995 through Spring 2001. Enrollment inconsistency is operationalized as the percentage of terms in which a given student did not enroll in courses from Fall 1995 through the last term that the student was observed in the system. Delay of first math is operationalized as the term number of first math enrollment, with Fall 1995 assigned a value of one and Spring 2001 assigned a value of seventeen. All three of these variables are treated as continuous.

Academic goal is a self-reported measure of a student's primary objective, collected at the time of application, which I collapsed into ten nominal categories: transfer to a four-year institution as an exclusive objective; transfer to a four-year institution with an allied objective of a nonvocational associate's degree; nonvocational associate's degree as an exclusive objective; vocational associate's

Table 1 Frequency distributions of the student-level variables addressed in this study ($N_{students} = 85,894$)

Variable	Values	N	%
Academic outcome	No credential and no transfer	50,996	59.37
	Certificate only	1,897	2.21
	Associate's degree with or without certificate	6,060	7.06
	Transfer without credential	16,092	18.73
	Transfer with credential	10,849	12.63
Math status	College math "completer"	13,391	15.59
	Remedial math "completer"	17,182	20.00
	College math "noncompleter"	2,664	3.10
	Remedial math "noncompleter"	52,657	61.30
Academic goal	Transfer	19,774	23.02
	Transfer with associate's degree	36,730	42.76
	Associate's degree	5,033	5.86
	Vocational degree	2,170	2.53
	Vocational certificate	1,488	1.73
	Other job-related goal	6,307	7.34
	Abstract	3,755	4.37
	Remediation	1,838	2.14
	Undecided	7,935	9.24
	Unreported	864	1.01
English competency	College-level	26,996	31.43
	Remedial writing	36,967	43.04
	Remedial reading	5,386	6.27
	ESL	7,670	8.93
	None	8,875	10.33
First math grade	A	12,236	14.25
	B	13,587	15.82
	C	14,037	16.34
	D	6,200	7.22
	F	9,807	11.42
	Withdrawal	21,030	24.48
	Credit	3,816	4.44
	No credit	2,067	2.41
	Ungraded	587	0.68
	Missing/unreported	2,527	2.94
Persistence	1–2 Semesters	12,172	14.17
	3–5 Semesters	21,882	25.48
	6–8 Semesters	23,673	27.56
	9–11 Semesters	17,658	20.56
	12–14 Semesters	8,751	10.19
	15–17 Semesters	1,758	2.05
Enrollment inconsistency	<20.1%	31,670	36.87
	20.1–40.0%	28,473	33.15

degree as an exclusive objective; vocational certificate as an exclusive objective; other job-related goals (e.g., acquiring or advancing job skills, maintenance of a professional license); abstract educational goals (e.g., discovering educational interests, personal development); remediation in fundamental academic subjects (including seeking credit for a high school diploma or GED); undecided;

Table 1 continued

Variable	Values	N	%
	40.1–60.0%	16,261	18.93
	60.1–80.0%	7,918	9.22
	>80.0%	1,572	1.83
Delay of first math	Fall 95–Spring 96	61,683	71.81
	Summer 96–Spring 97	12,555	14.62
	Summer 97–Spring 98	5,382	6.27
	Summer 98–Spring 99	3,001	3.49
	Summer 99–Spring 00	1,856	2.16
	Summer 00–Spring 01	1,417	1.65
Advising	Referred for advising	76,458	89.01
	Not referred for advising	9,436	10.99
	Received advising	63,543	73.98
	Did not receive advising	22,351	26.02
Fee waiver	Received fee waiver	29,311	34.12
	Did not receive fee waiver	56,583	65.88
Total $ value of grant(s)	Did not receive grant(s)	66,845	77.82
	<$501	1,187	1.38
	$501–1,000	2,300	2.68
	$1,001–1,500	3,312	3.86
	$1,501–2,000	2,544	2.96
	$2,001–2,500	5,097	5.93
	$2,501–3,000	1,971	2.29
	>$3,000	2,638	3.07
Race	White	37,128	43.23
	Black	7,661	8.92
	Hispanic	23,776	27.68
	Asian	10,132	11.80
	Pacific Islander	621	0.72
	Filipino	3,517	4.09
	Native American	830	0.97
	Other	983	1.14
	Unreported	1,246	1.45
Sex	Male	40,127	46.72
	Female	45,767	53.28
Age (years)	<18	8,096	9.43
	18–20	60,750	70.73
	21–25	7,318	8.52
	26–30	3,518	4.10
	31–35	2,439	2.84
	36–40	1,698	1.98
	41–50	1,613	1.88
	>50	462	0.54

and unreported. Academic goal is treated as a set of dummy variables, with "transfer to a four-year institution as an exclusive objective" excluded.

Grade in first math course includes ten nominal attributes: A, B, C, D, F, Withdrawal, Credit, No Credit, Ungraded, and missing/unreported. It is treated as a set of dummy variables, with "A" excluded.

English competency, like math competency, is set to the skill-level of a student's first English course. Through a process similar to that used to categorize math, I collapsed 6,625 substantive English courses into four categories: remedial reading, remedial writing, English-as-a-Second-Language (ESL), and college-level English. To these four categories, I added a fifth to account for students who did not enroll in any English coursework. English competency is treated as a set of dummy variables, with "college-level English" excluded.

Finally, interaction with academic advising services is measured using two dichotomous indicators of a given student's experience of being referred to, and/or receiving, advising at any point during the six-year observation period.

College-Level Control Variables

In addition to the student-level controls, I control for several variables measured at the level of the college, including: the size of each college, the degree of math competency of entering students, and the goal orientation of each college. Size is operationalized as the number of first-time freshmen who enrolled in a given college in the Fall 1995 term. Degree of math competency is operationalized as the percentage of the Fall 1995 first-time freshmen cohort at a given college whose first nonvocational math enrollment was remedial in nature. Goal orientation is operationalized using four variables, each of which measures the percentage of the Fall 1995 first-time freshmen cohort at a given college who indicated one of the following four goals: transfer, associate's degree, job-related goals, and abstract goals. All six of these contextual variables are treated as continuous.[4]

Strengths and Weaknesses of the Data

The data I assembled for this study have a number of strengths and weaknesses. Among the strengths are access to a population (rather than a sample), a population that is larger than any used in prior studies of this topic, the length of time over which academic careers are observed, the capacity to distinguish between temporary breaks in enrollment and long-term exit from the postsecondary system, and the capacity to observe course enrollments despite student movement across colleges. However, five weaknesses of the data also must be noted.

First, the definitions of "remedial math student" and "college math student" employed in this study assume perfect placement into remedial or college-level coursework. In other words, in these data the only consistent method of classifying students across the colleges is course-taking behavior. This is an unavoidable consequence of the absence of high school transcripts in the data and variation in matriculation processes across the colleges.

While there is no clear solution for this weakness of the data, it is of less serious concern than it might appear. To elaborate, students whose math skills are deficient, but who do not enroll in any math coursework, really are not of interest (methodologically speaking) in answering the question posed in this study. The problem arises when a student who needs remedial assistance with math instead enrolls in a first math course that is college-level and, thereby, is classified as a "college math student." Logically speaking, the most likely outcome for such a student is failure of, or withdrawal from, the math course. If the student does not pursue further math coursework, then the student is captured in the category of CN, which does not pose a problem for this study because the CN category is not central to the hypothesis tested here. On the other hand, if the student drops backwards into remedial math (where the student should have begun) and ultimately works his/her way up to complete successfully a college math course, then the student is identified as a CC when, in fact, he/she should be classified as an RC. This could be problematic because the hypothesis tested in this study compares the outcomes of CCs and RCs.

To explore the scope of this problem, I examined the data for such patterns and found that, of the 16,579 students classified as "college-level," only 847 exhibited the pattern of enrolling initially in a college math course, failing, withdrawing, or receiving "no credit" for that course, and then enrolling in remedial math. Of these 847 students, only 388 eventually achieved college-level math competency. Thus, methodologically speaking, any problem generated by classifying math status on the basis of first math course appears to be minor.

Second, in terms of completing a college math course, the data do not account for academic progress accomplished outside of California's semester-based community colleges. More specifically, students who enter one of the 107 colleges included in this analysis, enroll in a remedial math course (or enroll in and then fail, or withdraw from, a college math course), and subsequently transfer to one of the five quarter-system community colleges, to a private two-year college, or to a community college outside of California, effectively are treated as "noncompleters" in these data because academic progress that occurs outside of the 107 colleges is unobserved. Although such unobserved progress is expected to represent only a small fraction of the total progress, due consideration should be given to the possible impact on the findings.

Third, because the observation period for course enrollments is truncated at six years, some remedial math students may delay their first math course so long that remediating successfully within the observation period effectively is impossible. However, such a condition characterizes only a small percentage of this cohort. More specifically, 96.5% of the students enrolled in a first math course within the first four years following admission, allowing more than sufficient time to remediate successfully even for those who faced severe math deficiencies.

Fourth, the data do not address two control variables found to be important in prior studies of educational outcomes, namely employment intensity (e.g., hours worked per week) and credit course load (e.g., part-time versus full-time enrollment). Employment intensity has been found to be moderately negatively correlated with degree expectations, persistence, and other desirable outcomes (American Council on Education 2003; Carter 1999; Hoyt 1999; Toutkoushian and Smart 2001), although this finding is not entirely consistent across studies (Titus 2004). The findings concerning the effects of course load on academic outcomes are clearer and generally indicate that part-time students are somewhat less likely to experience desirable outcomes than are full-time students (Hoyt 1999; O'Toole et al. 2003; Stratton et al. 2007; Szafran 2001). While a variable measuring course load could be constructed from the transcript data, it would face the same problems and complications described by Adelman (2004a, p. 96).

The fifth weakness of the data concerns the generalizability of findings. While the use of a population has substantial advantages over the use of a sample, the population addressed here was drawn exclusively from California's community colleges. Although California's community college system, which has an annual enrollment of 2.9 million students (Turnage 2003), is the largest postsecondary system in the world, and while remediation in California is much like remediation in other states' systems in that placement procedures and exit standards vary from college to college (Boylan et al. 1999; Dougherty and Reid 2007; Hadden 2000; James et al. 2002; Jenkins and Boswell 2002; Kozeracki 2002; Oudenhoven 2002; Shults 2000), the generalizability of the findings of this analysis to other states is uncertain.

In addition, it should be noted that the population addressed in this study includes only first-time college freshmen, who constitute a segment of a larger population of first-time *and* returning students who enroll in remedial and/or college math. Consequently, any inferences drawn from this study are limited to first-time students, an important, but not all encompassing, segment of the population served by community colleges.

Method

I use two-level hierarchical multinomial logistic regression (Raudenbush and Bryk 2002) to model natural variation in the probability of each of the five possible outcomes. This model is specified according to the equations below, in which the left-hand side of the first equation represents the natural log of the odds of the probability of individual i, who is enrolled in college j, experiencing outcome 2, 3, 4, or 5, versus outcome 1. This outcome varies from the intercept for college j (B_{0j}) as a function of a set of three dummy variables that represent students' math status (RC, CN, and RN, with CC excluded as the comparison category), the corresponding coefficients for college j (B_{1j}, B_{2j}, B_{3j}), a set of k student-level control variables, and the coefficients associated with these control variables (B_{kj}). In turn, the intercept for college j (B_{0j}) varies from the intercept for all colleges (C_{00}) as a function of a set of q college-level control variables, the coefficients associated with these college-level variables (C_{0q}), and a random college-level error term (ε_{0j}). The coefficients associated with students' math status (B_{1j}, B_{2j}, B_{3j}) vary randomly and unconditionally at the college level (ε_{1j}, ε_{2j}, ε_{3j}), relieving the model of the assumption that the effect of math status is the same for all colleges. The coefficients associated with the student-level control variables (B_{kj}) are fixed across colleges. Students are assigned to the college in which they are observed to be enrolled in the Fall term of 1995, or, in the case of multiple institutions, to the college in which a given student enrolled in the greatest number of courses in that term.[5]

$$\ln \left(\frac{P(y_{ij} = m)}{P(y_{ij} = 1)} \right) = \beta_{0j} + \beta_{1j}(RC)_{ij} + \beta_{2j}(CN)_{ij} + \beta_{3j}(RN)_{ij} + \beta_{kj}(\textit{Student Level Controls})_{ij}$$

$$\beta_{0j} = C_{00} + C_{0q}(\textit{College Level Controls})_j + \varepsilon_{0j}$$

$$\beta_{1j} = C_{10} + \varepsilon_{1j}$$

$$\beta_{2j} = C_{20} + \varepsilon_{2j}$$

$$\beta_{3j} = C_{30} + \varepsilon_{3j}$$

$$\beta_{kj} = C_{k0}$$

Analyses

Bivariate Analysis

As discussed earlier, the ameliorative objective of remediation implies that the academic outcomes of successful remedial math students (RCs) should be comparable to the outcomes of students who attain college math skill without the need for remedial assistance (CCs). Conversely, one would expect that students who do not remediate successfully in math (RNs) experience outcomes that are much less favorable than either "completing" group. To begin the exploration of this hypothesis, I present in Table 2 a cross-tabulation of the outcomes of these three categories of students, plus the fourth category of students who enrolled initially in college math but did not complete a college math course successfully (CNs).

The most noteworthy finding presented in this table is the overall similarity of the outcomes of CCs and RCs. These two groups are approximately equally likely to complete only a certificate and approximately equally likely to transfer, although RCs are more likely to transfer *with* a credential, while CCs are more likely to transfer *without* a credential. RCs are somewhat more likely to complete an associate's degree (without transfer) than are CCs, but the absolute magnitude of the difference is small (approximately 4% points). Slightly more than one-fifth of CCs do not complete a credential and do not transfer, as compared with slightly less than one-fifth of RCs.

In contrast to the two successful groups, RNs experience outcomes that are much less favorable. In fact, more than four-fifths of RNs do not complete a credential and do not transfer. CNs have a more favorable transfer rate than do RNs, and a less favorable credential attainment rate (without subsequent transfer), but, globally speaking, the outcomes of CNs are relatively poor.

Regression Analysis

While the bivariate analysis supports my hypothesis that RCs exhibit patterns of credential attainment and transfer that are comparable to those of CCs (suggesting that remedial math programs are quite effective at resolving skill deficiencies for those who complete remediation), the internal validity of conclusions drawn from bivariate analyses is weak at best (Grubb and Gardner 2001). In particular, the absence of statistical controls makes it impossible to determine if the similarity of the outcomes of the two "completing" groups is a product of remediation working as intended or, alternatively, of average differences between the two groups on other predictors of attainment. Thus, it is important in this case

Table 2 Cross-tabulation of academic outcome and math status (cell sizes are provided in parentheses)

Math status		Academic outcome					
		No credential and no transfer	Certificate only	Associate's degree with or without certificate	Transfer without credential	Transfer with credential	Total
"Completer"	College math	21.77% (2,915)	0.69% (93)	6.53% (874)	45.16% (6,047)	25.85% (3,462)	100.00% (13,391)
	Remedial math	18.89% (3,246)	0.79% (136)	10.51% (1,805)	32.62% (5,604)	37.20% (6,391)	100.00% (17,182)
"Noncompleter"	College math	71.66% (1,909)	1.43% (38)	3.23% (86)	21.73% (579)	1.95% (52)	100.00% (2,664)
	Remedial math	81.52% (42,926)	3.10% (1,630)	6.26% (3,295)	7.33% (3,862)	1.79% (944)	100.00% (52,657)
Total		59.37% (50,996)	2.21% (1,897)	7.06% (6,060)	18.73% (16,092)	12.63% (10,849)	100.00% (85,894)

Table 3 Estimated coefficients and standard errors for the hierarchical multinomial logistic regression of academic outcome on math status and selected student-level and college-level control variables ($N_{students}$ = 85,894; $N_{colleges}$ = 107; control variables not shown)

Math status		Academic outcome				
		No credential and no transfer	Certificate only	Associate's degree with or without certificate	Transfer without credential	Transfer with credential
"Completer"	College math	Comparison category				
	Remedial math		−0.269 (0.143)	−0.048 (0.061)	−0.061 (0.050)	0.137** (0.044)
"Noncompleter"	College math		−0.114 (0.222)	−0.746*** (0.147)	−1.532*** (0.070)	−3.064*** (0.166)
	Remedial math		0.230 (0.119)	−1.027*** (0.061)	−2.460*** (0.050)	−3.477*** (0.063)

Note: ** $p \leq 0.01$; *** $p \leq 0.001$; standard errors provided in parentheses

Table 4 Predicted probabilities of each of the five academic outcomes for the "typical" student who is enrolled in the "average" community college, conditional on math status (calculated based upon the estimated coefficients of the model presented in Table 3)

Math status		Academic outcome					
		No credential and no transfer	Certificate only	Associate's degree with or without certificate	Transfer without credential	Transfer with credential	Total
"Completer"	College math	0.301	0.007	0.043	0.325	0.324	1.000
	Remedial math	0.294	0.005	0.040	0.298	0.363	1.000
"Noncompleter"	College math	0.729	0.015	0.049	0.170	0.037	1.000
	Remedial math	0.830	0.024	0.042	0.076	0.028	1.000

Note: The "typical" student, in this case, is a White female who was 20.46 years of age at the commencement of postsecondary attendance, whose first English course was a remedial writing course, who did not receive any financial aid, who indicated an academic goal of transfer in combination with achieving a nonvocational associate's degree, who was enrolled for 6.83 semester terms, who had an inconsistency of enrollment of 30.06%, whose first math enrollment occurred 2.89 semester terms into attendance, but who withdrew from her first math course, and who was both referred to, and received, academic advising

to employ a comprehensive set of statistical controls in order to disentangle the effect of remediating successfully from the effects of behaviors and experiences that promote successful remediation. To this end, I present in Table 3 estimated coefficients and standard errors for the hierarchical multinomial logistic regression of academic attainment on math status and selected controls.

In reviewing Table 3, one finding is immediately obvious. Although RCs *do* differ significantly from CCs in the relative likelihood of experiencing one of the four outcomes, the difference between these two groups is quite small, net of controls. For RCs, the odds of transferring *with* a credential versus neither completing a credential nor transferring are approximately one-seventh (15%) *greater* than the odds for CCs, all else being equal. Otherwise, RCs do not differ significantly from CCs in the odds of transferring without a credential, in the odds of completing an associate's degree (without transfer), or in the odds of completing a certificate only, versus neither completing a credential nor transferring. Thus, on the whole, the two "completing" groups experience outcomes that are nearly identical to one another, once other variables are controlled.

In contrast, it is not surprising to find that the outcomes of the two "noncompleting" groups differ substantially and negatively from the two "completing" groups. For example, the odds of transferring *with* a credential versus neither completing a credential nor transferring for CCs are 31 times (3,136%) greater than the odds for RNs and 20 times (2,041%) greater than the odds for CNs, net of controls. Smaller, but still sizeable, gaps are noted in the likelihood of transferring *without* a credential and in the likelihood of completing an associate's degree without transfer. Taken as a whole, it is clear that students who do not attain college math skill are at an enormous disadvantage in terms of academic outcomes within the community college, and remedial math "noncompleters" experience the worst outcomes of the two "noncompleting" groups.

Predicted Probabilities

While odds ratios are useful for interpreting nonlinear statistics, they are of little help in visualizing the practical size of differences in attainment. Therefore, I calculated the predicted probability of each outcome based upon the model presented in Table 3. These calculations were accomplished by setting all of the student- and college-level controls to their respective means (for continuous variables) or modes (for categorical variables), and then adjusting math status systematically. Conse-

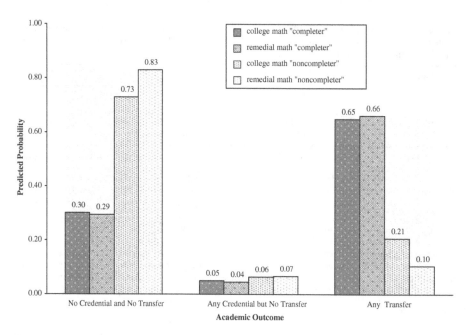

Fig. 1 Summary of the predicted probabilities of the various academic outcomes for the "typical" student who is enrolled in the "average" community college, conditional on math status (collapsed from the figures presented in Table 4)

quently, these predictions are based on what one might think of as the "typical" student who is enrolled in the "average" college. The results are detailed in Table 4 and summarized in Fig. 1.

While the results presented in Table 4 further illustrate the comparability of outcomes of CCs and RCs, they also demonstrate the favorable distribution of outcomes for these two groups. The "typical" CC and RC have roughly a 65% chance of transferring (with or without a credential), a 5% chance of completing a credential without subsequent transfer, and a 30% chance of neither completing a credential nor transferring. In contrast, the "typical" RN has a 10% chance of transferring, a 7% chance of completing a credential without transfer, and an 83% chance of neither completing a credential nor transferring. The "typical" CN has a greater chance of transferring, and a lesser chance of neither completing a credential nor transferring, but otherwise does not differ substantively from the "typical" RN.

Alternative Model Specifications

In the interest of thoroughness, three alternative specifications of the model were examined. In the first alternative specification, I removed from the model all control variables that address concepts that occurred subsequent to enrollment in college. I retained math status, sex, race, age, the three proxies of SES, English competency at college entry, academic goal, and the college-level controls. The purpose, in this case, is to ensure that I do not "over control" the outcome by including variables that might be influenced by the experience of remediating successfully itself. The results are presented in Table 5.

The primary differences between the full model (Table 3) and the simplified model (Table 5) involve increases in the magnitudes of the estimated effects of math status. For example, RCs have a greater estimated advantage over CCs in the likelihood of transfer with a credential, while the RNs and CNs have a greater estimated disadvantage. A similar change is noted in the completion of an associate's degree without transfer, for which RCs now have a statistically significant advantage, while CNs and RNs face a greater estimated disadvantage. Concerning the likelihood of transfer without a credential, RCs and CCs remain equal, while RNs and CNs experience a greater estimated

Table 5 Estimated coefficients and standard errors for a *simplified specification* of the hierarchical multinomial logistic regression of academic outcome on math status and selected student-level and college-level control variables ($N_{\text{students}} = 85,894$; $N_{\text{colleges}} = 107$; control variables not shown)

Math status		Academic outcome				
		No credential and no transfer	Certificate only	Associate's degree with or without certificate	Transfer without credential	Transfer with credential
"Completer"	College math	Comparison category				
	Remedial math		0.202 (0.141)	0.538*** (0.055)	0.028 (0.048)	0.473*** (0.041)
"Noncompleter"	College math		−0.533* (0.215)	−1.752*** (0.131)	−1.798*** (0.065)	−3.641*** (0.152)
	Remedial math		0.020 (0.116)	−1.380*** (0.057)	−2.618*** (0.048)	−3.837*** (0.061)

Note: * $p \leq 0.05$; *** $p \leq 0.001$; standard errors provided in parentheses

disadvantage. Only on the certificate-only outcome are the findings inconsistent, as the simplified model indicates that CNs face a significant disadvantage relative to CCs, while the full model indicates no significant differences. However, this coefficient barely reaches the threshold of statistical significance in the simplified model, which itself is a meaningful observation given the size of the analytical cohort, so this difference between the full and simplified models is not of great consequence.

By and large, these differences between the two specifications make sense in light of the variables that are excluded in the simplified model. For example, consider that first math grade is positively associated with the likelihood of achieving college math skill (Bahr n.d.; Wang 2001). In turn, achieving college math skill is positively associated with the outcomes examined here. Thus, in the simplified model, part of the estimated total effect of not achieving college math skill (CN and RN) includes the effect of first math grade, as one would expect that "noncompleters" performed more poorly, on average, in first math than did "completers." Likewise, some of the increased advantage of RCs over CCs observed in the simplified model likely is a product of greater average persistence among RCs (Kolajo 2004), which increases the likelihood of completing a credential of some sort (whether or not this is followed by transfer). Thus, on the whole, the results detailed previously in the full model (Table 3) appear to be logically consistent and fairly robust against this particular modification to the specification.

Concerning the second alternative specification, prior research indicates that the likelihood of successful remediation in math declines sharply with increasing skill deficiency at college entry (Bahr 2007, n.d.; Hagedorn and Lester 2006). Although not related directly to this pattern, one also might anticipate that students who exhibit the poorest math skills at college entry benefit less from remediating successfully in math than do remedial math students who exhibit stronger math skills at college entry. One might ask, does remediating successfully in math benefit students equally across the varying levels of initial math skill deficiency? For example, do basic arithmetic students who remediate successfully experience academic outcomes that are comparable to those of intermediate algebra students who remediate successfully, and do both of these groups achieve the various academic outcomes at rates that are similar to those of successful college math students? In other words, is remediation equally efficacious at every level of mathematical underpreparation?

To test the efficacy of remediation across levels of initial deficiency, I modified the operationalization of math status to include separate categories for each level of initial math skill, based upon a given student's first math course enrollment. This modified variable includes 10 categories, one for each of five levels of initial math skill multiplied by the two possible outcome conditions of achieving college math skill successfully or not. I then replicated the model presented in Table 3, replacing the simpler four-category indicator of math status with this new 10-category indicator. The pertinent results are presented in Table 6.

The results presented in Table 6 generally support the findings of the previous models. Although several statistically significant differences between CCs and the various categories of RCs emerge, no clear pattern of disadvantage for the poorest skilled RCs is evident, and all differences between CCs and RCs are comparatively small in magnitude. This suggests that, generally speaking, remediation is equally efficacious in its effect on academic outcomes across levels of initial math deficiency, net of controls.

In contrast, a progressive decline in the likelihood of achieving an associate's degree (without subsequent transfer) and transferring (with or without a credential) is observed among RNs as math skills at college entry decline. In other words, although it appears that the benefits of remediating successfully are fairly equal across levels of initial math skill deficiency, the consequences of *not* remediating successfully grow increasingly worse as math skills at college entry decline. This is an intuitively reasonable finding as one would anticipate that, in the absence of successful remediation, declining math skills progressively foreclose academic opportunities.

In the third and final alternative specification, I replicated the model presented in Table 6 using a different threshold of *successful* college math skill attainment. In particular, I treated a grade of "D" in a college math course as *unsuccessful*, in contrast to the inclusion of grades of "D" as *successful* in

Table 6 Estimated coefficients and standard errors for the hierarchical multinomial logistic regression of academic outcome on an *expanded math status variable* and selected student-level and college-level control variables ($N_{students}$ = 85,894; $N_{colleges}$ = 107; control variables not shown)

Math status		Academic outcome				
		No credential and no transfer	Certificate only	Associate's degree with or without certificate	Transfer without credential	Transfer with credential
"Completer"	College math	Comparison category				
	Intermediate algebra/geometry		−0.176 (0.174)	−0.127 (0.074)	−0.178** (0.056)	0.015 (0.054)
	Beginning algebra		−0.397* (0.185)	−0.085 (0.074)	−0.035 (0.070)	0.164** (0.058)
	Pre-algebra		−0.462 (0.334)	−0.303* (0.149)	0.052 (0.125)	0.207 (0.111)
	Basic arithmetic		−0.249 (0.284)	−0.460** (0.148)	−0.358* (0.145)	−0.003 (0.131)
"Noncompleter"	College math		−0.081 (0.214)	−0.684*** (0.145)	−1.487*** (0.069)	−3.028*** (0.166)
	Intermediate algebra/geometry		0.117 (0.146)	−0.699*** (0.081)	−2.023*** (0.063)	−3.139*** (0.092)
	Beginning algebra		0.287* (0.126)	−0.842*** (0.065)	−2.407*** (0.050)	−3.303*** (0.071)
	Pre-algebra		0.091 (0.139)	−1.475*** (0.091)	−2.806*** (0.068)	−3.838*** (0.103)
	Basic arithmetic		0.148 (0.135)	−1.783*** (0.095)	−3.070*** (0.080)	−4.128*** (0.106)

Note: * $p \leq 0.05$; ** $p \leq 0.01$; *** $p \leq 0.001$; standard errors provided in parentheses

Table 7 Percentage of students at various levels of initial math skill who successfully achieved college-level math skill under two competing definitions of *success* ($N_{students} = 85,894$; $N_{colleges} = 107$)

Initial math skill	N	Minimum "D" threshold (%)	Minimum "C" threshold (%)	Difference	Odds ratio
College-level math	16,055	83.41	79.59	−3.82	0.776
Intermediate algebra/geometry	15,119	50.13	47.36	−2.77	0.895
Beginning algebra	26,315	26.35	24.83	−1.52	0.923
Pre-algebra	11,417	13.36	12.56	−0.80	0.932
Basic arithmetic	16,988	6.74	6.23	−0.51	0.919
Total	85,894	35.59	33.72	−1.87	0.921

Note: Values in "Odds Ratio" column were calculated by dividing the odds of success under the "minimum C" definition of successful remediation by the odds of success under the "minimum D" definition. Thus, the values in this column gauge the *relative* change in the likelihood of successful remediation when switching from the "minimum D" threshold to the "minimum C" threshold. The odds ratio is useful in this case because it allows comparisons between the various levels of initial math skill. For example, although the absolute decrease in the likelihood of success under the "minimum C" definition for Basic Arithmetic students is one-third that of Beginning Algebra students, the relative decrease for the two categories of initial math skill is nearly equal.

the models presented in Tables 1–6. In Table 7, I compare the distributions of college math skill attainment as a function of math skill at college entry under these two competing definitions of success. In Table 8, I present the pertinent coefficients and standard errors for this third alternative regression model specification.

Regarding the overarching pattern of outcomes, the results presented in Table 8 parallel those presented in Table 6. Although RCs, relative to CCs, are slightly advantaged in some respects and slightly disadvantaged in other respects, the overall pattern of comparable outcomes for RCs and CCs is preserved. Likewise, as in Table 6, a similar pattern of increasing disadvantage with decreasing math skill is observed among RNs. Thus, neither of the two alternative thresholds of successful remediation appears to be more or less informative than the other with respect to the questions addressed in this study.

Discussion

This paper poses the question, "Does mathematics remediation work?" To answer this question, I used hierarchical multinomial logistic regression to model natural variation in a five-category nominal outcome measure of long-term student attainment as a function of a four-category nominal measure of student's entry to, and exit from, math and a set of student- and college-level control variables. In addition, I replicated this model using a more complex 10-category nominal measure of math status and two competing definitions of college-level math skill attainment. The answer to the question posed here clearly is affirmative, yet with one important caveat.

Within the context of the community college, students who remediate successfully in math exhibit attainment that is comparable to that of students who achieve college math skill without the need for remediation, and this finding generally holds true even across the various levels of initial math skill deficiency. In fact, the two groups effectively are indistinguishable from one another in terms of credential attainment and transfer, with the minor exception of small differences in the likelihood of completing a credential prior to transfer. This is a remarkable finding, as it indicates that remediation has the capacity to fully resolve the academic disadvantage of math skill deficiency, at least as far as these outcomes are concerned. Thus, as it pertains to students who remediate successfully in math, the primary goal of remediation clearly *is* being achieved.

However, the caveat is large and troubling. Three out of four (75.4%) remedial math students do not remediate successfully (Table 1), and the academic attainment of these students is abysmal: more than four in five (81.5%) do not complete a credential and do not transfer (Table 2). So, one

Table 8 Estimated coefficients and standard errors for the hierarchical multinomial logistic regression of academic outcome on an expanded math status variable and selected student-level and college-level control variables, *using an alternative definition of successful college-level math skill attainment* ($N_{students}$ = 85,894; $N_{colleges}$ = 107; control variables not shown)

Math status		Academic outcome				
		No credential and no transfer	Certificate only	Associate's degree with or without certificate	Transfer without credential	Transfer with credential
"Completer"	College math	Comparison category				
	Intermediate algebra/geometry		−0.193 (0.184)	−0.099 (0.076)	−0.146* (0.061)	0.043 (0.055)
	Beginning algebra		−0.427* (0.199)	−0.068 (0.078)	−0.004 (0.075)	0.191** (0.061)
	Pre-algebra		−0.388 (0.351)	−0.315* (0.159)	0.114 (0.130)	0.259* (0.114)
	Basic arithmetic		−0.214 (0.299)	−0.442** (0.154)	−0.317* (0.140)	0.024 (0.139)
"Noncompleter"	College math	Comparison category	−0.104 (0.199)	−0.796*** (0.132)	−1.480*** (0.072)	−2.956*** (0.142)
	Intermediate algebra/geometry		0.078 (0.144)	−0.799*** (0.078)	−2.089*** (0.062)	−3.128*** (0.083)
	Beginning algebra		0.245 (0.129)	−0.910*** (0.066)	−2.459*** (0.050)	−3.324*** (0.065)
	Pre-algebra		0.046 (0.141)	−1.529*** (0.094)	−2.883*** (0.069)	−3.847*** (0.094)
	Basic arithmetic		0.124 (0.138)	−1.843*** (0.096)	−3.139*** (0.080)	−4.161*** (0.101)

Note: * $p \leq 0.05$; ** $p \leq 0.01$; *** $p \leq 0.001$; standard errors provided in parentheses

must conclude that the answer to the question posed here is, "Yes, remediation does work for *some* students," or, perhaps, "*When* remediation works, it works extremely well."

Why does mathematics remediation work for some and not for others? Said another way, why do the majority of remedial math students *not* attain college-level math skill? In answer to this question, several strong correlates of successful remediation in math have emerged in the literature: grade in first math, depth of remedial need at college entry, and breadth of remedial need at college entry. The first of these—grade in first math—is a strong, positive predictor of the likelihood of successful remediation in math (Bahr n.d.; Wang 2001). The underlying reasons for this association are debatable, as a student's math grade is a product of a number of factors, including prior math preparation and the degree of effort applied to the topic by the student (Farkas 2003). It seems certain, however, that academic self-efficacy plays a role, as the relationships between performance, self-efficacy, and outcomes are well articulated (Britner and Pajares 2001; Chen and Kaplan 2003; Robbins et al. 2004; Santiago and Einarson 1998). More specifically, one would expect that poor performance in first math would discourage further pursuit of mathematical competency through the impact of the performance disappointment on academic self-efficacy.

Concerning the latter two correlates, depth of remedial need refers to the degree of deficiency in a given subject, while breadth of remedial need refers to the number of subjects in which a given student requires remedial assistance (Bahr 2007). A number of studies indicate that depth and breadth of remedial need are strongly and inversely associated with the likelihood of successful remediation (Bahr 2007, n.d.; Easterling et al. 1998; Hagedorn and Lester 2006; McCabe 2000; Weissman et al. 1997b). The effect of depth of remedial need, in particular, is startling evident in Table 7. For example, in this study only 1 in 15 basic arithmetic students achieved college-level math skill, while approximately one in two intermediate algebra and geometry students did so. Thus, the likelihood of successful remediation in math declines sharply as degree of deficiency (depth of remedial need) increases.

However, the mechanisms that underlie the relationships between depth/breadth of remedial need and successful remediation are, as of yet, unclear. For example, some have suggested that the stigma of placement in low ability groups influences negatively students' perceptions of themselves and the subject matter, and, thereby, academic outcomes (Hadden 2000; Maxwell 1997). One might extrapolate from this argument that the lower is a student's placement in the remedial hierarchy, the greater is the stigma attached to that placement, and, therefore, the lower is the likelihood that the student will remediate successfully. Yet, this explanation conflicts with Deil-Amen and Rosenbaum's (2002) finding of a shift toward "stigma-free" remediation in community colleges that tends to hide from underprepared students their remedial status. Alternatively, McCusker (1999) suggests that remedial students become discouraged at the prospect of taking numerous courses that do not result in credit towards a degree and/or lengthen the time required to achieve educational objectives, which is a problem that worsens the further down the remedial ladder one begins. Conversely, Rosenbaum (2001) suggests that some underprepared students view community college attendance as a personal educational "experiment," which contributes to undisciplined behavior with respect to coursework. One might reason that the students who are least prepared for college-level coursework are the most likely to view college attendance as an "experiment," which would contribute to the negative correlations between depth and breadth of remedial need and the likelihood of favorable outcomes. While these all appear to be plausible explanations, further research is needed to elaborate fully the relationships between depth and breadth of remedial need and successful remediation.

Policy Implications

At least three important implications for educational policy may be drawn from this work. First, as noted earlier, when mathematics remediation works, it works extremely well. Thus, although critics of remediation might continue to argue that this "second chance" is a "waste" of resources (Reising 1997), they may not argue that remedial math programs are failing to meet their objective for students who remediate successfully.

Nevertheless, critics legitimately may question the global success of programs in which three-quarters of the students who start a journey towards college-level math never arrive at that destination. Moreover, as noted earlier, it is those students who have the greatest deficiencies who are the least likely to remediate successfully. Thus, criticism of remedial programs may be justified on two fronts: comparatively few remedial math students remediate successfully, and those students who do remediate successfully are disproportionately those who require the least assistance.

Note, however, that the focus of the analysis presented here is *not* on the effect of remedial math coursework in general, but on the effect of remediating *successfully* in math. Therefore, one implication that should *not* be drawn from these findings is that remedial coursework is detrimental to the academic outcomes of some students. This distinction between the effect of remedial coursework and the effect of remediating successfully is an important one because studies that examine the effect of remedial coursework face a quagmire of problems associated with controlling confounding background characteristics of students.

In contrast, the only instance in which questions about unaddressed confounding variables would become prominent in a study such as this one is when the findings suggest that remediating successfully does *not* lead to outcomes that are comparable to those of college-prepared students. That is not the finding of this study. Rather, I find only negligible differences in outcomes between successful remedial math students and students who do not require remediation. Given that students who require remedial assistance disproportionately face other (additional) obstacles to academic success (including the many confounding background characteristics), this finding of only minor differences runs contrary to what one would anticipate if confounding background characteristics were analytically problematic in this study. Thus, a high level of confidence may be placed in the finding of this study, but this confidence extends only to the focus of this study (the effect of remediating successfully), and any inference drawn concerning some "general effect" of remedial math coursework likely would be erroneous.

Second, in this population more than four in five (81.3%) first-time freshmen who enrolled in nonvocational math enrolled specifically in remedial math (Table 1). Given this high rate of enrollment in remedial math coursework, one can see clearly that remediation is not simply one of many functions of the community college. Rather, it is so fundamental to the activities of the community college that significant alterations in remedial programs would change drastically the educational geography of these institutions. This should give pause to those who advocate the elimination of remediation or other substantial changes in the availability of remedial programs, as the implications of such changes would be profound indeed.

Finally, it is important to note that 59% of the first-time freshmen who enrolled in nonvocational math did not complete a credential and did not transfer, and 84% of the students who did not complete a credential and did not transfer were remedial math students who did not remediate successfully (Table 2). My analysis suggests that, all else being equal, assisting all remedial math students to remediate successfully may reduce the number of students who enroll in nonvocational math, but do not complete a credential and do not transfer, by as much as two-thirds (65%).[6] Thus, postsecondary remediation plays an indisputably central role both in the educational trajectories of students who require assistance with basic skills *and* in the "bigger picture" of educational attainment in the community college system. Given the growing attention on the performance of, and performance standards for, community colleges (Bahr et al. 2004, 2005; Bastedo and Gumport 2003; Boylan 1997; McMillan et al. 1997; Roueche and Roueche 1999; Roueche et al. 2002), it is exceedingly apparent in light of this analysis that identifying methods of increasing the rate of successful remediation in math should be a topic of central concern to all stakeholders in the community college system.

Conclusion

Postsecondary remediation is a hotly contested topic. Yet, remarkably few large-scale, comprehensive, multi-institutional evaluations of remediation have been put forward, leading to an astonishing lack of empirical evidence to inform this debate. In this study, I tested the efficacy of postsecondary remedial math programs, using data that address a population of 85,894 first-time college freshmen enrolled in 107 community colleges. I found that students who remediate successfully (achieve college-level math skill) exhibit long-term academic attainment (credential completion and transfer) that is comparable to that of students who achieve college-level math skill without the need for remedial assistance. Conversely, students who do not remediate successfully, who constitute both the majority of students who enroll in remedial math coursework and the majority of students who enroll in any nonvocational math coursework (remedial or college-level), experience outcomes that are considerably less favorable. Thus, it is clear that mathematics remediation is extremely effective for students who remediate successfully. However, further research is needed to elaborate the obstacles that are hindering successful remediation for so many.

Acknowledgments I am indebted to Tim Brown, Willard Hom, Myrna Huffman, Tom Nobert, Mary Kay Patton, and Patrick Perry of the Chancellor's Office of California Community Colleges for their assistance with the data employed in this study. I thank Elisabeth Bahr for her assistance with the editing of this manuscript. Finally, I am grateful to John C. Smart and the anonymous referees of *Research in Higher Education* for their respective recommendations concerning improving this work.

Notes

1. An alternative interpretation suggests that remedial coursework actually protects academic standards by allowing college-level courses to address college-level material (McCabe 2000).
2. It is possible that some students may begin at one community college and then transfer to another community college, or may simultaneously complete courses at two or more community colleges. To account for these possibilities, course enrollments for each student were observed across all semester-based community colleges without regard to the first institution of attendance.
3. While the data do not contain direct measures of SES, the receipt of financial aid serves as an indirect measure and is not without precedent as an indicator of SES in research on remediation (Koski and Levin 1998). DesJardins et al. (2002) offer a persuasive argument for using *offered* financial aid as an indicator of SES, but these data were not available.
4. The contextual variables were transformed as necessary to approximate a normal distribution.
5. Although movement from one college to another is not uncommon among community college students (Bach et al. 2000), this model cannot capture these changes. An alternative specification using a cross-classified data structure would allow the college in which a given student is enrolled to vary, but would treat a student enrolled in multiple colleges as different students (Raudenbush and Bryk 2002).
6. As this is a counterfactual argument, it is only a supposition based upon the evidence.

References

Adelman, C. (2004a). *Principal indicators of student academic histories in postsecondary education, 1972–2000*. Washington, D.C.: Institute of Education Sciences.

Adelman, C. (2004b). *The empirical curriculum: Changes in postsecondary course-taking, 1972–2000*. Washington, D.C.: Institute of Education Sciences.

American Council on Education. (2003). *Issue brief: Student success: Understanding graduation and persistence rates*. Washington, D.C.: American Council on Education.

Astin, A. W. (1998). Remedial education and civic responsibility. *National Crosstalk, 6*, 12–13.

Attewell, P., Lavin, D., Domina, T., & Levey, T. (2006). New evidence on college remediation. *Journal of Higher Education, 77*, 886–924.

Bach, S. K., Banks, M. T., Kinnick, M. K., Ricks, M. F., Stoering, J. M., & Walleri, R. D. (2000). Student attendance patterns and performance in an urban postsecondary environment. *Research in Higher Education, 41*, 315–330.

Bahr, P. R. (2007). Double jeopardy: Testing the effects of multiple basic skill deficiencies on successful remediation. *Research in Higher Education, 48*, 695–725.

Bahr, P. R. (n.d.). Preparing the underprepared: An analysis of racial disparities in postsecondary mathematics remediation. Manuscript under review. Department of Sociology, Wayne State University, Detroit, Michigan.

Bahr, P. R., Hom, W., & Perry, P. (2004). Student readiness for postsecondary coursework: Developing a college-level measure of student average academic preparation. *Journal of Applied Research in the Community College, 12,* 7–16.

Bahr, P. R., Hom, W., & Perry, P. (2005). College transfer performance: A methodology for equitable measurement and comparison. *Journal of Applied Research in the Community College, 13,* 73–87.

Bastedo, M. N., & Gumport, P. J. (2003). Access to what?: Mission differentiation and academic stratification in U.S. public higher education. *Higher Education, 46,* 341–359.

Bers, T. H. (1987). Evaluating remedial education programs. *AIR Professional File, 29,* 1–8.

Bettinger, E., & Long, B. T. (2004). Shape up or ship out: The effects of remediation on students at four-year colleges. National Bureau of Economic Research, Working Paper No. W10369.

Bettinger, E., & Long, B. T. (2005). Remediation at the community college: Student participation and outcomes. *New Directions for Community Colleges, 129,* 17–26.

Bickley, S. G., Davis, M. D., & Anderson, D. (2001). The relationship between developmental reading and subsequent academic success. *Research in Developmental Education, 16,* 1–4.

Boughan, K. (2001). Closing the transfer data gap: Using National Student Clearinghouse data in community college outcomes research. *Journal of Applied Research in the Community College, 8,* 107–116.

Boylan, H. R. (1997). Criteria for program evaluation in developmental education. *Research in Developmental Education, 14,* 1–4.

Boylan, H. R. (1999). Developmental education: Demographics, outcomes, and activities. *Journal of Developmental Education, 23,* 2–8.

Boylan, H. R., & Bonham, B. S. (1992). The impact of developmental education programs. *Research in Developmental Education, 9,* 1–4.

Boylan, H. R., & Saxon, D. P. (1999a). *Outcomes of remediation.* Boone, North Carolina: National Center for Developmental Education.

Boylan, H. R., & Saxon, D. P. (1999b). *Remedial courses: Estimates of student participation and the volume of remediation in U.S. community colleges.* Boone, North Carolina: National Center for Developmental Education.

Boylan, H. R., Saxon, D. P., & Boylan, H. M. (1999). *State policies on remediation at public colleges and universities.* Boone, North Carolina: National Center for Developmental Education.

Breneman, D. W., & Haarlow, W. N. (1998). *Remediation in higher education.* Washington, D.C.: Thomas B. Fordham Foundation.

Britner, S. L., & Pajares, F. (2001). Self-efficacy beliefs, motivation, race, and gender in middle school science. *Journal of Women and Minorities in Science and Engineering, 7,* 271–285.

Brothen, T., & Wambach, C. A. (2004). Refocusing developmental education. *Journal of Developmental Education, 28,* 16–33.

Burley, H., Butner, B., & Cejda, B. (2001). Dropout and stopout patterns among developmental education students in Texas community colleges. *Community College Journal of Research and Practice, 25,* 767–782.

Carter, D. F. (1999). The impact of institutional choice and environments on African-American and White students' degree expectations. *Research in Higher Education, 41,* 17–41.

Chen, Z., & Kaplan, H. B. (2003). School failure in early adolescence and status attainment in middle adulthood: A longitudinal study. *Sociology of Education, 76,* 110–127.

Cohen, C., & Johnson, F. (2004). *Revenues and expenditures for public elementary and secondary education: School Year 2001–02 (NCES 2004–341).* Washington, D.C.: National Center for Education Statistics.

Condron, D. J., & Roscigno, V. J. (2003). Disparities within: Unequal spending and achievement in an urban school district. *Sociology of Education, 76,* 18–36.

Costrell, R. M. (1998). Commentary. In D. W. Breneman & W. N. Haarlow (Eds.), *Remediation in higher education* (pp. 23–40). Washington, D.C.: Thomas B. Fordham Foundation.

Crews, D. M., & Aragon, S. R. (2004). Influence of a community college developmental education writing course on academic performance. *Community College Review, 32,* 1–18.

Curtis, J. W. (2002). *Student outcomes in developmental education: 1994–95 through 1999–2000.* Locust Grove, Virginia: Germanna Community College. ERIC No. ED459900.

Day, P. R. Jr., & McCabe, R. H. (1997). *Remedial education: A social and economic imperative.* Washington, DC: American Association of Community Colleges.

Deil-Amen, R., & Rosenbaum, J. E. (2002). The unintended consequences of stigma-free remediation. *Sociology of Education, 75*, 249–268.

DesJardins, S. L., Ahlburg, D. A., & McCall, B. P. (2002). A temporal investigation of factors related to timely degree completion. *Journal of Higher Education, 73*, 555–581.

Dougherty, K. J., & Reid, M. (2007). *Fifty States of achieving the dream: State policies to enhance access to and success in community colleges across the United States.* Community College Research Center, Teachers College, Columbia University.

Easterling, D. N., Patten, J. E., & Krile, D. J. (1998). Patterns of progress: Student persistence isn't always where you expect it. Paper presented at the annual forum of the Association for Institutional Research, May 19, Minneapolis, Minnesota.

Farkas, G. (2003). Racial disparities and discrimination in education: What do we know, how do we know it, and what do we need to know? *Teachers College Record, 105*, 1119–1146.

Gray-Barnett, N. K. (2001). *An analysis of the academic success achieved by five freshman cohorts through a community college developmental education program.* Unpublished dissertation manuscript. Department of Educational Leadership and Policy Analysis, East Tennessee State University, Johnson City, Tennessee.

Greene, J. P. (2000). *The cost of remedial education: How much Michigan pays when students fail to learn basic skills.* Midland, Michigan: Mackinac Center for Public Policy.

Grimes, S. K., & David, K. C. (1999). Underprepared community college students: Implications of attitudinal and experiential differences. *Community College Review, 27*, 73–92.

Grubb, W. N., & Gardner, D. (2001). *From black box to Pandora's Box: Evaluating remedial/developmental education.* New York, New York: Community College Research Center, Teachers College, Columbia University.

Hadden, C. (2000). The ironies of mandatory placement. *Community College Journal of Research and Practice, 24*, 823–838.

Hagedorn, L. S., & Lester, J. (2006). Hispanic community college students and the transfer game: Strikes, misses, and grand slam experiences. *Community College Journal of Research and Practice, 30*, 827–853.

Hagedorn, L. S., Siadat, M. V., Fogel, S. F., Nora, A., & Pascarella, E. T. (1999). Success in college mathematics: Comparisons between remedial and nonremedial first-year college students. *Research in Higher Education, 40*, 261–284.

Hoyt, J. E. (1999). Remedial education and student attrition. *Community College Review, 27*, 51–73.

Ignash, J. M. (1997). Who should provide postsecondary remedial/developmental education? *New Directions for Community Colleges, 100*, 5–20.

Illich, P. A., Hagan, C., & McCallister, L. (2004). Performance in college-level courses among students concurrently enrolled in remedial courses: Policy implications. *Community College Journal of Research and Practice, 28*, 435–453.

Immerwahr, J. (1999). *Taking responsibility: Leaders' expectations of higher education.* San Jose, California: National Center for Public Policy and High Education. Report No. 99-1.

James, J., Morrow, V. P., & Perry, P. (2002). Study session on basic skills. Presentation given to the Board of Governors of California Community Colleges, July 8–9, Sacramento, California.

Jenkins, D., & Boswell, K. (2002). *State policies on community college remedial education: Findings from a national survey.* Denver, Colorado: Education Commission of the States, Community College Policy Center. Publication No. CC-02-01.

Kerckhoff, A. C., Raudenbush, S. W., & Glennie, E. (2001). Education, cognitive skill, and labor force outcomes. *Sociology of Education, 74*, 1–24.

Kolajo, E. F. (2004). From developmental education to graduation: A community college experience. *Community College Journal of Research and Practice, 28*, 365–371.

Koski, W. S., & Levin, H. M. (1998). *Replacing remediation with acceleration in higher education: Preliminary report on literature review and initial interviews.* Stanford, California: National Center for Postsecondary Improvement.

Kozeracki, C. A. (2002). ERIC review: Issues in developmental education. *Community College Review, 29*, 83–101.

Kulik, C. C., Kulik, J. A., & Shwalb, B. J. (1983). College programs for high-risk and disadvantaged students: A meta-analysis of findings. *Review of Educational Research, 53*, 397–414.

Maxwell, M. (1997). *What are the functions of a college learning assistance center?* Kensington, Maryland: MM Associates. ERIC No. ED413031.

Mazzeo, C. (2002). Stakes for students: Agenda-setting and remedial education. *Review of Higher Education, 26*, 19–39.

McCabe, R. H. (2000). *No one to waste: A report to public decision-makers and community college leaders.* Washington, D.C.: Community College Press.

McCabe, R. H. (2003). *Yes we can!: A community college guide for developing America's underprepared.* Phoenix, Arizona: League for Innovation in the Community College.

McCusker, M. (1999). ERIC review: Effective elements of developmental reading and writing programs. *Community College Review, 27,* 93–105.

McMillan, V. K., Parke, S. J., & Lanning, C. A. (1997). Remedial/developmental education approaches for the current community college environment. *New Directions for Community Colleges, 100,* 21–32.

Mills, M. (1998). From coordinating board to campus: Implementation of a policy mandate on remedial education. *Journal of Higher Education, 69,* 672–697.

O'Toole, D. M., Stratton, L. S., & Wetzel, J. N. (2003). A longitudinal analysis of the frequency of part-time enrollment and the persistence of students who enroll part-time. *Research in Higher Education, 44,* 519–537.

Oudenhoven, B. (2002). Remediation at the community college: Pressing issues, uncertain solutions. *New Directions for Community Colleges, 117,* 35–44.

Overby, B. A. (2003). Reality versus perception: Using research to resolve misconceptions about developmental programs and promote credibility and acceptance. *Research in Developmental Education, 18,* 1–5.

Parsad, B., Lewis, L., & Greene, B. (2003). *Remedial education at degree-granting postsecondary institutions in Fall 2000 (NCES 2004-010).* Washington, D.C.: National Center for Education Statistics.

Phipps, R. (1998). *College remediation: What it is. What it costs. What's at stake.* Washington, D.C.: Institute for Higher Education Policy.

Pitts, J. M., White, W. G., Jr., & Harrison, A. B. (1999). Student academic underpreparedness: Effects on faculty. *Review of Higher Education, 22,* 343–365.

Purvis, D., & Watkins, P. C. (1987). Performance and retention of developmental students: A five-year follow-up study. *Research in Developmental Education, 4,* 1–4.

Raudenbush, S. W., & Bryk, A. S. (2002). *Hierarchical linear models: Applications and data analysis methods.* Thousand Oaks, California: Sage.

Reising, B. (1997). What's new in postsecondary remediation. *The Clearing House, 70,* 172–173.

Robbins, S. B., Lauver, K., Le, H., Davis, D., Langley, R., & Carlstrom, A. (2004). Do psychosocial and study skill factors predict college outcomes?: A meta-analysis. *Psychological Bulletin, 130,* 261–288.

Roberts, G. H. (1986). *Developmental education: An historical study.* ERIC No. ED276395. As cited in Tomlinson, L. M. (1989). *Postsecondary developmental programs: A traditional agenda with new imperatives.* Washington, D.C.: The George Washington University.

Rosenbaum, J. E. (2001). *Beyond college for all: Career paths for the forgotten half.* New York: Russell Sage Foundation.

Roueche, J. E., & Roueche, S. D. (1999). *High stakes, high performance: Making remedial education work.* Washington, D.C.: American Association of Community Colleges.

Roueche, J. E., Roueche, S. D., & Ely, E. D. (2001). Pursuing excellence: The community college of Denver. *Community College Journal of Research and Practice, 25,* 517–537.

Roueche, J. E., Roueche, S. D., & Johnson, R. A. (2002). At our best: Facing the challenges. *Community College Journal, 72,* 10–14.

Santiago, A. M., & Einarson, M. K. (1998). Background characteristics as predictors of academic self-confidence and academic self-efficacy among graduate science and engineering students. *Research in Higher Education, 39,* 163–198.

Saxon, D. P., & Boylan, H. R. (2001). The cost of remedial education in higher education. *Journal of Developmental Education, 25,* 2–8.

Seybert, J. A., & Soltz, D. F. (1992). *Assessing the outcomes of developmental courses at Johnson County Community College.* Overland Park, Kansas: Johnson County Community College. ERIC No. ED349052.

Shults, C. (2000). *Remedial education: Practices and policies in community colleges.* American Association of Community Colleges, Research Brief No. AACC-RB-00-2. Annapolis Junction, Maryland: Community College Press.

Southard, A. H., & Clay, J. K. (2004). Measuring the effectiveness of developmental writing courses. *Community College Review, 32,* 39–50.

Spring, J. (1976). *The sorting machine: National educational policy since 1945.* New York: David McKay.

Steinberg, L. (1998). Commentary. In D. W. Breneman & W. N. Haarlow (Eds.), *Remediation in higher education* (pp. 44–50). Washington, D.C.: Thomas B. Fordham Foundation.

Stratton, L. S., O'Toole, D. M., & Wetzel, J. N. (2007). Are the factors affecting dropout behavior related to initial enrollment intensity for college undergraduates? *Research in Higher Education, 48,* 453–485.

Szafran, R. F. (2001). The effect of academic load on success for new college students: Is lighter better? *Research in Higher Education, 42,* 27–50.

Tennessee Higher Education Commission. (2001). *An analysis of remedial and developmental education.* Nashville, Tennessee: Tennessee Higher Education Commission.

Titus, M. A. (2004). An examination of the influence of institutional context on student persistence at 4-year colleges and universities: A multilevel approach. *Research in Higher Education, 45,* 673–699.

Tomlinson, L. M. (1989). *Postsecondary developmental programs: A traditional agenda with new imperatives.* Washington, D.C.: The George Washington University.

Toutkoushian, R. K., & Smart, J. C. (2001). Do institutional characteristics affect student gains from college? *Review of Higher Education, 25,* 39–61.

Trombley, W. (1998). Remedial education under attack: Controversial plans for the City University of New York. *National Crosstalk, 6,* 2.

Trombley, W., Doyle, W., & Davis, J. (1998). The remedial controversy: Different states offer various solutions. *National Crosstalk, 6,* 1.

Turnage, R. (2003). 2004–05 Comprehensive five-year capital outlay plan. Presentation to the Board of Governors of California Community Colleges, July 14–15, Sacramento, California.

Walters, P. B. (2001). Educational access and the state: Historical continuities and discontinuities in racial inequality in American education. *Sociology of Education, 74,* 35–49.

Wang, W. (2001). Succeeding in transferable level math: The effects of procrastination and other variables. Paper presented at the annual meeting of the California Association of Institutional Researchers, November 14–16, Sacramento, California.

Waycaster, P. (2001). Factors impacting success in community college developmental mathematics courses and subsequent courses. *Community College Journal of Research and Practice, 25,* 403–416.

Weissman, J., Bulakowski, C., & Jumisko, M. (1997a). Using research to evaluate developmental education programs and policies. *New Directions for Community Colleges, 100,* 73–80.

Weissman, J., Silk, E., & Bulakowski, C. (1997b). Assessing developmental education policies. *Research in Higher Education, 38,* 187–200.

Worley, J. (2003). Developmental reading instruction, academic attainment and performance among underprepared college students. *Journal of Applied Research in the Community College, 10,* 127–136.

P. R. Bahr (✉)
Department of Sociology, Wayne State University, Detroit, MI 48202, USA
e-mail: peter.bahr@wayne.edu

COPYRIGHT INFORMATION

TITLE: Does Mathematics Remediation Work?: A Comparative Analysis of Academic Attainment among Community College Students

SOURCE: Res Higher Educ 49 no5 Ag 2008

REFERRAL, ENROLLMENT, AND COMPLETION IN DEVELOPMENTAL EDUCATION SEQUENCES IN COMMUNITY COLLEGES*

THOMAS BAILEY,** DONG WOOK JEONG, AND SUNG-WOO CHO

Community College Research Center, Teachers College, Columbia University, United States

Abstract. After being assessed, many students entering community colleges are referred to one or more levels of developmental education. While the need to assist students with weak academic skills is well known, little research has examined student progression through multiple levels of developmental education and into entry-level college courses. The purpose of this paper is to analyze the patterns and determinants of student progression through sequences of developmental education starting from initial referral. Our results indicate that fewer than one half of the students who are referred to remediation actually complete the entire sequence to which they are referred. About 30 percent of students referred to developmental education do not enroll in any remedial course, and only about 60 percent of referred students actually enroll in the remedial course to which they were referred. The results also show that more students exit their developmental sequences because they *did not enroll in* the first or a subsequent course than because they *failed or withdrew from* a course in which they were enrolled. We also show that men, older students, African American students, part-time students, and students in vocational programs are less likely to progress through their full remedial sequences. © 2009 Elsevier Ltd. All rights reserved.

Keywords: Developmental education, Community college

1. Introduction

Developmental education is designed to provide students who enter college with weak academic skills the opportunity to strengthen those skills enough to prepare them for college-level course-work.[1] The concept is simple enough—students who arrive unprepared for college are provided instruction to bring them up to an adequate level. But in practice, developmental education is complex and confusing. To begin with, experts do not agree on the meaning of being "college ready." Policies and regulations governing assessment, placement, pedagogy, staffing, completion,

*Funding for this study was provided by Lumina Foundation for Education as part of the Achieving the Dream: Community Colleges Count Initiative.
**Corresponding author at: Community College Research Center, Teachers College, Columbia University, Box 174, 525 W. 120th Street, New York, NY 10027, United States. Tel.: +1 212 678 3091.
E-mail address: tbailey@tc.edc (T. Bailey).

and eligibility for enrollment in college-level credit-bearing courses vary from state to state, college to college, and program to program. The developmental education process is confusing enough simply to describe, yet from the point of view of the student, especially the student with particularly weak academic skills who has not had much previous success in school, it must appear as a bewildering set of unanticipated obstacles involving several assessments, classes in more than one subject area, and sequences of courses that may require two, three, or more semesters of study before a student (often a high school graduate) is judged prepared for college-level work.

The policy deliberation and especially the research about developmental education give scant attention to this confusion and complexity. Discussions typically assume that the state of being "college ready" is well-defined, and they elide the distinction between students who need remediation and those who actually enroll in developmental courses. What is more, developmental education is often discussed without acknowledgement of the extensive diversity of services that bear that label. Any comprehensive understanding of developmental education and any successful strategy to improve its effectiveness cannot be built on such a simplistic view.

In this article, we broaden the discussion of developmental education by moving beyond consideration of the developmental *course* and focusing attention instead on the developmental *sequence*. In most colleges, students are, upon initial enrollment, assigned to different levels of developmental education on the basis of performance on placement tests.[2] Students with greater academic deficiencies are often referred to a sequence of two or more courses designed to prepare students in a step-by-step fashion for the first college-level course. For example, those with the greatest need for developmental math may be expected to enroll in and pass pre-collegiate math or arithmetic, basic algebra, and intermediate algebra, in order to prepare them for college-level algebra. We define the "sequence" as a process that begins with initial assessment and referral to remediation and ends with completion of the highest level developmental course—the course that in principle completes the student's preparation for college-level studies. Although a majority of students do proceed (or fail to proceed) through their sequences in order, some students skip steps and others enroll in lower level courses than the ones to which they were referred, so the actual pattern of student participation is even more complicated than the structure of courses suggests. (We will discuss this in more detail later.) At times we extend the notion of "sequence" into the first-level college course in the relevant subject area, since in the end the short-term purpose of remediation is to prepare the student to be successful in that first college-level course.

We examine the relationship between referral to developmental education and actual enrollment, and we track students as they progress or fail to progress through their referred sequences of remedial courses, analyzing the points at which they exit those sequences. We also analyze the demographic and institutional characteristics that are related to the completion of sequences and exits at different points along them.

We carry out this analysis using data collected as part of the Achieving the Dream: Community Colleges Count initiative, a multi-state, multi-institution initiative designed to improve outcomes for community college students. The sample includes over 250,000 students from 57 colleges in seven states. The sample is not representative of all community college students, so we check our results against an analysis using the National Education Longitudinal Study of 1988 (henceforth, NELS:88).[3] Results of that analysis are consistent with results derived from the Achieving the Dream database.

An exploration of the distinction between *the course* and *the sequence* reveals some startling conclusions. While the majority of individual course enrollments do result in a course completion, between 33 and 46 percent of students, depending on the subject area, referred to developmental education actually complete their entire developmental sequence. And between 60 and 70 percent of students who fail to complete the sequence to which they were referred do so even while having passed all of the developmental courses in which they enrolled.

This collection of articles is dedicated to Henry Levin and our article relates particularly to his influential Accelerated Schools Project (ASP). Remediation in college is necessary because students arrive at the end of high school without adequate academic skills. The ASP was of course designed to avoid just this type of problem. Many of the students who arrive at community college with weak academic skills fell behind their classmates early in elementary school. ASP is a strategy to strengthen the academic skills of elementary and secondary students more effectively than traditional approaches to "remediation." Thus widespread use of ASP would reduce the need for developmental education in college. Moreover, we will argue that the ASP approach makes sense for remediation at the postsecondary level as well.

The remainder of this paper is organized in the following manner: in Section 2 we provide some general background on the characteristics and outcomes of remediation; in Section 3 we describe the Achieving the Dream and the NELS:88 databases; Section 4 presents the results of the analyses on student placement and progression in developmental education; Section 5 shows the results of multivariate analyses of the student and college characteristics that are related to an individual's likelihood of progressing through developmental education; Section 6 summarizes the results and presents conclusions and recommendations.

2. Developmental education basics

More than one half of community college students enroll in at least one developmental education course during their tenure in college. In the National Postsecondary Student Aid Study of 2003–04 (NPSAS:04), 43 percent of first- and second-year students enrolled in public two-year colleges took at least one remedial course during that year (Horn & Nevill, 2006). Longitudinal data that allow a measure for the incidence of developmental education over multiple years of enrollment show even higher levels of enrollment. Attewell, Lavin, Domina, and Levey (2006) found that in the NELS:88 sample, 58 percent of community college students took at least one remedial course, 44 percent took between one and three remedial courses, and 14 percent took more than three such courses. In the Achieving the Dream database, which will be described in detail below, about 59 percent of the sample enrolled in at least one developmental course.

Developmental programs absorb sizable public resources. More than ten years ago, Breneman and Haarlow (1998) estimated that remediation cost more than one billion dollars a year. A more recent study calculated the annual cost of remediation at $1.9–2.3 billion at community colleges and another $500 million at four-year colleges (Strong American Schools, 2008). State reports cite expenditures in the tens of millions of dollars (Arkansas Department of Higher Education, n.d.; Florida Office of Program Policy Analysis and Government Accountability, 2006; Ohio Board of Regents, 2006).

The costs of remediation to the taxpayer are substantial, but the financial, psychological, and opportunity costs borne by the students themselves may be even more significant. While they are enrolled in remediation, students accumulate debt, spend time and money, and bear the opportunity cost of lost earnings. In some states, they deplete their eligibility for financial aid. Moreover, many students referred to developmental classes, most of whom are high school graduates, are surprised and discouraged when they learn that they must delay their college education and in effect return to high school. A recent survey of remedial students found that a majority believed that they were prepared for college (Strong American Schools, 2008). This can cause students to become frustrated and to give up and leave college (Deil-Amen & Rosenbaum, 2002; Rosenbaum, 2001). Many students referred to remediation try to avoid it by using loopholes and exceptions that can be found in many regulations and guidelines (Perin & Charron, 2006).

Although remediation has high costs, clearly some provision must be made for students who enter college unprepared. Proponents argue that it can be an effective tool to improve access to higher education, particularly for underprivileged populations (McCabe, 2006), while others argue that the costs of remediation, for both society and student, outweigh the benefits. The controversy about remediation has prompted some research on the effectiveness of remedial programs in preparing students for college-level courses, but, given the size and significance of the developmental education function, that research is surprisingly sparse. Some descriptive studies have compared different approaches to remediation (Boylan, 2002). But only a handful of studies have compared the success of students who enroll in developmental courses to the success of similar students who enroll directly in college courses. Bettinger and Long (2005) used different remediation assignment cutoff scores among community colleges in Ohio to compare similar students who were and were not referred to developmental education to measure the effect of the remedial instruction. They used the distance from the student's home to the college as an instrument. Their sample was restricted to students who had taken the SAT or ACT. They found that students placed in math remediation were 15 percent more likely to transfer to a four-year college and took ten more credit hours than similar students not placed in remediation. They found no positive effect for reading developmental placement. Calcagno and Long (2008) and Martorell and McFarlin (2007) analyzed the effects of remediation on subsequent outcomes in Florida and Texas, respectively, where statewide remedial assignment cutoff scores allowed regression discontinuity analyses. These studies find no positive effect of remediation on college credit accumulation, completion, or degree attainment. Calcagno and Long found a small positive effect on year-to-year persistence in Florida, but Martorell and McFarlin found no effect on any outcome variable. The Florida and Texas studies in particular provide reliable but discouraging results; nevertheless, these results are only relevant to students scoring near the remediation assignment cutoff scores. In terms of the concept of a sequence, these are the students referred to developmental classes only one level below college-level.[4]

What accounts for these discouraging results? Certainly one fundamental problem is that most students referred to remediation, even those referred to only one level below college-level, do not complete their sequences. In the rest of this article, we analyze the patterns and determinants of that problem.

3. Achieving the Dream initiative: data description

Achieving the Dream: Community Colleges Count is a multiyear, national initiative designed to improve outcomes for community college students. As of early 2009, 19 funders and over 80 colleges in 15 states participated in the initiative. One of its most important goals is helping participating colleges and state agencies to build "a culture of evidence"—to gather, analyze, and make better use of data to foster fundamental change in the education practices and operations of community colleges for the purpose of improving student outcomes. The Achieving the Dream initiative collects longitudinal records for all first-time credential-seeking students in specified cohorts at all of the colleges participating in the initiative, including data on cohorts starting two years before the college entered the initiative. These cohorts will be tracked for the life of the initiative (at least six years for participating colleges) and possibly beyond. The dataset includes student demographics, enrollment information, the number of credits accumulated, and the receipt of any degrees or certificates. It also includes detailed information on referral to developmental education; enrollment and completion of remedial courses in reading, writing, and mathematics; and enrollment and completion of "gatekeeper" courses—the first college-level courses corresponding to the developmental subject fields.[5] The initiative started in 2004 with five participating states: Florida, New Mexico, North Carolina, Texas, and Virginia. Twenty-seven colleges were chosen from those states. Each had student populations that were at least 38 percent Pell Grant recipients or 54 percent African American, Hispanic, or Native American. In 2005 and 2006, 31 colleges from Connecticut, Ohio, Pennsylvania, Washington, and Texas joined the initiative.[6] Although subsequently 26 colleges in eight states joined the initiative, we use data only from those who joined in 2004, 2005, or 2006, because we have at least three years of post-enrollment data on students from those colleges.

Table 1 describes institutional characteristics of 57 Achieving the Dream colleges in fall 2004.[7] We retrieved the data from the Integrated Postsecondary Education Data System (IPEDS) to compare Achieving the Dream colleges with national and state public two-year institutions. The first column represents national public two-year colleges, the second column represents public two-year colleges in Achieving the Dream states, and the third represents the colleges included in the sample. Compared to the national and state samples, Achieving the Dream colleges serve substantially higher proportions of African American and Hispanic students. Achieving the Dream colleges also enroll a larger number of students per college, and they make noticeably smaller instructional expenditures per full-time equivalent enrollment (FTE). They are also more likely to be located in urban areas. Thus the Achieving the Dream sample more closely represents an urban, low-income,

Table 1
Characteristics of Achieving the Dream colleges.

Variables	Public two-year (Nation)	Public two-year (Achieving the Dream states[a])	Achieving the Dream colleges[b]
Percent of Black students	14.22 (17.02)	14.13 (13.31)	16.56 (11.84)
Percent of Hispanic students	8.54 (13.67)	12.07 (17.07)	22.39 (20.71)
Full-time equivalent enrollments (FTE)	2114.2 (2142.2)	2150.7 (2216.8)	6609.5 (3350.6)
Percent of students receiving federal financial aid	43.94 (18.71)	41.41 (17.34)	38.45 (14.52)
Average amount of federal financial aid received per FTE (in dollars)	2708.2 (637.5)	2646.3 (633.4)	2878.98 (465.61)
Instructional expenditures per FTE (in dollars)	5261.5 (20,987)	5025.6 (12,675)	3339.47 (848.90)
Location			
Urban	39.47%	48.99%	80.94%
Suburban	23.72%	21.14%	14.77%
Rural	36.81%	29.87%	4.29%
Full-time retention rate (fall 2003–fall 2004)	57.73% (13.85)	56.30% (13.56)	57.61% (6.50)
Observations (N)	1169	307	57

Note: Standard deviations for continuous variables are in parentheses.

[a] Achieving the Dream states include Connecticut, Florida, Ohio, New Mexico, North Carolina, Pennsylvania, Texas, Virginia, and Washington.

[b] For the purpose of comparison, we excluded three four-year institutions from the Achieving the Dream colleges.

and minority student population than do community colleges in the country as a whole. The sample therefore characterizes an important sub-group of community colleges, but when possible we check our results against the national NELS:88 sample.

The Achieving the Dream database we used for this study was derived from 256,672 first-time credential-seeking students who began their enrollment in Fall 2003 to Fall 2004 in 57 colleges that provided detailed information on developmental education. We followed their enrollments in remediation through the summers of 2006 and 2007—three academic years. For simplicity, we focused on two common developmental education subjects: math and reading. The database contains information on student gender, race/ethnicity, age at entry, full- or part-time enrollment, major, all remedial courses taken, and the grades earned in those courses. One unique aspect of this dataset, particularly important for our purposes, is that it includes a variable indicating whether students were referred to developmental education and, for those who were referred, the level to which they were referred.[8]

4. Student progression through developmental education

4.1. Student placement in developmental education

Most Achieving the Dream colleges use a placement test and/or academic records to place beginning students into developmental education. Based on their performance on the test/records, many individuals are referred to a sequence of developmental courses. The Achieving the Dream database classifies all beginning students into four groups for each type of developmental education: students referred to (1) no developmental education, (2) developmental education one level below the entry-level college course (henceforth we will refer to this as Level I), (3) two levels below (henceforth Level II), and (4) three or more levels below (henceforth Level III). Some students are thus expected to finish three or more developmental courses before enrolling in college-level classes. Fifty-nine percent of students were referred to developmental math: 24 percent to Level I, 16 percent to Level II, and 19 percent to Level III. Far fewer students—only 33 percent—were referred to reading remediation: 23 percent, 7 percent, and 3 percent into the respective three levels.[9]

Different colleges provide different numbers of levels of developmental education. In Fall 2000, public two-year colleges reported to offer, on average, 3.6 remedial courses in math while offering 2.7 courses in reading. Among the 53 Achieving the Dream colleges in the sample that provided information on remedial math offerings, 35 offer three or more levels of remedial math, 9 offer two levels, and 9 offer one level. Among the 51 such colleges that provided information on remedial

Table 2
Developmental course offerings and student referrals of Achieving the Dream colleges.

Developmental course offerings	Level of developmental education referral					
	Number of colleges	3+ levels below	2 levels below	1 level below	Not referred	Number of students (N)
Math						
One level	9			51%	49%	29,714
Two levels	9		30%	17%	53%	22,381
Three or more levels	35	33%	18%	16%	33%	89,495
Reading						
One level	11			39%	61%	22,361
Two levels	20		11%	20%	69%	28,015
Three or more levels	20	8%	9%	17%	66%	27,773

Note: Among 57 Achieving the Dream colleges, four and six provided no information on developmental education in math and reading, respectively.

reading offerings, 20 offer three or more levels of remedial reading, 20 offer two levels, and 11 offer one level (see Table 2).

4.2. Student progression through developmental education

In colleges with multiple levels of developmental education, in principle, only those who passed the course into which they were originally referred can pursue a higher level developmental course. In reality, many students enroll in higher and even lower level courses than those to which they are referred or skip courses in the sequence. Some referred students skip remediation entirely and enroll directly in the first college-level course in the relevant subject area.

Overall, 46 percent of students referred to reading remediation and 33 percent of those referred to math remediation completed their sequence of developmental education. Students who passed the highest level developmental course in their referred sequence are defined as sequence completers (see Table 3). Not surprisingly, developmental education completion rates are negatively related to the number of levels to which a student is referred. Of those students in our Achieving the Dream sample who were referred to Level I remediation (Table 3), 45 percent and 50 percent completed developmental math and reading, respectively.[10] The corresponding figures are 17 percent and 29 percent for those referred to Level III.

Many of the students who failed to complete their remediation sequence did so because they never even enrolled in a developmental course to begin with. Just under one-third of all students referred to remediation in this sample did not enroll in any developmental course in the relevant subject area within three years.

Of those students who did enroll in a remediation course, many—29 percent of all students referred to math and 16 percent of those referred to reading—exited their sequences after failing or withdrawing from one of their courses. But a substantial number—11 percent for math and 8 percent for reading—exited their sequence never having failed a course. That is, they successfully completed one or more developmental courses and failed to show up for the next course in their sequence. Thus if one combines the number of students who never enrolled with those who exited between courses, more students did not complete their sequence because they did not enroll in the first or a subsequent course than because they failed a course. For example, for reading, 30 percent never enrolled, and 8 percent left between courses, while only 16 percent failed or withdrew from a course.

The goal of developmental education is to prepare students for college-level courses. How did sequence completers fare in those college-level courses? In the Achieving the Dream dataset, the first college-level courses are referred to as gatekeeper courses (see footnote 5 for a definition). Data displayed in Table 4 indicate that between 50 and 55 percent of sequence completers also completed a gatekeeper course. But to complete the gatekeeper course, students must first enroll and then pass

Table 3
Student progression among those referred to developmental education.

Developmental course referral	Student progression				Total (*N*)
	Never enrolled in developmental education	Did not complete—never failed a course[a]	Did not complete—failed a course	Completed sequence[b]	
Math					
Level I	37%	2%	17%	45%	59,551
Level II	24%	13%	32%	32%	38,153
Level III	17%	23%	44%	17%	43,886
Total	27%	11%	29%	33%	141,590
Reading					
Level I	33%	5%	12%	50%	54,341
Level II	21%	13%	24%	42%	16,983
Level III	27%	19%	25%	29%	6,825
Total	30%	8%	16%	46%	78,149

[a] The small percentage of those who were referred to Level I and never failed a course are likely to have enrolled in a lower level of remediation, passed that course, and left the system.
[b] Sequence completion refers to the completion of Level I.

Table 4
Enrollment and completion rates among developmental enrollees.

Developmental course referral	Students who enrolled in developmental education		Among developmental education completers		
	Remediation enrollment among those referred	Gatekeeper pass rate among those referred	Gatekeeper pass rate	Gatekeeper enrollment	Pass rate among those who enrolled in gatekeeper
Math					
Level I	76%	27%	48%	61%	78%
Level II	78%	20%	53%	66%	81%
Level III	83%	10%	53%	68%	78%
Total	79%	20%	50%	63%	79%
Reading					
Level I	64%	42%	56%	73%	75%
Level II	78%	29%	52%	68%	75%
Level III	70%	24%	55%	71%	78%
Total	67%	37%	55%	72%	75%

the course. About two thirds of the sequence completers enroll and three quarters of those who enroll pass, so once again, as was the case with developmental education completion, failure to enroll is a greater barrier than course failure or withdrawal.

The high pass rate is encouraging, but developmental education completers are already a selected group of students who have successfully navigated their often complicated sequences. When considered from the beginning of the sequence, only 20 percent of students referred to math remediation and 37 percent of those referred to reading complete a gatekeeper course in the relevant subject area within three years.

As we have seen, many of those referred to developmental education fail to complete a college course because they never even enroll in their first remedial course: between one quarter and one-third of referred students never enroll in developmental education (see Table 3). Table 5 presents data on what happened to those students. These students do not necessarily leave college. In some colleges or states, remediation is not mandatory and in most colleges, students can take courses in subjects for which the remedial course to which they were referred is not a prerequisite.[11] It may be that students, perhaps with the collaboration of some faculty or counselors, simply do not comply with the regulations (Perin & Charron, 2006).

Table 5
Enrollment and completion rates among developmental non-enrollees.

Developmental course referral	Students who did not enroll in developmental education					
	Never enrolled in remediation in that subject	Gatekeeper enrollment	Gatekeeper pass rate	Enrolled in another course within three years	No credits obtained after first term	Number of students who did not enroll (N)
Math						
Level I	24%	24%	18%	64%	38%	14,045
Level II	22%	14%	10%	62%	42%	8,338
Level III	17%	6%	4%	54%	51%	7,439
Total	21%	17%	12%	61%	42%	29,822
Reading						
Level I	36%	50%	36%	71%	36%	19,375
Level II	22%	29%	21%	61%	44%	3,800
Level III	30%	26%	17%	59%	49%	2,059
Total	33%	45%	32%	68%	38%	25,234

Many students ignored the advice (or instructions) of the placement and referral system and skipped their developmental sequence, enrolling directly in a gatekeeper course in the subject area for which they were presumably in need of remediation (see Table 5). Among those students who never enrolled in remediation, about 17 percent of students referred to math remediation and 45 percent of those referred to reading remediation enrolled directly in a gatekeeper course. These students passed their gatekeeper courses at a slightly lower rate than those students who enrolled in a gatekeeper course after they completed their sequences. But many students who comply with their placement never reach a gatekeeper course. Perhaps a more revealing analysis would compare the probability of completing a gatekeeper course for referred students who enter that college-level course directly to that probability for those who follow the recommendations of the counseling system and enroll in the course to which they are referred. About 72 percent of those who went directly to the college-level course passed that course, while only about 27 percent of those who complied with their referral completed the college-level course.

It appears that the students in this sample who ignored the advice of their counselors and proceeded directly to college-level courses made wise decisions. One interpretation is that the developmental education obstacle course creates barriers to student progress that outweigh the benefits of the additional learning that might accrue to those who enroll in remediation. This is at least consistent with the research cited earlier that suggested that remedial services do little to increase the chances that a student will be successful in their first college-level course. An alternative explanation is that these students have a better understanding of their skills than the counselors, armed with widely used assessments.

For other students, especially for those referred to math remediation, non-enrollment had a more negative effect. Of those students referred to math remediation who never enrolled, only 61 percent enrolled in another course and 42 percent never earned a college credit in three years after their first term.

Any multiple-step sequence of courses presents many possibilities for pathways through that sequence. Students can skip courses and of course they can pass or fail and they can move on or fail to move on to subsequent courses. For example, taking the 43,000 students in our sample who were referred to Level III math remediation, we counted 75 different pathways used by at least one student through (or more likely not through) the developmental maze.

4.3. National Education Longitudinal Study of 1988

In the remainder of this section, we provide a comparison to the Achieving the Dream data by using a national micro-level dataset taken from NELS:88. One of the key advantages that NELS provides

Table 6
Demographic characteristics of Achieving the Dream and NELS students.

Characteristics	Achieving the Dream college students	NELS students[a]
Female	56%	55%
White	50%	68%
Black	17%	7%
Hispanic	22%	16%
Other	8%	9%
Age at college entry	23.6 (8.48)	19.1 (1.75)
Observations	256,672	3410

Note: Standard deviations for continuous variables are in parentheses.
 [a] The sample consists of individuals who were enrolled in community college soon after high school and whose college transcripts are provided by their institutions. The sample does not include older students.

is the inclusion of more extensive information than the Achieving the Dream database on student characteristics. But there are disadvantages: the data refer to a period about ten years before the Achieving the Dream data era, NELS does not indicate whether a student was referred to developmental education, and the sample is much smaller. In 2000, the National Center for Education Statistics (NCES) collected the NELS:88 fourth follow-up survey respondents' college transcripts from approximately 3,200 postsecondary institutions. This set of transcripts is referred to as the Postsecondary Transcript Study (PETS) of 2000.[12] Our analytic sample consists of 3,410 students who started postsecondary education at community college and whose transcripts are available.[13] Table 6 contrasts demographic characteristics of the NELS and Achieving the Dream samples. Summary statistics indicate that African American and Hispanic populations are significantly overrepresented in the Achieving the Dream sample.[14] This overrepresentation may reflect the selection process under which colleges serving a high proportion of minority students were chosen to participate in Achieving the Dream. But it also reflects general changes in the demographic characteristics of community college students. In the past decade, there has been a significant increase in the proportion of minority populations attending community colleges: from 10 percent in 1990 to 14 percent in 2003 for African Americans, and from 8 percent to 14 percent for Hispanics over the same period (Snyder, Tan, & Hoffman, 2006). The table also shows that the NELS students are on average four years younger at college entry than the Achieving the Dream students. In contrast to NELS, the Achieving the Dream sample includes older students who entered college perhaps many years after high school.

College transcript records taken from PETS contain information on student enrollment and performance in developmental education courses. From these course-by-course and term-by-term records, we were able to identify a set of developmental math courses[15] that students ever enrolled in: (1) pre-collegiate math or arithmetic, (2) basic algebra, and (3) intermediate algebra.[16] Table 7 presents NELS students' first-time math course enrollment, whether developmental or college-level.[17] Among the 3410 NELS students, 25, 16, and 12 percent enrolled for their first math course in pre-collegiate math, basic algebra, and intermediate algebra, respectively. Almost 26 percent enrolled in a college-level course. The remaining 20 percent did not enroll in any math course during their college career.

NELS does not indicate whether a student was referred to developmental education. In order to compare the present analysis to our analysis of the Achieving the Dream data, we estimated the need for developmental education among NELS students using 12th grade standardized math test scores. Our estimation procedure is described in Appendix A.

Table 8 describes the NELS students' progression through developmental education in math. We first observe that few students whom we estimate to be in need of remediation actually completed their full sequences. For example, only 10 percent of those with test scores indicating that they needed pre-collegiate math enrolled in and passed all three courses in the sequence: pre-collegiate math, basic algebra, and intermediate algebra. The corresponding figures are only 24 percent

Table 7

Type of first enrollment in a math course for NELS students.

Enrollment/assignment	All students	First enrolled math course				
		Never enrolled in a math course	Pre-collegiate math	Basic algebra, plane geometry	Intermediate algebra[a]	College-level math course
Enrollment	3400[b] [100%]	690[20%]	860 [25%]	550 [16%]	420 [12%]	880 [26%]
Assignment	3400 [100%]	–	1100 [32%]	720 [21%]	520 [15%]	1060 [31%]

Notes: To be consistent with the Achieving the Dream sample, only student transcripts that captured three years or less of a student's academic performance were used. For the purposes of assignment, a student's 12th grade math scores were used for imputation.

[a] In this paper we consider intermediate algebra to be a developmental course.

[b] Ten observations were dropped from the original sample of 3410 due to missing data.

for individuals in need of basic algebra and 65 for those in need of intermediate algebra. When aggregating the data across the course levels, we see that only one-third of developmental students completed all of their necessary courses in math. This is very close to the same percentage as the corresponding Achieving the Dream students (33 percent). Among those completers, two out of three are reported to have enrolled in and passed at least one college-level math course. As was the case with the Achieving the Dream developmental education completers, the percent of NELS completers who passed a college-level course is similar across the three levels of developmental need: 51, 58, and 59 percent for those with a demonstrated need for pre-collegiate math, basic algebra, and intermediate algebra, respectively. Approximately 28 percent of all developmental education completers (regardless of first enrollment) did not even attempt to take any college-level math courses.

As was the case with the Achieving the Dream students, many developmental students in the NELS sample did not finish the first course in their sequence. More than a third of individuals estimated to be in need of pre-collegiate math failed to pass that course. The equivalent numbers are 41 percent for students in need of basic algebra and 35 percent for those in need of intermediate algebra. More than half of those non-completers never enrolled in the first course of their sequence throughout all of their tracked college years. This is very similar to analogous results from the Achieving the Dream data: 56 percent of the students who did not complete their developmental math sequence failed to do so because they did not enroll, often in the very first course to which they were referred, not because they tried and failed or dropped out of a course. Even for those who finished the first course in their sequence, many never enrolled in the next level. For example, of those with the greatest developmental need, 63 percent enrolled in and passed pre-collegiate math,

Table 8

Developmental math progression among NELS students.

Course level	Referred to		
	Pre-collegiate math	Basic algebra, plane geometry	Intermediate algebra
Pre-collegiate math			
Not enrolled	22%		
Not passed	15%		
[Sub-total]	[37%]		
Basic algebra, plane geometry			
Not enrolled	34%	23%	
Not passed	7%	18%	
[Sub-total]	[41%]	[41%]	
Intermediate algebra			
Not enrolled	10%	26%	19%
Not passed	3%	10%	16%
[Sub-total]	[13%]	[36%]	[35%]
Completed	10%	24%	65%
Observations[a]	1100	720	520

[a] NELS observations are rounded to the nearest 10 to protect the confidentiality of individually identifiable respondents.

but almost half of those who passed did not show up for the next course in the sequence, basic algebra. Two out of three of those developmental students who did not complete their full sequence of math courses never actually failed one of those courses.

In summary, the NELS data confirm the basic story that emerges from the Achieving the Dream analysis: (1) only a minority of students who need developmental education complete their full sequence of developmental courses, (2) many never pass their first developmental course in their sequence, and (3) a majority of those students who do not complete their full sequence of courses fail to do so because they do not enroll in their initial course or a subsequent course, not because they fail or drop out of any of the courses they attempt.

5. The determinants of developmental progression: multivariate analysis

In this section, we use the concept of a developmental sequence to analyze the determinants of educational outcomes for remedial students. Our analysis so far has shown that many students drop out of their developmental education sequences. But there is considerable variation in these outcomes among students who are referred to the same remedial level. Can we identify student or institutional characteristics that are related to a higher likelihood of reaching intermediate points in the sequence, of completing the sequence, and of moving successfully into college-level courses?

In the following analysis we supplement the individual-level data from Achieving the Dream with institution-level data from the Achieving the Dream and the IPEDS databases to conduct a multivariate analysis that allows us to differentiate the relationships between individual and institutional factors and student progress through developmental education.

5.1. Empirical model

To simplify our analysis, we focus on the step-by-step character of the remedial sequence. Developmental students are expected to enroll in and pass single or multiple developmental courses depending upon their placement. For those who are referred to the lowest level (three or more levels below college-level) of developmental education, their achieved outcome can be categorized into one of the following four types: (1) $Y = 0$, those who did not pass the third-level course (three or more levels below college-level); (2) $Y = 1$, those who passed the third-level course but did not progress any further; (3) $Y = 2$, those who passed the second-level course, but not the first-level; and (4) $Y = 3$, those who completed the entire sequence. The last three outcomes ($Y = 1, 2, 3$) are observed for those referred to two levels below while the last two ($Y = 2, 3$) are observed for those referred to one level below.

Compared to a binary definition of developmental education completion, the concept of a sequence allows us to treat non-completers differently depending on where they stop. For example, among individuals referred to three levels below college-level, those who finished the first course but not the next-level course ($Y = 1$) are presumed to be more successful in developmental education than those who did not even finish the first course ($Y = 0$). Consequently, we use an ordered logit regression. In this approach the ordinal variable is conceived of as the discrete realizations of an underlying continuous random variable, Y^*, indicating the degree to which the student completed developmental education. The unobservable Y^* can be expressed as a linear function of covariates X: $Y^* = \beta/X + \varepsilon$. The observed categorical variable, Y, is derived from unknown cutoff points $(\alpha_0, \alpha_1, \ldots, \alpha_j)$ in the distribution of Y^*: $Y = j$ if $\alpha_{j-1} \leq Y^* < \alpha_j$. Let the probability of $Y = j$ be $\text{Prob}(Y = j)$. Then, the proportional odds model is

$$\frac{\text{Prob}(Y \leq j)}{\text{Prob}(Y > j)} = \exp(\alpha_j - \beta'X)$$

where $\text{Prob}(Y \leq j)$ denotes the probability of having at most jth level of developmental completion and $\text{Prob}(Y > j)$ denotes the probability of having above the level j. The parameter β represents the relationship between the covariate and the dependent variable. In this model, the association is assumed not to be the same for every category j. The regression coefficient β_1 for a particular explanatory variable is the logarithm of the odds ratio for the dependent variable, holding others constant. To simplify the interpretation of the results, we transformed the raw coefficients into odds ratios.

5.2. Empirical specifications

We hypothesized that success in developmental education depends on student demographics, college characteristics, and state-specific effects. Student demographics include gender, race/ethnicity, age at entry, cohort year, intensity of first-term enrollment, major studied, developmental need in other subjects, and socioeconomic background. Gender, race/ethnicity, age, and cohort differences are commonly identified as determinants of postsecondary outcomes (Choy, 2002; Pascarella & Terenzini, 2005). Working while enrolled and attending part-time are also associated with a lower probability of retention and graduation. Students who major in academic areas including liberal arts are expected to succeed in developmental education at a higher rate than those studying in vocational areas. As a measure of pre-college ability, we added a dummy variable indicating whether the student was in need of remediation in other subjects.

We also used college-level variables from IPEDS to account for the influence of institutional characteristics on a student's likelihood of progressing through developmental education. College characteristics include school location, size, proportion of full-time students and minority students, tuition, average amount of federal aid received per FTE enrollment, instructional expenditure per FTE enrollment, and certificate orientation. College location, size, and student body demographics are commonly entered as covariates in the literature on student success in college (Bailey, Calcagno, Jenkins, Leinbach, & Kienzl, 2006). For example, students at large and urban colleges serving mainly minorities and economically disadvantaged populations are found to persist and/or graduate at lower rates than their counterparts. We included tuition as a cost of college attendance that is presumed to have a negative relationship with course completion. As a proxy for students' financial need, we entered the amount of financial aid received by students in the college per FTE enrollment. College resources devoted to instruction are expected to help students succeed in developmental education. In addition, certificate-oriented colleges may not stress developmental education as much as degree-oriented colleges. To control for certificate orientation, we included a dummy indicating whether the college awarded more certificates than associate degrees. Finally, we introduced into the analysis state-specific fixed effects to control for differences in state policy or funding systems that might influence outcomes for developmental students.

5.3. Results

Table 9 presents summary statistics of the Achieving the Dream college sample by level of developmental education to which they were referred. Regardless of the subject, female, young, Black, and Hispanic students tended to need more levels of developmental education. Full-timers were determined to have less need for developmental education than part-timers. Individuals studying in vocational areas tended to have more need for remediation than those studying in non-vocational areas. It is not surprising that students with a demonstrated developmental need for a particular subject tended to be referred to developmental education in the other subject. Finally, developmental students with greater need were more likely to enroll in colleges that were urban, large, certificate-oriented, and serving high proportions of minority students, particularly Hispanic and economically disadvantaged populations.

Now let us turn to the question of what determines developmental progression. Table 10 shows the results from the ordered logit regression for each group of students referred to a particular level of remediation. We first observe that there are substantial individual-specific differences in developmental progression. Female students tended to have significantly higher odds of progressing through developmental math education than their male counterparts. The results indicate that the odds of females passing to a higher level of developmental education were 1.53–1.56 times (depend-

Table 9

Summary characteristics of Achieving the Dream students.

Variables	Developmental math referred to				Developmental reading referred to			
	Not referred	1 level below	2 levels below	3+ levels below	Not referred	1 level below	2 levels below	3+ levels below
Student demographics								
Cohort 2004	0.516	0.503	0.488	0.496	0.501	0.507	0.517	0.531
Female	0.530	0.555	0.580	0.615	0.550	0.576	0.604	0.567
Age	24.98 (9.78)	21.82 (6.57)	22.42 (7.12)	23.34 (7.74)	24.44 (9.15)	21.40 (6.17)	22.26 (7.23)	22.37 (7.13)
White	0.548	0.473	0.473	0.335	0.550	0.374	0.263	0.145
Black	0.141	0.190	0.222	0.179	0.135	0.228	0.309	0.141
Hispanic	0.185	0.244	0.203	0.426	0.215	0.295	0.314	0.588
Other race/ethnicity	0.125	0.093	0.102	0.06	0.101	0.103	0.113	0.126
Full-time study in the 1st term	0.505	0.589	0.577	0.504	0.529	0.576	0.525	0.497
Major studied: vocational	0.349	0.327	0.349	0.312	0.327	0.307	0.343	0.357
Referred to math dev. ed.	0	1	1	1	0.440	0.838	0.871	0.891
Referred to reading dev. ed.	0.123	0.493	0.421	0.59	0	1	1	1
College characteristics								
Urban (=1)	0.760	0.760	0.853	0.884	0.790	0.758	0.843	0.865
Suburban (=1)	0.184	0.206	0.091	0.075	0.159	0.199	0.096	0.105
Rural (=1)	0.056	0.034	0.056	0.041	0.051	0.043	0.062	0.029
Small: 5000 or less (=1)	0.259	0.221	0.258	0.245	0.277	0.208	0.264	0.264
Medium: 5001–10,000 (=1)	0.138	0.112	0.089	0.107	0.133	0.102	0.088	0.173
Large: 10,000 or more (=1)	0.603	0.667	0.653	0.648	0.590	0.690	0.648	0.563
Offer 1 level of dev. ed. (=1)	0.294	0.499	0	0	0.227	0.411	0	0
Offer 2 levels of dev. ed. (=1)	0.258	0.139	0.369	0	0.411	0.337	0.571	0
Offer 3 levels of dev. ed. (=1)	0.448	0.362	0.631	1	0.362	0.252	0.429	1
Percentage of full-time students	22.71 (17.95)	24.49 (17.75)	22.72 (17.99)	26.73 (18.33)	23.72 (17.93)	23.19 (18.31)	21.36 (18.56)	35.55 (10.12)
Percentage of Black students	18.28 (12.77)	17.69 (11.85)	18.36 (11.83)	11.89 (9.36)	16.44 (11.64)	17.16 (11.55)	19.51 (16.28)	9.28 (9.53)
Percentage of Hispanic students	19.47 (18.39)	22.08 (19.60)	17.45 (17.91)	35.71 (26.59)	22.09 (20.40)	23.57 (20.79)	24.33 (24.84)	49.89 (24.14)
Tuition ($1000)	1.70 (0.67)	1.60 (0.55)	1.66 (0.66)	1.28 (0.43)	1.59 (0.61)	1.58 (0.58)	1.73 (0.81)	1.24 (0.25)
Average federal aid received/FTE	2.78 (0.62)	2.64 (0.79)	2.95 (0.40)	3.03 (0.40)	2.82 (0.57)	2.66 (0.80)	2.99 (0.41)	3.01 (0.45)
Instructional expenditure/FTE	3.53 (5.17)	3.21 (2.17)	3.87 (4.99)	3.84 (6.06)	3.55 (4.11)	3.58 (6.78)	3.86 (5.56)	3.57 (0.92)
Certificate orientation (=1)	0.024	0.029	0.030	0.059	0.033	0.025	0.052	0.084
Observations (N)	97,678	59,551	38,153	43,886	151,597	54,341	16,983	6825

Note: Standard deviations for continuous variables are in parentheses. Of the 256,672 Achieving the Dream students in the sample. Data on developmental math are missing for 42,088 students and on developmental reading for 45,452 students.

Table 10
Odds ratios estimated from ordered logit regressions for Achieving the Dream students.

Variables	Developmental math referred to			Developmental reading referred to		
	3+ levels below	2 levels below	1 level below	3+ levels below	2 levels below	1 level below
Cohort 2004	0.966 (0.034)	1.044 (0.051)	0.949 (0.056)	1.297 (0.230)	1.019 (0.084)	1.051 (0.086)
Female	1.561** (0.063)	1.535** (0.088)	1.527** (0.069)	1.768** (0.176)	1.706** (0.057)	1.519** (0.071)
Age	0.995 (0.003)	0.996 (0.003)	0.988** (0.003)	0.976** (0.006)	0.990* (0.005)	0.978** (0.004)
Black	0.669** (0.027)	0.753* (0.050)	0.906 (0.059)	0.864 (0.118)	0.866* (0.058)	1.105 (0.068)
Hispanic	1.125 (0.092)	1.196 (0.155)	1.108** (0.039)	1.048 (0.070)	1.167 (0.127)	1.094 (0.121)
Other race/ethnicity	1.258** (0.078)	1.172* (0.093)	1.277** (0.099)	1.130 (0.186)	1.249 (0.172)	1.359* (0.207)
Full-time study in the 1st term	1.502** (0.096)	1.684** (0.112)	1.681** (0.062)	1.531** (0.179)	1.744** (0.126)	1.672** (0.081)
Major studied: vocational	0.609** (0.043)	0.668* (0.028)	0.771** (0.067)	0.710** (0.076)	0.776** (0.053)	0.885 (0.067)
Referred to math/reading dev.	0.764** (0.041)	0.947 (0.085)	0.921 (0.074)	1.273 (0.308)	0.878 (0.089)	1.094 (0.165)
Suburban (=1)	0.786 (0.121)	0.550 (0.169)	0.656 (0.272)	0.313 (0.198)	0.778 (0.221)	0.870 (0.440)
Rural (=1)	0.831 (0.128)	0.989 (0.256)	0.974 (0.232)	0.633 (0.162)	0.607 (0.187)	1.025 (0.289)
Small: 5000 or less (=1)	0.768 (0.142)	0.770 (0.191)	0.709 (0.141)	0.433** (0.029)	0.697 (0.129)	0.783 (0.191)
Medium: 5001–10,000 (=1)	0.474** (0.067)	1.060 (0.249)	1.358 (0.429)	0.518 (0.273)	0.637* (0.131)	1.163 (0.381)
Percentage full-time students	0.990 (0.006)	0.980* (0.005)	0.989 (0.009)	1.012 (0.007)	0.996 (0.005)	0.996 (0.009)
Percentage Black students	1.010 (0.011)	0.987* (0.006)	0.990 (0.008)	0.955 (0.025)	0.998 (0.005)	0.974 (0.016)
Percentage Hispanic students	1.013 (0.005)	1.008* (0.004)	1.005 (0.007)	0.990 (0.012)	1.009* (0.004)	0.991 (0.008)
Tuition (in $1000 units)	0.530* (0.124)	0.985 (0.199)	0.854 (0.185)	0.395 (0.241)	1.270 (0.224)	0.764 (0.218)
Average federal aid received/FTE	0.977 (0.159)	0.938 (0.104)	0.954 (0.091)	1.022 (0.173)	0.813 (0.093)	0.822 (0.098)
Instructional expenditure/FTE	0.997 (0.004)	0.999 (0.003)	1.000 (0.007)	0.746 (0.113)	0.996 (0.002)	1.001 (0.003)
Certificate orientation (=1)	0.576 (0.201)	0.470* (0.168)	0.538 (0.183)	0.736 (0.119)	0.659 (0.189)	0.384** (0.137)
Offer 2 levels of dev. ed.		0.721 (0.185)	1.282 (0.460)		0.720 (0.141)	1.710 (0.688)
Offer 3 levels of dev. ed.			1.089 (0.262)			1.627 (0.717)
Log likelihood	-42,727.39	-36,238.18	-47,398.89	-8020.23	-15,942.93	-32,079.64
Chi-Squared	40,241.93	6,186.68	2,918.56	1694.61	10,110.64	3,790.55
Observations	35,189	32,151	49,865	6762	15,504	44,749

Note: Standard errors adjusted for college clusters are in parentheses. State dummies are commonly included in the regressions.

* Significant at 5 percent.
** Significant at 1 percent.

ing on the level) as large as the odds for males, holding other factors constant. The corresponding figures for developmental reading range from 1.52 to 1.77. Older students tended to have lower odds of passing to a higher developmental level than their younger counterparts. It is noteworthy that the odds of African American students passing to a higher level of developmental math were 0.67–0.91 times the odds of their White peers. The equivalent numbers vary from 0.86 to 1.11 for developmental reading. In contrast, there is no indication that Hispanic students had lower odds of developmental progression than their White peers. We also observe that both the intensity of first-term enrollment (whether the student attends full-time or part-time) and the type of major are related to the odds of developmental progression. The odds of passing to a higher level of developmental math were 1.50–1.68 times as large when individuals studied on a full-time basis. These numbers are very similar to those for reading. The results also indicate that the odds of passing to a higher level in developmental math were lower (0.61–0.77) when studying in vocational areas. Individuals with a demonstrated developmental need for reading seem to have had lower odds of progressing through developmental math. In sum, men, Black students, and those attending part-time or studying in a vocational area had lower odds of progressing through their developmental sequences. Black students had particularly low odds when they were referred to developmental math at two or three or more levels below college-level. The gender effect is strong throughout the entire sequence for both math and reading, but the negative effect of age applies mostly to reading.

The table also shows that institution-level variables—in particular, college size, student composition, and certificate orientation—are important for developmental progression even after adjusting for individual demographics. The results indicate that the odds of passing to a higher level of math remediation were 0.71–0.77 times as large when students attended small colleges. The corresponding figures range from 0.43 to 0.78 for reading. There seem to be similar associations among students at mid-size and large colleges. We also observe that student composition has some influence on the odds of progressing through developmental education. Individuals at institutions serving high proportions of Black and economically disadvantaged students (measured by receipt of federal aid) generally have lower odds of passing to a higher level of remediation than their peers at colleges serving low proportions of these populations. Tuition level seems to matter as well, particularly for individuals referred to the lowest levels of developmental education. Lastly, the results indicate that the odds of passing to a higher level of developmental education were lower when students enrolled in certificate-oriented colleges.

5.4. Robustness of the results and limitations of the analysis

Potential analytic problems may derive from the fact that our analysis depends on crude measures of individuals and institutions available in the Achieving the Dream and IPEDS databases. For example, we did not include any measures of individual-level socioeconomic background that are presumed to be important determinants of developmental progression. Fortunately, the Achieving the Dream database includes students' residential ZIP codes according to which we can derive socioeconomic measures from outside sources. Specifically, we exploited the 2000 Census to obtain two ZIP code-level measures of socioeconomic background: neighbors' income and educational attainment. But more than 20 percent of the Achieving the Dream sample had no or incomplete ZIP code information. These observations were therefore dropped from the sample for this analysis. Nonetheless, the results from the ordered logit regressions with the two socioeconomic measures are very similar to those presented in Table 10. As expected, neighborhood income and educational attainment were positively related to the odds of developmental progression.

Another possible problem is related to the assumption that the associations between the independent variables and the dependent variable are constant across the transitions through developmental levels. This assumption is required for the use of the ordered logit model. A particular covariate may have different relations with developmental progression depending on the transition, category j. In order to address this issue, we ran a set of generalized ordered logit regressions, the so-called generalized threshold model (Maddala, 1983), where the odds ratios are allowed to vary across the ordinal categories. We observed some differences in the odds ratios for several variables across the categories; nevertheless, the results for each category are qualitatively similar to those presented in Table 10.

A final specific concern is that the ordered logit model does not take full advantage of the sequential nature of developmental progression. A student's progression toward a higher level of remediation is predicated on the student's success in the previous level. We used a sequential response model (Amemiya, 1985; Maddala, 1983) that estimates probabilities of passing different transitions. At each transition, individuals determine whether to drop out or continue developmental education. Basically, the sequential model is analogous to a discrete time hazard rate model in duration analysis that estimates the probability of exit at a particular time conditional on survival. For simplicity, we assumed that the probability of passing a given transition is conditionally independent of passing previous transitions; in other words, all transitions are considered a conditionally independent series of binary processes. The results from the sequential logit regressions suggest that there are some differences in the estimated odds ratios across the transitions, but they are also qualitatively similar to those presented in Table 10.

Lastly, we point out that our multivariate analysis is exploratory, not definitive. It shows the relationships between the covariates and the developmental outcome. It is difficult to make causal inferences from the results due to multiple sample selections at transitions. There may be unobserved individual-specific heterogeneity that is correlated with student success in the previous and current transitions.

6. Conclusion

In this article we have focused attention on the sequence of developmental courses. What does the concept of a sequence help us learn?

First of all, a focus on the sequence makes immediately clear the daunting task confronting many of the nearly two thirds of all community college students who are referred to developmental education in at least one area. Students arriving with weak academic skills can face semesters of work before they can in effect start college—at least in relevant areas. This developmental "obstacle course" presents students with many opportunities to step out of their sequences, and students in large numbers take those opportunities. Fewer than one half of students complete their sequences, and only 20 percent of those referred to math and 40 percent of those referred to reading complete a gatekeeper course within three years of initial enrollment.

Should we be concerned about these low completion rates? Given the circumstances, what is the optimal developmental education completion rate? Research does suggest that there is economic value in college education even if it does not end in a degree (Grubb, 1993; Kane & Rouse, 1995). Students who complete one or two developmental courses have probably learned valuable skills even though they have not learned enough to be eligible for college-level work. Even very early exit may not necessarily indicate a problem. Manski (1989) argued that initial college attendance can be seen as an experiment in which students gather information about their aptitude and taste for college. Many students have little concrete knowledge about college before they start. During the early months of college, students learn whether they like college and how much work and effort they will have to exert in order to be successful. They can evaluate that against the likely benefits of persisting and perhaps completing college. Certainly the costs in time and money of a college education will be higher for students who must start in developmental courses. Thus their early exit may suggest that they had gathered enough information about the barriers that they faced to decide that the cost would be too high.

Without more information on these students and their motivations, it is difficult to make a judgment about this. Whether the low completion rates are in some sense optimal for individuals, we should remember that many of these students who exit the developmental sequence are high school graduates. Most high school graduates who enroll in remediation believe that they are prepared for college, so it seems reasonable that if high schools fail to carry out that preparation, some services ought to be available to do what the high schools should have done. Another problem with the optimal withdrawal argument is that withdrawals are still closely related to race and income. It is problematic from a social point of view to argue that the optimal withdrawal rate is higher for African American and low-income students than it is for middle-class White students. Finally, if there is a national goal to increase college success and graduation rates, that increase is going to have to come from among these types of students. The goal of educators therefore must be to try to lower the cost in time and resources to the student of successfully navigating the developmental sequence. If that can be done, then any cost benefit calculation would create incentives for a higher completion rate.

In addition to evidence on the overall completion rates, this article has presented information about the nature of the sequences and the places where students tend to exit the sequence. Analysis of developmental sequences makes clear that many students who exit their sequence do so even though they have never failed or withdrawn from a developmental course. This pattern extends into the first college-level course: among developmental completers in the sample, those who enrolled in a gatekeeper course had a good chance of passing it, but about 30 percent did not enroll in such a course within the three-year period of the study.

This article has also revealed the confusion and disarray that underlies the apparent orderliness of the developmental sequence. In theory, the system consists of an ordered set of courses into which students are placed with the assistance of assessments used by hundreds of thousands of students. But barely a majority of students actually follow their referral recommendations. For some students, deviation from the referral appears to be a wise decision, but others ignore the recommendations and disappear from the college altogether. And those who do enroll in remedial courses take a bewildering variety of pathways as they try to make progress toward college-level courses.

Given the confusion and ineffectiveness of the developmental system, one possible objective would be to reduce the length of time before a student can start college courses—to accelerate the remediation process. A system that used more accurate assessment that identifies the specific needs of students and focuses instruction on addressing those particular needs would be one way to minimize the time a student spends in remediation. It may be possible to provide that supplemental instruction, through tutoring for example, while the student is enrolled in an introductory college-level course. We have seen that students who choose to skip remediation do reasonably well. It might make sense to provide appropriate support so that more students could follow that path.

We have emphasized that more students fail to complete developmental sequences because they never enroll in their first or a subsequent course than because they drop out of or fail to pass a course in which they are enrolled. This insight suggests a wide variety of possible approaches. Perhaps colleges should combine two or three levels of instruction into one longer, more intensive, accelerated, course. At the very least, concerted efforts should be made to encourage students who complete one course in their sequence to go on to the next. This might involve abandoning the semester schedule to prevent gaps between courses, or registering and scheduling students for the next course in a sequence while they are still in the previous course.

Returning to the link between our work and Henry Levin's Accelerated Schools Project (ASP), like Levin we have focused on the poor outcomes for students in remediation, although our focus has been on postsecondary remediation. Here is what Levin (2007, pp. 1410–1411) states:

> *Webster's New Collegiate Dictionary* describes *remediation* as the "act or process of remedying" where *remedy* is defined as "treatment that relieves or cures a disease" or "something that corrects or counteracts an evil." Although such meanings may appear far-fetched from education, they are accurate metaphors for what happens in the educational remediation of low-income and minority students. Presumably, children who are put into remedial programs are children who arrive at school with "defects" in their development that require repair of their educational faults. But, even this metaphor falls short of its own meaning because the typical child is never repaired, but remains in the repair shop for many years in enclaves labeled as Title I, or special education, or other categorical programs. And, contrary to gaining needed academic prowess, this approach stigmatizes the child with a label of inferiority and constrains academic development to the limitations of the remedial pedagogy. Low-income children fall farther behind the academic mainstream the longer they are in school.

Of course postsecondary students are young adults, so rather than stay in school for years, they more often simply leave, but for many students, like its K-12 counterpart, remediation does little to help them "catch up." Levin argued that the remedy for this is a program of accelerated learning. He argued that students with weak academic skills do not need a different type of education, but rather one that looks very much like the type of education that we as a matter of course provide to more advanced students. He states that "a better strategy for success is not to slow down their development and learning through repetition of the lowest level skills, but to incorporate those skills into more meaningful educational experiences that will accelerate their growth and development to bring them into the academic mainstream."

When students with weak academic skills arrive at college they are directed toward a complicated and time-consuming set of services that have uncertain value. Certainly the needs of these students should be addressed, but college staff have something to learn from Levin's experience with ASP. He suggested that educators working with students with weak academic skills, should "accelerate, do not remediate." This is apt advice for remediation in college as well.

Appendix A. Imputation of need for developmental education for NELS students

The NELS data do not include a variable indicating whether a student is assigned to or needs remediation. We used an imputation technique (Royston, 2004) to predict whether a student would be in need of developmental instruction in math based on their 12th grade test scores. We first treated individuals with no math enrollment as if they had missing values for their first-time math courses. We then created a categorical variable that takes a value of 0 for students in no need of developmental math, 1 for those in need of intermediate algebra, 2 for those in need of basic algebra, and 3 for those in need of pre-collegiate math or arithmetic. A univariate technique based solely on the individuals' 12th grade math test scores was then employed to estimate the course into which they would have been placed had they taken a math course. For a given missing value of the categorical variable, the imputed value was selected to minimize the mean absolute difference in the logit of the predicted value probability between the non-missing observation and the target-missing observation. Given the ordinal nature of the variable, an ordered logit regression was used in the imputation. In order to carry out this analysis, we assumed that students who actually enrolled in developmental and college-level math courses were referred to those courses. We then used the relationship between the 12th grade math score and enrollment in the different math courses to predict, for the 20 percent who did not enroll in any math course, which course they would have been referred to given their 12th grade test score. As a result of imputation, the proportions of students in need of pre-collegiate math, basic algebra, and intermediate algebra increase from 25, 16, and 12 percent to 32, 21, and 15 percent, respectively. In other words, 69 percent of community college students in the NELS sample are predicted to have been referred to developmental education in math while only 54 percent actually enrolled. For the Achieving the Dream college students, 59 percent were referred to math developmental education while only 42 percent enrolled.

Notes

1. Most practitioners use the term "developmental" rather than "remedial" education. In general, developmental education is taken to refer to the broad array services provided to students with weak skills, while remediation is taken to refer specifically to courses given to such students. Moreover, the term "remedial" is often considered to carry a negative connotation. This paper discusses primarily developmental classes. To simplify the exposition and to avoid the overuse of either of these two words, we use "developmental" and "remedial" interchangeably. No positive or negative connotation is intended.
2. In fall 2000, 92 percent of public two-year colleges utilized placement tests in the selection process for remediation (Parsad, Lewis, & Greene, 2003).
3. A nationally representative sample of eighth-graders was first surveyed in the spring of 1988. A sample of these respondents was then resurveyed in four follow-ups in 1990, 1992, 1994, and 2000. On the questionnaire, students self-reported on a range of topics including: school, work, and home experiences; educational resources and support; the role in education of their parents and peers; neighborhood characteristics; educational and occupational aspirations; and other student perceptions. For the three in-

school waves of data collection (when most were eighth-graders, sophomores, or seniors), achievement tests in reading, social studies, mathematics, and science were administered in addition to the student questionnaire (National Center for Education Statistics, 2003).

4. For critical analysis of the research on remediation, see Grubb (2001), Bailey and Alfonso (2005), Perin and Charron (2006), Levin and Calcagno (2008), and Bailey (2009).

5. Colleges are asked to choose their own "gatekeeper" courses. Gatekeeper courses are formally defined in the data gathering instructions to the colleges as the first college-level courses the student must take after remediation. These may be different for students enrolled in different programs within one institution. For example, a student enrolled in a medical program may have a different college-level math requirement than a student in a business program.

6. These second- and third-round colleges include three open-admission, four-year institutions in Texas. However, these institutions were not included in our analysis.

7. One of the first 27 colleges dropped out of the initiative, so the sample consists of 26 colleges from the initial group, and 31 that joined in 2005 and 2006.

8. Participating institutions were given the following instructions on how to determine whether a student should be considered referred to remedial math or reading: "Student was referred for remedial needs in mathematics [reading]. Remedial courses are instructional courses designed for students deficient in the general competencies necessary for a regular postsecondary curriculum and educational setting. The student can be referred through a counselor, a developmental office, etc." Institutions with multiple levels of remedial education were asked to report the level to which the student was initially referred.

9. A sequence of developmental reading courses might include pre-college reading, textbook mastery, and college textbook material.

10. For simplicity, throughout the paper, individuals in need of remediation at colleges having only one level are treated the same as those in need of remediation one level below college-level at institutions having two or three or more developmental levels. Of course, there may be differences in student characteristics among these groups, but for analytic purposes, all the individuals in these groups have only a single transition to pass through. Similarly, individuals referred to remediation two levels below college-level are treated the same regardless of the number of developmental levels offered by the college.

11. In most colleges, students are required to take the sequence of courses to which they are referred before they are eligible for college-level courses, but in some states and colleges, remediation is voluntary. In 75 percent of public two-year colleges, students are in principle required to take remedial courses to which they are referred while in the remaining 25 percent students are only recommended by colleges to take those courses (Parsad et al., 2003).

12. In 1988, 24,599 eighth-graders were selected for the NELS sample that was followed up four times (in 1990, 1992, 1994, and 2000). In the end, 12,144 individuals survived the base-year and four follow-up surveys. Attewell et al. (2006) provide a detailed description of the NELS data for their analysis on developmental education.

13. Given the fact that transcript data were retrieved from a restricted-use source, all sample size numbers are rounded to the nearest ten throughout the paper in accordance with the NCES policy regarding confidentiality. Transcripts are limited to a three-year period of observation in an effort to be consistent with the Achieving the Dream sample.

14. Even the NELS sample does not represent the entire community college student population at that time because of individuals who delayed postsecondary education after high school.

15. The NELS transcripts only identify one reading/English course as remedial, so we were not able to use NELS to analyze progression through a sequence of developmental reading courses.

16. NCES considers intermediate algebra a pre-college course even though in a small number of cases, students are granted additive credits for the course (Snyder et al., 2006). In this paper, we consider intermediate algebra to be a developmental course.

17. The length of time for transcript observation for each student is three years from the start of postsecondary education.

References

Amemiya, T. (1985). *Advanced econometrics.* Cambridge: Harvard University Press.

Arkansas Department of Higher Education. (n.d.). *2003–04 Arkansas academic cost accounting system: A strategic management tool for higher education planning and campus decision-making.* AR: Author.

Attewell, P., Lavin, D., Domina, T., & Levey, T. (2006). New evidence on college remediation. *Journal of Higher Education, 77*(5), 886–924.

Bailey, T. (2009). Challenge and opportunity: Rethinking the role and function of developmental education in community college. *New Directions for Community Colleges, 145,* 11–30.

Bailey, T., & Alfonso, M. (2005). *Paths to persistence: An analysis of research on program effectiveness at community colleges.* Indianapolis: Lumina Foundation for Education.

Bailey, T., Calcagno, J. C., Jenkins, D., Leinbach, T., & Kienzl, G. (2006). Is student-right-to-know all you should know? An analysis of community college graduation rates. *Research in Higher Education, 47*(5), 491–519.

Bettinger, E., & Long, B. (2005). *Addressing the needs of under-prepared college students: Does college remediation work?* Cambridge, MA: National Bureau of Economic Research. (NBER Working Paper No. 11325).

Boylan, H. (2002). *What works: A guide to research-based best practices in developmental education.* Boone, NC: Appalachian State University, Continuous Quality Improvement Network with the National Center for Developmental Education.

Breneman, D. W., & Haarlow, W. N. (1998). Remedial education: Costs and consequences. *Fordham Report, 2*(9), 1–22.

Calcagno, J. C., & Long, B. (2008). *The impact of postsecondary remediation using a regression discontinuity approach: Addressing endogenous sorting and noncompliance.* New York: National Center for Postsecondary Research. (NCPR Working Paper).

Choy, S. P. (2002). *Access and persistence: Findings from 10 years of longitudinal research on students.* Washington, DC: American Council on Education, Center for Policy Analysis.

Deil-Amen, R., & Rosenbaum, J. (2002). The unintended consequences of stigma-free remediation. *Sociology of Education, 75*(3), 249–268.

Florida Office of Program Policy Analysis and Government Accountability. (2006). *Steps can be taken to reduce remediation rates; 78% of community college students, 10% of university students need remediation.* FL: Author. (OPPAGA Report No. 06-40).

Grubb, N. (1993). The varied economic returns to postsecondary education: New evidence from the class of 1972. *Journal of Human Resources, 28*(2), 365–382.

Grubb, N. (2001). *From black box to Pandora's box: Evaluating remedial/developmental education.* New York: Columbia University, Teachers College, Community College Research Center.

Horn, L., & Nevill, S. (2006). *Profile of undergraduates in U.S, postsecondary education institutions: 2003–04: With a special analysis of community college students.* Washington, DC: U.S. Department of Education, National Center for Education Statistics. (NCES 2006-184).

Kane, T., & Rouse, C. (1995). Labor-market returns to two- and four-year college. *American Economic Review, 85*(3), 600–614.

Levin, H. (2007). On the relationship between poverty and curriculum. *The University of North Carolina Law Review, 85*(5), 1381–1418.

Levin, H., & Calcagno, J. C. (2008). Remediation in the community college: An evaluator's perspective. *Community College Review, 35*(3), 181–207.

Maddala, G. (1983). *Limited dependent and qualitative variables in econometrics.* Cambridge, MA: Cambridge University Press.

Manski, C. F. (1989). Schooling as experimentation: A reappraisal of the postsecondary dropout phenomenon. *Economics of Education Review, 8*(4), 305–312.

Martorell, P., & McFarlin, I. (2007). *Help or hindrance? The effects of college remediation on academic and labor market outcomes.* Unpublished manuscript.

McCabe, R. (2006). *No one to waste: A report to public decision makers and community college leaders.* Washington, DC: American Association of Community Colleges.

National Center for Education Statistics. (2003). *National Education Longitudinal Study: 1988–2000 Data Files and Electronic Codebook System. Base year through fourth follow-up.* Washington, DC: U.S. Department of Education, Institute of Education Sciences. ECB/CD-ROM (2003-348).

Ohio Board of Regents. (2006). *Costs and consequences of remedial course enrollment in Ohio public higher education: Six-year outcomes for fall 1998 cohort.* OH: Author.

Parsad, B., Lewis, L., & Greene, B. (2003). *Remedial education at degree-granting postsecondary institutions in fall 2000.* Washington, DC: U.S. Department of Education, National Center for Education Statistics. (NCES 2004-010).

Pascarella, E. T., & Terenzini, P. T. (2005). *How college affects students: A third decade of research.* San Francisco: Jossey-Bass.

Perin, D., & Charron, K. (2006). Lights just click on every day. In T. Bailey, & V. S. Morest (Eds.), *Defending the community college equity agenda* (pp. 155–194). Baltimore: The Johns Hopkins University Press.

Rosenbaum, J. (2001). *Beyond college for all.* New York: Russell Sage Foundation.

Royston, P. (2004). Multiple imputation of missing values. *Stata Journal, 4*(3), 227–241.

Snyder, T. D., Tan, A. G., & Hoffman, C. M. (2006). *Digest of education statistics 2005.* Washington, DC: U.S. Department of Education, National Center for Education Statistics. (NCES 2006-030).

Strong American Schools. (2008). Diploma to Nowhere. Retrieved October 8, 2008, from http://www.edin08.com/.

CHAPTER 45

THE LOCATION OF DEVELOPMENTAL EDUCATION IN COMMUNITY COLLEGES: A DISCUSSION OF THE MERITS OF MAINSTREAMING VS. CENTRALIZATION

DOLORES PERIN

Ineffective high school education and increasing ethnic and linguistic diversity are combining to make developmental education critically important for individuals who wish to participate in postsecondary education. Developmental education has become an integral part of the community college mission (Carnevale & Desrochers, 2001; Levin, 2001). With their open admissions policy and commitment to serving a wide range of students in local communities, community colleges have historically played an important role in higher education by offering instruction in basic reading, writing, and math skills to enable academically underprepared students to master the college curriculum. As Levin (2001) stated,

> For many students in either large or small communities, the community college is the only public educational institution that will accept them for college-level studies given their high school academic performance. Furthermore, of the many types of postsecondary institutions facing students who are unprepared for college-level studies, the community college is the only institution whose legal and social mandate is remedial education. (p. xii)

Community college students display a number of academic and personal risk factors that are associated with low rates of persistence and achievement (McClenney, undated). In response, the colleges attempt to increase student preparedness for the college curriculum in a variety of ways including precollege level reading, writing, and math courses (variously termed "developmental education" and "remediation"); academic tutoring in learning assistance centers while students are enrolled in college-level courses; and instructional modifications such as writing-across-the-curriculum in discipline classrooms. Content-area remediation is also provided in some institutions in the form of supplemental instruction, a peer-tutoring model where students who have earned high grades in discipline courses (e.g. biology and history) lead study groups for students who are failing in those classes. However, among this complex array, developmental education courses are the most visible form of remediation in community colleges because these courses are clear catalog offerings in which basic skills instruction is formalized.

Organizational Approaches: Mainstreaming and Centralization

Given the importance of developmental education courses, the question has arisen as to whether they should be integrated into regular departments, here called *mainstreaming*, or housed in sepa-

674

rate organizational units, referred to as *centralization*. The distinction between maistreaming and centralization is an important issue for college policy because the organization of developmental education may have direct impact on its quality (Boylan, Bliss, & Bonham, 1997). When developmental education is mainstreamed, precollege level remedial courses are offered in academic departments, such as English or mathematics, whose main purpose is to offer college-level courses applicable to associate's degrees or certificates. Courses are numbered as part of a sequence that begins with noncredit, remedial level instruction and continues through advanced associate-level preparation. Instructors are all considered faculty of the department in question and are paid through its budget. Working in close proximity in a departmental context permits developmental education instructors to mingle with colleagues who teach college-level courses. In fact, some faculty teach both developmental and credit-bearing courses simultaneously. On the other hand, when remediation is centralized, the remedial courses are offered in a separate department whose sole function is to offer precollege-level courses. Course numbers reflect the separateness of the department, and the faculty may communicate more often with each other than with instructors from academic departments. In addition to courses, the centralized department may offer ancillary support services such as counseling and tutoring. Most of the instructors will be paid from the centralized department's budget although some may have joint appointments with academic departments and teach courses in both (see McKay et al., 1998).

The term "mainstreaming" is used here in the context of stand-alone developmental education courses. The current question is whether such stand-alone courses should be offered in a regular college department or in a separate remedial department. Arendale (1998, cit. Damashek, 1999) uses the term to refer to the replacement of stand-alone courses with a comprehensive system of support available to all students via a learning assistance center. Boylan et al. (1997) use the term "decentralized" for what we are calling mainstreamed developmental education.

Although there have been strong statements in favor of centralization (e.g., Roueche & Roueche, 1999), there is little direct evidence to support this policy. The purpose of this article is to consider the relative merits of each approach. Because there is a shortage of empirical evidence in the previous literature, the discussion is speculative, relying on practitioners' views and relevant data reported in the existing literature. Sources of information for this discussion were journal articles, book chapters, and technical reports on community college developmental education identified in a search of the ERIC and Educational Abstracts electronic data bases, as well as bibliographies, conference presentations, and personal communications with experts in developmental education. Some of the studies relate specifically to two-year colleges and others to four-year institutions but the organizational issues in both settings are identical.

Current Practices

Roueche and Roueche (1999) have reported that the majority of community colleges across the country mainstream their developmental education programs. Some community colleges have a separate remedial division that teaches their lower level developmental courses, with an academic department teaching the higher level courses. In other colleges, a mixed model may be used, for example, mainstreaming writing and math in their respective content departments, while offering reading courses in a separate developmental education department. According to NCES (1996, Table 10), 54% of community colleges mainstream remedial reading, 59% mainstream remedial writing, and 62% mainstream remedial math courses.

A study of 15 states by the Southern Regional Education Board (Abraham, 1992) found that in community and four-year colleges combined, most developmental education was mainstreamed: 41% of institutions delivered reading remediation in an academic department, (57% in writing, 58% in math) while only about one-third centralized remedial education. Since separate percentages were not provided for community colleges, it is difficult to compare these figures with the NCES data.

Similarly, Boylan, Bliss, and Bonham (1997) examined the organization of developmental education in two- and four-year colleges combined. In a national sample, they found that 52% centralized developmental education. In contrast, the findings of a national survey conducted by the

American Association of Community Colleges (Shults, 2000) indicated that only 25% of community colleges centralized their remedial courses, while 15% mainstreamed these courses within academic departments. Although a further 61% of institutions surveyed offered their courses "within their respective subject areas," a term not defined, it is notable that Shults' (2000) findings differ from the NCES (1996) data in finding a low incidence of mainstreaming. Similarly, Grubb and Associates (1999) reported that remediation tended to be centralized, stating, "Within community colleges, remediation is usually organized as an activity separate from the core purposes, isolated in a jigsaw puzzle of developmental reading and writing departments and tutorial programs" (p. 171). Taking into consideration all of these studies, it is not clear whether the trend is for colleges to mainstream or centralize remediation.

Drawing on NCES (1996), Roueche and Roueche (1999) note that community colleges with high proportions of minority students are more likely than are low-minority institutions to centralize rather than mainstream their developmental courses. People from ethnic and racial minority groups may predominate among the segment of students who are academically underprepared. In a national study of students who completed remedial programs, McCabe (2000) found that among individuals whose skills were "seriously deficient" (i.e., students who tested into reading, writing, and math remediation, including at least one lower level course), minority groups were overrepresented (56%). In particular, 51% of all students in this category were women from minority groups. McCabe found that only 20% of the seriously deficient students in his sample completed remediation, compared to 43% for higher functioning students. The tendency of minority-dominated institutions to provide centralized rather than mainstreamed developmental education suggests that this approach may be particularly helpful for lower achieving remedial students.

Beyond the prevalence of the two approaches, Boylan et al. (1997) studied the relation between organizational structure and student outcomes. Based on an analysis of academic data on a random sample of 6,000 developmental education students attending 300 community and four-year colleges, it was found that students attending institutions where developmental education was centralized had significantly higher first-term grade point averages, cumulative grade point averages, retention rates, and math and English grades, compared with students in colleges where remediation was mainstreamed. Unfortunately, the means were not reported so that it cannot be ascertained whether the group differences were in fact educationally meaningful or only an artifact of statistical power associated with large sample size.

Because other empirical evidence is lacking, the remainder of this discussion relies on descriptive studies and practitioner commentary that, although not providing direct evidence, help weigh the advantages and disadvantages of the two approaches. We frame the discussion in terms of a number of educational components that are frequently mentioned in discussions of remedial education: quality of instruction; availability of ancillary support services; teacher motivation and experience; students' reactions; and the reputation of developmental education in the larger college structure. How do the two models compare in those areas?

This discussion considers the organizational structure of remediation from the perspective of student learning. The issue could also be considered from philosophical, political, or budgetary perspectives. For example, Klicka (1998) claims that centralization protects program philosophy, makes remediation more visible, and ensures budget allocation and administrative representation in the college. The issue of student learning is considered here in terms of transfer of skill from the remedial context to college classrooms. However, whatever measure of learning is considered important, there are no empirical studies in the literature that determine the impact on student learning through direct comparison of mainstreamed and centralized developmental education.

Comparison of Mainstreamed and Centralized Developmental Education in Terms of Critical Educational Components

Quality of instruction. The main purpose of remedial education is to prepare students for the college-level academic demands. Therefore, the quality of remedial instruction can be considered in terms of its alignment with the college curriculum. Specifically, the skills and content taught in developmental reading, writing, and math classrooms should be related to those that students will later encounter in their subject-matter classrooms. From a cognitive perspective, close alignment of developmental and college-level instruction should promote students' generalization of learning beyond remediation to the college-level classroom. Transfer from learning to application is one of three major types of cognitive generalization (Simons, 1999) and is a central goal of education (Bereiter, 1995). An important factor in the transfer of learning is the reinforcement of students' original learning through the use of multiple examples in numerous contexts. As Haskell (2001) states, "Teaching that promotes transfer . . . involves returning again and again to an idea or procedure but on different levels in different contexts, with apparently 'different' examples." (pp. 26-27). The remedial classroom is where academic skills are learned and the various college-level classrooms that the student attends as he or she moves through the discipline program are the settings in which these skills are applied. Transfer of skill is more likely if learning and application occur close in time.

Remedial programs described as exemplary include the "integration of coursework within and beyond the developmental program" (McCabe & Day, 1998, p. 25). There are several ways to accomplish the integration of remediation and higher-level instruction, for example, through paired courses that create formal links between precollege developmental and college-level courses in discipline areas (Badway & Grubb, 1997). These pairings provide immediate opportunities for the application of newly learned reading, writing, and math skills. The alignment of remedial with occupational courses seems useful, since many remedial students plan to pursue career-related degree programs (McCabe, 2000). However, most alignment between developmental and college level curriculum involves general education courses such as freshman composition, history, and psychology, rather than specialized technical courses (Perin, 2001).

Irrespective of students' interests, course pairing may be ruled out when state or institutional policy mandates remedial completion prior to enrollment in college-level courses. That is, if students are prohibited from enrolling in college-level courses before they complete their remedial requirements, they are necessarily barred from participating in a paired course model since one of the courses bears college credit.

In situations where policy allows formal connections between remedial and college-level classes, is this innovation more likely when developmental education is mainstreamed or centralized? Instructional reform requiring the interdisciplinary collaboration necessary for course linking depends on positive working relationships among instructors (Perin, 2000). Centralizing developmental education may serve to marginalize it within the college, reducing the likelihood of regular interaction between developmental and college-course instructors. If this is the case, curricular alignment in the form of paired courses may be more likely to occur when developmental education is mainstreamed.

Apart from course pairing, instruction can also be aligned by matching exit levels of developmental education to entry levels of the college-level courses. Lining up these levels, at least for college composition and mathematics courses, seems more feasible when developmental education is mainstreamed, because in principle, at least some instructors who teach college-credit classes would also have as part of their teaching load some developmental-level classes.

In practice, as discussed below, discipline area instructors may decline developmental teaching assignments, and when taught in academic departments, the instruction of remedial courses may be left to part-time, adjunct faculty who may or may not also be teaching college-level courses. If this problem can be overcome administratively, mainstreamed developmental education may have better potential than centralized departments to align curriculum, at least in the subject areas of English and mathematics, thus facilitating the generalization of student learning.

The benefits of the greater use of full-time instructors in centralized rather than mainstreamed developmental education programs may be undermined by the lack of awareness of the academic demands and content of college-level study that such instructors may have as a result of isolation from the academic departments. The danger in this case is that even at the highest level remedial courses, students considered ready to exit remediation may actually remain underprepared for academic study in the content areas (Perin et al., in press).

Availability of ancillary support services. Overall, community colleges have a strong reputation for providing assistance to support learning and are perceived by students as more nurturing than four-year colleges (Carlan & Byxbe, 2001). A report by the Institute for Higher Education Policy (1998) suggested that the effectiveness of remediation in higher education could be improved by including "support services that rely on multiple intervention strategies" (p. 23). Roueche, Ely, and Roueche (2001) linked community colleges' effectiveness in educating remedial students to the provision of supplementary tutoring, mandatory participation in learning labs, and "case management models" (p. 33) that permit individualized attention. Programs described as exemplary by McCabe and Day (1998) provide support services including tutoring, academic and career advisement, and workshops in areas such as time management and study skills (Moriarty et al., 1998).

These ancillary services may be necessary to increase the persistence and performance of academically low functioning students, many of whom experience not only the family and financial difficulties typical of community college students in general but may also suffer from low self-esteem related to academic difficulties. Remedial students can feel lost in a college environment that they may perceive as impersonal. Support services seem especially important for students at the lower remedial levels who test into three or more remedial courses. In particular, students who enter the college with reading difficulties are at severe academic risk (Adelman, 1998; Roueche & Roueche, 1999).

Centralized developmental education departments may be more likely to recognize the need for support services for at-risk students. Since the sole purpose of a centralized department is remediation, chairs may be more willing than heads of regular academic departments to allocate funds to provision of support services. Further, because their teaching staff may be more attuned and sympathetic to the needs of academically low performing students, centralized departments may be more likely to implement an "early alert" system (Hebel, 1999) that identifies and refers at-risk students for counseling or other support services. However, taking into consideration both the need for curricular alignment and provision of support services, one can speculate that the lower level remedial student, marked by the need for reading instruction, is best served in a centralized department while the higher functioning student may benefit most from developmental courses in a mainstreamed department.

Teacher motivation and experience. Faculty in centralized developmental education departments see the teaching of remedial students as a primary task, while academic discipline instructors may view developmental teaching as a low status assignment and even a punishment. Developmental teachers seem more likely to be able to identify both strengths and weaknesses, rather than only deficiencies, in remedial students. Additionally, hiring criteria in centralized departments are more likely to include commitment to teaching remedial reading, writing or math. Professional development activities are more likely to focus expressly on remedial issues in a centralized than in a mainstreamed department. Thus, on the dimension of teacher motivation and experience, centralized departments seem superior to mainstreamed developmental education.

Students' reactions. Developmental education courses have been criticized as causing feelings of discouragement by reinforcing students' sense that they are at risk and forcing them to take longer to finish their degrees (McCusker, 1999). Alternatives to traditional remedial courses include tutoring and adjunct courses directly connected with regular college-level courses (Commander & Smith, 1995; Maxwell, 1997, both cited by McCusker, 1999). These options provide opportunities for academically underprepared students to interact with their higher achieving peers and participate more fully in college life. Locating remedial education in a regular academic department may hold similar promise. Course numberings indicating that remedial reading, writing, and math courses are part of a larger departmental sequence including college-level English and math may also have positive effects on students' feelings about education. In terms of student reactions to developmental education, mainstreaming appears to be superior to centralization.

In fact, when the mandate to attend remedial classes is weak, students may take it upon themselves to mainstream their remediation within their own programs of study by taking developmental education and credit bearing courses simultaneously, even where remediation is centralized administratively within the college. Since developmental education courses are intended as preparation for postsecondary-level study, it is surprising that students are rarely required to complete remediation prior to matriculating in college-level programs. NCES (1996) reported that only 2% of higher education institutions (community and four-year colleges combined) prohibited simultaneous enrollment in remedial and credit courses of any type. Among the other 98% of institutions, practices varied across the remedial areas of reading, writing, and math. Between 29% and 35% of institutions placed no restrictions on simultaneous course taking in any area, and between 64% and 69% of institutions imposed some restrictions in one or more remedial areas (NCES, 1996, Figure 4).

While NCES provides some information at the institutional level, little has been reported about state policy regarding completion of remediation prior to matriculation, although at the time of writing this report, the Education Commission of the States was in the process of surveying states on this among other issues (Boswell, 2001, personal communication). That state policy tends to be weak or nonexistent on this topic is suggested by findings of Boylan et al. (undated) that only one half of all states require remedial placement based on initial assessment. Where remedial placement itself is not mandatory, it seems unlikely that completion of remediation would be required for entry to college-level courses. In contrast, within institutions and states where remediation must be completed prior to program matriculation, developmental education serves as a vestibule that must be exited in order for credit-bearing college work to begin. Students may react to the long wait by simply dropping out. The mainstreaming of remedial courses either organizationally within the college or programmatically within students' own course selections seems more likely than centralization models to create positive student reactions.

Reputation of developmental education in the larger college structure. Centralizing developmental education in effect segregates it from the rest of the college (Eaton, 1994), which may make it difficult for remedial faculty to engage in discussion about curriculum and pedagogy that may occur in the rest of the college (Grubb & Associates, 1999, p. 206). Despite the sometimes unfavorable view of developmental education within academic departments, centralizing remediation may be worse by stigmatizing remediation in the whole college.

Summary. The following table summarizes the relative potential effectiveness of the centralized and mainstreamed structures in the five areas discussed above. Relative superiority is indicated as "+" and inferiority as "-."

Table 1

Relative potential effectiveness of centralized and mainstreamed structures

Educational Component	Centralized Model	Mainstreamed Model
Quality of instruction	--	+
Ancillary support services	+	--
Teacher motivation and experience	+	--
Student reactions	--	+
Reputation of developmental education	--	--

Conclusions and Recommendations

Both centralized and mainstreamed developmental education models show advantages and disadvantages. Among five critical features considered, mainstreaming appears to have the potential for higher quality instruction and more positive student reactions. Centralized departments seem superior regarding ancillary support services and teacher motivation and experience. Both models seem to suffer from the low reputation of developmental education in higher education.

One issue that emerged in this discussion is that lower level remedial students may benefit from a centralized department while students closer to the college level of academic performance may be better served in a mainstreamed department. The tendency of institutions with higher proportions of minority students to centralize developmental education provides indirect support for this speculation, since minority students show greater academic risk than do nonminority students. However, at-risk students are also particularly prone to drop out of community college altogether. One wants to prevent remedial education from driving them away. Any evaluation of the relative merits of centralized versus mainstreamed developmental education should include data from both successful completers and drop-outs.

Pending the availability of comparative evaluation studies, colleges in the process of selecting between centralized and mainstreamed approaches must weigh the severity of each disadvantage. On a more positive note, it is possible to incorporate the beneficial features of both models in either a centralized or mainstreamed setting. The following recommendations could be implemented within either model given the necessary level of administrative commitment and financial resources.

Whether mainstreamed or centralized, developmental reading, writing, and math curricula should be aligned with content and skills found in college-level courses. Remedial literacy and math practices should be authentic, utilizing actual material and examples from the college curriculum rather than drilling in skills that fragment the literacy process (Grubb & Associates, 1999; Levin, 1999). While alignment of remedial reading, writing, and math curricula may be easier when developmental education is mainstreamed in English and mathematics departments, there is no reason in principle why teachers in centralized departments could not incorporate meaningful, content-based, college-level reading, writing, and math material. Ideally, whether centralized or mainstreamed, the content of remedial reading, writing, and math instruction should be closely connected to the subject matter students will later study in degree programs. Many would benefit from being exposed to specific technical and career-related knowledge in the context of reading, writing, and math remediation.

Individualized attention and supplementary tutoring are important sources of support for academically underprepared students. Borrowing practices characteristic of centralized departments, colleges that mainstream developmental education should ensure that appropriate support services are available to students who need them. This may require setting up the early-warning system referred to above. A major challenge concerns the allocation of funds for these services in departments that are also committed to a wide range of college-level activities, as well as the administrative attention of program heads whose primary commitment may be to degree preparation. To overcome these challenges senior administrators need to work with relevant academic program chairs to ensure that remedial students are adequately supported and monitored. Whether developmental education is centralized or mainstreamed, it should "create conditions for learning," and provide the advisement and support needed to help students overcome the fear of failure (McClenney, undated).

Crowe (1998) asked, "Do colleges train and support developmental instructors or just throw them in the breach?" (p. 15). Professional development, with appropriate incentives for participation and application, would help improve teaching ability and motivation in both mainstreamed and centralized developmental education. In the mainstreamed model, collaborations between remedial and college-level instructors may help the latter develop the passion that the former feel for helping students who have failed in the past. Further, mainstreamed developmental faculty need to learn systematic techniques for teaching reading, writing, and math typical of the learning disabilities field, with which centralized faculty are often highly familiar. On the other hand, instructors in centralized departments may not be adequately familiar with the literacy requirements and content of the college-level, subject-matter curriculum. Contact with college-level English and math instructors would give them an opportunity to examine discipline curricula in order to identify content and skills that could improve the effectiveness of developmental courses in preparing students for college-level work.

There may be a trade-off between instructional quality and teacher motivation across the two models of developmental education. In the mainstreaming approach, instructors may dislike the assignment of teaching remedial courses, but within this same model there may be greater opportunities to link remedial instruction to college-level material. The challenge for institutions would be to raise instructor motivation within the mainstreaming model or to provide incentives for linking remedial and college-level content within the centralized model. Possible mechanisms for accomplishing this aim include incentive pay, caps on class size, and reduction in teaching load.

Whether in mainstreamed or centralized departments, developmental education students should be encouraged to participate in college activities, especially related to the majors and professions to which they aspire, to reduce their feelings of discouragement and self-perceptions as academic failures. Although their skill levels may preclude enrollment in college-level courses, developmental instructors could find ways to provide contact between developmental and college-level students that could raise the motivation of developmental students to persist in what may be a multiyear remedial endeavor. For example, developmental educational students could visit selected credit-level courses as guests, or peer-tutoring programs could be mounted in which students in credit courses work with developmental education students on basic academic skills needed in the degrees to which the latter aspire.

Learning experience is enhanced when students feel that they are connected with an endeavor that is respected in the college. Efforts should be made by academic departments and college administrators to integrate developmental education with the rest of the college program, rather than marginalizing it within departments or within the college. Colleges will have different ways of accomplishing this integration. Doing so seems appropriate given the extent of remedial need in the student body and the growing centrality of developmental education to the community college mission.

Although centralized models have been recommended by experts in the field, Boylan and his colleagues (Boylan et al., 1997; Boylan, 1999) suggest that it is not the centralization itself that might be responsible for superior outcomes but the fact that this structure makes it easier to coordinate services and promote communication among staff. Coordination and communication may come more easily in a centralized model but are, of course, entirely possible in a situation where remedial education is incorporated in a larger department. In conclusion, both mainstreamed and centralized models have good potential to prepare students for postsecondary academic work, as long as the college demonstrates commitment to the ongoing improvement of developmental education in whatever form is institutionally appropriate.

References

Abraham, A.A. (1992). College remedial studies: Institutional practices in the SREB states. Atlanta, GA: Southern Regional Education Board.

Adelman, C. (1998). The kiss of death: An alternative view of college remediation [Online]. Available: www.highereducation.org/crosstalk/ct0798/voices0798- adelman.html

Arendale, D. (1998). Trends in developmental education [Online]. Available: http://umkc.edu/cad/nade/nadedocs/trends.htm

Badway, N., & Grubb, W.N. (1997). A sourcebook for reshaping the community college: Curriculum integration and the multiple domains of career preparation, Vols. I and II. Berkeley, CA: National Center for Research in Vocational Education.

Bereiter, C. (1995). A dispositional view of transfer. In A. McKeough, J. Lupart, & A. Marini (Eds.). *Teaching for transfer: Fostering generalization of learning* (pp 21-34). Mahwah, NJ: Erlbaum.

Boswell, K. (2001, July 5). Education Commission on the States [personal communication].

Boylan, H.R. (1999). Developmental education: Demographics, outcomes and activities [Online]. Available: www.ncde.appstate.edu.

Boylan, H., Bliss, L., & Bonham, B. (1997). Program components and their relationship to student performance. *Journal of Developmental Education, 20* (3), 2-9.

Boylan, H., Saxon, P., & Boylan, H.M. (undated). State policies on remediation at public colleges and universities. Paper prepared for the League for Innovation in the Community College. Boone, NC: National Center for Developmental Education, Appalachian State University.

Carlan, P.E., & Byxbe, F.R. (2000). Community colleges under the microscope: An analysis of performance predictors for native and transfer students. *Community College Review, 28* (2), 27-43.

Carnevale, A.P., & Desrochers, D.M. (2001). *Help wanted, credentials required: Community colleges in the knowledge economy.* Princeton, NJ: Educational Testing Service.

Commander, N.E., & Smith, B.C. (1995). Development adjunct reading and learning courses that work. *Journal of Reading, 38,* 352-360.

Crowe, E. (1998, September). *Statewide remedial education policies: State strategies that support successful student transitions from secondary to postsecondary education.* Denver, CO: State Higher Education Executive Officers.

Damashek, R. (1999, fall). Reflections on the future of developmental education. *Journal of Developmental Education, 23* (1), 18-20, 22.

Eaton, J. (1994). *Strengthening collegiate education in community colleges.* San Francisco: Jossey Bass.

Grubb, W.N., & Associates (1999). *Honored but invisible: An inside look at teaching in community colleges.* New York: Routledge.

Haskell, R.E. (2001). *Transfer of learning: Cognition, instruction and reasoning.* San Diego: Academic Press.

Hebel, S. (1999, May 7). Community College of Denver wins fans with ability to tackle tough issues. *Chronicle of Higher Education,* A37.

Institute for Higher Education Policy (1998). College remediation: What it is, what it costs, what's at stake. Washington, DC: Author.

Klicka, M.A. (1998). Developmental education services at Bucks County Community College. In R.H. McCabe & P.R. Day, Jr. (Eds.). *Developmental education: A twenty-first century social and economic imperative* (pp 37-52). Mission Viejo, CA: League for Innovation in the Community College.

Levin, H. (1999). Improving remedial education. Paper prepared for the Social Science Research Council, New York.

Levin, J.S. (2001). *Globalizing the community college: Strategies for change in the 21st century.* New York: Palgrave.

Maxwell, M. (1997). What are the functions of a college learning assistance center? (ERIC Document Reproduction Service No. ED413031)

McCabe, R.H. (2000). *No one to waste: A report to public decision-makers and community college leaders.* Washington, DC: Community College Press.

McCabe, R.H., & Day, P.R., Jr. (1998). *Developmental education: A twenty-first century social and economic imperative* [Online]. Mission Viejo, CA: League for Innovation in the Community College. Available: www.league.org

McClenney, K.M. (undated). Teaching in a future that ain't what it used to be. [Online]. In Celebrations: An Occasional Publication of the National Institute for Staff and Organizational Development (NISOD). Austin, TX: University of Texas at Austin. Retrieved May 24, 2001, from: www.nisod.com

McCusker, M. (1999). ERIC review: Effective elements of developmental reading and writing programs. *Community College Review, 27* (2), 93-105.

McKay, S.E., Red Shirt, E.M., and Hickey, M.C. (1998). The Guilford Technical Community College Developmental Education Program. In R.H. McCabe & P.R. Day, Jr. (Eds.), *Developmental education: A twenty-first century social and economic imperative* [Online]. (pp 67-72). Mission Viejo, CA: League for Innovation in the Community College. Available: www.league.org

Moriarty, D.F., with Naigus, N., Wyckoff-Byers, N., Greenfield, T., & Mulligan, D. (1998). In R.H. McCabe & P.R. Day, Jr. (Eds.), *Developmental education: A twenty-first century social and economic imperative* [Online]. (pp 73-77). Mission Viejo, CA: League for Innovation in the Community College. Available: www.league.org

National Center for Education Statistics, Statistical Analysis Report (1996, October). Remedial education at higher education institutions in Fall 1995. Postsecondary education quick information system (PEQis). (NCES No. 97-584). Washington, DC: Author.

Perin, D. (2001). Academic-occupational integration as a reform strategy for the community college: Classroom perspectives. *Teachers College Record, 103,* 303-335.

Perin, D., Keselman, A., & Monopoli, M. (in press). The academic writing of community college remedial students: Text and learner variables. To appear in *Higher Education.*

Roueche, J.E., & Roueche, S.D. (1999). *High stakes, high performance: Making remedial education work.* Washington, DC: Community College Press.

Roueche, J.E., Ely, E.E., & Roueche, S.D. (2001). Challenges of the heart: Pursuing excellence at the Community College of Denver. *Community College Journal, 71* (3), 30-34.

Shults, C. (2000). Remedial education: Practices and policies in community colleges. AACC Report No. RB-00-2. [Online]. Washington, DC: American Association of Community Colleges. Available: http://www.aacc.nche .edu/initiatives/issues/Remedial.pdf

Simons, P. R. J. (1999). Transfer of learning: Paradoxes for learners. *International Journal of Educational Research, 31,* 577-589.

Dolores Perin is an associate professor of psychology and education in the Health and Behavior Studies Department and senior research associate in the Community College Research Center, Teachers College, Columbia University in New York.

CHAPTER 46

THE SOCIAL PREREQUISITES OF SUCCESS: CAN COLLEGE STRUCTURE REDUCE THE NEED FOR SOCIAL KNOW-HOW?

REGINA DEIL-AMEN AND JAMES E. ROSENBAUM

A study of fourteen colleges finds that community colleges require certain kinds of social know-how—skills and knowledge less available to disadvantaged students. They present seven obstacles: (1) bureaucratic hurdles, (2) confusing choices, (3) student-initiated guidance, (4) limited counselor availability, (5) poor advice from staff, (6) delayed detection of costly mistakes, and (7) poor handling of conflicting demands. However, we find that a very different kind of college—the private occupational college—takes steps to structure out the need for this social know-how and address the needs of disadvantaged students. We speculate about possible policy implications.

Keywords: community colleges, proprietary, cultural capital, higher education, college students, dropout

In recent decades, community colleges have vastly changed higher education, and they have adapted in amazing ways. In addition to offering two years of a college education at low cost, they offer unprecedented flexibility to meet the diverse needs of nontraditional college students. For working students, community colleges offer satellite campuses and convenient class schedules (Saturday, Sunday, and evening classes). For students with poor high school skills, they offer remedial coursework, sometimes even below eighth-grade level. For immigrants, they offer English language training. Community colleges enroll high school students, high school dropouts, older students, working students, and students from diverse backgrounds and with diverse goals.

Despite these amazing accommodations, we find that community colleges still pose hidden obstacles that present difficulties for nontraditional college students. Similar to the four-year colleges on which they are modeled, community colleges require certain kinds of social know-how—skills and knowledge that are more available to middle-class students than to the lower-income students who are a large portion of community colleges. These social know-how requirements constitute a hidden curriculum of social prerequisites necessary for navigating and succeeding in a college environment. The community college staff we interviewed are barely aware that these obstacles present systematic problems for students; they assume that students have the social know-how necessary to succeed. While these requirements may not be difficult for middle-class students who get help from college-educated parents, we find that they pose great difficulties for nontraditional students who lack this know-how and who face additional outside commitments and pressures, the very students these colleges were created to serve.

We find that community colleges present seven obstacles for students with less access to knowledge about college: (1) bureaucratic hurdles, (2) confusing choices, (3) student-initiated guidance,

(4) limited counselor availability, (5) poor advice from staff, (6) slow detection of costly mistakes, and (7) poor handling of conflicting demands. Based on case studies in public and private two-year colleges, we find that community colleges implicitly demand social know-how about how to navigate a college environment and its bureaucratic structures. Our research identifies what social know-how students must possess, and it illustrates the deleterious consequences for students who lack this know-how. We suggest that students' social know-how—their knowledge about how to handle enrollment, class registration, and financial aid; to initiate information gathering; to access sound and useful advice; to avoid costly mistakes; and to manage conflicting demands—is likely to affect their ultimate college success.

However, we find that these social know-how requirements are not inevitable. Indeed, we report a study of a very different kind of college—the occupational college—that takes steps to structure out the need for this social know-how. These practices specifically address the needs of disadvantaged students who must face difficult decisions, strong competing pressures, little availability of crucial information, and large risks from even small mistakes. If community colleges are to serve nontraditional students, they must address this emerging issue of social know-how.

Background and Previous Research

Community colleges have rightly been praised for democratizing higher education and making it accessible to all people, regardless of economic or educational background. Since 1960, while enrollment in four-year colleges has nearly doubled, enrollment in two-year schools has quintupled (National Center for Educational Statistics 1998, 206). The low tuition and open-access admissions policies of these institutions have reduced the barriers to higher education for disadvantaged populations.

While high schools used to be the last schools attended by most students, colleges have increasingly taken that role. While only 45 percent of high school graduates enrolled in college in 1960, 67 percent enrolled by 1997 (National Center for Educational Statistics 1998), and more than 60 percent of undergraduates participated in subbaccalaureate education (Bailey 2002, 4). Moreover, two-year colleges focus on serving disadvantaged students and on providing occupational preparation (Brint and Karabel 1989).

Much prior research on community colleges has been quantitative, focusing on degree completion (Dougherty 1994). A few ethnographies have examined behaviors, practices, and experiences within community colleges (London 1978; Neumann and Riesman 1980; Richardson, Fisk, and Okum 1983; Weis 1985), but these studies have not systematically explored the institutional mechanisms that affect retention across multiple institutions.[1] While Tinto (1993) provided a model explaining student persistence at four-year colleges, few of Tinto's factors exist at two-year colleges—residential dormitories, extensive extracurricular activities, and so forth.

Private two-year colleges are even more neglected. The best studies are either old (Wilms 1974) or purely quantitative (Apling 1993). However, a recent statistical analysis also described a single for-profit college and suggested practical lessons for community colleges (Bailey, Badway, and Gumport 2001). Our study explores that suggestion in greater detail.

This article also provides a new view of the sociological concept of cultural capital. Bourdieu and Passerson (1977) contended that schools have implicit requirements of certain knowledge and skills (cultural capital) that low socioeconomic status students often lack, and these hard-to-see requirements interfere with their educational attainments. This study examines community college practices that generate these requirements and private college practices that avoid these requirements and seem to remove cultural capital obstacles to students' attainments.

Sample and Data

Our sample includes two types of colleges: seven community colleges and seven private occupational colleges in a large Midwestern city and surrounding suburbs. Our research uses interviews, analyses of written materials, observations, and surveys in these colleges. Four of the occupational colleges are for-profit, or proprietary, colleges. The other three are nonprofit colleges. All offer accredited two-year degrees.

We focus on accredited programs leading to applied associate's degrees in a variety of business, health, computer, and technical occupational programs. We conducted more than 130 semistructured, one-hour interviews with administrators, administrative staff, program chairs, and deans. We interviewed 80 community college students and 20 occupational college students. Surveys of more than 4,300 students indicate strong similarity in the types of students at the two types of colleges: both enroll large proportions of low-income and racial minority students.[2]

Findings

Community colleges provide a vast array of programs: transfer to four-year colleges, two-year occupational degrees, remedial classes, General Equivalency Diploma preparation, English as a second language, adult basic education, vocational skills, contract training, continuing education, and lifelong learning. These institutions offer something for every segment of the population, and the diversity of students is a testament to their success in making higher education accessible.

However, attrition has long been a serious problem. More than 42 percent of high school graduates leave two-year colleges without a degree (Dougherty 1994). In Illinois, state data indicate that roughly 45 percent of the students who begin in community colleges do not return by the following year (excluding transfers),[3] and the rate is similar in the community colleges we studied (40 percent).[4]

Although more options sometimes leads to better decisions, they can also increase the need for information and may create confusion and mistaken choices. Multiple options make it difficult to coordinate college offerings and to allocate fixed resources. The career dean at one community college stated, "It's a balancing act, and we have these external pressures on us to do 14 million things." A dean of instruction noted that part of the challenge is "knowing exactly what our role is." These multiple missions may limit community colleges' capacity to serve as an avenue of social mobility.

While low-income, relatively young minority students face many cultural barriers (Zwerling and London 1992), choice itself can be another obstacle. Community colleges offer many program options and give students the autonomy to steer their own route through the educational process. This can be liberating for some but overwhelming for others. We find that disadvantaged students with limited time and finances to devote to education are often confused about their choices. They do not know how to get the information they need, and small amounts of confusion can evolve into large problems of wasted time and poor decisions. Students often come from public schools where counseling services are limited, and they lack the know-how they need to make the required choices.

We find that many students are first-generation students whose parents have not attended college. In some of these cases, families may not provide financial or other support. Beatriz, for instance, reported,

> Getting myself into college was not an easy task at all to accomplish. Since I came from a Mexican family of eight, it was almost impossible to think of finishing high school, much less enter college. In my house, school was not really emphasized. Work, on the other hand, was all my parents talked about. . . . Many times, my father would yell at me, telling me I was just wasting my time and money and I was gonna go nowhere.

Other families provide emotional support but not information or financial help. For example, when asked if his parents encourage college, Derrick said, "Basically, it's my decision. They give me a pat on the back and say 'I'm glad you're doing it.' " However, his family cannot provide financial help, so Derrick works two part-time jobs to pay tuition and living expenses. Many students' families cannot provide guidance, information, or savings.

As we note below, we find that these community colleges pose seven obstacles for students with less social know-how, and occupational colleges have devised ways to reduce the need for this social know-how.

Bureaucratic Hurdles

While community colleges' size allows them to offer a broad range of courses and degrees, their complexity demands that students acquire and assess a great deal of information about courses, requirements, and options. Students who lack the social know-how needed to navigate through college are at risk of making serious mistakes that imperil their college careers.

First, bureaucratic hurdles arise from the size and complexity of community colleges. Students find their complicated class schedules and college catalogs difficult and time consuming to understand. At a community college that serves a high poverty area, the academic support center dean notes that many students make mistakes in selecting classes on their own, and they later learn that their degree will take longer than they had anticipated.

> [Students] were constantly saying to us, "Nobody told me. I didn't know." . . . We can claim that . . . everything that they need to know we write down [somewhere]. [laughs] . . . It doesn't work that way. So they were getting frustrated, we were getting frustrated.

The college's reputation was suffering, as prospective students and their parents began asking questions. The dean of career programs noted that students want to know "how long it's going to take me" and say, "I don't wanna take a lot of unnecessary courses. I need to have a time line." He hears parents saying, "This is how much money I got. How much is it going to cost? They got two years, they'd better be at the end of the road."

This was a problem at the other community colleges in our sample as well, where the issue includes transfer. A student at another urban college commented, "One of my friends went [here], and she told me, 'Don't go there because you're going to waste your time. You're going to take classes that you won't need when you transfer.' "

In addition, students face other hurdles: filling out enrollment forms, registering for classes, applying for financial aid, making choices that efficiently accumulate credits toward a degree, and fitting in work and family obligations. Students must figure out how to overcome these obstacles each semester. One student complained about his seven-hour registration ordeal: "I went to registration at 12, and I didn't get out until 7," and he became so frustrated that he did not register the second semester and did not return until four years later.

Information is hard to obtain. Students report having to search all over campus to get information about specific program requirements, to learn which courses lead to their desired goals and meet requirements most quickly. Many students are not aware of the state and federal financial aid options available. Some wrongly assume they would not qualify for aid because they are working full- or part-time or because the tuition is low. Students who apply for financial aid complain about the difficulty of the forms and the lack of assistance at these colleges. Unfortunately, many students faced unpleasant and even hostile encounters with financial aid staff in their attempts to complete the financial aid process. Two weeks after she started, Rosa still had not finished the financial aid process. She said of the financial aid department,

> They're rude. This lady kicked me out. . . . I didn't have . . . my security card. She said, "Ah, just get out of here. Just go. You don't have anything ready. Go." . . . I understand they get frustrated, but they don't have to be rude.

Corrie, who grew up in "the projects" and is now living with friends while she puts herself through school to become an occupational therapist, also faced hostility:

> The financial aid office wasn't what I expected. . . . I've had a bad experience with them. They're just very nonchalant about your funding, and I feel like a lot of them don't care because it's like, "It's not me getting the money, and I don't really care." And I've been yelled at a couple of times in financial aid by my counselor.

Bureaucratic hurdles continue in other domains. Because of problems with community college staff, when Lisette needed more information about transfer, she went directly to the college to which she planned to transfer to get information. Many students had similar problems getting correct information, and some, like Lisette, learned through other students or older siblings to seek information directly from the four-year colleges. Unfortunately, students who lack this know-how often found that poor information extended their time in college.

Confusing Choices

Second, students face a confusing array of hard-to-understand choices because of the wide variety of programs, each having different requirements for their various degrees and certificates. Students may not even have a clear picture of their goals, which makes it harder to get good advice. Indeed, in our interviews, most students who had not chosen a major had not sought counselor advice about their course selections in their first year. In the words of one administrator, this often results in students' "wandering aimlessly through the curriculum, amassing large numbers of hours but not making progress toward a degree." He feels this explains the fact that a third of the college's students failed to complete 75 percent of their courses, which is considered unsatisfactory academic progress and threatens their financial aid eligibility.

Even after students have chosen a program, choosing classes is still a daunting task. It can be difficult to schedule all the required courses in the correct order while still paying attention to prerequisites and general education courses and synchronizing course schedules with work and family schedules. We encountered many students who were confused about general education requirements and the necessary prerequisites for their major courses. If students do not fulfill a course requirement, they may have to wait an entire year before the course is offered again. These mistakes can be overwhelming setbacks for students with limited resources and constrained timetables, and they can lead to disappointment, frustration, and eventual dropout.

Given the complex course catalogs and class schedules and the lack of structured guidance, these are surprisingly easy mistakes to make. Even sophisticated observers could have difficulty: the authors, both Ph.D.s, spent many hours trying to understand some of the catalogs' labeling systems for classes and degrees, and several interviews were necessary to clarify the information. Not surprisingly, disadvantaged students rarely know what questions to ask. Due to the catalog's lack of clarity and her misunderstanding of how these classes fit into her program requirements, Annette was not aware that the remedial courses she had to take would not count toward her degree:

> Why didn't anyone tell me that? . . . They had me registering and everything. . . . This is going to hold me back. . . . So I still have two years to go 'cause none of these classes here even count. So I was a little upset about that because it was really misleading.

Apparently, Annette is not alone in her uncertainty. Our surveys find that many community college students, especially from low-income families, were uncertain of their program and degree requirements and course prerequisites.

The Burden of Student-Initiated Assistance

Third, the burden of student-initiated guidance also raises obstacles, especially for disadvantaged students. Although community colleges make guidance available to students, the colleges require that students initiate the process of seeking out guidance. The consequences of this situation for at-risk students are fourfold. First, students must be aware of what kind of help they need and when they need it. Second, they must be informed about how and where to get this help. Third, they must actually go get it. Fourth, students must seek this information well in advance.

Unfortunately, these conditions do not serve first-generation college students well. Those students whose parents have not attended college cannot easily get advice about how to succeed, what pitfalls to avoid, or how to plan their pathway through college. These students are left to navigate college on their own.

Often, students do not even know that they need help, so they do not take the initiative to seek it out, particularly for long-range planning. Although students know they must ask counselors or faculty to approve their course selections for the next semester, students do not seek information about long-term plans, such as figuring out how to meet their degree requirements efficiently or discussing their educational or career goals. As a result, students are often left without a plan of action, and they make seemingly arbitrary decisions about their classes, the direction of their education, and their career goals.

Even for students who talk to counselors, first-generation students' limited knowledge of college and career paths often make these interactions ineffective. Students often cannot see the pathway for how to get to their occupational goal, and they ask questions and gather information based on wrong assumptions. Putting the burden of initiating advice on inexperienced students leads to poorly directed college strategies, particularly when counseling assistance is focused on selecting classes, not on mapping out long-range plans. Sonia, for instance, is a first-generation college student who comes from a low-income family of eight. In her interview, it was clear that her only source of career advice had been her older brother, who was in his early twenties. She is following the requirements for a math major although she wants to be an accountant or possibly major in computer science. When we asked what career she is considering, Sonia told us accounting. However, in her brief meeting with a counselor, he only asked about her course interests, which led him to suggest only a math major.

> Sonia: Well, I was confused. . . . I had to talk to a counselor. . . . He wanted to know what I was going to major in. . . . I told him I liked math, so I'm taking math courses. . . . So that's it.
>
> Regina: Did you try to go through other degrees, like accounting?
>
> Sonia: No.
>
> Regina: Did you tell him that you were interested in those things, too, or just math?
>
> Sonia: Just math. I figured math and accounting were maybe the same. I'd never taken accounting.

In the brief session, Sonia did not think to mention her career interests, so she is pursuing only one option. If it becomes too difficult or uninteresting, she has no plan for considering alternatives, and her courses were not chosen to provide prerequisites for other majors.

Limited Counselor Availability

Fourth, the limited availability of counselors is a serious obstacle to getting good advice. Counselors at community colleges are typically overburdened, responsible for advising students not only about academic planning but also about the transfer process, career exploration, part-time job placement, and personal issues. They are vastly understaffed, with typically 800 students per counselor. According to one counselor, "We don't have a command performance. Obviously, we couldn't have with just 8 of us for over 6,000 students." This 1:750 ratio is actually better than many of the other community colleges in our sample, and it can be compared with high schools where a ratio of 1:400 is common and is widely believed to be inadequate.

In fact, some administrators report that students need to schedule appointments months in advance to see a counselor. Counselors typically schedule thirty minutes for each appointment, and times fill up quickly, especially around registration time when counseling is needed most. One administrator highlighted the need for students to plan far ahead of time: "they're going for preregistration and they go make an appointment, and then it's October, and the counselors say, 'Well, you could come in December sixth.'" Students report being "too busy" to see counselors, but that should not be mistaken for indifference. For instance, Dan tried to see a counselor several times, but each time, he had to schedule one far in advance, and then he either forgot or could not make the appointment.

None of the community colleges involved in the study required students to meet with counselors even once during their schooling. The majority of students we interviewed had not spoken with a counselor because of the difficulties and delays entailed. Although she is conscientious about meeting the various demands on her, Lauren is completing her second semester and yet reports, "I haven't talked directly to counselors."

Even when they meet, inadequate staffing also affects the students' interactions with counselors. If students do not know exactly what they need help with, then the counseling experience can be ineffective and anxiety ridden. Rolanda described her unsuccessful experience:

> I talked to one of the counselors, but since there was a lot of people waiting, it was kind of fast. We didn't have much time to talk. Also, when you go to a counselor, many times you don't really know what you're going to talk about. You have an idea, but you don't know what questions to ask. I think counselors should ask more questions of us. They just answer our questions then say, "OK, you can go, since you don't know what to ask." It's hard. There are things we don't know.

As a result of her negative experience, Rolanda has avoided seeking further advice from counselors. Instead, she picks classes on her own from a transfer form that she noticed on the wall outside the counselors' offices.

Poor Advice from Staff

Fifth, poor advice is common. The complexity is so daunting that information proves to be challenging even for counselors and administrators. Students in search of information report that they often got conflicting opinions, which directs them to radically different actions. Many students report being guided into courses that were unneeded and thus a waste of their time and tuition money. Unfortunately, for students with limited resources, the time wasted and mistakes involved in figuring things out on their own can prevent them from completing their educational goals.

Even when students see a counselor, the information is sometimes wrong. Counselors might fail to get sufficient information about program offerings and requirements from departments, and their information is also often out of date. Some department chairs admitted that they had little communication with counselors:

> Interviewer: How much direct contact does your department have with the counselors?
>
> Department Chair: Very little. . . . I would say it's pretty much just "hello" in the hallway or something. There's no real . . . contact with them, unless they have some kind of question or something or we find out they're giving out bad info, we'll go down there from time to time to straighten them out or something.

Some administrators complain that counselors often have mistaken notions about their programs. With so many programs to understand and so many other responsibilities, counselors sometimes have difficulty keeping track of all the changes in requirements and curriculum. One department chair reports that students sometimes come to him complaining that the counseling office is giving incorrect information, which appears to make their plans unachievable. This chair will send these students back down to speak with the counselors again; "I tell them, . . . You know, stick to your guns and tell them, 'This is my life.' Or, don't go to them at all. Have me sign the darn registration and I'll do it!"

Other students' transfer plans are delayed due to poor and contradictory counseling from different counselors, who rarely have a long-term relationship with students. For example, Deanna spent four years at community college before she actually transferred, and although she was extremely happy with her teachers and classes, she complained about the counseling system:

> The only thing I had a problem with was the counselors weren't very helpful . . . not at all. . . . You go to them for what classes you need to take. I feel I took a lot of wasted classes. You didn't get much help. Now that I'm in a university, I realize if I would have just had a good counselor I probably would have avoided a lot of this. You had a different one every time you went. I would have graduated in the two years like I should have if I had a better counselor. . . . I feel like [students] just don't get out of there. It's a rut you can get into. . . . Counselors don't tell you what you need to do. People are walking around blindfolded. . . . They don't know what to do.

Although counselors can see students' transcripts, they often lack detailed knowledge about students other than their grades. They also may not understand the program requirements.

Because counselors' advice is often inadequate, many students get advice from worse sources—faculty in other programs unrelated to their own. Although students must have their registration forms signed before they can register, this form can be signed by "any full-time faculty"—not just counselors. Often, this signing takes place during extremely busy and chaotic open registration periods, which are not conducive to careful guidance. Only students who know the value of counseling, who show initiative, and who make plans in advance manage to get counselors' time. Thus, most advising is done by faculty, who have no counseling training and who may not know the requirements for the student's particular program. Within this system, there is no assurance that the individual who signs the form can assess whether students are on track for graduation or whether a course will transfer or even count in the student's major. Anyone can sign their cards, and as a result, students are often entirely responsible for mapping out their own academic progress. For students with little knowledge about the college process, this responsibility can lead to small mistakes, which result in major setbacks.

Like many students we interviewed, Carlos's experience with his urban public high school's guidance counselors was limited to discipline problems. "[In high school] the only time you got to see a counselor was when you were in trouble. It was like that. Like, for cutting or whatever you did." So, when he first began community college, Carlos thought that a good student is one who manages to avoid seeing counselors. He did not seek out any additional help to determine what courses he should take:

> Nobody told me to go see a counselor. No. They just had that open registration. You go talk to anybody. The teachers are like, "What classes do you want? Here, go register. You've got your financial aid? Go take care of it." Things like that.

In hindsight, he realized that getting a counselor's advice would have been important "so you don't waste your time here." He thinks the fact that they leave it up to the student to seek assistance contributed to his initial difficulties:

> Like, for example, they gave me a Biology 101. This was my first semester here . . . when I was first out of high school. I didn't know anything about college. . . . I thought I was getting credit for it, but I wasn't. Now when I dropped it, I got an F because I didn't see a counselor. I didn't even know you were supposed to go see a counselor. . . . Then when I went to go retake the class, the class isn't even offered anymore. Then I find out that you don't even need the class. I saw my GPA. . . . It brought me down.

This bad experience in his first semester led to his decision to drop all his classes and quit altogether. He did not return until several years had passed. Five years later, Carlos, twenty-three years old at the time of our interview, was starting his sixth semester of community college, yet he had accumulated only about two semesters of college credits. Having learned the value of seeking advice the hard way, he now speaks to counselors at four-year colleges for information about transfer:

> Everything I've done was because I went to visit counselors at other schools. They helped me. They're the ones telling me what classes to take and this and that. Here, I don't know what the problem is, but they're not doing their job.

Carlos's lack of exposure to academic or career advising in high school was similar to that of many of the low-income students we interviewed. They lacked cultural capital regarding the value of counseling and therefore faced difficulties seeking this type of assistance in community college.

Delayed Detection of Costly Mistakes

Sixth, students' mistakes are easy to make and hard to detect, and even a few simple mistakes can be devastating. Given the complexity of choices and the inaccessibility of guidance, students often make mistakes. An admissions counselor says that first-generation college students face many difficulties because information about the system is not apparent. "They don't even know what type of degree they're getting. They're not aware of whether the degree they're getting is a terminal degree or not." Ivette, who is in her second full-time semester and aiming for an A.A. degree, responded to the question about when she expects to complete her degree by saying, "I still haven't seen what credits I need for the classes." Although her classes had been mostly remedial and do not count toward her degree, she assumed she could finish a two-year associate's degree within the "promised" two years.

Although their choices are crucial, students often do not understand their situation. The risks of student error are increased because they do not know what they do not know. Many students we interviewed did not know how to distinguish between different types of degrees and different types of credits. Considerable background knowledge is required to make these distinctions, and failure to see crucial distinctions can have serious repercussions. For example, Raymond had trouble distinguishing between credit, noncredit, and remedial classes, and he did not understand the difference between required and optional courses. Because he did not seek counselors' advice at registration, he signed up for a reading class, after finding that a math class he needed was closed. He did not realize that the reading class was remedial, and he was paying for a course that would not count for degree or transfer credit.

Students' mistakes are often not detected for some time. Many students reported that they subsequently discovered that they had wasted time and money in courses that do not contribute toward their educational goals and that they had made less progress than they expected. Denise's problems, for instance, resulted from problematic counselor advice and her own mistakes. In her second year, she realized that she cannot finish this year—a major adjustment given her financial and child care constraints:

> I took it upon myself to be my own counselor. I took five unnecessary classes because I thought I knew everything. . . . The first counselor I had, the one that gave me those wrong classes, . . . wasted my time, so I took it upon my myself and I didn't go see a counselor anymore. She gave me wrong classes, but I messed up more.

Such discoveries are disappointing and may lead students to drop out of college. Although we did not interview dropouts, our respondents described struggles that led them to contemplate dropping out, and they reported that many of their friends did drop out in comparable circumstances.

Community colleges are expected to be all things to all people. They have made concerted efforts to remain flexible, preserve choice, and minimize the constraints on students. However, without good counseling, a multitude of options can lead to poor choices for students without the necessary know-how. For students who are not familiar with the system and do not seek out appropriate help, higher education can pose overwhelming choices. By the time these students have learned how to navigate the system, many may have lost valuable time and tuition dollars or may have given up and dropped out.

Disadvantaged students are especially harmed by the lack of accessible and reliable information. Often, no one in their family or social circle has attended college, so they may not be aware of how colleges work or even what programs are offered. In our interviews, administrators and faculty often spoke about students who lacked clear direction or goals:

> I think when a lot of students come in, they don't know what they want to do. And a lot of them, I think, are like pinballs. They're bouncing from one thing to another, you know, before they find something that they actually like.

Our results help explain why many students who intend to transfer to four-year colleges take courses that do not count for transfer credit at four-year colleges (Dougherty 1994).

In addition, low-income students generally have limited time and money for college and may often have parents pressuring them to take full-time jobs. For such students, the longer they take to choose their program, the greater the chance that they will run out of time or money and be forced to drop out of school with only an array of unrelated courses to show for their efforts. For such students, confusing choices and poor guidance create frustration and disappointment, which may lead students to give up on the pursuit altogether.

Poor Handling of Conflicting Demands

Seventh, colleges poorly handle conflicting outside demands. Compared with other students, nontraditional students usually face more numerous and more severe conflicts with outside demands. Students report many problems that pull them away from school: parent illness, financial need, child care crises, unanticipated pregnancies, automobile breakdowns, and work obligations. Unlike young, full-time students, nontraditional students often have less flexible outside prior commitments and crises that impinge on their studies, and some lack know-how about how to balance school with other demands.

Administrators, faculty, and staff at these community colleges boasted that the variety of morning, afternoon, evening, and weekend class times allowed students to arrange their school schedule around their outside obligations. However, although this approach clearly adds flexibility, it ironically imposes further problems. Class schedules are driven by student demand rather than planned sequencing, and course schedules change every term, so students cannot anticipate their class schedule from semester to semester. Given the vast array of course options that community colleges offer, administrators cannot create coordinated schedules for students. Students report that the courses they need to take are often scheduled at vastly different times of day, and some are not offered for several semesters. This makes their education extremely difficult to coordinate with outside work and family commitments. Moreover, their course schedules in the spring term are invariably quite different than those in the prior term, so the work and child care arrangements created in one semester fail to work in the next. In addition, some students find that necessary courses are already closed to additional students, conflict with other necessary courses, or are not being offered in the term originally expected. Ironically, community colleges' attempts at flexibility may delay students seeking to finish their degrees.

Moreover, even though these conflicts are common, community colleges do not systematically provide students with advice or assistance to handle these conflicts. This failure to provide know-how that will help students cope with conflicts is not limited to just course selection and degree planning.

Community colleges view work as an unfortunate necessity that competes with school. One program chair described this view: "Well, in the best of all possible worlds, I think a student should not work. But, that is not an option for most of our students. . . . They have to make money." Although community college administrators are proud of their nontraditional student body, their comments about work commitments imply that the traditional student model is the ideal. When asked why students do not succeed, faculty members often suggested that students need to reduce their work hours to solve the problem.

Viewing the problem as external to the college, they do not focus on institutional strategies for improving retention. Rather than helping students incorporate school and work, they merely tolerate work as an economic necessity. These community colleges help students find part-time jobs, but they are often unrelated to students' area of study (cf. Grubb 1996).

Many students are in desperate need of career counseling and advice about how to explore opportunities that will best prepare them for their desired career. For example, one student sought a career in film, but he did not understand how to gain experience in that industry: "I'm going to be starting at Blockbuster Video . . . because I want to . . . make movies, work in film. Blockbuster seems like a pretty good place to get some knowledge." This student was trying to incorporate his need to work while in school with his desire to gain some experience related to his chosen field of study. However, he has received no guidance from the college about how to do that.

In fact, most community college faculty members believe that students should try to minimize work hours. Working is seen as an impediment to success in school. Other than offering classes at different times and minimizing out-of-class group projects, the community colleges do little to help students manage their work and school responsibilities.

The New Private Occupational Colleges

Given students' many problems at community colleges, it is useful to examine alternatives. While most two-year college students are at public colleges, about 4 percent attend private colleges (Bailey, Badway, and Gumport 2001). Like community colleges, the private colleges we studied offer accredited two-year degrees, and we selected colleges that offer similar applied programs such as business, accounting, office technology, computer information systems, electronics, medical assisting, and computer-aided drafting. Each college offers degrees in three or more of these program areas, which are intended to lead directly to related jobs.

Although for-profit colleges acquired bad reputations due to past abuses and even fraud, 1992 federal legislation led to the demise of 1,500 schools and compelled the remaining schools to improve (Apling 1993). We selected occupational colleges that passed the same accreditation standards as community colleges and offer associate's degrees of similar quality to community colleges. As such, they are comparable to community colleges but dissimilar to 94 percent of other business and technical schools, which offer no degree above a certificate (Apling 1993). These private colleges should not be considered a random sample: they are some of the best programs in these fields and may be considered to represent an ideal type.[5]

We focus on the ways these colleges structure out the need for much of the social know-how that the community colleges require. They have developed original structures and processes that appear to reduce barriers to disadvantaged students with limited know-how by helping them navigate the administrative obstacles in college.

Structuring Out the Need for Social Know-How

The occupational colleges in this study have found ways to transform implicit rules into explicit organizational structures and policies. They create programs that students can easily understand, master, and negotiate, even if students know very little about how college works. In fact, many of these occupational colleges have found that they can improve student success by making their curriculum more structured, not less. By structuring students' choices, they have found that they also reduce the likelihood that students will make mistakes in their course choices. These colleges also implement strong guidance and tight advisory relationships with their students, which facilitates completion and successful work entry.

While community colleges have become overburdened with competing priorities and functions, occupational colleges continue to provide a limited number of clearly structured programs that lead disadvantaged students to a two-year degree and a stable job in the primary labor market. They accomplish this by procedures that address the seven above-noted problems in community colleges, as we detail below.

Eliminating Bureaucratic Hurdles

First, occupational colleges minimize bureaucratic hurdles. Enrolling is a simple process handled mainly by a single individual who makes all the arrangements for a student. Every student is then assigned to a single adviser who assists in selecting courses. Information is available in one place, and students do not have to run around the college getting information. Students deal with one staff person, not a bureaucratic tangle of scattered offices. Furthermore, registration each term is a simple matter, and as noted later, course choices are simple and offered in the same time slots over the year, avoiding schedule conflicts. Students choose a package of coordinated courses, rather than selecting from a long menu of individual course choices with fluctuating and conflicting time slots.

Occupational colleges also reduce the bureaucratic hurdles to financial aid. At community colleges, obtaining financial aid is largely up to students, and little help is provided. Heckman (1999) has noted the low take-up rate on federal and state financial aid programs, and he speculated (based on no empirical data) that it was due to students' decisions not to seek aid. Our interviews with community college staff and students indicate that students do not apply because they do not know about it or they cannot figure out the complex forms. In contrast, occupational colleges help students through the application process to get the best aid package possible. Admissions staff physically walk applicants to the financial aid office, where a staff person answers all questions and fills out the financial aid application with each student (and their parents, if desired). Occupational colleges treat financial aid as an integral part of the application process, and college staff members explain and simplify the process. This is rarely done by the community colleges we studied or by those studied by others (Orfield and Paul 1994).

Reducing Confusing Choices

Second, while community college students face a confusing array of hard-to-understand course and program choices with unclear connections to future career trajectories, occupational colleges offer a clear set of course sequences aimed at efficient training for specific career goals.

When students first arrive at community colleges, they are often uncertain about what degree or program to pursue. Community colleges encourage students to explore, yet their model for exploration is based on that of four-year colleges—sample from a wide variety of unrelated courses that are highly general, do not specify clear outcomes, and may count for some programs but not for others. Much like a cafeteria where the customer is supposed to choose from the seven different food groups, students are encouraged to sample from five or more academic disciplines without much regard for future career goals.

This nondirective approach may work well for middle-class students who can count on four years of college, but it presents difficulties for many nontraditional students with a shorter time frame. Exploration at some community colleges is largely confined to liberal arts courses, in which many of these students have done poorly in the past. Confusion also arises from the lack of clarity about the implications and relevance of specific choices to future careers. For students with limited resources who must obtain a marketable degree with a minimum of forgone wages or tuition dollars, this approach is problematic (Wilms 1974). Many disadvantaged students do not understand college offerings, face strong pressures to get through school quickly, and seek an efficient way to improve their occupational qualifications and get better jobs.

Occupational colleges help students to determine from the outset what degree program best coincides with their abilities, interests, and needs. When they enroll, every student is required to sit down with an admissions counselor who will go through all the degree programs and the courses they entail, with an explanation of implications, sequences, requirements, and job outcomes. Students' achievement and goals are assessed. In the words of one student,

> You go through all the programs, and they evaluate you, and you take some tests. They just interview you, what you like, what you don't like. . . . They get a feel for you, and they tell you, you know, "We recommend this one. We think you'd be good at it."

In some cases, students are advised not to attend the college since their occupational goals do not coincide with program offerings. For students unsure of their future goals, this personal attention from a counselor who is familiar with all the degree possibilities can be very helpful.

While this approach lacks the breadth of exploration in community colleges, it does entail exploration. Obviously, for these nontraditional students, many of whom did poorly in high school, the very effort to try out college is a daring and risky exploration, and each college course provides a challenge that could end their effort. In addition, while these occupational programs are far more directive than community colleges, they allow some exploration and some redirection of career trajectory after the first semester or after the first year. Moreover, at some occupational colleges, students who do well in the associate's program are encouraged to transfer to a bachelor's degree program in a related field.[6]

College-Initiated Guidance and Minimizing the Risk of Student Error

Third, in contrast to the burden of student-initiated guidance, occupational colleges have actually structured out the need for students to take the initiative to see a counselor when they need assistance. Instead, the colleges take the initiative by developing systems that provide guidance without students having to ask for it. They automatically assign each student to a specific counselor who monitors his or her academic progress. Students must meet with their advisor each term before registering for courses, and advisors provide assistance that is specific to each student's needs. One administrator explained the typical way that these meetings work. An advisor will sit down with the student and tell him or her,

> Next quarter, you're going to take these classes, you have these options. . . . In this time slot, you can take this class or this class. Now, do you want to take psych., . . . soc., . . . political science, or . . . history? Here is why you are taking these classes. This is required here.

In addition, the occupational colleges have registration guides that tell students exactly what courses to take each term to complete their degree in a timely manner. Although this limits course flexibility, most students appreciate the system because it helps them to complete a degree quickly and prevents them from making mistakes. According to one student,

> I think it's a good idea; a lot of people start taking classes that they don't really need and it throws them off. I think it's good . . . it's simple . . . all you have to do is follow it. There's no, "Oh my god, I didn't know I had to take that class!" There's a lot of classes where you have prerequisites. But if you go in that order, you have no problem.

In our survey of 4,300 students, we asked, "Have you ever taken any course which you later discovered would not count toward your degree?" While 45 percent of the community college students responded, "yes," this had happened to them, only 16 percent of the private occupational college students reported the same.[7]

Investing in Counselors and Eliminating Poor Advice

Fourth, while community colleges offer very few counselors, occupational colleges have invested in counseling services and job placement staff. For example, one of the occupational colleges we studied has four academic advisors and one dean devoted exclusively to counseling 1,300 first-year students, a ratio of 260 students to each staff person. Moreover, this college has five additional advisors for assisting with job placement. This provides a sharp contrast to community colleges, where counselors perform many counseling tasks, including personal, academic, and career counseling, and typically have 800:1 ratios for all these services.

Unlike community colleges, all of the occupational colleges devote substantial resources to job placement, separate from the other counseling and advising functions. Job placement offices are well staffed with low student-to-staff ratios, ranging from 90:1 to 122:1 at all these colleges. In contrast, none of these community colleges have any full-time staff devoted to job placement, and other research suggests that may be typical (Grubb 1996; Brewer and Gray 1999). Occupational colleges believe these investments are essential to their mission of helping students complete degrees and get good jobs.

Fifth, in contrast with community colleges, at occupational colleges, instructors communicate with advisors to exchange information about students' progress. Advisors are regularly informed about departmental requirements and faculty talk with advisors about particular students, a simple process given the highly explicit organization of programs.

Quick Detection of Mistakes

Sixth, in contrast to the difficulty of detecting student mistakes at community colleges, occupational colleges require students to meet with their advisors frequently—usually every term. At one college, students must meet with their advisor three times each term.

Occupational colleges also tend to have good student information systems that keep advisors informed about students' progress or difficulties. At several occupational colleges, attendance is regularly taken, advisors are quickly informed of absences, and students are contacted by their advisors before the problem gets serious. After midterms, instructors notify advisors of those students who are performing poorly in class. If the student seems to be having problems, the advisor is responsible for mediating between student and teacher to find a solution to existing problems and make sure the student receives academic support. Through the scheduled interactions, students get to know their advisors on a personal basis, and they are more likely to approach them for help even when they are not required to do so. This is a stark contrast to the more anonymous community college system of advising.

Reducing Conflicts with Outside Demands

Seventh, occupational colleges make efforts to alleviate external pressures that increase the chances of dropping out. These schools have adapted to students' needs by compacting the school year. In an old study, Wilms (1974) estimated that proprietary schools have competitive cost-benefit ratios, despite much higher tuitions, because of their speed at getting students to a degree that raises their earnings sooner. If an associate's degree raises students' wage rates, and if completing school increases students' work hours each week, then getting the degree nine months earlier increases earnings in two ways.

In addition, many students face strong pressures from parents, spouses, children, and jobs to complete schooling quickly. Private occupational colleges respond to these pressures by creating year-round schooling, which leads more quickly to degrees. Several schools have altered their school year to consist of year-round courses with only two one-week vacations in December and July. Students attend classes year round, and in one school, they can obtain a fifteen-month associate's degree.

Since disadvantaged students face many pressures and crises that cause students to lose the benefit of their prior work for the term, occupational colleges reduce the cost of such discontinuities by shortening the length of the school term. If outside pressures force students to suspend their studies and lose one term, it is a relatively short term, and they can resume their studies in a very short time. In addition, prospective students do not have to wait long before a new term begins. Instead of offering classes in relatively long semesters, one school has altered the school year so that it now consists of a series of five ten-week terms, and several other schools have short terms.

Moreover, unlike community colleges, which have complex class schedules in noncontinuous time slots, occupational colleges schedule two courses back-to-back that would typically be taken in a program. This blocking of courses decreases commuting time and makes it easier for students to attend school while they continue to work. Also, while community colleges' class schedules change from term to term, occupational colleges offer the same time schedules from one term to the next. As a result, work and child care arrangements made for one term will continue to work out in the following term.

In addition, while community colleges offer so many courses that they cannot promise to offer needed courses each term, occupational colleges preplan sequences of courses for each program, and they make sure that every program has the courses necessary to make progress every term. Obviously, when all students in a program are taking the same courses, this is relatively easy and economically efficient, but the commitment of these colleges goes beyond that. In several cases, a few students fell out of their cohort's sequence in their course taking, and the colleges offered classes with only three students, just so students could finish their degree within the promised time frame. This is very expensive, but the colleges prized their promise that students can complete the degree in the customary time. In the community colleges, classes below a minimum enrollment were routinely cancelled.

In contrast to community colleges' futile attempt to downplay students' jobs, occupational colleges essentially turn what is viewed as something negative into something that can advance students' career goals. Students receive detailed guidance on how to combine their need to work with their educational goals. These occupational colleges consider work a valuable experience related to their degrees, and they help students find relevant jobs, even if they may pay less. Advisors encourage students to get jobs related to their goals:

> We tell them in the first quarter . . . try to get a job, even if you're just answering the phone, let's say, at Arthur Andersen, but you're an accounting student. One day you can say, "Here's my resume, I want to see if there's something for me here." And then you can be a clerk, you know; you've just got to move your way up.

Instead of lamenting the reality of students' need to work, occupational colleges try to guide students toward using their work to advance their career goals.

Conclusion

While we have seen that community colleges pose some serious problems for students who lack know-how, some occupational colleges have found ways to address these problems. While the answer is not to turn community colleges into occupational colleges, community colleges can better help students by borrowing some lessons from occupational colleges—(1) creating clear curriculum structures, (2) vastly improving counseling, (3) closely monitoring student progress, (4) implementing an information system that would quickly show signs of student difficulties, and (5) alleviating conflicts with external pressures.

This article has addressed an issue in community colleges that may influence the outcomes of low-income, first-generation, and nontraditional students. We show how the structure of community colleges we studied creates a need for students to have extensive know-how about the college process. We have also found that by making the implicit explicit, some occupational colleges eliminate the know-how prerequisite that community colleges seem to require for students to be successful in completing their educational and career goals.

Although most people in our society must learn to cope with bureaucratic complexities eventually, students' ability to cope and learn from them may improve with experience—they may be able to adapt to complexities better as they proceed through college, after acquiring social know-how and academic successes.[8] An individual's capacity to adapt to complexities may depend on attainment of basic skills or increased maturity. It is also possible that procedures that gradually introduce the complexities in small steps may make them easier to manage, and strong advising and school supports may also make adaptation easier.

The occupational college model is not for everyone. Although these occupational colleges offer degrees in several fields, students' options are limited. On the other hand, community colleges offer a more diverse range of programs and courses. For students who have the know-how for making these decisions and who do not face strong external competing pressures, community colleges may provide an inexpensive version of a four-year college education that works very well. However, community colleges pose challenges that often require students to devote additional time (and tuition) obtaining information, puzzling among choices, exploring, and making false starts and mistakes in pursuit of a degree in this complex system. For students who lack social know-how, their attempts at college may amount to nothing more than a series of unrelated credit hours and failed dreams.

Notes

1. A more recent study by Shaw (1997) does compare institutional cultures and ideologies across several community colleges, and it is an excellent example of the value of such comparative qualitative work. Yet her focus is on remedial programs and not on the general experiences of credit-level students. Furthermore, her work does not specifically connect qualitative data with issues of persistence.

2. Surveys were administered to students in class; therefore, the response rate approached 100 percent. Classes were selected to target a cross section of credit-level students in comparable occupationally focused programs across the various colleges. Surveys asked about students' goals, background, attitudes, experiences, course-taking patterns, and perceptions. In both types of colleges, students' families are generally lower and middle income, with 41 percent of community college students and 45 percent of occupational college students reporting parents' annual incomes less than $30,000 (and nearly one-quarter less than $19,000 in each type of college). Approximately 83 percent of community college students and 89 percent of occupational college students have parents with less than a bachelor's degree. At community colleges, 25 percent reported grades of Cs or lower in high school, and at occupational colleges, 28 percent reported these low grades. Moreover, at both, students want similar things from college, with just less than 70 percent at community colleges and slightly more than 80 percent at occupational colleges indicating that they were in college to "get a better job." These findings confirm well-established findings of prior research (Dougherty 1994; Grubb 1996).

3. In the fall of 1999, 121,573 undergraduate freshmen were enrolled, but only 57,670 undergraduate sophomores were enrolled in the fall of 2000. Since only 12,286 students were reported to have transferred from community colleges in that same semester and 4,391 transferred to community colleges, and freshman enrollments increased by only 799, these data suggest that roughly 45 percent of the 1999 freshmen did not return the following year as sophomores. Some, especially part-timers, may have returned as freshmen again, but since this same pattern persists from 1997 to 2000, it is likely that this percentage reflects attrition during the first two years. This percentage is likely to be higher than in longitudinal studies since it does not account for students' degree intentions or follow the same students over time.

4. Sophomores are 41.5 percent of the previous year's freshman enrollments, and the fall 2000 transfer percentage was doubled to 20 percent, assuming that each of the fall and spring semesters would include 10 percent of students transferring.

5. These colleges, which we termed "occupational colleges" (Deil and Rosenbaum 2001), are similar to what Bailey, Badway, and Gumport (2001) referred to as "Accredited Career Colleges." They have very low loan default rates, unlike many former proprietary schools that were closed as a result of new legislation. Two-year business colleges and technical colleges can be found in every major city and are widely advertised in local media.

6. Two of the colleges in our sample have their own accelerated bachelor's degree programs in business, computer, and technology fields.

7. This analysis includes only those students who had not attended a previous college.

8. While this entire discussion has focused on community colleges, similar issues arise at other levels of education, such as high schools, where students make choices about courses in increasingly complex "shopping mall high schools," where curricula are unstructured and implications of choices are unclear. For instance, failure to choose algebra by ninth grade precludes precalculus by twelfth grade, which makes science majors difficult in college, yet these implications of ninth-grade choices do not become apparent for many years.

References

Apling, Richard N. 1993. Proprietary schools and their students. *Journal of Higher Education* 64 (4): 379-416.

Bailey, Thomas. 2002. Director's column. *CCRC currents*, April.

Bailey, T., N. Badway, and P. Gumport. 2001. *For-profit higher education and community colleges*. Stanford, CA: Center for Postsecondary Improvement.

Bourdieu, Pierre, and John C. Passeron. 1977. *Reproduction in education, society and culture*. Beverly Hills, CA: Sage.

Brewer, Dominic J., and Maryann Gray. 1999. Do faculty connect school to work? Evidence from community colleges. *Educational Evaluation and Policy Analysis* 21 (4): 405-16.

Brint, Steven, and J. Karabel. 1989. *The diverted dream: Community colleges and the promise of educational opportunity in America, 1900-1985*. New York: Oxford University Press.

Deil, Regina, and James Rosenbaum. 2001. How can low-status colleges help young adults gain access to better jobs? Practitioners' applications of human capital vs. sociological models. Paper presented to the American Sociological Association, Los Angeles, 19 August.

Dougherty, Kevin J. 1994. *The contradictory college: The conflicting origins, impacts, and cultures of the community college*. Albany: State University of New York Press.

Grubb, Norton W. 1996. *Working in the middle: Strengthening education and training for the mid-skilled labor force*. San Francisco: Jossey-Bass.

Heckman, James J. 1999. Doing it right: Job training and education. *Public Interest* 135:86-107.

London, Howard B. 1978. *The culture of a community college*. New York: Praeger.

National Center for Educational Statistics. 1998. *Total first-time freshman enrolled in institutions of higher education and degree-granting institutions, 1955-1996*. Washington, DC: Government Printing Office.

Neumann, R. W., and D. Riesman. 1980. The community college elite. In *New directions in community colleges #32: Questioning the community college role*, edited by G. Vaughan, 53-71. San Francisco: Jossey-Bass.

Orfield, Gary, and Faith G. Paul. 1994. *High hopes, long odds: A major report on Hoosier teens and the American dream*. Indianapolis: Indiana Youth Institute.

Richardson, R. C., E. A. Fisk, and M.A. Okum. 1983. *Literacy in the open-access college*. San Francisco: Jossey-Bass.

Shaw, Kathleen M. 1997. Remedial education as ideological background: Emerging remedial education policies in the community college. *Education Evaluation and Analysis* 19 (3): 284-96.

Tinto, Vincent. 1993. *Leaving college.* Chicago: University of Chicago Press.

Weis, Lois. 1985. *Between two worlds: Black students in an urban community college.* Boston: Routledge Kegan Paul.

Wilms, Wellford W. 1974. *Public and proprietary vocational training: A study of effectiveness.* Berkeley, CA: Center for Research and Development in Higher Education.

Zwerling, L. Steven, and Howard B. London. 1992. First-generation students: Confronting the cultural issues. In *New directions in community colleges 80.* San Francisco: Jossey-Bass.

Regina Deil-Amen, Ph.D., is an assistant professor in the Department of Education Policy Studies at Pennsylvania State University. She completed her Ph.D. in sociology at Northwestern University and continues to serve as a consultant for the College to Career study at their Institute for Policy Research. This study explores institutional differences between public and private colleges in how they prepare students for jobs in the subbaccalaureate labor market. Her main fields of interest are higher education access and inequality, institutions, race, and culture.

James E. Rosenbaum, Ph.D. is a professor of sociology, education, and social policy at Northwestern University. His interests include education, work, careers and the life course, and stratification. He has just completed a book in the Rose monograph series on the high school to work transition, and he is now conducting studies of the transition between community colleges and work.

NOTE: The authors wish to thank Steven Brint, Stefanie DeLuca, Kevin Dougherty, John Meyer, and the editors of this volume for comments on earlier versions of this article. They are also indebted to the Sloan Foundation, the Spencer Foundation, and the Institute for Policy Research at Northwestern University for financial support. Of course, this article does not necessarily reflect their views.

CHAPTER 47

Is Developmental Education Helping Community College Students Persist? A Critical Review of the Literature

Tatiana Melguizo,[1] Johannes Bos,[2] and George Prather[3]

Abstract. There is considerable debate about the effects and benefits of developmental/basic skills/remediation education in college. Proponents argue that it enables poorly prepared high school students to attain the necessary preparation to succeed in college while critics contend that the benefits of remediation are not clear. The main objective of the article is to provide a critical review of the literature on the impact of developmental math on the educational outcomes and persistence of community college students. The authors first describe three types of summative quantitative evaluations. The authors then review a number of studies that have used these techniques to evaluate the impact of developmental math on a number of educational outcomes of community college students nationwide. In the last section, the authors propose the use of regression discontinuity (RD) design as a feasible evaluation tool that institutional researchers at community colleges can use to identify the level (i.e., number of levels below college level courses), subpopulations (i.e., gender, race/ethnicity, and age), and institutions (i.e., multicampus district) that are doing a better job in teaching the developmental courses needed to persist in college.

Keywords: community colleges, remedial math, basic skills, evaluation

A large proportion of the high school graduates who attend a postsecondary institution take at least one developmental/basic skills/remedial course in either mathematics or English.[1] Between 25% and 40% of first-year students at public two-year colleges enroll in remedial courses (Parsad & Lewis, 2003; Spann, 2000). However, there is evidence from national longitudinal studies that this percentage might be even higher; according to transcript data, in the early 1980s about 64% of the students who started at a community college were assigned to remedial courses (Wirt et al., 2001). In addition, estimates suggest that by 1995 almost all public two-year institutions offered remedial education and almost 75% of four-year colleges offered at least one remedial course (Parsad & Lewis, 2003).

[1]University of Southern California, Los Angeles, CA, USA

[2]Berkeley Policy Associates, Oakland, CA, USA; American Institutes for Research, Palo Alto, CA, USA

[3]Los Angeles Community College District, Los Angeles, CA, USA

Corresponding Author:

Tatiana Melguizo, 3470 Trousdale Pkwy, WPH 702G, Rossier School of Education, Los Angeles, CA, 90089

Email: melguizo@usc.edu

There is considerable debate on the effects and benefits of remediation in college. Proponents argue that it enables poorly prepared high school students to attain the necessary preparation to succeed in college (Lazarick, 1997), while critics contend that the benefits of remediation are not clear (Calcagno & Long, 2008). One of the major criticisms is that remediation is too costly. Estimates of the cost of remediation in community college vary considerably. Rough estimates presented by Breneman and Haarlow (1998) suggest that the annual cost is more than $1 billion for public colleges. However, according to Merisotis and Phipps (2000) this represents less than 1% of their total $115 billion budget. The cost of remediation is also incurred by the students. Recent estimates by Melguizo, Hagedorn, and Cypers (2008) suggest that despite the relatively low tuition and fee costs of community colleges in California, the real cost for students is the substantial amount of time that they spend enrolled before transferring to a four-year college. Students with deep developmental needs who successfully transfer to a four-year college spent on average 5 years before transferring and transferred only 1 year's worth of courses. In summary, a substantial number of students arrive to college with deep remediation needs, and the cost of remediation is high not only for the states, districts, and local governments that need to pay at least twice for a course that students should have taken in high school but also for the students who cannot progress toward a baccalaureate degree on time.

The main objective of the article is to provide a critical review of the literature on the impact of basic skills math on the educational outcomes and persistence of community college students.[2] We start by briefly describing three different summative quantitative evaluation techniques (i.e., descriptive, quasi-experimental, and experimental) commonly used to estimate the effect of basic skills math on student success. We then present a review of the evaluations that have used these techniques. The last section describes in detail the benefits and limitations of regression discontinuity (RD) and presents it as a promising evaluation technique for individual colleges and community college districts in the context of one of the recent largest basic skills initiatives in California. In the next section we briefly describe three summative quantitative evaluation techniques. We are aware that there are other qualitative or mixed-methods types of evaluations that are also promising. But for the purposes of this study we will only focus on summative quantitative evaluations.

Descriptive, Quasi-Experimental, and Experimental Design

After a thorough review of the literature we can identify three main types of summative evaluation techniques: descriptive studies, quasi-experimental design, and experimental design. For a thorough review of the statistical techniques for evaluation, see Schneider, Carnoy, Kilpatrick, Schmidt, and Shavelson (2007). In this section we briefly describe them and highlight their main advantages and limitations.

Descriptive Studies

Most of the descriptive or correlational studies usually compare the outcomes of students in basic skills with those who did not take basic skills. Their main limitation (and a reason why they produce inconsistent results) is that the results may be biased because of uncontrolled preexisting differences between students who take remedial courses versus those who do not (Bettinger & Long, 2005). The most common statistical procedures used to identify group differences are: t tests, chi-square tests, analysis of variance (ANOVA), and regression analysis. The main limitation of this type of evaluation is that due to preexisting differences and lack of appropriate controls, the estimates are likely to be biased. In addition, it is not possible to make any causal inferences.

Quasi-Experimental Design Studies

The studies that have used quasi-experimental design attempted to control for the preexisting differences between the students who take basic skills courses and those who do not. The most common statistical procedures used are: two-stage regression analysis with instrumental variables

(Heckman, 1979) and propensity score matching (PSM) techniques (Dehejia & Wahba, 1999, 2002; Rosenbaum & Rubin, 1983; Winship & Morgan, 1999). The main advantage of two-stage regression analysis is that with an appropriate instrument (i.e., a variable that is related to the explanatory variable but not with the error term), and if properly implemented, this technique can substantially reduce the bias of the estimates. The main advantage of the PSM technique is that as Heckman, LaLonde, and Smith (1999) noted, nonparametric methods, if rigorously applied, force analysts only to compare comparable people. An additional advantage is that cross-section estimates based on matching, like experiments, balance the bias.

Experimental Design

Experimental design or randomized trials are the only design that enables the evaluator to fully control for the preexisting differences between the students (Campbell & Stanley, 1963; Rubin, 1974). The idea is to take a sample of individuals who do not differ significantly in background and academic preparation characteristics and randomly assign them to the treatment (i.e., basic skill course) or the control (i.e., college-level course). By doing this the evaluator is removing the bias that arises when students with some characteristics that are difficult to control by the evaluator, such as being very persistent or motivated, decides to enroll in the remedial course. The main advantage of randomly assigning students is that it is possible to make causal inferences. One limitation of experimental design in this context is that it defeats the purpose of placement testing.

Similar to randomized control trials, one evaluation technique that also enables the researcher to do causal inferences is regression discontinuity design (Bloom, Michalopoulos, & Hill, 2005; Cook & Campbell, 1979; Lipsey & Garrard, 2007; Schochet, 2006). The primary purpose of this design is to eliminate selection bias. As mentioned earlier, the best remedy to control for the selection of students into programs and therefore to establish causality is randomization. Random assignment of students to different levels of math would make all unobserved and observed factors equal between control (nonremediated/nonparticipants) and treatment (remediated/participants) groups. However, such randomization is not feasible because as mentioned earlier, it would compromise math instruction and would defeat the purpose of placement testing. A regression discontinuity design replaces true random assignment with assignment according to an exogenously determined cutoff score on a continuous predictor variable. Specifically, RD design is the closest nonexperimental research design to a random assignment experiment in which a portion of entering students would be assigned to one level of math and a portion would be assigned to the next higher level. Finally, by focusing on students who score close to the cut point, RD design will most closely resemble a true randomized experiment as the actual underlying difference in the ability of those taking the tests will vary little within the study sample. In other words, many of the students who test below the cut point might have tested above on a different day or different test form and vice versa. Thus, the assignment to different math levels will be determined largely by testing error, not by differences in the actual underlying ability of the students taking the test.

The following section provides examples of the three types of evaluations described previously.

Existing Evidence of the Impact of Basic Skills Math on Educational Outcomes of Community College Students

The evidence of descriptive studies is mixed. In the early 1990s a number of evaluations were conducted by the National Center for Developmental Education (Boylan, Bliss, & Bonham, 1994, 1997). Boylan and his colleagues conducted an evaluation of a random sample of 160 two- and four-year institutions. Within this sample they identified a random sample of students in developmental programs to test the effectiveness of these courses on first semester retention, GPA, and success in subsequent developmental courses. Their results for community college students in developmental mathematics showed that (a) retention rates in math were higher for students when remediation placement was mandatory and (b) remedial math success rates were higher in programs where counseling was available and in programs engaged in evaluation of the educational outcomes of their students. Following these findings, Boylan (2002) identified 33 best practices for institutions to follow. These became the benchmarks that are currently used in a substantial number of evaluations at the institutional and state levels, including the California Basic Skills Initiative (CBSI). It is important to clarify that even though Boylan chose a random sample of institutions and a random sample of developmental students within these institutions, this is not a randomized control trials experiment because students selected themselves into the remediation courses. This is probably the largest nationwide study performed to date, but it did not attempt to address issues of selection.

In California, James, Morrow, and Perry (2002) compared the retention and success rates of a cohort of first-time freshmen in 1995 tracked for six years. They compared students who had been placed in basic skills with non–basic skills students. According to them, 37.7% of the basic skills students stated a goal of degree/certificate or transfer, compared to 31.1% for the non–basic skills students. Of those with stated goals, about 17.4% of basic skills students earned an associate's degree (AA) or certificate in 6 years, compared to 13.1% of the non–basic skills students. Finally, of those with stated goals, about 21% transferred to a four-year institution in 6 years, compared to 27.5% of the non–basic skills students. These results are not surprising given that students with lower remediation needs were more successful in completing the college-level courses necessary to transfer. The findings of this study clearly illustrate the problem of using two nonanalogous comparison groups.

In terms of the effect of basic skills mathematics programs on student success on college-level mathematics, the results of three studies suggest that taking these courses makes no difference. O'Connor and Morrison (1997) found that developmental mathematics had no effect on students entering more advanced undergraduate mathematics courses. Similarly, Baxter and Smith (1998) found that participation in developmental mathematics courses does not lead to success in college-level mathematics. Waycaster (2001) also found no difference in a longitudinal study in five community colleges in Virginia. He compared the educational outcomes of students who had been placed in remedial math with those who enrolled directly in college-level courses. He found comparable success rates between students who had taken developmental courses and those who had been placed directly in college-level courses.

Finally, Adelman (1999), who tested the impact of taking more remedial courses on college completion, found a negative impact. He used data from the National Center of Education Statistics (NCES) to compare the graduation rates of students who had taken remedial courses versus those who have not and found lower graduation rates for the students who took more remedial courses. The wide disparity in the findings of these studies confirm that descriptive studies present conflicting evidence that makes it really hard to understand the impact of basic skills math on students' educational outcomes.

The evidence of remediation in studies that use more advanced quasi-experimental designs is limited. Attewell, Lavin, Domina, and Levey (2006) used the National Education Longitudinal Study class of 1992 (NELS:88) to test the effect of remediation on students' educational outcomes. They used propensity score matching to better control for differences in students' observed characteristics. They found no negative effect of remediation on either certificate or AA degree completion, but they found that remediated students were 6% less likely to attain a bachelor's degree. Jepsen (2006) tested the effect of basic skills instruction on a sample of students from 12 community colleges in California. He compared students who had been assigned to basic skills through the conventional assessment process (i.e., placement test in combination with other transcript information) with those who enrolled in a basic skills course below the one assigned in their placement. He found that participation in remedial courses was positively associated with second term enrollment as well as completing transfer-level courses. He found that the positive effects of basic skills instruction were greater for non–traditional age (older) students. In a recent study, Doyle (2009) used student-level data from a 1995-2004 Tennessee sample to estimate the impact of increased academic intensity on community college student transfer. He used matching estimators to overcome the problem of selection of students. The findings revealed that taking 12 or more credit hours increased the probability of transfer by 11% to 15%.

Even though these studies used advanced statistical methods to control for heterogeneity in students' observed characteristics, the results could still be biased because the groups might have differed in terms of unobserved characteristics such as motivation or aptitude. There have been only a handful of studies that have used quasi-experimental techniques to explicitly control for the selection problem. Lavin, Alba, and Silberstein (1981) exploited a change in the admission policies at the City University of New York (CUNY) to test the effect of remediation on educational outcomes. They found that success in remedial courses increased persistence to the following academic year by 7% to 8%. In addition, success in basic skills courses increased the probability of transfer to a four-year institution by 2% to 3%.

Bettinger and Long (2004) found negative effects of remediation on the outcomes of students at nonselective four-year colleges and universities in Ohio. To account for selection bias, they used a variation in remediation placement policies across institutions and distance from high school to college as instruments for placement in remediation. The results suggested that placement into remediation increases the likelihood of dropout or transfer to lower level courses. In a subsequent study, Bettinger and Long (2005) used data from the Ohio Board of Regents (OBR) to explore the effects of remediation on a 1998-2003 sample of first-time community college students. They found that students in remediation performed as well as similar individuals who did not enroll in remedial courses. They also found that math remediation appeared to improve some of the students' outcomes. Despite differences in the findings reported previously, it is important to note that the populations of these studies were different. Therefore, the differences between the studies in New York City and Ohio might be reflecting that CUNY was doing a better job than four-year nonselective institutions and community colleges in Ohio in providing basic skills.

Finally, Abou-Sayf (2008) reported the findings of a one-semester experiment at Kapiolani Community College in Honolulu, Hawaii. Instructors in the college decided to voluntarily waive the mathematics and English prerequisites from 12 courses in the community college in fall 2006. The study compared the enrollment rates, GPA, and persistence rates of these students with an analogous group in fall 2005. The findings suggest that waiving of the mathematics prerequisites led to an increase in enrollment in the target courses. According to the author, an unexpected finding was that there was no difference in the performance of the students. These findings suggest that there is no evidence that the enforcement of prerequisites leads to improved performance. However, the author argues that the lack of difference might be explained by changes in the grading practices of the voluntary instructors.

Regression Discontinuity

As described previously, it is not possible to evaluate basic skills doing a randomized control trial since it would defeat the purpose of placement. The technique that enables the researcher to make causal inferences is RD design. In recent years a handful of studies have used this evaluation technique to evaluate basic skills in individual colleges and statewide systems. Lesik (2006) used regression discontinuity design to estimate the effect of a developmental mathematics program on student success in college-level mathematics for a sample of students in a single four-year college in the Northeast. Her results suggest that participating in a developmental program significantly increases the odds of passing a college-level course on the first try.

Two recent studies that analyzed state-level data from Florida and Texas using regression discontinuity design did not find a positive impact of remediation in passing college-level courses and degree attainment. Scholars (Calcagno, 2007; Calcagno & Long, 2008) used a unique data set from the Florida department of education to test the effect of basic skills instruction on college course passing rates and transfer rates of community college students. These studies used a large sample of 140,000 students. They found a positive effect of remediation on the likelihood of enrolling in the following fall term for students on the margin of passing the cutoff. However, no significant differences were found in terms of passing first college-level courses, associate's degree completion, or transfer rates. Martorell and McFarlin (2007) analyzed a large sample of community college and four-year college students in Texas using regression discontinuity design in the early 1990s. They found limited evidence of a positive effect of remedial math on persistence and educational out-comes. They also concluded that aside from weak evidence that remediation improves the grades received in college-level math courses, there was little evidence that students benefit from remedia-tion. In summary, the results of the two recent state-level evaluations suggest major problems with the current state of basic skills in Florida and Texas.

However, these results are probably masking course-, subpopulation-, and institutional-level dif-ferences. In other words, some community colleges might be doing a better job in the provision of the basic skills courses that are just below the college-level courses than the courses that are the high school prerequisites. In terms of group differences, some subpopulations, like the older students in the Jepsen (2006) study, might be benefitting more than traditional age students. Some community colleges might be doing a better overall job in their basic skills sequences that is reflected in greater student success in either passing to the next level, passing a college-level course, or transferring to a four-year college. In the next section, we describe the promises and limitations of this evaluation technique.

Regression Discontinuity Promises and Limitations

One of the main advantages of regression discontinuity is that it is an intuitive technique that is eas-ily understood by a lay audience, and it enables the evaluator to make causal inferences. This is a useful technique for institutional researchers at the institutional, district, and state levels because they have access to large longitudinal samples of students that guarantee the statistical power nec-essary to implement the evaluation. If properly implemented, this evaluation has the potential of identifying specific colleges that are doing a good job in providing basic skills. This is a technique that also enables the researcher to look at different outcomes of interest. For example, a college might be doing a good job with basic skills in terms of success in the subsequent college-level course, but the college might still have dismal transfer rates. This is a very important piece of infor-mation because it will enable the college to focus efforts and direct resources toward enhancing the college-level courses. Similarly, RD design with sufficient sample sizes enables the researcher to look for differences by gender, race/ethnicity, or age. Once again, being able to identify the popula-tions that are facing greater challenges is a very useful policy tool.

Despite the advantages of this technique, there are many obstacles to its implementation. The first is the issue of compliance: Do students who are assigned to remediation follow the recommen-dation? Even though this is a significant concern for this design there are some variants of RD (i.e., fuzzy regression) design that address this problem. Second, if colleges enable students to retake a placement test, this compromises the validity of the design, constituting a major threat to validity because it changes the assignment process. Savvier and more motivated students will probably end up in the higher level courses, thus biasing the estimates of the evaluation.

Discussion and Recommendations

The review of the literature suggests that current evidence on the state of basic skills math in the United States is contradictory and mixed at best. There is evidence that this is a large and probably growing problem that is costly for the states (Breneman & Haarlow, 1998), as well as the students and their families (Melguizo et al., 2008). In the next part we briefly describe the California Basic Skills Initiative and how RD is a promising evaluation technique for colleges, districts, and the state.

California is currently undergoing a major statewide initiative to strengthen the delivery of basic skills courses.[3] The CBSI was a result of three major events. First, the California Community College Board of Governors (BOG) adopted a new strategic plan in 2006 with basic skills as a key component to achieve student success. Second, the BOG approved statewide minimum English and mathematics graduation requirements for associate's degrees for all students entering in Fall 2009. Third, the academic senate for California Community Colleges (CCC) and the state instructional and student service officers presented the CBSI to the CCC chancellor. The total funds allocated to support the initiative in the past 3 years are approximately $100 million (California Legislative Ana-lyst Office, 2008).

The CBSI is definitely the largest statewide initiative to address this growing problem. This is an unprecedented effort that is providing substantial state administrative support as well as additional funding for all the community colleges in California. We believe that RD can be a very useful tool to be employed to evaluate this initiative. As described previously, it can be used by individual colleges to identify course levels and student populations who benefitted from changes in the courses that resulted from the initiative. It can also be used by the districts to make comparisons between institutions. Finally, at the state level, regression discontinuity design could be used as an ex post evaluation tool of the whole CBSI initiative. Given the substantial amount of resources invested under one of the most difficult economic times for the state economy, it would be important to test whether the institutional support and resources provided by the California chancellor's office translated into student success in basic skills.

Declaration of Conflicting Interests

The author(s) declared no conflicts of interest with respect to the authorship and/or publication of this article.

Funding

The author(s) disclosed receipt of the following financial support for the research and/or authorship of this article:

The research reported here was supported by the Institute of Education Sciences, U.S. Department of Education, through grant R305A100381 to University of Southern California. The opinions expressed are those of the authors and do not represent views of the Institute or the U.S. Department of Education.

Notes

1. We use the definition of *basic skills education* used in California community colleges. They use this term to refer to courses that are two or more levels below transfer and include English as a Second Language (ESL) courses. We use the terms *basic skills* and *developmental* and *remedial education* interchangeably.
2. For a more detailed review of the literature, see: Boylan and Saxon (1999), O'Hear and MacDonald (1995, 1996), and Research and Planning Group of California Community Colleges (2005).
3. For a thorough description of the initiative, see Illowsky (2008) as well as the Web page of the California community college chancellor.

References

Abou-Sayf, F. (2008). Does the elimination of prerequisites affect enrollment and success? *Community College Review, 36*, 47-62.

Adelman, C. (1999). *Answers in the tool box: Academic intensity, attendance patterns, and bachelor's degree attainment* (Monograph). Washington, DC: Office of Education Research and Improvement, U.S. Department of Education.

Attewell, P., Lavin, D., Domina, T., & Levey, T. (2006). New evidence on college remediation. *Journal of Higher Education, 77*, 886-924.

Baxter, J., & Smith, S. (1998). Subsequent grades assessment of pedagogies in remedial mathematics. *Primus, 8*, 276-288.

Bettinger, E. P., & Long, B. T. (2004). *Shape up or ship out: The effects of remediation on students at four-year colleges* (NBER Working Paper 10369). Cambridge, MA: National Bureau of Economic Research.

Bettinger, E. P., & Long, B. T. (2005). Remediation at the community college: Student participation and outcomes. *New Directions for Community Colleges, 129*, 17-26.

Bloom, H. S., Michalopoulos, C., & Hill, C. J. (2005). Using experiments to assess nonexperimental comparison-group methods for measuring program effects. In H. S. Bloom (Ed.), *Learning more from social experiments* (pp. 173-235). New York: Russell Sage Foundation.

Boylan, H. R. (2002). *What works: Research-based best practices in developmental education*. Boone, NC: National Center for Developmental Education.

Boylan, H., Bliss, L., & Bonham, D. (1994). Characteristics components of developmental programs. *Review of Research in Developmental Education, 11*(1), 1-4.

Boylan, H., Bliss, L., & Bonham, D. (1997). Program components and their relationship to students' performance. *Journal of Developmental Education, 20*(3), 1-8.

Boylan, H., & Saxon, D. (1999). *What works in remediation: Lessons from 30 years of research*. Retrieved from http://www.ncde.appstate.edu/reserve_reading/what_works.htm

Breneman, D. W., & Haarlow, W. N. (1998). Remedial education: Costs and consequences. *Remediation in higher education*. In *Fordham report: Volume 2(9). Remediation in higher education: A symposium* (pp. 1-50). Washington, DC: Thomas B. Fordham Foundation.

Calcagno, J. C. (2007). *Evaluating the impact of developmental education in community colleges: A quasi-experimental regression-discontinuity design*. Unpublished doctoral dissertation, Teachers College, Columbia University.

Calcagno, J. C., & Long, B. T. (2008). *The impact of remediation using a regression discontinuity approach: Addressing endogenous sorting and noncompliance* (NBER Working Paper 14194). Cambridge, MA: National Bureau of Economic Research.

California Legislative Analyst Office. (2008). *From back to basics: Improving college readiness of community college students*. Retrieved on from http://www.cos.edu/eli/files/ccc _readiness_0608.pdf

Campbell, D., & Stanley, J. (1963). Experimental and quasi-experimental designs for research on teaching. In N. Gage (Ed.), *Handbook of research on teaching* (pp. 171-246). Chicago: Rand McNally.

Cook, T. D., & Campbell, D. T. (1979). *Quasi-experimentation: Design and analysis for field settings*. Chicago: Rand McNally.

Dehejia, R. H., & Wahba, S. (1999). Causal effects in non-experimental studies: Re-evaluating the evaluation of training programs. *Journal of the American Statistical Association, 94*, 1053-1062.

Dehejia, R. H., & Wahba, S. (2002). Propensity score matching methods for non-experimental causal studies. *Review of Economics and Statistics, 84*, 151-161.

Doyle, W. (2009). Impact of increased academic intensity on transfer rates: An application of matching estimators to student-unit record data. *Research in Higher Education, 50*, 52-72.

Heckman, J. J. (1979). Sample selection bias as a specification error. *Econometrica, 47*, 153-161.

Heckman, J., LaLonde, R., & Smith, J. (1999). The economics and econometrics of active labor market programs. In O. C. Ashenfelter & D. Card (Eds.), *Handbook of labor economics* (pp. 1865-2097). Amsterdam, the Netherlands: Elsevier.

Illowsky, B. (2008). The California Basic Skills Initiative. *New Directions for Community Colleges, 144*, 83-91.

James, J., Morrow, V. P., & Perry, P. (2002). *Study session on basic skills*. Sacramento, CA: Board of Governors California Community Colleges.

Jepsen, C. (2006, April). *Basic skills in California's community colleges: Evidence from staff and self referrals*. Paper presented at the meeting of the American Education Research Association (AERA), San Francisco, CA.

Lavin, D., Alba, R., & Silberstein, R. (1981). *Right versus privilege: The open admissions experiment at City University of New York*. New York: Free Press.

Lazarick, L. (1997). Back to the basics: Remedial education. *Community College Journal, 68*(2), 10-15.

Lesik, S. A. (2006). Applying the regression discontinuity design to infer causality with nonrandom assignment. *Review of Higher Education, 30*, 1-19.

Lipsey, M. W., & Garrard, W. M. (2007, June). *Evaluating a school-level statewide conflict resolution education program for middle schools*. Paper presented at the annual meeting of the Society for Prevention Research, Washington, DC.

Martorell, P., & McFarlin, I. (2007). *Help or hindrance? The effect of remediation on academic and labor market outcomes*. Unpublished manuscript.

Melguizo, T., Hagedorn, L. S., & Cypers, S. (2008). The need for remedial/developmental education and the cost of community college transfer: Calculations from a sample of California community college transfers. *Review of Higher Education, 31*, 401-431.

Merisotis, J. P., & Phipps, R. A. (2000). Remedial education in colleges and universities: What's going on? *Review of Higher Education, 24*, 67-85.

O'Connor, W., & Morrison, T. (1997). Do remedial mathematics programmes improve students' mathematical ability? *Studies in Educational Evaluation, 23*, 201-207.

O'Hear, M. F., & MacDonald, R. B. (1995). A critical review of research in developmental education: Part I. *Journal of Developmental Education, 19*(2), 2-6.

O'Hear, M. F., & MacDonald, R. B. (1996). A critical review of research in developmental education: Part II. *Journal of Developmental Education, 19*(1), 8-10.

Parsad, B., & Lewis, L. (2003). *Remedial education at degree-granting postsecondary institutions in fall 2000* (NCES Publication No. 2004-010). Washington, DC: National Center for Education Statistics, U.S. Department of Education.

Research and Planning Group for California Community Colleges. (2005). *Environmental scan: A summary of key issues facing California community colleges pertinent to the strategic process.* Retrieved from http://ftp .rpgroup.org/documents/projects/CCC-StrategicPlan/EvScanCCC-StrategicPln-RPCSS-07-05.pdf

Rosenbaum, P. R., & Rubin, D. B. (1983). The central role of the propensity score in observational studies for causal effects. *Biometrika, 70,* 41-55.

Rubin, D. (1974). Estimating causal effects of treatments in randomized and non-randomized studies. *Journal of Educational Psychology, 66,* 688-701.

Schneider, B., Carnoy, M., Kilpatrick, J., Schmidt, W., & Shavelson, R. (2007). *Estimating causal effects using experimental and observational designs* (Governing Board of the American Educational Research Association Grants Program White paper). Washington, DC: American Educational Research Association.

Schochet, P. A. (2006). *Regression discontinuity design case study: National evaluation of early reading first.* Princeton, NJ: Mathematica Policy Research.

Spann, M. G. (2000). *Remediation: A must for the 21st century learning society* (Policy paper). Denver, CO: Education Commission of the States.

Waycaster, P. (2001). Factors impacting success in community college developmental mathematics courses and subsequent courses. *Community College Journal of Research and Practice, 25,* 406-416.

Winship, C., & Morgan, L. M. (1999). The estimation of causal effects from observational data. *Annual Review of Sociology, 25,* 659-707.

Wirt, J., Choy, S., Gerald, D., Provasnik, S., Rooney, P., Watanabe, S., . . . & Glander, M. (2001). *The condition of education 2001* (NCES Publication No. NCES 2001-072). Washington, DC: National Center for Education Statistics, United States Department of Education.

Tatiana Melguizo is an assistant professor at the University of Southern California. She studies college trajectories leading to college completion for low-income and racial/ethnic minorities.

Johannes Bos is a vice-president at the American Institutes for Research. He specializes in research methodology and in research in the transitions between secondary and post-secondary education.

George Prather is chief of the Office of Institutional Research in the district office at the Los Angeles Community College District where he has worked for the past twenty years.

SECTION IX

GLOBALIZATION, TECHNOLOGY, AND POLICY ISSUES FACING 21ST CENTURY COMMUNITY COLLEGES

SECTION IX: GLOBALIZATION, TECHNOLOGY, AND POLICY ISSUES FACING 21ST CENTURY COMMUNITY COLLEGES

Section IX of the *Reader* touches on the role of local, state, and federal governmental policies that influence the institutional context for community colleges. In Chapter Forty-Eight, "Governmental policies affecting community colleges: A historical perspective," Cohen provides early antecedents, origins, and offers a historical perspective on policy issues in the two-year sector. More specifically, Chapter Forty-Eight outlines how salient organizational control, administration, governance, financing, curriculum, and enrollment are impacted by various levels of government—especially the role of states in the policy context of community colleges. Cohen offers readers a useful appraisal of how state governance structures shape the direction of programmatic efforts and policy implementation over the past 50 years.

Chapter Forty-Nine, "Public policy, community colleges, and the path to globalization," by John Levin builds on the role of the state in higher education and considers public policy relative to community colleges in lieu of internationalization reaching the two-year sector. The borders of community have been extended beyond the local context as the open door concept has far-reaching influence in many countries seeking to promote access to postsecondary education. The author shares the path to globalization and how the process of globalization has ignited increased competition among higher learning institutions. Hence, in correspondence to this paradigm shift of increased competition, greater diversity, and the need for highly skilled training, the international emphasis at many community colleges has taken root. Chapter Forty-Nine proposes that the community college is not exempt from the manifestation and residual effects of economic globalization and reflects on the ramifications and functionality of globalization theory for community colleges.

Raby's work in Chapter Fifty, "Globalization and community college model development," highlights the nexus among policy, globalization, and technological issues challenging community college education. The author shares the dichotomy that exists, as there is a global-local binary in how the institutions are compressed and homogenized. Raby discusses the need for connecting the positive aspects of globalization in terms of accessibility and social equity to support the local function as well as foster global standards in educational opportunities.

The last two chapters in this section share a common thread of positioning the use technology in community colleges. Garza Mitchell's Chapter Fifty-One, "Online education and organizational change," explores organizational change and online learning. The author affords the reader with an in-depth case study that examined faculty and administrator perceptions regarding organizational culture shifts due to the onset of online education. Garza Mitchell's findings support that there are various logistical, structural, and procedural challenges that online education present. In addition, the first and second order changes that are necessary in delivering online education impacted the exchange of teaching and learning, the nature of faculty and administrator roles, and presented organizational transformation at multiple levels.

Just as online courses provide students with innovative opportunities to learn, they are especially attractive for community college students given their multiple roles and responsibilities (e.g., work hours, family obligations, transportation issues, etc.). Bambara, Harbour, Davies, and Athey wrote Chapter Fifty-Two "Delicate engagement: The lived experience of community college students enrolled in high-risk online courses," which serves as the concluding work in this volume.

This chapter sheds light on an overlooked aspect of online education—how students engage and experience online learning in courses considered high risk (i.e., courses with withdrawal or failure rates of 30% and higher). This exploratory qualitative study found across four different high-risk online courses, that the academic rigor and feelings of isolation affected meeting the academic challenges of the course. The authors contend there is a delicate balance between academic and social integration in online learning that shapes student involvement or disengagement.

CHAPTER 48

GOVERNMENTAL POLICIES AFFECTING COMMUNITY COLLEGES: A HISTORICAL PERSPECTIVE

ARTHUR M. COHEN

Government affects every enterprise. In the private sector it provides subsidies; levies taxes; mandates rules governing employment, wages, hours, and workplace safety; and, through numerous other measures, advances or retards the course of all types of industry. Government influence is even more pronounced in the public sector, where various organizations are developed and supported under governmental aegis. Federal, state, and local governments create, build, merge, and collapse agencies and institutions dedicated to myriad endeavors.

This chapter traces the influence of governmental forces on several aspects of the nation's public community colleges. It considers college organization and governance, finance, staffing, enrollments, and curriculum, pointing up how different levels of government, especially the states, have affected the colleges at different stages of their development.

College Organization and Governance

The American community colleges started as neighborhood schools. Subsequently, state plans guided their development. The federal government had little to do with them. In fact, excepting special circumstances such as a college for the deaf, a college for blacks, and the military academies, the federal government was not involved in the establishment of colleges at any level. Its only direct connection with junior colleges was during the Great Depression of the 1930s when it organized a few colleges as part of its workforce development effort. But in the main, the building of institutions was left to local, and then state, governments.

A community college is defined as any institution accredited to award the associate degree as its highest degree. Although private junior colleges and two-year proprietary schools are included in that definition, the 1,050 or so publicly supported comprehensive institutions are the dominant form; hence, this discussion concentrates on them. Located in every state, these colleges provide occupational programs, the first two years of baccalaureate studies, basic skills development, and a variety of special interest courses to nearly half the students beginning postsecondary education.

The community colleges' main contribution has been to expand access to postsecondary studies for the millions of students who would otherwise not have an opportunity to participate. The first question then becomes, why did the states not expand their universities sufficiently to accommodate the rising tide of demand that has been apparent since early in the twentieth century? Why form an entirely new type of institution? Many interpretations have been brought forward attributing the organization and growth of the community colleges to broad social forces. One contention is that the colleges were sponsored by upper classes wishing to maintain their social position by restricting access to the universities that their offspring attended. Accordingly, they supported institutions that would deflect the aspirations of lower-class youths. This argument is bolstered by quotations from university presidents who sought to convert their institutions into research and graduate schools exclusively. And its proponents use as evidence the differential progress into society made by young people from families of high- and low-socioeconomic status. The thesis is especially appealing to people seeking reasons to account for a class-based society and for the inequitable distribution of social goods.

A reciprocal thesis resting on social forces contends that the community colleges arose out of an alliance between working-class groups and middle-class reformers seeking to counter the upper-class effort to stratify and limit educational opportunity. This position holds that the working class has always supported publicly funded education that allows its youth to progress to higher levels of schooling through access to education that has a common or general curriculum, not just a vocational orientation. Thus, community colleges, emphasizing both occupational studies and collegiate curriculum, provided an avenue of opportunity that young people from the lower classes could travel. Accordingly, working-class groups welcomed them and lobbied for their establishment.

A tangential argument holds that the colleges were built because of the desires of professional educators. Here the proponents point to the support for community colleges exhibited by university presidents in the early years. Since the universities wished to distance themselves from the students they did not care to serve, they sponsored community colleges in their own interest. Complementarily, public school officials advocated community colleges for the prestige and higher-status professional positions they yielded, as teachers became professors and superintendents became presidents. This position that the education community itself created the colleges has been supported especially by those who contend that the colleges were transformed from prebaccalaureate to vocational institutions in the 1970s because their leaders were seeking a secure niche in the structure of higher education.

At one level it is engaging to consider broad social forces, especially when a writer can postulate a conspiracy of the elite, a populist alliance, or a clique of professional educators. But great and complex developments typically have great and complex causes, and no one set of arguments seems more plausible than any other. It is perhaps more informative to cast the discussion in the context of specific legislative acts and institutional development that can be supported by the evidence of history.

The Colleges Emerge

Educational institutions in the United States grew from the bottom and the top, with a gap in the middle that was not filled until more than a century had passed after the formation of the nation. In the colonial era and until well in the nineteenth century, public schooling for the vast majority of youth stopped at the sixth or eighth grade. For a few it picked up again at the college level. In the late nineteenth and early twentieth centuries, however, the center was filled in as public high schools were built in every state and education was made mandatory through age 16 in most states. Meanwhile the universities were expanding upward. Enamoured with the German research and freedom-of-inquiry model, the universities added master's and doctoral programs featuring selective admissions and an independently functioning faculty. This was as true of the vocationally oriented universities that had been formed under the Morrill Act 1862, as of the older institutions. Rather than reach out to the rapidly growing numbers of high school graduates, many universities attempted to excise the freshman and sophomore classes. Where they opened to most high school graduates, as in Midwest, universities endeavoured to maintain collegiate standards by dismissing a sizable proportion of the matriculants before the end of their freshman year.

These moves toward upper division and graduate study left the lower-school districts to engage in their own form of upward mobility by adding grades 13 and 14 to the high schools. Rationalized as completing the students' general education, that is, helping them become good citizens, homemakers, or workers, the schools were actually filling in the gap. As state after state passed child labor legislation, the number of students staying in school and graduating high school grew rapidly. Since a primary benefit of a year of schooling is to provide a ticket enabling a person to attend the next year of schooling, the pressure for postsecondary education became evident. Accordingly, in many states the community colleges were organized and funded by local school districts following the model already in place for their elementary and secondary schools. Community colleges rose into a vacuum, as it were, well ahead of state authorization or planning.

Although, over the past 40 years, responsibility for funding and governance has moved in the main to the state level, community colleges still reflect their lower-school roots. The policy of admitting all students who apply, the patterns of funding on the basis of student attendance, the qualifications and working life of the faculty, and the generality of the curriculum all betray their origins. Even where the colleges were organized originally under state legislation, the authorizing acts usually directed the local district to petition for the establishment of a college, and state support typically was provided on an average-daily-attendance or full-time-student-equivalent basis.

The other major form of development, although a distant second in terms of number of institutions, was the two-year college built by the universities. Some were formed as branch campuses and others as colleges within colleges, responsible to the parent university but with their own staff and admissions policies (with the latter always proving more liberal).

Early State Legislation

Prior to mid-century, statewide plans for organizing, community colleges were hardly seen and national influence was even less apparent. Even though President Harry Truman's Commission on Higher Education (President's Commission on Higher Education, 1947) concluded that half of the nation's young could benefit from extending their formal education through grade 14, tangible federal support was slow to develop. Most of the states, however, were considering ways of coordinating college organization. And although the head of the American Association of Junior Colleges (formed in 1920) could still say that the colleges "had been growing without plan, general support, or supervision" (Bogue, 1950, p. 137), change was imminent.

By the 1960s state plans were mushrooming across the nation, leading to a period of tremendous expansion with some 50 new colleges opening each year. Half the states in the nation were commissioning studies, writing master plans, passing legislation, and building toward statewide systems of community colleges. The early leaders in statewide planning and development included California, Florida, Illinois, Michigan, and North Carolina. Indeed, these became the states with the most comprehensive sets of colleges. A review of developments in 15 states reveals the patterns.

Maryland had had public junior colleges since 1927 but in the 1960s it moved toward a state system by authorizing local boards of education to establish colleges that would be partially funded by the state and by authorizing the issuance of bonds. Furthermore, state funds for campus construction would be provided to the local districts on a matching basis.

Oregon's first community college opened in 1949 under a law stating that a public school district could be reimbursed for providing grade 13 and 14 classes. With a new law passed in 1961, the state provided funds for full time equivalent (FTE) operations plus 75 percent of building costs. Supervision was manifested in a community colleges section of the state department of education.

North Carolina's Community College Act was passed in 1957, providing construction funds (on a matching basis) and other small grants to the four municipally supported community colleges then functioning. The public community colleges emphasized prebaccalaureate programs, while a separate system of industrial education centers offered vocational training. In 1963 a law stated that a department of community colleges, operating within the state board of education, would combine the two systems. The state would match local funds for capital construction and would pay up to 65 percent of the operating costs.

New Jersey had been the recipient of six colleges funded by the federal government under the Emergency Relief Administration, beginning in 1933. However, federal support was withdrawn toward the end of the 1930s, and four of the six colleges closed. Not until 1962 did New Jersey pass legislation establishing county colleges. The costs for capital would be shared equally by state and county, and the state would provide a maximum of $200 per FTE student toward operation. The colleges were directed to provide both prebaccalaureate and technical studies. By the end of the 1960s, 12 colleges had been established.

In Washington some of the high schools had tried extending secondary programs as early as 1915, but these proved unsuccessful. Beginning in 1925 independent junior colleges were established, but not funded, by the state. In 1945 the legislature enabled the junior colleges to again become part of school districts, and in 1961 a law was passed designating community colleges, with strict control from the legislature. The state was to provide around 80 percent of the operating budgets, with the remainder coming from tuition. The colleges were formed from the local school districts but because prior to 1961 the districts were not allowed to organize colleges in counties that had state colleges or universities already there, the institutions were slow in developing. By 1967 the legislature divided the state into community college districts, each with a board of trustees. A separate coordinating council for occupational education was also established.

Michigan's first junior college opened in 1914 with a traditional liberal arts curriculum. The colleges that opened over the years were locally controlled and funded. By 1961 an amendment to the state constitution was passed providing for the establishment and financial support of community colleges that would be supervised by locally elected boards. The amendment further stated that a state board for community colleges should advise the state board of education on the general planning for such colleges and their requests for annual appropriations. Thus Michigan became unusual among American states by naming the community colleges in its constitution. In subsequent years the state provided somewhat less than half the cost of capital outlay and operating expenses, but in 1964 a legislative act was passed authorizing the local boards to offer both collegiate and noncollegiate programs, award associate degrees, and, in general, maintain flexibility in the types of students that they might matriculate and for whom state support would be provided. The law also allowed the local boards to levy property taxes and issue bonds for the support of the colleges. In the latter 1960s most of the community colleges broke away from the lower-school districts and established their own districts.

In Texas several junior colleges were originally founded as two-year church colleges dating from 1898. Others grew out of the public secondary schools. Well into the 1960s, the colleges were making moves toward becoming baccalaureate-granting institutions. Prior to the 1940s, the 22 public junior colleges in operation were still financed entirely from local funds. Subsequently, the legislature agreed to pay a portion of the operating costs on a per-student basis. Still, the majority of the funds for capital construction were local and most of the operating costs were carried by the sponsoring districts and the students. Not until the mid-1960s did state appropriations nearly approximate the operating costs for the colleges, and by the end of the 1960s the state was, for the first time, paying the full instructional costs in the colleges.

Pennsylvania's Community College Act was passed in 1963. Prior to that time, the state's higher education included an abundance of 164 institutions, public and private, many with branches or extension centers. When the community colleges were formed under the new act, local boards of trustees were elected, and operating expenses were shared on a one-third basis by the local districts, the state, and the students. This expectation put Pennsylvania among the states with the highest tuition right from the start. The Community College Act also divided governance powers among the state board of education and other state agencies and the local school districts. A subsequent amendment directed that capital expenses were to be shared equally by the state and local districts. The law noted that the community college instructional program should include "preprofessional liberal arts and sciences, semiprofessional business studies and technology, trade and industrial education, developmental training and adult education" (Yarrington, 1969, p. 154).

California's two-year colleges date from 1907, when a legislative act authorized high schools to offer postgraduate courses, and they were given impetus in 1921, when an act authorized establishment of separate junior college districts. Subsequent acts dealt with state support and included the junior colleges within the state's constitutional definition of free public education. In 1961 state funds were authorized to be used for capital construction. However, the California Master Plan, enacted into law early in the 1960s, added a provision to the education code stating that "the public junior colleges are secondary schools and shall continue to be a part of the public school system of this State." Another part of the same act said that public higher education included each campus of the University of California, all state colleges, and "all public junior colleges heretofore and hereafter established pursuant to law" (Yarrington, 1969, p. 159). The state provided around one-third of the funding for operations through the middle 1970s, with the balance made up by the local districts. At the end of the 1970s a proposition effectually eliminated the colleges from the likelihood of finding funds from their local tax base, and funding subsequently reverted almost entirely to the state.

The succession of legislative acts authorizing junior colleges in California led to some institutions being formed by high school districts, some by unified districts, and some by separate junior college districts. The latter split between those having an administration shared with the public school districts and those having a separate board of trustees. In the 1960s this duality was overturned when the local districts were directed to separate from the unified schools and to form independent community college districts. The state board of education set rules for forming a district that mandated a certain minimum student potential and a certain local assessed valuation. In the late 1960s a state-level board of governors was created with members appointed by the governor to assume all of the responsibilities previously vested in the state board of education and most of its staff and most of its rules were transferred over directly from the state department of education. The dual status of community colleges as part of both the lower schools and higher education has continued as subsequent acts guaranteed funding for the community colleges just as for the lower schools, while others gave much more latitude to the colleges in terms of staffing. The state continued to mandate admissions expectations and to set student fees, which have remained the lowest in the nation.

Illinois claims the first public community college in the nation (Joliet Junior College), dating from 1902. Over the next 30 years the state's community colleges grew, despite the absence of specific legal sanction. State aid for operating costs was provided in 1955 and, ten years later, for capital construction. In 1965 the Illinois Junior College Board was formed and took over the functions formerly carried out by the state superintendent of public instruction. It designated the junior colleges as part of the higher-education system, in contrast to their former status as an element in the lower school system.

Minnesota's local school districts had started junior colleges as early as 1915, with financial support entirely the responsibility of the local school district. In 1957 the legislature authorized state aid for operating costs, and in 1963 the legislature created a State Junior College Board to manage the system: to determine the location of new colleges, prescribe tuition rates, provide for uniform faculty salaries, and find funds for construction. Thus, Minnesota established the most restrictive state system, which endured into the 1990s when the community colleges were merged with the technical institutes and the state colleges into an even more comprehensive statewide system.

The Kansas legislature passed the first enabling act for junior college in 1917; it was a permissive law authorizing boards of education in local school districts to add grades 13 and 14 to their schools. In 1965 the state passed a Community Junior College Act providing for the superintendent of public instruction to be the state authority, naming various state agencies as oversight groups, enabling the junior colleges to have their own separate boards with taxing powers, and authorizing state aid, including tuition, to be paid by counties lacking community colleges, whose residents had to attend classes outside the district. By 1968 the state was providing operating funds on a per-credit-hour basis, but 40 percent of the operating costs were being borne by the local districts and 10 percent by the students.

In Virginia the community colleges were funded entirely by the state, including operating costs and capital outlay. No local funds were needed, although student tuition carried some of the burden. The colleges themselves were either two-year branches of state universities or vocational schools operated as extensions of the public schools. In 1966 a State Board for Community Colleges was established and the Virginia Community College System began operations. The board, appointed by the governor, was responsible for creating local community college boards for each institution. The state provided operating funds and capital construction, but the local units were responsible for site development. According to the state rules, the community colleges were to include occupational education, prebaccalaureate education, general education, adult education, remedial programs, special training for new industries, and noncredit community service—in short the entire range of community college activities.

When the public colleges of Georgia were organized into a system under the control of the board of regents in the 1930s, eight junior colleges were in existence. Four of those were converted to senior colleges during the ensuing 25 years, and no new junior colleges were established. Subsequent to 1958, seven new junior colleges were opened and two community-operated colleges were taken into the system. By 1968, four more junior colleges were converted to senior colleges. The Junior College Act of 1958 authorized local communities to develop and operate colleges with the assistance of state funds for operating expenses. No provision was made for site development or construction.

The public junior colleges of Mississippi were established with local districts and the state sharing responsibility. Most of them were an outgrowth of county agricultural high schools, dating from 1908. Legislation enacted in 1922 provided that any such high school located not less than 20 miles from a state college could add freshman and sophomore courses. The law also set standards for instructors and library holdings, but made no state appropriation to support college work. A 1928 law established a Junior College Commission as a regulatory agency for the colleges and provided some state funds for support. The local counties were placed into junior college districts in 1964 and allowed to levy local taxes. The state provided funds on a matching basis for constructing vocational-technical facilities.

State Plans

In the late 1960s additional legislation was passed in several states, much under the impetus of the federal Higher Education Act of 1965, which directed the states to create higher-education coordinating commissions if they wished to qualify for various federal aid programs. State master plans for community college development continued evolving. By the end of the 1960s, comprehensive plans specifically detailing college development and support were in place or imminent in 19 states, while legislation providing generalized guidelines had been passed in several others (Hurlbert, 1969). The state plans typically described organized systems, including the ways in which the colleges would be funded, and pointed out what separate communities had to do in order to develop their own institutions. One of the main arguments in favor of state planning was the recognition of the states' responsibility for equalizing the financing of community colleges so that students from low-income districts would be less disadvantaged. Another was the realization that for the community college to be a player within a higher-education system, some guidelines for curriculum, student access, and professional standards had to be established. The imminence of federal funding and regulation was also recognized, and contentions were raised that only through statewide coordination could the requirements and opportunities set down by the federal government be realized.

The plans were always rationalized with the idea of providing equal opportunity for all of the state's residents and a sense of the importance of preparing them to take their place within the state's workforce. Access for the widest number of the state's population was usually mentioned, along with the characteristics of the community colleges that would serve both prebaccalaureate and occupational aspirants. Typically, although the plans might have referred to remedial and general education, those terms were not well defined. In some instances the state plans stated specifically that the community colleges were to serve commuters, with the institutions cautioned not to build residence halls. However, this expectation was not universal, and residence halls were developed in many states where students were attracted from distant locations.

Equity throughout a state was also furthered by plans showing districts or regions where community colleges would be developed. Especially noted were areas where opportunities for postsecondary education were limited. Here the plans pointed toward the special necessity of developing colleges so that all of the state's residents would have an opportunity to attend. The goal in all cases was that 95 percent of the population would be within reasonable commuting distance of a junior college.

By way of ensuring that communities build colleges only where there were sufficient numbers of potential students, many state plans specified minimum enrollment expectations: 300 in Massachusetts; 400 in Virginia; 500 in New Hampshire and Texas; 600 in Colorado; 1,000 in Illinois, Michigan, and Ohio. Maximum enrollments were rarely specified. Admission was often noted as being open for everyone, including high school dropouts. Some of the plans noted faculty qualifications: for example, Kansas and Oregon endorsed the master's degree or equivalent for instructors in prebaccalaureate areas. Other plans noted minimum years of experience in the vocational areas in which instructors were teaching. Some plans recommended funding for prospective faculty members who could obtain additional graduate school credits.

Many of the plans indicated the percentage of operating costs that the state would pay; this was usually around half the total cost, ranging from 30 percent in California to 65 percent in North Carolina. Several states adopted minimum foundation plans in which each district would contribute in accordance with its ability to pay.

State contributions to capital outlay were quite vaned. Michigan called for funding for up to 100 percent of the initial building program; Illinois, 75 percent; and New Hampshire and Colorado, 100 percent of building construction, provided that the local community purchase and prepare the site. Virginia and Oregon also did not permit the use of state funds for site acquisition. In Kansas, state funds could not be used for constructing residence halls. The plans typically also commented on tuition. At one extreme was California, with tuition-free higher education, while at the other was New Hampshire, which took a stand against low tuition as being a subsidy to students that disregarded family income. Most states allowed tuition to vary from around 10 to 50 percent of operating costs.

As for organization, state departments and state boards were often recommended, with local boards filling in with additional responsibilities. It is possible to see the trend developing toward separate boards for community colleges even as the statewide authority was vested in a state board of education or a state board of higher education. In some cases the state boards for junior colleges had representatives on a coordinating council for all of higher education: California, Illinois, and Pennsylvania exemplify that type of coordination. Overall, the state plans had to create systems of community colleges out of uncoordinated groups of institutions.

Inserted in most of the plans was the expectation that the state supervisory agency would conduct a continuing study of student access and college operations. This put a research responsibility into the state departments, but one that depended on local cooperation, that is, the individual colleges were going to have to supply the data that the state agency needed to summarize trends and events in the colleges. This expectation proved difficult to bring about because it demanded a uniform set of reporting, which was, in effect, a violation of the idea that each college would be able to determine its own categories and criteria. At the same time, few state agencies developed a capacity for collecting data according to consistent criteria. Every time a state agency tried to define a category, a number of local college leaders typically responded that the criteria did not recognize the unique circumstances within their own institutions.

Research at the local level was rarely mentioned. The understanding was that the junior college staff should not have research as part of its responsibilities but would only provide data to the state agencies. Over the years this proved to be a weakness, as the collection of data required local staff to understand its importance and the ways of collecting it. Other weaknesses in the plans were that they rarely specified how staff were to be recruited, leaving that to the local institutions. Nor did the plans suggest specifics regarding transfer procedures and requirements, leaving that to be worked out between the local institutions and the universities to which their students aspired.

The state plans purported to reduce the further development of underfunded, marginally viable colleges, but they confronted some widely held views that the growth of junior colleges depended less on state-level decrees than on the healthy formation of institutions in response to local needs and conditions. The concept of locally controlled community colleges was still firmly in place, and many commentators viewed with suspicion the development of institutions controlled from distant state capitals. As Hurlbert noted, "Without the aspirations, pride, and initiative of local communities, many community colleges would never have come into existence" (1969, p. 5). He recognized the delicacy of balancing state and local control and proposed master plans that would coordinate systems even while allowing for a significant portion of grass-roots management and goal setting. Lombardi (1968) also commented on the care taken in the legislation establishing California's board of governors to mention that local boards of trustees would maintain a sizable proportion of responsibility. Even as control and funding moved steadily toward state capitals over the next 30 years, the belief in the value and importance of local control would not die. It became rather like the nostalgia for the ivy-covered, autonomous four-year college, free of external interference, a nostalgia that persisted long into an era when every aspect of institutional management and support was influenced by court rulings and civil legislation.

Later State Legislation

Reviews of state legislation passed in the 1970s and 1980s demonstrate the evolution of state policy. In 1976, the first of Martorana and colleagues' (Martorana & McGuire, 1976) many reports on legislation affecting community colleges classified the legislative actions under the headings of finance, state-level concerns, institutional concerns, personnel, students, and academic concerns. Predictably, most of the legislation dealt with finance: appropriations for operations, capital funds, and financial procedures. State-level administration and statewide coordination also came in for a share of concern, along with institutional administration and tuition. A total of 334 legislative enactments among the thirty states was reviewed.

Increases in appropriations were seen in most of the states at a time of enrollment growth. The states authorized bond issues to fund capital improvement in many cases. Legislation affecting financial procedures tended toward yielding greater financial flexibility, on the one hand, and legislative control of expenditures, on the other. Some states were going one way and some the other. Several bills related to coordination, with two states (California and Florida) proposing the establishment of regional coordinating councils. A few states passed laws establishing a legal basis for community colleges so that the local districts would have taxing and bonding authority: Texas, Connecticut, and Arkansas were among them.

Under institutional concerns the legislation dealt with issues of liability, and either permissive or mandatory actions related to what local boards and administrators might do. Among the latter, five states dealt with provisions for electing trustees. Laws were also passed in Oklahoma and Mississippi authorizing or providing for the establishment of new colleges. Name changes during this era were also authorized, generally moving the institutions from the category of "junior" to "community."

Several states authorized collective bargaining for faculty during the mid-1970s, including Connecticut, Michigan, Washington, and Florida. Other states expanded protection for faculty members, extending due process procedures for those terminated. Nevada, in effect, granted tenure to the faculty.

Among laws affecting students included those providing for tuition waivers for veterans, disadvantaged students, and senior citizens. The continuing tendency toward access is revealed in these types of bills. Scholarship funds were increased in Michigan, Hawaii, and Arizona, while Iowa and Illinois opened up their student aid programs to part-time students.

Several enactments related to curriculum tended to be proscriptive. Tennessee required all students to complete a minimum number of credits in U.S. or state history; Hawaii resolved that environmental education should be required; Texas required nursing programs to grant credit for experience. Other laws dealt with establishing economic education or law enforcement centers.

The states reacted to the federal Higher Education Acts of 1965 and 1972, which directed them to establish procedures for coordinating public higher education within their boundaries. Community colleges were typically represented on the so-called 1202 commissions (state planning commissions) established during this era, but there was much foot-dragging as questions of state and local responsibility and of public versus independent higher education were considered. Still, several states created governing or coordinating boards covering all of public higher education. The states also reacted to federal influence on student financial aid, as when they provided for veterans' benefits and for administering federal aid to students.

The legislative activity of the late 1970s continued to focus especially on finance and administration, with more than half the legislation falling into those two areas. General appropriations for community colleges were increasing, with operational costs and capital funding bills being enacted across the board. Much of the legislation related to procedural matters and taxing structures, but the trend toward state control of finances was definitely in place.

The legislation affecting governing local and state governing bodies "focused on board composition and procedural execution of policy rather than substantive issues of authority" (Martorana & Broomall, 1981, p. 27). Massachusetts established a state board, and New Jersey and Arizona passed legislation affecting the composition of local boards. The legislatures were also enacting bills providing for various types of studies and surveys, including general studies of the role of the community college and specific surveys of subcategories of students, such as those with learning disabilities (Virginia) and foreign and out-of-state students (Tennessee). However, in general there was "a continued trend among state legislators to view the community college more as an element within postsecondary education or state government and less as a unique educational entity" (p. 60).

Other trends were that legislative attention to academic affairs focused increasingly on occupational education and that legislation directed toward students came in the form of bills providing for tuition waivers for special groups, such as senior citizens, the academically gifted, people unemployed due to the closure of major industries, and those for whom English was a second language. Notable for its absence was legislation directed toward enhancing community or adult education or toward strengthening the articulation between community colleges and secondary schools.

The level of legislative activity increased through the 1980s, with an average of 18 pieces of legislation affecting community colleges passed in each state. Finance and administration accounted for five out of every eight laws; the others dealt with personnel, students, and academic programs, while physical facilities and institutional growth seemed lowest in levels of activity. A growing concern for quality was apparent as legislators passed more bills concerned with academic programs.

Although several studies examining community college mission were conducted, few changes were occurring. These commissions recommended increases in vocational education and economic development, but the provision of funds or directives to establish particular types of programs was slow in coming. Most of the commissions stated the major functions of the community colleges but left to the institutions the magnitude of emphasis that they would place on one function or another. Nonetheless, some states recommended strongly that the community colleges be involved with economic development. As an example, in its 1982 Master Plan for Higher Education in Ohio, the state board of regents suggested that two-year colleges become partners in local efforts at economic revitalization, establish adult learning programs related to employment, and contract for training employees of local businesses. The question of when the states became concerned particularly with the access and progress of ethnic minorities can be raised in association with these reports of legislation. Apparently, the federal government was much more concerned about such matters at this time. Another question is when the states became interested in distance education; nothing in the reports from the mid-1980s and earlier suggests that they were.

By 1990 the tempo had picked up, with almost twice as many pieces of legislation being passed as in prior years (an average of 32 per state). The topical areas were similar across state lines, as though imitation was guiding the policy makers. Governance issues remained prominent, with seven states enacting legislation to change or substantially modify governance structures. Academic issues were gaining in attention, now running a close third to administration and finance, and laws concerned with students were now fourth.

The trends toward access remained intact. Several states considered legislation that would establish funds for prepaid tuition or tax credits. Michigan was the first state to create a guaranteed tuition savings plan, followed by similar legislation in Alabama, Louisiana, and Massachusetts. Texas created a college savings bond program.

The requests for data continued taking specific turns. Pennsylvania was first to require that colleges report the level of crime on their campus. Coordinating bodies also continued to evolve. For example, the boards for state technical colleges and community colleges in Connecticut were merged into a single board. However, some states acted to ease bureaucratic controls on specific institutional functions: Arkansas, New Jersey, and New York were in this group.

In academic affairs, top concern was given to occupational training, but there also seemed to be a growing interest in program articulation with high schools and with universities. Much attention was being given to the ability of community college students to transfer to senior public universities, while other policies were enacted to allow high school students to matriculate in community colleges. At the same time that articulation between community colleges and universities was being laboriously streamlined in some states, the two-year upper-division universities that had been built in Texas, Florida, and Illinois were being expanded so that they could include freshman and sophomore students. Nonetheless, institutional competition in general was not a public policy issue. Interest in tracking students on a statewide basis was growing, along with issues related to the use of part-time faculty.

The number of states seeking institutional accountability grew gradually during the 1990s. In 1997 the Kentucky Postsecondary Improvement Act included provisos for educational quality as revealed by data on student outcomes, including pass rates on licensure examinations; student progress, with data on time to degree; the effectiveness of remedial programs; and persistence and graduation rates (Kentucky Council on Postsecondary Education, 1997). South Carolina attempted to base its appropriations to higher education on performance indicators that included 37 criteria for judging institutional performance (Schmidt, 1997).

Moves toward uniformity in curriculum and graduation requirements were revealed in a 1992 law passed in Indiana that required colleges and universities to jointly identify at least 30 credit hours of comparable general education courses fulfilling graduation requirements (Indiana State Commission for Higher Education, 1996). Florida also attempted to standardize requirements for baccalaureate programs and general education by mandating that common degree program prerequisites be established and that general education requirements be stabilized at 36 hours at all colleges and universities (LeMon & Pitter, 1996).

Issues of personnel qualifications, employment, and dismissal continued to be codified. A bill enacted into law in California in 1990 removed the requirement that instructors possess a state teaching credential and allowed local districts to set standards for instructors and policies for employing and evaluating them. It put forth the concept of shared governance, stating that groups representative of faculty, administrators, students, and classified staff (business officers, custodians) be consulted on all policy decisions. Faculty were to be involved in evaluating administrators.

The California pattern of responsibility shared by a state board and local trustees points up how the evolution of community colleges from local institutions to state controlled institutions has proceeded fitfully. A merit system administered by a state personnel commission has authority over the local trustees in matters involving the classified staff. The state board of governors, working within the framework of the state education code, defines rules relating to administrators with responsibility for academic affairs and student services. The local boards employ the administrators, who can be dismissed at any time (as long as due process is followed) unless they have been granted an expressed contract, which is limited by the code to four years. The state does not provide for administrative employment rights except to say that administrators must be notified if they are to be terminated (Lau, 1997).

To summarize, the flurry of state legislation that began in the early 1960s had several effects. It typically spelled out the responsibilities, funding, and management issues shared by state and local authorities, while separating the colleges from the public school districts, which had constructed many of them. Despite assurances that local boards would maintain certain prerogatives, it is obvious that control was gravitating toward the state capitals. Under federal prodding, nearly all the states created coordinating bodies for all public higher education, including community colleges. The states sponsored studies of need and feasibility that projected population growth, employment opportunities, and college demand. They also set tuition policies, reimbursement schedules, and guidelines for capital expenditures, often leaving a portion of the latter to the local districts. A few built state systems encompassing all governance and funding, but most sustained hybrids.

Other areas, such as course requirements and staff responsibilities, were less strictly controlled. But by the 1990s, more micromanagement was apparent, as the state agencies sought evidence of college effects, especially in remedial and occupational education. Various groups lobbying on behalf of their members were active in gaining state approval for all sorts of special action, from faculty salaries to intercollegiate athletics. Oregon's State Board of Education set instructor standards. The Texas Higher Education Coordinating Board mandated an academic skills test and began linking approval of new associate degrees to the college's job-training record. Florida's state board of regents set uniform general-education requirements across all colleges and universities and limited the number of credit hours toward degrees for which it would provide reimbursement. Having established rules for college formation and support, the states moved steadily toward more detailed regulations. Little fell outside their purview.

Federal Policies

Federal policies affecting community colleges may be clustered under headings of access, funding, and curriculum. Under access the primary policy was the Servicemen's Readjustment Act of 1944, commonly known as the GI Bill. By placing funds for college-going in the hands of the veterans of World War II, the bill marked a major shift in the direction of federal influence. For the first time federal monies were given to individuals rather than to the institutions. Each veteran was authorized to attend any college or university that would admit him, and the government agreed to pay the tuition, pay for books and supplies, and pay a monthly stipend for living expenses. Since many veterans did not qualify for university admission or chose to attend the community colleges in their hometown, veteran enrollment swelled the two-year college campuses.

A second set of acts affecting access came in subsequent years as numerous forms of antidiscrimination legislation were passed. The civil rights acts of the 1960s and 1970s forbade discrimination in college admissions on the basis of race. Title IX of the Education Amendments of 1972 prohibited gender bias in college admissions. The Rehabilitation Act of 1973 and the Americans with Disabilities Act of 1990 mandated access and special facilities for individuals with disabilities who otherwise met academic and technical standards. The Age Discrimination Act of 1975 prohibited discrimination on the basis of age in programs or activities receiving federal financial assistance.

Numerous court rulings pointed to the specifics in these acts enhancing access. In the 1970s a federal district court ruled in favor two 16-year-old plaintiffs who had sought entrance to Sonoma County Junior College in California. The court reasoned that the institution's requirement that students be 18 years old was not rational in relationship to the state's interest in educating qualified students. Also in the 1970s the U.S. Supreme Court ruled that Southeastern Community College (North Carolina) was within its rights in denying the admission of a severely deaf student to its nursing program because the student's disability would preclude her taking part in the clinical aspects of the nursing program and would create serious difficulties in practicing the profession. However, in other cases the courts have ruled that students must he admitted if reasonable accommodations can be made that would enable them to participate in educational programs. Accordingly, the colleges were directed to build access ramps for physically disabled students and to make accommodations in science laboratories so that visually handicapped students might participate.

Federal funding for students was continued through the Pell Grant program, along with supplemental educational opportunity grants, guaranteed student loans, and college work-study aid. Since the Pell Grant program began in the early 1970s, students in community colleges have received between 18 and 26 percent of the awards each year. It is more difficult to estimate an exact federal contribution to students in the form of guaranteed loans because students who receive the loans are expected to repay them. The contribution of the federal government appears in the form of interest that is paid while the student is enrolled and when the government pays the banks if the student defaults. Because, compared to students in the universities, the students in community colleges tend to be from lower socioeconomic classes and the dropout rates are higher, default rates in the community colleges have been higher than those for university students. This, then, represents a type of student subsidy.

Amendments to the Higher Education Act of 1965 have been made several times, most recently in 1998. A review of these amendments shows some effects on community colleges, of which a few are direct but most are tangential. Among the direct effect, the 1992 amendments established a Community College Liaison Office in the U.S. Department of Education and provided Presidential Access Scholarships for students in two-year programs. Among the less direct effects, the amendments extended Pell Grant eligibility for students attending part time, authorized grants to colleges enrolling high proportions of Hispanic students, and allowed colleges to petition for funds to support child care services for disadvantaged students.

The 1998 amendments sharply increased the maximum Pell Grant award while denying Pell Grants to students in colleges with 25 percent or greater default rates over a three-year period. Some community college students were affected because their colleges were struggling to keep from crossing the 25 percent default line. The amendments also demanded more disclosure of campus crime rates and mandated that colleges distribute a voter registration form to each enrolled student.

Federal government influence on community college curriculum has been felt primarily in the occupational areas. Beginning with the Vocational Act of 1963, which authorized federal funding of occupational programs in postsecondary institutions, the community colleges have been handsomely supported by this form of federal financing. Actually, the Vocational Education Act was not the first piece of legislation to authorize federal funds for community colleges. In the 1930s several colleges were receiving federal money for occupational education that had been appropriated under the 1917 Smith-Hughes Act and the 1937 George-Deen Act. The colleges slipped in under those acts because, as Eells (1941) pointed out, they did not "mean that the *institution* must be of less than college grade—only that the particular *work offered*, for which federal aid is received, must be of less than college grade" (1941, p. 29). However, the 1963 act and the amendments of 1968 and 1972 vastly augmented federal funds for vocational education. The Carl D. Perkins Vocational Education Act of 1984 further modified the guidelines for distributing federal funding, and by 1985 the community colleges were receiving around 22 percent of the Perkins money. Other federal programs providing funds for community college vocational education include Job Training Partnerships, Job Opportunities and Basic Skills, Omnibus Trade and Competitiveness, Worksite Literacy, and Cooperative Education.

Compared with the federal funds running to occupational education, federal support for other studies has been minuscule. The National Endowment for the Humanities (NEH) has sponsored a few programs addressed to community college education, but funding does not reach more than a couple of percentage points of that which the federal government makes available for occupational studies. Some colleges have taken advantage of programs sponsored by the Fund for the Improvement of Postsecondary Education and the National Science Foundation. Most federal legislation does not specify institutional type; however, Title III (Developing Institutions) has benefited the colleges. Also, the Tribally Controlled Community Colleges Act singles out a particular group for direct support. Other funds appropriated by the federal government often loop through the states for administration. Many are block grants that can be used by the states to assist the colleges in developing curriculum, providing funds to various categories of students, training teachers, and so on. The federal interest in these areas goes all the way back to the various types of vocational education support appropriated early in the century.

Conclusion

The history of state and national policy affecting community colleges points up how the institutions have developed within a federated system, ranging from the U.S. government to the local school districts. But without a doubt, the state governments have been most influential, especially since the 1960, when nearly all of them stepped up efforts to coordinate public higher education within their borders. State policies allocate decision-making authority to state agencies and college officials. State regulations promote or inhibit institutional growth. State databases reveal college operation and compliance with regulations. State funds provide for operating expenses and capital outlay. Some states have imposed standards for associate degrees and certificates and for the types of courses qualifying for reimbursement; others have established staff qualifications. Although the colleges are still localized institutions, drawing their students and character from their neighborhood, they operate within a myriad state regulations. The influence of the federal government pales in light of state rules and support.

A stable set of institutions has been the main effect of state control. From the start, the states have demanded minimum numbers of students and reliable funding sources. The college leaders know what to expect; their communities are not faced with unforeseen closures, mergers, or reconstitutions as different types of schools. There is little tolerance for weak, drifting colleges that are hardly worthy of the name. The community colleges are reliable players in each state's education system.

Some of the other consequences of state influence have been institutional expansion and a lateral curriculum. Most states fund on the basis of student enrollment. Since enrolling more students results in the receipt of more money, the college leaders have developed a mindset favoring growth, which stems from the knowledge that without augmented enrollment, leaders cannot fund salary increases, new programs, and all the changes that make their colleges appear innovative. The institutions are reimbursed for students taking classes, whether these are, from one term to another, the same or different students. There have been few incentives for increased rates of program completion; thus, the leaders react with alarm when states impose enrollment caps or request data on graduation or job-attainment rates. The federal government has colluded in this "growth is good" presumption through its ever-expanding student grant and loan programs.

Curricular breadth is a corollary of the growth dogma; more courses designed to serve more students with different aspirations enhance enrollments. Here again the federal government is a contributor. If it had not funded occupational education heavily, the colleges could not have developed the numerous vocational programs that have expanded their curriculums. Taken together, the enrollment growth and the curricular breadth have yielded the community colleges' greatest contribution to American postsecondary education, access, and their second greatest contribution, workforce development.

In the coming years, governmental influence will continue along the channels developed over the past several decades: federal support for students and state support for the colleges on a broader basis. The trend toward state-level coordination, in place for over one-third of a century, will continue. The requests for data on program outcomes will increase, and pressures for funding on the basis of outcomes will become ever more insistent. Perhaps the latter evidences public distrust of the colleges; perhaps it suggests that they are so important a part of the social system that it is unconscionable for their staff to imply, "Send us the funds and don't ask questions." In any event, a set of institutions attuned historically to process is being turned laboriously, gradually, toward a concern for product. Are community colleges players in the global economy? Purveyors of education to people around the world? They began as schools serving their local communities, and there they will remain, as public perceptions hold them in the place from which they arose.

References

Bogue. J. P. (1950). *The community college* New York: McGraw Hill.

Eells, W. C. (1941). *Prevent status of junior college terminal education.* Washington, DC: American Association of Junior Colleges.

Hurlbert, A. S. (1969). State master plans for community colleges. *ERIC Clearinghouse for Junior Colleges Monograph Series* (Number 8), Los Angeles.

Indiana State Commission for Higher Education (1996). *Transferring Ivy Tech credit to public institutions: 1996 progress report.* Indianapolis.

Jones, D. Ewell, P. and McGuinness, A. (1998). *The challenges and opportunities facing higher education.* San Jose, CA: National Center for Public Policy and Higher Education.

Kentucky Council on Postsecondary Education. (1997). *The status of Kentucky postsecondary education: In transition, 1997.* Frankfort.

Lau R. (1997, April 2). *Employment rights of administrators in the California community colleges.* Compton, CA: Compton Community College District.

LeMon, R. E., & Pitter, G. W. (1996). *Standardizing across institutions: Now that we all look alike, what do we look like?* Tallahassee, FL.

Lombardi, J. (1968, October). *Unique problems of the inner city colleges.* Speech presented to California Junior College Association, Anaheim, CA ERIC ED 026057.

Martorana, S. V. & Broomall, J. K. (1981, June). *State legislation affecting community and junior colleges, 1980* (Report Number 37). Pennsylvania State University Center for the Study of Higher Education.

Martorana, S. V., & Garland, P. H. (1986). *State legislation and state-level public policy affecting community, junior, and two-year technical college education, 1985.* Pennsylvania State University.

Martorana, S. V., & McGuire, W. G. (1976). *State legislation relating to community and junior colleges, 1973-75.* State College: Pennsylvania State University Press.

Martorana, S. V., et al. (1991). *State legislation and state-level public policy affecting community, junior, and two-year technical college education, 1989.* Pennsylvania State University.

President's Commission on Higher Education. (1947). *Higher education for American democracy. Washington, DC:* U.S. Government Printing Office.

Schmidt, P. (1997, April 4). Rancor and confusion greet a change in South Carolina's budgeting system. *Chronicle of Higher Education,* pp A26-A27.

Yarrington, R. (1969). *Junior colleges: 50 states, 50 years.* Washington, DC: American Association of Junior Colleges.

CHAPTER 49

PUBLIC POLICY, COMMUNITY COLLEGES, AND THE PATH TO GLOBALIZATION

JOHN S. LEVIN, THE UNIVERSITY OF ARIZONA, ARIZONA, U.S.A.

Abstract. This study addresses the nature of government policy toward community colleges in the 1990s and the responses of institutions to these policies. This is an examination of Canadian and U.S. community colleges in two Canadian provinces and three U.S. states as well as analysis of government policy in two countries, at the federal, state and provincial levels. Government policies are viewed as directing community colleges toward economic goals, emphasizing workforce training and state economic competitiveness as outcomes, compelling colleges to improve efficiencies, increase productivity, and to become accountable to government and responsive to business and industry. Government responses to economic concerns at the provincial and state levels resulted in economic development policies applicable to community colleges. Institutional responses among community colleges, evident in behaviors such as marketization and productivity and efficiency, altered college missions, resulting in the pursuit of economic ends by these institutions.

Keywords: community colleges, globalization, interventionary state, mission, public policy

In the 1990s, public policy applicable to community colleges in both Canada and the U.S. directed these institutions to global competitiveness and to a re-fashioning of institutional mission. Government policies clearly endeavored to direct community colleges toward economic goals, emphasizing workforce training and state economic competitiveness as outcomes, compelling colleges to improve efficiencies, increase productivity, and to become accountable to government and responsive to business and industry. Pressures for efficiency and productivity accompanied claims of government restraint on public sector funding and directed colleges to behave like globally competitive businesses. Pressures to orient institutions to the marketplace, evident in the emphasis placed upon vocationalism and commercialism (Kenway 1998), were consistent with the needs of global capital. Furthermore, government responsiveness to economic concerns at the provincial and state levels became economic development policies applicable to community colleges. Institutional responses, evident in behaviors such as marketization and productivity and efficiency, altered community college missions, resulting in the pursuit of economic ends by these institutions.

The domain of politics was the arena where government policy and policy behaviors on the one hand and institutional responses on the other hand interacted. Policy can be seen as government efforts to control decisions and actions of institutions in accord with the objectives of governments (Goedegebuure et al. 1993). Policy regulates institutions, permitting, requiring, or forbidding actions, which include those of both institutional members and government officials (Schlager and Blomquist 1996). Simply, policy reflects government objectives. Institutional responses are formally connected to policy implementation. For community colleges, the economic objectives of the 1990s overshadowed and in some cases replaced earlier objectives of accessibility, personal and social development, and a liberal or general education (Schugurensky and Higgins 1996). Institutional responses to policy were varied, although in general colleges altered structures, processes, and institutional mission to align these more with economic interests.

The Community College

Since the 1960s, the community college in North America has been viewed and conceived as a social and educational institution that responds to its local community, offering open-access to postsecondary education and providing comprehensive education and training programs to meet the needs of individual students. Its image is based upon its mission: to serve the underserved and to expand access to postsecondary education and training. Historically, community colleges have prided themselves on fulfilling the needs of individual students and serving their local communities (Cohen and Brawer 1996; Dennison and Gallagher 1986; Roueche and Baker 1987).

Yet, within the last decade, with the rise in public and government emphasis and attention upon a global economy, the community college became not only a more prominent regional and national institution but also an institution that was affected by macro-level changes in the external environment. These changes include government policies to reflect both societal and economic concerns such as the training of a globally competitive workforce and private sector demands for an increase in workbased training and specific skill acquisition for workers.

Global forces, particularly economic ones, contributed to organizational change in the 1990s, and colleges in response to these forces altered their missions and structures. These alterations in effect moved colleges away from local community social needs towards local market needs and in line with national and international agendas of dominant influencers such as governments and businesses, suggesting a more pronounced economic role for community colleges.

In this multi-case investigation of community colleges in the United States and Canada, I refer to the process of change as globalization. Organizational behaviors in response to globalization, and to others' responses to globalization, affected both education and work within these institutions. Community colleges changed in significant fashion in the 1990s, and there was a considerable role of public policy in stimulating and sustaining these alterations. College missions expanded, encompassing a greater economic development and workforce training role, and institutional behaviors became more fiscally acquisitive. The pursuit of new sources of revenues and the maintenance of existing levels of revenues became major institutional activities. In part a consequence of government funding behaviors and in part a result of government policy, college managers became more economically focused and colleges became more entrepreneurial in their behaviors.

Globalization

As a practical term, globalization reflects a perception "that the world is rapidly being moulded into a shared social space by economic and technological forces and that developments in one region of the world can have profound consequences for the life chances of individuals or communities on the other side of the globe" (Held et al. 1999, p. 1). It may be that consciousness of a global society, culture, and economy and global interdependence are the cornerstones of globalization (Robertson 1992), and these—consciousness and interdependency—have saliency in knowledge-based enterprises. Institutional theory identifies organizational "Fields," or institutional types, such as higher education institutions or hospitals, for example, where patterns of institutional behaviors become similar across institutions (DiMaggio and Powell 1983). Higher education institutions, because of their cultural, social, and economic roles, are caught up in and affected by globalization.

The process of globalization has been connected to numerous alterations in higher education. For example, with emphasis upon international competitiveness, economic globalization is viewed as moving postsecondary institutions into a business-like orientation, with its attendant behaviors of efficiency and productivity. At the level of universities in both the U.S. and Canada, globalization can be equated with corporatism, with the marketplace playing a more pronounced role than in the past. Furthermore, education is vocationalized, and training is driven by the demands of business and industry. Conceptually, training and education are synonymous, much like the interchangeability of "knowledge" and "skills" (Aronowitz and DiFazio 1994; Currie 1998; Leslie and Slaughter 1997; Levin 1999a; Newson 1994; Slaughter 1997; Slaughter and Leslie 1997). The placement of higher education institutions in closer proximity to the marketplace, especially in fields connected to techno-science, through corporate partnerships and associations, is an obvious manifestation of economic globalization.

Globalization literature either implicitly or explicitly suggests a number of institutional behaviors that are influenced by globalizing processes (Appadurai 1990; Bridges 1994; Castells 1993; Rifkin 1995; Slaughter and Leslie 1997). These processes include not only economic globalization but also cultural and social. I have identified behaviors in this literature that are relevant to higher educational institutions. These identified behaviors characterize how institutions (their members) respond to global forces as well as to the behaviors of the state in its responses to global forces such as global competitiveness. These behaviors are *internationalization, multiculturalism, commodification, homogenization, marketization, re-structuring, labor alterations, productivity and efficiency*, and *electronic communication and information*.

These organizational behaviors are not only consistent with globalization but also reflect both the impact of global forces upon higher education institutions and the reproduction of the globalization process (Alfred and Carter 1996; Aronowitz and Di Fazio 1994; Currie 1998; Dudley 1998; Levin 1999b; Leslie and Slaughter 1997; Marginson 1997; Newson 1994; Ritzer 1998; Schugurensky and Higgins 1996; Slaughter 1997; Slaughter and Leslie 1997).

Nine sets of organizational behaviors are connected to globalization (see Table 1). One set of behaviors includes both internationalizing the curriculum and the campus and extending the campus in other nations. Specific behaviors are the recruitment of students from other countries, the delivery of college curriculum in other nations, and the inculcation of others' cultural values, including the promotion and display of international images, symbols, and practices. I refer to this set of behaviors as *internationalization*. Related to some extent to internationalization, institutions and their members adopt an ideology that on the one hand promotes equality among groups along the lines of ethnic origins, class, and gender orientation, and favors strategies that give special status to underrepresented or historically less privileged groups. This set of behaviors is labeled *multiculturalism*. Higher education institutions create products and establish services that they take to the marketplace to sell, or private individuals or companies approach the college to purchase goods and services. This entails the development of programs to fit the requirements of a specific business. It also includes the delivery of instruction or training to the specifications, such as duration or place, of private business and industry. This set of behaviors represents *commodification*. Along these same

Table 1. Globalization behaviors

	Category	Abbreviation Code
A.	internationalization	[I]
B.	multiculturalism	[MC]
C.	commodification	[COM]
D.	homogenization	[HOM]
E.	marketization	[MRK]
F.	re-structuring	[R]
G.	labor alterations	[LA]
H.	productivity and efficiency	[P/E]
I.	electronic communication and information	[ET]

lines, institutions make their products and services similar; they routinize work; they standardize practices, such as educational delivery; and most importantly, they attempt to objectify curriculum so that it approaches quantification or reduction to its basic elements. I refer to this set of behaviors as *homogenization*. Institutions also align themselves closer to the private sector, and they compete with other institutions and organizations for revenues. They form associations with private business and industry. They solicit private donations of money, goods, and services, which they acknowledge through publicity and tax benefits. I refer to this set of behaviors as *marketization*. Organizations make structural alterations to change work patterns and to change how and what they produce and the services they provide. This usually entails elaborate modifications that lead to job change, job loss, and the reallocation of resources. Indeed, resources and their scarcity generally motivate these behaviors. I refer to this set of behaviors as *restructuring*. Related are those institutional behaviors that change work patterns, including the nature and duration of work. These behaviors may entail additional students in classrooms or the implementation of online management systems—technological change—that modify workloads and work practices. I refer to these behaviors as *labor alterations*. To address and satisfy revenue needs, often the consequence of constrained government funding, higher education institutions exhibit two behaviors: they turn to the private sector, including fee-payers, a marketization behavior, and they pursue greater efficiency in work, including raising productivity of existing workers or lowering costs by reducing the work force. I refer to this latter set of behaviors as *productivity and efficiency*. Institutions adopt technologies that are perceived as both labor saving and normative. Higher education institutions use electronic technologies both for work processes, such as communications and information processing, and for education, such as online instruction. I refer to this set of behaviors as *electronic communication and information*.

With the role of the state increasing in the affairs and operations of public higher education institutions, the state has become a more noticeable institutional actor, intervening or interfering in colleges actions. I refer to this set of behaviors as *state intervention*, although it is not an institutional behavior but needs to be recognized that it is a behavior of the state acting upon higher education institutions. Some of these sets of behaviors are not present in all organizations, not present simultaneously in an organization, and not enacted in all areas of an organization.

The State and Higher Education

There is considerable evidence in government policy that in the 1990s the state was largely preoccupied with economic issues, specifically with improving its economic competitiveness on a global scale and with reducing its public sector costs. Workforce training was the major focus of government policy directed to community colleges. And governments, particularly state and provincial governments, directed community colleges to alter institutional practices and become more productive and efficient, for example increase the number of students served, graduate more workplace-ready students, and reduce per unit costs.

Goedegebuure et al. (1993) conceptualize two types of state influence or state behaviors related to higher education: the interventionary state and the facilitatory state. In the former, government is actively involved in institutional activities and actions, intervening directly to ensure such outcomes as "economic efficiency . . . student access and accountability" (Goedegebuure et al. 1993, p. 1). The interventionary state can be viewed as an instrument of economic interests and particularly capitalism. Thus, promotion of workforce training and emphasis upon economic competitiveness are behaviors of government consistent with the state as an "expression . . . of social-class relations . . . [that] . . . imply domination of one group by another . . ." (Carnoy 1984, p. 250). If the state is an actor independent of capital and labor, and state officials are relatively autonomous, then the interventionary state may be seen as an agent of policy influencers of higher education—these include the interests of business and students as well as state and institutional officials (Carnoy 1984; Dougherty 1994; Skocpol 1985). Thus, in this latter case, government social policy as well as economic policy and other actions that "attempt to reinforce the authority, political longevity, and social control of the state" (Skocpol 1985, p. 15) find a vehicle in higher education institutions.

Slaughter (1990) advances an integrative view of the state and higher education: that the state is *de facto* inseparable from higher education institutions, and therefore not an autonomous entity; and that the state is not monolithic, not a simple source of money or authority but a multifaceted resource. That is to say that at some levels, the state does reflect class and social struggles while at other levels the state is independent of capital and labor. This view suggests that although workforce training and economic competitiveness may indeed reflect the state's imposition of capitalistic behaviors on institutions, student policies and funding behaviors that support access could be seen as expressions of social policy that may not be in accord with capitalism or the domination of one group over another.

In my analysis of government documents, which includes Canadian federal and provincial documents and U.S. federal and state documents, government policies clearly endeavored to direct community colleges toward economic goals. The state was clearly interventionary rather than facilitatory. Policy emphasized workforce training and state economic competitiveness as outcomes, compelling colleges to improve efficiencies and to become accountable to government and responsive to business and industry. These findings are more consistent with the view that the state preserves and expands modes of production. But, there were also areas of compatibility that support the view of a multifaceted resource. There was little or no support for the view that favors autonomous decision-makers as drivers of policy.

The Study

In the most general terms, the study addresses the nature of government policy toward community colleges in the 1990s and the responses of institutions to these policies. A qualitative, multiple case study design and the use of field methods—including document analysis, interviews, informal conversations, observations, and the use of informants—were viewed as appropriate methodologies to collect the necessary data and to understand organizational behaviors, as well as government policy (Berg 1995; Eisenhardt 1989; Yin 1984). A comprehensive discussion of research methods is contained in another document (Levin 1999a).

Analytical Frameworks

Two theoretical domains guide this research study: globalization theory and organization theory. Globalization theory is used as an analytical tool for categorizing those institutional behaviors that have contributed to or defined organizational change. Organization theory provides several analytical frameworks for examining the ways in which organizations change, specifically changes in formal structure, organizational culture, goals, programs, or missions in institutions (DiMaggio and Powell 1983; Levy and Merry 1986; Mintzberg 1983).

Investigative Strategy

The investigation began in the spring of 1996, and its strategy was to study multiple sites in depth through interviews and informal conversations with college personnel and students, through the review and analysis of institutional documents, and through observations. Seven community colleges—four Canadian and three American—comprised the multiple sites. Colleges were given fictitious names during the investigation and in subsequent reports, in accordance with institutional agreement to participate in the study. Approximately 430 individuals were interviewed at the seven sites (60 people at each site). These individuals included: the president or chief executive officer, the president's assistant or secretary, the chief business officer, the chief academic officer, the chief student services officer, the chief human resources/personnel officer, samples of mid-level administrators (deans, directors), samples of full-time faculty—including departmental chairs—and part-time faculty, the faculty union president and/or vice-president, support staff union president, and one to two board members (if available, the board chair was interviewed). Additionally, if a college was part of a multicollege district, the district chancellor was interviewed as well as other district office executives. A group of researchers undertook site visits—from three to five investigators at one site at the same time. The use of a group approach not only assisted in data collection but also in analysis during collection. The multiple viewpoints, the discussion of individual on-site observations, and the confirming and disconfirming of preliminary hunches all contributed to a richer and more accurate understanding of the site (Eisenhardt 1989). Site visits occurred twice, with a one-year to eighteen-month separation between the first and second visit.

The study also included the collection and analysis of documents. Documents included Canadian provincial and U.S. state legislation and policy and higher education, labor, and finance reports. Also included were national (Canada and U.S.) federal policies and policy reports. Other government agency documents (local or regional) on the economy, labor markets, or population demographics were collected and reviewed.

Furthermore, institutional documents covering the period of 1989–1998 were collected and analyzed. These documents included collective bargaining agreements, college catalogues, college policies, strategic and financial plans, and communication documents such as newspapers as well as letters and memos to employees.

In addition to existing public documents, each college was surveyed and asked to provide quantitative information on budgets, students, programs, and graduate employment placements. This survey was intended to provide a comparative guide for the sites as well as a quantitative measure against which qualitative assessments could be compared within sites.

Data Analysis

In order to determine the ways and the extent to which globalizing forces affected and influenced community colleges, interview data, document data, observational data, institutional questionnaire data, and government document data were analyzed using an analytical framework drawn from globalization literature and then pattern coded (Miles and Huberman 1984). Furthermore, national and provincial and state policy document data, which included government document data, underwent a second iteration of coding and thus another analysis process. First, documents were categorized according to their jurisdiction: federal Canada; federal U.S.; Canadian province, U.S. state. Second, documents were categorized according to their source, and these categories included government; government affiliate; non-government body; non-government organization; institution; and private. Finally, documents were categorized by type, including legislation; formal policy; policy discussion; policy background; policy draft; review of legislation; review of policy; research; or report.

After pattern coding, content analysis of the extracted data included counting of coded data by category and the identification and explanation of specific themes. Counting ensured that there was a substantial quantity of data for the established patterns. Thematic analysis led to a clearer understanding of the meaning of the patterns.

Interview and journal data were coded thematically, relying upon patterns identified as those connected to college mission and college structure changes, such as mission alteration that favors higher level programming in instruction and structural changes to institutional decision-making. These themes and patterns were then used to explain alterations to institutional mission and structures. The concepts of mission and structures were drawn from higher education literature, specifically community college literature.

The Policy Jurisdictions

In order to understand the explicit intentions of government policy for community colleges and to determine if these were consistent with globalization, I reviewed and analyzed policy documents of the 1990s from seven jurisdictions. These included federal Canada, Alberta, British Columbia, federal U.S., California, Hawaii, and Washington. Documents ranged from government legislation to government reports and strategic plans. I identified themes and coded documents by using the categories of globalizing behaviors noted earlier. These categories are displayed in Table 1. Findings from each jurisdiction are displayed in Table 2.

Table 2. Themes of globalizing behaviors in policy documents

Jurisdiction	Dominant Themes	Explicit Intent
Federal Canada	I, MRK, P/E, ET	Reduce unemployment nationally and train for marketplace
Alberta	MRK, P/E, ET	Offer less expensive education, provide greater responsiveness to business and industry, and achieve greater productivity of institutions, with less reliance upon public funds
British Columbia	MRK, P/E, ET	Provide workforce training to meet the needs of business and industry and assist province in global economic competitiveness
Federal U.S.	MRK, P/E	Meet national economic needs for global competitiveness through workforce training
California	MRK, R, P/E	Achieve economic competitiveness for business and industry through workforce training and increased institutional productivity to assist state economy
Hawaii	MRK, R, P/E	Assist economic performance of state by increasing productivity and efficiency and train a globally competitive workforce
Washington	I, MRK, P/E	Improve economic condition of the state within a globally competitive environment by training and re-training the workforce

In this analysis of government documents, which included Canadian federal and provincial documents and U.S. federal and state documents, government policies clearly endeavored to direct community colleges toward economic goals, emphasizing workforce training and state economic competitiveness as outcomes, compelling colleges to improve efficiencies and to become accountable to government and responsive to business and industry. Each of the separate jurisdictions, federal or state or province, tell the same story.

Government Policy for Community Colleges

There were remarkably similar emphases across jurisdictions, from province to province, from state to state, and from one country to another. The global economy occupied center-stage in government initiatives and directions for community colleges.

In the United States, the "Carl D. Perkins Vocational and Applied Technology Education Act, as amended through July 1995" emphasized global competition and the acquisition of skills.

> It is the purpose of this Act to make the United States more competitive in the world economy by developing more fully the academic and occupational skills of all segments of the population. This purpose will principally be achieved by concentrating resources in improving educational programs leading to academic and occupational skill competencies needed to work in a technologically advanced society. (Section 2)

Education and training are clearly viewed as instrumental in this Act. Other federal policies and state policies on higher education reflected this view as well. Higher education institutions, specifically community colleges, were directed and coerced to serve the needs of capital through supplying business and industry with a trained workforce. At the same time, these institutions were asked and pushed to increase efficiency, that is reduce per unit costs. Restrictions upon, even reductions of, government's public spending were strategies to cope with both declining revenues and increasing demands for government services. This was particularly evident in the policy documents and governmental behaviors in the states of Washington and California. These policy directives suggest that public education is intended to serve private interests in at least two ways: first by supplying labor for the private sector and second in containing private taxation.

However, in some cases, most specifically in U.S. federal policy, and in Washington, Hawaii, and British Columbia policy, there were signs that social not economic issues were significant to the state. Here, social programs had a noticeable place in policy. For example, within policies on workforce training, the U.S. federal government highlighted the importance of serving underrepresented groups—for example, American Indians and Native Hawaiians. In the "Carl D. Perkins Vocational and Applied Technology Act," Part H, Section 381 permits the federal government "to provide grants for the operation and improvement of tribally controlled, postsecondary vocational institutions to ensure continued and expanded educational opportunities for Indian students . . . ." In Washington State, workforce training policy featured dislocated workers, minorities, and women. In British Columbia, the social and economic needs of special groups—women, aboriginal peoples, and the disabled—were addressed along with the needs of the provincial economy. As noted as early as 1992 in British Columbia's *Human Resource Development Project Report*, the adult learning system in that province was exhorted and pushed to achieve greater equity.

> We must take the steps necessary, at all levels and in all aspects of our learning system, to ensure that the needs of aboriginal British Columbians, women, people with disabilities, members of ethnocultural communities and visible minorities, the unemployed and other emerging groups are addressed . . . (Report of the Steering Committee 1992, p. 31)

A similar sentiment is reiterated in *Charting a New Course* (Government of British Columbia 1996), the policy document of the government department responsible for postsecondary education in British Columbia.

> Attitudinal and physical barriers will be reduced and learning opportunities provided for equity groups, non-traditional learners and other learners who may face systemic barriers . . . (p. 41)

"Aboriginal people," "females," "marginalized students," "learners with disabilities," "students with children," "non-English speaking families," "low literate adults," "unemployed and workers who need retraining," and "Income Assistance recipients" (pp. 42–43) are those who constitute those groups for whom access to education is problematic. The presence of social issues in these jurisdictions may suggest that the state had influence and power distinct from the power of capital or of a dominant economic class. These directives served to promote organizational behaviors consistent with *multiculturalism*. Surprisingly, in the U.S. jurisdictions there was no specific reference in policy documents to multiculturalism *per se* even though the three colleges in these jurisdictions featured multiculturalism in curriculum, extracurricular activities, and in institutional value statements.

Other non-economic issues were not forgotten entirely in government policy. Independent of business and industry and capital, government promoted social issues, even though these were largely tied to economic matters such as employment and training for employment. Alberta was clearly the only jurisdiction where social issues were not topics of government policy related to higher education. British Columbia in contrast not only promoted issues of equity but also acted in its legislation to democratize institutional governance. This was achieved by altering government legislation in the mid–1990s to grant formal decision authority to employees of colleges and institutes. In the U.S., while there were fiscal pressures to close the doors of community colleges, access for all was maintained as a primary value. For all three U.S. states, expanding, even maintaining, access, according to government policy, required "doing more with less." In Canada, consistent with federal policy which expressed a devolution of responsibility for training to provinces, there was a pronounced emphasis upon provincial priorities in government policy related to higher education in general and community colleges in particular. In both Alberta and British Columbia, planning documents assumed that community colleges were part of a provincial system, serving the needs of provincial citizens and aiding the provincial economy, with access to education and training as a key goal.

Government policy in the 1990s clearly favored the interests of business, industry, and capital. The state's attention to issues of equity, access, and an informed citizenry—issues that could be held up as critical to the community college movement—was marginal. In Canada, the rather narrow perspective of community colleges as training sites is underscored in a recent report from the Council of Ministers of Education, Canada (1999).

> [Colleges and technical institutes] are rooted in their communities and are designed to serve as the primary vehicle for adult education and training. Normally, their principal mandate is to respond to the training needs of business, industry, and the public sector, as well as to the educational needs of vocationally oriented secondary school graduates. (p. 5)

In the United States, the "Workforce and Career Development Act of 1996" proposed to integrate adult education programs "into a streamlined, coherent, and accountable statewide system designed to . . . meet the needs of employers in the United States to be competitive" (p. 3). This is similar to an earlier act, "Job Training Partnership Act" (1992).

> It is the purpose of this Act to establish programs to prepare youth and adults facing serious barriers to employment . . . thereby improving the quality of the work force and enhancing the productivity and competitiveness of the Nation. (p. 1)

The state—province, state, and federal government in the U.S.—used the community college as a vehicle of government economic policy and as a model of production, directing these institutions to greater efficiencies and less reliance upon the public purse. Furthermore, government policy fashioned the community college as an economically globalized institution, adhering to global competitiveness and its attendant behaviors.

Government Effects upon Community Colleges

The role of government in changing community colleges was significant, and organizational change was influenced by the responses of government to a global economy. Hartmark and Hines (1986) identify five areas where government policy can influence higher education institutions. These pertain to the goals and purposes of higher education, values and norms, programs, management, and resources. Government policy and policy implementation affected goals and purposes through legislation; values and norms through major social policies, such as access and affirmative action; programs through planning documents, the budgetary process, and targeted funding; management through collective bargaining; and resources through fiscal allocation. In all cases, government was interventionary, endeavoring to influence community colleges directly in programs, management, and resources and indirectly in goals and purposes. To conform to government policy, community college norms and values were expected to alter. The path to globalization for government policy was a path of economic growth.

The behaviors and influences of governments were also dualistic in regards to the colleges. Governments persuaded and coerced colleges to increase their productivity, to respond to workplace and business needs, and at least to affect an accountability posture to the public. Colleges responded to workplace demands but also neglected aspects of their mission and thus their communities because their focus and their resources were directed to government priorities. Colleges endeavored to increase productivity but in so doing precipitated tensions in labor relations, where management asked for and expected, for example, faculty to teach greater numbers of students and to use technology to support their added responsibilities. In this sense, governments directed colleges to become more efficient and more oriented toward global competition. But, governments also shielded or detached colleges from global forces not only by translating these forces for colleges but also by mediating between global conditions and local conditions, for example in collective bargaining. Governments used colleges as instruments of policy and they also protected colleges from market forces by subsidizing their operations. These actions were significant contributors to the conditions of colleges as buffered from or buffeted by global forces.

The British Columbia provincial government was the principal agent for City Center College to deal with global forces, as well as with social, cultural, and political issues. The government and its agencies interpreted global forces for the college, for example declining revenues as a result of decreasing exports, such as lumber, to Asian countries. City Center College was the recipient of government initiatives that responded to global forces: policies on productivity and efficiency; proposals and incentives to engage in private sector partnerships; and no measurable increases in overall government grants to the college. At the same time that government constricted its fiscal support of City Center College, it increased its oversight and directing of the college. The government's interpretation of global forces was balanced with its ideology as a social democratic government. As one senior college administrator noted in an articulation that expressed the sentiments of others, "the government is schizoid, contradictory, combining politics and economics: they want productivity and efficiency but also want to protect union jobs; they also want more entrepreneurship." Government thus acted within the context of a global economy as a neo-liberal, capitalistic force trying to respond by legislating productivity and economic growth. But government also acted within the province with a socialist ideology promoting its embrace of multiculturalism, equity, and the underprivileged. On the one hand, the provincial government directed colleges to "freeze tuition" so that students could have access and that a lesser financial burden was placed upon students than the college deemed necessary for their productivity. On the other hand, government required colleges to seek alternate sources of revenue to public sector funds, captured from taxation. The president of City Center College noted that in "freezing tuition, the [provincial] government was micromanaging the college. [Such action] will result in employee and program cuts." The government supported the worker, for example assisted in raising the salaries of faculty unions, and yet the government asked for greater institutional productivity, which may indeed have meant the displacement of workers either by technology or because of financial exigency.

At Pacific Suburban Community College in Hawaii, the state was accused of "micro-managing the university and college system," according to a college administrator, and college observers noted that the college was viewed "as another department of state government." The intrusive role and influence of government in higher education began with the governor's office: the governor not only appointed board members but also became involved in labor relations through collective bargaining. The state legislature influenced the college through policy, through funding, and through championing of specific programs: "downsizing is politically popular," noted one college senior official showing the impact of political behaviors upon college funding reductions from the state.

City South Community College in Washington was treated as a branch plant, similar to how large corporations behave toward foreign production sites. The state established funding policies and used targeted funding for an agenda not favorable to colleges or students, set tuition fees, used its agency to demand specific forms of accountability, and controlled collective bargaining, in part, by its state salary allocations. "The state has a strong role through its funding," noted a district office executive. The use of performance indicators by the state means that "we will lose funding if we don't reach expected levels of course completion," noted a faculty member. But, enrollments, even without the imposition of performance indicators, were down in the 1990s and state funding allocations decreased. The state passed on its loss of revenues during the late 1980s and early 1990s to its community colleges. As a consequence, there were retrenchment actions, including the elimination of faculty and staff positions.

> There is a smaller workforce on campus. Faculty have to sit on too many committees. There are not enough full-time faculty. Everybody is overworked. It has been difficult to keep the energy and enthusiasm up around campus. (Student services administrator, City South Community College)

The state's Welfare-to-Work program was, from the perspective of college faculty and administrators, a regressive action that moved students out of the classroom and onto the streets looking for work, even below poverty level wage work.

Enrollments are affected by changes in Welfare-to-Work legislation . . . Enrollment drop [is a consequence] of welfare reform: hurts us badly. (Administrator, City South Community College)

We are funded at a lesser rate for workforce training. (Faculty, City South Community College)

Students are segregated: state funded and welfare funded, with short term programs [for welfare students]. (Faculty, English as a second language training, City South Community College)

This Welfare-to-Work policy was viewed as a contributor to the loss of those programs that could help students attain careers and occupations rather than temporary or unstable jobs in a global economy. The program encouraged short-term training and thus detracted from the more educational and long-term employment orientation of a two-year Associate degree programs. At City South, in 1998, between 500–600 full time equivalency students were categorized as Welfare-to-Work, close to 20% of the college's total student body.

Also at City South Community College, state influence was largely fiscal, directing programs through enrollment based funding and operations through the use of performance indicators. Increased government oversight and accompanying decreases in state appropriations placed other stresses upon the institution as its enrollments in traditional vocational programs declined and enrollments in academic and other occupational programs did not rise enough to offset declines. Thus, emphasis upon increasing productivity, on competition with other institutions, and on bureaucratic procedures to conform to state demands (e.g., performance indicators) along with decreasing revenues pushed the college to the category of marginality in the "winners and losers" dichotomy of the global economy.

In Washington State, educational policies that might benefit students, such as university transfer articulation policies that facilitate student mobility or support for excellence of student performance, were either non-existent or below the level of institutional consciousness. Neither organizational members nor institutional documents referred to state policy that had educational salience.

At East Shoreline College in British Columbia, although there was less government funding relative to institutional expenditures over a ten year period, there was evidence to suggest increased government influence and control over college behaviors and actions. Government funding behaviors had considerable influence over college actions and in the development of college structures and processes. The president of East Shoreline College noted that government behaviors were responsible for the college's fiscal problems. "The government has the power and they want to keep it." A recent freeze by the provincial government of tuition raises was viewed as part of power wielding. The college's director of finances suggested that government funding of the college is "tied to political whims." A department chair concurred.

The college is an extension of government as a public institution—structural changes are brought about by fiat . . . The government is involved in the management of the institution.

Others echoed these perceptions. "The government is micro-managing the college," noted a faculty member who was vice-chair of a college governing body.

Government behaviors were identified as productivity incentives and targeted funding for specific programs, government intervention in the collective bargaining relationship between faculty and the college, most evident in the establishment of a provincial-wide bargaining structure, and government legislative action. This legislative action was evident in the change of governing board composition and in the establishment of a formal, senate-type body to share governance with the governing board and administration. Moreover, government permissive legislation for baccalaureate degree programs at East Shoreline affected not only growth but also academic culture and institutional purpose.

There is a schism between university and vocational programs. (Adult basic education department head)

Faculty now want deans elected from faculty . . . We now have a felt need to become credible, to offer credible degree programs. We pursue status such as title and rank. (Faculty union president)

We are trying to keep what has been good, but we cannot help change . . . Nurses now have to have baccalaureate degrees . . . We are in a phase of identity change. (Nursing faculty)

Everything that goes on around here is about degrees. (Science department chair)

In California, the role of the state was evident at Suburban Valley Community College in at least two areas: college finances and accountability. The California system of education funding was based upon limits to property tax assessments (Schrag 1998). This led to a shortage of funds to support the demands of higher education. Furthermore, the state targeted funding to support specific areas of its interests, but faculty salaries were not among those interests, to the consternation of faculty. College enrollments either grew or remained stable and costs rose, but government funding did not keep pace with increased costs.

Also at Suburban Valley, the state intervened in college management and operations through its demands for greater productivity and its requirements for increasing accountability. Mandates in the 1990s included a "pay for performance" administrative plan, enrollment fees, performance indicators, and various laws that constrained both the offering of distance education and student registration. As a major action, the college endeavored to increase enrollments because state funding was enrollment driven.

Overall, community college responses to policy and to government actions differed not only along institutional lines, but also along national lines. A marked difference between Canadian institutions and U.S. institutions was particularly evident in institutional association with government ideology. In Canada, the institutions in Alberta and British Columbia exhibited close ties to provincial government departments and the ideology of provincial governments. Funding behaviors of government influenced institutional behaviors and government policy was evident in institutional behaviors. In Alberta, government policy to shift the financial burden of government to taxpayers (Smith 1992) and reduce public sector funding (Andrew et al. 1997) had a dramatic effect upon the actions of North Mountain College. The college made a deliberate shift away from reliance upon government funds, altered its programming to reduce dependency and to increase its opportunities to secure private sector revenues. Additionally, college tuition fees rose so that students paid a greater percentage of the costs. Government behaviors actually led to a change in thinking on the part of many organizational members, especially managers, including consideration of privatization of the institution at the extreme.

Particularly noteworthy were governance alterations in the province of British Columbia in the 1990s and the evidence from City Center College, Rural Valley College, and East Shoreline College where organizational members repeatedly acknowledged significant changes to decision processes and structures. Government legislation in the mid-1990s formally established a role for college faculty, support staff, and students in decision-making in British Columbia colleges (Government of British Columbia 1994). The legislative alteration clearly moved these groups from an advisory-only role to a decision-making role. The legislation provided for an educational body with powers that not only paralleled the administrative bureaucracy but also in some cases superseded administrative authority.

> Governance has changed from night to day: the board now discusses and debates. (City Center College faculty union president)

> The Educational Council (Senate) increasingly seems as a co-governance structure. (Faculty member and Chair of Educational Council, City Center College)

While governance changes were not rationalized responses to global forces, they can be associated with globalizing behaviors promoted by government including worker productivity and labor-management stability, both of which promoted investment, especially international investment.

In the U.S., college members did not exhibit the same association with government ideology as in Canada. Although U.S. colleges were affected by financial allocations, and not as much by government policy, other external organizations, primarily businesses and industries and universities, had more influence upon college behaviors in the U.S. than in Canada. The board chair at Suburban Valley Community College noted that the business approach to education had become the norm.

> The college is becoming more corporate and business-like. Corporate America is moving in. We need to be efficient. We are being charged to run like a business.

Consistent with business-like behaviors, the U.S. community colleges reported challenges from private and public educational institutions as well as from corporations' own educational branches.

> We have a wide array of competitors like Motorola University and the University of Phoenix. Walt Disney and AT&T are all eager to enter the education market. All competitors are well-funded. (District Chancellor, Suburban Valley Community College)
>
> Our competitors are Harley Davidson U., Motorola U., and a state university. (Dean, Suburban Valley Community College)
>
> The University of Phoenix is our rival, as is City University and Governor's University. (President, City South Community College)

Because Pacific Suburban Community College was a legal component of the state university—that university was the only public higher education institution in the state—university behaviors and policies had considerable impact on college attitudes and behaviors.

> There is frustration aimed at the university structure which is large and bureaucratic. (Department chair)
>
> The bureaucratic procedures of the university stifle us—it is a slow and deep bureaucracy. (Association Dean)
>
> We have an unresolved transfer credit problem with the university. (Department chair, Health sciences)
>
> We supply the most transfer students to the university. The [main campus] of the university has a poor reputation—not friendly, not welcoming. (Counselor)
>
> Because university students do not complete [their general education requirements] in five years . . . this impacts Pacific Suburban Community College because the college then has to offer general education courses that line up with the university. (Faculty senate chair)

These responses suggest an important difference between the two countries and the role of government policy in institutional behaviors. In Canada, community colleges are extensions of the state, and provincial institutions conform in large part to the ideology of the government in power. In the U.S., community colleges are vehicles or recipients of government policy, but affected as well by business and industry and other higher education institutions, such as state universities.

Notwithstanding these national differences, in both Canada and the U.S., government—especially state and provincial—served as what Wheeler calls efficient managers or facilitators for "a world governed by global markets" (Wheeler 1999, p. 11). Cultural and knowledge-related issues, those matters associated with a liberal education, were superfluous in government policy. College purposes and mission, values and norms, programs, management, and resources were affected by an interventionary state. In large part, the state, directly or indirectly, reproduced globalization (with special emphasis upon economic globalization), and was a responsible force for the creation of a globalized institution.

Re-fashioning Institutional Mission

Community colleges, at least since the 1970s and perhaps in their entire history, have not been the institutions that McGrath and Spear (1991) suggest they were: academically-oriented and disciplined based. Indeed, there has always been ambiguity over the purposes and identity of the community college, and its predecessor, the junior college (Cohen and Brawer 1982; Dougherty 1994; Frye 1992). The impetus for the rise of the junior college at the beginning of the twentieth century in the U.S. as a consequence of social pressures, such as immigration and changing family structures, or as the extension of an American ideal of personal achievement through social mobility is somewhat in dispute (Brint and Karabel 1989; Dougherty 1994; Diener 1986; Frye 1992). Arthur Cohen, at the end of the 1960s, captures the comprehensive and convoluted identity for the community and junior college in an articulation that looks both forward and backward:

> The community junior college . . . is viewed variously as democracy's college, as an inexpensive, close-to-home alternative to the lower division of a prestigious university; as a place to await marriage, a job, or the draft; and as a high school with ashtrays. For many of its enrollees, it is a stepping stone to the higher learning; for most, it is the last formal, graded, public education in which they will

be involved. The community college is—or attempts to be—all things to all people, trying valiantly to serve simultaneously as a custodian, trainer, stimulant, behavior-shaper, counselor, adviser, and caretaker to both young and old (Cohen 1969, p. xvi).

In Canada, Dennison and Gallagher acknowledge that jurisdiction's reliance upon an earlier U.S. tradition in higher education, suggesting a similar pattern of institutional development. Yet, they emphasize that community colleges in Canada were decidedly unlike other postsecondary institutions, and primarily established by provincial governments to serve the public and the needs of the public in all its ramifications, from recreational to advanced credential requirements (Dennison and Gallagher 1986).

The multiple purposes of community colleges in both countries run parallel to heterogeneity of their students who have both diverse abilities and diverse expectations (Dennison and Gallagher 1986; Grubb 1999). The re-fashioning of mission at the community college, consistent with the responsive character of these institutions in addressing local community needs and the alteration in demographic and economic conditions (Cohen and Brawer 1996; Dennison and Gallagher 1986; Grubb 1999), is both a consequence of government pressures and institutional responses to these pressures as well as to global forces. These global forces include, most prominently, a global economy, but also global cultural flows (Appadurai 1990) and global forms of communication, epitomized by the concept of a "networked society" (Castells 1996). Economic ends dominated the mission of community colleges in the 1990s, re-fashioning traditional missions of access and responsiveness to community educational and training needs so that these became means not ends. Instead, improving economic conditions of regions and nations became priorities through such activities as workforce training, both for the state to compete in production globally and to attract investors with a competitive economic environment. Furthermore, by "economizing," by operating institutions more efficiently, colleges imitated the behaviors of businesses or corporations and became participants in the global economy. This was precisely the intent of government policy for community colleges in the two nations.

Government policy and government behaviors in the 1990s shaped community colleges as instruments and extensions of the state. Serving the community—a foundational principle of community colleges in both countries—can be viewed as a euphemism for supporting the interests of a neo-liberal state with its devotion to private sector business and industry. This state favors markets over community and defines its citizens as economic entities rather than as social citizens (Marginson 1997; Ralston Saul 1995). In this sense a new vocationalism has entered the community college. Program areas, such as Adult basic education, may remain from earlier decades but they have new purposes, such as supplying labor for the private sector and new curricular emphases such as workplace skills in the global economy along with an employer-friendly work ethic. At the same time, higher level credentials, notably the baccalaureate degree, are pursued both to attract and retain students and thus capture government funding. This behavior, too, conforms to government policy expectations for a globally competitive workforce provided by the public sector for the private.

Acknowledgements

This research was supported by funding from the Social Sciences and Humanities and Research Council of Canada. The article draws upon *Globalizing the Community Colleges: Strategies for Change in the Twenty-first Century* (Palgrave, 2001).

References

Alfred, R. and Carter, P. (1996). 'Inside track to the future', *Community College Journal* 66(4), 10–19.

Andrew, M., Holdaway, E. and Mowat, G. (1997). 'Postsecondary education in Alberta since 1945', in Jones, G. (ed.), *Higher Education in Canada*. New York: Garland Publishing, pp. 59–92.

Appadurai, A. (1990). 'Disjunctures and difference in the global cultural economy', in Featherstone, M. (ed.), *Global Culture: Nationalism, Globalization and Modernity*. Newbury Park: Sage Publications, pp. 295–310.

Aronowitz, S. and DiFazio, W. (1994). *The Jobless Future: Sci-tech and the Dogma of Work*. Minneapolis: University of Minnesota Press.

Berg, B. (1995). *Qualitative Research Methods for the Social Sciences*. Boston: Allyn and Bacon.

Bridges, W. (1994). *Job Shift*. Reading, MA: Addison Wesley.

Brint, S. and Karabel, J. (1989). *The Diverted Dream: Community Colleges and the Promise of Educational Opportunity in America, 1900–1985*. New York: Oxford University Press.

'Carl D. Perkins Vocational and Applied Technology Education Act, as amended through July 1995' (1995). Washington, DC: Government Printing Office.

Carnoy, M. (1984). *The State and Political Thought*. Princeton, NJ: Princeton University Press.

Carnoy, M., Castells, M., Cohen, S. and Cardoso, F. (1993). *The New Global Economy in the Information Age*. University Park: The Pennsylvania State University.

Castells, M. (1993). 'The informational economy and the new international division of labor', in Carnoy, M., Castells, M., Cohen, S., and Cardosa, F. (eds.), *The New Global Economy in the Information Age*. University Park: The Pennsylvania State University, pp. 15–43.

Castells, M. (1996). *The Rise of the Network Society*. Cambridge, MA: Blackwell Publishers.

Clowes, D. and Levin, B. (1989). 'Community, technical and junior colleges: Are they leaving higher education?', *The Journal of Higher Education* 60(3), 349–355.

Cohen, A. (1969). *Dateline '79: Heretical Concepts for the Community College*. Beverly Hills, CA: Glencoe Press.

Cohen, A. and Brawer, F. (1982). *The American Community College*. San Francisco: Jossey-Bass.

Cohen, A. and Brawer, F. (1996). *The American Community College*. San Francisco: Jossey-Bass.

Coleman, W. and Skogstad, G. (1990). 'Policy communities and policy networks: A structural approach', in Coleman, W. and Skogstad, G. (eds.), *Policy Communities and Public Policy in Canada*. Mississauga, Ontario: Copp Clark Pitman Limited.

Council of Ministers of Education, Canada. (1999). A report on public expectations of postsecondary education in Canada. Toronto, Ontario: Council of Ministers of Education, Canada, February.

Cross, P. (1985). 'Determining missions and priorities for the fifth generation', in Deegan, W., Tillery, D. & Associates (eds.), *Renewing the American Community College*. San Francisco: Jossey-Bass Publishers, pp. 34–50.

Currie, J. (1998). 'Introduction', in J. Currie and J. Newson (eds.), *Universities and Globalization*. Thousand Oaks: Sage Publications, pp. 1–13.

Currie, J. and Newson, J. (eds.) (1998). *Universities and Globalization*. Thousand Oaks, CA: Sage Publications.

Deegan, W. and Tillery, D. (1985). 'The process of renewal: An agenda for action', in Deegan, W., Tillery, D. & Associates (eds.), *Renewing the American Community College*. San Francisco: Jossey-Bass Publishers, pp. 303–324.

Dennison, J. and Gallagher, P. (1986). *Canada's Community Colleges*. Vancouver: University of British Columbia Press.

Dennison, J. and Levin, J. (1989). Canada's Community College in the Nineteen Eighties. Willowdale, Ontario: Association of Canadian Community Colleges.

Diener, T. (1986). *Growth of an American Invention: A Documentary History of the Junior and Community College Mission*. New York: Greenwood Press.

DiMaggio, P. and Powell, W. (1983). 'The iron cage revisited: Institutional isomorphism and collective rationality in organizational fields', *American Sociological Review* 48, 147–160.

Dougherty, K. (1994). *The Contradictory College*. Albany: State University of New York.

Dudley, J. (1998). 'Globalization and education policy in Australia', in J. Currie and J. Newson (eds.), *Universities and globalization*. Thousand Oaks, CA: Sage Publications, pp. 21–43.

Eisenhardt, K. (1989). 'Building theories from case study research', *Academy of Management Review* 14(4), 532–550.

Frye, J. (1992). *The Vision of the Public Junior College, 1900–1940*. New York: Greenwood Press.

Goedegebuure, L., Kaiser, F., Maassen, P. and De Weert, E. (1993). 'Higher education policy in international perspective: An overview', in Goedegebuure, L., Kaiser, F., Maassen, P., Meek, L., Van Vught, F., and De Weert, E. (eds.). *Higher Education Policy*. New York: Pergamon Press, pp. 1–12.

Government of British Columbia (1996). *Charting a New Course*. Victoria, British Columbia: Ministry of Advanced Education, Training and Technology.

Government of British Columbia (1994). *College and Institute Amendment Act.* Victoria, BC: Queen's Printer.

Grubb, W. (1999). *Honored But Invisible.* New York: Routledge.

Hartmark, L. and Hines, E. (1986). 'Politics and policy in higher education: Reflection on the status of the field', in Gove, S. and Stauffer, T. (eds.), *Policy Controversies in Higher Education.* New York: Greenwood Press, pp. 3–26.

Held, D., McGrew, A., Goldblatt, D. and Perraton, J. (1999). *Global Transformations.* Stanford, CA: Stanford University Press.

'Job Training Partnership Act as Amended: Public Law 102–367' (1992). Employment and Training Administration, U.S. Department of Labor.

Kenway, J. (1998). *Fast Capitalism, Fast Feminism and Some Fast Food for Thought.* Paper presented at the annual meeting of the American Educational Research Association, April, San Diego.

Kempner, K. (1991). *The Community College as a Marginalized Institution.* Paper presented at annual meeting of Association for the Study of Higher Education, November, Boston.

Leslie, L. and Slaughter, S. (1997). 'The development and current status of market mechanisms in United States postsecondary education', *Higher Education Policy* 10, 238–252.

Levin, J. (1999a). *Mission and Structure: The Community College in a Global Context.* Report for the Social Sciences and Humanities Council of Canada. Tucson, Arizona: Center for the Study of Higher Education.

Levin, J. (1999b). 'Missions and structures: Bringing clarity to perceptions about globalization and higher education in Canada', *Higher Education* 37(4), 377–399.

Levy, A. and Merry, U. (1986). *Organizational Transformation: Approaches, Strategies, and Theories.* New York: Praeger.

Lipsey, R. (1991). 'The case for trilateralism', in Globerman, S. (ed.), *Continental Accord: North American Economic Integration.* Vancouver: The Fraser Institute, pp. 89–123.

McGrath, D. and Spear, M. (1991). *The Academic Crisis of the Community College.* Albany, NY: State University of New York Press.

Marginson, S. (1997). *Educating Australia: Government, Economy and Citizen Since 1960.* Melbourne: Cambridge University Press.

Miles, M. and Huberman, M. (1984). *Qualitative Data Analysis: A Sourcebook of New Methods.* Beverly Hills, CA: Sage Publications.

Mintzberg, H. (1983). *Power In and Around Organizations.* Englewood Cliffs, NJ: Prentice Hall, Inc.

National Center for Educational Statistics (1994). *Digest of Education Statistics.* Washington, DC: U.S. G.P.O.

Newson, J. (1994). *NAFTA and Higher Education in Canada.* Unpublished paper, York University, Toronto, Ontario.

Phillipe, K. (ed.) (1995). *National Profile of Community Colleges: Trends and Statistics.* Washington, DC: American Association of Community Colleges.

Ralston Saul, J. (1995). *The Unconscious Civilization.* Concord, Ontario: House of Anansi Press.

Report of the Steering Committee (1992). *Human Resource Development Project Report.* Victoria, BC: Government of British Columbia.

Richardson, R. and Bender, L. (1987). *Fostering Minority Access and Achievement in Higher Education.* San Francisco: Jossey-Bass Publishers.

Rifkin, J. (1995). *The End of Work.* New York: G.P. Putnam's Sons.

Ritzer, G. (1998). *The McDonaldization Thesis: Explorations and Extensions.* Thousand Oaks, CA: Sage Publications.

Robertson, R. (1992). *Globalization: Social Theory and Global Culture.* London: Sage Publications.

Roe, M. (1989). *Education and U.S. Competitiveness: The Community College Role.* Austin, Texas: IC2 Institute, University of Texas at Austin.

Roueche, J. and Baker III, G. (1987). *Access and Excellence.* Washington, DC: The Community College Press.

Schlager E. and Blomquist, W. (1996). 'A comparison of three emerging theories of the policy process', *Political Research Quarterly* 49(3), 651–672.

Schrag, P. (1998). *Paradise Lost: California's Experience, America's Future.* New York: The New Press.

Schugurensky, D. and Higgins, K. (1996). 'From aid to trade: New trends in international education in Canada', in Raby, R. and Tarrow, N. (eds.), *Dimensions of the Community College: International, Intercultural, and Multicultural.* New York: Garland Publishing, pp. 53–78.

Skocpol, T. (1985). 'Bring the state back in: Strategies in current research', in Evans, P., Reuschemeyer, D. and Skocpol, T. (eds.), *Bring the State Back In*. New York: Cambridge University Press, pp. 3–37.

Slaughter, S. (1990). *The Higher Learning and High Technology*. Albany: State University of New York.

Slaughter, S. (1997). *Who Gets What and Why in Higher Education? Federal Policy and Supply-Side Institutional Resource Allocation*. Presidential address, Association for the Study of Higher Education annual meeting, Memphis, TN.

Slaughter, S. and Leslie, L. (1997). *Academic Capitalism, Politics, Policies, and the Entrepreneurial University*. Baltimore: The Johns Hopkins University Press.

Smith, P. (1992). 'A province just like any other', in M. Howlett, M. and Brownsley, K. (eds.), *The Provincial States*. Mississauga, Ontario: Copp Clark Pitman, pp. 242–264.

Statistics Canada (1991). *Profile of Higher Education in Canada*. Report 81–222, Department of the Secretary of State. Ottawa: Ministry of Supply and Services.

Tapscott, D. (1996). *The Digital Economy: Promise and Peril in the Age of Networked Intelligence*. New York: McGraw Hill.

Vallas, S. (1993). *Power in the Workplace: The Politics of Production at AT&T*. Albany: State University of New York.

Waters, M. (1995). *Globalization*. New York: Routledge.

Wheeler, W. (1999). *A New Modernity? Change in Science, Literature and Politics*. London: Lawrence and Wishart.

Weis, L. (1985). *Between Two Worlds: Black Students in an Urban Community College*. Boston: Routledge and Keegan Paul.

'Workforce and Career Development Act of 1996' (1996). Conference report. H.R. 104–707 Congress, 2nd Session.

Yin, R. (1984). *Case Study Research*. Newbury Park: Sage Publications.

CHAPTER 50

GLOBALIZATION AND COMMUNITY COLLEGE MODEL DEVELOPMENT

ROSALIND LATINER RABY

Globalization serves as the impetus for sociopolitical and economic change. As a dynamic force, globalization perpetuates a borderless world where practices and ideas are shared across space and time aided by technology, mobility, communication, socioeconomic relationships, and environmental interdependence. As an identified concept, globalization impacts institutional mission and curricula that internationalize the campus, and in so doing, supports intercampus and intercountry relationships as a "requisite seed for internal change that reflects how the institution responds to [globalization] pressures" (Levin, 2001, p. x). This chapter profiles how community college models are affected by, and perpetuate conditions that advance, globalization in terms of (a) a global–local dichotomy; (b) economic and humanitarian philosophical influences upon which models are based; and (c) positive and negative consequences that result from the globalization process.

The Global-Local Dichotomy of Globalization

Globalization embodies a global–local dichotomy that enacts a sameness through a "compression of the world" (Robertson, 1992, p. 8), while simultaneously preserving a local identity (McLaren, 1999). Throughout this book, examples illustrate a condition whereby globalization affects two trajectories: one in which community college models share common qualities that illustrate a universality of experience, and the other in which applications are inexplicitly tied to local communities which endows their uniqueness.

Homogenization Influences

Homogenization promotes a sense of universal sameness in which boundaries are permeable and are heightened by economic linkages, population shifts, informational flows, and interconnections of technology and popular culture. Resulting interdependency enhances a "global system of societies," a process that is sustained by emulation (Robertson, 1992, p. 8; Clayton, 2004). Permeability defines the community college models movement since most are either self-generated or purposefully marketed abroad by those who view the economic and humanitarian construct as desirable and adaptable.

Homogenizing influences are different for those who transmit the flow and for those who receive it. External flows support a borderless, transcultural and post-national world where external pressures force the local to respond. This is seen in the increase of cross-national accreditations (Alleyne, 1978) in which colleges confer status to others. Internal flows connect students and staff via communication and even adoption of popular culture and mass-produced products. Combined, homogenization provokes social change through the creation of hybrid identities. A north–south modality mostly governs the direction of these flows as "north" community colleges seek out others through student mobility, international curricula, and transfer of career skills pedagogy by international development projects. As a result, "north" ideas of community colleges are purposely transferred across borders.[1]

Not all the flows stem from the United States, although some claim that the US model is the most adaptable (Elsner, 2008). Canadian community colleges have 25 years of institutional partnerships in over 60 countries (ACCC, 2008). Models in Iran, Mexico, and Senegal were patterned on French technical institutes; King Mongkut's Institute of Technology's (Thailand) initial partnership was with German technical colleges; and the Royal Melbourne Institute of Technology (Australia) now offers associate degrees in institutions throughout Southeast Asia. In 1991, World Bank's vocational training policy in Asia was largely based on Japanese community college models (Lauglo, 2004), and Japan International Cooperation Agency currently with Mpumalanga Provincial Department of Education (South Africa) (World Congress, 2008).

A south–south modality is redefining globalization as influence flows from one developing country to another. Examples include Kein Giang College (Vietnam), which receives course work and certification from NIIT Technologies, an Indian IT training institute; Malaysian colleges which collaborate with Chinese colleges; and Caribbean Community Regulations (CARICOM), which is redefining local certification from one Caribbean nation to another via the Caribbean CAPE Degree. Distance education via the Internet, curricular development, and staff training all sustain south–south flows (De Siqueira, 2004).

Homogenization is at the core of cross-national community college collaboration. In 1975, 14 countries signed resolutions that regulate the field today (Eskow and Caffrey, 1974). In 1998, the International Association of Community and Further Education Colleges created a base to exchange ideas and resources, and in 1999, the World Federation of Colleges and Polytechnics refined this process with 30 members representing nine colleges. In 2008, both cosponsored the 4th World Congress to "provide opportunities for developing partnerships with colleges around the world." As a result, community colleges circumvent the world, which has allowed them to become "learning centers for the whole community . . . [that] weave together people and projects that reach beyond traditional educational boundaries" (Gordon, 1999, p. 1).

Localizing Influences

Despite proclamations of a flat world (Friedman, 2005) globalization is building boundaries by reinforcing local identities. Eskow (1989) refers to the local emphasis as a "global paradox," for when the polity and economy grow larger, the needs of the local become more manifest. This manifestation is intensified by a need for perpetuation of local stories and collective memories that define the individual (de Courtivron, 2008).

This paradox is seen in the constant struggle of mission and curricula to prepare students for local employment, but whose context is defined by a global economy. The question of what is the meaning of *community* in a global space remains important. As a geographic term, the local accentuates the singularity of experience as college programs link to specified spaces within its borders. Globally, *community* accentuates a universality of experience that stems from economic globalization. As similar policies, programs, and structures transverse across countries, community college models share common qualities as the global and local become "mutually constituted parts of contradictory social wholes" (McLaren, 1999, 10).

The localized application sustains the uniqueness of each community college as convergence of global connections is rooted locally. Despite decades of globalization, sameness has not replaced national identity or purpose (de Courtivron, 2008; Steiner-Khamsi, 2003). Indeed, community college models have a long history of asserting "globalization from below" which challenges hegemonic "globalization from above" (Kneller, 2005, p. 61). In 1975, Hawke's Bay Community College (New Zealand) refocused its mission from lifelong education to serve local Maori community needs (Kintzer, 1979). In the 1980s, Japanese junior college reforms distanced themselves from the US model upon which they were based. In 1996, Madras and Stella Maris Colleges (India) developed small business curricula in Tamil for semiliterate and illiterate rural women. In 1998, the International Consortium for Economic and Educational Development initiated programs in Mexico to support local needs. Finally, many missions continue to emphasize the local, such as College of North Atlantic Qatar "helping to serve the needs of the general community," Nong Bualumpu Community College (Thailand) "using local resources to provide opportunities for social mobility" and Scottish Further Education "providing education and training for local communities to make colleges accessible to local students."

Globalization supports unique conditions that support educational reform through decentralization, competency-based curriculum, occupational certification, and student-centered pedagogy (Raby and Tarrow, 1996). The impact of globalization accentuates localized connections that accentuate singularity of experience.

Developmental Philosophical Influences

Two philosophies influence the creation of community college models. The first is based on economic principles of neoliberalism which sees the global market as redefining technical and career sectors so that colleges are a supplier of human capital. The second philosophy employs humanitarian principles that view education as a key link in overcoming inequalities that stem from differential access to higher education.

Economic Rationale

The economic rationale claims that training, credentialization, and international development secure new workplace skills that correspond to overall social prosperity.

Training is at the core of market-oriented policies, and links relevant skills with lifelong learning to serve the economy and reduce unemployment[2] (Schugurensky and Higgins, 1996; Lin-Liu, 2001; Levin, 2005; and Carnoy and Luschei, 2008). Globalization is causing lower-level skills to be needed less, while competition for higher-level postsecondary education is increasing. Since few universities offer study in occupational and technical fields, community college models are filling this gap[3](Wolf, 2008). Mexican technological universities "offer education as a strategic means to develop human capital and contribute to increase competitiveness of a knowledge-based economy" (CGUT, 2008), and Mozambique's (ISPs) Polytechnic Institution Mission "fulfills their role as a Strategy for Economic Development" (Massinga et al., 2008). Missions tend to support an economic rationale that links education with employment that is increasingly affiliated with transcultural and transnational mobility. Credentialization demands minimum competencies for the local workforce (Lim, 2008). A basic characteristic of the community college is that it easily and quickly can modify work-based and trade credentials to respond to the changing demands of the global economic marketplace (Elsner, 2008). In Hungary, community college models "provide improved access to low-cost, relevant, work-related training for large numbers of people" (CCIDa, 2008). In India, community college models "aim at empowerment of the disadvantaged through appropriate skills development leading to gainful employment" (ICRDCE, 2008). Using education to provide credentials for workforce development is at the core of Association Liaison Office for University Cooperation in Development–Community Colleges for International Development (CCID) projects in 12 countries.[4] It must be noted that since many of these projects are relatively new, their impact has yet to be fully realized.

International development and training projects transfer the community college characteristics worldwide (Smith, 2007). Although the United States is not the only exporter, most projects stem from there (CCID, 2008a; Elsner, 2008). Early examples include the 1982 Paramaribo conference for Caribbean cooperative job skills acquisition and the 1990s; and the United States Agency for International Developments (USAID) and the American Association for Community Colleges' (AACC) "Building International Workforce Development Partnerships Grants" to support projects in Brazil, Ethiopia, India, Mexico, South Africa, Sri Lanka and Tanzania.[5] In 2006, 11 US community colleges formed the Global Corporate College to share best practices to service international clients and influence what and how community college models teach. On a systems level, the memorandum with the Bundesinstitut für Berufsbildung (Federal Institute for Vocational Training) "have workers trained by common standards [so that] jobs can be transferred to different countries and companies can relocate factories. It is an occupational area that knows no borders" (McKenney, 2004, p. 1). In 2005, AACC developed an explicit campaign to help transfer the US model abroad. Hence, whether the vision is local or global, there remains a common belief in the support of the link between community college models and economic improvement.

Humanitarian Influences

Humanitarian philosophy depicts community colleges as imparting democratic ideals as it models sociopolitical reform through equity of opportunity. Social mobility is enhanced as institutions offer opportunities for participation to the widest margins of society, and in so doing, challenge traditional higher education elitism (Kintzer, 1998). Despite evidence that "the process of globalization is often accompanied by efforts at de-democratization" (McLaren, 1999, p. 11), this philosophy continues to dominate the development and sustaining of community college models.

Community college models do, in many countries, allow a postsecondary option to those who previously have been denied access due to minority status or lowered income. While not consistent in all countries, low tuition, lack of entrance exams, and local location do provide access for nontraditional students, many of whom have "suffered social and political disorder"and who need to be "reintegrated back into society" (Smith, 2007). Indeed, many students do come from less-advantaged backgrounds (Lowe and Gayle, and 2007). Increasingly, community college models do offer, what the humanitarian philosophy proposes, life-transforming educational opportunities.

The humanitarian philosophy alleges that education delivers opportunities that lead to employment, which supports economic development and improves social conditions (Strydom and Lategan, 1998; Kintzer, 1998; Koltai, 1993, Jones, 2002). As an example, mission statements reinforce this philosophy: Norway Regional Colleges "fills undemocratic gaps between districts, generations and sexes" (Kintzer, 1979, p. 73); United Arab Emeritus Higher Colleges of Technology "builds leadership potential to make the fullest possible contribution to the development of the community for the good of all its people"; Riverdale Community College (Ireland) "gives each pupil opportunity to develop his/her aptitudes and talents fully"; Nova Scotia Community College (Canada) "builds economy and quality of life through education and innovation"; and Thai community colleges "provides locals with a chance for post-secondary education that they otherwise would be denied." In turn, education enhances social change.

Humanitarian assistance has been the cornerstone of many Canadian and US international development projects. Empowerment and literacy programs, health and technological assistance services circumvent the globe such as Middlesex Community College's (Massachusetts) development project in Cambodia and Georgia for conflict-resolution training (Cowan and Falcetta, 1996), and CCID (2008b) Sustainable Systems Programs in Romania and First Global Community College Nong Khai–Udon Thani in Thailand. In this context, international development is not for a profit, but rather as a "contribution to humanitarian efforts" (Smith, 2007). World educators choose to emulate because of "social mobility that has characterized America, and they accept the idea that society can be better, just as individuals can better their lot within it" (Cohen and Drawer, 2003, p. 36). On the donor side, aid supports national interests to "apply our ideals, our sense of decency and our humanitarian impulse to the repair of the world, [as] investment in development is indeed investment in prevention" (Koltai, 1993, p. 2), such as is seen in current US State Department grants whose primary design is to use education to create social stability. This philosophy maintains that human capacity is built through education, which in turn strengthens democracy and the socioeconomic future of world citizens that sustains the global community college movement. The link between the two philosophies, economic and humanitarian, cannot be underestimated. Increased economics stimulates and reinforces sociopolitical reform. Several chapters in this book, such as the ones on Uzbekistan, Mexico, and Belize, illustrate college beliefs that providing knowledge required by market and development of the skills for future employment will lead to the socioeconomic well-being of the population. The Ghanaian mission "provides support to industry and commerce in areas of human resource" to communities in which they are located (Nsiah-Gyabaah and Obour, 2008), while the Thai network of colleges "creates open-access to higher education in order to support an equalitarian and democratic social structure and promotes economic development in the outlying provinces through the development of a skilled and entrepreneurial workforce" (East-West, 2008). Finally, Caribbean community college models enhance local, regional, and international flows through collaborations on research, curriculum development, and technological expansion. Whether community college models are succeeding at their humanitarian efforts is not as significant as the fact that these institutions are repositioning themselves in this global space.

Consequences of the Globalizing Process

Globalization has negative repercussions that include (a) neocolonial influences, (b) vocational fallacy, (c) socioeconomic inequity, and (d) lowered status, as well as a positive impact that increases (a) accessibility, (b) adaptability, and (c) social equity.

Negative Consequences

Globalization has various imprints, one being that some education does not have the same market value or social prestige as others. The unidirectional flows from the "north" tend to perpetuate inequity which heightens "disadvantages to whom the community college model should serve" (Strydom and Lategan, 1998, p. 98).

Neocolonial Influences

Neocolonial influences prevail when the local does "not have the same market value, social prestige or general reception in the society as other degrees or diplomas" (Kintzer, 1979, p. 75; Humphrys, 1994; Cohen, 1995; Levin, 2005). Unlike traditional neocolonialism, community college models are not imposed upon other countries, but rather emerge as a result of exchange visits. A 1969 visit to US community colleges by Sri Lanka's Minister of Education led to shared projects that now span decades. A 1980 visit from Taiwan's Minister of Education resulted in a network of new colleges (Harper, 1978). A visit by President of Jilin Institute of Architecture and Civil Engineering (Changchun, China) to Humber College (Toronto) created a joint interior design program to help students improve English skills and learn western design techniques and software packages. Thai colleges seek "U.S. assistance so they can develop a strong community college system that will help them meet these needs" (East-West, 2001). Thousands of educators visit US and Canadian colleges and most result in bilateral agreements for supply services to develop mid-level management, paraprofessional, career curriculum, and English language programs.

A quintessential manifestation of globalization is the international contract program that utilizes defined curriculum and even course numbers to develop branch colleges abroad. The Observatory on Borderless Higher Education claims that in 2006, 51% of the defined 82 branch campuses were affiliated with US universities, 12% in Australia, and 5% each in Britain and Ireland, and that one third of branch campuses offer degrees in single subjects that intersect with community college models business and technology programs (Jasshik, 2007). Many of these programs have international certification for full adoption of entire programs and courses (syllabus and textbooks), such as Houston Community College District's contract with Saigon Institute of Technology, Ford Foundation US–China Education Foundation Community College Development Project, First Global Community College (Nong Khai-Udon Thani) in Thailand, Yong-In Technical College in Korea, and Japan MEXT college project. In the south-south modality, an increasing number of branch campuses from India and Pakistan are now operating in Dubai and North Africa (OBHE, 2008). However, due to political change, cultural confusion, and lack of funding, few sustained programs exist (Yamano ahd Hawkins, 1996).

While literature emphasizes global connections that build interdependency, critics see globalization as reinforcing dependent relationships that support "western imperialism, whether economic political, technological or broadly cultural" (Mosa, 1996, p. 1). Altbach (2003) questions who defines quality control and accreditation. For example, cultural hegemony, as shown in many chapters in this book, has the conflict of building global identities while trying to preserve and maintain the status quo. Governments adhering to poverty argument that devise low-cost alternatives will not work unless they accommodate children at work (night schools, flexibility in timings, seasonal variations, and parallel structures). Cultural definitions of community, academic standards, and faculty preparation make neo-colonial patterns puzzling at best. Cultural intolerance arises from strained relationships between indigenous staff, counterparts abroad, and indigenous financial backers, all of whom have their own, oftentimes conflicting agendas. It is still too early to discern whether or not community college models will promote social reconstruction or social fragmentation. The questions of who controls what is defined as knowledge, what gets taught and acted upon in a global culture, and if a global culture becomes one of repression or liberation, therefore, is of extreme importance.

Vocational Fallacy

Vocational fallacy insinuates that institutions with a weak general education foundation may not be an optimal means for solving manpower needs (Foster, 1965, 2002; Selvarathuam, 1998; Ishumi, 1998). These colleges are often cost-ineffective and offer irrelevant and inflexible curricula which reinforce student perception and actual attainment of jobs in occupations other than those for which they were trained (Lauglo, 2008). When combined with poor national planning, corruption, and an unstable economy, there is often a lack of jobs upon graduation. Community college models are easily victim to this fallacy (St. George, 2006), but as Cohen and Brawer (2003, p. 21) note, this should not be a surprise since the original intent of the US community college was to "divert unsuitable candidates into appropriate vocational training while making it possible for traditional universities to maintain selective admissions requirements." Today, privatization and corporatization can create a situation in which only a select cohort of students is served. Societal and economic reform is limited as degrees do not always lead to employment. When this occurs, the future of community colleges as a potential for human resources development is placed at risk and these institutions thus do not always evoke economic or social reform (Raby, 1996). Actualization of socioeconomic reform depends on the type of education exported (technical–vocational, personal development, professional, or academic), the type of student targeted, the relationship of the type of education to the college's mission, and what students actually do with this education (i.e., transfer to a university, work, or drop out).

Socioeconomic Inequity

Socioeconomic inequity occurs when community college models do not provide access or their education or their education does not translate to greater social mobility. Brint and Karabel (1989) claim that emphasis on a vocational mission relegates students to low- and middle-class occupations, which then limits opportunities for social advancement. Indeed, restricting students to "short" or "career" programs results in segmentation, which is intensified in models that have no avenues for transfer to four-year institutions. The consequences are what Clark (1960) refers to as "cooling-out" in which an illusion of openness veils a lack of opportunities. While more students attend US colleges, fewer transfer or graduate, which results in limited economic and social class mobility[6](Archer et al., 2003). In Egypt, Iran, Curacao, and Zimbabwe limiting community college access heightens competition. Hence, even colleges with low tuition, such as those in Chile, Malaysia, or the Russian Natural-Technical Colleges, access is still out of reach for the poorest students. While community college models do provide an array of educational opportunities, they do not necessarily increase access for disenfranchised and may merely perpetuate an already unequal higher educational system (Kintzer, 1979; El Mallah et al., 1996; Madden, 1998; McMurtrie, 2001). Hence, instead of fulfilling a democratizing function through education, these models result in greater stratification.

Lowered Status and Corresponding Change in Institutional Orientation

A prevailing community college characteristic is a low status that is compounded by chronic under-funding and faculty with low status. Since these institutions often service rural and urban poor, they share economic dependency characteristics which influence the development of vocational training and cause many to have a rate of return to investment (Lauglo, 2004). For example, employers in

Ghana discriminate against holders of Polytechnic qualifications because of their low second-rate status, and as a result 30% of graduates are unemployed (Nsiah-Gyabaah and Obour, 2008). Despite the verbiage that appreciates the local, when local and global conflict, due to this low status, the global predominates. Finally, lack of sufficient resources continues to plague colleges in Vietnam, Zimbabwe, and in many Caribbean countries. Although community college models are consistently overlooked by policymakers, worldwide, their share of the education student population merits greater attention (Lowe and Gayle, 2007).

To gain status and a place in national budgets, commonly, some community college models are transforming into University Colleges. While this process is not new, the magnitude in which these changes are occurring today is noteworthy. In the 1970s, nationalization of Nigerian universities converted Nigerian colleges of arts, science, and technology to State Universities. From 1968 to 1975 the Helwan Higher Institute of Technology in Egypt (based on the German *Fachochschule* model) became Helwan University. In 1989, the Unified National System of Higher Education converted Australian Technical Institutes into universities. In the late 1990s, community pressures in countries throughout Africa resulted in more closure due to declining low status. Several chapters in the book illustrate more current transformations. Some fear that these changes will now produce a "professional class in need of BA degrees . . . [as community colleges] no longer are simply a sub-baccalaureate institution, no longer a postsecondary institution that serves marginalized and undeserved groups as its primary client or customer" (Levin 2002, p. 19). Nonetheless, even the changing mission is itself inherently a community college characteristic in which reform itself is an institutional responsiveness to local demands.

In conclusion, negative influences from globalization create obstacles which prohibit community college models from effecting social or economic reform. Compounding these obstacles is the continued low ranking, dearth of academic studies, and disenfranchisement of the models themselves. Future issues of concern are those of overall access, women enrollment, participation of local authorities in funding, and status. Key in this process is defining the relevance of education itself and whether or not it equipped the poor to play any useful role in the local community.

Positive Consequences

Expansion beyond borders as a result of globalization, while limiting the original mission of the community college, exemplifies how institutions respond to the changing world around them (Valeau and Raby, 2007). Community college models continue to gain popularity, and students attend these institutions in increasing numbers. Support persists because these institutions are (a) less expensive and more accessible than universities; (b) adaptable to provide needed curriculum and pedagogy that meets the demands of emerging local population; and (c) able to contribute towards social equity.

Accessibility

The widespread growth of community college models connects institutions to local communities and meets national and global interest by laying a foundation for higher educational opportunities to nontraditional student groups that provides a context for social mobility. In some countries, when traditional universities are unwilling or unable to change to meet new global standards, the community college models fill that gap. In Senegal, the inability of the French model to sustain societal needs caused Regional University Centers to emulate the US and Canadian models, which was seen as a commitment to human resource investment. In other countries, it is the transferability element that is the most attractive feature as compared with terminal credentials that limit opportunities as seen in models in India and Singapore. By serving their communities, "the most crucial function of the community colleges then has been to provide students with training and retraining programmes which help them to achieve social mobility and contribute to the economic well-being of a country" (Ural, 1998, p. 119; Smith, 2007). Worldwide, countries are utilizing the community college models to provide a *window of opportunity* which has then changed the structure of postsecondary education.

Adaptability

The ability of community college models to respond to the local economy by adopting product-oriented curricula and flexible short-term programming for differentially skilled laborers and career education helps to maintain their viability. For some colleges, success lies in the adaptation of student-centered pedagogy, such as the Aga Khan Humanities Project in Tajikistan and Nong Bualumpu Community College in Thailand, both of which use local resources to create organic relationships between teachers and learners. Adaptability is increasingly important for as technology changes so do literacies that cross mathematic–scientific and writing competencies that support even the most rudimentary positions. Since the community college model is connected to the local, it not only can easily recognize this change, but respond accordingly (Dellow and Romano, 2006). Facilitating change efforts are projects funded by the Asia Development Bank, Canadian International Development Agency, Ford Foundation, United States Agency for International Development, World Bank, bilateral and unilateral banks, and private industry, all of which seek to "bring together local workforce training providers to develop services that bridge the gap between elementary/secondary school systems and the tertiary institutions and targets acute workforce and education needs" (ALO/USAID, 2004). Increasing globalization has led to a realization in developing countries that education is key and is, in force, adopting U.S. models of tertiary education (Guess, 2007).

Social Equity

Community college models continue to pride themselves as a significant form of "community education in the context of redressing inequalities" (Ural, 1998, p. 199). Access to postsecondary education for nontraditional students lays a foundation for social mobility change. Evidence shows that many community college models do serve the least affluent and least politically influential segments of the population. Even faculty who teach at these institutions are frequently not academics, but rather are professionals who work in fields to which their students aspire. At the core is a belief in change and prosperity, which Vaughan (1989, p. 7) relates to "the right to pursue the American Dream; we must never forget that the community college represents the only hope millions of Americans have to achieving that Dream." In this way, community college models throughout the world serve both the people and their communities by training and retraining, by appealing to unique student sectors, and allowing them to contribute to the economic well-being of the country and to achieve social mobility (Cohen, 1995; Ratcliff and Gibson-Berninger, 1998; Tonks, 1999; Vasquez, 2003; Evelyn, 2005).

There is also evidence that community college models can be effective in reducing cultural conflict in multicultural societies (Van der Linde, 1996; Mellander and Mellander, 1994; Lowe and Gayle, 2007). The ubiquitous ideal that community college models can utilize postsecondary education to counter socioeconomic inequities, while not proven in academia, is sufficient to encourage educators abroad to enter into agreements that facilitate transplanting community college models to their own countries (Strydom and Lategan, 1998; Gallacher, 2006). In so doing, community college models mirror Kneller's (2005, p. 61) call for multiple literacies which he defines as "an oppositional democratic, pedagogical, and cosmopolitan globalization, which supports individuals and groups using information and multimedia technologies to create a more multicultural, egalitarian, democratic and ecological globalization."

Conclusion

Proliferation of the community college model impacts educational systems globally, as it attracts those who demand to break out of traditional university patterns and promote nontraditional educational models. Illustrate, investment in community college models supports the conviction that they provide opportunities for the disenfranchised and assist with social and economic restructuring by empowering students with economic and social opportunities. The mass migration of rural to urban centers and the global transmigration patterns underscores this need to provide increasing access to higher education. Hence, the process of introducing a community college model into a society instigates socioeconomic change that is cultivated at both global and local levels. This change offers access, helps promote career–personal advancement opportunities, impacts local business and industry by reinforcing new curricular emphasis, and can provoke reduction of culture-conflict in multicultural societies resulting from the education of the underprivileged.

Implications for countries interested in creating or revising characteristics of this model are not clearly defined. It is critical to highlight both community college ideals and to understand their realities as they apply to a varying set of circumstances. Care must be taken as reverberations from globalization can force countries to abandon key elements of community college models, such as open access, or to be unable to sustain the educational ideals envisioned and expected by diverse sections of the society. While one country's model experience yields insights that might benefit other countries, the appropriate response may not be wholesale duplication but rather selective adaptation. As such, variations of the community college model may be a reaction to globalization as each country conforms to this ideal. Increasingly, therefore, the challenge facing the community college will be to create a climate that nurtures institutions that target civic engagement. What better way than to have institutions that in curriculum and the interactions among students, faculty, and staff model the best of community life? This model, in turn will prevail because its programs are often strongly workplace-oriented and supportive of upward mobility.

Notes

1. "North" community colleges are typically seen as colleges from Australia, Canada, Great Britain, and the United States (Kintzer, 1998; Raby, 2000; Romano, 2002; De Siqueira, 2004; Raby and Thomas, 2006).
2. From 1962 to 1980, the World Bank linked education with manpower forecasting, with the bulk of funding going to vocational and technical schools (which are a small part of education sector) (Heyneman, 2003).
3. Jobs requiring an "associate degree" are the fastest-growing job group with 49% of future US jobs (U.S. Department of Labor Monthly Labor Review), 80% of future Canadian jobs (AACC, 2008), and 50% of new British jobs (United Kingdom White Paper) (quoted in Wolf, 2008).
4. ALO/CCID projects were conducted in China, Egypt, El Salvador, Ethiopia, Guyana, India, Namibia, Nepal, Romania, South Africa, Suriname, and Tomsk.
5. Early CCID (2008b) bilateral educational agreements include memoranda of understanding (MOUs) with Republic of China, Taiwan (1976), Republic of Suriname (1979), Dominican Republic, Saudi Arabia, Thailand, Korea, Greece, Grenada, Guyana, Jamaica, Netherlands Antilles, Saint Vincent (1981); Technical University of Budapest and Czech Technical University in Prague (1986); National Kaoshiung Institute of Technology (Taiwan) (1987); began connections with Educational Foundation in India (USEFI) (1988); Kazan Technical Institute in USSR (1989); Vocational Research Institute of the Pedagogical Science Academy of the USSR (1989); Teachers' Training Institute, Bhopal, India (1992); Guyana Ministry of Education (1997); Universidad Don Bosco, El Salvador (1998); Stella Maris College, Madras, India (1998); Addis Ababa Commercial College, Ethiopia (1998); Polytechnic of Namibia Center for Entrepreneurial Development (1999): New University-Partnership College, South Africa (1999); Egypt Agricultural Technician Training Institute (2000): Nepal Pedagogical Institute (2002); Kien Giang Community College, Vietnam (2006); Puntland State University, Somalia (2007); Tomsk Polytechnic Institute Workforce Development Center (2007); Sustainable Systems Program, Romania (2007); Suriname Telecommunications Company (2007).

    Non-CCID community colleges also conduct international development programs. In 2007, 37% of California community colleges offered curricular development and/or staff training to institutions in other countries, such as Riverside Community College's collaboration with the University of Asmara (Eritrea) that shares curriculum and pedagogy on information technologies and distance education and the San Diego Community College District's "Borderlands Project" which helps to improve the employability of workforce in Mexico by developing curriculum and instructional materials for US certification training.
6. Due to significant tuition increases from California community colleges, it is estimated that 90,000 students were shut out of the system in Spring 2003 (Evelyn, 2003, p. A43.)

References

Abbey Community College, Wicklow. Accessed May 1, 2008. http://www.abbeycc.net/mission.htm

Alleyne, M.H. (February 1978). Educational Objectives in Latin American and the Caribbean and the Role of Community Colleges. Conference Paper: Postsecondary Education in the International Community Florida.

AACC/ALO/USAID. (2004). *Building International Workforce Development Partnerships Grants: 1999–2002.* Retrieved March 4 from the AACC/ALO/USAID database. http://www.aascu.org/alo/WD/

Altbach, P.G. (Summer 2003). American Accreditation of Foreign Universities. Colonialism in Action. *IHE* 32: 5–7.

American Association for Community College. (AACC). Accessed May 1, 2008: www.aacc.nche.edu/-7.

Archer, L., Hutchings. M., and Ross, A. (April 2003). Higher Education and Social Class: Issues of Exclusion and Inclusion. *Widening Participation and Lifelong Learning* 5(I).

Association Liaison Office for University Cooperation in Development. Accessed March 4, 2008. http://www.aascu.org/alo/lP/proposals.htm

Association of Canadian Community Colleges (ACCC). (2008). Key Priorities 2006-2007. Accessed May 1, 2008. www.accc.ca/english/about/strat_focus06-07.htm

Ayr Community College (Scotland) Home Page. Accessed May 1, 2008. http://www.ayrcoll.ac.uk/

Brint, S. and Karabel, J. (1989). *The Diverted Dream: Community Colleges and the Promise of Educational Opportunity in America.* 1900-1985. New York: Oxford University Press.

Caribbean Advance Proficiency Exam (CAPE). Accessed May 1 2008. http://www.cxc.org/Exams/Exams_CAPE.htm

Carnoy, M. and Luschei, T.F. (March 2008). Skill Acquisition in 'High Tech' Export Agriculture: A Case Study of Lifelong Learning in Peru's Asparagus Industry. *Journal of Education Work* 21(1): 1-25.

CGUT (2008). Accessed: May 1, 2008. http://cgut.sep.gob.mx/

Clark, B.R. (1960). The 'Cooling-Out' Function in Higher Education. *American Journal Sociology* 65(6): 569-576.

Clayton, T. (August 2004). Competing Conceptions of Globalization Revisited: Relocating the Tension Between World-Systems Analysis and Globalization Analysis. *Comparative Education Review* 48(3): 274-294.

Cohen, A. (1995). Accommodating Postcompulsory Education Seekers Around the World. *Community College Review* 21(2): 65-75.

Cohen, A.M. and Brawer, F.B. (2003). *The American Community College.* 4th edition. San Francisco, CA: Jossey-Bass.

College of the North Atlantic Qatar. Accessed May 1, 2008. www.cna-qatar/cnaqatar/home.asp

Community Colleges for International Development (CCID) (2008a). Home Page. Accessed May 1, 2008. http://www.ccid.cc/

Community Colleges for International Development (CCID) (2008b). Exemplary Projects. Accessed May 1, 2008. http://ccid.kirkwood.cc.ia.us/projects.htm

Cowan, C.A. and Falcetta, F.M. (Fall 1996). Community College of the World Connection. *New England's Journal of Higher Education & Economic Development* 11(3): 30-32.

de Courtivron, I. (April 2008). Meditations on the Meaning of Home: Where Is Home? And Does It Matter? Keynote presentation: Forum Meeting. Boston, MA, www.forumea.org

De Siqueira, A. (2004). The Regulation of Education Through the WTO/GATS: Path to the Enhancement of Human Freedom? Conference Paper: CIES National, Salt Lake City, UT.

Dellow, D.A., and Romano, R.M. (2006). Globalization, Offshoring, and the Community College. *Community College Journal* August/September: 30 (I): 18-22.

East-West Consortium for Community College Development (2001). ERIC Documents: #ED475799. http://eric.ed.gov

East-West Consortium for Community College Development (2008). Web-site: http://eric.ed.gov

El Mallah, A.A., Kal, G., and Hassan, A.H.S. (1996) Egyptian Community Colleges: A Cast Study. In R.L. Raby and N. Tarrow (Eds.), *Dimensions of the Community College: International, Intercultural, and Multicultural Perspectives.* New York: Garland.

Elsner, P. (2008). Plenary Session Address. CCID 2008 Conference, Long Beach, CA.

Eskow, S., (Fall 1989). Toward Tellecommunity College: From Open Admission to Open Learning. In E. Harlacher (Ed.), *Cutting Edge Technologies in Community Colleges*. Washington, DC: American Association of Community and Junior Colleges.

Eskow, S. and Caffrey, J. (Autumn 1974). World Community College: A 2020 Vision. *Class to Mass Learning. New Directions for Community Colleges*. No. 7 V/4 Autumn. San Francisco. CA: Jossey-Bass.

Evelyn, J. (2003). 2-Year Enrollments Drop in California. *Chronicle of Higher Education*, Sept 26: A43.

Evelyn, J. (2005). Community Colleges Go Globe-Trotting. *Chronicle of Higher Education*, February 11.

First Global Community College Nong Khai–Udon Thani in Thailand. Accessed May 1, 2008. http://www.fgcc.ac.th/

Foster, P.J. (1965). The Vocational School Fallacy in Development Planning. In C.A. Anderson and M.J. Bowman (Eds.), *Education and National Development*. Chicago, IL: Aldine.

Foster, PJ. (2002). The Vocational School Fallacy Revisited: Education, Aspiration and Work in Ghana 1959-2000. *International Journal of Educational Development*, 22 (1): 27-28.

Friedman, T. (2005). *The World Is Flat: A Brief History of the Twenty-First Century*. New York: Farrar, Straus & Giroux.

Gallacher, J. (February 2006). Blurring the Boundaries or Creating Diversity. The Contribution of Further Education Colleges to Higher Education in Scotland. *Journal of Further and Higher Education*, 30 (11): 43-58.

Global Corporate College. http://globalcorporatecollege.com/global.asp

Gordon, M. (1999). International Programs at Middlesex Community College. Pioneering Leadership Exemplary Programs Occasional Papers Series. CCID Web Page. Accessed May 1, 2008. http://ccid.kirkwood.cc.ia.us/examp.htm

Guess, A. (2007). House Panels Study Abroad. Accessed May 1, 2008. http://insidehighered.coin/news/2007/07/27/global

Harper, W.A. (1978). Trip to Taiwan. *Community and Junior College Journal*, September, 1978. 49 (1) (February): 23-37.

Heyneman, S.P. (2003). The History and Problems of Making Education Policy at the World Bank, 1960-2000. *International Journal of Education Development*, 23: 315-337.

HKU School of Professional and Continuing Education (SPACE) Community College. Accessed May 1, 2008. http://hkuspace.hku.hk/index.php

Holland College - Prince Edward Island, Canada. Accessed May 1, 2008. www.holland pe ca/About/htm

Humber College Institute of Technology & Advanced Learning in Toronto. Accessed March 1, 2004. http://www.humberc.on.ca/

Humphrys, J.G. (1994). History of CCID 1976-92. Accessed February 11, 2003. http://www.ccid.cc/history/index.htm

Indian Center for Research and Development of Community Education (ICRDCE). Concept of Community College in India. Accessed May 1, 2008. http://www.tcrdce.com/concept.html

International Association of Community and Further Education Colleges. Accessed May 1, 2008. http://www.iaoc.org/

International Consortium for Economic and Educational Development (ICEED). Accessed May 1, 2008. www.iceed.com

Ishumi, A.G.M. (1998). Vocational Training as an Educational and Development Strategy Conceptual and Practical Issues. *International Journal of Educational Development* 83: 163-174.

Japan MEXT (Ministry of Education, Culture, Sports, Science and Technology) (2005). Higher Education. Accessed April 16, 2005. http://mext.go.jp/english/org/f_formal_22.htm

Jasshik, S. (2007). Overseas Outposts. Inside Highered. Accessed February 20, 2007. http://www.insidehighered.com/news/2007/02/15/branch

Jikei Group, Japan Home Page. (2004). Japanese Technical Colleges: How They Serve the Educational World. Accessed March 1, 2004. www.jikeigroup.net/english/aboutTec/index.html

Jones, P. (2002). Globalization and Internationalism: Democratic Prospects for World Education. In Nelly P. Stromquist and K. Monkman (Eds.), *Globalization and Education: Integration and Contestation Across Cultures* (pp. 27-43). Lanham, M.D.: Rowman & Littlefield.

Kenan Institute Asia, A.I. ASIA. Capacity Building for Community Colleges in Thailand. Accessed May 1 2008. http://www.kiasia.org/En/Group5

King Mongkut's Institute of Technology, North Bangkok. Accessed May 1, 2008. www.kmitnb.ac.th/

Kintzer, F. (1979). World Adaptations to the Community College Concept. In M.C. King and R.I. Breuder (Eds.), *Advancing International Education* (pp. 65-79). New Directions for Community Colleges Nu. 26. San Francisco, CA: Jossey-Bass.

Kintzer, F. (June 1998). Community Colleges Go International: Short-Cycle Education Around the World. *Leadership Abstracts World Wide Web Edition*, 11(6): 1-4.

Kneller, D. (2005). The Conflicts of Globalization and Restructuring of Education. In M.A. Peters (Ed.). *Education, Globalization, and the State in the Age of Terrorism*. Boulder, CO: Paradigm.

Koltai, L. (5-6 November 1993). Are There Challenges and Opportunities for American Community Colleges on the International Scene? Keynote address: CIES Western Region, Los Angeles, CA.

Lauglo, J. (2004) Vocationalize Secondary Education Revisited. Conference Paper: CIES National, Salt Lake City from Education, Training Contexts. Bern/Frankfurt: Peter Lang.

Lauglo, J. (2008). Revisiting the Vocational School Fallacy: A tribute to Philip Foster. Conference Paper: CIES, Columbia University. Accessed June 1, 2008. www.cies.us/newsletter.htm

Levin, J.S. (2001). *Globalizing the Community College: Strategies for Change in the Twenty-First Century*. New York: Palgrave (ED 450 856).

Levin, J.S. (2002). *Institutional Identity: The Community College as a Baccalaureate Degree Granting Institution*. Paper for symposium at annual meeting of the Association for the Study of Higher Education. Sacramento, CA. November 21, 2002. ERIC ED# 474 578.

Levin J.S. (2005). The Business Culture of the Community College: Students as Consumers; Students as Commodities. *New Directions for Higher Education*, 129, 11-26.

Lim, D. (March 2008). Enhancing the Quality of VET in Hong Kong: Recent Reforms and New Initiatives in Widening Participation in Tertiary Qualifications. *Journal of Education and Work*, 21 (1): 25-41.

Lin-Liu, J. (14 November 2001). China Plans to Build Network of Community Colleges. *Chronicle of Higher Education*. Accessed September 14, 2007. http://chronicle.com/daily/2001/11.htm

Lowe, J. and Gayle, V. (August 2007). Exploring the Work/Life/Study Balance: The Experience of Higher Education Students in a Scottish Further Education College. *Journal of Further and Higher Education*, 31(3): 225-239.

McKenney, J.F. (4 March 2004). *International Education & Economic Development Programs*. Conference Paper: California Colleges International Education, Monterey, CA.

McLaren, P. (1999). Introduction: Traumatizing Capital: Oppositional Pedagogies in the Age of Consent. In M. Castells, R. Flecha, P. Freire, H. Giroux, D. Macedo, and P. Willis (Eds.), *Critical Education in the New Information Age*. Boulder, CO: Rowman & Littlefield.

McMurtrie, B. (25 May 2001). Community Colleges Become a Force in Developing Nations Worldwide. *Chronicle of Higher Education*, 47(37): A44-A45.

Madden, L. (1998). The Community College Experiment in Latin America. *Community College Journal*, 69(2): 10-15.

Madras Community Colleges. Education in India. Accessed June 24, 2004. http://prayatna.typepad.com/education/2004/06/community_colle.html

Massinga, R.A., Menete, M.Z., and Bene, B.B. Polytechnic Institutions in Mozambique (2008). Presentation at World Congress, 2008. Accessed May 1, 2008. http://www.worldcongress2008.com/Session%202%20-%20Mozambique.ppt

Mellander, G.A. and Mellander, N. (Eds.) (August 1994). *Towards an Hungarian Community College System*. ERIC Document Reproduction Service No. ED 375870.

Mosa, A.A. (1996). Why Globalization? Conference Paper: 9th Comparative and International Education Conference. Sydney.

Netherlands Community College. Accessed May 1, 2008. www.arup.com/netherlands/project.htm

NIIT. Accessed May 1, 2008. http://www.niit.com/

Nova Scotia Community College (Canada). Accessed May 1, 2008. http://www.nscc.ns.ca/

Nsiah-Gyabaah, K., and Obour, S.A. (2008). Developing Industry and College Partnerships: The Dilemma of Ghanaian Polytechnics. Conference Paper: World Federation of Colleges and Polytechnics. New York City. http://www.worldcongress2008.com/Table %2014.pdf

Observatory on Borderless Higher Education (OBHE). Accessed May 1, 2008. http://www.obhe.ac.uk/

Raby. R. (1996). Introduction to Part 11. In R.L. Raby and N. Tarrow (Eds.). *Dimensions of the Community College: International, Intercultural, and Multicultural Perspectives.* New York: Garland.

Raby, R. (2000). Globalization of the Community College Model: Paradox of the Local and the Global. In Nelly P. Stromquist and K. Monkman (Eds.), *Globalization and Education: Integration and Contestation Across Cultures* (pp. 149-173). Lanham, M.D.: Rowman & Littlefield.

Raby, R.L. and Tarrow, N. (Eds.) (1996). *Dimensions of the Community College: International, Intercultural, and Multicultural Perspectives.* New York: Garland.

Raby, R.L. and Thomas. D. (2006). Equity, Access and Democracy: The Community College Model. *Education and Society* 24(1): 57-77.

Ratcliff, J. and Gibson-Beminger, B. (1998). Community Colleges in a Global Context. In A.H. Strydom and L.O.K. Lategan (Eds.), *Introducting Community Colleges to South Africa.* Bloemfontein: University of the Free State.

Riversdale Community College. Accessed March 1, 2008. http://indigo.ie/-rdalecc

Robertson, R. (1992). *Globalization Social Theory and Global Culture.* London: Sage.

Romano, R.M. (Ed.) (2002). *Internationalizing the Community College.* Washington, DC: Community College.

Royal Melbourne Institute of Technology. Accessed May 1, 2008. http://www.rmit.edu.au/

Schugurensky, D. and Higgins, K., (1996). From Aid to Trade: New Trends in International Education in Canada. In R.L. Raby and N. Tarrow (Eds.), *Dimensions of the Community College: International, Intercultural, and Multicultural Perspectives.* New York: Garland.

Selvarathuam, V. (August 1998). Limits to Vocationally-Oriented Education in the Third World. *International Journal of Educational Development,* 8(8): 1-35.

Smith. D.J. (23 October 2007). How Community Colleges Can Work for World Peace. *Chronicle of Higher Education. Community Colleges,* 54(9):B30, http://chronicle.com

St. George, E. (2006). Positioning Higher Education for the Knowledge Based Economy. *Higher Education,* 52: 589-610.

Steiner-Khamsi, G. (2003). Discourse Formation in Comparative Education. In J. Schriewer (Ed.), *Discourse Formation in Comparative Education,* 2nd edition. Frankfurt am Main: Peter Lang.

Strydom, A.H. and Lategan, L.O.K. (Eds.) (1998). *Introducing Community Colleges to South Africa.* Bloemfontein: University of the Free State Publications.

Thai East-West Community College Workshop (2001). [Report.] Bangkok, Thailand. Found on CCID website. Accessed May 1, 2008. www.ccid.org

Tonks, D. (August 1999). Access to Higher Education, 19991-1998: Using Geodemographics. *Widening Participation and Lifelong Learning.* 1(2):6-15.

United Arab Emirates, Higher Colleges of Technology. Accessed May 1, 2008: www.hct.ac.ae/hctweb/index.asp

Unites States Agency for International Development (USAID) (1995). *Seeking a New Partnership: Task Force Report on U.S. Community Colleges.* Washington, DC: Government Printing Office (ERIC Document Reproduction Service No. ED 398 942).

Ural, I. (1998). International Community College Models: A South African Perspective. In A.H. Strydom & L.O.K. Lategan (Eds.), *Introducing Community Colleges to South Africa* (pp. 106-119). Bloemfontein: University of the Free State.

Valeau, E.J., and Raby, R.L. (2007). *International Reform Efforts and Challenges in Community Colleges.* New Directors for Community Colleges (138. Summer). San Francisco, CA: Jossey-Bass.

Van der Linde, C.H. (1996). The Role of the Community College in Countering Conflict in Multicultural Societies. In R.L. Raby and N. Tarrow (Eds.), *Dimensions of the Community College: International, Intercultural, and Multicultural Perspectives.* New York: Garland.

Vasquez, G.H. (2003). Peace Corps and Community Colleges: A Twenty-First Century Partnership. *Community College Journal.* 73(5): 62-66.

Vaughan, G.B. (1989). *Leadership in Transition.* New York: Macmillan.

Wolf, L. (2008). Global Trends in Training Middle-Level Manpower.

World Bank (2003). *Constructing Knowledge Economies: New Challenges for Tertiary Education.* Washington, DC: World Bank.

World Congress (2008). Accessed May 1, 2008. www.worldcongress2008.com/index.html

World Federation of Colleges and Polytechnics. http://www.wfcp.org/about-us-biz-plan.pdf

Yamano, T. & Hawkins, J. (1996). Assessing the Relevance of American Community College Models in Japan. In R.L. Raby and N. Tarrow (eds.). *Dimensions of the Community College: International, Intercultural, and Multicultural Perspectives.* New York: Garland.

CHAPTER 51

ONLINE EDUCATION AND ORGANIZATIONAL CHANGE

REGINA L. GARZA MITCHELL, CENTRAL MICHIGAN UNIVERSITY, MOUNT PLEASANT

An in-depth case study examined faculty and administrator perceptions of how online education affected the organizational culture of a large, suburban community college. Findings suggest that in addition to structural and procedural changes, online education had an impact on faculty and administrator roles, teaching and learning (in both online and face-to-face settings), and the community of students and faculty members who comprise the college. The result was a new perception of the organization itself.

Keywords: online courses, faculty roles, administrator roles, organizational culture

Community colleges are known for their ability to change quickly, and their adoption of online education is no exception. Since this instructional form emerged in the 1990s, community colleges have consistently been on the forefront of offering online education. Currently, over half of the 3.9 million students taking at least one online course do so at a 2-year college (Allen & Seaman, 2008), a larger percentage than their share of overall higher education enrollments (American Association of Community Colleges, 2008). Growth in online education has remained steady since its inception, and we are just beginning to understand its organizational impact.

When online education is implemented, structural and procedural changes occur. Though surface changes are a natural outgrowth of any new component introduced to an institution, there also exists the potential for change in organizational culture. It is important to understand how this change is experienced by those who are affected because organizational structure and dynamics, along with the lenses through which organizational participants view the organization, contribute to culture (Harris, 1994; Kezar, 2001; Schein, 2004). Much of the literature regarding online education focuses on surface-level changes rather than its cultural impact. This study sought to better understand the impact of online education on organizational culture from the perspectives of faculty members and administrators.

Online Education and Change

Online education does not neatly fit into a college's existing structure because it involves technology, academic administration, academic departments, and student services, blurring traditional boundaries between units (Jones & O'Shea, 2004). Though changes at the structural level are disruptive, they are only first-order, surface-level changes that affect positions, procedures, and processes while leaving the culture of the institution intact (Harris, 1994; Kezar, 2001). The longer-term effects of online education, however, are far reaching and may achieve deeper, second-order or cultural changes because the philosophies behind those changes challenge underlying values and beliefs.

Structural and Procedural Changes

Implementing online education involves immediate changes to technological and organizational structures. On the physical side, technology is necessary to create an infrastructure that supports and promotes online education. Organizationally, a structure must be in place to handle the day-to-day administrative functions. It is possible that either technological or structural components of the infrastructure for online education may be incorporated into existing systems but processes and procedures will be affected.

The technological infrastructure for online education includes, at a minimum, computers, networks, online student services, and a course management system (Hanna, 2003; Moore & Kearsley, 2005). Instructional technologies available for use within a college may also be used for online course delivery. However, online education requires a much higher usage of these resources (Diaz & Cheslock, 2006). In addition, teaching and learning in an online environment require different processes, policies, and procedures. For example, online courses are generally developed as part of a process involving the faculty member as a content expert working with technology and multimedia experts to produce a course package for student delivery (Hanna, 2003; Moore & Kearsley, 2005). Course development in this manner differs from the traditional process in which a single faculty member has autonomy over a course. Furthermore, course development and instruction in an online format tend to require more time and effort on behalf of faculty members (Lenz, Jones, & Monaghan, 2005; Mupinga & Maughan, 2008; Tomei, 2004).

As noted above, online education involves technology, academic administration, academic departments, and student services (Jones & O'Shea, 2004). Thus, changes made in regard to online education have a ripple effect across a college, and the intentional or unintentional incorporation of the philosophies behind those changes have the potential to transform the underlying values and beliefs of an organization, resulting in cultural or second-order change.

Second-Order Change

Second-order change occurs when guiding frameworks, or schemas, are altered (Bartunek & Moch, 1987; Harris, 1994; Kezar, 2001). The integration of online education has the potential to alter ingrained beliefs about technology, teaching, and learning. Hence, paradigmatic shifts in relation to technology and pedagogy may occur as online education becomes ingrained in a college.

Principles guiding online education are derived from constructivist views of teaching and learning that differ from traditional views of lecture-driven instruction (Meyer, 2002). Although early models of distance education did not require changes to traditional views of teaching, more current models focus on connecting teachers and students through collaborative discussions, assignments, and group projects (Hanna, 2003). There is an increased emphasis on interaction between teachers and students and among students (Palloff & Pratt, 2004, 2007), and more responsibility for learning is placed on students (Meyer, 2002). Despite the enhanced focus on student learning, the quality of online courses is often called into question, even among schools with robust online programs. Yet, no single definition of quality guides the development and instruction of online courses (Meyer, 2002). One tendency is to compare online courses with face-to-face courses. The "no-significant-difference" phenomenon was postulated in the 1990s, with a compilation of studies showing no significant difference between distance and face-to-face instruction (Russell, 1999). Although some research continues to compare online and face-to-face instruction (e.g., Fortune, Shifflett, & Sibley, 2006), other studies have begun to put a greater focus on teaching methods over delivery (e.g., Basu Conger, 2005; McDonald, 2002; Sener, 2004). Thus, there is no single accepted method for measuring the quality of online courses, which remains a challenge for those engaged in online education.

The move toward online education requires an acceptance of technology in relation to teaching. The idea that teaching and learning can legitimately occur without regard to time, place, or proximity may require a rethinking of idealized conceptions of teaching and learning. Thus, organizational schemas about teaching, learning, and technology may be altered to accept online education as legitimate.

Theoretical Lens

Transformational change occurs on multiple levels, affects many aspects of the organization, and results in paradigmatic shifts (Bartunek & Moch, 1987; Kezar, 2001; Levy & Merry, 1986). This type of change takes longer to accomplish and is intentional (Eckel, Hill, & Green, 1998; Kezar, 2001). One way to gauge transformational change is through a cultural lens. Organizational culture provides a context for those within it but is also shaped by individual beliefs and values.

Drawing on Schein's (2004) depiction of culture as a construct with three levels, Eckel, Hill, and Green (1998) likened culture to an onion's layers, with artifacts comprising the outermost layers, espoused values making up the middle layers, and underlying assumptions constituting the deepest layers. These elements of culture are complex, overlapping, and intertwining on different levels. Becoming aware of culture involves looking at patterns of interaction, at language, at images and themes in conversations, and at rituals, rites, and ceremonies (Morgan, 1997). Culture in colleges may also be viewed through the broad categories of governance, educational philosophy, teaching and learning, academic community, commitment to students, architecture, rituals and ceremonies, behavior patterns and processes, and implicit and explicit values and beliefs (Peterson & Spencer, 1993). This study used a cultural lens to examine changes as perceived by faculty members and administrators at Leading Edge Community College (LECC).

Method

This research involved a single-site, in-depth case study that investigated changes in culture that emerged as the result of a growing online education program at LECC.[1] LECC provided a unique case (Yin, 2003) in which a college with an already robust online education program received permission from its accrediting agency and board of trustees to offer all of its courses and programs in an online format.

Data were collected through individual interviews, document analysis, and site observations. Documents were defined as any written, electronic, or otherwise recorded material that was not prepared specifically for the researcher or for this research project (Lincoln & Guba, 1985; Merriam, 1998; Whitt, 2001). Prior to and during my visits to the college, I obtained documentation regarding the growth of online education at LECC. Documentation consisted of vision and mission statements, newsletters, research conducted by the college, self-study reports, accreditation documents, and other documents that helped paint a picture of LECC's online program and the college's culture. Interviews were conducted with faculty members and administrators who had been employed at the college for at least 2 years at the time of the study. Random purposeful sampling was used to identify participants (Creswell, 2008). Reduction and analysis of the data were performed on an ongoing basis throughout the study, and common themes were derived from interviews (Merriam, 1998). Findings from this study were intended to present a portrait of how change was perceived by different groups at the college. To ensure quality and validity, data were triangulated through different collection methods, member checks, and through the comparison of findings between methods (Huberman & Miles, 2001; Patton, 1990; Yin, 2003).

Participants included 13 administrators and 8 full-time faculty members. An attempt was made to speak with employees who worked directly with online education and with those who did not. However, all participating faculty members taught online. Every effort was made to present findings from the participants' perspectives by sharing their stories and words (Creswell, 2007). Interview summaries were sent to participants to ensure proper interpretation and context of information. Although perspectives belong to those who participated in the study, findings were categorized in an attempt to delineate organizational, group, and individual perceptions of change.

The Leading Edge

LECC is a very large, suburban community college serving just under 60,000 students per year, 7,000 of whom took courses online during 2008.[2] The college has been in operation for over 50 years and is one of the largest associate's degree–granting institutions in the nation. LECC is situated within a state that is facing severe economic challenges, including a high unemployment rate. Over 1,800 faculty members, staff members, and administrators, including 200 full-time faculty members, support the college. College employees are represented by nine unions; all employees except for senior administrators belong to a bargaining unit.

The college has three campuses, two of which were represented in this study. The college also houses a university center where students can take courses from partner institutions toward bachelor's or master's degrees. In addition to its physical campuses, LECC has a robust online education program with more than 200 courses and five complete degree programs. Enrollment at LECC has been on an upswing for the past several years, with enrollment in online courses alone increasing 22% between 2007 and 2008.

LECC prides itself on being a comprehensive community college and on being at the leading edge of change. In line with the college's vision statement, which stipulates that the institution will "be a leading edge community college and the community's preferred choice for lifelong learning, cultural enrichment, and community development opportunities," the college and community retain close ties. Community outreach and support are essential to the college's mission, vision, and culture. Yearly satisfaction surveys are conducted to assess the community view of the college. The community, in turn, supports the college through a voter-approved millage and donations to the college's foundation. LECC is the college of choice for county residents, with four out of five high school seniors attending within 5 years of graduation.

LECC is also the college of choice for its faculty, staff, and administrators. A large number of LECC employees are former students, and most have a long tenure at the college. The college president has spent his entire career at LECC, moving up the ranks from adjunct faculty member to president. A faculty member who had been at the college for 3 years commented, "If you're not here 20 years, you're new." Despite their longevity, faculty and staff members have remained energetic and innovative. The president encourages creativity and innovation as long as "it [made] sense" for the college. An associate dean with a personal interest in online education heralded the college's move toward online education. Concerning the work of this associate dean, the president remarked, "We were very fortunate that she was here, because it was almost an avocational interest of hers, but she was able to drive the agenda and we were able to start moving."

Online Education at LECC

LECC was one of the first community colleges in its state to successfully put online education into practice. According to a college document, LECC implemented online education in 1998 "with four online certificated faculty, four courses, and 80 students (duplicated)[3]." The LECC culture demands not only that the college do creative things but also that faculty and staff members do those things well. The president realized that funding would be needed for online education, so he sought and was successful in receiving approval from the community for a technology bond in 1998 and for a millage in 2000 to support technology. These technology funds allowed the college to create and maintain a supportive infrastructure for online education.

Following the first experimental year, the college reached an agreement with its faculty union and implemented a 3-year pilot program. By 2008, a total of 210 online and 11 hybrid course sections were offered. During the winter semester of 2008, just over 3,400 students (duplicated) enrolled in courses that were offered completely online, and 205 students (duplicated) enrolled in hybrid course sections. The online program has seen consistent growth since its inception, as illustrated in

Figure 1, and the college anticipates that growth will continue, as enrollment in online courses usually fills within hours after registration is open. LECC implemented a wait-list system in 2008 to track the demand for online courses, and initial indications were that students placed themselves on wait lists for online courses rather than enrolling in comparable on-site sections. Despite high enrollment, a study conducted by the college found that the attrition rate in online courses was seven percentage points higher than the attrition rate of face-to-face courses, a statistically significant difference. The attrition rate is of concern to the college, and measures are being taken to increase persistence in online courses. However, the study also found that rather than the delivery method, the three variables most likely to affect persistence and success were the academic discipline, the course, and the instructor.

Structural Changes Regarding Online Education

Numerous structural and procedural changes were associated with online education at LECC. The online education infrastructure has undergone several incarnations and is currently headed by the Vice Provost of Learning Outreach and a support staff that includes an associate dean and director. Though administrators head the unit, decisions are made in conjunction with the faculty. For example, policies and procedures regarding online education were initially developed by a steering committee of faculty members, staff members, and administrators. This group was recently resurrected as an advisory group that continues to provide input.

Instructors who teach online are required to complete a college-run training course before they are allowed to teach online or develop an online course. This requirement is part of the contracts for both full-time and adjunct faculty members. The 6-week training course is conducted online and teaches faculty members how to develop and teach courses online while giving them the experience of being a student in an online course. Participants felt strongly that online courses are not a good fit for all students or for all faculty members, and not all faculty members who take the training course

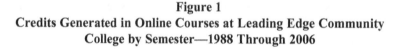

Figure 1
Credits Generated in Online Courses at Leading Edge Community
College by Semester—1988 Through 2006

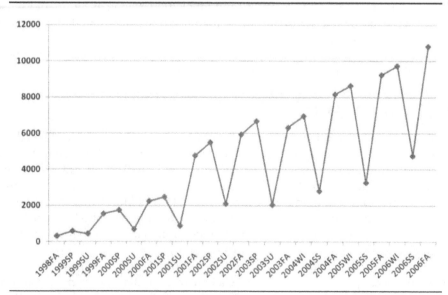

Note: FA = fall semester; SP = spring semester; SU = summer semester; WI = winter semester; SS = spring and summer semester combined. Starting in 2004, LECC changed its academic calendar, moving from spring, summer, and fall semesters to a calendar with winter, spring/summer, and fall semesters.

choose to teach online. Many administrators have also taken the course so that they can better understand what faculty members and students go through during these courses.

In contrast with official college documents that refer to faculty members as "faculty" or "instructors," contracts and other documents refer to online instructors as "facilitators." Enrollment in online courses is limited to 23 students; this limit was increased from an initial limit of 18 and was also written into the faculty contracts. The rationale for the cap on student enrollment related to concerns regarding teaching and learning. LECC mandates a high level of interaction between students and instructors in online courses, and instructors wanted that interaction to remain personal.

"Facilitator expectations" are in place, mandating how certain elements of online courses are taught. Instructors and students are allowed to "check in" to online courses when it is convenient to do so; however, the college's guidelines specify that both instructors and students must participate in their online courses at least five times per week "with engaging, purposeful, and well thought contributions." Faculty members and administrators lauded this policy as a means of ensuring an interactive, engaging experience. A dean stated,

> Faculty and students have to be online at least 5 days a week, and they have to be interacting, doing active, engaging things. Again, it's not something where the faculty or students can just disappear for days or weeks at a time. If they think that's going to be the case, then they're not a candidate for our online program.

Faculty members and administrators speculated that the participation requirements might be a contributing factor to the high attrition rate in online courses. Participants described a misconception that online courses require little work and function as an independent study rather than a structured course.

Online courses were implemented and have continued to operate over an 8-week period rather than the traditional 16-week format used in face-to-face courses. Administrators and faculty members expressed concern that the condensed format may be another factor adding to the high attrition rate for online courses. Attrition in online classes also created a financial dilemma. The course limit of 23 students is lower than the limit imposed for on-campus sections, and students are not allowed to enroll in an online class after the first week. Thus, if a student drops the course after it has started, there is only a slim chance that the empty seat will be filled by another student, and the potential for revenue loss exists. As a result of these concerns, some faculty members are now piloting 12- and 16-week online courses.

Full-time faculty members must maintain on-site office hours at least 2 days a week, even if their entire course load is taught online. Although some faculty members expressed displeasure with this requirement, it was acknowledged as necessary to keep faculty members actively involved in college activities and governance. One faculty member who teaches mostly online stated that it would be easy to teach completely online and never come to campus at all, but coming to campus twice a week "keeps us in touch with our on-ground community and the college body itself."

Faculty members and administrators initially expressed disproportionate resistance to online education, but opinions have changed over the past 10 years. Online instruction is now described as "just another avenue of teaching." Online education has been ingrained into the college culture, and college personnel view it as an integral part of the institution. An administrator commented, "You know, it's just become part of the culture. You talk about online education just like you do graduation or taking courses. It's just embedded in the culture." Both groups viewed online education as an extension of the college's mission of being a comprehensive community college. As one faculty member put it,

> I think this is the future of education . . . Our students no longer have nine-to-five jobs. They don't have the opportunity to be in one place at one time any longer. That's just the way our society is, and we have to change with that society.

A dean concurred, stating, "We always did try to provide alternate delivery systems, personalized options, community-based learning . . . It's a community college, so we try to reach the community in any way that we can." There is an overarching belief that providing online education is a necessary way of reaching out to students, particularly those who may not be able to come to campus. Online education allows the college to expand and support its student base, to provide community outreach, and to expand or enhance the college mission.

Role Expansion

Both faculty members and administrators felt that their roles expanded because of online education, but the effects were experienced more deeply by the faculty. Administrators perceived that changes in relation to online education were mainly procedural, but they also found themselves placed in the role of advocate for online education.

From the administrative perspective, there was a college-wide focus on online education, a push from senior administrators, and a high demand from students to offer courses in this format. Regardless of personal views, administrative participants felt that online education was necessary to the college, and they felt a subtle push toward it. Cathy, an associate dean, explained, "It's not like somebody is saying, 'You must do this.' It's highly encouraged." Due to the collegewide interest in online education, administrators felt a need to stay informed and to learn as much as they could about it. A number of administrators went through the faculty online training course. Cathy stated,

> I feel that it's incumbent upon me to learn as much about [online education] as I can so that I can facilitate the needs of the faculty in that regard and also to encourage the development where there is initiative to do so.

In addition to fully online courses, administrators also felt a push to Web-enhanced classroom courses by encouraging instructors to use Internet-based instruction as a supplement for face-to-face classes.

Though the college had a "designated champion" for online education in the form of the Vice Provost for Learning Outreach, other administrators felt that their roles expanded to include advocating for online instruction and Web enhancement because of the perceived push from the college. Leonard, an academic vice provost, stated, "I continue to preach the Web-enhanced philosophy. Once people get in, I think they'll get hooked." Simon, a dean, concurred, "I try to do what I can to cajole and convince and promote, and that sort of thing, to get folks moving along that continuum." Although administrators viewed their role as "trying to be a cheerleader and a proponent for the system," they were cautious about forcing faculty members into teaching online. Dorothy, another associate dean, pointed out that not everyone wants to teach online, and that she will not push someone who does not want to teach in that format: "What I've done is sit back and waited for them to come to me, because we've done a great job of communicating that this training is available, that the online classes are there." Administrative participants believed that the decision to teach online or to develop an online course must come from faculty members themselves; thus, the final decisions about which courses and programs should be offered online were up to the faculty.

On the faculty side, role changes were experienced on a deeper level. The faculty role at LECC has become more complex and less autonomous as the result of online education. At LECC even the faculty title has changed, as instructors who teach online courses are now referred to as facilitators in both contractual language and everyday terminology. The shift to facilitator reflects the influence of constructivist and cognitive philosophies of teaching that undergird online instruction (Meyer, 2002). There are also different expectations in place for teaching face-to-face, online, or in a hybrid format, with online courses having the most stringent requirements.

Not surprisingly, online instruction requires more time and effort on behalf of the instructor. This has led to the feeling of "nonstop teaching" and "inundation of online." It takes more time to set up the course, to teach, and to communicate with students. An instructor who has taught online for about 10 years noted, "One of the things I have noticed about being online is that it's nonstop." Another faculty member explained, "As a faculty member, it's much more work. I always tell my colleagues, 'Yeah, you guys walk out of class and you're done. My students never go away.'" Thus, online instruction and course development were viewed as more labor and time intensive than traditional methods (Lenz et al., 2005; Mupinga & Maughan, 2008; Tomei, 2004). The faculty at LECC did not perceive the extra time or work as a negative but as a natural effect of this type of teaching and learning.

Another role assumed by many faculty members was that of mentor to new online instructors. This was not required by the college but arose from a feeling that the online environment was not suitable for everyone.

> When selecting [faculty] it is very important to have a proper selection criteria for online. It can't just be somebody who wants to spend their time at home teaching in their jammies. It's got to be somebody who understands the online process.

Several voluntary mentoring programs were created on the basis of this understanding, and three participants in this study acted as mentors in these programs. A business instructor acknowledged that it requires a bit of extra work on her part, but she likes to assist new online faculty members: "In addition to them having to go through the online class and learn[ing] it themselves, I am even more adamant about making sure that there are certain standards that they maintain." Two other faculty members described a mentoring situation that involved the new faculty member shadowing a more experienced online instructor after going through the college's online training program. The type of mentoring exhibited by this group of faculty members was not required, but those who carried out this mentoring role claimed that it was necessary. Faculty members perceived mentoring to be a means of ensuring quality and making sure that courses are taught the "Leading Edge way." It was very important to the LECC faculty that those who want to teach online understand the amount of work involved and the level of quality that is expected, and some departments subsequently adopted formal mentoring models.

The college encouraged the growth of online education and the use of online elements in face-to-face classrooms, yet this type of instruction still faced high scrutiny by administrators and faculty members. A strong theme that emerged from both the faculty and administrator groups was the desire to ensure that online students received the same quality of instruction as onsite students and that all online courses were taught in a similar manner. Although online education was "just another avenue of teaching" at LECC, there was a noticeable difference in how instruction was perceived in online and on-ground courses. Furthermore, online courses were subject to strict requirements in terms of how instruction was to be offered.

Both administrators and faculty members perceived that online education had had an impact on their roles. Though some of the changes were procedural, there was evidence that individual schemas were altered. In acting as advocates for online courses and programs, administrators found themselves having to learn more about how this type of education worked and what the implications were for the faculty; they perceived that they needed a deeper understanding of this type of education. This changed the way administrators perceived online education, moving from initial resistance to the belief that it was a positive and necessary avenue for LECC. Faculty members shifted from instructors to facilitators and willingly assumed the role of mentor for new faculty members who chose to teach in this manner, either through formal or informal programs.

Teaching and Learning

In addition to the workload, online education affected the approach to teaching at LECC. The design and instruction of online courses at LECC deliberately positioned faculty members in the role of facilitator versus expert (Barr & Tagg, 1995). Overall, there was a greater use of instructional technology, and a greater emphasis was placed on the use of technology in the classroom, whether online or on-ground. Faculty participants indicated that lecturing was the prevailing mode of instruction in on-ground courses, but those who had taught online indicated that they now perceived students as more autonomous and that they have accommodated students by becoming more interactive in face-to-face settings. Online courses had a focus on a student-centered rather than an instructor-centered classroom, reflecting the notion that students were very much at the heart of LECC. Although it was not a change for faculty members to focus their instruction on the needs of students, instructional methods used by instructors were different after teaching online.

> I've taken some of the things from the online class, and we do those in the on-ground class. But more importantly, it gives me time to work on those individual skills that the students require rather than just listening to me gab.

Instructors consciously moved from a "SAGE-on-the-stage" approach to a "guide-on-the-side" approach. With this shift, instructors felt that they were able to provide more individualized attention to their students than in the past.

Edgar, who had taught at LECC for 33 years, talked about how teaching online renewed his interest and energy in teaching: "I've kind of gone into a different mode from a pure lecture-mode situation to a more participatory mode and more of a one-on-one tutoring. I'm getting to know my students more than I ever did in the past." The overall feeling of all faculty members in the study, despite the extra work involved, was a renewed enthusiasm for teaching and interacting with students, particularly among those faculty members who have been at the college for a number of years.

A New Type of Community

A change perceived by both faculty and administrator groups was the type of student being served by the college, particularly in online courses. One faculty member remarked, "We're growing a greater variety of students than we would have been able to do physically." Instructors who taught online at LECC for 7 or more years commented on the change in students taking those courses. Initially, online instruction served students who had no other way to come to campus. At LECC that population was mostly women who were homebound or who were returning to work and had family obligations that prevented them from coming to campus. Today, online students at the college reflect a more traditional college population, including male students, dual-enrolled students, and students from 4-year institutions:

> It seemed to be that in the past I had the moms and the people who said, "Okay, I want to go to school and I can't be on campus. This is my only option." I think I found those people gave it their all more so than our current students. You still have your dedicated students in there, but I'm also finding there's a broader range of students. Now it's just another class to take as opposed to "I really want to go to college, but I can't be on campus at any of these times."

This change was viewed as evidence that online courses had "caught on" and become a more acceptable form of instruction. "This is how the student body has changed. It went from single moms who just couldn't get out of the house to anybody, now, is willing to take them." In addition to the change in student backgrounds, there came a change in motivation. Some instructors felt that students turned to online courses as a matter of convenience rather than need.

Administrators credited online education as being a venue for expanding college services to students who are homebound or who otherwise may not be able to come to campus for classes. Yet, the administrators also saw online education as providing avenues for expansion in terms of new markets and new opportunities. They perceived students who took online courses as a mixed bag that included current students who see online courses as merely another option, those who need the online format for various reasons, and students who took the courses at a geographical distance outside of the college's service area. Several participants mentioned students in the military— some stationed in Iraq—who took online courses through LECC. One administrator mentioned specific instances he was aware of in which students enrolled in online courses after joining the military because they wanted to keep their affiliation with LECC and only needed one or two more courses to finish a degree. Several administrators spoke about students who were enrolled in online courses but lived in other states. One associate dean knew of students taking courses from as far away as Hawaii and Australia, though she emphasized that these students were the exception and not the rule. The director of enrollment services commented,

> We've had students from across the country that will jump in and get registered. They may have been a Leading Edge student and got transferred someplace else and need to pick up a course or two. And what better way to do it than to go online?

Participants also mentioned a number of faculty members who moved out of state but continued their affiliation with LECC by teaching online. Thus, online education has provided a necessary service to existing LECC students who need or want the option of taking courses in this format and has expanded the range of those served by LECC to include those who are not in the immediate geographic service area but who want to either extend or build an affiliation with the college.

Challenges of Integrating Online Education

LECC provides a picture of successful cultural change in the integration of online education, and many positives have been associated with this change. However, change does not come easily, and challenges to this change continue to be raised. Although it is acknowledged that the majority of the college is in favor of online education, some still fear and distrust this type of education. Departments offering courses and programs online struggle to maintain a balance between the numbers of sections offered online and on-site for fear of losing on-campus students.

Implications

LECC provides an example of a community college that was successful in implementing transformational change. Although the resources available to implement online education successfully will vary from college to college, the actions taken by LECC illustrate elements of best practice for institutionalizing online education. Other colleges contemplating expansion of online education programs should plan for changes in key areas, including physical and organizational structures.

Also key to implementing change was the motivation of all employee groups at LECC. Administrators and faculty members worked together to create the initial policies and procedures regarding online education, and both groups continued to have input into how online education functioned. This level of participation fostered buy-in from employees (Black & Gregersen, 2003) and helped them to see how online education supported institutional mission, vision, and core values (Levy, 2003). Faculty members, staff members, and administrators involved in online education must be part of the process of its institutionalization, and they should establish guidelines and procedures together.

Professional development played a large part in altering faculty and administrator opinions about online education. At the request of the faculty, training in online instruction was mandatory for full- and part-time faculty members who taught online, and administrators also chose to participate in the training. The first-hand experience in an online setting allowed participants to address their concerns related to teaching and learning in a new environment. Thus, rather than relying on early adopters to shepherd the online movement, professional development made it possible for faculty members and administrators at different levels to test the environment and their comfort level with it, reducing the anxiety related to learning a new process (Schein, 2004). An unanticipated effect of the training was a shift toward more student-centered teaching both in the physical and virtual settings. Hence, colleges can be intentional in providing professional development opportunities that will allow employees to learn about the online environment and incorporate specific instructional methods.

Discussion and Conclusion

Like other colleges, LECC has experienced steady enrollment increases in online education over the past 10 years. LECC places high importance on being a comprehensive community college and perceives online education as an enhancement of its mission. Structural and procedural changes occurred in the college, resulting in significant changes in attitudes and beliefs regarding online education. Intentionality played a large part in changes that occurred at LECC. Administrators felt a push from the senior levels to incorporate this type of education and to become familiar with it to support the faculty. Through their efforts, administrators viewed themselves as champions of online education, a role that is essential in achieving transformational change (Black & Gregersen, 2003;

Kotter & Cohen, 2002). As online education became more ingrained in the college culture, participants noticed changes in administrative and faculty roles, in teaching and learning, in the students and faculty members involved with the college, and in overall perceptions regarding online education.

A key indicator of the shift toward faculty facilitators involved language. The word *facilitator* replaced *instructor* or *teacher* in official documents for online instructors, including the faculty contract, and in everyday conversation. In addition, faculty members at LECC found that online instruction required more time and effort because of the increased interaction with students and the requirement that instructors and students be involved with the online class at least five times per week. Though the expectations for online instruction, including training and required participation, were agreed on by faculty members and administrators, such stringent stipulations were not placed on face-to-face instruction. Yet, the basis of comparison for online courses was their face-to-face counterparts, indicating that the perception of quality may be based on the status quo rather than on a defined measure of quality (Meyer, 2002).

Teaching and learning were affected in an unexpected manner at LECC. The expectation was that online education would be of lower quality than face-to-face courses. Yet, the training intended for teaching in an online setting was applied independently by faculty members in their on-site courses as well. Formal training programs or certifications for teaching online are becoming more common at community colleges. Of interest is how faculty members are using (or not using) this training and how training of this sort can be used intentionally to enhance teaching and learning in all settings.

Faculty members who taught online indicated that they tried new methods of instruction both online and in the physical classroom. Instructors assumed the role of learning facilitator rather than expert or lecturer, and students were expected to be active in constructing their own learning during the course (Barr & Tagg, 1995; Meyer, 2002). The general feeling was that online instruction required more time and effort on behalf of the instructor, and individual parameters had to be set to avoid being overwhelmed. Despite the perceived increase in work, faculty members in this study demonstrated enthusiasm for teaching online and a renewed enthusiasm for teaching in general.

Online education was institutionalized at LECC, and the ensuing changes went beyond the surface level to affect schemas at different levels. The changes reflected a range of beliefs about teaching, learning, and what it means to be a comprehensive community college. Change was experienced across the institution and demonstrated the tightly coupled nature of an online education system. The college's existing culture made it possible for this change to occur without being overly traumatic for faculty members and administrators.

An important finding lies in the fact that this college incorporated online education and deliberately expanded its service area while attempting to remain true to its mission of responding to local community needs and demands. Just as community colleges changed from being physical parts of secondary schools to stand-alone institutions, the definition of the communities that they serve is now evolving. In this era of globalization, in which information is transferred over distances with a speed previously unimagined, the idea of community is not limited to physical geography. Students choose which communities they belong to in the virtual world and that choice may extend to community colleges that offer online education. Colleges that make changes in ways that align with their core mission and values may find that students choose to remain connected to that community despite other available options. What does this mean in terms of financial support that ties back to a college's service area? The implications of choosing one's community should be explored in more depth.

LECC provided a single example of changes to institutional culture stemming from online education. Changes at LECC, overall, were positive. Enrollment has increased, technology is being used in ways that are designed to engage students, and there is a large focus on both serving students and maintaining high educational quality. LECC used a combined lens of social and institutional logic in making decisions related to online education (Gumport, 2003), but it strived to keep its local community at the center of decision making. In light of recent economic upheavals, ever-tightening governmental restrictions, and an increasing number of students taking courses at community colleges, LECC and other institutions will continue to struggle to maintain the balance between serving local communities and growing the funding needed to do so.

Notes

1. Pseudonyms are used for the names of the college and its personnel.
2. Student numbers are duplicated counts. Approximately 40% of online students take their courses solely online. The majority take courses at one or both of the campuses as well as online.
3. Duplicated headcount indicates that enrollment counts were conducted per course rather than per student.

References

Allen, I. E., & Seaman, J. (2008). *Staying the course: Online education in the United States, 2008.* Needham, MA: Sloan Consortium.

American Association of Community Colleges. (2008). *Community college fact sheet.* Retrieved December 14, 2008, from http://www.aacc.nche.edu/AboutCC/Pages/fastfacts .aspx.

Barr, R. B., & Tagg, J. (1995). A new paradigm for undergraduate education. *Change, 27*(6), 13-25.

Bartunek, J. M., & Moch, M. K. (1987). First-order, second-order, and third-order change and organization development interventions: A cognitive approach. *Journal of Applied Behavioral Science, 23,* 483-500.

Basu Conger, S. (2005, July). If there is no significant difference, why should we care? *Journal of Educators Online, 2*(2). Retrieved March 14, 2007, from http://www.thejeo.com/Basu%20Conger%20Final.pdf

Black, J. S., & Gregersen, H. B. (2003). *Leading strategic change: Breaking through the brain barrier.* Upper Saddle River, NJ: Prentice Hall.

Creswell, J. W. (2007). *Qualitative inquiry and research design: Choosing among five approaches.* Thousand Oaks, CA: SAGE.

Diaz, V., & Cheslock, J. (2006). Faculty use of instructional technology and distributed learning. In J. S. Levin, S. Kater, & R. Wagoner (Eds.), *Community college faculty: At work in the new economy* (pp. 63-79). New York: Palgrave Macmillan.

Eckel, P. D., Hill, B., & Green, M. (1998). *On change: En route to transformation.* Washington, DC: American Council on Education.

Fortune, M. F., Shifflett, B., & Sibley, R. E. (2006). A comparison of online (high tech) and traditional (high touch) learning in business communication courses in Silicon Valley. *Journal of Education for Business, 81,* 210-214.

Gumport, P. J. (2003). The demand-response scenario: Perspectives of community college presidents. *Annals of the American Academy of Political and Social Science, 568,* 38-61.

Hanna, D. E. (2003). Organizational models in higher education, past and future. In M. G. Moore & W. G. Anderson (Eds.), *Handbook of distance education* (pp. 67-78). Mahwah, NJ: Lawrence Erlbaum Associates.

Harris, S. G. (1994). Organizational culture and individual sensemaking: A schema-based perspective. *Organizational Science, 5,* 309-321.

Huberman, A. M., & Miles, M. B. (2001). Data management and analysis methods. In C. F. Clifton, J. G. Hayworth, & L. R. Lattuca (Eds.), *Qualitative research in higher education: Expanding perspectives* (2nd ed., pp. 553-572). Boston: Pearson Custom.

Jones, N., & O'Shea, J. (2004). Challenging hierarchies: The impact of e-learning. *Higher Education, 48,* 379-395.

Kezar, A. (2001). *Understanding and facilitating organizational change in the 21st century: Recent research and conceptualizations.* San Francisco: Jossey-Bass.

Kotter, J. P., & Cohen, D. S. (2002). *The heart of change: Real-life stories of how people change their organizations.* Boston: Harvard Business School Publishing.

Lenz, T. L., Jones, R. M., & Monaghan, M. S. (2005). Faculty workload comparison between a campus-based and Internet-based patient assessment course. *American Journal of Pharmaceutical Education, 69*(4), 67-68.

Levy, A., & Merry, U. (1986). *Organizational transformation: Approaches, strategies, theories.* New York: Praeger.

Levy, S. (2003). Six factors to consider when planning online distance learning programs in higher education. *Online Journal of Distance Learning Administration, 6*(1). Retrieved March 12, 2007, from http://www.westga.edu/~distance/ojdla/search_results_id.php?id=185

Lincoln, Y. V., & Guba, E. G. (1985). *Naturalistic inquiry.* Beverly Hills, CA: SAGE.

McDonald, J. (2002). Is "as good as face-to-face" as good as it gets? *Journal of Asynchronous Learning Networks, 6*(2), 10-23. Retrieved March 30, 2008, from http://www.sloan-c.org/publications/jaln/v6n2/v6n2_macdonald.asp

Merriam, S. B. (1998). *Qualitative research and case study applications in education* (2nd ed.). San Francisco: Jossey-Bass.

Meyer, K. (2002). *Quality in distance education: Focus on online learning* (ASHE-ERIC Higher Education Report, Vol. 29, No. 4). San Francisco: Wiley.

Moore, M. G., & Kearsley, G. (2005). *Distance education: A systems view* (2nd ed.). Belmont, CA: Thomson/Wadsworth.

Morgan, G. (1997). *Images of organization* (2nd ed.). Thousand Oaks, CA: SAGE.

Mupinga, D. M., & Maughan, G. R. (2008). Web-based instruction and community college faculty workload. *College Teaching, 56*(1), 17-21.

Palloff, R. M., & Pratt, K. (2004). *Collaborating online: Learning together in community.* San Francisco: Jossey-Bass.

Palloff, R. M., & Pratt, K. (2007). *Building online learning communities: Effective strategies for the virtual classroom* (2nd ed.).San Francisco: Jossey-Bass.

Patton, M. Q. (1990). *Qualitative evaluation methods.* Beverly Hills, CA: SAGE.

Peterson, M. W., & Spencer, M. G. (1993). Qualitative and quantitative approaches to academic culture: Do they tell us the same thing? In J. C. Smart (Ed.), *Higher education handbook of theory and research* (Vol. 9, pp. 344-388). New York: Agathon Press.

Russell, T. L. (1999). *The no significant difference phenomenon.* Raleigh: North Carolina State University.

Schein, E. H. (2004). *Organizational culture and leadership* (3rd ed.). San Francisco: Jossey-Bass.

Sener, J. (2004). Escaping the comparison trap: Evaluating online learning on its own terms. *Innovate, 1*(2). Retrieved January 17, 2008, from http://innovateonline.info/index.php?view=article&id=11&action=article

Tomei, L. A. (2004). The impact of online teaching on faculty load: Computing the ideal class size for online courses. *International Journal of Instructional Technology & Distance Learning.* Retrieved May 4, 2008, from http://www.itdl.org/journal/Jan_04/article04.htm

Whitt, E. J. (2001). Document analysis. In C. F. Clifton, J. G. Haworth, & L. R. Lattuca (Eds.), *Expanding perspectives: Qualitative research in higher education* (2nd ed., pp. 447-454). Boston: Pearson Custom.

Yin, R. K. (2003). *Case study research: Design and methods* (3rd ed.). Thousand Oaks, CA: SAGE.

Regina L. Garza Mitchell is an assistant professor at Central Michigan University, Mount Pleasant, MI.

For reprints and permission queries, please visit SAGE's Web site at http://www.sagepub.com/journalsPermissions.nav.

CHAPTER 52

DELICATE ENGAGEMENT: THE LIVED EXPERIENCE OF COMMUNITY COLLEGE STUDENTS ENROLLED IN HIGH-RISK ONLINE COURSES

CYNTHIA S. BAMBARA, CLIFFORD P. HARBOUR, TIMOTHY GRAY DAVIES AND SUSAN ATHEY

This article reports the findings of a phenomenological study that examined the lived experience of community college students enrolled in high-risk online courses (HRCs) at a community college in the American Southeast. HRCs were defined as college courses with withdrawal or failure rates of 30% or more. In-depth interviews were conducted with 13 students enrolled in four different HRCs. Isolation, academic challenge, ownership, and acquiescence emerged as structural themes that framed the experience of participants. These structural themes intermingled in discrete ways that led to the survival or surrender of these HRC participants and formed the essence of the phenomenon that is referred to as delicate engagement, which speaks to the vulnerable threads of academic and social involvement that permeated the HRC student experience.

Keywords: online courses, student success, phenomenology

Nationwide, the number of students enrolled in online courses has grown at a rapid rate. Student enrollment from the fall of 2004 to the fall of 2005 increased from 2.3 million to nearly 3.2 million (Allen & Seaman, 2006). The 2005 online enrollment represented 17% of all higher education students. Allen and Seaman (2006) found that 96% of all higher education public institutions provided opportunities for online learners. Associate's degree-granting institutions, such as community colleges, enrolled more than half of all online learners.

Online courses provide many community college students with new opportunities to participate in postsecondary education (Cox, 2005; Dalziel, 2003; Kozeracki, 1999; Young, 2008). Online courses are especially attractive to many community college students because work and family obligations limit attendance in traditional synchronous, on-campus classes. Some students enroll in online courses to expand their schedule of classes or limit the cost of commuting. Health care workers, fire fighters, and police officers find online learning compatible with their dynamic shift schedules. In addition, parents of small children can reduce child care expenditures by taking online classes.

As online learning options expand, however, these new opportunities are accompanied by higher attrition rates (Berge & Mrozowski, 2001; Carr, 2000). Carr's (2000) inquiry into online learning at several community colleges indicated that student attrition increases when the instructor and the student are in different locations. Studies of online student attrition and persistence conducted at individual community colleges confirm Carr's findings, reporting dropout rates that are 15% to 50% higher in online classes than in the same synchronous face-to-face options (Crabtree, 2000; Kennedy, 2001; Pedone, 2003; York, 2003). As community colleges continue to expand opportunities for students through online learning, it is essential to understand why large numbers of these students withdraw or fail these courses.

This article reports on a qualitative study that used the phenomenological method to examine the lived experiences of students enrolled in challenging online courses at a community college in the American Southeast. Our main objective was to determine if participants in such online courses shared a common experience that superseded their individual successes or failures. We discuss our study in the following manner. First, we briefly review the relevant literature on community college online learners. Second, we explain our research method, phenomenology, and discuss data collection and analysis procedures. Third, we present and interpret our findings in a section that outlines four structural themes that describe the experiences reported by our student participants. We then describe and explain the essence of the phenomenon that we refer to as a "delicate engagement". Finally, we close with a summary and recommendations for practice and research.

Literature Review

The literature regarding distance education at the community college has confirmed its rapid growth. Kozeracki's (1999) research provided a baseline for examining the early development of distance education at community colleges. Kozeracki based her work on several sources, including statistical data from United States Department of Education reports and documentary data collected from community college course listings, catalogs, and enrollment reports. She found that in the late 1990s only a small portion of the curriculum was offered via distance technologies. However, she reported that between 58% and 79% of the institutions surveyed in two national studies offered at least some courses via distance technology. More recently, Cox (2005) examined the adoption of online education at 15 community colleges in six states. Cox's work, based primarily on documentary and interview data, found that the institutions' adoption of online courses was driven to a large extent by myths regarding the utility of online courses as a means of satisfying student interests and demands, the need to adopt online education to survive greater competition in the higher education marketplace, and the notion that online education was enhancing students' technological literacy. Cox maintained that these myths were not supported by empirical data and instead reflected context-specific institutional forces and interests. These two studies (Cox, 2005; Kozeracki, 1999) showed how researchers are attempting to describe and understand the development of this important innovation in the community college curriculum.

Since Kozeracki's (1999) study, the literature has focused more specifically on various aspects of community college online courses and on the students enrolled in them. Dissertation research has reported on student performance (Bangurah, 2004; Crabtree, 2000), the experience of student learning (Harbeck, 2001; Pedone, 2003; Schilke, 2001), student satisfaction (Aljarrah, 2000; Reed, 2001), and student retention (York, 2003). Research concerning student performance in online courses at 4-year colleges and universities is progressing along similar lines (e.g., Dupin-Bryant, 2004; Morris, Wu, & Finnegan, 2005; Schreck, 2003). For example, Schreck (2003) reported on efforts made by one university's faculty and staff to retain students in online courses. Morris et al. (2005) described their work to identify student record variables that came closest to predicting retention in one university's general education online courses. Researchers in both community college and university settings are still seeking to identify and then understand the variables most likely to predict retention (e.g., Dupin-Bryant, 2004; Morris et al., 2005) and the complex life experiences of students enrolled in online courses (e.g., Harbeck, 2001; Pedone, 2003; Schilke, 2001). Our specific interest was in understanding the life experiences of community college students enrolled in high-risk online courses (HRCs), that is, courses in which 30% or more of the students withdraw from the course or earn final course grades of D or F (Pascarella & Terenzini, 2005). An extensive review of the literature revealed no research on this topic

Method

We selected phenomenology as our qualitative method for research. This approach allowed for an in-depth inquiry of participants sharing a common experience (Moustakas, 1994). Phenomenology also afforded us an opportunity to examine the interrelated dimensions of the human experience and address our universal research question: What is the lived experience of community college students enrolled in HRCs?

The community college selected for our study published a distance learning research report providing an analysis of enrollment in all online courses offered in 2003-2004. The report compared 25 courses delivered online and on campus. Following Pascarella and Terenzini's (2005) definition of an HRC, we identified 13 online courses in which 30% or more of the students withdrew or earned final course grades of D or F. From the list of HRCs, we selected the four courses with the highest rates (40%-76%) of withdrawal or final course grades of D or F. The HRCs selected for this study were the following: principles of accounting I, precalculus, statistics, and basic computer skills.

All students enrolled in these four HRCs from the spring of 2005 through the summer of 2006 were sent an e-mail invitation to participate in the study. All participants were required to be enrolled in a program leading to a degree or certificate at the college. Thirteen students who met this criterion volunteered to participate in our study. Our primary researcher collected data through private, face-to-face, in-depth interviews to gain a rich understanding of their experiences (Fontana & Frey, 2000). Interviews lasted 60 to 90 minutes each. A standard but flexible protocol with broad discussion topics was used to guide the interviews (Moustakas, 1994). Questions asked participants to describe their experiences as community college students enrolled in an HRC, what the experiences meant for them, how the experiences affected them, and what opportunities and obstacles were encountered in the HRC. E-mail and brief telephone conversations were used for follow-up conversations with participants to clarify and check data for accuracy.

Of the 13 community college students who participated, three had experience in two HRCs. This allowed us to collect data from sixteen course experiences. Eight participants were women and five were men. Participants ranged in age from the early 20s to the early 60s. Eight participants completed their HRCs and two of the eight completed two different HRCs. This allowed for a total of 10 completed HRC experiences. Five participants withdrew from or failed their HRCs. The participants' experiences included both completion and withdrawal or failure in principles of accounting I, statistics, and basic computer skills. One experience in precalculus was reported; in this instance, the participant withdrew from the course.

The interview transcriptions and follow-up e-mail messages were used to create typed, electronic data sets for all 13 participants. Pseudonyms were assigned to each participant, assuring confidentiality. Moustakas's four major processes were used to analyze and interpret data: epoche, phenomenological reduction, imaginative variation, and synthesis of composite textural and structural descriptions. As we followed these processes, we developed a procedure to organize, analyze, and synthesize the individual portions of our data. Adaptation of Moustakas's method allowed us to articulate our participants' collective voices and the essence of the phenomenon that emerged in those voices.

Findings and Interpretation

Participants' voices (presented here through pseudonyms) combined to form four structured themes that defined the participants' lived experiences in their HRCs. These were isolation, academic challenge, ownership, and acquiescence. All participants experienced isolation and academic challenge in some way and to some degree. Where they differed, however, was in how they responded to these experiences. Data analysis revealed that some responded through ownership. Others responded through acquiescence.

Isolation

The structural theme of isolation describes the loneliness participants felt as they experienced their HRCs. Data analysis confirmed that four dimensions of the students' HRC experience contributed to their sense of isolation: the surreal HRC classroom, the lack of student-instructor interaction, the void in student-to-student connections, and the possibility of a different experience.

The Surreal HRC Classroom. Participants' voices portrayed the HRC classroom as a surreal and intangible place. They articulated the difficulty of interpreting an abstract concept in a virtual world and then attempting to apply it in their real world. To make the classroom feel real, they needed to connect the virtual world to their real world through an inanimate object, a computer, and intangible technology. As they logged into their course management system, their connection to this virtual world occurred through downloading course documents, interacting with other students on the class discussion board, interacting with their instructors through the courseware e-mail, and dropping assignments into a digital drop box. Many participants knew the virtual classroom could be a lively, dynamic place, but it was not so in these HRCs. On the contrary, these virtual classrooms were static. Participants reported that the discussion board was used minimally with no meaningful student or instructor interaction. Responses from instructors to e-mails or discussion board postings were often cryptic and incomplete. Without a requirement to interact with other students or the instructor, many participants downloaded the course documents and essentially took the class offline. Alyson and Carly both said, "It's not the same as being in a regular class, you don't have a teacher." Sandy described the isolation she felt by saying, "I thought that it was a lot of teaching myself . . . I was by myself a lot. I remember feeling left out." Samantha added, "I don't feel like HRC is a real class." Tom echoed, "What class? What professor? What assignments? . . . The online courses seem almost surreal." The experience of isolation tempted HRC participants to believe there was no class at all.

The Lack of Student–Instructor Interaction. Struggling to find life within their classrooms, participants reached out to establish a relationship with others. Unlike traditional campus classes where, as Keith said, "there are other people around you to talk to, [where] you can figure out what is going on," HRC participants did not see anyone, and they did not have a sense that anyone was present. David explained, "I don't feel like there was an instructor presence . . . I don't feel like there was anything that I was learning from the instructor. The instructor was simply there as a Web administrator or as a grader." When our participants tried to contact their instructors, some received very limited and unhelpful replies. Geraldine explained that whenever anyone would ask a question, the instructor would respond monosyllabically: "It was so 'yes, no.' . . . It was a two word answer . . . you sort of felt slapped." In some cases participants received no reply at all. In many instances, the only feedback they received on class assignments was a score in the electronic course grade book. Participants reported that the interaction between the instructors and participants decreased as the semester progressed, leaving the students with a greater sense of isolation. Keith said:

> It is kind of like leaving home for the first time and Mom and Dad aren't going to help you . . . you learn it on your own . . . you figure it out . . . you are on your own. And that is how I felt . . . Good luck!

The Void in Student-to-Student Connections. Participants explained that they had little or no contact with other students in their HRC classrooms. There was no chance to hear the perspectives of others, no opportunity to learn from each other. Geraldine summarized the importance of student-to-student connections, "I think the interaction among students is everything!" David echoed the value of student-to-student connections and said, "Not only are you learning from yourself, from the manual, from the instructor, but you are also learning from the other people in the class." What our participants found was aptly described by Samantha as follows: "No interaction between the students, student interaction is nonexistent! I know nothing about these people!" They had no sense of community within the HRCs, no peer interaction. Geraldine remarked, "I was just sort of on this island, all by myself." David echoed her sentiments when he said, "I felt like, specifically in that [HRC] class, I was alone and adrift." For some participants, the need to have a student community was in David's words "ultimate", and for others like Julie "a huge obstacle to try to overcome." The void in student-to-student interaction intensified the sense of isolation felt by our participants.

The Possibility of a Different Experience. Through their experiences in other online classes, many participants realized virtual classrooms could be vibrant, interactive, and filled with life. Participants knew there were ways to reduce the feelings of isolation that ran rampant throughout the HRCs. The remedy for their isolation was human interaction. Participants saw the instructor–student interaction and student-to-student connections as the conduit to reduce the isolation and bring life to their virtual classrooms. When they did not find the human element within their HRCs, their feelings of isolation became an important aspect of their experience.

Academic Challenge

Academic challenge articulates the sometimes overwhelming feelings participants faced as challenges were posed by course content and delivery. For many participants, expectations for their HRCs were not realized. In most cases, they believed the academic content would be easy to understand. Instead, they often found course material unfamiliar, complex, and nonintuitive. In addition, participants reported that the content of the HRCs was cumulative. To progress, participants often needed to grasp and understand the content in sequential order. The way HRCs were organized affected the learning experience of participants. In addition, technology hurdles surfaced for many participants throughout their HRC experience. The nature and extent of the problems varied. Academic challenge emerged as a structural theme defined by four areas in participants' experience: unrealistic expectations, academic content, course organization, and technology frustrations.

Unrealistic Expectations. The participants' unrealistic expectations framed their experience of academic challenge within the HRCs. Many participants believed it would be easy to understand course content and navigate the online environment. For example, Alyson was very direct about her unrealistic expectations: "Honestly, I didn't know how difficult it was going to be." David made a similar observation when he said, "I didn't know that the HRC was going to be so tough for me . . . I didn't have a clue . . . I didn't really know what I was getting into." Participants entered the HRCs thinking, as Julie did, that the course "would be a breeze." Instead they found that the classes were far more complex and difficult than they had expected.

Academic Content. Participants were challenged by the academic content of their HRCs, and this was evident in four respects. They struggled with new terminology, nonintuitive content, sequential content, and in some cases, a disdain for the course. As Helen expressed, "It is hard . . . when you don't understand what the words mean. So, that was a big problem for me." Without a background in the subject matter or a context in which to ground new information, some participants struggled to understand course content. The absolute, nonintuitive content also was difficult for some participants to master. Tom described this aspect of academic challenge when he said the following:

> With the HRC course . . . there is only one way to do it. There is a right or a wrong way . . . when you are taking an online course, it is very difficult to determine what [that] is.

The cumulative nature of the course content was problematic when participants did not focus on thoroughly learning the material in sequence. They were unable to complete advanced material when they did not master foundational content. Sandy, who completed two HRCs, said, "If I hadn't done well at the beginning, I know I definitely would not have been able to grasp the end." Finally, several participants entered their HRCs with a distinct disdain for the subject matter. Carly commented, "HRC and me do not get along." Keith echoed, "HRC and me, we just don't play nice together." Helen was anticipating the challenge of her HRC and said, "I think that is why I have avoided it." She was clear about why she saved her HRC for last: "The HRC was the hard course . . . it is my least favorite. Anything dealing with HRC . . . I avoid the things I don't know, and what I am afraid of. I just hate HRC." The sentiments from Carly, Keith, and Helen expressed the discordant attitudes of some participants toward their HRC. The lack of interest in the content presented a barrier to their learning.

Course Organization. For some participants, the organization of the HRCs also adversely affected their learning experiences. In some cases, HRCs that were condensed into a shortened summer-semester format advanced at a rapid pace. The condensed summer semester was especially challenging for some and simply beyond the capability of others. As David pointed out, "Do you realize you are taking a 16-week class inside of 10 weeks, and you are taking it online? Do you know what kind of time that is going to be?" The sequence of course content presented additional obstacles. Even during semester-long courses, participants were challenged to maintain interest in the subject matter when practical applications were delayed until the later portion of the course. Participants described some HRCs as beginning with a great deal of theory and little practical application. They had difficulty maintaining interest in the course when they were unable to connect the material to meaningful applications. The lack of clarity of course assignments was also noted by participants. Inaccurate directions, confusing assignments, and misinformation within some of the HRCs further complicated an already ambiguous virtual environment, adding to the academic challenge of the courses.

Technology Frustrations. Our participants told us that a myriad of technology hurdles surfaced throughout their HRC experience. Some related to academic assignments and others to more general issues concerning software and hardware. A challenge for some was simply navigating the course management system. Participants were especially vulnerable when technology issues occurred in the beginning of the semester. Technology concerns left them feeling anxious, and this threatened their ability to keep pace with the course. These difficulties caused frustration among participants, adding to the other areas of academic challenge that they were experiencing.

The academic challenge experienced by participants as they attempted to learn the academic content left them surprised by their unrealistic ideas of what to expect in the course. They were overwhelmed by the difficulty of the content, inundated and confused by aspects of the course organization, and frustrated by technology challenges.

Ownership

On the other hand, ownership explains how some participants prized their HRCs and how they embraced the demands of the course. Although the experience of ownership was not always associated with success, it usually was, and it was less common with those students who failed or withdrew from their HRCs. Participants demonstrated their HRC ownership in two ways: a positive stance toward the HRC and the investment made in the class. The positive stance of participants was reflected as they described their motivation, commitment, independence, self-direction, and resourcefulness. Participants invested in their HRCs through preparation and a commitment of their time, effort, focus, and organizational skills. Participants' personal stances toward their HRC, combined with their investment in the course, enabled them to prize and own their experience.

A Positive Stance toward the HRC. Participants illustrated their positive stance by explaining how their motivation, commitment, independence, self-direction, and resourcefulness enabled them to survive and in some cases thrive in their HRCs. As Kay said, "It takes a lot of motivation to take time away from your kids after not seeing them all day." Keith described his commitment to his HRC in his statement, "I started it and I had to finish it." The independence described through several voices propelled the self-direction and resourcefulness of HRC participants. Samantha articulated independence when she said, "I am independent by nature anyway, so it's not a huge thing for someone to say, here is the book, you need to learn this." Although some participants perceived working alone as a debilitating feature of the HRC (as mentioned above in the discussion of the structure of isolation), others like Samantha were also motivated by this independence.

Our participants also articulated the need to be self-directed learners within their HRCs. To complete the HRCs, they needed to teach themselves. Tim described his learning experience as "having to piece it all together myself." He went on to say, "It was basically something that was all going on with me." Sandy added that her instructor was not "linking the material very well. I remember things if I write them down. So, every chapter I would outline and then go through all of the problems. I thought that it was a lot of teaching myself." Alyson described a similar perspective and observed the following:

> I like being self-driven . . . I like to work on my own instead of having someone stand over me and tell me OK, this is what you are doing. I just like for them to say, OK, this is what you need to do, and leave me alone.

Resourcefulness also emerged as a personal quality that contributed to the positive stance of participants within their HRC experience. Geraldine shared, "one thing I learned by taking an HRC was, really, what you need to learn, if you are patient enough, you can usually find your answers on your own." We found that those who were resourceful in finding the help they needed to solve problems independently were able to progress in the course. Participants equipped with a positive stance toward their HRCs—a stance marked by motivation, commitment, independence, self-direction, and resourcefulness—completed their courses. Those without such personal qualities did not.

The Investment Made in the Class. Personal investment, the second dimension of ownership, describes how participants allocated the resources required to meet the demands of their HRCs. Many participants were surprised by the time and effort required to complete their courses. They described how they invested the extra time, extra effort, and total focus required by the HRCs. Most participants were experienced students. They were well aware that a certain amount of time, effort, and sacrifice was required to complete any class. Some participants had online class experience, and they knew this environment often required extra resources. What came as a surprise to many, however, was that the HRCs required even more time and effort than they anticipated. With lives already filled with commitments, they had to make adjustments and reallocate personal resources to their HRCs. Tim described this part of his experience when he said, "I think it was just that this needed extra effort. And I couldn't even allow myself to be distracted. I just needed to attack this for a long period of time." Alyson shared a similar observation when she stated the following:

> An online course as difficult as my HRC would take twice as much time as it would in a campus setting . . . because you spend more time trying to teach yourself how to do the certain problems . . . once I understood that, I knew that I had to spend more time.

Participants also described how their approach to preparing, organizing, and managing their resources contributed to their HRC experience. They found that their HRCs required more time and effort than they planned to invest. To comprehend the material, participants had to "work it and work it and work it" as Alyson described and as Keith said, "repeat things, and repeat things, and repeat things." Kay articulated how she invested her time and effort,

> When I actually . . . started reading the book, you couldn't just read it like it was a book. You had to really read it and do the exercises . . . and think about it critically as you are going through the whole chapter.

The investment of extra time, effort, and focus was required to excel in the HRC experience. Participants who were able to demonstrate ownership through their personal stance and their investment in their HRC advanced in their course and completed it with a positive outcome. For some, completing the HRC meant more than added credits to their transcript. They were empowered by the experience to realize their goals and change their lives.

Acquiescence

Acquiescence emerged as a structure that described the subtle ways participants submitted to their HRC and slowly surrendered to their experience. The experience of acquiescence was not always associated with a student's failure or withdrawal in the HRC, but this was usually the case. Acquiescence was seen in three ways: silent submission, compromise, and loss.

Silent Submission. Silent submission was experienced and represented through the quiet self-acknowledgement of lost motivation, a sense of diminishing returns, lackluster commitment, and a realization that there was no going back to a time without the HRC experience. For example, David voiced how he lost motivation and commitment for the course when he said, "I honestly believe it was a much harder challenge for me to do the HRC. I found the time that I was putting into it was less enjoyable. Yes, that certainly has an effect on my motivation." Similarly, Julie stated, "Motivation is a very big issue for me. I did not have the motivation." Some were not able to adjust to the independence and self-direction required to complete their HRC courses. Julie also offered,

> Learning from other students as well as from what the instructor is providing for you, and the textbook. To me, that is a huge learning thing . . . and a huge obstacle to try to overcome . . . with not having contact with other students.

The retreat to acquiescence was imminent when participants' investment in their HRC did not reap tangible rewards. This led to erosion in personal commitment to the HRC and a sense that the effort invested was not producing the desired returns. David explained this aspect of his experience when he said "It was just taking me a lot of time. That was a growing source of frustration for me because I knew the more time that I was putting into HRC, the worse my grade was getting . . . the more important that time was to me to be able to put into other [classes] where I was strong."

When participants realized that their effort was not rewarded with satisfactory learning and good grades, they began to see the experience as a losing proposition and pulled back in their effort and commitment. Whether evidenced by a lack of motivation, a sense of diminishing returns, or lackluster commitment, students recognized that the HRC was not what they bargained for and they responded by silently submitting to the requirements of the course and their experience.

Compromise. Compromise represents an element of acquiescence experienced by those participants who completed their HRCs but who made concessions to survive the experience, if not the course. They settled for an undesirable experience as the cost of completing a requirement or earning credit. Keith shared, "I know I like college. I like to learn. I like the classroom. I did not have a positive experience. I could tell you, yea, I learned this, I learned that. But it wasn't what I like." Geraldine, disappointed by the lack of interaction in her HRC, summed up her experience: "That is the price that you pay for the convenience of not having to go to school." Scott's focus on earning his degree propelled him to complete his HRC despite his disappointment in the course. He was disappointed in the lack of interaction in the class and the way in which the content was presented. He described this experience as "kind of lame." He went on to say "maybe it was because I had five or six other classes. And I have way more interest in other subjects than learning HRC." Scott compromised his standards by pursuing a class that he felt was uninspiring because he needed the course to complete his degree. The HRC was a convenient way for him to complete a degree requirement.

Loss. Although the encounter with acquiescence was brief for these participants, their concessions were lasting. The silent submissions and subtle compromises left some participants with a sense of loss that they expressed through feelings of defeat, shame, and resentment. As Carly described, "I got myself in deeper, where I couldn't catch up." As the withdrawal date approached, she realized it was beyond her to succeed and finish. Participants shared their shame and how withdrawal from the HRCs, in Julie's words, was "devastating." The challenges they experienced left them feeling humiliated and embarrassed.

Julie voiced feelings echoed by several other participants when she said, "I was embarrassed . . . when I withdrew from the HRC, I was really ashamed." David was painfully aware of his loss and said, "I knew that I had paid for it, I knew I didn't have the money to pay for it, and I didn't want to face the failure of, oh yeah, you wimped out, you washed out." Resentment also emerged in participant voices when the promise of access presented by the HRC was not fulfilled. Participants enrolled in their HRCs with high hopes of making progress toward their educational goals through these online opportunities. But, some lost hope when they had to withdraw. Julie stated that at the beginning of the semester, "I was excited to see [the HRC] there. Once I had taken it, I was like, why do they offer that online?" When she withdrew from her HRC, her hopes of completing her degree online were shattered. David voiced his resentment about the advice he received to take the HRC online. He said, "I spoke to three different counselors for different things, and they all saw what I was taking and none of them were like, so let's talk it out, you know, what have you got going on? . . . What are you thinking?"

He added, "I feel resentful in that [the college] is just saying, give me your money!" Some of the HRC participants escaped acquiescence through their resolve. Some participants realized they needed to accept the concessions they made as the price for the convenience of their HRCs. A few learned that they needed to make adjustments to complete other HRCs in the future. Others realized that they were not suited for online learning and indicated that in the future, they would only enroll in campus classes.

Delicate Engagement

The four structural themes of isolation, academic challenge, ownership, and acquiescence framed the HRC student experience. These structures interplayed in positive and negative ways that led participants to survive or surrender to the HRC experience. We characterized survivors as either empowered or compromised. Empowered survivors successfully completed their HRCs. They persevered through the experience of isolation and academic challenge and responded by successfully taking ownership of the courses. Compromised survivors also successfully completed the HRCs but did not respond positively to the isolation. Although they took some degree of ownership of the HRC, their experience also was characterized by acquiescence.

We characterized surrenderers as either reluctant or misplaced. Surrenderers did not complete their HRCs successfully. Reluctant surrenderers responded positively to their experience of isolation but were unable to meet the academic challenge posed by the HRC. They did not exhibit ownership and ultimately demonstrated their acquiescence to the experience of the HRC. Misplaced surrenderers responded negatively to both isolation and academic challenge and, in the end, only exhibited acquiescence, therefore leading us to conclude that of all four groups, these were the students who never should have enrolled in the HRC. They were truly misplaced. Table 1 illustrates the ways in which participants responded to the four structures of the phenomenon under study.

The subtle ways the structures of isolation, academic challenge, ownership, and acquiescence intermingled formed a delicate engagement, the essence of their HRC experience. Delicate engagement speaks to the strength and resilience of participants who brought ownership to their experience and embraced the isolation and academic challenge of the HRCs. Delicate engagement also

Table 1
Delicate Engagement

	Survivors		Surrenderers	
Structure	Empowered Survivors	Compromised Survivors	Reluctant Surrenderers	Misplaced Surrenderers
Responded positively to isolation	Yes	No	Yes	No
Responded positively to academic challenge	Yes	Yes	No	No
Exhibited ownership	Yes	Yes	No	No
Exhibited acquiescence	No	Yes	Yes	Yes

describes the fragility and vulnerability of those who retreated to acquiescence, unable to overcome the isolation and academic challenge of the HRCs, and ultimately surrendered to their HRC experience. In addition, delicate engagement also describes the vulnerable threads of academic and social connection that permeated the experience of HRC participants. It represents how only some were able to persevere with a lack of contact with others. For many, this void adversely affected the quality and satisfaction of their learning experience. Our participants valued interaction with fellow students and with their instructors, and without such meaningful associations, many participants expressed dissatisfaction. Connection to the HRCs was fragile, and for some the engagement was too delicate to retain their involvement.

Summary of Findings and Recommendations

Online learning is rapidly expanding in community colleges. It is also a relatively new form of distance education delivery, and relatively little is known about the community college student experience in online courses. The literature reports high rates of student withdrawal and failure in community college online courses. This study focused on how one group of community college online students experienced their HRCs. To be sure, this research cannot be generalized to a larger population of community college students. But, of course, this was not our objective in conducting a phenomenological inquiry. Instead we sought to understand if in-depth interviews with a small group of students might help illuminate an overarching experience that was shared by those who were and were not successful in completing an online HRC. Our findings indicate that for these students at one community college, a shared experience did reflect a discernable phenomenon. Insights gained from the study allowed us to offer recommendations for practice and future research.

Recommendations for Practice

In our study, we examined the experience of HRC students who completed their courses and those who did not. By looking at both groups of students, we were able to gain a holistic understanding of this shared experience for both completers and noncompleters. This was an essential feature of our study. The following are recommendations for practice and are intended to aid all students who might enroll in HRCs, that is, those who are well prepared and those who are not:

1. Identify HRCs and develop targeted retention programs for students enrolled in them.
2. Provide prospective students with orientation sessions that alert them to the course expectations and the personal investment of time, effort, and focus required to complete the HRC.
3. Examine institutional policies and practices to ensure student services and academic support programs are prepared for a range of students enrolled in HRCs.
4. Provide mentoring for HRC instructors and require participation in professional development that promotes best practices in instructional design and delivery of online courses.

The recommendations above are only some of the ways online opportunities for community college students can be maximized and obstacles minimized. Continued assessment of courses and services can provide community college administrators and faculty members additional strategies to enhance the student experience.

Recommendations for Future Research

The findings of our study demonstrated a need for additional research and we suggest inquiry along the following lines:

1. There is a need for research examining how community colleges can mitigate the isolation experienced in HRCs while also enhancing student ownership.

2. There is a need for research examining online teaching strategies along with associated high and low completion rates in HRCs. Such studies could identify both effective and ineffective teaching strategies.

3. There is a need for research examining how student advising, learning communities, and other student learning and support strategies affect retention and positive completion in HRCs.

4. There remains a need for research examining the relationship between enrollment in HRCs and degree completion and successful transfer.

Conclusion

In this research we provided a forum for participants to share their perspectives of what worked for them in their HRCs and a chance for them to voice their ideas on what can be improved in HRCs. Their willingness to share their experiences provides a valuable contribution to the future of community college online learning. The importance of these student experiences was heard through their voices as they shared why they enrolled. For some, the HRCs and other online classes were their only access to higher education. For others, these classes afforded the chance to better manage their many obligations and responsibilities. The insights gained through the voices of HRC participants offer all of us an opportunity to identify ways that might improve the quality of the online learning experience for future community college students.

References

Aljarrah, A. A. (2000). *Distance education: Community college student perspectives and attitudes toward online course.* Unpublished doctoral dissertation, Colorado State University, Fort Collins.

Allen, I. E., & Seaman, J. (2006, November). *Making the grade: Online education in the United States, 2006.* Needham, MA: The Sloan Consortium. Retrieved May 29, 2007, from http://www.sloan-c.org.

Bangurah, F. M. (2004). *A study of completion and passing rates between traditional and web-based instruction at a two-year community college in northeast Tennessee.* Unpublished doctoral dissertation, East Tennessee State University, Johnson City.

Berge, Z. L., & Mrozowski, S. (2001). Review of research in distance education, 1990 to 1999. *American Journal of Distance Education, 15*(3), 5-19.

Carr, S. (2000, February 11). As distance education comes of age, the challenge is keeping the students. *The Chronicle of Higher Education.* Retrieved March 11, 2002, from http:// chronicle.com/weekly/v46/ i23/23a00101.htm

Cox, R. D. (2005). Online education as institutional myth: Rituals and realities at community colleges. *Teachers College Record, 107,* 1754-1787.

Crabtree, L. F. (2000). *A comparison of community college student performance, retention, and demographics in online and onground courses.* Unpublished doctoral dissertation, University of Missouri, Columbia.

Dalziel, C. (2003). Community colleges and distance education. In M. G. Moore & W. G. Anderson (Eds.), *Handbook of distance education* (pp. 663-671). Mahwah, NJ: Lawrence Erlbaum.

Dupin-Bryant, P. A. (2004). Pre-entry variables related to retention in online distance education. *American Journal of Distance Education, 18,* 199-206.

Fontana, A., & Frey, J. H. (2000). The interview: From structured questions to negotiated text. In N. K. Denzin & Y. S. Lincoln (Eds.), *Handbook of qualitative research* (2nd ed., pp. 645-672). Thousand Oaks, CA: Sage.

Harbeck, J. D. (2001). *Community college students taking on-line courses: The student point of view.* Unpublished doctoral dissertation, Virginia Polytechnic Institute and State University, Blacksburg.

Kennedy, C. M. (2001). *The experiences of online learning at a community college in South Texas: A case study.* Unpublished doctoral dissertation, Texas A & M University, College Station.

Kozeracki, C. (1999). Scratching the surface: Distance education in the community colleges. In G. Schuyler (Ed.), *Trends in community college curriculum* (New Directions for Community Colleges, No. 99, pp. 89-99). San Francisco: Jossey-Bass.

Morris, L. V., Wu, S., & Finnegan, C. L. (2005). Predicting retention in online general education courses. *American Journal of Distance Education, 19,* 23-36.

Moustakas, C. (1994). *Phenomenological research.* Thousand Oaks, CA: Sage.

Pascarella, E. T., & Terenzini, P. T. (2005). *How college affects students: Vol. 2. A third decade of research.* San Francisco: Jossey-Bass.

Pedone, M. D. (2003). *A qualitative analysis of student learning experiences in online community college undergraduate education courses.* Unpublished doctoral dissertation, University of Central Florida, Orlando.

Reed, T. E. (2001). *Relationship between learning style, internet success, and internet satisfaction of students taking online courses at a selected community college.* Unpublished doctoral dissertation, Northern Illinois University, DeKalb.

Schilke, R. A. (2001). *A case study of attrition in web-based instruction for adults: Updating Garland's model of barriers to persistence in distance education.* Unpublished doctoral dissertation, Northern Illinois University, DeKalb.

Schreck, V. (2003). *Successful online course retention at Marylhurst University: Constructing a model for online course retention using grounded theory.* Unpublished doctoral dissertation. Portland State University, Oregon.

York, D. L. (2003). *Falling through the net: Implications of inherent characteristics in student retention and performance at a community college.* Unpublished doctoral dissertation, University of Missouri, Columbia.

Young, J. R. (2008, July 8). Gas prices drive students to online courses. *The Chronicle of Higher Education.* Retrieved July 8, 2008, from http://chronicle.com/free/2008/07/3704n.htm

Cynthia S. Bambara is vice president of student success at Lord Fairfax Community College, Middletown, VA.

Clifford P. Harbour is an associate professor in the Department of Adult Learning and Technology at the University of Wyoming.

Timothy Gray Davies is a professor in the School of Education at Colorado State University.

Susan Athey is an associate dean for undergraduate programs in the College of Business at Colorado State University.

Appendix A — List of Recommended Works

Compiled with assistance from Cheyenne Luzynski, Eastern Michigan University

Section I – Historical Foundations, Theoretical Perspectives, and Sociological Approaches

Alba, R. D., & Lavin, D. E. (1981). Community colleges and tracking in higher education. *Sociology of Education, 54*, 223–237.

Alexander, K., Bozick, R., & Entwisle, D. (2008). Warming up, cooling out, or holding steady? Persistence and change in educational expectations after high school. *Sociology of Education, 81*, 371–396.

Alfonso, M. (2006). The impact of community college attendance on baccalaureate attainment. *Research in Higher Education, 47*, 873–903.

Anderson, G. M., Alfonso, M., & Sun, J. C. (2006). Rethinking cooling out at public community colleges: An examination of fiscal and demographic trends in higher education and the rise of statewide articulation policies. *Teachers College Record, 108*, 422–451.

Bahr, P. R. (2008). *Cooling out* in the community college: What is the effect of academic advising on students' chances of success? *Research in Higher Education, 49*, 704–732.

Brand, J. E., Pfeffer, F. T., & Goldrick-Rab, S. (2012). *Interpreting community college effects in the presence of heterogeneity and complex counterfactuals*. Retrieved from http://wiscape.wisc.edu/Publications/Publication.aspx?ID=f067637b-c646-47c0-8361-c6e1aadf017e

Brint, S., & Karabel, J. (1989). *The diverted dream: Community colleges and the promise of educational opportunity in America, 1900-1985*, New York, NY: Oxford University Press.

Callan, P. M. (1997). Stewards of opportunity: America's public community colleges. *Daedalus The American Academic Profession, 126*(4), 95–112.

Chaves, C. (2006). Involvement, development, and retention: Theoretical foundations and potential extensions for adult community college students. *Community College Review, 34*, 139–152.

Cohen, A. M., & Brawer, F. B. (2008). *The American community college, 5th ed*. San Francisco, CA: Jossey-Bass.

Cohen, A. M., & Kisker, C.B., (2009*). The shaping of American higher education: Emergence and growth of the contemporary system, 2nd ed*. San Francisco, CA: Jossey-Bass.

Dougherty, K. J. (1987). The effects of community colleges: Aid or hindrance to socioeconomic attainment? *Sociology of Education, 60*, 86–103.

Dougherty, K. J. & Kienzl, G. S. (2006). It's not enough to get through the open door: Inequalities by social background in transfer from community colleges to four-year colleges. In A. M. Cohen, J. C. Palmer, & K. D. Zwemer (Eds.), *Key resources on community colleges: A guide to the field and its literature* (pp. 452–487). San Francisco, CA: Jossey-Bass.

Dougherty, K. J., & Townsend, B. K. (2006). Community college missions: A theoretical and historical perspective. *New Directions for Community Colleges, 136*, 5–13.

Eaton, J. S. (2006). Recreating America's community colleges: Implications of the substantive issues in their future. *Community College Journal of Research and Practice, 30*, 91–95.

Gilbert, C. K., & Heller, D. E. (2013). Access, equity, and community colleges: The Truman Commission and federal higher education policy from 1947 to 2011. *The Journal of Higher Education, 84*(3), 417–443.

Goffman, E. (1952). On cooling the mark out: Some aspects of adaptation to failure. *Psychiatry, 15*, 451–463.

Goldrick-Rab, S. (2010). Challenges and opportunities for improving community college student success. *Review of Educational Research, 80*(3), 437–469.

Karabel, J. (1972). Community colleges and social stratification. *Harvard Educational Review, 42*, 543–558.

Labaree, D. (1997). The rise of the community college. In D. Labaree (Ed.), *How to succeed in school without really trying* (pp. 190–223). New Haven, CT: Yale University Press.

Levin, J. S. (2000). The revised institution: The community college mission at the end of the 20th century. *Community College Review, 28*(2), 1–25.

Morest, V. S. (2013). From access to opportunity: The evolving social roles of community colleges. *The American Sociologist, 44*(4), 319–328.

Treat, T., & Barnard, T. C. (2012). Seeking legitimacy: The community college mission and the honors college. *Community College Journal of Research and Practice, 36*(9), 695–712.

Vaughn, G. (1995). *The community college story: A tale of innovation.* Washington, DC: The American Association of Community Colleges.

Wells, R. (2008). The effects of social and cultural capital on student persistence: Are community colleges more meritocratic? *Community College Review, 36*, 25–46.

Zamani-Gallaher, E.M., Bazile, S., & Stevenson, T.N. (2011). Segmentation, capital, and community college transfer students: Exploring community colleges as agents of currency. In R.D. Bartee (Ed.), *Contemporary perspectives on capital in educational contexts* (pp. 101–132). Charlotte, NC: Information Age Publishing.

Section II – Divergent Goals and Institutional Diversity Among Two-Year Institutions

Bahr, P. R. (2013). Classifying community colleges based on students' patterns of use. *Research in Higher Education, 54*(4), 433–460.

Bahr, P. R., Gross, J. L., Slay, K. E., & Christensen, R. D. (2013). First in line: Student registration priority in community colleges. *Educational Policy*, 0895904813492381.

Bailey, T. R., & Alfonso, M. (2005). Paths to persistence: An analysis of research on program effectiveness at community colleges. *Lumina Foundation for Education: New Agenda Series, 6*(1). Retrieved from http://www.achievingthedream.org/_images/_index03/CCRC_Report_Paths_to_Persistence.pdf

Bailey, T., Jenkins, D., & Leinbach, T. (2005). *Graduation rates, student goals, and measuring community college effectiveness* (CCRC Brief, No. 28). Retrieved from Community College Research Center, Teachers College, Columbia University website: http://ccrc.tc.columbia.edu/Publication.asp?UID=336

Bailey, T. R., & Morest, V. S. (2006). *Defending the community college equity agenda.* Baltimore, MD: John Hopkins University Press.

Calcagno, J., Crosta, P., Bailey, T., & Jenkins, D. (2007). Does age of entrance affect community college completion probabilities? Evidence from a discrete-time hazard model. *Educational Evaluation and Policy Analysis, 29*, 218–235.

Clotfelter, C. T., Ladd, H. F., Muschkin, C. G., & Vigdor, J. L. (2013). Success in community college: Do institutions differ? *Research in Higher Education, 54*(7), 805–824.

Cofer, J., & Somers, P. (2001). What influences student persistence at two-year colleges? *Community College Review, 29*, 56–76.

Conway, K. M. (2010). Educational aspirations in an urban community college: Differences between immigrant and native student groups. *Community College Review, 37*, 209–242.

Cox, R. D. (2009). "I would have rather paid for a class I wanted to take": Utilitarian approaches at a community college. *Review of Higher Education, 32*, 353–382.

Cox, R. D., & McCormick, A. C. (2003). Classification in practice: Applying five proposed classification models to a sample of two-year colleges. *New Directions for Community Colleges, 122*, 103–121.

Dougherty, K. J., & Townsend, B. K. (2006). Community college missions: A theoretical and historical perspective. *New Directions for Community Colleges, 136*, 5–13.

Dowd, A. C. (2007). Community colleges as gateways and gatekeepers: Moving beyond the access "saga" toward outcome equity. *Harvard Educational Review, 77*, 407–419.

Fike, D., & Fike, R. (2008). Predictors of first-year student retention in the community college. *Community College Review, 36*, 68–88.

Green, D. (2006). Historically underserved students: What we know, what we still need to know. *New Directions for Community Colleges, 135*, 21–28.

Grubb, N., Badway, N., & Bell, D. (2003). Community colleges and the equity agenda: The potential of noncredit education. *Annals of the American Academy of Political and Social Science, 586*, 218–240.

Grubb, N. W., & Lazerson, M. (2004). Dilemmas of the community college. In N. Grubb, & M. Lazerson (Eds.), *The education gospel: The economic power of schooling*, (pp. 84–106). Cambridge, MA: Harvard University Press.

Hagedorn, L., Maxwell, W., Cypers, S., Moon, H., & Lester, J. (2007). Course shopping in urban community colleges: An analysis of student drop and add activities. *Journal of Higher Education, 78*, 464–485.

Horn, L. (2009). *On track to complete? A taxonomy of beginning community college students and their outcomes 3 years after enrolling: 2003-04 through 2006.* (NCES 2009-152). Washington, DC: U.S. Department of Education. Retrieved from National Center for Education Statistics, Institute for Education Sciences website: http://nces.ed.gov/pubs2009/2009152.pdf

Jepsen, C., Troske, K., & Coomes, P. (2014). The labor-market returns to community college degrees, diplomas, and certificates. *Journal of Labor Economics, 32*(1), 95–121.

Kolesnikova, N. (2009). *Community colleges: A route of upward economic mobility.* Federal Reserve Bank of St. Louis. Retrieved from http://www.stlouisfed.org/community_development/assets/pdf/Community-Colleges.pdf

Leslie, D. W., & Grappa, J. M. (2002). Part-time faculty: Competent and committed. *New Directions for Community Colleges, 118*, 59–67.

Lovell, C.D., & Trouth, C. (2002). State governance patterns for community colleges. *New Directions for Community Colleges, 117*, 91–100.

Moeck, P. G., Hardy, D.E., & Katsinas, S.G. (2007). Residential living at rural community colleges. *New Directions for Community Colleges, 137*, 77–86.

National Governors Association. (2011). *Using community colleges to build a STEM-skilled workforce.* Issue Brief. Washington, DC: National Governors Association. Retrieved from NGA Center for Best Practices website: http://www.nga.org/cms/home/nga-center-for-best-practices/center-publications/page-edu-publications/col2-content/main-content-list/using-community-colleges-to-buil.html

Romano, R. M. (2011). A brief look at what economists are saying about the community college. *Community College Review, 39*(1), 69–87.

Scott, M. A., & Kennedy, B. B. (2005). Pitfalls in pathways: Some perspectives on competing risks event history analysis in education research. *Journal of Educational and Behavioral Statistics, 30*, 413–442.

Shaw, K. M., & Jacobs, J. A. (2003). Community colleges: New environments, new directions. *The Annals of the American Academy of Political and Social Science, 586*, 6–15.

Smart, J. C., Kuh, G. D., & Tierney, W. G (1997). The roles of institutional cultures and decision approaches in promoting organizational effectiveness in two-year colleges. *The Journal of Higher Education, 68*(3), 256–281.

Strauss, L. C., & Volkwein, J. F. (2002). Comparing student performance and growth in 2- and 4-year institutions. *Research in Higher Education, 43*, 133–161.

Townsend, B. K. (2001). Redefining the community college transfer mission. *Community College Review, 29*, 29–42.

Townsend, B. K. (2002). Transfer rates: A problematic criterion for measuring the community college. *New Directions for Community Colleges, 117*, 13–23.

Townsend, B. K. (2007). Interpreting the influence of community college attendance upon baccalaureate attainment. *Community College Review, 35*, 128–136.

Zamani-Gallaher, E. M. (2005). Proprietary schools: Beyond the issue of profit. *New Directions for Institutional Research, 124*, 63-79. San Francisco, CA: Jossey-Bass.

Section III – Organization, Administrative Leadership, and Finance

Allen, K. W. (1973). *Organization and administration of the learning resources in the community college.* North Haven, CT: Linnet Books.

Anderson, S. K., & Davies, T. G. (2000). An ethical decision-making model: A necessary tool for community college presidents and board of trustees. *Community College Journal of Research and Practice, 24*(9), 711–28.

Bailey, T., Calcagno, J, Jenkins, D., Leinbach, T., & Kienzl, G. (2006). Is student right-to-know all you should know? An analysis of community college graduation rates. *Research in Higher Education, 47*, 491–519.

Baldridge, V., & Riley, G. (1997). *Governing academic organizations.* Berkley, CA: McCutchan Publishing Company.

Breneman, D. W., & Nelson, S. C. (1981). *Financing community colleges: An economic perspective.* Washington, DC: The Brookings Institution.

Cohen, A. M., & Brawer, F. B (1994). *Managing community colleges: A handbook for effective practice.* San Francisco, CA: Jossey-Bass.

Committee on Measures of Student Success. (2001). *Committee on measures of student success: A report to secretary of education Anne Duncan.* Washington DC: U.S. Department of Education retrieved from http://www2 .ed.gov/about/bdscomm/list/acmss.html

D'Amico, M. M., Katsinas, S. G., & Friedel, J. N. (2012). The new norm: Community colleges to deal with recessionary fallout. *Community College Journal of Research and Practice, 36*(8), 626–631.

Dougherty, K. J., Hare, R., & Natow, R. S. (2009). *Performance accountability systems for community colleges: Lessons for the voluntary framework of accountability for community colleges.* (CCRC Working Paper). New York, NY: Community College Research Center, Teachers College, Columbia University. Retrieved from http:// ccrc.tc.columbia.edu/Publication.asp?UID=728

Dougherty, K. J., & Hong, E. (2006). Performance accountability as imperfect panacea: The community college experience. In T. Bailey, & V. S. Morest (Eds.), *Defending the community college equity agenda* (pp. 51-86). Baltimore, MD: Johns Hopkins University Press.

Dowd, A. C., & Coury, T. (2006). The effect of loans on the persistence and attainment of community college students. *Research in Higher Education, 47*, 33–62.

Eagly, A. H., & Karau, S. J. (2002). Role congruity theory of prejudice toward female leaders. *Psychological Review, 109*, 573–597.

Eddy, P. L. (2003). Sensemaking on campus: How community college presidents frame change. *Community College Journal of Research and Practice, 27*(6), 453–471.

Eddy, P. L. (2005). Framing the role of leader: How community college presidents construct their leadership. *Community College Journal of Research and Practice, 29*(9-10), 705–727.

Eddy, P. L. (2013). Developing Leaders: The role of competencies in rural community colleges. *Community College Review, 41*(1), 20–43.

Frederick, A. B., Schmidt, S. J., & Davis, L. S. (2012). Federal policies, state responses, and community college outcomes: Testing an augmented bennett hypothesis. *Economics of Education Review, 31*(6), 908–917.

Frost, R. A., Raspiller, E., & Sygielski, J. J. (2011). The role of leadership: Leaders' practice in financing transformation. In S.E. Sutin, D. Derrico, R. Latiner Raby, & E. J. Valeau (Eds.), *Increasing effectiveness of the community college financial model: A global perspective for the global economy* (pp. 49–64). New York, NY: Palgrave Macmillan.

Garms, W. I. (1977). *Financing community colleges.* New York, NY: Teachers College Press.

Gillett-Karam R. (2001). Community college leadership: Perspectives of women as presidents. *Community College Journal of Research and Practice, 25*(3), 167–170.

Gumport, P. J. (2003). The demand-response scenario: Perspectives of community college presidents. *The Annals of the American Academy of Political and Social Science, 586*, 38–61.

Gleazer, E. J. (1980). *The community college: Values, vision and vitality.* Washington, DC: American Association of Community and Junior Colleges.

Herbert-Schwarzer, C. A., & McNair, D. E. (2010). Linking scholarship and practice: Community college leaders, state mandates, and leadership competencies. *Journal of Research on Leadership Education, 5*(2), 23–42.

Holmes, S. (2004). An overview of African American college presidents: A game of two steps forward, two steps backward, and standing still. *The Journal of Negro Education, 73*(1), 21–39.

Hom, W. C. (2009). The denominator as the "target". *Community College Review, 37*, 136-152.

Jenkins, D. (2007). Institutional effectiveness and student success: A study of high- and low-impact community colleges. *Community College Journal of Research and Practice, 31*, 945–962.

Kenton, C., Huba, M., Schuh, J., & Shelley, M. (2005). Financing community colleges: A longitudinal study of 11 states. *Community College Journal of Research and Practice, 29*(2), 109–122.

Kezar, A., & Eckel, P. D. (2004). Meeting today's governance challenges: A synthesis of the literature and examination of a future agenda for scholarship. *Journal of Higher Education, 75*(4), 371–399.

Kienzl, G. S., Alfonso, M., & Melguizo, T. (2007). The effect of local labor market conditions in the 1990s on the likelihood of community college students' persistence and attainment. *Research in Higher Education, 48,* 751–774.

Kubla, T. S. (1999). A national study on the community college presidency. *Community College Journal of Research and Practice, 23*(2), 183–93.

Leinbach, D. T., & Jenkins, D. (2008). *Using longitudinal data to increase community college student success: A guide to measuring milestone and momentum point attainment* (CCRC Research Tools No. 2). New York, NY: Teachers College, Columbia University. Retrieved from Community College Research Center website http://ccrc.tc.columbia.edu/Publication.asp?uid=570

Levin, J. S., Beach, J. M., & Kisker, C. B. (2009). Educational attainment skewed in California community colleges? *Community College Journal of Research and Practice, 33,* 256–269.

Marcotte, D. E., Bailey, T., Borkoski, C., & Kienzl, G. S. (2005). The returns of a community college education: Evidence from the national educational longitudinal survey. *Educational Evaluation and Policy Analysis, 27,* 157–175.

Marti, C. N. (2008). Latent postsecondary persistence pathways: Pathways in American two-year colleges. *Research in Higher Education, 49,* 317–336.

McKenney, C. B., & Cejda, B. D. (2000). Profiling chief academic officers in public community colleges. *Community College Journal of Research and Practice, 24*(9), 745–62.

McNair, D. E., Duree, C., & Ebbers, L. (2011). If I knew then what I know now: Using the leadership competencies developed by the American association of community colleges to prepare community college presidents. *Community College Review, 39,* 3–25.

Melears, K. B., & Least. (2006). Community college governance: A compendium of state organizational structures. In D. D. Gehring & D. P. Young (Eds.), *The higher education administration series.* Asheville, NC: College Administration Publication.

Merisotis, J. P., & Wolanin, T. R. (2000). *Community college financing: Strategies and challenges. New expeditions: Charting the second century of community colleges. Issue paper No. 5.* Annapolis Junction, MD: Community College Press. Retrieved from http://www.aacc.nche.edu/Resources/aaccprograms/pastprojects/Pages/ccfinancing.aspx

Miller, M. T. (2000). The department chairs as speaker of the house: Shared authority in the community college. *Community College Journal of Research and Practice, 23*(8), 739–47.

Mullin, C. M. (2011). The road ahead: *A look at the trends in educational attainment by community college students.* (2011-04PBL). Washington, DC: American Association of Community Colleges.

Mullin, C. M., & Honeyman, D. S. (2008). Statutory responsibility for fixing tuition and fees: The relationship between community colleges and undergraduate institutions. *Community College Journal of Research and Practice, 32*(4-6), 284–304.

Nevarez, C., & Wood, J. (2010). *Community college leadership and administration: Theory, practice, and change.* New York, NY: Peter Lang.

Oliver, D. E., & Hioco, B. (2012). An ethical decision-making framework for community college administrators. *Community College Review, 40*(3), 240–254.

Pope, M. L., & Miller, M. T. (2000). Community college faculty governance leaders: Results of a national survey. *Community College Journal of Research and Practice, 24*(8), 627–39.

Provasnik, S., & Planty, M. (2008). *Community colleges: Special supplement to the condition of education 2008* (NCES 2008-033). Washington, DC: U.S. Department of Education. Retrieved from National Center for Education Statistics, Institute of Education Sciences website: http://nces.ed.gov/programs/coe/2008/analysis/2008033.pdf

Romano, R. M. (2012). Looking behind community college budgets for future policy considerations. *Community College Review, 40*(2), 165–189.

Smart, J. C., Kuh, G. D., & Tierney, W. G. (1997). The roles of institutional cultures and decision approaches in promoting organizational effectiveness in two-year colleges. *The Journal of Higher Education, 68*(3), 256–281.

Stange, K. (2012). Ability sorting and the importance of college quality to student achievement: Evidence from community colleges. *Education Finance and Policy, 7*(1), 74–105.

VanDerLinden, K. (2002). *Credit student analysis: 1999 and 2000*. Annapolis Junction, MD: Community College Press. Retrieved from American Association of Community Colleges website: http://www.aacc.nche.edu/Publications/Briefs/Documents/04192002creditstudent.pdf

Voorhees, R. A., & Zhou, D. (2000). Intentions and goals at the community college: Associating student perceptions and demographics. *Community College Journal of Research and Practice, 24,* 219–232.

Zamani, E. M. (2003). African American student affairs professionals in community college settings: A commentary for future research. *NASAP Journal, 6,* 91–103.

Section IV – The Instructional Core – Community College Faculty

Chang, J. C. (2005). Faculty student interaction at the community college: A focus on students of color. *Research in Higher Education, 46,* 769–802.

Eagan, M. K., Jr., & Jaeger, A. J. (2009). Effects of exposure to part-time faculty on community college transfer. *Research in Higher Education, 50,* 168–188.

Eddy, P. (2005). Faculty Development in community colleges: Surveying the present, preparing for the future. *Journal of Faculty Development, 20*(3), 143–152.

Eddy, P. (2010). New faculty issues: Fitting in and figuring it out. Hiring the next generation of faculty. *New Directions for Community Colleges, 152,* 15–24.

Flowers, L. A. (2005). Job satisfaction differentials among African American faculty at 2-year and 4-year institutions. *Community College Journal of Research and Practice, 29,* 317–328.

Fujimoto, E. O. (2012). Hiring diverse faculty members in community colleges: A case study in ethical decision making. *Community College Review, 40*(3), 255–274.

Hardre, P. L. (2012). Community college faculty motivation for basic research, teaching research, and professional development. *Community College Journal of Research and Practice, 36*(8), 539–561.

Hardy, D. E., & Laanan, F. S. (2006). Characteristics and perspectives of faculty at public 2-year colleges. *Community College Journal of Research, 30*(10), 787–811.

Harris, A., Joyner, S., & Slate, J. (2010). Hispanic faculty members in Texas community colleges. *Community College Enterprise, 16*(2), 63–75.

Hughes, K. L., & Scott-Clayton, J. (2011). Assessing development in community colleges. *Community College Review, 39,* 327–351.

Isaac, E. P., & Boyer, P. G. (2007). Voices of urban and rural community college minority faculty: Satisfaction and opinions. *Community College Journal of Research and Practice, 31,* 359–369.

Jeffcoat, K., & Piland, W. E. (2012). Anatomy of a community college faculty diversity program. *Community College Journal of Research and Practice, 36*(6), 397–410.

Keim, M. C., & Murray, J. P. (2008). Chief academic officers' demographic and educational backgrounds. *Community College Review, 36*(2), 116–132.

Kisker, C. B., & Outcalt, C. L. (2005). Community college honors and developmental faculty: Characteristics, practices, and implications for access and educational equity. *Community College Review, 33,* 1–21.

Lester, J. (2009). Not your child's playground: Workplace bullying among community college faculty. *Community College Journal of Research and Practice, 33*(5), 446–464.

Levin, J. S., Walker, L., Haberler, Z., & Jackson-Boothby, A. (2013). The divided self: The double consciousness of faculty of color in community colleges. *Community College Review, 41*(4), 311–329.

McArthur, R. C. (2005). Faculty-based advising: An important factor in community college retention. *Community College Review, 32,* 1–18.

Moye, M. J., Henkin, A. B., & Floyd, D. J. (2006). Faculty-department chair relationships: Examining the nexus of empowerment and interpersonal trust in community colleges in the context of change. *International Journal of Educational Reform, 15*(2), 266–288.

Murray, J. P. (2005). Meeting the needs of the new faculty at rural community colleges. *Community College Journal of Research and Practice, 29*(3), 215–232.

Murray, J. P. (2005). Why faculty development? Enhancing faculty knowledge in the community college. Retrieved from http://www.texascollaborative.org/cpmodules.htm.

Murray, J. P. (2007). Rural community college faculty satisfaction. In P. Eddy, & J. P. Murray (Eds.), *Rural community colleges: teaching, learning, and leading in the heartland: New Directions in Community Colleges* (pp. 57–64). San Francisco, CA: Jossey-Bass.

Murray, J.P. (2007). Recruiting and retaining rural community college faculty. *New Directions in Community Colleges, 137*, 57–64.

Murray, J. P., & Kishur, J. (2008). Crisis management in the community college. *Community College Journal of Research and Practice, 32*(7), 480–495.

Murray, J. P. (2010). Preparing to hire the best. In B. D. Cejda, & J. P. Murray (Eds.), *Hiring the next generation of community college faculty: New Directions in Community Colleges* (pp. 5-14). San Francisco, CA: Jossey-Bass.

Nora, A., Crisp, G., & Matthews, C. (2011). A reconceptualization of CCSSE's benchmarks of student engagement. *The Review of Higher Education, 35*(1), 105–130.

Opp, R. D., & Gosetti, P. P. (2002). Women full-time faculty of color in 2-year colleges: A trend and predictive analysis. *Community College Journal of Research and Practice, 26*, 609–627.

Opp, R., & Smith, A. (1994). Effective strategies for enhancing minority faculty recruitment. *Community College Journal of Research and Practice, 18*, 147–163.

Ottenritter, N. (2012). Crafting a caring and inclusive environment for LGBTQ community college students, faculty, and staff. *Community College Journal of Research and Practice, 36*(7), 531–538.

Palmer, J. (1991). Nurturing scholarship at community colleges. *New Directions for Community Colleges 76*, 69–77.

Perna, L. (2003). The status of women and minorities among community college faculty. *Research in Higher Education, 44*(2), 205–240.

Pope, M. L. (2002). Community college mentoring: Minority student perception. *Community College Review, 30*(3), 31–45.

Spaid, R., & Parsons, M. (2011). Engaging community college faculty. *Academic Exchange, 15*(1), 20–24.

Wood, J. L., & Turner, C. S. V. (2011). Black males and the community college: Student perspectives on faculty and academic success. *Community College Journal of Research & Practice, 35*, 1–17.

Section V – Diverse Students at Two-Year Institutions of Higher Learning

Adelman, C. (2005). Educational "anticipations" of traditional age community college students: A prolegomena to any future accountability indicators. *Journal of Applied Research in the Community College, 12*, 93–107.

Adelman, C. (2005). *Moving into town – and moving on: The community college in the lives of traditional-age students.* Washington, DC: U.S. Department of Education. Retrieved from http://www.ed.gov/rschstat/research/pubs/comcollege/movingintotown.pdf

Ammon, B. V., Bowman, J., & Mourad, R. (2008). Who are our students? Cluster analysis as a tool for understanding community college student populations. *Journal of Applied Research in the Community College, 16*, 32–44.

Angell, L. R. (2009). Construct validity of the community college survey of student engagement (CCSSE). *Community College Journal of Research and Practice, 33*, 564–570.

Bailey, T., Jenkins, D., & Leinbach T. (2005). *What we know about community college low income and minority student outcomes: Descriptive statistics from national surveys.* (NCES-BPS: 96/01). New York, NY: Teachers College, Columbia University.

Becker, L. A. (2011). Noncredit to credit transitioning matters for adult ESL learners in a California community college. In E. M. Cox & J. S. Watson (Eds.), *Marginalized Students* (pp. 15-26). San Francisco, CA: Jossey-Bass.

Bers, T. (2005). Parents of traditionally aged community college students: Communications and choice. *Research in Higher Education, 46*, 413–436.

Bush, E. C., & Bush, L. (2010). Calling out the elephant: An examination of African American male achievement in community colleges. *Journal of African American Males in Education, 1*(1), 40–62.

Cejda, B. D., & Rhodes, J. H. (2004). Through the pipeline: The role of faculty in promoting associate degree completion among Hispanic students. *Community College Journal of Research and Practice, 28*(3), 249–262.

Conway, K. M. (2009). Exploring persistence of immigrant and native students in an urban community college. *Review of Higher Education, 32*, 321–352.

Cox, E. M., & Watson, J. S. (Eds.). (2011). *Marginalized students. New Directions for Community Colleges, 155.* San Francisco, CA: Jossey-Bass.

Crisp, G., & Nora, A. (2010). Hispanic student success: Factors influencing the persistence and transfer decisions of Latino community college students enrolled in developmental education. *Research in Higher Education, 51*, 175–194.

Cummins, P. A. (2013, May). *Credential attainment by older workers: The role of community colleges and the dislocated worker program in successful employment outcomes.* Retrieved from http://c.ymcdn.com/sites/www.ncwe .org/resource/resmgr/ncwe_awards/cummins_dissertation_summary.pdf

Dougherty, K. J. (1994). *The contradictory college: The conflicting origins, impacts, and futures of the community college.* Albany, NY: State University of New York.

Ethington, C. A. (2000). Influences of the normative environment of peer groups on community college students' perceptions of growth and development. *Research in Higher Education, 41,* 703–722.

Fairlie, R., Hoffmann, F., & Oreopoulos, P. (2011). *A community college instructor like me: Race and ethnicity interactions in the classroom.* (Working Paper No. 17381). Cambridge, MA: National Bureau of Economic Research.

Flowers, L. A. (2006). Effects of attending a 2-year institution on African American males' academic and social integration in the first year of college. *Teachers College Record, 108,* 267–286.

Gardenhire-Crooks, A., Collado, H., Martin, K., & Castro, A. (2010). *Terms of engagement: Men of color discuss their experience in community college.* New York, NY: MDRC. Retrieved from http://achievingthedream.org/sites/default/files/resources/TermsOfEngagement_MenOfColorDiscussTheir-ExperiencesInCommunityCollege.pdf

Garrison-Wade, D. F., & Lehmann, J. P. (2009). A conceptual framework for understanding students' with disabilities transition to community college. *Community College Journal of Research and Practice, 33,* 415–443.

Glenn, F. S. (2003-2004). The retention of black male students in Texas public community colleges. *Journal of College Student Retention, 5,* 115–133.

Greene, T. G., Marti, C. N., & McClenney, K. (2008). The effort-outcome gap: Differences for African American and Hispanic community college students in student engagement and academic achievement. *Journal of Higher Education, 79,* 513–539.

Hagedorn, L. S., & Horton, D., Jr. (Eds.). (2009). *Student-athletes and athletics. New Directions for Community Colleges, 147.* San Francisco, CA: Jossey-Bass.

Hagedorn, L. S., & Lester, J. (2006). Hispanic community college students and the transfer game: Strikes, misses, and grand slam experiences. *Community College Journal of Research and Practice, 30,* 827–853

Hagedorn, S. L., Maxwell, W., & Hampton, P. (2001-2002). Correlates of retention for African American males in the community college. *Journal of College Student Retention, 3*(3), 243–263.

Harris III, F., & Wood, J. L. (2013). Student success for men of color in community colleges: A review of published literature and research, 1998–2012. *Journal of Diversity in Higher Education, 6*(3), 174.

Hoffman, J. L., & Horton, D., Jr. (2011). State gender law and athlete participation among community college in Washington State. *Community College Journal of Research and Practice, 35*(1), 165–178.

Horton, D. (2009). Class and cleats: Community college student athletes and academic success. *New Directions for Community Colleges, 147,* 15–27.

Horton, D., Jr. (2011). Developing an institutional culture toward degree attainment for student athletes. In E. M. Cox & J. S. Watson (Eds.), Marginalized students. *New Directions for Community Colleges,* 27–33. San Francisco, CA: Jossey-Bass.

Jain, D. (2010). Critical race theory and community colleges: Through the eyes of women student leaders of color. *Community College Journal of Research and Practice, 34,* 78–91.

Joshi, P. V., Beck, K. A., & Nsiah, C. (2009). Student characteristics affecting the decision to enroll in a community college: Economic rationale and empirical evidence. *Community College Journal of Research and Practice, 33,* 805–822.

Kim, K. A. (2002). ERIC review: Exploring the meaning of "nontraditional" at the community college. *Community College Review, 30,* 74–89.

Kissinger, D. B., Newman, R., Miller, M. T., & Nadler, D. P. (2011). Athletic identity of community college student athletes: Issues for counseling. *Community College of Education Journal of Research and Practice, 35,* 574–589.

Levine, A., & Nidiffer, J. (1996). The odds against going to college. In A. Levine, & J. Nidiffer *Beating the odds: How the poor get to college* (pp. 29–53). San Francisco, CA: Jossey-Bass.

Marti, C. N. (2009). Dimensions of student engagement in American community colleges: Using the community college student report in research and practice. *Community College Journal of Research and Practice, 33,* 1–24.

Mason, H. P. (1998). A persistence model for African American male urban community college students. *Community College Journal of Research and Practice, 22*(8), 751–760.

McClenney, K. M. (2007). Research update: The community college survey of student engagement. *Community College Review, 35*, 137–146.

Melguizo, T. (2009). Are community colleges an alternative path for Hispanic students to attain a bachelor's degree? *Teachers College Record, 111*, 90–123.

Mendoza, P., Horton, D., & Mendez, J.P. (2012). Retention among community college student athletes. *Community College Journal of Research and Practice, 36*(3), 201–219.

O'Connor, N. (2009). Hispanic origin, socio-economic status, and community college enrollment. *Journal of Higher Education, 80*, 121–145.

O'Connor, N., Hammack, F. M, & Scott, M. A. (2010). Social capital, financial knowledge, and Hispanic student college choices. *Research in Higher Education, 51*, 195–219.

Offstein, J., & Shulock, N. (2009). *Community college student outcomes: Limitations of the integrated postsecondary education data system (IPEDS) and recommendations for improvement.* Sacramento, CA: Institution for Higher Education Leadership and Policy. Retrieved from http://www.csus.edu/ihelp/PDFs/R_IPEDS_08-09.pdf

Ornelas, A., & Solorzano, D. (2004). The transfer condition of Latina/o community college students in California: Policy recommendations and solutions. *Community College Journal of Research and Practice, 28*, 233–248.

Palazesi, L.M., Bower, B.L., & Schwartz, R.A. (2007). Underlying consumer valuing structures of baby boomers as older adults in community colleges: A grounded analysis. *Journal of Marketing for Higher Education, 17*(2), 256–291.

Park, V., Cerven, C., Nations, J., & Nielsen, K. (2013). What matters for community college success? Assumptions and realities concerning student supports for low-income women. Retrieved from http://pathways.gseis.ucla.edu/publications/201302_WhatMattersPR.pdf

Pascarella, E. T., Wolniak, G. C., & Pierson, C. T. (2003). Influences on community college students' educational plans. *Research in Higher Education, 44*, 301–314.

Perin, D., & Charron, K. (2006). Lights just click on every day. In T. Bailey & V. S. Morest (Eds.), *Defending the community college equity agenda* (pp. 155-194). Baltimore, MD: Johns Hopkins University Press.

Philibert, N., Allen, J., & Elleven, R. (2008). Nontraditional students in community colleges and the model of college outcomes for adults. *Community College Journal of Research and Practice, 32*, 582–596.

Pierson, C. T., Wolniak, G. C., Pascarella, E. T., & Flowers, L. A. (2003). Impact of two-year and four-year college attendance on learning orientations. *Review of Higher Education, 26*, 299–321.

Pope, M. L. (2002). Community college mentoring: Minority student perception. *Community College Review, 30*, 31–45.

Price, D. B., Hyle, A. E., & Jordan, K. V. (2009). Ties that blind: Perpetuation of racial comfort and discomfort at a community college. *Community College Review, 37*, 3–33.

Rendon, L. I. (1993). Eyes on the prize: Students of color and the bachelor's degree. *Community College Review, 21*(2), 3–13.

Rumann, C., Rivera, M., & Hernandez, I. (2011). Student veterans and community colleges. *New Directions for Community Colleges, 155*, 51–58.

Sanlo, R. (2004). Lesbian, gay, and bisexual college students: Risk, resiliency, and retention. *Journal of College Student Retention: Research, Theory and Practice, 6*(1), 97–110.

Schlossberg, N. K., Lynch, A. Q., & Chickering, A. W. (1989). Moving in: Adults' needs on entering higher education. In N. Schlossberg (Ed.), *Improving higher education environments for adults* (pp. 34-55). San Francisco, CA: Jossey-Bass.

Schoenecker, C., & Reeves, R. (2008). The national student clearinghouse: The largest current student tracking database. *New Directions for Community Colleges, 143*, 47–57.

Strayhorn, T. L. (2011). Traits, commitments, and college satisfaction among Black American community college students. *Community College Journal of Research and Practice, 35*(6), 437–453.

Suarez-Balcazar, Y., Orellana-Damacela, L., Portillo, N., Rowan, J. M., & Andrews-Guillen, C. (2003). Experiences of differential treatment among college students of color. *Journal of Higher Education, 74*, 428–444.

Townsend, B., & Twombly, S. (2007). Accidental equity: The status of women in community college. *Equity & Excellence in Education, 40*(3), 208–217.

Wang, W. W., Chang, J. C., & Lew, J. W. (2009). Reasons for attending, expected obstacles, and degree aspirations of Asian Pacific American community college students. *Community College Journal of Research and Practice, 33*, 571–593.

Wassmer, R., Moore, C., & Shulock, N. (2004). Effect of racial/ethnic composition on transfer rates in community colleges: Implications for policy and practice. *Research in Higher Education, 45*(6), 651–672.

Weissman, J., Bulakowski, C., & Jumisko, M. (1998). A study of white, black, and Hispanic students' transition to a community college. *Community College Review, 26,* 19–32.

Whitt, E., Edison, M., Pascarella, E., Nora, A., & Terenzini, P. (1999). Women's perceptions of a 'chilly climate' and cognitive outcome in college. *Journal of Student Development, 20,* 163–177.

Wilson, K.B., & Cox, E.M. (2011). No kids allowed: Transforming community colleges to support mothering. *NASPA Journal About Women in Higher Education, 4*(2).

Wood, J. L., Hilton, A. A., & Lewis. C. (2011). Black male collegians in public two-year colleges: Student perspectives on the effect of employment on academic success. *National Association of Student Affairs Professionals Journal, 14*(1), 97–110.

Wood, L. J., & Vasquez Urias, M. C. (2012). Community college v. proprietary school outcomes: Student satisfaction among minority males. *Community College Enterprise, 18*(2), 83–100.

Wood, J. L., & Williams, R. C. (2013). Persistence factors for Black males in the community college: An examination of background, academic, social, and environmental variables. *Spectrum: A Journal on Black Men, 1*(2), 1–28

Zamani-Gallaher, E. M., & Bazile, S. (2011). Multicultural student services at community colleges. In D.L. Stewart (Ed.), *Building brides, revisioning community: Multicultural student services on campus* (pp. 154–166). Sterling, VA: ACPA/Stylus Publishing.

Zamani-Gallaher, E.M., & Choudhuri, D.D. (2011). A primer on LGBTQ students at community colleges: Considerations for research and practice. *New Directions for Community Colleges, 155,* 35–49.

Section VI – Career-Technical and Workforce Education

Alssid, J.L., & Goldberg, M. (2011). *Workforce strategies for America's future: Community college contributions. 21st century commission on the Future of Community Colleges.* Retrieved from http://www.ilcccp.org/sites/default/files/pictures/aacc_briefs.pdf#page=74

Barnett, E. (2011). Faculty validation and persistence among nontraditional community college students. *Enrollment Management Journal, 5*(2), 1–161.

Barnett, E. (2011). Validation and persistence among community college students. *Review of Higher Education, 32*(2), 193–230.

Barnett, E., & Hughes, K. (2010). *Issue brief: Community college and high school partnerships.* Prepared for the white house community college summit. New York, NY: Community College Research Center, Teachers College, Columbia University.

Boswell, K., & Wilson, C. D. (2004). *Keeping America's promise: A report on the future of the community college.* Denver, CO: Education Commission of the States. Retrieved from http://www.ecs.org/html/Document.asp?chouseid=5309

Bragg, D. D., Bremer, C., Castellano, M., Kirby, C., Mavis, A., & Schaad, D. (2007). *A cross case analysis of career pathway programs that link low-skilled adults to family-sustaining careers.* St. Paul, MN: National Research Center for Career and Technical Education University of Minnesota. Retrieved from http://www.nrccte.org/resources/podcasts/career-pathway-programs-link-low-skilled-adults-family-sustaining-wage-careers

Bragg, D. D. (2002). Contemporary vocational models and programs: What the research tells us. *New Directions for Community College, 117,* 25–34.

Bragg, D. D., & Taylor, J. L. (2014). Toward college and career readiness: How different models produce similar short-term outcomes. *American Behavioral Scientist, 0002764213515231.*

Floyd, D. L., Falconetti, A. M., & Felsher, R. A. (2012). Applied and workforce baccalaureate models. *New Directions for Community Colleges, 158,* 5–11.

Floyd, D. L., Maslin-Ostrowski, P., & Hrabak, M. L. (2010). Beyond the headlines: Wounding and the community college presidency. In D. L. Wallin (Ed.), *Leadership in an era of change. New Directions for Community College, 149,* 65-72. San Francisco, CA: Jossey-Bass.

Floyd, D. L., & Walker, K. P. (2009). The community college baccalaureate: Putting the pieces together. *Community College Journal of Research and Practice, 33*(2), 90–124.

Gordon, H. R. (2014). *The history and growth of career and technical education in America.* Long Grove, IL: Waveland Press.

Grubb, W. N. (2002). Learning and earning in the middle, part I: National studies of pre-baccalaureate education. *Economics of Education Review, 21*(4), 299–321.

Jackson, D. L. (2013). A balancing act: Impacting and initiating the success of African American female community college transfer students in STEM into the HBCU environment. *The Journal of Negro Education, 82*(3), 255–271.

Jacobs, J., & Dougherty, K. J. (2006). The uncertain future of the community college workforce development mission. *New Directions for Community Colleges, 136,* 53–62.

Jenkins, D., & Cho, S. (2012). *Get with the program: Accelerating community college students' entry into and completion of programs of study* (CCRC Working Paper No. 32). New York, NY: Community College Resource Center, Teachers College, Columbia University.

Katsinas, S., D'Amico, M., & Friedel, J. (2011). Jobs. Jobs. Jobs. Challenges community colleges face to reach the unemployed. *The Education Policy Center at the University of Alabama, 1–8.*

Kim, J., & Bragg, D. D. (2008). The impact of dual and articulated credit on college readiness and retention in four community colleges. *Career and Technical Education Research, 33*(2), 133–158.

Laanan, F. S., Starobin, S. S., Compton, J. I., & Friedel, J. N. (2009). Assessing post college earnings of career and technical education students in Iowa community colleges. *Enrollment Management Journal, 3*(4), 68–94.

Lester, J. (2010). Women in male-dominated career and technical education programs at community colleges: Barriers to participation and success. *Journal of Women and Minorities in Science and Engineering, 16*(1), 51–66.

Marcotte, D. E. (2010). The earnings effect of education at community colleges. *Contemporary Economic Policy, 28*(1), 36–51.

Maslin-Ostrowski, P., Floyd, D. L., & Hrabak, M. R. (2011). Daunting realities of leading complicated by the new media: Wounding and community college presidents. *The Community College Journal of Research and Practice, 35*(1), 29–42.

Mattis, M. C., & Sislin, J. (Eds.). (2005). *Community college enhancing the community college pathway to engineering careers.* Washington, DC: Academies Press. Retrieved from http://books.nap.edu/catalog.php?record_id=11438

National Research Council of the National Academies. (2008). *Using American community survey for the National Science Foundation's science and engineering workforce statistics programs.* Washington, DC: National Academies Press. Retrieved from http://www.nap.edu/catalog.php?record_id=12244

Packard, B. W. L., Gagnon, J. L., LaBelle, O., Jeffers, K., & Lynn, E. (2011). Women's experiences in the STEM community college transfer pathway. *Journal of Women and Minorities in Science and Engineering, 17*(2), 129–147.

Roksa, J. (2006). Does the vocational focus of community colleges hinder students' educational attainment? *Review of Higher Education, 29,* 499–526.

Rudd, C.M., Bragg, D.D., & Townsend, B.K. (2010). The applied baccalaureate degree: The right time and place. *Community College Journal of Research and Practice, 34*(1-2), 136–152.

Speroni, C. (2011). *Determinants of students' success: The role of advanced placement and dual enrollment programs.* (An NCPR Working Paper). New York, NY: National Center for Postsecondary Research, Teachers College, Columbia University.

Starobin, S. S., & Laanan, F. S. (2008). Broadening female participation in science, technology, engineering, and mathematics: Experiences at community colleges. *New Directions for Community Colleges, 141,* 37–46.

Starobin, S. S., Schenk Jr, T., Laanan, F. S., Rethwisch, D. G., & Moeller, D. (2013). Going and passing through community colleges: Examining the effectiveness of Project Lead the Way in STEM pathways. *Community College Journal of Research and Practice, 37*(3), 226–236.

Strawn, C., & Livelybrooks, D. (2012). A five-year University/Community college collaboration to build STEM pipeline capacity. *Journal of College Science Teaching, 41*(6), 47–51.

Zeidenberg, M., Cho, S., & Jenkins, D. (2010). *Washington states integrated basic education and skills training program (I-BEST): New evidence of effectiveness.* (CCRC Working Paper No. 20). New York, NY: Community College Resource Center, Teachers College, Columbia University.

Section VII – Community College Transfer

Bailey, T., & Weininger, E. B. (2002). Performance, graduation, and transfer of immigrants and natives in City University of New York community colleges. *Educational Evaluation and Policy Analysis, 24,* 359–377.

Bensimon, E., & Dowd, A. (2009). Dimensions of the transfer choice gap: Experiences of Latina and Latino students who navigated transfer pathways. *Harvard Educational Review, 79*(4), 632–658.

Boswell, K., & Wilson, C. D. (2004). *Keeping America's promise: A report on the future of the community college.* Denver, CO: Education Commission of the States. Retrieved from http://www.ecs.org/html/Document.asp?chouseid=5309

Boughan, K. (2001). Closing the transfer data gap: Using National Student Clearinghouse data in community college outcomes research. *Journal of Applied Research in the Community College, 8,* 107–116.

Bradburn, E. M., & Hurst, D. G. (2001). *Community college transfer rates to 4-year institutions using alternative definitions of transfer* (NCES 2001-197). Washington, DC: National Center for Education Statistics. Retrieved from http://nces.ed.gov/pubs2001/2001197.pdf

Carlan, P. E., & Byxbe, F. R. (2000). Community colleges under the microscope: An analysis of performance predictors for native and transfer students. *Community College Review, 28,* 27–42.

Cejda, B. D., Kaylor, A. J., & Rewey, K. L. (1998). Transfer shock in an academic discipline: The relationship between students' majors and their academic performance. *Community College Review, 26*(3), 1–14.

Clark, B. R. (1980). The 'cooling-out' function revisited. *New Directions for Community Colleges, 32,* 15–31.

Cohen, A. M., & Brawer, F. (1987). *The collegiate function of community colleges: Fostering high learning through curriculum and student transfer.* San Francisco, CA: Jossey-Bass.

Cohen, A. M., & Ignash, J. M. (1994). An overview of the total credit curriculum. *New Directions for Community Colleges, 86,* 13–29.

Crisp, G. & Nora, A. (2010). Hispanic student success: Factors influencing the persistence and transfer decisions of Latino community college students enrolled in developmental education. *Research in Higher Education, 51*(2), 175–194.

Desai, S. (2012). Is comprehensiveness taking its toll on community colleges? An in-depth analysis of community colleges' missions and their effectiveness. *Community College Journal of Research & Practice, 36*(2), 111–121.

Dougherty, K. J., & Kienzl, G. S. (2006). It's not enough to get through the open door: Inequalities by social background in transfer from community colleges to four-year colleges. *Teachers College Record, 108*(3), 452–487.

Dowd, A. C., & Melguizo, T. (2008). Socioeconomic stratification of community college transfer access in the 1980s and 1990s: Evidence from HS&B and NELS. *Review of Higher Education, 31,* 377–400.

Dowd, A. C., Pak, J. H., & Bensimon, E. M. (2013). The role of institutional agents in promoting transfer access. *Education Policy Analysis Archives, 21*(15). Retrieved from http://cue.usc.edu/Dowd_Role%20if%20Institutional%20Agents%20in%20Promoting%20Transfer%20Access_EPAA_2013.pdf

Doyle, W. R. (2009). Impact of increased academic intensity on transfer rates: An application of matching estimators to student-unit record data. *Research in Higher Education, 50,* 52–72.

Eaton, J. S. (1993). General education in the community college: Developing habits of thought. *New Directions for Community Colleges, 81,* 21–30.

Ethington, C. A., & Horn, R. A. (2007). An examination of Pace's model of student development and college impress. *Community College Journal of Research and Practice, 31,* 183–198.

Ellis, M. M. (2013). Successful community college transfer students speak out. *Community College Journal of Research and Practice, 37*(2), 73–84.

Falconetti, A. M. G. (2009). 2+2 statewide articulation policy, student persistence, and success in Florida universities. *Community College Journal of Research and Practice, 33,* 238–255.

Illinois State University. (2012). *Grapevine: An annual compilation of data on state fiscal support for higher education.* Bloomington, IL: ISU. Retrieved from grapevine website http://grapevine.illinoistate.edu/index.shtml

Hagedorn, L. S., Cypers, S., & Lester, J. (2008) Looking in the rearview mirror: A retrospective look at the factors affecting transfer for urban community college students. *Community College Journal of Research and Practice, 32*(9), 643–664.

Hodara, M., & Rodriguez, O. (2013). Tracking student progression through the core curriculum. CCRC Analytics. *Community College Research Center, Columbia University.*

Ishitani, T. T. (2008). How do transfers survive after "transfer shock"? A longitudinal study of transfer student departure at a four-year institution. *Research in Higher Education, 49,* 403–419.

Laanan, F. S. (2001). Transfer student adjustment. *New Direction for Community Colleges, 114,* 5–13.

Laanan, F. S. (2007). Studying transfer students: Part II: Dimensions of transfer students' adjustment. *Community College Journal of Research and Practice, 31,* 37–59.

Lee, V. E., & Frank, K. A. (1990). Students' characteristics that facilitate the transfer from two year to four-year colleges. *Sociology of Education, 63,* 178–193.

Lester, J., Leonard, J. B., & Mathias, D. (2013). Transfer student engagement blurring of social and academic engagement. *Community College Review, 41*(3), 202–222.

Lockwood, P., Hunt, E., Matlack, R., & Kelley, J. (2013). From community college to four-year institution: a model for recruitment and retention. *Community College Journal of Research and Practice, 37*(8), 613–619.

Long, B. T., & Kurlaender, M. (2009). Do community colleges provide a viable pathway to a baccalaureate degree? *Educational Evaluation and Policy Analysis, 31,* 30–53.

Mattis, M. C., & Sislin, J. (Eds.). (2005). *Community college enhancing the community college pathway to engineering careers.* Washington, DC: Academies Press. Retrieved from http://books.nap.edu/catalog.php?record_id=11438

Melguizo, T., & Dowd, A. C. (2009). Baccalaureate success of transfers and rising 4-year college juniors. *Teachers College Record, 111*(1), 55–89.

Moser, K. M. (2013). Exploring the impact of transfer capital on community college transfer students. *Journal of The First-Year Experience & Students in Transition, 25*(2), 53–76.

National Research Council of the National Academies. (2008). *Using American community survey for the National Science Foundation's science and engineering workforce statistics programs.* Washington, DC: National Academies Press. Retrieved from http://www.nap.edu/catalog.php?record_id=12244

Nutting, A. W. (2011). Community college transfer students' probabilities of baccalaureate receipt as a function of their prevalence in four-year colleges and departments. *Education Economics, 19*(1), 65–87.

Pascarella, E., Bohr, L., Nora, A., & Terenzini, P. (1995). Cognitive effects of 2-year and 4-year colleges: New evidence. *Educational Evaluation and Policy Analysis, 17,* 83–96.

Peter, K., & Cataldi, E. F. (2005). *The road less traveled? Students who enroll in multiple institutions (NCES 2005-157).* Washington, D.C.: National Center for Education Statistics. Retrieved from http://nces.ed.gov/pubs2005/2005157.pdf

Phelps, A. L., & Prevost, A. (2012). Community college-research university collaboration: Emerging student research and transfer partnerships. *New Directions for Community Colleges, 157,* 97-110.

Roksa, J., & Keith, B. (2008). Credits, time, and attainment: Articulation policies and success after transfer. *Educational Evaluation and Policy Analysis, 30,* 236–254.

Roksa, J. (2009). Building bridges for student success: Are higher education articulation policies effective? *Teachers College Record, 111,* 2444–2478.

Roksa, J. (2010). Bachelor's degree completion across state contexts: Does the distribution of enrollments make a difference. *Research in Higher Education, 51,* 1–20.

Romano, R. M., & Wisniewski, M. (2005). Tracking community college transfers using national student clearinghouse data. *AIR Professional File, 94,* 1–11.

Schuetz, P. (2008). A theory-driven model of community college student engagement. *Community College Journal of Research and Practice, 32,* 305–324.

Shaw, K. M., & London, H. B. (2001). Culture and ideology in keeping transfer commitment: Three community colleges. *Review of Higher Education, 25,* 91–114.

Starobin, S. S., Hagedorn, L. S., Purnamasari, A., & Chen, Y. A. (2013). Examining financial literacy among transfer and nontransfer students: Predicting financial well-being and academic success at a four-year university. *Community College Journal of Research and Practice, 37*(3), 216–225.

Strauss, L. C., & Volkwein, J. F. (2004). Predictors of student commitment at two-year and four year institutions. *Journal of Higher Education, 75,* 203–227.

Summers, M. D. (2003). ERIC Review: Attrition research at community colleges. *Community College Review, 30,* 64–84.

Townsend, B. K. (2001). Redefining the community college transfer mission. *Community College Review, 29,* 29–42.

Wang, X. (2009). Baccalaureate attainment and college persistence of community collegetransfer students at four-year institutions. *Research in Higher Education, 50*(6), 570–588.

Wirth, R. M., & Padilla, R. V. (2008). College student success: A qualitative modeling approach. *Community College Journal of Research and Practice, 32,* 688–711.

Yang, X., Brown, K. J., & Brown, J. K. (2008, May). Enrollment patterns and completion status: Students in North Carolina public postsecondary institutions. Paper presented at the annual forum of the Association for Institutional Research, Seattle, WA. Retrieved from http://ocair.org/files/presentations/Paper2007_08/Xiaoyun_Yang/AIR_Paper.pdf

Section VIII – Remediation and Developmental Education

Armstrong, W. B. (2000). The association among student success in courses, placement test scores, student background data, and instructor grading practices. *Community College Journal of Research and Practice, 24*(8), 681–695.

Bahr, P. R. (2010). Revisiting the efficacy of postsecondary remediation: The moderating effects of depth/breadth of deficiency. *The Review of Higher Education 33*(2), 177–205.

Bahr, P. R. (2010). The bird's eye view of community colleges: A behavioral typology of first time students based on cluster analytic classification. *Research in Higher Education, 51*(8), 724–749.

Bahr, P. R. (2012). Deconstructing remediation in the community college: Exploring associations between course-taking patterns, course outcomes, and attrition from the remedial math and remedial writing sequences. *Research in Higher Education, 53*, 661–693.

Bailey, T. (2009). Challenge and opportunity: Rethinking the role and function of developmental education in community college. *New Directions for Community Colleges, 145*, 11–30.

Bremer, C. D., Center, B. A., Opsal, C. L., Medhanie, A., Jang, Y. J., & Geise, A. C. (2013). Outcome trajectories of developmental students in community colleges. *Community College Review, 41*(2), 154–175.

Burley, H., Butner, B., & Cejda, B. (2001). Dropout and stopout patterns among developmental education students in Texas community colleges. *Community College Journal of Research and Practice, 25*, 767–782.

Callahan, M. K., & Chumney, D. (2009). "Write Like College": How remedial writing courses at a community college and a research university position "at-risk" students in the field of higher education. *Teachers College Record, 111*(7), 1619–1664.

Cohen, A. M., & Brawer, F. B. (2008). *The American community college (5th ed.).* San Francisco, CA: Jossey-Bass.

Collins, M. L. (2008). *It's not about the cut score: Redesigning placement assessment policy to improve student success.* Boston, MA: Jobs for the Future.

Conley, D. (2005). *College knowledge: What it really takes for students to succeed and what we can do to get them ready.* San Francisco, CA: Jossey-Bass.

Cortes-Suarez, G., & Sandiford, J. R. (2008). Causal attributions for success or failure of students in college algebra. *Community College Journal of Research and Practice, 32*, 325–346.

Crews, D. M., & Aragon, S. R. (2007). Developmental education writing: Persistence and goal attainment among community college students. *Community College Journal of Research and Practice, 31*, 637–652.

Deil-Amen, R. (2011). Beyond remedial dichotomies: Are underprepared college students a marginalized majority? *New Directions for Community Colleges, 155*, 59–72.

Deil-Amen, R., & Rosenbaum, J. E. (2002). The unintended consequences of stigma free remediation. *Sociology of Education, 75*, 249–268.

Ewell, P., Boeke, M., & Zis, S. (2008). *State policies on student transitions: Results of a fifty state inventory.* Boulder, CO: National Center for Higher Education Management Systems.

Fong, K., Melguizo, T., Prather, G., & Bos, J. M. (2013). A different view of how we understand progression through the developmental math trajectory. *Los Angeles, CA: The University of Southern California.*

Gerlaugh, K., Thompson, L., Boylan, H., & Davis, H. (2007). National study of developmental education II: Baseline data for community colleges. *Research in Developmental Education, 20*(4), 1–4.

Grubb, W. N., & Cox, R. D. (2005). Pedagogical alignment and curricular consistency: The challenges for developmental education. *New Directions for Community Colleges, 129*, 93–103.

Hadden, C. (2000). The ironies of mandatory placement. *Community College Journal of Research and Practice, 24*, 823–838.

Hoachlander, G., Sikora, A. C., & Horn, L. (2003). *Community college students: Goals, academic preparation, and outcomes* (NCES 2003-164). Washington, DC: U.S. Department of Education. Retrieved from National Center for Education Statistics, Institute of Education Sciences website: http://nces.ed.gov/pubs2003/2003164.pdf

Horn, C., McCoy, Z., Campbell, L., & Brock, C. (2009). Remedial testing and placement in community colleges. *Community College Journal of Research and Practice, 33*, 510–526.

Howell, J. S., Kurlaender, M., & Grodsky, E. (2010). Postsecondary preparation and remediation: Examining the effect of the Early Assessment Program at California State University. *Journal of Policy Analysis and Management, 29*(4), 726–748.

Hughes, K. L., & Scott-Clayton, J. (2011). *Assessing developmental assessment in community colleges.* (CCRC Working paper No. 19). New York, NY: Community College Research Center, Teachers College, Columbia University.

Jenkins, D., & Boswell, K. (2002). *State policies on community college remedial education: Findings from a national survey*. Denver, CO: Education Commission of the States.

Karabel, J. (1972). Community colleges and social stratification. *Harvard Educational Review, 42*, 543–558.

Kozeracki, C. A. (2002). ERIC review: Issues in developmental education. *Community College Review, 29*, 83–101.

Lesik, S. A. (2007). Do developmental mathematics programs have a causal impact on student retention? An application of discrete-time survival and regression discontinuity analysis. *Research in Higher Education, 48*, 583–608.

Levin, H. M., & Calcagno, J. C. (2008). Remediation in the community college: An evaluator's perspective. *Community College Review, 35*, 181–207.

Melguizo, T., Hagedorn, L. S., & Cypers, S. (2008). Remedial/developmental education and the cost of community college transfer: A Los Angeles County sample. *Review of Higher Education, 31*, 401–431.

Moss, B. G., & Yeaton, W. H. (2006). Shaping policies related to developmental education: An evaluation using the regression-discontinuity design. *Educational Evaluation and Policy Analysis, 28*, 215–229.

Oudenhoven, B. (2002). Remediation in the community college: Pressing issues, uncertain solutions. *New Directions for Community Colleges, 117*, 35–44.

Parsad, B., Lewis, L., & Greene, B. (2003). *Remedial education at degree-granting postsecondary institutions in Fall 2000* (NCES 2004-010). Washington, DC: U.S. Department of Education. Retrieved from National Center for Education Statistics website: http://nces.ed.gov/pubs2004/2004010.pdf

Perin, D. (2006). Can community colleges protect both access and standards? The problem of remediation. *Teachers College Record, 108*(3), 339–373.

Perin, D., Keselman, A., & Monopoli, M. (2003). The academic writing of community college remedial students: Text and learner variables. *Higher Education, 45*, 19–42.

Roksa, J., & Calcagno, J. C. (2008). *Making the transition to four-year institutions: Academic preparation and transfer* (CCRC Working Paper No. 13). New York: NY: Community College Research Center, Teachers College, Columbia University. Retrieved from http://ccrc.tc.columbia.edu/Publication.asp?UID=618

Sheldon, C. Q., & Durdella, N. R. (2010). Success rates for students taking compressed and regular length developmental courses in the community college. *Community College Journal of Research and Practice, 34*, 39–54.

Valeri-Gold, M., Kearse, W., Deming, M. P., Errico, M., & Callahan, C. (2001). Examining college developmental learners' reasons for persisting in college: A longitudinal retention study. *Research and Teaching in Developmental Education, 17*, 27–40.

Venezia, A., Bracco, K. R., & Nodine, T. (2010). *One shot deal? Students' perceptions of assessment and course placement in California's community colleges*. San Francisco, CA: WestEd.

Wolfle, J. D., & Williams, M. R. (2014). The impact of developmental mathematics courses and age, gender, and race and ethnicity on persistence and academic performance in Virginia community colleges. *Community College Journal of Research and Practice, 38*(2-3), 144–153.

Section IX – Globalization, Technology, and Policy Issues Facing 21st Century Community Colleges

Alfred, R., & American Council on Education. (2009). *Community colleges on the horizon: Challenge, choice or abundance*. Lanham, MD: Rowman & Littlefield Education.

Ayers, D. F. (2011). Community colleges and the politics of sociospatial scale. *Higher Education: The International Journal of Higher Education and Educational Planning, 62*(3), 303–314.

Benson, A., Johnson, S., Duncan, J. Shinkareva, O., Taylor, G., & Treat, T. (2008). Community college participation in distance learning for career and technical education. *Community College Journal of Research and Practice, 32*(9), 665–687.

Boggs, G. R., & Irwin, J. T. (2007). What every community college leader needs to know: Building leadership for international education. In E. J. Valeau, & R. L.Raby (Eds.), *International reform efforts and challenges in community colleges*. New Directions for Community Colleges, 138, 25–30. San Francisco, CA: Jossey-Bass.

Boyarkski, J. S., & Hickey, K (Eds.). (1994). *Collection management in the electronic age: A manual for creating community college collection development policy statements*. Chicago IL: Community and Junior College Libraries Section, Association of College and Research Libraries, American Library Association.

Bradshaw, G. W. (2013). Internationalization and faculty-led service learning. *New Directions for Community Colleges, 161*, 39–53.

Brown, N, J., & Burke, K. P. (2007). New rules for business in a flat world: A call to action. *Community College Journal of Research and Practice, 31*(4), 441–448.

Bunnell, T. (2006). The growing momentum and legitimacy behind an alliance for international education. *Journal of Research in International Education 5*(2), 155–76.

Connell, C. (2010). *Global community international educator.* Retrieved from http://www.nafsa.org/_/File/_janfeb10_commcolleges.pdf

Cox, R. (2005). Online education as institutional myth: Rituals and realities at community colleges. *Teachers College Record, 107*(8), 1754–1787.

Dellow, D. A. (2007). The role of globalization in technical and occupation programs. In E. J. Valeau, & R. L. Raby (Eds.), *International reform efforts and challenges in community colleges. New directions for community colleges, 138.* San Francisco, CA: Jossey-Bass.

Elsner, P. A., Boggs, G. R., & Irwin, J. R. (2006). *Global development of community colleges, technical colleges, and further education programs.* Washington, DC: Community College Press.

Emert, H. A., & Pearson, D. L. (2007). Expanding the vision of international education: Collaboration, assessment, and intercultural development. In E. J. Valeau, & R. L. Raby (Eds.), *International reform efforts and challenges in community colleges. New directions for community colleges, No. 138.* San Francisco, CA: Jossey-Bass.

Ewell, P, & Jenkins, D. (2008). Using state student unit record data to increase community college student success. *New Directions for Community Colleges, 143,* 71–81.

Fetzner, M. (2000). One college's response to online needs. *Community College Week, 12*(15), 35.

Frost, R. (2009). Globalization contextualized: An organization-environment case study. *Community College Journal of Research and Practice, 33*(12), 1009–1024.

Frost, R., & Latiner Raby, R. (2009). Creating global citizens: The democratization of community college open access. In R. Lewin (Ed.) *The handbook of practice and research in study abroad: Higher education and the quest for global citizenship.* New York, NY: Routledge.

Green, M. F. (2007). Internationalizing community colleges: Barriers and strategies. In E. Valeau & R. L. Raby (Eds.). *International reform efforts and challenges in community colleges. New Directions in Community College, 138.* San Francisco, CA: Jossey-Bass.

Gumport, P. J. (2003). The demand-response scenario: Perspectives of community college presidents. *The Annals of the American Academy of Political and Social Science, 586,* 38–61.

Hagedorn, L. S., & Kress, A. M. (2008). Using transcripts in analyses: Directions and opportunities. *New Directions for Community Colleges, 143,* 7–17.

Hagedorn, L. S., & Mezghani, W. T. (2013). Bringing community colleges to Tunisia. *New Directions for Community Colleges, 161,* 101–111.

Harrell, I. & Bower, B. L. (2011). *Student characteristics that predict persistence in community college online courses. American Journal of Distance Education, 25, 178–191.*

Jaggars, S. S. (2013). Choosing between online and face-to-face courses: Community college student voices. *Community College Research Center Working Paper No, 58.*

Jenkins, D., & Weiss, M. J. (2011). *Charting pathways to completion for low-income community college students.* (CCRC Working Paper, No. 34). New York, NY: Community College Research Center, Teachers College, Columbia University.

Kuo, Y. C., Walker, A. E., Belland, B. R., & Schroder, K. E. (2013). A predictive study of student satisfaction in online education programs. *International Review of Research in Open & Distance Learning, 14*(1), 16–39.

Laanan F. S. (2003). Older adults in community colleges: Choices, attitudes, and goals. *Educational Gerontology, 29*(9) 757–776.

Le, A. T. (2013). The history and future of community colleges in Vietnam. *New Directions for Community Colleges, 161,* 85–99.

Leinbach, D. T., & Jenkins, D. (2008). *Using longitudinal data to increase community college student success: A guide to measuring milestone and momentum point attainment* (CCRC Research Tools, No. 2). New York, NY: Community College Research Center, Teachers College, Columbia University. Retrieved from http://ccrc.tc.columbia.edu/Publication.asp?uid=570

Levin, J. (2001). The buffered and the buffeted institution: Globalization and the community college. In B. Townsend, & S. Twombly (Eds.). *Community Colleges,* (pp. 81–96). Norwood, NJ: Ablex.

Levin, J. S. (2001). *Globalizing community college.* New York, NY: Palgrave.

Levin, J. (2007). Neoliberal policies and community college faculty work. In J. Smart (Ed.), *Higher education: Handbook of theory and research, Vol. XXII*, (pp.451-496). New York, NY: Springer.

Levin, J. (2007). Neo-liberal policies and community college faculty work. In J. Smart, & W. Tierney (Eds.), *Handbook of higher education, Vol. XXII*, (pp.451-496). Norwell, MA: Kluwer Academic Publishers.

Levine, J. S., Montero-Hernandez, V., Cerven, C., & Shaker, G. (2011). Welfare students in community colleges: Policy and policy implementation as barriers to educational attainment. In A. Kezar (Ed.), *Recognizing and serving low income students in postsecondary education: An examination of institutional policies, practices, and culture* (pp. 139-158). New York, NY: Routledge.

Lovell, C.D., & Trouth, C. (2002). State governance patterns for community colleges. *New Directions for Community Colleges, 117*, 91–100.

Mamiseishvili, K. (2011). Characteristics, job satisfaction, and workplace perceptions of foreign born faculty at public 2-year institutions. *Community College Review, 39*, 26–45.

Margolin, J., Miller, S. R., & Rosenbaum, J. E. (2013). The community college website as virtual advisor a usability study. *Community College Review, 41*(1), 44–62.

Mars, M. M., & Ginter, M. B. (2007). Connecting organizational environments with the instructional technology practices of community college faculty. *Community College Review, 34*(4), 324–343.

Milliron, M. D. (2007).Transcendence and globalization. Our education and workforce development challenge. *New Directions for Community Colleges, 138*, 31–38.

Pusser, B., & Levin, J. S. (2009*). Re-imagining community colleges in the 21st century*. Washington, DC: Center for American Progress.

Raby, R. L. (2006). Using technology to internationalize the community college curriculum. New York, NY: Institute for International Education Publications.

Raby, R. L. (2008). Expanding education abroad at U.S. community colleges. (White Paper Series 3 September). New York, NY: Institute for International Education Press. Institute for International Education Study Abroad.

Raby, R. L, Kaufman, J. P., & Rabb, J. (2012). The international negotiation modules project: Using simulation to enhance teaching and learning strategies in the community college. In R. Clothey, S. Austin-Li, & J. Weidman (Eds.), *Post-secondary education and technology: A global perspective on opportunities and obstacles to development*. New York: Palgrave Macmillan.

Raby, R. L., Rhodes, G. M., & Biscarra, A. (2014). Community college study abroad: implications for student success. *Community College Journal of Research and Practice, 38*(2-3), 174–183.

Raby, R. L., Sawadogo, G. (2006). Community colleges and study abroad. In W. Hoffa, & J. Pearson (Eds.), *NAFSA's guide to education abroad for advisors and administrators (3rd ed.)*. Washington, DC: NAFSA Association of International Educators.

Raby, R. L., & Valeau, E. (2009). *Community college models: Globalization and higher education reform*. Dordrecht (Ed.). The Netherlands: Springer Publishers.

Raby, R. L., & Valeau, E. (2007). International reform efforts and challenges in community colleges. *New Directions in Community College, 138*. San Francisco, CA: Jossey-Bass.

Sax, L. J., Gilmartin, S. K., Lee, J. J., & Hagedorn, L. S. (2008). Using web surveys to reach community college students: An analysis of response rates and response bias. *Community College Journal of Research and Practice, 32*, 712–729.

Shulock, N., & Moore, C. (2007). *Rules of the game: How state policy creates barriers to degree completion and impedes student success in the California community colleges*. Sacramento, CA: Institute for Higher Education Leadership and Policy.

Smith, D., & Ayers, D. (2006). Culturally responsive pedagogy and online learning: Implications for the globalized community college. *Community College Journal of Research and Practice, 30*(5-6), 401–415.

Sullivan, L.G. (2007). Preparing Latinos/as for a flat world: The community college role. *Journal of Hispanic Higher Education, 6*(4), 397–422.

Treat, T., & Hagedorn, L. S. (2013). Resituating the community college in a global context. *New Directions for Community Colleges, 161*, 5–9.

APPENDIX B—RECOMMENDED WEB-BASED RESOURCES

COMPILED WITH ASSISTANCE FROM CARRIE KLEIN, GEORGE MASON UNIVERSITY RECOMMENDED WEB-BASED RESOURCES

Achieving the Dream, Inc.

8455 Colesville Road, Suite 900
Silver Spring, Maryland 20910
TEL: 240.450.0075
FAX: 240.450.0076
EMAIL: info@achievingthedream.org
WEB: http://achievingthedream.org/

From their website: Achieving the Dream, Inc. is a national nonprofit that is dedicated to helping more community college students, particularly low-income students and students of color stay in school and earn a college certificate or degree. Evidence-based, student-centered and build on the values of equity and excellence, Achieving the Dream is closing achievement gaps and accelerating student success nationwide by guiding evidence-based institutional improvement; influencing public policy; generating knowledge; and, engaging the public.

American Association of Community Colleges

One Dupont Circle, NW, Suite 4210
Washington, DC, 20036
TEL: 202.728.0200
FAX: 202.833.2467
WEB: www.aacc.nche.edu/

From their website: This mission statement captures AACC's commitment to advance the recognition of the role of community colleges in serving society today. By providing advocacy, leadership, and service for community colleges, the Association will play a key role in assisting the nation as it passes from the industrial era of the twentieth century to the new knowledge-based society of the twenty-first century.

The AACC's offers competencies for community college leaders on the resources section of their website at http://www.aacc.nche.edu/Resources/leadership and research and project briefs at http://www.aacc.nche .edu/Publications/Briefs/Pages/default.aspx.

Association for Career and Technical Education Research (ACTER)

Department of Educational Leadership and Policy Studies
N243 Lagomarcino Hall
Ames, Iowa 50011-3195
TEL: 515.294.7292
FAX: 515.294.4942
WEB: www.public.iastate.edu/~laanan/actermain/home.shtml

From their website: ACTER is the premier professional organization for researchers, faculty, graduate students, administrators, policy-makers, and all others with global interests in workforce education research, education, issues and policy.

Center for the Study of Community Colleges

9544 Cresta Drive
Los Angeles, California 90035
TEL: 310.951.3565
FAX: 425.671.2276
EMAIL: info@centerforcommunitycolleges.org
WEB: www.centerforcommunitycolleges.org

From their website: The Center for the Study of Community Colleges is a non-profit 501(c)(3) research and policy center based in Los Angeles, California, whose mission is to improve community college effectiveness and student success by engaging in relevant and applicable research related to community college practice and policy. The Center also houses the Council for the Study of Community Colleges (www.cscconline.org), a scholarly community affiliated with the American Association of Community Colleges.

College Board Advocacy & Policy Center

45 Columbus Avenue
New York, NY 10023-6917
TEL: 212.713.8000
WEB: http://advocacy.collegeboard.org

From their website: The College Board Advocacy & Policy Center was established to help transform education in America. Guided by the College Board's principles of excellence and equity in education, we work to ensure that students from all backgrounds have the opportunity to succeed in college and beyond. We make critical connections between policy, research and real-world practice to develop innovative solutions to the most pressing challenges in education today. Addressing the broad needs of our membership of education professionals from more than 6,000 institutions, our priorities include: College Preparation & Access; College Affordability & Financial Aid; and College Admission & Completion.

Community Colleges for International Development, Inc.

CCID Executive Offices
P.O. Box 2068
Cedar Rapids, Iowa
52406-2068 USA
TEL: 319.398.1257
EMAIL: ccid@kirkwood.edu
WEB: https://programs.ccid.cc/cci/

From their website: CCID is a consortium of 160 two year colleges in the U.S. and twelve other countries, and is the pre-eminent two-year college organization in the United States working on all aspects of global vocational/professional education, and training overseas. The mission of CCID is to take the community college model and share it internationally, while internationalizing it as well. Established in 1976, CCID has worked throughout the world during its 30 -year history, and through its member colleges represents over 500 technical and vocational programs and 15,000 faculty and staff. Developing the community college model for overseas clients, workforce development, and undertaking needs assessment are specialties. CCID also initiates and manages student study abroad programs, international faculty development programs, senior administrator visits overseas, and conferences and videoconferences focused on global issues in the two-year college.

Community College Research Center (CCRC)

Institute on Education and the Economy, Teachers College
Columbia University
Box 174
525 West 120th Street
New York, NY 10027
TEL: 212.678.3091
FAX: 212.678.3699
EMAIL: ccrc@columbia.edu
WEB: http://ccrc.tc.columbia.edu/

From their homepage: "The CCRC's mission is to conduct research on the major issues affecting community colleges in the United States and to contribute to the development of practice and policy that expands access to higher education and promotes success for all students." The CCRC produces publications, coordinates events and services, and provides fellowships in support of this mission.

Community College Survey of Student Engagement

c/o Center for Community College Student Engagement
3316 Grandview Street
Austin, TX 78705
TEL: 512.471.6807
FAX: 512.471.4209
EMAIL: info@cccse.org
WEB: www.ccsse.org

From their website: The Community College Survey of Student Engagement (*CCSSE*), a product and service of the Center for Community College Student Engagement, is a well-established tool that helps institutions focus on good educational practice and identify areas in which they can improve their programs and services for students. Administered during the spring to mostly returning students, *CCSSE* asks about institutional practices and student behaviors that are highly correlated with student learning and retention. *CCSSE* serves as a complementary piece to the Survey of Entering Student Engagement (*SENSE*), with a more broad focus on the student experience.

Community College Week

Box 1305
Fairfax, VA 22038
TEL: 703.978.3535
FAX: 703.978.3933
WEB: www.ccweek.com

From their website: Since 1988, Community College Week has been the independent source of in-depth information for and about two-year college faculty, administrators and trustees. Published biweekly, Community College Week's readers include college presidents, chief academic officers, faculty, student-service professionals, librarians, and other educators. In each edition, our readers find news and features not provided by other news sources, including analyses of critical academic trends and issues, vital statistics, technology updates and employment opportunities.

Council for the Study of Community Colleges (CSCC)

c/o UCLA Graduate School of Education and Information Studies
2128 Moore Hall, Box 951521
Los Angeles, CA 90095-1521
WEB: www.cscconline.org

From their website: The Council for the Study of Community Colleges (CSCC) is an affiliate of the American Association of Community Colleges (AACC) and a project of the Center for the Study of Community Colleges (centerforcommunitycolleges.org). Council members include university-based researchers and community college practitioners who further scholarship on the community college enterprise. The purposes of the Council are to: contribute to the development of pre-service and in-service education for community college professionals; conduct and disseminate research pertaining to community colleges; serve as a forum for dialogue between university professors, graduate students, and community college practitioners who study community colleges; disseminate information about related conferences and events; provide research and other services to the American Association of Community Colleges and its affiliate councils; recognize outstanding service to, research in, and publication about community college education; and provide a unified and formal base of participation for CSCC members in AACC affairs.

CSCC International Affairs

WEB: csccinternationalaffairs.wordpress.com/

From their website: The International Affairs Committee was established in April 2010 to promote global awareness among community college researchers, faculty, administrators, and students. Our purpose is to support student and faculty programs abroad, to better connect Council for the Study of Community Colleges (CSCC) members to Fulbright exchange opportunities, and to help community college curricula become more globally focused. We are a committee of CSCC and we collaborate with and support efforts by the American Association of Community Colleges (AACC) to accomplish these objectives.

Education Commission of the States Community (ECS)

700 Broadway, #810
Denver, CO 80203-3442
TEL: 303.299.3600
FAX: 303.296.8332
EMAIL: ecs@ecs.org
WEB: www.ecs.org

From their website: The mission of the Education Commission of the States is to help states develop effective policy and practice for public education by providing data, research, analysis and leadership; and by facilitating collaboration, the exchange of ideas among the states and long-range strategic thinking.

Grapevine: An Annual Compilation of Data on State Fiscal Support for Higher Education

Center for the Study of Education Policy
Illinois State University
Campus Box 5900
Normal, IL 61790-5900
TEL: 309.438.2041
FAX: 309.438.8683
EMAIL: jcpalmer@ilstu.edu
WEB: http://grapevine.illinoisstate.edu/index.shtml

From their website: Since 1960, *Grapevine* has published annual compilations of data on state tax support for higher education, including general fund appropriations for universities, colleges, community colleges, and state higher education agencies. Each year's *Grapevine* survey has asked states for tax appropriations data for the new fiscal year and for revisions (if any) to data reported in previous years.

Instructional Technology Council (ITC)

426 C Street, NE
Washington, DC 20002-5839
TEL: 202.293.3110
FAX: 202.293.3132
EMAIL: cmullins@itcnetwork.org; aweingfurter@itcnetwork.org
WEB: www.itcnetwork.org

From their website: ITC is a leader in advancing distance education. ITC's mission is to provide exceptional leadership and professional development to its network of eLearning experts by advocating, collaborating, researching, and sharing exemplary, innovative practices and potential in learning technologies. ITC tracks federal legislation that will affect distance learning, conducts annual professional development meetings, supports research, and provides a forum for members to share expertise and materials. The ITC online searchable library is located at http://www.itcnetwork.org/resources/articles-abstracts-and-research.html.

Jobs for the Future

88 Broad St., 8th Floor
Boston, MA 02110
TEL: 617.728.4446
FAX: 617.728.4857
EMAIL: info@jff.org
WEB: www.jff.org

From their website: Jobs for the Future aligns education with today's high-demand careers. With its partners, JFF develops policy solutions and new pathways leading from college readiness to career advancement for struggling and low-income populations in America. By 2020, JFF, working with our partners, is committed to doubling the number of low-income youth and adults who attain postsecondary credentials.

League for Innovation in the Community College

1333 South Spectrum Boulevard, Suite 210
Chandler, Arizona 85286
TEL: 480.705.8200
FAX: 480.705.8201
WEB: www.league.org

From their website: The League is an international organization dedicated to catalyzing the community college movement. We host conferences and institutes, develop Web resources, conduct research, produce publications, provide services, and lead projects and initiatives with our member colleges, corporate partners, and other agencies in our continuing efforts to make a positive difference for students and communities.

Office of Community College Research and Leadership (OCCRL)

c/o College of Education
University of Illinois at Urbana-Champagne
51 Gerty Drive, 129 CRC
Champaign, IL 61820
TEL: 217.244.9390
FAX: 217.244.2087
EMAIL: occrl@illinois.edu
WEB: http://occrl.illinois.edu

The OCCRL provides publication, newsletters, project information, and helpful links for those interested in community college research and leadership. From their website: Our mission is to use research and evaluation methods to improve policies, programs and practices to enhance community college education and transition to college for diverse learners, at the state, national, and international levels. Over the years, OCCRL has conducted its work with support from the ISBE and the Illinois Community College Board (ICCB) and other state agencies, the United States Department of Education, the National Science Foundation (NSF), and numerous private, not-for-profit foundations. In 2003, OCCRL partnered with the ICCB on various policy and programmatic initiatives, and this partnership continues to be a major focus of OCCRL's agenda today.

Current initiatives focus on partnerships between community colleges and high schools, including studies of programs of study, academic and career pathways, applied baccalaureate degree programs, and college and career readiness programs, all initiatives that support youth or adult learners' transition to college and careers.

Pathway to a STEM Baccalaureate Degree from Community College to University

c/o Department of Educational Leadership and Policy Studies
College of Human Sciences
Iowa State University
N243 Lagomarcino Hall
Ames, Iowa 50011-3195
TEL: 515.294.7292
FAX: 515.294.4942
WEB: www.public.iastate.edu/~laanan/

From their website: We are the Office of Community College Research and Policy (OCCRP) at Iowa State University. We create, share, and apply knowledge in the context of community college education. Our mission is "to articulate and analyze the issues affecting policy and practice by conducting rigorous research." We seek to assist community college practitioners and policy makers strengthen governance structures, develop leadership competencies, and make informed decisions to improve educational opportunities and academic success for students in community colleges in Iowa and nationwide.

Pathways to College Network

Institute for Higher Education Policy
1320 19th St., NW, Suite 400
Washington, DC 20036
TEL: 202.861.8223
FAX: 202.861.8307
EMAIL: abowles@ihep.org
WEB: www.pathwaystocollege.net

From their website: The Pathways to College Network (PCN) is an alliance of national organizations that advances college opportunity for underserved students by raising public awareness, supporting innovative research, and promoting evidence-based policies and practices across the K-12 and higher education sectors. Pathways promotes the use of research-based policies and practices, the development of new research that is both rigorous and actionable, and the alignment of efforts across middle school, high school, and higher education in order to promote college access and success for underserved students. The PCN offers an online library with a searchable database of publications, research reports, websites, and other resources related to improving college access and success for underserved populations at http://www.pathwaystocollege.net/PCNLibrary/.

The Pathways to College Network is directed by the Institute for Higher Education Policy (IHEP, www.ihep.org). IHEP is an independent, nonprofit organization in Washington, DC, dedicated to increasing access and success in postsecondary education around the world.

Sacramento State Institute for Higher Education Leadership & Policy

California State University
6000 J Street
Sacramento, California 95819-6081
TEL: 916.278.3888
FAX: 916.278.3907
EMAIL: ihelp@csus.edu
WEB: www.csus.edu/ihelp/

The Institute for Higher Education Leadership & Policy (IHELP) seeks to enhance leadership and policy for higher education in California and the nation, with an emphasis on community colleges in recognition of their importance to providing an educated and diverse citizenry and workforce. Our work is aimed at producing information and services relevant to policy makers, practitioners, and educators. We believe that policy matters, and our work is intended to contribute to the development of state policies that ensure access to and success in California's public higher education institutions as a means of ensuring the continued social and economic health of the state.

The Texas Collaborative for Teaching Excellence Modules

EMAIL: info@texascollaborative.org
WEB: www.texascollaborative.or/cpmodules.htm

From their website: The Texas Collaborative for Teaching Excellence is a statewide professional development resource for community and technical college faculty. The goal of the Collaborative is to enable colleges to share resources and avoid duplication. Resources offered on this their site were developed by the Collaborative's clearinghouse and regional centers at partner colleges across Texas. From on-demand modules ranging from discipline-specific to teaching and learning foundational topics, to professional development planning tools, the Collaborative's resources were created with busy faculty members in mind.

Among the modules offered is Dr. J.P. Murray's *Why faculty development? Enhancing faculty knowledge in the community college*, which is designed to help practitioners explore the reasons for implementing professional development programs at their campus and ways to make these programs efficient and effective.

Publications

Cross, T. (1995). *An oasis of order: The core curriculum at Columbia College.* New York: Columbia College Office of the Dean. Chapter Six, "College instructors are rare." Available at: http://www.college.columbia.edu/core/oasis/history6.php

From the website: One of the most intractable problems facing the core curriculum over the years has been staffing. The MacMahon, Truman, and Belknap committees, along with Daniel Bell, all pointed to problems in staffing both CC and the Humanities. Finding full-time faculty willing to teach in the core was proving increasingly difficult in the 1960s, and the burden of teaching both courses fell more and more upon preceptors, full-time graduate students who became part-time faculty, teaching the course while completing their dissertations. This situation was unsatisfactory for many faculty and students—and, though few bothered to ask, for many preceptors—but it had not developed overnight. It was a result of the history and the underlying educational philosophy of the core. In all the discussions of texts and requirements and committee reports, it is easy to lose sight of an essential truth—that both CC and the Humanities rise or fall because of what goes on in the classroom.

Gardenhire-Crooks, A., Collado, H., Martin, K., & Castro, A. (2010). *Terms of Engagement: Men of color discuss their experiences in community college.* Available at: http://www.mdrc.org/publications/547/full.pdf.

This study is published by MDRC (mdrc.org) and Achieving the Dream, Inc., and funded by the Lumina Foundation (luminafoundation.org). Per the publication's overview, the study gleans information from the experiences of male members of racial minority groups enrolled in math courses at four Achieving the Dream schools, looking primarily at motivation, prejudice, and identities. Recommendations include ways in which community colleges can work to meet the needs of male students of color and support their success at community colleges.

Gonzalez, J. (2012). Multiyear study of community-college practices asks: What helps students graduate? *The Chronicle of Higher Education*. Available at: http://chronicle.com/article/Community-College-Study-Asks-/130606/

The article investigates which programs and policies aid student completion rates, why they work and how they can be implemented to include all students.

Heller, D. & Gilbert, C. (2010). *Working paper no. 9, The Truman Commission and its impact on federal education policy from 1947 to 2010.* University Park, PA: Penn State College of Education, Center for the Study of Higher Education. Available at: http://www.personal.psu.edu/deh29/papers/papers_index.html.

From the introduction: This paper describes the Commission's recommendations in three key areas: 1) improving college access and equity; 2) expanding the role of community colleges; and 3) restructuring and expanding the federal government's role in funding higher education institutions, including an analysis of subsequent federal policy initiatives that have evolved in response to these recommendations.

Humphreys, D. (1998). *The impact of diversity on college students: The latest research.* The Ford Foundation Campus Diversity Initiative. Available at: http://www.diversityweb.org/research_and_trends/research_evaluation_impact/benefits_of_diversity/impact_of_diversity.cfm

From the website: The study provides a summary of research related to campus diversity on efforts to improve access, retention and success of traditionally underrepresented students and the impact of demographic, cultural and social changes on college and university campuses. Findings include the impact of diversity on students.

Hurtado, S. (n.d.). *How diversity affects teaching and learning: Climate of inclusion has a positive effect on learning outcomes.* Available at: http://www.diversityweb.org/research_and_trends/research_evaluation_impact/benefits_of_diversity/sylvia_hurtado.cfm

From the website: The article connects the transformations in teaching and learning activity with understanding and serving a diverse student body, requiring changes in thinking about institutional practices.

Iijima Hall, C. (2009). Learning from number two: Diversity in community college leadership. *Association of American College and Universities, On Campus with Women.* Vol 38, No 2. Available at: http://www.aacu.org/ocww/volume38_2/national.cfm

Explores the advantages in the diversity of community colleges for higher education leadership.

Latimore, R.S. (2009). *Rising to the top: A national study of black women community college presidents.* Athens, GA: The University of Georgia. Available at: https://getd.libs.uga.edu/pdfs/latimore_robbie_s_200905_edd/latimore_robbie_s_200905_edd.pdf

From the abstract: The purpose of this study was to understand how African American women community college presidents in the USA ascend to the presidency. Three major conclusions were indicated from the findings. First, the career preparation of African American women community college presidents is different because the women were held to higher standards than their counterparts because of racism and sexism and therefore the women "over achieved" and "over prepared" and "over-credentialed" in an effort to counteract these implicit societal forces. Second, African American women community college presidents developed a deliberate yet flexible approach to their careers that was consistently cognizant of managing their images and that was informed by a mentoring collective. Third, African American women presidents were engaged servant leaders who constructed and nurtured a politically savvy persona that they used to engage the community as a base and support system.

Kelly, R. (2008). Integrating adjuncts into the community college through professional development support. *Faculty Focus.* Available at: http://www.facultyfocus.com/uncategorized/integrating-adjuncts-into-the-community-college-through-professional-development-support/

Article discusses best practices and professional development programs used to integrate adjuncts into community colleges, as well as outcomes of such supported integration.

Kirkpatrick, L. (2001). *Multicultural strategies for community colleges: Expanding faculty diversity.* ERIC Digest. Available at: http://www.ericdigests.org/2002-2/faculty.htm

From the abstract: Multiculturalism is of great importance in the community college, for it is the community college that provides the initial exposure to higher education for most non-traditional students. Adopting a multicultural stance in the community college is helpful in facing the challenge of serving a diverse student clientele (Burstein, 1997). However, undertaking such an endeavor is not an easy task. Students that come from a variety of cultural and lifestyle backgrounds need role models on their college campuses (Erkut & Mokros, 1984). Increasing the diversity of the administration and faculty is one promising way to provide role models and establish the kind of rapport needed for effective mentoring. To be effective, mentoring must include people that listen to each other, care about each other, and have a willingness to strive toward mutually rewarding experiences leading to the satisfaction of individual and group needs (ACE/AAUP, 2000).

National Science Foundation. (2008). *Using the American community survey for the National Science Foundation's science and engineering workforce statistics programs.* Washington, DC: The National Academies Press. Available at: http://www.nap.edu/catalog.php?record_id=12244#d

From the website: The National Science Foundation (NSF) has long collected information on the number and characteristics of individuals with education or employment in science and engineering and related fields in the United States. An important motivation for this effort is to fulfill a congressional mandate to monitor the status of women and minorities in the science and engineering workforce. Consequently, many statistics are calculated by race or ethnicity, gender, and disability status. For more than 25 years, NSF obtained a sample frame for identifying the target population for information it gathered from the list of respondents to the decennial census long-form who indicated that they had earned a bachelors or higher degree. The probability that an individual was sampled from this list was dependent on both demographic and employment characteristics. But, the source for the sample frame will no longer be available because the census long-form is being replaced as of the 2010 census with the continuous collection of detailed demographic and other information in the new American Community Survey (ACS). At the request of NSF's Science Resources Statistics Division, the Committee on National Statistics of the National Research Council formed a panel to conduct a workshop and study the issues involved in replacing the decennial census long-form sample with a sample from the ACS to serve as the frame for the information the NSF gathers. The workshop had the specific objective of identifying issues for the collection of field of degree information on the ACS with regard to goals, content, statistical methodology, data quality, and data products.

Offenstein, J., & Shulock, N. (2009). *Community college student outcomes: Limitations of the integrated postsecondary education data system (IPEDS) and recommendations for improvement.* Sacramento, CA: Institute for Higher Education Leadership and Policy. Available at: http://www.csus.edu/ihelp/PDFs/R_IPEDS.

Rutschow, et al. (2011). Turning the tide: Five years of Achieving the Dream in community colleges. *MDRC Publications.* Available at: http://www.mdrc.org/publications/578/overview.html

From the website: The report examines the first 26 colleges to join Achieving the Dream in 2004, and tracks their progress through spring 2009. Finding include adoption of practices associates with a moderate to strong culture of evidence; shared characteristics of colleges that made the greatest strides; strategies instituted to improve student achievement; Achieving the Dream had an important influence on most colleges; trends in student outcomes remained relatively unchanged.

Women in Higher Education. (n.d.). *Making the most of expected high presidential turnover.* Available at: http://www.wihe.com/displayNews.jsp?id=439

Women in Higher Education's perspective on the American Council of Education's 2007 report, The American College President. The review of the ACE's data looks into diversity and gender in college presidential hiring and comments on what changes will be necessary to ensure diversity within the upper ranks of higher education administration.

ABOUT THE EDITORS

Eboni M. Zamani-Gallaher, is a Professor of Higher Education/Community College Leadership in the Department of Education Policy, Organization, and Leadership at the University of Illinois at Urbana-Champaign. She holds a Ph.D. in Higher Education Administration with a specialization in Community College Leadership and Educational Evaluation from the University of Illinois at Urbana-Champaign. Prior to joining the College of Education at Illinois, she previously held appointments as a faculty member at Eastern Michigan University, West Virginia University, a former fellow at ACT, Inc. and Mathematica Policy Research Institute (MPR) in Washington, DC. Her teaching, research and consulting activities largely include psychosocial adjustment and transition of marginalized collegians, transfer, access policies, women in leadership and institutional practices affecting work and family balance.

Dr. Zamani-Gallaher was the 2009 Recipient of the Association for the Study of Higher Education (ASHE) Council on Ethnic Participation Mildred B. Garcia Senior Scholar Award. Her research has been published in various journals and scholarly texts, including *Equity and Excellence in Education, Higher Education Policy, and New Directions for Student Affairs*. Dr. Zamani-Gallaher is the co-author of *The case for affirmative action on campus: Concepts of equity, considerations for practice* (Stylus Publishing) and co-editor of *The state of the African American Male: A courageous conversation* (Michigan State University Press), *Organization and governance in higher education: An ASHE Reader, Sixth Edition* (Pearson Publications) and *African American females: Addressing challenges and nurturing the future* (Michigan State University Press). Her most recent work is entitled *Working with student in community colleges: Contemporary strategies for bridging theory, research, and practice* (Stylus Publishing).

Jaime Lester, Associate Professor of Higher Education, George Mason University. Lester holds a Ph.D. and M.Ed. in higher education from the Rossier School of Education at the University of Southern California. Lester also holds a dual B.A. from the University of Michigan in English and Women's studies. Dr. Lester received the Barbara Townsend Emerging Scholar Award from the Council for the Study of Community Colleges in 2009. She was also the Mason state council rising star nominee in 2011 and received the Mason Excellence in Teaching Award. Dr. Lester is the Editor of Community College Review.

The overarching goal of her research program is to examine the relationship between workplace practices and identity to promote the equitable and effective leadership of higher education institutions. Dr. Lester's research is defined by three primary areas of inquiry: identity-based practices in organizational contexts; work-life balance in higher education as an organizational norm; and, organizational change and non-positional leadership.

Dr. Lester has published articles in the Community College Journal of Research and Practice, Community College Review, Journal of Higher Education, Research in Higher Education, Liberal Education, National Women's Studies Association Journal, and NEA: Thought & Action. She also has five books on gendered perspectives in community colleges, family-friendly policies in higher education, ways to restructure higher education to promote collaboration, non-positional leadership, and workplace bullying.

Debra D. Bragg, is the Gutgsell Endowed Professor in the Department of Educational Policy, Organization, and Leadership at the University of Illinois. In addition to being Director of the Office of Community College Research and Leadership (OCCRL), Dr. Bragg is Director of the Forum on the Future of Public Education, a strategic initiative of the College of Education at Illinois. She is also responsible for coordinating the Higher Education and Community College Executive Leadership programs. Her research focuses on P-20 policy issues, with a special interest in the transition of youth and adults to college. She has directed research and evaluation studies funded by federal, state, local, and foundation sponsors, including examining the participation of underserved students in college transition and career pathways initiatives. Recent investigations include studies of the implementation and impact of bridge-to-college programs for youth and adults funded by the Joyce Foundation and the United States Department of Education (USDE) and applied baccalaureate programs for adults funded by Lumina Foundation. She is co-editor of the *ASHE Reader Series on Community Colleges, Third Edition* (Pearson Publications).

Linda Serra Hagedorn is Associate Dean of the College of Human Sciences and Professor in the Department of Educational Leadership and Policy Studies at Iowa State University. Hagedorn's research focuses on community college student success, retention, and transfer. She is also a researcher in the area of international students. Prior to joining the faculty at Iowa State University, she directed the Institute of Higher Education at the University of Florida. She was also the Director of the Transfer and Retention of Urban Community College Students Project (TRUCCS); a longitudinal study of over 5,000 students enrolled in the Los Angeles Community College District. Although Dr. Hagedorn performs both quantitative and qualitative research, she is especially known for developing techniques to analyze enrollment and other college files. She has created new rubrics and designs for the longitudinal analyses of transcript data (transcript analysis). Her most recent published works include; *Redefining Nontraditional Students: Exploring the Self-Perceptions of Community College Students;* and *The Community College Transfer Calculator: Identifying the Course-Taking Patterns that Predict Transfer.* Dr. Hagedorn is currently president of the Association for the Study of Higher Education.